A HISTORY OF
NARRATIVE FILM

A HISTORY OF
NARRATIVE FILM

David A. Cook
Emory University

W · W · Norton & Company · New York · London

Typographical design by Maria Epes.
Page design and original artwork by Edwina Gluck.

Library of Congress Cataloging in Publication Data
Cook, David A
  A history of narrative film
  Bibliography: p.
  Includes index.
  1. Moving-pictures—History. I. Title.
PN1993.5.A1C65 1981   791.43'09   79–25862
ISBN 0–393–01370–7
ISBN 0–393–09022–1 pbk.

For Diane,
my constant collaborator
in productions both
literary and human

Contents

We spend much of our waking lives surrounded by moving photographic images. They have come to occupy such a central position in our experience that it is unusual to pass even a single day without encountering them for an extended period of time, through either film or television. In short, moving photographic images have become part of the total environment of modern industrial society. Both materially and psychologically, they have a shaping impact on our lives. And yet few people in our society have been taught to understand precisely how they work. Most of us, in fact, have extremely vague notions about how moving images are formed and how they are structured to create the multitude of messages sent out to us by the audio-visual media on an almost continual basis. If we made an analogy with verbal language, we should be forced to consider ourselves barely literate—able to assimilate the language form without fully comprehending it. We would, of course, be appalled to find ourselves living in a culture whose general verbal literacy level corresponded to that of a three-year-old child. Most persons living in such a culture would, like small children, be easy prey to whomever could manipulate the language. They would be subject to the control of any minority which understood the language from the inside out and which could therefore establish an authority of knowledge over them, just as verbally literate adults establish authority over children. Such a situation would be unthinkable in the modern industrial world, of course, and our own culture has made it a priority to educate its children in the institutions of human speech so that they can participate in the community of knowledge which verbal literacy sustains.

Imagine, though, that a new language form came into being at the turn of the twentieth century, an audio-visual language form which first took the shape of cinema and became in time the common currency of modern television. Imagine that because the making of statements in this language depended upon an expensive industrial process, only a handful of elite specialists were trained to use it. Imagine, too, that although public anxiety about the potentially corrupting influence of the new language was constant from its birth, it was *perceived* not as a language at all but as a medium of popular entertainment—that in this guise the language was gradually allowed to colonize us, as if it were the vernacular speech of some conquering foreign power. Finally, imagine waking up one day in the last quarter of the twentieth century to discover that we had mistaken language for a mode of dreaming and in the process become massively illiterate in a primary language form, one which had not only surrounded us materially but which, as language forms tend to do, had invaded our minds as well. What would we do if that happened? We could choose to embrace our error and lapse into the anarchic mode of consciousness characteristic of pre-literate societies, which might be fun but would most certainly be dangerous in an advanced industrial society. Or we could attempt to re-instruct ourselves in the language form from the ground up and from the inside out. We could try to learn as much of its history, technology, and aesthetics as possible. We could trace the evolution of its syntactic and semantic forms from their birth through their present stages of development, and try to forecast the shapes they might take in the future. We could, finally, bring the apparatus of sequential logic and critical analysis to bear on the seemingly random structures of the language in order to read them in new and meaningful ways.

This scenario conforms quite accurately, I believe, to our present situation in the modern world. The language of the moving photographic image has become so pervasive in our daily lives that we scarcely notice its presence. And yet it *does* surround us, sending us messages, taking positions, making statements, and constantly redefining our relationship to material reality. We can choose to live in ignorance of its operations and be manipulated by those who presently control it. Or we can teach ourselves to read it, to appreciate its very real and manifold truths, to recognize its equally real and manifold deceptions. As a life-long student and teacher of language forms, both verbal and audio-visual, I believe that most intelligent and humane persons in our culture will opt for the latter. It is for them that I have written this book.

Acknowledgments

A full account of the debts incurred during the seven years it took to write and produce this book would fill one of its longer chapters, so I am forced to be more selective in these acknowledgments than I have any right to be. First, I must thank the two primary readers of the manuscript, Ronald Gottesman (director, Center for the Humanities, University of Southern California) and Ernest Callenbach (editor of *Film Quarterly* and film editor for the University of California Press), without whose immense knowledge of film history and seasoned critical judgment this book would have perpetuated many errors of the past. I would also like to thank Dean Charles Lester of Emory University, whose understanding and good counsel sustained me through many difficult years of writing this book while teaching simultaneously, and Jean Firstenberg of the American Film Institute, whose support and encouragement in several capacities assisted me greatly during the final stages of the project. Dennis DeNitto (City College of New York) and Elisabeth Weis (Brooklyn College of New York) read the manuscript in a nearly final stage and made many helpful comments.

Next, I would like to thank my Norton editors, John Benedict and Emily Garlin, for their steadfast guidance, and Edwina Gluck for her discriminating coordination of text and illustrations. I would also like to thank Mary Corliss of the Museum of Modern Art/Film Stills Archive for her assistance in compiling the great majority of the production stills which illustrate the text, and Joseph Berry and the staff of the Emory University Audio-Visual Department for their help in securing frame enlargements and other essential photographic materials. Timothy J. Corrigan's contributions to the Glossary and Bibliography were also significant.

This project was sustained at various points over its seven-year growth by grants from the National Endowment for the Humanities and the Emory University Research Committee, for which I would now like to express my gratitude. In addition, I must thank the John and Mary R. Markle Foundation, whose grant to write a cultural history of television also enabled me to see the present book through its latter editorial stages.

Personal debts are the hardest to express of all. But to Cecil Lang, who taught me that intellect and compassionate understanding need never be opposed (and to whom the sections on Josef von Sternberg and Luis Buñuel in the present volume are affectionately dedicated), and to Al Fulton, whose work as one of America's first film history teachers and film historians at Purdue University from 1940 to 1971 provided the inspiration for this book, thanks many times over. Above all, I owe thanks to my wife, Diane Cook, who worked with me in close collaboration on every stage of the project from inception through page proofs. She became during this period my most persuasive editor and critic, and her contributions to the book are quite literally immeasurable. Thanks, finally, to my parents, Allen and Sara Cook, whose love for the movies when I was growing up planted the seeds of my own life-long passion, and to my children, Lindsay, Gregory, and Jessica, whose love for life and everything it contains made all of the effort worthwhile.

A Note on Method

For reasons which will become apparent in the course of this book, I believe that the history of film as we have experienced it to date is the history of a narrative form. Many of the greatest films ever made were created by artists seeking to break the constraints of this form as it defined itself at different points in time, and there is much evidence to suggest that since the 1950's the cinema has been moving in an increasingly non-narrative direction. But the fact remains that the language common to the international cinema from the last decade of the nineteenth century through the present has been narrative in both aspiration and structural form. For this reason, I have excluded documentary cinema, animated cinema, and the experimental avant-garde from consideration in this book except where they have influenced narrative form to a demonstrable and significant extent. This is not to suggest that any of these excluded forms is unimportant but, rather, that they are each important and distinctive enough to warrant separate histories of their own (several of which, in fact, already exist).

A Note on Dates, Titles, and Stills

Wherever possible, the date given for a film is the year of its theatrical release in its country of origin. Unless otherwise noted (as in the case of intermittent production or delayed release), the reader may assume a lapse of six months between the start of production and the date of release. This is important in correlating the history of film with the history of human events (for instance, many American films with the release date of 1942 went into production and were completed before the Japanese attack on Pearl Harbor on December 7, 1941).

As for the titles of films in languages other than English, those in French, Italian, Spanish, Portuguese, and German are given in the original language, followed, in parentheses, by a literal English translation (and an alternate English language release title, if one exists), followed by the date of release. After the initial reference, the original foreign-language title is used, except in the case of a film that is best known in the English-speaking world by its English title (for example, Jean-Luc Godard's *Breathless* [*À bout de souffle,* 1959]). For Scandinavian, Eastern European, Asian, and African languages the convention is reversed: the initial reference is given in English, followed by the original title in parentheses (a transliteration is supplied if the original title is in an alphabet other than our own). All subsequent references use the English title, unless the film is best known here by its foreign-language title (as in the case, for instance, of Akira Kurosawa's *Ikiru* [*Living/To Live,* 1952] and *Yojimbo* [*The Bodyguard,* 1961]). In the case of films for which the original foreign-language title was unavailable, only the English title is given.

The photographs used to illustrate the book represent a combination of production stills and frame enlargements. Since they are taken on the set by professional photographers, production stills yield a higher quality of reproduction; but since they are made initially for the purpose of publicity, they sometimes "beautify" the shots they are intended to represent to the point of distortion. Frame enlargements, on the other hand, are blown-up photographically from 16mm prints of the films themselves, so that they represent the actual images as composed and shot by the film-makers. Their quality of reproduction is often lower than that of production stills, since several extra steps of photographic transference are involved in printing them, but their correspondence with the film images is exact. Whenever shot sequences have been reproduced for discussion or when lengthy analysis accompanies an individual image or series of images, I have tried to use frame enlargements. When less analytical procedures are involved, I have used production stills. (Many films of the fifties and most films of the sixties, seventies, and eighties were shot in some type of widescreen process, with aspect ratios varying from 2.55:1 to 1.85:1. For reasons of typography and design, most of the stills in this volume have been reproduced in the 1.33:1 aspect ratio of the Academy frame.) Though photographs can never replicate cinema, lacking as they do the essential component of motion, they *can* be made to represent it. Throughout the book, I have attempted to integrate the stills with the written text in a manner that will provide for maximum delivery of information. The reader is therefore encouraged to regard both photographic and verbal information as part of the same critical fabric, although neither, finally, can substitute for the audio-visual information contained in the films themselves.

The illustrations in this book were obtained from the following sources (frame enlargements supplied by the author are not listed):

The Academy of Motion Picture Arts and Sciences: 10.30

Cinema 5: 17.31

Cinemabilia: 10.24, 10.26

Howard Cramer: 2.7

The Library of Congress: 1.12, 1.13, 1.21(a), 2.1, 2.2

New Line Cinema: 17.28, 17.29

The New York Film Festival: 17.35

New Yorker Films: 17.27, 17.34

Unifilm: 17.1, 17.4, 17.5, 17.9, 17.10, 17.11, 17.12, 17.13

The Museum of Modern Art/Film Stills Archive: 1.2, 1.3, 1.4, 1.6, 1.8, 1.9, 1.10, 1.11, 1.14, 1.16, 1.17, 1.18, 1.19, 1.22, 1.23, 1.25, 1.27, 1.29, 2.5, 2.6, 2.8, 2.9, 2.13, 2.15, 2.17, 2.19, 2.20(a), 2.22, 2.25, 2.26, 2.27, 2.28, 3.1, 3.2, 3.3(a,b), 3.5, 3.6, 3.7, 3.9, 3.12, 3.15, 3.17, 3.20, 3.21, 3.24, 3.25, 3.26, 3.27, 3.28, 3.29, 3.30, 3.31, 3.32, 3.34, 3.35, 3.36, 3.37, 3.38, 3.39, 4.2, 4.3, 4.4, 4.5, 4.6, 4.7, 4.8, 4.9, 4.10, 4.11, 4.12, 4.13, 4.14, 4.17, 4.18, 4.19, 4.20, 4.21, 4.22, 4.23, 4.24, 4.25, 4.26(a), 4.27, 4.28, 4.29, 4.30, 4.31, 4.32, 5.2, 5.3, 5.4, 5.8(a), 5.12(a), 5.13, 5.15(c), 5.16(b), 5.19(a), 5.20 (7, 24, 34, 84, 88, 93, 120), 5.21(s), 5.22, 5.24(a,b,c), 5.25, 5.27, 5.28(b), 5.29, 5.30(c), 5.31, 5.33(a), 5.39(a), 5.41(e,f), 5.42, 5.43, 5.45, 6.5, 6.6, 6.7, 6.8, 6.9, 6.10, 6.11, 6.12, 6.14, 6.17, 6.18, 6.20, 6.21, 6.22, 6.23, 6.24, 6.25, 6.27, 6.28, 6.29, 6.30(b), 6.31, 6.32, 6.33, 6.36, 6.37, 6.38, 6.39, 6.40, 6.41, 6.42, 6.43, 6.44, 6.45, 6.46, 6.47, 6.48, 6.49, 6.51, 6.52, 7.1, 7.2, 7.4, 7.5, 7.7, 7.12, 7.15, 7.18, 7.19, 7.20, 7.21, 7.23, 8.1, 8.2, 8.3, 8.5, 8.6, 8.7, 8.8, 8.9, 8.10, 8.11, 8.12, 8.13, 8.14, 8.15, 8.17, 8.18, 8.20, 8.21, 8.23, 8.25, 8.26, 8.27, 8.28, 8.29, 8.30, 8.31, 8.33, 8.34, 8.35, 8.36, 8.37, 8.38, 8.39, 8.40, 8.41, 8.43, 8.45, 8.46, 8.48(a), 8.49, 8.50, 8.51, 8.53, 8.54, 8.55, 8.59, 8.60, 8.61, 8.62, 9.1, 9.2, 9.3, 9.5, 9.6, 9.7, 9.8, 9.9, 9.10, 9.11(b,c,g), 9.13, 9.14(b), 9.15(b,f), 9.19, 9.21, 9.22, 9.23, 9.27, 9.31(a,c), 9.32, 9.33, 9.34, 9.37, 9.38, 9.39(a), 9.42, 9.43, 9.44, 9.45, 9.48, 9.50, 9.53, 9.54, 9.55(a), 9.57, 9.58, 9.59, 9.61, 10.2, 10.3, 10.4, 10.5,

10.10(a), 10.11, 10.17, 10.19, 10.20, 10.21, 10.22, 10.27, 10.29, 10.33, 10.35, 10.37, 10.39, 10.40, 10.41, 10.47, 10.48, 10.51(b), 10.52(b), 10.61(b), 10.62(a), 10.64, 10.67, 10.72, 10.76, 10.79, 11.1, 11.2, 11.4(a), 11.6, 11.8, 11.9, 11.10, 11.11(a), 11.12, 11.13, 11.14, 11.16, 11.17, 11.18, 11.19, 11.20, 11.21, 11.22, 11.23, 11.24, 11.25, 11.26, 11.27, 11.28, 11.29, 11.31, 11.32, 11.33, 11.34, 11.35, 12.2, 12.3, 12.4, 12.5, 12.6, 12.7, 12.8, 12.10(a), 12.11, 12.12, 12.13, 12.14, 12.15, 12.17, 12.18, 12.19, 12.20, 12.21, 12.22, 12.23, 12.24, 12.25, 12.26, 12.27, 12.28, 12.29, 12.30, 12.31(a), 12.32, 12.33, 12.34, 12.38, 12.39(b), 12.40, 12.41, 12.43, 12.44, 13.1, 13.2, 13.4, 13.6, 13.7, 13.9, 13.10, 13.12, 13.13, 13.14, 13.15, 13.17, 13.18, 13.19, 13.21, 13.22(a), 13.23, 13.24, 13.25, 13.26, 13.27, 13.28, 13.30, 13.31, 13.32(a), 13.33(a), 13.34, 13.36, 13.37, 13.39, 13.40, 13.41, 13.42, 13.44, 13.45, 13.46, 13.47, 13.48, 13.50, 13.52, 13.53, 13.54, 14.1, 14.2, 14.3, 14.4, 14.5, 14.6, 14.7, 14.8, 14.9, 14.10, 14.11, 14.12, 14.13, 14.14, 14.15, 14.22, 14.23, 14.24, 14.25, 14.26, 14.27, 14.29, 14.31, 14.32, 14.33, 14.34, 14.35, 14.37, 14.38, 14.39, 14.40, 14.41, 14.42, 14.43, 14.44, 14.45(b), 14.47, 14.51, 14.52, 14.53, 14.54, 14.55, 14.56, 14.57, 14.58, 14.59, 14.60, 14.61, 14.62, 14.64, 14.65, 14.66, 14.67, 14.68, 14.69, 14.70, 14.71, 14.72, 15.4, 15.7, 15.8, 15.9, 15.14, 15.15, 15.16, 15.17, 15.21, 15.22, 15.27, 15.30, 15.31, 15.34, 15.37, 15.38, 15.39, 15.40, 15.42, 15.43, 15.44, 15.48, 15.49, 15.50, 15.51, 15.55, 15.56, 15.58, 15.59, 15.65, 15.66, 15.67, 15.68, 15.71, 16.1, 16.2, 16.5, 16.7, 16.8, 16.9, 16.10, 16.11, 16.12, 16.13, 16.14, 16.15, 16.16, 16.17, 16.18, 16.19, 16.20, 16.22(a), 16.24, 16.27, 16.28, 16.29(a), 16.32, 16.33, 16.34, 16.35, 16.36, 16.37, 16.38, 16.39, 16.40, 17.2, 17.3, 17.6, 17.7, 17.14, 17.15, 17.19, 17.21, 17.22, 17.23, 17.24, 17.25, 17.26, 17.30, 17.32, 17.36, 17.37, 17.38, 17.39, 17.41, 17.42, 17.43, 17.44, 17.45, 17.46, 17.47, 17.48, 17.51, 17.54, 17.56, 17.57, 17.58.

Origins

OPTICAL PRINCIPLES

The beginning of film history is the end of something else: the successive stages of technological development throughout the nineteenth century whereby simple optical devices used for entertainment grew into sophisticated machines which could convincingly represent empirical reality in motion. Both toys and machines were dependent for their illusions upon an optical phenomenon known as persistence of vision. This is a characteristic of human perception, known to the ancient Egyptians but first described scientifically by Peter Mark Rogêt in 1824, whereby the brain retains images cast upon the retina of the eye for approximately one-twentieth to one-fifth of a second beyond their actual removal from the field of vision. It is this phenomenon which causes us to see the individual blades of a rotating fan as a unitary circular form or the different hues of a spinning color-wheel as a single, homogeneous color. Persistence of vision also allows us to see a succession of static images as a single unbroken movement and permits the illusion of continuous motion upon which cinematography is based.* The frames of a strip of film are a series of individual still photographs which the motion picture camera, as it was first perfected by the Edison Laboratories in 1889 and as it exists today, imprints a single frame at a time. The succession of frames recorded in the camera, when projected at the same or similar speeds, creates the illusion of continuous motion essential to the cinema. (Individual frames are actually held longer before the projector's lens than before the camera's, but the movement *between* frames is more rapid in projection, so that the speeds of both instruments remain synchronized.)

Illusion is the operative term here. Most motion picture cameras today expose individual frames at the approximate speed of one-thirtieth of a second and can therefore record up to thirty frames per second. But the illusion of continuous motion can be induced in our brains at rates as low

* For a provocative but unsubstantiated argument that Rogêt's conception has been badly misinterpreted by film historians and that, in fact, very little is really known about the cognitive processes involved in the perception of motion, see Joseph Anderson and Barbara Fisher, "The Myth of Persistence of Vision," *Journal of the University Film Association*, 30, 4 (Fall 1978), 3–8. See also *Journal of the University Film Association*, 32, 1 and 2 (Winter–Spring 1980 [double issue: "Cinevideo and Psychology"]).

as twelve frames per second, although speeds have traditionally been set at about sixteen frames per second for silent film and twenty-four for sound. A large part of any film strip, then (25 to 50 percent, varying with the number of frames exposed per second and with shutter speeds), is comprised of the unexposed blank spaces between the frames. When we "watch" a film in a theater, we actually spend as much as 50 percent of the time in darkness, with the projector's shutter closed and nothing before us on the screen. Thus the continuity of movement and light that seems to be the most palpable quality of the cinema exists only in our brains, making cinema the first communications medium to be based upon psycho-perceptual illusions created by machines.* The second, of course, is television.

Persistence of vision was exploited for the purpose of optical entertainment for many years before the invention of photography. A popular child's toy of the early nineteenth century was the Thaumatrope (from the Greek for "magical turning"), a paper disk with strings attached to either side so that it could be twirled between finger and thumb. A different image was imprinted on each face, and when the disk was spun the images seemed to merge into a single unified picture (a rider would mount a horse, a parrot enter his cage, etc.). Between 1832 and 1850, hundreds of optical toys were manufactured which used rotating "phase drawings" of things in motion to produce a crude form of animation. Drawings representing successive phases of an action would be mounted on a disk or cylinder and rotated in conjunction with some type of shutter apparatus (usually a series of slots in the disk or cylinder itself) to produce the illusion of motion. Joseph Plateau's Phenakistiscope (from the Greek for "deceitful view"—1832) and George Horner's Zoetrope ("live turning"—1834) were among the most popular of these toys, which reached increasing stages of refinement as the century progressed. When still photography was invented by Louis-Jacques Mandé Daguerre (1789–1851) in 1839† and perfected throughout the next decade, it was

1.1 The Thaumatrope.

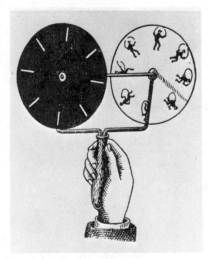

1.2 The Phenakistascope.

1.3 The Zoetrope.

---

* It might be argued that photography and telephony are no less illusory. But when we look at a photograph, there *is* a materially real, light-encoded representation of reality before us, and when we use the telephone, there *is* a materially real human voice behind the electronic pulses transmitting it through the wire. When we watch a film in a theater, on the other hand, the movement we perceive on the screen does not exist materially on the screen but solely in our heads. The only empirically real movement in the "movies" is the motion of the film strip through the camera and projector. Television compounds this illusion by dematerializing the screen and relocating it *inside* our heads, so that neither movement nor screen are materially "there" before us.

† The very first photographs were actually made by Daguerre's business associate Joseph Nicéphore Nièpce (1765–1833) in 1826 using a *camera obscura*. This device, whose name literally means "dark room," was invented during the Renaissance and consisted of a sealed chamber or box with a tiny hole in one wall. The hole acted as a lens to focus light from the outside (and therefore the image of the objects before the hole) onto the opposite wall. This is the simple optical principle on which all photography is based. Nièpce added the final step by fixing the image thus projected on a pewter plate covered with chemical emulsions. But the exposure time for Nièpce's process was eight hours, and he died in 1833 without making further innovations. Daguerre's contribution was the introduction of silvered copper plates, which reduced the exposure time to fifteen minutes and made photography a practical reality. Daguerrotypy popularized photography throughout Western Europe, but

1.4 Muybridge's glass-plate series photographs.

a relatively simple step to replace the phase drawings in the motion-simulation devices with individually posed "phase photographs." At this point, live action could be *simulated photographically,* but not *recorded spontaneously and simultaneously as it occurred.* This required the drastic reduction in photographic exposure time from fifteen minutes to one one-thousandth of a second that was achieved by the replacement of collodion wet plates with gelatine dry plates between 1876 and 1881, and the introduction of "series photography" by the Anglo-American photographer Eadweard Muybridge (1830–1904).

SERIES PHOTOGRAPHY

In 1872 Muybridge was hired by Governor Leland Stanford of California to prove that at some point in its gallop a race-horse lifts all four hooves off the ground (a convention of nineteenth-century graphic illustration required that running horses always be pictured with at least one foot on the ground). After several years of abortive experiments, Muybridge accomplished this in the summer of 1877 by setting up a battery of twelve electrically operated cameras (later studies used twenty-four) along a Sacramento racetrack and stretching wires across it which would trip the cameras' shutters. As a horse came down the track, its hooves

---

its prints were positive and could not therefore be reproduced. A rival process developed by the Englishman William Henry Fox Talbot (1800–1877) during the eighteen-forties imprinted photographic images on negative paper stock coated with silver chloride, from which an infinite number of positive prints could be reproduced. Talbot ultimately replaced his paper negatives with collodion film stock and by mid-century had reduced the exposure time to one-hundredth of a second, giving photography its modern form.

1.5 A seventeenth-century illustration showing the magic lantern.

1.6 Marey's chronophotographic gun.

tripped each shutter individually and caused the cameras to photograph it in successive stages of motion during the gallop. Muybridge subsequently discovered that by mounting glass-plate photographs of the galloping horse on an enlarged Phenakistiscope, which he called the Zoopraxiscope, and projecting them successively on a screen with a magic lantern,* he could reproduce live action as it had actually and spontaneously occurred. Muybridge devoted the rest of his life to refining his process of series photography,† but he was not "the man who invented moving pictures," as a recent biography proclaims. He recorded live action continuously for the first time in history, but he did so with a series of twelve or more cameras; until the separate functions of these machines could be incorporated into a single instrument, the cinema could not be born.

It was the French physiologist Étienne-Jules Marey (1830–1904) who recorded the first series photographs of live action in a single camera which, as it happens, was also portable. Marey, a specialist in animal locomotion, invented the "chronophotographic gun" in 1882 in order to take series pictures of birds in flight. This instrument was a camera shaped like a rifle which took twelve instantaneous photographs of a movement per second and imprinted them on a rotating glass plate. A year later Marey switched from the cumbersome plates to paper roll film, which had the effect of introducing the film strip to cinematography. But, like most of his contemporaries, Marey was not interested in cinematography as such. In his view, he had invented a machine for the dissection of motion similar to Muybridge's apparatus but more flexible, and he never intended to project his results. (In 1892, however, after the idea of projection had gained currency, Marey did attempt to design a projector that used celluloid roll film on a continuous belt; he was unsuccessful.)

The next step was taken in 1887, when an Episcopalian minister named Hannibal Goodwin first used celluloid roll film as a base for light-sensitive emulsions. Goodwin immediately sold his idea to the American entrepreneur George Eastman, who in 1888 began to mass-produce and market celluloid roll film on an international scale. Both men were interested solely in the advancement of still photography, but it was the introduction of a *plastic* recording medium (in the generic sense of both durable and flexible), coupled with the technical breakthroughs of Muybridge and Marey, that enabled the Edison Laboratories in Menlo Park, New Jersey, in 1889 to invent the Kinetograph, the first true motion picture camera.

---

* The optical, or magic, lantern was a simple projection device invented in the seventeenth century, consisting of a light source and a magnifying lens. It enjoyed great popularity as a projector of still transparencies (or slides) throughout the eighteenth and nineteenth centuries and became a major component in motion picture projection after the invention of the first practical camera in 1889.

† Muybridge ultimately became a professor at the University of Pennsylvania, where he undertook motion studies of a wide assortment of men, women, children, and animals. The resulting series photographs—in excess of 100,000—were published by the university in 1887 in an eleven-volume edition that sood for five hundred dollars. This work, *Human and Animal Locomotion,* was republished as a three-volume set by Dover Books in 1979.

CINEMATOGRAPHY

Like his predecessors, Thomas Alva Edison was not interested in cinematography in and of itself. Rather, he wished to provide a visual accompaniment for his vastly successful phonograph, and in 1888 he commissioned a young laboratory assistant named William Kennedy Laurie Dickson (1860–1937) to develop a motion picture camera for that purpose. Edison, in fact, envisioned a kind of "home-entertainment machine," similar in appearance to the modern television set, in which motion pictures made by the Kinetograph would illustrate the sound from the phonograph.* This aspect of the Kinetograph's genesis is important to note for two reasons. In the first place, it shows that the idea of making motion pictures was never divorced from the idea of recording sound. The movies were intended to talk from their very inception, so that in some sense the silent cinema represents a thirty-year aberration from the medium's natural tendency toward a total representation of reality. More significant is the fact that the first viable motion picture camera was invented as an accessory to a sound recording device and not for its own sake. The advent of the Kinetograph thus completes a pattern which has been emerging throughout this chapter and which should now be apparent: cinema was born as an independent medium only *after* the cinema machines had been evolved for purposes other than the establishment of such a medium. That is, the invention of the machines preceded any serious consideration of their documentary or aesthetic potential; and this relationship has remained constant throughout the history of film because the cinema at its material base is a technological form—one in which technological innovation *necessarily* precedes the aesthetic impulse.

Dickson "invented" the first motion picture camera in a brilliant synthesis of already existing principles and techniques which he had learned

* Perhaps Edison's most original invention, the phonograph was a combined product of certain principles of telegraphy (invented in 1839) and telephony (invented in 1876), although until very recently phonographic technology was mechanical rather than electrical. Edison discovered the technique of phonographic reproduction while attempting to design an automatic telegraph which would inscribe Morse code signals by needle onto continuously moving rolls of paper tape. In the process, he discovered the technology of voice and sound transcription, in which sound waves are recorded as physical vibrations in the grooves of a revolving wax cylinder or disk and redeemed as sound by a vibrating stylus and diaphragm in the phonographic performance. Like the motion picture camera, the phonograph was a mechanical rather than an electrical invention: its sound was amplified by a simple horn, its power provided by a hand-turned crank. Edison patented the phonograph on December 15, 1877, and he initially conceived of it as a dictating machine. But it was as a home-entertainment device that the phonograph enjoyed its first great success. (In fact, it was the so-called phonograph craze of 1878 that first brought Edison to international attention.) By the 1890's, however, sophisticated coin-operated phonographs had become extremely popular and lucrative, and it was in this context that Edison conceived of the Kinetograph camera and the coin-operated viewing device which pre-dated the projector by several years.

1.7 W. K. L. Dickson (with violin) recording sound for an early Kinetophone experiment.

from studying the work of Muybridge, Marey, and others.* After some ineffectual attempts to record photographic images microscopically on the photograph cylinder itself, Dickson began to experiment with the use of celluloid roll film in a battery-driven camera† similar to Marey's chronophotographic gun, and he arrived at the Kinetograph in 1889. The machine incorporated what have come to be recognized as the two essentials of motion picture camera and projector engineering: 1) a stop-motion device to insure the discontinuous but regular motion of the film strip through the camera (at first, at the rate of forty frames per second, but ultimately, at sixteen and twenty-four frames per second for silent and sound film respectively), and 2) a perforated celluloid film strip (initially consisting of four sprocket-holes on each side of each frame on a one-and-a-half-inch-wide strip). The former permits the unexposed film strip in its rapid transit through the camera to be stopped for a fraction of a second (one-fortieth, one-sixteenth, one-twenty-fourth, etc.) before the lens while the shutter opens to *admit* light from the photographed object and expose the individual frames. In projection, the process is exactly reversed: each frame, now developed, is held intermittently before the projection lamp while the shutter opens to *emit* light through the lens and project the film image onto the screen. Without a stop-motion device in both camera and projector the film image would blur. The synchronization of film strip and shutter (which insures the exact regularity of this discontinuous movement) and the synchronization of the camera and projector is accomplished by means of the regular perforations in the film strip which a system of clawed gears pulls through both machines.

But Edison was not interested in projection. He mistakenly believed that the future of moving pictures lay in individual exhibition, so he commissioned Dickson to perfect the small viewing machine he had already designed for private use in the laboratory. The first moving pictures recorded in the Kinetograph were viewed by the public individually through the magnified lens of a box-like peep-show machine in which a continuous forty- to fifty-foot film loop ran on spools between an electric lamp and a shutter. This device was dubbed the Kinetoscope. True to Edison's original intention, Dickson had designed both viewer and camera so that sound and image could be synchronized and recorded simultaneously. Only a very few Kinetoscope films (called "kinetophones") were

---

* As often happened, Edison took intellectual credit for his employee's work after it had proved successful, and for decades he allowed himself to be eulogized as the "inventor of the motion pictures." The film historian Gordon Hendricks restored Dickson to his rightful creative place with *The Edison Motion Picture Myth* (Berkeley: University of California Press, 1961), and no one has since doubted Dickson's crucial role in the development of the Kinetograph. For his own account, see W. K. L. Dickson and Antonia Dickson, *History of the Kinetograph, Kinetoscope, and Kinetophonograph* (New York: Albert Bunn, 1895; reprinted, New York, Arno Press, 1970).

† Edison's faith in electricity notwithstanding, hand-cranked cameras proved the most popular and efficient of the silent era, since their operators could vary the speed of the film strip and rewind it at will to create special effects such as dissolves (the simultaneous fading out of one image and fading in of another). Hand-cranked cameras were also much lighter and more reliable than their electric counterparts.

made with sound, however, and a few years later, when speculative emphasis shifted to projection, the reproduction of sound became technically infeasible because there was as yet no means of amplifying it for a large audience. (It would remain so until amplification and recording technologies were invented in the Bell Laboratories early in the twentieth century.) Edison applied for patents on his new machines in 1891 but had so little faith in their ability to turn a profit that he decided against paying the extra $150 to secure an international copyright. When patents were granted in 1893, Edison began to market Kinetoscopes through a company established by Norman C. Raff and Frank R. Gammon for $250 to $300 apiece (later models brought as much as $500), and the Edison Corporation went into the film-making business by establishing its own Kinetograph studio at West Orange, New Jersey.*

MOTION PICTURES

On April 14, 1894, a Canadian entrepreneur named Andrew Holland opened the first Kinetoscope parlor in a converted shoe store at 1155 Broadway, in New York City. Holland charged twenty-five cents per person for access to a row of five Edison peep-show viewers,† each of which contained a single film loop shot with the Kinetograph, and he became the first man in history to make a living from the movies. Others followed his lead, and soon Kinetoscope parlors were opened across the country, all supplied with fifty-foot shorts produced for them exclusively by the Edison Corporation's West Orange studio at the rate of ten to fifteen dollars outright per print. This first motion picture studio had been constructed by Dickson in 1893 for just over six hundred dollars; it was an unusual edifice, to say the least. Called the "Black Maria" (after contemporary slang for what was later known as a "paddy-wagon") because it was covered with protective tar-paper strips, Dickson's studio was a single room measuring about twenty-five by thirty feet. A section of its roof could be opened to admit the sunlight—for decades the cinema's only effective lighting source—and the whole building could be rotated on a circular track to follow the sun's course across the sky. Here, from 1893 to 1894, Dickson was the producer, director, and cameraman for hundreds of brief films distributed by the Edison Corporation to the Kinetoscope parlors.

These first films seem extremely primitive today in both content and form. The fifty-foot maximum format (approximately sixteen seconds at a speed of forty frames per second; sixty at the later standard rate of sixteen) militated strongly against the construction of narratives but was eminently suitable for recording quick vaudeville turns, slapstick comedy

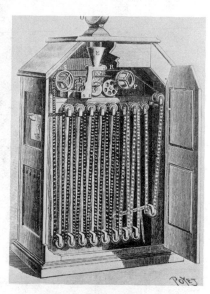

1.8 The Edison Kinetoscope.

1.9 Andrew Holland's Kinetoscope parlor.

1.10 The "Black Maria."

---

* For a more detailed account in the context of Edison's whole career as an inventor and entrepreneur, see Robert Conot, *A Streak of Luck: The Life and Legend of Thomas Alva Edison* (New York, 1979), pp. 320–33.

† The admission price fell quickly to ten and then to five cents as the novelty of the Kinetoscope wore off. In 1894, twenty-five cents was a skilled worker's hourly wage.

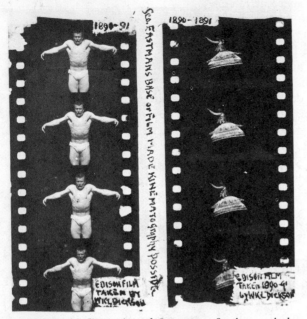

1.11 Original film strips of Strongman Sandow and the dancer Carmencita shot in the Black Maria, 1894. The handwriting and (inaccurate) dating are Dickson's. Reproduced to scale.

1.12 Typical Vitascope fare: *Parisian Dance* and *Black Diamond Express No. 1* (both 1897).

1.13 One of the most popular films made in the Black Maria, *Corbett and Courtney Before the Kinetograph* (1894).

1.14 A contemporary drawing (c. 1894) of a motion picture being made in the Black Maria, showing the bulk and awkwardness of the Kinetograph.

skits, and other kinds of brief performance. Some characteristic titles are *Fred Ott's Sneeze* (the first motion picture ever made in the Kinetograph, which depicts an Edison Laboratory mechanic sneezing), *Chinese Laundry, The Gaiety Girls Dancing, Trained Bears, Blacksmith, Dentist Scene, Bucking Broncos,* and *Highland Dance.* Taken together, the earliest Kinetoscope shorts preserve a series of standard theatrical routines whose only requisite content is motion. Structurally, the films are even cruder, consisting of continuous, unedited footage of what occurred before the lens of Dickson's stationary camera. This stasis was partially the result of technological limitations—especially the small enclosure of the Black Maria studio and the cumbersomeness of the Kinetograph, which resembled a small icebox in shape and size and initially weighed over five hundred pounds. But it was also the result of a natural ignorance of the ways in which the cinema machines might be used. The first impulse was simply to turn the camera on some interesting subject, staged or real, and let it run. So in terms of structure the earliest films, like Edison's shorts and those of his Continental counterparts the Lumière brothers, are simply brief recordings of entertaining or amusing subjects in which the camera was made to obey the laws of empirical reality. That is, it was treated as an unblinking human eye, and there was no concept of editing because reality cannot be edited by the human eye. At this point in the history of film, the camera was never permitted to record more than could be seen by a single individual standing in one fixed spot and focusing on a single event for a given length of time.

PROJECTION: EUROPE AND AMERICA

Before the invention of the Kinetograph, experimental interest had centered on the picture-recording device, with the picture-viewing device coming as an afterthought if it was thought of at all. But when it became clear to the industrial nations of the Western world in 1889 that the recording of motion pictures was a viable proposition, the search for an effective camera merged with the search for an equally effective projector, and Edison was left far behind. The basic requirements of projection engineering were 1) the enlargement of the images for simultaneous viewing by large groups and 2) a means of ensuring the regular but intermittent motion of the developed film strip as it passed between the projection lamp and the shutter (which would correspond with the discontinuous movement of the strip through the camera). The first requirement was easily and rapidly met by applying the principle of magic-lantern projection to film; the second proved more difficult but was eventually fulfilled by a variety of cams, shutters, and gears—and ultimately by the Maltese-cross system used in most projectors today. This system was perfected by the German film pioneer Oskar Messter (see Chapter 4); as indicated by the diagram, it has two basic parts: a) a gear in the shape of a Maltese cross connected directly to the sprocket wheels which pull the film through the projector, and b) a circular disk attached to the projector's drive mechanism which carries a metal pin at its outer edge.

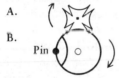

A.

B.

Pin

The disk rotates continuously and the pin is so located that it enters one slot of the cross per cycle and propels it through a quarter of a revolution; but when the disk makes contact again with the edge of the cross itself, the gear is tightly locked until the pin rotates around to the next slot. This ensures the regular stop-and-go motion of the film strip through the projector. *

Many of the people credited with having perfected the first workable projectors through these means left no concrete proof of their endeavors. The English inventor William Friese-Green (1855–1921) is supposed to have invented a combined camera and projector in 1887, but no evidence of successful projection has survived. Similarly, a French scientist named Louis Aimé Augustin Le Prince (1842–1890?) patented a camera-projector in 1888 and apparently did project moving pictures for French government officials at the Paris Opera in 1890, but he disappeared two months later and was never heard from again. Finally, an American living in France, Jean Aimé Leroy (1854–1937?), is known to have

---

* Today, the Maltese cross appears as the imprimatur of the AFL-CIO in the credits of every American film produced with union labor.

1.15 The Lumière Cinématographe in operation, c. 1895.

1.16 *La sortie des ouvriers de l'usine Lumière* (Lumières, 1895).

1.17 *L'arroseur arrosée* (Lumières, 1895).

projected Edison Kinetoscope shorts commercially in Paris in 1893–94, but he too dropped from sight before his machine became generally known. It was actually the year 1895 which witnessed the most significant developments in projection technology, and these occurred almost simultaneously in every country in Western Europe, and in the United States. Ironically, the majority of projection devices brought forth in that year were modeled (quite legally and ethically, since there was no European copyright) upon the Edison Kinetograph and Kinetoscope.

By far the most important of these devices was perfected by two brothers, Auguste and Louis Lumière (1862–1954; 1864–1948), who operated a factory for the manufacture of photographic equipment in Lyon, France (and whose family name was, appropriately, the French word for "light"). After a thorough study of the workings of the Edison machines, the Lumières invented a similar apparatus which could serve as camera, projector, and film printer and which was finally patented as the Cinématographe, thus coining the term which attaches to the medium of film to this day.* (It is generally acknowledged today that only the youngest Lumière, Louis, was responsible for the actual design and construction of the machine.) The Cinématographe was built to run at a speed of sixteen frames per second and established the standard for silent film.† On March 22, 1895, the Lumière brothers projected their first film to a private audience in Paris. Many film historians designate *La sortie des ouvriers de l'usine Lumière (Workers Leaving the Lumière Factory)* as the world's first moving picture;‡ certainly this was the first effective theatrical projection of a film made specifically for that purpose. On December 28, 1895, the Lumières rented a basement room in the Grand Café, on the Boulevard des Capucines in Paris, to project a program of about ten films for the first time to a paying audience. Some of the titles from that program were *L'arrivé d'un train en gare (Arrival of a Train at*

---

* One distinct advantage of the Cinématographe was its portability. Whereas the Kinetograph was battery-driven and weighed several hundred pounds, the hand-cranked Lumière machine weighed just under sixteen. This fact and the Cinématographe's treble function as camera, projector, and printer freed it from the studio confinement of the Kinetograph and enabled Lumière cameramen to travel all over the world to film "local *actualitè.*" See Robert C. Allen, "Vitascope/Cinématographe: Initial Patterns of American Film Practice," *Journal of the University Film Association,* 31, 2 (Spring 1979), 13–18.

† Sixteen frames per second (fps) was the *intended* standard for silent films, but the speed was hardly universal. As Kevin Brownlow points out in "Silent Film: What Was the Right Speed?" (*Sight and Sound,* 49, 3 [Summer 1980], 164–67), exhibitors would frequently speed up or slow down projection to accommodate their schedules, and cameramen would overcrank or undercrank during shooting for a variety of reasons, including, most prominently, the absence of speed indicators from cameras until well into the twenties. In practice, speeds among and even within silent films could vary by as much as 10 fps, from 14 to 24. (Indeed, several sequences in D. W. Griffith's *The Birth of a Nation* [1914] were so undercranked by Billy Bitzer that they could only be projected at 12 fps.) For practical purposes, then, 16 fps should be thought of as the *average* and not the uniform speed of silent film recording and projection. The motorization of cameras in the late twenties made it possible for sound speed to be internationally standardized at 24 fps.

‡ The oldest known print of *La sortie des ouvriers,* dating from 1895, was discovered beneath the floorboards of a bank building in Perth, Australia, in October 1979. Twelve Lumière films were found in all, including three which had been previously unknown.

a Station), which dramatically marked the beginning of the cinema's long obsession with that particular icon of the Industrial Revolution; *Le répas de bébé* (*Baby's Lunch*), a record of brother Auguste feeding his infant daughter; and *L'arroseur arrosée* (*The Sprinkler Sprinkled*), a bit of slapstick in which a young boy steps on a hose which then squirts a gardener in the face when he peers at the nozzle. *L'arrivé* was a visual tour de force, and audiences are said to have stampeded at the sight of the locomotive barreling toward them from a distant prospect into the foreground on the screen. Due to its relative lightness, the Cinématographe could be taken out of doors more easily than the Kinetograph, and for this reason the early Lumière films have a much higher documentary content than do Edison's (the Lumières called their films *"actualités,"* or documentary views).* Structurally, however, the Lumière and Edison films are precisely the same—the camera and point of view are static and the action continuous from beginning to end, as if editing "reality" was unthinkable to their makers.

Admission to the Lumière program was one franc per customer, and the receipts for the first day totaled only thirty-five francs. But within a month the Cinématographe showings were earning an average of seven thousand francs a week, and motion pictures had become, overnight, an extremely lucrative commercial enterprise. The most important aspect of the Cinématographe projections, however, was the fact that they marked the end of the period of technological experimentation which began with Muybridge's series photography in 1872: the two machines upon which the cinema is founded had been perfected at last. In Germany, the Skladanowsky brothers, Max and Émile (1863–1939; 1859–1945) developed almost simultaneously with the Lumières a projector for celluloid film strips called the "Bioskop" or Bioscope (a common term for many early cameras and projectors) and projected films of their own making in a public performance at the Berlin Wintergarten on November 1, 1895. Projection reached England immediately thereafter, in 1896, when a manufacturer of scientific instruments named Robert W. Paul (1869–1943) patented the Theatrograph (later renamed the Animatographe), a projector based on the Kinetoscope—although the Lumière Cinématographe was soon to capture both the British and the Continental markets.

When Edison became aware of the vastly promising financial future of projection through the European success of the Cinématographe, and aware as well of a substantial decrease in the sales of his Kinetoscope viewers (all told, just over nine hundred of them were sold), he commissioned the invention of a projection device in the summer of 1895. In September of that year, however, Edison learned that an amateur inventor named Thomas Armat (1866–1948) had projected a program of Kinetograph shorts at the Cotton States Exposition in Atlanta, Georgia, with an electrically powered machine which incorporated a stop-motion

1.18 *L'arrivé d'un train en gare* (Lumières, 1895).

1.19 A poster advertising an early Cinématographe projection, c. 1895.

---

* By the turn of the century, both firms were competing heatedly for both markets, Edison turning his attention to Lumière-like *actualités* on the American subcontinent and the Lumières shooting studio-bound domestic stage performances.

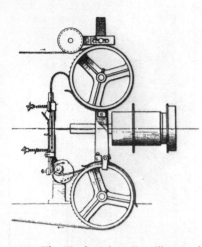

1.20 The "Latham loop," as illustrated in the Armat patent application, 1901.

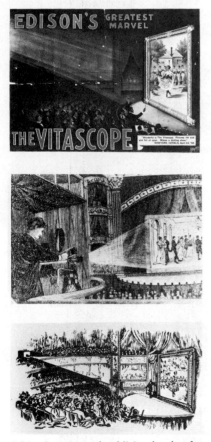

1.21 A poster and publicity sketches for an Edison Vitagraph projection in a music hall, c. 1896.

mechanism superior to anything then under patent.* Armat's projector also made the first practical use of a small but extremely important device discovered earlier in the year by the Latham brothers, Georgia-born entrepreneurs who formed the Kinetoscope Exhibition Company in New York City to make motion pictures of prizefights and other sporting events; this device merits special consideration here.

One of the chief practical problems of early projection was that of film breakage. At lengths of greater than fifty to one hundred feet, the inertia of the take-up reel would frequently cause the film strip to tear or snap in the projector. The Lathams had discovered that by placing a small loop in the film strip just above and below the projection lens, and maintaining it with an extra set of sprockets, the stress could be redistributed in such a manner as to permit films of greater length in the magazine. This relatively simple technological innovation had far-reaching aesthetic consequences, since without it the cinema could never have evolved as an art form. Obviously, there can be very little creative potential in a medium whose basic form is the one-minute short subject. The "Latham loop" (named for its inventors, Greg and Otway Latham, and also called the "American loop") is yet another dramatic example of the way in which technology and art are inextricably wed in cinema. Here, as so often in film history, the meeting of a rather minor technological exigency created a whole new aesthetic dimension for the medium.

Edison was so impressed with the features of Armat's machine that he abandoned his own research project and bought the apparatus outright under a scandalous agreement whereby Edison would himself manufacture the machine and take full credit for its invention while Armat would be allowed a small plate on the back crediting him with "design." Edison dubbed the new machine the Vitascope and gave it its first public exhibition on April 23, 1896, at the popular Koster and Bials Music Hall in New York City, where it received top billing as "Edison's latest marvel." Some representative titles from the program of twelve short films were *Sea Waves; Umbrella Dance* (apparently the first color-tinted print); *The Barber Shop; A Boxing Bout; Venice—Showing Gondolas; Kaiser Wilhelm—Reviewing His Troops; Skirt Dance;* and *The Bar Room.* Like their predecessors, Edison's Vitascope films (some of which had originally been produced for the Kinetoscope, some of which had been illegally copied from the Lumières) offered nothing more than unmediated glimpses of real action as it unfolded before the camera from a single point of view; but these rather crude "living pictures," as they were soon labeled, proved novel and engaging enough to satisfy the public's taste for several years to come. After all, the world had never seen their like before.

The Vitascope and Cinématographe projections mark the culmination of the cinema's prehistory. By 1896, all the basic technological principles of film recording and projection had been discovered and incorporated

---

* An improved version of the Phantascope, developed with Charles Francis Jenkins (1867–1934) in 1894. (The Kinetoscope, unlike the Kinetograph, ran continuously rather than intermittently.)

into existing machines—machines which, with certain obvious exceptions like the introduction of light-sensitive sound, have remained essentially unchanged from that day to this. Conversely, the history of cinema as an art form begins with these events, for if our understanding of the machines was sophisticated, knowledge of how to use them was primitive indeed. In fact, the kind of documentary recording practiced by Edison and the Lumières was to become the mainstream tendency of the cinema until the turn of the century because there was as yet no notion that the camera might be used to tell a story—i.e., to *create* a narrative reality rather than simply *record* some real or staged event which occurred before its lens. It is true that during this period films were able to grow in length to one thousand feet, or approximately sixteen minutes, thanks to the Latham device, but they remained static in terms of form until their narrative dimension was discovered and articulated on the screen. Nevertheless, by the late 1890's cinema was already on its way toward becoming a mass medium with the then unimaginable power to communicate without print or speech.

THE EVOLUTION OF NARRATIVE: GEORGES MÉLIÈS

The man usually given credit for discovering the narrative potential of film is Georges Méliès (1861–1938), a professional magician who owned and operated the Théâtre Robert-Houdin in Paris. Méliès had been using magic-lantern projections in his conjuring acts for years, and when he attended the first Cinématographe programs in 1895 he immediately recognized the vast illusionist possibilities of the "living pictures."* Accordingly, in early 1896 he attempted to buy a Cinématographe from the Lumières for ten thousand francs but was promptly refused, since the brothers recognized potential competition when they saw it. Méliès, however, who had also been a mechanic, an actor, an illustrator, a photographer, and a stage designer, was not easily discouraged. Several months later, he bought an Animatographe projector from the English inventor Robert W. Paul and simply reversed its mechanical principle to design his own camera, which was constructed for him by the instrument-maker Lucien Korsten. By April 1896, the Théâtre Robert-Houdin had become the first public film theater in the world and Méliès the cinema's first independent producer-director. In time, he would become its first important narrative artist as well, but not before he had done some apprentice work in the manner of the Lumières and Edison by filming a series of *actualités,* comic episodes, and staged conjurer's tricks for projection in his theater.

---

* For a detailed account of the reciprocal relationship between professional magic shows and primitive cinema, see Erik Barnouw, "The Magician and the Movies," Parts I and II, *American Film,* April and May 1978. See also Katherine Singer Kovács, "Georges Méliès and the *Feérie," Cinema Journal,* 16, 1 (Fall 1976), 1–13.

One afternoon in the fall of 1896, while Méliès was filming a Parisian street scene, his camera jammed in the process of recording an omnibus as it emerged from a tunnel. When he got the machine working again, a funeral hearse had replaced the omnibus, so that in projection the omnibus seemed to change into the hearse.* By this accident, Méliès came to recognize the possibilities for the manipulation of real time and real space inherent in the editing of exposed film. He had discovered that film need not obey the laws of empirical reality, as his predecessors had supposed, because film was in some sense a separate reality with structural laws of its own. Unfortunately, Méliès put his discovery to only limited use. Although he went on to make hundreds of delightful narrative films, his model for them was the narrative mode of the legitimate theater since it was what he knew best. That is, he conceived all of his films in terms of dramatic *scenes* played out from beginning to end rather than in terms of *shots,* or individual visual perspectives on a scene; the only editing, therefore, aside from that used in optical illusions of disappearance and conversion, occurs *between* scenes rather than *within* them. The scenes themselves are composed of single shots taken with a motionless camera from a fixed point of view, that of a theater spectator sitting in the orchestra center aisle with an excellent eye-level view of the action; and the actors move across the film frame from left to right and right to left as if it were the proscenium arch† of a stage. A viewer experiences no more narrative manipulation within a Méliès film than in watching a stage play of the same action; one sees a significant amount of stage illusion, of course, but changes in time and space coincide precisely with changes in scene, and the narrative point of view is rigidly static.

Méliès was nevertheless the cinema's first narrative artist. By adapting certain techniques of still photography, theater spectacle, and magic lantern projection to the linear medium of the film strip, he innovated significant narrative devices like the fade-in (the gradual appearance of an image as the screen becomes light), the fade-out (the gradual disappearance of an image as the screen becomes dark), the overlapping, or "lap," dissolve (the simultaneous fading-out of one image and fading-in of another, accomplished through superimposition and used to indicate narrative transitions or the passage of time), and stop-motion photography (the technique whereby film is shot a frame at a time rather than continuously, making possible all forms of animation and many types of special effects). To put his discoveries into effect, Méliès, in late 1896, organized the Star Film Company, and, by the spring of 1897, he had constructed a small production studio on the grounds of his house in the Paris suburb

1.22 The interior of Méliès' studio at Montreuil.

* According to Paul Hammond, in his authoritative study *Marvelous Méliès* (London: Gordon Fraser, 1974), this frequently recounted incident derives from Méliès' notoriously unreliable *Mes mémoires* (Rome, 1938) and may well be apocryphal (p. 34). But if the tale was fabricated, it at least suggests that Méliès was consciously aware of his own inventiveness.

† In a theater, the part of the stage in front of the curtain (sometimes including the curtain). The proscenium provides a static framing device for the action on the stage and marks the borders between stage illusion and the real world.

of Montreuil. The building measured fifty-five by twenty feet and was glass-enclosed like a greenhouse to admit maximum sunlight, the cinema's only effective lighting source until the advent of mercury-vapor lamps in 1908. Here Méliès produced, directed, photographed, and acted in some five hundred films* between 1897 and 1913, when, like so many other film pioneers, he was forced out of business by his competitors (principally Charles Pathé; see Chapter 2) because he had lost touch with the rapid development of both the medium and the industry. Representative titles, in translation, are *The Cabinet of Mephistopheles* (1897), *Cinderella* (1899), *The Man with the India-Rubber Head* (1901), *A Trip to the Moon* (1902), *The Palace of the Arabian Nights* (1905), *Twenty Thousand Leagues Under the Sea* (1907), and *The Conquest of the Pole* (1912). Although he also made many films based on historical and contemporary events (*actualités reconstituées,* or "reconstructed newsreels," he called them), Méliès' most memorable productions concern the fantastic and bizarre and are acted out before lush, phantasmagoric backgrounds which he himself designed and painted. Many were released in color, since at the height of his very substantial success Méliès employed twenty-one women at the studio of Madame Tuillier to hand-tint his films individually, frame by frame (a practice apparently initiated by Edison for the first Vitascope projection and continued with some regularity throughout the early silent period). Although Méliès went bankrupt in 1923 due to his ruin at the hands of Pathé Frères and other rivals, his films had immense popular appeal at the turn of the century. Indeed, by 1902 Star Film had become one of the world's largest suppliers of motion pictures and had nearly driven the Lumières out of production.

By far the most successful and influential film Méliès made at Montreuil was *Le voyage dans la lune* (*A Trip to the Moon*). Produced in 1902, this film achieved nearly international distribution within a year of its production, albeit as much through piracy as through legitimate means.† *Le voyage dans la lune,* loosely adapted by Méliès from the Jules Verne novel of the same title, was 825 feet long (a little under fourteen

---

* Fewer than 140 of these survive today. Four hundred films were requisitioned by agents of the French army in 1917 and melted down to produce a chemical necessary in the manufacture of boot-heels. When he went bankrupt in the summer of 1923, Méliès himself destroyed a batch of negatives and sold his own stock of prints by the kilo to a second-hand film dealer.

† These were maverick times for the small but burgeoning film industry. Where international copyrights had been secured, they were frequently not enforced, and patents on equipment were ignored by almost everyone. Despite massive counterfeiting, however, *A Trip to the Moon* was so popular that Méliès made a fortune during its first year of distribution—a fact explained by the circumstance that films were not leased to exhibitors but sold to them outright until the advent of the first permanent theaters, the nickelodeons (see below).

To prevent further piracy and to promote his films abroad, Méliès established an American branch of Star Film in New York in 1903 under the management of his older brother Gaston (1852–1915). Gaston founded his own production company and joined the Edison Patents Trust (see Chapter 2) in 1908; between 1909 and 1913 he produced over 150 one-reel films—most of them Westerns and war "epics"—at the Star Film Ranch in San Antonio, Texas, and at Santa Paula, California, on the Pacific coast. Before going out of

minutes at standard silent speed), or three times the average length of the contemporary Edison and Lumière products (one of Méliès' achievements was increasing the standard length of fiction films). Utterly characteristic of both the strengths and weaknesses of Méliès' theatrical narrative mode, the film is composed of thirty separate scenes,* which he appropriately called *"tableaux,"* all photographed from the same angle and connected by means of lap dissolves. The scenes are arranged in precise chronological sequence, as follows:

1. The scientific congress at the Astronomic Club.
2. The planning of the trip itself.
3. The construction of the projectile in the workshop.
4. The casting of the cannon in the foundry.
5. The boarding of the projectile by the astronomers.
6. The loading of the cannon (complete with female "Marines" in short pants and tights).
7. The firing of the cannon.
8. The flight of the projectile through space.
9. The landing in the eye of the moon.
10. The earth viewed from the moon.
11. A view of the moon's topography.
12. The astronomers' dream (visions of the Pleiades and Zodiac signs).
13. A snowstorm on the moon.
14. The astronomers' descent into a crater.
15. A grotto of giant mushrooms in the interior of the moon.
16. Encounter with the moon creatures, or Selenites (acrobats from the Folies-Bergère).
17. The astronomers taken prisoner.
18. The astronomers brought before the King of the Moon and his Selenite army.
19. The astronomers' escape.
20. The Selenites' pursuit.
21. The astronomers' departure in the projectile.
22. The projectile falling vertically through space.
23. The projectile splashing into the sea.
24. The projectile at the bottom of the ocean.
25. The rescue and return to land.
26. The astronomers' triumphal return.
27. The decoration of the heroes.
28. Procession of "Marines."
29. The erection of the commemorative statue.
30. Public rejoicing.[1]

business in 1913, Gaston Méliès employed as directors both Wallace C. McCutcheon, the son of Biograph's George "Old Man" McCutcheon (see Chapter 3), and Francis Ford, John Ford's eldest brother, who later convinced him to go into the motion picture business (see Chapter 8). For more, see Patrick McInroy, "The American Méliès," *Sight and Sound,* 48, 4 (Autumn 1979), 250–54.

* Most circulating prints today have fewer, but they generally preserve the original sequence.

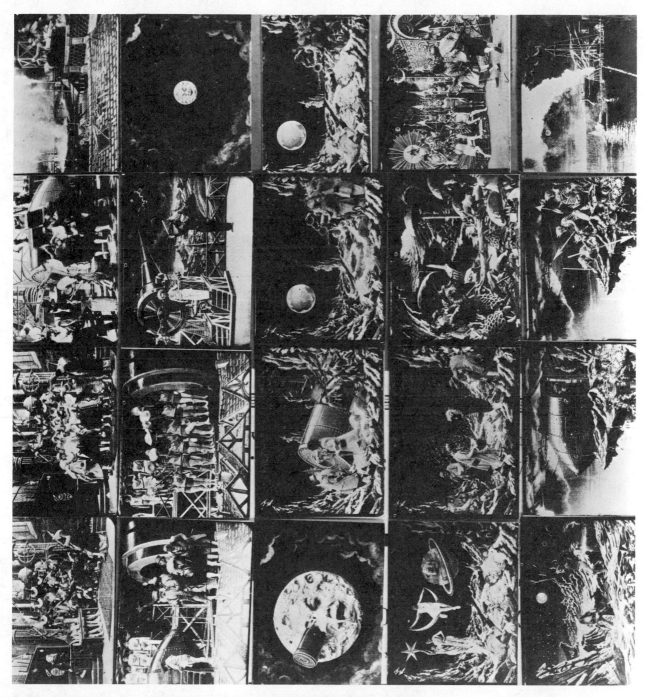

1.23   Twenty of the original *tableaux* from *Le voyage dans la lune* (Georges Méliès, 1902).

As the description suggests, the whole film very much resembles a photographed stage play, save for the inclusion of some of the optical tricks which were a Méliès trademark. Some of these, such as the disappearance of the Selenites in a puff of smoke when they are struck by the astronomers' umbrellas, were accomplished cinematically, through the use of stop-motion photography, but are not terribly important in terms of narrative. Many others, however, the product of nineteenth-century stage illusion pure and simple, serve to illustrate how very far Méliès really was from tapping the full potential of the medium. The classic example of Méliès' lack of vision in this respect is that when he wished to show the astronomers' projectile crashing dramatically into the face of the moon (shot 9), he moved the papier-mâché moon into the lens of the camera on a dolly rather than moving the camera into the moon.

Méliès, in fact, never moved his camera once in any of his more than five hundred films. Neither did he alternate the point of view within scenes or even between them by changing camera angles. His films were, as he once called them, "artificially arranged scenes," or "moving *tableaux*," and his camera functioned as the inert eye of a theater spectator from the beginning to the end of his career. Yet Méliès discovered, if he did not exploit, the enormous potential inherent in the editing of exposed film, and through his influence on contemporary film-makers he pointed the cinema well on its way toward becoming an essentially narrative rather than a documentary medium, as Edison and Lumière cameramen had originally conceived it. Furthermore, Méliès was an artist of unique and individual talent, and his films endure every bit as much for their distinctive imaginative power as for their contributions to cinematic form. He had stumbled onto the narrative dimensions of the cinema very much as cinema had stumbled into being—arbitrarily, almost by accident—and he had appropriated a conventional and unimaginative narrative model because it was what he knew best; yet those who came after him would understand. Charlie Chaplin called him "the alchemist of light," but D. W. Griffith put it best when he said of Méliès at the end of his own monumental career in 1932, "I owe him everything."*

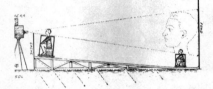

1.24 A drawing (c. 1896) illustrating the way in which Méliès simulated camera movement in his films.

THE DISCOVERY OF THE SHOT: EDWIN S. PORTER

While Méliès was leading the French film to international prominence with his stylish but static narratives, an American film-maker named Edwin S. Porter (1870–1941) was carrying Méliès' discovery of the cinema's narrative potential to its logical conclusion. Porter began his career

---

* The contemporary avant-garde also owes him a considerable debt. The American experimentalist Stan Brakhage (b. 1933), for example, has written, "I took my first senses of the individual frame life of a film from Méliès" (*Art Forum,* January 1973, p. 76). For a brilliant appreciation and revaluation of this aspect of Méliès' singular artistry, see Paul Hammond's *Marvelous Méliès,* cited above.

as a Vitascope projectionist and mechanic for the Edison Corporation in 1896, but by 1900 he had risen to become cameraman, then director, and finally production head at the new Edison skylight studio on East Twenty-first Street, in New York City. His first films were brief skits and *actualités,* such as *Kansas City Saloon Smashers* (1901) and *New York City in a Blizzard* (1901), which simply continued the Edison and Lumière tradition. Sometime after 1901, however, Porter encountered the films of Méliès and those of the two British pioneers G. A. Smith (1864–1959) and James Williamson (1855–1933), who had been experimenting with the use of interpolated close-ups in their studio at Brighton.

Smith and Williamson were the principal members of the "Brighton school" of film-makers, which flourished in England from 1900 to 1908 and which some film historians (notably Georges Sadoul, Kenneth Macgowan,[2] and Barry Salt) have credited with making major contributions to cinematic narrative technique. The claim is difficult to substantiate since few of the films in question have come down to us, but surviving prints clearly indicate that Smith experimented with the systematic insertion of close-ups.[*] It also seems likely that in several films—*Attack on a Chinese Mission Station* (1900), *Stop Thief!* (1901), and *Fire!* (1901)—Williamson practiced a crude form of parallel editing by cutting from an exterior shot of a building to an interior shot and then back again to the exterior. The standard product of the Brighton school at this point, however, was the fantastic theatrical narrative in the Méliès vein, and it is impossible to state with any accuracy which of the Brighton films Porter might have seen. Yet it is clear that what influence did exist between the two was mutual, since several later productions of the Brighton school were plainly in debt to the continuity editing of Porter's *The Great Train Robbery* (1903)—especially Cecil Hepworth's chase film *Rescued by Rover* (1905), which many critics feel to be the most skillfully edited film produced before Griffith.[†]

No one can state with certainty just what and how much Porter imbibed from either source, but it was enough, combined with his own gifts, to make him the next major link in the chain between the animated photographs of Edison-Lumière and the fully elaborated cinematic

---

[*] In 1978 the International Federation of Film Archives (FIAF, Brussels), at its annual conference at Brighton, made the first complete survey of surviving films from a single period. It was concluded that some fifteen hundred films made between 1900 and 1906 have been preserved and that at least three times that number have been lost.

[†] Barry Salt claims that Porter's *The Life of an American Fireman* (1903) is an imitation of Williamson's *Fire!* (1901), which in turn was modeled on late-nineteenth-century narrative lantern slide sequences (fire was a very popular subject of the early screen). He also suggests that Porter's *The Great Train Robbery* (1903) was based on the Sheffield Photographic Company's *Daring Daylight Robbery* (1903). But as Charles Musser points out in his painstakingly researched "The Early Cinema of Edwin Porter" (*Cinema Journal,* 19, 1 [Fall 1979], 1–38), ". . . Porter's borrowings tended towards the pro-filmic elements of set construction and gesture (which were themselves highly conventionalized and obviously did not originate with Williamson) rather than specifically cinematic strategies of decoupage" (p. 28). See Barry Salt, "Film Form, 1900–1906," *Sight and Sound,* 47, 3 (Summer 1978), 148–53. See also Martin Sopocy, "A Narrated Cinema: The Pioneer Story Films of James A. Williamson, *Cinema Journal,* 28, 1 (Fall 1978), 1–20.

syntax of Griffith.* Porter's first important narrative film—and one of the first sustained narrative films made in the United States †—was *The Life of an American Fireman,* produced in late 1902 and released in January 1903. Impressed with Méliès' and the Brighton directors' technique of building films up out of several separate sequences, Porter decided to assemble a documentary-like narrative about the activities of a fire engine company out of stock footage (i.e., film which had already been shot and printed) from the Edison archives. In the process, Porter hit upon the idea of combining this "found" footage with staged scenes of a dramatic rescue from a burning building‡ and came up with a uniquely cinematic form: a fiction constructed from recordings of empirically real events (which is, of course, a good definition of cinema itself). About the sequencing of these events, however, there is much controversy. On the basis of the standard print distributed by the Museum of Modern Art Department of Film, it was long thought that in the final sequence of the film Porter intercut, or cut together, interior shots of a blazing room with exterior shots of a fireman climbing a ladder to rescue its occupants, creating a radically innovative effect—the illusion of separate but simultaneous and parallel actions, which was to become the basic structural element of cinematic narrative. *The Life of an American Fireman* was a lost film until 1944, when the Museum of Modern Art acquired a 35mm nitrate print from Pathé News, Inc. Although the Museum has never claimed that this print, known today as the "Cross-Cut Version," was the original, it conforms in principle to the editing continuity of the original as it has been described by American film historians from Terry Ramsaye (*A Million and One Nights* [1926]) through Lewis Jacobs (*The Rise of the American Film* [1939]) and beyond. Ramsaye's description was based either on memory or on Porter's own account of the film (more recently set forth by Budd Schulberg in *Variety,* May 9, 1979). Jacobs' description was based on a combination of Ramsaye's version, the *Edison Catalogue* description, and a sequence of

---

* The point should be made that film narrative evolved *gradually* and *internationally* during the medium's first two decades, 1889–1909. But the very clear succession of influence that has been outlined above can be demonstrated empirically, whereas the influence of random innovations by anonymous film-makers cannot, especially given the 1:4 survival ratio for prints from the period. Porter's own sense of things at least was clear. In a newspaper interview some years after *The Life of an American Fireman,* he said: "From laboratory examination of some of the popular films of the French pioneer director, George Méliès—trick films like 'A Trip to the Moon'—I came to the conclusion that a picture telling a story in continuity form might draw the customers back to the theatres and set to work in this direction" (quoted in Musser, p. 25).

† Musser (above) argues for the priority of Porter's own *Jack and the Beanstalk,* released July 1902 (p. 25).

‡ From the *Newark News,* November 15, 1902: "TO SAVE WOMAN AND PUT OUT FIRE. And While East Orange Firemen Perform Kinetoscope [sic] Machine Will Record Scene. There will be a fire on Rhode Island Avenue, East Orange, this afternoon, or at least the East Orange firemen will be called out and go through the motions of extinguishing a fire and rescuing a woman from the upper story of a house for the benefit of the Edison Kinetoscope Company, which will have one of its chain-lightning cameras there to reproduce the scene" (Musser, p. 28).

1.25 A possible editing sequence of Porter's *The Life of an American Fireman* (1902).

production stills made for copyright purposes by the Edison Company, which seem to suggest intercutting at the film's climax.

The Cross-Cut Version, which has wide circulation, is 378 feet long (just over six minutes at standard silent speed) and consists of twenty separate* shots linked together by dissolves or straight cuts as follows:

1. The fire chief asleep, dreaming of his wife and child, who appear in a circular vignette at the upper-right-hand corner of the screen (Porter may have invented this device, later called the "dream balloon").

2. Close-up of a fire-alarm box and an anonymous hand pulling its lever (probably the first close-up in American cinema to be completely integrated with its narrative context). All other shots in the film are long shots.

3. Interior of the firemen's dormitory, with the men waking up, dressing, and sliding down the pole (apparently stock footage, since this scene doesn't match what follows, which was staged).

4. Interior ground floor of the firehouse, actually an outdoor set, with the pole in the center upon which no one has yet appeared; workers harness the horses to the engines, and the firemen finally slide down the pole from above at the conclusion of the scene.

5. Exterior of the firehouse as the doors are flung open and the engines charge out (stock footage as well, apparently, since it's snowing in this scene but nowhere else in the film).

6. Suburban street scene: eight engines rush past the camera from right to left, passing a crowd of bystanders.

7. Street scene: four engines rush past the camera, which pans (moves horizontally on its vertical axis) slightly to follow the fourth and comes to rest on the front of a burning house.

8. Interior of the house: mother and child in an upstairs room filled with smoke.

9. Exterior of the house: the mother approaches an upstairs window and calls for help.

10. Interior: the woman collapses on a bed.

11. Exterior: a fireman enters the front door.

12. Interior: the same fireman runs into the room through a door at the right and breaks the window (which was open in shots 9 and 11, but closed in 8 and 10).

13. Exterior: firemen on the ground place a ladder against the broken window.

14. Interior: the fireman carries the woman to the ladder, which has appeared at the window.

15. Exterior: the fireman and the woman descend the ladder.

16. Interior: the fireman enters the window by the ladder and picks up the child.

17. Exterior: the woman becomes hysterical.

18. Interior: the fireman exits through the window with the child.

---

* The museum also has a print with five fewer shots of the rescue but intercut in precisely the same sequence

19. Exterior: the fireman descends the ladder with the child and re-unites it with the mother.
20. Interior: firemen enter the room through the window to extinguish the fire with a hose.

By intercutting (or, synonymously, crosscutting) seven shots of an interior with seven shots of an exterior to depict parallel actions occuring simultaneously, Porter seems to have achieved for the first time in motion picture history the unique kind of narrative omniscience which only the cinema among all art forms is capable of sustaining. No other medium permits the rapid alternation of multiple perspectives without destroying point of view.*

In recent years, however, another print of *The Life of an American Fireman* has come to light which is based on the paper print filed for copyright at the Library of Congress by the Edison Company in 1903. This so-called Copyright Version is 400 feet long, and it simply repeats the entire interior sequence (shots 8, 10, 12, 14, 16, 18, and 20) and the entire exterior sequence (shots 9, 11, 13, 15, 17, and 19) continuously without intercutting them at all. Intercutting these sequences, as the Cross-Cut Version does, creates the illusion of simultaneous actions occurring from simultaneously accessible points of view, but merely repeating them from two separately accessible points of view, as does the Copyright Version, serves only to create a confusing situation of visual redundancy. In the first instance, Porter's film becomes a vastly significant cinematic document, rather spectacularly pre-dating by five years Griffith's first use of intercutting in *The Lonely Villa*. In the latter case, *The Life of an American Fireman* is no more cinematic than *A Trip to the Moon*. There is substantial evidence for the priority for both prints, although contemporary opinion seems to favor the Copyright Version.† Like so many other issues of early film history, this one is complicated by the fact that 1) producers sometimes filed prints for copyright with the

---

*There were precedents for parallel editing, or crosscutting, in late-nineteenth-century melodrama, fiction, magic lantern projections, stereopticon slide shows, and newspaper comic strips. See Nicholas A. Vardac, *Stage to Screen* (Cambridge: Harvard University Press, 1949); Alan J. Spiegel, *Fiction and the Camera Eye* (Charlottesville: University of Virginia Press, 1976); John L. Fell, *Film and the Narrative Tradition* (Norman: University of Oklahoma Press, 1975); Burns Hollyman, "Alexander Black's Picture Plays: 1893–1894," *Cinema Journal*, 16, 2 (Spring 1977), 26–33; William C. Darrah, *The World of Stereographs* (Gettysburg, Pa.: W. C. Darrah, 1977); Pierre Couperie et al., *A History of the Comic Strip,* trans. Eileen B. Henessy (New York: Crown, 1968); Windsor McCay, *Little Nemo* (New York: Nostalgia Press, 1972); and Francis Lacassin "The Comic Strip and Film Language" (translated with "Supplementary Notes" by David Kunzle), *Film Quarterly*, 26, 1 (Fall 1972), 11–23.

†For more on the controversy, see Roman Gubern, "David Wark Griffith et l'articulation cinématographique," and Barthélemy Amengual, "*The Life of an American Fireman* et la naissance du montage," *Cahiers de la Cinématheque*, 17 (Christmas 1975); and Charles Musser, "The Early Cinema of Edwin Porter," and André Gaudreault, "Detours in Film Narrative: The Development of Cutting," *Cinema Journal*, 19, 1 (Fall 1979). For an engaging ideological approach both to Porter's films and to the historiography of the primitive period, see Noël Burch, "Porter, or Ambivalence," *Screen*, 19, 4 (Winter 1978–79), 91–105. (A third print of the film, which seems to support the authenticity of the Copyright Version, was found in 1978 but hadn't been dated at the time of publication.)

scenes spliced together in the order in which they had been shot rather than as they were edited for final release, and 2) after 1910 the public demand for films became so great that distributors and pirates would frequently re-edit older films to conform with contemporary tastes and re-distribute them as completely new productions. At the very least, however, *The Life of an American Fireman* brought the narrative methods of Méliès and the Brighton school into the American cinema; Porter's next film was to show how much further beyond them the cinema was capable of going.

There are no disputes about *The Great Train Robbery* (Edison, 1903): it exists in a single authoritative version and is agreed to be Porter's finest achievement. Although it was shot entirely in Paterson, New Jersey, *The Great Train Robbery* was simultaneously the cinema's first Western and, as Kenneth Macgowan has observed,[3] the first film to exploit the violence of armed crime. The most significant thing about the film for us, however, is its editing continuity. Although *The Great Train Robbery* contains no intercutting *within* scenes, Porter cut *between* his scenes without dissolving or fading and—most important—*without playing them out to the end*. In Méliès, and in early Porter for that matter, all scenes are played out to their logical dramatic conclusion and all new scenes are begun in the studied and gradual manner of nineteenth-century theater. There are no ellipses between scenes and no omissions in the action, just as there would and could be none on the legitimate stage. But Porter discovered that a filmmaker could in fact cut away from one scene before it was dramatically or logically complete and simultaneously cut into another after it had already begun. The reputed intercutting of *The Life of an American Fireman* notwithstanding, this was the beginning of a truly cinematic narrative language, because it posited that the basic signifying unit of film—the basic unit of cinematic meaning—was not the *scene*, as in Méliès, and not the continuous unedited film strip, as in the earliest Edison and Lumière shorts, but rather the *shot*, of which, as Griffith would later demonstrate, there may be a virtually limitless number within any given scene.

Written, directed, photographed, and edited by Porter, *The Great Train Robbery* is 740 feet long (a little over twelve minutes at standard silent speed) and consists of fourteen separate *shots*—not scenes—of actions which are themselves dramatically incomplete. These are connected by straight cuts in the following sequence:

1. Interior of the railroad telegraph office: two bandits enter and bind and gag the operator while the moving train, visible through the office window, comes to a halt.
2. Railroad water tower: the other members of the gang board the train secretly as it takes on water.
3. Interior of the mail car with scenery rushing by through an open door; the bandits break in, kill a messenger, seize valuables from a strong box, and leave.
4. Coal tender and interior of the locomotive cab: the bandits kill the

1.26   The editing sequence of Porter's *The Great Train Robbery* (1903).

fireman after a fierce struggle, throw his body off the train, and compel the engineer to stop.

5. Exterior shot of the train coming to a halt and the engineer uncoupling the locomotive.
6. Exterior shot of the train as the bandits force the passengers to line up along the tracks and surrender their valuables; one passenger attempts to escape, runs directly into the camera lens, and is shot in the back.
7. The bandits board the engine and abscond.
8. The bandits stop the engine several miles up the track, get off, and run into the woods as the camera tilts slightly to follow them.
9. The bandits scramble down the side of a hill and across a stream to mount their horses; the camera follows them in a sweeping vertical movement, or panning shot.
10. Interior of the telegraph office: the operator's daughter arrives and unties her father, who then runs out to give the alarm.
11. Interior of a crowded dance hall: a "tenderfoot" is made to "dance," as six-guns are fired at his feet; the telegraph operator arrives and a posse is formed.
12. Shot of the mounted bandits dashing down the face of a hill with the posse in hot pursuit; both groups move rapidly toward the camera; one of the bandits is killed as they approach.
13. Shot of the remaining bandits examining the contents of the stolen mail pouches; the posse approaches stealthily from the background and kills them all in a final shoot-out.
14. Medium close-up (a shot showing its subject from the mid-section up) of the leader of the bandits firing his revolver point blank into the camera (and, thus, the audience), a shot which, according to the Edison Catalogue, "can be used to begin or end the picture."[4]

In addition to cutting away from scenes (or shots) before they were dramatically concluded, *The Great Train Robbery* contained other innovations. Although the interior sequences were shot in the conventional manner of Méliès, the camera placement in many of the exterior sequences was fresh and dynamic. In shot 4, for example, the camera looks down on the action in the engine cab from the coal tender, and in shot 6 an actor moves diagonally across the frame into the camera lens rather than horizontally across it. There is effective use of back projection in shot 1 (the moving train coming to a halt, seen through the telegraph office window) and shot 3 (the landscape rushing past the express car door).* More significant, there are two authentic panning shots—a

---

* Back projection is accomplished in the following manner: The primary action of a scene is shot before a backdrop, all or part of which (for instance, the telegraph office window, the express car doorway) is a translucent screen. Films of moving objects or scenery are projected synchronously onto this screen from *behind* it, so that the camera photographing the primary action also photographs the projection. This has become a standard technique for simulating location scenes and movement, as from a car or horse, and has been used extensively, if not always imperceptibly, by such major directors as Alfred Hitchcock. (Porter may also have achieved his special effects by in-camera matting: blacking out the window and door spaces on the first exposure and then double-exposing his film to imprint the projected sequence. See Raymond Fielding, *The Technique of Special Effects Cinematography* [New York, 1972], and John Brosnan, *Movie Magic: The Story of Special Effects in the Cinema* [New York, 1976]).

rather perfunctory tilt following the bandits as they dismount the engine in shot 8, and an impressively cinematic pan following the sweep of their flight through the woods in shot 9.* Finally, there is a suggestion of parallel editing reminiscent of the Cross-Cut Version of *The Life of an American Fireman* when Porter cuts from the bandits' getaway back to the bound telegraph operator in shot 10.

Nevertheless, *The Great Train Robbery* is not a great film aside from its contributions to the medium. All of the interior scenes are photographed in the stage-like fashion of Méliès, with the actors moving from left to right, or vice versa, across the "proscenium" of the frame, and the actors' gestures themselves are exaggerated and stilted. Furthermore, Porter never uses more than one camera angle or position in any one setting, and, like those of Méliès, most of his shots are long shots showing the actors at full length. On the other hand, by building up a continuity of dramatic action out of thirteen separate shots, not counting the final close-up, Porter had shown that the narrative structure of cinema need not be that of *scenes* arranged according to the dicta of the legitimate stage, which must observe the unities of time and place, but could and should be that of *shots* arranged according to the laws which film generates for itself. It remained for D. W. Griffith and others to elaborate these laws, but Porter had hit upon the absolutely essential fact that cinematic narrative depends not upon the *arrangement of objects or actors within a scene* (as does the theater and, to a large extent, still photography) but upon the *arrangement of shots in relation to one another*. As we shall see, it is the creative arrangement of the infinitely variable relationships among shots that makes later films like *The Birth of a Nation* (1915) and *Potemkin* (1925) great cinema over and above anything beautiful or moving in the specific content of their frames, however great this may be as well.

Contemporary audiences understood none of this, but they loved the dramatic excitement generated by Porter's editing and by what amounted at the time to his "special effects." So spectacular was the commercial success of *The Great Train Robbery* that the film was studied and imitated by film-makers all over the world. It is frequently credited with establishing the realistic narrative, as opposed to the fantastic narrative of Méliès, as the dominant cinematic form from Porter's day to our own and with temporarily standardizing the length of that form at a single reel—one thousand feet or ten to sixteen minutes, depending on the speed of projection (as pointed out earlier in this chapter, films could grow in narrative sophistication only in proportion to their growth in length). Furthermore, *The Great Train Robbery* probably did more than any film made before 1912 to convince investors that the cinema was a money-making proposition, and it was directly instrumental in the spread of

---

* Panning was a relatively difficult operation before the introduction of the geared pan head for the camera tripod later in the decade. Charles Musser, however, points out that the technique had a long-established precedent in the photographic panoramas of the nineteenth century ("The Early Cinema of Edwin Porter," p. 17).

permanent movie theaters, popularly called "nickelodeons" or "store theaters," across the country.*

Judged by the standards of *The Great Train Robbery,* Porter's subsequent films are disappointing, for he seems to have grasped only vaguely the significance of his own narrative innovations. Like Méliès before him, he was given to see only so far, and most of his later films, which number in the hundreds, are as static and stagebound as anything produced by his contemporaries. Only a handful are worthy of note and these not primarily for cinematic reasons. Several months after *The Great Train Robbery,* for example, the man who had so recently helped to liberate the cinema from the conservative theatrical model mounted a painfully stagebound production of *Uncle Tom's Cabin,* complete with painted backdrops and a cakewalk, in fourteen *"tableaux"* linked together by descriptive subtitles (which he may, however, have used for the first time in the cinema). Porter does seem to have practiced parallel editing in *The Ex-Convict* (1904) and *The Kleptomaniac* (1905) but in a manner that simply repeated the formula of *The Great Train Robbery* rather than enlarging upon it; and, while his 1906 fantasy *The Dream of a Rarebit Fiend* is an amusing compendium of contemporary cinematic tricks, most of its successors are as retrograde technically as the majority of film narratives that followed *A Trip to the Moon.* The reason for this decline in power seems to have been at least in part the rigorous production schedule under which Porter was placed by Edison after the astonishing financial success of *The Great Train Robbery.* With the rampant growth of the nickelodeons, public demand for story films had reached a level that far exceeded supply, and Porter found himself caught up in a commercial boom that he, more than any other single film-maker of the day, had helped to create. Faced with the task of turning out films for Edison on an assembly-line basis, Porter had little time to experiment with narrative technique. He became, in fact, the founding father of that uniquely American category of film directors—those who barely miss greatness by being forced to work within the confines of a highly routinized production system and end up, broadly speaking, as proficient hacks.

1.27 *The Dream of a Rarebit Fiend* (Edwin S. Porter, 1906).

1.28 The original "Nickelodeon," Pittsburgh, 1905.

* Before the advent of the nickelodeon (named after the "Nickelodeon" theater which opened in Pittsburgh in 1905), films in America had been exhibited almost exclusively in vaudeville theaters like Koster and Bials or in penny arcades, where in both cases the steady diet of Edison and Lumière *actualités* caused the popularity of the movies to decline. There had been permanent store theaters (i.e., movie-houses converted from storefronts) in Europe since 1896, but the first American version didn't appear until Thomas H. Tally opened his Electric Theater in Los Angeles (where else?) in 1902. Significantly, the date coincides with the beginnings of narrative film in the work of Méliès and Porter. Indeed, the idea of permanent theaters and that of narrative cinema caught on simultaneously, and by 1907 there were between eight and ten thousand nickelodeons all over the country offering film programs of approximately fifteen minutes for the admission price of five to ten cents, depending on the amenities (such as piano accompaniment and cushioned seats) and the location. It should be added that the spread of the nickelodeons caused a shift in the means of motion picture distribution from selling outright to trading and then leasing, since the owners of permanent theaters had to offer their clientele a much larger variety of films than did the traveling showmen, vaudeville theaters, or penny arcades.

One of Porter's later films did, however, accomplish something immensely important to the history of cinema. The otherwise undistinguished film *Rescued from an Eagle's Nest* (1907—see Chapter 2) provided a needy young actor named David Wark Griffith with his first role in films and marked the beginning of a career which was to last forty years and bring the embryonic narrative cinema to a high point of development. Before he came to Porter, Griffith had tried his hand at almost everything, from hop picking to selling the *Encyclopedia Britannica* door-to-door, but he wanted most desperately to become a writer. A chain of rejected stories and failed plays had led him inexorably to the door of the Edison Corporation studios with a scenario based upon a work by the French playwright Victorien Sardou (1831–1908), *La Tosca*. This Porter flatly rejected as having too many scenes, but he offered Griffith a salary of five dollars a day to appear in a wildly improbable little film of his own. In it, Griffith, who was more than a little ashamed to have accepted work as a film actor, played a heroic woodcutter who rescues his infant child from the mountain aerie of a large and vicious eagle, wrestling the bird to its death in the process. (Appropriately, the struggle was emblematic of Griffith's simplistic vision of human experience, which he depicted in his own films as one long, arduous battle between the forces of darkness and the forces of light.) When *Rescued from an Eagle's Nest* first appeared on the screen in 1907, Porter had already abdicated his position of creative leadership in film, but the technology of cinema had long been born and the rudiments of its narrative language discovered. The cinema now awaited its first great narrative artist, who would refine that language, elaborate it, and ultimately transcend it.

1.29 D. W. Griffith in Porter's *Rescued from an Eagle's Nest* (1907).

International Expansion, 1907–1918

AMERICA

The Exchange System of Distribution

At approximately the same time that D. W. Griffith was beginning his work in the cinema under Edwin S. Porter at the Edison Company, the film industry began to assume its characteristic modern form. Since 1903, the conventional system of motion picture distribution, under which theater-owners were forced to buy their prints outright from the producer at the rate of ten to twelve cents per foot (or approximately a hundred dollars per reel), had discriminated economically against the exhibitor. In that year, Harry J. and Herbert Miles of San Francisco established a film exchange which bought prints from producers and leased them to exhibitors for 25 percent of the purchase price. As Lewis Jacobs has pointed out, the Miles operation was an immediate and tremendous success since all concerned profited handsomely by it: the producers gained a well-organized and dependable new customer for any film they could turn out, the new middlemen, or "distributors," made a killing by renting the same print over and over again to individual exhibitors, and the exhibitors who used the exchange could both lower their overheads and vary their programs with relatively little risk.[1]

The exchange system of distribution pioneered by the Miles brothers caught on rapidly, and its rise coincided with the spread of permanent theaters, or "nickelodeons," across the country and with the accelerated growth of film production companies. As the number of permanent film theaters multiplied, the demand for program changes and thus for new films became greater. This in turn stimulated producers to make more films more rapidly than ever before. Indeed, the three components of the new enterprise stimulated one another economically to the extent that by 1908 the cinema had risen from the status of a risky commercial venture to that of a permanent and full-scale, if not yet a major and respectable, industry. In that year, there were ten thousand nickelodeons and one hundred film exchanges in operation all over the United States, and nine major production companies plus scores of minor ones were churning out films at the rate of two one-reelers per director per week. A similar situation existed on the Continent and in Britain, and by the time Griffith entered the cinema the studios or "factories" (as they were then called) of the Western world could scarcely keep up with the public demand for

2.1 The exterior and interior of a typical nickelodeon, c. 1909.

2.2 A storefront theater in Tacoma, Washington, c. 1903.

2.3 J. Stuart Blackton's rooftop studio in New York City, c. 1903.

2.4 British film pioneer G. A. Smith's studio in Brighton, c. 1900.

new films. Furthermore, the novelty of the medium was such that almost anything the studios could produce, regardless of quality, was gobbled up by the international network of distribution and exchange.

Not surprisingly, industry emphasis on speed and quantity of production militated against creative experimentation, and the years 1903 to 1912 witnessed little formal innovation in American film, save in the Biograph shorts of D. W. Griffith (see Chapter 3). Although the introduction of mercury-vapor lamps led several companies to construct indoor studios, films were generally shot out of doors in a single day on budgets of two hundred to five hundred dollars and rigorously limited to one reel of about one thousand feet in length, with a running time of ten to sixteen minutes, depending on projection speed. Nearly all of them were put together on an assembly-line basis according to the stage-bound narrative conventions of Méliès and late Porter, with natural backgrounds and few, if any, retakes. Lewis Jacobs captures the crudity of the early production process:

Action was divided into scenes, and these were photographed in consecutive order. The number of scenes was limited to seven or eight, each 100 to 150 feet long, in order to keep the story within the 1,000-foot length in which the raw film came. . . . Increased production necessitated more people and a division of duties to speed the output. By 1908 directing, acting, photographing, writing, and laboratory work were separate crafts, all of equal status. Each worker regarded himself as a factory hand, lacking only a time-clock ritual for concrete evidence of his position. No one received any screen credit for the work he did, for, as the employers realized, a public reputation would mean higher wages. Besides, most of the directors, actors, and cameramen who had come to the movies were more or less ashamed of their connection with them; they stayed in their jobs because they needed work, and they gave little thought to the medium's possibilities or opportunities. Nearly everyone still regarded movie making as a shabby occupation.[2]

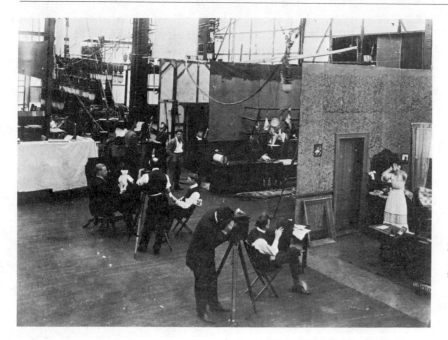

2.5 The interior of the Edison studio (c. 1912), showing the shooting of several separate films.

Jacobs' last point is an important one: early film-makers felt that they were doing little more than grinding out cheap entertainment—a perception that on an economic plane was entirely true; hence the serious development of the medium was retarded for nearly a decade. As so often happened in the history of the cinema, the rigors and banalities of the production system itself forced these people to take a workaday attitude toward their craft, which inhibited stylistic innovation and the free exchange of ideas. There was none of the intellectual excitement and creative ferment which we might expect to find at the birth of an art form, because no one was yet equipped to acknowledge that birth, and so between 1903 and 1912 the industry's level of artistic and technical competence scarcely ever rose above the marginally adequate.*

2.6 *The Starving Artist* (Vitagraph, 1907).

Nevertheless, financial competition among rival production companies was fierce and frequently lawless. Though Thomas Edison owned the sole American rights to the Kinetograph and, less clearly, to the "Latham loop," many companies were using versions of his machines without paying royalties. Hundreds of suits and countersuits were filed by Edison and his competitors during this renegade period of rampant growth, and security agencies like Pinkerton's were employed by all parties to the dispute. This was because many contenders employed strong-arm tactics when the legal process proved too slow or resulted in decisions not to their liking, and it was not unusual for the "agents" (or goons) of one production company to raid the shooting location of another, stealing equipment and injuring personnel. Indeed, as the first decade of the century wore on, every new embellishment to cinema technology became the

2.7 The office staff of the Selig Polyscope Company, Western Avenue, Chicago, c. 1906. (The staff members frequently doubled as extras.)

* For the several minor exceptions to this statement, see Lewis Jacobs' chapter on the "First School of Directors: Specialization of Crafts," in *The Rise of the American Film,* 2nd ed. (New York, 1948), pp. 120–35.

subject of a similarly bitter and unprincipled dispute. At the other end of the industry, relationships between distributors and exhibitors became increasingly strained. Since copyright laws technically did not yet apply to motion pictures, films were more or less in the public domain, and prints were stolen, pirated, and illicitly duplicated, just as printed material had been before 1893. Theoretically, of course, what a production company made it owned, even if its product had been made with pirated equipment, but legal and professional standards for the film industry during this period of rapid international expansion were ill-defined, and their enforcement was difficult.

None of this should surprise us, since the same problems of ownership and duplication rights have arisen in our own day in connection with magnetic audio and video recording tape. The dispute over film patents and copyrights was perhaps more ruthless because it was conditioned by the mercenary social Darwinism of the Gilded Age, which operated on the principle that might makes right. The period 1880 to 1904 was the era of the great American "robber barons," and it is not in the least incongruous that Edison goon squads were wrecking the equipment of rival production companies during the same years that witnessed bloody strikebreaking by police, National Guardsmen, and Pinkertons all over the country, as well as race-riots and lynchings. As one might expect, however, it took a counterforce of considerable intensity to turn the young industry from the anarchic competitiveness of *laissez-faire* capitalism toward a more orderly pursuit of profit.

This counterforce was provided by attacks from what were to become the American cinema's two classical antagonists: organized religion and the political Right. These institutions had tolerated "living pictures" so long as they promised to be a short-lived novelty, but when it became clear that the cinema was well on its way to becoming a major social and economic force in the nation, they took the offensive. In early 1907, for example, an editorial appeared in the conservative and influential *Chicago Tribune,* accusing the "Five Cent Theatre" of "ministering to the lowest passions of children" and being "wholly vicious." "Proper to suppress them at once," the editorial said. "They cannot be defended. They are hopelessly bad." The question basically was and is the ancient one, dating from Plato's *Republic,* of the state's right of censorship. But the fact that film is a mass medium of popular entertainment as well as an art form—and a medium which bypasses language to communicate directly with the senses through moving photographic images of reality— makes the issue more complex than perhaps it has ever been in Western culture.* There was no complexity as far as the *Tribune* and its allies were concerned; between 1907 and 1909 it became obligatory in many parts of the country for ministers, businessmen, and politicians to inveigh against the movies as a corrupter of youth and a threat to public morality. Yet the issue at this point was perhaps less ideological than economic; in becoming a major entertainment industry overnight, the

---

* The superabundance of moving photographic images made possible by television in our own day further compounds the problem.

movies suddenly threatened the very substantial revenues of churches, saloons, and vaudeville theaters from coast to coast. The situation was not unlike the sudden emergence of television as a formidable rival to the movies in the late forties, for in both cases the older institutions sought to take social and economic sanctions against the newer ones and fell on their faces in the process. Like television, the movies came to stay, and no amount of mud-slinging or moralizing was going to change that fact.

The Motion Picture Patents Company

On January 1, 1909, the major components of the film industry joined together under Edison leadership in a protective business association called the Motion Picture Patents Company, or the MPPC. As Arthur Knight points out, the Patents Company was a trust "in the full Rooseveltian sense" of the term.[3] It attempted, that is, to place total control of the international film industry in the hands of nine "manufacturers" (the American companies Edison, Biograph, Vitagraph, Essanay, Selig, Lubin, and Kalem, and the American branches of the French companies Star and Pathé) and one distributor (George Kleine, the largest domestic importer of foreign films). Between them, these companies held all of the disputed patents for camera and projection technology, and by pooling their rights they became for a while the most powerful economic force in the industry.

For one thing, the trust refused to sell camera equipment or patents to any non-member. This meant that no manufacturer outside of the Patents Company could legally produce films in the United States; but to insure complete monopolistic control of production, the MPPC made a deal with the largest single manufacturer of raw film stock in the Western world, the Eastman Kodak Company, to sell its stock exclusively to members of the trust. Worse, the Patents Company refused to sell or lease either films or projectors to exhibitors who did business with non-member companies, and levied a tax of two dollars per week upon its own licensed exhibitors for the right to rent its projectors and films. Distribution was carried on initially through 116 licensed exchanges around the country, which were independently operated and owned. In 1910, however, in order to extend its dominion over every aspect of the industry, the Patents Company forced the sale of the largest of these exchanges to its recently established distribution subsidiary, the General Film Company, and drove the rest out of business by refusing to supply them with films.

In the days when clarity of image and synchronization of camera and projector were still highly unreliable, the Patents Company producers naturally made the best films in the business because of their monopoly on the best equipment and film stock. Patents Company films were generally static, stolid, and unimaginative in terms of narrative, but they guaranteed their viewers a degree of technical competence that few other manufacturers could match in the absence of patented equipment; for this reason, and because the trust could guarantee good distribution,

2.8 A typical Laemmle advertisement from the trade journal *Motion Picture World* attacking the Patents Company's monopoly on the industry.

many foreign distributors who had Lumière equipment and were therefore immune to the coercive machinery of the trust did business with it of their own volition. Had things gone according to plan, the MPPC would have completely monopolized the film industry of the United States and a large part of the West by 1911 or 1912. As so often happens, however, paranoid thoroughness produced its own reaction.

The ten thousand licensed exhibitors who had signed with the Patents Company in 1910 bitterly resented paying the weeky license fee of two dollars demanded by the trust and were prepared to bolt whenever they got the chance. More important, several independent distributors had managed to survive the MPPC's pressure to sell out by going into production themselves with foreign equipment and film stock. At least two of these distributor-producers, Carl Laemmle (1867–1939) of the Independent Motion Picture Company (IMP) and William Fox (1879–1952) of the Greater New York Film Rental Company, successfully challenged the trust and became major Hollywood powers (as the chief executives of Universal Pictures and the Fox Film Corporation, respectively) for many years after the Patents Company and its members were defunct. By 1912, in fact, there were over forty independent producers, large and small, openly aligned against the Patents Company. Their collective competition involved the trust in continuous legal and illegal warfare against them—patent-infringement suits on the one hand and goon-squad assaults on the other. At first the Patents Company won these battles in both the courts and the streets, but by 1912 anti-trust feelings were running high, and in early 1913 the Justice Department of the new Wilson administration brought suit against the MPPC for violating the Sherman Anti-Trust Act of 1890 in an illegal conspiracy to restrain trade. The proceedings were drawn out by countersuits, interrupted by World War One, and not completely resolved until 1917, when the courts ruled against the defendants and ordered the Patents Company to disband. But the trust had actually lost control of the film industry through its own shortsightedness and conservatism long before the decision.

In the first place, the Patents Company clung tenaciously to the notion that the public had a negligible attention span and would not sit still for films above one reel in length. It is true, of course, that a majority of early filmgoers were untutored laborers, many of them non-English-speaking immigrants, lacking sophisticated verbal skills; but the processes of verbal and visual cognition are quite distinct from one another (recent scientific research, in fact, has demonstrated them to be functions of separate hemispheres of the brain). Furthermore, there are few things more compelling in human perceptual experience than the cinematic image in projection. Nevertheless, the entire Patents Company system was geared toward the production of one-reelers, and its licensees were expressly forbidden to make or to distribute films of greater length. Since the chief sources of story material for early films were novels and plays, this dictum produced such anomalies as one-reel versions of fifteen Shakespearian plays, including *King Lear* (1909) and *The Tempest* (1911); five Dickens novels; three Wagner operas; and *The Scarlet Letter* (1909), *Vanity Fair* (1911), and *Ben Hur* (1907). When films like J. Stuart Blackton's five-reel *The Life of Moses* (1909) and D. W. Griffith's two-reel *His Trust* (1910) were produced, they were released to exhibitors in serial fashion at the rate of one reel a week, which seriously damaged their continuity. In open revolt against this practice, many exhibitors began to hold up the first reel of a multi-reel film until they had received the others and could show them sequentially on the same bill—a procedure which ultimately forced the Patents Company to release Griffith's second two-reeler, *Enoch Arden* (1911), as a single film.

2.9 Vitagraph's one-reel *Romeo and Juliet* (1908).

The Advent of the Feature Film

At the same time that this revolt against the Patents Company was taking shape among theater-owners and the public, a few members of the trust ventured into the production of two- and three-reelers, and the independent producer-distributors began to import multi-reel French and Italian features into the United States, with unexpected commercial success. The first important foreign importation was the three-and-one-half-reel French film *La reine Elizabeth* (*Queen Elizabeth*), directed by Louis

2.10 The original offices of Zukor's Famous Players Company, New York City, c. 1912.

2.11 An "arty" advertisement for an early American feature, from a 1912 issue of the *New York Dramatic Mirror*.

Mercanton for the Histrionic Film Company in 1912. Imported and distributed by Adolph Zukor's Famous Players Company, *Queen Elizabeth* starred Sarah Bernhardt and was a "filmed play" in the very worst sense of the term (for a discussion of the narrative defects of *films d'art* like *Queen Elizabeth,* see below); but its remarkable commercial success (Zukor realized eighty thousand dollars on an investment of twenty-eight thousand before the year was out) did a great deal to convince the industry that feature-length films could make money in America.

Even more persuasive was the huge American success of the nine-reel Italian super-spectacle *Quo vadis?* (see below) in the spring of 1913. Directed by Enrico Guazzoni (1876–1949) for the Cines Company, this film contained vast crowd scenes and lavish special effects which kept audiences entranced throughout its running time of more than two hours, and it proved to American producers beyond question that the future of cinema lay at least in part in the feature film. *Quo vadis?* also established another important precedent: it was shown exclusively in first-class legitimate theaters rather than nickelodeons (a policy which Griffith would later adopt for his features) and thus attracted a more prosperous and sophisticated audience than the American cinema had enjoyed at any time since its birth. The international success of *Quo vadis?* was so great that it permitted Italy to capture the world market until the outbreak of the war, and the film was followed in late 1913 by another nine-reel historical blockbuster, Giovanni Pastrone's (1883–1959) masterly *Cabiria.* In its liberal camera movement, elaborate sets, and skillfully constructed narrative, *Cabiria* anticipated the great epics of Griffith; in fact, Griffith saw both Italian films while he was working on his own four-reel feature *Judith of Bethulia* in 1913.

A substantial portion of the film-going public had also been affected by the Italian spectacles, and soon a feature craze was sweeping the country and the industry, challenging the Patents Company's conservative leadership and the very existence of its one- and two-reel films. The trust remained adamant in its opposition to features, but it was engaged in a losing battle. The final blow was struck in 1914, when the Paramount Pictures Corporation was formed by some of the nation's most powerful independent distributors and exhibitors. Paramount was created to commission, finance, and distribute feature films in a controlled market and was as monopolistic in its intentions as the Patents Company itself, but it signaled the permanent arrival of the feature-length film as the major product of the industry. Appropriately, the first producers to become associated with Paramount, and the men who would later guide it to a position of supreme leadership within the American industry, were Adolph Zukor (1873–1976) of the Famous Players Company and Jesse L. Lasky (1880–1958) of the Feature Play Company.

For several interrelated reasons, the coming of the feature film (arbitrarily defined in this era as any film of five reels or more) was a major step in the evolution of cinematic narrative art. Feature films made the movies respectable for the middle class. The production companies of the century's first decade saw themselves as manufacturers of cheap entertainment for a generally uneducated mass public, and the Patents Company had rigidly systematized this conception of film-making in its five-year domination of the industry. Audiences who aspired to more than short, simple action stories and comedies could provide were unlikely to find it on the screen, so they stayed home or went to plays instead, and their absence was demoralizing to the small but growing number of film-makers within the system—most notably D. W. Griffith—who were coming to regard their medium as a serious form of expression. The advent of the feature, however, opened up the possibility of a more varied and complex kind of expression than the one- and two-reelers could afford. As a form, the feature is analogous to the novel or the symphony in that it is relatively open-ended and provides a large scope for the elaboration and interaction of its elements. Thus, the new feature length offered film-makers a form commensurate with serious artistic endeavor and made possible the narrative sophistication which the cinema attained under Griffith and those who came after him. It also gradually expanded the cinema's regular audience to include large sections of the middle class and placed a new premium on the quality of production as well as its quantity. Longer films had to be made more slowly, with larger budgets and greater care than the one- and two-reelers, and, once the feature was popularly accepted, high artistic and technical standards became a new locus of competition within the industry.

To accommodate the new films and their new audiences, a new kind of movie theater sprang up across the country, the first of which was the thirty-three-hundred-seat Strand opened by Mitchell L. Marks in the heart of the Broadway district of Manhattan in 1914. No longer converted storefronts with sawdust floors and hard seats, the new theaters were the earliest of the big, comfortable, and elegantly appointed urban "dream palaces" which came to be controlled by the major Hollywood studios in the 1920's.* The Strand, for example, featured a two-story gilt and marble interior hung with tapestries and crystal chandeliers, plush pile carpeting, numerous lounges, a thirty-piece orchestra, and a monumental Wurlitzer organ—all for the respectably expensive admission price of twenty-five cents. By 1916 there were over twenty-one thousand such new or remodeled film theaters in the country; their arrival signaled the close of the nickelodeon era.

The Rise of the Star System

Another point upon which the Patents Company had stubbornly refused to yield to popular demand had to do with publicity for its creative personnel; it feared that if the real names of its actors, actresses, and directors appeared in screen credits or in any other form of advertisement, they would acquire a public following and be able to demand higher salaries from their employers. (This shows a surprising amount of foresight, since only a decade after the trust's effective demise stars like

2.12 "Dream palace" architecture in the twenties: the auditoriums of the Ambassador Theater, St. Louis, and the Oriental Theater, Chicago.

---

* For a thoroughgoing account of the demographics of "dream palace" proliferation in the twenties, see Douglas Gomery, "The Picture Palace: Economic Sense or Nonsense?" *Quarterly Review of Film Studies*, 3, 1 (Winter 1978), 23–36.

Charlie Chaplin were commanding salaries of one million dollars per film and dictating terms to the studio chiefs who had once been their bosses.) For years the most popular of early performers were known to audiences only by the names of the characters they played (Mary Pickford was "Little Mary") or the production company in whose films they appeared (Florence Lawrence was "the Biograph girl"). Production companies were constantly deluged with inquiries into the private lives of their leading players. The Patents Company was unmoved, but the producer Carl Laemmle of the Independent Motion Picture Company saw behind each letter a fan who would pay over and over again, not merely to watch a movie but to see his or her favorite player on the screen. An empire might be built, he reasoned, on a pretty face or a handsome grin.

In 1910, Laemmle lured the extremely popular Florence Lawrence from Biograph by raising her salary and immediately circulated anonymous press reports of her death, using her real name in public for the first time.* Then he undertook an extensive advertising campaign to denounce the story as a "black lie" spread by the Patents Company to conceal the fact that Miss Lawrence had come over to IMP; and, as proof of her continued existence, Laemmle promised that King Baggott, IMP's leading man (also named publicly for the first time), would escort Miss Lawrence to St. Louis on the day that their first IMP picture together opened in that city. There was a near riot as what seemed to be half of St. Louis crowded into the train station to get a glimpse of the former Biograph girl's still earthly presence, and the star system was born. Laemmle's publicization of players like Florence Lawrence and King Baggott proved so successful that other independent producers soon adopted star policies of their own. As usual, the Patents Company members resisted innovation until the eleventh hour, losing many popular players to the authentic if primitive stardom promised by the independents. But by 1913, Vitagraph, Lubin, and Kalem had all begun to publicize their performers, and Biograph was even touting its directors and cameramen—pre-eminently D. W. Griffith and G. W. "Billy" Bitzer, who were both soon to join the ranks of the independents in any case. The production companies now suddenly subjected their audiences to a publicity blitz of photographs, posters, postcards, and fan magazines featuring their favorite stars; and stardom rapidly began to acquire the mythic dimensions which would make it the basis of production policy in the American cinema for the next fifty years.

The Move to Hollywood

Those fifty years were spent almost exclusively in the Los Angeles suburb (originally a small industrial town) called Hollywood—the result of a mass migration of production companies from the East which oc-

2.13 A Laemmle advertisement in *Motion Picture World.*

---

* In *Stardom: The Hollywood Phenomenon* (New York, 1970), Alexander Walker maintains that Miss Lawrence had *already* been dismissed from Biograph for publicizing herself and had been blacklisted by all other licensed film companies when Laemmle hired her, which, if true, only serves to heighten the spectacular opportunism of the producer's coup.

2.14 Hollywood, c. 1919 and 1915.

2.15 A Selig Polyscope Company stage, Hollywood, 1913. Note the compartmentalized sets and muslin sun diffusers overhead.

curred between 1908 and 1913. The reasons why a full-scale Eastern-based industry* moved its entire operation to Southern California during these years have never been completely clear, but it is generally thought that most of the independents went West to escape the subpoenas and wrecking crews of the Patents Company, for Hollywood's distance from MPPC headquarters in New York City and its proximity to the Mexican border made it an ideal sanctuary. The region held attractions for film-makers other than mere refuge, however, and companies like Selig had been enjoying them as early as 1907, two years before the formation of the trust.

   For one thing, films could be shot out of doors in Southern California all year round and all day long, because of the region's sunny, temperate climate—a fact of major economic importance since the sun was still the

* For a fascinating account of the early motion picture industry in the East, see Paul C. Spehr, *The Movies Begin: Making Movies in New Jersey, 1887–1920* (Newark; Newark Museum, 1977).

cinema's only effective lighting source, and since films were being made in an ever more industrial mode, requiring efficient daily scheduling. The film historian Kenneth Macgowan notes that even interiors could be shot out of doors in Hollywood if sheets of muslin were placed overhead to soften the shadows.[4] The second great attraction was the wide range of topography. Almost every type of scenery imaginable—mountains, valleys, lakes, islands, seacoast, and desert—was available to film-makers within a fifty-mile radius of Hollywood. The Mediterranean could be simulated on the Pacific coastline, and Griffith Park in Los Angeles could stand in for the forests of the Rockies. Southern California also offered low taxes, cheap labor, and cheap land. Local real estate developers sold tens of thousands of acres to the newly arrived production companies, on which they subsequently built vast studios and backlots. * Between 1908 and 1912, many of the independents moved permanently to Hollywood, and even the Patents Company members began to shoot films there on a seasonal basis. D. W. Griffith, for example, first took his Biograph crew west for the winter in 1910, and he continued this practice until he left Biograph in 1913 to work in Southern California year round with the independent Mutual Film Company.

The New Studio Chiefs and Industry Re-Alignment

By 1914, the independents had completely colonized Hollywood, and several Patents Company members had moved west as well. But the trust was badly ailing by this time, and it was the independent companies which founded the studios that would make Hollywood the capital of world cinema for the next five decades. It is important to understand that the men who controlled these companies and who would come to dominate the American film industry during this period were all first- and second-generation Jewish immigrants with little formal education—Carl Laemmle of Universal Pictures, Adolph Zukor of the Famous Players Company and Jesse L. Lasky of the Feature Play Company (both later merged with several smaller production companies and the Paramount distribution exchange as the Famous Players–Lasky Corporation), Samuel Goldfish (later "Goldwyn") of the Goldwyn Picture Corporation, Louis B. Mayer of the Metro Picture Corporation, Marcus Loew and Nicholas and Joseph Schenck of Loew's, Incorporated (a national exhibition chain which became the parent company of Metro-Goldwyn-Mayer), Lewis J. Selznick of the Selznick Picture Company, William Fox of the Fox Film Corporation, and, after the war, Harry, Abe, Sam, and Jack Warner of Warner Brothers Pictures, Incorporated. Most of these men had been small tradesmen who had gambled on the movie business in the anarchic first decade of the cinema, hoping to turn a quick profit. From penny-arcade showmen and nickelodeon operators they became "manufacturers" of their own films, then producer-distributors, and finally Hol-

---

* Large tracts of open land owned by the studios and used to simulate various locations.

lywood studio chiefs. Thus, equipped with little more than common business sense, uncommon ambition, and sound instincts for survival, these men became the moguls of a multi-million-dollar empire and the temporary custodians of the twentieth century's most influential and culturally significant art form—a circumstance which goes far toward explaining the strange blend of crassness, materialism, and vitality that has always charactered Hollywood films.*

The year 1914 was a crucial one for the American film industry. The feature film had by this time triumphed almost completely over the one- and two-reeler, or "short," which survived only in the cartoon, newsreel, and serial installment (and, until the mid-twenties, as the vehicle for some of America's greatest comic talent—see Chapter 6); and this development coincided with a general economic boom created by the outbreak of war in Europe. Profits soared, along with costs, and the industry expanded rapidly in all directions, making and breaking fortunes in the process. Those companies—most notably Paramount—which had placed their faith in feature films became prosperous and powerful, while those which had cast their lot with the shorts were destroyed. The pioneers—Kalem, Star Film, General Film, Biograph, the Edison Company itself—were all wiped out by the new public hunger for feature films, and the MPPC dwindled to insignificance during the war years. Vitagraph, Lubin, Selig, and Essanay survived temporarily by merging as VLSE, and the independents Mutual, Reliance, and Keystone combined to form the short-lived but important Triangle Film Corporation, which simultaneously employed the talents of the American cinema's three top directors—D. W. Griffith, Thomas H. Ince, and Mack Sennett (see Chapters 3 and 6). Meanwhile, Paramount—and, to a lesser extent, Universal and Fox—had begun to produce features as never before. Jacobs estimates that by 1915 Paramount alone was releasing three to four features *per week* to some five thousand theaters across the nation.[5]

The vast new market for feature-length films produced far-reaching changes in both the structure and scale of the industry. As films quintupled in length, and star salaries and screen-rights payments increased dramatically, production costs rose from between five hundred and one thousand dollars per film to between twelve thousand and twenty thousand—and the figures would triple in the post-war years. Production profits were ensured during this period through promotion of the star system and through advertising on a grand scale to increase demand, but producers also sought some means of national distribution to multiply the return on their increasingly large investments. As usual, it was Adolph Zukor who led the way.

---

* For example, before his ouster as head of the corporation in 1930, William Fox personally approved every picture released by Fox Film: "No picture ever produced by the Fox Film Corporation was permitted to be viewed by the general public, until every title it contained had been approved and passed by me, and I don't remember a single picture ever made by the company that the titles contained therein were not corrected, edited, and rewritten by me" (quoted in Upton Sinclair, *Upton Sinclair Presents William Fox* [Los Angeles: Upton Sinclair, 1933], p. 5). Fox had quit school at the age of eleven in order to help support his family.

The "Block Booking" Dispute and the Acquisition of Theaters

In 1916, Zukor merged his Famous Players Company with the Paramount distribution exchange and twelve smaller companies to form the Famous Players–Lasky Corporation (later Paramount Pictures)* which briefly came to dominate the industry by inventing the practice of "block booking." The block booking system of distribution forced exhibitors to accept a production company's films in large groups, or "blocks," tied to several particularly desirable titles (usually prestigious star vehicles) in advance of production. This all-or-nothing distribution policy quite obviously favored the producer, who was provided with a constant outlet for his films regardless of their quality, and soon every production company in the business had adopted it. Within a year's time, however, the practice of block booking had led to such abuses that the nation's leading exhibitors rebelled against the Hollywood-based production companies in much the same way that independents like Zukor had only several years earlier rebelled against the Patents Company monopolists.

In 1917, executives of twenty-six of the largest first-run exhibition chains established the First National Exhibitors Circuit, whose purpose was to challenge Paramount Famous Players–Lasky Corporation by producing and/or distributing its own features. It was an attempt to gain control over the means of film production and distribution, just as block booking represented an attempt on the part of producers to gain control over the means of distribution and exhibition. In short, both parties to the struggle, like Edison before them, recognized that whoever controlled distribution controlled the industry. Under the skillful management of W. W. Hodkinson (1881–1971), who had originally founded the Paramount exchange in 1914, First National was able to eliminate block booking temporarily by 1918 and to acquire sole distribution rights to the films of the industry's number one star, Charlie Chaplin. In retaliation, Paramount Famous Players–Lasky Corporation in 1919 entered the theater business itself and bought up first-run houses and exhibition circuits all over the country. Zukor's campaign to acquire exhibition outlets was as aggressive and ruthless as the MPPC's war against the independent procedures had been a decade before. His agents became known as "the wrecking crew" and "the dynamite gang" among independent theater owners from New England to Texas to Colorado, and by 1921 Paramount Famous Players–Lasky owned 303 theaters compared to First

* From 1916 to 1927, Zukor retained the corporate name of "Paramount Pictures" for the distribution and exhibition components of his empire. From 1927 to 1930, the company was called Paramount Famous Lasky Corporation, and in 1930, with the acquisition of the huge Publix theater chain, it became the Paramount Publix Corporation. When the firm went bankrupt in 1933, it was re-organized as Paramount Pictures, Incorporated, which name it retains today as a wholly owned subsidiary of Gulf and Western Industries (since 1966). In the text, I refer to Zukor's production-distribution-exhibition conglomerate of the teens and twenties as Paramount Famous Players–Lasky (or simply Paramount, as it was commonly known during the twenties), although each component was separately incorporated in a bid (ultimately unsuccessful; see Chapter 11) to avoid anti-trust suits.

National's 639. Its war with First National—and, later, Loew's, Incorporated, the parent firm of MGM—for control of distribution and exhibition extended well into the twenties, culminating in Paramount's bankruptcy and First National's absorption by Warner Brothers. Before that occurred, however, First National had become a major power in its own right, and Fox, Goldwyn, and Universal had all joined Zukor's corporation in the race for theater acquisition.*

This race, which naturally required huge capital for real estate investment over and above normal production costs, was financed by the great Wall Street banking houses: Kuhn, Loeb, and Company were backing Paramount Famous Players–Lasky; the Du Ponts and the Chase National Bank stood behind Goldwyn; Fox was supported by the John F. Dryden–Prudential insurance group and Universal by Shields and Company. Stock issues were floated for the production companies and listed on the New York Exchange for public investment, and trained financiers began to assume managerial positions within the industry to protect their own investments. The continuing involvement of American big business in motion pictures had begun, and, less than a decade after the demise of the storefront theater, the cinema had become a large-scale industry. By the arrival of sound in the late twenties, it had become, by some accounts, the fourth largest in the nation (see final note, Chapter 6).

The Rise of Hollywood to International Dominance

Hollywood rose to power largely because of the First World War, which temporarily eliminated the European competition (mainly French and Italian) and gave America dominion over the world film market for the next fifteen years (and even after, though the configuration of the market changed with the coming of sound). Before August 1914, the American film industry had been forced to compete on the open market with all of the major European industries and for some years had actually lagged behind those of Italy and France. Just prior to the war, however, France had slipped into a kind of cinematic reactionism under the constricting influence of Méliès and Film d'Art (see below), and Italy's world-famous spectacles had already degenerated into turgid clichés. But in America, the arrival of the big-budget feature had resulted in

---

* Despite temporary victories, block booking persisted into later decades, in one form or another, and there is still a tendency for producer/distributors to coerce exhibitors (including, since the sixties, television networks) into accepting their less desirable titles as part of package deals. In the mid-seventies, the film companies instituted the practice of "blind bidding," whereby first-run exhibitors are required to put up a lump sum rental fee for a major film four to eight months in advance of its release (the revenues, in fact, are often used to finance the film's production). Like block booking, blind bidding insures a profitable rate of return for the producer/distributor regardless of a film's box office success, and leaves the exhibitor with a disproportionate burden of financial risk. In 1979, the National Association of Theater Owners (NATO), a trade organization representing eight thousand U.S. exhibitors, drafted an anti-blind-bidding bill for introduction in about thirty state legislatures; but, as of this writing, only five states had adopted it.

a considerable rise in the standards of motion picture production in the immediate pre-war years, and the audience had been growing rapidly. In some sectors, the American film was even gaining respectability as an art form: serious books were written about it (for example, the poet Vachel Lindsay's *The Art of the Moving Picture* [1915] and the philosopher Hugo Münsterberg's *The Film: A Psychological Study* [1916][6]), and newspapers established regular columns for "photoplay" reviews.

When war broke out on the Continent in the late summer of 1914, the European industries were virtually shut down since the same chemicals used in the production of celluloid were needed to manufacture gun powder, but the American cinema prospered throughout the war in unchallenged economic and political security. Jacobs estimates that while in 1914 the United States produced just a little over one half of the world's motion pictures, by 1918 it was making nearly all of them.[7] Thus, for four years America exercised complete control over the international market and set up a formidable worldwide distribution system, and between 1914 and 1918 the world at large, including Asia and Africa (but excepting the belligerent Germany), saw nothing but American films if it saw films at all. In 1919, immediately following the Treaty of Versailles, 90 percent of all films screened in Europe were American, and the figure for South America was, and would remain for years, 100 percent. During the twenties, of course, the European figures would decline drastically as Germany and the Soviet Union became major powers in world cinema and as other nations attempted to shield their industries with protective laws. Nevertheless, the First World War had placed the American film industry in a position of undisputed economic and artistic leadership — a position it would maintain until the coming of sound and in some respects forever after.

EXPANSION ON THE CONTINENT

The German and Scandinavian film industries were still embryonic when war came to Europe in 1914,* and the British cinema, after taking an early lead through the work of the Brighton school (see Chapter 1), had failed to evolve industrially at all. But the industries of France and Italy had reached fairly advanced states of development in the first decade of the century, and together they led the world cinema commercially and artistically until the American industry usurped them.

The Empire of Pathé Frères

From 1896 to 1905, the French cinema was dominated by Georges Méliès, whose stagebound fantasies became so widely popular that all other producers were forced to imitate his techniques in order to compete

---

* An exception was Denmark's Nordisk Films Kompagni, founded in 1906 and still in existence (making it the world's oldest production company), which was well organized and actively competitive in the world market, largely due to the international popularity of its leading lady, Asta Nielsen (1882–1972).

with him. This meant that trick photography and the static camera became key features of French films until the end of the First World War. Nevertheless, Méliès' commercial influence began to decline in the latter half of the decade as his Star Film Company, basically a small-scale artisanal business, was driven into competition with the ruthless and monopolistic Pathé Frères, founded in 1896 by the former phonograph manufacturer Charles Pathé (1863–1957).

The French film historian Georges Sadoul has called Charles Pathé "the Napoleon of the cinema,"[8] because in just over a decade he created a vast industrial empire which gave France control of the international film market until the eve of the war. Financed by several of France's most powerful corporations, Pathé Frères built vast production studios at Vincennes in 1901 and then became the largest single manufacturer of film equipment and raw film stock in Europe. Huge capital investments allowed Pathé to extend its control over distribution exchanges and film theaters in every part of the Continent, and soon there were agents of the company all over the world. (Indeed, Pathé Frères distribution and production units are credited with pioneering the film industries of Australia, Japan, Brazil, and India.) Thus, while he did not totally eliminate his competition, Charles Pathé realized within the structure of a single organization what Edison was unable to achieve through the conglomerate MPPC (of which Pathé and Star formed the Continental wing)—a complete vertical monopoly over every aspect of the industry. In 1908 Pathé marketed twice as many films in the United States as all the American production companies put together, and by 1909 the same situation existed in Great Britain.

Pathé's profits of 5,000 to 10,000 percent enabled it to subsume the Star Film Company in 1908 and become Méliès' distributor for several stormy years until 1913, after which the "alchemist of light" abandoned his alchemy altogether. In 1923, Méliès was forced to sell his negatives for the chemical value of the celluloid (the reason that less than 140 of his five hundred films survive—see note, p. 15), and in 1929 he was found operating a gift kiosk in a Paris Mètro station*—like so many of the cinema's great pioneers, utterly forgotten. Happily, though, Méliès spent the remaining nine years of his life in the relative comfort of a rent-free apartment provided by Mutuelle du Cinéma, a rest home for retired cinematographers, and had the satisfaction of seeing his achievements revaluated by the first real historians of the cinema in the thirties.

The director-general of Pathé's huge studios at Vincennes was a former music-hall singer named Ferdinand Zecca (1864–1947) whose canny instincts for what the public would pay to see contributed fundamentally to his employers' enormous financial success. Like Méliès, Zecca specialized in story films, and he was thoroughly conversant with the former magician's cinematic tricks, but in most of his productions Zecca broke away from the Méliès tradition of filmed theater by shooting out of doors and

---

*This story may also be apocryphal, deriving as it does from Méliès' now-discredited *Mes mémoires* (see note, p. 14).

2.16 Pathé's *La passion* (Ferdinand Zecca and Lucien Nonguet, 1903).

2.17 Max Linder as Pathé's "Max."

2.18 A poster for *Fantômas*, c. 1914.

occasionally panning his camera to follow an action. His first films were realistic one-reel melodramas of the lower classes such as *L'histoire d'un crime* (1901) and *Les victimes d l'alcöolisme* (1902—a five-minute version of Émile Zola's novel *L'assommoir*), but he went on to become a master of many genres, including the historical romance, fantasy, farce, religious spectacle, and the highly popular *actualité reconstituée,* or "reconstructed newsreel," innovated by Méliès. Furthermore, borrowing freely from the chase films of England's Brighton school, Zecca developed a uniquely Gallic version of the type—the *course comique* ("comic chase"), in which cutting for parallel action was combined with trick photography *à la Méliès* to achieve not suspense but laughter. With titles like *Dix femmes pour un mari* (*Ten Wives for One Husband*), *La course à la perruque* (*The Pursuit of the Wig*), *La course aux tonneaux* (*The Pursuit of the Beer Barrels*)—all 1905—most of these films were shot in the streets of Paris and had a vitality and inventiveness which impressed the young Mack Sennett, among others, who found in them the model for his own Keystone Kops (see Chapter 6).

Zecca remained with Pathé until its dissolution in 1939* but never evolved beyond an intelligent synthesizer of the discoveries of others. Like his German counterpart Oskar Messter (see Chapter 4), he is best remembered as an authentic primitive who upgraded and varied the content of his nation's films and who worked toward the refinement of the medium generally, without making any unique personal contributions. Another Pathé talent was the comedian Max Linder (1883–1925), who became world famous for his subtle impersonation of an elegant but disaster-prone young-man-about-town in pre-war Paris. Linder wrote and directed most of his four hundred films and had a profound influence upon the work of Charlie Chaplin in the next decade (see Chapter 6). Finally, it should be remarked that in 1910 Pathé inaugurated the first regular newsreel, the "Pathé Gazette," which acquired an international weekly following in the years before the war.

Louis Feuillade and the Rise of Gaumont

Pathé's only serious rival on the Continent was another French firm, Gaumont Pictures, founded by the engineer-inventor Léon Gaumont (1864–1946) in 1898. Gaumont offered little competition for Pathé during the first decade of the century, but—largely through the work of a single director, Louis Feuillade (1873–1925)—it was able to dominate the French cinema from 1913 to 1920. Formerly a scriptwriter for Pathé, Feuillade had begun his career at Gaumont in 1906 by directing comic shorts and chase films in the manner of Zecca. He made hundreds of narrative films over the next few years and finally came into his own with the serial detective film *Fantômas,* shot in five episodes of four to six parts

* The company was revived in 1944—*sans* Charles Pathé, who had sold his interest in the business to Bernard Natan in 1929—as the Société Nouvelle Pathé-Cinéma, which today specializes mainly in distribution (see Charles Pathé, *De Pathé Frères à Pathé Cinéma* [Lyons, 1970]).

each between 1913 and 1914. This type of film had been originated by Victorin Jasset (1862–1913), an ex-sculptor directing for Gaumont, in the *Nick Carter* series of 1908. Feuillade brought to the form a sense of plastic beauty and visual poetry which allowed his serials to achieve the status of an art.

Fantômas was based on the popular serial novel by Pierre Souvestre and Marcel Allain about the adventures of the mysterious French super-criminal Fantômas, "Master of Terror," and the attempts of a ratiocinating police detective named Juve to track him down. The incredible exploits of Fantômas and his pursuer are all beautifully photographed on location in the streets, houses, sewers, and suburbs of pre-war Paris and offer a strangely lyrical blend of naturalism and fantasy. Feuillade's other detective serials—the ten-episode *Les vampires* (1915–16), the twelve-episode *Judex* (1916), *La nouvelle mission de Judex* (1917), *Tih Minh* (1918), and *Barabbas* (1919)—all manifest this same combination of mystery and the quotidian real, and their atmospheric beauty had a direct and continuing influence upon French film in the work of Jean Durand, Abel Gance, Jacques Feyder, and René Clair (see Chapter 9).

2.19 *Fantômas* (Louis Feuillade, 1913–14): composition in depth.

2.20 *Les vampires* (Louis Feuillade, 1914–15): density and depth.

Yet Feuillade was himself a conservative in terms of cinematic structure. As David Robinson has very aptly pointed out, Feuillade consistently rejected the serially arranged shots, or montage, of Griffith (see Chapter 3), in favor of *tableaux* elaborately composed in depth.[9] This circumstance makes Feuillade not only a legitimate heir to Méliès but the progenitor of *mise-en-scène** (literally, "putting-in-the-scene") aesthetics, first articulated after World War II by the French film theorist André Bazin and the young critics of *Cahiers du cinéma* (see Chapter 13), which puts major emphasis on the creative use of movement and space *within*

2.21 *Judex* (Louis Feuillade, 1916).

* In theater, the arrangement of actors, scenery, and props in preparation for a performance. In cinema, that which occurs before the lens of the camera, as opposed to the effects created by editing.

2.22 Pearl White in Pathé's *The Perils of Pauline* (Louis Gasnier, 1914).

2.23 Advertisements for the Gaumont Palace Theatre and the Gaumont studio, c. 1912.

the shot rather than upon the relationship *between* shots, as does montage. At the height of his fame during World War I, Feuillade was recognized as a genius. Extremely successful with audiences all over the world, his serials were also admired by contemporary intellectuals—especially the surrealists André Breton, Louis Aragon, and Guillaume Apollinaire, who saw in his skillful amalgamation of realistic detail, dense poetic imagery, and pure fantasy an analogue for their own attempts to "re-spiritualize" modern art. But because montage aesthetics dominated film theory from the era of Griffith and Eisenstein (see Chapter 5) until the writings of Bazin began to appear in the late forties, Feuillade's reputation was in total eclipse from 1918 to this latter date, when the *Cahiers* critics (who would later become the *auteurs* ["authors," or directors with a personal style] of the French New Wave) finally recognized Feuillade as the first great *metteur-en-scène* (practitioner of *mise-en-scène* aesthetics), as seminal to their theory of film art as Griffith was to montage.

The success of Feuillade's serials led to widespread acceptance of the form throughout the world: *Fantômas* is the father of the American *Perils of Pauline* series (actually directed for Pathé by the French director Louis Gasnier), Britain's *Ultus,* Germany's *Homunculus,* and Italy's *Tigris,* all well received in their day. And their popularity allowed Gaumont to succeed Pathé as the most powerful French studio of the century's second decade, although by 1914 France's monopoly on the international market had begun to weaken considerably as a result of the approaching war and of American competition. In 1910 approximately 60 to 70 percent of all imported films in the West derived from French studios, making France's domination of world cinema as nearly complete as Hollywood's was to be. When the war began, however, France lost much of its market at a time when the rate of Hollywood production was multiplying almost monthly.

The Gaumont studio commanded the talents not only of Feuillade but of his protégé Jean Durand (1882–1946), whose comedy series *Onésime, Calino,* and *Zigoto,* made between 1907 and 1914, influenced the work of both Mack Sennett and René Clair (see Chapters 6 and 9). Gaumont also had under contract Alice Guy-Blaché (1873–1968), the world's first woman director (*La vie du Christ* [*The Life of Christ,* 1906]; *Fanfan la tulipe* [*Fanfan the Tulip,* 1907]), and the cartoonist Émile Cohl (1857–1938), who applied the principle of stop-motion photography to the drawing-board and became the father of modern animation. The practice of animating concrete objects by photographing them one frame at a time and changing their position between frames had first been used by the American director J. Stuart Blackton (1875–1941) in a 1907 Vitagraph film called *The Haunted Hotel* and was already known in France as *mouvement américain* when Cohl began to refine it near the end of the decade. In cartoons like the *Fantoche* series and *Les joyeaux microbes* (*The Jolly Germs,* 1909), Cohl pioneered the frame-by-frame animation of line drawings, puppets, and natural objects, and also became the first director to combine large-scale animation with live action. Finally, despite the French cinema's fall from international pre-eminence, Gaumont was able to establish a huge production studio and exhibition circuit in

England, called Gaumont-British, which remained under French control until 1922 and had a substantial impact on the development of British film (many of Alfred Hitchcock's first films, for example, were shot for Gaumont-British).*

The Société Film d'Art

The most influential phenomenon to occur in French cinema during the period of international expansion, however, came in the first decade of the century and was only remotely connected with a major production company (Pathé had partial control of the venture). This was the work of the Société Film d'Art, founded by the Parisian financiers Frères Lafitte in 1908 for the purpose of transferring prestigious stage plays starring famous performers to the screen. The idea was to attract the theater-going middle classes to the cinema by increasing its aesthetic and intellectual appeal—a revolutionary notion at a time in which the medium had only just emerged from the nickelodeon and the fairground tent.

2.24 *Les joyeaux microbes* (Émile Cohl, 1909)

The film historian Kenneth Macgowan has called Film d'Art "the first highbrow motion picture movement,"[10] and that description applies in both its positive and negative senses. On the one hand, the company used the best creative talent of the stage to mount its productions, commissioning original plays from members of the esteemed Académie Française and employing stars of the Comédie Française to act in them. Leading composers wrote original scores for these plays and eminent stage directors were contracted to direct them. From a literary and dramatic perspective, in fact, the credentials of Film d'Art were impeccable. From the standpoint of cinema, on the other hand, the Film d'Art productions were regressive in the extreme.

For all their intellectual pedigree (and perhaps because of it), the lavishly staged productions of the Société Film d'Art were merely photographed plays; their directors made no concessions whatever to the filmic medium. Like a theater spectator in an orchestra seat, the camera occupied a central position with regard to the action and remained rigidly static throughout, so that the film frame assumed the function of a proscenium arch. All takes were long or medium-long shots which permitted the players to appear at full length on the screen, just as they would on the stage. Each shot was made to correspond to an entire dramatic scene played out from beginning to end, and the acting itself was full of wild gesticulation and bombast. Finally, as if to assure the spectators that they were indeed watching a "high-art film" (as American distributors billed the product), and not just an ordinary "living picture," Film d'Art sets

---

* Léon Gaumont retired in 1928, selling his distribution and theater chains to MGM. The production company became part of the Gaumont-Franco Film-Aubert consortium, which went bankrupt in the early thirties, but the Gaumont name persists today in the Société Nouvelles des Établissements Gaumont, an international producer/distributor. Gaumont-British prospered independently under the stewardship of the producer Michael Balcon until he left in 1936 (see Chapter 9), when it collapsed as a production/distribution firm. The exhibition chain was absorbed by the J. Arthur Rank Organization in the late forties, but newsreels continued to be made under the Gaumont-British logo until 1959.

2.25 *L'assassinat du duc de Guise*
(Charles LeBargy and André Calmettes,
for the Societé Film d'Art, 1908).

were constructed of papier-mâché and plaster, and the backgrounds were
painted canvas. As cinematic narratives, then, the Film d'Art productions
were more primitive than the films of Méliès and considerably less imaginative. Nevertheless, for several years they enjoyed an immense popular
success and were imitated throughout the Western world.

The screening of the first Film d'Art production, *L'assassinat du duc de
Guise* (*The Assassination of the Duc de Guise*), on November 17, 1908,
met with nearly universal acclaim. Directed by Charles le Bargy and
André Calmettes of the Comédie Française, with a script by Académician
Henri Lavédan and a score by Camille Saint-Saëns, *L'assassinat du duc
de Guise* was hailed by France's leading intellectual journals as a great
cultural landmark; and one drama critic wrote that its premiere would
prove as significant to the history of film as the first Cinématographe
projection on December 28, 1895. In subsequent years, the Société Film
d'Art filmed plays by Edmond Rostand, Francois Coppée, and Victorien
Sardou, as well as versions of Dickens' novel *Oliver Twist, Madame
Sans-Gêne* (a play by Sardou and Moreau), and Goethe's novel *The Sorrows of Young Werther,* before the company was killed off by the introduction of sound. In its prime, however, the Société Film d'Art had so
many imitators in France, Italy, Great Britain, Germany, Denmark, and
ultimately the United States that it could scarcely compete with them.
France, for example, had not only the Société Cinématographiques des
Auteurs et Gens de Lettres but the Série d'Art Pathé, Gaumont's Film
Esthétique, Éclair's Association Cinématographique des Auteurs Drama-
tiques, and two independent companies, Film d'Auteurs and Théatro-
Film.

For several years, the rage for lengthy adaptations of "classical" novels
and plays—now known generically as *films d'art*—swept across Western

Europe, stifling experiment and enshrouding the new medium of film in the literary orthodoxies of the century past. For a while it seemed as if everything written, sung, or danced (for photographed ballet and opera formed a large part of the *film d'art* corpus) in Western Europe between 1900 and the Renaissance, and Greek tragedy as well, found its way into one of these stagebound and pretentious productions. Sophocles, Shakespeare, Goethe, Dumas *père* and *fils,* Hugo, Dickens, Balzac, Wagner, and Bulwer-Lytton were all represented, side by side with the "modern classics" of contemporary authors like Antole France and Henrik Sienkiewicz. Even Eastern Europe was affected: David Robinson maintains that the great Russian vogue for historical costume films, which reached its aesthetic peak in Eisenstein's two-part *Ivan the Terrible* (1944–46), was born during this period, as was the Hungarian cinema's permanent fascination with literary subjects[11] (see Chapters 5 and 15).

Although the *film d'art* vogue died out almost as rapidly as it had come into being, the movement's financial success had revealed a vast new audience which preferred serious screen stories to comic chases and vaudeville acts, convincing producers all over the world to upgrade the content of their films. Not surprisingly, when directors like Griffith and Feuillade began to cast serious stories into visually sophisticated form through montage on the one hand and *mise-en-scène* on the other, *film d'art* productions rapidly lost their audience, and the topsy-turvy state into which World War I threw the international market helped to accelerate the process.

Still, the *film d'art* movement had made the medium socially and intellectually respectable for the first time in its brief history, and had heightened the respect of the industry for itself. It also made a number of people, again notably Griffith and Feuillade, aware of the necessity for developing a unique style of film acting which would eschew the broad gestures and facial grimaces of nineteenth-century theater in favor of a more subtle and restrained kind of playing. These contortions were important components of the grand theatrical style, appropriate and even necessary on a stage which is distant from its audience and fixed in space. In the cinema, however, a fixed distance between the figures on the screen and the audience cannot be maintained because spatial relationships are in a constant state of flux due to editing and camera movement. Furthermore, even in the most conservative of filmed plays—those photographed in long shot from a single camera angle and edited only between scenes—the figures in the arranged *tableaux* appear much larger on the screen than they would on the legitimate stage, and theatrical gestures easily become exaggerated to the point of absurdity. In short, by attempting to impersonate the eye of a theater spectator, the *film d'art* camera taught a generation of film-makers how very little like an eye it really was. The human eye sees, but it also distorts, compensates, and errs. The scrutiny of the camera lens, however, is mercilessly accurate: it records all blemishes and is capable of magnifying the slightest facial mannerism to grotesque proportions on the screen. For this reason, film acting has had to develop conventions of its own in recognition of the perverse thoroughness with which the camera records certain aspects of reality,

2.26 Sarah Bernhardt in *La reine Elizabeth* (Louis Mercanton, for Histrionic Films, 1912).

and it might well be said that *film d'art* performances provided a negative model for these conventions.

Finally, *film d'art* productions were directly responsible for increasing the standard length of films from a single reel to five reels and above. As *films d'art* grew increasingly popular, they turned to ever weightier source material and grew proportionally in length. *L'assassinat du duc de Guise* (1908) had been only 921 feet, or a little less than fifteen minutes long at standard silent speed. One of the last and most prestigious *films d'art*, Louis Mercanton's *La reine Elizabeth* (*Queen Elizabeth*, 1912), ran three and one-half reels, or about fifty minutes—just one and one-half reels under the standard feature length. The story of how Adolph Zukor imported *Queen Elizabeth* into the United States and proved to the MPPC that Americans would sit through a film above a single reel in length (and pay a dollar each for the experience) has already been told. But it should be pointed out that the success of *film d'art* productions was also responsible for increasing film length in Great Britain, France, Italy, Germany, and Scandinavia, where the industries were less rigidly controlled than in America but equally conservative with regard to length. Thus, it fell to the *film d'art* movement to inaugurate the feature-length film in the West, though its advent had probably been inevitable since the invention of the Latham loop.

The Italian Super-Spectacle

No country was more responsible for the rapid rise of the feature film than Italy, whose lavishly produced costume spectacles brought its cinema to international prominence in the years immediately preceding World War I. The Italian film industry may be said to have begun with the construction of the Cines studios in Rome, 1905–6, by the former inventor Filotea Alberini (1865–1937). This firm gave the Italian cinema its first costume film, *La presa di Roma* (*The Capture of Rome* [1905]) but devoted most of its first years to the production of short comedies in the French vein and modishly "decadent" melodramas starring the archetypal *femme fatale* Lyda Borelli (1884–1959—the model for America's own definitive vamp Theda Bara [1890–1955]). As major Italian financiers became increasingly interested in the film business, however, rival production companies began to proliferate. When Ambrosio Films of Turin released Luigi Maggi's (1867–1946) six-reel *Gli ultimi giorni di Pompei* (*The Last Days of Pompeii*) in 1908, Cines once again turned its attention to historical themes, producing Mario Caserini's (1874–1920) feature-length *Catilina* and *Beatrice Cenci* in 1909, and his *Lucrezia Borgia* and *Messalina* in 1910. Concurrently, Pathé founded Film d'Art Italiana in Milan to produce historical costume dramas on its own, and suddenly the boom was on.

The years 1909 to 1911 saw a flood of historical films with titles like *Il sacco di Roma* (*The Sack of Rome* [Enrico Guazzoni, 1909]), *Giulio Cesare* (*Julius Caesar* [Giovanni Pastrone, 1909]), *La caduta di Troia* (*The Fall of Troy* [Giovanni Pastrone, 1910]), *Bruto* (*Brutus* [Enrico Guazzoni, 1910]), and *San Francisco* (*Saint Francis* [Enrico Guazzoni, 1911]); but 1912 witnessed the advent of the Italian super-spectacle in a ten-reel remake of Maggi's *Gli ultimi giorni di Pompei,* produced and directed by Ernesto Pasquali (1883–1919). As Vernon Jarratt points out, however, this film is entitled to its designation as the first of the great "blockbusters" only by virtue of its length and its cast of one thousand extras.[12] It was actually the nine-reel *Quo vadis?,* directed by Enrico Guazzoni for Cines in late 1912, that established the conventions of the

2.27 The chariot race from Enrico Guazzoni's *Quo vadis?* (1913).

2.28 Giovanni Pastrone's *Cabiria* (1914).

super-spectacle and captured the world market for the Italian cinema. Adapted from the novel by the Nobel laureate Henryk Sienkiewicz, *Quo vadis?* featured enormous three-dimensional sets designed by Guazzoni himself, crowd scenes with five thousand extras, a real chariot race, a real fire representing the burning of Rome, and a Coliseum full of real lions to devour the Christians. In terms of narrative, the film was a series of arranged scenes, but its spectacle properly made it an international hit, returning its producers twenty times their very substantial investment of 480,000 lire (about $48,000 in the currency of the period). So phenomenal was the success of *Quo vadis?* that the Cines technical staff was forced to work in twenty-four-hour shifts for some months to keep up with the worldwide demand for prints.

The successor to *Quo vadis?* was a film of even greater extravagance, grandeur, and distinction—the Italia Company's *Cabiria,* directed in 1914 by Giovanni Pastrone (under the name of Piero Fosco) and produced for the staggering sum of over one million lire (about $100,000 in the currency of the period). Pastrone wrote the script himself after twelve months of research in the Louvre and hired the famous Italian novelist Gabriele d'Annunzio to lend his name to it and to write the titles. Shot in Turin over a period of six months amid the most monumental and elaborate three-dimensional sets yet created for a motion picture, with exteriors filmed on location in Tunisia, Sicily, and the Alps, *Cabiria* is an epic saga of the Second Punic War between Rome and Carthage; it has been called by Vernon Jarratt "the dizziest peak of the Italian cinema."[13] Its twelve reels develop a dramatically sophisticated narrative against an historical reconstruction of the entire struggle from the burning of the Roman fleet at Syracuse (accomplished through some of the best special effects* to appear on the screen for the next twenty years) to Hannibal crossing the Alps and the sack of Carthage.

Spectacle aside, *Cabiria* contains some important innovations in film technique which may very well have influenced directors like Cecil B. DeMille and Ernst Lubitsch, as well as D. W. Griffith (see Chapters 3 and 6). The film is most notable for its use of extended, slow-moving tracking (or traveling) shots, which permitted the camera to roam about freely among the vast sets, moving in to isolate the characters in close-up and moving out again to re-frame the shifting action. Pastrone and his innovative Spanish cameraman Segundo de Chomón (1871–1929) improvised a dolly and a primitive crane to achieve these shots. Although Griffith was to use this process much more dynamically in *The Birth of a Nation* (1915) and *Intolerance* (1916), there is no question that Pastrone was the first director anywhere to attempt it on such a grand scale. *Cabiria*'s other significant innovations were the use of artificial (electrical) lighting to create dramatic effects (a technique later dubbed "Rembrandt lighting" and adopted by Griffith, DeMille, and Lubitsch), its use of careful and convincing process photography,† its relatively restrained acting, and its painstaking reconstruction of period detail (subsequently a hallmark of Griffith's and Lubitsch's historical films).

Released on the eve of the war and overshadowed by the recent international triumph of the much less distinguished *Quo vadis?*, *Cabiria* was not the financial success for which its producers had hoped. Indeed, the Italian cinema's brief period of commercial and aesthetic dominance was abuptly ended by World War I, and the nation's subsequent descent into Fascism prevented a renaissance until after World War II. Nevertheless, it seems clear today that this last and greatest of the Italian super-spectacles provided DeMille and Lubitsch with the model for their post-war historical spectacles and substantially influenced the narrative form of Griffith's epic masterworks. In fact, Griffith spoke of seeing both *Quo vadis?* and *Cabiria* while *The Birth of a Nation* was still in the planning stages, and there can be little doubt of their impact upon his development at a time when he was searching for an appropriate cinematic form into which to cast his epic vision of American history.‡

---

* Any shots which cannot be obtained through normal cinematography, including matte shots, front and rear projection, split-screen effects, shots using miniatures (model shots), and, more recently, explosions, ballistic effects, and computer graphics (see Glossary).

† The generic term for a number of special-effects techniques which combine studio action and backgrounds shot elsewhere into a single screen image. Back projection, the Schüfftan process, the glass shot, the matte shot, and the model shot are all types of process photography (see Glossary).

‡ By some accounts, Griffith is said to have purchased his own print of *Cabiria* and studied it intensively during the shooting of *The Birth of a Nation*.

D. W. Griffith and the Consummation of Narrative Form

The achievement of David Wark Griffith (1875–1948) is unprecedented in the history of Western art, much less Western film. In the brief span of six years, between directing his first one-reeler in 1908 and *The Birth of a Nation* in 1914, Griffith established the narrative language of the cinema as we know it today and turned an aesthetically inconsequential medium of entertainment into a fully articulated art form. He has been called, variously, and, for the most part, accurately, "the father of film technique," "the man who invented Hollywood," "the cinema's first great *auteur*," and "the Shakespeare of the screen." Yet in the fifty years since his most important work was completed, Griffith's stature as an artist has been the subject of continuous debate among film scholars, and his critical reputation has suffered more fluctuation than that of any other major figure in film history. The problem is that Griffith was essentially a figure of paradox. He was unquestionably the seminal genius of the narrative cinema and its first great visionary artist, but he was also a provincial Southern romantic with pretensions to high literary culture and a penchant for sentimentality and melodrama that would have embarrassed Dickens. Griffith was the film's first great technical master and its first legitimate poet, but he was also a muddleheaded racial bigot, incapable of abstract thought, who quite literally saw all of human history in the black-and-white terms of nineteenth-century melodrama. In one sense, Griffith presents the paradox of a nineteenth-century man who founded a uniquely twentieth-century art form, and this tension between ages accounts for many disparities of taste and judgment that we find in his films today. But there is another contradiction in Griffith which is less easy to rationalize and which raises issues central to the nature of film art itself, and that is the very existence of such staggering cinematic genius side by side with the intellectual and emotional shallowness described above. Given the peculiar limitations of his vision, Griffith was never dishonest or hypocritical, but he was intellectually narrow to an alarming degree for a major artist in any medium.

How is it, then, that the man who created films comparable in literature to Tolstoi's *War and Peace* (in their epic sweep and grandeur) and Joyce's *Ulysses* (in their revolutionary technical virtuosity) in these same

3.1 D. W. Griffith during his Biograph years.

films only rarely rose above the conceptual level of the dime novel? How can the man who created the apocalyptic, gut-churning racism of *The Birth of a Nation*, second in its manipulative distortion only to the Nazis' *Der ewige Jud* (*The Eternal Jew*, 1940),* deserve to be called an artist at all? On Griffith's death in 1948, his friend and one-time colleague, Eric von Stroheim, wrote that he alone among his peers had "put beauty and poetry into a cheap and tawdry sort of amusement," and yet, as the film historian Jay Leyda has observed, "None of Griffith's frustrating conflicts with the banks and the exhibitors was as bloody as the conflict with his own inadequacies."[1] The significance of Griffith to film history lies somewhere between the terms of this paradox, and by examining them we shall attempt to discover it.

FORMATIVE INFLUENCES

David Wark Griffith, the seventh child of a Confederate Army colonel, Civil War hero, and local character, Jacob "Roaring Jake" Griffith, was born in a rural district of Kentucky near the Indiana border in 1875. Never affluent, the Griffiths had been impoverished by the Reconstruction, but they clung to the ideals of the past, and David Wark grew up steeped in the romantic mythology of the Old South, with its codes of honor, chivalry, and purity intact. This regionalism combined well with Griffith's penchant for the more popular Victorian poets and novelists to produce a set of naïvely romantic values which the young man was never to outgrow. When Jacob Griffith died of an old war wound in 1885, Griffith's mother moved the family to Louisville, where she attempted to operate a boarding-house with scant success, adding urban poverty to the list of formative influences upon her son. Like Dickens in similar circumstances (and there are more than a few resemblances between the two artists), Griffith was forced to quit public school and work to help support the family.

After a succession of menial jobs in Louisville, he became stage-struck and began to tour the Midwest with traveling stock companies. Griffith's acting career was probably less a matter of aptitude than of zeal and good looks (he was strikingly handsome and statuesque throughout his life), but between 1897 and 1905 he pursued this career from Minneapolis to New York to San Francisco by jumping freights, living in flophouses, and working his way to his next engagement at all manner of jobs, from shoveling ore to picking hops. From San Francisco, Griffith returned to the East in 1906 with a respectable part in the Nance O'Neill Company's production of *Elizabeth the Queen of England*, after which he married the company's ingenue, Linda Arvidson (1884–1949), and began to write his own play, *The Fool and the Girl*, a serious melodrama

---

* A vicious but compelling anti-Semitic tract, purporting to be a documentary on the conspiratorial and verminous nature of European Jewry, which the Nazis used widely to indoctrinate the occupied nations into their extermination program (see Chapter 9).

derived from his recent experience of migratory workers in the California hop fields.

His acting career notwithstanding, Griffith's lifelong ambition had been to become a writer in the lofty and cultivated Victorian mode of his boyhood favorites. Unfortunately, he had little facility with language, and most of his literary productions were stilted and rhetorical. Miraculously, however, he sold his first play for one thousand dollars to the impresario James K. Hackett, who produced it in Washington, D.C., in the fall of 1907. *The Fool and the Girl* opened to hostile reviews and closed after two weeks, but Griffith was convinced of his talent and used his royalties to embark upon a new literary career. Within a year, he had managed to publish a handful of poems and short stories in mass-circulation middle-class magazines like *Collier's Weekly, Good Housekeeping,* and *Cosmopolitan,* and he had completed another play—a four-act epic drama of the American Revolution entitled *War,* based entirely on diaries and letters of the period which he found in the New York Public Library. Although much of its factual material was later incorporated into his film epic *America* (1924), *War* was never produced, and Griffith began to cast about again for steady employment.

It was under these circumstances in New York in late 1907 that he ran into Max Davidson, an old friend and acting colleague from Louisville, who advised him that a living might be made selling stories to the motion picture companies which had suddenly sprung up in the city. Griffith was initially opposed to the idea, fearing that his literary reputation would be damaged by association with the vulgar new medium. He knew very little about the movies at this time and in all probability had never seen one, but he held them in utter contempt. Nevertheless, he had to eat, and screen stories were then selling for around five dollars apiece; so he tossed off an uncredited version of Victorien Sardou's play *La Tosca* under his stage name, Lawrence Griffith, and offered it to Edwin S. Porter at the Edison Company studios. Porter rejected the scenario on the grounds that it had too many scenes for a movie, but, impressed with the young man's looks, he offered Griffith a job as an actor in his current film, *Rescued from an Eagle's Nest,* at a salary of five dollars per day. Griffith ruefully accepted. When the film was completed, Porter had no further use for the actor-scenarist, so Griffith approached the American Mutoscope and Biograph Company, at 11 East Fourteenth Street, with some of his screen stories.

THE BEGINNING AT BIOGRAPH

The American Mutoscope and Biograph Company had been founded in 1895 as a partnership among E. B. Koopman, Henry Marvin, Herman Casler, and William Kennedy Laurie Dickson, the inventor of the Kinetograph and Kinetoscope, as the K.M.C.D. Syndicate. Disaffected from the Edison Laboratories by a quarrel with the business manager, Dickson had combined with the others to perfect a motion picture technology which would rival Edison's without infringing his patents. (Interestingly enough, they envisioned their product chiefly as a marketing device for industrial manufacturers, whereby salesmen could demonstrate the operation of machinery such as looms and turbines to prospective clients.) Dickson invented a portable peepshow device (the "Mutoscope"*) for the syndicate, and later a camera and projector (both called the "Biograph"), all of which legally circumvented Edison patents. Though American Biograph (the word "Mutoscope" was dropped shortly after Griffith was hired) joined the Motion Picture Patents Company in 1909, the firm for years provided Edison with his only significant American competition and employed several of the most talented persons in the business—including the man who was to become Griffith's personal cinematographer, G. W. "Billy" Bitzer (1872–1944).

In 1908, however, the company was in serious trouble: it was $200,000 in debt to its bankers, and the public had begun to lose interest in its films. Furthermore, the health and energy of its director, George "Old Man" McCutcheon, were flagging rapidly, and the company had fallen below its standard production rate of two one-reel films per week. The need to hire a new director was clear, but the handful of experienced motion picture directors in the world at this time were all employed. Griffith, who was hired initially as an actor and story writer, was offered his first opportunity to direct a month afterwards on the basis of some perceptive remarks he had made to the Biograph cameraman, Arthur Marvin.

At first, Griffith was disinclined to take the job because he feared being fired from Biograph altogether if he failed. But his employers guaranteed him against this possibility and promised him his choice of story material and a free hand in selecting actors and locations. Characteristically, Griffith chose as the subject of his first film a melodramatic (and racist) little tale of a child kidnapped by Gypsies and improbably rescued after shooting the rapids in an empty water cask. Called *The Adventures of Dolly,* it was *Rescued from an Eagle's Nest* without the eagle. Griffith shot the film in two days on location at Sound Beach, Connecticut, in June 1908, with a great deal of advice and moral support from Bitzer and from Marvin, who was the cameraman. Though the film was scarcely innovative, it was respectable enough to garner Griffith a forty-five-dollar-a-week director's contract with Biograph and a royalty of one mil per foot on every print sold. By the time *The Adventures of Dolly* was given its first screening in July, Griffith had already directed five more films and completed one begun by another director.

3.2 K.M.C.D.'s Mutoscope, c. 1897.

---

* Rather than using a perforated film strip like the Kinetoscope, the Mutoscope mounted photographic impressions of individual film frames on cardboard cards and arranged them successively on a rotary wheel. When turned by a crank, the wheel would put the photographs in motion, flipping them rapidly one by one, to create "moving pictures" according to the same optical principles which govern the operation of camera and projector. Many Mutoscopes survive today in penny arcades and designated museums of Americana, official (the Smithsonian) and otherwise (Disneyland, Disney World). Due to the deterioration of so many early paper and nitrate prints, these Mutoscopes provide a rare opportunity to experience the images of primitive cinema at first hand.

INNOVATION, 1908–1909: INTER-FRAME NARRATIVE

In the five years that followed, Griffith directed over four hundred and fifty one- and two-reelers* for American Biograph, experimenting with every narrative technique which he would later employ in *The Birth of a Nation* (1915) and *Intolerance* (1916) and which would pass into the classical lexicon of the cinema. Yet Griffith seems to have been scarcely aware of his innovations. They were for him the unformulated results of practical problem-solving rather than of abstract theorizing, and his method of proceeding was always intuitive and empirical rather than formalistic. Unrestricted by narrative conventions, since there were very few at the time,† Griffith simply adopted for his Biograph films what worked best in the particular circumstances, according to the dynamics of the tale. If he had any methodology at all, it consisted in creating analogies between the conventions of stage narrative, which he knew implicitly from his long experience as an actor, and certain uniquely cinematic structural devices which he discovered as he went along. The narrative devices of the Victorian novels Griffith had loved in his youth also provided models for his innovations. Ultimately, Griffith combined his own analogies between dramatic/novelistic modes and cinematic modes with those of others, like Porter and Pastrone, and molded them into the visual narrative language which we call generically "film." In the course of his career, in fact, Griffith effected a nearly complete translation of nineteenth-century narrative modes into cinematic terms, insuring through the intensity, stature, and prestigiousness of his films that the cinema would remain a predominantly narrative form until some new technology or ideology was born to liberate it.

Griffith's first true innovation, besides the new seriousness he brought to his craft, occurred in a one-reel film entitled *For Love of Gold* (1908), adapted by Griffith from a short story by Jack London just four months after *The Adventures of Dolly*. In it, Griffith needed to show that two thieves, previously partners, had begun to mistrust one another. Because nearly all scenes in dramatic films of the day were photographed in *long shots,* showing the actors at full length from head to foot (as they would

---

*The vast majority are one-reelers, and, remarkably, all but eight of Griffith's Biograph films are known to have survived. In 1975, the Museum of Modern Art held a retrospective screening of nearly one hundred of them to commemorate the centennial of Griffith's birth.

† In his recent book *A History of Films* (New York, 1979), John L. Fell makes the claim that "film narrative was well organized when Griffith appeared" (p. 54). My own survey of recent research in film form prior to 1908 (for instance, Barry Salt, "Film Form, 1900–1906," *Sight and Sound,* 47, 3 [Summer 1978], 148–153) suggests that this is a gross overstatement of the facts. It is true that there were precedents for some of the "innovations" which Griffith and others have claimed were his alone, but that scarcely makes their application and elaboration in his hands any less significant or brilliant. I am inclined to agree with Edward Wagenknecht, who writes in *The Films of D. W. Griffith* (New York, 1975) that ". . . absolute priority in these matters is of very little interest; what counts in art is not who did it first but who does it best" (p. 17). See also John Fell, "Motive, Mischief and Melodrama," *Film Quarterly,* 33, 3 Spring 1980), 30–37.

appear on the stage), the only way of conveying a character's thoughts was to double-expose* a "dream balloon" of the type used by Porter in *The Life of an American Fireman* (1903) to show the fire chief's dream of home. But Griffith had a different notion: changing the position of his camera in mid-scene, he moved it into a *full* or *medium shot* of his actors from the waist up, so that the audience could read the actors' emotions in their faces rather than having to infer them from broad gestures. In so doing, Griffith had not only broken his scene up into a number of shots (which Porter seems to have done at least once before him) but had broken down the standard distance between the audience and the action, violating the canonical dictum of Charles Pathé: "In the cinema an actor must be photographed so that his feet touch the bottom of the screen and his head the top." The cut from long to medium shot worked effectively to solve a major narrative problem, and Griffith used it again and again in the next few months, with very positive results.

Griffith's next innovation was a logical extension of the first. In a 1908 screen version of Tennyson's narrative poem *Enoch Arden* entitled *After Many Years,* Griffith introduced what some regard as the first true narrative close-up in the history of cinema, the novelty close-ups and inserts of earlier directors notwithstanding. In a scene showing Annie Lee waiting for her husband's return from the sea, Griffith cut from a medium shot of the heroine to a large close-up of her brooding face; and, as if the psychological impact of this cut were not sufficient, he followed it with an associational cut from the close-up to the object of the woman's thoughts—her husband shipwrecked on a desert island. This was a revolutionary innovation, prefiguring not only the "subjective camera" of F. W. Murnau and Karl Freund but Eisenstein's "montage of attractions" (see Chapters 4 and 5, respectively). Griffith would use it for the rest of his Biograph career in films like *A Corner in Wheat* (1909), where he cut from a shot of the wheat tycoon gorging himself at a sumptuous meal to a shot of poor sharecroppers standing in a breadline.† He also employed the technique to effect the *flashback,* or "switchback," as he called it—a shot or sequence of shots which interrupts the narrative present and returns us momentarily to the past.

In fact, what Griffith had begun to do in *After Many Years* and would continue to do more and more successfully throughout his career was to *alternate shots of different spatial lengths,* none of which was dramatically complete in itself, to create cinematic "sentences" within scenes, cutting long shots, medium shots, and close-ups together in order to render a single dramatic scene from multiple points of view or angles of vision—i.e., from multiple camera set-ups. In the process, Griffith came to learn the immense symbolic and psychological value of the close-up, especially the close-up unexpectedly interpolated between shots of other

---

* To photograph separate images on the same strip of film which when projected appear simultaneously.

† See Eileen Bowser, "The Reconstitution of *A Corner in Wheat,*" *Cinema Journal,* 15, 2 (Spring 1976), 42–55, and "Addendum to the Reconstitution of *A Corner in Wheat,*" *Cinema Journal,* 19, 1 (Fall 1979), 101–2.

spatial lengths. Phenomenologically, the close-up has the effect of isolating a detail from its background and giving it greater dramatic emphasis by making it fill the frame.* In subsequent Biograph films like *Ramona* (1911) and *The Battle of Elderbush Gulch* (1912), Griffith would also learn the importance of the *extreme long shot* in rendering panoramic or epic action sequences of the type essential to *The Birth of a Nation* and *Intolerance*.

Now, however, the Biograph executives, who had opposed the production of *After Many Years* in the first place on the grounds that it had no action and no chase (and one of Griffith's many great achievements was to upgrade the intellectual content of contemporary films), were deeply and vocally shocked by this experiment which violated every known canon of film-making in its disregard for the dramatic unities of time and space and for strict chronological sequence. Griffith's response to their criticism, as reported by Linda Arvidson Griffith, tells us a great deal about his attitude toward his new craft:

> When Mr. Griffith suggested a scene showing Annie Lee waiting for her husband's return to be followed by a scene of Enoch cast away on a desert island, it was altogether too distracting.
> "How can you tell a story jumping about like that? The people won't know what it's about."
> "Well," said Mr. Griffith, "doesn't Dickens write that way?"
> "Yes, but that's Dickens; that's novel writing; that's different."
> "Oh, not so much, these are picture stories; not so different." [2]

As Griffith saw it, films were narratives, or stories, which were told through the arrangement not of words but of moving photographic images. Nevertheless, Biograph's managers felt Griffith had gone too far, and they closely watched the film's public reception. To their astonishment, *After Many Years* was hailed as a masterpiece, and, according to Lewis Jacobs, it was the first American film to be widely imported into foreign markets. [3] In his first year as Biograph's director, in fact, Griffith's films had substantially, if anonymously, improved the company's fortunes, and the Biograph product was soon enjoying the kind of critical prestige normally reserved for successful stage plays. In May 1909, for example, the *Dramatic Mirror* wrote of Biograph: "This progressive film company follows one high-class feature† production with another so rapidly as to make us wonder when and where the upward advance is to end." [4] Or, as Edward Wagenknecht puts it more meaningfully, "Even we children sensed that Biograph pictures were 'different,' though we could not, for the life of us, have told you wherein their difference might consist." [5]

Griffith's next step was even more radical, for it involved spatial and temporal fragmentation of the reality continuum to create the illusion of parallel action and achieve a new kind of dramatic suspense. In his 1909

---

* For an informative article on the historical evolution of the close-up, see Andrew Sarris, "About Faces," *American Film*, 4, 8 (June 1979), 54–61.

† In the sense of "premier" or "top of the line," and not "feature-length."

3.3 Four shots of parallel action from the three-way rescue which concludes *The Lonely Villa* (1909): the besieged family, and the husband rushing to the rescue. Missing are exterior shots of the robbers trying to break into the villa.

melodrama *The Lonely Villa,* Griffith wished to show three actions occurring simultaneously: a band of robbers attempting to break into a suburban villa from without, a frightened woman and her children desperately attempting to forestall the attack from within, and the husband rushing from town to rescue his family and drive away the robbers. In a logical extension of the technique he had employed in *After Many Years,* Griffith simply cut back and forth between one action and another, gradually increasing the tempo of alternation until all three actions converged in the dramatic climax of the tale. The effect of this *crosscutting* or *intercutting* was to transform the *dramatic* climax of his film into the *visual* or *cinematic* climax as well, so that the tale and the telling of the tale (i.e., the narrative technique) became the vehicles for one another—so that the medium, in effect, became the message. It is possible that Porter had used a rudimentary form of intercutting in *The Life of an American Fireman* in 1903 (as discussed in Chapter 1), and it seems clear that the filmmakers of the Brighton school and even Griffith himself (in films like *The Fatal Hour* [1908]) had experimented with the technique prior to 1909.* But *The Lonely Villa* was probably the first dramatic film to employ the device as its basic structural principle, and after its debut the practice of intercutting passed rapidly and permanently into the cinema's narrative lexicon.

In fact, so powerful was the impact of this film that its intercutting was widely imitated throughout the industry and came to be known generically as the "Griffith last-minute rescue." The term underscores an important element of this technique—its generation of suspense not simply through the rapid alternation of shots to portray simultaneous action but through the rapid alternation of shots of shorter and shorter duration. As Arthur Knight has noted, Griffith had discovered that the length of time a shot remained on the screen could create significant psychological tension in the audience—that the shorter the length of time a shot was held on the screen, the greater the tension it was capable of inducing.[6] This is the chief principle of the intercut rescue sequences for which Griffith became world famous, though of course this kind of editing is not restricted to the chase. It became, in fact, the structural foundation of the narrative cinema from *The Birth of a Nation* to the present. In the intercut rescues of the type that conclude *The Birth of a Nation* and *Intolerance,* for example, the alternating shots of the simultaneous actions grow shorter and shorter as the dramatic climax mounts, until we end with the visual counterpart of a musical crescendo. In other words, the visual tempo of the cutting for simultaneous action parallels the dramatic tempo of the action photographed, so that content is perfectly embodied in form. Griffith's second major innovation, then, is the syntactical corollary of the first—to the alternation of shots of varying *spatial lengths,* he added the alternation of shots of varying *temporal lengths,* creating the basis for

---

* In *A History of Films,* for example, John L. Fell notes that intercutting was practiced in Vitagraph's 1906 short *The Hundred-to-One Chance,* where the film-makers cut back and forth several times between a racing car and events taking place at its destination (p. 38).

montage and the montage aesthetics which came to dominate the first fifty years of narrative cinema.

Once again, public approval of Griffith's innovations was resounding (although his name was still not associated with them because of the MPPC's screen credit policy), and he was offered his second contract with Biograph in August 1909. Though he still had misgivings about "working for the nickelodeons," as he called it, Griffith accepted the job and continued to pursue his vigorous experiments in film narrative.

INNOVATION, 1909–1911: INTRA-FRAME NARRATIVE

The discoveries of 1908–9 (the alternation of shots of varying spatial and varying temporal lengths) had all been functions of editing, of the dynamic relationship *between* the clusters of frames we call shots (*inter*-frame narrative), but Griffith soon showed himself equally concerned with what occurred *within* the frames and shots of his films (*intra*-frame narrative). For one thing, he began to insist upon stories of high quality for his films, many of them derived from literary sources. To be sure, Griffith directed a fair number of chase films, melodramas, and potboilers during his tenure at Biograph, but he also adapted dramatic films from Shakespeare, Poe, Tennyson, Browning, Dickens, and Tolstoi, and some of his films, such as *A Corner in Wheat* (1909), even had serious (if simplistically treated) contemporary social themes. By making the content of his films more serious, Griffith was attempting to dignify the medium of motion pictures itself. Another aspect of this concern was the care he took in selecting and directing his actors.

Griffith was in fact the first great actor's director. Because he had been an actor himself and understood the psychology of the profession, he knew the value of careful rehearsals and rigidly imposed them upon his cast and crew, even though most other directors shot their films "cold." For their efforts, however, Griffith often paid his actors four times what they might receive at a rival studio, and by 1913 he had built his own stock company of ensemble players with such future luminaries as Mary Pickford and Lionel Barrymore (both soon to leave Griffith), Mae Marsh, Dorothy and Lillian Gish, Blanche Sweet, Henry B. Walthall, Bobbie Harron, Donald Crisp, and Wallace Reid. Griffith also understood, as no director had before him, how immensely revealing the motion picture camera is of exaggeration and artificiality in characterization, and he coached his performers for naturalness and subtlety of expression. Griffith's attention to detail extended even to his sets, whose design and construction he frequently supervised. To his employers, the care he lavished on his "nickelodeon" productions must at first have seemed a waste of time and money. Nevertheless, as early as 1909 audiences and critics alike were praising the "naturalness" and "authenticity" of films bearing the "AB" (American Biograph) trademark—as yet the only distinguishing mark of a Griffith production. Soon trade papers were writing enthusiastic articles on his motion pictures, and Biograph became the

3.4 Lighting for dramatic effect in *Pippa Passes* (1909).

3.5 Blanche Sweet in *The Lonedale Operator* (1911).

first studio to receive fan mail for individual films (Griffith's) rather than for individual stars.

Griffith's concern for the content of his films, however, went far beyond the care he bestowed upon his actors and sets. In late 1908, for example, in a film called *The Drunkard's Reformation,* he had begun to experiment with expressive lighting by illuminating a scene with firelight. At a time when electric mercury-vapor lamps had just been introduced for indoor shooting, this was a radical step because convention then dictated the flat and uniform illumination of every portion of the set. But the results of the effort were impressive, and Griffith went on to experiment with lighting more elaborately in a 1909 film version of Browning's dramatic poem *Pippa Passes* (the first film, incidentally, to be reviewed by the *New York Times*). The events of this one-reeler take place in a single day, and the passage of time is effectively rendered by changes in directional lighting which simulate the movement of the sun across the sky. In Griffith's first all-California film, *The Thread of Destiny* (1910), interior scenes of an old Spanish mission were lit solely by the slanting rays of the sun as they came through a high window, illuminating some objects, like the pulpit, and leaving others in darkness. (This shaft of light later reappeared in *Intolerance* to illumine the "endlessly rocking" cradle of the transitional scenes.) Griffith went on to become a master of tonal or atmospheric illumination (dubbed "Rembrandt lighting" by Cecil B. De-Mille's cameraman Alvin Wyckoff around 1915), which characterizes a given scene through patterns of highlight and shade. Moreover, although Griffith was forced, for financial reasons, to shoot most of his two great epics in direct sunlight, lighting for dramatic effect was soon established and elaborately refined by directors like Giovanni Pastrone in Italy, Ernst Lubitsch in Germany (and later the United States), and Cecil B. DeMille in the United States.

By far the most important of Griffith's contributions to intra-frame narrative, however, were made after he began to move his company to Southern California on a regular seasonal basis in early 1910. (Griffith was not the first film-maker to locate in Hollywood: in the fall of the previous year, the Selig Polyscope Company had built a small studio there.) Here, in films like *The Lonedale Operator* (1911) and *The Battle of Elderbush Gulch* (1912), he discovered the importance of camera movement and placement to the dramatic expressiveness of film. Before Griffith went to Hollywood, the film camera had been largely static. There had been *panning* (horizontal) and *tilting* (vertical) movements in films like *The Great Train Robbery,* but most of these were purely functional.* Griffith had begun to experiment with narrative panning shots as early as 1908 (*The Call of the Wild*) and 1909 (*The Country Doctor*). But in 1910 most film narratives—even those of Griffith—were structured mainly through editing, whether the units edited together were scenes or shots. In California, Griffith became increasingly interested in

---

*For some exceptions, see Jon Gartenberg, "Camera Movement in Edison and Biograph Films 1900–1906," *Cinema Journal,* 19, 2 (Spring 1980), 1–16.

structuring his films through intra-frame as well as inter-frame movement. In the horizontal sweep of the panning shot, Griffith was able not only to follow the movement of his principals through any given scene but to engage the audience in the total environment of his films. Moreover, in the *tracking* or *traveling shot,* in which the camera—and thus the audience—actively participates in the action by moving with it, Griffith brought a new kind of movement to the screen. In *The Lonedale Operator,* for example, in order to convey the breathless momentum of a locomotive speeding to the rescue of a young woman trapped by thieves, Grifith and Bitzer mounted their camera in the moving engine cab and crosscut between traveling shots of the engine plunging through the landscape and the desperate plight of the girl. In later years, Griffith and Bitzer would mount their camera in an automobile to follow moving action during the gathering of the Klan and the climactic riot sequence in *The Birth of a Nation,* and in the rescue sequence from the Modern story of *Intolerance.* (The Babylonian story of the latter film contains one of the longest and most elaborate tracking shots even made. In order to move their camera from an extreme long shot of the mammoth set of Belshazzar's feast straight into a full shot of the action, Griffith and Bitzer built an elevator tower that rolled on rails and tracked it slowly forward in a single unbroken shot which lasts nearly sixty seconds onscreen.) With these additions to film language, the whole notion of the frame as a proscenium arch, pervasive since Méliès, began to break down, and by the time Griffith finished *The Birth of a Nation* in 1914 it had nearly disappeared.

Griffith also discovered the dramatic expressiveness of camera placement during his early California years, becoming the first director to compose his shots in depth, with simultaneous action in background, middleground, and foreground rather than on a single plane. As early as 1910, he found that the perspective from which a shot was taken could be used to comment upon its content or to create dramatic emphasis for certain of its elements. A great deal can be said about a person's character metaphorically, for example, when he is photographed from a very low camera angle in a back-lit shot instead of a naturally lit head-on medium shot. The actor in a shot like this would seem to tower over the audience, and the lighting would create seemingly sinister shadows on his face. The reverse angle might be used to characterize someone who is helpless or weak, like Mae Marsh in the courtroom scene from the Modern story of *Intolerance.* Thus Griffith, who had already learned to create visual metaphors through associative editing (*After Many Years; A Corner in Wheat*), was now learning to create visual metaphors *within* the frame through camera placement. The logical extension of Griffith's metaphoric or symbolic style, seen at its height in *Intolerance* (1916) and *Broken Blossoms* (1919), occurs in the angular perspectives of German Expressionism and the subjective camera technique of F. W. Murnau and Karl Freund (see Chapter 4).

Griffith began other technical innovations at Biograph which seem decidedly minor by comparison with his breakthroughs in editing and in camera movement and placement, but which are important nonetheless. For one thing, he perfected the *dissolve* and the *fade,* both very crude transitional devices derived from Méliès before Griffith rendered them more fluid. Since the twenties, dissolves and fades have been synthetically processed in a machine called an optical printer, but in Griffith's time they were all accomplished in the camera. The scene which was to dissolve *out* was shot with a slowly closing shutter; then the film was stopped and rewound, and the scene which was to dissolve *in* was shot over the prior scene with the shutter slowly opening at the same speed. The *fade-in* and the *fade-out,* used by Griffith for the first time to begin and end film narratives, were accomplished by performing the same two processes separately.

Griffith perfected the dissolve and the fade, like so many other devices he brought to general recognition, simply by exercising more care in their achievement than earlier directors had done. Indeed, Griffith's greatest attribute as a film-maker aside from his cinematic genius was his compulsion to take everything about the cinema seriously once he had cast his lot with it. Many of his "discoveries" were not discoveries at all but simply the result of bestowing a degree of care on operations which earlier directors had performed in a slapdash manner, either through unconcern or because of the necessity of meeting their weekly quota of one-reelers for the MPPC. Griffith, in fact, "invented" very little in a literal sense. His greatness lay rather in his ability to self-consciously elaborate existing techniques into a new narrative language whose model was neither the reality continuum nor the stage.

Several innovations do belong solely to Griffith or to the Griffith-Bitzer collaboration. These include the *flashback,* the *iris shot* (a shot in which a circular lens-masking device either contracts or expands to isolate or reveal an area of the screen for symbolic or narrative emphasis), the *mask* or *matte shot* (a shot in which a masking device or diaphragm somehow changes the shape of the screen to achieve a dramatic visual effect), the *split-screen shot,* and the *soft-focus shot* (a blurring of the image for romantic effect, achieved through the use of a greased lens or a diffusion filter such as gauze). Like the dissolve and the fade, these devices were all essentially *graphic* embellishments, and today they are little used except by way of allusion to the Griffith era; but we shall soon see how important they were in creating the rich visual texture of *The Birth of a Nation* at a time when they were uncommon.

GRIFFITH'S DRIVE FOR INCREASED FILM LENGTH

Griffith's apprenticeship, as his Biograph period is often called, reached its peak in 1911 when he was offered his third contract at the extravagant salary of seventy-five dollars a week plus royalties and finally changed his working name back from Lawrence to David Wark (D. W.) Griffith. The change signaled Griffith's increased pride in his work and

3.6 An iris shot of Lillian Gish, from *The Birth of a Nation* (1915).

3.7 *The Musketeers of Pig Alley* (1912): Lillian and Dorothy Gish. Note the depth of the image.

his new conviction that motion pictures were a significant art form. The odd job he had taken three years earlier to keep from starving had finally become a career. As Griffith saw his one-reelers grow increasingly popular between 1911 and 1912, he opted for narratives of greater and greater complexity, like the tale of small-town hypocrisy, *The New York Hat* (1912), written by Anita Loos, and the contemporary street drama *The Musketeers of Pig Alley* (1912), shot on location in the streets of New York and often cited as a predecessor of Italian neo-realism. Yet, by late 1911 Griffith had begun to chafe under the constraints of the one-reel (ten-to-sixteen-minute) limit imposed by the MPPC upon all contemporary films. He felt that he had exhausted the one-reel form and could continue his experiments in narrative only by increasing the length of his films. He also seems to have understood that for the cinema to achieve the status of an art it would have to evolve a form commensurate with that of other narrative arts, and that such a form would have to be an expansive one which could provide for the dynamic interplay of its own components. The idea of a serious novel, opera, or play which takes only ten or fifteen minutes to apprehend is ludicrous, and Griffith reasoned that the same was true of cinema.

Accordingly, against the wishes of his employers, Griffith decided to remake his successful one-reeler *After Many Years* (1908) as the two-reel *Enoch Arden* in late 1911. Griffith had attempted a two-reeler in 1910 (*His Trust*), but Biograph had titled each reel separately and released them both as separate films. After the completion of *Enoch Arden*, the studio tried to do the same thing by releasing the film in two parts, but the public, through the film's exhibitors, demanded the full version, and Biograph ultimately yielded. In an ironic turnabout the following year, Biograph actively encouraged Griffith to make two-reelers instead of the standard product in order to compete with an influx of two-reel films from Europe. This pleased Griffith well enough for a time, and in 1912 he made three two-reel films in California (in addition to many others) which prepared both him and his audience for his 1913 feature *Judith of Bethulia*.

The first of these was *Man's Genesis* (remade the following year as *The Wars of the Primal Tribes,* or *Brute Force*), which the Biograph catalogue describes as "a psychological study founded upon the Darwinian theory of the Evolution of Man." While its allegorical account of intelligence triumphing over brute strength in prehistoric times is simplistic by contemporary standards, *Man's Genesis* was unique for its day. In the same year, Griffith also made *The Massacre,* which Lewis Jacobs has called "America's first spectacle film."[7] This two-reeler offered an historical reconstruction of a wagon train massacre with overtones of Custer's Last Stand, and it presented Griffith with his greatest technical challenge to date. Nevertheless, its large-scale battle scenes look forward to those of *The Birth of a Nation* in their fluid editing continuity and their striking photographic composition, and Griffith had reason to expect that *The Massacre* would be hailed as a great achievement. Instead, it was barely noticed, for in the interim between the film's production and its release, *Queen Elizabeth* and other *films d'art* had come to America and touched off "feature fever" in a market once solely geared to shorts.

Except for its relative length, Griffith saw little to admire in *Queen Elizabeth,* which contained only twelve separate shots or camera set-ups in its entire fifty-three-minute running time. (Griffith's one-reel *The Sands of Dee,* produced concurrently with *Queen Elizabeth,* used sixty-eight separate shots in less than ten minutes.) But he did not like being upstaged, and immediately began production of what he hoped would be a new masterpiece, *The Mothering Heart,* a contemporary melodrama whose extravagant budget was a source of deep concern to Biograph's president, J. J. Kennedy. Before the film was finished, however, Italy's spectacular *Quo vadis?* arrived in America, and *The Mothering Heart* fell into obscurity while audiences stood in line, naturally enough, to see the longest and most expensive motion picture ever made. Griffith was beside himself, for now he had been not only upstaged but outclassed. *Quo Vadis?* was scarcely innovative in terms of its narrative technique and today looks archaic next to Griffith's more sophisticated two-reelers, but it was the elaborate, big-budget feature that he had longed to make for the past two years. Now he was determined to best his new European rivals; he set to work frenetically upon a lavish new production which he vowed would clinch his title as supreme master of the cinema.

JUDITH OF BETHULIA AND THE MOVE TO MUTUAL

It is uncertain whether or not Griffith had actually seen *Quo vadis?* when he began shooting *Judith of Bethulia* in the secrecy of Chatsworth Park, California, in June 1913, but he had read enough about the film in

3.8 *The Massacre* (1912).

3.9 *Judith of Bethulia* (1913).

the trade press to know that its essence was epic spectacle. Griffith's own film was based on a story from the Apocrypha about the Bethulian widow Judith who feigned love for the Assyrian conqueror Holofernes in order to assassinate him and save her besieged city. The film was budgeted at eighteen thousand dollars, a very large sum for its day, but Griffith ended up spending more than twice that amount in his compulsive quest for dramatic authenticity and grandeur of scale. A substantial portion of the film's budget was spent rehearsing elaborate battle sequences on the twelve-mile-square set at Chatsworth, which housed, among other wonders, a full-scale reconstruction of Bethulia. Griffith's penchant for accuracy of detail in costuming and production design accounted for another large chunk of the budget. But the most expensive aspect of the film was its length: Griffith shot six full reels of film stock for *Judith of Bethulia,* which he later edited into four reels.

This film represents the summation of Griffith's Biograph career. Like that of *Intolerance,* its complex story is divided into four contrapuntal movements and employs nearly every narrative device Griffith had discovered or perfected in his five years with the studio. Nevertheless, the economy of the film's narrative development is often quite remarkable given the sophistication of its technique. As spectacle, *Judith of Bethulia* moved beyond anything seen on the screen to date, with its mass scenes of sieges, open-field battles, and chariot charges; and yet, as in Griffith's later masterpieces, the personal drama of the protagonists is never lost amid the epic scale of the action. Despite occasional lapses of taste (the pseudo-orgiastic dance of the Fish Maidens, for example), *Judith of Bethulia* is the greatest American film made before 1914. As Jacobs has remarked, "Even if Griffith had done nothing further than *Judith of Bethulia,* he would still be considered a sensitive and outstanding craftsman."[8]

Griffith's employers at Biograph, however, were stunned at their director's extravagance and audacity, and they resolved to take action against him. When Griffith returned to New York with his six unedited reels of

Judith of Bethulia, Biograph vice-president and general manager Henry Marvin informed him that he had been "promoted" to production chief of the studio, from which position he would supervise the work of other directors but not direct films or handle budgets himself. Moreover, caught up in the *film d'art* craze produced by *Queen Elizabeth,* Biograph had signed an ill-fated contract with the theatrical producers Klaw and Erlanger to film their stage plays as five-reel features. The meaning of Griffith's new "promotion" was all too clear: he could stay at Biograph only if he would agree to supervise his former assistants in the mechanical reproduction of stage plays. This was impossible for him, and so he let it be known among the independent producers that he was looking for a new job.

Because his Biograph shorts had come to epitomize successful film craftsmanship in the American industry, Griffith was almost immediately offered fifty thousand dollars a year by Adolph Zukor, but he turned it down because he rightly saw that Zukor's company would offer him no more creative freedom that Biograph had. More to his liking was the proposition of Harry E. Aitken (1870–1956), the president of a new film distributing company called Mutual, to come to work for his subsidiary firm of Reliance-Majestic as an independent producer-director at a salary of one thousand dollars per week. Aitken promised to let Griffith make two independent feature films a year, in addition to the conventional program features he would be required to direct under his contract, and Griffith accepted the offer without hesitation. On December 3, 1913, Griffith announced his departure from Biograph in an advertisement in the *New York Dramatic Mirror* which correctly proclaimed him to be "Producer of all great Biograph successes, revolutionizing Motion Picture drama and founding the modern technique of the art." The advertisement went on to enumerate, with some exaggeration, his specific technical contributions to the form ("the large or close-up figures, distant views, . . . the 'switch-back,' sustained suspense, the 'fade out,' and restraint in expression") and to list 151 of his most important and successful Biograph films from *The Adventures of Dolly* through the still unreleased *Judith of Bethulia.* In this manner, Griffith publicly and legitimately laid claim to the hundreds of films he had directed for Biograph in almost complete anonymity between 1908 and 1913; but more important was the fact that the man who had once been so ashamed of working for the "living pictures" now proclaimed himself to be the founding father of the narrative cinema and its first great personal artist or, to borrow a term from contemporary criticism, its first great *auteur.*

Griffith took with him to Mutual/Reliance-Majestic most of the stock company of ensemble players he had built up during the years at Biograph, but his brilliant and invaluable cameraman, Billy Bitzer, at first refused to follow him on the grounds that there was more security in working for a Patents Company member than for an independent. After several months, however, Bitzer was finally persuaded to join Griffith as his director of photography. He was to stay with Griffith throughout his career and to work on at least twenty-four of the thirty-five feature films

3.10 D. W. Griffith's advertisement for himself.

3.11 Bitzer and Griffith examining a shot on the set of Biograph's *The Avenging Conscience* (1913) shortly before their departure from the company.

he made between 1914 and 1931. With this, the Griffith company was once again complete and ready to embark upon the production of two of the most important and influential motion pictures ever made.*

THE BIRTH OF A NATION

Production

Before he turned to his first independent project in late 1914, Griffith took his company to Hollywood and hurried through four minor program features for Reliance-Majestic, one of which, a potboiler entitled *The Battle of the Sexes,* was shot in four days. Griffith nevertheless insisted that Mutual's president, Harry Aitken, promote each film with expensive advance publicity and rent a Broadway legitimate theater for its opening. So committed had Griffith become to cinema that even the reception of his potboilers was a matter of serious concern to him. But he was still haunted by the success of the Italian super-spectacles, and he sought everywhere for an epic subject that would enable him at last to rival them. He found it when one of his writers, Frank E. Woods, told him about a modestly successful play entitled *The Clansman,* adapted by a Southern clergyman, Thomas Dixon, from his own novel, which concerned the return of a Confederate soldier to his ravaged home in South Carolina after the Civil War and his role there in the organization of the Ku Klux Klan. Both novel and play were decidedly mediocre as literature and openly racist in their depiction of the Reconstruction period as one in which renegade mulatto "carpetbaggers" and Negro thugs joined with unscrupulous white politicians to destroy the social fabric of the South. Yet this material had a natural fascination for Griffith, whose romantic image of the South and the Civil War had stayed with him since childhood. In fact, some of his most spectacular Biograph films had dealt with incidents from the Civil War, and now he seized the opportunity to do a feature-length epic on the subject.

Aitken was induced to buy the screen rights to the story from Dixon for $10,000,† and Griffith and Woods collaborated on a loose scenario, supplementing *The Clansman* with material from another Dixon book entitled *The Leopard's Spots* and with Griffith's own idealized vision of the South. When they were done, the story covered not only the Reconstruction period but the years immediately preceding the Civil War and the war itself. The film was initially budgeted by Aitken at $40,000, or four times the usual rate for a conventional feature, but as Griffith became more and more obsessively involved with the project that figure grew until it nearly tripled. By the time the film was completed at a cost of $110,000, Griffith's entire personal fortune, including his weekly pay-

---

* After Griffith and his company left Biograph, the production company rapidly declined, and in 1915 it was liquidated.

† Dixon accepted a $2,500 down-payment and later opted for a percentage of the film's profits rather than the $7,500 balance, whereby he became very rich.

checks, had been pumped into the enterprise, along with the savings of many associates and friends.

Shooting began in total secrecy in late 1914, and, despite the rough scenario put together with Woods, Griffith worked wholly without a written script. Through six weeks of rehearsal and nine weeks of shooting—a remarkable schedule in an era when most features were cranked out in a week—Griffith carried around in his head every detail of the editing continuity, titles, settings, costumes, and props. So personal an undertaking was his Civil War epic, in fact, that no one involved in the production but Griffith had any clear idea of what the film was about. The cast and crew were astonished at the number of camera set-ups he would demand for a single scene, and no one could imagine how the director intended to assemble into a single film the thousands of separate shots he was taking. As Lillian Gish wrote of the filming: "We were rarely assigned parts, and the younger members of the company always rehearsed for the older members when the story was being developed, as all the 'writing' was done by Griffith as he moved groups of characters around. . . . When the story was ready to go before the camera, the older players . . . came forward and acted the parts they had been watching us rehearse for them. . . . Very often we would play episodes without knowing the complete story. . . . Only Griffith knew the continuity of *The Birth of a Nation* in its final form."[9] Griffith did indeed have a grand design for his film, because he was quite consciously involved in creating "the greatest picture ever made," but this should not obscure the fact that he was a great *practical* genius whose finest effects were often improvised on the set to meet some specific requirement of the narrative or the shooting process. Griffith was also tenacious to the point of monomania: the shooting was finished in the winter of 1914 only because he had personally forced the film to completion against some very difficult odds, including a shortage of production materials created by the First World War, his own huge budget deficit, and industry-wide hostility toward his project's revolutionary nature.

Originally composed of over 1,544 separate shots—in an era in which the most sophisticated of foreign spectacles contained fewer than 100—*The Clansman* (as it was initially called) took Griffith some three months to edit and score. When the job was done, he had achieved on a vast scale the nearly total integration of every narrative technique he had ever used and, in collaboration with the composer Joseph Carl Breil* (1870–1926), had synthesized an orchestral score from the music of Grieg, Wagner, Tchaikovsky, Beethoven, Liszt, Rossini, Verdi, and American folk and period songs (e.g., "Dixie," "Marching Through Georgia"), which dramatically paralleled the editing continuity of the film. He had also produced the longest (twelve reels) and most expensive ($110,000) motion picture yet made in America, and because of its

---

*Breil had composed scores for the American versions of *Queen Elizabeth* (1912) and *Cabiria* (1914), and he later collaborated with Griffith to score *Intolerance* (1916), *The White Rose* (1923), and *America* (1924)

length the existing exchanges refused to distribute it. Griffith and Aitken were forced to form their own company, the Epoch Producing Corporation, to handle distribution of *The Clansman* amid widespread predictions that Griffith's "audacious monstrosity," as one Trust member called it, would be a box-office disaster.* But within five years of its opening, Griffith's "monstrosity" would return more than fifteen million dollars.

The Clansman had its premiere on February 8, 1915, at Clune's auditorium in Los Angeles, and its first public opening on March 3, 1915, at the Liberty Theater in New York, where it was retitled *The Birth of a Nation* and ran for an unprecedented forty-eight consecutive weeks. At Aitken's insistence, it was the first film ever to command the two-dollar admission price of the legitimate theater, and its phenomenal popularity made it one of the top-grossing films of all time. By 1948, *The Birth of a Nation* had been seen in theaters by an estimated 150 million people all over the world and, according to trade legend, had grossed nearly forty-eight million dollars, or more than any film made anywhere in the world up to that time.† From its very first screening in Los Angeles, the critics were unanimous in their praise of the film's technical brilliance. As the trade paper *Variety* remarked on March 12, 1915, "Daily newspapers pronounced it the last word in picture-making," and for a while it seemed that no critical hyperbole was too strong to describe Griffith's achievement. "Epoch-making" and "prestigious" were the terms most frequently applied to his film, and after a special White House screening (the first of its kind), President Woodrow Wilson, who was himself a professional historian, is reputed to have said, "It is like writing history with lightning."

But combined with the film's success there was also controversy and scandal. Several weeks after the New York opening, Griffith yielded to pressure from the National Association for the Advancement of Colored People (founded in 1908) and city officials to cut the film's most blatantly racist sequences. He grudgingly removed some 558 feet, reducing the

---

* The film was opened at first-class legitimate theaters in all of the major cities to garner publicity and two-dollar admissions (a marketing strategy later known as "road showing") and then distributed to small towns and cities on a "states' rights" basis. In this latter arrangement, regional distributors would buy the exclusive rights to control exhibition of the film in a given state or group of states, with Epoch receiving a percentage of the box-office grosses. In *D. W. Griffith: His Life and Work* (New York: Oxford University Press, 1972), Robert M. Henderson points out that Aitken's failure to set up an accurate accounting system for the states' rights returns (which he wrongly thought would be small) caused Mutual to lose millions of dollars in concealed profits to regional distributors (pp. 158–59). Operating as the states rights' distributor for Massachusetts, Louis B. Mayer alone made a million dollars in rake-offs from *The Birth of a Nation* (a fortune which would later enable him to become the driving force behind Metro-Goldwyn-Mayer).

† According to *Variety*'s Seventy-Fourth Anniversary edition for January 9, 1980, the true figure is closer to ten million dollars. But the business practices described in the note above suggest that the actual grosses far exceeded those reported by regional distributors (see, for example, Janet Wasko, "D. W. Griffith and the Banks," *Journal of the University Film Association*, 30, 1 [Winter 1978], 15–20).

total number of shots from 1,544 to 1,375. This excised material has never been recovered,* but it apparently included scenes of white women being sexually attacked by renegade blacks as well as an epilogue suggesting that the solution to America's racial problems was the deportation of the Negroes to Africa. No sooner had Griffith made this compromise than historians, President Wilson notwithstanding, began to assail his distorted view of Reconstruction; and prominent citizens and community leaders such as the president of Harvard University, Jane Addams of Hull House, and the editors of progressive urban weeklies started to attack *The Birth of a Nation* for its racial bigotry and to demand its suppression. Oswald Garrison Villard, the editor of the *Nation,* called the film "improper, immoral, and injurious—a deliberate attempt to humiliate ten million American citizens and portray them as nothing but beasts,"[10] and the governor of Massachusetts attempted to have the film banned throughout the state after a race riot had attended its Boston premiere. Riots also occurred when the film opened in Chicago and Atlanta, where it was directly instrumental in the birth of the modern Ku Klux Klan.† So extreme was the antagonism created by Griffith's epic that it was ultimately refused licenses for exhibition in Connecticut, Illinois, Kansas, Massachusetts, Minnesota, New Jersey, Wisconsin, and Ohio; and President Wilson was forced to retract his praise publicly and to suggest that the film had used its brilliant technique in the service of specious ends.‡

Griffith was shocked and deeply injured by the unexpectedly hostile reaction to *The Birth of a Nation.* From his point of view, he had struggled for a full year against nearly insurmountable odds to bring forth what he considered to be not only "the greatest picture ever made" but a great epic of the American nation. The widespread public attacks upon his film seemed to him like attacks upon American civilization itself, and he

---

* Some of it exists on the original nitrate stock at the Library of Congress but is unavailable for research purposes.

† One immediate response within the black community was an attempt to create an indigenous Afro-American cinema, which ultimately resulted in Selig Polyscope's swindle-ridden, fragmentary epic of black history *The Birth of a Race* (1918). A complete six-reel nitrate print of this rare all-black film was discovered near Canyon, Texas, in 1980 by representatives of the American Film Institute and will soon be available for public screening. See Thomas Cripps, *Slow Fade to Black: The Negro in American Film, 1900–1942* (New York: Oxford University Press, 1977), pp. 70–75. In another black counter-offensive, a brief epilogue was in some cities added to *The Birth of a Nation* itself, filmed on the campus of the Hampton Institute, Hampton, Virginia, apparently by professional photographers on the Hampton staff. This "Hampton Epilogue" stressed the advancement of the Negro race since Reconstruction and its contributions to American social and industrial progress. Griffith permitted the addition to silence protest against his film, but its mitigating effect was negligible. See Nickie Fleener, "Answering Film with Film: The Hampton Epilogue, a Positive Alternative to the Negative Black Stereotypes Presented in *The Birth of a Nation,*" *The Journal of Popular Film and Television,* 7, 4 (Summer 1980), 400–425.

‡ For more on the public reaction to *The Birth of a Nation* and on its historical context, see Daniel J. Leab, "*The Birth of a Nation* as a Public Event," and A. Marshall Deutelbaum, "Reassessing *The Birth of a Nation,*" in *"The Birth of a Nation" and 1915"* (Society for Cinema Studies, 1976), pp. 4–11 and 12–14.

struck back by publishing a pamphlet, entitled *The Rise and Fall of Free Speech in America,* which vigorously defended *The Birth of a Nation* against censorship by attacking the practice itself but which offered no answers to the specific charges of racism. The charges were in fact unanswerable, for race was central to Griffith's interpretation of American history.

Epics are concerned with the origins of races, and the "nation" born out of Griffith's epic was quite clearly White America. It may be true, as a recent biographer has remarked, that Griffith's "racial bias was almost totally unconscious,"[11] but regional conditioning had so perverted his understanding of American history that his film became in many ways a pseudo-historical tract whose collective hero is the "Aryan" race (Griffith's term). In another sense, though, Griffith was simply confirming the stereotypes of his age, for *The Birth of a Nation* accurately incarnates the myth of Reconstruction propagated by politicians and historians alike in the late nineteenth and early twentieth centuries. The social economist and philosopher Thorstein Veblen remarked, after viewing the film in 1915, "Never before have I seen such concise misinformation"; but much of the misinformation contained in *The Birth of a Nation* belonged to an entire generation of Americans. If Griffith distorted history, then so did Woodrow Wilson in his five-volume *History of the American People* (1902), written while he was president of Princeton University, which tells pretty much the same story as *The Birth of a Nation* in Volume V, even to the point of spelling "negro" with a small "n"—a practice for which Griffith is still vilified.

In its monumental scale, in its concentration upon a crucial moment in American history, in its mixture of historical and invented characters, in its constant narrative movement between the epochal and the human, and, most significantly, in its chillingly accurate vision of an American society predicated on race, *The Birth of a Nation* is a profoundly *American* epic. We can fault Griffith for badly distorting the historical facts of Reconstruction, for unconscionably stereotyping the American Negro as either fool or brute, and for glorifying a terrorist organization like the Klan, but we cannot quarrel with his basic assumption that American society was, and is, profoundly racist. That he endorses and encourages this situation rather than condemns it is properly repellent to contemporary audiences, as it was to many persons in 1915. But *we* must not allow our sympathies to obscure our own critical judgment, for then we make the same mistake as Griffith. And, as Americans, we must never overlook the possibility that the impetus for our most hostile reactions to Griffith's racism lies somewhere within our most deeply cherished illusions about ourselves.*

---

* It is instructive in this regard to compare the extreme reactions to *The Birth of a Nation* with the public outcry over *The Deer Hunter* (Michael Cimino, 1978), which portrays Vietnamese in a manner similar to Griffith's depiction of American blacks. In fact, the parallels between the two films, separated by sixty-five years, are striking. Both are lengthy, emotional epics about American involvement in wars which most of us would like to forget—not merely because they were brutal but because they brought Americans into bloody conflict with one another. Both films attempt to reconcile the breach between Amer-

Structure

3.12 A classically structured Griffith battle sequence from *The Birth of a Nation,* moving from extreme long shot to long shot to medium shot to close shot: Henry B. Walthall as Ben Cameron.

The Birth of a Nation tells the story of the American Civil War and its aftermath from a southern point of view, treating, as an inter-title states, "the agony which the South endured that a nation might be born." It is well to remember that the events it depicts were recent history to the audiences of 1915, only fifty years distant. Like Griffith himself, many persons seeing the film in the year of its release knew intimate details of the war from parents who had survived it, and the political and social divisions produced by the conflict still ran very deep.

The film begins with a prologue explaining that the seeds of the tragedy were sown not by the South but by the seventeenth-century New England traders who first brought the slaves to America and who, ironically, Griffith claims, were the ancestors of the nineteenth-century abolitionists. There follows a brief pre-war interlude in which two northern boys, both sons of the powerful abolitionist senator Austin Stoneman (modeled on Thaddeus Stevens, Republican congressman from Pennsylvania and leader of the radical Reconstructionists in the House of Representatives), visit their former boarding-school friends, the Cameron brothers, on the family's modest plantation in Piedmont, South Carolina. During this idyll, which is intended to show the grace and charm of southern culture as well as the general beneficence of plantation life, Phil Stoneman falls in love with the Cameron daughter, Margaret, while young Ben Cameron discovers his ideal of feminine beauty in a daguerreotype of Phil's sister, Elsie. Immediately following the visit, civil war breaks out, and both the northern and southern brothers heed the call to arms of their respective governments.

The next portion of *The Birth of a Nation* deals with the war itself and is very nearly self-contained. It is this part of the film which most truly merits the description "epic," for it combines a sophisticated narration of historical events with spectacle on a colossal scale. From the moment the Piedmont regiment marches off gaily and naïvely to its first battle, to the assassination of President Lincoln at Ford's Theater, we are swept along on a narrative current so forceful and hypnotic that it is impossible even today to escape its attraction. The siege of Petersburg, the burning of Atlanta, and Sherman's march to the sea are all recreated in battle scenes whose intensity is still compelling, despite six decades of technological refinement. Griffith and Bitzer composed these scenes after Mathew Brady's Civil War photographs and shot them from many different perspectives, combining extreme long shots of the battlefields with medium and close shots of bloody hand-to-hand fighting to evoke the chaotic violence of combat itself. Griffith increased the tension of these sequences by radically varying the duration of each shot and by cutting on contrary

---

icans by appealing to the racial prejudices of the majority, and both fictionalize history in the process. Finally, *The Birth of a Nation* and *The Deer Hunter* have both provoked—and will no doubt continue to provoke—highly ambivalent public responses because, however manipulative or wrong-headed they may be, the two films deal openly with matters about which our society is itself extremely ambivalent.

movements: at one point in the Battle of Petersburg, Griffith cuts from a group of Confederate soldiers charging across the screen from the left side of the frame to a band of Union soldiers charging across from the right, while a third cut shows their ferocious head-on collision on the field. For the burning of Atlanta sequence, Griffith used a diagonally split screen containing blazing buildings in the upper half and Sherman's relentlessly marching troops in the lower half, all illuminated by bursting shells and flames (according to Bitzer, the only artificially lit sequence in the film).

3.13 The wounded Ben Cameron is carried across the Union lines at Petersburg.

Griffith continues the personal story of the Stonemans and the Camerons against this panoramic overview of the Civil War. The families' two youngest sons die in each other's arms on the battlefield; and Ben Cameron, the "little Colonel," is wounded and captured by federal troops after leading a daring charge against the Union lines at Petersburg. Meanwhile, in the South, a band of renegade Negro militiamen ransacks the Cameron homestead in Piedmont, leaving the family with little but their lives, and Atlanta is destroyed as Sherman marches to the sea. Griffith renders the devastating impact of this march in a striking iris shot. A small iris at the upper left-hand corner of the frame gradually opens to disclose a sorrowful mother with her children gathered about her on a hillside. As the iris opens further, the source of the woman's misery is revealed to be Sherman's troops marching like columns of black ants through the valley below: cause and effect are thus dramatically and visually linked.*

3.14 Sherman marches to the sea.

Concurrently, in a Union military hospital in Washington, D.C., Ben Cameron once again meets Elsie Stoneman, who nurses him back to health in her capacity as a volunteer. Mrs. Cameron soon joins her son in the hospital when she learns that he is under a death sentence for guerrilla activities, and she successfully intercedes for his life with a reverently portrayed President Lincoln. Despite their sentimentality, the detailed composition in depth of these hospital scenes, whose action in foreground, middleground, and background is autonomous, has long impressed critics with its verisimilitude. Equally authentic is the reconstruction of the Confederate surrender at Appomatox which follows—one of the several effective "historical facsimiles" that Griffith introduced from time to time into the narrative. As the war ends, the Camerons begin to rebuild their ravaged home, and Ben returns to Piedmont in a moving and understated homecoming scene.

3.15 The surrender at Appomattox, an "historical facsimile" from *The Birth of a Nation:* Howard Gaye as Lee, Donald Crisp as Grant.

In Washington, Phil and Elsie Stoneman attend a performance of *Our American Cousin* at Ford's Theater and witness the assassination of President Lincoln. Since the assassination sequence is one of Griffith's great

3.16 The homecoming.

---

* In his autobiography, *Billy Bitzer: His Story* (New York, 1973), Bitzer says that the mother and children were an actual family group which happened to stop along the hillside while the crew was setting up the Sherman's march sequence below. Griffith ordered him to sneak up the hill and shoot them unawares. This shot was later combined with the long shot of the marching troops through matting to create the single iris shot composition described above. As Bitzer comments, it was touches like this "that made *The Birth* so real and convincing to audiences accustomed to stilted acting and stock shots, especially in costume movies" (p. 108).

set pieces and provides an excellent example of his continuity editing, it is worth examining in some detail. The following excerpt from the script of the film prepared by Theodore Huff for the Museum of Modern Art[12] illustrates Griffith's brilliant use of parallel editing to achieve tension in the scene:

TITLE
The gala performance to celebrate the surrender of Lee, attended by the President and staff.
THE YOUNG STONEMANS PRESENT.
An historical facsimile of Ford's Theater as on that night, exact in size and detail with the recorded incidents, after Nicolay and Hay in *Lincoln, a History.*   24 feet*

SCENE 444
Iris-in to circle bottom of screen
Elsie and her brother come to seats—speak to acquaintances—
Iris opens to full screen to long shot of theater (from above one side showing stage 1—orchestra, boxes, gallery, etc.)   18 feet

SCENE 445
Semi-close-up of Phil and Elsie
She looks through her opera glasses.   3 feet

TITLE
"The play: *Our American Cousin,* starring Laura Keene."   4 feet

SCENE 446
As 444
The painted curtain rises—maid dusting table.   7 feet

SCENE 447
Medium-long shot of stage
Star enters grandly.   3 feet

SCENE 448
As 446
Star bows to audience's applause.   4½ feet

SCENE 449
As 445
Elsie with fan—applauds—smiles at brother.   6 feet

SCENE 450
As 447
Star blows kisses to audience—bows.   3½ feet

SCENE 451
As 448
Star comes forward to footlights—receives flowers—
applause—   9 feet

TITLE
"Time, 8:30
The arrival of the President, Mrs. Lincoln, and party."   4½ feet

---

* "The figure at the right of each scene is the footage; it also can be taken as the number of seconds the scene lasts. When scenes were under three feet, they were measured exactly—the figure in parentheses being the number of *frames.* Thus 2 (4) means two feet plus four frames, or a total of thirty-six frames (sixteen frames per foot-second)" [*Preface to the script*].

SCENE 452
Three-quarter shot of stairs back of box (sides rounded)
Stairs dark and shadowy—guard leads man, two women, and
Lincoln up stairs.   8 feet

SCENE 453
Medium shot of theater box
First of party enter.   3 feet

SCENE 454
As 452
Lincoln hands hat and coat to man—enters box door right.   5 feet

SCENE 455
As 453
Lincoln comes forward in box.   4½ feet

SCENE 456
Semi-close-up of Phil and Elsie
They see Lincoln—applaud—rise.   6 feet

SCENE 457
Long shot of theater
Audience standing up, cheering.   2½ feet

SCENE 458
As 453
Lincoln bows.   2 (6)

SCENE 459
As 457
Audience cheering.   2½ feet

SCENE 460
As 458
Lincoln and party sit down.   6½ feet

TITLE
"Mr. Lincoln's personal bodyguard takes his post outside the
presidential box."   6 feet

SCENE 461
Three-quarter shot of hall back of box (corners rounded)
Guard enters—sits in chair in front of box door.   10½ feet

SCENE 462
As 459
Audience still standing—play tries to go on—   4 feet

SCENE 463
As 460
The box—President and Mrs. Lincoln bowing.   8 feet

SCENE 464
Medium-long shot of audience and box (corners soft)
Cheers—waving handkerchiefs.   3 feet

SCENE 465
Medium shot of stage
Old-style footlights—painted scenery—people leave stage—couple
alone, come forward—spotlight follows them.   9 feet

TITLE
"To get a view of the play, the bodyguard leaves his post."   2 (10)

SCENE 466
Medium shot of hall, rear of box (edges rounded)
Guard tries to see play.   3½ feet

SCENE 467
Medium shot of stage   3 feet

SCENE 468
As 466
Guard gets up—opens rear door to gallery.   6½ feet

SCENE 469
Long shot of theater   Iris-up toward boxes and gallery
Guard comes.   3 feet

SCENE 470
Medium shot of gallery (circle)
The guard seats himself at edge.   4 feet

TITLE
"Time, 10:13
Act III, scene 2"   2 feet

SCENE 471
Long shot of theater   Iris at upper right corner of screen
The gallery—man in shadows.   4 feet

SCENE 472
Semi-close-up of Phil and Elsie
Watching play—Elsie laughing behind fan—points with
fan to man in balcony—asks who he is.   7 feet

TITLE
"John Wilkes Booth."   (14)

SCENE 473
Semi-close-up of Booth (circle iris)
(Napoleon pose) in the shadows of gallery.   2 (2)

SCENE 474
As 472
Elsie is amused by his mysterious appearance—laughs
behind fan—looks at him through opera glasses.   6 feet

SCENE 475
As 473
Booth waiting.   2 (3)

SCENE 476
Medium-long shot of gallery and audience (sides rounded)
Booth waiting   5½ feet

SCENE 477
As 475
Booth waiting.   4 feet

SCENE 478
Medium shot of stage play
Comedy line—man waves arms.   3½ feet

SCENE 479
Medium shot of Lincoln's box
They laugh—Lincoln feels draught—reaches for shawl.   6½ feet

SCENE 480
As 477
Booth watches.   3 feet

SCENE 481
As 479
The box—Lincoln drawing shawl around shoulders.   5½ feet

SCENE 482
Long shot of theater as 471   *Iris opens*
Booth goes to box door.   5 feet

SCENE 483
Medium shot (circle)
Guard in gallery—Booth opens door behind him.   1 (7)

SCENE 484
Medium shot of hall back of box (corners softened)
Heavy shadows—Booth enters softly—closes and locks door—peeks
through keyhole at box door—stands up majestically—pulls out
pistol—tosses head back—actor-like—   12½ feet

SCENE 485
Close-up of pistol (circle vignette)
He cocks it.   3 feet

SCENE 486
As 484
Booth comes forward—opens door to box—enters.   9 feet

SCENE 487
The box as 479
Booth creeps in behind Lincoln.   4½ feet

SCENE 488
The play as 478
The comic chases woman out—cheers.   4 feet

SCENE 489
Medium shot of box
Lincoln is shot—Booth jumps from left side of box.   4½ feet

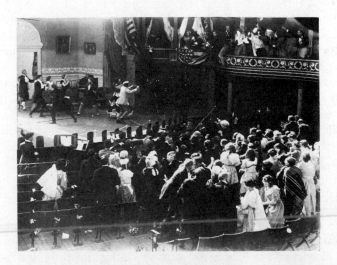

3.17   The assassination of Lincoln: Raoul Walsh as
Booth, Joseph Henabery as Lincoln.

SCENE 490
Long shot of theater
Booth jumps on stage—shouts. 2½ feet

TITLE
"Sic semper tyrannis!" 2 feet

SCENE 491
Medium shot of Booth on stage
Holds arms out—limps back quickly. 3 feet

SCENE 492
Medium shot of box
Lincoln slumped down—Mrs. Lincoln calls for help. 2 (6)

SCENE 493
Semi-close-up of Phil and Elsie
They hardly realize what has happened—rise. 4½ feet

SCENE 494
Long shot of theater
Audience standing up in turmoil—Elsie in foreground faints—Phil
supports her— 4 feet

SCENE 495
As 492
Man climbs up into box to Lincoln's aid. 5 feet

SCENE 496
Medium-long shot of theater and boxes
Audience agitated. 3½ feet

SCENE 497
Long shot of excited throng
Phil and Elsie leave.
Fade-out 11½ feet

SCENE 498
Medium shot of box
They carry Lincoln out.
Fade-out 10½ feet

The sequence is composed of fifty-five shots, some held for only a few
seconds; it establishes dynamic *visual* relationships among Lincoln,
Booth, the bodyguard, the audience, and the play long before their *dramatic* relationship is energized by the assassination. One has only to
imagine how a Porter or a Zecca might have handled this sequence in a
single shot or perhaps several to understand the breadth of Griffith's
achievement.

Lincoln's assassination, much lamented in the South, concludes the
"War" section of *The Birth of a Nation* and inaugurates the most controversial part of the film—that dealing with Reconstruction. This section opens with the ascendancy of Senator Austin Stoneman to "the
power behind the throne" after Lincoln's death. Determined, as a title informs us, to crush "the White South under the heel of the Black South" (a
phrase from Wilson's *History of the American People,* incidentally, and
not an invention of Griffith's), Stoneman leads the radical Reconstructionists to victory in Congress and sends his fawning but secretly

3.18 In Piedmont, the Camerons learn
of Lincoln's death: Ben, Flora (Mae
Marsh), Dr. Cameron (Spottiswoode Aitken), Mrs. Cameron (Josephine Crowell),
and Margaret (Miriam Cooper).

ambitious mulatto protégé, Silas Lynch, to Piedmont to administer a program of universal Negro suffrage there. Lynch and his lieutenants, however, organize the recently freed slaves into a mob, and commit a series of outrages against the white community ranging from mere insult to bogus imprisonment and sexual assault.

Lynch subsequently becomes lieutenant governor of South Carolina and goes on to preside over a moronic all-Negro legislature which enacts statutes providing for the disenfranchisement of prominent whites and for interracial marriage. One of Griffith's most masterful uses of the dissolve appears in the state legislature scene. He opens it with a still photograph of the actual chambers and slowly dissolves to a replica of the hall swarming with raucous, gin-swilling Negro solons. The sequence concludes with a revoltingly effective iris-in. After the legislature has enacted its racial intermarriage bill, an iris begins to slowly close upon a group of Negroes on the assembly floor who are leering at something above them; then the iris moves like the lens of a telescope to reveal the object of this lustful attention: a group of frightened white women and children in the gallery.

3.19 Griffith's version of the South Carolina legislature.

While this travesty is enacted in the state capital, back in Piedmont Ben Cameron decides that the "Black Empire" of Lynch and his cronies must be combated by an "Invisible Empire" of white southern knights, organized, as a title tells us, "in defense of their Aryan birthright." This is Griffith's account of the birth of the Ku Klux Klan, and it must be said that the account is not much different from that offered by the historians of his era, including Woodrow Wilson, who wrote in the fifth volume of his *History of the American People:*

> The white men of the South were aroused by the mere instinct of self-preservation to rid themselves, by fair means or foul, of the intolerable burden of governments sustained by the votes of ignorant negroes and conducted in the interest of adventurers. . . . They could act only by private combination, by private means, as a force outside the government, hostile to it, proscribed by it, of whom opposition and bitter resistance was expected, and expected with defiance.[13]

Meanwhile, Austin Stoneman has come to Piedmont with his family to oversee the implementation of his policies. The senator has fallen ill in the interim, however, and becomes an easy dupe of the vicious Lynch and of Stoneman's own mulatto mistress, Lydia Brown. The Elsie Stoneman–Ben Cameron and Phil Stoneman–Margaret Cameron romances start to blossom again in Piedmont but are cut short by the bitter residues of war. In one particularly striking scene, Phil proposes to Margaret, and Griffith intercuts the proposal with a flashback to an earlier shot of her young brother lying dead on the field at Petersburg. Griffith once said, "You can photograph thought," and in this flashback sequence, and many others like it sprinkled throughout *The Birth of a Nation,* he demonstrated his point remarkably well. Finally, after another wave of indignities committed by blacks against whites, the terrorist reprisals of the Klan begin in earnest, and Elsie rejects Ben when she learns of his involvement with the organization.

At this point, the film takes an extremely nasty turn as young Flora Cameron, the family's darling, is attacked (but not actually raped) and driven to take her life by Gus, a "renegade negro" who wants to marry her. Gus chases Flora through a forest and up a cliff from which she plummets to her death rather than submit to his embraces, even as brother Ben races desperately to the rescue. Filmed amid the beautiful pine forests and foothills of Big Bear Lake, California, this sequence is perhaps the most skillfully edited three-way chase Griffith ever conceived. But, like a similar sequence in Ingmar Bergman's *The Virgin Spring* (1962; see Chapter 14), it is the most disturbing in the entire film, for there is no rational way for a viewer to defend against its wrenching images of racial violence and attempted violation. Here we see Griffith, like Eisenstein after him, a master of sensational manipulation, assaulting our sensibilities beyond the bounds of decency in order to drive home an ideological point. It is among the cinema's most compelling and horrifying sequences, as unforgettable—though by no means as forgivable—as the Odessa steps massacre in Eisenstein's *Potemkin* (1925; see Chapter 5) and the bullet-riddled death agony of Arthur Penn's protagonists in *Bonnie and Clyde* (1967; see Chapter 17).

After Flora's death, Gus is tracked down by the Klan and summarily executed in a scene which is dramatically apposite but morally loathsome for the legitimacy it accords the practice of lynching. The body is dumped on the lieutenant governor's doorstep as a warning, and Lynch's reply is to call out the Negro militia for a roundup of suspected Klansmen. Old Dr. Cameron, head of the family, is arrested in the process but is ultimately rescued by two "faithful" black "souls," his daughter Margaret, and Phil Stoneman (now turned against his father) and taken to the sanctuary of a small woodland cabin. Meanwhile, Elsie Stoneman attempts to intercede with Lynch on Cameron's behalf only to find herself being forced into an interracial marriage with the vicious mulatto, who has become "drunk with power and wine" (Griffith's phrase) as the troops of his "Black Empire" run amok in the streets of Piedmont, arbitrarily assaulting and killing whites.

Now the film starts to build to its climax as the Lynch-Elsie sequence is intercut with the "Summoning of the Clans" sequence in which two hooded Klansmen, or "Night Hawks," ride through the countryside far and wide, spreading news of the Piedmont rampage and sounding the call to arms. As their wild ride progresses, Klansmen are drawn to the Night Hawks like tributaries flowing into a central stream, until a vast army pours down the road to the rescue, in the words of the poet and critic Vachel Lindsay, like "an Anglo-Saxon Niagara."[14] Meanwhile, Negro militiamen have discovered the cabin containing Dr. Cameron, Margaret, and Phil, and have besieged it with every intention of murdering its occupants. Shots of this action are now intercut with shots of the

3.20 Gus (Walter Long) about to be lynched by the "Invisible Empire."

3.21 The torrential ride of the Klan.

---

* V. I. Pudovkin (see Chapter 5) used a similar montage sequence for the climax of *Mother* (1925), in which individual workers flow together from the side streets and byways of St. Petersburg into a mighty revolutionary stream heading toward the factories.

torrential ride of the Klan, Negroes rioting in the streets of Piedmont, and what has become by this time Lynch's impending rape of Elsie Stoneman; so that we have a suspense-filled, multi-pronged "last-minute rescue" elaborately wrought of four simultaneous actions converging toward a climax. Griffith heightens the tension of his montage by decreasing the temporal length of each shot and increasing the tempo of physical movement as the sequence moves toward its crescendo. When at last the Klan arrives in town to clear the streets, there follows an action sequence that rivals the battle scenes of the war section. Its dynamic continuity cutting and breathlessly moving camera caused Vachel Lindsay to describe this episode as "tossing wildly and rhythmically like the sea." [15]

3.22   The arrival in Piedmont.

After Piedmont is secured and Elsie Stoneman rescued from Lynch, the Klan learns of the besieged cabin in the woods and begins its second ride. Though anticlimactic, this second rescue is more urgent than the first since the band of Negroes has almost succeeded in breaking into the little stronghold when the ride begins, and danger to the principals is imminent. After a flurry of intercutting in which the Negroes finally enter the house and actually grasp Margaret Cameron by her long tresses, the Klan arrives to disperse them and save the whites from violation and/or murder. There follows a parade of the Klan and the rescued parties through the streets of Piedmont, and a new election, easily dominated by the whites. A title tells us that the "Black Empire" has collapsed in the face of the "Invisible Empire," and that "the establishment of the South in its rightful place is the birth of a new nation." The two Cameron-Stoneman marriages take place, and the film concludes with a symbolic epilogue in which the God of War dissolves into the Prince of Peace and we are told, somewhat prematurely, that "the new nation, the real United States, as the years glided by, turned away forever from the blood lust of war and anticipated with hope the world millennium in which the brotherhood of love should bind all the nations."

3.23   Ben Cameron leads a charge of liberators in a rapid backward tracking shot.

3.24   The triumphal march: Margaret Cameron, Elsie Stoneman (Lillian Gish), and friends.

Impact

It should be obvious by this point that, whatever it represents ideologically, *The Birth of a Nation* is a technical marvel. Griffith created it in the absence not only of established narrative conventions but of modern cinematic technology—what he might have accomplished with wide-screen color cameras and stereophonic sound is beyond imagining.* And to have articulated these conventions and anticipated this technology in a film of epic proportions so early in the medium's history is a monumental achievement that no one can gainsay. Furthermore, in his symbolic use of objects in close-shot (inedible parched corn in the plate of a Confederate defender of Petersburg; a bird in the hands of the gentle "Little Colonel" during a rendezvous with Elsie Stoneman) and what might be called the "psychological" or "subjective" intercut (the image of Margaret Cameron's dead brother appearing during Phil Stoneman's proposal of marriage; flashbacks depicting recent Negro outrages in Piedmont as Ben Cameron narrates them to his family), Griffith moved the cinema in the direction of "symbolic realism," or the representation of reality which suggests a symbolic—i.e., a psychological or universal—meaning. Even without cutting, Griffith frequently manages to endow reality with symbolic significance. At the most rudimentary level, for example, Silas Lynch's cruelty to animals implies his capacity for evil, while Senator Stoneman's limp suggests his moral weakness and impotence. Griffith's approach to symbolic realism often degenerates into sentimentality, as when the "Little Colonel" and Elsie kiss the bird held in Ben's hand instead of each other, but his discovery and elaboration of the mode made possible the infinitely more sophisticated symbolic methods of Eisenstein and the school of Soviet montage (see Chapter 5).

The influence of *The Birth of a Nation* was not, of course, all benign. For one thing, it is a matter of historical record that the film's glowing portrait of the Ku Klux Klan was directly responsible for the modern revival and expansion of that organization, whose membership had reached five million by the time of World War II.† Indeed, according to the Klan's current leaders, *The Birth of a Nation* was used as a key instrument of recruitment and indoctrination well into the nineteen-sixties. Less pernicious socially, but perhaps ultimately more destructive, was the enormous financial success of the film, which gave Hollywood at the moment of its birth a permanent taste for the emotional, sensational, and melodramatic as opposed to the rational, philosophical, and discursive. As a supremely manipulative film, *The Birth of a Nation* showed the American industry how effectively and lucratively the movies could pander to public frustration, anxiety, and prejudice—a lesson that Hollywood has hardly ever forgotten in its seventy-year history, as the recent

---

* The film was in fact shot with a single camera—a three-hundred-dollar hand-cranked Pathé with two interchangeable lenses (a 2.52-inch and a wide-angle).

† See Maxim Simcovitch, "The Impact of Griffith's *Birth of a Nation* on the Modern Ku Klux Klan," *Journal of Popular Film,* 1, 1 (Winter 1972), 45–54.

3.25 Sensationalistic posters, Peoria, Illinois, 1916.

crop of disaster-and-mayhem and grisly horror films demonstrates. Thus, "the man who invented Hollywood" gave that institution not only its initial direction and its emotional tenor but its first successful formula as well.

Yet, precisely because of its remarkable emotional power, its tendency to incite and inflame rather than to persuade, *The Birth of a Nation* marked the emergence of film as a potent social and political force in the modern world. As Harry M. Geduld writes:

> It was the first film to be taken seriously as a political statement and it has never failed to be regarded seriously as a "sociological document." . . . People who had previously dismissed the movies as nothing more than a crude entertainment suddenly realized that they had become the century's most potent and provocative medium of expression: the mechanized age had produced mass communications, mass entertainment, and also the possibility of mass indoctrination.[16]

At the same time, *The Birth of a Nation* was so clearly a work of genius, however flawed, that it conferred great prestige upon the new medium of the feature film when it most needed it. The first film ever to be widely acclaimed as a great work of art and simultaneously reviled as a pernicious distortion of the truth, *The Birth of a Nation* is the cinema's seminal masterpiece, and its paradox is the paradox of cinematic narrative itself. Whereas literary narrative tells invented tales through the deliberate manipulation of verbal signs which exist at a third remove from reality, film constructs its fictions through the deliberate manipulation of photographed reality itself, so that in cinema artifice and reality become quite literally indistinguishable. Perhaps the final comment on *The Birth of a Nation* and the whole narrative tradition it founded belongs to Woodrow Wilson, despite his subsequent retraction. It was, he said, "like writing history with lightning,"[17] and lightning is powerful, illuminating, even magical. But it is also unpredictable, potentially destructive, and highly imprecise.

INTOLERANCE

Production

More persons saw *The The Birth of a Nation* in the first year of its release than had seen any single film in history. Attendance in the Greater New York area alone was over 825,000, and nationally the figure was close to three million. Griffith had achieved his goal of outdoing the Italian super-spectacles on their own terms, and he was universally acknowledged to be the supreme master of the screen. But his victory was not unmixed with bitterness. Attacks on *The Birth of a Nation*'s content continued (indeed, they have never stopped), and the accusation that he was a bigot disturbed Griffith deeply. In *The Rise and Fall of Free Speech in America* (1915), his counterblast to the film's detractors, he had declared:

> The integrity of free speech and publication was not . . . attacked seriously in this country until the arrival of the *motion picture,* when this new art was seized by the powers of intolerance as an excuse for an assault on our liberties. . . . Intolerance is the root of all censorship. Intolerance martyred Joan of Arc. Intolerance smashed the first printing press. Intolerance invented Salem witchcraft.

Early in 1916, still stinging from charges of racism, Griffith determined to produce a massive cinematic polemic against these "powers of intolerance" as they had endangered civilization throughout human history. The resulting film, *Intolerance,* was not—as is sometimes claimed—Griffith's "liberal" atonement for his "reactionary" Civil War epic but rather a spirited defense of his right to have made it. Both films are cut from the same cloth, and their liabilities and assets are quite similar.

Just after *The Birth of a Nation* was released, Griffith had gone to work on a modest contemporary melodrama entitled *The Mother and the Law.* A relatively low-budget feature by its predecessor's standards, more on the scale of *The Battle of the Sexes* (1914) than *The Birth of a Nation,* it was based upon a recent case in which Pinkerton guards had killed nineteen workers during a strike at a chemical plant. *The Mother and the Law* had already been completed when Griffith conceived the idea of combining it with three other tales into an epic exposé of intolerance through the ages. One tale would be set in ancient Babylon during the invasion and conquest of Cyrus the Persian (538 A.D.), another during the St. Bartholomew's Day Massacre in sixteenth-century France (1572), and another in Judea during the Crucifixion of Christ (we can guess which story Griffith saw as most closely paralleling

3.26 The Babylonian set of *Intolerance* (1916) prepared for the Belshazzar's feast sequence and the lengthy tracking shot.

his own recent martyrdom). This promised to be an expensive undertaking, but Griffith had been so elevated by the success of *The Birth of a Nation* that no project, however extravagant, could be denied him. He was now working for the Triangle Film Corporation, which his producer, Harry Aitken, had formed with Griffith, Mack Sennett, and Thomas H. Ince (see Chapter 6) in late 1915, after he had been ousted from Mutual as the result of an internal power struggle. Triangle was not wealthy enough to produce Griffith's new epic, but Aitken incorporated the Wark Producing Corporation to finance the film, and investors fought one another for the privilege of betting on a second Griffith blockbuster.

It was well that they did, for with no standards left to exceed but his own, Griffith conceived of *Intolerance* on a scale so vast as to dwarf all of his previous work combined. Sparing no expense, financial or human, he threw up mammoth sets designed by the previously uncredited Walter W. Hall* for each of the four periods represented in the film, the most elaborate of which was a full-scale model of ancient Babylon covering more than ten acres of land and standing some three hundred feet above the ground. He hired sixty principal players and eighteen thousand extras to people the film, and at one point the production's payroll alone exceeded twenty thousand dollars a day. Among his eight assistant directors (*The Birth of a Nation* had none) were four who would later have significant Hollywood careers of their own—Allan Dwan, Christy Cabanne, Tod

---

* Hall surfaced as the production designer of *Intolerance*, apparently his only film, with the publication of Karl Brown's *Adventures with D. W. Griffith* (New York, 1973). Brown was Bitzer's assistant and provides a lively and detailed account of the making of *The Birth of a Nation*, *Intolerance* and other Griffith features.

3.27   The Babylonian set under construction, seen from behind.   3.28   The walls of Babylon besieged.

Browning, and Erich von Stroheim. When the project was finally completed, Griffith had spent fourteen months and nearly two million dollars on it.* *The Birth of a Nation,* by comparison, had been put together in seven months for one-twentieth the sum. Indeed, a single banquet scene in the Babylonian section of *Intolerance* cost more than $250,000 to film, or well over twice the entire budget of its predecessor. This unprecedented extravagance caused alarm among Griffith's backers, and he was forced to plow back a substantial portion of his profits from *The Birth of a Nation* (ultimately about one million dollars) into *Intolerance* in order to keep the project afloat. If the film had been the popular success he expected, Griffith would have become one of the richest men in Hollywood. As it was, *Intolerance* nearly ruined him.

The rough cut† of *Intolerance* ran for eight hours, and Griffith toyed with the notion of distributing the film at this length in two separate parts. Practicality got the better of him, however, and he cut the release print from 200,000 to 13,500 feet, approximately three and one-half hours. After the box-office failure of *Intolerance* became apparent, Griffith rashly cut into the negative and re-edited *The Mother and the Law* and *The Fall of Babylon* for release as separate films to recoup his losses. Later, when he attempted to reconstruct the negative, nearly two thousand feet had been permanently lost, so that today we can never see *Intolerance* in its original form, which, according to the custom of the day, also included tinting in blue, red, green, and sepia to achieve atmospheric effects (blue for melancholy and night, red for war and passion, green for the pastoral and for calm, and sepia for interiors). Nevertheless, the

---

* The total cost of production, publicity, and distribution. A Price-Waterhouse audit in 1916 set the negative cost at $485,000, a figure still forty times the budget of a conventional feature in that year.

† The "first draft" of a film—the preliminary linking together of shots and sequences into coherent dramatic and cinematic form.

version which has come down to us closely resembles the original in terms of its formal structure, and this is the most important aspect of the film from our standpoint.*

Structure

For *Intolerance,* Griffith conceived the revolutionary notion of cross-cutting not only between parallel actions occurring simultaneously in separate spatial dimensions, as in his earlier films, but between parallel actions occurring on separate temporal planes—those of the four stories—as well. Thus, the plots of the four stories are interwoven like movements in a symphony until they converge in a crescendo at the film's climax. Before this quadruple climax, actions occurring in the separate historical periods are episodically self-contained and are drawn together by the recurrent transitional symbol of a mother rocking a cradle, emblematic of human continuity. This image is illuminated by a shaft of sacred light and accompanied by Walt Whitman's line "Out of the cradle endlessly rocking. . . ." As the separate stories move toward their conclusions, however, Griffith largely abandons this transitional device and cuts back and forth directly between incomplete climactic actions in the process of unfolding on all four temporal planes. He told a contemporary interviewer: "[The] stories will begin like four currents looked at from a hilltop. At first the four currents will flow apart, slowly and quietly. But as they flow, they grow nearer and nearer together, and faster and faster, until in the end, in the last act, they mingle in one mighty river of expression."[18] Although the Biblical and St. Bartholomew's Day plots are resolved before the more complicated Babylonian and Modern stories, for the better part of the film's last two reels Griffith involves us in three separate three-way rescues and a dramatically excoriating Crucifixion. In these passages, Christ's progress toward Calvary, the desperate ride of the "Mountain girl" across the Euphrates plain to warn Babylon of its impending destruction, the massacre of the French Huguenots, and the modern wife's race against time to save her innocent husband from execution are all rapidly intercut in shots of shorter and shorter duration to create what is even today among the most exciting and unusual climactic sequences in motion picture history. As Iris Barry said of it, "History itself seems to pour like a cataract across the screen."[19] Like *The Birth of a Nation, Intolerance* concludes with a symbolic montage in which prison walls dissolve into flowered meadows and a grim place of battle becomes a field of frolicking children.

Contemporary audiences, who had only recently been exposed to the conventional if striking narrative intercutting of *The Birth of a Nation,* found this essentially metaphorical or symbolic intercutting difficult to understand—not surprisingly, for Griffith was cinematically years ahead of his time. He was already practicing in *Intolerance* the kind of abstract

3.29 Transition: "Out of the cradle endlessly rocking. . . ." Lillian Gish as The Woman Who Rocks the Cradle.

---

* The reconstructed version of *Intolerance* is currently available for rental in a 16mm tinted print.

3.30 Christ on the road to Calvary: Howard Gaye.

3.31 The St. Bartholomew's Day Massacre begins.

3.32 Griffith and Bitzer shooting the climactic chase in the Modern story: Mae Marsh (center) as The Dear One.

or "expressive" montage that Eisenstein and his Soviet colleagues would bring to perfection a decade later (see Chapter 5). Furthermore, the film contains the ultimate refinement of every narrative device Griffith had employed from *The Adventures of Dolly* through *The Birth of a Nation*. It uses revolutionary continuity editing, of course, but also huge close-ups, sweeping panoramas, assorted dissolves, irises, and masks (including a widescreen effect used for large battle sequences), dramatically expressive camera angles, and, finally, tracking movement that anticipates the elaborate maneuvers of F. W. Murnau and the German *Kammerspielfilm* (see Chapter 4) eight years later. For the climactic rescue of the Modern story, for example, Griffith mounted his camera in a moving automobile to follow a suspenseful chase between it and a train, just as he had done for the riot sequences in *The Birth of a Nation*. More important, Griffith built for *Intolerance* a huge elevator tower that rolled on rails to track the camera gradually from an extreme long shot of Babylon down into a full shot of actors on the set itself. The shot occurs several times in the film and is still one of the longest and most elaborate tracking shots in the American cinema.

Influence and Defects

For sheer technical virtuosity and inventiveness, then, *Intolerance* must rank as Griffith's greatest film. Moreover, Griffith's handling of massive crowd and battle scenes, as well as more intimate personal ones, surpassed anything he had ever done before or would attempt again. For the past decade, however, it has been customary to praise *Intolerance* far beyond its intrinsic worth because it went on to have such a powerful influence upon the Soviet film-makers who articulated and refined montage. It is also a relatively "safe" film to like compared to its volatile predecessor, and some critics have even tried (incorrectly) to make of it

3.33 Shot sequence from the "last-minute rescue" in the Modern story intercut with the Crucifixion: Bobby Harron as the Boy.

an apology for *The Birth of a Nation*. Yet, as an aesthetic experience rather than a narrative structure, *Intolerance* is something of a white elephant. Its spectacular proportions are unwieldy, and its elaborate intercutting apparatus does not always work. There are moments of incoherence: the St. Bartholomew's Day story sometimes gets lost in the shuffle, and the precise sequence of events in the Babylonian episode occasionally becomes unclear. Worse, Griffith's case-pleading in both his images and his titles becomes nearly hysterical at times, and his expressed intention to show "how hatred and intolerance, through the ages, have battled against love and charity" is scarcely germane to either the Babylonian or the Modern sequences. Indeed, Griffith hardly seems to have known what he meant by the term "intolerance," except that he associated it with the bitter outcry against *The Birth of a Nation*. In the context of the film itself, "intolerance" is simply an omnibus word encapsulating any form of human evil; and evil, of course, has never been a difficult or an unpopular subject to attack.

Intolerance is, in fact, the most Manichean of Griffith's feature films: in portraying the melodramatic struggle of Good against Evil through the ages, Griffith allowed his sentimentality to become distinctly overripe. Indeed, there are so many pious, pompous titles in *Intolerance* that Iris Barry was led to describe the film as "an epic sermon."[20] Ultimately, *Intolerance* is an erratic but brilliant film of undeniable importance whose decisive influence upon figures as diverse as Cecil B. DeMille, Sergei Eisenstein, V. I. Pudovkin, Fritz Lang, and Abel Gance is a matter of historical record. As a self-contained work of art, it is by turns ponderous, awe-inspiring, obsessive, and thrilling. The film historian Jay Leyda, in an essay written on the occasion of Griffith's death in 1948, called *Intolerance* "a towering compound of greatness and cheapness,"[21] but the film-maker John Dorr put it more precisely: "*Intolerance* succeeded as a film of spectacle and as a film of narrative action, but not as a film of ideas."[22]

For the audiences of 1916, which cared little for ideas in any event, *Intolerance* was simply too much—too big, too complicated, too serious, and too solemn. Ironically, the film's commercial failure was probably conditioned by its predecessor's enormous success. The millions who had been swept away by *The Birth of a Nation* expected Griffith's second epic to carry them off in the same tumultuous and inflammatory manner. Emotional appeal, however, was not one of *Intolerance*'s strong points, for Griffith had deliberately subordinated personal involvement with its characters to spectacle and historical process. Furthermore, the United States was about to enter the war in Europe when the film was released in September 1916, and a bellicose mood was sweeping the country. By a crushing historical irony, Griffith's rejoinder to the suppression of *The Birth of a Nation* was itself censured and suppressed in many American cities as a pacifist statement, despite the obvious enthusiasm of its battle scenes (many of them shot at night and illuminated by magnesium flares). Finally, after twenty-two weeks of distribution, the film was taken out of circulation and re-edited as two separate films, as described above. This attempt by Griffith to salvage his enormous financial investment was only partially successful; he would continue to pay his debts on *Intolerance* until his death in 1948.*

GRIFFITH AFTER *INTOLERANCE*

The failure of *Intolerance* did not by any means end Griffith's career. It curtailed his independence as a producer and dampened his enthusiasm as a creator, but he went on to direct another twenty-six feature films between 1916 and 1931. Most critics see this period as one of marked decline in power. It is true that Griffith made no significant narrative innovations after *Intolerance,* but it could reasonably be argued that there were very few left to make before the coming of sound. What seems to have happened is that Griffith lost touch with the prevailing tastes of the post-war era and, therefore, with the popular audience. Though the failure of *Intolerance* had convinced him of the necessity of catering to popular tastes, he experienced increasing difficulty in locating them after 1917. This was partially the result of rapid social change. Industrialization, modernization, and our involvement in the First World War had caused an inversion of traditional American attitudes and values (see note, Chapter 6). The nineteenth-century virtues of morality, idealism, and purity, incarnated by the Cameron family in *The Birth of a Nation,* had given way to the pursuit of sensation and material wealth in the disillusioned post-war era. The verities of rural romanticism, so crucial to Griffith's pre-war epics, were replaced by the sophistication, urbanity, and wit of film-makers like C. B. DeMille and Ernst Lubitsch (see Chapter 6), whose cynical amorality was all but incomprehensible to a director who had never permitted his lovers to so much as kiss on the screen. Griffith continued to make interesting films—he produced one masterpiece, *Broken Blossoms*—but most of his post-war features are either disappointingly conventional or hopelessly old-fashioned.† In effect, the movies had entered the Jazz Age, while Griffith still lived in the afterglow of the nineteenth century.

A great artist's failures, however, are as interesting as his successes, and Griffith's are worth recording briefly here. Before *Intolerance* had even started to sink at the box office, Griffith was invited to England by the British government to make a propaganda picture in support of the war effort. Financed largely by the War Office Committee of the Ministry of Information, *Hearts of the World* (1917) was an anti-German

---

* The crumbling Babylonian set stood for years at the intersection of Sunset and Hollywood Boulevards, becoming a familiar local landmark, because there was not enough money returned on *Intolerance* to have the structure torn down. It was finally removed by the WPA in the late thirties.

† There has been a recent tendency to revaluate Griffith's later work (e.g., *True-Heart Susie* [1919]; *Sally of the Sawdust* [1925]) for the better. See William Cadbury, "Theme, Felt Life, and the Last-Minute Rescue in Griffith After *Intolerance,*" *Film Quarterly*, 28, 1 (Fall 1974), 39–48; Edward Wagenknecht and Anthony Slide, *The Films of D. W. Griffith* (New York, 1975); and John L. Fell, *A History of Films* (New York, 1978).

3.34 A "Hun" prepares to flog a French peasant girl (Lillian Gish) in *Hearts of the World* (1917). (Studio publicity still.)

film shot on location in France and England which depicted the effects of "Hunnish" occupation on a small French town. Griffith shot another film while he was in England—*The Great Love,* a morale-booster designed to show "the regeneration of British society through its war activities," according to advance publicity. This feature, which hasn't survived, was produced by Adolph Zukor's Paramount-Artcraft Company,* which had agreed to become the American distributor for *Hearts of the World.* Before leaving for England, Griffith had signed a contract with Zukor to direct six films for his company and to oversee the production of several others—a wise decision since Triangle was about to be bankrupted through mismanagement and the depredations of rival production companies, Zukor's among them. Neither English film was a critical success; *Hearts of the World* seems especially crude today in its stereotyping of all German soldiers as beasts, although that, of course, was its avowed intention in the year it was made. Returning to Hollywood, Griffith directed five feature films for Zukor in rapid succession between 1917 and 1919—*True-Heart Susie, The Romance of Happy Valley, The Greatest Thing in Life, The Girl Who Stayed at Home,* and *Scarlet Days* (his only feature-length Western, which also hasn't survived), all of them (except the last) dated, idyllic romances with little popular appeal. Next Griffith signed a contract to direct three quickie potboilers for First National in order to raise money for his newest project—the building of an independent studio on a large estate he had purchased near Mamaroneck, New York, where he hoped to become his own producer. According to one of Griffith's biographers, Robert Henderson,[23] First National was interested only in the Griffith imprimatur and permitted him to leave the direction of these films to his assistants, which he apparently did. *The Greatest Question* (1919), a melodrama about spiritualism, and *The Idol Dancer* (1920; released 1922) and *The Love Flower* (1920), both exotic South Seas adventures, were of indifferent quality and did little to enhance the reputation of "the Master," as Griffith had recently been dubbed by the press. Between *The Greatest Question* and *The Idol Dancer,* however, Griffith independently produced *Broken Blossoms,* his last masterpiece and his first great commercial success since *The Birth of a Nation.*

Based on a story called "The Chink and the Child," from Thomas Burke's *Limehouse Nights, Broken Blossoms* concerns a young waif of the London slums, brutally mistreated by her father, who finds brief sanctuary in the chaste love of a gentle Chinese boy.† When her father

---

* Part of Zukor's Paramount Famous Players–Lasky empire, founded in 1916, originally to distribute Mary Pickford's films.

† Griffith's sympathetic treatment of the Chinese boy in *Broken Blossoms,* during the height of anti-Oriental, "Yellow Peril" sensationalism in the United States, has troubled critics who prefer to see him as an unreconstructed and irredeemable racist. In fact, the historical record shows that Griffith took great pains in both the production and promotion of the film not to pander to the popular (and, by then, stereotypically Hollywood) image of the Oriental as inscrutable villain. Apparently, he was a man who at least could learn from his own mistakes. See Vance Keply, Jr., "Griffith's *Broken Blossoms* and the Problem of Historical Specificity," *Quarterly Review of Film Studies,* 3, 1 (Winter 1978), 37–48.

learns of the relationship, he beats the child to death with a whip-handle; the boy then kills the father and commits suicide. Griffith shot this film entirely in the studio in eighteen days (with much prior rehearsal, however) on such a rigorously economical schedule that—according to Lillian Gish, who played the girl—there were no retakes and only two hundred feet of printed stock were left unused[24] (the normal ratio of footage printed to footage used in a commercial film was about fifteen to one in 1919 and is ten to one today). Yet *Broken Blossoms* shows no evidence of its hasty construction and is simultaneously Griffith's most richly evocative and tightly controlled film. Despite some ludicrously sentimental touches (such as the wretched young girl's attempts to counterfeit a smile by propping up the corners of her mouth with her fingers), *Broken Blossoms* succeeds admirably as pathos and is probably the closest Griffith ever came to incarnating his Victorian sensibilities in an appropriate dramatic form. But more important than its dramatic structure is the film's dreamlike atmospheric context—its mood-drenched *mise-en-scène*. Griffith derived the film's ambiance from a series of watercolors of London's Limehouse district, the city's Chinatown, by the English artist George Baker; but both photography and lighting in *Broken Blossoms* are distinctly Continental, probably because of the efforts of Billy Bitzer's recently acquired assistant, Hendrik Sartov,* a specialist in mood lighting and soft focus, or "impressionistic," photography. Griffith, Bitzer, and Sartov together created out of brooding London fogs, smoke-filled opium dens, and the petal-like delicacy of the boy's rooms a *mise-en-scène* worthy of—and probably contributory to—the studio-produced *Kammerspielfilm* of the German cinema (see Chapter 4).

For its release in May 1919 *Broken Blossoms* was tinted entirely in soft pastels, which further enhanced its visual lushness. Unpredictably, the film was a smashing commercial and critical success. Produced for the now modest sum of ninety thousand dollars, it made nearly a million and was widely hailed as a masterpiece. One critic wrote that Griffith "had far exceeded the power of the written word," while others gave "the Master" a new title: "the Shakespeare of the screen." This praise was well deserved, for *Broken Blossoms* is Griffith's most highly integrated film, as well as his most personal and poetic. There are indications that the chief appeal of *Broken Blossoms* to contemporary audiences was nostalgic. Whether or not Griffith understood this is unclear, but it is certain that the resounding accolades for his film convinced him more than ever

---

* Sartov was Lillian Gish's personal photographer and cameraman, brought into the production at her insistence, and Griffith quickly came to admire his work. In addition to assisting Bitzer on *Broken Blossoms* (1919), *Way Down East* (1920), and, with Hal (H. S.) Sintzenich, *The White Rose* (1923), Sartov was the principal cinematographer for *Dream Street* (1921), *Orphans of the Storm* (1922, with Paul Allen), *One Exciting Night* (1922), *America* (1924, with Bitzer, Marcel Le Picard, and Sintzenich), and *Isn't Life Wonderful?* (1924, with Sintzenich). In 1924 Sartov followed Gish to MGM (where, for example, he photographed her in Victor Seastrom's *The Scarlet Letter* [1926]), and Griffith continued to work with some combination of Sintzenich, Harry Fischbeck, and Karl Struss in consultation with Bitzer, whose alcoholism and domestic problems left him increasingly unreliable.

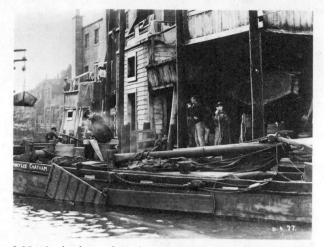

3.35 A wharf scene from the studio-produced *Broken Blossoms* (1919): Lillian Gish at the right of the frame.

3.36 The climactic rescue in *Way Down East* (1920): Lillian Gish, Richard Barthelmess.

before that he was a natural genius who could do no wrong on the screen.

Broken Blossoms was released through United Artists Corporation, the producing-distributing company that Griffith had formed with Charlie Chaplin, Mary Pickford, and Douglas Fairbanks in the spring of 1919, and the film's financial success made it possible for Griffith to equip his own studio at Mamaroneck as planned. His first project there was an adaptation of a creaky Victorian stage play of seduction and betrayal, *Way Down East,* for the rights to which he paid $175,000. Once again Griffith was emotionally in tune with his material, and he produced an exciting and credible melodrama. Shot on location in New York, Connecticut, and Vermont, *Way Down East* (1920) possesses an unexpectedly cinematic vitality and concludes with a skillfully edited last-minute rescue equal to anything Griffith had ever done before. After an elaborate chase through a real blizzard, the heroine collapses on an ice-floe moving rapidly downriver toward a steep falls (actually Niagara, cut into the sequence from stock shots). The hero emerges from the storm, leaps downstream from one ice cake to another, and finally rescues her on the very brink of the plunging falls in a sequence which most certainly influenced Pudovkin's ice-floe montage at the conclusion of *Mother* (1925; see Chapter 5). The audiences, if not the critics, were enthusiastic about *Way Down East* and made it Griffith's last great popular success. In fact, the film grossed four and one-half million dollars, returning the largest profit of any Griffith film after *The Birth of a Nation.*

DECLINE

Griffith took his share of the profits and plowed it back into his Mamaroneck studios. But he knew that the days of independent producing were rapidly drawing to a close, and there is evidence that with this knowledge he was driven to consider film-making more and more as a

3.37 Griffith directing the guillotine scene in *Orphans of the Storm* (1921).

business activity and less and less as an art. His next several films confirmed this new preoccupation. *Dream Street* (1922) was a misbegotten effort to re-create the misty poetic ambiance which had proved so lucrative with *Broken Blossoms.* * *Orphans of the Storm* (1921) was a spectacular attempt to capitalize on the new vogue for historical costume films created by Ernst Lubitsch's *Madame Du Barry* (*Passion,* 1919) by setting a dated Victorian melodrama against the background of the French Revolution. The film was expensively produced at Mamaroneck and well received by the critics, but it lost so much money that it nearly terminated Griffith's dream of independence. In an effort to recoup his losses, he made two more potboilers—a haunted-house mystery entitled *One Exciting Night* (1922) and an old-fashioned piece of Deep South exoticism called *The White Rose* (1923). Both films were failures that served only to deepen Griffith's financial crisis.

Now Griffith began to dream of saving his company by duplicating the phenomenal success of *The Birth of a Nation.* He remembered *War,* the drama of the American Revolution which he had written years before he had ever seen a movie, and decided to produce an epic film on the subject. This costly attempt to remake *The Birth of a Nation* in other terms was called *America* (1924), and it succeeded admirably as spectacle. Its enormous battle scenes easily rival anything Griffith ever produced, but its dull textbook account of the Revolution and its heavy-handed patriotism made it a museum-piece even in its own time. Like every film he had

---

* Nevertheless, Griffith was still experimenting technically: *Dream Street* contained several songs recorded (not very successfully) with the early Photokinema sound-on-disk system (see Chapter 7) and featured a prologue with Griffith himself speaking from the screen (not very audibly) on "the Evolution of the Motion Pictures."

made since *The Love Flower,* except *Way Down East, America* lost money, and the Mamaroneck studios were doomed. Griffith was now facing extinction as a producer and simultaneously being squeezed for more films by his United Artists partners. Accordingly, in the summer of 1924 he traveled to Germany to make *Isn't Life Wonderful?,* his last film as an independent producer for United Artists. Based on contemporary events with exteriors shot entirely on location, the film is a semi-documentary account of the ravages of post-war inflation upon the German middle class. It is thought to have influenced both G. W. Pabst's *Die freudlose Gasse (The Joyless Street;* see Chapter 4), made in Germany the following year, and the neo-realist cinema which sprang up in Italy after World War II (see Chapter 11). Part of the film's uniqueness surely stemmed from the fact that before leaving America Griffith had secretly signed a contract to direct three fast films for Paramount Famous Players–Lasky in an attempt to stave off bankruptcy. He must have realized that *Isn't Life Wonderful?* would be his last independent project.

Sadly, it was. Zukor had just lost Cecil B. DeMille as his premier director, and he promptly hired Griffith for the job, which meant that for the first time since his early Biograph days Griffith was unable to choose his own material. The apathy this produced in him was very nearly fatal. At Paramount's Astoria, New York, studios he made two limp W. C. Fields vehicles, *Sally of the Sawdust* (1925) and *That Royle Girl* (1926), and a studio-contrived fantasy-spectacle, *The Sorrows of Satan* (1926), which had originally been intended for DeMille; but his direction of these unappealing projects was so pedestrian that his Paramount contract was not renewed when it expired in late 1926. At this point, Joseph Schenck (1878–1961), now president of United Artists, offered Griffith a job directing films for his independently owned Art Cinema Corporation in exchange for the voting rights to Griffith's United Artists stock (a swindle nearly as flagrant as Edison's theft of Thomas Armat's Vitagraph projector), but Griffith was foundering rapidly and was forced to accept.

For Art Cinema, Griffith made three undistinguished films—*Drums of Love* (1928), a medieval Italian melodrama based on the Paolo and Francesca legend; *The Battle of the Sexes* (1928–29), a humorless remake of his old Reliance-Majestic farce with a synchronized sound-on-film score; and *Lady of the Pavements* (1929), a romantic "women's picture" released in both silent and sound versions which completely miscast the sexy Lupe Velez as an ingenue. Schenck was ready to fire Griffith (who, in addition to his other worries, had developed a drinking problem) when Griffith proposed that he direct a sound-film biography of Abraham Lincoln. The old *Birth of a Nation* mystique worked for Griffith one last time, and Schenck approved the project. The resulting film, *Abraham Lincoln* (1930), with a script by the American poet Stephen Vincent Benét, is a shadow of Griffith's great Civil War epic. The battle sequences and even the assassination look devitalized and grotesquely under-budgeted by comparison with analogous scenes in *The Birth of a Nation;* and, like most early sound films, *Abraham Lincoln* is visually wooden and static. But Griffith had turned in a respectable and intelligent performance in the most difficult years of the transition from silent pictures to

3.38 The last epic: *America* (1924).

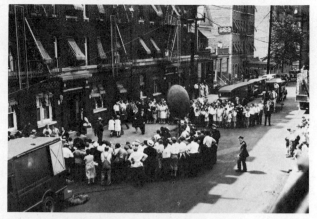

3.39 Griffith directing his last film, *The Struggle* (1931), on location in New York City. The large disk is part of the sound-recording equipment.

sound, and he was rewarded for it. Several influential trade journals named him "Director of the Year," and the film itself was on most "Ten Best" lists for 1930.

Griffith now felt that he was one film away from complete rehabilitation, but he knew that he could never make that film for Schenck; so he quit Art Cinema and floated a bank loan—his last—in order to produce what he hoped would be his first sound-era masterpiece—a version of Zola's *L'assommoir* (*The Drunkard*) written by Anita Loos and entitled *The Struggle* (1931). It turned out, instead, to be his last film. Thinly capitalized and shot for reasons of economy in semi-documentary fashion in and around New York City, *The Struggle* was an abject failure with both contemporary critics and the public. Like all Griffith films, it was visually impressive and had a soundtrack far above average quality for its time, but in terms of drama *The Struggle* was as archaic as "The Face on the Bar-Room Floor." The film was released in January 1932 and permanently withdrawn after a week of exhibition: audiences had walked out on its opening night, and the critics were mocking it, although some today regard it as a much better film than *Abraham Lincoln.** Sixteen years after *The Birth of a Nation,* "the Shakespeare of the screen" had become a figure of ridicule, and Griffith was forced to retire in humiliation from the industry that he, more than any single figure in its brief history, had helped to create. He lived out the remainder of his life in modest comfort on an annuity he had purchased for himself in more prosperous times, overseeing retrospective exhibitions of his greatest films and attending testimonial banquets in his honor. He died in Los Angeles in 1948, only five months after Sergei Eisenstein in Moscow, and was eulogized around the world as "the man who invented cinema." None were more moving in their praise than those who had for the past sixteen years refused him employment.

---

* For example, see Edward Wagenknecht and Anthony Slide, *The Films of D. W. Griffith* (cited above).

THE IMPORTANCE OF GRIFFITH

Griffith remained until the end of his career the same paradoxical figure he had been at its beginning. To borrow Jay Leyda's terminology for *Intolerance,* the greatness and the cheapness of the man were inextricably mixed. By his own candid admission, Griffith derived most of his major narrative innovations from the techniques of nineteenth-century fiction and melodrama, but he also imbibed the simplistic world-view of these two popular forms, to the everlasting detriment of his art. In his famous essay entitled "Dickens, Griffith, and the Film Today,"[25] Sergei Eisenstein pointed out that Griffith's constant resort to parallel editing was a function of his dualistic vision of human experience, in which an entire civil war or twenty centuries of human history were reducible to a melodramatic struggle between the forces of Good and Evil. As a dramatist, in fact, Griffith was less "the Shakespeare of the screen" than its Thomas Middleton. But Griffith was also perhaps the greatest cinematic genius in history—the man who discovered (sometimes, admittedly, in the work of others), synthesized, and articulated the narrative language of film as it is practiced even today. In effect, the way he structured the cinema is the way most of us still perceive it.

His genius, however, was fundamentally innovative and intuitive, rather than critical or analytic. When the days of innovation ceased and intuition was no longer essential to the film-making process, Griffith was thrown back upon a world-view which was hopelessly inappropriate to the post-war era and which had never been intellectually respectable, even in its own century. To compound the misfortune, the lionization of Griffith which followed *The Birth of a Nation* and continued well into the twenties produced in him a kind of megalomania which permanently impaired his judgment. When Griffith began to think of himself as the prophet and philosopher of the film medium, he ceased to be its leading artist. And yet he achieved so much in so short a time with such limited means that to dwell upon the defects of his work or his character, however serious, is more than ungenerous. It is simply irrelevant, for the greatest of Griffith's achievements in a lifetime of achievement was that this fundamentally nineteenth-century man ultimately managed to transcend his defects of vision, judgment, and taste to become one of the great artists of the twentieth century.

German Cinema of the Weimar Period, 1919–1929

THE PRE-WAR PERIOD

Prior to the First World War, the German cinema had reached a less advanced state of development than the cinemas of France, Italy, England, and the United States. Although the Skladanowski brothers had unveiled their "Bioskop" projector in the Berlin Wintergarten in November 1895, almost simultaneously with the first Lumière Cinématographe projection, an indigenous German film industry had somehow failed to evolve in the fifteen years that followed. One reason for this seems to have been the fact that in Germany, more than in the other nations of the West, the cinema became a cultural refuge for the illiterate, disenfranchised, and unemployed. Consequently, very few educated Germans took films or film-making seriously during these years, and most of the films shown in the early tent-shows (*Wanderkinos*) and nickelodeons (*Laden-kinos*) were either imported from other countries or produced in Germany by fly-by-night showmen. Many early native films were frankly pornographic; almost all were technically crude.

One notable exception to this general tendency was the work of Oskar Messter (1866–1943), an inventor who had been instrumental in perfecting the Maltese cross movement for projection systems (see Chapter 1). In 1897, Messter established a small studio in the Berlin Friedrichstrasse and went on to produce hundreds of short entertainment films and *actualités* of a reasonably high caliber and some technical sophistication. He used close shots as early as 1903 and became one of the first directors anywhere in the world to light his sets artificially. Messter, who also experimented with synchronized sound using the phonograph, helped to upgrade the content of German films by featuring famous stars of cabaret and, ultimately, the legitimate stage in his productions between 1904 and 1908. In 1909 he ventured into the production of feature films (*Gross-filme*) with *Andreas Hofer,* directed by Carl Froelich, and devoted his energies to that form almost entirely until 1917, when his company and most others in Germany came under the control of the new government-subsidized conglomerate Universum Film Aktiengesellschaft (UFA). The main historical interest of Messter's features is that they provided the film debut of performers like Henny Porten, Emil Jannings, Lil Dagover, and Conrad Veidt, who became major stars in the twenties.

A more important development, however, began in the following year when, in response to the great success of the French *film d'art* movement, directors, actors, and writers associated with the German theater began to take a serious interest in the cinema for the first time. In 1912 the first *Autorenfilm* ("famous author's film," and thus the German version of *film d'art*) was brought to the screen by the former stage director Max Mack (1884–?). This predictably static adaptation of Paul Lindau's highly successful stage play *Der Andere* (*The Other One*), about the split personality of a Berlin lawyer, starred the world-famous German actor Albert Bassermann (1867–1952). The following year, the great stage director and producer Max Reinhardt (1873–1943) filmed versions of the plays *A Venetian Night* and *The Isle of the Dead,* and the poet-playwright Hugo von Hofmannsthal wrote the "dream-play" *Das fremde Mädchen* (*The Strange Girl*), the first serious German feature film to express a purely supernatural theme. The influx of literary and theatrical people into German film had the effect of radically elevating its social status, but, as in France, the movement also retarded the development of true cinematic narrative by binding it tightly to the narrative conventions of the stage.

The first pre-war German film to break with stage conventions was the Danish director Stellan Rye's production of *Der Student von Prag* (*The Student of Prague*) in 1913, starring a former Reinhardt actor, Paul Wegener (1874–1948), in the title role. Based collectively on variants of the Faust legend in the work of E. T. A. Hoffmann, Edgar Allan Poe, and Oscar Wilde, the film concerns a young student who sells his mirror reflection, and thus his soul, to a sorcerer who in turn causes the image to become a murderous incarnation of the student's evil second self. Much of the film was shot on location in Prague, and it is distinguished by atmospheric lighting and many effective photographic illusions, as well as by Wegener's subtle performance in the double role of the student and the student's alter ego. The film's immediate impact, however, was felt more in terms of its content than of its technical virtuosity, for, as Siegfried Kracauer has noted, *Der Student von Prag* introduced the morbid theme of "deep and fearful concern with the foundations of the self,"[1] which was to obsess the German cinema from 1913 to 1933, at which point it was nationalized and anesthetized by the Nazis.* Moreover, as a tale of psychological horror in a specifically supernatural setting, *Der Student von Prag* prefigures the German Expressionist cinema which began in earnest after the war; and, indeed, the film was itself remade in the Expressionist manner in 1926 by some of its original collaborators.

4.1 *Der Student von Prag* (Stellan Rye, 1913).

THE WAR YEARS

In 1915, after the outbreak of war, Wegener and the scriptwriter Henrik Galeen (1882–?; later to direct the 1926 version of *Der Student*

---

* It should be pointed out, however (as Kracauer does not), that German literature had been preoccupied with the notion of the *Doppelgänger* ("double") since the Middle Ages

von Prag) jointly directed another precursor of the Expressionist movement, *Der Golem* (*The Golem*), which was also set in Prague. The film has not survived, but it too was remade after the war (by Wegener and Galeen in 1920) and we now know from the later version that it was based upon a Jewish legend in which a sixteenth-century rabbi brings to life a clay statue to guard his people against a pogrom. In the film, the giant statue is rediscovered in modern times, is infused with life, and becomes a raging monster who must be destroyed when his resuscitator's daughter rejects him (cf. *Frankenstein,* U.S.A. [1931]; *King Kong,* U.S.A. [1932]). The pre-Expressionist theme of soullessness embodied in *Der Golem* appears in another German film of the era, the six-part serial *Homunculus,* directed by Otto Rippert in 1916. The most popular film of the war years, *Homunculus* deals with an artificially created being of great intellect and will who has no soul. Like the Golem, he turns his energies to destruction when he discovers his synthetic origins, becoming a ruthless dictator who avenges himself upon the human race by means of war and mass murder.

Taken together, *Der Student von Prague, Der Golem,* and *Homunculus* provide a clear indication of the direction the German cinema was to take after the war, but they also indicate the radically stepped-up pace of domestic production during the war itself. Between 1914 and 1919, Germany was cut off from its normally large supply of British, French, and American films. The only foreign productions it was able to import were those from neutral Sweden and Denmark, and consequently the Scandinavian and German industries grew very close during these years. Scandinavian films at this point were generally static and literary but often beautifully photographed by directors like Victor Sjöström and Mauritz Stiller;* their visual clarity had a pronounced influence on post-war German cinema, which, with *film d'art* and the *Autorenfilm,* they helped to make intellectually respectable. Their popularity was also responsible for bringing a Danish production company (German Nordisk, a subsidiary of Nordisk Films Kompagni, until it was absorbed by UFA) and a whole colony of Scandinavian film artists, including the famous Danish actress Asta Nielsen and the great Danish director Carl Dreyer (see Chapter 7), to Germany during World War I.

(witness the Faust legends); and *Der Andere,* the first German feature film of any merit, had, of course, provided a treatment of the theme.

* Victor Sjöström (1879–1960), a Swede, and Mauritz Stiller (1883–1928), born in Finland of Russian parents who moved to Sweden in 1904, were the founding fathers of the Scandinavian cinema. Both began directing in 1912 for Charles Magnusson's (1878–1948) newly formed Svenska Biografteatern company (later to become Svensk Filmindustri), and many of the films they made between 1914 and 1920 received international acclaim. A number of these films, like Sjöström's *The Girl from Marsh Croft* (*Tösen från Stormytorpet,* 1917) and *The Phantom Carriage* (*Körkarlen,* 1920), and Stiller's *Sir Arne's Treasure* (*Herr Arnes pengar,* 1919) and *The Saga of Gösta Berling* (*Gösta Berlings saga,* 1924), were adapted from the work of the great Swedish novelist Selma Lagerlöf (1858–1940). The work of both directors has been described as stately, solemn, and static (terms which might be used to characterize the Scandinavian cinema generally until very recently), but Sjöström was the more ponderous of the two. Nevertheless, in his best dramas of pastoral life Sjöström managed to integrate the rugged Swedish landscape into the texture of his

4.2 *The Saga of Gösta Berling* (Mauritz Stiller, 1924): Ellen Cederström, Greta Garbo.

THE FOUNDING OF UFA

Nevertheless, there simply weren't enough Swedish and Danish motion pictures to fill the void created by the disappearance of other imported films from the German screen, and so the Germans renewed efforts to increase the quantity and quality of domestic production. The first major step was the establishment of the nationally subsidized film conglomerate Universum Film Aktiengesellschaft (UFA) by government decree in 1917. Aware of the depressed state of the domestic industry, and also of the growing number of effective anti-German propaganda films emanating from the Allied countries, General Erich Ludendorff, commander-in-chief of the German army, on December 18, 1917, ordered the merger of the main German production companies, as well as exhibitors and distributors, into a single unit for the making and marketing of high-quality nationalistic films to enhance Germany's image at home and abroad. Huge new studios were built near Berlin, at Neubabelsberg, and UFA immediately set about the task of upgrading production and distribution methods by assembling a team of first-rate producers, directors, writers, and technicians. Perhaps the best comment on the organization's effectiveness in this regard is that, by the end of the war, German production facilities were ten times what they had been at the outset, and the German film industry was ready to compete commercially with that of any other nation in the world. (It became in fact the only industry to successfully compete with Hollywood in foreign markets, including the American, for a brief time during the twenties.) When the war ended in a German defeat in November 1918, the government sold its shares in the company to the Deutsche Bank and to corporations like Krupp and I. G. Farben, and UFA was transformed into a private company. This caused little change in the studio's internal organization, which was fundamentally authoritarian, but its mission was altered slightly because of the compelling necessity of competing in a new international market.

It is often said that the German cinema as an art form was born with the founding of UFA, which was to become the greatest and largest single

---

films with an almost mystical force—a feature noted and much admired by film-makers in other countries. Stiller, who had a lighter touch, excelled at comedy, of which his *Erotikon* (1920), an acknowledged influence on Ernst Lubitsch, remains an impressive example. He must also be credited with introducing Greta Garbo (b. 1905) to the screen in *The Saga of Gösta Berling* and with helping to mold her early career. Both men went to Hollywood to work for MGM in the mid-1920's, where Sjöström (renamed Seastrom) made two neglected masterpieces—*The Scarlet Letter* (1926) and *The Wind* (1928)—and Stiller was reduced to directing trashy star vehicles. Sjöström returned to a life of semi-retirement in Sweden in 1928, working occasionally as a director and an actor, and Stiller died in the same year, fatigued and disillusioned, some have said, by the Hollywood experience (see Chapter 6). The Swedish film industry, virtually monopolized by Magnusson's Svensk Film-industri after 1919, fell into a period of stagnation during the twenties from which it was not to emerge until the outbreak of the Second World War. The slump, during which Sweden produced only a handful of films for export, has been blamed primarily on competition from Hollywood, which, as in the case of Sjöström, Stiller, Garbo, and actors such as Lars Hanson and Nils Asther, siphoned off its major talent to work in the American film industry.

4.3   The UFA studios at Neubabelsberg.

studio in Europe before World War II,* but, as Kracauer points out,[2] UFA was merely the instrument of this birth, which had its deeper causes in the *Aufbruch*—a wave of revolutionary intellectual excitement that swept over the whole of Germany in the wake of the war. Germany's crushing defeat resulted in a complete rejection of the past by much of its intelligentsia and a new enthusiasm for the progressive, experimental, and avant-garde. A liberal-democratic republic was established, with its capital at Weimar. Marxism became intellectually respectable for the first time in German history; expressionism† became popular in the arts; and in early 1919 the Council of People's Representatives abolished national censorship.‡ In this creatively charged atmosphere, the last shreds of intellectual resistance to the cinema disappeared, and Germany's radical young artists were ready to accept it as a new means of communicating with the masses.

---

* The impression is often given that UFA was the only production organization in Germany during the twenties and thirties, or nearly so. In fact, during the twenties at least, it functioned more as a distributor than as a producer. According to Eric Rhode in *A History of the Cinema from Its Origins to 1970* (New York: Hill & Wang, 1976), UFA produced only 12 of the 185 German features for 1926, 15 of 222 for 1927 (while distributing 105 of these), 16 of 224 for 1928 (distributing 18), and 13 of 183 for 1929 (distributing 68). The reason for the confusion is that, of the small number of films UFA did produce during the twenties, nearly one and all became the classics of the German cinema's so-called Golden Age.

†Expressionism, a movement that began in German painting, music, architecture, and theater before the war in reaction to the pervasive naturalism of late-nineteenth-century art, found a large public during the revolutionary *Aufbruch*. Expressionism attempted to represent not objective reality, as naturalism had done, but the subjective feelings of the artist in response to objective reality. It employed a variety of non-naturalistic techniques, including symbolism, abstraction, and perceptual distortion, to achieve this end. Expressionism was one of the first recognizably modernist movements in the arts.

‡The new freedom of expression manifested itself most immediately in a series of well-mounted pornographic films (*Aufklärungsfilme*) with titles like *Prostitution, Vom Rande des Sumpfes (From the Verge of the Swamp), Verlorene Töchter (Lost Daughters), Hyänen der Lust (Hyenas of Lust),* and *Fräulein Mutter (Maiden Mother).* Like the Scandinavian sex films which glutted the world market in the late nineteen-sixties, the post-war German productions masqueraded as vehicles of sex education and social reform. Their only significant effect, however, was to stir up anti-Semitic sentiments against their supposedly Jewish producers and to cause the National Assembly to re-institute state censorship through the Reich Film Act in May 1920. Significantly, it was this act which would later enable the Nazis to assert ideological control over the German cinema.

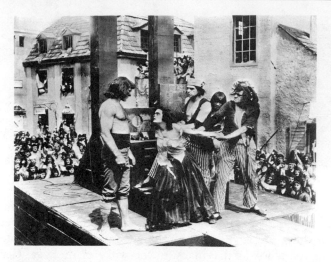

4.4 Pola Negri in *Madame du Barry* (Ernst Lubitsch, 1919).

UFA's first peacetime productions were lavish costume dramas (*Kostümfilme*), initially made to compete with Italian spectacles like *Quo vadis?* and *Cabiria* (see Chapter 2). Joe May's *Veritas vincit* (1918), an elephantine drama about the transmigration of souls through three different historical ages, probably established the conventions of the genre, but Ernst Lubitsch (1892–1947) was to become its master. Lubitsch had worked as an actor for Max Reinhardt and directed a popular series of short comedies before coming to UFA in 1918. In that year, he directed the Polish actress Pola Negri (b. 1894) in two lush costume films, *Die Augen der Mumie Ma* (*The Eyes of the Mummy Ma*) and *Carmen* (English title: *Gypsy Blood*), both of which were successful enough for Lubitsch and his producer Paul Davidson to attempt a third in 1919. This was *Madame Du Barry* (English title: *Passion*), a story of the French Revolution, which became an international success and launched the famous series of historical pageants with which we associate the first part of Lubitsch's career. In rapid succession, Lubitsch directed *Anna Boleyn* (English title: *Deception,* 1920), *Das Weib des Pharao* (English title: *The Loves of Pharaoh,* 1921), and *Sumurum* (English title: *One Arabian Night,* 1921). These historical films—and Lubitsch directed many other types during his German period—were distinguished technically by his dynamic handling of crowd scenes and his brilliant use of artificial lighting, both of which he seems to have learned from Reinhardt. Furthermore, he made innovative use of camera angles and rapid cutting, which impressed American critics like Lewis Jacobs as "revolutionary,"[3] though in fact D. W. Griffith had already advanced the narrative syntax of film far beyond anything Lubitsch contributed. (Lubitsch emigrated to the United States in 1922, where he enriched the American cinema with his sophisticated comedies of wit, urbanity, and sexual innuendo; see Chapter 6.)

Nevertheless, Lubitsch's technical virtuosity was the first thing of its kind the German screen had witnessed, and this expertise coupled with his painstakingly accurate rendition of period detail (called "historical realism" by contemporary critics) in film after film made Lubitsch's spectacles among the most popular of the post-war years, not simply in Germany but all over the world. Other UFA directors successfully practiced the Lubitsch formula, among them Dmitri Buchowetski in *Danton* (1921), *Othello* (1922), and *Sappho* (1922), and Richard Oswald in *Lady Hamilton* (1922) and *Lucrezia Borgia* (1922), all of which exploited the post-war mania for craftsmanlike reconstructions of the past. Yet there was more to the popularity of the German historical spectacles than a simple fascination with the past, for, as Kracauer has suggested, they tended to present history as a slave to individual passions and psychoses rather than as a process dependent upon a wide range of social and economic variables.[4] Thus, the films of German "historical realism" are antihistorical in an important sense, and Romantic to the point of nihilism. Significantly, their popularity in Germany died out in 1924, the year which witnessed the rise of an undisguised and unabashed nihilistic realism in the triumph of the *Kammerspielfilm* (see below). Until this occurred, however, it was not the historical spectacle but another type of film entirely which was to dominate the German cinema.

DAS KABINETT DES DR. CALIGARI

In late 1918, a Czech poet, Hans Janowitz, and a young Austrian artist named Carl Mayer, who was later to become one of the most influential creative figures of the Weimar cinema, collaborated in writing a scenario based upon certain shared experiences of psychic phenomena and mysterious coincidence, as well as a bizarre sex-slaying in Hamburg known personally to Janowitz. In it, a strange mountebank named Dr. Caligari comes to the North German town of Holstenwall with a traveling fair. His "act" consists of interrogating an apparently hypnotized somnambulist named Cesare, who can forecast the future. Shortly after their

4.5 *Das Kabinett des Dr. Caligari* (Robert Weine, 1919): Caligari (Werner Krauss), Cesare (Conrad Veidt), and prey (Lil Dagover).

4.6 *Caligari:* Cesare carries his victim over the rooftops of Holstenwall.

arrival, a series of brutal, inexplicable murders is committed in Holstenwall, which the young student Francis later discovers to be the work of Cesare, done at the evil Caligari's bidding. Francis gives the alarm and pursues Caligari into the countryside and finally to his refuge in a state insane asylum, where, it turns out, the showman is not an inmate but the director. Papers found in his study indicate that the director had become obsessed with a homicidal eighteenth-century hypnotist named Caligari to the point of assuming his identity and causing one of his own patients (Cesare) to commit murders for him. Confronted with these proofs, the director goes mad and must be incarcerated in his own asylum. The script, entitled *Das Kabinett des Dr. Caligari** (*The Cabinet of Dr. Caligari*)—a reference to the coffin-like box in which Cesare is kept by his master—was clearly anti-authoritarian if not subversive in its equation of power and madness.

Nevertheless, when Janowitz and Mayer submitted the scenario to Erich Pommer (1889–1966), chief executive of Decla-Bioscope (an independent production company which was to merge with UFA in 1920), it was immediately accepted. Whether Pommer grasped the script's radical nature is unclear, but he certainly saw in it an opportunity for upgrading the artistic content of his studio's films. The young Austrian director Fritz Lang (see below) was initially assigned to the project but was replaced by Robert Wiene (1881–1938) due to a prior commitment on Lang's part. At this point, and against the authors' violent opposition, Pommer decided to put a frame around the original story which utterly inverted its meaning: Francis is made the narrator of the tale and introduced as a madman in an asylum which, we discover at the film's conclusion, is operated by the benevolent Dr. Caligari himself. Thus, the body of the film was transformed from an anti-authoritarian fable into the recounting of a paranoid delusion which ultimately justifies and glorifies the very authority it was intended to subvert. Still, in terms of its production design, *Das Kabinett des Dr. Caligari* became strikingly experimental under Wiene's direction.

Wiene hired three prominent Expressionist artists—Hermann Warm, Walter Röhrig, and Walter Reimann—to design and paint the sets for the film, which were to embody the tortured state of the narrator's psyche. Thus, the visual word of *Caligari* became a highly stylized one of exaggerated dimensions and deranged spatial relationships—an unnatural, sunless place in which buildings pile on top of one another at impossible angles, jagged chimneys reach insanely into the sky, and the very flesh of its inhabitants seems frozen under pounds of make-up. But the decision to use artificial backdrops was pragmatic as well as thematically appropriate, since in the economic recession which immediately followed the war the film studios, like all other German industries, were allocated electric power on a quota basis. In a film like *Caligari* which required many dramatic lighting effects, it was cheaper and more convenient to simply

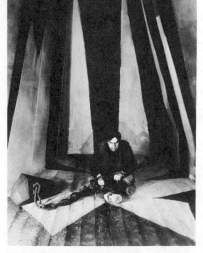

4.7 *Caligari:* a villager falsely imprisoned for Cesare's crimes.

---

* Originally *Das Cabinet des Dr. Caligari,* the title was officially "Germanized" in the thirties to disguise its French derivation (a National Socialist policy), and the latter title stuck.

paint light and shadow onto the scenery itself than to produce the effect electrically (yet another instance of the way in which technological necessity fosters aesthetic innovation in the cinema). Nevertheless, the angular distortion of the sets was clearly intended by Wiene to provide an objective correlative for the narrator's insanity, and for this reason *Caligari* became the progenitor and exemplar of the German Expressionist cinema.

The classic study of this cinema, written by Lotte H. Eisner, is entitled *The Haunted Screen,*[5] and the screen of German Expressionism was indeed a haunted one; but its terrors were those of morbid psychological states and troubled dreams rather than the more concrete horrors that Hollywood's Universal Studios was to offer us in the thirties (although Universal's horror films were the lineal descendants of Expressionism, created in many cases by the same artists—see Chapter 8). The nightmarishly distorted decor of German Expressionist films and their creation of *stimmung* ("mood") through shifting chiaroscuro lighting were *expressive* of the disturbed mental and emotional states they sought to portray. The setting for *Caligari* is warped and out of joint because the film itself, we learn at its conclusion, occurs largely in the twisted mind of its narrator. Thus, the creators of *Caligari* and its successors made a deliberate effort to portray subjective realities in objective terms, to render not simply narratives but states of mind, moods, and atmosphere through the medium of the photographic image (a task more difficult than Expressionist representation in the other arts, since there is, seemingly, nothing more objective than a photographic image but the object itself). German Expressionism, then, attempted to express interior realities through the means of exterior realities, or to treat subjective states in what was widely regarded at the time as a purely objective medium of representation. This was perhaps as radical an innovation for the cinema as Porter's discovery of the shot, since it added a non-narrative and poetic dimension to what had been, even in the hands of Griffith, an almost wholly narrative medium.

In terms of narrative, however, *Caligari* was extremely conservative; its expressiveness was fundamentally a matter of decor and staging. We must remember that the years during which Germany was denied access to American films (1914–19) were precisely those in which Griffith made his most significant contributions to film language. Wiene practiced cinema in ignorance of the lessons of Griffith, and so the editing continuity of *Caligari* is essentially that of arranged scenes, though there is some rudimentary intercutting and some camera movement. In fact, the film is as stagy as any Méliès or Film d'Art production, despite its wildly avant-garde design. *Caligari* imported Expressionism into the cinema but did not exploit it in cinematic terms and, as a *narrative* structure, did nothing to advance the medium. Thus, despite international acclaim (Lewis Jacobs has called it "the most widely discussed film of the time"[6]), *Caligari* had little direct impact on the course of other national cinemas. Yet in terms of its set design, its psychological probing and thematic ambiguity, its sinister and morbid subject matter, and, above all, its attempt to render the internal and subjective through the external and objective,

4.8 *Caligari:* in a forest of the mind.

Caligari had an immense influence upon the German films which followed it.

The production of *Caligari* marked the beginning of the German cinema's great decade. This era was to be characterized by films which, like *Caligari* itself, were completely studio-made, and by intense admiration for the German studio product all over the world. The emphasis on studio production seems to have stemmed less from economic considerations, as it did in Hollywood, than from aesthetic ones. German directors found that they could exercise complete authority over every aspect of the film-making process when they worked in the controlled environment of the studio, as they could not when they worked on location. As Arthur Knight has noted,[7] these directors ultimately preferred to create their settings in the studio from the ground up rather than to discover them in reality at large; as a result, between 1919 and 1927 UFA became the largest and best equipped studio in the Western world. During this period, there was no set so extravagant that it could not be constructed on the vast backlots of the UFA studio at Neubabelsberg, which offered some forty thousand square meters for exteriors alone. Mountains, forests, cities, and entire ages were all recreated with such astonishing fidelity that the critic Paul Rotha coined the term "studio constructivism" to characterize "that curious air of completeness, of finality, that surrounds each product of the German studios."[8] The "realistic" *Kammerspielfilm* (see below) no less than the aggressively artificial Expressionist film profited aesthetically from the large measure of control that studio production permitted a director, and the great cinema of the Weimar Republic could almost certainly not have existed without it. And yet, as we shall see later, UFA's very organizational completeness ultimately led to its own destruction.

4.9 *Der Golem* (Paul Wegener, 1920): art direction by Hans Poelzig.

THE FLOWERING OF EXPRESSIONISM

In any case, between 1919 and 1924 many successors to *Caligari* appeared upon the German screen. Most of these *Schauerfilme* (films of fantasy and terror) used horrific plots and Expressionist decor to embody the theme of the human soul in search of itself. Some representative titles are: F. W. Murnau's *Der Januskopf* (*Janus-Faced,* 1920—adapted from Robert Louis Stevenson's *Dr. Jekyll and Mr. Hyde*), Paul Wegener's remake of *Der Golem* (1920), Arthur Robison's *Schatten* (*Warning Shadows,* 1922), Robert Wiene's *Raskolnikov* (1923—a bizarrely stylized but utterly convincing version of Dostoevsky's *Crime and Punishment*), Paul Leni's *Das Wachsfigurenkabinett* (*Waxworks,* 1924), and Henrik Galeen's remake of *Der Student von Prag* (1926). All of *Caligari*'s spiritual descendants were technically proficient and superbly designed, but two of them deserve special notice, both for their individual accomplishments and because their directors went on to become major figures in the cinema of the Western world. These are Fritz Lang's *Der müde Tod* (1921—literally, "The Weary Death," but usually entitled *Destiny* in English) and F. W. Murnau's *Nosferatu* (1922).

4.10 *Raskolnikov* (Robert Weine, 1923): art direction by Andrei Andreiev.

4.11 *Der müde Tod* (Fritz Lang, 1921): the bereaved lover (Lil Dagover) in the cemetery garden. Art direction by Robert Herlth, Walter Röhrig, and Hermann Warm.

4.12 *Der müde Tod:* the Chinese episode.

Fritz Lang

Fritz Lang (1890–1976) had already directed several feature films and serials (such as the recently reconstructed *Die Spinnen* [*The Spiders,* 1919]) when he and his wife, the scriptwriter Thea von Harbou (1888–1954), collaborated in the production of *Der müde Tod* for UFA. The film is a Romantic allegory, set in the Middle Ages, about a girl whose lover is snatched away by Death himself. She seeks this figure out and demands her lover's return, but Death refuses and instead offers her three fantastic narratives in which lovers attempt unsuccessfully to triumph over Death. These episodes are set in ninth-century Bagdad, in Renaissance Venice, and in a dream-like, mystical China;* and in all of them the lovers are destroyed by cruel and insatiable tyrants. At the end of these *exempla*, Death tells the girl that only by offering her own life or that of another can she insure the return of her lover. Later, in saving a baby from a burning hospital, she is killed, but she is reunited with her dead lover by Death in fulfillment of his pledge. Kracauer sees *Der müde Tod* as a manifestation of Germany's post-war obsession with doom and *Götterdämmerung,* the logical culmination of the cultural pessimism of the late nineteenth century, as expressed in such works as Oswald Spengler's *The Decline of the West* (1918, 1922);[9] and certainly the film's relationship to the major thematic concerns of Expressionism is clear. Lang added something new to the cinema, however, in his striking use of lighting to emphasize architectural line and space.

Lang had in fact been trained as an architect, and he was to carry over

4.13 *Siegfried* (Fritz Lang, 1923): geometrical stylization of space. Art direction by Otto Hunte, Erich Kellethut, and Karl Vollbrecht.

* Douglas Fairbanks claimed that the Chinese episode of *Der müde Tod* inspired him to make *The Thief of Bagdad* (1924), which features similar cinematic sleight-of-hand.

4.14 The forest for *Siegfried* under construction at UFA-Neubabelsberg.

4.15 *Siegfried:* the forest.

4.16 An Expressionistic poster for Lang's *Metropolis* (1926).

his facility for stylized architectural composition as opposed to a purely graphic Expressionism into his other major films of the silent period. These were not intellectualized films in the manner of, say, *Caligari,* but they were all overwhelmingly impressive in terms of sheer plastic beauty and decorative design. *Dr. Mabuse, der Spieler* (*Dr. Mabuse, the Gambler,* 1922) offers an Expressionistic treatment of a Caligariesque master criminal intent upon destroying the fabric of post-war society. In *Siegfried* (1922–24) and *Kriemhilds Rache* (*Kriemhild's Revenge,* 1923–24), Lang again exercised his penchant for legendary romance and compositional majesty in a massive retelling of the Nordic Nibelungen saga,* complete with studio-constructed mountains, forests, and a full-scale fire-breathing dragon. Finally, in his last major silent film, *Metropolis* (1926), Lang presented a terrifying if simplistic vision of a twenty-first-century totalitarian society whose futuristic architecture and technology were rendered brilliantly concrete through the process and model work of the cinematographer Eugen Schüfftan.† Lang made two other silent films (*Spione* [*The Spies,* 1928] and *Die Frau im Mond* [*The Woman in the Moon,* 1929]) before shooting his early sound masterpiece *M* (see Chapter 9).‡ Many of his silent films were made for UFA and written by Thea von Harbou, who later became an ardent Nazi, and Lang himself was offered the leadership of the German film industry by the Nazi propaganda minister, Josef Goebbels, in early 1933 (*Metropolis* was Hitler's favorite film—for all the wrong reasons, of course). Half-Jewish and a political liberal, Lang refused the offer and fled Germany for Hollywood, where he became an important director of American sound films.

---

* In Teutonic mythology, the Nibelungen are a race of dwarfs who possess a magic ring and a great hoard of gold. The *Nibelungenlied* ("song of the Nibelungen") is an anonymous thirteenth-century Middle High German epic in which Siegfried and Kriemhild, the archetypal Teutonic hero and heroine, become fatally involved with the Nibelungen and their treasure, bringing on cosmic chaos—the *Götterdämmerung,* or "Twilight of the Gods." The German classical composer Richard Wagner (1813–83) wrote a monumental tetralogy of music dramas based on the *Nibelungenlied,* but Lang's primary source was the original epic.

† Eugen Schüfftan (1883–1977) left Germany in 1932 after shooting only a few films and (as Eugene Schuftan) became a successful cinematographer, director, and technical advisor in England, France, and the United States. For *Metropolis* he invented the trick-shot technique, still universally used and known today as the "Schüfftan process," which works as follows: Miniatures are reflected onto a glass with a magnifying mirrored surface which is placed at a forty-five-degree angle relative to the camera lens. This surface is scraped away from the areas in which live action is to take place, leaving holes behind which the actual sets are constructed and lit to correspond with the lighting of the model. Alfred Hitchcock was fond of this particular process and used it to achieve some of his most spectacular visual effects (such as the Mount Rushmore sequence in *North by Northwest* [1959]; see Chapter 12).

‡ Many of Lang's films have not been seen in their original versions in the United States. *Metropolis,* for example, was cut from seventeen to ten reels for its 1927 American release, and a full hour is missing from *Kriemhilds Rache.* However, the Munich Film Museum is in the process of restoring Lang's German films, along with other classics of the Weimar period. See John Gillet, "Munich's Cleaned Pictures," *Sight and Sound,* 47, 1 (Winter 1977–78), 37–39.

4.17 *Metropolis:* the quarters of the ruling class. Art direction by Hunte, Kellethut, and Vollbrecht.

4.18 The subterranean city of the robot-like workers.

4.19 The electric Moloch which powers Metropolis and which the workers serve.

4.20 Lang shooting *Metropolis:* the mad scientist Rotwang creates "the False Maria."

4.21 Lang creating an "architecturalized" crowd.

4.22 Realization: the workers' revolt and flood which conclude *Metropolis.*

F. W. Murnau and the *Kammerspielfilm*

The second major figure to emerge from the Expressionist movement was F. W. (Friedrich Wilhelm) Murnau (1888–1931), whose highly stylized vampire film *Nosferatu, eine Symphonie des Grauens* (*Nosferatu, a Symphony of Horrors,* 1922)* has become a classic of the genre. Trained as an art historian, Murnau became fascinated by the theater and began to write for films shortly after the war, collaborating with both Carl Mayer and Hans Janowitz. When he began to direct his own films, Murnau worked almost exclusively in the Expressionist vein, making films like *Der Bucklige und die Tänzerin* (*The Hunchback and the Dancer,* 1920—written by Mayer), *Der Januskopf* (*Janus-Faced,* 1920—written by Janowitz), and *Schloss Vogelöd* (*Castle Vogelod,* 1921—written by Mayer). It is *Nosferatu,* however, adapted loosely (and without credit) by Henrik Galeen from Bram Stoker's novel *Dracula* (1897), that represents the high point of Murnau's Expressionist period.

One of the remarkable things about *Nosferatu* is the apparent naturalness of its stylization, achieved, it should be noted, with a minimum of resources since the film was independently produced. Like the Scandinavian directors whose films flooded Germany during the war, Murnau had an affinity for landscapes, and he had most of *Nosferatu* shot on location in Central Europe by the great cinematographer Fritz Arno Wagner (see note, below), whose specialty was a kind of low-contrast, realistic photography which exchanged stark black-and-white for a whole range of intermediate grays. While the film is essentially a thriller and is more than a bit creaky in terms of narrative structure, it nonetheless provides a succession of haunting visual images more authentically "expressive" of horror than those of *Caligari*. Whereas *Caligari*'s Expressionism was mainly graphic, *Nosferatu*'s is almost purely cinematic, relying upon camera angles, lighting, and editing rather than production design. Nosferatu, the vampire king, is frequently photographed from an extremely low angle which renders him gigantic and monstrously sinister on the screen (a device not lost upon Orson Welles, who would employ it obsessively throughout *Citizen Kane* eighteen years later; see Chapter 10). A number of these shots are lit so that the vampire's vast and angular shadow is cast across every object in the frame.† Many of the film's images are strikingly composed in depth, with action sharply in focus in the foreground, middleground, and background simultaneously. This mode of composing the frame has the effect of integrating character and landscape, and much of *Nosferatu*'s "naturalness" derives from it. Composition in depth also produces some memorable expressive effects. Near the film's conclusion, its heroine, who is situated in the foreground of the frame, gazes through her window at a mass funeral procession for the vampire's victims, which is shot so that it seems to stretch away end-

4.23 *Nosferatu* (F. W. Murnau, 1922): Max Schreck as the vampire. Art direction by Albin Grau.

**Nosferatu* was remade under the same title by the brilliant German director Werner Herzog in 1978 (see Chapter 17).

†A minor *gaffe*—a vampire casts no shadow, as all horror buffs are well aware.

lessly from the middleground to infinity, suggesting the enormity of Nosferatu's crimes. Less impressive today, perhaps, are the cinematic tricks that Murnau and Wagner used to create a supernatural atmosphere for the film. The forests surrounding Nosferatu's castle, for example, are made to seem ghostly through the use of negative footage, and the vampire's supernatural strength is rendered in terms of jerky accelerated action achieved through stop-motion photography (see Chapter 1). Nevertheless, *Nosferatu* as a whole remains one of the most ominous and expressive horror films ever made; as the Hungarian film critic Béla Balázs (see Chapter 15) wrote, "a chilly draft from doomsday" passes through its every scene.[10]

Murnau's next important film was made in the genre which superseded Expressionism—that of the *Kammerspiel* (literally, "intimate theater") or "instinct," film. The scriptwriter Carl Mayer, of *Caligari* fame, was the founding father and chief practitioner of this genre, which dealt realistically with the oppressiveness of contemporary lower-middle-class life and, by extension, with the irresistibility of fate in a disintegrating society. All of Mayer's scripts for the "instinct" films showed great compression of form and were specifically tailored to the technical requirements of cinema. They generally avoided the use of inter-titles altogether and contained only a few characters, each of whom represented a destructive and uncontrollable impulse. Mayer began writing *Kammerspiel* scripts in the heyday of Expressionism, and there is no question that they contain Expressionist elements. Indeed, the whole realistic cinema which grew out of the *Kammerspielfilm* can be seen as both an extension of and a reaction against the Expressionist cinema, in that it retained the morbid psychological themes of the earlier films but cast them in realistic form (and, furthermore, a realistic form which was the product of UFA studio shooting rather than documentary technique). The films made from Mayer's early *Kammerspiel* scripts are Leopold Jessner's *Hintertreppe* (*Backstairs*, 1921), and Lupu Pick's *Scherben* (*Shattered*, 1921) and *Sylvester* (1923); but it was *Der letzte Mann* (literally, "The Last Man," but usually entitled *The Last Laugh* in English), written by Mayer and directed by Murnau, which incarnated the type and inaugurated a new period of German realism in 1924.

Der letzte Mann, produced by Erich Pommer for UFA, is a distinguished film in every respect, and an extremely important one in terms of the enormous influence it exercised, especially upon German and American cinema. The script by Mayer, the acting by Emil Jannings (1884–1950), and the production design by Walter Röhrig and Robert Herlth are all impressive; but it is the innovative use of camera movement that makes *Der letzte Mann* so important to the history of film, and this was achieved largely by Murnau and his cinematographer, Karl Freund.*

---

* Karl Freund (1890–1969) was director of photography for many of Germany's most distinguished silent films, including Murnau's *Januskopf* (1920), *Der letzte Mann* (1924), *Tartuffe* (1925), *Faust* (1926), and *Sunrise* (1927—an American motion picture produced almost exclusively by UFA personnel); Lang's *Metropolis* (1926); Walter Ruttmann's *Berlin, die Symphonie einer Grosstadt* (Berlin, Symphony of a Great City, 1927); and E. A.

4.24 *Der letzte Mann* (F. W. Murnau, 1924): Emil Jannings as the proud porter.

4.25 Expressionistic set design: the porter's tenement.

It was Mayer who suggested that the camera be put into nearly continuous motion (the "unchained camera," he called it), and he specified its involvement in the action in his script. Freund, however, was responsible for the brilliant tactical maneuvering that permitted this movement, and, as director, of course, Murnau executed it.

Like all *Kammerspielfilme, Der letzte Mann* has a fairly simple plot. It is also unrelievedly grim until the sudden appearance of a happy ending, which is emotionally satisfying in a primitive sort of way but wholly out of key with what has gone before. The film concerns an aging doorman (Jannings) in a fashionable Berlin hotel who loses his job and, more important, his resplendent uniform to a younger man. Within the lower-middle-class tenement where he lives with his daughter, the uniform has brought him prestige and dignity; its unexpected loss elicits a kind of furious ridicule from his neighbors that is chillingly sadistic. Demoted to the position of washroom attendant at the hotel and utterly humiliated in his own home, the old man begins to come apart. He becomes stoop-shouldered and slovenly overnight; he gets raging drunk at his daughter's wedding and experiences delusions of persecution; he even makes a desperate attempt to steal his uniform back out of a hotel locker. As the film nears its conclusion, we discover him crouched furtively against the wall of the hotel lavatory like a trapped beast, terrified of the entire world outside himself and apparently as mad as Caligari. But no: the film's single title flashes on the screen to explain that whereas in the real world things would end at this point, the film-makers have decided to take pity on the ex-doorman. There follows a farcical conclusion in which he inherits a vast sum of money by an outlandish coincidence and shows up in the hotel dining room to flaunt his wealth before his former employers in a grandly vulgar but good-natured manner. It is thought that this contrived ending was tacked onto the film either to pander to the American audience's taste for such sentimental optimism or to parody it; no one is quite sure which. (The American cinema had finally begun to influence the German cinema by 1924 and was to have considerably more influence as the decade progressed.) But, whatever the case, the incongruity of the ending is the only notable flaw in what is both cinematically and thematically a nearly perfect film.

Indeed, *Der letzte Mann* was the most technically innovative film to come out of Weimar cinema. Prior to it, most camera movement had been panning and tilting (see Chapter 1) wedded to a fixed tripod. With several significant exceptions (in the films of Griffith and the Italian film *Cabiria* [1914]), there had been little sustained *tracking* movement—i.e.,

Dupont's *Varieté* (*Variety*, 1925). He also worked with Reinhardt, Lubitsch, Wegener (*Der Golem*, 1920), and Dreyer (see Chapter 7). With Fritz Arno Wagner (1894–1958: Murnau's *Nosferatu* [1922]; Lang's *Der müde Tod* [1921], *Spione* [1928], *M* [1931], and *Das Testament des Dr. Mabuse* [1933]; and Pabst's *Die Liebe der Jeanne Ney* [1927; see below], *Westfront 1918* [1930], and *Kameradschaft* [1931]), Freund was one of the two great cinematographers of the Weimar period. After emigrating to Hollywood in 1930 he scored major successes both as a cinematographer (for Rouben Mamoulian's *Dr. Jekyll and Mr. Hyde* [1932], Tod Browning's *Dracula* [1931], George Cukor's *Camille* [1935], etc.) and as a director (*The Mummy* [1932], *Mad Love* [1935], etc.).

movement in which the whole camera apparatus participates, either to follow another moving object or to isolate a static one by moving in close upon it. What is necessary to achieve this kind of fluidity is a *dolly*—a small wheeled cart on which to mount the camera during shooting, which may or may not use tracks (thus "tracking"). Today, the boom crane and a variety of sophisticated dollies (not to mention Steadicams*) are available to permit such freedom, but these devices could only be improvised in 1924. (Murnau did, however, have access to motor-driven cameras which allowed their operators to concentrate full attention on movement and focus.) Griffith, of course, had put his camera in the back of an automobile to follow the motion of the chase in *The Birth of a Nation* and *Intolerance,* and he had used an elevator tower that rolled on rails to track his machine into the gigantic set of Belshazzar's feast in *Intolerance;* other American directors had improvised dollies in order to follow the movement of actors within a scene without cutting; but *Der letzte Mann* was the first film in history to move its camera backward and forward, as well as up and down and from side to side, in scenes of substantial duration.†

These are scenes held for a single shot and kept alive almost solely through camera movement, rather than scenes built up out of a number of separate shots and kept alive through editing, as in the work of Griffith and Eisenstein. In the frequently cited opening scene, for example, we ride via the camera down the hotel elevator, move through the bustling lobby, approach the revolving door (a major symbol of life's randomness in the film—a sort of existential roulette wheel), and move out to the doorman on the sidewalk in what appears to be a single unbroken shot (there is actually a discreet dissolve between the rain-covered glass door and the street‡). The film is replete with shots like this, and their accomplishment was by no means simple in the absence of modern cranes and dollies. For the shot described above, Freund mounted his camera on a bicycle in the descending elevator, rolled it out into the lobby, and tracked it several hundred feet to the revolving door. In other shots, the camera rode the ladder of a fire truck, anticipating the boom crane, and traveled on overhead cables. Indeed, Freund's camera seems to move almost continuously throughout *Der letzte Mann,* although there are actually many shots taken with the camera at full rest which provide an appropriate counterpoint for the others.

But of equal importance with the camera mobility achieved by Murnau and Freund was their use of the *subjective camera*—the technique whereby the camera lens becomes the eyes of a player in the film, usually the protagonist, so that the audience sees only what he sees and only

---

* The trade name for a device which serves to stabilize the movement of hand-held cameras, introduced in 1976.

† For an ambitious, thoroughly researched history of camera movement "executed with the action or related to it for dramatic purposes," see Lutz Bacher, *The Mobile Mise-en-Scène* (New York: Arno Press, 1978).

‡ This uncannily resembles the dissolve Orson Welles would use in *Citizen Kane* (1940; see Chapter 10), when he had Gregg Toland track his camera straight through the El Rancho nightclub sign and through a rain-drenched skylight down into the club below.

from his angle of vision. Griffith's "objects of attention" intercut with facial close-ups are a rudimentary form of this technique: when he cuts from a character looking at something to a shot of what the character sees as he sees it, Griffith is practicing a kind of short-hand subjectivity. These are called "motivated point of view" shots, and they were brought to a state of extreme refinement by the UFA director G. W. Pabst later in the twenties (see below). No one before Murnau and Freund, however, had understood the full range of possibilities inherent in the subjective camera and the way in which it might be used to create multiple perspectives on a single narrative.

The most famous subjective camera shot in *Der letzte Mann* occurs in the scene in which the doorman gets falling-down drunk in his apartment. To render the character's point of view at this moment, Freund strapped a lightweight camera to his chest and stumbled drunkenly about the room. This is a fairly typical and straightforward use of the technique, but in *Der letzte Mann* the camera is subjective in another sense too, a sense which demonstrates the roots of German realism in Expressionism. Quite frequently, in addition to assuming the position of the doorman's *physical eye,* the camera assumes the position of his *mind's eye* as well. During the same drunken scene, he feels acutely humiliated at the loss of his job and his prestigious uniform, and he imagines himself to be the object of ridicule and scorn which he will in fact become on the following day, when his misfortune becomes known to all. At the height of his despair in this sequence, we see on the screen not the doorman (as with the objective camera), nor what he sees, but a visual embodiment of what he *feels*—a long lap-dissolved montage of malicious laughing faces in close-up. Later, after he has stolen his old uniform and run out of the hotel into the street, the doorman looks back on the building, which seems to tremble and sway as if about to fall and crush him. We might say, then, that Murnau shows his Expressionist roots by using the subjective camera in a highly expressive way—to embody the morbid psychological state of his protagonist in terms of visual images. But there is more.

In scenes like these Murnau showed that he had grasped the concept that the camera was capable of first-person as well as third-person narration; that this first-person narration had both inner and outer modes; and, finally, that a director could alternate between these several modes of narration at will to create multiple perspectives on a given subject. Thus, while *Der letzte Mann* is simple in terms of plot, it has an extremely elaborate structure in which the narrative point of view is in constant rotation between the third-person objective camera and the two modes of first-person subjective camera. This was an innovation at least as significant for cinematic narrative as, say, Griffith's realization that a dramatic sequence could be built up from shots of varying temporal and spatial lengths. Like Griffith's innovations, both modes of subjective camera have now passed into the conventional lexicon of the cinema, but in 1924 they were virtually unprecedented, and the influence of *Der letzte Mann* upon contemporary cinema was immense. As *The Last Laugh,* it enjoyed worldwide success and had a greater effect upon Hollywood technique than any other single foreign film in history, in terms of both

4.26 Subjective camera: the porter imagines ridicule at his daughter's wedding feast.

4.27 *Der letzte Mann:* down and out.

its fluidity and its titleless narration. As Murnau's biographer Lotte H. Eisner puts it, "It was the almost universal decision of Hollywood that this was the greatest picture ever made";[11] Murnau was to leave Germany for a Hollywood career after completing two final super-productions for UFA (*Tartuffe* [1925], and *Faust* [1926]).

Hollywood was to be almost equally impressed in the following year with *Der letzte Mann*'s immediate successor, E. A. (Ewald André) Dupont's (1891–1956) *Varieté* (1925), also produced by Erich Pommer for UFA and photographed by Karl Freund. The film deals with a love triangle among trapeze artists (Emil Jannings, Lya de Putti, Warwick Ward) at the Berlin Wintergarten which ends in murder, and it contains camera movement even more breathlessly dynamic than that of *Der letzte Mann*. In almost documentary fashion, Freund's camera penetrates everywhere the human eye can go. It darts frenetically from face to face in a crowded room; it flies through the air with the acrobats, focusing subjectively on the swaying audience below; and at one point it seems to plummet to the floor of the Wintergarten as a performer falls to his death. Much of this movement is less functional than that of *Der letzte Mann* and gives the impression of having been contrived for its own sake. Moreover, the film is highly derivative of *Der letzte Mann* in terms of atmosphere and theme as well as technique. Nevertheless, as Lewis Jacobs writes, "*Variety* put American movie-goers into a white heat of enthusiasm over film art,"[12] and it insured the permanence of German influence upon the Hollywood studios until the end of the silent era (which was soon matched by a tendency to "Americanize" the German film, as we shall see). For the German cinema, on the other hand, *Varieté* provided a bridge between the introspective *Kammerspiel* genre and a more objective kind of realism which was to emerge after 1924.

4.28 Decadence in *Varieté* (E. A. Dupont, 1925).

THE PARUFAMET AGREEMENT AND THE MIGRATION TO HOLLYWOOD

In 1924 the German mark had been stabilized and the spiral of postwar inflation halted by Germany's acceptance of the Dawes Plan (named for the American banker Charles E. Dawes, who presided over an international committee set up to monitor Germany's war reparations payments). This provided for the long-term payment of reparations and admitted Germany back into the economic system of the Allies. The effect was to create in the German Republic a stabilized period of false confidence and even prosperity which lasted until the stock market crash of 1929. Ironically, however, the German film industry, which had survived rampant inflation, was seriously threatened by stabilization, because the Dawes Plan stipulated the curtailment of all exports. Thus, between 1924 and 1925 many independent production companies folded, and the surviving ones found it very difficult to borrow money from German banks. Sensing a chance to cripple its only European rival, Hollywood began to pour American films into Germany, founding its own distribution agencies and buying up theaters. By late 1925, UFA was on the brink of collapse due to external conditions and to the extravagance of its own recent productions; at this point the American studios Paramount and Metro-Goldwyn-Mayer offered to subsidize UFA's huge debt to the Deutsche Bank by lending it four million dollars at 7.5 percent interest in exchange for collaborative rights to UFA studios, theaters, and personnel—an arrangement which clearly worked in the American companies' favor. The result was the foundation of the "Parufamet" (Paramount-UFA-Metro) Distribution Company in early 1926. Within a year, however, UFA was showing losses of twelve million dollars and was forced to seek another loan, this time from the Prussian financier Dr. Alfred Hugenberg (1865–1951). Hugenberg, who was chairman of both Krupp and the right-wing German National Party, subsequently bought out the American companies and became chairman of the UFA board as well. Without fanfare, he established a nationalistic production policy which gave increasing prominence to Nazi Party rallies in UFA newsreels and which finally permitted the Nazis to subvert the German film industry in 1933. While the republic survived, however, Hugenberg was content to wait.

The most immediate effect of the Parufamet agreement was the migration of UFA film artists and technicians to Hollywood, where they worked for a variety of studios. Ernst Lubitsch had left for America in 1922 to direct *Rosita* for Mary Pickford and was joined in 1926–27 by the directors E. A. Dupont, Ludwig Berger, Dmitri Buchowetski (Russian-born), Lothar Mendes, Lupu Pick (Rumanian-born), Berthold Viertel, Paul Leni, F. W. Murnau, and Mihály Kertész (a Hungarian working for UFA, who became Michael Curtiz in America and went on to direct over one hundred films for Warner Brothers between 1927 and 1960, including the legendary *Casablanca* [1942]); the cinematographers Karl Freund and Karl Struss; the performers Emil Jannings, Conrad Veidt (Cesare in *Caligari*), Werner Krauss (Caligari), Pola Negri (Polish-born), Greta Garbo (Swedish), and Lya de Putti (Hungarian); and the producer Erich Pommer and the scenarist Carl Mayer.* This migration

___

* Other German and Central European film artists who ultimately emigrated to Hollywood, most of them to escape Hitler, were the directors Fritz Lang, Max Öphüls, Detlef Sierck (who would become Douglas Sirk, master of that quintessential fifties genre, the widescreen melodrama, and a formative influence upon the work of Rainer Werner Fassbinder, a leading figure in the New German Cinema of the seventies; see Chapter 17), Kurt and Robert Siodmak, William Dieterle, Billy Wilder, Edgar G. Ulmer, Fred Zinnemann, Max Reinhardt, Otto Preminger, Reinhold Schünzel, William Thiele, Ernö Metzner, Hermann Kosterlitz (Henry Koster), Gustav Machatý, Stephan Székely, Joe May, Richard Oswald, Henrik Galeen, Kurt (Curtis) Bernhardt, Hans (John) Brahm, Paul Czinner, Charles Vidor, and André De Toth, and the cinematographers Eugen Schüfftan and Rudolph Maté. Other important *émigrés* are as follows. Actors and actresses: Albert Basserman, Elizabeth Bergner, Helmut Dantine, Marlene Dietrich, Peter van Eyck, Hugo Haas, Paul Henreid, Oscar Homolka, Hedwig Kiesler (Hedy Lamarr), Fritz Kortner, Franz (Francis) Lederer, Peter Lorre, Paul Lukas, Luise Rainer, Sigfried Rumann, S. Z. Sakall, Joseph Schildkraut, and Walter Slezak. Writers: Bertolt Brecht, Lion Feuchtwanger, Bruno Frank, Georg Fröschel, Heinz Herald, Hans (John) Kafka, Fritz (Frederic) Kohner, Emil Ludwig, Alfred Neumann, Wolfgang Reinhardt, Walter Reisch, and Franz Schulz (Francis Spencer). Composers: Paul Dessau, Hanns Eisler, Bronislau Kaper, Erich W. Korngold, Miklós Rózsa, Hans Salter, Max Steiner, Franz Wachsmann (Waxman), and Kurt Weill. There

didn't decimate UFA, since it was random and temporary. Yet many German technicians, actors, and minor directors did settle in Hollywood and pursue modestly successful careers. Karl Freund, for example, not only became one of the most able Hollywood cinematographers of the thirties but also directed a handful of superbly atmospheric horror thrillers for Universal Studios (see note, p. 121) which conferred a substantial legacy of German Expressionism upon the Hollywood horror film as a sound film genre. But the fate of the major German directors in Hollywood was similar to that of the Scandinavians Sjöström and Stiller (see note, p. 109).

To put it simply, Hollywood didn't want them to film the kinds of subjects that had made them great directors in their native industries. In effect, the American studios had bought a boatload of foreign talent that they literally didn't know how to employ. The major artists rapidly became bored with their dull assignments and returned to Germany (some only to return to America later as refugees from the Nazis). Only Lubitsch was able to successfully adapt himself to the complexity and vapidity of the Hollywood production process, and his American career proved much more significant than his German one. Murnau stayed on too, and it is conceivable that he might have brought his American career to greatness had his life not been cut short by an automobile accident in 1931 (see Chapter 6). As it was, after he made the visually exquisite but saccharine *Sunrise* in 1927 (produced by Pommer for Fox, written by Mayer, and shot by Freund, but devoid of the thematic power of *Der letzte Mann*), the quality of Murnau's work declined.* His last film, the independently produced South Seas tragedy *Tabu* (1931), was an aesthetic success, but the director died before it reached the screen.

4.29 *Caligari*'s American children: the Universal horror films of the thirties. Tod Browning's expressionistic *Dracula* (1931), photographed by Karl Freund.

G. W. PABST AND "STREET" REALISM

Another effect of the Dawes Plan on the German film industry was less direct than the Parufamet agreement but more important to the general trend of domestic production. This was the fact that the period after 1924 produced, superficially at least, a return to social normalcy in Germany. As a consequence, the German cinema began to turn away from the morbid and mannered psychological themes of Expressionism and *Kammerspiel* and toward the kind of literal (but still studio-produced) realism exemplified by the "street" films of the second half of the decade—G. W. Pabst's *Die freudlose Gasse* (*The Joyless Street*, 1925), Bruno Rahn's *Dirnentragödie* (*Tragedy of the Street*, 1927), Joe May's *Asphalt*

---

were many, many others less prominent. All told, Hollywood managed to absorb more talent from the German cinema than was left to the Nazis when they took over the industry in 1933, and, for a while, Los Angeles became known as "the new Weimar." See the Exhibition Catalogue *German Film Directors in Hollywood: Film Emigration from Germany and Austria,* ed. Ernst Schürmann (San Francisco: The Goethe Institutes of North America, 1978).

* See, for example, Murnau's *Our Daily Bread* (completed 1928, released by Fox as *City Girl* [1930]).

4.30 *Die neue Sachlichkeit: Die freudlose Gasse*
(G. W. Pabst, 1925).

(1929), and Piel Jutzi's *Berlin Alexanderplatz* (1930). Named for their prototype, Karl Grune's *Der Strasse* (*The Street*, 1923), these films all dealt realistically with the plight of ordinary people in the post-war period of inflation and incarnated the spirit of *die neue Sachlichkeit* ("the new objectivity") which entered German society and art at every level during this period. Cynicism, resignation, disillusionment, and a desire to accept "life as it is" were the major characteristics of *die neue Sachlichkeit*, and these translated into a type of grim social realism in the street films.*

The undisputed master of the new realism was the Austrian-born director G. W. (Georg Wilhelm) Pabst (1885–1967). Trained in the theater, Pabst was a latecomer to the Weimar cinema who directed his first film, *Der Schatz* (*The Treasure*), rather perfunctorily in 1924. His next film, however, was *Die freudlose Gasse* (*The Joyless Street*, 1925), which achieved world recognition as a masterpiece of cinematic social realism. (In some countries recognition came in the form of censorship—England banned *Die freudlose Gasse*, and the prints seen in Italy, Austria, and France were substantially cut.) The film concerns the financial and

---

* While the shift to social realism of some sort was fairly general in the German cinema at this point, two other more popular genres deserve mention here. The *Kulturfilme* were feature-length escapist documentaries on esoteric subjects, expensively produced by UFA. With titles like *Wege zu Kraft und Schönheit* (*Ways to Health and Beauty*, 1925), these films became a German specialty on the international market and were a vast financial success for the studio. The other popular genre was an exclusively national phenomenon—the mountain films of Dr. Arnold Fanck (1889–1974), which exploited the Germanic predilection for heroic scenery and winter sports in vehicles like *Berg des Schicksals* (*Peak of Destiny*, 1924), *Der heilige Berg* (*The Holy Mountain*, 1927), and *Die weisse Hölle von Piz Palü* (*The White Hell of Pitz Palu*, 1929; co-directed by Pabst). These were all fiction films, stunningly photographed on location by the best talent money could buy (the actress Leni Riefenstahl—see Chapter 9—and the director G. W. Pabst were among Fanck's collaborators), which relied heavily upon spurious sentiment and inflated plots for their dramatic effect. Nevertheless, they enjoyed quite a cult among the German audience, and, according to Kracauer, their popularity was a harbinger of the heroic and irrational appeal of Nazism.

spiritual ruin of the middle classes through inflation in post-war Vienna, focusing upon the lives of several destitute bourgeois families struggling to preserve their dignity and decency in the face of secret star-vation. The misery of their existence is contrasted with the extravagant pleasure-seeking of the war profiteers. Daughters of the middle class—the most prominent played by the Swedish actresses Asta Nielsen and Greta Garbo (in her German screen debut)—sell themselves into prostitution to save their families, while the wealthy amuse themselves at opulent black-market nightclubs where these girls must eventually come to be "bought." Yet there is no sentimentality or symbolism in the presenta-tion. Pabst captures "life as it is" with a kind of photographic realism that completely rejects the subjective camera of Murnau and Freund. Like theirs, of course, Pabst's camera does move, but the essential dyna-mism of his films is generated through cutting and, more specifically, cutting on a character's movement.

Pabst was the first German director to be substantially influenced by Eisenstein's theory and practice of montage (see Chapter 5). In fact, prior to Pabst, the German cinema had evolved through its various phases as essentially a cinema of *mise-en-scène* rather than of montage, since it had developed in isolation from the innovations of Griffith and his Russian successors. Pabst's own contribution to film technique was the discovery that the perceptual fragmentation created by editing within scenes could be effectively concealed for the purpose of narration by cutting a shot in the midst of a motion which is shown to be completed in the next shot. The spectator's eye follows the character's movement and not the film's (not, that is, the cut itself), which renders the whole process of montage more fluid and comprehensible. Thus, a director who wished to cut smoothly from a full shot of an actor to a medium shot from the waist up might require the actor to begin some incidental movement or gesture in the full shot which could be completed in the medium shot after the cut—e.g., lighting a cigarette, answering a phone, or even rising from a chair. This kind of cutting (sometimes called "invisible editing" or "conti-nuity editing") became fundamental to the sound film, where it is often necessary to create visual bridges between shots corresponding to aural bridges on the soundtrack (for instance, a character may move from one shot into several others while speaking continuous dialogue, so that the visual sequence must be made to seem continuous as well). Ironically, by neutralizing the perceptual fragmentation inherent in narrative montage, Pabst actually increased its potential for use in any given sequence, and one hallmark of his later films is the large number of barely perceptible cuts he uses per scene. Another hallmark is his increasing use of the mo-tivated point of view shot, in which the camera angle simulates the per-spective of a character's glance from the immediately preceding shot. Typically, a close-up of some character's directed attention will be fol-lowed by a shot of the object of that attention from his point of view, and so on for each participant in the scene. Pabst would build up entire conti-nuity sequences in this manner, enabling the audience to experience the unique perspectives (both visual and psychological) of major characters

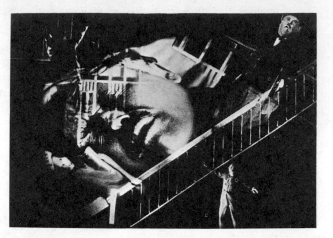

4.31 *Geheimnisse einer Seele* (G. W. Pabst, 1926): Freud on film.

in his films.* The combination of cutting on movement with motivated point of view shots produced elaborate—but seemingly effortless—continuity structures. In *Die Liebe der Jeanne Ney* (*The Love of Jeanne Ney,* 1927), for example, one two-minute narrative sequence contains over forty fluid cuts representing the perspectives of three separate characters as they move about a room during a heated argument. Pabst refined these techniques increasingly with each successive film, and it seems correct to say that he brought to its logical conclusion Edwin S. Porter's discovery that a scene may be broken down into more than one shot and that the shot is the basic signifying unit of the cinema.

Pabst's later films continue his involvement with social realism, although they are sometimes diluted by melodrama and fantasy from the inescapable heritage of Expressionism. *Geheimnisse einer Seele* (*Secrets of a Soul,* 1926), for example, a cinematic case history of an anxiety neurosis (produced in collaboration with two disciples of Sigmund Freud [1856–1939], the founder of psychoanalysis: Dr. Hans Sachs and Dr. Karl Abraham) contains some of the most vivid dream sequences ever recorded on film. In *Die Liebe der Jeanne Ney* Pabst returned to the social arena to film the progress of a love affair caught up in the turmoil of the Russian Revolution and its aftermath. Photographed in semidocumentary fashion with natural lighting by Fritz Arno Wagner, often using real locations, the film portrays post-war European society in the process of rapid disintegration; in it Pabst carried his sophisticated cutting techniques to new heights. Pabst's last two silent films,† *Die Büchse der Pandora* (*Pandora's Box,* 1929) and *Tagebuch einer Verlorenen* (*Diary of a Lost One,* 1929), both concern the lives of prostitutes (played by the striking American actress Louise Brooks [b. 1906] in each case) and the way in which their degraded roles relate to the general decadence of society. Pabst adapted himself readily to sound and became one of the

---

* For the fullest exposition/analysis of filmic point of view available in English, see *Film Reader 4,* ed. Blaine Allan et al. (Evanston, Ill., 1979), which contains twelve individual essays on the subject (pp. 105–236).

† Excluding the melodramatic "mountain film" *Die weisse Hölle von Piz Palü* (1929), which Pabst co-directed with Arnold Fanck.

foremost masters of the early sound film (his pacifist films *Westfront 1918* [1930] and *Kameradschaft* [*Comradeship,* 1931] are both among the most important works of the period). Indeed, Pabst's career extended well into the fifties, but his greatest work was done between 1924 and 1931—a time, ironically, when what has been called the Golden Age of German film was drawing to a close and the German cinema was about to begin its long decline.

DOWN AND OUT

In the past, it was fashionable to blame this decline upon the Nazis, who did indeed subvert UFA immediately after coming to power in 1933, turning the studio into a factory for the mass production of light entertainment and an instrument of propaganda for the state, under the direction of Josef Goebbels. Recently, however, it has come to be recognized that the German cinema was dying of internal disorders long before the Nazi takeover, long before even the coming of sound. This is not to suggest that it was completely moribund by the end of the silent era. Far from it; for Germany produced three of the most distinguished early sound films made anywhere in the world: Josef von Sternberg's *Der blaue Engel* (*The Blue Angel,* 1930; see Chapter 8), Fritz Lang's *M* (1931), and Pabst's *Westfront 1918* (1930; see Chapter 9). Yet there is no doubt that the general quality of production declined sharply after 1924 and that the causes were deep-seated and manifold.

For one thing, it seems certain that the emphasis on studio production, so important to the aesthetic quality of the German cinema between 1919 and 1924, had proved stifling by the end of the silent period. The UFA style of architectural composition and pictorial lighting was becoming an end in itself, and the sheer extravagance of its productions had substantially diminished the studio's economic stability (Murnau's *Faust,* for example, was rumored to have overrun its costs by four times the budgeted amount). It is significant in this regard that the last two important films of the Weimar cinema were "montage documentaries" shot on location in and around Berlin. Walter Ruttmann's *Berlin, die Symphonie einer Grosstadt* (*Berlin, the Symphony of a Great City,* 1927), written by Mayer and photographed by Freund, employed the candid camera and rhythmic montage techniques of Dziga Vertov's "kino-eye" group (see Chapter 5) to create an abstract portrait of the city and its teeming life from dawn to midnight on a late spring day.* *Menschen am Sonntag* (*People on Sunday,* 1929), a semi-documentary account of two young couples on a holiday at a lake outside Berlin, was the collaborative effort of several young men who would later become major directors of the sound era in America—Robert Siodmak, Fred Zinnemann, Edgar G. Ulmer, and Billy Wilder (Eugen Schüfftan, who would also emigrate to Hollywood, was the cinematographer). Like its wholly documentary

4.32 *Berlin, die Symphonie einer Grosstadt* (Walter Ruttmann, 1927).

---

* The film was edited by Ruttmann to parallel the rhythms of a score by the German Marxist composer Edmund Meisel, whose stirring revolutionary music for Eisenstein's *Potemkin* had helped to get that film banned in Germany.

cessor, *Menschen am Sonntag* showed the marked influence of Vertov and Russian montage.

It was the American influence, however, which proved most powerful, and many film historians have blamed the decline of Weimar cinema on the intrusion of Hollywood money and manners into Germany after the Parufamet agreement was signed. It is well known, for example, that Pabst was ordered by UFA executives to direct *Die Liebe der Jeanne Ney* in the "American style" and that the film barely survived the attempt.* Indeed, the American style in Neubabelsberg proved even less successful than the UFA style in Hollywood. Other film scholars have argued that the German cinema was artistically impoverished by the talent raids which Hollywood made upon UFA in 1926; certainly the loss of Murnau and so many of his associates was significantly detrimental to the studio. Finally, UFA was literally impoverished by American competition, both international and domestic, in the wake of the Dawes Plan, so that it had to be bailed out by the political Right. It seems clear, however, that the most important reasons for Germany's decline as a major cinematic power run deeper than those put forth here already.

Lotte H. Eisner gets closer to the heart of the matter in the final chapter of *The Haunted Screen,* in which she suggests that the thematic legacy of Expressionism was tragedy and despair. Indeed, as Siegfried Kracauer shows time and time again in *From Caligari to Hitler,* the struggle for control of the self which provided the great theme of the Weimar cinema was always *lost* on the screen; and this had the effect of increasing the insecurity and thus the authoritarian tendencies of the masses, which in the post-war era included large segments of the middle class brought low by inflation. Since the German form of government was republican and Germany was a conquered nation, however, this authoritarian impulse had no means of expression, and the collective mind of the society was paralyzed by its inability to articulate itself. Thus, if Eisner and Kracauer are correct, and I believe that they are, the decline of the German cinema was due to multiple external factors underwritten by a nationwide inner paralysis which in some sense the German cinema, at least as an organ of German society, had helped to create. It was not the Nazis who destroyed the German cinema, then, but the cultural pre-conditions which permitted their rise to power; and though UFA managed to produce a handful of truly distinguished films between 1929 and 1933, the vital spark of the German screen had been extinguished. Thanks to the virulence of the Nazi plague and the partitioning of Germany which followed World War II, it could not be rekindled until the generation of Germans born after the war came to artistic and political consciousness in the late sixties. Since that time, the West German cinema has become one of the most exciting and influential in all of Europe, and, in the work of brilliant young film-makers like Werner Herzog, Rainer Werner Fassbinder, Wim Wenders, and Jean-Marie Straub, it stands once again on the very cutting edge of the international avant-garde (see Chapter 17).

*Ilya Ehrenburg, from whose novel the screenplay was adapted, provides an interesting account of the film's production in Volume III of *Men, Years—Life* (London: McGibbon & Kee, 1963), pp. 124–30.

Soviet Silent Cinema and the Theory of Montage, 1917–1931

THE PRE-REVOLUTIONARY CINEMA

Before the Bolshevik Revolution of 1917, the film industry in Russia was mainly European. Agents of Lumière Frères, Pathé, Gaumont, and Danish Nordisk had established large distribution branches in several cities at the turn of the century, and almost all films shown in Russia between 1898 and the outbreak of World War I were imported. The first native Russian studio was not founded until 1908, and by 1917 there were still only four major production companies in the entire country (Ermoliev, Khanzhonkov, Russ, and Neptune). Ninety percent of all film-making activity was concentrated in the major cities of Moscow and Petrograd.* All technical equipment and film stock were imported from Germany or France.

The smallness of the industry was due to the fact that in Russia the cinema had not yet become a popular form, as it had in the West. Unlike their German counterparts, the Russian working classes were too impoverished to attend the movies, and the ultra-conservative ruling classes simply didn't care to. Still, the pre-revolutionary cinema produced several films of note. In 1913, the Futurist poet Vladimir Mayakovsky (1893–1930) and his colleagues made a unique avant-garde manifesto in film entitled *Drama in Futurist Cabaret 13* (*Drama v futuristicheskom kabare 13*). Between 1915 and 1916, the great stage director Vsevolod Meyerhold (1874–1942) adapted three famous literary works for the screen—Oscar Wilde's novel *The Picture of Dorian Gray* (*Portret Doriana Greya,* 1915), Alexander Ostrovsky's play *The Storm* (*Groza,* 1916) and Pshibuishevsky's *The Strong Man* (*Silnyi chelovek,* 1917)—all of which show a uniquely cinematic conception of *mise-en-scène.* By far the most impressive film of the period, and the last important one made before the October Revolution, was Yakov Protazanov's production of Lev Tolstoi's *Father Sergius* (*Otets Sergei,* 1918), whose acting, photography, and narrative construction surpassed anything made to date. Most films of the period, however, were distinctly mediocre, consisting

---

* The city's more Germanic name, "St. Petersburg," had been changed to "Petrograd" when Russia entered the war against Germany in 1914. In 1924 it was renamed "Leningrad" by the Bolsheviks.

mainly of costume melodramas, horror thrillers, and an occasional farce.

When Russia entered the war in 1914, foreign films could no longer be imported, and the tsarist government established the Skobelev Committee (named for its chairman) to stimulate domestic production. The commercial film industry continued to make escapist entertainment, but the committee specifically encouraged the production of propaganda films to stem growing discontent with the tsarist regime. The committee was not and could not have been successful, because social conditions in Russia had become so bad by the second year of the war that a revolution was imminent. The armed forces, under-fed and under-equipped, had suffered heavy losses. There were shortages of food and fuel everywhere, and the civilian population was completely demoralized.

THE BIRTH OF THE SOVIET CINEMA

In March 1917, the tsarist regime was replaced by a provisional parliamentary government under Alexander Kerensky (1881–1970), who unwisely attempted to continue Russia's involvement in the war. Kerensky's government immediately abolished film censorship and reorganized the Skobelev Committee to produce anti-tsarist propaganda. But only two films (*Nicholas II* [*Tsar Nikolai II*] and *The Past Will Not Die* [*Proshloye ne umryot*]) were made under this new dispensation, because the Provisional Government itself was overthrown by the Bolsheviks, led by Vladimir Ilyich Lenin (1870–1924), in the October Revolution of 1917. There followed the establishment of the Soviet government at Petrograd; a bitter three-year civil war between the "Red" and "White" factions of the Russian army; an invasion by France, Britain, the U.S.A., Japan, and others; a crippling foreign trade embargo; and, finally, economic collapse and famine. In the midst of this chaos, the Bolshevik leaders looked to film as a means of re-unifying their shattered nation. As a party of 200,000 which had assumed the leadership of 160 million people, most of them illiterate, scattered across the single largest contiguous land mass in the world and speaking well over one hundred separate languages, the Bolsheviks' most immediate task was one of communication and consolidation, and they saw film as the perfect medium for this endeavor. Lenin himself declared, "The cinema is for us the most important of the arts."

Unfortunately, most producers and technicians of the pre-revolutionary commercial cinema were capitalists openly hostile to the Bolshevik government (and vice versa). They emigrated to Europe, taking their equipment and film stock with them and, in the process, often wrecking the studios they left behind. No new equipment or film stock could be imported into Russia because of the foreign blockade, and massive power shortages severely restricted the use of what few resources remained.* Nevertheless, in the very face of these obstacles, the Soviet government

---

* Recognizing the urgent necessity for film stock, the Soviet government hired an Italian named Roberto Cibrario as an international purchasing agent for the film industry in 1918. He was sent to New York City, where he was to use $1 million in pre-war Russian bank deposits to buy film stock. Cibrario turned out to be a con man; he pocketed most of the funds

scrapped the Skobelev Committee and set up a special subsection on cinema under the new Ministry of Education, whose commissar was the playwright and literary critic Anatoly Lunacharsky (1875–1933). In August 1919 the Soviet film industry was nationalized and the Cinema Committee placed under the People's Commissariat of Propaganda and Education. Headed by Lenin's wife, Nadezhda Krupskaya, the Cinema Committee founded a film school in Moscow to train actors and technicians for the cinema (another was established briefly at Petrograd): the VGIK (Vsesoyuznyi Gosudarstvenyi Institut Kinematografia—"All-Union State Institute of Cinematography"), or State Film School. This school was the first of its kind in the world; its initial purpose was to train people in the production of *agitki*—newsreels edited for the purpose of agitation and propaganda, or "agit-prop." Starting in 1918, these *agitki* toured Russia on specially equipped agit-trains and agit-steamers designed to export the Revolution from the urban centers to the provinces—an immense undertaking in a country containing one-sixth of the world's land mass and one-twelfth of its population.* Indeed, because of the severe shortage of film stock and the chaotic conditions of the new Soviet state, almost all films made during the years of the Civil War (1918–21) were newsreels of this sort. Thus, the Soviet cinema was at its birth a cinema of propaganda in documentary form. And its first major artist was, appropriately, the first great practitioner and theorist of the documentary form, Dziga Vertov.

DZIGA VERTOV AND THE *KINO-EYE*

Dziga Vertov (b. Denis Kaufman,† 1896–1954) was born in Bialystok, Poland, then part of the Russian Empire. In 1917 he became an editor of newsreels for the Moscow Cinema Committee. Cameramen traveling about the country to record the progress of the Red Army in the Civil War and the activities of the new government would send their footage back to Moscow, where it was edited into newsreels by Vertov and

---

by forging invoices and bills of lading. Though he was arrested at the Soviet government's request, he was never brought to trial and was actually able to keep most of the stolen money because the United States did not recognize the Soviet government. (A comic dramatization of these events entitled *Thank You, Comrades,* by Jim Hawkins, was produced for the BBC and broadcast in the United States on PBS in 1978.)

* Ironically, after 1922 much of this activity was financed by box-office receipts from American films imported for the purpose by the Soviet Commissariat of Foreign Trade on the orders of Lunacharsky and Lenin. See Vance Kepley, Jr., and Betty Kepley, "Foreign Films on Soviet Screens, 1922–1931," *Quarterly Review of Film Studies,* 4, 4 (Fall 1979), 429–42.

† "Dziga" is a Ukrainian word meaning "spinning top" or "restless, fidgety, bustling person." "Vertov" is derived from a Russian word meaning "to turn, spin, rotate, or fidget." The pseudonym, adopted around 1915, suggests the sound of a hand-cranked movie camera; it is also, perhaps, Vertov's comment on the film-maker's profession.

Vertov's brothers also earned places in film history. Boris Kaufman (1907–80) was acclaimed as one of the world's great black and white cinematographers. He worked with Jean Vigo in France (see Chapter 9) and with Elia Kazan, Sidney Lumet, and other American directors. Mikhail Kaufman (b. 1897) began as Vertov's cinematographer but later produced a number of distinguished documentaries of his own.

others. At first, Vertov was content to assemble the footage in a purely functional manner, but he gradually began to experiment with more expressive kinds of editing. By 1921, Vertov had made three feature-length compilation documentaries from his weekly newsreel footage: *Anniversary of the Revolution* (*Godovshchina revoliutsii,* 1919—the first Soviet feature film), *The Battle at Tsaritsyn* (*Srazhenie v Tsaritsyne,* 1920), and a thirteen-part *History of the Civil War* (*Istoriya grazhdenskoi voini,* 1921). In all of them he experimented with subliminal cuts of one to two frames each, color tinting by hand, expressive titles,* and the dramatic reconstruction of documentary events.

Since the period immediately following the revolution was one of extraordinary creative fervor in the arts, Vertov's experiments were actively encouraged by the Cinema Committee, and he began to gather about him a small band of committed young documentarists who came to call themselves the *Kinoki* (from *kino-oki*—"cinema-eyes"). This group published a series of radical manifestoes in the early twenties denouncing conventional narrative cinema as "impotent" and demanding that it be replaced by a new cinema based on the "organization of camera-recorded documentary material" (Vertov). The key terms here are "camera-recorded" and "organization," for Vertov and his colleagues believed both in the absolute ability of the cinema apparatus to reproduce reality as it actually exists *and* in the necessity of editing to arrange this reality into an expressive and persuasive whole. This doctrine, called by Vertov *kino-glaz* ("cinema-eye"), contributed significantly to the montage aesthetics which came to dominate the Soviet silent cinema after 1924 (see below). But it also produced a number of stunning documentary achievements in its own right.

In 1922, Lenin ordered that a fixed ratio (dubbed the "Leninist film-proportion") be established between Soviet fiction films and documentary films. Shortly thereafter, Vertov launched a new series of consciously crafted newsreel-documentaries collectively entitled *Kino-pravda* ("film truth"), which were specifically designed to test his theories. The twenty-three *Kino-pravda* films Vertov made between 1922 and 1925 employed a wide variety of experimental techniques, but none was as startling as his first independently shot non-archival feature, *Kino-glaz* (1924), which used trick photography, animation, microphotography,† multiple exposure, and "candid camera" techniques to create what one critic has called "an epic vision of actuality."[1] Between 1925 and 1929 Vertov made three similar features—*Stride, Soviet!* (*Shagai, Soviet!,* 1926), *A Sixth of the World* (*Shestaya chast mira,* 1926), and *Eleventh Year* (*Odinnadtsati,* 1928)—but his most exhaustive essay in the "*kino*-eye" technique was his major work, *The Man with a Movie Camera* (*Chelovek s kinoapparatom,* 1928).

This film utilizes every resource of editing and camera manipulation known to silent cinema to create a portrait of "life as it is lived" on a

5.1 A poster by Alexander Rodchenko for *Kino-Glaz* (Dziga Vertov, 1924).

---

* Often, gigantic revolutionary slogans in capital letters that seemed to shout at the audience from the screen.

† Also called "photomicrography": shooting film through a microscope.

typical day in Moscow from dawn to dusk. But *The Man with a Movie Camera* is less about Moscow than about cinema itself, for it constantly seeks to reveal the process of its own making. The film contains recurrent images of cameramen shooting it, Vertov editing it, and people in a theater watching it. Point of view is manipulated to such an extent that it breaks down, and the camera's power to transform reality is flaunted in a continuous burst of cinematic pyrotechnics which include variable camera speeds, dissolves, split-screen effects,* the use of prismatic lenses, multiple superimposition, animation, microphotography, and elaborately structured montage. In *The Man with a Movie Camera*, in fact, Vertov had progressed from documentarist to *ciné*-poet, creating a kind of meta-cinema, or self-reflexive cinema, which prefigures the work of the French New Wave (see Chapter 13). To quote critic David Bordwell, "Long before the Marxist film theorists of *Cahiers du cinéma* . . . called for a cinema which declares its sources in a context of production and consumption, Vertov was mounting a continuous *autocritique* of film-making."[2]

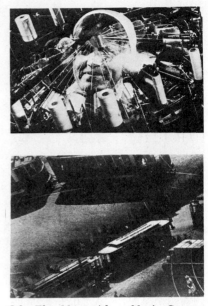

5.2 *The Man with a Movie Camera* (Dziga Vertov, 1928).

Unlike most other serious film-makers of his day, Vertov welcomed the coming of sound (see Chapter 7), seeing it as a means of augmenting the "*kino*-eye" with the "radio-ear," and he continued to make films through 1944. Although his international influence throughout the thirties on both the avant-garde and the conventional documentary was strong, his own work became increasingly doctrinaire, but nevertheless, like so many of his compatriots; he fell into disfavor with Stalin and his government for "formalist" error—the sometimes deadly sin of exalting the aesthetic form of a work above its ideological content. In the sixties and seventies, however, Vertov has come to be regarded as a prophet of *cinéma vérité* (a term derived by translating *kino-pravda* into French; see Chapter 13) and the father of the new non-fiction film (see Chapter 17). Recently, the French New Wave director Jean-Luc Godard (b. 1930) and his political followers associated themselves with Vertov's work by naming their production cooperative after him: all of Godard's films between 1968 and 1973 were made collectively under the auspices of the Dziga-Vertov Group (see Chapter 13). More important, however, it is clear today that Vertov was a co-founder of the Soviet silent cinema, which gives him a major role in one of the greatest movements in the history of film.†

LEV KULESHOV AND THE KULESHOV WORKSHOP

The other recognized co-founder was Lev Kuleshov (1899–1970), one of the few pre-revolutionary film-makers to remain in Russia after 1917.

---

* Division of the screen (and therefore of the film frame) into two or more separate images which do not overlap. In Vertov's time all such effects were accomplished in the camera; today they are more easily obtained by using an optical printer.
† See Vlada Petric, "Dziga Vertov as Theorist," *Cinema Journal,* 28, 1 (Fall 1978), 29–44.

Kuleshov began his career as a set designer at the Khanzhonkov studios for the director Yevgeni Bauer (188?–1917) in 1916, at the age of seventeen, and actually completed Bauer's last feature, *After Happiness* (*Posle schastya*) after the director died unexpectedly a year later. During the Civil War, he became a cameraman for the agit-trains and was active in establishing the VGIK in 1919. Like Vertov, Kuleshov was interested in the theory as well as the practice of cinema; he had published his first articles on the subject in the academic journal *Vestnik kinematographia* ("cinematographic messenger") in 1917. But Kuleshov's superiors at the film school lacked confidence in the zealous twenty-year-old's ability to work within an orthodox curriculum, and they permitted him to found his own workshop outside the formal structure of the institute. This "Kuleshov Workshop" drew the most radical and innovative young students at the film school, Sergei Eisenstein and V. I. Pudovkin among them (see below), and concerned itself mainly with experiments in editing.

Because of the severe shortage of raw film stock and equipment which afflicted the Soviet Union in the immediate post-revolutionary period, the workshop's initial experiments involved the production of "films without celluloid." Kuleshov and his students would write scenarios, direct and act them out as if before cameras, and then—on paper—assemble the various "shots" into completed "films." By a happy historical accident, however, Kuleshov soon had another subject and model for experimentation in the most sophisticatedly constructed film made to date— D. W. Griffith's *Intolerance* (1916).

How a print of Griffith's epic came to be smuggled through the foreign blockade of Moscow in early 1919 is unclear,* but the film's enormous influence upon the fledgling Soviet cinema is a matter of historical record. Apparently, Lenin saw the film soon after its arrival and, impressed with what he took to be the proletarian sympathies of the Modern story, ordered that it be shown throughout the Soviet Union—where, according to Iris Barry, it ran continuously for almost ten years.[3] All available film stock was gathered up to be used in duplicating prints, and there are reports that Lenin actually cabled Griffith and offered him the directorship of the Soviet film industry, which Griffith supposedly declined only because of the opening of his new Mamaroneck studio. In any case, as Jay Leyda points out in *Kino,* his monumental history of the Russian and Soviet film, *Intolerance* went on to become the Soviet film industry's first great popular, political, and aesthetic success. To quote Leyda: "We know for certain of the popular success of *Intolerance,* and we know as certainly of the tremendous aesthetic and technical impetus given to *all* young Soviet film-makers by this and subsequently-shown Griffith films. No Soviet film of importance made within the following ten years was to be completely outside *Intolerance*'s sphere of influence."[4]

That influence was imbibed, elaborated, and disseminated largely through the Kuleshov Workshop, where prints of *Intolerance* (and, after the lifting of the blockade in 1920, *The Birth of a Nation*) were screened

* In fact, the print may have been imported before the Revolution. See Vance Kepley, Jr., "*Intolerance* and the Soviets: A Historical Investigation," *Wide Angle,* 3, 1, 22–27.

continuously until, according to legend, they fell apart. Kuleshov and his students spent months studying the precise manner in which Griffith had built up his complicated multiple narrative out of thousands of separate shots, until they had mastered the principle themselves. Then, they re-assembled his sequences in hundreds of different combinations to test the ways in which an arrangement of shots produces meaning. As raw film stock began to dribble back into the Soviet Union between 1922 and 1923 as a result of a Soviet-German trade agreement and the success of Lenin's New Economic Policy (NEP), Kuleshov struck out on his own and carried the analysis of film structure far beyond anything that had gone before.

Though the form of Kuleshov's initial experiments was dictated by the relative scarcity of raw stock, his ultimate goal was to discover the general laws by which film communicates meaning to an audience—to discover, that is, the way in which film *signifies.* In his most famous experiment, as recounted by V. I. Pudovkin in *Film Technique and Film Acting,* Kuleshov took unedited footage of a completely expressionless face (that of the pre-revolutionary matinee idol Ivan Mozhukhin, who had emigrated to Paris after the revolution) and intercut it with shots of three highly motivated objects: a bowl of hot soup, a dead woman lying in a coffin, and a little girl playing with a teddy bear. When the film strips were shown to randomly selected audiences, they invariably responded as though the actor's face had accurately portrayed the emotion appropriate to the intercut object. As Pudovkin recalled: "The public raved about the acting of the artist. They pointed out the heavy pensiveness of his mood over the forgotten soup, were touched and moved by the deep sorrow with which he looked on the dead woman, and admired the light, happy smile with which he surveyed the girl at play. But we knew that in all three cases the face was exactly the same."[5] Kuleshov concluded from these results, known today as the "Kuleshov effect," that the shot, or cinematic sign, has two distinct values: 1) that which it possesses in itself as a photographic image of reality, and 2) that which it acquires when placed in relationship to other shots. In another experiment, Kuleshov cut together a shot of a smiling actor with a close-up of a revolver and a second shot of the same actor looking frightened. Audiences naturally interpreted the sequence as portraying cowardice, but when Kuleshov reversed the position of the two shots of the actor within the sequence, the opposite interpretation was made. He reasoned from this that the second value of the shot implicit in the "Kuleshov effect," that which it acquires when juxtaposed with other shots, was infinitely more important in the generation of cinematic meaning than was the first. He concluded, that is, that meaning in cinema is a function of the celluloid strip, not of the *photographed reality,* and that it arises from the sequential arrangement of its parts. Griffith, of course, had practiced this principle instinctively in all of his major films, but Kuleshov was the first to give it a theoretical articulation and to suggest that it is the basis for the process of cinematic signification.

A further experiment involved the creation of "artificial landscapes" through "creative geography"—the juxtaposition of separate shots taken at separate places and times. In one of these, a shot of a man moving from right to left across the frame in one part of Moscow is cut together with a shot of a woman moving from left to right across the frame in another section of the city, while a third shot shows them suddenly meeting in yet another part of Moscow to shake hands. At the conclusion of this shot, the man points offscreen, and a fourth shot reveals the object of his attention to be the White House in Washington, D.C. The fifth and final shot of the sequence shows the two ascending the steps not of the White House, but of a well-known Moscow church. Kuleshov had thus created the cinematic illusion of spatial and temporal unity by cutting together five separate shots taken at five separate places and times. In yet another experiment, he synthesized the body of a woman out of shots of the face, torso, hands, and legs of several separate women.

What Kuleshov demonstrated in these and similar experiments was that in cinema "real" time and space are absolutely subordinate to the process of editing, or *montage,* as the Soviets came to call it, after the French verb *monter,* "to assemble." Furthermore, as Ron Levaco points out, Kuleshov had shown that the associational power of montage was not inherent in the edited film strip itself but was the result of the viewer's *perception* of the edited film strip, which makes the montage process an act of consciousness for film-maker and audience alike.[6] Griffith, of course, had been the first to discover the profound psychological impact which editing could have upon an audience, and Soviet film-makers had distilled many of their theoretical insights from his practice. But Kuleshov's theory of montage went beyond Griffith's editing in a manner described later by his former pupil Sergei Eisenstein: "Griffith's . . . close-ups create atmosphere, outline traits of character, alternate in dialogues of leading characters, and close-ups of the chaser and the chased speed up the tempo of the chase. But Griffith at all times remains on a level of representation and objectivity and nowhere does he try through the juxtaposition of shots to shape import and image."[7] In other words, editing was, for Griffith, primarily a narrative and representational mode. It generally served to advance a plot or tell a tale, and the "metaphorical" style of *Intolerance* was largely an aberration. As a result of their experiments, however—and, paradoxically, of their countless screenings of *Intolerance*—Kuleshov and his pupils conceived of montage as an expressive or symbolic process whereby logically or empirically dissimilar images could be linked together synthetically to produce metaphors (to produce, that is, non-literal meaning). Building upon this fundamental notion, Eisenstein and Pudovkin, Kuleshov's two most brilliant students, went on to elaborate distinctly individual theories of montage in their own theoretical writings and films. But before this occurred, the Kuleshov Workshop had an opportunity to put its theories into practice.

By 1923, the workshop had secured enough equipment and film stock to begin work upon its first feature film—a parody of American detective thrillers entitled *The Extraordinary Adventures of Mr. West in the Land of the Bolsheviks* (*Neobychainiye priklucheniya Mistera Vesta v stranye bolshevikov,* 1924), directed by Kuleshov. *Mr. West* was first and foremost a showcase for the workshop's newly acquired cinematic sophis-

tication, but it was also a very intelligent and amusing satire on popular
American misconceptions about the effects of the Bolshevik Revolution.
The zany plot concerns an American senator and YMCA official who
journeys to Soviet Moscow on business, expecting it to be inhabited by
brigands and thieves. Ironically, a street gang (composed of "counter-
revolutionary degenerates") does kidnap him, and proceeds to act out the
horror show that Mr. West has expected to see all along. Just as he is
about to pay a large ransom for his release, he is rescued by the state
police and shown the "real" Bolshevik Moscow. The film was an enormous success with Russian audiences, and it remains today a minor classic of silent comedy. The original Kuleshov group made only one final
feature together, a science-fiction mystery thriller called *The Death Ray*
(*Luch smerti,* 1925), directed by Kuleshov and written by Pudovkin. *The
Death Ray* was a technically dazzling but ultimately sterile attempt to
synthesize material from several popular serials, including the American
Perils of Pauline series and Feuillade's *Fantômas* and *Judex,* and it came
under attack from the Communist Party leadership for not being sufficiently ideological.

His workshop was disbanded in 1925, apparently as a result of these
attacks, but Kuleshov himself went on the following year to direct his
greatest film, *By the Law* (*Dura lex/Po zakonu,* 1926), for the newly
centralized state cinema trust, Sovkino, which had been established in
1924 to control the film affairs of the entire Soviet Union through government financing. Adapted from Jack London's short story "The Unexpected" with the collaboration of the Formalist poet Viktor Shklovsky,
By the Law achieved an extraordinary blend of emotional intensity and
geometrical stylization on the smallest budget ever allocated for a Soviet
feature film. Set entirely in a one-room cabin in a desolate region of the
Yukon during the winter, it tells the story of two people who are com-

5.3 *Dura lex* (Lev Kuleshov, 1926).

pelled by social conditioning to try, condemn, and execute a third person
for the murder of two friends. There are no parallel lines of action and no
changes of locale, but Kuleshov achieves an expansion of dramatic space
through montage which is remarkable in a film of such narrowly defined
scope and which clearly influenced the style of Carl Dreyer's *La Passion
de Jeanne d'Arc* (1928; see Chapter 7) two years later. Indeed, the precision and economy of the film are such that one Soviet critic could write
on its release, "*By the Law* was worked out in the spirit of an alge-
braic formula, seeking to obtain the maximum of effect with the minimum of effort." Unfortunately, the film was poorly received by most of
the official critics, and Kuleshov's three subsequent silent features were
unsuccessful. He made only one sound film of note, *The Great Consoler*
(*Velikii uteshitel,* 1933), loosely based on some O. Henry short stories,
which he may in fact have intended as an allegory of the plight of Soviet
artists under Stalin. Like Vertov, Kuleshov was himself denounced for
"formalist error" at the 1935 Congress of Film Workers and forced to
recant much of his earlier work. He continued to make films until 1944,
when he was rewarded for his Party loyalty by appointment to the position of head of the State Film School (VGIK), where he taught and lectured until his death in 1970.

Though Kuleshov contributed a number of important films to his country's great cinema, it is as a theorist rather than a practitioner of cinema that he will be most prominently remembered. He was in fact the first theorist of the cinema, as Pudovkin recognized when he wrote, in an introduction to Kuleshov's theoretical study *Art of Cinema* in 1929, "We make films—Kuleshov made cinematography."[8] Ron Levaco estimates that more than half of the major Soviet directors since 1920—including Eisenstein, Pudovkin, and Boris Barnet (see below), and Mikhail Kalatozov and Sergei Paradzhanov (see Chapter 15)—had been his students at the Film School at one time or another.[9] His legacy to them and to us is again best articulated by Pudovkin:

> All he said was this: "In every art there must be first a material, and secondly, a method of composing this material specifically adapted to this art. . . ." Kuleshov maintained that the material in filmwork consists of pieces of film, and that the method of composing is their joining together in a particular creatively conceived order. He maintained that film-art does not begin when the artists act and the various scenes are shot—this is only the preparation of the material. Film-art begins from the moment when the director begins to combine and join together the various pieces of film. By joining them in various combinations, in different orders, he obtains differing results.[10]

The discovery and articulation of this notion was the enabling act of the Soviet silent cinema and the montage aesthetics upon which it was founded.*

SERGEI EISENSTEIN

Sergei Mikhailovich Eisenstein (1898–1948) was, with D. W. Griffith, one of the two pioneering geniuses of the modern cinema. Yet, though their syntactical methods were similar and both worked on an epic historical scale, as artists the two men could hardly have been less alike. Griffith was a sentimentalist whose values were typically those of the Victorian middle class. His films were modernist in form, reactionary in feeling; and he made too many of them. Eisenstein, by contrast, was a contemporary Marxist intellectual whose vibrantly revolutionary films left an indelible mark on history and cinema alike. Where Griffith was unschooled and narrow, Eisenstein was a modern Renaissance man whose intellectual breadth astonished all who knew him. Though he completed only seven films in his twenty-three-year career, the impact of these films and of his theoretical writings on the film form itself has been

5.4 Sergei Eisenstein seated on the tsar's throne in the Winter Palace during the shooting of *October* (1927).

* It would be wrong to assume, as so many past accounts have done, that the montage idea came solely from the Kuleshov Workshop, or the influence of *Intolerance*, or the economies imposed upon Soviet film-makers by the scarcity of raw stock. The idea had in fact been very much alive in avant-garde art between 1910 and 1918. As David Bordwell has pointed out (in "Dziga Vertov: An Introduction," *Film Comment*, Spring 1972, p. 38), this was the great period of Futurist and Formalist experimentation, and the notion of fragmentation and re-assembly as a means of artistic construction was distinctly in the air. Furthermore, the analogies between montage structure and the Marxist historical dialectic are impressive, as we shall see.

greater than that of any other body of work in the history of the medium save Griffith's. Griffith had discovered, in editing, the fundamental narrative structure of the cinema, but he and his followers had used it conservatively to tell nineteenth-century tales. Eisenstein formulated a completely modernist theory of editing, based on the psychology of perception and the Marxist historical dialectic, which made it possible for the cinema to communicate on its own terms for the first time, without borrowing either matter or form from other media. And, like Griffith, Eisenstein gave the world a handful of films which will always rank among the highest aesthetic achievements of the cinema.

The Formative Years

Eisenstein was born in Riga, Latvia, in 1898; his father was a well-to-do architect and city engineer. Despite an early interest in art and the process of artistic creation, Eisenstein was sent to the Institute of Civil Engineering in Petrograd, where he was a nineteen-year-old student when the tsarist regime began to crumble in February 1917. The institute immediately disbanded, Eisenstein's parents departed for Europe, and Eisenstein himself joined the Red Army as an engineer. After two years of building bridges during the Civil War, he decided to follow his natural impulse and become an artist. He worked throughout 1919 as a poster artist on an agit-train; then, through a chance meeting with an old friend, he became first a set designer and then a director for the Moscow Proletkult* Theater. This institution, with a union of more than two hundred local branches, had been established during the Revolution for the purpose of replacing the bourgeois culture of tsarist times with a purely proletarian one. When Eisenstein joined the Proletkult Theater in 1920, it was a virtual clearinghouse for avant-garde experiment and modernist ideas. The world-famous stage director Konstantin Stanislavsky (1863–1938) lectured daily on his naturalistic acting "method" here, while the equally prominent director Vsevolod Meyerhold railed against Stanislavsky's naturalism and called for an anti-traditional theater—a stylized, nonverbal, and popular theater which would use pantomime, acrobatics, Meyerhold's own system of "bio-mechanics" (see below), and all the resources of circus spectacle and *commedia dell'arte*† to create "a machine for acting." Here too the Futurist‡ poet and playwright Vladimir Mayakovsky expounded his radical aesthetic doctrines, Mikhail Chekhov lectured on Hindu philosophy and yoga, and weekly seminars were held on Marxism, Freudian psychology, and Pavlovian reflexology.**

---

* An acronym for "proletarian culture."

† A form of drama which originated in sixteenth-century Italy, *commedia dell'arte* employs standard characters (Pantaloon, Harlequin, Columbine), improvised dialogue, and action based on a written script.

‡ Futurism was a revolutionary movement in the arts, closely allied with Constructivism, which glorified power, speed, and technology at the expense of more traditional cultural forms. It had a natural affinity for the cinema and its mechanized apparatus.

** The science founded by the Nobel Prize–winning physiologist Ivan Pavlov (1849–1936) which interprets all behavior as consisting of simple and complex physiological reflexes.

Eisenstein fell first under the influence of Meyerhold, who had not worked in the cinema again after his two pre-revolutionary films; but Eisenstein spoke of him as his "artistic father" long after Meyerhold had been discredited and imprisoned during the Stalin-era purge trials. Meyerhold, for his part, claimed that "all Eisenstein's work had its origins in the laboratory where we once worked together as teacher and pupil."[11] What Eisenstein learned from Meyerhold was, essentially, the possibility of mixing two ostensibly contradictory artistic approaches—that of rigorous systematization and spontaneous improvisation. Under Meyerhold's method for acting, which he called "bio-mechanics," spontaneity was systematically conditioned. According to Peter Wollen, the notion drew upon such varied sources as Pavlovian reflexology, Taylorism (the study of workers' physical movements, invented in America to increase production), the Italian *commedia dell'arte,* the philosophy of pragmatism articulated by William James, the acrobatic Douglas Fairbanks films, the German Romantic puppet theater, and the highly stylized Oriental theater.[12] Eisenstein's encounter with bio-mechanics marks the beginning of his life-long theoretical concern with the psychological effects of the aesthetic experience: specifically, the question of what combination of aesthetic stimuli will produce what responses in the perceiver under what conditions.

Eisenstein's preoccupation with this phenomenon was encouraged by his friend and colleague at the Proletkult Theater, Sergei Yutkevich (b. 1904), himself to become a prominent Soviet director during the sound era. It was Yutkevich who involved Eisenstein in designing sets for the Futurist Workshop Theater, run by a former German baron named Foregger, where the use of parodic masks introduced him to the notion of "typage" so important to his early films, and it was he who later introduced Eisenstein to the FEX group in Petrograd. The Factory of the Eccentric Actor, or FEX, was a Futurist theatrical movement run by Grigori Kozintsev and Leonid Trauberg (later to collaborate as director and scenarist on many important Soviet films of the twenties and thirties) which combined elements of the circus, cabaret, and music hall, as well as of American adventure films and slapstick comedy films. Eisenstein's contact with the FEX group clearly influenced the form of his first stage production for the Proletkult in 1923, an adaptation of a work by the nineteenth-century dramatist Alexander Ostrovsky (1823–86) entitled *Even a Wise Man Stumbles,* or simply *The Wise Man* (*Mudrets*). Eisenstein took the bare bones of the plot and organized them not into acts or scenes but into a series of "attractions," as in a circus or cabaret. The stage, in fact, was laid out like a circus arena, with trapezes, tightropes, and parallel bars, and the audience was treated to a long procession of acrobatic acts, satirical sketches, "noise bands" reproducing the sounds of the "new industrial age," and, finally, firecrackers exploding beneath every seat in the house. At one point in the performance, Eisenstein even projected a short film (his first) parodying Dziga Vertov's *Kino-Pravda* newsreel.

Eisenstein called this assault on the audience's sensibility the "montage of attractions," and to elaborate the concept he published his first

5.5 A scene from *The Wise Man* (1923).

theoretical manifesto in Mayakovsky's radical literary journal *Lef** in 1923 (the same issue contained Vertov's first manifesto on the *"kino-eye"*). Eisenstein wrote that he had long sought a scientific "unit of measurement" for gauging the emotional effects of art and had found it at last in the "attraction":

> [A] roll on the kettledrums as much as Romeo's soliliquy, the cricket on the hearth no less than the cannon fired over the heads of the audience. For all, in their individual ways, bring us to a single idea—from their individual laws to their common quality of *attraction. The attraction . . . is every element that can be verified and mathematically calculated to produce certain emotional shocks.* [13]

Eisenstein said further that the montage of attractions ("units of impression combined into one whole") could be used to introduce " a new level of tension" into the aesthetic experience which would produce a theater "of such emotional saturation that the wrath of a man would be expressed by a backward somersault from a trapeze." Thus, before he ever attempted to make a serious film, Eisenstein had articulated a rudimentary theory of montage as a process whereby independent and arbitrary units of "attraction" or "impression" were assembled to produce a total emotional effect different from the sum of its parts. As Eisenstein came more and more under the influence of Freud and of Ivan Pavlov, discoverer of the conditioned reflex, he replaced the notion of "attractions" with that of shocks or stimuli, and, as Peter Wollen notes, this dovetailed neatly with his Marxist concern for the agitational aspects of his work. [14]

Eisenstein's next effort for the Proletkult was a production of *Listen, Moscow! (Slushai Moskvu!)*, Sergei Tretyakov's play about recent revolutionary events in Bavaria, which Eisenstein termed "agit-Guignol." Like *The Wise Man,* it had many cinematic elements, including a device for shifting the spectators' attention rapidly from one focal point on stage to another. As Yon Barna points out in his recent biography, *Eisenstein,* [15] it was becoming apparent that Eisenstein had approached the limits of what he could achieve in the theater by cinematic means, and the cinema itself was exerting increasing appeal for him. In his last theatrical production for the Proletkult, however, Eisenstein went ever farther afield in his effort to produce a chain of aesthetic shock effects by staging Tretyakov's agitational play *Gas Masks (Gazovye maski)* in the Moscow gas-works. The audience sat on benches amidst the machinery and the grand finale was the arrival of the actual night-shift workers to light their gas jets as the actors departed. The play was not a success because the actors were dwarfed by the machinery, but the failure convinced Eisenstein that the theatrical form—however stylized, modernized, or revolutionized—could no longer contain his developing notions of montage. As he had written in *Lef* in 1923, with characteristic impatience: "The theater as an independent unit within a revolutionary framework . . . is out of the question. It is absurd to perfect a wooden plough; you must order a tractor."

---

* An acronym for "artistic left front."

5.6 *Strike!* (Sergei Eisenstein, 1924): the workers' leaders call a strike after a secret meeting in the factory scrap-iron heap.

From Theater to Film

The "tractor" was ordered for Eisenstein by the Proletkult Theater it-self when in early 1924 it decided to sponsor a series of eight films, to be collectively entitled *Toward the Dictatorship of the Proletariat* (*K dikta-ture proletariata*), which would trace the rise of the Communist Party from the late nineteenth century through 1917. One of the scripts was being written by Valeri Plentyov, director of the Proletkult, and he in-vited Eisenstein to collaborate with him on the project, which ultimately became the Proletkult-Goskino* production *Strike!* (*Stachka!*, 1924), Eisenstein's directorial debut. *Strike!* was intended as the fifth film in the series, but it was the first and only one to be made since, according to Eisenstein, it contained "the most mass action" and was therefore "the most significant."[16] Between 1920 and 1924, Eisenstein had seen countless German Expressionist and American films in Moscow, includ-ing the major works of Griffith,† and had apprenticed himself for several weeks in 1924 to his friend Esther Shub (1894–1959), the skillful *agitki* editor and, later, director of Goskino documentaries, when she was re-editing a print of Fritz Lang's *Dr. Mabuse, der Spieler* (see Chapter 4) for general release in Moscow as *Gilded Putrefaction*.‡ But in fact Eisenstein knew very little about the technical aspects of film-making when he began to work on *Strike!* Nevertheless, like Griffith before him, Eisen-stein quickly apprenticed himself to the very best cinematographer at the Goskino studios, Eduard Tisse (1897–1961), and inaugurated a lifelong

---

* Goskino (an acronym for "state film") was a major division of Sovkino ("Soviet film"), the state film enterprise established in 1924 under Lenin's New Economic Policy.

† Eisenstein later wrote that Griffith had played "a massive role in the development of mon-tage in the Soviet film," concluding that "all that is best in the Soviet cinema has its origins in *Intolerance*" (quoted in Yon Barna, *Eisenstein* [Bloomington, Ind., 1973], p. 74). Indeed, several scholars have recently argued that the Modern story of *Intolerance* provided the inspiration for Eisenstein's *Strike!*

‡ Shub transformed the concluding battle between Mabuse and the police into a class-inspired street rebellion.

artistic collaboration whose importance is equaled only by the Griffith-Bitzer association. Yet even before he had learned how to use Goskino's technical equipment, Eisenstein undertook an exhaustive program of research into his subject from which he produced a minutely detailed scenario.

5.7 *Strike!*: after a sumptuous meal, the owners resolve to act.

In it, Eisenstein conceived his film as a revolutionary assault upon the "bourgeois cinema," i.e., the narrative cinema as practiced in the West thus far. To this end, though all sequences were shot against natural backgrounds, the strike of the title was itself made typical and representative rather than historical. Furthermore, Eisenstein abandoned the traditional individual hero for a collective one—his film's aggregate protagonist was the striking workers in their struggle against the brutal and oppressive factory system, and no single one of them was shown to be more socially valuable or thematically significant than another. Finally, in an effort to forge an "unbreakable link" between the Marxist dialectic and cinematic form, Eisenstein planned the entire film as an extended montage of "attractions" or "shock stimuli" which would agitate the audience into identification with the striking workers. In the completed film, as in his theater productions, some of Eisenstein's "attractions" are mere tricks designed to seize the audience's attention in the most direct and forceful manner, but much of the time he is engaged in creating uniquely cinematic metaphors through the juxtaposition of two (or more) images which suggest a meaning different from and greater than them both. He is engaged, that is, in practicing the first stage of the highly complex and sophisticated montage process on which his greatest films are built.

Although it contains many grotesque and circus-like elements from Eisenstein's theater days, *Strike!* evolves in a non-narrative chronicle form which was clearly influenced by Vertov's doctrine of the "kino-eye" (though, to underscore the agitational aspect of his work, Eisenstein would later say, "I don't believe in the kino-eye; I believe in the kino-fist"[17]) and the editing experiments of Kuleshov. The film opens with a montage of smokestacks, industrial machinery, evil factory owners, and

5.8 *Strike!*: local criminals hired as strike-breakers emerge from hiding to receive instructions from the police.

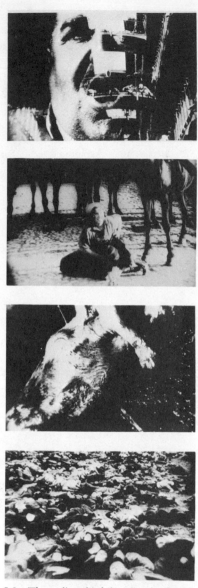

5.9 The police chief (lap-dissolved with the workers' tenement) orders the final slaughter.

noble but horribly oppressed workers. We soon discover that the workers are planning a strike and that the management has hired *agents provocateurs* and informers to infiltrate their ranks. After a worker's suicide triggers the strike, the factory is temporarily shut down and the strikers enjoy the first leisure they have known in their lives—but only briefly, for their grievances are ignored by the owners, who finally resolve to break the strike by violent means. The police are enlisted to "interrogate" strike leaders and to stage provocations with the help of local criminals, but the workers refuse to be intimidated despite counter-insurgency and a general famine among them. Frustrated with intrigue, the police chief orders an armed invasion of the workers' apartments and the massacre of all strikers and their families. The famous concluding montage intercuts graphic footage of this atrocity with shots of cattle being slaughtered in an abbatoir, and the film ends with a long shot of the ground before the apartment block littered with the bodies of hundreds of adults and children.

Strike! was the first revolutionary mass-film of the new Soviet state, and, although some critics accused it of formalism, its agitational impact upon the populace was great (Eisenstein himself, with characteristic immodesty, proclaimed it "the October of the cinema").* More important, however, *Strike!* inaugurated the classical period of Soviet silent cinema at a time when the silent cinemas of the West had very nearly reached their peaks. In America, by 1924, D. W. Griffith had already produced his greatest work, and Griffith, Erich von Stroheim, Robert Flaherty, Charlie Chaplin, and Buster Keaton were all at work on major films (*America, Greed, Moana, The Gold Rush,* and *Sherlock, Jr.,* respectively; see Chapter 6). The German cinema was passing from Expressionism to the "new realism" with F. W. Murnau's *Der letzte Mann* (1924), and the careers of Murnau, Ernst Lubitsch, and Fritz Lang were flourishing. In France, the avant-garde cinema had reached its height with the films of Germaine Dulac, Louis Delluc, Jean Epstein, Marcel L'Herbier, Jacques Feyder, and René Clair (Clair's influential *Entr'acte* and Fernand Léger's famous *Ballet mécanique* both appeared in 1924; see Chapter 9). The Italian silent cinema had peaked with its series of pre-war super-spectacles and had declined long before 1924, but in Sweden the silent film was still enjoying the twilight of its great masters, Victor Sjöström and Mauritz Stiller (*The Phantom Chariot* [1920]; *The Saga of Gösta Berling* [1924]). Thus, Soviet silent cinema was a latecomer compared to the silent cinemas of the West, in large part because of the socio-economic chaos created by the 1917 Revolution and the Civil War. But by 1924, though raw film stock and equipment were still in scant supply, the means of film distribution had once more been stabilized and all pre-revolutionary cinema theaters (some twenty-five hundred of them) had been re-opened: the Soviet film industry was at last prepared to embark upon a period of creative growth.

---

* Though *Strike!* was not exported for commercial distribution, the film's excellence was recognized abroad when it won a major prize at the Exposition des Arts Decoratifs in Paris in 1925.

The Production of *Battleship Potemkin*

The year 1925 was the twentieth anniversary of the abortive 1905 Revolution against tsarism, and the Jubilee Committee decided to sponsor a series of films to commemorate it. On the basis of *Strike!,* Eisenstein was selected to direct the keynote film, *Year 1905 (1905 God),* which was to provide an historical panorama of the entire uprising from the Russo-Japanese War in January to the crushing of the armed rebellion in Moscow in December. Eisenstein and Nina Agadzhanova-Shutko (b. 1889), a professional agitator who had actively participated in the 1905 revolt, collaborated on a hundred-page scenario covering dozens of events that had taken place in at least thirty separate locations from Moscow to Siberia to the Caucasus. Shooting began in Leningrad in March 1925, but bad weather forced Eisenstein's company to move south for sunnier (and therefore better lit) locations. Eisenstein took his crew first to Baku and then to the port of Odessa, on the Black Sea, where a short sequence of forty-two shots was to be made representing the mutiny of the tsarist battleship *Potemkin* and its bloody aftermath.* When Eisenstein arrived in Odessa, however, he became obsessed with the cinematic possibilities of the vast flight of marble steps leading down to the city's harbor, where Cossacks had massacred citizens supporting the mutineers. He made the fateful decision to limit his treatment of the Revolution to this single representative episode.

Battleship Potemkin (*Bronenosets Potyomkin,* 1925), the film which emerged, has been called the most perfect and concise example of film structure in the history of the cinema. With *The Birth of a Nation* (1915) and *Citizen Kane* (1941), *Potemkin* is clearly one of the most important and influential films ever made, and its montage represents a quantum leap from the relatively simple juxtapositions of *Strike!* Indeed, Eisenstein created a completely new editing technique merely foreshadowed in his first film—one based upon psychological stimulation rather than narrative logic, which managed to communicate physical and emotional sensation directly to the audience. Furthermore, the film's revolutionary impact inaugurated a whole new school of film-making and caused the Soviet cinema to burst full-blown upon the international screen, where it has retained a powerful position ever since.

Potemkin took ten weeks to shoot (the Odessa steps sequence was finished in seven days) and two weeks to edit, and, contrary to the prevailing mythology, its montage was *not* constructed according to some carefully pre-arranged and systematic plan. Eisenstein himself lent credence to this notion through his intricate structural analyses of the film in his later theoretical writings, but the truth is that, like its two great counterparts *The Birth of a Nation* and *Citizen Kane, Potemkin* was less a matter of careful planning than an intense release of creative energy. The completed version of the film ran 86 minutes at silent speed (sixteen frames per second) and contained 1,346 shots—a remarkably high

5.10 A revolutionary poster for *Battleship Potemkin* (Sergei Eisenstein, 1925), designed by Rodchenko.

---

* For a full historical account of the incident, see Richard Hough, *The Potemkin Mutiny* (Englewood Cliffs, N.J., 1960).

number when we consider that the released version of *The Birth of a Nation,* with a running time of 195 minutes, contained only 1,375 shots. Clearly, the most important aspect of *Potemkin* is its editing, but it would be wrong to assume that Eisenstein's interest in montage caused him to neglect the pictorial or compositional aspects of his film. In fact, Eisenstein composed every single frame of *Potemkin* with a painter's eye for the distribution of light, mass, and geometric design (the triangle, circle, and diagonal intersection were his basic visual motifs).

Nevertheless, the film Eisenstein created from these beautifully composed frames was first and foremost a political film intended to possess the broadest possible audience appeal. Though *Potemkin* is hardly the "efficiently engineered political cartoon" that one recent critic has called it, the film *is* intensely manipulative of audience response. Furthermore, though Eisenstein, like Griffith, was obsessed with the accuracy of historical detail in his work (to the extent of interviewing large numbers of survivors of the *Potemkin* mutiny and the Odessa massacre), he was also, like Griffith, wholly capable of distorting historical events to suit a specific set of ideological assumptions. This should serve to remind us that Soviet "realism" was at its root a popular ideological cinema whose announced purpose was primarily agitational and didactic. It was, in other words, a cinema of political propaganda and indoctrination. That Eisenstein so often yielded to this tendency should not surprise us, because he was at the time a committed Marxist whose film-making activity was completely subsidized by and dependent upon the state. It should surprise us, rather, that he so consistently and gloriously managed to transcend it.

The Structure of *Potemkin*

Like *Strike!*, *Potemkin* is a drama of mass action with a collective hero, and it was shot entirely with non-actors against naturalistic backgrounds. (According to Eisenstein's theory of "typage," actors were important not as individuals but as "types"—elements within the composition of the frame which acquire meaning only through montage.) Of its recognizably documentary surface Eisenstein would later write, "*Potemkin* looks like a chronicle or newsreel of an event, but it functions as a drama." Indeed, unlike its relatively formless predecessor, *Potemkin* is divided into five movements or acts whose structural symmetry is very nearly perfect.* The first act, entitled "Men and Maggots," begins with an image of natural turbulence as large waves break violently over an anonymous harbor jetty, creating a metaphor for the social tumult we are soon to witness aboard the battleship. A title quoting Lenin ("Revolution is the only lawful, equal, effectual war. It was in Russia that this war was declared and begun") introduces us to a night of unrest aboard the

5.11 *Battleship Potemkin:* "Revolution is the only lawful, equal, effectual war."

---

* Tragically, *Potemkin* was Eisenstein's last silent film to be completed as he intended. He was forced to revise both *October* (*Ten Days That Shook the World*, 1928) and *Old and New* (original title: *The General Line*, 1929) as a result of political pressure (see below).

Potemkin at sea, during which a petty officer beats a sleeping sailor in random anger, and Seaman Vakulinchuk urges his comrades to join their striking brothers on the shore and rise against tsarist oppression.

In the morning, the situation worsens as sailors on deck gather angrily around a maggot-ridden piece of meat intended for their consumption. Led by Vakulinchuk, they protest, "We have had enough of rotten meat," but the supercilious ship's surgeon, Dr. Smirnov, soon arrives to inspect the infested carrion through his pince-nez and, as the screen fills with a close-up of the swarming maggots, proclaims them to be "merely dead fly eggs that will wash off with salt-water." Dispersed by senior officers, the outraged sailors go about their duties until the call for mid-day meal, which most refuse to eat. The ship's officers are furious, but their anger is purely institutional. The anger of the sailors, on the other hand, is deep and real, as we see from the scene which concludes this section of the film. A young sailor, washing dishes from the officers' mess, suddenly realizes that the plate in his hands bears the hypocritical inscription "Give us this day our daily bread." In a fit of rage which defies the laws of empirical time and space, he smashes this same plate against the table not once but *twice* in a four-second montage sequence which joins together nine separate but overlapping shots of the uncompleted action, ranging in length from one-quarter to three-quarters of a second, in order to emphasize the extreme violence of the sailor's response. By creating a cinematic metaphor for impotent fury erupting into violent action, this sequence leads us into *Potemkin*'s second movement, "Drama on the Quarterdeck."

This section opens with an assembly of officers and crew on the open quarterdeck of the battleship. Commander Golikov, the ship's captain, orders, "Those satisfied with the food . . . two paces forward," and only a handful of petty officers obey. Enraged, Golikov orders the mass execution of all protesters and calls up the Marines to carry out punishment. Seaman Matyushenko breaks ranks and successfully rallies most of the men to the gun-turret as the Marines arrive on deck, but several remain in the prow, where they are covered with a tarpaulin by officers in preparation for the firing squad. Group shots are juxtaposed with extreme close-ups as the situation becomes increasingly tense: the sailors massed around the gun-turret are anxious about their comrades, the officers become nervous about their own safety, and the Marines show signs of reluctance to carry out their orders. The ship's priest, a white-bearded Russian Orthodox monk, appears from below, offers pompous prayers for the condemned, and begins to count off the seconds by tapping his palm with a crucifix. In a much-quoted sequence, Eisenstein intercuts a close shot of this action with another of a junior officer nervously tapping the hilt of his sword, suggesting the unholy alliance which existed between Church and State in tsarist Russia.

Tension reaches its height when the order is given to fire. The Marines take aim, and the sailors under the tarpaulin fall to their knees in terror. Suddenly Vakulinchuk cries out from the gun-turret: "Brothers! Do you realize who you are shooting?" The rifles waver, and one after another

5.12   The rotting meat.

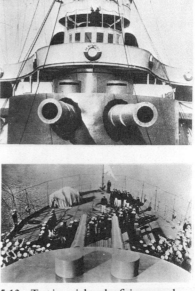

5.13   Tsarist might; the firing squad.

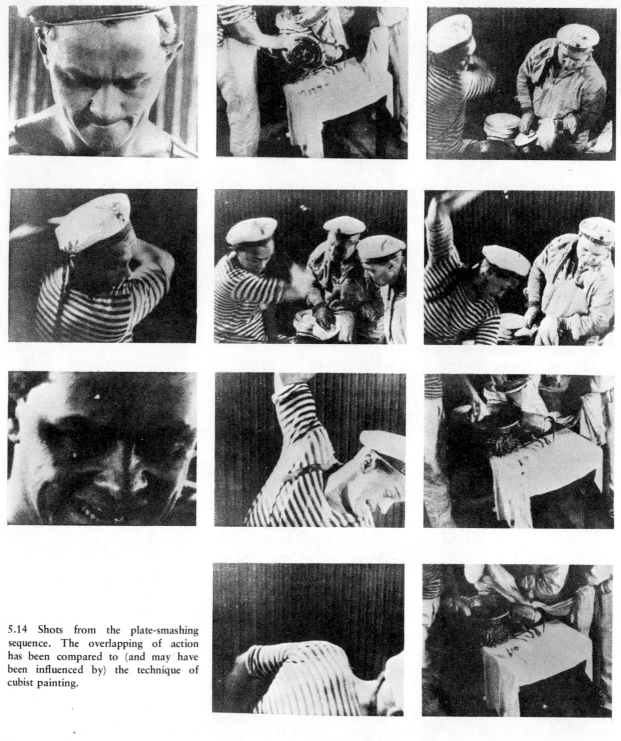

5.14 Shots from the plate-smashing sequence. The overlapping of action has been compared to (and may have been influenced by) the technique of cubist painting.

5.15   Mutiny: crushing the symbols of oppression.

the Marines lower their arms. It is important to note that although the incidents which occur between the mustering of the Marines and their refusal to fire on their shipmates would take only a few seconds in empirical reality, they last nearly three full minutes on the screen. Like Griffith and those who came after him, Eisenstein frequently used editing to compress time for the sake of narrative economy, but here and in the fourth section of *Potemkin,* "The Odessa Steps," he employs editing to *expand* time in order to create certain aesthetic and emotional effects. In "Drama on the Quarterdeck," by rendering the events described above into fifty-seven separate shots of varying temporal and spatial lengths, Eisenstein draws out the Marines' moment of decision for what seems an eternity, generating maximum psychological tension in the audience and achieving a highly expressive effect. After the firing squad has balked, the senior officers continue to scream the order to shoot, but it is too late: the mutiny has begun.

The quarterdeck is suddenly swarming with confusion. Sailors attack the officers and beat them to their knees. The melee spreads rapidly through the entire ship, as one by one the symbols of tsarist tyranny are chased down and killed by the crew. The old priest is knocked through a hatchway, and his fallen crucifix sticks upright in the wood of the deck like the instrument of oppression to which it has been recently compared. The ship's surgeon is dragged from his hiding-place and thrown overboard, raising an eddy of white foam on the dark surface of the ocean. Eisenstein cuts abruptly to a close-up of white maggots swarming on a dark field of meat and follows it with another of the surgeon's pince-nez dangling pathetically from the riggings where he has gone over, reminding us of the gross moral indifference which produced the mutiny. The bloodshed on deck continues until finally the cry goes up: "Comrades! The ship is in our hands!" But in another part of the ship a brutal senior officer has cornered Vakulinchuk, leader of the rebellion, and shot him in the head. As the sailor topples from the yardarm, he is caught in a cradle of ropes and hangs suspended above the water as though crucified. Vakulinchuk's body is carefully recovered and given a martyr's funeral by his comrades. That evening a launch bearing the dead hero's corpse and attended by an honor guard of seamen steams slowly toward the port of Odessa. There, in a tent at the end of the quay, Vakulinchuk's remains

5.16 Vakulinchuk's martyrdom and canonization.

5.17 Shots from the fog montage.

5.18 Vakulinchuk on his bier. The hand-lettered sign reads: "For a spoonful of soup."

come to lie in state, an inspirational symbol of the revolution for which he perished. A mood of somber calm prevails as night descends on both the harbor and the bier.

This mood is sustained through the famous "fog montage" which opens the third section of the film, "An Appeal from the Dead." In it, Eisenstein joins together a sequence of shots depicting various aspects of the harbor just before daybreak—sailing vessels and steamships at anchor, a gull-covered buoy, dockside cranes, Vakulinchuk's tent outlined against the sky—each of which grows progressively lighter as the sun rises and gradually disperses the thick Odessa fog. By the end of this lyrical sequence, dawn has fully broken and the harbor resumes its normal walking activity. Now the tent begins to attract attention. At first only a handful of Odessa's citizens come to pay homage to the fallen hero, but as the day grows lighter a large procession of mourners starts to descend the steps to the quay and file past the bier. Soon the crowd has grown into a vast, classless multitude which surges excitedly toward the quay from all quarters of the city.

At this point, Eisenstein begins to intercut extreme close-ups of individual mourners with long shots of the masses as they stream endlessly across the breakwater and swarm about the tent, the tempo of the cutting increasing with the anger of the crowd as agitators begin to harangue it. Suddenly, to a student's cry of "Down with the executioners!" a supercilious bourgeois responds, "Down with the Jews!" Heads turn in unison; a paroxysm of violent emotion grips the crowd, and the bourgeois is beaten to the ground. In Odessa, the masses continue to surge convulsively across and under a huge stone viaduct toward the quay, where raised fists now bristle into the sky in a show of solidarity. A delegation of workers from the shore arrives on the quarterdeck of the battleship to assure the mutineers of their support. As one of the delegates proclaims his mission from the bridge of the ship, a large red flag* is raised on the mainmast, to the jubilant cheers of both the sailors and the masses assembled on the quay.

The fourth section of *Potemkin,* "The Odessa Steps," is constructed around what is probably the single greatest and most influential montage

---

* In the original release prints of *Potemkin,* this revolutionary flag was actually hand-tinted bright red.

5.19   The gathering on the quay. Accelerated intercutting of long shots and close-ups produces agitational frenzy on the screen, but compositional continuity is preserved in the geometrical motifs which dominate the individual shots—here, as throughout the film, the circle, the triangle, and the diagonal intersection.

sequence in the history of the cinema—that depicting the massacre of the Odessa citizens by tsarist troops on the stone steps leading down to the harbor. This was the incident which had gripped Eisenstein's imagination from the outset of the production, for he saw it as a virtual paradigm of tsarist treachery, brutality, and oppression. Part Four begins on the same joyful note of solidarity with which Part Three concluded, as dozens of yawls sail out to the battleship from Odessa, laden with food and supplies for the mutineers. Citizens of the town are massed along the quay, shouting encouragement to the men on the ship and cheering on the yawls. Close-ups reveal individuals in the crowd who will later figure prominently in the mass action of the massacre—a white-bloused woman with dark bobbed hair, accompanied by a bearded man in black; a well-dressed elderly woman wearing pince-nez, with her arm about a schoolgirl; an ardent young student in wire-rimmed glasses.

As they approach the *Potemkin* at anchor, the yawls are seen as photographed from a launch moving with them across the bay. One by one, the sailboats overtake the camera and glide past it toward the battleship, where cheering sailors greet the boatmen and help the gift-bearing civilians on board. On shore, the inhabitants of Odessa watch this fraternal encounter from the harbor steps and signal their enthusiastic support by waving. On the deck of the battleship, civilians and sailors embrace. The townspeople on the steps continue to wave and cheer en masse, and Eisenstein again cuts to close shots of individual members of the crowd. We see the old woman in pince-nez once more, an elegantly attired lady with an open white parasol, a legless child—premonitory of the horror soon to come—who scoots along the steps with one hand and hails the ship with the other, a young mother directing her son's attention toward the anchored ship and urging him to wave, two children held up above the crowd by adult hands to get a better view.

Then, a single, sinister title—"Suddenly"—and a chilling close shot of a row of jackbooted feet stepping in perfect unison onto the first flight of stone stairs. The dark bobbed hair of the women in white fills the screen from one edge of the frame to the other and jerks backward so violently that the image is blurred by the motion. Through a series of jump cuts* which abruptly eliminate the forward return, she yanks her head back again and again in utter horror at what she sees (which, however, Eisenstein doesn't permit the audience to see yet). The cripple leaps wildly on his hands down the steep balustrades which flank the steps, and the lady with the open parasol dashes madly into the camera, filling the entire screen with its white, beribboned fabric. Eisenstein pulls back to a long shot from below of townspeople scrambling pell-mell down the vast sweep of the stairs, and then reverses the angle to show the object of their terror from above: at the top of the stairs, a line of white-jacketed troops

---

* A jump cut is an abrupt cut within a shot whose action would normally be continuous, made to create an effect of perceptual shock and/or dislocation. The technique was decidedly unconventional outside of the European avant-garde, until it came to be widely practiced by the young directors of the French New Wave in the early sixties (see Chapter 13).

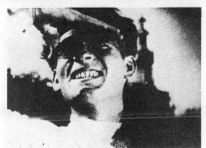

5.20 Shot sequence from the Odessa steps massacre (continues through page 166).

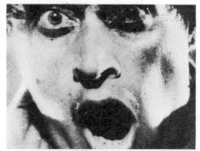

'Let us appeal
to them!'

  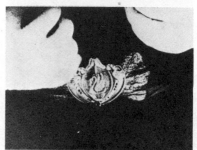
 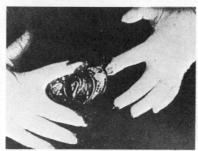 
 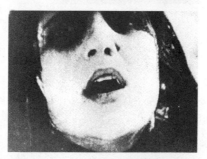 

carrying rifles with fixed bayonets has started its murderous descent. Another long shot from below of townspeople pouring down the stairs, and the slaughter begins.

Eisenstein cuts to close shots of knees buckling, of bodies falling through the air and sprawling across the steps in heaps. Now a second line of troops has appeared and begun its descent, and the camera starts to track laterally with the escaping civilians down the side of the steps. When the militiamen fire downward into the fleeing mass, the small boy we have seen earlier on the quay falls wounded. His mother screams in horror as he is trampled by the stampeding crowd: her face and then her eyes in extreme close-up fill the screen. She gathers his body into her arms to march up the corpse-littered steps against both the downward flight of the masses and the inexorable advance of the troops. Meanwhile, the woman in pince-nez, who has sought refuge with several others behind a parapet, decides to appeal to the troops. Now two groups are moving up the death-strewn stairs in opposition to the troops—the enraged mother with her dead son, screaming at the troops in anguish, and the woman in pince-nez and her followers, who attempt to supplicate them. The camera moves up the steps with both groups, and the troops move rhythmically and irresistibly down. The mother with the child stops on a landing so close to the bristling of rifles of the troops that their shadows fall upon her. There is a pause as she madly entreats the soldiers to help her son. Instead they fire, she falls with her son, and the troops sweep calmly over their bodies. At the bottom of the steps, more horror: saber-slashing Cossack horsemen appear from nowhere and charge into the crowd as it reaches the quay, cutting off the only line of escape. On the steps, volley after volley is fired into the crowd, and the long line of troops continues its implacable, orderly descent, in complete contrast to the chaotic flight of the masses below.

Now Eisenstein begins the tour de force of his sequence, cutting to yet another young mother as she pushes her baby's carriage hurriedly across a landing in advance of the firing troops. Fleeing civilians rush past her, jolting the carriage, which she is clearly afraid to push down the next steep flight of steps. Above her, the troops march relentlessly on. Trapped between them and the steps, she hesitates and screams. We see a line of jackboots in close shot slowly descend the stairs and then a line of rifles against the sky erupting into smoke. The mother's head sways back in close-up; another close shot shows the wheels of the baby carriage teetering on the edge of the steps. The mother's white-gloved hands clutch the silver buckle of her belt, while on the quay below we see people being trampled, slashed, and beaten indiscriminately by Cossacks. Now a close-up returns us to the mother as blood begins to drip over her gloves and belt. Her body starts to sway forward and sink slowly off-screen. Behind her, the baby in the carriage reaches into the air; before her, the troops continue their measured cadence down the stairs. Slowly, the mother sways back against the carriage and pushes it off-screen. From a lower level of the steps, the woman in pince-nez screams in horror as the rear wheels of the carriage roll over the edge of the landing and the steps. Now, through a series of quick cuts, we see the carriage bounce its way unevenly down the stairs past the dead and wounded, slowly at first, then with gathering speed. The camera moves with it from the side, as Eisenstein intercuts its fatal progress with medium shots from above of the baby jostling violently inside and with close reaction shots of the horror-stricken woman in pince-nez and the student with wire-rimmed glasses. On the steps above the carriage, we see a line of soldiers from the waist down firing their bayonetted rifles into a heap of supplicating wounded. Below, the student screams as the carriage fairly leaps across the steps, then suddenly tilts and flips end over end.

The wrenching "agit-Guignol" of the massacre ends as it began, with a series of violent jump cuts. On the quay below, we see a ferocious young Cossack slash his saber down again and again in a series of four discontinuous close shots—some no longer than a few frames apiece—which eliminate his backward strokes and intensify the shocking violence of his action. Then Eisenstein cuts to the object of this murderous assault in the final shot of the massacre sequence—a close-up of the elderly woman in pince-nez beneath whose shattered glasses blood spurts from a slashed and blinded eye.

In the harbor, the muzzles of the *Potemkin*'s two huge turret guns swing slowly into the camera. A title informs us: "The brutal military power answered by the guns of the battleship. . . ." Onshore, the decorative stone sculpture of the Odessa Theater, headquarters of the tsarist generals, stands silhouetted against the sky. White smoke erupts from the *Potemkin*'s battle cannon, and Eisenstein cuts again to the sculptured parapet of the theater. Then, from several angles, we see the ornamental iron gate and heavy stone columns of the theater burst asunder and topple in a billowing cloud of debris and smoke. Finally, in a brief but justly famous three-shot montage sequence, a sculptured stone lion rises from his sleep and roars, symbolizing the outrage of the Russian people at the atrocity just committed on the steps and their awakening anger against the regime which perpetrated it. The shots, of course, are of three separate stone lions posed in three separate positions and located in three different places, but by joining them together in the manner of Kuleshov's "creative geography" to create the illusion of a continuous action impossible in empirical reality, Eisenstein generates a cinematic metaphor for rage much more forcefully and economically than he could have done in a straightforward narrative sequence.

Eisenstein created another cinematic metaphor in the timing of the massacre sequence itself. Even though the rate of the cutting in this sequence is terrifically accelerated (the average shot length is fifty-two frames, or just over two seconds, as opposed to eighty-eight frames, or nearly four seconds, for the rest of the film), it takes much longer for the massacre to occur on the screen than it would take in actuality. This is because Eisenstein wished to suggest a *psychological* duration for the horrible event that far exceeded its precise chronological duration. As Arthur Knight writes, "Eisenstein realized that for the people trapped on the steps these would be the most terrifying (and, for many, the final) moments of their lives."[18] By drawing out, through the montage process, the time it would normally take for the militiamen and their victims to reach the bottom of the stairs, Eisenstein manages to suggest destruction of a much greater magnitude than we actually witness on the screen, just as at the end of Part One he had suggested the black rage of the oppressed seamen by drawing out the time it takes the sailor to smash the officer's plate.

Part Five of *Potemkin*, "Meeting the Squadron," is both literally and aesthetically anticlimactic after the dynamic, emotionally draining Odessa steps sequence. It begins with a contentious shipboard meeting in which the citizens of Odessa urge the sailors to land and join forces with the army in rebellion against the tsar. But it is learned that the Admiralty squadron has been sent out against the *Potemkin*, and the sailors vote unanimously to face it at sea. Here Eisenstein cuts to the empty deck of the battleship some time later, and a title tells us: "A night of anxiety begins." Now a montage of sixty-eight shots evokes the calm which precedes the storm. From a variety of camera angles we see the ship at anchor in the moonlight, the watch moving slowly about across the deck, a searchlight directed on the water, the motionless needles of the pressure gauges in the engine room, and sailors sleeping fitfully below deck. Meanwhile, the squadron creeps up stealthily in the darkness. At last, a seaman with a telescope spots the squadron on the horizon and sounds the alarm. Agitated sailors leap from their berths and assume their battle stations. The cannon are loaded with heavy shells. A title appears—"Full speed ahead"—and yet another breathless montage sequence begins.

At an ever-increasing tempo Eisenstein intercuts close shots of the churning pistons, rotating cam shafts, and plunging piston heads of the powerful ship's engines with Matyushenko giving orders from the bridge, the ship's funnels belching smoke, the *Potemkin* itself cutting rapidly through the waves, and the port cannons seeking the range of the squadron, which has begun to mass on the horizon. As the *Potemkin* draws

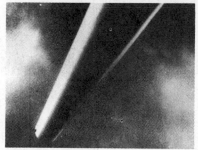

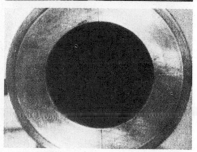

closer and closer to the squadron, Eisenstein increases the tension by accelerating the cutting rate to fever pitch. Suddenly the sequence is augmented by shots of two large battleships bearing down on the *Potemkin*. The *Potemkin*'s cannon swing slowly toward them as they steam into firing range. From the bridge, Matyushenko orders the semaphorist to run up the signal "Don't fight—join us." Billowing signal flags are now injected into the sequence, as the squadron remains mute, drawing ever nearer. The *Potemkin*'s gigantic cannon stretch diagonally across the screen, outlined against the sky; the gunners await their signal.

Now the *Potemkin* swings the muzzles of its huge cannon directly into the camera, filling the entire screen. The cannon of the squadron ships are raised menacingly toward those of the *Potemkin*. On the mast, the mutineers' red flag is whipped by the wind. Cannon confront each other across a brief expanse of sea, and the intent faces of sailors peer forth from the gun-turrets in a painfully drawn-out agony of suspense. Suddenly, one of them smiles, and a title exclaims, "Brothers!" The faces of elated seamen crowd the screen. The *Potemkin*'s deserted quarterdeck begins to swarm with cheering, laughing sailors. The ship's cannon are lowered as the tsarist ships, their decks packed with friendly, cap-waving sailors, steam past within a thousand yards. A title reads: "Over the heads of the tsarist admirals roared a brotherly cheer. . . ." Without a shot being fired, the *Potemkin* is allowed to pass unmolested through the ranks of the squadron. Caps fly in the air, and shots from all angles show the jubilant mutineers crowding the decks of their ship. The red flag flutters victoriously above them, and from the waterline we see the *Potemkin*'s giant prow steam straight into the camera and seemingly break through the frame in enormous close-up as it carries its crew to safety and freedom.

Potemkin was given a gala public opening in Moscow on January 18, 1926, but it was soon met by a storm of protest. Eisenstein's political enemies within the Communist Party—a category which continued to grow in direct proportion to his fame—again charged him with "formalism,"* a preference for aesthetic form above ideological content. Rival film-makers claimed that the film was a glorified documentary, inaccessible to the average audience. But the Soviet public loved the film from the start,† and, when it began to be exported, so too did the foreign audiences and press. In the spring of 1926, the German Marxist composer Edmund Meisel worked closely with Eisenstein to prepare a stirring revolutionary score for *Potemkin* (a collaboration which Eisenstein later described as his "first work in the sound film"[19]) which made the film's agitational appeal very nearly irresistible. *Potemkin* was officially banned in many European countries but shown underground to large audiences, and its fame spread rapidly throughout the Western world. The film's triumphs abroad (at its Berlin screening the great stage director Max Reinhardt, whose styles of lighting had so influenced German Expressionism, observed, "After viewing *Potemkin,* I am willing to admit that the stage will have to give way to the cinema"[20]) earned Eisenstein the temporary favor of Soviet officials. Critical attacks on *Potemkin* ceased, and the film began to play in the best theaters all over the Soviet Union. As Eisenstein later wrote, "I awoke one morning and found myself famous."[21]

Eisenstein's Theory of Dialectical Montage

Part of Eisenstein's growing fame was as a theorist of film as well as a practitioner. The body of his writings on the medium—later collected into two volumes, *The Film Sense* (1942) and *The Film Form* (1948)—had been steadily accumulating since 1923, and after the resounding international success of *Potemkin,* he began to articulate his most important contribution to film theory—his notion of dialectical montage. To summarize briefly, Eisenstein saw film editing, or montage, as a process which operated according to the Marxist dialectic. The dialectic is a way of looking at human history and experience as a perpetual conflict in which a force (*thesis*) collides with a counterforce (*antithesis*) to produce from their collision a wholly new phenomenon (*synthesis*) which is not the sum of the two forces but something greater than and different from them both. The process may be diagrammed thus:

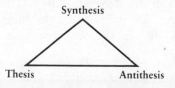

Synthesis

Thesis   Antithesis

---

* As distinct from "Formalism," a contemporaneous movement in literature which took the position that language had no inherent relationship with the reality it purported to signify.

† The official attendance figures indicate this, at least. But they may have been exaggerated by the authorities, who had a stake in demonstrating to the rest of the world that there was

The synthesis emerging from the thesis-antithesis conflict will ultimately become the thesis of a new dialectic which will in turn generate a new synthesis, and so on until the end of historical time. Eisenstein maintained that in film editing the shot, or "montage cell," is a thesis which when placed into juxtaposition with another shot of opposing visual content—its antithesis—produces a synthesis (a synthetic idea or impression) which in turn becomes the thesis of a new dialectic as the montage sequence continues.* This visual opposition between shots may be a conflict of linear directions, planes, volumes, lighting, etc., and need not extend to the dramatic content of the shot. Thus, Eisenstein defined montage as a series of ideas or impressions which arise from "the collision of independent shots," and in a characteristically industrial metaphor he compared its process to "the series of explosions of an internal combustion engine, driving forward its automobile or tractor." Similarly, he wrote, "the dynamics of montage serve as impulses driving forward the total film."[22] Another of Eisenstein's favorite analogies was linguistic: just as the individual words in a sentence depend for their meaning upon the words which surround them, so the individual shots in a montage sequence acquire meaning from their interaction with the other shots in the sequence.

The underlying cognitive assumption of this theory is that the viewers of a film perceive the shots in a montage sequence not *sequentially,* or one at a time, but rather *simultaneously,* or one on top of another. That is, they respond not to an incremental or additive process in which each shot is modified by the ones which precede it (ABC ≠ A + B + C) but to a *Gestalt*—a totality or a whole which is different from and greater than the sum of its parts (ABC = x). This is so because shots A, B, and C can be strictly said to follow one another only on the film strip; when the film strip is projected, however, the viewer's mind puts the shots together in a manner analogous to photographic superimposition. Thus at the end of the Odessa steps section of *Potemkin,* when we are shown three consecutive shots of a stone lion sleeping, a stone lion awakening, and a stone lion rising, we see the sequence not as a combination of its parts but as something quite different—a single unbroken movement with a specifically ideological signification.

Although Griffith's two great epics and Kuleshov's experiments in editing clearly stand behind these notions, Eisenstein developed many of them from his study of the psychology of perception; and to illustrate the process of dialectical montage, he would frequently use the example of the Japanese pictograph or ideogram. In Japanese character-writing, completely new concepts are formed by combining the symbols for two separate older ones. Moreover, the new concept is never merely the sum

a large Soviet audience for Soviet films. See the casebook of contemporary reviews and documents, *The Battleship Potemkin: The Greatest Film Ever Made,* ed. Herbert Marshall (New York, 1978).

* In a very important sense, as Eisenstein realized, the dialectic can also be used to describe the psycho-perceptual process of cinema itself: in projection, two (or more) independent still photographs on a film strip collide to produce something different from and greater than them both—the illusion of continuous motion.

of its parts and is invariably an abstraction which could not be represented graphically on its own terms. For example, the symbol for "dog" plus the symbol for "mouth" create an ideogram meaning not "dog's mouth," as one might expect, but "bark." Similarly,

child + mouth = scream
bird + mouth = sing
knife + heart = sorrow
water + eye = weep
door + ear = listen

Thus, in every case the combination of two distinct signs for concrete objects produces a single sign for some intangible or abstraction. What Eisenstein was attempting to suggest by these examples was the way in which film, whose signs are moving photographic images and therefore *wholly* tangible, can communicate conceptual abstractions on a par with other art forms. Griffith had intimated as much when he said, "You can photograph thought," but he was referring specifically to the narrative use of close-ups and flashbacks. Eisenstein characteristically went far beyond Griffith, to suggest that the cinema contains within its most essential structuring process (editing) a mechanism for creating conceptual abstractions (dialectical montage) which need only be exercised to be perceived.

Eisenstein conceived that whole films, as well as autonomous sequences within them, could be constructed according to the dialectic. In theoretical essays like "A Dialectical Approach to Film Form" (1929) and "The Structure of the Film" (1939),[23] he wrote lengthy post-factum analyses of the dialectical structure of *Potemkin*. Eisenstein claimed that each part or act of *Potemkin* was broken into two equal halves by a "caesura," a term (borrowed from poetry and music) denoting a strong medial pause in the action, and that the film as a whole was similarly divided by the harbor mist sequence which begins the third act. The dialectical pattern of each act (and of the film itself) was one of mounting tension followed by a resolution or exploding of tension, which together produced a synthesis that became the thesis of the next act. Eisenstein diagrammed the structure of Acts II through V as follows:

  II. Scene with the tarpaulin ⟶ mutiny
  III. Mourning for Vakulinchuk ⟶ angry demonstration
  IV. Lyrical fraternization ⟶ shooting
  V. Anxiously awaiting the fleet ⟶ triumph

He also described the transition-point or caesura peculiar to each act:

In one part (III), this is a few shots of clenched fists, through which the theme of mourning the dead leaps into the theme of fury.

In another part (IV), this is a sub-title—"SUDDENLY"—cutting off the scene of fraternization, and projecting it into the scene of the shooting.

The motionless muzzles of the rifles (in Part II). The gaping mouths of the guns (in Part V). And the cry of "Brothers," upsetting the awful pause of waiting, in an explosion of brotherly feeling—in both moments.[24]

Finally, Eisenstein outlined the ideological dialectic of sequences within acts. At the outset of the Odessa steps massacre, for example, he perceives the following dialectical structure:

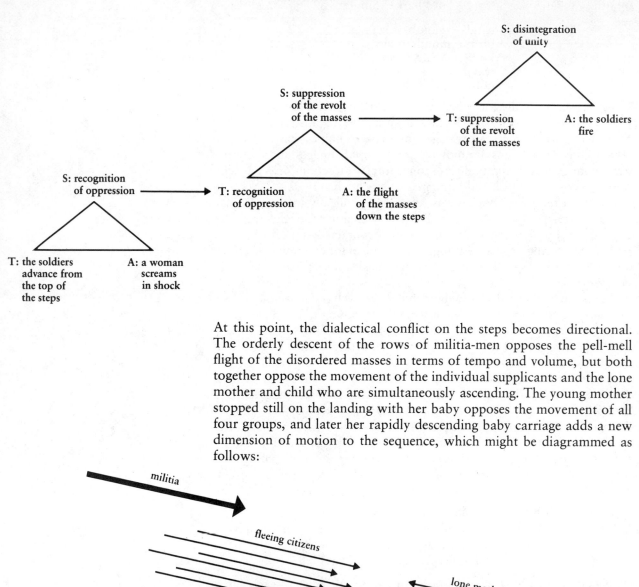

At this point, the dialectical conflict on the steps becomes directional. The orderly descent of the rows of militia-men opposes the pell-mell flight of the disordered masses in terms of tempo and volume, but both together oppose the movement of the individual supplicants and the lone mother and child who are simultaneously ascending. The young mother stopped still on the landing with her baby opposes the movement of all four groups, and later her rapidly descending baby carriage adds a new dimension of motion to the sequence, which might be diagrammed as follows:

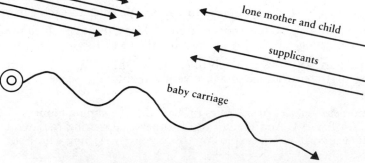

As the sequence ends at the bottom of the steps, the young Cossack savagely swinging his saber collides with the bloodied face of the woman in pince-nez to produce the synthesis: rage. Then, the guns of the *Potemkin* collide with the generals' headquarters to produce the ultimate synthesis: collective action.

Eisenstein distinguished five separate types or "methods" of montage, all of which may be used simultaneously within any given sequence: 1) the metric, 2) the rhythmic, 3) the tonal, 4) the overtonal, and 5) the intellectual or ideological. Metric montage is concerned solely with the tempo of the cutting, regardless of the content of the shots. The basis for editing is thus the temporal length or duration of each shot, and these lengths are determined by the imposition of a regular metrical pattern upon the cutting rate. In this method, shots of one length may alternate regularly with shots of another, or the shots may progressively increase or decrease in length as the sequence moves forward, but the proportional relationship of one shot to another must remain constant throughout the sequence. A good example of accelerating metric montage would be the Griffith intercut chase sequence, in which the climax is reached by alternating shots of progressively shorter duration.* Eisenstein felt that metric montage was both mechanical and primitive, and he identified it (in the main, unfairly) with his major Soviet rival, V. I. Pudovkin (see below).

Rhythmic montage is an elaboration of metric montage in which the cutting rate is based upon the rhythm of movement *within* the shots as well as upon predetermined metrical demands. This rhythm may be used either to reinforce the metric tempo of the sequence or to counterpoint it. As an example of the latter Eisenstein cites the Odessa steps sequence from *Potemkin,* in which the steady rhythm of the soldiers' feet as they descend the stairs within the frame is made to regularly violate the metric tempo of the cutting. This type of editing sets up a counterpoint between rhythmic and metric movement which sustains the high tension of the sequence.

Tonal montage represents a stage beyond the rhythmic in which the dominant emotional *tone* of the shots becomes the basis for editing. Eisenstein makes the following distinction between the two modes:

> In rhythmic montage it is movement within the frame that impels the montage movement from frame to frame. Such movements within the frame may be of objects in motion, or of the spectator's eye directed along the lines of some immobile object.

> In tonal montage, movement is perceived in a wider sense. The concept of movement embraces *all affects* of the montage piece. Here montage is based on the characteristic *emotional sound* of the piece—of its dominant. The general *tone* of the piece.[25]

---

* As Griffith wrote of his own method in 1925: "The action must quicken to a height in a minor climax, then slow down and build again to the next climax, which should be faster than the second and on to the major climax, where the pace should be fastest. Through the big moments of the story, the pace should be like the beat of an excited pulse." ("Pace in the Movies," *Liberty,* April 18, 1925.)

As an example of tonal montage, Eisenstein cites the fog sequence at the beginning of the third act of *Potemkin*. Here, the basic tonal dominant of the shots is the quality of their light ("haze" and "luminosity"), which all the other plastic elements of the shots subserve. Tonal montage has to do not with the narrative content of the shots but rather with their formal, plastic content, and it predicates a tenuous psychological or associative relationship between emotional and visual tones.

Overtonal montage, according to Eisenstein, is basically a synthesis of metric, rhythmic, and tonal montage which emerges in projection rather than in the editing process (where only the "undertones" are visible). This is not really a distinct category but another way of looking at montage based upon the totality of stimuli. Eisenstein writes of it: "The visual *overtone* cannot be traced in the static frame, just as it cannot be traced in the musical score. Overtonal conflicts, foreseen but unwritten in the score, cannot emerge without the dialectical process of the passage of the film through the projection apparatus, or that of the performance by a symphonic orchestra."[26]

Intellectual or ideological montage was the type that most fascinated Eisenstein in both his theory and his practice. All of the above montage methods are concerned with inducing emotional and/or physiological re-actions in the audience through a sophisticated form of behavioristic stimulation. But Eisenstein also conceived that montage was capable of expressing abstract ideas and making direct intellectual statements. Thus, in intellectual montage, cutting is based primarily upon neither tempo, rhythm, nor tone (although all of these components may be present in a given sequence) but upon the *conceptual* relationship between shots of opposing visual content, i.e., upon their ability to create metaphors for ideas and abstractions. The intercutting of the massacre of the workers with the slaughter of an ox at the end of *Strike!* and the intercutting of the priest tapping his crucifix with the ship's officer tapping his sword in the second act of *Potemkin* are simple manifestations of intellectual montage. But the most sophisticated use of this metaphorical technique occurs in Eisenstein's third film, *October (Oktiabr;* alternatively titled *Ten Days That Shook the World,* 1928), a magnificent failed attempt to recount the events of the Bolshevik Revolution in terms of pure intellectual cinema. Eisenstein himself cited the "gods" sequence of this film, omitted from most American prints, as a prime example of the method. In it, he offers a montage of various religious icons, beginning with a baroque statue of Christ and concluding with a hideous primitive idol, to debunk the traditional concept of God. As Eisenstein pointed out later: "These pieces were assembled in accordance with a descending intellectual scale—pulling back the concept of God to its origins, forcing the spectator to perceive this 'progress' intellectually."[27] A more complex example of intellectual montage in *October* is the famous sequence depicting the rise to power of Alexander Kerensky, head of the Provisional Government which preceded the Bolshevik Revolution. Eisenstein presents successive shots of Kerensky solemnly climbing the baroque marble staircase of the Winter Palace and intercuts them with grandiose

5.22 Final frames from the "gods" sequence in *October* (Sergei Eisenstein, 1928).

titles announcing his ascent through the ranks of the government ("Minister of the Army," "And the Navy," "Generalissimo," "Dictator") and with shots of military flunkies bowing and scraping before him on the landings. At one point, Kerensky passes beneath a statue of Victory that seems about to place a crown of laurels on his head. Then, as he reaches the top of the stairs and stands before the doorway to his office, Eisenstein cuts from his highly polished military boots to his gloved hands, and finally to a mechanical peacock spreading its tail in prideful splendor. The whole sequence is meant to suggest the inflated vanity, monumental pride, and dictatorial ambition of Kerensky and his government.

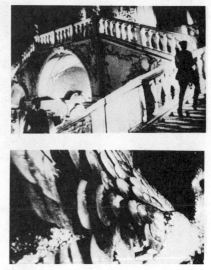

5.23 Intellectual montage: Kerensky and the peacock in *October*.

All of Eisenstein's thinking on montage worked toward the establishment of a uniquely cinematic language based upon psychological association and stimulation which had little or nothing to do with narrative logic. Deriving from his lifelong study of the dynamics of aesthetic perception, this language, which Eisenstein chose to call "dialectical montage," operated according to a precise manipulation of audience psychology on both the emotional and cerebral levels of experience. Some recent critics, notably followers of the French film theorist André Bazin, have claimed that dialectical montage is *too* manipulative, even "totalitarian," in its selective ordering of the viewer's response. Their objection is largely philosophical, for they believe that the analytical fragmentation of a filmed event through montage, as in the Odessa steps sequence, destroys "the reality of space" (Bazin[28]) which provides the necessary relationship between the cinematic image and the real world. They believe, in other words, that dialectical montage substitutes artificial and contrived spatial relationships for natural ones. And yet it is precisely its lack of dependence upon "real" or "natural" spatial relationships which renders dialectical montage a symbolic and metaphoric—and, therefore, a *poetic*—language rather than a narrative one. As Paul Seydor points out in an essay intended to be highly critical of Eisenstein: "Eisenstein's early cinema is quintessentially a cinema of (though not necessarily for) the mind. Space and movement are not literally seen, that is, are not on the screen; they exist only in the viewer's imagination, his eye serving to register the details with which his mind will make the 'proper' points."[29] And as Eisenstein himself wrote in *The Film Sense:* "The strength of montage is this, that it includes in the creative process the emotions and mind of the spectator. The spectator is compelled to proceed along the selfsame creative road that the artist travelled in creating the image."[30] Whether or not such a process is ideologically appropriate is a moot point when it works as well aesthetically as it does, say, in *Potemkin*. But, for Eisenstein and for others, it didn't always work, and his third film provides a measure of its limitations.

October (*Ten Days That Shook the World,* 1928): A Laboratory for Intellectual Montage

In the fall of 1927, Eisenstein was commissioned by the Central Committee of the Communist Party and by Sovkino to make a film commem-

5.24 Heroic metaphor and documentary realism: the storming of the Winter Palace in *October*.

5.25 *October:* Kerensky hiding in the Winter Palace.

orating the tenth anniversary of the Bolshevik Revolution. Using hundreds of personal memoirs and interviews, newsreel and newspaper accounts, and John Reed's book *Ten Days That Shook the World* (the title by which the film was known in America and Great Britain), Eisenstein and his co-scenarist, Grigory Alexandrov (b. 1903),† wrote a meticulously detailed shooting script, entitled *October,* which initially covered the history of the entire revolution. But, as with *Potemkin,* Eisenstein ultimately narrowed his scope to focus on a single representative episode— the events in Petrograd (now Leningrad) from February to October 1917. Vast resources, including the Soviet army and navy, were placed at Eisenstein's disposal, and life in Leningrad was completely disrupted during the six months of shooting as mass battles like the storming and bombardment of the Winter Palace were restaged with casts of tens of thousands. When editing was completed in November 1927, the film ran approximately thirteen thousand feet, or just under four hours, with a carefully integrated score composed by Edmund Meisel. But during its production Leon Trotsky (1870–1940), who as commissar of war had played an enormously important role in the Revolution and Civil War, was expelled from the Politburo (executive committee) of the Communist Party and forced into exile by Iosif Stalin (1879–1953), and Eisenstein was compelled to cut *October* by over four thousand feet in order to

* For an account of Alexandrov's own career as a director in the thirties and forties, see Norman Swallow, "Alexandrov," *Sight and Sound,* 48, 4 (Autumn 1979), 246–49.

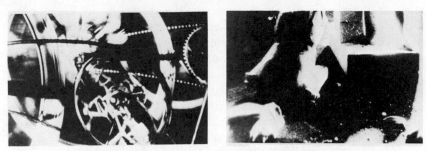

5.26 Synecdoche and symbol in *October:* wheels spinning, a broken statue.

eliminate all references to the ousted leader. (For the same reason, Reed's book was banned in the Soviet Union from late 1927 until after Stalin's death in 1953.) When this truncated version* was finally released to the public in March 1928, it was poorly received. Audiences could not understand its abstract intellectual montage, and Party critics attacked it bitterly for "formalist excess"—a charge which publicly announced the widening rift between Eisenstein's aesthetics and the new Stalinist establishment.

Yon Barna has called *October* "an experimental film of immense proportions,"[31] and indeed it was, for Eisenstein used it as a laboratory in which to test his theories of intellectual montage upon an actual audience. In *October,* Eisenstein employed intellectual montage on the order of the stone lion sequence in *Potemkin* to comment upon each and every aspect of the Revolution depicted in the narrative portion of the film. Thus, Kerensky is compared to a peacock and his militia to tin soldiers and empty wineglasses through the insertion of shots from outside the dramatic context of the film. Similarly, the treacherous pleading of the Mensheviks is intercut with shots of soft female hands stroking harps, and the union of the motorcycle battalion with the Bolsheviks is juxtaposed with shots of spinning bicycle wheels. At one point, Eisenstein suggests the stolid emptiness of the tsarist regime through a series of still shots of elaborate ornamental façades and heavily beribboned military tunics. Synecdoche—the use of a part to symbolize the whole—is everywhere apparent: rifles waving in the air tell us that the army has joined the Bolshevik cause; the hands of bureaucrats frantically clicking their telephone receivers indicate that the Kerensky government has lost control.

Countless other rhetorical devices are used by Eisenstein to maximize the film's ideological effect, from complicated inter-frame symbolism (as when the history of religion is condensed into a series of shots proceeding from the most "civilized" of icons to the most primitive and barbarous) to simple cinematic trickery (as when a statue of Tsar Alexander III,

---

* The version released as *Ten Days That Shook the World* in Britain and North America was even further shortened through the elimination or abridgement of key montage sequences. For the Fiftieth Anniversary celebration of the Revolution in 1967, Grigory Alexandrov reconstructed the original version of *October* on the basis of Eisenstein's notes, with a new score by Dmitri Shostakovich.

5.27 The faces of the Soviet people: typage in *October.*

5.28 *October:* shots from the draw-bridge sequence.

demolished earlier in the film to represent the success of the Revolution, is magically reassembled through reverse projection to represent the monarchists' vain hopes of returning to power). In a much-discussed sequence, Eisenstein uses the agonizingly slow raising of a drawbridge to suggest that the city of Petrograd has been split asunder by the revolution. From one side of the rising bridge dangles a live horse still harnessed to a cart, from the other the flaxen hair of a dead girl, shot during a demonstration, and this hair for a long time spans the crevice between the two halves before falling into the breach. In narrative terms, the drawbridge has been raised by the police in order to cut retreating workers off from their quarters, but Eisenstein turns the event into a poetic metaphor by lingering on the slowly widening gulf between the two sides and by drawing out the moment of their separation far beyond the time it would naturally take in reality. As in the plate-smashing sequence and the Odessa steps massacre of *Potemkin,* Eisenstein here expands time to represent the psychological duration of an event as opposed to its chronological duration.

In its publicly released form *October* does appear to be, as its critics charged, excessively formalistic—concerned more with the intricacies of its own cinematic mechanisms than with its revolutionary content. Furthermore—and, by Eisenstein's own standards, most damning of all—the film's intellectual montage does not always work. There is sometimes a disturbing disparity between the idea Eisenstein seeks to communicate and its technical expression. Eisenstein wrote in 1929: "The hieroglyphic language of the cinema is capable of expressing any concept, any idea of class, any political or tactical slogan, without recourse to the help of a rather suspect dramatic or psychological past."[*32] And yet a cinema of

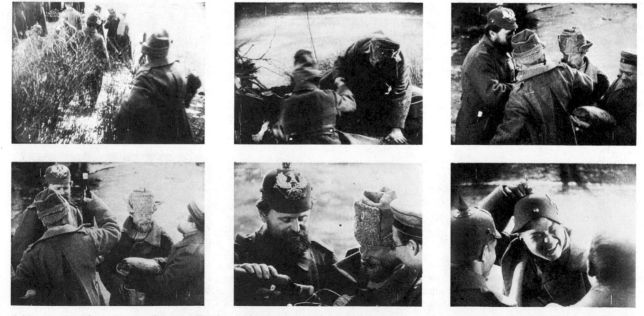

5.29 *October:* fraternization between Russian and German soldiers at the front.

5.30   Lenin addresses his supporters at the conclusion of *October*.

pure intellectual abstraction, excepting certain specialized forms of animation, can never really exist, since cinematic statements can be made only through the juxtaposition of concrete images. Eisenstein's notion, of course, was that concrete images properly arranged can *suggest* abstract ones, and this is true. But all available evidence indicates that the technique of intellectual montage will work only when it is firmly grounded in some specific narrative or dramatic context. When intellectual montage usurps its narrative context, as it often does in *October,* it tends to create a class of non-referential symbols which have meaning neither as abstractions nor as objects.

Eisenstein after *October*

Eisenstein's next film was a continuation of a project begun just prior to the commissioning of *October,* Initially entitled *The General Line* (*Generalnaya linya*)—i.e., the "general line" or policy of the Communist Party—and renamed *Old and New* (*Staroye i novoye,* 1929) when Stalinist bureaucrats disavowed it, the film was conceived by Eisenstein as a lyrical hymn of praise, in semi-documentary form, to the collectivization of Soviet agriculture. It tells the didactic tale of the evolution of a typical Russian peasant village from backwardness and poverty to prosperity through the establishment of a collective farm. For the first time, Eisenstein told his story through a central character, Marfa Lapkina, a simple peasant woman (played in the film, according to Eisenstein's theory of typage, by a real peasant) who becomes a devoted supporter of the cooperative effort and is instrumental in its ultimate success. Like all Eisenstein films, *Old and New* was carefully researched and shot mainly on location, and, as with *October,* Eisenstein used it as a laboratory for experiment—this time not with "intellectual" but with "overtonal" montage, and much more successfully than before. According to this technique, which Eisenstein also called "polyphonic montage" and "the filmic fourth dimension," a film is assembled through the harmonic orchestration of tonal dominants—i.e., through what André Bazin would

5.31   The ultimate typage: Marfa Lapkina as Marfa Lapkina in Eisenstein's *Old and New* (1929).

5.32   Overtonal montage: old and new.

---

* An index of how firmly Eisenstein believed this statement is that between 1927 and 1928 he seriously considered making a film of Marx's massive socio-economic dissection of capitalism, *Das Kapital* (1867), which he hoped would raise intellectual montage "into the realm of philosophy." (Quoted in Yon Barna, *Eisenstein* [Boston, 1973], p. 126.)

5.33 Hostile kulaks, superstitious peasants.

later term *mise-en-scène* as opposed to wholly analytic editing (see Chapter 13). Unlike the intellectual montage of *October,* all the shots in this method arise naturally out of the dramatic context of the film, and they are carefully composed in depth within the frame to orchestrate the "thematic major" and "thematic minor" keys.

Eisenstein's analogy, of course, was with the composition of symphonic music. As he wrote of *Old and New* in *The Film Form,* "The whole intricate, rhythmic and *sensual* nuance scheme of the combined pieces (of certain sequences) is conducted almost exclusively according to a line of work on the 'psychophysiological' vibrations of each piece."[33] Famous sequences include Marfa's first encounter with a mechanized cream separator, the arrival and mating of the village bull, and the final "dance" of the tractors; but Eisenstein's cutting throughout the film is the most sophisticated and subtle he was ever to achieve. In fact, many critics have come to regard it as his most beautiful silent film. Sounding like one of his Italian neo-realist successors, Eisenstein wrote that his purpose in *Old and New* was "to exalt the pathos of everyday existence."[34] And indeed the film's extraordinary lyrical quality—its feeling for sky, sun, and soil, and for humanity itself—works in tandem with its superb visual form to create a kind of "total cinema" that Eisenstein was never to attain again. However, when the film was completed in the spring of 1929, Soviet officials were dissatisfied, and Eisenstein was forced to shoot another ending at Stalin's command. Despite this adjustment and much popular acclaim, *Old and New* was bitterly denounced by party critics, who dissociated themselves from its politics and again raised the old charge of formalism. This reaction portended serious trouble for Eisenstein, but in 1929 he stood at the height of his international fame, and the party could not afford to overlook the prestige he was bringing to the Soviet Union from all parts of the globe.

With *Old and New,* Eisenstein had taken the silent film form about as far as it would go, just as six years earlier he had reached the outer limits of the legitimate stage and "fallen into the cinema."[35] He now stood at the peak of his artistic powers on the very brink of the sound film, in

5.34 Marfa transformed by the operation of the cream separator.

5.35 Marfa's vision of fertility: a cow decked with bridal flowers on her way to mate with a bull.

whose aesthetic prospects he had become almost insatiably interested. Sadly, Eisenstein's contributions to the art of the sound film were for the next decade to be almost solely theoretical, for this great architect of the Soviet silent cinema was not permitted to complete another motion picture until *Alexander Nevsky* in 1938. A political tragicomedy was about to be enacted in the Soviet Union which would make it impossible for Eisenstein to practice cinema in his own country for nearly nine years. For the moment, however, Eisenstein was an internationally acclaimed master with several huge successes to his credit, and many persons throughout the West looked to him as the supreme arbiter of cinematic form. Accordingly, in August 1929, at the age of thirty-one, Eisenstein set out with scenarist Alexandrov and cinematographer Tisse on a goodwill tour of Western Europe and America, where, between 1930 and 1931, he was to work on several abortive projects for Paramount before journeying to Mexico to shoot his remarkable unfinished epic *Que viva México!* (1931–32). Eisenstein's American sojourn marked his first practical encounter with the new technology of sound recording and the beginning of a series of tragic complications which would plague him until his early death in 1948; these will be examined in Chapter 9.

5.36 The dream parade of the tractors which concludes *Old and New*.

VSEVOLOD PUDOVKIN

Vsevolod I. Pudovkin (1893–1953), the second great director of the Soviet silent cinema, had been trained as a chemist, but he decided to renounce his profession and become a film-maker after seeing D. W. Griffith's *Intolerance* in Moscow in 1920. He joined the State Film School and spent two years as a member of the Kuleshov Workshop, where he participated in the famous editing experiments described earlier in this chapter and was directly involved in the production of *The Extraordinary Adventures of Mr. West in the Land of the Bolsheviks* (1924) and *The Death Ray* (1925). Pudovkin's first solo film was a feature-length documentary on Pavlovian reflexology entitled *The Mechanics of the Brain (Mekhanika golovnova mozga,* 1926), in which he successfully used editing principles discovered by Kuleshov as a pedagogical device to explain conditioning theory to an unsophisticated audience. Shortly afterward, Pudovkin shot *Chess Fever (Shakhmatnaya goryachka,* 1926; co-directed with Nikolai Shpikovsky), a two-reel comedy in the manner of Mack Sennett's Keystone films (see Chapter 6), but constructed according to Kuleshovian principles (woven into the plot is footage of the chess champion José Capablanca obtained by one of Pudovkin's cameramen posing as a newsreel photographer). Both films were photographed by Anatoli Golovnya (b. 1900), who was to become Pudovkin's constant collaborator from 1925 to 1950, and both were popular with domestic audiences, but it was Pudovkin's first dramatic feature film, *Mother (Mat,* 1926), that thrust him into the international limelight as Eisenstein's closest Soviet rival.

Loosely adapted by Pudovkin and the scenarist Nathan Zarkhi (another frequent collaborator) from Maxim Gorky's novel of the same title,* and photographed by Golovnya, *Mother* is set during the time of the 1905 Revolution. It tells the story of a politically naïve woman married to a brutal (and brutalized) drunkard who works with their son, Pavel, in a factory. The family leads a life of abject poverty, and to finance his drinking the father joins the ranks of the Black Hundreds, a secret organization of counter-revolutionary terrorists in the pay of the tsarist government. During a violent confrontation between striking workers and the Black Hundreds in the factory yard, the father discovers that Pavel is one of the strikers. They fight, and the father is accidentally killed by one of Pavel's friends. Later, the police come to Pavel's home searching for weapons, and the mother, in her naïveté, betrays her son, believing that he will be exonerated. Instead, Pavel is arrested and sentenced to prison in a rigged trial; the mother is first anguished and then radically politicized by this experience of tsarist tyranny. She maintains close contact with Pavel's friends and later helps him to escape from jail. At the conclusion of the film, they meet again, on May Day, at the head of a workers' demonstration. A regiment of Cossacks attacks the demonstrators, and mother and son die in each other's arms.

Mother enjoyed an immediate international success similar to that of *Potemkin,* and for some of the same reasons.† It is a beautifully proportioned film, carefully photographed by Golovnya and brilliantly edited by Pudovkin himself. Its action proceeds rhythmically through four symmetrical parts, and its montage effects are masterfully controlled. Yet *Mother* is in many ways a quieter, less spectacular film than its predecessor. Though it is essentially a political parable dealing with violent action, it eschews the epic proportions of *Potemkin* to concentrate on the

---

* The German playwright Bertolt Brecht (1898–1956) dramatized the novel for the stage in 1932; his highly stylized adaptation (which includes songs) provides an interesting contrast with Pudovkin's film.

† In a poll of 117 film critics from twenty-six countries to choose the twelve best films of all time at the 1958 Brussels World's Fair, *Potemkin* ranked first and *Mother* eighth.

human drama played out against the backdrop of a great historical moment. Eisenstein's film was about that moment itself, Pudovkin's about the people caught up in it. This is the pattern which appeared throughout Pudovkin's silent films and which above all others made them more popular with the Soviet masses than Eisenstein's. Whereas Eisenstein was the grand master of the mass epic, Pudovkin's approach to film-making was more personal. As the French critic Léon Moussinac would later write, "A film of Eisenstein's resembles a scream, one of Pudovkin a song."[36] Pudovkin had learned from Griffith to contrast scenes of mass action with the more intimate drama of the "little people" whose lives are transfigured by it. Though he subscribed in part to current theories of "typage," Pudovkin had also learned from Griffith the importance of emotionally credible film acting, and he coaxed magnificent performances from his two leading players, Vera Baranovskaya (n.d.) as the mother and Nikolai Batalov (1898–1937) as the son. Their presence alone imbues the film with a kind of emotional lyricism completely alien to Eisenstein's work, with the sole exception of parts of *Old and New*.

But despite the more direct emotional appeal of his film, Pudovkin's montage was every bit as sophisticated as that of Eisenstein, from whom, of course, he and all Soviet film-makers had learned a great deal (Pudovkin always said that the second major film experience of his life, after *Intolerance,* was *Potemkin*[37]). Some of the great montage sequences from *Mother* include that in which the mourning mother keeps vigil over her husband's corpse while water drips slowly into a bucket beside her; Pavel's lyrical fantasy of escape from prison, in which images of spring coming to the land are intercut with his smiling face; and Pavel's actual escape from prison over the ice floes, which eventually modulates into the concluding massacre. The sequence on the ice derives from Griffith's *Way Down East* (1920) rather than from Gorky's novel, but Pudovkin reveals the heritage of the Kuleshov Workshop by making the montage metaphorically as well as narratively functional. As the sequence begins, ice cakes floating downriver are intercut with workers marching toward the factory and their heroic confrontation with the troops. As the river becomes more and more clogged with ice, the ranks of the workers swell, until they overflow the curbs of the street. The narrative function of the ice floes becomes apparent when we see that the river runs past the prison and will provide Pavel with the medium for his escape. He joins the marchers on the oppposite bank by leaping across the floes like the hero at the climax of *Way Down East,* but the metaphorical function of the sequence reasserts itself as the floes smash suddenly and violently into the piers of a stone bridge—the very bridge upon which moments later the workers will clash head-on with the troops. The complex montage of the massacre itself, second only to the Odessa steps sequence of *Potemkin* in conveying the plight of individuals caught up in violent action, provides an emotionally gripping, revolutionary climax to an intensely affecting film.

From the foregoing account it should be clear that Pudovkin's montage, even at its most symbolic, usually serves some narrative purpose.

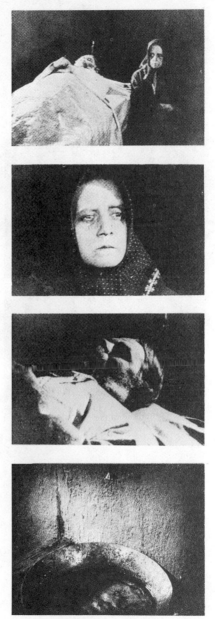

5.37 Shots from the mourning sequence in *Mother* (Vsevolod Pudovkin, 1926).

5.38 Shots from the concluding massacre in *Mother*.

Unlike Eisenstein, Pudovkin rarely engaged in intellectual abstraction. He had good theoretical reasons for this, believing that the process of montage operated differently from the way Eisenstein conceived it. For Pudovkin, the key process of montage was not collision but *linkage.* As he wrote in the introduction to the German edition of his book *Film Technique and Film Acting* (1926): "'The expression that the film is 'shot' is entirely false, and should disappear from the language. The film is not *shot,* but *built,* built up from the separate strips of celluloid that are its raw material."[38] Thus, Pudovkin chose an architectonic model for film structure and Eisenstein a dialectical one, though in practice both frequently mixed effects. Ultimately, however, the argument between Eisenstein and Pudovkin was less about the formal aspects of montage than about the psychology of the viewer, with Eisenstein believing that cinematic meaning is generated through the cognitive collision of frames within the viewer's mind and Pudovkin that it is generated through the cognitive linkage of frames. The opposition between these two points of view has never been resolved, and it will not be until we know a good deal more about the processes of perception involved in watching films. By August 1928, however, confronted with the imminent introduction of sound, Eisenstein and Pudovkin had managed to resolve their aesthetic differences well enough to issue a joint manifesto (with Grigory Alexandrov) endorsing the use of asynchronous, or contrapuntal, sound as opposed to lip-synchronized dialogue, which they correctly saw as a threat to the art of montage as practiced in the silent film.

Pudovkin's next film, like Eisenstein's *October,* was commissioned by the Central Committee to commemorate the tenth anniversary of the Bolshevik Revolution. It was entitled *The End of St. Petersburg (Konyets Sankt-Peterburga,* 1927), and, as he had done in *Mother,* Pudovkin once again chose to focus upon the personal drama of individuals caught up in the Revolution. The first half of the film tells the story of a peasant boy who comes to the tsarist capital, St. Petersburg, on the eve of World War One to find employment. Because he is politically unenlightened, the boy takes work as a strike-breaker and informer. When he later comes to understand the plight of the workers under capitalism, however, he attacks his employer in a frenzy and is tossed into jail, from which he is conscripted into the army when war is declared. Then the focus of the film shifts to the war itself and to the revolution as experienced by the young soldier. The second part of *The End of St. Petersburg,* covering the years 1915 to 1917, often resembles Eisenstein's work in its use of expressive montage to communicate the historic impact of great events. But in Pudovkin's films the human element is always intertwined with the epic and symbolic. He uses montage brilliantly throughout this section to contrast the profiteering of the capitalists with the human misery caused by war. As he had done in *Mother,* Pudovkin also makes use of expressive camera angles in the manner of Griffith. When the boy comes to St. Petersburg for the first time, the camera observes him from an extremely high angle, so that he seems dwarfed by the great buildings and monuments of the city. But when he returns as a Bolshevik soldier at the conclusion of the film to storm the Winter Palace, the angles are effectively reversed. *The*

5.39 A bombastic tsarist orator addressing a mindless crowd in *The End of St. Petersburg* (Vsevolod Pudovkin, 1927).

End of St. Petersburg was very successful in the Soviet Union and was hailed as a masterpiece abroad. Many critics today consider it superior to Eisenstein's film as an analysis of the revolution, although *October* is such a singular and eccentric work that it is difficult to compare them.

Pudovkin's last great silent film, *Heir to Genghis Khan* (*Potomok Chingis-Khan,* 1928; English title: *Storm over Asia*), continued the narrative pattern, begun in *Mother,* in which a politically naïve person is galvanized into radical action by tsarist tyranny. But *Heir to Genghis Khan* is set in Soviet Central Asia in 1920, and its protagonist is a Mongol trapper who is exploited not by Russians but by the foreign armies of intervention which fought against the Red Army in Asia during the Civil War.* As this most exciting of Pudovkin films opens, the young Mongol Bair attacks an English fur trader who has badly cheated him and flees to join the Soviet partisans in the north. The British army of intervention eventually tracks him down, shoots him, and leaves him gravely wounded; but a colonel finds an amulet among Bair's belongings which declares him to be a direct descendant of Ghenghis Khan. The British nurse Bair back to health and set him up as a puppet ruler over Buryat Mongolia. The Mongol accepts his role at first but ultimately realizes that he is being used to oppress his own people, and he turns against the British with a fury that assumes nearly cosmic proportions as the film concludes: like Samson, Bair literally pulls the British headquarters down upon the heads of his captors; then he leaps on a pony, and gathers an impossibly vast horde of Mongol horsemen who ride in wave after wave after wave against the British oppressors, becoming finally an apocalyptic windstorm that hurls the interventionists helplessly about and literally blows them from the face of the land.

This magnificent symbolic conclusion initially contained hundreds of shots (some prints derived from the German version shorten it to twenty-seven) and was roundly attacked by Party-line critics who considered it unrealistic—which, of course, it was meant to be—and insufficiently ideological. Critics also found fault with the luxuriant pictorial beauty of the film, shot on location by Golovnya, which they thought indulgently formalistic. *Heir to Genghis Khan* was a great popular success, and foreign audiences were much taken with its technical virtuosity; but Pudovkin had been shaken by the bitterness of official Soviet criticism, and his next film, an attempt to put his theory of contrapuntal sound into practice, was a failure. Entitled *A Simple Case* (*Prostoi sluchai,* 1932), it was released in a silent print only and Pudovkin was publicly charged with formalism, signaling again that the great experimental period of Soviet art was drawing to a close. Reactionary forces had gained control of the Politburo, and though Pudovkin managed to weather the storm of criticism that was about to engulf the great montage artists of the Soviet cinema—he went on to make several respected sound films (*Deserter* [*Dezertir,* 1933]; *Suvorov* [co-directed with Mikhail Doller, 1941])—he would never again achieve the stature of his three silent masterpieces.

5.40 Heir to *Genghis Khan* (Vsevolod Pudovkin, 1928).

---

* Political pressure from foreign ministries made it necessary to label the British "White Russians" in many exported versions of the film, but they remain unmistakably British.

ALEXANDER DOVZHENKO

The third major artist of the Soviet silent film, and perhaps the most unconventional, was Alexander Dovzhenko (1894–1956). The son of Ukrainian peasants, Dovzhenko had been a teacher, a diplomat, and a painter before joining the Odessa Studios in 1926 at the age of thirty-two. Like Griffith, he knew little about cinema when he began his career in it ("I very rarely saw films," Dovzhenko wrote of his former life[39]), and his first three productions for Odessa were of indifferent quality. But in 1928 he made a film which revealed a remarkable depth of poetic feeling and which was so technically unconventional that officials of the Ukrainian film trust asked Eisenstein and Pudovkin to preview it in order to certify its coherence. The film was *Zvenigora,* a collection of richly symbolic tales about a legendary Scythian treasure, which contained within it a contemporary political allegory; Eisenstein and Pudovkin immediately recognized its importance. Eisenstein wrote later that its striking blend of fantasy, reality, and "profoundly national poetic invention" was reminiscent of the work of the Russian writer Nikolai Gogol (1809–52).[40] Dovzhenko himself called the film "a catalogue of my creative possibilities,"[41] and indeed it was, for in its bold stylization of narrative form, its emotional lyricism, and its passionate sensitivity to Ukrainian life, *Zvenigora* prefigured *Arsenal* (1929) and *Earth* (*Zemlya,* 1930), the two great silent masterpieces to come.

Arsenal is an epic film poem about the effects of revolution and civil war upon the Ukraine. Beginning with the world war and ending in a violent strike by workers at the arsenal in Kiev, the film does not so much tell a story as create an extended visual metaphor for revolution encom-

5.41 The absurd horror of war in *Arsenal* (Alexander Dovzhenko, 1929).

passing the nightmarish horrors of war, the miseries of economic oppression, and, finally, the ineradicable spirit of freedom in the hearts of the Ukrainian people. Structurally, *Arsenal* provides a synoptic view of the Ukrainian revolution through a series of imagistic vignettes in which history, caricature, folklore, allegory, and myth are combined. In the beautifully composed frames of cameraman Danylo Demutsky, people not only live and die, but horses talk, portraits come to life, and, at the end of the film, the protagonist himself bares his breast to volley after volley of White Russian bullets and miraculously continues to stand, a symbol of the irrepressible revolutionary spirit. Of the film's highly symbolic, non-narrative organization, Eisenstein remarked that it was the prime example in cinema of a "liberation of the whole action from the definition of time and space."[42] Indeed, the official critics experienced some difficulty with *Arsenal,* and yet, according to Jay Leyda, the public seemed to accept the film almost intuitively upon its own terms.[43]

Dovzhenko's next film, *Earth (Zemlya,* 1930), is universally acknowledged to be his masterpiece. Though its scant plot concerns a commonplace manifestation of the class struggle, the film is essentially a non-narrative hymn to the continuity of life and death in Dovzhenko's beloved Ukraine. Unfolding with a slow, natural rhythm, like the processes of life itself, *Earth* tells the simple story of the tension between a family of wealthy landowners (kulaks) and the young peasants of a collective farm in a small Ukrainian village. When the kulaks refuse to sell their vast land holdings to the collective, Vasyl, the village chairman, commandeers the property, buys a new tractor, and turns the collective into a thriving enterprise. One evening, after making love to his betrothed, Vasyl is shot dead on the way home by the kulaks' deranged son. In his grief, Vasyl's father sends away the village priest and demands a "modern" funeral for his son "with new songs about new life," and the film concludes with an ecstatic funeral celebration for the young man, after which rain begins to descend upon the crops. Lewis Jacobs has accurately described *Earth* as

5.42 *Earth* (Alexander Dovzhenko, 1930): visual poetry.

5.43 *Earth:* Vasyl dances by moonlight.

"a luminous contribution to the realm of lyric cinema."[44] It is a rare film of mysterious beauty that perpetually transcends its contemporary political context to exalt the everlasting fecundity of the soil and the inevitable cyclic recurrence of birth, life, love, and death. The film begins with an old man joyfully biting into an apple as he dies and concludes with the mystically sensuous funeral procession, during which Vasyl's fiancée rips her clothes from her body in grief, his mother goes into labor with her last child, and warm rain falls to replenish the earth.

The central sequence of *Earth* follows the plenteous harvest and is dominated by what Dovzhenko called a "biological, pantheistic conception." Young couples lie in ecstasy under the moonlit summer's night, the hands of the boys on the girls' breasts. Vasyl and his fiancée are among them. They part, and, alone on the dusty road, Vasyl breaks spontaneously into a dance celebrating his deep spiritual joy in life and love. Suddenly, in the middle of a slow-motion pirouette, he falls dead, pierced by the bullet of his hidden assassin. But what would be tragedy in the work of other directors becomes jubilant affirmation in Dovzhenko, for Vasyl has died at the moment of his young life's most perfect self-expression, and life will continue to renew itself as ever before. Ivor Montagu has written: "Dovzhenko's films are crammed with deaths. . . . But no death in Dovzhenko was ever futile. . . . The sum of his films instead is beauty and glory. He is saying to the widow: 'Glory in your children,' and to the childless widow: 'Glory in all the children of man.' "[45]

Though it was later twice voted among the twelve greatest films of all time by panels of international film experts, when first released *Earth* was poorly received by the Soviet critics, who denounced it as "defeatist," "counter-revolutionary," and, in one case, "fascistic." Dovzhenko's domestic reputation, like those of Eisenstein and Pudovkin, was about to enter a period of political eclipse. He adapted his talents readily to the new demands of the sound film (*Ivan* [1932]; *Aerograd* [1935]; *Shchors* [1939]), but increasing pressure to conform to the Party line made it impossible for him to ever again reach the lyric heights of *Arsenal* and *Earth*. though for the rest of his life he courageously continued to try.

5.44 *New Babylon* (Grigory Kozintsev and Leonid Trauberg, 1929).

5.45 *Women of Ryazan* (Olga Preobrazhenskaya, 1927).

OTHER SOVIET FILM-MAKERS

Before examining the reasons for the dramatic decline of the Soviet cinema in the nineteen-thirties and the selective suppression of its major artists, it is necessary to mention several other film-makers who played an important role in the great decade of experiment that followed the Revolution. Most notable, perhaps, was the team of Grigory Kozintsev, director (1905–1973) and Leonid Trauberg, scenarist (b. 1902), who had founded FEX, the Factory of the Eccentric Actor, in 1921. Kozintsev and Trauberg together produced a number of ebullient, wildly experimental shorts like *The Adventures of Octyabrina* (*Pokhozhdeniya Oktyabrini*, 1924) before turning to an extremely successful expressionistic adaptation of Gogol's *The Overcoat* (*Shinel*) in 1926. Their masterpiece, however, magnificently scored by the great modernist composer Dmitri Shostakovich, was *New Babylon* (*Novyi Vavilon,* 1929), a highly stylized drama of the rise and fall of the Paris Commune,* set in a luxurious Parisian department store. (In his later years, Kozintsev worked on his own to produce three masterful literary adaptations: *Don Quixote* [1956], *Hamlet* [1964], and *King Lear* [*Korol Lira,* 1972].) Trauberg's younger brother, Ilya (1905–48), after working as an assistant to Eisenstein on *October,* made a remarkable feature debut with *The Blue Express* (*Goluboi ekspress,* 1929), an exciting adventure film set in the Far East which also functions as a political allegory of China's movement toward Communism.

Boris Barnet (1902–65), a pupil of Kuleshov, directed several impressive comedies of contemporary manners in the late silent era, among them *The House on Trubnaya Square* (*Dom na Trubnoi,* 1928), a gently satiric tale of everyday life in Moscow under the New Economic Policy. Two pre-revolutionary directors returned from exile to make significant films during the period: Yakov Protazanov (1881–1945) created a science-fiction fantasy entitled *Aelita* (1924) which is notable as the only Soviet film ever designed completely in the Constructivist† style, and the former Protazanov actress Olga Preobrazhenskaya (1884–1966) directed a somber and poetic evocation of traditional Russian peasant life, *Women of Ryazan* (*Babi Ryazanskye,* 1927). *Bed and Sofa* (*Tretya meshchanskaya,* 1927), directed by Abram Room (1894–1976) and designed by Eisenstein's friend Sergei Yutkevich, was a witty social comedy about a *ménage à trois* caused by the housing shortage. Yutkevich himself, who had helped to form the FEX and was to become an important figure in

---

* After the siege of Paris which ended the Franco-Prussian war of 1870–71, many of the inhabitants of the city rebelled against the government of the Third Republic and established their own council of municipal self-government, called the Commune of Paris. Ostensibly socialist, the Commune governed for two months, until it was brutally suppressed by the French army. Karl Marx hailed the Paris Commune as the first great revolt of the proletariat against the bourgeoisie, and in Marxist-Leninist dogma the Commune is thought to have prefigured the Bolshevik Revolution of 1917.

† Constructivism was a movement in the theater arts closely related to Futurism. It advocated production methods featuring architectural and/or mechanical structures on the stage to give a three-dimensional effect to scenic design.

the sound film, produced two lively features at the end of the silent era, *Lace* (*Kruzheva*, 1928) and *The Black Sail* (*Chyorni parus,* 1929). Three other directors who were to become major figures in the Soviet sound film began their careers during this period: Friedrich Ermler (1898–1967) with *Fragment of an Empire* (*Oblomok imperii,* 1929), Mikhail Kalatozov (1903–73) with *Salt for Svanetia* (*Sol Svanetia,* 1930), and Mark Donskoi (1901–81) with *In the Big City* (*V bolshe gorode,* 1927).

Finally, some mention must be made of the documentaries of the Ukrainian director Viktor Turin (1895–1945) and those of Eisenstein's friend and teacher Esther Shub. Turin's *Turksib* (1929), a dynamic feature-length account of the building of the Turkistan-Siberian Railway, won international acclaim and influenced the development of the British documentary tradition, but his other films are uneven. The work of Shub is broader, more substantial, and more consistent. From her early experience as a Goskino editor she originated the compilation film, a documentary form which mixes together existing newsreel footage from other films, and her remarkable sense of rhythm and tempo in cutting allowed her to create several brilliant feature-length chronicles of Russia's revolutionary past. Her greatest films are *The Fall of the Romanov Dynasty* (*Padeniye dinasti Romanovikh,* 1927) and *The Great Road* (*Velikii put,* 1927), both made to commemorate the tenth anniversary of the Bolshevik Revolution.*

SOCIALIST REALISM AND THE DECLINE OF SOVIET CINEMA

The fate of that revolution was also the fate of the Soviet cinema, whose decline coincided with the coming of sound but was not directly attributable to it. Some Soviet directors, of course, had difficulty adjusting to the new technology of sound, but on the whole its arrival was greeted enthusiastically as a means of expanding the medium's artistic potential. Dziga Vertov had eagerly anticipated the introduction of sound since the mid-twenties; in August 1928 Eisenstein, Pudovkin, and Alexandrov published a manifesto collectively endorsing the creative use of sound in motion pictures; and Eisenstein, Alexandrov, and Tisse journeyed to Western Europe and America in 1929 primarily to investigate developments in the sound film. The truth seems to be that the Golden Age of Soviet cinema, like that of German cinema, came to an end less for technological reasons than for political ones.

At the Fifteenth Communist Party Congress in 1927, Iosif Stalin, who had been the general secretary of the Central Committee since 1922, succeeded in out-maneuvering his opponents to become dictator of the Soviet Union for the next twenty-six years. Unlike his predecessors, Lenin (died 1924) and Trotsky (exiled 1928), Stalin and many of the men who

---

* See Vlada Petric, "Esther Shub: Cinema Is My Life" and "Esther Shub's Unrealized Project," *Quarterly Review of Film Studies,* 3, 4 (Fall 1978), 429–56.

surrounded him were insular, provincial, and highly intolerant of the arts—especially of the avant-garde experiments of the past decade. As a ruthlessly practical politician, Stalin recognized the enormous importance of film as a means of mass communication, but whereas Lenin had said, "The cinema is for us the most important of the arts," Stalin was more blunt: "The cinema," he wrote, "is the greatest medium of mass agitation. The task is to take it into our hands." And this is precisely what happened.[46]

At the Sixteenth Party Congress in 1928, Stalin demanded greater state control of the arts in order to make them both more accessible and more relevant to the masses. Shortly thereafter, in 1929, the open-minded Anatoly Lunacharsky was replaced as commissar of information by the doctrinaire bureaucrat Boris Shumyatsky, who openly discouraged all manner of "formalism," symbolism, and montage experiment in favor of didactic plots and, ultimately, blatant propaganda. Where Lunacharsky had suggested, Shumyatsky decreed, and as the Soviet leadership grew more and more authoritarian, the arts were pushed increasingly toward the narrow ideological perspective known as "socialist realism." This was a prosaic and heavy-handed brand of didacticism which idealized the Soviet experience in order to inspire the masses with the glories of life under Lenin and Stalin. When socialist realism was declared the official style of all Soviet art at the Twentieth Party Congress in 1932, the genius of the Soviet cinema was devastated, since anything unique, personal, or formally experimental was explicitly forbidden to appear upon the screen.*

Tragically, if characteristically, it was the founders of that cinema who were most injured by this reactionary decree. Eisenstein, Pudovkin, Dovzhenko, Kuleshov, and Vertov were all variously denounced and, in some cases, publicly humiliated for their past "formalist aberrations." They continued to work under the burden of official disfavor for the rest of their lives, their visions and their methods strait-jacketed by Stalinist paranoia from that time forth. With the sole exception of Eisenstein, none of them produced work in the sound era equal to their greatest silent films because (as the Nazis would discover almost simultaneously with the Stalinists) art shackled by ideology ceases to be art and becomes something else. Great art may sometimes be ideological, as *Potemkin,* *Mother,* and *Arsenal* clearly illustrate, but ideology in the service of itself alone can never be great art. The film in the Soviet Union has only recently begun to recover from the creative sterility induced by Stalinism, and so long as totalitarian attitudes prevail over the arts, it will be some time before we witness a recurrence of the Soviet cinema's Golden Age.

---

* Socialist realism was officially defined as the "artistic method whose basic principle is the truthful, historically concrete depiction of reality in its revolutionary development, and whose most important task is the Communist education of the masses."[47] It was, in other words, an artistic method which demanded the "socialization" of Soviet art as a propaganda medium for Communist Party policy. For a detailed scholarly account of how the Soviet cinema was turned from a revolutionary agitational movement into "a mouthpiece for Stalinist orthodoxy," see Richard Taylor, *The Politics of the Soviet Cinema, 1917–1929* (London, 1979).

Hollywood in the Twenties

By the end of World War I, the American film industry had assumed the structure it would retain for the next forty years. The independent producers, led by Adolph Zukor, William Fox, and Carl Laemmle, had triumphed over the monopolistic Motion Picture Patents Company to become vertically integrated monopolies themselves, controlling their own theater chains and distributorships. With the refinement of the feature film, motion picture audiences became increasingly middle-class, and exotic "atmospheric" theaters which could seat up to three thousand patrons spread to cities small and large across the country. Thanks to increased film length, monetary inflation, and the monumental salaries newly commanded by stars, production budgets rose by as much as ten times their pre-war level, and the movies became a major national industry in the span of several years. Film-making practices and narrative formulas were standardized to facilitate mass production, and Wall Street began to invest heavily in the industry for both economic and political gain (i.e., it was in the material interest of the wealthy and the powerful to have the new mass medium of the movies—and later of radio—under their control). New money, new power, and the "new morality"* of the post-war Jazz Age all combined to make Hollywood in the twenties the modern Babylon of popular lore.

The industry giants at the beginning of the twenties, known collectively as the "Big Three," were Zukor's Famous Players–Lasky Corporation, which had acquired Paramount Pictures as its distribution and exhibition wing in 1916 and was commonly known as "Paramount"; Loew's, Incorporated, the mammoth theater chain owned by Marcus

6.1 A typical "atmospheric" theater interior of the twenties, with Moorish decor and cloud machine.

6.2 A drawing of the auditorium of the Roxy Theater—"the Cathedral of the Motion Picture"—in New York City, c. 1927.

---

* The mood of post-war America was one of bitterness, disillusionment, and cynicism not unlike that of the post-Watergate era. The "new morality" was an adjunct of this mood. It rejected the "old morality" of Victorian idealism for a fashionable materialism which emphasized wealth, sensation, and sexual freedom. The "new morality" encouraged the widespread use of drugs (mainly nicotine and alcohol; in Hollywood, cocaine), female liberation (women won the vote in 1920), and sexual promiscuity. Its spread was facilitated by the decade's relative economic prosperity and by simultaneous revolutions in communications (mass distribution of films; the booming of network radio) and transportation (mass marketing of the private automobile).

6.3 The formation of United Artists, 1919: Fairbanks, Griffith, Pickford, and Chaplin.

Loew which had moved into production with the acquisition of Metro Pictures in 1920; and First National (after 1921, Associated First National)—the company founded in 1917 by twenty-six of the nation's largest exhibitors to combat the practice of block booking by financing its own productions (see Chapter 2). United Artists was formed in 1919 by the era's four most prominent film artists—D. W. Griffith, Charlie Chaplin, Mary Pickford, and Douglas Fairbanks—in order to produce and distribute their own films, and it was a major force in the industry until the advent of sound (and became so again, in the seventies). Metro-Goldwyn-Mayer emerged as a powerful new studio combine in 1924 through the merger of Metro Pictures, Goldwyn Pictures, and Louis B. Mayer Productions under the auspices of Loew's, Incorporated. Hollywood's second string in the twenties, the "Little Five," consisted of the Fox Film Corporation; Producers Distributing Corporation (PDC); Film Booking Office (FBO); Carl Laemmle's Universal Pictures; and Warner Brothers Pictures, which would force the industry to convert to sound by introducing the Vitaphone process in 1926 and would absorb First National in the process. Below these were about thirty thinly capitalized minor studios, of which only Columbia, Republic, and Monogram survived the coming of sound.

THOMAS INCE, MACK SENNETT, AND THE STUDIO SYSTEM OF PRODUCTION

6.4 The original Inceville at Santa Ynez, with the Pacific Ocean in the background, c. 1912.

It was in the twenties that the studios became great factories for the large-scale production of mass commercial entertainment, and this was mainly due to the example of Thomas Harper Ince (1882–1924) in the previous decade. Like Griffith, Ince had begun his career as an actor-director at American Biograph in 1910 and ultimately established his own studio, "Inceville," in the Santa Ynez Canyon near Hollywood in 1912. Here Ince directed over a hundred films, ranging in length from two to five reels, before turning exclusively to production in late 1913. Between 1914 and 1918, he built Inceville into the first recognizably modern Hollywood studio, complete with five self-contained shooting stages; his mode of production became the prototype for the highly organized studio system that was to dominate the American film industry for the next forty years. Ince's practice was to set up a number of production units on his lot, each headed by a director. Writers, working in close collaboration with both Ince and the directors, would prepare detailed shooting scripts (also known as continuities or scenarios) in which the entire production was laid out shot by shot. Ince would then approve the script, and the film would go into production according to a strict timetable. When the shooting was finished, Ince would supervise the editing and retain authority over the final cut.* This kind of film-making was very

---

* For an economic analysis of the Ince system and the central role of the continuity script, see Janet Staiger, "Dividing Labor for Production Control: Thomas Ince and the Rise of the Studio System," *Cinema Journal*, 28, (Spring 1979), 16–25.

much the opposite of Griffith's mode of improvisation, but it represented the wave of the American cinema's heavily capitalized future, and it helps to explain why Griffith was not to be a part of that future for very long. Still, Ince was like Griffith in his genius for visualizing narrative, and most of his productions—the vast majority of them action-packed Westerns—tended to be well-paced, tightly constructed features which bore the strong stamp of his personality.

Ince and Griffith actually became business partners for several years with Mack Sennett in the ill-fated Triangle Film Corporation, founded by Harry Aitken after he left Mutual in 1915. In conception, this organization was sound: each of the three directors was to supervise the production of films of the type that had made him popular and famous—action films and Westerns for Ince, two-reel slapstick comedies for Sennett, melodrama and spectacle for Griffith. In practice Triangle failed after three years due to miscalculation of the public's taste and misguided attempts to bring stars of the legitimate stage to the screen. When the failure occurred, Ince built himself a large new studio at Culver City (which would become the physical plant of MGM some ten years later) and continued to produce features there until his death in 1924. In the course of his career, Ince had introduced the detailed scenario, or continuity script, to the film-making process and pioneered the studio system of production. He had also given many talented actors and directors their first opportunities to work in film: William S. Hart, Sessue Hayakawa, Billie Burke, Frank Borzage, Henry King, Lloyd Ingraham, Fred Niblo, Rowland V. Lee, Lambert Hillyer, and Francis Ford all got their start at Inceville. Finally, Ince had contributed to the cinema a number of tautly constructed feature films, such as *The Battle of Gettysburg* (1913), *The Typhoon* (1914), *The Coward* (1915), *Hell's Hinges* (1916), *The Aryan* (1916), *Civilization* (1916), *The Patriot* (1916), *The Beggar of Cawnpore* (1917), *Human Wreckage* (1923), and *Anna Christie* (1923), which are for the most part models of fast-paced and economical narrative form. As John Ford remarked, "Ince had a great influence on films, for he tried to make them move."[1]

Another architect of the American studio system, and the founder of silent screen comedy, was Ince's and Griffith's partner in the Triangle Film Corporation, Mack Sennett (1880–1960). Sennett had worked as an actor in many of Griffith's Biograph films and set himself consciously to study the director's methods. He began to direct films for Biograph himself in 1910, but was given very little creative freedom. So in 1912 Sennett founded the Keystone Studios in Hollywood with the financial backing of two New York bookies named Kessel and Bauman. Here, between 1913 and 1935, he produced thousands of one- and two-reel films and hundreds of features which created a new screen genre—the silent slapstick comedy—that was to become the single most vital American mode of the twenties. Influenced by circus, vaudeville, burlesque, pantomime, the comic strip, and the chase films of the French actor Max Linder, Sennett's Keystone comedies posited a surreal and anarchic universe where the logic of narrative and character was subordinated to purely visual humor of a violent but fantastically harmless nature. It is a world of

6.5 Part of the Ince studio at Culver City (later MGM).

6.6 Keystone mayhem in an unidentified Sennett film.

inspired mayhem—of pie-throwing, cliff-hanging, auto-chasing, and, pre-eminently, of blowing things up. The slam-bang comic effect of these films depended upon rapid-fire editing and the "last-minute rescue" as learned from Griffith, and also upon Sennett's own incredibly accurate sense of pace. He had a genius for timing movement, both the frenetic physical activity which filled the frames of his films and the breathless editing rhythms which propelled them forward at breakneck speed. Sennett's films often parodied the conventions of other films, especially those of Griffith (e.g., *Teddy at the Throttle* [1916]), or satirized contemporary America's worship of the machine (*Wife and Auto Trouble* [1916]). Just as often, they would develop a single improvised sight gag involving the Keystone Kops or the Sennett Bathing Beauties into a riotous series of visual puns whose only logic was associative editing (*The Masquerader* [1914]; *The Surf Girl* [1916]).

In the first two years at Keystone, Sennett directed most of his films himself, but after 1914 he adopted the Inceville model and began to function exclusively as a production chief in close association with his directors, actors, and writers. Unlike Ince, however, Sennett preferred simple story ideas to detailed shooting scripts, and he always left room in his films for madcap improvisation. The number of great comedians and directors who began their careers at Keystone is quite amazing. Sennett discovered and produced the first films of Charlie Chaplin, Buster Keaton, Harry Langdon, Fatty Arbuckle, Mabel Normand, Ben Turpin, Gloria Swanson, Carole Lombard, Wallace Beery, Marie Dressler, and W. C. Fields. He also provided the training ground for some of the most distinguished directors of comedy in the American cinema: Chaplin and Keaton, of course, but also Malcolm St. Clair, George Stevens, Roy Del Ruth, and Frank Capra. Furthermore, the enormous international popularity of Sennett's Keystone comedies contributed substantially to America's commercial dominance of world cinema in the years following World War I. Sennett's realization that the cinema was uniquely suited to acrobatic visual humor established a genre which in the twenties would become perhaps the most widely admired and vital in the history of American film. Many serious critics, at least, regard it as such. And yet Sennett's conception of comedy was wed to the *silent* screen. Purely visual humor loses a great deal to the logic of language and naturalistic sound; and when silence ceased to be an essential component of the cinema experience, the genre that Sennett had founded vanished from the screen. Sennett himself continued to make films after the conversion to sound, but by 1935 Keystone was bankrupt, and its founder did not produce another film before his death in 1960.

CHARLIE CHAPLIN

Sennett's most important and influential protégé was Charlie Chaplin (1889–1977). Chaplin, the son of impoverished British music hall entertainers, had spent his childhood on stage. Like Charles Dickens and D. W. Griffith, both of whom he greatly resembles, Chaplin's vision of the world was colored by a youth of economic deprivation, and he felt deeply sympathetic toward the underprivileged all of his life. Chaplin was already a veteran performer when he was engaged by Keystone Studios during an American vaudeville tour. In his first film for Sennett, *Making a Living* (1914), he played a typical English dandy, but by his second, *Kid Auto Races at Venice* (1914), he had already begun to develop the character and costume of "the little tramp" which would make him world-famous and become a kind of universal cinematic symbol for our common humanity. Chaplin made thirty-four shorts and the six-reel feature *Tillie's Punctured Romance* (Mack Sennett, 1914) at Keystone, progressively refining the character of the sad little clown in oversized shoes, baggy pants, and an undersized coat and derby.

But Chaplin's gifts were meant for a more subtle style of comedy than the frenetic rhythms of the Keystone films allowed, so in 1915 he signed a contract with Essanay to make fourteen two-reel shorts for the enormous sum of $1,250 a week. He directed these and all of his subsequent films himself, based on his experiences at Keystone. In fact, in terms of narrative technique, Chaplin scarcely ever advanced *beyond* what he had learned from Sennett. With the possible exception of *A Woman of Paris* (1923), which was unavailable in the West until 1978, his films are interesting not for their form but for their content—specifically, for his brilliant characterization of the little tramp, totally at odds with the world about him, through the exquisite art of mime. Chaplin's best Essanay films were *The Tramp, Work, The Bank,* and *A Night at the Show* (all 1915), and they made him so popular that in the following year he was able to command a star salary of $10,000 a week plus an annual bonus of $670,000 in a contract for twelve films with Mutual, of which the greatest are *The Floorwalker* (1916), *The Fireman* (1916), *One A.M.* (1916), *The Pawnshop* (1916), *The Rink* (1916), *Easy Street* (1917), *The Immigrant* (1917), and *The Adventurer* (1917). These two-reelers were produced with infinite care and constitute twelve nearly perfect masterpieces of mime. They also made Chaplin internationally famous and first showed his great gift for social satire—a satire of the very poor against the very rich, of the weak against the powerful, which endeared him to the former but not to the latter, especially during the Depression. In *The Immigrant,* for example, one of the most memorable sequences is predicated upon the hypocrisy of American attitudes toward immigration and upon the brutality of the immigration authorities themselves. As Charlie's ship arrives at Ellis Island, he looks up with hope and pride at the Statue of Liberty. Then a title announcing "The Land of Liberty" is followed by a shot of the New York port police forcibly herding together a large number of immigrant families for processing like so many cattle. In the next shot, Charlie casts another glance at the Statue of Liberty—this one suspicious, even disdainful.

By June 1917 Chaplin had gained such star-power that he was offered a one-million-dollar contract with First National to produce eight films for the company, regardless of length. This deal enabled him to establish his own studios, where he made all of his films from 1918 until he left the country in 1952. His cameraman for all of these productions was Rollie

6.7   The final shot of Chaplin in *The Tramp* (Charles Chaplin, 1915).

6.8 Chaplin with Jackie Coogan in *The Kid* (Charles Chaplin, 1921).

6.9 *A Woman of Paris* (Charles Chaplin, 1923): Edna Purviance, Adolphe Menjou.

Totheroh (1891–1967), whom he had first met in 1915 at Essanay. Most of Chaplin's First National films were painstakingly crafted two-reelers, like *A Dog's Life* (1918), *Shoulder Arms* (1918), *The Idle Class* (1921), and *Pay Day* (1922), which continued the vein of social criticism begun at Mutual. But Chaplin's most successful effort for First National was the first feature-length film he directed, *The Kid* (1921). This was an autobiographical comedy/drama about the tramp's commitment to an impoverished little boy in the slums of Victorian London which combined pathos with tender humor and became an international hit, earning over 2.5 million dollars for its producers in the year of its release and making its child lead, the five-year-old Jackie Coogan, a star. Chaplin's last film under the First National contract was the four-reel feature *The Pilgrim* (1923), a social satire in which an escaped prisoner (Chaplin) is mistaken for a minister by the venal parishioners of a small Texas town, with hilarious results. The film is a brilliant comic assault on religious hypocrisy, and it may well have been the catalyst for the venomous personal attacks launched against Chaplin by religious groups a few years later.

After he had fulfilled his obligation to First National, Chaplin was free to release his films through United Artists, the distributing company which he had founded with D. W. Griffith, Mary Pickford, and Douglas Fairbanks in 1923. His first United Artists film was the much-admired *A Woman of Paris* (1923), a sophisticated "drama of fate" whose subtle suggestiveness influenced film-makers as diverse as Ernst Lubitsch (see below) and René Clair (see Chapter 9). Chaplin appeared only briefly as a porter in *A Woman of Paris,* which like all of his films after 1923 was a full-length feature, but in his comic epic *The Gold Rush* (1925) he returned to the central figure of the little tramp. Set against the Klondike gold rush of 1898, this film manages to make high comedy out of hardship, starvation, and greed as three prospectors fight it out for the rights to a claim. In the subtlety of its characterization, the brilliance of its mime, and its blending of comic and tragic themes, *The Gold Rush* is Chaplin's most characteristic work. It is as popular today as it was in 1925, and it remained his personal favorite. *The Circus* (1928), in which the tramp attempts to become a professional clown, is a beautifully constructed silent film released during the conversion to sound. In honor of it, Chaplin was given a special award at the first Academy Awards ceremony in 1929 for "versatility and genius in writing, acting, directing, and producing." During the filming of *The Circus,* however, Chaplin was involved in a divorce suit brought by his second wife, and he became the target of a vicious campaign of personal abuse on the part of religious and "moralist" groups which nearly drove him to suicide. It was the first of many clashes between Chaplin and the established order in America.

Characteristically, Chaplin's first two sound films were produced with musical scores (written by Chaplin) and sound effects but no spoken dialogue: it was his way of extending the great art of silent mime into the era of sound.* *City Lights* (1931) is a sentimental but effective film in which

---

* For more on Chaplin's sound films, see "Chaplin and Sound," *Journal of the University Film Association,* 31, 1 (Winter 1979 [special issue]).

6.10 Chaplin makes a meal of a boot in *The Gold Rush* (Charles Chaplin, 1925).

the unemployed tramp falls in love with a blind flower girl and goes through a series of misadventures, including robbery and a jail term, in order to raise money for the operation which can restore her sight. Chaplin called the film "a comedy romance in pantomime," and it is, but *City Lights* is also a muted piece of social criticism in which the cause of the poor is defended against that of the rich. If there were any remaining doubts about the nature of Chaplin's social attitudes, they were dispelled by *Modern Times* (1936), a film about the dehumanization of the common working man in a world run for the wealthy by machines. In it, Chaplin plays a factory worker who is fired for inefficiency, holds a variety of other jobs, and ends up unemployed but undefeated. The film's satire on industrialization and inequity in the "modern times" of the Great Depression earned it little popularity among the powerful in the United States, where in some quarters it was called "Red propaganda," or in Germany and Italy, where it was banned. But *Modern Times* was enormously successful in the rest of Europe, and it remains today one of Chaplin's funniest, best structured, and most socially committed works.

In *The Great Dictator* (1940) Chaplin produced his first full talkie and one of the first anti-Nazi films to come out of Hollywood. A satire on European dictatorships, the film chronicles the rule of Adenoid Hynkel, dictator of Tomania, as he persecutes the Jews and plunges Europe into another war. Chaplin played the dual role of Hynkel and an amnesiac Jewish barber who is Hynkel's double. Released some eighteen months before Pearl Harbor, the film was not well received: many thought its politics too serious, others found them not serious enough. Chaplin's next film was the dark and cynical *Monsieur Verdoux* (1947), "a comedy of murder" based upon the exploits of the infamous French mass-murderer Landru. In it, a Parisian bank clerk (Chaplin) loses his job and takes up the practice of marrying and then murdering rich, middle-aged women in order to support his invalid wife and small son. He is caught, and while awaiting execution Verdoux states the film's theme concisely in an argument with a fellow prisoner: "Wars, conflict, it's all business. One murder makes a villain; millions a hero. Numbers sanctify." The film was bitterly attacked in the United States, where it was released on the eve of the hysterical anti-Communist witch-hunts of the Cold War era; it was withdrawn from circulation after six weeks but had great success in France. The relationship between Chaplin and his American

6.11 *Modern Times* (Charles Chaplin, 1936).

6.12 Chaplin in *The Great Dictator* (Charles Chaplin, 1940).

audiences had grown increasingly strained since the disappearance of the little tramp and the emergence of the liberal social critic, but resentment of Chaplin went back at least as far as the moralistic campaigns of the twenties. Some of this animosity had to do with the fact that Chaplin had retained British citizenship since coming to the United States and had not been consistent in paying his federal income tax.

In his last American film, *Limelight* (1952), Chaplin returned to the London music-halls of his childhood to tell the bittersweet tale of an aging performer who triumphs over the fact of his own declining power and imminent death by curing a young ballet dancer of paralysis and starting her on her career. The film is long (two and a half hours), slow, and cinematically archaic, but it is one of Chaplin's finest testaments to that dignity and decency of human nature which he felt the twentieth century had done so much to destroy. In early 1953, Chaplin and his family were granted six-month exit visas to attend a royal premiere of *Limelight* in London. On the first day at sea, Chaplin received a cablegram from the U.S. State Department denying him re-entry unless he would consent to appear before a board of inquiry to answer charges of political and moral turpitude. In this manner, the highest-paid and most popular star in the history of American film was forcibly ushered from his adopted country. Chaplin chose to take up residence in his homeland (and, later, in Switzerland). Four years later he responded to the cable with *A King in New York* (1957), a strained political parable about a European head of state visiting the United States who is ruined, as Chaplin himself had been, by the malicious charges of the House Un-American Activities Committee (see Chapter 12). The film is understandably bitter and indifferently directed, but it does contain some fine satire on life in America during the fifties.

Chaplin's last film was a limp bedroom farce, *The Countess from Hong Kong* (1966), starring Marlon Brando and Sophia Loren. The film is misconceived in terms of both script and direction, and it underscores the conventionality of Chaplin's cinematic intelligence as distinguished from his great intelligence as a performer. His genius was as an actor and a mime. So long as his little tramp character stood at the center of his films, they were masterworks of comedy and pathos. When the tramp disappeared, the limitations of Chaplin's directorial ability became increasingly apparent. With few exceptions, it was Chaplin's *presence* in his films, rather than anything in their formal structure, that made them interesting, important, and distinguished. During the twenties, the image of the little tramp became a worldwide symbol for the general excellence of the American cinema. When Chaplin the man began to replace Chaplin the persona in the late thirties and forties, Chaplin the film-maker became what he had always been—a competent, conventional director with some unconventional ideas.

BUSTER KEATON

It's useful to compare Chaplin's essentially theatrical cinema with the films of his fellow Keystone graduate Buster Keaton (1895–1966). Like Chaplin, Keaton had been raised in vaudeville by his parents; he made his first stage appearance with them at the age of three. From earliest youth, he was involved in solving complicated problems of *mise-en-scène* for the family act, and his later skill in direction may be traced to this experience. Though his reputation was eclipsed by Chaplin's throughout the twenties, it seems clear today that Keaton was Chaplin's equal as an actor and his superior as a director. When the family act broke up in 1917, the twenty-one-year-old Keaton was already a star. He was offered a contract to appear in the Shuberts' popular *Passing Show of 1917,* but he decided to enter the movies instead by going to work as a supporting player at Roscoe "Fatty" Arbuckle's Comicque Studios. Here he made fourteen two-reel shorts with Arbuckle—from *The Butcher* in 1917 to *The Garage* in 1919—in which the quality and sophistication of the studio's product increased notably in both form and substance.

In 1919, Joseph Schenck formed Buster Keaton Productions to produce two-reel comedy shorts starring Keaton and acquired the former Chaplin studios for the purpose. Schenck handled all of the financing but gave Keaton complete creative freedom in writing and directing at a salary of one thousand dollars per week plus 25 percent of the profits. The resulting twenty shorts, made between 1920 and 1923, represent, with Chaplin's Mutual films, the high point of American slapstick comedy. The best of them are films like *One Week* (1920), *The Goat* (1921), *Playhouse* (1921), *The Boat* (1921), *Cops* (1922), and *The Balloonatic* (1923), whose complexity of structure and fine visual sense make them unique among slapstick shorts. Keaton always maintained that comedy must be funny without being ridiculous, and for this reason he took great pains to make his films credible in dramatic as well as comic terms. Unlike Sennett and his many imitators, much of Keaton's excellence as a film-maker stemmed from a strict adherence to the dramatic logic of his narratives and the use of gags which progress in a geometrical pattern

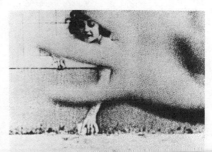

6.13 *One Week* (Buster Keaton, 1920): a hand blocks the lens for privacy.

6.14 Keaton bumbles into a police parade in *Cops* (Buster Keaton, 1922).

6.15 Perfect timing: part of a trajectory gag from *Cops*.

grounded in character and plot. Keaton's first feature was the seven-reel *The Saphead,* directed by Herbert Blaché (b. 1907) for Metro in 1921. This rather limp adaptation of an 1887 comedy about a family of Wall Street brokers was important to Keaton's development since it gave him his first opportunity to create a continuous dramatic characterization in film. By 1923, two-reelers were becoming increasingly unprofitable to produce due to the public's mania for features, and Schenck changed the Keaton studio's production output from eight shorts to two independent features per year. Keaton's salary was raised to star level (twenty-five hundred dollars per week plus 25 percent of the profits), and he entered the period of his greatest creativity.

It has been said that after 1923 Keaton was as important as any director practicing in Hollywood, and so strong was his creative personality that this is true even of the films which do not bear his name on the direction credits. His first independent feature for Keaton Productions, *The Three Ages* (1923), was a sparkling parody of Griffith's *Intolerance* directed by Keaton in collaboration with Eddie Cline (1892–1961) which depicted the trials of courtship through the ages by intercutting stories from three separate historical periods: the Stone Age, ancient Rome, and contemporary America. Though its *mise-en-scène* is not as elaborate nor its narrative as tightly integrated as those of his subsequent films, *The Three Ages* is a successful comedy whose hilarious conclusion introduced a classical Keaton device—the "trajectory" gag, in which the perfect timing of acting, directing, and editing propels the Keaton character through an extended series of dramatically connected sight gags ending in the denouement of a sequence or of an entire film. At the conclusion of the modern sequence of *The Three Ages,* for example, Keaton in long shot leaps from the fire-escape of a six-story building toward an adjacent building, misses the ledge, and falls. A second long shot shows him falling through two canvas window-awnings and catching hold of a third. In the next shot, Keaton uses the awning for ballast as he grabs hold of a drainpipe which comes loose in his arms. Another long shot shows him, still holding the pipe, pivoting into an open window two stories down. We cut here to a medium shot of the interior of a firehouse dormitory, with Keaton hurtling through the window, catching hold of the firemen's pole, and sliding down it. In the next shot, he arrives at the ground floor below and leaps onto the back of a fire engine about to answer an alarm. The final shot of the sequence shows Keaton arriving at a burning building and recognizing it as the police station from which he has just escaped as a wanted man. He slips quietly away, thus completing the trajectory.

Keaton's second independent feature, *Our Hospitality* (1923), represents a tremendous advance over *The Three Ages* and is one of his greatest films. Directed by Keaton in collaboration with Jack Blystone (1892–1938), it concerns a young man's involvement in a bloody family feud in the American South in the early days of the railroad. The film is a nearly perfect example of Keaton's ability to create serious narrative situations and then cause the gags to grow naturally out of them. It is also a film of great pictorial beauty which makes significant use of the long take, or sequence shot,* composed in depth with dramatic action in the foreground, middleground, and background of the frame. As always, Keaton's editing is fluid and perfectly timed, but unlike the followers of Griffith (Henry King, King Vidor, Rowland V. Lee, Frank Borzage) he does not exploit the montage effect for its own sake. And, as in many of Keaton's later films, location shooting (on Lake Tahoe)† and close attention to the details of period costume and setting give *Our Hospitality* a realistic surface which both involves us in the narrative and lends credibility to the action.

Sherlock Junior (1924), directed and edited solely by Keaton, is perhaps his most extraordinary feature-length work. In it, Keaton plays a projectionist in a neighborhood theater who is accused of theft by his girlfriend's father. Later, he falls asleep at work, slides down the projection beam, and enters the screen to become a part of the action, which has been transformed into the real-life drama of the framing story. At first, Keaton is thrown out of the frame by the villain. As he scrambles back into it, the scene changes through a cut and he is suddenly standing in front of a door. As he reaches to open it, the scene changes again and he finds himself in a garden. As he tries to sit down on a garden bench, there is a cut to a crowded street scene and Keaton tumbles into a stream of rushing traffic. This routine continues for several minutes before leading us into a more continuous dream narrative in which Keaton becomes "Sherlock Junior" and clears himself of all false charges, finally waking to his girlfriend's embrace in the projection room. The film is full of breathtakingly complicated (and dangerous) trajectory gags, but the sequence which depicts a real person trapped inside a movie is in many ways a comment on the process of film editing itself; the French avant-

6.16 Keaton projects himself onto the screen within the screen in *Sherlock Junior* (Buster Keaton, 1924).

---

* A "sequence shot," or "long take," is a single unedited shot containing an entire dramatic sequence. It usually involves camera movement and composition in depth as a surrogate for montage.

† "Location shooting" is any filming done away from the studio, no matter where the action is set in the script.

garde director René Clair (see Chapter 9) called attention to its surrealistic aspects as early as 1925, when he compared *Sherlock Junior* to Luigi Pirandello's play *Six Characters in Search of an Author* (1921).*

Keaton's next film, *The Navigator* (1924), directed in collaboration with Donald Crisp (1880–1974), was another virtuoso piece of sustained comic narrative. In it, Rollo Treadway (Keaton), a useless millionaire who can't even shave himself, and his scatterbrained fiancée are set adrift on an ocean liner by foreign spies. Alone, "these beautiful spoiled brats—the most helpless people in the world," as Keaton called them in a contemporary newspaper interview, must chart their survival through some hilarious adventures at sea. Unlike Chaplin, Keaton did not play the same character over and over again, but the narrative situation in which his characters find themselves was always pretty much the same: a vulnerable but plucky human hero, as in *The Navigator,* is confronted with some vast and seemingly insurmountable problem, usually involving objects and machines rather than other humans. It is a classical absurdist situation, and the comic effect arises from the hero's spirited but futile attempts to surmount the insurmountable, at which he ultimately—and for totally arbitrary reasons—somehow succeeds. Remarkably, Keaton never once repeated a narrative formula in his entire career.

Seven Chances (1925), directed by Keaton and adapted from an old David Belasco† farce, concerns a young man who stands to inherit a fortune if he can marry within twenty-four hours. The news is made public, and Keaton soon finds himself being pursued through the Southern California hills by hundreds of rampaging prospective brides. The chase ends in one of Keaton's most striking and dangerous trajectories, as he is forced to run down the sheer face of a hill dodging a landside of fifteen hundred papier-mâché boulders which range in diameter from one to eight feet. Once the sequence was set up, the rest was left to chance and to Keaton's great improvisatory talent as both director and performer: the conclusion of *Seven Chances* remains one of the most stunning of any slapstick comedy. Keaton's next two films were somewhat gag-impoverished, perhaps because he had lost the team of writers who had been collaborating with him since the days of the shorts—Clyde Bruckman, Jean Havez, and Joseph Mitchell. *Go West* (1925), a parody of the popular Western genre, misfires through uncharacteristic sentimentality and disunity, while *The Battling Butler* (1926) is a tale of a spoiled rich boy who pretends to be a boxing champion in order to impress his girlfriend. The latter film concludes with an unaccountably brutal fight

---

* In fact, Keaton's films were widely admired among European avant-gardists of the era, dadaists, surrealists, and absurdists alike. His work was known not only to Pirandello (1867–1936) but to Eugène Ionesco (b. 1912), Federico Garcia Lorca (1899–1936—who wrote the short surrealist farce *El paseo de Buster Keaton* [*Buster Keaton Takes a Walk*] in 1930), and Samuel Beckett, who is said to have written *Waiting for Godot* (1952) with Keaton in mind and who later cast him in the leading role of his original screenplay *Film* (directed by Alan Schneider, 1965).

† David Belasco (1854–1931) was an extremely successful writer, director, and producer of spectacular stage melodrama at the turn of the century. Griffith may have borrowed certain styles of lighting and decor from Belasco's *mise-en-scène*.

sequence which reminds us that Keaton's comedy, like Chaplin's, could occasionally turn bitter, melancholy, and surprisingly unpleasant.

In 1927, Keaton returned to the top of his form with *The General,* which he directed in collaboration with his former scriptwriter Clyde Bruckman. Many critics regard this film as his masterpiece, and Walter Kerr[2] has linked it with Chaplin's *The Gold Rush* (1925) as one of the two great comic epics of the cinema. Based on a real incident from the American Civil War in which Union undercover agents hijacked a Southern locomotive,* *The General* achieved a nearly perfect integration of dramatic action and comedy. Keaton plays Johnny Gray, a civilian railroad engineer during the war who has been unjustly accused of cowardice. His locomotive, "The General," and his fiancée are seized by Union spies and driven northward. Johnny singlehandedly pursues the train into the heart of enemy territory, recaptures it along with his fiancée, and speeds back to the South with what seems to be the entire Union army in hot pursuit. At Rock River, he burns a railroad bridge behind him and precipitates a spectacular comic catastrophe, as a Union locomotive hurtles onto the bridge, causing its collapse, and plunges thirty feet into the river, creating a huge geyser of smoke and steam. In sheer pictorial beauty *The General* surpasses even *Our Hospitality* (1923). Shot on location in the forests of Oregon, its battle scenes are lit and composed, like those of *The Birth of a Nation,* to resemble the Civil War photographs of Mathew Brady. But Keaton achieves a more authentic re-creation of the era than either Griffith or John Huston twenty-five years later in *The Red Badge of Courage* (1951) through the impeccable verisimilitude of his costumes and sets. As for comedy, the timing and structure of *The General*'s trajectories have never been equaled. The film seems to validate the statement by his biographer that Keaton "could perform miracles as easily as he breathed."[3]

Keaton made only two more independent features before his studio was acquired by the MGM conglomerate. *College,* co-directed with James W. Horne (1880–1942), has Keaton as a contemporary college student, a bookworm who aspires to the hand of the most popular girl in school by constantly attempting to prove his nonexistent athletic prowess. The film is conventionally structured and photographed (perhaps because of the interference of the studio's new business manager), but it is as crammed full of energetic gags and trajectories as any Keaton short. *Steamboat Bill Jr.* (1928), the last film Keaton produced himself, was one of his finest. The plot is classical Keaton: an effeminate youth returns from college to his burly father's Mississippi riverboat and falls in love with the daughter of his father's rival, wreaking havoc on both families. The film concludes with a spectacularly realized cyclone that blows away the whole town, a sequence that contains Keaton's most dangerous stunt: in the midst of the storm, an entire house front collapses on him,

6.17 Keaton examines a mortar in *The General* (Buster Keaton, 1927).

6.18 The collapse of the railroad bridge in *The General.*

*Walt Disney Productions made an adventure film based on the same incident, entitled *The Great Locomotive Chase* (Francis D. Lyon, 1956). The Keaton film itself was remade once, by MGM, as *A Southern Yankee* (Edward Sedgwick, 1948), with Red Skelton in the Keaton role.

6.19 Two shots from the cyclone sequence in *Steamboat Bill Jr.* (Charles F. Reisner, 1928).

but he is saved by virtue of standing precisely at the point of a window opening in the façade, the frame clearing his head and body by inches on either side. As Keaton remarked to an interviewer, "It's a one-take scene. . . . You don't do those things twice."[4] Co-directed with Charles F. Reisner (1887–1962), *Steamboat Bill Jr.* is one of Keaton's most technically polished films, full of fluid camera movement and striking composition in depth, as well as the perfectly edited cyclone sequence.

In 1928, Keaton allowed his company to be absorbed by MGM with the promise that Joseph Schenck's brother Nicholas, the newly installed president of Loew's Incorporated, would allow him to continue his creative mode of production. There was little hope that the promise would or could be kept within the factory-like system of the world's largest studio, and Keaton soon found his team of directors, writers, and technicians dispersed to work on other MGM projects. Keaton himself was cast in a film about a bumbling Hearst newsreel cameraman trying to win the hand of another Hearst employee (Hearst owned large shares of MGM stock, and his papers could be counted on for good reviews). The improbable result was *The Cameraman* (1928), Keaton's last great film, co-directed with Edward Sedgwick (1892–1953), which has been described as "a newsreel by Buster Keaton of a newsreel by Buster Keaton."[5] In many ways, *The Cameraman* is as self-reflexive as *Sherlock Junior,* mixing documentary footage of real events with footage of dramatically staged events and at some points integrating the two completely—as when Keaton and his sweetheart are showered with confetti in a New York ticker-tape parade and the camera pulls back to reveal the world-famous aviator Charles Lindbergh, who had made the first transatlantic flight the year before, seated in the car behind them. Keaton's last silent feature, *Spite Marriage* (Edward Sedgwick, 1929), was a great popular success, even though it was released at the height of the public's new mania for sound. It contained a great many subtle gag routines growing out of the situation in which a lowly pants-presser marries a beautiful actress, but the film was not the equal of its predecessors and showed signs of interference by MGM executives.*

There is no question that Keaton's talent could have survived and even profited from the conversion to sound, but in 1933, after appearing in seven witless talking features for MGM, he was fired from the studio by vice president and general manager Louis B. Mayer.† Simultaneously, his

---

* Like *The General,* Keaton's last two silent features were remade by MGM as Red Skelton vehicles—*Spite Marriage* as *I Dood It* (Vincente Minnelli, 1943) and *The Cameraman* as *Watch the Birdie* (Jack Donohue, 1950).

† Keaton always insisted that he had been dismissed because of a personal insult to Mayer; but, according to his most recent biographer, Tom Dardis, the situation was more complex. The evidence shows that Keaton's sound films (e.g., *Doughboys* [Edward Sedgwick, 1930]; *Sidewalks of New York* [Jules White, 1931]; *The Passionate Plumber* [Edward Sedgwick, 1932]; *What! No Beer?* [Edward Sedgwick, 1933]), however bad, were quite successful at the box office, and no one at MGM, from Schenck through Thalberg through Mayer, *wanted* to fire him. But Keaton could simply not adapt himself to working within the restrictive environment of the studio system, and his unhappiness manifested itself in heavy drinking. His increasingly erratic behavior and long absences from the set caused costly

6.20 *The Cameraman* (Buster Keaton and Edward Sedgwick, 1928): a riot in Chinatown.

personal life fell apart, and though he played bit parts in numerous talkies, his career as a film-maker effectively ended in 1929. It seems clear today that of the two great silent clowns, Chaplin and Keaton, Keaton was the superior director. Like Chaplin, he had a great gift for timing, but he had an even stronger sense of narrative structure and *mise-en-scène*. Keaton's films are often formally beautiful where Chaplin's are not, and one has only to compare Chaplin's epic masterpiece *The Gold Rush* (1925) in purely visual terms with any of Keaton's features after *The Three Ages* (1923) to discover why. Furthermore, Keaton's technical genius for setting up and filming his strenuously elaborate gags, and the reckless physical courage with which he performed them, were extraordinary. (Keaton never used a stunt man once in all of his films, although he did employ an Olympic champion to run the decathlon for him in *College*.) Yet, like Chaplin, Keaton was a magnificently subtle actor. His "great stone face" was actually capable of suggesting a vast range of emotion, and there was very little that he could not express with his body. Like Chaplin, Keaton knew that great comedy always exists close to the brink of tragedy, but sentimentality does not play an important part in Keaton's work, as it does in Chaplin's. For both artists, comedy was a strange blend of logic and fantasy in which the impossible was made to seem real. But Keaton alone seems to have understood how dreamlike and surreal was the process of film itself.

HAROLD LLOYD AND OTHERS

Another important architect of silent comedy was Harold Lloyd (1893–1971). Lloyd was working as an extra for Universal Pictures in 1914 when he met Hal Roach (b. 1892), who was to become Sennett's

production slowdowns, and Mayer finally decided to fire him on February 2, 1933, less for personal reasons (although he loathed Keaton as he loathed all artists) than for corporate ones. See Tom Dardis, *Keaton: The Man Who Wouldn't Lie Down* (New York, 1979), pp. 158–227.

only major rival in the production of comic shorts in the twenties. Roach had just established his own production company on the basis of a three-thousand-dollar inheritance, and he hired Lloyd as a comic at three dollars per week. Between 1915 and 1917 Lloyd played tramp figures called "Lonesome Luke" and "Willie Work" that were highly imitative of Chaplin's tramp. But in a 1917 two-reeler entitled *Over the Fence* he discovered for the first time his very own comic persona—the earnest, mild-mannered boy-next-door with his horn-rimmed glasses. Over the next decade Lloyd developed this character into an archetype of American "normalcy" and niceness. Like all Americans, "Harold" was eager to succeed and could become quite aggressive in competition, but beneath it all there was a sound core of decency and innocence.

When he began to do feature work in the twenties, Lloyd specialized in the "comedy of thrills"—a bizarre variant of Keystone mayhem in which the protagonist placed himself in real physical danger to elicit shocks of laughter from the audience. Lloyd's most famous film of this sort was *Safety Last* (directed by Fred Newmeyer and Sam Taylor, 1923), in which he scales the sheer face of a twelve-story building, apparently without safety devices, and ends up hanging above the rushing traffic thousands of feet below, suspended from the hands of a large clock. Other important Lloyd features were *Grandma's Boy* (Fred Newmeyer, 1922), *Dr. Jack* (Fred Newmeyer, 1922), *Why Worry?* (Fred Newmeyer and Sam Taylor, 1923), *Girl Shy* (Newmeyer and Taylor, 1924), and *The Freshman* (Newmeyer and Taylor, 1925). By the mid-twenties, Lloyd had become more popular with American audiences in box office terms alone than either Chaplin or Keaton. But, as with so many of the great silent clowns, his highly kinetic brand of humor did not survive the coming of sound, although he managed to make four sound films (including Preston Sturges' *Mad Wednesday* [1947]) before retiring in 1952. Lloyd's comic genius had neither the intellectual depth of Keaton's nor the emotional depth of Chaplin's. But as a slam-bang, razzle-dazzle acrobat Lloyd had no peers, and, as Walter Kerr has put it, his comedy of pure sensation made a whole generation of Americans feel good about themselves.[6]

Two other popular Hal Roach comedians were Stan Laurel (1890–1965) and Oliver Hardy (1892–1957). Laurel was an Englishman who had first come to America in the same vaudeville troupe as Chaplin and had become a minor comic star for a variety of studios in the teens. Hardy was a native of Georgia who made his living as a singer and bit player until he was signed to a long-term acting contract by Roach in 1926. Laurel was signed shortly afterwards, and in 1927 the two were teamed together in a two-reeler called *Putting the Pants on Philip* (Clyde Bruckman, 1927), initiating a comic partnership which lasted another thirty-four years. Between 1927 and 1929, Laurel and Hardy made twenty-seven silent shorts for Roach, including the minor classics *You're Darn Tootin'* (Edgar Kennedy, 1928) *Two Tars* (James Parrott, 1928), *Liberty* (Leo McCarey, 1929), *Wrong Again* (Leo McCarey, 1929), *Big Business* (James Horne, 1929), *Men of War* (Lewis Foster, 1929), *Bacon Grabbers* (Lewis Foster, 1929), and *The Hoosegow* (James Parrott,

6.21 Harold Lloyd in *Safety Last* (Fred Newmeyer and Sam Taylor, 1923).

6.22 Laurel and Hardy in *Leave 'Em Laughing* (Clyde Bruckman, 1928).

1929); and they became the first important comic team in the history of film.

Since Laurel and Hardy had both been trained for the stage, they made an easy transition to sound, and as a consequence of two-reel talkies like *Hog Wild* (Parrott, 1930), *Another Fine Mess* (Parrott, 1930), *Laughing Gravy* (Horne, 1931), *Helpmates* (Parrott, 1931), *The Music Box* (Parrott, 1932), *Scram* (Raymond McCarey, 1932), *Busy Bodies* (Lloyd French, 1933), and *Them Thar Hills* (Charles Rogers, 1934), the team became extremely popular in the thirties. They also survived the inevitable conversion from shorts to features in *Pardon Us* (Parrott, 1931), *Pack Up Your Troubles* (George Marshall and Raymond McCarey, 1932), *Fra Diavolo* (Hal Roach and Charles Rogers, 1933), *Sons of the Desert* (William A. Seiter, 1933), *Babes in Toyland* (Gus Meins and Charles Rogers, 1934), *Our Relations* (Harry Lachman, 1936), *Way Out West* (Horne, 1937), *Blockheads* (John G. Blystone, 1938), and *A Chump at Oxford* (Alfred Goulding, 1940). Though they frequently worked with such fine directors as George Stevens and Leo McCarey, Laurel was the guiding genius of the team. He wrote many of their scripts and produced some of their major films of the thirties. The careers of Laurel and Hardy effectively ended after 1940, when they stopped working for Roach and were absorbed into the megalithic studio system. At Fox and MGM they were unable to shape their own material, and the features which they made after 1940 were weak attempts to recycle the great humor of their heyday.

Like Harold Lloyd's comedy, that of Laurel and Hardy was in the visually violent tradition of Keystone and usually ended in some form of anarchic destruction. Unlike the randomly organized Sennett shorts, however, Laurel and Hardy films always had a kind of structural logic whereby a single misbegotten incident would be progressively multiplied toward some catastrophic infinity. As characters, both comedians were simply overgrown children whose naked aggression and vengefulness was mirrored in the middle-class world about them. And the physical contrast they presented on the screen was undeniably funny. Laurel, the weak, whimpering, and barely coordinated little fool, and Hardy, the inept, self-important, and grossly inflated bully, offered a comic version of bourgeois stupidity which Flaubert might have admired.

Two other silent comics deserve mention here, although, like Laurel and Hardy, both are decidedly minor by comparison with Chaplin, Keaton, and Lloyd. Harry Langdon (1884–1944) came to work for Mack Sennett from vaudeville in 1924. In numerous shorts at Keystone between 1924 and 1926 he developed the haunting character of a middle-aged, baby-faced innocent whose pathetic naïveté was somewhat reminiscent of Chaplin without Chaplin's dignity. Langdon rose briefly to stardom in a series of three popular features made between 1926 and 1928—*Tramp, Tramp, Tramp* (Harry Edwards, 1926), *The Strong Man* (Frank Capra, 1926), and *Long Pants* (Frank Capra, 1927). Since the first of these films was written and the latter two were directed by Frank Capra, it has been suggested that he alone was responsible for the appeal of Langdon's whimsical comic presence. But Langdon was a brilliant

6.23 Harry Langdon in *The Strong Man* (Frank Capra, 1926).

pantomimist in his own right, and there was something uncanny in his infantile foolishness that belonged exclusively to the character he first created at Keystone. Nevertheless, Langdon's own features as a director, *Three's a Crowd* (1927), *The Chaser* (1928), and *Heart Trouble* (1928), were not as successful as the Capra films, and his career did not survive the coming of sound.

Roscoe "Fatty" Arbuckle (1881–1933), tipping the scales at 270 pounds, also began at Keystone, where he worked successfully with Chaplin from 1914 to 1916 and became Sennett's principal star after Chaplin's departure for Essanay. Arbuckle's comic appeal rested almost solely upon the broad base of his fatness, his childishness, and a certain Sennettesque flair for mayhem. But his popularity was second only to Chaplin's during the brief course of his career. In 1917, Arbuckle founded his own Comicque Studios with the backing of Joseph Schenck and gave Buster Keaton his first job in films as a supporting player. In the earliest Arbuckle-Keaton collaborations, the latter was clearly the foil, but by 1919 Keaton had totally usurped Arbuckle as a comic talent and gone on to form a production company of his own. Arbuckle was still extremely popular and made eight successful features for Paramount between 1919 and 1921, when his career ended in a catastrophic scandal that rocked the movie industry and changed the course of Hollywood history.

6.24 Fatty Arbuckle in a Sennett short.

HOLLYWOOD SCANDALS AND THE CREATION OF THE MPPDA

Since the earliest days of the nickelodeon, moralists and reformers had agitated against the corrupting nature of the movies and their effects upon American youth, much as similar groups are concerned about the effects of television in our own era. Powerful pressure groups, often working through religious organizations, had been formed to protect American audiences from the display of morally pernicious materials on the screen. Though differently motivated, the storm of well-organized protest which greeted *The Birth of a Nation* in 1915 and caused its suppression in twelve states is a good example of how effective such pressure groups could be. (And Griffith's response to the protest—outrage followed by an attempted vindication in the shape of *Intolerance*—is a good example of how American film-makers have characteristically reacted to such pressure.) All of this is to say that the American film industry has been threatened by the specter of external censorship since its very beginnings; and to describe the attitude of Hollywood towards its audiences as one of paranoia would not be at all extreme, especially considering that those audiences were overwhelmingly Christian and that the moguls of Hollywood were virtually all immigrant Jews. But World War I, the coming of Prohibition, and increasing middle-class patronage of the movies had alleviated some of this tension; and after the war, the content of American films became increasingly sophisticated and risqué, reflecting the "new morality" of the Jazz Era—a compound of materialism, cynicism, and sexual license. The sentimental conventions of Griffithian melodrama were abandoned by all but a few, as films suddenly began to depict and even glorify adultery, divorce, drinking, and drug-taking. Simultaneously, the Hollywood of Babylonian legend was born of the impossibly extravagant production budgets and star salaries which mushroomed in the late teens—the Hollywood of baronial mansions, orgiastic parties, sexual promiscuity, and multiple divorce which has fascinated the American tabloid press from that day to our own. For a while, the stars were worshiped by the public from afar as a kind of new American royalty, a race of beautiful demigods basking in the sun-drenched splendors of Beverly Hills. But it transpired that many of the stars were human after all, some quite scandalously so, and producers soon sought to play down the publicity given to their private lives, properly fearing a moralistic backlash against the amorality of their life-styles, which frequently involved the abuse of drugs, alcohol, and sex.

These fears were realized with a vengeance in September 1921, when Fatty Arbuckle was charged with the rape and murder of a young starlet named Virginia Rappe in the aftermath of a Labor Day weekend drinking party at a hotel suite in San Francisco. Arbuckle was indicted for manslaughter and stood trial three times before he was finally aquitted for lack of evidence in 1923. Miss Rappe had a history of peritonitis and had apparently died of a ruptured bladder aggravated by alcohol, but there were widespread allegations in the press that Arbuckle had raped her with a champagne bottle and crushed her beneath his great weight. Tabloids across the country portrayed him as a perverted beast, and the public outcry became so violent during this period that his pictures had to be withdrawn from circulation. To appease the moralists, Arbuckle was fired by Paramount and was permanently barred from working in the industry again, even after he was exonerated by the courts. But Hollywood had more to account for than Fatty's indiscretions. During Arbuckle's second trial in February 1922, the chief director of Famous Players–Lasky and current president of the Screen Directors Guild, William Desmond Taylor (1877–1922), was found murdered in his Beverly Hills apartment. It seems that he had been conducting simultaneous affairs with the actress Mary Miles Minter (b. 1902) and the popular Keystone comedienne Mabel Normand (1894–1930), who had been the last person to see him alive. Hungry for more scandal, the tabloid press implicated both women in the murder, though they were manifestly innocent, and destroyed their careers in the process. Within a year, Wallace Reid (1891–1923), a handsome actor who was a prototype of the clean-living American male, died of a drug overdose and was revealed to have been a long-term narcotics addict. These three scandals, as well as many smaller ones which were unearthed by the sensational press, produced a storm of public outrage against the depravity of Hollywood which was unprecedented in the film industry's brief history. Editorial denunciations by respectable publications like *Good Housekeeping* became commonplace; ministers and priests across the nation forbade their parishioners to go to the movies; women's clubs and reform groups demanded a mass boycott; and, by early 1922, thirty-six states and the federal government itself were considering the enactment of censorship laws. (U.S. courts did not rule that films were protected from censorship by the First Amendment until the late fifties.) The threat was rendered even more serious by a steep decline in film attendance in 1922, a result less of the scandals than of two new sources of competition for Americans' leisure time—the radio, which began commercial broadcasting in 1922, and the family automobile, which became available through installment credit loans at about the same time. In brief, 1922 was the dawning of the age of mass communications and mass consumption in America, and Hollywood, whose chief business was both, found itself in the embarrassing position of having deeply offended its audience.

Following the example of major-league baseball, which had recently whitewashed a national bribery scandal by appointing a conservative federal judge to oversee its operations, the frightened Hollywood producers formed a self-regulatory trade organization, the Motion Picture Producers and Distributors of America (MPPDA) in March 1922, amid much publicity, and hired President Warren G. Harding's postmaster general, Will Hays (1879–1954), for $150,000 a year to head it. Hays was an ultra-conservative Republican, Mason, Kiwanian, Rotarian, and Presbyterian elder from the state of Indiana, and his presence made the film industry's gesture of self-censorship convincing to the public and the government alike. In practice, the Hays Office, as the MPPDA* came to be called for the next twenty years, was a public relations and lobbying organization which engaged in little real censorship, although it did help producers to compile a blacklist of 117 stars who were banned from the industry because of unfavorable publicity about their personal lives. There was a gently chiding "Purity Code" known facetiously as the "Don'ts and Be Carefuls," and producers were required to submit summaries of their screenplays to the Hays Office for approval. But the only "censorship" consisted of informal advising according to the principle of "compensating values" whereby, to paraphrase Arthur Knight, vice could be flaunted for six reels so long as virtue triumphed in the seventh.[7] The main task of the Hays Office in the twenties was to stave off the threat of government censorship by mollifying pressure groups, managing news, deflecting scandal, and generally discouraging close scrutiny of the industry. In the early thirties, when sound helped to produce a new wave of excess in American films and touched off another round of national protest concerning the way in which the sounds of violence and vulgar language were exploited by early sound producers (see Chapter 8), the Hays Office became the medium for a very rigid form of censorship indeed, as administrator of the Draconian "Production Code." But in the twenties it merely provided whitewash for overly enthusiastic manifesta-

---

* Hays was succeeded as "movie tsar" by Eric A. Johnston (1896–1962) in 1945, when the organization's name was changed to the Motion Picture Association of America (MPAA). Johnston was ultimately replaced by Jack Valenti (b. 1921) in 1966, and the Production Code was scrapped in favor of a ratings system instituted in 1968 (see Chapter 12). Like Hays, both successors have had close ties with the White House.

tions of the "new morality" and helped producers subvert the careers of stars whose personal lives might make them too controversial. Today, it is clear that Hays himself was one of the more crooked members of the corrupt Harding administration, but he was an undeniably effective figurehead for the MPPDA who lent Hollywood a much-needed aura of respectability, sobriety, and moral rectitude at a time when its "sinfulness" had become a major national issue. (Hays was also an effective lobbyist for the industry in Washington, where he helped to minimize federal taxes and forestall anti-trust litigation.)*

CECIL B. DeMILLE

The most successful and flamboyant representative of the "new morality" in all of its manifestations was Cecil B. DeMille (1881–1959). A virtual incarnation of the values of Hollywood in the twenties, DeMille had an uncanny ability to anticipate the tastes of his audiences and give them what they wanted before they knew they wanted it. He began his career by directing *The Squaw Man* (1914), the first feature-length Western ever made in Hollywood, for Jesse Lasky's Feature Play Company. The film was a great popular and critical success, and DeMille followed it with a series of Western features (*The Virginian* [1914]; *Call of the North* [1914]) and stage adaptations (*Carmen* [1915]) that made him famous. Like Griffith, DeMille had been trained in the melodramatic theatrical tradition of David Belasco, and these early films were striking for their expressive chiaroscuro lighting effects (known as "Lasky lighting" at the time) and vivid *mise-en-scène*. During the war, DeMille made a group of stirringly patriotic films—*Joan the Woman* (1917); *The Little American* (1917); *Till I Come Back to You* (1918)—and then shifted gears to pursue the post-war obsession with extramarital sex among the leisure class. In a series of sophisticated comedies of manners aimed directly at Hollywood's new middle-class audience—*Old Wives for New* (1918), *Don't Change Your Husband* (1919), *Male and Female* (1919), *Why Change Your Wife?* (1920), *Forbidden Fruit* (1921), *The Affairs of Anatol* (1921), *Fool's Paradise* (1921), *Adam's Rib* (1922), and *Saturday Night* (1922)—DeMille made the bathtub a mystic shrine of beauty and the act of disrobing a fine art, as "modern" marriages collapsed under the pressure of luxuriant hedonism. These films did not simply embody the values of the "new morality"; they also legitimized them and made them fashionable.

When the Hays Office was established, DeMille embraced the "compensating values" formula and made it uniquely his own in *The Ten Commandments* (1924), a sex- and violence-drenched religious spectacle that made him internationally famous. Costing over 1.5 million dollars to produce, with Biblical sequences in two-color Technicolor (generally

6.25 "Rembrandt" or "Lasky" lighting in Cecil B. DeMille's *The Woman God Forgot* (1917).

6.26 *The Ten Commandments* (Cecil B. DeMille, 1923).

---

* See J. Douglas Gomery, "Hollywood, the National Recovery Administration, and the Question of Monopoly Power," *Journal of the University Film Association*, 31, 2 (Spring 1979), 47–52.

lost today—see Chapter 7), this film became one of the most profit-able motion pictures of the era, and it offers a good example of the way in which the Hays Office worked to permit the lurid depiction of "sin" so long as it was shown to be ultimately punished. This successful formula for religious spectacle became a DeMille trademark, and he used it time and again throughout his career—in *King of Kings* (1927), *The Sign of the Cross* (1932), *Samson and Delilah* (1949), and finally in his last film, *The Ten Commandments* (1956), a full-color widescreen remake of the prototype. But DeMille excelled at other forms of spectacle as well: his-torical (*Cleopatra* [1934]; *The Crusades* [1935]; *The Buccaneer* [1938]), Western (*The Plainsman* [1938]; *Union Pacific* [1939]), and circus (*The Greatest Show on Earth* [1952]). With the exception of a brief venture into independent production between 1925 and 1929, DeMille worked all of his life for some incarnation of Paramount—first the Lasky Feature Play Company, then Famous Players–Lasky, and finally Paramount it-self after 1930. A frequent collaborator was the scenarist Jesse Lasky, Jr. (b. 1908—*Union Pacific, Samson and Delilah*), son of the studio's co-founder, and in the sound era DeMille became closely identified with the Paramount "style" as described in the next chapter. A few of his films, such as *Male and Female* (1919) and *Union Pacific* (1939), are classics of their genres, but on the whole DeMille was a great showman, rather than a great director, who incarnated the values of Hollywood in the twenties throughout his career. He was extravagant, flamboyant, and vulgar, but he possessed a remarkable instinct for the dualistic sensibilities (some would simply say "hypocrisy") of his middle-class American audiences, who paid by the millions for over fifty years to sit through his kinetic spectacles of sex, torture, murder, and violence so long as some pious moral could be drawn from them at the end.

THE "CONTINENTAL TOUCH": LUBITSCH AND OTHERS

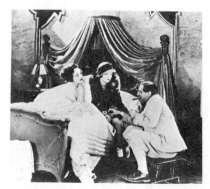

6.27 Ernst Lubitsch directing Marie Prevost and Charlotte Vidor in *The Marriage Circle* (1924).

Another director of sophisticated erotica during the twenties, but a film-maker of much greater taste and refinement than DeMille, was Ernst Lubitsch (1892–1947). Lubitsch, a German Jew, was the origina-tor of the lavish post-war *Kostümfilm* at UFA (see Chapter 4) and had come to Hollywood in late 1922 with the scenarist Hans Krähly (1885–1950) to direct Mary Pickford in *Rosita* (1923). Once there, he embarked upon a series of stylish sex comedies which made him famous for his subtle visual wit. In films like *The Marriage Circle* (1924), *Three Women* (1924), *Forbidden Paradise* (1924), *Kiss Me Again* (1925), *Lady Windermere's Fan* (1925), *So This Is Paris* (1926), and *The Stu-dent Prince* (1927), Lubitsch pioneered the functional use of decor to avoid titles and became a master of sexual innuendo. Soon all Hol-lywood spoke of the "Lubitsch touch"—the use of symbolic detail, such as a meaningful glance or gesture, or the closing of a bedroom door, to suggest sexual activity which could not have been depicted with impun-ity upon the screen. In sum, Lubitsch brought a touch of Continental elegance and irony to Hollywood in the twenties which was widely imitated by other directors. He went on to become an important innovator of the early sound film with *The Love Parade* (1929), *Monte Carlo* (1930), and *The Smiling Lieutenant* (1931), and by 1935 he had become production chief of Paramount. As a French critic of the day wrote of Lubitsch, "He set about bringing to the Americans the European comedy in all its charm, decadence, and frivolity."

There were other Europeans in Hollywood during the twenties, most of them Germans who had come to work for the American film industry as a result of the Parufamet Agreement of 1926. Between 1926 and 1927, Hollywood saw the arrival of the UFA directors F. W. Murnau (*Sunrise* [1927]; *Tabu* [1931]), Paul Leni (*The Cat and the Canary* [1927]), Lother Mendes (*A Night of Mystery* [1927]), Ludwig Berger (*The Sins of the Fathers* [1928]), Dmitri Buchowetski (*Crown of Lies* [1926]), Mihaly Kertesz (*Noah's Ark* [1928]), and Alexander Korda (*The Private Life of Helen of Troy* [1927]); the UFA cinematographers Karl Freund and Karl Struss; the UFA performers Emil Jannings, Conrad Veidt, Werner Krauss, Pola Negri, Greta Garbo, and Lya de Putti; and the UFA producer Erich Pommer and scenarist Carl Mayer. The Hungarian director Paul Fejos (b. Pál Fejös, 1898–1963) made *The Last Moment* (1927) and the experimentally naturalistic *Lonesome* (1928) for Universal before returning to Europe in 1930;* the French Jacques Feyder (1885–1948) directed some mediocre melodramas for MGM (*The Kiss* [1928]; *Daybreak* [1931]; *Song of India* [1931]); and the Dane Benjamin Christensen (1879–1959), famous for his Swedish film *Häxan* (*Witchcraft Through the Ages* [1922]), directed a fine series of horror films for MGM (*The Devil's Circus* [1926]; *Mockery* [1927]) and First National (*The Hawk's Nest* [1927]). The great Swedish directors Victor Sjöström and Mauritz Stiller (see note, p. 109) were both imported in the mid-twenties by MGM, where Sjöström—renamed Seastrom—produced three neglected masterpieces—*He Who Gets Slapped* (1924), *The Scarlet Letter* (1926), and *The Wind* (1928)—and Stiller was reduced to directing star vehicles, although his atmospheric *Hotel Imperial* (1926) remains a distinguished film. Sjöström returned to a life of semi-retirement in Sweden in 1928, and Stiller died in the same year, fatigued and disappointed by the Hollywood experience.

The fate of most foreign directors in Hollywood during the twenties was similar to that of the Swedes. The American industry had imported them to lend Continental elegance and class to the standard studio product, but it had in fact refused to let them tamper with the nature of the product itself; and so, bitterly disillusioned, most went home. Of the directors, only Lubitsch and the Hungarian-born Mihály Kertész (Michael Curtiz) stayed on to adapt themselves to the Hollywood production system. Murnau stayed too but was killed in an auto accident in 1930, before he had achieved his promise. Yet the European, and especially

6.28 *Sunrise* (F. W. Murnau, 1927).

---

*For more on Fejös and other European directors working in Hollywood during this period, see Graham Petrie, "Paul Fejos in America," *Film Quarterly*, 32, 2 (Winter 1978–79), 28–37; and "Fejos," *Sight and Sound*, 47, 3 (Summer 1978), 175–77.

the Germanic, presence in Hollywood during the twenties influenced the American cinema far more deeply than a purely descriptive account might suggest. The Germans taught American film-makers at first hand the Expressionistic use of lighting and camera that had helped to produce their native cinema's greatest works. The UFA cinematographers Freund and Struss made long, successful careers in Hollywood, and soon, in the early years of sound, they were joined by their distinguished countrymen Max Reinhardt, Fritz Lang, Max Ophüls, Detlef Sierck (Douglas Sirk), Kurt and Robert Siodmak, William Dieterle, Billy Wilder, Edgar G. Ulmer, Eugen Schüfftan (Eugene Schuftan), Hans (John) Brahm, Otto Preminger, and Fred Zinnemann, after the collapse of the Weimar Republic. All told, the Germanic influence upon Hollywood camera style, lighting, and decor was a permanent, if understated, one, and it contributed substantially to the visual texture of American cinema in the sound era before the advent of widescreen.

IN THE AMERICAN GRAIN

Despite the sophisticated cinema of the "new morality" and all of the European incursions discussed above, there was still a homegrown American tradition of sentimental melodrama and rural romance based upon the uncomplicated narrative montage of Griffith's pre-war films. Griffith had established this tradition in his Biograph shorts and continued it well into the twenties in features like *True Heart Susie* (1919), *A Romance of Happy Valley* (1919), *The Love Flower* (1920), *Way Down East* (1920), *The White Rose* (1923), and *Sally of the Sawdust* (1925). Other practitioners were Henry King (*The White Sister* [1923]; *Stella Dallas* [1925]; *The Winning of Barbara Worth* [1926]), whose narrative montage in *Tol'able David* (1921) was much admired and analyzed by V. I. Pudovkin; King Vidor (*The Jack-Knife Man* [1919]; *Happiness* [1923]; *The Big Parade* [1925]); William Wellman (*The Vagabond Trail* [1923]; *Beggars of Life* [1927]); Clarence Brown (*Smouldering Fires* [1924]; *The Goose Woman* [1925]); Rowland V. Lee (*Alice Adams* [1923]; *Doomsday* [1925]); Allan Dwan (*Robin Hood* [1922]; *The Iron Mask* [1927]); and Frank Borzage (*Humoresque* [1920]); *Seventh Heaven* [1927]).

Side by side with the Griffith tradition, which was extinguished by the coming of sound, there grew up two native genres—the Western and the action spectacle. The Western had been a major component of the American cinema since Edwin S. Porter's *The Great Train Robbery* in 1903, and Thomas Ince had become a master of the tough, realistic Western as exemplified in the films of William S. Hart in the teens (*Hell's Hinges* [Ince, 1916]; *The Aryan* [Ince, 1916]; *The Narrow Trail* [Lambert Hillyer, 1917]. But it wasn't until the twenties that the Western came into its own as a unique feature genre; as David Robinson suggests, this may well have been a function of collective public nostalgia for the lost frontier.[8] When Porter made the first Western in 1903, the American West was still an authentic borderland between civilization and the wilderness. By the mid-twenties, America had become an urbanized, industrialized mass society predicated upon mass consumption, mass communications, and rapid transit; and the Edenic potential of the frontier had been permanently circumscribed by a mushrooming corporate economy. So it was during the twenties that the classical form of the Western genre was codified and given its first epic expression in films like King Baggott's *Tumbleweeds* (1925), James Cruze's *The Covered Wagon* and *The Pony Express* (1925), and John Ford's *The Iron Horse* (1924).

The adventure spectacle was largely the province of a single performer, Douglas Fairbanks (1883–1939), whose star personality so influenced the character of his films that he deserves to be called an *auteur*. Fairbanks began his career at Griffith's Triangle Company, where he starred in comedies like *Manhattan Madness* (Allan Dwan, 1916), *Reaching for the Moon* (John Emerson, 1917), and *The Mollycoddle* (Victor Fleming, 1920), which debunked contemporary manners and parodied current film genres and fads. In these films, most of them written by Anita Loos (b. 1893), Fairbanks played an all-American boy—boisterous, optimistic, and athletic—who detested weakness, insincerity, and social regimentation in any form. After Fairbanks became a super-star and formed United Artists with Griffith, Chaplin, and Mary Pickford (his wife from 1919 to 1929), he cast himself as the protagonist in a series of lavish costume-adventure spectacles, including *The Mark of Zorro* (Fred Niblo, 1920), *The Three Musketeers* (Fred Niblo, 1921), *Robin Hood* (Allan Dwan, 1922), *The Thief of Bagdad* (Raoul Walsh, 1924), *Don Q, Son of Zorro* (Donald Crisp, 1925), *The Black Pirate* (Albert Parker, 1926), *The Gaucho* (F. Richard Jones, 1927), and *The Iron Mask* (Allan Dwan, 1929). In these extravagant serio-comic "swashbucklers," the very first of their kind, Fairbanks displayed the full gamut of his energetic athleticism to contemporary audiences, thrilling them with a nearly continuous succession of breathtaking stunts. Fairbanks' physical agility was his major virtue as a performer, and he was forced into retirement in 1934 under the twin pressures of sound and advancing age. But during his meteoric ascent to stardom he had initiated a perennially popular genre (witness the success of Richard Lester's *The Three Musketeers* [1974], *The Four Musketeers* [1975], *Royal Flash* [1975], and *Robin and Marion* [1976]; John Milius' *The Wind and the Lion* [1975]; and John Huston's *The Man Who Would Be King* [1976]; see Chapter 17), and he incarnated for millions of Americans Hollywood's obsession with physical culture and glamor.

A third genre, which might be called the "narrative documentary," was founded in the twenties by the American explorer and amateur cameraman Robert Flaherty (1884–1951). Flaherty was originally a mineralogist in the Canadian Arctic who had surveyed the Belcher Islands in 1917 and became interested in the harsh lives of the Eskimos who populated them. In 1920, sponsored by the Revillon Fur Company, Flaherty returned to the islands to live with an Eskimo family and make a film about the daily lives of its members. After fifteen months he returned to the United States with the footage and edited it into the fifty-minute feature documentary *Nanook of the North* (1922), which was distributed internationally by Pathé with great commercial and critical success.

6.29   *The Iron Horse* (John Ford, 1924).

6.30   *The Thief of Bagdad* (Raoul Walsh, 1924), produced and written by Douglas Fairbanks for United Artists.

6.31 *Nanook of the North* (Robert Flaherty, 1922).

6.32 *Moana* (Robert Flaherty, 1925).

One source of *Nanook*'s popularity was its exoticism: it represented the first sustained encounter between the civilized world and the Eskimo, outside of professional ethnographic circles. But *Nanook* was also unique in using the editing syntax of narrative film to portray a documentary reality. Flaherty had shot close-ups, reverse angles, tilts, and pans on location to be intercut later with the rest of his footage, and he had assumed a third-person point of view toward his subject throughout the film. He had also directed the Eskimos in enacting or re-enacting certain scenes before the camera to accord with a loosely constructed story line which was true to the spirit if not the letter of their lives

The American industry was so impressed with *Nanook*'s audience appeal that Jesse L. Lasky of Paramount commissioned Flaherty to make another such film anywhere in the world on a subject of his choice. The result was *Moana* (1926), an idyllic documentary of life on the South Seas island of Samoa, which Herman G. Weinberg described in a contemporary review as an "intensely lyrical poem on the theme of the last paradise." Once again, Flaherty had edited his film as a narrative and had reconstructed reality instead of simply recording it. The film was attacked by anthropologists as poetic fantasy (which it was) rather than an accurate representation of Samoan life, and it was acclaimed by critics on precisely the same grounds.* But audiences stayed away this time, despite Paramount's crude attempt to bill the film as "The Love Life of a South Sea Siren." Flaherty was next commissioned by MGM to collaborate with W. S. Van Dyke (1889–1943) on the production of *White Shadows in the South Seas* (1929), a dramatic feature to be shot on location in Tahiti, but he quit the project in revulsion at its commercialism. A subsequent collaboration with F. W. Murnau on the independently pro-

---

* It was in an anonymous review of *Moana,* later discovered to have been written by the British documentarist John Grierson, that the term "documentary" was first coined to describe formally structured non-fiction films like Flaherty's. The term derives from the French *documentaire,* meaning an educational travel film.

duced *Tabu* (1931), a narrative about the lives of Tahitian pearl-divers, proved more successful, but Flaherty became disillusioned with Murnau's melodramatic approach to the material and withdrew from the film after supervising its photography. At this point in his career, thoroughly disgusted with the Hollywood studio system, Flaherty emigrated to England, where he exercised a decisive influence upon John Grierson and the British social documentary movement of the thirties, contributing both *Industrial Britain* (1932, edited by Grierson) and the lyrical *Man of Aran* (1934).* Flaherty was far too personal and individual an artist to ever work again in Hollywood, but he did return to the United States in later life to make two more powerful films for non-theatrical release— *The Land* (1942), produced for the U.S. Information Service under the auspices of another documentarist, Pare Lorentz (b. 1905), and *Louisiana Story* (1948), produced for Standard Oil—both among the finest achievements in documentary narrative.

6.33 The Hollywood boom: the castle set for Douglas Fairbanks' extravagant 1922 production of *Robin Hood* (directed by Allan Dwan), made six years after Griffith's *Intolerance*, at twice the cost.

Despite the presence of so much individual talent in Hollywood in the twenties, most American films were produced according to formula. Soaring production costs throughout the decade forced the studios toward a rigid standardization of product. Whereas Griffith had spent just over $100,000 to produce *The Birth of a Nation* in 1914, MGM spent more than $4.5 million to produce *Ben Hur* (Fred Niblo, 1925) only ten years later. In fact, Benjamin Hampton estimates that there was a 1,500 percent across-the-board increase in the cost of feature production during this period, which meant that the pressure to make films according to tried-and-true formulas was extreme.[9] Experimenting with public taste (never very advanced) for the sake of art could result in a crippling capital loss, and it was during the twenties that "Play It Safe" became the enduring First Commandment and Golden Rule of the American film industry. Consequently, of the more than five thousand American features produced between 1920 and 1929, only a handful made contributions either to the "literature" of world cinema or to the evolution of narrative form; and most of these, as we have seen, were in the realm of slapstick comedy. But there was a towering exception to this general law in the work of a single man—the enigmatic, distasteful, and finally tragic figure of Erich von Stroheim (1885–1957).

6.34 The interior of the castle set.

ERICH VON STROHEIM

Von Stroheim was born Erich Oswald Stroheim in Vienna, the son of a Jewish merchant from Silesia, and emigrated to the United States at some time between 1906 and 1909. Little is known of his early life here, but he eventually came to Hollywood, where he affixed the "von" to his surname and propagated the myth that he was descended from the Austrian aristocracy and had been a cavalry officer in his youth. As Erich von

---

* The subject of *Aran* (1979), a documentary about Flaherty's film and the "myth of Aran" by the French film-maker Georges Combe.

6.35 Erich von Stroheim as "The Man You Love to Hate" in Griffith's *Hearts of the World* (1918).

Stroheim, he first went to work as an extra and established himself as a regular member of the Griffith acting company after a brief appearance in *The Birth of a Nation* (1915) in blackface. He subsequently became an assistant to Griffith on *Intolerance* (1916) and, between 1915 and 1917, to Triangle Company directors John Emerson (1878–1946), Allen Dwan (b. 1885), and George Fitzmaurice (1885–1941). In 1917, von Stroheim served as assistant director and military advisor on Griffith's World War One epic, *Hearts of the World,* in which he also played his first feature role as a brutal Prussian officer—the kind of role that later made him famous to American audiences as "The Man You Love to Hate."*

Von Stroheim was given his first chance to direct by Carl Laemmle of Universal Pictures, who permitted him to adapt his original screenplay, *The Pinnacle,* as *Blind Husbands* in 1918. The film concerns the seduction of a naïve American wife by a cynical Prussian officer (played by von Stroheim) at a resort in the Austrian Alps, and it was among the very first American post-war films to deal with sex in a sophisticated way. Despite its rather conventional melodramatic plot, *Blind Husbands* is full of subtle psychological insights and visual wit, and it was a tremendous popular success. Von Stroheim's next two films repeated the pattern of *Blind Husbands* with something like obsessiveness: each concerns a sexual triangle in which an American wife in Europe is seduced by an army officer, and each is rendered with unsparing documentary and psychological realism. Moreover, the three films among them brought together the production team with which von Stroheim was to work for the duration of his career—the cameraman Ben Reynolds, and the performers Gibson Gowland, Sam de Grasse, May Busch, and Maude George. There are no surviving prints of *The Devil's Passkey,* which was made for Universal in 1919, but it ran to the amazing length of twelve full reels (over two hours) and forecast von Stroheim's desire to expand the narrative cinema to a form commensurate with that of the great realistic novels of the nineteenth century. It was also the last film that the director was ever permitted to finish as he had planned.

To complete his trilogy of adultery (although, according to the formula of the day, the act of adultery itself was never shown to be consummated), von Stroheim made *Foolish Wives* (1922), which most critics consider to be his first great film. This sordid and satiric tale of a lecherous Russian "count" (von Stroheim) who makes his living on the Riviera by bilking rich American tourists was budgeted by Laemmle at over a million dollars. To augment its realism, von Stroheim constructed an elaborate full-scale reproduction of the main square of Monte Carlo on the Universal backlot, with hotels, cafés, and casinos represented in minute detail. In its original form, the film ran twenty-one reels (approximately 315 minutes), and von Stroheim planned to release it in two parts. But the Universal production manager, Irving Thalberg (1899–1936), ordered it cut to fourteen reels (210 minutes) and changed many of its

---

* The title of a feature-length documentary on von Stroheim's life and work, directed by Patrick Montgomery and written by Richard Koszarski, is *The Man You Loved to Hate* (1979).

6.36   The casino, the hotel, and the Café de Paris in Monte Carlo reconstructed to scale on the Universal backlot in the San Fernando Valley for *Foolish Wives* (Erich von Stroheim, 1922).

titles to read less candidly than its director intended. Even in its mutilated version,* *Foolish Wives* remains a brilliant, brutal film, full of studied vignettes of post-war European decadence and rich psychological characterization. *Foolish Wives* was an international popular and critical success, but, given its huge budget, the film just barely broke even. Von Stroheim's last film for the studio was *Merry-Go-Round* (1922), the beginning of another erotic trilogy, set this time in pre-war Austria during the decline of the Hapsburg Empire. Midway through the shooting, Thalberg removed the director from the film because of his lavish and expensive attention to detail (including the construction of a full-scale model of the Prater, Vienna's mammoth amusement park) and replaced him with Rupert Julian (1889–1943), terminating von Stroheim's association with Universal. But on the basis of his first three films von Stroheim had become a star in his own right, as both an actor and a director, and so in 1923 he was able to persuade the Goldwyn studios to back him in the realization of a long-cherished project—an adaptation of Frank Norris' naturalistic American novel *McTeague* (1899).

Norris' novel, like Zola's *L'assommoir* (1877), was a model of the nineteenth-century naturalist convention by which some hereditary flaw or character trait brings its protagonists to ruin through a steady process of degeneration. In *McTeague,* the title character is a young man with a family heritage of brutality who sets up as a dentist in San Francisco and eventually marries Trina Sieppe, the daughter of lower-middle-class

---

* The film survives today only in eight-reel (Museum of Modern Art) and eleven-reel (American Film Institute) versions, although von Stroheim had originally shot at least thirty-two.

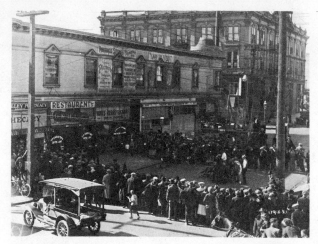

6.37 Von Stroheim and crew shooting *Greed* (1924) on location in the streets of San Francisco, 1923.

6.38 *Greed:* Prologue, 1908. McTeague (Gibson Gowland) as a car-boy in the Big Dipper gold mine in the California mountains. Note the composition-in-depth.

6.39 Ten years later: McTeague with a patient in his "dental parlours" on Polk Street, San Francisco (seen through the bay windows, below).

6.40 Von Stroheim directing Cesare Gravina and Dale Fuller as Zerkow the junkman and Maria Macapa the scrub-lady in a bizarre sub-plot cut entirely from the released version of *Greed.* Their story echoed that of McTeague's degenerate parents (also cut) and foreshadowed McTeague and Trina's decline.

German immigrants. Trina wins five thousand dollars in a lottery and becomes a monster of avarice in her attempts to retain the entire sum without spending a penny. McTeague loses his job through trusting a rival, and the couple sinks lower and lower in the socio-economic scale until they are reduced to a state of total degradation. McTeague begins to drink; finally, his hereditary brutishness asserts itself and he murders Trina for her gold. The novel ends in Death Valley, where the fugitive McTeague encounters his rival Marcus and beats him to death with a pistol butt. But McTeague too is doomed, for in the process of his struggle

6.41 Zerkow and Maria set out in the junk-wagon to bury their dead child. Like the deranged McTeague, Zerkow will later murder his wife because of his lust for gold. Note the density and depth of the frame.

6.42 Saturday dinner at the Sieppes' (cut from the released version). Far right: McTeague's friend Marcus Schouler (Jean Hersholt) and Marcus' cousin, Trina Sieppe (Zasu Pitts), with whom McTeague will soon become infatuated.

6.43 After he has repaired her broken tooth in his "parlours," McTeague pays court to Trina and visits the Sieppe house with Marcus.

with Marcus he has become handcuffed to the corpse. This grim tale was unlikely raw material for Hollywood commercial entertainment, but it was von Stroheim's intention to translate the novel, sentence-by-sentence, into cinematic terms and to render its naturalism photographically meaningful.

The film was shot entirely on location in the streets and rooming-houses of San Francisco, in Death Valley, and in the California hills, on the basis of von Stroheim's own script. The process took nine months and cost over half a million dollars. After von Stroheim had personally edited the film in early 1924, he presented Goldwyn with a forty-two-reel epic running over ten hours. He was asked to reduce it to a reasonable length for commercial distribution in two parts. This five-hour version was still too

6.44 McTeague contemplates a gigantic golden molar, a birth-day gift from Trina, meant to hang in his window to advertise his trade. Like other objects and/or symbols of gold in the film, it was hand-tinted gold-yellow in the original release print to emphasize the obsessive nature of greed.

6.45 Meticulous *mise-en-scène:* McTeague and Trina's wedding feast, an orgy of feeding.

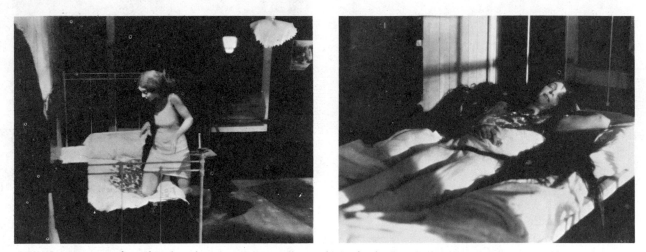

6.46 A sequence cut from the released version: Trina madly worshiping her lottery winnings, converted now to gold coin.

long for Goldwyn, so with the collaboration of his friend, the Metro director Rex Ingram (1892–1950), von Stroheim further reduced the print to eighteen reels, or approximately four hours, which both men considered the absolute minimum to which the film could be cut without destroying its continuity. In the meantime, Goldwyn Pictures had merged with Metro Pictures and Louis B. Mayer Productions to become MGM, and Mayer replaced Goldwyn as executive in charge of production. Among Mayer's first acts as studio chief was to turn von Stroheim's epic over to his new assistant and the director's old adversary, Irving Thalberg, for further editing. The film was eventually cut to ten reels by an MGM story editor, June Mathis, who had read neither the novel nor the

6.47 Von Stroheim, with the cinematographer Ben Reynolds, directing the final scenes of *Greed* in Death Valley during the summer of 1923. The other cameramen on the film were William H. Daniels and Ernest B. Schoedsack.

6.48 Marcus alone in the desert, in desperate pursuit of McTeague.

6.49 From the final frames of *Greed:* McTeague bludgeons Marcus with his revolver, sealing his destiny—to die like a beast in the wild.

shooting script, and the excised footage was destroyed. Retitled *Greed* (1924), this mutilated version of the film was the only one ever publicly seen, and it opened to great critical acclaim, despite its incoherence.*

At one-fourth of its original length, *Greed* is a fragmentary masterpiece with vast gaps in continuity bridged by lengthy titles, but it is a masterpiece nonetheless. Because von Stroheim was an original master of the long take and built up his most powerful effects *within* shots rather than editing between them, many of the film's greatest sequences have

---

* In 1971, von Stroheim's close friend, the film critic Herman G. Weinberg, published *"Greed": A Reconstruction of the Complete Erich von Stroheim Film from Stills,* using 348 still photographs left to him by the director, together with 52 production stills. Weinberg has performed the same valuable service for *The Wedding March* (1974) and the other films in the von Stroheim canon (1975).

survived intact. Even as it stands, *Greed* is overwhelming in its psychological intensity, for von Stroheim used strikingly clear deep-focus photography and a documentary-like *mise-en-scène* to totally immerse us in the reality of the film. His camera moves very little, and, in a manner forecasting the work of Michelangelo Antonioni (see Chapter 14), the narrative proceeds through a gradual accretion of detail in which the time and space of the characters in the film become our own. Palpably real photographic objects—a caged canary, a funeral cortège, a huge gold tooth, cuts of meat—acquire symbolic value through composition-in-depth rather than expressive montage or the Griffithian intercut close-up. Finally, despite *Greed*'s structural disunity and its unpleasant subject matter, the atmospheric density of the film holds us from beginning to end. *Greed* is not a "realistic" film, as, for example, G. W. Pabst's *Die freudlose gasse* (1925) strives to be, but rather a "naturalistic" one in the literary sense of the term. In its uncompromising depiction of degradation and despair, it raises reality to the level of symbol and asks profound questions about the nature of human experience.

Von Stroheim, who had mortgaged his home and his car to support himself during the editing of *Greed* (he was paid only for direction), disowned the film and refused to see it after it was released.* Incredibly, he was hired back by MGM in 1925 and given a free hand in adapting the Franz Lehar operetta *The Merry Widow* (1925), although he was forced to use the stars John Gilbert and Mae Murray against his will. By reducing the operetta to less than one-half of the film's running time and adding his own material, von Stroheim was able to turn this purely commercial venture into the second film in his darkly satiric trilogy on the corruption of the Viennese aristocracy. Although technically set in an imaginary Ruritanian kingdom named Monteblanco, *The Merry Widow* clearly reflects the decadence of the Hapsburg Empire at the turn of the century and reveals the rottenness and perversion concealed beneath its elegant façade. The studio deleted a few scenes from the release print due to their explicit sexual content, but *The Merry Widow* came closer to realizing its director's intentions than any film he had made since *The Devil's Passkey* in 1919. It was an international success, both critically and commercially, and it made a fortune for MGM.

At this point in his career, von Stroheim left MGM for good to make a film of his choice for Pat Powers' independent Celebrity Pictures. The result was *The Wedding March* (1928), von Stroheim's last great film and the concluding section of his trilogy on the decadence of Imperial Austria. It tells the bitterly sardonic tale of a forced marriage between an impoverished Viennese nobleman (von Stroheim) and the crippled daughter of a wealthy industrialist; and it is among the most visually extravagant films ever made. *The Wedding March* was also to have finally realized von Stroheim's perennial desire to make a long film in two parts, whose

---

* Von Stroheim finally saw what was left of his epic in 1950, at the instigation of Henri Langlois of the Cinémathèque Française. Immediately afterwards he commented: "This was like an exhumation for me. In a tiny coffin I found a lot of dust, a terrible smell, a little backbone and shoulder-bone."

6.50 Ruritanian decadence: Crown Prince Mirko of Monte-blanco (John Gilbert) and his party prepare for an evening of mirth in *The Merry Widow* (Erich von Stroheim, 1925).

6.51 The wedding in *The Wedding March* (1928): Erich von Stroheim, Zasu Pitts.

form would approximate that of the great nineteenth-century novels. *Part I* was completed as von Stroheim had intended, but midway through the filming of *Part II* he was removed from the project by Paramount, to whom Powers had been forced to sell his option when von Stroheim over-ran his original budget of $750,000 by $400,000. Paramount turned the footage over to Josef von Sternberg (see Chapter 8) to edit into a single film. Between them, von Stroheim and von Sternberg were able to put together a version of *The Wedding March* for release in 1928 which corresponded roughly to the original *Part I* and concluded with the wedding of the protagonists in St. Stephen's Cathedral. Paramount editors then combined footage from *Parts I* and *II* into a hodgepodge entitled *The Honeymoon* which was released in Europe in 1929 and subsequently disowned by von Stroheim. Just before his death in 1957, the director recut both parts of the film to conform more closely to his original intention, and there is now preserved in the archives of the Cinémathèque Française an authoritative reconstruction of this most lavish and erotic masterpiece of *mise-en-scène*.

After the *Wedding March* debacle, as after *Greed,* von Stroheim's reputation among Hollywood producers was not good, but his singular talent was indisputable. In 1928, he was commissioned by Joseph Kennedy (an independent producer and father of the future president) to write and direct a star vehicle for Gloria Swanson (b. 1897) for release through United Artists. The script, which was approved by the Hays Office, can only be described as bizarre. An Imperial German prince, betrothed to the queen of a small Bavarian state, falls in love with a young commoner named Kitty Kelly (Swanson). She is subsequently shipped off to German East Africa, where her guardian aunt runs a bordello and where she is forced to marry a rich old degenerate. In the meantime, the prince follows her to Africa, the queen is assassinated at home, and the husband dies. Recalled to ascend the throne, the prince returns to Germany and marries Kitty, who becomes "Queen Kelly," institutionalizing

6.52 "Queen Kelly" imprisoned in an African brothel.

the regal spirit she has carried within her all along. Von Stroheim had shot more than half of this fantastic film, including some harrowing African sequences, when production was halted in January 1929. Like *The Wedding March, Queen Kelly* had been conceived as a silent film with a synchronized orchestral score, but during production it became clear to both Swanson and Kennedy that the "talkies" were the new way to fame and fortune in the American cinema, and so they simply abandoned the project as a bad investment, leaving von Stroheim in the lurch. Worse, the footage he had already shot* was crudely padded with out-takes, given a tacked-on ending (directed by Irving Thalberg!), and released by United Artists as an "original von Stroheim" in Europe and South America in the early thirties. Like the mutilated *Greed* and *The Honeymoon,* this remnant was disowned by von Stroheim.

The cancellation of *Queen Kelly* was a professional disaster for von Stroheim. It seemed to confirm his vastly inflated reputation for excess and perversity in the eyes of all Hollywood, and the conversion to sound became a pretext on the part of his many enemies for squeezing him out of the industry. After an abortive attempt to remake *Blind Husbands* for Universal in sound and color, he was reduced to writing screenplays (*The Tempest* [1927]; *East of the Setting Sun* [1929]) and acting in other people's films (*The Great Gabbo* [James Cruze, 1929]; *Three Faces East* [Roy del Ruth, 1930]; *As You Desire Me* [George Fitzmaurice, 1932]) to make a living. Von Stroheim was given his last chance to direct by Winfield Sheehan, a producer for the Fox Film Corporation, who signed him to adapt the Dawn Powell play *Walking Down Broadway* in early 1932. Though this popular story of two girls rooming together in contemporary New York City was conceived as a modest program picture† by Fox, von Stroheim lavished infinite care upon its visual texture, working in close collaboration with the cinematographer James Wong Howe (b. 1899). *Walking Down Broadway* was completed in an exemplary manner, under budget and under schedule, in October 1932, and in the process it seems to have become a study of morbid psychology with crypto-lesbian undertones. When Fox vice president Sol Wurtzel saw the film, he was outraged and halted its release. Von Stroheim was fired, the script rewritten, and the film turned over to Alan Crosland (1894–1936) and other directors to be reshot. The revised version, containing about one-half of the original, was released in March 1933 as *Hello, Sister!* without von Stroheim's name appearing on the credits. Fired by Universal, MGM, Paramount, United Artists, and Fox in turn, von Stroheim's reputation as a film-maker was completely destroyed, and he was never permitted to direct again. He worked for a while as a dialogue writer at MGM before turning his career completely to acting. Between 1934 and 1955, von Stroheim appeared in some fifty-two films for other directors

---

* Von Stroheim had shot ten reels of a projected thirty when the film was canceled. Eight reels of this footage constituted the prologue, set in pre–World War I Bavaria; the other two contained scenes set in Dar-es-Salaam, East Africa. Miss Swanson used only the prologue in her "released version."

† A cheaply produced second feature—the bottom half of a double bill (also called a "B-film").

and gave many distinguished performances (for instance, in Jean Renoir's *La grande illusion* [1937] and Billy Wilder's *Sunset Boulevard* [1950]). He made a fair living at this profession, and he was still a celebrity when he died in France in 1957.

Simultaneously a romanticist, a determinist, and a cynic, Erich von Stroheim was Hollywood's last great independent director and its last great personal *auteur*. For most of his films he was his own scenarist, art director, costume designer, editor, assistant cameraman, and star. His obsessive realism became a Hollywood legend, and yet realism for von Stroheim was always a means toward the end of symbolic naturalism—a mode practiced by late-nineteenth-century novelists like Zola, Maupassant, Crane, and Norris, in which the accumulation of surface detail ultimately leads us beneath the surface of things to some deeper human meaning. To this end as well, von Stroheim rejected Griffithian montage in favor of the long take, or sequence shot, composed in depth from a relatively static camera—shots which have the naturalistic effect of linking characters with their environment. In his classic essay "The Evolution of the Language of the Cinema," André Bazin has described von Stroheim as "the creator of the virtually continuous cinematic story, tending to the permanent integration of the whole space. . . . He has one simple rule for direction. Take a close look at the world, keep doing so, and in the end it will lay bare for you all its cruelty and its ugliness."[10] But if von Stroheim was a naturalist, he was also, often simultaneously, an ironic fantasist. His fascination with sexual perversion is a case in point. He did not use it to titillate, as DeMille might have done, or even to display his worldliness, as might have been expected of Lubitsch. Like Luis Buñuel after him (see Chapter 14), von Stroheim used sexual pathology as a metaphor for a more pervasive cultural decadence which was his major philosophical concern. The corruption of the European aristocracy, the corruptibility of the American bourgeoisie, and the degradation of the masses are the recurrent themes of von Stroheim's major work. They bespeak a profound cultural pessimism born of late-nineteenth-century Europe—the bitter dregs of a failed idealism—which is balanced in the films themselves by an obvious sympathy for the individual humans caught up in the self-destructive impulses of the race.

"Self-destructive" is an adjective which many persons have applied to von Stroheim himself, and it is true that he was in some sense a victim of his own temperament and his own myth. But he was also a casualty of Hollywood's transformation from a speculative entrepreneurial enterprise into a vertically and horizontally integrated big business, and his beleaguered career as a director from 1918 to 1932 is a virtual paradigm of that transformation. What happened to von Stroheim in Hollywood during the twenties was the same thing that happened to Griffith, Chaplin, and Keaton, those three other great independent producer-directors of the American silent film. When von Stroheim and Griffith first began to make feature films in Southern California in the teens, there was no established procedure for producing them since they were an unprecedented commodity. As things evolved at the time, some individual or group of individuals with investment capital—a Harry Aitken or a

Carl Laemmle, for example—would provide the financial backing, and Griffith and von Stroheim would "produce" their own films in the most literal sense of the term. Script-writing, casting, locations, set design, art direction, and the general logistics of shooting the film, in addition to the shooting and editing itself, were all directorial responsibilities; and this assured a high degree of personal artistic freedom for the individual director. As American film production grew into what its promoters claimed to be the nation's fourth largest industry* between 1919 and 1927, this system of independent production yielded first to the privately owned studio (Triangle Films, Keaton Productions, Chaplin Productions) and finally to the monopolistic industrial combines of Paramount, Fox, First National, and MGM. By 1927, the studio film-making process had been standardized under the supervisory production system pioneered by Thomas Ince and Mack Sennett a decade before, and there was little place within the system for such an individual and eccentric talent as a von Stroheim or a Keaton or a Griffith.

The coming of sound was to clinch the matter. The studios had to borrow huge sums of money to pay for the conversion on the very eve of the Great Depression, which spurred them to increase the efficiency of their production process by totally effacing the concept of the personal director and replacing it with the concept of the executive producer, modeled on MGM's Irving Thalberg, the man who had done such injury to *The Wedding March* and *Greed*. Thus, the coming of sound meant a great deal more for the American cinema than the transformation of those dreamlike, hallucinatory demigods of the silent screen into mere mortals with accents, drawls, and lisps—more even than the regressive inertia temporarily caused by the early technology of recording sound. It meant the transformation of a wildcat business run largely by film-makers fascinated with the process of film itself into a large-scale technological industry controlled by corporate managers who exercised supreme authority over all artistic variables in order to maximize profits. Like so many other aspects of modern American life—including mass communications, mass consumption, and rapid transit—gigantic corporate capitalism was born of the twenties. That decade was the only time in the history of American film that so much talent has ever been allowed to display itself so extravagantly and magnificently, and then has been so ruthlessly destroyed.

---

* This "fourth largest industry" claim, long accepted as gospel by film historians (and, apparently, for at least a decade by the U.S. Chamber of Commerce), has recently been challenged by J. Douglas Gomery. In "Hollywood, the National Recovery Administration, and the Question of Monopoly Power" (*Journal of the University Film Association,* 31, 2 [Spring 1979], 49), he maintains that on the basis of total sales for 1933, the industry ranked somewhere between the thirty-seventh and forty-fifth, so that it could hardly have been the fourth largest a decade before. Gomery believes that the industry began circulating this specious claim to power during the twenties as a form of self-advertisement and, perhaps, intimidation of government regulatory agencies. This may be so, but in terms of its *social* as opposed to its economic influence—in terms of the sheer number of persons deeply and permanently affected by its values—the American film industry was surely among the most powerful since the Industrial Revolution. Only radio and television would exceed its power as a medium of mass persuasion and social control.

The Coming of Sound, 1926–1932

SOUND-ON-DISK

The development of sound recording systems for films runs parallel to the evolution of the cinema itself. In fact, the idea of combining motion pictures with some type of synchronized sound had been present since their inception. Thomas Edison originally commissioned the invention of the Kinetograph with the notion of providing a visual accompaniment for his phonograph, and W. K. L. Dickson had actually achieved a rough synchronization of the two machines as early as 1889. Many other inventors, such as Georges Demeny and Auguste Baron in France, and William Friese-Greene in England, experimented with devices for coupling sound and image before the turn of the century. At the Paris World Exposition of 1900 three separate systems which synchronized phonograph recordings with projected film strips were exhibited: the Phonorama of L. A. Berthon, C. F. Dussaud, and G. F. Jaubert; Léon Gaumont's Chronophone; and the Phono-Cinéma-Théâtre of Clément-Maurice Gratioulet and Henri Lioret, which offered minute-long performances by great stars of the theater, opera, and ballet. In Germany, Oskar Messter began to produce short synchronized sound films as novelty items in 1903, and by 1908 he was supplying exhibitors with recorded musical scores for nearly all of his productions. In Britain, Gaumont's Chronophone proved popular, as did Cecil Hepworth's system, Vivaphone; and in the United States the Edison Corporation achieved some popular success with two phono-film systems—Cinephonograph and Kinetophone.

All of these early systems relied on the phonograph to reproduce the sound component of the filmed performance. The earliest ones used wax cylinders and the later ones disks, but all had three difficulties in common: the problem of synchronizing the sound recording with the filmed event, of amplifying the sound for presentation to a large audience, and of the brevity of the cylinder and disk formats in relation to the standard length of motion pictures. The first problem was partially solved by a number of regulatory devices which were intended to insure an exact correspondence of sound and image but were usually imperfect in operation. If the phonograph stylus skipped a groove in performance, for example, or if the film strip broke in the projector, regaining synchronization was nearly impossible. The problem of amplification was generally dealt with by concealing a battery of single-horn speakers behind the screen, although experiments with compressed-air speakers of the sort used today began around 1910. The third problem was the most difficult. By 1905, the length of the standard narrative film had far exceeded the four-minute playing time of the phonograph cylinder and the five-minute time of the twelve-inch disk. The introduction of automatic changers and multiple phonographs did not resolve the difficulty, since changing records frequently caused a loss of synchronization, and the use of oversized disks only resulted in poor sound quality. In the years before the First World War, as the standard length of films grew even longer and their inter-frame structure more complex, experimental interest in the imperfect phono-film sound systems died out. They remained extant through the war mainly as a means of making short novelty films in single takes.

But the imperfection of the phono-film systems did not leave the motion pictures soundless. In fact, the "silent" cinema was rarely that. Sound effects provided by individual performers or by sound-effect machines like the Allefex and Kinematophone were a standard feature of films after 1908, and live music had been a part of the cinema since its beginnings. A pianist had accompanied the first commercial motion picture exhibition, the Lumière Cinématographe program at the Grand Café, Paris, December 28, 1895, and Méliès personally provided piano accompaniment for the Paris debut of *Le voyage dans la lune* in 1902. Pianists were employed in most storefront theaters and nickelodeons in the first decade of this century to improvise music to fit the scenes. As the standard film length increased from one reel (about one thousand feet, or fifteen minutes) to six-to-ten reels ((ninety to 150 minutes) between 1905 and 1914, film narratives grew increasingly sophisticated; and, according to Harry M. Geduld, the practice of musicians playing intermittently during film programs gave way to continuous musical accompaniment in which the nature of each scene determined the kind of music played with it.[1]

During this period, the nickelodeons and storefronts began to be replaced by "dream palaces" that could seat thousands of movie-goers and accomodate hundred-piece orchestras, or, at the very least, a mighty Wurlitzer organ that could produce a wide range of orchestral effects. By the time the feature film had become the dominant cinematic form in the West, many producers were commissioning original scores for their class-A productions;* and during the twenties all features, regardless of quality, were accompanied by cue sheets suggesting appropriate musical selections to be played at designated points in the film. The first original piece of film music was composed in 1907 by Camille Saint-Saëns for the Film d'Art Company's *L'assassinat du Duc de Guise* (1908). Other memorable and distinguished scores of the "silent" era were Joseph Carl Breil's scores for Griffith's *The Birth of a Nation* (1915) and *Intolerance* (1916), Victor Schertzinger's score for Thomas H. Ince's *Civilization* (1916), Hugo Riesenfeld's score for James Cruze's *The Covered Wagon* (1925), Louis F. Gottschalk's scores for Griffith's *Broken Blossoms*

7.1 A Wurlitzer organ at the Roxy Theater, New York City, with the theater's owner, S. L. "Roxy" Rothapfel.

---

* Big-budget first features, as opposed to "B-films," or "program pictures."

(1919) and *Orphans of the Storm* (1921), Mortimer Wilson's score for Douglas Fairbanks' *The Thief of Bagdad* (1923), William Frederick Peters' score for Griffith's *Way Down East* (1921), Erno Rapee's score for John Ford's *The Iron Horse* (1924) and F. W. Murnau's *Sunrise* (1927), and Leo Kempinski's score for Erich von Stroheim's *Greed* (1924). In Europe, Edmund Meisel wrote brilliant revolutionary scores for Eisenstein's *Potemkin* (1925) and *October* (1928), and Gottfried Huppertz composed for Fritz Lang's *Siegfried* (1923) and *Metropolis* (1926). Other European composers who scored films during the twenties include George Antheil, Erik Satie, Darius Milhaud, Arthur Honegger, Jacques Ibert, Jean Sibelius, Roger Desormière, Paul Hindemith, and Dmitri Shostakovich.

SOUND-ON-FILM

The notion that sound could complement and vivify the experience of cinema, then, came of age with the cinema itself. But since only a handful of exhibitors in major cities could afford full-scale orchestras or even Wurlitzer organs, the search for an inexpensive and effective means of recording sound for films continued during and after the war, when experimental emphasis shifted from sound-on-disk to sound-on-film systems.* It was reasoned at this point that the massive problems of synchronization encountered in the disk systems could be solved by recording the sound on the same strip of film as the images. The potential for recording sound photographically, or optically, by converting sound waves into patterns of light and shade had been understood a decade before the invention of the Kinetograph, but the first successful attempt to record sound directly on a film strip, side-by-side with the image track, was made by Eugen Augustin Lauste, a former mechanical assistant to W. K. L. Dickson, in 1907. Lauste's experiments were to become the basis for RCA Photophone, one of the two major sound-on-film systems adopted by Hollywood in the early sound era, but the first workable sound-on-film, or optical sound, systems were not perfected until after the war.

In 1919, three German inventors—Josef Engl, Joseph Massole, and Hans Vogt—patented the "Tri-Ergon" (literally, "the work of three") process, a sound-on-film system which used a photo-electric cell to convert sound waves into electric impulses and electric impulses into light waves which were then recorded photographically on the edge of the film strip. Built onto their projector was a "reader," composed of an incan-

---

* Around 1916 there was a brief flurry of interest in a groove-on-film system known alternatively as Proptjectophone or Madalatone, after its inventors, Katherina and Ferdinand von Madaler. This was a variation of the sound-on-disk systems, in which a single continuous groove impressed directly onto the film strip served the same function as the concentric grooves of a disk recording, so that a stylus and sound box on the projector could convert fluctuations in the groove into sound waves for amplification. Madalatone was marketed on the Continent from 1927 to 1928 but was too imprecise to compete with the optical sound-on-film systems.

descent light and another photo-electric cell, which re-translated the patterns of light and shade back into sound waves as the film strip passed through the projector, insuring perfect synchronization of sound and image. The Tri-Ergon process also incorporated a flywheel mechanism on a sprocket which prevented variations in film speed as the strip passed through the projector—a device necessary to maintain the continuous reproduction of sound without distortion. This flywheel was heavily protected by international patents, so that between 1920 and 1927 all other manufacturers of optical sound equipment had to either pay royalties to Tri-Ergon, infringe the patent, or market an inferior product. Tri-Ergon eventually sold its American rights to William Fox of Fox Film Company in 1927 (a sale ruled illegal by the U.S. Supreme Court in 1935) and its Continental rights to UFA, which in 1928 sold them to Tonbild Syndicat AG, merged as Tobis-Klangfilm in 1929.*

In 1923, independently of the German inventors, an American inventor who had been active in the development of radio broadcasting, Dr. Lee De Forest (1873–1961), patented a sound-on-film system, very similar to the Tri-Ergon process, which also decisively solved the problem of amplification. In 1907, to improve radio reception, De Forest had patented the Audion 3-Electrode Amplifier Tube, a vacuum tube which magnified or amplified the sound it received and drove it into a speaker. The audion tube became essential to the technology of all sound systems requiring amplification—radio, public address, sound film, and, ultimately, high-fidelity recording and television—because it is to sound reproduction what the lens is to projection; that is, it enables its message or signal to reach large numbers of people simultaneously. De Forest became preoccupied with the development of "talking pictures" in 1919, when he realized that incorporating his audion tube into an optical sound-on-film process would provide more amplification than was possible with any other system of the period. By 1922, De Forest had worked enough of the bugs out of his system to test it commercially, and in November of that year he founded the De Forest Phonofilm Company to produce a series of short sound films in cooperation with Dr. Hugo Riesenfeld, a composer of silent film scores.

Working at the Norma Talmadge Studios in New York City, De Forest made several one- and two-reel Phonofilms each week, and their success was such that by the middle of 1924 some thirty-four theaters in the East had been wired to show them and another fifty were in the process of being wired elsewhere in the United States, in Britain, and in Canada. The content of De Forest's films was varied, but they all somehow exploited sound. They included set-pieces from grand opera, instrumental performances by famous musicians, popular vaudeville acts, scenes from current plays, speeches by prominent persons such as President Calvin Coolidge, Senator Robert La Follette, and George Bernard Shaw, and

---

*On the corporate history of Tobis-Klangfilm, see Douglas Gomery, "Tri-Ergon, Tobis-Klangfilm, and the Coming of Sound," *Cinema Journal,* 16, 1 (Fall 1976), 51–61, and "Economic Struggle and Hollywood Imperialism: Europe Converts to Sound," *Yale French Studies,* 60 (1980), 80–93.

even an original narrative from time to time. (It is also possible that De Forest used the Phonofilm process to provide full-length recordings of Riesenfeld's scores for James Cruze's *The Covered Wagon* in 1924 and Fritz Lang's *Siegfried* in 1925, but the historical record on this point is unclear.) Although De Forest experienced some popular success with the more than one thousand short sound films he made in New York between 1923 and 1927, his attempts to interest Hollywood producers in the Phonophone process proved fruitless, because they did not want to spend the money required to convert their entire system of production and exhibition. As early as 1923, he had offered it to moguls like Carl Laemmle of Universal and Adolf Zukor of Paramount, only to be ignored. The studio chiefs tended to regard "talking pictures" as an expensive novelty that had no future beyond causing financial ruin for its backers, and not a single Hollywood executive showed the slightest interest in Phonofilm until the phenomenal success of a rival sound-on-disk system called Vitaphone forced them to reassess their options in 1926.

VITAPHONE

Vitaphone was a sophisticated sound-on-disk system developed at great expense by Western Electric and Bell Telephone Laboratories, a subsidiary firm of American Telephone and Telegraph Corporation, in blithe ignorance of (or at least indifference to) Hollywood's antipathy toward sound. When representatives of Western Electric attempted to market the system to the major studios in 1925, they were politely refused. But the financially venturesome and, at the time, emphatically minor Warner Brothers Pictures decided to take a chance on sound. Warner Brothers was not on the verge of bankruptcy, as is frequently claimed. In fact, it had embarked upon an aggressively expansionist campaign against its larger competitors and was having temporary cash-flow problems. The studio's executives conceived the acquisition of sound as an offensive rather than a defensive maneuver. So, in April 1926, Warner Brothers established the Vitaphone Corporation, formally leased the sound-system from Western Electric, and for $800,000 secured the exclusive right to sublease it to other studios. There was at first no question of making "talking pictures." Warner Brothers' notion was that Vitaphone could be used to provide synchronized musical accompaniment for all Warner Brothers films. As an official statement prepared for Vitaphone's debut put it, "The invention will make it possible for every performance in a motion picture theater to have a full orchestral accompaniment to the picture regardless of the size of the house." Having cast its lot with Vitaphone, Warner Brothers decided to promote it on a spectacular scale at a total cost of over three million dollars. For its world premiere at the "Refrigerated Warner Theater" at Broadway and Fifty-Second Street in New York City on August 6, 1926, Warners presented *Don Juan* (Alan Crosland, 1926), the latest and most lavish John Barrymore costume drama, with an elaborate recorded orchestral score performed by the New York Philharmonic. The feature was preceded by a

7.2 The Western Electric Vitaphone projection system.

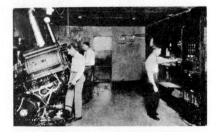

7.3 An actual Vitaphone projection in progress.

one-hour, one-million-dollar program of sound shorts, featuring the stars of the Metropolitan Opera and the New York Philharmonic Orchestra, which was preceded by a brief filmed speech by Will Hays, president of the Motion Picture Producers and Distributors of America, announcing "the beginning of a new era in music and motion pictures."

Again, it was as a revolutionary way of providing synchronized musical accompaniment for "silent" films that Vitaphone was initially promoted, and its debut as such was enormously successful. The first Vitaphone program ran eight weeks in New York, where it was seen by more than 500,000 people who paid nearly $800,000. It went on to have record-breaking runs in Chicago, Los Angeles, Boston, Detroit, St. Louis, and many European cities. The critics were unanimous in their praise of the Vitaphone system, describing it as "uncanny in its excellence," "impossible to imagine," and "the eighth wonder of the world." Of Hays' filmed speech before the program, Professor of Physics Michael Pupin of Columbia University remarked, "No closer approach to resurrection has ever been made by science."[2] Nevertheless, the future of Vitaphone was still uncertain in late 1926. No one could determine at this point whether its warm public and critical reception was the result of a passing fancy or a legitimate interest in sound films. But, as Harry M. Geduld writes, "Warners had too much at stake to accept the idea that Vitaphone might be an ephemeral novelty—while the rest of the film industry had too much at stake to entertain the notion that it might not."[3]

The rest of the film industry had a very good reason for hoping that the enthusiasm for Vitaphone would pass. It was understood among studio chiefs that a full-scale conversion to sound would cost an incalculable amount of money and perhaps even bring the industry to financial collapse. New sound studios would have to be built and costly recording equipment installed.* Thousands of cinema theaters across the country, many of them now owned by the studios, would have to be wired for sound and perhaps wired twice due to the incompatibility of competing systems. (In 1927 the installation of Vitaphone equipment alone could cost as much as twenty-five thousand dollars per theater.) Each studio would suddenly have a huge backlog of silent films representing millions of dollars in capital investment, and the industry's vast overseas market would be decimated if easily translated inter-titles gave way to spoken dialogue. The star system which sustained the American studios and helped to sell their product all over the world would also be thrown into disarray when actors and actresses trained solely in the art of mime suddenly had to start speaking dialogue. Finally, as *Variety,* the industry trade paper, asked, "What would happen to the class theatres with expensive orchestras and stage shows, if any jerk-water movie joint was able to give

7.4 A billboard in New York City, 1926.

---

* Alexander Walker: "For most studios sound did not mean adaptation but wholesale replacement. Glass and plywood came down and the California sunshine that had been one of the lures for the early pioneers was shut out by thick walls of brick and concrete. All wood used had to be kiln-dried, to get rid of resin which generated electric static. Doors were of intimidating thickness and rubber-sealed. In the very early days the main stages on some lots were surrounded by a twenty-foot moat to eliminate vibrations." (*The Shattered Silents: How the Talkies Came to Stay* [London, 1978], p. 74.)

7.5 *Variety* proclaims the arrival of a new era in film.

its patrons gorgeous feasts of music via the screen?" In short, conversion to sound threatened the entire economic structure of the American (and, therefore, the Western) film industry, and the industry had every reason to resist it. Accordingly, in December 1926 the major studio heads (executives of the "Big Three"—MGM; Famous Players–Lasky, soon to become Paramount; and First National—and the largest of the "Little Five"—Universal and Producers Distributing Corporation) held a "council of war" in Hollywood in which they agreed first to try to destroy Warner Brothers' initiative and, failing that, to adopt a uniform competing sound system which Warners could not use. They resolutely refused to buy Vitaphone sub-licenses, and it was this agreement that ultimately led to the promotion of rival systems and the eventual triumph of sound-on-film over sound-on-disk.

For the time being, however, Vitaphone was still the best system on the market, and, buoyed by the success of the *Don Juan* program, Warners announced that all of its silent films for 1927 would be produced with synchronized musical accompaniment. It also announced plans to buy one major theater in every large American city and wire it for sound. By April 1927, the Vitaphone Corporation had completed 150 installations, an average of twelve per week. In the same month, Warners completed construction of the first sound studio in the world, where, a month

7.6 A contemporary poster for *The Jazz Singer* (Alan Crosland, 1927).

7.7 Al Jolson in *The Jazz Singer*.

later, production began on the picture that would insure the triumph of the sound film and determine its future direction: Alan Crosland's *The Jazz Singer* (1927). Although Warners had been recording synchronized scores for its pictures and providing with them programs of sound shorts since August 1926, *The Jazz Singer* was to be the start of the studio's regular production of Vitaphone features for distribution to Vitaphone theaters. It was planned as a prestigious production ("Warner Brothers' Supreme Triumph," said the publicity posters), and the popular vaudeville star Al Jolson (1886–1950) was hired for twenty thousand dollars to play the lead.

The Jazz Singer, adapted from a successful Broadway play which had originally starred George Jessel (b. 1898), told the sentimental story of the son of a Jewish cantor who undergoes an anguished conflict between his religion, his family, and his career as a music-hall singer.* Like previous Vitaphone productions, it was conceived as a silent picture with a synchronized orchestral score, some Jewish cantorial music, and seven popular songs performed by Jolson. It was conceived, that is, as a "singing" rather than a "talking" picture, and all dialogue was to be provided by interpolated titles (inter-titles). But, during the shooting of two musical sequences, Jolson ad libbed some dialogue on the set which Warners shrewdly permitted to remain in the finished film. At one point near the beginning of the picture, Jolson speaks to his audience in the middle of a nightclub act and delivers his famous "Wait-a-minute. . . . Wait-a-minute. . . . You ain't heard nothin' yet!" Later in the film, as he sits at a piano in his mother's parlor, he has a sentimental exchange with her that lasts several minutes, between verses of "Blue Skies." This was the only spoken dialogue in the film, yet its impact was sensational. Audiences had heard synchronized speech before, but only on formally contrived and easily anticipated occasions, such as the speech which preceded *Don Juan.* Suddenly, though, here was Jolson not only singing and dancing but speaking informally and spontaneously to other persons in the film as someone might do in reality. The effect was not so much of *hearing* Jolson speak as of *overhearing* him speak, and it thrilled audiences bored with the conventions of silent cinema and increasingly indifferent to the canned performances of the Vitaphone shorts. Thus, we say that the "talkies" were born with *The Jazz Singer* not because it was the first feature-length film to employ synchronized dialogue but because it was the first to employ it in a realistic and seemingly undeliberate way.

The combination of Jolson, Vitaphone, and synchronized dialogue made *The Jazz Singer* an international success, eventually earning over three million dollars. By the end of 1927, it was playing to huge crowds in cities all over the world, and Warner Brothers was already starting to recoup its massive investment in the Vitaphone system. Most important, the film's success had convinced the other Hollywood studios that sound was here to stay in the form of "talking" pictures, and a mad scramble began on their part to acquire sound-recording equipment of their own.

* *The Jazz Singer* has been twice remade as a theatrical film—once in 1952, with Michael Curtiz directing Danny Thomas in the Jolson role, and again in 1980, with Richard Fleischer directing Neil Diamond. There have also been several television versions.

FOX MOVIETONE

Another organization that found itself in a good position to convert to sound was the Fox Film Corporation, like Warner Brothers a minor studio at the time. In 1927 its president, William Fox, secretly acquired the American rights to the Tri-Ergon sound-on-film process, including the flywheel mechanism, for fifty thousand dollars. A year earlier he had bought the rights to an American sound-on-film system from Theodore W. Case and Earl I. Sponable; this system was similar in almost every respect to De Forest's Phonofilm and had, in fact, been stolen from him. Neither knowing nor caring about the latter,* Fox formed the Fox-Case Corporation in the summer of 1926 to make short sound films with the system and exhibit them in his theaters under the name of Fox Movietone. Fox-Case experimented with Movietone for nearly a year before presenting its first program in New York City on January 21, 1927 (some six months after the premiere of Vitaphone), a short series of canned performances by a Spanish singer, followed by the silent feature *What Price Glory?* (Raoul Walsh, 1926). The second Movietone program opened on May 25, 1927, and was more ambitious. It offered three short performance films, including a brief dialogue sketch by comedian Chic Sale entitled "They're Coming to Get Me," followed by the feature film *Seventh Heaven* (Frank Borzage, 1927), with a synchronized orchestral score by Erno Rapee.

But it was the third Movietone program, offered on June 14, 1927, some four months before the opening of *The Jazz Singer,* that received international acclaim and convinced Fox of the value of the "talkies." On a bill with a conventional silent feature, Fox presented Movietone shorts of Charles A. Lindbergh's reception at the White House by President Coolidge and of a speech by Italian dictator Benito Mussolini. These shorts of famous personalities speaking directly and clearly from the screen electrified the audience, and popular reaction to them was so favorable that Fox established the Fox Movietone News that autumn in response to it. This was the first regular sound newsreel series, and its success was phenomenal. Within the year, Fox Movietone was sending camera crews around the world to interview everyone from George Bernard Shaw to the Pope, and delivering three to four newsreels to Fox theaters per week.

When he inaugurated the Movietone News, Fox was certain that sound was on its way in, so he negotiated a reciprocal contract between Fox-Case and Vitaphone in which each corporation licensed the other to use its sound systems, studios, technicians, and theaters. This had the effect of covering both Fox and Warners if one sound system won out over the other, and of combining their resources to insure survival in the face of any rival system which might be promoted by their competitors. As it turned out, though, most of the competition came over to their side. Nineteen-twenty-seven had been a very bad year financially for every

---

* He should have done both, since De Forest's suit against Fox for patent infringement helped to cause the mogul's downfall a decade later.

Hollywood studio but Warners, and 1928 was already looking worse. Movie audiences had been dwindling since 1926, when the public apparently began to tire of Hollywood's retrograde production formulas and its heavily promoted stars. In addition, the ready availability of the automobile and the radio to the average American family since the early twenties had created considerable competition for the silent cinema, much as television would challenge the sound film in the late forties and fifties. In 1927, only sound films had been able to regularly attract large audiences, and, according to the film historian Richard Griffith, by the spring of the next year the worst sound film would outdraw the best silent picture in any given community in the country.[4]

THE PROCESS OF CONVERSION

By 1928, then, the American public had clearly chosen sound, and the studios could only acquiesce or be damned. So on May 15, 1928, Electrical Research Products, Incorporated (ERPI), the newly created merchandising subsidiary of Western Electric, issued licenses to Paramount, MGM, and United Artists permitting them to use Western Electric equipment with Movietone sound-on-film. First National, Universal, Columbia, Tiffany-Stahl, Hal Roach Comedies, and Christie Comedies would soon make similar agreements with ERPI. At the same time, the Radio Corporation of America (RCA) acquired the theater chains of B. F. Keith and Orpheum and merged them to form the Radio-Keith-Orpheum Corporation (RKO) for the production of sound films with the RCA Photophone system, a sound-on-film process which had grown out of Eugen Lauste's experiments mentioned earlier in this chapter. Thus, by the summer of 1928 every studio in Hollywood, willingly or not, had somehow prepared itself for the conversion to sound.

Warner Brothers, however, continued to lead the way. Having produced the first "part-talkie"—*The Jazz Singer*—it went on to produce the first "100 percent all-talkie"—*Lights of New York* (Brian Foy, 1928), a clumsily plotted tale of two small-town barbers who come to the city to seek their fortunes and become dangerously involved with a gang of bootleggers. *Lights of New York* ran only fifty-seven minutes and was awkwardly directed, but twenty-two of its twenty-four sequences contained recorded dialogue, making it the first film in history to rely entirely upon the spoken word to sustain its narrative. The enormous popular success of *Lights of New York* demonstrated to Hollywood that all-dialogue films not only could be made but could draw huge audiences as well. In fact, the talkies (or "audible photo-plays," as the trade press called them) were drawing so well by the end of 1928 that it was clear to all that the silent cinema was dead. This was an unexpected blow to the film industry, since it had been assumed by nearly everyone in Hollywood that sound and silent pictures would be able to coexist, for a while at least. Now, suddenly, Hollywood became aware that the public would no longer pay to see silent films.

7.8 The first all-dialogue film: Warner Brothers' *Lights of New York* (Brian Foy, 1928). Enormously popular, it returned its producers' $75,000 investment more than fourteen times.

The upshot was a nearly total conversion to sound by the end of 1929 which radically changed the structure of the film industry and revolutionized the practice of cinema all over the world. In that year, fully three-fourths of all films made in Hollywood were released with some kind of pre-recorded sound. *Film Daily Yearbook* for 1929 lists the production of 335 all-dialogue features, ninety-five features with a mixture of dialogue and subtitles, and seventy-five features with musical scores and sound effects. The films in the last two categories were silent pictures to which some sound had hastily been added to satisfy public demand, a common way of salvaging expensively produced silent features during the year of transition. Hollywood also released 175 straight silent features in 1929 for exhibition in those provincial theaters which had not yet been wired for sound (an operation costing between eighty-five hundred and twenty thousand dollars, depending on the seating capacity and the sound process); but by the end of the year, almost every American theater of any size had installed sound equipment. In fact, the number of theaters wired for sound increased more than fifty times between December 31, 1927, and December 31, 1929. As Alexander Walker writes, "There has never been such a lightning retooling of an entire industry—even wartime emergencies were slower. . . ."[5]

7.9 MGM's *Our Dancing Daughters* (Harry Beaumont, 1928), a silent film hastily salvaged by the addition of Movietone sound effects and a musical score. Joan Crawford is the actress in the center.

The cost of this conversion was staggering, requiring that the studios borrow huge sums of money from Wall Street. In July 1929, Fox's general manager, Winfield Sheehan, estimated that Hollywood had invested more than fifty million dollars in the changeover. The final figure would be in excess of three hundred million—nearly four times the market valuation of the entire industry for fiscal year 1928.* Much of this capital was lent to the studios by the two corporate giants of the era, the Morgan and the Rockefeller groups, which also controlled Western Electric and RCA, thus strengthening the alliance between Hollywood and Wall Street which had begun in the early twenties and which exists ever more visibly today. As Arthur Knight remarks, representatives of the financiers were soon sitting on the boards of the motion picture companies, making policy decisions and giving power to sound engineers imported from the broadcasting and telephone industries who knew nothing about film.[6]

Nevertheless, the prodigious borrowing of 1928–29 was offset by the prodigious profits of the same year. Weekly attendance shot up from sixty million in 1927 to ninety million in 1930, with an increase in box office receipts of 50 percent. After a deficit of over one million dollars in 1927 owing to its heavy investment in Vitaphone, Warner Brothers reported profits of over two million dollars for 1928 and over seventeen million for 1929, when the production company was able to gain control of five hundred exhibition outlets by buying the Stanley theater chain and

---

* This estimate is from Alexander Walker's well-researched *The Shattered Silents* (cited above), and it includes the costs of wiring theaters as well as converting production. Other estimates vary, and the true figure will probably never be known owing to the untrustworthy, if creative, accounting procedures of the day. See also *Sound and the Cinema: The Coming of Sound to American Film,* ed. Evan W. Cameron (Pleasantville, N.Y., 1980).

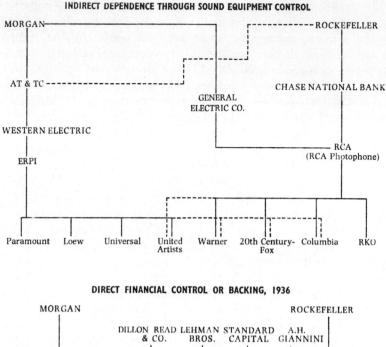

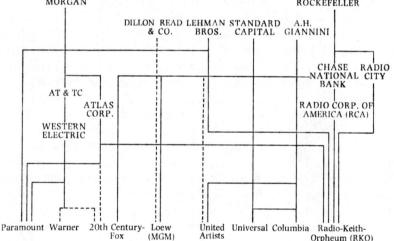

7.10 Charts showing direct and indirect financial control of the American sound film (and thus of the American film industry) during the thirties. (From F. D. Klingender and Stuart Legg, *Money Behind the Screen* [London, 1937]. Reprinted by permission of Lawrence & Wishart Ltd.)

First National (one of the "Big Three" with which, two years earlier, Warners had been in such unequal competition) to become for over a decade one of the most powerful studios in Hollywood. In 1929, Fox's profits had soared high enough for the company to build itself a new multi-million-dollar studio and for Fox himself to pay fifty million dollars for a controlling interest in Loew's, Inc., which owned MGM, and another twenty million dollars for a 45-percent share of Gaumont-British, England's largest producer/distributor/exhibitor.* Most of the other studios' profits doubled between 1928 and 1930 due to the public's

---

* This bid on Fox's part to control the largest production companies and theater chains in the United States and England respectively, as well as to control of all of the West's sound-on-film patents through Movietone, was nothing less than an attempt to consolidate the film industries of the entire English-speaking world under his personal control. This ex-

mania for the talkies, and it is probably true that the introduction of sound, more than any other single factor, enabled Hollywood to survive the Great Depression, which began with the stock market crash of October 1929.* As Kenneth Macgowan aptly comments: "If the producers had waited till late October 1929—as they might well have done except for the daring of Warner Brothers and Fox—sound would have been impossible for ten more years, and receiverships [bankruptcy] would have come quite some time before 1932."[7]

When the Depression finally did hit Hollywood in 1932, the silent cinema was a distant memory. All sound equipment had been standardized by international agreement in 1930. Sound-on-film—Fox Movietone and RCA Photophone in the United States, Tobis-Klangfilm's Tri-Ergon process on the Continent—had won out over sound-on-disk because of the superior quality of reproduction in the former and the massive problems of synchronization posed by the latter. Sound-on-film had also proved the most flexible system for recording on location, as the naturalistic soundtrack of Fox's *In Old Arizona* (Raoul Walsh, 1928), the first all-talkie shot outdoors, had demonstrated. The immense profits Warners had reaped from Vitaphone enabled it to switch systems in its studios and theaters without risk. And in 1935, after nine years of litigation, Dr. Lee De Forest, who had spent $200,000 of his own funds developing the sound-on-film system that Hollywood eventually adopted, but who had lacked the resources to promote it, was finally awarded the sum of $100,000 for patent infringement by the Fox-Case and Vitaphone Corporations. Even with the compensation, De Forest had to borrow money to pay his legal fees, but he had at least won the right to call himself the inventor of the process that changed forever the aesthetic configuration of the cinema.

THE INTRODUCTION OF COLOR

Color entered the cinema at approximately the same time as sound, although, like sound, it had been around since the beginning of things. Méliès had employed twenty-one women at Montreuil to hand-tint his most spectacular films frame by frame (Charles Pathé would later employ

---

traordinarily ambitious and avaricious plan collapsed about Fox's ears within months of its implementation, when the Justice Department of the newly elected Hoover administration (notoriously chummy with Louis B. Mayer, who stood to lose a fortune in the Fox-Loew's deal) ordered Fox to divest himself of the Loew's stock. The stock market crashed simultaneously, killing the Gaumont-British deal and forcing Fox to sell his shares in Loew's at a thirty-million-dollar loss. In 1931, Fox was ousted from his company by a coalition of executives and stockholders, and he finally declared bankruptcy in 1936. His legal entanglements continued until 1941, when he was sentenced to a year in prison for attempting to bribe a federal judge at his bankruptcy hearing. After serving six months of the term in 1943, he retired to live reasonably well on the several sound film patents he had managed to retain through the court battles of the thirties. Fox's apologia for this incredible career is contained in *Upton Sinclair Presents William Fox* (Los Angeles, 1933).

* Some characteristic studio profits for fiscal year 1929 were: Warner Brothers $17,271,805; Fox $9,469,050; Paramount $15,544,544; and MGM $11,756,956.

over three hundred), and Porter and Griffith both used tinted sequences in their films. By the twenties, over 80 percent of all American features were tinted in some fashion by means of chemical baths. The first natural color process, however, was an unreliable three-color system, called Kinemacolor, invented by the British film pioneer Charles Urban (1871–1942) in 1908. Two years later, G. A. Smith of the Brighton school used it to film the coronation of King George V and other subjects. Soon, similar systems were patented in England, France, and Germany, but the Motion Picture Patents Company managed to suppress them in this country until Dr. Herbert Kalmus (1881–1963) founded his Technicolor Corporation in 1918.

All color systems work by separating natural colors into several primary colors, recording these primary colors on different emulsion layers, or film strips, and then re-synthesizing them on the screen. Urban's system had been *additive*—that is, the natural colors on the screen were synthesized by adding lights of different colors—but additive systems require more light than film projectors can readily provide. Kalmus' major contribution was to invent a two-color *subtractive* system in 1922, in which natural colors on the screen were synthesized by subtracting their complementary color from the white light of the projector. This was achieved by shooting two negatives in the same camera—one sensitive to the red-orange-yellow portion of the spectrum (magenta) and another to the green-blue-purple portion (cyan)—and bonding them together through a chemical process known as "imbibition" into a single positive print which would reproduce a limited color scale. The first film shot in this process was MGM's *Toll of the Sea* (1922), which made over a quarter of a million dollars in the year of its release.

Kalmus' two-color Technicolor process was used by the studios throughout the twenties to provide color sequences for blockbusters like *Ben Hur* (Fred Niblo, 1925) and *The Phantom of the Opera* (Rupert Julian, 1925), as well as to produce novelty features like Douglas Fairbanks' *The Black Pirate* (1926), but it was not until the coming of sound that producers began to consider color seriously. Then, in a flush of enthusiasm for the sensational new realism made possible by sound (and, more practically, to distract the public's attention from the poor quality of early sound reproduction), studios began to produce their "all-talking, all-singing, all-dancing" pictures in "all-color" too (there were also scattered experiments with widescreen processes). The first all-color sound film in two-color Technicolor was Warner Brothers' *On with the Show* (Alan Crosland, 1929). It was followed in the boom year of 1930 by a large number of Technicolor talkies, including *Whoopee!* (Thornton C. Freeland), *The Vagabond King* (Ludwig Berger), *No, No, Nanette* (Clarence Badger), *Rio Rita* (Luther Reed), *Paramount on Parade* (Dorothy Arzner and Otto Brower), and *Rogue Song* (Lionel Barrymore). Yet by 1932 the production of Technicolor films had nearly ceased. The sudden rush to color failed because audiences grew increasingly bored with the poor registry of the two-color process, in which flesh tones varied from pink to orange, and also because the process itself was expensive to work with (in 1935, shooting in Technicolor added 30 percent to the production costs of the average feature). By contrast, recent improvements in black-and-white stock had made it sensitive to a wider range of tones than ever before, so black-and-white became the standard medium for sound films through the early fifties.

Nevertheless, in 1932 Kalmus perfected the three-color Technicolor system, variants of which are still in use today. This system employed three negatives*—one sensitive to blues, another to reds, and another to yellows—and offered a great deal more verisimilitude than its predecessor. It was first used in Walt Disney's animated short *Flowers and Trees* (1932) and the experimental live-action short *La Cucaracha* (1933), but the first feature shot in this process was Rouben Mamoulian's *Becky Sharp* (1935), a version of Thackeray's novel *Vanity Fair*. Three-color Technicolor was still so expensive and tricky to work with that throughout the thirties it was used primarily for Disney animation (for instance, *Snow White and the Seven Dwarfs* [1937]), where all the variables could be controlled, and for costume spectacles like *The Garden of Allah* (Richard Boleslawski, 1936), *Elizabeth the Queen* (Michael Curtiz, 1939), *The Wizard of Oz* (Victor Fleming, 1939), and, quintessentially, *Gone with the Wind* (Victor Fleming, 1939). (An exception in the next decade, when World War II generally prevented the expense of Technicolor shooting, was Laurence Olivier's vastly intelligent, patriotic adaptation of *Henry V* [1944], which uses its color scheme emblematically to embody the images of Shakespeare's play.) The Technicolor Corporation provided its own cameramen, "consultants," and equipment for these productions, and it monopolized the field of color cinematography in the United States almost completely until the cheaper, faster, but less stable Eastmancolor system was introduced in 1952 (see Chapter 12).

PROBLEMS OF EARLY SOUND RECORDING

It is important to note that the introduction of sound is analogous in almost every respect to the invention of the cinema itself. In each case, the technological principles upon which the invention was based had been known for decades prior to their combination into a workable apparatus. In each case, the apparatus was developed and exploited for the purposes of novelty and commerce without a thought to aesthetic ends (early "movies" are comparable to early "talkies" in that both initially exploited their most novel feature at the expense of proportion and common sense). Finally, there was a long delay between the introduction of the sophisticated machine and the sophisticated artistic use of it.

The aesthetic and technical problems caused by the introduction of sound to the cinema were immense. It is almost axiomatic to say that the movies ceased to move when they began to talk, because between 1928

---

* The Technicolor three-strip camera exposed each negative simultaneously through a single lens by means of a prismatic beam-splitter located directly behind it. A fourth negative, imprinted independently, provided the optical soundtrack.

7.11 On an unidentified Vitaphone set, 1927. Note the camera booth and microphone.

7.12 A Vitaphone camera in its soundproof booth.

7.13 Sound men inside a studio monitor booth.

7.14 An early recording room.

and 1931 they virtually regressed to their infancy in terms of editing and camera movement. In large part this was because the early microphones that were used to record sound had two substantial defects. First, they had a very limited range, so that to be heard on the soundtrack at all actors were forced to speak directly into them. This had the regressive effect of rendering actors motionless within the frame while they delivered their lines, and led to some remarkable exercises in concealing microphones on the set in flowerpots, ship's lanterns, and clumps of sagebrush. The second major defect of the microphones was, paradoxically, that within their limited range they were highly sensitive and omnidirectional—they picked up and recorded *every sound* made within their range on the set. This characteristic not only created problems in sound engineering but rendered the camera almost totally inert: in order to avoid distortion in the synchronized soundtrack, all cameras were motorized to run at a standard speed (twenty-four frames per second) in 1929. This meant, for one thing, that cameras could no longer be undercranked or overcranked by their operators to achieve expressive effects. But motorization also caused cameras to make a noisy, whirring clatter which would inevitably be picked up by the microphones. To prevent this, early sound cameras and their operators had to be imprisoned in soundproof glass-paneled booths where they could neither tilt nor track, and for this reason the earliest sound films resembled the "filmed theater" of Méliès and *film d'art* far more than they resembled their immediate silent predecessors.

In fact, sound recording rendered the cinema even *more* static than the filmed plays of its first decade because actors had to keep within range of both a static microphone *and* a static camera. Not only was the frame or camera itself rendered motionless, but the actors had to remain motionless *within* the frame (that is, within a given camera set-up) if they were to have their voices picked up by the crude recording equipment. In filmed plays like *Queen Elizabeth* (1912) the actors, at least, could move around on the set, even though the cameras didn't move at all, but now

7.15 On the set of *Lummox* (Herbert Brenon, 1930). Before the advent of post-synchronization, any sounds to be heard simultaneously in the finished film had to be recorded simultaneously on the set. Here, a mother (right) listens to her daughter (left) singing in the room next door, which required that the two scenes be photographed and recorded at the same time.

they too were rendered immobile. To make things worse, montage, or creative editing of any sort that might have compensated for this new stasis of the camera (as Soviet montage compensated for the Soviet camera's lack of fluidity), was prohibited by the procedures of early sound recording. It was virtually impossible to edit a sound-on-film track which had been recorded and synchronized simultaneously with the images (it was, obviously, out of the question with sound-on-disk recordings). If the images of a synchronized dialogue sequence were intercut, the continuity of the soundtrack would be destroyed,* and so, in the earliest sound films, editing, like camera movement, became purely functional rather than expressive. Cuts could be made, just as the camera could be moved, only when no sound was recorded on the set (and thus on the track), so that most early sound editing was strictly *transitional*—a device (as in Méliès) for changing linearly from one scene to the next, rather than a mode for expressing multiple points of view. Crosscutting between actors speaking to one another, close-ups intercut with shots of other focal

---

* Since it is mechanically impossible for the lens and the sound head of a projector to be located in the same place, there must be a displacement between image and soundtrack on composite sound-on-film exhibition prints. In 35 mm filming, the soundtrack runs twenty frames in advance of the corresponding image track, making it impossible to edit a composite print without eliminating portions of the relevant sound. From a production standpoint, this problem was resolved by the introduction and refinement of post-sychronization, or dubbing, between 1929 and 1932 (see below). But to keep very early dialogue scenes from lapsing into inertia, the same sequence was frequently filmed by as many as four cameras simultaneously and later intercut. In this way, the images could be varied while the soundtrack remained constant, but the method was prohibitively expensive.

lengths, all the editing syntax of Griffith, the montage structure of Eisenstein, and the fluid, expressive camera movement introduced by Murnau and Freund—all were effectively, if temporarily, eliminated by the clumsy technology of early sound recording. They were replaced by a series of talking photographs taken from the same angle at medium range and varied only when the talking stopped. Ironically, Edison's original conception of the film as a sequence of moving pictures to accompany and illustrate sound recordings was fully realized in the first few years of the sound era.

To make matters worse, the studios were so anxious to exploit the novelty of sound that they turned to scripts (called "properties") which emphasized and even exaggerated the cinema's new inertia. Many producers assumed that the sound film would provide a perfect medium for photographing stage hits with their original casts and bringing them to a mass audience; between 1929 and 1931 much of the American cinema became "canned theater" in which Broadway plays and musicals were transferred from stage to screen verbatim with little or no adaptation. The impulse to record stage performances live on film at the beginning of the sound era was the same as that which had motivated the *film d'art* craze of 1908–12, and its failure was no less emphatic. The public rapidly tired of these "100 percent all-talking" productions (or "teacup dramas," as they were sometimes called), but they had the lasting effect of bringing Broadway players and directors to Hollywood.*

7.16 "Canned theater": Warner Brothers' *Disraeli* (Alfred E. Green, 1929). George Arliss, Anthony Bushell.

Actors with stage experience were especially valuable during the early sound era, because directors could no longer shout out instructions on the set as they had done before and therefore needed players who could work on their own through long dialogue sequences. They also needed players with good voices and clear articulation, which meant that stage actors, and film actors with stage experience,† rapidly replaced many silent stars who spoke with heavy foreign accents (like Emil Jannings, Pola Negri, and Lya de Putti) or whose voices somehow did not match their screen images (like Norma Talmadge and John Gilbert). Other silent stars, such as Greta Garbo, Gary Cooper, and Janet Gaynor, were able to make the transition with the aid of voice specialists and diction coaches from the theater world. The advent of sound caused other new

---

* Among the Broadway players who came to stay were George Arliss, Helen Hayes, Humphrey Bogart, Fredric March, Leslie Howard, Clark Gable, Sylvia Sidney, Fred Astaire, Paul Muni, Spencer Tracy, and Katharine Hepburn. The directors included Richard Boleslawski, George Cukor, and Rouben Mamoulian.

For a brief period in 1928, it even seemed as though the migration might be reversed and that the film industry might shift its production base back to New York City in order to be close to Broadway talent (it took nearly four days to cross the country by train in this era; only the super-rich could afford to fly) and to the sophisticated audio technology of the recording and broadcasting industries. By mid-summer of that year, Paramount, MGM, First National, and Warners had all set up soundstages in New York, but after a brief flurry of film-making activity there, economies of scale brought the conversion back home to Hollywood. See Alexander Walker, *The Shattered Silents*, pp. 90–106.

† These included Ronald Colman; Claudette Colbert; William Powell; Ethel, John, and Lionel Barrymore; George Bancroft; Marie Dressler; Clive Brook; Boris Karloff; and Charles Laughton.

arrivals in Hollywood. Sound technicians from the broadcasting and tele-phone industries who had no understanding of film-making suddenly ap-peared on the studio sets endowed with tremendous authority to deter-mine camera and microphone placement. Arthur Knight writes of their brief but dictatorial rule: "[The] experts, concerned with nothing beyond the sound quality of the pictures they worked on, continually simplified their problems by insisting that scenes be played in corners, minimizing long-shots for the more readily controllable close-up. In no time at all the techniques, the artistry that directors had acquired through years of silent films were cast aside and forgotten in the shadow of the microphone."[8]

THE THEORETICAL DEBATE
OVER SOUND

Indeed, so great a threat to the cinema as a creative form did sound recording seem at the outset that many directors and theorists of film violently opposed its arrival. They were appalled that the cinema, which was currently in its most advanced state of articulation, might be perma-nently retarded by the public's passing fancy for a crude novelty. Paul Rotha spoke for this group in 1930:

> No power of speech is comparable to the descriptive value of pho-tographs. The attempted combination of speech and pictures is the direct opposition of two separate mediums, which appeal in two ut-terly different ways. . . . [A] silent visual film is capable of achieving a more dramatic, lasting, and powerful effect on an audience by its sin-gleness of appeal than a dialogue film. . . . Immediately a voice begins to speak in a cinema, the sound apparatus takes precedence over the camera, thereby doing violence to natural instincts.[9]

Others, like Eisenstein and Pudovkin, perceived the threat posed by sound but also recognized its potential for adding a new dimension to the medium. In "Sound and Image," a manifesto published on August 5, 1928, Eisenstein, Pudovkin, and Alexandrov correctly predicted:

> The sound film is a two-edged sword, and it is very probable that its users will follow the path of least resistance, that is, they will attempt simply to satisfy the public's curiosity. First we shall see commercial exploitation of the merchandise which is easiest to manufacture and sell: the talkie, the film in which the recorded word coincides most ex-actly and realistically with the movement of lips on the screen, in which the public enjoys the illusion that it is really listening to an actor, an automobile horn, a musical instrument, etc.
> This first period of sensationalism will not prejudice the new art's development, but there will be a second period—a terrible period. With the decline of the first exploration of practical possibilities, peo-ple will try to substitute dramas taken from "good literature" and will make other attempts to have theatre invade the screen.
> Used in this way, sound will destroy the art of montage.

Then, they offered an antidote to the situation:

Only the use of sound as counterpoint to visual montage offers new possibilities of developing and perfecting montage. The first experiments with sound must be directed toward its "noncoincidence" with visual images. Only this method can produce the feeling we seek, the feeling which, with time, will lead to creation of a new orchestral counterpoint of image-vision and image-sound.

Finally, they pointed out that the sound film provided one distinct technical advantage over the silent cinema:

The new technical discovery is not a chance factor in the history of cinema but is a natural way out for the cinema's avant-garde, thanks to which filmmakers can escape from a large number of dead ends which probably had no exit.

The title, despite innumerable attempts to incorporate it into the movement or images of a film, is the first such dead end.

The second is the explanatory hodgepodge which overloads the composition of scenes and slows the film's rhythm. . . .

Sound, treated as a new element of montage (and as an element independent of the visual image), will inevitably introduce a new, extremely effective means of expressing and resolving the complex problems which we have not been able to solve so far. It is impossible to find the necessary solutions if we have only visual elements with which to work.[10]

Eisenstein, especially, spoke from a long and generally negative experience of trying to integrate his titles with his images. Titles were a definite liability to the silent cinema, since they interfered with the flow of its narratives and the rhythms of its montage.* It is often pointed out, for example, that one of the last great films of the silent era, Carl Theodor Dreyer's *La passion de Jeanne d'Arc* (1928; see Chapter 9), was seriously flawed by the insertion of dialogue titles at crucial positions within the narrative and would have profited immensely from a recorded soundtrack. By eliminating the necessity for titles, the sound film had liberated the cinema from its thirty-year bondage to the printed word and provided it with a narrative dimension that need not interfere with the visual dynamics of montage. The task now was not to re-shackle the medium to the spoken word of the talkie.

Another European cinematic formalist had similar feelings about sound. The young French director René Clair (1898–1981) wrote in 1929 that he was opposed to the "100 percent talkie" but could see distinct possibilities for the creative use of sound in films (a potential which he would later realize in 1931 with his own films *Le million* and *À nous la liberté*): "The film is not everything. There is also the sound film—on which the last hopes of the advocates of the silent film are pinned. They count on the sound film to ward off the danger represented by the advent of talkies. . . . [If] *imitation* of real noises seems limited and disappointing, it is possible that an *interpretation* of noises may have more of a future in it."[11] Clair reserved special praise for the first American musical, MGM's *Broadway Melody* (Harry Beaumont, 1929), as a

---

* For an engaging essay on the structural function of intertitles in silent films, see William F. Van Wert, "Intertitles," *Sight and Sound,* 49, 2 (Spring 1980), 98–105.

film which used its soundtrack with great intelligence. He particularly admired a sequence in which the noise of a door being slammed and a car
driving off are heard on the soundtrack but not illustrated on the image
track, which contains only a close-up of the heroine's anguished face wit-
nessing the departure. In another sequence the heroine is on the verge of
tears, and as her face disappears in a fade-out we hear a single sob from
the blackened screen. Clair concludes from this: "In these two instances
the sound, at an opportune moment, has replaced the shot. It is by this
economy of means that the sound film will most probably secure original
effects."

What the three Soviet film-makers and Clair had all realized was that
sound recording posed a threat to the cinema *only* if the microphone became as slavishly subservient to the spoken word, or to "naturalistic"
sound, as the early camera had been to empirical reality in its unwillingness to disrupt the natural continuity of time and space. So they
denounced *synchronous* or *"naturalistic"* sound, whereby the audience
hears exactly what it sees on the screen as it sees it and *sees* exactly what
it hears on the soundtrack as it hears it, as a non-creative form of recording which threatened the formal achievement of the silent cinema. And
they advocated instead the use of *asynchronous* or *contrapuntal*
sound—sound which would counterpoint the images that accompanied it
for expressive effect, in the same way that conflicting shots in a silent
montage sequence counterpointed one another. That is, they endorsed
sound recording as an extension and expansion of montage, in which
noise, dialogue, and music were all to be used in counterpoint to visual
images like individual shots in a montage sequence. As Pudovkin wrote,
"Sound and human speech should be used by the director not as literal
accompaniment, but to amplify and enrich the visual image on the
screen."[12]

7.17 MGM's *Broadway Melody* (Harry
Beaumont, 1929): innovative use of sound.
The film won the Academy Award for
Best Picture of 1929, certifying the new
medium's ascendancy.

The controversy between the advocates of synchronous versus
asynchronous sound became the great theoretical debate of the early
sound era, and it was precisely analogous to that which we may imagine
to have occurred in the first decade of film itself. The question became
whether the soundtrack, like the early camera, should simply record reality "naturalistically" or whether it should create a synthetic reality of its
own. Practically speaking, the question was whether sound should be
synchronized with the images to produce "naturalistic" or *literal* sound,
or whether it should be placed in creative conflict with the image track.
Because of the large middleground between these two poisitions, there
was clearly an either/or fallacy involved in the debate: in fact, the best
cinema mixes both practices, as all the pioneers of creative sound recording were to discover. But for the first several years, at least, it seemed that
the future of the sound film lay in one direction or the other.*

Most American producers believed that an absolute pairing of sound
and image was the only feasible way to use the new process. They felt
that to separate sound and image—even to the small extent of recording

---

* For more on the theoretical and practical aspects of the debate, see Lucy Fischer, "René
Clair, *Le Million,* and the Coming of Sound," *Cinema Journal,* 16, 2 (Spring 1977), 34–50.

naturalistic sound but not visualizing it (for example, having a door slam offscreen, as in *Broadway Melody*)—would disorient audience perception, just as their predecessors had thirty years earlier been loath to fragment the visual reality continuum. Thus the huge number of "100 percent talkies" (films like *Lights of New York*) which were little more than illustrated radio plays. On the other side of the issue were the cinematic formalists like Eisenstein, Pudovkin, and Clair who saw contrapuntal sound as the only way to use the new technique—sound in which music, choruses, sound effects, and perhaps a bare minimum of dialogue would be used to counterpoint and comment upon the visuals. The controversy was ultimately resolved through the discovery of a process known as *post-synchronization*, or *dubbing*, which permitted synchronous and asynchronous sound to be used together consistently and simultaneously within the same film.

THE ADJUSTMENT TO SOUND

Post-synchronization was first used by the American director King Vidor (b. 1894) for his first talking picture, *Hallelujah!* (1929), which is also generally regarded as the first major film of the sound era. *Hallelujah!* was shot on location in and around Memphis, Tennessee, with an all-black cast, and its final sequence depicts a wild chase through an

7.18 MGM's *Hallelujah!* (King Vidor, 1929).

7.19 Universal's *All Quiet on the Western Front* (Lewis Milestone, 1930): Lew Ayres and comrade.

Arkansas swamp. Vidor shot the entire sequence silent with a continuously moving camera, and then later in the studio he added a soundtrack to it containing naturalistic noises of the pursuit—breaking branches, screeching birds, heavy breathing, etc.—all of which had been separately recorded.* Given the crudity of early sound-recording equipment, this

---

* This was in part the result of a happy accident: Vidor's sound truck failed to show up when the crew arrived in Memphis, so he started to shoot the movie silent out of necessity and simply continued the practice when he realized how liberating it was. The post-dubbing process itself was extremely difficult, and Vidor's editor is said to have suffered a nervous breakdown in the midst of it. See Alexander Walker, *The Shattered Silents* (cited above).

7.20   On the set of Paramount's *The Love Parade* (Ernst Lubitsch, **1929**).

was a technically brilliant achievement. But since the soundtrack was physically separate from the image track, though printed beside it on the same strip of film,* the potential for post-dubbing sound had existed in the sound-on-film systems from the time of their invention. Lewis Jacobs explains: "The detachment of sound and its reproduction in a film are made possible by the mechanical nature of the recording apparatus and the editing process. Microphone and camera are independent instruments, recording what is seen and heard either together simultaneously or separately at different times."[13] Vidor, however, was the first to realize this and to realize simultaneously that sound could create a psychological impact quite independent of the images. Another American director, Lewis Milestone (1895–1980), used post-dubbing for the battlefield sequences of his great pacifist film *All Quiet on the Western Front* in 1930, shooting them with a mobile silent camera on location and dubbing in the battle sounds later. In 1931, Milestone was able to keep his camera constantly in motion during the fast-talking dialogue comedy *The Front Page,* adapted from the stage play by Ben Hecht and Charles MacArthur. Ernst Lubitsch also used dubbing in his first sound films: in both *The Love Parade* (1929) and *Monte Carlo* (1930) he shot moving camera sequences silent and added sound effects and music later.

Rouben Mamoulian (b. 1898), a stage director imported from Broadway, introduced a new element into sound recording when he used two

---

* But see note on displacement, p. 249.

7.21 Paramount's *Applause* (Rouben Mamoulian, 1929), the first film to use a double-channel soundtrack. Helen Morgan.

7.22 On the set of Warner Brothers' *Mammy* (Michael Curtiz, 1930). The camera is still enclosed, but the microphone is suspended from an improvised boom.

separate microphones to record overlapping dialogue in a single scene of *Applause* (1929) and mixed them together on the soundtrack. Earlier soundtracks had consisted of a single channel, which meant that there was no way to isolate one type of sound from another. Everybody on the set spoke into the same microphone, and there could be no background music or sound effects while dialogue was being delivered unless these were provided off-camera simultaneously as the lines were spoken. By introducing two microphones and mixing the sound from each, Mamoulian opened up the possibility of multiple-channel recording and post-recording which would permit the precise manipulation of all sounds on the track—a possibility realized for four-channel recording as early as 1932. Two years later, in *City Streets* (1931), Mamoulian introduced the first sound "flashback," as snatches of dialogue spoken earlier in the film recur on the soundtrack accompanied by a close-up of the heroine, suggesting the process of memory.

The practice of post-synchronization was a prime force in liberating the sound film camera from its glass-paneled booth and the sound film generally from the single-minded notion that everything seen on the screen must be heard on the soundtrack, and vice versa. In its infancy, sound recording had bound film to the laws of empirical reality more securely than ever before, but post-synchronization re-introduced the plastic, manipulative element. From the experience of dubbing, directors gradually came to understand that the most "cinematic" soundtrack was neither wholly synchronous nor asynchronous but a composite of many different types of sound, all of which were under their control—perhaps even more so than the visuals, since sound could be synthetically produced.* Arthur Knight writes: "Each sound could be independently distorted, muffled, exaggerated or eliminated at will. The director could

---

* In certain sound-on-film processes employed today, a special stylus can be used to scrape light patterns directly onto the surface of the soundtrack, creating synthetic sound effects and music.

shoot his scene with a silent camera and dub in the sound later. He could reinforce dialogue passages with music, combine them with noises or bury them under other, post-synchronized sounds. . . . Post-synchronization became the first point of departure in the development of a new art." [14]

Other developments which helped to liberate the sound film from its initial stasis were more purely technological. By 1931, the camera could record dialogue sequences outside the glass-paneled booth owing to the invention of the camera "blimp," a lightweight, soundproof housing which encased the camera and muffled the clatter of its motor. A few years later, improvements in the sound camera, such as the replacement of noisy metal gears with fiber ones, greatly diminished the whirring noise of its drive mechanism, freeing it permanently from the booth. The camera simultaneously became smaller and more physically mobile. Microphones also became increasingly sophisticated and mobile. The invention of the microphone boom, a long radial arm that suspended the mike just above the set and allowed it to follow the movements of the actors, eliminated the stationary microphones of the early years. Microphones also ceased to pick up every sound on the set as they became more directional—better able to "hear" at one frequency or in one direction only. Finally, in 1932, a system of re-recording four different soundtracks or channels onto one master track was introduced, which permitted the simultaneous orchestration of different kinds of sound: close dialogue, distant dialogue, sound effects, and music. Since the introduction of magnetic sound in the early fifties, any number of separate channels can be re-recorded onto a single track or stereophonically re-recorded onto as many as six tracks, and it was not uncommon for widescreen epics in the nineteen-fifties and sixties to use as many as fifty channels for mass scenes. In the seventies, sound quality was further enhanced through the adoption of a wireless eight-track recording system which uses radio microphones and, increasingly, the non-magnetic stereo-optical Dolby noise-reduction system for playback in exhibition.*

7.23 A "blimped" camera shooting a scene whose sound is recorded by an off-frame boom microphone. (The film is Warner Brothers First National's *Lilies of the Field* [Alexander Korda, 1930], with Corinne Griffith and Ralph Forbes; behind the camera are Lee Garmes, the cinematographer [left], and William Goetz, the producer [right].)

* See Charles Schreger, "The Second Coming of Sound," *Film Comment,* 14, 5 (September–October 1978), 34–37.

The Sound Film and the American Studio System

NEW GENRES AND OLD

Sound radically changed the configuration of the Western cinema. In the United States, it gave rise to important new genres and a system of production which determined the character of American films for over a decade. The most significant of the new genres was the musical film, whose development parallels that of the sound film itself. Photographed versions of Broadway musicals were among the first sound films ever made, and *The Jazz Singer* (1927), of course, was one of them. At first, these movie musicals were little more than filmed theater, but within a few years the form had grown enough in cinematic sophistication to become the major genre of thirties cinema. This was largely the work of two men—Busby Berkeley (1895–1975) and Fred Astaire (b. 1899).

A dance director from the New York stage, Berkeley came to Hollywood to work for Samuel Goldwyn in 1930 but did not reveal his genius until he moved to Warner Brothers in 1933. There, as dance director for musicals* like *42nd Street* (Lloyd Bacon, 1933), *Gold Diggers of 1933* (Mervyn LeRoy, 1933), *Footlight Parade* (Lloyd Bacon, 1933), *Dames* (Roy Enright, 1934), *Gold Diggers of 1935* (Busby Berkeley, 1935), *In Caliente* (Busby Berkeley, 1935), and *Gold Diggers of 1937* (Lloyd Bacon, 1937), he developed a flamboyant visual style which turned the production numbers of pedestrian backstage romances into surreal fantasias for the eye. Based upon the use of swooping aerial photography (or "crane choreography"†), kaleidoscopic lenses, highly expressive camera movement, and sophisticated montage techniques, Berkeley's production numbers come closer to an experimental cinema of abstract impressionism than to anything in the traditional narrative film.

Fred Astaire, by contrast, achieved a much greater integration of music and dance with narrative in the series of RKO musicals in which he played opposite Ginger Rogers between 1933 (*Flying Down to Rio*, Thornton Freeland) and 1939 (*The Story of Vernon and Irene Castle*, H. C. Potter). Beginning as a performer, Astaire went on to direct and choreograph his dance sequences in *The Gay Divorcee* (Mark Sandrich,

---

* Most of which starred some combination of Dick Powell, Joan Blondell, and Ruby Keeler.
† Aerial photography accomplished by means of a large boom crane.

8.1 Busby Berkeley's choreography: *Gold Diggers of 1933* (Mervyn LeRoy, 1933). Warner Brothers.

8.2 Berkeley choreography: *Dames* (Ray Enright, 1934). Warner Brothers.

8.3 *Gold Diggers of 1935* (Busby Berkeley, 1935). Warner Brothers.

8.4 *Gold Diggers of 1937* (Lloyd Bacon, 1937): Joan Blondell heads the Berkeley formation. Warner Brothers.

1934), *Roberta* (William Seiter, 1935), *Top Hat* (Mark Sandrich, 1935), *Swing Time* (George Stevens, 1936), *Shall We Dance?* (Mark Sandrich, 1937), and *Carefree* (Mark Sandrich, 1938), and he developed a sophisticated but highly functional camera style in which the camera itself became a partner in the dance through both cutting and movement. Furthermore, Astaire's RKO musicals contributed significantly to the development of creative recording techniques through their rhythmic pairing of sound and image.

Another contribution to sound film genres was made by Walt Disney (1901–66), whose "Silly Symphony" series, begun in 1929 with *The Skeleton Dance*, pioneered what might be called the "animated musical," or the musical cartoon. Unhampered by the restrictions of early sound-filming procedures, Disney could combine sound and image in an expressive manner impossible for his peers in the live-action narrative cinema and nevertheless achieve perfect frame-by-frame synchronization (today,

8.5 Fred Astaire and Ginger Rogers in a dance sequence from *Top Hat* (Mark Sandrich, 1935). RKO.

the precise coordination of sound and image in animation is still called "Mickey Mousing"). The success of his first musical cartoon, *Steamboat Willie* (1928), which introduced Mickey Mouse to the world, and his "Silly Symphony" shorts, in which all of the action is set to music and which culminated in 1933 with the immensely popular all-color hit *The Three Little Pigs,* led Disney to produce three extraordinary animated color features before World War II—*Snow White and the Seven Dwarfs* (1937), *Pinocchio* (1940), and the experimental *Fantasia* (1940), which attempted a total fusion of animated visuals and classical orchestral scores.

8.6 Mickey Mouse in *Steamboat Willie* (Walt Disney, 1928).

At the other end of the spectrum, the new realism permitted by sound bred a cycle of tersely directed urban gangster films which exploited armed violence and tough vernacular speech in a context of social alienation. There were a handful of silent antecedents in the work of Lewis Milestone (*The Racket* [1928]) and Josef von Sternberg (*Underworld* [1927]), but sound films like Mervyn LeRoy's *Little Caesar* (1930), William Wellman's *The Public Enemy* (1931), and Howard Hawks' *Scarface* (1932) forged a new generic tradition extending through Arthur Penn's *Bonnie and Clyde* (1967) and Francis Ford Coppola's *The Godfather, Parts I* (1972) and *II* (1974). In 1933–34, however, the brutal violence of these films provoked a public outcry which caused producers to shift emphasis from the gangster as "tragic hero," to borrow Robert Warshow's

8.7 *Pinocchio* (Walt Disney Productions, 1940).

8.8 Edward G. Robinson in *Little Caesar* (Mervyn LeRoy, 1930). Warner Brothers.

8.9 *The Public Enemy* (William Wellman, 1931): Jean Harlow, James Cagney. Warner Brothers.

8.10 The "biopic": Paul Muni in *Juarez* (William Dieterle, 1939). Warner Brothers.

phrase,[1] to the gangster as social victim.* This produced a cycle of prison films (such as Lloyd Bacon's *San Quentin* [1937]) and socially oriented crime films (among them William Wyler's *Dead End* [1937], Fritz Lang's *You Only Live Once* [1937], Lloyd Bacon's *Marked Woman* [1937], and Michael Curtiz's *Angels with Dirty Faces* [1938]) later in the decade.

Another tough-talking, realistic film cycle which emerged from the early sound years was that of the newspaper picture. Comprised of films like *The Front Page* (Lewis Milestone, 1931), *Five Star Final* (Mervyn Le Roy, 1931), *Scandal Sheet* (John Cromwell, 1931), and *Platinum Blonde* (Frank Capra, 1931), the cycle was immensely popular during the thirties and important for helping to refine the technique of the dialogue film. While many newspaper films were made according to formula (*Front Page Woman* [Michael Curtiz, 1935]; *Libeled Lady* [Jack Conway, 1936]), the cycle produced several comic masterpieces (such as Howard Hawks' *His Girl Friday* [1940]) and influenced the content of many more, including Orson Welles' *Citizen Kane* (1941), whose central figure is a newspaper magnate (see Chapter 10). (In the seventies, the genre resurfaced in the form of Alan J. Pakula's *The Parallax View* [1974] and *All the President's Men* [1975], Peter Hyams' *Capricorn One* [1978], and James Bridges' *The China Syndrome* [1979], which latter use TV news reporting as a central element of plot.)

The historical biography, or "biopic," was another important sound genre. The vogue began in 1933 with the international triumph of Alexander Korda's *The Private Life of Henry VIII,* the first British film to achieve success in the United States. *Henry VIII* had its origins in the lavish *Kostümfilm* pioneered by Ernst Lubitsch (*Madame DuBarry* [1919]; *Anna Boleyn* [1920]) in post-war Germany, but there can be no question that the addition of sound enhanced the historical verisimilitude of the genre so enormously as to transform it. Perhaps the popularity in the thirties of films about the private lives of famous persons stems from the impact of the first Fox Movietone newsreels (c. 1927), in which audiences heard the actual voices of prominent celebrities. In any case, between 1934 and 1940, historical biographies became staple products of every major American and British studio; and films like *Queen Christina* (Rouben Mamoulian, 1933), *Viva Villa!* (Howard Hawks† and Jack Conway, 1934), *House of Rothschild* (Alfred Werker, 1934), *Catherine the Great* (Paul Czinner, 1934), *Rembrandt* (Alexander Korda, 1936), *Lloyd's of London* (Henry King, 1936), *Marie Antoinette* (W. S. Van Dyke, 1938), *The Private Lives of Elizabeth and Essex* (Michael Curtiz, 1939), and William Dieterle's *The Story of Louis Pasteur* (1936), *The Life of Émile Zola* (1937), *Juarez* (1939), and *Dr. Ehrlich's Magic Bullet* (1940) were very successful on the international market.

In addition to creating new genres, sound permanently changed some older ones. Perhaps the most vital of silent genres, slapstick comedy, with its fundamental visual component, was replaced in the thirties by the

---

* A similar sort of critical outrage was vented against the violence of *Bonnie and Clyde* in 1967 (see Chapter 17).

† Uncredited.

8.11 Dialogue comedy: the Marx Brothers in *Horse Feathers* (Norman Z. McLeod, 1932). Paramount.

8.12 W. C. Fields and Mae West in *My Little Chickadee* (Eddie Cline, 1940). Universal.

anarchic dialogue comedies of the Marx Brothers (*The Cocoanuts* [Robert Florey and Joseph Santley, 1929]; *Animal Crackers* [Victor Heerman, 1930]; *Monkey Business* [Norman Z. McLeod, 1931]; *Horse Feathers* [Norman Z. McLeod, 1932]; *Duck Soup* [Leo McCarey, 1933]; *A Night at the Opera* [Sam Wood, 1935]; *A Day at the Races* [Sam Wood, 1937]) and W. C. Fields (*The Golf Specialist* [Monte Brice, 1930]; *The Dentist* [Leslie Pierce, 1932]; *Million Dollar Legs* [Eddie Cline, 1932]; *The Fatal Glass of Beer* [Arthur Ripley, 1933]; *Sin of a Kind* [Leo McCarey, 1934]; *The Man on the Flying Trapeze* [Clyde Bruckman, 1935]; *You Can't Cheat an Honest Man* [George Marshall, 1939]; *The Bank Dick* [Eddie Cline, 1940]), and the "screwball" comedies of such directors as Frank Capra (*Platinum Blonde* [1931]; *Lady for a Day* [1933]; *It Happened One Night* [1934]; *Mr. Deeds Goes to Town* [1936]; *You Can't Take It with You* [1938]) and Howard Hawks (*Twentieth Century* [1934]; *Bringing Up Baby* [1938]; *His Girl Friday* [1940]). The screwball comedy was a film type characterized by wisecracking dialogue, furious pacing, and a certain element of visual burlesque carried over from the silent slapstick days. The focus of the action was usually a couple in a bizarre predicament. Some other memorable screwball comedies of the decade were: *Private Lives* (Sidney Franklin, 1931) and *Design for Living* (Ernst Lubitsch, 1933), both adapted from plays by Noël Coward; *The Good Fairy* (William Wyler, 1935); *My Man Godfrey* (Gregory La Cava, 1936); *Theodora Goes Wild* (Richard Boleslawski, 1936); *Nothing Sacred* (William Wellman, 1937); *Easy Living* (Mitchell Leisen, 1937); *The Awful Truth* (Leo McCarey, 1937); and *Midnight* (Mitchell Leisen, 1939).*

The careers of Mack Sennett, Harold Lloyd, Harry Langdon, and Buster Keaton all declined rapidly with the coming of sound, and even

* In the forties, screwball comedy provided a precedent for the darker social satire of the writer-director Preston Sturges (1898–1959), who between 1940 and 1944 produced eight

Chaplin's two features of the thirties, *City Lights* (1931) and *Modern Times* (1936), were basically silent films with synchronized soundtracks. Some silent comedians, such as Laurel and Hardy, survived by creating a unique blend of slapstick and dialogue, but purely visual comedy was necessarily destroyed by sound, except insofar as it found a new home in the animated sound cartoon. Another important silent genre, the Western, went underground in the early years of sound, when it existed largely as a "B" form, only to emerge at the end of the thirties with renewed vitality and realism in John Ford's *Stagecoach* (1939). From 1939 to 1950, however, the Western would experience a renaissance. Finally, sound provided a new impetus for films of mystery and detection like *The Thin Man* (W. S. Van Dyke, 1934) and its sequels, and for the horror-fantasy genre. Hollywood's three great horror classics—*Dracula* (Tod Browning, 1931), *Frankenstein* (James Whale, 1931), and *The Mummy* (Karl Freund, 1932)—were all early sound films.

STUDIO POLITICS AND THE PRODUCTION CODE

It is impossible to comprehend the American film during the thirties without understanding the mechanisms of the Hollywood studio system. The great studios were founded in the era before World War I when the Motion Picture Patents Company was destroyed and the independents moved to assume monopolistic control over film production, distribution, and exhibition. Through a series of complicated business maneuvers, both legal and illegal, they succeeded, and by the end of the war the studios were on the brink of becoming the vast industrial empires of popular mythology. In the period of economic growth that followed the war, Wall Street began to invest heavily in the studios for both financial and political reasons. It was clear, in the first place, that motion pictures were on their way to becoming a major industry; it was equally clear during these years of the "Red Scare" that the movies were a medium of mass persuasion and propaganda par excellence. For Hollywood films to extol the virtues of corporate capitalism and "the American way of life" was to erect an impenetrable barrier against Bolshevism.* This perception encouraged Wall Street to invest massive sums in the Hollywood studios

8.13 The screwball comedy as satire: Veronica Lake and Joel McCrea in *Sullivan's Travels* (Preston Sturges, 1941). Paramount.

films, mainly for Paramount, that are recognized today as important and highly original contributions to the American comic tradition. The objects of Sturges' satire, however, were much more serious than the frivolous rich of the screwball comedy: American politics (*The Great McGinty* [1940]), American materialism and avarice (*Christmas in July* [1941]; *The Palm Beach Story* [1942]), American sexual attitudes (*The Lady Eve* [1941]), American small-town life (*The Miracle of Morgan's Creek* [1943]; *Hail the Conquering Hero* [1944]), and American cinema (*Sullivan's Travels* [1941]). At a time when Hollywood was unabashedly extolling the virtues of American society for the purposes of war propaganda (see Chapter 11), Sturges' films offered audiences a vision of a corrupt, ridiculous, but often vital people whose chief flaw was a profound lack of self-knowledge.

* On the whole, the decade from the end of World War I in 1919 to the stock market crash of 1929, which began the Great Depression, was one of the least liberal in American history. In the early twenties, America's business leaders were panicked by the success of the

immediately following the war. The capital of Adolf Zukor's Famous Players–Lasky (soon to become Paramount) alone rose from ten to twenty million dollars in two years, and every important studio received large corporate loans from American big business.

Lewis Jacobs describes the inevitable results: "New men from Wall Street, educated in finance, became the overseers of the motion picture business. Characteristic of the new managerial figures were two directors of a new and powerful company, Loew's: W. C. Durant, at that time also head of General Motors Corporation, and Harvey Gibson, president of the Liberty National Bank."[2] Naturally enough, the leadership of these men left its permanent imprint upon the process of production. As David Robinson puts it, "The bureaucrats and accountants, eager to overcome the unpredictable and intractable element in the creation of films, began to codify certain principles of commercial production that still prevail in the industry: the attempt to exploit proven success with formula pictures and cycles of any particular genre which temporarily sells, at the expense of other and perhaps unorthodox product; the quest for predictable sales values—star names, best-selling success titles, costly and showy production values—which have little to do with art."[3] Films came to be made according to the most efficient production method American industry had ever devised—the standardized assembly-line technique. The producer's role as supervisor became enormously important in this process, while the director's role declined, and by the time sound was introduced film-making in America had become a fairly conventionalized and predictable operation.

It was to become even more so through the intervention of the Hays Office and the Catholic Church in 1933. By that year, the new wave of grim and often violent realism created by the coming of sound had produced yet another public outcry against the "immorality" of Hollywood films. This time, the reaction led to the formation of the Catholic "Legion

---

Bolshevik Revolution in Russia and by the attempted organization of labor at home. The attorney general of the United States, A. Mitchell Palmer, played upon these fears by declaring the country to be in the grip of a Communist conspiracy, much as Senator Joseph McCarthy would do thirty years later. In January 1920 he authorized the infamous "Palmer raids," in which over five thousand persons in thirty-three different American cites were rounded up and held without trial for alleged revolutionary activities (most were not "revolutionaries" at all, but labor organizers). Many were imprisoned for long periods of time; great numbers of those who were not native-born were deported; and Palmer became a national hero. This latter fact provides some indication of the temper of the times: the country was in a nasty, insular mood, and aliens of all sorts were regarded with hostility. Patriotism became a façade for racism of murderous intensity. Immigrants, blacks, and Jews were openly persecuted for not being "100 percent American," and the Ku Klux Klan's membership grew so rapidly that by 1925 the organization had nearly attained the status of a third political party. Organized crime also grew, thanks to the Eighteenth Amendment (1918) and the Volstead Act (1921), providing for federal enforcement of Prohibition. During the same period the average weekly film attendance was fifty million Americans per week, making the cinema a mass medium on a par with network radio and the tabloid press (or with television today). It was therefore essential to the maintenance of the status quo that the ideological content of films be as carefully controlled as the ideological content of other mass media.

of Decency," an organization committed to fight for better and more "moral" motion pictures. Supported by elements of both the Protestant and Jewish communities, the Legion persuaded members of the Catholic Church to boycott films listed by the organization as offensive or indecent. As usual, the threat of boycotts and the specter of state censorship intimidated Hollywood studio executives into imposing self-censorship before it was too late to act autonomously. In 1929, a Motion Picture Production Code had been drafted based upon the "Don'ts and Be Carefuls" formula of the late silent era, but it had never been effectively enforced. Now, Hays assured the industry's critics that the Code would be enforced by creating the Production Code Administration (PCA) out of an existing MPPDA (later MPAA) committee and appointing his assistant, a Catholic layman, Joseph I. Breen, as its head. Under the new provisions, no studio belonging to the MPPDA was to distribute or release any film without a certificate of approval signed by Breen, as director of the PCA, and bearing the PCA's seal. Failure to comply would cause a fine of twenty-five thousand dollars to be levied by the MPPDA against the offending company (the fine was never imposed, but it proved an effective sanction for over thirty years). The process whereby this certification was obtained was a long and sometimes humiliating one for film-makers. Raymond Moley has outlined its major stages:

1. A preliminary conference between Breen or other members of the staff of the PCA and the producer, to consider the basic story before the screen adaptation is written or purchased; at this point the plot as a whole is discussed in its relation to the Code.
2. Careful scrutiny of the script submitted by the producing company.
3. Scenario conference with writers and others to effect necessary changes in the script.
4. Approval in writing by Breen of the script for production.
5. Continued conferences during production, so that any change made in the script as well as all lyrics, costumes and sets may be observed and passed upon.
6. Preview of separate sequences during the course of production, whenever the producer is in doubt about their conformity with the Code; this is done upon the request of the producer.
7. Preview of the completed picture in the PCA viewing theatre by the same two staff members who worked on the script and by a third staff member who comes to the picture with a fresh mind.
8. After deletion of scenes, dialogue, etc., which violate the Code, issue of its certificate of approval by the Production Code Administration.[4]

Under Breen's auspices, this code was written by Father Daniel A. Lord, a Jesuit priest, and Martin Quigley, a prominent trade publisher and Catholic layman. Its provisions, which dictated the content of American films for over twenty years, were awesomely repressive. The Code prohibited the showing or mentioning of almost everything germane to the situation of normal human adults. It forbade depicting "scenes of passion" in all but the most puerile terms, and it required that the sanctity of the institution of marriage and the home be upheld at all times (married couples, however, were never to be shown sharing a bed). Adultery, illicit sex, seduction, or rape could never be more than suggested, and then only if they were absolutely essential to the plot and were severely punished at the end (a favorite means was death from accident or disease). Also prohibited were the use of profanity (a term extended to include "vulgar" expressions like "cripes," "guts," and "nuts") and racial epithets; any implication of prostitution, miscegenation, sexual aberration, or drug addiction; nudity of all sorts; sexually suggestive dances or costumes; "excessive and lustful kissing"; and excessive drinking. It was forbidden to ridicule or criticize any aspect of any religious faith, to show cruelty to animals or children, or to represent surgical operations, especially childbirth, "in fact or in silhouette."

But the Code's most labyrinthine strictures were reserved for the depiction of crime. It was forbidden to show the details of a crime, or to display machine guns, submachine guns, or other illegal weapons, or to discuss weapons at all in dialogue scenes. It was further required that law enforcement officers never be shown dying at the hands of criminals, and that all criminal activities within a given film were shown to be punished. Under no circumstances could a crime be shown to be justified. Suicide and murder were to be avoided unless absolutely necessary to the plot, and the suggestion of excessive brutality or wholesale slaughter of any kind was absolutely prohibited. The anti-violence strictures of the Code seem positively civil in this age of the cinema of cruelty, but the Code as a whole was obviously restrictive and repressive. From 1934 until the mid-fifties it rigidly dictated the content of American films, and in a very real sense kept them from becoming as noxious as they might have, and, perhaps, should have, been.

THE STRUCTURE OF THE STUDIO SYSTEM

The most significant force shaping the American sound film, however, was economic. In 1928, the studios had greatly increased their debt to Wall Street by borrowing vast sums of capital for the conversion to sound (see business chart, Chapter 7). Wall Street was happy to oblige, since the novelty of sound had nearly doubled weekly admission figures over the previous year. By 1930, a series of mergers and re-alignments had concentrated 95 percent of all American film production in the hands of eight studios, five "majors" and three "minors." The major studios were organized as vertically integrated corporations, controlling the means not only of production but of distribution and exhibition (or consumption) as well, through their ownership of film exchanges and theater chains. These studios were, in order of relative economic importance, Metro-Goldwyn-Mayer (founded in 1924 by the merger of Metro Pictures Corporation, Goldwyn Pictures, and Louis B. Mayer Productions, under the auspices of the vast theater chain Loew's, Incorporated); Paramount (the ultimate manifestation of Adolph Zukor's Famous Players–

Lasky Corporation, formed by a merger with the Paramount distribution exchange and twelve smaller companies in 1916); Warner Brothers (which had risen from the minor to the major league in two short years due to the success of Vitaphone, absorbing First National on the way up); Twentieth Century–Fox (technically the Fox Film Corporation until its merger with Twentieth Century Pictures in 1935); and RKO (Radio-Keith-Orpheum, formed by Joseph P. Kennedy in 1928 for the Radio Corporation of America [RCA] to produce, distribute, and exhibit sound films using the RCA Photophone system). The minor studios—which owned no theaters and were dependent upon the majors for first-run exhibition outlets—were Universal (founded by Carl Laemmle in 1912 and personally controlled by him until 1936), Columbia (founded in 1924 by its president and production chief, Harry Cohn), and United Artists (formed by Charlie Chaplin, Mary Pckford, Douglas Fairbanks, and D. W. Griffith in 1919 to distribute their own productions and still a distributor for independent producers in the thirties).

All eight studios were themselves under the financial sway of the two corporate giants of the era, the Morgan and Rockefeller groups, which also, between them, controlled all of the major sound patents through their respective ties to American Telephone and Telegraph (which owned and licensed the Western Electric Vitaphone system) and the Radio Corporation of America (which owned and licensed the RCA Photophone system, as well as owning the RKO studio and its exhibition chains).* As David Robinson points out, this nearly total domination of the studios by Wall Street had far-reaching consequences for the organization of the American film industry and for the character of the American film in the period between the introduction of sound and the Second World War, especially when the Depression finally took effect in Hollywood:

> Depression in the industry, which reached its peak in 1933, when a third of the nation's cinemas were closed down, only served to tighten the financiers' control over the organisation of film production. There was even less place for imponderables. Emphasis was laid upon achieving the highest possible standards in those aspects of film-making which could be controlled: quality of equipment, techniques, photography, staging and costuming. Every step was taken to eliminate those unpredictable elements which are of the nature of art.[5]

---

* The source of this information and of the charts reprinted on page 244 is F. D. Klingender and Stuart Legg, *Money Behind the Screen* (London, 1937). Discussing the impact of Wall Street control in *Movie-Made America: A Cultural History of the American Movies* (New York, 1976), Robert Sklar suggests that it makes much less difference who *owns* a movie company (or eight of them) than who operates it. He argues that although four of the eight Hollywood studios (Paramount, Twentieth Century–Fox, RKO, and Universal) experienced major changes in management during the thirties, the character of American film-making did not significantly change, since all of the studio managers, old and new—if not the studio owners—were entertainment industry veterans intimately familiar with their product and its consumers. But it also seems likely, as David Robinson implies (in *The History of World Cinema* [New York, 1973]), that financial concentration brought with it a much more relentless emphasis on economies of scale than the industry had experienced in its first three decades, resulting in an unprecedented standardization of production and a high-quality product.

Charles Higham describes how these results were achieved at Warner Brothers, perhaps the most typical American studio of the era:

> The writers [of whom as many as twenty would frequently work on a single script] . . . unquestionably occupied first place: they set the entire tone of the pictures of the time. The scripts were prepared in detail, even down to specific compositions of the shots, and the writers were almost invariably present on the sets during the shooting. Once a producer had approved a finished screenplay, he cast the stars of the picture. The director was called in, and in rare instances helped with casting of minor roles or changes in the writing. For economic reasons, he had orders to rehearse his players, then only use one take for a scene. The producer or studio manager selected the art directors, the composers, the cameramen, the cutters. These were seldom the choice of the directors, and all conformed to studio style.[6]

Between 1930 and 1945, the Hollywood studios mass-produced some seventy-five hundred feature films in which every stage of production from conception to exhibition was carefully controlled. These films took their styles and values as much from the studios that made them as from the individual artists involved in their production, and so it is important to understand how these studios were composed.

MGM

MGM was the biggest, most prosperous, and most prolific of American studios in the thirties. At mid-decade, it was producing an average of one feature per week, which, as John Baxter notes, was the largest output of any studio in the history of the cinema.[7] Its parent firm, Loew's, Incorporated, ruled from New York by Nicholas Schenck (1881–1969), provided MGM with the largest exhibition outlet in the world, and its close affiliation with the Chase National Bank gave the studio access to nearly unlimited capital. There was no film so big that MGM couldn't produce it, no talent so large that MGM couldn't buy it. The studio had under contract some of the greatest film talent of the thirties—the directors Frank Borzage, Clarence Brown, King Vidor, George Cukor, Sidney Franklin, W. S. Van Dyke, Jack Conway, Sam Wood, and Victor Fleming; the cinematographers Karl Freund, William Daniels, George Folsey, and Harold Rosson; the design director Cedric Gibbons; and, finally, a cast of stars unparalleled in Hollywood history ("More stars than there are in Heaven," as the MGM publicity slogan had it)—Greta Garbo, Jean Harlow, Norma Shearer, Joan Crawford, Margaret Sullavan, Myrna Loy, Clark Gable, Spencer Tracy, Robert Montgomery, the Barrymores, Marie Dressler, Wallace Beery, William Powell, James Stewart, Robert Taylor, Nelson Eddy, Jeanette MacDonald, Judy Garland, and Mickey Rooney. MGM was run during this period (and until his ouster in 1951) by its vice president in charge of production, Louis B. Mayer (1885–1957), a ruthless businessman with little concern for art, or even entertainment, except insofar as it could be merchandised; but the

8.14 An aerial view of the MGM studio complex, Culver City, c. 1935.

8.15 A ballroom scene from *Marie Antoinette* (W. S. Van Dyke, 1937), illustrating the MGM style of high-key lighting and elaborate production design.

studio's canny young production manager, Irving Thalberg (1899–1936), was able to maintain a consistently high level of achievement in MGM films until his early death. Mayer's son-in-law, David O. Selznick (1902–65), who was hired from RKO to assist Thalberg in 1933, also acquired the reputation of an artistic producer, and between them the two men produced some of the most prestigious MGM films of the decade.

The predominant visual style of these films was characterized by high-key lighting and opulent production design (the one employed to reveal the other), and their cultural values were the typically American middle-class ones of optimism, materialism, and romantic escapism. MGM's major genres in the thirties were the melodrama, the musical, and the prestigious literary or theatrical adaptation; some of its most characteristic films were *Anna Christie* (Clarence Brown, 1930); *Grand Hotel* (Edmund Goulding, 1932); *Dinner at Eight* (George Cukor, 1933); *Viva Villa!* (Jack Conway, 1934); *Mutiny on the Bounty* (Frank Lloyd, 1935); the Marx Brothers' *A Night at the Opera* (1935) and *A Day at the Races* (1937), both directed by Sam Wood; *David Copperfield* (George Cukor, 1935); *Anna Karenina* (Clarence Brown, 1935); *Romeo and Juliet* (George Cukor, 1936); *San Francisco* (W. S. Van Dyke, 1936); *Libeled Lady* (Jack Conway, 1936); *Rose Marie* (W. S. Van Dyke, 1936); *The Great Ziegfeld* (Robert Z. Leonard, 1936); *Camille* (George Cukor, 1937); *The Good Earth* (Sidney Franklin, 1937); *Captains Courageous* (Victor Fleming, 1937); *Boys Town* (Norman Taurog, 1938); *Too Hot to Handle* (Jack Conway, 1938); *The Citadel* (King Vidor, 1938); *Marie Antoinette* (W. S. Van Dyke, 1938); *Goodbye, Mr. Chips* (Sam Wood, 1939); and *Broadway Melody of 1940* (Norman Taurog, 1940).

MGM also produced some of the most popular low-budget cycles of the decade, including the Andy Hardy, Tarzan, and "Thin Man" series, as well as a few controversial and/or technically innovative productions like King Vidor's *Hallelujah!* (1929) and Fritz Lang's *Fury* (1936). Yet the studios' ambience and attitudes during the thirties are best summed up by its two super-productions of 1939, both nominally

directed by Victor Fleming, *The Wizard of Oz* and *Gone with the Wind.* *
Neither film has the depth or force of personal artistic vision, but both
are opulent, epic, and spectacularly entertaining products of the studio
system at its most efficient, spinning out beautifully crafted fairy tales for
children and adults alike. (In 1973 MGM ceased to exist as a studio, although it has remained marginally involved in the production of theatrical films through investment; see Chapter 17.)

Paramount

If MGM was the most "American" of the American studios, Paramount was the most "European." Many of Paramount's directors, craftsmen, and technicians had come to it directly from Germany via the Parufamet agreement of 1926, and the UFA influence on the Paramount style
was substantial. For this reason, Paramount made the most sophisticated
and visually ornate films of the thirties. The studio's German art director,
Hans Dreier, and its German cinematographers, Karl Struss and Theodor
Sparkuhl (as well as their American colleague Victor Milner), created for
its films a baroque pictorial style which was counterpointed by their
subtlety of content. As John Baxter remarks, "Paramount's was the cinema of half-light and suggestion; witty, intelligent, faintly corrupt."[8] The
studio was controlled throughout the thirties (and some twenty years
beyond) by its president, Adolph Zukor, and though it never achieved the
financial stability of MGM it produced almost as many films. And, because Paramount was less tightly organized than its rivals, these films
bore the personal imprint of their directors far more than the standard
thirties studio product.

8.16 The Paramount studios, Hollywood, c. 1935.

Cecil B. DeMille (see Chapter 6) continued to turn out the lavish sex-
and-violence-soaked spectacles that had made him the star talent of
Famous Players–Lasky in the silent era. His most profitable films for Paramount in the thirties were *The Sign of the Cross* (1932), *Cleopatra*
(1934), *The Crusades* (1935), *The Plainsman* (1937), *The Buccaneer*
(1938), and *Union Pacific* (1939). At the other extreme were the films of
the urbane Ernst Lubitsch (see Chapter 4), innovator of the UFA *Kostümfilm* and the silent comedy of manners, who had come to America in
1922 to direct Mary Pickford in *Rosita* (United Artists) and stayed on to
become Paramount's most prestigious director of the thirties. In the
sound era, Lubitsch specialized in musical comedy, light opera, and, once
again, the comedy of manners. His major films of the decade were *The
Love Parade* (1930), *Monte Carlo* (1930), *The Smiling Lieutenant*
(1931), *One Hour with You* (1932), *Trouble in Paradise* (1932), *Design
for Living* (1933), *The Merry Widow* (1934), and *Ninotchka* (1939),† to
all of which he lent a distinctly European lightness of touch and a vaguely

---

* *Gone with the Wind* was actually a Selznick International production which was released
and partially financed by MGM and which used a lot of MGM personnel and stars (notably
Clark Gable). See note on independent producers, p. 280.

†The last two were produced for MGM; Lubitsch's Paramount contract permitted him to
direct one outside film per year.

8.17 "Erotic-historical baroque": Cecil B. DeMille's *The Sign of the Cross* (1932). Claudette Colbert, Fredric March. Paramount.

8.18 Paramount's Continental touch: Ernst Lubitsch's *Design for Living* (1933). Miriam Hopkins, Fredric March, Gary Cooper.

decadent charm. Equally decadent but far more bizarre were the Paramount films of Josef von Sternberg (1894–1969; see below), all of which cast his protégé Marlene Dietrich (b. 1901) as the archetypal *femme fatale* in some impossibly exotic setting: *Morocco* (1930), *Dishonored* (1931), *Shanghai Express* (1932), *Blond Venus* (1932), *The Scarlet Empress* (1934), and *The Devil Is a Woman* (1935). In these virtually (and deliberately) content-less films, von Sternberg achieved a degree of visual elegance which has led one critic to describe them as "poems in fur and smoke." Paramount was also the producer of the mannered, technically innovative films of the Armenian-born director Rouben Mamoulian, including *Applause* (1929), *City Streets* (1931), *Dr. Jekyll and Mr. Hyde* (1932), *Love Me Tonight* (1932), *Queen Christina* (1933), and *Becky Sharp* (1935), the first feature to be shot in the three-color Technicolor process. Other notable Paramount directors of the thirties were Mitchell Leisen (1898–1972), whose stylish films *Death Takes a Holiday* (1934), *Hands Across the Table* (1935), *Easy Living* (1937), and *Midnight* (1939) are much admired today for their sense of visual design; Henry Hathaway (b. 1898), who demonstrated a high degree of technical polish in such handsome productions as *Lives of a Bengal Lancer* and *Peter Ibbetson* (both 1935); and Dorothy Arzner (1900–1979), one of the industry's few women directors (*Working Girls* [1931], *Christopher Strong* [1933], *Nana* [1934], *Craig's Wife* [1936], *The Bride Wore Red* [1937], *Dance, Girl, Dance* [1946]), who was famous for her editing skills. Finally, the best and most anarchic of the Marx Brothers' comedies, *The Cocoanuts* (Robert Florey and Joseph Santley, 1929), *Animal Crackers* (Victor Heerman, 1930), *Monkey Business* (Norman Z. McLeod, 1931), *Horsefeathers* (Norman Z. McLeod, 1932), and *Duck Soup* (Leo McCarey, 1933) were made for Paramount, as were the thirties films of W. C. Fields (1879–1946) and Mae West (1892–1980).

Major Paramount stars of the decade were George Raft, Ray Milland, Fredric March, Claudette Colbert, Miriam Hopkins, Herbert Marshall, Sylvia Sidney, Gary Cooper, Cary Grant, Kay Francis, Bing Crosby, Dorothy Lamour, Fred MacMurray, and Carole Lombard. (As a subsidiary of Gulf and Western Industries, Paramount remains today a major producer of theatrical films [*The Godfather*, 1972; *Saturday Night Fever*, 1977; *Star Trek*, 1979] and television series; see Chapter 17.)

Warner Brothers

In the cultural hierarchy of American studios in the thirties, Warner Brothers fell below the sophisticated Paramount and the respectably middle-class MGM. It was in fact the studio of the working class, specializing in low-life melodramas and musicals with a Depression setting throughout the decade. Conditioned by its origins as a minor studio, Warner Brothers imposed a strict code of production efficiency on its directors, technicians, and stars alike. Directors were expected to produce at least five features a year. Actors and actresses were hired at low salaries and held to them long after they had become stars. Sometimes, when a film was being prepared for distribution, Warners' editors were required to cut single frames from every shot simply to tighten the film's structure and increase its speed. (The process was salutary: Warners' editor-in-chief, Ralph Dawson, won three Academy Awards for the studio during the thirties.) Finally, the Warners cinematographers, Hal Mohr, Ernest Haller, Tony Gaudio, and Sol Polito, were required to adopt a style of flat, low-key lighting in order to obscure the spareness of the studio's economical sets.

8.19 The Warner Brothers First National studios, Hollywood, c. 1935. Warners purchased First National in 1929 with the windfall profits from its early Vitaphone films.

This emphasis on maximum economy of means, enforced by executives like Hal B. Wallis (b. 1899) and Henry Blanke (b. 1901), produced a group of films which were models of fast-paced, disciplined narrative construction. Warners in the thirties was pre-eminently the home of the gangster cycle (*Little Caesar* [Mervyn LeRoy, 1930]; *Public Enemy* [William Wellman, 1931]) and the Busby Berkeley backstage musical (*42nd Street* [1933]; the *Gold Diggers* series); but it also undertook some major works of social realism like William Wellman's *Wild Boys of the Road* (1933), Mervyn LeRoy's *I Am a Fugitive from a Chain Gang* (1932), and Michael Curtiz's *Black Fury* (1935). Warners was also responsible (and rather courageously so) for the first American anti-Nazi film, Anatole Litvak's *Confessions of a Nazi Spy* (1939), as well as for a series of prestigious biographical films directed by the former UFA actor William Dieterle (b. 1893) which included *The Story of Louis Pasteur* (1936), *White Angel* (1936—a biography of Florence Nightingale), *The Life of Émile Zola* (1937), *Juarez* (1939), and *Dr. Erhlich's Magic Bullet* (1940). Dieterle also directed a marvelously expressionistic and, for Warners, utterly uncharacteristic version of *A Midsummer Night's Dream* in collaboration with the great German stage director Max Reinhardt in 1935. Other top directors at Warners in the thirties were Michael Curtiz, the Hungarian film-maker who had worked for UFA in the twenties, and

8.20 Warner Brothers realism: Paul Muni in *I Am a Fugitive from a Chain Gang* (Mervyn LeRoy, 1932).

8.21 Warner Brothers fantasy: *A Midsummer Night's Dream* (Max Reinhardt and William Dieterle, 1935). Titania (Anita Louise) and the Indian Prince (Kenneth Anger).

Mervyn LeRoy (b. 1900). Given the studio's rigid organization and tight production schedule, neither Dieterle, Curtiz, nor LeRoy was able to pursue a personal vision in their Warners films, but all three proved themselves to be remarkably versatile professional film-makers who could function as master craftsmen within a system which militated strongly against creative freedom. Warners was also distinguished in the thirties for its art directors,* Anton Grot and Robert Haas, and its two great composers, Erich Wolfgang Korngold and Max Steiner, both of whom joined the studio in 1935. Among the major Warners stars of the period were Bette Davis, Barbara Stanwyck, Paul Muni, James Cagney, Humphrey Bogart, Pat O'Brien, Edward G. Robinson, and Errol Flynn—players who seemed to embody the tough vernacular pragmatism of the studio's films themselves. (Warner Brothers survives today as the film [*The Exorcist,* 1973; *Superman,* 1978] and television production division of Warner Communications, Inc.; see Chapter 17.)

Twentieth Century–Fox

Twentieth Century–Fox was a studio born of financial difficulties. In March 1935, the U.S. Supreme Court ruled against William Fox in his all-or-nothing attempt to retain complete control of the U.S. patent rights to the Tri-Ergon sound-on-film process which was the basis for the Fox Movietone system. Had Fox won, he would have been due incalculable sums in damages from every producer of sound films in the country and would have come very close to his dream of monopolizing the entire American film industry. As it was, he lost his personal fortune of one

8.22 The Fox Movietone studios, built in 1928–29 to produce sound films; from 1935 through the present, the home of Twentieth Century–Fox.

---

* For a brilliant, authoritative history of art direction, see Léon Barsacq, *Caligari's Cabinet and Other Grand Illusions: A History of Film Design,* revised and edited by Elliott Stein (New York, 1978).

8.23 The gloss of Fox: Lionel Barrymore and Shirley Temple in *The Little Colonel* (David Butler, 1935).

hundred million dollars in bankruptcy proceedings and was ousted as president of Fox Film Corporation by Sidney Kent,* who arranged a merger with Joseph M. Schenck's Twentieth Century Productions in late 1935, forming Twentieth Century–Fox and securing Twentieth Century's executive producer, Darryl F. Zanuck (1902–79), as the new company's vice president in charge of production.

The studio's films of the thirties acquired a reputation for hard, glossy surfaces produced through careful budgeting and production control. Fox's major director at this time was John Ford (1895–1973; see below), although he also worked sporadically for other studios. Ford's most important films for Fox during the period were *Dr. Bull* (1933), *Judge Priest* (1934), and *Steamboat Round the Bend* (1935)—all three staring the popular vaudeville wit Will Rogers; *The Prisoner of Shark Island* (1935), *Young Mr. Lincoln* (1939), *Drums Along the Mohawk* (1939), *The Grapes of Wrath* (1940), and *How Green Was My Valley* (1941). Fox also specialized in musicals like Henry King's *Alexander's Ragtime Band* (1938), and American period nostalgia like the same director's *State Fair* (1933) and *In Old Chicago* (1938), but its fortunes in the thirties were also built in large part upon the films of its popular child star Shirley Temple,† which included *Stand Up and Cheer* (Hamilton McFadden, 1934), *Curly Top* (Irving Cummings, 1935), *Captain January* (David Butler, 1935), *The Littlest Rebel* (David Butler, 1935), *The Little Colonel* (David Butler, 1935), *Wee Willie Winkie* (John Ford, 1937), *Heidi* (Allen Dwan, 1937), *Rebecca of Sunnybrook Farm* (Allen Dwan, 1938), and *The Blue Bird* (Walter Lang, 1940). Other Fox stars of the thirties were Tyrone Power, Charles Boyer, Alice Faye, Don Ameche,

---

*Not consecutively. Fox was forced out of his own company in 1931; he didn't declare bankruptcy until 1936.

† She had so endeared herself to the American public by 1937 that Louis B. Mayer offered Clark Gable and Jean Harlow to Twentieth Century–Fox in exchange for the child star, whom he wanted to play the lead in *The Wizard of Oz*. Negotiations were terminated by Miss Harlow's sudden death in 1937, and Judy Garland was cast in the role.

Warner Baxter, Henry Fonda, Loretta Young, and Janet Gaynor. The studio's major cinematographers were Bert Glennon and Arthur Miller, and its music director was the brilliant arranger Alfred Newman. Finally, Fox was noted for having the best special effects department of all the major studios—a reputation borne out by the disaster sequences of *Dante's Inferno* (Harry Lachman, 1935) and *The Rains Came* (Clarence Brown, 1939). (Twentieth Century–Fox remains today an important producer of film [*Star Wars,* 1977; *Alien,* 1979] and television [*M.A.S.H.*]; with Columbia, it is only major Hollywood studio not under the control of a corporate conglomerate; see Chapter 17.)

RKO

The smallest of the majors was RKO, which remained financially unstable through the thirties and forties and finally ceased production in 1953, when it sold its entire twenty-four-year output of features to television. (Two years later, RKO was sold to the General Tire and Rubber Company, which in turn sold the studio facilities to Desilu Television Productions in 1957; today, as RKO General, it holds broadcasting and cable television franchises for its parent firm.) RKO was ruled by eight successive regimes from 1929 to 1952 (the last being that of millionaire Howard Hughes, who is credited with wrecking it), and it was the most volatile and risk-taking of all studios of the era; the decade of the thirties, however, was its most stable period. In 1934, RKO became the home of the Fred Astaire–Ginger Rogers musical with the success of their first film together, *Flying Down to Rio* (Thornton C. Freeland, 1933), in which they had second billing. From 1934 to 1939, the studio made eight Astaire-Rogers vehicles under the auspices of its innovative young producer Pandro S. Berman (b. 1905) and star directors like Mark Sandrich (1900–1945) and George Stevens (1904–75). Films like *The Gay Divorcee* (Sandrich, 1934), *Top Hat* (Sandrich, 1935), and *Swing Time* (Stevens, 1936) made the Astaire-Rogers team one of the most popular box-office attractions in America and gave RKO a reputation for stylishness and sophistication throughout the decade, although it produced its share of B-films for the second half of double bills.

The studio also had a penchant for literary adaptations like *Little Women* (George Cukor, 1933), *Of Human Bondage* (John Cromwell, 1934), and *The Hunchback of Notre Dame* (William Dieterle, 1938). John Ford directed three such films for RKO in the thirties: adaptations of two plays—Maxwell Anderson's *Mary of Scotland* (1936) and Sean O'Casey's *The Plough and the Stars* (1936)—and a masterly, expressive rendition of Liam O'Flaherty's novel *The Informer* (1935), which some historians regard as the first recognizably modern sound film in its symbolic, non-literal use of the medium. RKO's most extraordinary production of the decade and one of its most successful was the monster thriller *King Kong* (Merian C. Cooper and Ernest B. Schoedsack, 1933), whose brilliant stop-motion photography and special effects by Willis O'Brien

8.24 The RKO studios, Los Angeles, c. 1935.

8.25 RKO's spectacular *King Kong* (Merian C. Cooper and Ernest B. Schoedsack, 1933).

(1886–1962) are still a marvel of technical achievement. The studio's major star during this period was Katharine Hepburn (b. 1907), who made fourteen films for RKO between 1932 and 1938, including *A Bill of Divorcement* (George Cukor, 1932), *Little Women* (Cukor, 1933), *Mary of Scotland* (John Ford, 1936), *A Woman Rebels* (Mark Sandrich, 1936), *Stage Door* (Gregory La Cava, 1937), and the classic screwball comedy *Bringing Up Baby* (Howard Hawks, 1938). RKO's art director from 1930 to 1943 was the distinguished Van Nest Polglase (b. 1898), whose genius was equally responsible for the stylish elegance of the Astaire-Rogers musicals and the murky expressiveness of Ford's *The Informer* and *Mary of Scotland*. In addition to its own films, RKO also released independent productions for Samuel Goldwyn and David O. Selznick and became the distributor for Walt Disney's animated features with the release of *Snow White and the Seven Dwarfs* (1937). The studio ended the decade with bravado by signing the *enfant terrible* of broadcasting, Orson Welles, to a highly publicized six-film contract in 1939, the first product of which was *Citizen Kane* (1941; see Chapter 10).

The Minors

Universal Pictures, which remained under the control of its founder, Carl Laemmle, until 1936, had been a leading studio in the twenties, producing for such talents as Erich von Stroheim, Lon Chaney, and Rudolph Valentino, but by the thirties the company had slipped into a minor position. It produced a number of prestigious films during the decade, including Lewis Milestone's *All Quiet on the Western Front* (1930), James Whale's *Showboat* (1936), and George Marshall's *Destry Rides Again* (1939), and it achieved some commercial success with the popular melodramas of John M. Stahl (1886–1950—*Back Street* [1932], *Imitation of Life* [1934], and *Magnificent Obsession* [1935]), but its standard product was the low-budget feature designed for double bills. Nevertheless, Universal did manage to distinguish itself in the horror-fantasy genre during

8.26 Universal horrors: *Dracula* Tod Browning, 1931): Bela Lugosi, Dwight Frye. *Frankenstein* (James Whale, 1931): Boris Karloff.

the thirties, drawing upon the UFA tradition of Expressionism and the talents of the directors James Whale (1889–1957) and Tod Browning (1882–1962), and the former UFA cameraman Karl Freund.

Tod Browning's *Dracula,* broodingly photographed by Freund, began the Universal horror cycle in 1931, and it was continued by James Whale's powerful and chilling version of *Frankenstein* in the same year. Whale, an Englishman of great sophistication with a fine feeling for Gothic atmosphere, became Universal's star director of the thirties on the basis of his elegantly mounted horror films. He went on to direct *The Old Dark House* (1932), *The Invisible Man* (1935), and the oddly baroque *The Bride of Frankenstein* (1935) for the studio before turning to other genres. Other important Universal horror films of the thirties were Robert Florey's Caligariesque *Murders in the Rue Morgue* (1932), photographed by Freund; Edgar G. Ulmer's bizzare essay in Expressionist mayhem, *The Black Cat* (1934); Karl Freund's evocative thriller *The Mummy* (1932); Stuart Walker's *Werewolf of London* (1935); and Lambert Hillyer's *The Invisible Ray* (1935) and *Dracula's Daughter* (1936). The latter concluded the cycle of serious horror films begun with *Dracula* in 1931. A second cycle was begun at Universal in 1939 with *Son of Frankenstein,* stylishly directed by Rowland V. Lee, and George Waggoner's atmospheric *The Wolfman* (1941). These were worthy successors to the Whale series, but the films of the second cycle quickly lapsed into imitation and self-parody with titles like *The Invisible Man Returns* (1940), *The Mummy's Hand* (1940), *The Ghost of Frankenstein* (1942), and *Frankenstein Meets the Wolfman* (1943). When the first horror cycle ended, Universal discovered the teenage singing star Deanna Durbin and featured her in a series of musical comedies made by the producer-director team of Joe Pasternak and Henry Koster (*Three Smart Girls* [1936]; *Mad About Music* [1938]) which kept the studio from bankruptcy until the second horror cycle began to pay off. Other stars under contract to Universal during the thirties included, appropriately, Boris Karloff, Bela

Lugosi, and Lon Chaney, Jr. (As a subsidiary of the entertainment conglomerate MCA, Universal is today Hollywood's leading studio, producing more theatrical films [*Jaws*, 1975; *The Deer Hunter*, 1978; *1941*, 1979] and prime-time television series than anyone else in the industry; see Chapter 17.)

Columbia Pictures was the brainchild of a single man, Harry Cohn, who founded the organization in 1924 and ruled over it absolutely until his death in 1958. Columbia's staple product was the low-budget co-feature, but Cohn had a policy of hiring, for single pictures, stars who were temporarily disaffected from their regular studios, and he managed to produce a number of first-class films in this manner, including George Cukor's *Holiday* (1938); Rouben Mamoulian's *Golden Boy* (1939); and Howard Hawks' *Twentieth Century* (1934), *Only Angels Have Wings* (1939), and *His Girl Friday* (1940). The studio's star director was Frank Capra (b. 1897), whose New Deal and screwball comedies written by Robert Riskin were largely responsible for keeping Columbia solvent during the thirties. The prototype of the form was the enormously successful *It Happened One Night* (1934), written by Riskin and starring Clark Gable (on loan from MGM) and Claudette Colbert (on loan from Paramount). This romantic comedy concerns the adventures of a runaway heiress and a newspaperman who discovers her identity and ends by marrying her. The film is full of witty, fast-talking dialogue, ingenious gags, and incredible twists of plot that established a new style in Hollywood comedy for the rest of the decade. Other Capra-Riskin films— the social comedies *Mr. Deeds Goes to Town* (1936) and *You Can't Take It with You* (1938), the more serious *Mr. Smith Goes to Washington* (1939), and the utopian fantasy *Lost Horizon* (1937)—possess the same qualities of refreshing informality mixed with New Deal optimism and populism, constituting what one critic has called "fantasies of good will."[9] Other Columbia assets were the gifted comedienne Jean Arthur

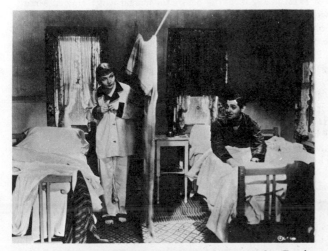

8.27 Columbia's "sleeper" *It Happened One Night* (Frank Capra, 1934): Claudette Colbert, Clark Gable.

8.28 *Mr. Deeds Goes to Town* (Frank Capra, 1936): Gary Cooper on the tuba. Columbia.

and the opera star Grace Moore, whose popular series of musicals—*One Night of Love* (Victor Schertzinger, 1934), *Love Me Forever* (Schertzinger, 1935), and *I'll Take Romance* (Edward H. Griffith, 1937)—put Columbia well on its way to becoming a major studio in the forties and fifties. (Today, as Columbia Pictures Industries, Inc., Columbia is still an independently-owned producer of theatrical films [*Shampoo*, 1975; *Close Encounters of the Third Kind*, 1977; *Kramer vs. Kramer*, 1979] and television; see Chapter 17.)

United Artists was not, strictly speaking, a production studio at all but a distributor for the films of independent producers.* It had been founded by Charlie Chaplin, Mary Pickford, Douglas Fairbanks, and D. W. Griffith in 1919 to distribute their own films, and in the thirties it handled the independent productions of Samuel Goldwyn, David O. Selznick, Walter Wanger, Hal Roach, and the Hungarian-born British producer-director Alexander Korda, among others. United Artists was unique in that it owned no production facilities and no exhibition chains, so production and distribution of its films were negotiated on an individual basis. Because United Artists had no studio and no stars, it did not fare well financially during this period of Hollywood's massive corporate growth, but by the same token the absence of a huge overhead enabled it to survive hard times. Its most important releases of the thirties were Chaplin's *City Lights* (1931) and *Modern Times* (1936), King Vidor's *Street Scene* (1931) and *Our Daily Bread* (1934), Lewis Milestone's *The Front Page* (1931), Howard Hawks' *Scarface* (1932), René Clair's *The Ghost Goes*

---

* There were a handful of independent producers in Hollywood during the heyday of the studio system, most of whom released their films through United Artists or RKO. The two most influential were Samuel Goldwyn of Samuel Goldwyn Productions and David O. Selznick of Selznick International Pictures. As Samuel Goldfish, Goldwyn had founded the Goldwyn Pictures Corporation with Edgar Selwyn (1875–1944) in 1917, combining the first and last syllables of their respective names into the famous surname that Goldfish legally took as his own in 1918. In 1923, shortly before the merger which created Metro-Goldwyn-Mayer (and which simultaneously dealt him out of the new corporation), Goldwyn formed Samuel Goldwyn Productions, a completely independent company, and he went on to become one of the most prestigious producers of the thirties and forties. The logo "Samuel Goldwyn Presents" became synonymous with high-quality family entertainment during these years and served to introduce much new talent to the industry. Although he produced the films of many important directors (e.g., King Vidor, John Ford), Goldwyn's most fruitful association was with William Wyler (see below), who provided him with some of his biggest hits (*Dodsworth* [1936]; *Dead End* [1937]; *Wuthering Heights* [1939]; *The Little Foxes* [1941]; *The Best Years of Our Lives* [1946]). David O. Selznick left MGM to found Selznick International Pictures in 1936 and became the very type of creative independent producer that so many film-makers enmeshed in the cogs and gears of the studio system longed to be. His motto "In a tradition of quality," Selznick produced a series of lavish but tasteful films whose meticulous attention to detail borders on the obsessive: William Wellman's *A Star Is Born* (1937) and *Nothing Sacred* (1937); Alfred Hitchcock's *Rebecca* (1940), *Spellbound* (1945), and *The Paradine Case* (1948); John Cromwell's *Since You Went Away* (1944); King Vidor's *Duel in the Sun* (1946); William Dieterle's *Portrait of Jenny* (1948); and, as co-producer with Alexander Korda, Carol Reed's *The Third Man* (1949). Although like Goldwyn he released mainly through United Artists and RKO, Selznick's most famous film, *Gone with the Wind* (1939), was produced for MGM so that he could cast MGM contract star Clark Gable in the role of Rhett Butler.

West (1936), William Cameron Menzies' *Things to Come* (1936), and Alexander Korda's *The Private Life of Henry VIII* (1933), *Rembrandt* (1936), and *Elephant Boy* (1937)*—the last five all products of a long-term contract with Korda's London Films production company. United Artists also had a distribution contract with Samuel Goldwyn, who released through the company, as an independent producer, *Stella Dallas* (King Vidor, 1937), *Dead End* (William Wyler, 1937), and *Wuthering Heights* (William Wyler, 1939), among other films. (As a subsidiary of Transamerica Corporation, United Artists today produces films [*One Flew Over the Cuckoo's Nest*, 1975; *Rocky*, 1976] and television entertainment, and owns a small chain of first-run theaters; see Chapter 17.)

"Poverty Row"

Below even the minor studios were the "B" studios. These came into existence in the thirties as the result of a uniquely American movie phenomenon: the double bill. When the novelty of sound had worn off and the Depression had set in, audiences began to stay away from the movies. From ninety million admissions a week in 1930, the figure dropped to sixty million by 1932. By midsummer of 1935, five thousand of the sixteen thousand movie theaters in the U.S. were closed. To combat this situation Hollywood invented the double bill, which offered two features, a cartoon, and a newsreel for the price of a single admission. By 1935, 85 percent of all American theaters were offering double bills, and from 1935 to around 1950 American audiences expected three-hours-plus worth of entertainment every time they went to the movies. The B-studios were created by the rental system which the major studios devised for double features. Whereas the producer/distributor and the exhibitor would split the box-office receipts for the main feature, or the A-film (usually sixty/forty or eighty/twenty), the B-film was rented to the exhibitor at a flat rate. This meant that there was very little financial risk involved in producing B-films (since distribution was guaranteed), but that there was also very little profit in it since the film would never make more money than the fixed rate allowed. For this reason the major studios had scant interest in producing B-features (although the minors produced their share), and so in the mid-thirties a handful of small studios sprang up in Hollywood for the specific purpose of producing cheap, hour-long genre films† for the bottom half of double bills.

Collectively known as "The B-Hive," or "Poverty Row," these studios operated on an extremely thin profit margin with very little capital. A B-feature might cost seventy-five thousand to eighty thousand dollars to produce and make a profit of ten thousand to fifteen thousand dollars nation-wide. Shooting schedules ranged from seven to fourteen days,

---

* Co-directed by Zoltan Korda and Robert Flaherty.

† Films like Westerns, gangster films, and science-fiction films which adhere to formulaic structures of plot and character with little variation. For a detailed history of the American B-film from 1933 to 1945, see Don Miller, *"B" Movies* (New York, 1973).

depending on the material, and were rigidly followed: to keep a cast and crew on tap for a single day beyond the scheduled completion date would often destroy the small profit margin. The most important B-studios were Republic, Monogram, Grand National, and—in the forties—Producers Releasing Corporation (PRC) and Eagle-Lion. At their peak, each studio produced forty to fifty films per year, most of which were trash. But the B-studios also provided the training ground for many a director who went on to better things (Lambert Hillyer, Edward Dmytryk, and, more recently, Curtis Harrington and Phil Karlson), and they produced a number of extraordinary films in their own right (e.g., Edgar G. Ulmer's *Detour* [1946]; Orson Welles' *Macbeth* [1948]; Joseph H. Lewis' *Gun Crazy* [1949]). When the major studios lost their theater chains in the late forties, the double bill was no longer profitable. The B-studios folded, and the B-film found a new home in the form of the television series.

The studio system of production could exist only so long as the majors maintained their monopolistic control of the means of exhibition.* Without a guaranteed weekly audience, films would have to be made and sold on terms other than the system allowed. In July 1938, in *The United States* v. *Paramount Pictures,* the federal government began litigation against the five major studios for combining and conspiring to restrain trade unreasonably and to monopolize the production, distribution, and exhibition of motion pictures. The three minors were charged with combining and conspiring with the majors for the same purpose. When war seemed imminent in 1940, a consent decree was issued permitting the studios to retain their exhibition chains, with minor restrictions, but the case was re-activated in 1945 and concluded in May 1948, when the U.S. Supreme Court ruled that the vertical integration of the majors violated federal anti-trust laws and ordered the five companies to divest themselves of their theaters over a five-year period (see Chapter 11). The divestiture order, known as the "Paramount decrees" or "consent decrees," destroyed the studio system by eliminating the guaranteed distribution and guaranteed weekly audience which were its mainstay.

MAJOR FIGURES OF THE STUDIO ERA

The period 1930 to 1939 saw the production of some five thousand feature films in the United States and was, in many ways, a Golden Age for the American cinema. Despite the rigors and impersonality of the Hollywood production system, at least four directors working in America in the thirties emerged as major figures of the sound film. They were Josef von Sternberg, John Ford, Howard Hawks, and Alfred Hitchcock.

---

* The studios actually owned only 17 percent of the nation's theaters, but that 17 percent comprised 70 percent of the first-run houses in the ninety-two largest cities. This de facto monopoly on first-run theaters guaranteed the studios bookings for all new productions. Today, without that guarantee, film-making in America has become a much greater speculative risk than it was during the years of the studio system.

Josef von Sternberg

Born Jonas Stern in Vienna, Josef von Sternberg (1894–1969) began his career in the United States during World War I as a maker of training and indoctrination films for the Army Signal Corps. He spent his apprenticeship as a technical assistant, scenarist, and cameraman for a variety of film-makers in America and England before directing his first film, the independently produced *The Salvation Hunters,* in 1925. Constructed according to the principles of the German *Kammerspielfilm* and strongly influenced by the psychological naturalism of von Stroheim, whose *The Wedding March* (1928) he would later re-edit for Paramount, this highly symbolic tale of low life on the San Pedro mud flats was shot on location in three weeks for the extremely small sum of forty-five hundred dollars. Distributed by United Artists, *The Salvation Hunters* established von Sternberg as an important new director in Hollywood.

In 1927, after several failed attempts at films for Charlie Chaplin (*The Sea Gull* [1926]) and MGM (*The Exquisite Sinner* [1926]), von Sternberg went to work for Paramount, where he made *Underworld* (1927), generally considered to be the first modern gangster film, although its realism was tempered by the lush visual poetry which would soon become a von Sternberg trademark. Based on a contemporary story idea by Ben Hecht,* this sumptuously photographed film was an immediate international success and had a great influence on European directors, especially Jacques Prévert, Marcel Carné, and Julien Duvivier (see Chapter 9), in its treatment of the gangster as modern anti-hero. *Underworld* was so popular that it made von Sternberg and everyone connected with it world-famous. In 1928, after directing Emil Jannings in an immensely successful melodrama of the Russian Revolution entitled *The Last Command,* von Sternberg returned to *Kammerspielfilm* with *The Docks of New York.* This brooding tale of an encounter between a ship's stoker and a prostitute along the New York waterfront is renowned as a masterpiece of pictorial composition. The film was produced entirely in the studio, and its visually complex *mise-en-scène* creates a dreamlike atmosphere, reminiscent of Griffith's *Broken Blossoms* (1919), which was resurrected a decade later in Carné and Prévert's *Quai des brûmes* (*Port of Shadows,* 1938).

Von Sternberg made the transition to sound with the realistic gangster/prison drama *Thunderbolt* in 1929, and in that year he was summoned to Germany by Erich Pommer to direct, for UFA, Emil Jannings' first talking picture, a version of Heinrich Mann's novel *Professor Unrat* (1905); it became the first real classic of the sound film, *Der blaue Engel* (*The Blue Angel,* 1930). Adapted from the novel by von Sternberg himself, *Der blaue Engel* is a powerful film on the theme of sexual domination

---

*Ben Hecht (1894–1964) was a journalist and playwright who collaborated with Charles MacArthur (1895–1956) on some of the best Hollywood screenplays of the thirties, including an adaptation of their own popular stage play *The Front Page* (1931); *Scarface* (1932); *Twentieth Century* (1934); *Soak the Rich* (1936); *Nothing Sacred* (1937); and *Wuthering Heights* (1939).

8.29   Marlene Dietrich as Lola-Lola in Josef von Sternberg's *Die blaue Engel* (1930).

8.30   "High cinema-baroque": Anna May Wong and Dietrich in von Sternberg's *Shanghai Express* (1932).

8.31   Dietrich in von Sternberg's *Blonde Venus* (1932).

in which a middle-aged bourgeois teacher, played by Jannings, becomes enslaved to a sensual cabaret singer named Lola-Lola. The singer was played by Marlene Dietrich (b. 1902), a stage and film actress under contract to UFA whom von Sternberg chose for the part and subsequently brought to stardom in America. *Der blaue Engel* is striking for its creative use of sound and its impressive recreation of the sleazy atmosphere of cabaret life; it owed a great deal in this regard to the *Kammerspiel* tradition. But it is also the film in which von Sternberg first began his career-long struggle with the problem of "dead space," that is, the space that separates the camera from its subject and the subject from its background. (Initially, as in *Der blaue Engel*, he attempted to occupy this space with a variety of streamers, nets, posters, veils, and even cardboard cutouts hanging from the ceiling above the stage, but in his later films he realized that only by thickening the air with camera filters, diffusers, and gauzes could he achieve the gradations of light necessary to fill the screen as he wished.) Though Dr. Alfred Hugenberg, the right-wing head of UFA, denounced the film as an attack on the German bourgeoisie (which, in passing, it was), *Der blaue Engel* was an instant international success.

In 1930, von Sternberg returned with Dietrich to the United States to begin the series of five films for Paramount that were to make her one of Hollywood's most glamorous and sought-after stars and simultaneously to wreck his career. The first of these was the successful *Morocco* (1930), the story of a romance between a European cabaret singer and a Foreign Legionnaire in Mogador, North Africa, written by Jules Furthman (1880–1960). Photographed by Lee Garmes and designed by Hans Dreier, *Morocco* presents Dietrich in all of her seductive, androgynous charm, and was one of the most innovative of early American sound films. Upon its release, Sergei Eisenstein, then visiting Hollywood, sent von Sternberg a telegram stating: "Of all your great works, *Morocco* is the most beautiful."[10] After making a sardonic and not particularly inspired spy thriller, *Dishonored* (1931), set in pre-war Vienna, von Sternberg directed a low-budget version of Theodore Dreiser's novel *An*

American Tragedy (1931), a project originally meant for Eisenstein but abandoned when his Hollywood visit ended in a debacle (see Chapter 9). Characteristically, von Sternberg turned Dreiser's great work of social criticism into a tale of erotic obsession, much to the disgust of the author. By this time, von Sternberg's reputation had grown so large that his name was appearing on theater marquees with the titles of his films—a rare practice in America at that time—and he was frequently ranked with Eisenstein as one of the foremost directors of the era.

With *Shanghai Express* (1932), written by Furthman, von Sternberg entered his richest period of creativity. Herman G. Weinberg has called this film "high cinema-baroque,"[11] and it is certainly one of the most visually evocative that the director ever made. It concerns the interactions of a group of passengers on an express train running from Peking to Shanghai which is hijacked by a rebellious warlord, and it focuses on a glamorous prostitute, "Shanghai Lily" (Dietrich), and her former lover, a glacial British army officer played by Clive Brook. Essentially a melo-drama of deception and desire, *Shanghai Express* is a film in which decor becomes a theme in itself. From the hypnotic chiaroscuro photography of Lee Garmes, the incredibly exotic costumes of Travis Banton, and the lavish production design of Hans Dreier, von Sternberg created a mytho-logical China where "dead space" is virtually absent. The tour-de-force opening sequence in which the train leaves the chaotic, flag-draped Pek-ing station, the poetic encounters between Dietrich and Brook on the ob-servation deck of the express, and the long lateral tracking shots down the latticed corridors of the cars themselves—all constructed in the studio—achieve a visual saturation rare outside of German Expres-sionism and the later work of Eisenstein.

Von Sternberg's next Dietrich vehicle was the bizarre *Blonde Venus* (1932), another stylistically striking film with a weak narrative concern-ing the broken life of yet another beautiful cabaret singer. (Dietrich's "Hot Voodoo" production number in this film may well contain the most outrageous variation upon the "beauty and the beast" metaphor in the history of modern culture: she comes onstage as a snarling gorilla and strips off the costume slowly, piece by piece, to reveal her own blonde loveliness and another costume of feathers and sequins beneath.) Then followed a fantastic and beautiful film "based on episodes from the pri-vate diaries of Catherine the Great," *The Scarlet Empress* (1934). This film re-created eighteenth-century Russia with as much poetic license as *Shanghai Express* had re-created contemporary China, and yet was vis-ually more sumptuous than the original could have ever been. With gro-tesque statues and gargoyles by the Swiss sculptor Peter Balbusch, By-zantinesque icons and portraits by the German painter Richard Kollorsz, impossibly magnificent costumes by Travis Banton, and perhaps the most lavish production design ever undertaken by Hans Dreier, *The Scarlet Empress* apotheosized Dietrich as the ultimate symbol of sexual domina-tion and degradation. The operatic grandeur and massive scale of the film are thought to have influenced Eisenstein's stylized design for *Ivan the Terrible, Parts I* and *II* (1944, 1946). Enormously expensive to pro-duce, *The Scarlet Empress* failed at the box office (predictably so in a

8.32 *Shanghai Express:* Dietrich, War-ner Oland, Clive Brook.

8.33 Von Sternberg's *The Scarlet Em-press* (1934): Dietrich as Catherine the Great, with John Lodge.

year whose smash hit was Frank Capra's populist fantasy *It Happened One Night*), and its director's favored status at Paramount was abruptly ended. Von Sternberg's final film with Dietrich for the studio and the one which virtually ended his career was *The Devil Is a Woman* (1935), based on the novel *La femme et le pantin* (*Woman and Puppet*) by the decadent French romanticist Pierre Louys.* It tells the now familiar Sternbergian tale of a middle-aged man—this time an aristocratic member of the Spanish Civil Guard at the turn of the century—who is dominated and humiliated by a temptress. Thought by many critics to be among the most beautiful films ever made, *The Devil Is a Woman* is the only film for which von Sternberg took credit for cinematography (with Lucien Ballard), although he had supervised the photography and lighting of all his other films. In it, he achieved the ultimate in his attempt to make the two-dimensional cinema frame three-dimensional by filling dead space with decor and subtle gradations of light.

Sadly, *The Devil Is a Woman* was suppressed by Paramount shortly after its release due to protests by the Spanish government that it insulted the Spanish armed forces; it was not resurrected until after World War II. Simultaneously, the sympathetic B. P. Shulberg (1892–1957) left his post as production manager of Paramount to go to work for Columbia and was replaced by Ernst Lubitsch, who had a deep personal and cultural antipathy toward von Sternberg. This was the end for the director. Destroyed by his refusal to compromise with the studio system and by his own profligate style, his contract was canceled, and von Sternberg and Dietrich went their separate ways. After a wretched term at Columbia during which he directed a limp modern version of Dostoevsky's *Crime and Punishment* (1935) and a silly Grace Moore vehicle entitled *The King Steps Out* (1936), von Sternberg went to London to direct an epic version of Robert Graves' novel *I, Claudius* for Alexander Korda. This star-crossed production failed financially and aesthetically at midpoint and was never completed, though the surviving footage, preserved in the BBC television documentary *The Epic That Never Was* (1966), confirms von Sternberg's photographic genius. Returning to America, von Sternberg directed a low-grade police thriller for MGM entitled *Sergeant Madden* (1939) and the independently produced *Shanghai Gesture* (1941), a baroque attempt to evoke the stylish eroticism of the Paramount-Dietrich cycle in forties terms. After several abortive projects in the forties and an unhappy two-picture contract with RKO, von Sternberg ended his career with the Japanese co-production *The Saga of Anatahan* (1952). This unusual film, the only one over which the director had total artistic control, tells the story of the tensions between twelve Japanese sailors shipwrecked on an isolated Pacific jungle island and a man and his mistress—an Asian variant of the typical Sternbergian seductress—who already inhabit the atoll. Produced, directed, photographed, designed, written, and narrated by von Sternberg alone, *The Saga of Anatahan* was

---

*Also the source for Julien Duvivier's *La femme et le pantin* (English title: *A Woman Like Satan*, 1958) and Luis Buñuel's *Cet obscur objet du désir* (*That Obscure Object of Desire*, 1977); see Chapter 14.

shot in black-and-white, in a lush artificial jungle constructed on a soundstage in Kyoto. It is utterly appropriate that the last film by this master of cinematic artifice should have been made in a studio, when real jungles were available not far away.

The British documentarist John Grierson objected to one of von Sternberg's more visually extravagant productions by remarking, in a contemporary review, "When a director dies, he becomes a photographer."[12] (Von Sternberg *was,* in fact, a photographer, having begun as a cameraman and having maintained his membership in the prestigious American Society of Cinematographers throughout his career.) Von Sternberg would have considered this a compliment because, for him, the image was the only true medium of cinematic art. Strongly influenced by graphic art, his greatest films constituted a kind of painting with light. It is fruitless to maintain that his plots are trivial or frivolous, because von Sternberg was not attempting to create a narrative cinema. In fact, he had little but contempt for the American tradition of narrative film as exemplified by the work of Griffith, Ince, and DeMille. Von Sternberg's great achievement, on the contrary, was to create *within* the American narrative cinema a cinema of mood and atmosphere based upon European styles of camera composition and lighting and his own eccentric vision of human passion and desire. It was a cinema of exoticism, eroticism, and, ultimately, cultural decadence, but one of astounding sensuous beauty which is unique in the history of film and modern art.

John Ford

Like von Sternberg, John Ford (b. Sean Feeney, 1895–1973) began his career in the silent film, but beyond that similarity it would be difficult to imagine two more different directors. Whereas von Sternberg had contempt for American narrative cinema and for American values, Ford was a staunch proponent of both. Whereas von Sternberg contributed to the cinema a handful of exotic and eccentric masterworks between 1927 and 1935, Ford directed over 125 films, most of them popular and commercial products of the studio system, in a career that extended from 1917 to 1970.

John Ford first came to Hollywood in 1913 to work as a prop man for his older brother, Francis, a contract director* at Universal. From 1917 to 1921, Ford was employed by Universal as a director of short Westerns and adventure dramas. In 1922 he went to work for Fox, winning fame as a stylist with *The Iron Horse* (1924), a feature-length epic on the building of the first transcontinental railroad, and a sweeping drama of the Dakota land-rush entitled *Three Bad Men* (1926). Ford's first important sound film was *Men Without Women* (1930), a submarine drama in which one man must die to save the rest of the crew. This film marked the beginning of Ford's long and fruitful collaboration with

---

* A director who works on projects from contract to contract, rather than on the regularly salaried basis which was common in the studio system.

the scenarist Dudley Nichols* and the cameraman Joseph August (1890–1947) on many a successful project. Other notable Ford films of the early sound era were his version of Sinclair Lewis' novel *Arrowsmith* (1931), his trilogy starring the famous humorist Will Rogers (1879–1935)—*Dr. Bull* (1933), *Judge Priest* (1934), and *Steamboat Round the Bend* (1935)—and a desert adventure called *The Lost Patrol* (1934). But he was not regarded as a major figure until *The Informer,* his first great critical success, cheaply and quickly produced for RKO in 1935. Adapted by Nichols from the novel by Liam O'Flaherty (1922) and ingeniously, if frugally, designed by Van Nest Polglase, it tells the symbol-laden story of an ignorant hulk of a man who betrays a fellow member of the Irish Republican Army to the British for money during the Irish Rebellion of 1922 and is psychologically tormented by his act until the IRA finally kills him in retribution. The film was photographed by Joseph August in a brooding manner reminiscent of German Expressionism and the *Kammerspielfilm,* and much use was made of subjective camera techniques to portray the informer's tortured state of mind, as when a crumpled "wanted" poster for the friend he has betrayed appears to pursue him down a foggy Dublin street like his own guilty conscience. Though it looks somewhat less impressive today, *The Informer* became one of the most highly regarded films of the decade, winning unanimously the New York Critics' Award for Best Film of the Year and four awards from the Academy of Motion Picture Arts and Sciences.†

After this success, Ford was given projects with a more social and historical orientation than his action films had possessed. *The Prisoner of Shark Island* (1936) told the true story of the fate of Dr. Samuel Mudd, who was imprisoned for unwittingly treating Lincoln's assassin. *Mary of Scotland* (1936) was an intelligent political tragedy adapted by Nichols from the Maxwell Anderson play. *The Plough and the Stars* (1936) was a rather ineffectual version of the Sean O'Casey play about the Easter Ris-

---

* Dudley Nichols (1895–1960) was another important scriptwriter of the thirties and forties, working not only with Ford but also with Howard Hawks (*Bringing Up Baby* [1938]; *Air Force* [1943]); Fritz Lang (*Man Hunt* [1941]; *Scarlet Street* [1945]); and Jean Renoir (*Swamp Water* [1941]; *This Land Is Mine* [1943]).

† The Academy of Motion Picture Arts and Sciences (AMPAS) was founded in 1927 by Louis B. Mayer and other film industry leaders—including Cecil B. DeMille, Douglas Fairbanks, and Mary Pickford, in their roles as producers—with the expressed purpose of advancing the educational, cultural, and technical standards of American movies. (Its real, and, ultimately, unsuccessful, purpose was to combat trade-unionism among the growing ranks of directors, technicians, and performers who were pressing for higher wages and better working conditions as film-making became one of the nation's largest industries.) Its membership (originally 36, now 4,120) is drawn from prominent individuals in every branch of the industry, and its chief function is, and always has been, the annual presentation of "Oscars" (Academy Awards) for distinguished film achievement in the previous year. In actual practice, the correlation between Academy Awards and cinematic achievement is not at all precise. For one thing, the winning of Oscars involves a great deal more than prestige, since they inevitably increase the earning power of the films and performers that receive them. Each year, expensive campaigns are mounted by studios and other financial backers to "lobby" Academy members for votes which can be translated into profit in the marketplace. (For a detailed account of Universal Pictures' $300,000

ing of 1916, when a small group of IRA troops seized control of Dublin and held off the huge British garrison for twenty-four hours. Ford's most unusual film of the period was probably *The Hurricane* (1937),* which concerned the sadistic imprisonment of a South Seas islander by a brutal European governor and concluded with a spectacularly realized tropical storm.

The year 1939, however, witnessed the release of three of Ford's finest films. In *Stagecoach,* Ford returned to the Western for the first time in more than ten years and produced a film that was to revitalize the genre, largely in his own hands, for another twenty. Written by Dudley Nichols and photographed by Bert Glennon, this tale of a dangerous coach ride through hostile Indian territory by a group of misfits from every level of frontier society embodies what was to become a classical Fordian theme—the convolutions of human character under the pressure of extreme stress. Its stark and awesome setting in Monument Valley, Arizona—a location to which Ford would return time and time again— creates a symbolic landscape of the individual alone in an alien environment.† The film was a great popular and critical success, receiving awards from both the New York Film Critics and the Academy of Motion Picture Arts and Sciences (it also made John Wayne [1907–79] a star). *Young Mr. Lincoln,* whose formal qualities have been much admired in recent years, provided a dignified and somber treatment of the Maxwell Anderson play and succeeded in raising the story of Lincoln's early career as a small-town lawyer to the level of national myth. Ford's final film of 1939, *Drums Along the Mohawk,* dealt with yet another aspect of the American past. His first work in color, the film is a visually

8.34 Henry Fonda in *Young Mr. Lincoln* (John Ford, 1939).

promotion to impress Academy members with the merits of *The Deer Hunter* [Michael Cimino, 1978], see *Advertising Age,* April 16, 1979, pp. 1, 80.) Furthermore, Hollywood is a closed and really rather small community, many of whose members have known one another for a long time. The Academy's judgment is often colored by personal sentiment, both positive and negative, and there is always the implicit bias that what is good for the community in material terms (financially successful films and film careers) is good in critical terms as well. In short, it would be a mistake to assume that Academy Awards invariably signal excellence in films or performances. In fact, the Awards are probably best regarded as a company town's certification of the company product, and in this regard they do at least provide some indication of Hollywood's ever-changing image of itself as fabricator of American dreams. (For more, see Andrew Sarris, "The Importance of Winning Oscar," *Film Comment,* 15, 2 [March–April, 1979], 53–56.) In addition to giving its annual Awards, the Academy also maintains a large collection of printed matter relating to film, and an extensive film archive with screening facilities open to the public in Hollywood; retrospectives are common.

* Remade under the same title by Jan Troell in 1979.

† There is a story that when Ford was a boy in Portland, Maine, his older brother would earn pocket money in the summer by ferrying picnickers back and forth to a small coastal island in a rowboat. One summer, the brother fell ill, and the ferry business devolved upon John at a very young age. Among his clients for that summer was an elderly artist who would stay on the island all day long painting landscapes. According to the story, Ford was so fascinated by the painter that he spent the entire summer watching him work. The artist was the great American landscape painter Winslow Homer (1838–1910). (Related to the author by Murray Golden, Hollywood, May 1979.)

8.35 *Stagecoach* (John Ford, 1939).

8.36 The Welsh mining village in *How Green Was My Valley* (John Ford, 1941).

8.37 *The Grapes of Wrath* (John Ford, 1940): Henry Fonda as Tom Joad.

striking re-creation of the American Revolution in New York State which was shot on location in the forests of Utah's Wasatch Mountains.*

Ford's new burst of creative energy continued into the forties with *The Grapes of Wrath* (1940), perhaps the most important Hollywood film of the Depression era. Adapted by Nunnally Johnson (1897–1977) from the John Steinbeck novel, it concerns a family of dispossessed farmers migrating to California across the Dust Bowl of the Southwest during the Depression. Although the film sentimentalizes the suffering of the Joad family, it is notable for the stark documentary texture of its exteriors, achieved through the beautifully restrained camerawork of the cinematographer Gregg Toland. Like *The Informer* and *Stagecoach*, *The Grapes of Wrath* was recognized as a distinguished film by both the New York Critics and the American Academy (although Ford himself never particularly liked it). After lukewarm adaptations of Eugene O'Neill's play *The Long Voyage Home* (1940) and Erskine Caldwell's novel *Tobacco Road* (1940), Ford directed his last commercial film before World War II, *How Green Was My Valley* (1941), adapted from the novel by Richard Llewellyn. This romantic and nostalgic film, for which an elaborate Welsh village was constructed on the Twentieth Century–Fox backlot, deals with the disintegration of a Welsh mining family and the communal society in which it lives at the turn of the century.

During the war, Ford joined the Navy and made documentaries for the Marine Corps, including the famous *Battle of Midway* (1942), which he photographed himself during the attack, losing the use of his left eye in

---

* Original plans to shoot on location in the Mohawk Valley itself had to be scrapped when it was learned that industrialization had completely destroyed the landscape. See John E. O'Connor, "A Reaffirmation of American Ideas: *Drums Along the Mohawk* (1939)," *American History/American Film,* ed. John E. O'Connor and Martin A. Jackson (New York, 1979), pp. 97–120.

the process.* Ford's first post-war film, *They Were Expendable* (1945), was a moving tribute to the unstinting courage and discipline of the men with whom he had served. Exquisitely photographed by Joseph August, it tells the story of the sailors who pioneered the use of the PT boat during the American evacuation of the Philippines, and it is one of Ford's most intensely personal films. His next film, *My Darling Clementine* (1946), is among the most classically beautiful Westerns ever made. It concerns the events leading up to the legendary gunfight between the Earp brothers, here assisted by Doc Holliday, and the Clanton family at the OK Corral in Tombstone, Arizona; and it contains scenes of frontier communal life (like the lyrical dedication ceremony of Tombstone's first church) which are among Ford's most visually poetic creations. *My Darling Clementine* was succeeded by the final Ford-Nichols collaboration—a version of Graham Greene's novel *The Power and the Glory* entitled *The Fugitive* (1947), photographed by the distinguished Mexican cameraman Gabriel Figueroa, which in both theme and technique was reminiscent of *The Informer*. After 1947, Ford produced many of his own films, the greatest of which were *The Quiet Man* (1952), a nostalgic paean to Irish village life shot on location at the Feeney family homestead in Connemara, and a series of epic Westerns: the so-called Cavalry trilogy shot in Monument Valley—*Fort Apache* (1948), *She Wore a Yellow Ribbon* (1949), and *Rio Grande* (1950); *Wagon Master* (1950); *The Searchers* (1956); *The Horse Soldiers* (1959); *Two Rode Together* (1961); and the elegiac *The Man Who Shot Liberty Valance* (1962) and *Cheyenne Autumn* (1964).

8.38 A communal celebration in *My Darling Clementine* (John Ford, 1946): Linda Darnell, Henry Fonda.

Sometimes racist (the Indians in most of his Westerns are bloodthirsty devils—with the notable exception of *Cheyenne Autumn*), frequently sentimental, and always culturally conservative, John Ford was nevertheless a great American director. His accommodation with the studio system did not prevent him from making films of great technical virtuosity and strong personal vision. In his Westerns, he created a coherent mythology of the American past which brings him close to Griffith—for both men, in fact, history was the embodiment of moral rather than empirical truth, and their visions of the past do not often conform to fact. Historical inaccuracy notwithstanding, all of Ford's major films sustain a world-view based upon his admiration for the traditional values of community life—for honor, loyalty, discipline, and, finally, courage—and it is a world-view as consistent and compelling as any the cinema has to offer.

Howard Hawks

Another important director who dealt with typically American themes was Howard Hawks (1896–1979). Less a stylist than either von Sternberg or Ford, Hawks characteristically concerned himself with the construction of tough, functional narratives that embodied his personal ethic of

---

* For a detailed account of Ford's obsession with the military and his own military career, see Andrew Sinclair's biography *John Ford* (New York, 1979). For a more intimate portrait, see his grandson Dan Ford's *Pappy: The Life of John Ford* (New York, 1979).

professionalism, quiet courage, and self-respect. He directed major films in every popular American genre, during a career that spanned nearly half a century.

Hawks had been an aviator in World War I before entering the cinema in 1919 as a prop man for the Mary Pickford Company. There he rose to editor, scriptwriter, and, finally, assistant director between 1920 and 1925, when he went to work as a contract director for the Fox Film Corporation. He made seven silent films at Fox, one of which, *A Girl in Every Port* (1928), was modestly successful in France, but Hawks' career did not begin in earnest until the arrival of sound, when he began to work independently of long-term studio contracts. His first all-talking picture was *The Dawn Patrol* (1930), a grim World War I drama about the awesome death-toll among Air Force flyers, which featured some splendid aerial photography. After a fine prison picture entitled *The Criminal Code* (1931) and a motor racing drama called *The Crowd Roars* (1932), Hawks directed his most important work of the early thirties—the classical gangster film *Scarface—Shame of a Nation* (1932). Loosely based by screenwriter Ben Hecht upon the career of Al Capone and superbly photographed by Lee Garmes (1898–1978), this violent, cynical film portrays the rise and fall of a Chicago mobster named Tony Camonte whose gang is like a dynasty of murderous Renaissance princes. *Scarface,* the greatest of the thirties gangster films, marked the beginning of the brilliant Hecht-Hawks collaboration that was to continue throughout the decade.

Hawks' next important project was *Viva Villa!* (1934), a distinguished MGM biopic written by Hecht and Hawks but completed by Jack Conway owing to the interference of Louis B. Mayer. The subsequent Hecht-Hawks collaboration for Columbia, *Twentieth Century* (1934), however, was a smashing success. It tells the story of a tyrannical Broadway producer (John Barrymore) who spends the entire film, much of which takes place aboard the Twentieth Century Limited Express from Chicago to New York, attempting to cajole his estranged actress-wife (Carole Lombard) into appearing in his next show. With its rapid-fire dialogue and fast-paced editing, *Twentieth Century* became the prototype of the screwball comedies of the later thirties and forties. Perhaps Hawks' most distinguished film of the thirties was *Road to Glory* (1936),* which ranks with Lewis Milestone's *All Quiet on the Western Front* (1930) and Stanley Kubrick's *Paths of Glory* (1957) as one of the strongest anti-war statements ever made on celluloid. The film was the product of an unusual combination of talents. Directed by Hawks, written by William Faulkner, photographed by Gregg Toland, and superbly acted by Fredric March and Warner Baxter, it tells a searing tale of the horrors of trench warfare during World War I and ultimately suggests that professionalism, comradeship, and devotion to duty are the only forces that will sustain men in such a brutally hostile environment.

A similar theme pervades *Only Angels Have Wings* (1939), which

8.39 *Only Angels Have Wings* (Howard Hawks, 1939): Rita Hayworth, Cary Grant, Jean Arthur. Note the framing and eye-level composition.

* Not to be confused with his 1926 directorial debut, which has the same title but a completely different subject.

Hawks wrote with Jules Furthman on the basis of his own experience as a flyer during World War I. Thought to be his most beautiful aviation film, this tale of a small commercial airline pioneering the delivery of airmail in Latin America is a classical Hawksian parable of the necessity of professionalism and *esprit de corps* in the face of daily peril and death. Hawks enlarged his contribution to the screwball comedy with the anarchic *Bringing Up Baby* (1938), which provided the model for Peter Bogdanovich's rather pallid *What's Up, Doc?* (1972; see Chapter 17), and *Ball of Fire* (1941). He also successfully remade Lewis Milestone's *The Front Page* (1931) as *His Girl Friday* (1940), replete with fast-paced overlapping dialogue, before returning to more serious themes in the quietly patriotic biography of America's greatest World War I hero, *Sergeant York* (1941).

8.40 *Bringing Up Baby* (Howard Hawks, 1938): Cary Grant, Katharine Hepburn.

During World War II, Hawks made the tough combat drama *Air Force* (1943) and the hard-boiled romantic melodrama *To Have and Have Not* (1944), adapted from an Ernest Hemingway novel by William Faulkner and teaming Humphrey Bogart for the first time with Lauren Bacall (in her screen debut). The couple also starred in Hawks' bizarre and atmospheric *film noir** *The Big Sleep* (1946), whose plot is so convoluted that even the director and his screenwriters (Faulkner and Furthman, working from a Raymond Chandler novel) claimed that they didn't understand it. Hawks' last serious film of the forties was the epic Western *Red River* (1948), which sets the psychological duel between a man (John Wayne) and his adopted son (Montgomery Clift) against the sweeping backdrop of the first cattle drive from Texas to Kansas in 1865. Hawks returned to comedy with *I Was a Male War Bride* (1948) and *Monkey Business* (1952), which endeavored to resurrect the screwball genre, and he continued to make films sporadically throughout the fifties and sixties. Most of these were disappointing in the light of his achievements of the thirties and forties, but several, such as the Westerns *Rio Bravo* (1959) and *El Dorado* (1967), still contain the vital spark of hard-hitting, fast-paced Hawksian narrative.

8.41 *To Have and Have Not* (Howard Hawks, 1944): Lauren Bacall, Humphrey Bogart.

Like one of his own heroes, Howard Hawks was a versatile professional who distinguished himself in every major American film genre and virtually inaugurated several of them. Having begun his career as a screenwriter, he worked on the script of almost every film he ever made. Hawks was no visual stylist—he generally composed his scenes into the eye-level medium shots favored by the studios and worked within the frame as much as possible, avoiding both spectacular montage effects and self-conscious camera movement. As for lighting, he left it to his cameramen, who were among the most distinguished Hollywood has ever known: Gregg Toland, Lee Garmes, James Wong Howe, Tony Gaudio, Ernest Haller, Russell Harlan, and Sid Hickox. But Hawks was a great visual storyteller with an urbane wit and a nearly existential concern with the condition of men in extreme situations. His films are

---

* A French term (literally, "black film") for an American genre of the forties and early fifties which dealt with crime and corruption in dimly lit urban settings. See the complete discussion in Chapter 11.

frequently characterized as "masculine," and there is no question that his heroes prize the company only of women who, like the characters played by Lauren Bacall, seem to share the code by which these men live. But it is probably more accurate to call his films simply "American," in the sense expressed by the French film archivist Henri Langlois: "He [Hawks] is the embodiment of modern man. It is striking how his cinema anticipates his time. An American he certainly is, no less than a Griffith or a Vidor, but the spirit and physical structure of his work is born from contemporary America and enables us to better and more fully identify with it, both in admiration and criticism."[13]

Alfred Hitchcock

The fourth major figure of the American sound film in this period was an Englishman trained within the British studio system, Alfred Hitchcock (1899–1980). Like Ford and Hawks, he was a brilliant craftsman; like von Sternberg, a subtle stylist. He spent most of his career working in a single genre—the suspense-thriller—but his mastery of film form transcended it. Indeed, Andrew Sarris has called him the only contemporary director whose style unites the divergent classical traditions of Murnau (camera movement and *mise-en-scène*) and Eisenstein (montage).[14]

After receiving his formal education from the Jesuits, Hitchcock joined the London branch of Famous Players–Lasky as a title writer in 1921. He became a scriptwriter, set designer, and finally, assistant director; and when producer Michael Balcon formed Gainsborough Pictures at Islington in 1924, Hitchcock joined the company as a contract director. Because of a reciprocal agreement between Balcon and Erich Pommer of UFA, Hitchcock's first completed features were made in German studios, where he fell under the spell of Expressionism; this influence was to last throughout his silent period and linger on considerably beyond it. Appropriately, his first major success, *The Lodger* (1926), was in the genre that he was to make so uniquely his own. This expressionistic suspense thriller, based on Marie Belloc-Lowndes' sensational Jack-the-Ripper novel of the same title, earned Hitchcock a high reputation at the age of twenty-seven. The young director made six more silent films (*The Lodger* had been his third) before returning to the genre again in his (and Britain's) first talkie.

Blackmail (1929) was initially made as a silent film but re-shot and partially dubbed as a sound film in the midst of the transitional period (the voice of the heroine, played by a Czech actress, had to be dubbed by an English actress). It is one of the best films of its era, notable for its expressive use of both naturalistic and non-naturalistic sound. The plot concerns a woman who is being blackmailed for the murder of an attempted rapist, and Hitchcock used the new medium of sound to inaugurate his characteristic theme of the nightmarish amidst the commonplace. At one point, for example, the heroine's subjective feelings of guilt are conveyed by the seemingly endless clanging of a shop-bell; later the word "knife," recalling the murder weapon, emerges from a harmless conversation to haunt her long after the conversation itself has become an indis-

8.42 Hitchcock on the set of *Blackmail* (1929), attempting to record Anny Ondra's voice. Note the camera enclosed in the soundproof booth.

tinct murmur on the soundtrack. Hitchcock's freedom to achieve such creative effects arose from the necessity of post-synchronizing scenes which had already been shot silent. For the same reason, the action sequences of *Blackmail*, especially those of the first and last reels, manifest a fluidity quite remarkable for an early sound film. And *Blackmail* concludes with what would become a characteristic Hitchcock motif: a spectacularly realized chase through famous settings—in this case, the pursuit of the blackmailer by police across the dome of the British Museum.

8.43 The British Museum chase from the conclusion of *Blackmail*.

After directing portions of a musical review entitled *Elstree Calling* (1930) and an uninspired version of Sean O'Casey's *Juno and the Paycock* (1930), Hitchcock returned to the thriller form with *Murder* (1930; adapted by Alma Reville* from a play by Helen Simpson and Clemence Dane) and again proved himself an innovator in the creative use of sound. This story of a famous actor who, convinced of a condemned girl's innocence, solves a murder to prove it, contains the first improvised dialogue sequence, the first use of the soundtrack to convey a character's stream of consciousness, and many other experiments with non-naturalistic sound. Hitchcock was by now regarded as Britain's most important director. After three films of varying quality, including *Rich and Strange* (1932) and the schmaltzy *Waltzes from Vienna* (1933), he launched the series of thrillers for Gaumont-British which was to make him internationally famous; the first was *The Man Who Knew Too Much* (1934). This complicated film, the only one that Hitchcock ever remade, concerns a couple on holiday in St. Moritz who learn of a plot to assassinate a visiting statesman in London. Their daughter is kidnapped by the assassins (led by Peter Lorre, in his first English-speaking role), and the couple must simultaneously recover their child and foil the murder plot without telling the police. The film is a classical Hitchcockian parable of horror asserting itself in the midst of the ordinary and innocent. Its famous set pieces include the concert in the Royal Albert Hall (shot by using the Schüfftan process), where the assassination is aborted by the mother's scream, and the gun battle in the East End, with which the film concludes.

8.44 *The Man Who Knew Too Much* (Alfred Hitchcock, 1934): the scream that prevents a murder in the Royal Albert Hall.

Hitchcock's next film, *The Thirty-Nine Steps* (1935), freely adapted from the John Buchan novel, is among his finest achievements. Suspenseful but light of touch, it deals with yet another classical Hitchcock situation—that of an innocent man who must prove his innocence while being simultaneously pursued by both villains and police. In *The Thirty-Nine Steps*, a female secret service agent is mysteriously murdered in the apartment of Richard Hannay (Robert Donat), who flees London to the north by train and arrives in Scotland. There, he inadvertently walks into the hands of the villain himself, escapes, and then walks into the hands of the police. After a series of further misadventures, he finds himself being pursued across the Scottish moors by both groups while handcuffed to a pretty young teacher (Madeleine Carroll) who believes him a murderer.

---

*Hitchcock's wife, Alma Reville (b. 1900), provided screenplays, adaptations, or continuities for many of his films from 1927 to 1950.

This exciting chase, with its superb ensemble playing by Donat and Carroll, eventually ends in London, where all secrets are revealed and all problems resolved. Witty, fast-paced, and technically brilliant, *The Thirty-Nine Steps* is narrative film-making at its very best.* It also contains some classic examples of audio-visual montage, as when the scream of Hannay's cleaning lady on discovering the secret agent's corpse becomes the shriek of the whistle on the locomotive of the train carrying Hannay to Scotland.

Hitchcock's next film was an unexceptional version of a play by Campbell Dixon, based on Somerset Maugham's "Ashenden" adventure stories, entitled *Secret Agent* (1936). It was followed by the remarkable *Sabotage* (1936). This film was a contemporary version of Joseph Conrad's novel *The Secret Agent* (confusingly enough), in which Verloc, an anarchist bent on destroying London, poses as the owner of a cinema theater. *Sabotage* contains some of Hitchcock's most masterful sequences. The film's high-point occurs when Verloc sends his wife's young brother out to plant a time bomb, without the boy's knowledge. The child is waylaid through circumstance at almost every point in his journey—here a crowd, there a puppet-show. As the time for detonation grows closer and closer, Hitchcock's montage becomes increasingly complex until at last the tension is released in a spectacular audience-alienation effect: the bomb explodes, and the boy and all the passengers on an omnibus are killed. Later, Mrs. Verloc learns of the death and her husband's responsibility for it, and she murders him at the dinner-table with a carving knife. The editing of the dinner scene which immediately precedes this act is among the most powerful and restrained in all of Hitchcock's work: Mrs. Verloc's mounting determination to kill her husband is gradually shown to coincide with his own desire to die for his crime.† After a light double-chase film entitled *Young and Innocent* (1937), which contained a 145-foot tracking movement from a long shot into a close-up of a character's eye, Hitchcock made *The Lady Vanishes* (1938), the last of his British thrillers.‡ This was a stylish film of espionage and intrigue in central Europe, set largely aboard a train. It revealed the same deftness as *The Thirty-Nine Steps* and was a clear parable of England's blindness to the Nazi threat.

At this point in his career, having brought international prestige to the British film industry, Hitchcock decided to come to America. He made one more British film, a melodramatic adaptation of Daphne du Maurier's *Jamaica Inn* (1939), and began a seven-year contract with David O. Selznick by adapting another du Maurier novel for the film *Rebecca* (1940).** The stately rhythms of this highly polished film

8.45 The famous sound match from *The Thirty-Nine Steps* (1935).

8.46 *The Lady Vanishes* (Alfred Hitchcock, 1938): Linden Travers, Naunton Wayne, Basil Radford.

---

* *The Thirty-Nine Steps* has been remade twice—first by Ralph Thomas in 1959, then by Don Sharp in 1978. Neither production (both are British) even approaches the stature of the original.

† See the shot sequence on pages 298–99.

‡ Remade in 1978, with a script by George Axelrod and direction by Anthony Page.

** Only three films were realized for Selznick International under the contract (*Rebecca* [1940], *Spellbound* [1945], and *The Paradine Case* [1947]), but Selznick himself profited handsomely by hiring Hitchcock out to other producers and studios (Walter Wanger, RKO,

marked a change of pace for Hitchcock, who now had the vast technical resources of the American studios at his disposal. His second American film was a tour-de-force of anti-isolationist propaganda (the war had been going on in Europe for several months when production began) cast in the mold of his very best British thrillers, *Foreign Correspondent* (1940). After a weak screwball comedy entitled *Mr. and Mrs. Smith* (1941) and the murder mystery *Suspicion* (1941)—his first film with Cary Grant—Hitchcock returned to the subject of espionage with *Saboteur* (1942), a spectacular double-chase film which concludes with a mad pursuit at the top of the Statue of Liberty. In 1943 Hitchcock made what he considers his best American film, *Shadow of a Doubt,* a restrained tale of a psychotic murderer's visit to relatives in a small California town who believe him to be normal. The film is distinguished by its subtle camera work, superb performances, and intelligent screenplay; and the soundtrack employs overlapping dialogue mixes of the type first used by Orson Welles, in *Citizen Kane* (1941) and *The Magnificent Ambersons* (1942; see Chapter 10). Hitchcock returned to the war with *Lifeboat* (1944), an allegory of the world conflict in which a group of people representing a wide cultural and political spectrum are trapped together in a lifeboat after a Nazi U-boat attack. The film was shot in a studio tank at Twentieth Century–Fox and is constructed mainly of close shots.

8.47 *Lifeboat* (Alfred Hitchcock, 1943).

Hitchcock's first post-war film was the psychological thriller *Spellbound* (1945), in which the head psychiatrist of an asylum comes to believe that he is in reality a murderous amnesiac. This expensively produced movie was cluttered with Freudian symbols and contained many spectacular technical effects, including a dream sequence designed by the artist Salvador Dali. *Notorious* (1946), a tale of atomic espionage by Nazis set in Rio de Janeiro, was equally well-produced, and its elegant black-and-white photography by Ted Tetzlaff was an aesthetic triumph. There are several splendid sequences in the film, but the most stunning involves a swooping crane shot that begins at the top of a ballroom staircase and proceeds through a whole series of chambers before finally coming·to rest in close-up on a key held in the heroine's hand.

After directing a weak courtroom melodrama called *The Paradine Case* (1947) for Selznick, Hitchcock briefly formed his own production company, Transatlantic Pictures, with Sidney Bernstein (b. 1899), a British baron and film enthusiast who had long admired the director's work. Hitchcock's first Transatlantic film was also his first film in color—the boldly experimental *Rope* (1948—adapted from a play by Patrick Hamilton), in which two young intellectuals murder a friend in order to prove their Nietzschean superiority to conventional morality,* and then stage a party for his relatives in the presence of his concealed corpse. The film was shot in a single large room of a penthouse apartment in ten-

Universal, and Twentieth Century–Fox) between 1940 and 1944—a period during which Selznick International was in liquidation for tax purposes.

* Friedrich Wilhelm Nietzsche (1844–1900) was a German philosopher who emphasized the will to power as the driving force of all organisms, individual and social. The posthumous debasement of his thought by Right-wing German ideologues created the myth of the

8.48 The master shot for the dinner-table scene in Hitchcock's *Sabotage* (1936), followed by the shot sequence of the murder.

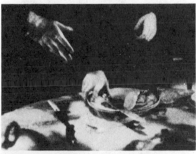

8.49 The murderers confronted in Hitchcock's *Rope* (1948): James Stewart, Farley Granger, John Dall.

8.50 The collapse of the merry-go-round in *Strangers on a Train* (Alfred Hitchcock, 1951).

minute takes with a continuously moving camera, for which Hitchcock developed tracking shots of extraordinary complexity. The few cuts were concealed by invisible editing and confined to reel changes, and there were no time lapses in the narrative, so the running time of the film and dramatic time of the action coincide, and the film appears to have been shot as a single continuous take. *Rope* was a critical and popular failure because the ten-minute take didn't work to sustain dramatic tension as Hitchcock had intended.

After two more relative failures in which he continued to experiment with the long take—*Under Capricorn* (1949) and *Stage Fright* (1950)—Hitchcock entered his second major period with *Strangers on a Train* (1951). This psychological thriller concerns a murder pact jokingly made between two young men, Bruno and Guy, who meet on a train, each agreeing to kill someone who stands in the other's way. Bruno, a psychotic, unexpectedly fulfills the pact by murdering Guy's troublesome wife, and then expects Guy to murder his (Bruno's) father. Horrified and consumed with guilt, Guy refuses to carry out his end of the deal, and Bruno attempts to frame him for the murder already committed. Photographed on location by Robert Burks, who with a single exception became Hitchcock's constant collaborator from 1951 until his death in 1968, this film contains some of Hitchcock's most psychologically subtle characterizations (especially in Robert Walker's Bruno) and concludes with a spectacular fight between Bruno and Guy on a merry-go-round that careens out of control and collapses. *I Confess* (1952), shot on location in the city of Quebec, concerns a priest who hears the confession of a murderer and is then accused of committing the murder himself. *Dial M For Murder* (1953) was a literal adaptation of a stage play filmed in 3-D* but released "flat" when the vogue for the process had died away (see Chapter 12).

Hitchcock's next four films were made for Paramount. In *Rear Window* (1954) he restricted his scope of action even more rigidly than he had done in either *Lifeboat* or *Rope*. The entire film is shot from a camera confined within the apartment of a professional photographer who is recovering from a broken leg, and during most of the film the camera records what he sees through his rear window. To pass the time, the photographer begins to spy on his neighbors through his telescopic lenses and gradually forms the conviction that one of them has murdered his wife, dismembered the corpse, and buried it in the courtyard garden. *Rear Window* is a disturbing and profoundly modern film: its theme of the moral complicity of the voyeur (and, by extension, the film spectator) in what he watches anticipates both Antonioni's *Blow-Up* (1966; see

superman—the notion that certain people could *will* themselves out of normal moral categories and commit with impunity acts that would ordinarily be regarded as crimes (mass murder, say, or other forms of barbarism).

* A desperate attempt to compete with the burgeoning popularity of television, 3-D, or "Natural Vision," was a cumbersome stereoscopic process for producing three-dimensional moving pictures which enjoyed a brief vogue between 1953 and 1954. Only sixty-nine films were made in 3-D, and some, like *Dial M for Murder,* had to be released "flat" because of audience disenchantment with the process.

8.51 The photographer as voyeur: Hitchcock's *Rear Window* (1954).

8.52 *Rear Window:* "We've become a race of peeping Toms. . . ." James Stewart, Grace Kelly, Thelma Ritter.

Chapter 14) and Francis Ford Coppola's *The Conversation* (1973; see Chapter 17), to say nothing of Hitchcock's own *Psycho* (1960).* In 1955 (the year he became a naturalized American citizen) Hitchcock directed *To Catch a Thief,* a stylish comedy-thriller about a cat burglar, shot on location on the French Riviera in Paramount's new widescreen process, VistaVision. He became one of the first directors to use the wide screen effectively for pictorial and dramatic composition, and all of his subsequent films were made in some variant of the process. *The Trouble with Harry* (1956) used VistaVision to capture the autumn splendor of the Vermont woods as a background to a sophisticated and witty black comedy about a corpse which refuses to stay buried because someone keeps digging it up. In the same year, Hitchcock turned out a splashy commercial remake of *The Man Who Knew Too Much* in color and VistaVision; and then, as if to expiate his extravagance, he made a grim semidocumentary film of false arrest and imprisonment, *The Wrong Man* (1957), shot on location in black-and-white in New York City.

In 1958 Hitchcock directed *Vertigo,* which many critics consider his most visually poetic film. Cast in the form of a detective thriller, *Vertigo* is actually a tale of romantic obsession adapted from the novel *D'entre des mortes* (*Between the Dead*), by Pierre Boileau and Thomas Narcejac. Scottie, a detective with a pathological fear of heights (vertigo), is hired to trail Madeleine, the wife of an old college associate, who believes herself to be a reincarnation of her Spanish grandmother; and he gradually falls in love with her. She dies—or seems to—by falling off the tower of an old Spanish mission, in part because of Scottie's negligence. Later he meets a woman in the streets who resembles Madeleine uncannily, and he spends the rest of the film attempting to re-create the image of the dead woman in the living one, who finally meets her death on the same tower

* For interesting treatments of the voyeurism theme in Hitchcock, see David Thomson, *Movie Man* (New York, 1967), and Donald Spoto, *The Art of Alfred Hitchcock* (New York, 1976).

8.53 *Vertigo* (Alfred Hitchcock, 1958): James Stewart, Kim Novak.

8.54 Cary Grant pursued by a crop-duster in Hitchcock's *North-by-Northwest* (1959).

8.55 Archetypal horror: Norman Bates (Anthony Perkins) stands before his mother's house in *Psycho* (Alfred Hitchcock, 1960).

at the film's conclusion. The two women are actually the same woman, who has acted as a foil in an extraordinary murder plot—a fact which Hitchcock reveals to the audience two-thirds of the way through the film, destroying suspense in order to concentrate our attention on mood and ambience. Shot on location in San Francisco in VistaVision and highly stylized color, *Vertigo* is Hitchcock's most atmospheric work, a successful attempt to re-create *film noir* (see Chapter 11) in late-fifties terms. *North by Northwest* (1959) is, by contrast, a return to the playful double-chase mode of *The Thirty-Nine Steps* (1935), which at times it seems intended to parody. And yet this film of a New York advertising-man pursued across America by both government authorities and nuclear spies contains some classic Hitchcock sequences, most notably the (literally) cliff-hanging conclusion on Mount Rushmore and the superbly constructed machine-gun attack on the hero by a crop-duster in the middle of an Indiana cornfield.

In 1960 Hitchcock directed *Psycho* (from the novel by Robert Bloch), his coldest, blackest, and most brilliant Hollywood film, shot in black-and-white widescreen with economical television production techniques. Before one-third of the film is over, the beautiful heroine (Janet Leigh), who is on the run from the police, is stabbed to death in a motel shower in a harrowing forty-five-second montage sequence which many critics think rivals the Odessa Steps sequence of Eisenstein's *Potemkin* (1925). *Psycho* is an outrageously manipulative film and is thus, like *Potemkin*, a stunningly successful experiment in audience stimulation and response. Hitchcock's precisely planned knife murder sequence is in fact a masterful vindication of the Kuleshov-Eisenstein school of montage: in a series of eighty-seven rapidly alternating fragmentary shots, we seem to witness a horribly violent and brutal murder on the screen, and yet only once do we see an image of the knife penetrating flesh, and that image is completely bloodless.* A second murder is so perfectly and unpredictably

---

*The sequence is perfectly complemented by the shrieking staccato violins of Bernard Herrmann's edgy score. Hitchcock had wanted to use only naturalistic sound effects for the murder, but Herrmann, felicitously, talked him out of it—an impressive example of artistic collaboration in a professional relationship which lasted from *The Trouble with Harry* (1956) through *Marnie* (1964).

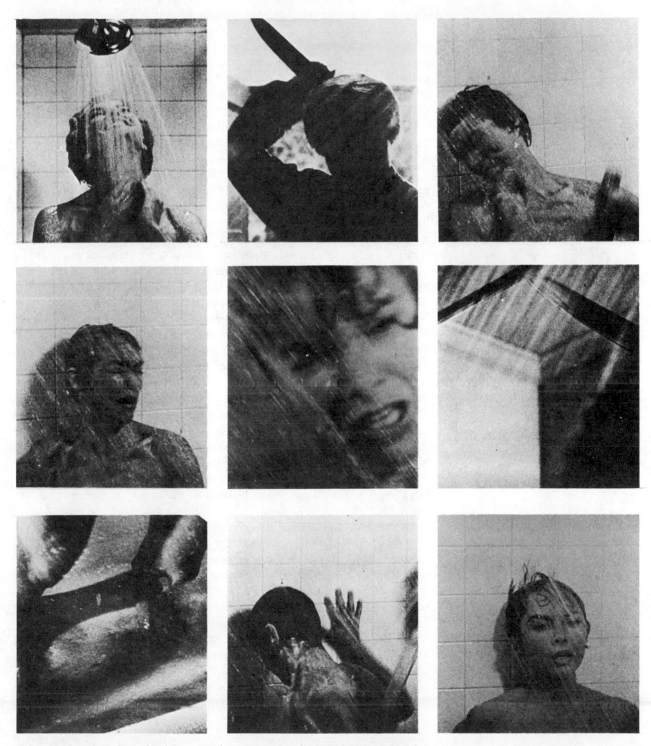

8.56 *Psycho:* shots from the shower murder sequence. Anthony Perkins, Janet Leigh.

8.57 A shot from the second murder sequence in *Psycho:* Martin Balsam, Anthony Perkins.

8.58 *The Birds* (Alfred Hitchcock, 1963).

timed that it delivers a large perceptual shock, even after many viewings. Time and again, Hitchcock uses his camera and his montage to deceive the audience by leading it up cinematic blind alleys and strewing the screen with visual red herrings. He also offers the most morbid narrative of his career—the knife murderer is a lunatic transvestite who lives in a gothic house with the rotting corpse of his mother, some twelve years dead by his own hand (or so we are told at the end, by the police psychiatrist). Many critics in 1960 were revolted by *Psycho* and appalled at its cynicism, but today its technical brilliance places it among the most important of post-war American films, and its blackness and bleakness look decidedly modern.

Hitchcock's next film, *The Birds* (1963), seemed to many an exercise in pure technique. Adapted from a Daphne du Maurier short story, it concerns a savage assault by the millions of birds in the vicinity of Bodega Bay, California, upon the human population of the area. The special effects (consisting of 371 trick shots) by Hitchcock and Ub Iwerks (1901–71), one of Disney's greatest animators, are remarkable, as is the menacing electronic soundtrack produced and recorded by Rení Gossman and Oskar Sala, but the film lacks depth and dramatic intensity. After *The Birds,* Hitchcock made a series of films which seemed to mark his decline. *Marnie* (1964), *Torn Curtain* (1966), and *Topaz* (1969) were all deficient in the cinematic vitality and technical ingenuity which had always been Hitchcock's personal signature. In 1972, however, he staged a strong comeback with *Frenzy,* which combined the lightness of the British double-chase films with the psychological introspection, kinetic violence, and technical virtuosity of *Psycho.* With *Family Plot* (1976), his fifty-third and last film, Hitchcock returned to black humor in a bizarre tale of kidnapping, phony spiritualism, and murder which contained distinct overtones of *The Man Who Knew Too Much* (1956 version) and *North by Northwest.* He was working on the screenplay of *The Short Night,* an espionage thriller based on the real-life case of the British double agent George Blake, when he died at his home in Beverly Hills on April 29, 1980.

The tendency to see Hitchcock as merely a brilliant craftsman, long the prevailing critical trend, has recently given way to a more judicious assessment of him as both a formalist and a moralist* (a status acknowledged by the American Film Institute's presentation to him of its Life Achievement Award in 1979). About his commitment to style there can be no question—during the thirties he was one of the few directors to use Eisensteinian montage, in an era of primarily functional editing; his mastery of the long take and the moving camera have been apparent since the forties; and his achievements in widescreen composition in the fifties are of major historical importance for the contemporary film. Beyond form, however, there is Hitchcock the moralist and fatalist who created an image of the modern world in which the perilous and the monstrous lurk

---

* For a persuasively argued opposing viewpoint, see David Thomson, "The Big Hitch," *Film Comment,* 15, 2 (March–April 1979), 26–29. Here, Hitchcock is neither "moral scientist nor teacher" but "a torturer."

within the most ordinary circumstances of everyday life. It is a world that shares much with the work of Franz Kafka and comprehends what Hannah Arendt termed "the banality of evil."[15]

George Cukor and William Wyler

Two other directors of historical importance emerged from Hollywood in the thirties, although their work has been less substantial and cohesive than that of the four major figures discussed above. George Cukor (b. 1899) first came to Hollywood from Broadway as a dialogue director, working with both Lewis Milestone and Ernst Lubitsch before directing his first film, *A Bill of Divorcement*, starring Katharine Hepburn and John Barrymore, in 1932. Since that time, with a series of stylish comedies and sophisticated literary adaptations he has established himself as one of the foremost craftsmen of the American cinema. Cukor has a flair for elegant decor and witty dialogue, and a facility for directing female stars which has typed him as a "women's director," but his talent

8.59 *Camille* (George Cukor, 1936): Greta Garbo, Robert Taylor.

8.60 Cukor's *Philadelphia Story* (1940): Cary Grant, Katharine Hepburn, James Stewart.

is really more versatile than the term implies. Cukor worked exclusively under contract to MGM in the thirties and forties but began to freelance in the post-war era. Among his most important films are *Dinner at Eight* (1933), *Little Women* (1933), *David Copperfield* (1935), *Camille* (1936), *Holiday* (1938), *The Philadelphia Story* (1940), *Gaslight* (1944),* *Adam's Rib* (1949), *Born Yesterday* (1950), *Pat and Mike* (1952), *It Should Happen to You* (1954), *A Star Is Born* (1954), *Bhowani Junction* (1956), and *My Fair Lady* (1964). These are all handsome, graceful productions which feature brilliant performances by some of the

---

* A remake of the 1940 British version of Patrick Hamilton's play directed by Thorold Dickinson. MGM purchased the rights to the play and withdrew the British film from circulation in the United States.

most talented actors and actresses in the American cinema: John Barrymore, Jean Harlow, Marie Dressler, Greta Garbo, Katharine Hepburn, Cary Grant, James Stewart, Ingrid Bergman, Charles Boyer, Judy Holliday, Spencer Tracy, Judy Garland, Jack Lemmon, James Mason, and Audrey Hepburn. Cukor's work reveals no strong personal vision, but it is remarkably consistent in its intelligence, sensitivity, and taste.

William Wyler (1902–81) was another fine American film-maker. He began his career by directing B-Westerns and shorts for his uncle, Carl Laemmle, at Universal Pictures. In 1935 he went to work for Samuel Goldwyn and earned a reputation as an accomplished adaptor of other people's work—most notably Lillian Hellman's play *The Children's Hour,* which Wyler filmed as *These Three* in 1936 and remade under its original title in 1962; Sidney Kingsley's play *Dead End,* with a screenplay by Hellman (1937); and Hellman's play *The Little Foxes* (1941). He also directed adaptations of novels—*Dodsworth* (1936), *Wuthering Heights* (1939), *Mrs. Miniver* (1942), and *The Heiress* (1949—from Henry James' *Washington Square*)—and other plays (*Jezebel* [1938]; *The Letter* [1940]). His collaborator for much of this period was the brilliant cinematographer Gregg Toland, who experimented with deep-focus photography in Wyler films like *Wuthering Heights* and *The Little Foxes* before he used the process so magnificently in Orson Welles' *Citizen Kane* (1941; see Chapter 10). Wyler's *The Best Years of Our Lives* (1946) was hailed as a masterpiece in the year of its release, although it is really a rather conventional, if intensely felt, drama of the problems of servicemen attempting to adjust to post-war American life. The inflated reputation brought him by this film led Wyler to pursue ever more inflated projects in the fifties, culminating in the widescreen blockbusters *The Big Country* (1958) and *Ben Hur* (1959). Nevertheless, he continued to pro-

8.61 William Wyler's version of *Wuthering Heights* (1939), shot by Gregg Toland on the moors of the San Fernando Valley: Merle Oberon and Laurence Olivier as Cathy and Heathcliff.

8.62 Wyler's adaptation of *The Little Foxes* (1941), photographed by Toland. Note the depth of the image and how the action occurs on several planes at once. Herbert Marshall, Bette Davis.

duce interesting work during this period, such as his tough, cynical action film *Detective Story* (1951), his literate adaptation of Dreiser's *Sister Carrie* (*Carrie* [1952]), and his delightful romantic comedy *Roman Holiday* (1953). In the sixties, Wyler staged something of a critical comeback with a powerful adaptation of John Fowles' novel *The Collector* (1965), but *Funny Girl* (1968) and *The Liberation of L. B. Jones* (1969) have since done little to confirm his renewed reputation. Nevertheless, Wyler was selected for the American Film Institute's Life Achievement Award, in recognition of his past contributions, in 1975.

The coming of sound threatened to destroy the international market that film had enjoyed since Méliès by introducing the language barrier between national industries. During the first few years of sound, Frenchmen would hiss and boo the dialogue in German films, and vice versa; the British and Americans found each other's accents incomprehensible; and there was the problem of regional dialects within a single nation. To overcome this barrier, films were for several years shot in different language-versions at the time of production. This expensive practice was soon abandoned when a whole new branch of the industry was evolved for the dubbing and subtitling of films for foreign markets. The American industry, long accustomed to international dominion, was able to maintain its control of the world market by virtue of its vast capital and, for a while at least, its wholesale ownership of the major patents for sound equipment.* But because of the economic domination of the American studios themselves by the country's largest corporate interests, the American cinema of the thirties had a specifically ideological orientation, which the Breen Code incarnated.

The central tenets of the Code were that the Depression, if it existed at all, had little impact on most people's lives; that there was no crime in the streets or corruption in government; that the authority of the police and the military were absolute; that religion and the nuclear family were sacred, coextensive institutions; and, finally, that most Americans in the thirties lived in bungalows behind white picket fences on peaceful streets in Anytown, U.S.A. By regulating the "moral" content of American films, the Breen Code was regulating their social content as well, so that what purported to be a blueprint for "cleaning up the movies" was actually an instrument of social control in a period of economic chaos. Thus, however great its aesthetic achievements—and they are clearly manifold—the American cinema of the thirties consistently concealed the *reality* of the Depression and, later, of the war in Europe from the American people. This is a matter not of opinion but of historical record: with several notable exceptions (e.g., Mervyn LeRoy's *I Am a Fugitive from a Chain Gang* [1932]; King Vidor's *Our Daily Bread* [1934]), Hollywood did not seriously confront the social misery caused by the Depression

---

* The Paris Sound Film Conference of 1930 awarded the rights for most of Europe to Tobis-Klangfilm and its French subsidiary, Films Sonores Tobis.

until the release of John Ford's *The Grapes of Wrath* in 1940; the first Hollywood film to acknowledge the Nazi threat in Europe, Anatole Litvak's *Confessions of a Nazi Spy,* did not appear until 1939.* So perhaps the final comment on Hollywood in the thirties should be this: Sound had been added to the cinema as the result of a bitter economic struggle between competing American production companies; the technology of sound recording had first been perfected by American engineers; and the creative use of sound had been pioneered almost exclusively by American film-makers. Yet, with regard to the social, sexual, and political dimensions of human experience, the American sound film throughout the thirties remained quite effectively "silent."

---

* One reason for the latter was that studio executives did not wish to antagonize Axis or neutral countries where their corporations had major markets and/or holdings.

Europe in the Thirties

BRITAIN

The British cinema had always been a stepchild of the American industry, and during the twenties it had almost ceased to exist. But in 1927 Parliament passed the Cinematograph Film Act, setting strict quotas on the number of foreign films that could be shown in the country; this had the effect of stimulating domestic production and investment. The British film industry doubled in size from 1927 to 1928, and the number of features it produced rose from 20 to 128. The expansion continued well into the thirties and enabled the British to compete with Hollywood not merely nationally but internationally for the first time in its history. Many of the films produced by the new boom were "quota quickies"— the British equivalent of the low-budget American B-film—but many more were distinguished undertakings by serious producers such as Alexander Korda (b. Sándor Kellner, 1893–1956) and Michael Balcon (1896–1977).

The producer-director Korda and his two younger brothers, the director Zoltán (1895–1961) and the art director Vincent (1897–1979), were

9.1 The original "biopic": Alexander Korda's *The Private Life of Henry VIII* (1933). Charles Laughton's performance as the gluttonous monarch made him internationally famous.

9.2 London Films' spectacular *The Thief of Bagdad* (Ludwig Berger, Michael Powell, and Tim Whelan, 1940): Sabu and the genie's foot. The film won American Academy Awards for art direction, color cinematography, and special effects.

Hungarians who settled in England and founded London Film Productions there in the early thirties. They collaborated on many outstanding costume spectacles, including *The Private Life of Henry VIII* (Alexander Korda, 1933), *Rembrandt* (Alexander Korda, 1936), *Elephant Boy* (Robert Flaherty and Zoltán Korda, 1937), *The Four Feathers* (Zoltán Korda, 1939), *The Thief of Bagdad* (Ludwig Berger, Michael Powell, Tim Whelan, 1940), and *The Jungle Book* (Zoltán Korda, 1942), which did much to establish Great Britain's position in the international market. Michael Balcon was successively director of production for the most important and discriminating British studios of the era: Gainsborough (which he founded in 1924), Gaumont-British (where he produced for Hitchcock), Ealing Studios, and the Rank Organisation. This was the era in British cinema which witnessed the flowering of Hitchcock's thrillers, the elegant period films of Anthony Asquith (1902–68), and the excellent social documentaries of John Grierson (1898–1972) and his school of socially "committed" cinema. By 1937, the British industry had the second largest annual output in the world (225 features), and British films were competing strongly with American films on an international scale.*

GERMANY

The German industry entered the sound era from a position of relative strength due to its ownership of the Tobis-Klangfilm recording patents, although the Weimar Republic was already on the brink of collapse. As in the United States, the first German sound films were unremarkable popular musicals, and the trend toward escapist entertainment grew as the nation sank ever more deeply into economic and political trouble. Yet some very important and distinguished films came out of the early sound period in Germany. Josef von Sternberg made *Der blaue Engel* (*The Blue Angel*) for Erich Pommer in Berlin in 1929. G. W. Pabst made his two great pacifist films—*Westfront 1918* and *Kameradschaft* (*Comradeship*)—in 1930 and 1931, as well as a highly successful version of Brecht's *Die Dreigroschenoper* (*The Threepenny Opera,* 1931). Leontine Sagan's anti-authoritarian parable of life within the confines of a Prussian girls' school, *Mädchen in Uniform* (*Girls in Uniform*), achieved international acclaim in 1931, as did Gerhard Lamprecht's gentle comedy *Emile und die Detektiv* (*Emile and the Detective*). But perhaps the most significant and influential work of Germany's early sound period was Fritz Lang's *M* (1930), with a script by Thea von Harbou (Lang's wife) based on the famous Dusseldorf child-murders.

In *M*, Peter Lorre (1904–64) plays a psychotic murderer of little girls in a large German city who is ultimately tracked down not by the police but by members of the local underworld. Through cutting, Lang establishes a clear parallel between the two groups. Lorre is brilliant as the tortured

---

* For a fascinating social analysis of British films of this period, see the "Cinema of Empire" section in Jeffrey Richards' *Visions of Yesterday* (London, 1973).

psychopath who wants desperately to stop killing but is constantly over-powered by his uncontrollable compulsion, and *M* is very much in the gloomy tradition of *Kammerspiel*. Studio-produced and highly stylized in its realism, the film contains no musical score but is distinguished by its expressive use of non-naturalistic sound, as in the recurring theme from Grieg's *Peer Gynt* suite which the murderer whistles offscreen before commiting his crimes. Not the least amazing thing about *M* is the way in which it deals with a revolting subject in a subtle and tasteful manner. Lang achieves this primarily through editing and the fluid camera style of Fritz Arno Wagner. Near the beginning of the film, for example, Lorre entices a little girl with a balloon; Lang cuts to shots of the girl's worried mother waiting for her return in an apartment; then he cuts to a shot of the balloon floating out and away from a small forest thicket to become entangled in some utility wires, and we know that the child has been murdered. At another point, to establish the identity between the bosses of the local underworld and the police, Lang contrives to have the chief of police complete a gesture begun by the chief of thieves in the previous shot. This persistent equation of authority with criminality, and a brood-ing sense of destiny, make *M* a film as much about the crisis of German society at the time it was made as about child-murder. One has the con-stant sense in watching *M* that one is in the presence of a culture on the brink of utter collapse. (Indeed, there is grim irony in the fact that the state which so diligently pursues the child-murderer in Lang's film would itself become responsible for the murder of millions of children in death camps little more than a decade later.)

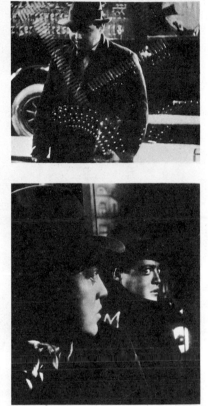

9.3   Peter Lorre in *M* (Fritz Lang, 1930).

Lang's next film was a sequel to his popular silent thriller about the master-criminal Dr. Mabuse, *Dr. Mabuse, der Spieler* (*Dr. Mabuse, the Gambler*, 1922). In *Das Testament des Dr. Mabuse* (*The Last Will of Dr. Mabuse*, 1932), the arch-tyrant directs his league of world crime from a lunatic asylum. Lang later claimed to have modeled Mabuse on Hitler and put Nazi slogans into the mouths of his criminal minions. This claim may be the result of hindsight, but the Nazis apparently recognized some-thing of themselves in the film and banned it when they came to power in 1933. Almost simultaneously, Lang, whose *Nibelungen* films (*Siegfried* and *Kriemhilds Rache*) and *Metropolis* were much admired by Hitler, was offered the position of artistic director of UFA—a position tan-tamount to leadership of the entire German film industry—by the Nazi propaganda minister, Josef Goebbels. Lang refused. He escaped to France on the next train (leaving behind his wife, a devout Nazi) and later emigrated to America, where he made two brilliant films before the war. *Fury* (1936) is a compelling indictment of mob violence that probes as deeply into the complex relationship between will and fate as had Lang's German films. *You Only Live Once* (1937) is another powerful tale of in-justice and destiny: a young ex-convict is falsely accused of murder and sentenced to death; with his wife's help he escapes from prison hours before his execution, and together the two flee across America until they are hunted down and killed at a roadblock on the Canadian border. Expressionist in atmosphere, composition, and lighting, *You Only Live Once* became the model for Joseph Lewis' *Gun Crazy* (1949) and Arthur

9.4 Nazi cinema: Werner Krauss in *Jud Süss* (Veit Harlan, 1940).

9.5 A camera crew shooting *Triumph des Willens* (Leni Riefenstahl, 1935) in Nuremberg, 1934.

Penn's *Bonnie and Clyde* (1967; see Chapter 17). The couple's desperate flight through nocturnal America has a tragic, brooding character that both later films preserve. Lang directed another twenty-one films in the United States between 1938 and 1956, but only his *film noir* masterpiece *The Big Heat* (1953) achieved the quality and depth of his greatest work.*

The German film industry which Lang had left was controlled from 1933 to 1945 by Goebbels, who spent considerable energy banning undesirable and "unhealthy" films like *Kameradschaft* and *M*. He mounted a rigorous campaign to rid the industry of its many Jews, but he saw no reason to nationalize the German cinema until well into the war, in 1942. Like the Soviet leaders, Goebbels regarded film as the century's most important communications medium, but unlike them he was not much concerned with agit-prop. Under his regime, Goebbels encouraged German films to remain well made but primarily trivial and escapist, since he wished the populace entertained rather than enlightened.† Of the eleven hundred features produced under Nazi rule, only fifty contain overt propaganda. Most propaganda was confined to newsreels and *Stattsauftragsfilme*—films conceived and financed by the state. These included biographical and historical films of the great national past like *Bismarck* (Wolfgang Liebeneiner, 1940) and *Der grosse König* (Frederick the Great,* Veit Harlan, 1942); dramatic films directly adulatory of the Nazi Party, like *S. A. Mann Brandt* (Franz Seitz, 1933) and *Hitlerjunge Quex* (Hans Steinhoff, 1933); and, finally, scurrilous racial propaganda films like the infamous *Jud Süss* (*Jew Süss,* Veit Harlan, 1940) and *Der ewige Jude* (*The Eternal Jew,* Fritz Hippler, 1940).

The only great films to emerge from Nazi Germany were two propaganda-"documentaries," both personally commissioned by Hitler for the Nazi Party. The first, *Triumph des Willens* (*Triumph of the Will,* 1935), is a film of nearly mythic dimensions, assigned to the direction of Leni Riefenstahl (b. 1902; see Chapter 4) at Hitler's insistence, which portrays the 1934 Nazi Party Congress at Nuremberg as a quasi-religious, mystical experience. Working with virtually limitless financial resources, thirty cameras and a crew of 120 persons, and her own utter ideological commitment, Riefenstahl shot the film in six days with the active cooperation of party leaders. (She later wrote, "The preparations for the party congress were made in concert with the preparations for the camera work,"[1] but recent studies document the fact that the entire congress was *staged* for her cameras and that nothing was left to chance.)

---

* See Don Willis, "Fritz Lang: Only Melodrama," *Film Quarterly,* 33, 2 (Winter 1979–80), 2–11, for a recent revaluation of Lang's Hollywood career.

† For an interesting, informed account of the German escapist cinema, 1933–45, see Richard Traubner, "The Sound and the Führer," *Film Comment,* 14, 4 (July–August 1978), 17–23; and "Berlin II. The Retrospective," *American Film,* 4, 7 (May 1979), 67–69. See also Julian Petley, *Capital and Culture: German Cinema 1933–45* (London, 1979), where it is argued (against the conventional wisdom) that the reorganization of the German film industry during the Third Reich was not an act of "subversion" but a collective undertaking "by the government and the most powerful sectors of the industry . . . working in closest co-operation and very much to the latter's advantage" (p. 1).

It took her eight months to edit the footage into a powerfully persuasive and visually beautiful piece of propaganda. Hitler is depicted as the new Messiah descending from the clouds in his airplane to succor his people. Once on earth, he begins a god-like procession to the congress hall, where his impassioned rhetoric rings through the chamber. The rest is all pseudo-Wagnerian music, monumental Nazi architecture, mass rallies, and torchlight parades choreographed for Riefenstahl's camera.

Triumph of the Will was effective enough to be banned in Britain, the United States, and Canada, and Hitler was so impressed that he commissioned Riefenstahl to make a spectacular film of the 1936 Berlin Olympics.* Again, unlimited resources were placed at her disposal, and her team of cameramen shot one and a half million feet of film which took her eighteen months to edit. The completed motion picture was released in two parts as *Olympische Spiele 1936* (*Olympiad/Olympia*) in 1938, and it stands even today as a great testament to athletic achievement, a forerunner of Kon Ichikawa's *Tokyo Olympiad* (1965) and the omnibus film of the 1972 Munich Olympics, *Visions of Eight* (Juri Ozerov, Mai Zetterling, Arthur Penn, Michael Phleghar, Kon Ichikawa, Miloš Forman, Claude Lelouch, and John Schlesinger, 1973). Riefenstahl's innovative use of slow-motion photography and telephoto lenses created images of compelling kinetic beauty, but, like *Triumph of the Will,* the film is steeped in the Nazi mystique which makes a cult of sheer physical prowess. Beyond these two powerful and disturbing films, the Nazi cinema produced few films of note, probably because most of the major filmmakers of the Weimar period had been either deported to prison camps or forced into exile.

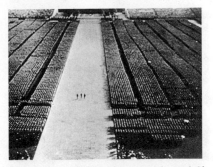

9.6 Leni Riefenstahl's (and Adolf Hitler's) *Triumph des Willems.*

9.7 *Olympiad* (Leni Riefenstahl, 1936).

THE SOVIET UNION

Sound came relatively late to the Soviet Union because the Soviet film industry chose to develop its own recording systems; the Tager sound-on-film process eventually became standard. The first Soviet feature-length sound film was not produced until 1930, which permitted Soviet directors to profit from the mistakes of their Western counterparts through benefit of hindsight and made their early talkies relatively fluid. They also had, at the time, a more thoughtful and theoretical approach to sound than the film-makers of any other country (see Chapter 7). Dovzhenko's *Ivan* (1932) provides a fine example of how rapidly they mastered the techniques of creative sound recording. Moreover, it was

---

* Riefenstahl has always maintained that *Olympiad* was financed by her own production company, Olympic Film Company, and commissioned by the International Committee for the Olympic Games, over Goebbels' protests. But official documents recently brought to light reveal that the Olympic Film Company was a front for the Nazi government and that the film was made with the full approval of Goebbels. The same documents show that the government made a handsome profit by distributing *Olympiad* internationally through Tobis-Klangfilm (See Hans Barkhausen, "Footnote to the History of Riefenstahl's *Olympia,*" *Film Quarterly,* 28, 1 [Fall 1974], 8–12; Glenn B. Infield, *Leni Riefenstahl: The Fallen Film Goddess* [New York, 1976]; Susan Sontag, "Fascinating Fascism," in *Women and the Cinema,* ed. Karyn Kay and Gerald Peary [New York, 1977], pp. 35–76; and David B. Hinton, *The Films of Leni Riefenstahl* [Metuchen, N.J., 1978].)

Soviet directors like Vertov who pioneered the sound documentary and sound montage. Nevertheless, sound arrived in the Soviet Union, as it had in Germany, during a period of reactionary political terror. The first of the purges in which millions of loyal Soviet citizens, as well as government functionaries, were imprisoned or executed during the decade begun in 1934. Fear and xenophobia were rife, and, again as in Germany, the Soviet cinema became increasingly escapist as the government became increasingly repressive. The bold revolutionary experiments of the past decade were dead. They were replaced by Hollywood-influenced musicals like Grigory Alexandrov's *The Jolly Fellows/Jazz Comedy* (*Vesyolye rebyata*, 1934); historical spectacles like Vladimir Petrov's *Peter the Great, Parts I* and *II* (*Pyotr Pervyi*, 1937–38); and biographies of revolutionary heroes, like the Vasiliev brothers' *Chapayev* (1934) and Dovzhenko's *Shchors* (1939). Related to the latter genre were dramatic reconstructions of revolutionary events in the stolid style of socialist realism, such as Mikhail Romm's *Lenin in October* (*Lenin v octiabrye*, 1937) and *Lenin in 1918* (*Lenin v 1918 godu*, 1939). Perhaps the most vital Soviet films of this period were two trilogies. The first, directed by Grigori Kozintsev and Leonid Trauberg, depicted the experiences of a young party worker during the revolutionary period in *The Youth of Maxim* (*Yunost Maxima*, 1935), *The Return of Maxim* (*Vozvrashcheniye Maxima*, 1937), and *The Vyborg Side* (*Vyborgskaya storona*, 1939). All three films were shot by the brilliant cinematographer Andrei Moskvin (1901–61), who would later work closely with Eisenstein. Mark Donskoi (b. 1901) contributed a robust adaptation of the three-volume autobiography of the Soviet writer Maxim Gorky (1863–1936)—*The Childhood of Maxim Gorky* (*Detstvo Gorkovo*, 1938), *My Apprenticeship* (*V lyudyakh*, 1939), and *My Universities* (*Moi universiteti*, 1940).

During most of this period, the man who might have returned the Societ cinema to its former glory remained inactive. Sergei Eisenstein had returned to Moscow from his American sojourn badly discouraged. All of his Paramount projects had been abortive, so in 1930 he had signed a contract with the Mexican Film Trust; a corporation formed by the American novelist Upton Sinclair (1878–1968)* and other investors to produce an Eisenstein film in Mexico. Eisenstein had long been interested in Mexico as both a cultural and a revolutionary phenomenon, and he later wrote that the film he had envisioned would have been "four novels framed by prologue and epilogue, unified in conception and spirit, creating its entity."[2] Provisionally entitled *Que viva México!*, the film would have been an attempt to encapsulate revolutionary Mexican history and evoke the spirit of the culture and the land. Eisenstein (working with Alexandrov and Tisse) had shot all of the film's sections except the last by 1932, when, as the climax of a series of misunderstandings, Sinclair

9.8 *Chapayev* (Sergei and Georgi Vasiliev, 1934): Boris Babochkin as the famous Red Army commander.

9.9 *The Youth of Maxim* (Grigori Kozintsev and Leonid Trauberg, 1935): Boris Chirkov.

9.10 *The Childhood of Maxim Gorky* (Mark Donskoi, 1938): Alexei Lyarsky.

---

* Sinclair was an internationally prominent socialist writer and a friend of the Bolshevik Revolution. Like Lenin, he believed that film was the most powerful medium of ideological persuasion in modern times, and he saw in the Eisenstein venture a chance to produce a sort of Latin American *Potemkin*.

9.11 Stills from Eisenstein's aborted epic *Que viva México!* (1930–32, uncompleted and unreleased).

abruptly ordered him to abandon the project, claiming correctly that Eisenstein had far exceeded his budget. All of the footage was in Hollywood for processing, and it was never restored to Eisenstein. Although Sinclair had promised to send the negative to Moscow for Eisenstein to edit into a feature film, he sold it immediately to the independent producer Sol Lesser (1890–1980), who cut parts of one episode into a silent melodrama of revenge entitled *Thunder Over Mexico* (1933), with a recorded orchestral score by Hugo Riesenfeld. Parts of the epilogue, also edited by Lesser, were released in 1934 as *Death Day*. Both films were critical and commercial failures, and there was a heated controversy among American artists and intellectuals over the question of who was to blame.* The rest of the footage ultimately found its way into various documentaries about the making of the film, and into the archives of the Museum of Modern Art in New York. From what is left of it, we can surmise that *Que viva México!* might have been Eisenstein's greatest film and the ultimate vindication of his theories of montage. Its dismemberment disturbed Eisenstein deeply, and it remains, with von Stroheim's *Greed* (1924; see Chapter 6) and Welles' *The Magnificent Ambersons* (1942; see Chapter 10), one of the great lost masterworks of the cinema.†

In Moscow again, Eisenstein conceived a number of projects, but they were systematically thwarted by Boris Shumyatsky, the commissar of information, who with full official sanction began a campaign of slander and humiliation against Eisenstein designed to discredit him and reduce his influence within the Soviet cinema. The Stalin government believed that Eisenstein had grown too independent during his American tour and that he set a dangerous example for other Soviet artists. Also, Shumyatsky hated Eisenstein personally, a not uncommon response to the director's eccentric personality and irreverent sense of humor. In 1934 Eisenstein was publicly insulted at the Congress of Party Film Workers and attacked in the official press. He was also deliberately offered projects by Shumyatsky which he was bound to reject, but the most flagrant abuse committed against him was the suppression of what would have been his first sound film, *Bezhin Meadow (Bezhin lug)*, which had been approved for production in 1935. Based in part on a short story by the nineteenth-century writer Ivan Turgenev, this film was to have presented the tragedy of a wealthy peasant who kills his son for supporting collectivization. Shooting began in the spring of 1935 but was interrupted in September when Eisenstein fell ill with smallpox. Upon Eisenstein's return to the set, Shumyatsky demanded major revisions in the script to force it in the direction of socialist realism. Eisenstein complied, and he had nearly completed the film before he fell ill again. This time, Shumyatsky halted production and published an attack on Eisenstein in *Pravda* so vicious that the director was forced to publicly recant the film and confess to ideological errors which, in fact, had little to do with its content.‡ This act of self-abasement apparently satisfied the party

9.12 Stills from Eisenstein's suppressed *Bezhin Meadow* (1935, uncompleted and unreleased).

* See Ivor Montagu, *With Eisenstein in Hollywood* (New York, 1969), and Harry M. Geduld and Ronald Gottesman, *The Making and Unmaking of "Que Viva México!"* (Bloomington, Ind., 1971).

† In 1973 the Soviet state film archive Gosfilmofond negotiated a deal with the Museum and the Sinclair estate to secure copies of all extant footage of Eisenstein's Mexican film. In August 1979, Sovexport released an "official" restoration of *Que viva México!* by Grigory Alexandrov, Eisenstein's assistant on the production, who claims to possess Eisenstein's original cutting schedule. Reviews were unenthusiastic, but the Alexandrov reconstruction is as close as we are ever likely to come to the film Eisenstein intended.

‡ About 60 percent of *Bezhin Meadow* had been shot when the project was canceled. The official Soviet position is that this footage was stored in a Mosfilm vault which was destroyed by German bombardment in 1942. In all likelihood, it was destroyed by Shumyatsky in 1937. Whatever happened to the original, Elfir Tobak, the film's editor, pre-

bureaucrats: a year later Shumyatsky was deposed and Eisenstein was entrusted with the production of a big-budget historical film of major political importance, *Alexander Nevsky* (1938).

On what many observers felt was the eve of a Nazi invasion, Eisenstein was chosen to make a film about how the great Slavic culture hero Prince Alexander Nevsky of Novgorod had rallied the Russian people to repel an invading force of Teutonic Knights in the thirteenth century. It was Eisenstein's first sound film and the consummate realization of his theories of contrapuntal sound. According to Georges Sadoul, Eisenstein conceived the entire film as an opera in which Sergei Prokofiev's brilliant score would alternately complement and conflict with the film's visual rhythms.[3] And these rhythms are among the most beautiful the director ever achieved. Every shot in *Alexander Nevsky* is painstakingly composed in terms of the plastic arrangement of space, mass, and light within the frame. The Teutonic Knights, for example, always appear in strictly geometrical formations, while the Russian ranks are asymmetrical, suggesting the monolithic rigidity of the Germans as contrasted with the vital but disorganized Russians. Eisenstein managed every detail of the production, including costume design and make-up, and one of his most striking conceptions was the battle dress of the German invaders. Probably influenced by the sinister headgear of the Ku Klux Klansmen in *The Birth of a Nation*, Eisenstein costumed his Teutonic Knights throughout

9.13 Nikolai Cherkassov in *Alexander Nevsky* (Sergei Eisenstein, 1938).

9.14 *Alexander Nevsky:* Teutonic barbarism in the captured city of Pskov.

the film in menacing steel helmets with tiny slits for eye-holes, so that their faces were never visible as were those of the Russians. The barbaric military regalia which adorned these helmets, the symbol of the red cross on the Knights' white tunics and capes (cleverly positioned to resemble armbands with swastikas), and the atrocities which they commit upon the people of Pskov in the first reel all serve to clearly identify the Teutons with the Nazis.

The film's most impressive sequence is the famous battle on the ice on

served a number of frames which were assembled into a montage of stills by Eisenstein's friends Sergei Yutkevich and Naum Kleiman in 1956. Released as *Bezhin Meadow*, this film was provided with a score from the symphonies of Prokofiev and had a running time of twenty-five minutes. Its continuity was based on the original script.

9.15 *Alexander Nevsky:* the battle on the ice is joined.

frozen Lake Ilmen at Novgorod, actually shot in the outskirts of Moscow in midsummer with artificial snow and ice. Here the decisive battle between the Teutons and the Russian defenders is rendered in a spectacular audio-visual montage complete with swish pans and a jolting, rough-and-tumble camera style that would not be seen again until the early days of the French New Wave. (The battle on the ice in *Nevsky* greatly influenced the staging of the Battle of Agincourt in Laurence Olivier's *Henry V* [1944], a film with similar nationalistic/patriotic motives.) Eisenstein appropriately called *Alexander Nevsky* "a fugue on the theme of patriotism," and, despite the fact that some foreign critics balked at its operatic structure, the film was an enormous critical and popular success in many Western countries as well as in the Soviet Union, where it temporarily restored Eisenstein to his position of esteem within the Soviet cinema.

9.16 *Alexander Nevsky:* the Russians celebrate their victory.

Alexander Nevsky was suppressed in its native land in the year following its release due to the false friendship inspired by the Nazi-Soviet Non-Aggression Pact of 1939, but it was revived with a great display of patriotism after Hitler's invasion of Russia in 1941. In the meantime, to commemorate a state visit by the Nazi propaganda minister, Goebbels, Eisenstein produced a remarkable version of Wagner's massive Teutonic music-drama *Die Walküre* at the Bolshoi Opera in which he attempted, as he later wrote, to achieve "a fusion between the elements of Wagner's score and the wash of colors on the stage" through lighting.[4] The psychologist of perception was still very much alive in Eisenstein, but he had advanced from reflexology to synesthesia.* And just as he had used the Proletkult Theater as a testing ground for his developing theories of montage, he used his 1940 production of Wagner's opera as a laboratory for his new ideas on the dramatic interplay of sound, space, and color, so important to his last two films.

Sometime in 1940, Eisenstein conceived the notion of making an epic film trilogy about the life of Tsar Ivan IV, known in Russian as *grozny* ("awesome," "terrible"), the Nevsky-like figure who had first unified all of Russia in the sixteenth century. This project was to be the consummation of all his theory and practice, and Eisenstein spent two full years studying his subject. Production began at the Alma-Ata studios in Central Asia in 1943. Instead of a shooting script, Eisenstein used a series of his own sketches as his scenario. *Part I, Ivan the Terrible (Ivan Grozny)*, was completed and released in early 1945, and it immediately won the Stalin Prize for artistic achievement. *Part II, The Boyars' Plot (Boyarskii zagovor)*, shot in Moscow between 1945 and 1946, was released in 1946 and promptly banned by the Party Central Committee for "ignorance in the presentation of historical fact." (Eisenstein had apparently been too critical of the *oprichnina*, Ivan's secret police, for Stalin's paranoid taste.) When this happened, Eisenstein was already planning *Part III, The Battles of Ivan*, but he suffered a heart attack in 1946, and the film was never

---

* The use of one mode of sensory stimulation to produce responses in other senses.

9.17 Eisenstein's *Ivan the Terrible, Part I* (1945): the coronation of Ivan Vasilievich as tsar of Moscow, autocrat of all the Russias, in the Ouspensky Cathedral, January 16, 1547. Nikolai Cherkassov as Ivan.

9.18 The wedding feast of Ivan and the Tsarina Anastasia.

9.19 Ivan in his study with an ambassador to England.

9.20 Ivan and his subjects at Anastasia's bier in the cathedral; she has been poisoned by the tsar's scheming aunt, Euphrosinia.

9.21 Retired to a provincial palace, the grief-stricken Ivan is petitioned to return to Moscow by his people.

produced. Eisenstein did not recover from his illness—perhaps because he didn't wish to—and he died only a few months before D. W. Griffith, on February 11, 1948.

His last bequest to the cinema was a two-part film of incomparable formal beauty of which Eisenstein himself wrote, "The grandeur of our theme necessitated a grandiose design."[5] *Ivan the Terrible, Parts I* and *II*, is quintessentially a film whose meaning *is* its design. The montage aesthetics of the great silent films are subordinated here, like all other plastic elements, to elaborate compositions within the frame photographed by Tisse and Moskvin in which even the actors become part of the decor (much as they were part of the montage patterns of the silent films). Eisenstein demanded highly expressive and even contorted performances from his actors—especially from Nikolai Cherkassov (1903–66), who had also played Nevsky, in the role of Ivan—and achieved a *mise-en-scène* whose hieratic stylization is deliberately reminiscent of the work of the sixteenth-century painter El Greco. Like *Alexander Nevsky, Ivan the Terrible* is an operatic film with a magnificent Prokofiev score employed

9.22 *Ivan the Terrible, Part II* (1946): in the pompous throne-room of King Sigismond of Poland, the conspirators against the tsar learn of his return to Moscow.

9.23 In Moscow, Pimen, archbishop of Novgorod, plots with Euphrosinia to murder Ivan and place her weak-minded son Vladimir on the throne.

9.24 The tsar is informed.

9.25 Having plied Vladimir with drink, Ivan convinces the simpleton to wear his robes and regalia in a religious procession.

contrapuntally throughout. Furthermore, in his quest for synesthesia and total sensory saturation Eisenstein even used a color sequence (his first—made with Agfacolor stock captured from the Germans) in *Part II* to create a certain emotional tonality for the wild dance of the *oprichniki*.

Ivan the Terrible may seem a strange ending to a career that began with *Strike!* and *Potemkin*. It is heavy, ornate, and static where they are light and fast. But, ultimately, all of Eisenstein's films are cut from the same cloth. His devotion to pictorial beauty, his fascination with the psychology of perception, and his epic aspirations pervade everything he undertook. If Eisenstein turned from agit-prop to grand opera in his later years, it was perhaps because, after nearly two decades of bitter experience under the Stalin regime, he no longer believed in any cause beyond the nobility and necessity of art.

9.26 Vladimir is murdered in the tsar's stead, the plotters are arrested, and Ivan ascends his throne as absolute monarch of all Russia.

FRANCE
Avant-Garde Impressionism, 1921–1929

Next to America's, the film industry with the most prominent national image in the thirties was that of France. After World War I, Paris had become the center of an international avant-garde encompassing cubism, surrealism, dadaism, and futurism, and many intellectuals involved with these movements had become intensely interested in the possibilities of film to embody dream states and to express modernist conceptions of time and space. The most prominent among them was the young author and editor Louis Delluc (1890–1924), who founded the journal *Cinéma* and became, long before Eisenstein, the first aesthetic theorist of the film. Delluc's practical mission was the founding of a truly French national cinema which would be authentically cinematic. To this end, he rejected much of French cinema as it had evolved before the war—especially the theatrical abuses of *film d'art*—and turned instead to the models of Sweden (Sjöstrom and Stiller), America (Chaplin, Ince, and Griffith), and Germany (Expressionism and *Kammerspiel*). Delluc began to write original scenarios and gathered about him a group of young film-makers which became known as the French "impressionist" school,* or the first avant-garde—Germaine Dulac, Jean Epstein, Marcel L'Herbier, and Abel Gance.

Delluc himself directed a handful of important films, including *Fièvre* (*Fever,* 1921) and *La femme de nulle part* (*The Woman from Nowhere,* 1922), both of which are reminiscent of *Kammerspiel* in their concern with creating atmosphere and preserving the unities of time and place. Germaine Dulac (1882–1942), one of cinema's first female artists, directed Delluc's first scenario *La fête espagnole* (*The Spanish Festival,* 1919) and went on to become an important figure in the avant-garde and documentary cinema. Her most significant impressionist films were *La souriante Madame Beudet* (*The Smiling Madame Beudet,* 1922), an intimate psychological portrait of middle-class marriage in a drab provincial setting, and *La coquille et le clergyman* (*The Seashell and the Clergyman,* 1928), a Freudian study of sexual repression. Jean Epstein (1897–1953), like Delluc, began his career in film as a theorist but contributed a major work to the impressionist cinema in 1923 with *Coeur fidèle* (*Faithful Heart*), the story of a working-class love triangle in Marseille with a fine feeling for landscape and atmosphere. According to the film historian Georges Sadoul, this film, for all its sophisticated use of the moving camera and rapid cutting, incarnates the quality of *populisme* which may be seen in French films as early as the Lumière shorts† and which was the major legacy of impressionism to the French cinema—a

9.27 *Le femme de nulle part* (Louis Delluc, 1922).

9.28 *La souriante Madame Beudet* (Germaine Dulac, 1922).

---

* Unrelated to the late-nineteenth-century movement in painting known as French Impressionism. See Eugene C. McCreary, "Louis Delluc, Film Theorist, Critic, and Prophet," *Cinema Journal,* 16, 1 (Fall 1976), 14–35.

† Later (and, predominantly, Marxist) French critics, however, have found little *populisme* in the Lumière films. Vincent Pinel writes of them, for example: "The image which these

fascination with ordinary people and settings, with dramas of the working class, and with outdoor shooting in natural settings such as seaports, fairgrounds, and bistros.[6] Epstein's later *La chute de la maison Usher* (*The Fall of the House of Usher,* 1928) used a variety of brilliant technical effects to create for the tale by Edgar Allan Poe what Henri Langlois called "the cinematic equivalent of Debussy."[7] The most faithful follower of Delluc's theories was Marcel L'Herbier (1890–1979), who had been a prominent symbolist poet before turning to film-making in 1917. The most cerebral member of the impressionist group, L'Herbier was concerned largely with abstract form, and with the use of visual effects to express inner states. His *L'homme du large* (*The Big Man,* 1921) was an adaptation of a novel by the nineteenth-century realist Honoré de Balzac set on the coast of Brittany, whose frames were composed to resemble Impressionist paintings. The visual texture of *Eldorado* (1922), a drama of Spanish low-life set in a café, recalls the paintings of Claude Monet, and *Don Juan et Faust* (*Don Juan and Faust,* 1922) used cubism to the same end. L'Herbier's most extravagant impressionist film, *L'inhumaine* (*The Inhuman,* 1923), with a score by Darius Milhaud and sets by the cubist painter Fernand Léger and by Robert Mallet Stevens, was an essay in visual abstraction thinly disguised as a narrative about a sort of cosmic *femme fatale.*

9.29 *Eldorado* (Marcel L'Herbier, 1922).

Abel Gance (b. 1889) is, like Erich von Stroheim, one of the great maverick talents of the cinema, and his affiliation with the impressionists was fleeting at best. Born into a bourgeois family, Gance had been a poet, an actor, and a scriptwriter before forming his own production company in 1911. Despite some impressive experimental work, including the Caligariesque *La folie du Docteur Tube* (*Dr. Tube's Mania,* 1916), Gance did not achieve fame until the success of his beautifully photographed melodramas *Mater Dolorosa* (1917) and *La dixième symphonie* (*The Tenth Symphony,* 1918). Then he struck out on his own to pursue a dual obsession with technical innovation and epic form. Deeply influenced by *Intolerance,* Gance practiced complex metaphorical intercutting in his symbolic anti-war narrative *J'accuse* (*I Accuse,* 1919), and then contributed the extraordinary modern epic *La roue* (*The Wheel,* 1922) to the impressionist movement. Written, directed, and edited by Gance, *La roue* was shot almost entirely on location, from the railway yards at Nice to the Alps at St. Gervaise, and took nearly three years to complete. It tells the tragic story of an engine driver and his son who are both in love with the same woman—their adopted daughter and sister, respectively—and deliberately resonates with the myths of Oedipus, Sisyphus, Prometheus, and Christ. Like von Stroheim's *Greed* (1924), the film was intended for

9.30 Sisif (Séverin-Mars) blinded by a steam valve in *La roue* (Abel Gance, 1922).

'views' give of appearances (by the choice of subjects more than by a bias caused by any deliberate rhetoric or deformation) is the image that the dominant class of the end of the century seeks to give of the world and itself. An image of self-satisfaction, a clear conscience, a quiet certainty, and values posited (or imposed) as universal and eternal. Lumière's films praise in their way—and admirably—the virtues of Work, Family, and Fatherland. Which after all is surely a normal effect of the historical situation. . . ." ("Louis Lumière," *Anthologies du cinéma,* No. 78 [Paris, 1974], p. 447.)

release in an eight-hour version but was cut by its producer (Pathé) to two and a half hours. Even in the shortened version, Gance's intercutting approaches Eisenstein's in its sophistication and metaphorical power, and its atmospheric evocation of life in the railway yards is close to the spirit of the nineteenth-century epic naturalist Émile Zola. Monumental, technically dazzling, hyper-romantic, and frequently tasteless, *La roue* influenced a whole generation of French avant-garde film-makers, including Fernand Léger and Jean Cocteau (see below), and its editing was widely studied in the Soviet film schools during the twenties.*

Gance's next film, *Napoléon vu par Abel Gance: première époque: Bonaparte* (*Napoleon as Seen by Abel Gance: First Epoch: Bonaparte,* 1927), is, with *Intolerance* (1916) and *Greed* (1924), one of the great eccentric masterpieces of the silent cinema. Twenty-eight reels in its original version but reduced to eight by subsequent distributors, *Napoléon* required four years to produce and was only the first part of a projected six-part film of the life of Bonaparte which was never completed. As it stands, it covers his youth, the revolution, and the opening of the Italian campaign, and there is scarcely a passage in the film which does not make use of some innovative and original device. From beginning to end, Gance assaulted his audience with the entire arsenal of silent-screen techniques, and the effect is impressive. As in *La roue,* he used sophisticated metaphorical intercutting to inundate the viewer with significant images, many of them lasting only a few frames; and at times he superimposed as many as sixteen simultaneous images on the screen. At several points in *Napoléon,* Gance also used a widescreen process called Polyvision which expanded the frame to three times its normal width, but the most original achievement of *Napoléon* was the astonishing fluidity of its camera work.

The recent manufacture in France of light, portable cameras made possible many extraordinary subjective camera shots and traveling shots which went far beyond the pioneering work of Murnau and Freund in *Der letzte Mann* (1924; see Chapter 4) and which would not be seen again until the advent of the hand-held thirty-five-millimeter (35 mm) sound camera some twenty-five years later. In the Corsican sequence, for example, the camera was strapped to the back of a galloping horse to shoot the landscape as it would have been seen by the rider. Later, encased in a waterproof box, the camera was hurled from a steep cliff into the Mediterranean to approximate the impressions of Napoléon as he dived. To film the tumultuous Paris Convention, Gance mounted the camera on a huge pendulum to convey the radical swaying back and forth between Girondist and Jacobin factions, and he intercut this shot with one of Napoléon's boat on its way to France pitching to and fro in a storm at sea. Finally, in scenes from the siege of Toulon, a small camera was even mounted in a football and tossed into the air to simulate the perspective of a cannonball.

---

* *La roue* also attracted the intense admiration of Griffith, who saw the eight-hour version at a special screening arranged for him in New York City during Gance's five-month visit to the United States in the latter half of 1923.

9.31　Polyvision tryptichs from *Napoléon vu par Abel Gance* (1927).

The Polyvision process, developed by Gance specifically for *Napoléon*, anticipated the modern Cinerama process in that it employed a triptych, or three-panel screen, to show three standard 35 mm images side by side. Gance used the process in two distinct ways. Often he would supplement the primary image on the middle screen with complementary and/or contrapuntal images on either side. At several points during the Italian campaign, for instance, huge close-ups of Bonaparte's head or of a symbolic eagle dominate the middle screen while marching troops of the Grand Armée stream across the side panels. (This widescreen triptych effect was not used again successfully until Michael Wadleigh's documentary *Woodstock* in 1969; see Chapter 17.) At other times, Gance used Polyvision more naturalistically to explode the screen into a single vast panoramic image for mass scenes, as during the Italian campaign and the

Convention. This image was photographed by a battery of three cameras running concurrently side by side. Like so many other elements of *Napoléon,* Polyvision was twenty-five years ahead of its time (and, by his own admission, it gave Professor Henri Chrétien, the father of modern wide-screen processes, the idea for inventing the anamorphic lens* in 1941).

Gance made nothing comparable to *Napoléon* for the rest of his career, although he constantly returned to it, adding stereophonic sound for an Arthur Honegger score, some dialogue scenes, and, as late as 1971, an introductory color sequence. Yet audiences in only eight European cities saw *Napoléon* in its original form. It was cut to less than one third of its length for overseas distribution, and there was no definitive print of the original silent film until a complete restoration was done by the British film-maker and film historian Kevin Brownlow (b. 1938) in 1979. A seventeen-reel reconstruction by the Cinémathèque Française excited the passionate admiration of the young *cinéastes*† of the French New Wave when it was shown in Paris in the late fifties and contributed substantially to a resurrection of Gance's critical reputation. But Brownlow's full-triptych reconstruction runs the original twenty-eight reels, or six hours. It was premiered at the Telluride (Colorado) Film Festival in September 1979—with Gance present, in honor of his ninetieth birthday‡—demonstrating with finality what Brownlow has maintained all along: "The visual resources of the cinema have never been stretched further than in *Napoléon vu par Abel Gance.* The picture is an encyclopedia of cinematic effects—a pyrotechnical display of what the silent film was capable of in the hands of a genius."[8]

The "Second" Avant-Garde

Louis Delluc died of tuberculosis in 1924, and the French impressionist film entered a period of decadent formalism shortly thereafter; but Delluc's influence survived him and the school he had founded, in the rise of serious French film criticism and the *ciné-club* (film society) movement. By the mid-twenties, film reviews had become a standard feature of almost every newspaper published in France, and professional film writers like Léon Moussinac were establishing a tradition of cinema studies in France which was to make that country the home of the most advanced and subtle thinking on film from 1925 through the present. As Georges Sadoul has written: "This group of men was the first in Europe to assert the stature of the film as an art—the equal (or even the superior) of

---

* A distorting lens which on the camera "squeezes" a wide image onto standard (usually 35 mm) film and on the projector "unsqueezes" it for widescreen projection. It is the technical basis for Cinemascope, Panavision, and other widescreen processes (see Chapter 12).

† A French term for film-makers of great artistic commitment.

‡ In Telluride, Gance announced plans for another film epic, to be entitled *Christopher Columbus.* "Right now the cinema is dead," he said; "*Columbus* will bring it back to life." (*Variety,* September 18, 1979, p. 28.) On the general difficulty of seeing Gance films in the United States, see William M. Drew, "Abel Gance: Prometheus Bound," *Take One,* 6, 8 (July 1978) 30–32, 45.

music, literature and the theatre—and to obtain recognition for it as such. With the creation of independent film criticism they gave body and substance to their claim. . . . Henceforward the cinema became a subject of dinner-table conversation like the novel or the play, and there emerged a group among the intellectual elite for whom it was a major artistic preoccupation."[9] The *ciné-club* movement was founded by Delluc, Moussinac, and Ricciotto Canudo (1879–1923) in Paris, where it achieved great success and spread rapidly to the provinces. Some *ciné-clubs* ultimately became specialized film theaters where a knowledgeable public could see serious films unavailable to it in conventional cinemas. Since French commercial film production reached a new low point during the twenties, both financially and aesthetically, it was largely these specialized theaters and *ciné-clubs* that kept the creative tradition of French cinema alive and that transmitted it into the sound era by enabling a second wave of French avant-garde film-makers to find an audience.

The "second" avant-garde had its roots in the literary and artistic movements of dadaism and surrealism. Like the impressionists, the members of this later group wished to create a pure cinema of visual sensation divorced from conventional narrative—or, as they put it in their manifestoes, to make films without subjects. The first to attempt this was an American photographer living in Paris, Man Ray (b. 1890), whose brief *Le rétour à la raison* (*Return to Reason,* 1923) offered its audience a kaliedoscopic succession of barely discernible images. A year later the cubist painter Fernand Léger and his American technical collaborator Dudley Murphy produced *Ballet méchanique,* in which isolated objects, pieces of machinery, posters, and newspaper headlines were animated into a rhythmic ballet of plastic forms. The most famous of the early avant-garde films was indisputedly René Clair's *Entr'acte* (1924), made to be shown at the intermission of Francis Picabia's dadaist ballet *Relâche* (*Performance Suspended*). With a score by Erik Satie, who also wrote the music for the ballet, *Entr'acte* was a logically meaningless succession of outrageous images, many derived from the tradition of prewar slapstick comedy and the serials of Feuillade (see Chapter 2). Clair's *Paris qui dort* (English title: *The Crazy Ray,* 1924) was an irreverent but lyrical story of a mad scientist who invents an invisible ray to immobilize all of Paris except for six persons who eventually take up residence on the Eiffel Tower. Clair went on to become a major figure in the sound film, as did Luis Buñuel (b. 1900), whose *Un chien andalou* (*An Andalusian Dog,* 1928) represents the avant-garde at its most mature, most surreal, and most Freudian.

Written in collaboration with the surrealist painter Salvador Dali (b. 1904), *Un chien andalou* provides a seemingly incoherent stream of brutal, erotic images from the unconscious which Buñuel himself called "a despairing, passionate call to murder." In the course of the film, we witness in close-up a woman's eyeball being slashed in two with a razor, two priests in harness pulling a grand piano upon which are draped the rotting carcasses of two donkeys, swarms of ants crawling from a hole in a man's palm, and a whole succession of gratuitous murders, severed limbs, and symbolic sexual transformations. Designed to create a series

9.32 Part of a film loop from *Ballet méchanique* (Fernand Léger, 1924) in which a woman seems to endlessly climb a flight of stairs.

9.33 *Entr'acte* (René Clair, 1924): a ballet dancer shot from a subterranean perspective.

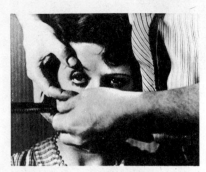

9.34 *Un chien andalou* (Luis Buñuel, 1928).

of violent antagonisms within the viewer through shock, titillation, and repulsion, *Un chien andalou* is the prototype of film surrealism. Yet Buñuel later added a recorded score to the film comprised of popular contemporary tangos and the *Leibestod* from Wagner's opera *Tristan und Isolde*, as if to suggest that *Un chien andalou* was as much about the collapse of European culture between the wars as a subterranean voyage through the recesses of the unconscious mind. A subsequent Buñuel-Dali collaboration in the early sound period produced *L'âge d'or* (*The Golden Age*, 1930), a film no less surreal than its predecessor but one whose attacks upon religion and the established social order were so violent as to excite the wrath of the French Fascists, who ultimately succeeded in having it banned. Buñuel made no more overtly surrealist films after *L'âge d'or*, but the surrealistic strain has remained strong in his films of the past forty-five years (see Chapter 14).

One of the most remarkable works of the new avant-garde was Dmitri Kirsanoff's *Ménilmontant* (1924), which employed elaborate montage effects nearly a year before the release of Eisenstein's *Strike!* and *Potemkin* (see Chapter 5). Kirsanoff (1899–1957) was a Russian émigré who apparently knew nothing of the montage experiments of Kuleshov, Pudovkin, and Eisenstein. But *Ménilmontant* clearly anticipates the rapid metaphorical cutting of Kirsanoff's Soviet counterparts in many ways. The film itself tells the story of two young women from the country whose lives are ruined by the brutal murder of their parents. The women come to the Parisian suburb of Ménilmontant, where they drift into prostitution, and the remainder of the film recounts their sordid existence there. Some scholars see Kirsanoff's film as a precursor of Italian neo-realism (see Chapter 11) in its sensitive use of on-location photography and natural settings.

The poet and playwright Jean Cocteau (1889–1963) turned to the avant-garde cinema for the first time as the director of *Le sang d'un poète* (*Blood of a Poet*, 1930), a collage of intensely personal poetic symbols which attempts to evoke the sacrificial nature of art. By the end of the decade, however, the avant-garde had taken an abrupt turn away from introspection toward social commitment. Abstract films continued to be made by artists such as Man Ray (*Les mystères du château du Dé* [*The Mysteries of the Château du Dé*, 1929]) and Jean Grémillon (*Un tour au large* [1927]), but the main tendency after 1927 was toward documentary cinema.

Influenced by the screening of the officially banned films of Vertov, Eisenstein, and Pudovkin in the *ciné-clubs*, French avant-garde *cinéastes* turned from abstractionism to the poetry of everyday life in a group of films that anticipated both the British documentary school of John Grierson and Italian neo-realism. As early as 1926, the Brazilian-born filmmaker Alberto Cavalcanti (b. 1897), later to become a major figure in the British documentary and narrative cinemas (*Coal Face* [1936]; *Dead of Night* [1945]), directed *Rien que les heures*, a chronicle of a typical day in the life of Paris which may well have influenced Ruttmann's *Berlin, die Symphonie einer Grosstadt* (1927; see Chapter 4). Georges Lacombe (b.

1902), in *La zone* (1928), offered a moving account of the lives of rag-pickers in the shantytowns of Paris, while the first film of Marcel Carné (b. 1909), *Nogent, Eldorado du dimanche* (*Nogent, Sunday's Eldorado,* 1929), was a short documentary about Sundays at a popular working-class resort on the Marne. During this same period, Jean Painlevé (b. 1902) began to produce the series of beautiful nature films which culminated in *L'hippocampe* (1934), a poetic documentary on the life cycle of the seahorse. A bit later, Luis Buñuel combined surrealism with social commitment in the powerful and subversive *Las Hurdes* (English title: *Land Without Bread,* 1932), which depicts the degradation, misery, and ignorance of the denizens of Spain's poorest district in the coolly ironic tones of a conventional travelogue. But the indisputable master-piece of the French avant-garde documentary movement was the first film of Jean Vigo (see below), *À propos de Nice* (1929), which used the *kino-eye* techniques of Dziga Vertov—whose brother Boris Kaufman was Vigo's cameraman—to create a lyrical but angry polemic against bourgeois decadence in a fashionable resort town.

9.35 *À propos de Nice* (Jean Vigo, 1929).

The general bleakness of the French commercial cinema during this period of widespread independent experimentation was illuminated here and there by the films of Jacques Feyder, René Clair, and Carl Dreyer. Feyder (1885–1948) was a Belgian who made dozens of French commercial films before establishing his reputation with *L'Atlantide* (1921), an opulent tale of the lost continent of Atlantis with exteriors shot in the Sahara desert. His critical and popular success continued through *Crain-quebille* (1922), a semi-impressionistic version of the novel by Anatole France which was much admired by Griffith, and a highly praised adaptation of Zola's *Thérèse Raquin* (1928) which has not survived. But when his gently satiric sound film *Les nouveaux messieurs* (*The New Gentlemen,* 1928) was unfairly banned for impugning "the dignity of Parliament and its ministers," Feyder left France temporarily for Holly-wood, where he spent four years working on melodramas (among them two Garbo films: *The Kiss* [1930] and the German-language version of Clarence Brown's *Anna Christie* [1932]). The Danish director Carl Theo-dor Dreyer (1889–1968) made his late silent masterpiece *La passion de Jeanne d'Arc* (*The Passion of Joan of Arc,* 1928) in Paris between 1927 and 1928. This austere and anguished film, which condenses the trial, torture, and execution of St. Joan (Marie Falconetti) into a single ten-sion-charged twenty-four-hour period, was based on actual trial records and shot largely in extreme close-ups against stark white backgrounds to enhance its psychological realism. To the same end, its actors and ac-tresses wore no make-up. Dreyer had intended to make *La passion de Jeanne d'Arc* a sound film, but he abandoned the notion for lack of equipment, so the film remains the last great classic of the international silent screen. Jean Cocteau wrote of it: *"Potemkin* imitated a documen-tary and threw us into confusion. *La passion de Jeanne d'Arc* seems like an historical document from an era in which the cinema didn't exist."[10] Dreyer also made his first sound film in France, the hauntingly atmos-pheric *Vampyr* (1932), which does, however, seem less distinctly Gallic

9.36 *Les nouveaux messieurs* (Jacques Feyder, 1929).

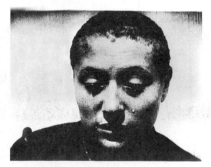

9.37 Marie Falconetti in *La passion de Jeanne d'Arc* (Carl Theodor Dreyer, 1928).

9.38 Dreyer's *Vampyr* (1932): Julian West.

than *La passion.** René Clair had turned from the avant-garde to the commercial cinema in 1925 but did not achieve artistic success until he made the delightful *Un chapeau de paille d'Italie* (*The Italian Straw Hat,* 1927), which transformed a popular nineteenth-century farce by Eugène Labiche into a highly cinematic comic chase film in the manner of Mack Sennett and Jean Durand.

Sound, 1929–1934

The coming of sound spelled the end for the French avant-garde cinema. The French mode of production during the twenties had been one in which a large number of small studios leased their facilities to independent companies formed to produce single films, and this method had lent itself readily to experimentation. But production costs soared with the introduction of sound because France, unlike the United States and Germany, possessed no patents for the new process. Thus, the French studios were at the mercy of Western Electric and Tobis-Klangfilm, both of which exacted crippling sums for the rights to use their sound equipment. But the success of American and German sound films in France was such that financiers were eager to invest in the foreign patent rights; through a complicated series of mergers and liquidations, they were able to group most existing studios into two large combines around the old trade names of Gaumont and Pathé, thereby replicating the monopolistic structure of the American film industry. Hollywood and Tobis attempted to further plunder the French industry by establishing huge production facilities in the suburbs of Paris. Paramount built a vast plant at Joinville, but the quality of its mass-produced multi-lingual films fell to such a low level that the facility eventually became a dubbing studio for American-made films. The Tobis operation in Epinay was a much more respectable affair; its very first production was a motion picture praised around the

---

* Dreyer is an important director, the major body of whose work lies outside the main-stream of film history. Like that of Robert Bresson (see Chapter 13) and Yasujiro Ozu (see Chapter 16), Dreyer's art has been called religious and his style "transcendental" because of its simplicity and austerity (see Paul Schrader, *Transcendental Style in Film* [Berkeley, 1972]). Originally a journalist and a scriptwriter for Danish Nordisk, Dreyer began by making films in direct imitation of Griffith (such as *Blade af Satans bog* [*Leaves from Satan's Book,* 1921]), but by the late twenties he was making films (like *La passion de Jeanne d'Arc*) of such an extraordinary character as to defy classification. Because of the physical confinement he imposed on his dramas, Dreyer has sometimes been accused of theatricality (*Du skal aere din hustru* [*Master of the House,* 1925], for example, was shot entirely in a small four-room house). But, typically, Dreyer's subject is deep human emotion, frequently suffering, and his ability to evoke spiritual intensity through concentration and confinement is perhaps his greatest gift as a film artist. Dreyer's greatest films are characterized by luminous photography (often by great cinematographers like Rudolf Maté, Karl Freund, and Gunnar Fischer), expressive decor, deliberately paced editing, and a nearly total immobility of camera. His painstaking production procedures and his fierce artistic integrity led him to make only fourteen films in a career that spanned forty-five years. The most significant are *Michaël* (1924), *Du skal aere din hustru* (1925), *La passion de Jeanne d'Arc* (1928), *Vampyr* (1932), *Vredens dag* (*Day of Wrath,* 1943), *Ordet* (*The Word,* 1954), and his last film, *Gertrud* (1964).

world as the first artistic triumph of the sound film: René Clair's *Sous les toits de Paris* (*Under the Roofs of Paris,* 1930).

As with several other French directors making the transition to sound, Clair's involvement with the avant-garde of the twenties had predisposed him to experiment with the new process. *Sous les toits de Paris* was a brisk musical comedy about ordinary people set in a delightfully designed Parisian *faubourg* (residential district); it used a bare minimum of dialogue and vindicated Clair's own theoretical defense of asynchronous or contrapuntal sound. Advertised as "the most beautiful film ever made," *Sous les toits de Paris* was an international triumph, and its stunning integration of sound with sophisticated visuals earned Clair a somewhat inflated reputation as a master of the sound film. His next Tobis film was another ebullient musical comedy, *Le million* (*The Million,* 1931), which employed a whole range of non-naturalistic effects on the soundtrack and a wild chase through an opera house to create what many historians feel is the best European musical comedy of the period between the wars. With *À nous la liberté* (*Liberty Is Ours,* 1931), Clair turned to the more serious themes of industrialization and economic depression, still, however, using the musical-comedy form. Based loosely on the life of Charles Pathé (see Chapter 2), the film tells the story of an escaped convict who becomes a fabulously wealthy industrialist; he is subsequently discovered and blackmailed by a prison buddy, but in the utopian conclusion he gives up his role as a captain of industry to become a happy vagabond. The buoyant wit of this film, its great visual precision, and its brilliant use of asynchronous sound have made it a classic. But it is also notable for its humanistic indictment of mechanized modern industry, which Clair, through parallel editing, consistently equates with the experience of imprisonment. *À nous la liberté* has many similarities with Chaplin's *Modern Times* (1935; see Chapter 6)—so many, in fact, that Tobis pressed Clair to sue Chaplin for copyright infringement after the latter film's release. Clair declined, saying that he could only be honored to have inspired so great a film-maker as Chaplin.

9.39 The bleakly futuristic assembly-line in *À nous la liberté* (René Clair, 1931), and the open road of possibility with which the film concludes.

Clair's next film for Tobis, another Parisian musical entitled *Quatorze juillet* (*The Fourteenth of July*, 1932), was less successful aesthetically than his earlier films; the old formula was beginning to wear thin. Clair changed modes with *Le dernier milliardaire* (*The Last Millionaire*, 1934), a satire on dictatorship which was begun for Tobis but completed for Pathé when Goebbels, head of the German film industry since 1933, terminated the project. The film was not up to Clair's best work, but it was maliciously defamed by France's increasingly powerful Right-wing press upon its release. Deeply disturbed by this reaction, Clair accepted a contract to direct *The Ghost Goes West* (1936), a fantasy-satire about an American millionaire who buys a haunted Scottish castle and takes it home with him, for Alexander Korda in London. After this project, Clair himself went west, to Hollywood, where he worked on a series of fantasy-comedies (*I Married a Witch* [1942]; *It Happened Tomorrow* [1943]) until the end of World War II, when he returned to France.

Another important figure of the early sound film in France, although his total output amounts to little over three hours of viewing time, was Jean Vigo (1905–34). The son of a famous anarchist who was jailed and probably murdered by the French government during World War I, Vigo spent his youth as an orphan in a series of wretched boarding schools. He later became an assistant cameraman and met one of Dziga Vertov's brothers, the cameraman Boris Kaufman, with whom he made his first feature—the forty-five-minute masterpiece *Zéro de conduite* (*Zero for Conduct*, 1933). This much-admired film concerns the revolt of the boys of a rundown provincial boarding school against their petty, mean-spirited teachers; it is autobiographical in both its anarchic spirit and many of its specific details. The film is simultaneously lyrical, surrealistic, comical, and profoundly serious. Important sequences include the balletic, slow-motion pillow fight during the dormitory rebellion in which feathers swirl about the room like snowflakes in a blizzard; the official visit of the schools-inspector—a dwarf wearing a top hat; and the final assault on the courtyard, in which the boys stand on the school roof and bombard dignitaries at a pompous assembly with rubbish. By pitting the free and rebellious spirit of the children against the bourgeois repressiveness of the adults, Vigo was sounding a classical anarchist theme, and French authorities acknowledged this by banning *Zéro de conduite* from public viewing until the Liberation in 1944. This intensely personal film, with its subtle blend of poetry, fantasy, and realism, has had a great impact upon succeeding generations of directors, especially that of French New Wave film-makers such as François Truffaut. Truffaut's *Les quatre cents coups* (*The Four Hundred Blows*, 1959), and the British director Lindsay Anderson's *If . . .* (1968), for example, both owe a great deal to it in terms of structure, style, and theme (see Chapters 13 and 14).

Vigo's third film, and his last, *L'Atalante* (1934), was another utterly unique masterpiece. Based upon a commissioned script about the life of two young newlyweds aboard a river barge, it was planned as an eighty-nine-minute commercial feature; Vigo turned it into a powerful lyric poem about life and love. By blending realistic details of life on the barge, and of the bleak industrial landscape through which it passes, with sur-

9.40 The pillow fight in *Zéro de conduite* (Jean Vigo, 1933). 9.41 The newlyweds in Vigo's *L'Atalante* (1934).

real fantasy and bizarre exaggeration of character, Vigo created a film which both revived the tradition of *populisme* from the twenties and announced the "poetic realism" of the brief but glorious era of French cinema that was about to begin. Georges Sadoul speaks correctly of "the astonishing quality of poetry [*L'Atalante*] engenders from a world superficially ordinary and drab."[11] Poetry meant little to the film's distributors, however, who cut and re-edited *L'Atalante* as *Le chaland qui passe* (*The Passing Barge*) in order to exploit a popular song by that title which was added to the soundtrack as its theme. Vigo died of tuberculosis complicated by heart disease on the day of the film's premiere in Paris; he was twenty-nine. In a tragically brief career he had made two great films whose influence on future generations would be immense, and there can be no question that the French cinema lost one of its geniuses when he died.

Poetic Realism, 1934–1940

Except for the work of Clair and Vigo, the French cinema of the early sound era had not been in good health either aesthetically or financially, and in 1934—the year of Clair's departure for England and Vigo's death—the industry experienced a major economic crisis. In that year, because of worldwide depression and internal mismanagement, domestic production dropped from 160 to 120 features per year, the two giant combines of Gaumont and Pathé collapsed, and the end of French cinema was widely prophesied. What happened instead was that French cinema entered its period of greatest creative growth, because the fall of the studio combines necessitated a return to the system of independent production which had prevailed before the coming of sound. The predominant style of this period (1934–40) has been characterized by Georges Sadoul as "poetic realism"—a blend of lyricism and realism which derives from "the influence of literary naturalism and Zola, certain traditions of Zecca, Feuillade, and Delluc, certain lessons also from René Clair and Jean Vigo."[12] Poetic realsim seems to have had two phases—one born of the

9.42 *La kermesse héroique* (Jacques Feyder, 1935).

9.43 Jean Gabin in *Pépé le Moko* (Julien Duvivier, 1937).

optimism created by the Popular Front movement* of 1935–37, the other a product of the despair created by the movement's failure and the realization that Fascism in some form was at hand. The same directors and scriptwriters contributed films to both phases.

Among the first practitioners of poetic realism was Jacques Feyder, who had returned to France from self-imposed exile in the United States in 1934 as if to compensate for the loss of Vigo and Clair. Feyder made his most important films of the period in collaboration with Charles Spaak (1903–75), the screenwriter who, with Jacques Prévert (1900–1977), contributed most to the development of poetic realism. Together, Feyder and Spaak produced *Le grand jeu* (*The Great Game*, 1934), a brooding melodrama of life in the Foreign Legion; the beautiful costume film *La kermesse héroique* (English title: *Carnival in Flanders*, 1935), set in sixteenth-century Flanders, with a *mise-en-scène* based on the paintings of the great Flemish masters; and *Pension mimosas* (1935), a grim, naturalistic drama of gambling in high society and low, which provided the foundation for poetic realism as practiced later by Feyder's assistant Marcel Carné.

During this period, Spaak also collaborated successfully with Julien Duvivier (1896–1967), a prolific director of commercial films who did his best work under the influence of poetic realism. Together, Duvivier and Spaak produced *La bandera* (English title: *Escape from Yesterday*, 1935), the story of a criminal seeking refuge in the Foreign Legion, and *La belle équipe* (English title: *They Were Five*, 1936), which tells how five unemployed Parisian workers make a cooperative effort to open a restaurant on the banks of the Marne. Both films starred Jean Gabin (1904–76), who later became the archetype of the doomed modern hero in Duvivier's internationally successful *Pépé le Moko* (1937). Written by Henri Jeanson (and influenced by Howard Hawks' 1932 film *Scarface* and other American gangster films), *Pépé le Moko* concerns a Parisian gangster (Gabin) hiding out with his gang in the Casbah in Algiers while the police wait outside for the move that will betray him. The love of a woman draws Pépé out of his sanctuary, and he is gunned down by the police. As a genre film, *Pépé le Moko* can compete with the very best of the Hollywood gangster cycle, but in its muted violence and fatalism it is highly representative of the pessimistic side of poetic realism.†

The greatest exponent of this darker aspect of poetic realism was the

---

* In 1934, the coalition of Radicals and Socialists which had taken control of the Chamber of Deputies in 1932 was in serious jeopardy. By that year, Right-wing agitation, much of it overtly Fascist, had become so violent that there was a threat of civil war. As an emergency measure, all of the parties of the Left, including the Communists, banded together into a "Popular Front" in 1935 and re-asserted their control of the country and the government by delivering the premiership to the Socialist leader Léon Blum early in 1936. This alliance was never very sound, but it was effective until 1937, when the Blum government was overthrown by a coalition of Rightist and Centrist parties. With Hitler arming his legions just across the Rhine, many Frenchmen saw the collapse of the Popular Front as a sign that Fascism was inevitable.

† *Pépé le Moko* was remade twice in Hollywood—first as the romantic thriller *Algiers* (John Cromwell, 1938), then as the semi-musical *Casbah* (John Berry, 1948).

young Marcel Carné, who had made the avant-garde documentary *Nogent, Eldorado du dimanche* in 1930 and had begun his career in the sound film as an assistant to Feyder. Carné's great collaborator was the surrealist poet Jacques Prévert, with whom he produced a series of films in the late thirties which incarnate the romantic pessimism of the French cinema in the latter part of its great creative decade. Influenced by the films of von Sternberg and the German tradition of *Kammerspiel, Quai des brumes (Port of Shadows,* 1938) deals with a deserter from the colonial army (Jean Gabin) who finds himself trapped in the port of Le Havre. Like Pépé le Moko, he becomes involved with the underworld and is doomed to die through his love for a woman. Photographed entirely in the studio by Eugen Schüfftan, *Quai des brumes* is an ominously gloomy film which exudes such a pervasive sense of fatality that a spokesman for the collaborationist Vichy government later declared, "If we have lost the war, it is because of *Quai des brumes.* . . ." (Carné replied that the barometer shouldn't be blamed for the storm.)[13] In the Carné-Prévert film *Le jour se lève (Daybreak,* 1939), released just before the war, a man (Gabin) commits murder and locks himself in an attic room to await the inevitable police assault at dawn. Through the night (in what is perhaps the most structurally perfect flashback ever filmed) he remembers the love affair which led to his crime, and at daybreak he commits suicide. Simultaneously metaphysical and realistic, *Le jour se lève* exploits the metaphor of a decent man irreversibly trapped by fate more persuasively and powerfully than any other French film of the period, and it had enormous influence abroad during the war, even though it was banned in Nazi-occupied Europe.

9.44 *Quai des brumes* (Marcel Carné, 1938): Jean Gabin, Michele Morgan.

During the Occupation, the Carné-Prévert association produced two of the most spectacular films ever made in France. *Les visiteurs du soir* (English title: *The Devil's Envoy,* 1942), an adaptation of a medieval legend about a failed attempt by the Devil to intervene in a human love affair, provided a stunning re-creation of fifteenth-century France. (Carné and Prévert intended the Devil in the film to represent Hitler, but the allusions were necessarily so indirect as to be unrecognizable.) *Les enfants du paradis (The Children of Paradise,** 1945), more than three hours long, evoked the world of the nineteenth-century theater. Inspired by the great French novelists of that era, the film explores the classic theme of the relationship between life and art, and, more specifically, between reality, cinema, and theater, in the context of a complicated love affair between a beautiful woman (who has been, successively, the mistress of an actor, a criminal, and a count) and a famous professional mime. Elaborate, intelligent, superbly acted, and beautifully mounted, *Les enfants du paradis* has become a classic of the French cinema.† It is clearly Carné's and Prévert's masterpiece, and though they collaborated

---

* A reference to theatergoers who can afford only the cheapest seats in the theater, those at the very top (known in theatrical slang as "Paradise," or "the gods").

† In 1979, *Les enfants du paradis* was voted the best French film since the coming of sound by the French Academy of Cinema Arts and Techniques. Second was Jean Renoir's *La grande illusion* (1937), followed by Jacques Becker's *Casque d'or* (1952), Renoir's *La règle du jeu* (1939), Jacques Feyder's *La kermesse héroïque* (1935), Jean-Luc Godard's *Pierrot le*

9.45 Carné's *Les enfants du paradis* (1945): Jean-Louis Barrault.

several times more after the war, they never again produced a work equal to this one.

Some mention must also be made of the films of Marcel Pagnol (1895–1974), the famous playwright who built his own studio in the south of France in order to transfer his stage plays to film. An outspoken advocate of "canned theater" who saw film primarily as an actor's medium, Pagnol produced a series of robust and vigorous comedies which probably did much to establish the reputation of French cinema in English-speaking countries. His trilogy of life among the ordinary people of Marseille—*Marius* (directed by Alexander Korda, 1931), *Fanny* (directed by Marc Allégret, 1932), and *César* (directed by Pagnol, 1936)—and the delightful farce *La femme du boulanger* (*The Baker's Wife,* directed by Pagnol, 1938), also set in Marseille, are flavored by a kind of populist realism (or *populisme*) which brings them very close to the mainstream of poetic realism in its more optimistic days. Another French film-maker with roots firmly in the theater was the actor and playwright Sacha Guitry (1885–1957), who, even more than Pagnol, saw film as essentially a means of preserving his own stage plays and performances. Guitry's most important cinematic achievement was the feature *Le roman d'un tricheur* (*The Story of a Cheat,* 1936), in which he used a voice-over commentary by the protagonist (Guitry himself) to describe the action on the screen, which occurred wholly in pantomime.

Jean Renoir

By far the greatest and most influential director to emerge from French poetic realism was Jean Renoir (1894–1979). Son of the Impressionist

fou (1965), Alain Resnais' *Hiroshima, mon amour* (1959), René Clément's *Jeux interdits* (1952), Marcel Carné's *Quai des brumes* (1938), and Henri-Georges Clouzot's *Le salaire de la peur* (1953). (All are discussed in either Chapter 9 or Chapter 13.) For more on *Les enfants du paradis,* see Edward Baron Turk, "The Birth of *Children of Paradise,*" *American Film,* 4, 9 (July–August 1979), 42–49.

painter Pierre-Auguste Renoir (1841–1915),* he began his career in cinema with an uneven series of eight silent films, including a brilliant adaptation of Zola's novel *Nana* (1927); *La petite marchande d'allumettes* (1927), a modern-dress version of Hans Christian Andersen's fairy-tale *The Little Match Girl*; and *Tire-au-flanc* (1928), a farce that compares well with Clair's *Un chapeau de paille d'Italie*, combining slapstick, satire, and poetic fantasy. Renoir's other silent films were strictly commercial vehicles, and it was not until the coming of sound that he began to distinguish himself as an artist. His first sound film was *On purge bébé* (*Purging the Baby*, 1931), adapted from a play by Georges Feydeau and starring Renoir's frequent collaborator during this period, Michel Simon (1895–1975). This relatively trivial domestic comedy was nevertheless a great commercial success and permitted Renoir to make his first important sound film, *La chienne* (*The Bitch*, 1932), a year later. This melodrama of a middle-class bank clerk and Sunday painter (Simon) who has an affair with a prostitute and later kills her for deceiving him owed much to the example of von Sternberg's *Der blaue Engel* (1929; see Chapter 4), and it achieved a degree of social realism in evoking its mileau which exceeded even that of its German predecessor.†

After the suspenseful detective film *La nuit de carrefour* (*Night at the Crossroads*, 1932), adapted from a work by Georges Simenon, and the lightweight comedy *Chotard et cie* (*Chotard and Company*, 1932), Renoir once again returned to the theme of *La chienne*, pitting the bourgeois life against the anarchic values of a tramp in *Boudu sauvé des eaux* (*Boudu Saved from Drowning*, 1932). In this film, a respectable Parisian book-dealer saves a moody vagabond named Boudu (Michel Simon) from drowning in the Seine and insists that he move in with him. After seducing both the wife and mistress of his benefactor, and generally wreaking havoc on the household, Boudu leaves happily to resume his wanderings. Produced independently with complete creative freedom, *Boudu*, like *La chienne*, was a commercial failure. Renoir's next film was a fine adaptation of Flaubert's *Madame Bovary* (1934) in which he attempted to translate the novel's symbolic sub-structure into cinematic terms. Originally more than three and a half hours long, but cut to two hours by its distributors, *Madame Bovary* was another commercial failure; happily, Renoir was given a chance in the following year to undertake a much-cherished project by producer Marcel Pagnol. This was *Toni* (1934), a story of immigrant Italian workers in the quarries of southern France. Shot entirely on location and making extensive use of non-actors, *Toni* harks back to Soviet realism and is a forerunner of Italian neo-realism (see Chapters 5 and 11).

After this attempt to make a film, in Renoir's words, "as close as possible to a documentary,"[14] he entered into his only collaboration with the scriptwriter Jacques Prévert; the resulting film marks a major turning

9.46 *Nana* (Jean Renoir, 1926): Catherine Hessling, Valeska Gert.

9.47 A shot in depth from Renoir's *La nuit de carrefour* (1932).

9.48 Renoir's *Boudu sauvé des eaux* (1932): Marcelle Hainia, Charles Granval, Michel Simon, Séverine Lerczinska.

9.49 Depth perspective in *Madame Bovary* (1934): Valentine Tessier.

---

* Renoir is also the uncle of the cinematographer Claude Renoir (b. 1914) and the brother of the actor Pierre Renoir (1885–1952), with both of whom he worked frequently in the thirties.

† *La chienne* was remade in the United States by Fritz Lang as *Scarlet Street* (1945).

9.50 Experimenting with depth in *Toni* (Jean Renoir, 1934).

9.51 Two shots from *Le crime de Monsieur Lange* (Jean Renoir, 1935) emphasizing depth.

point in his work. Shot during the great electoral triumphs of the Popular Front in 1935, *Le crime de Monsieur Lange* (*The Crime of Monsieur Lange,* 1935) is in many ways a political parable of the need for collective action in the face of capitalist corruption. The employees of a publishing house form a co-operative to run the business when they learn of the accidental death of their lecherous and exploitative boss. The co-op experiences great success until the boss unexpectedly returns to claim his business. One of the workers, a writer of Wild West serials named M. Lange (his name is a pun on the French *l'ange,* "angel"), shoots him and flees the country for freedom. Shot largely on a single set representing the courtyard of a Parisian working-class tenement, *Le crime de Monsieur Lange* announced the new spirit of social commitment which would pervade Renoir's work through his last pre-war films. The strength of this commitment was demonstrated in *La vie est à nous* (*Life Is Ours*/*People of France,* 1936), an election propaganda film for the French Communist Party which mixes newsreel footage with dramatic episodes to show the necessity of presenting a united front against Fascism. Financed solely by public subscription, the film was banned from French commercial theaters but enjoyed a lively underground reputation in the *ciné-clubs* and specialist theaters. It was thought to have been destroyed during the war, but a copy came to light in 1969, and *La vie est à nous,* appropriately, had its first commercial success in France during the height of the student-worker rebellion of the late sixties.*

Renoir's next two films were literary adaptations. *Une partie de campagne* (*A Day in the Country*) was a version of a brief Maupassant story shot in 1936 but not edited and released until 1946. Just forty minutes long, *Une partie* is the bittersweet tale of an 1880 Parisian bourgeois who takes his wife, his daughter, and her fiancé to the country for a Sunday outing. At a restaurant on the banks of the Marne they meet two men who take the women for a short boat ride up the river. In the process, the daughter falls in love with one of them. They embrace briefly but realize that they must return to their separate worlds. The pictorial quality of the film—its unique feeling for landscape and nature—is reminiscent of the paintings of Renoir's father and of his fellow Impressionists Manet, Monet, and Degas. Renoir's other adaptation of 1936 was a somewhat inconclusive version of Maxim Gorky's play *The Lower Depths* (*Les bas-fonds,* 1936), written by Renoir and Charles Spaak, set not in late-nineteenth-century Russia but in some unidentified time and place.

Renoir's next film, *La grande illusion* (*Grand Illusion,* 1937), also written in collaboration with Spaak, has proved to be an enduring masterpiece. It portrays European civilization on the brink of cultural collapse and pleads for the primacy of human relationships over national and class antagonisms, simultaneously asserting the utter futility of war and the necessity of international solidarity to combat this most destructive and degrading "grand illusion" of the human race. One winter during World War I, three downed French pilots—an aristocrat (Pierre Fres-

---

*See note, p. 472. On Renoir's political sympathies, see Elizabeth Grottle Strebel, "Renoir and the Popular Front," *Sight and Sound,* 49, 1 (Winter 1979–80), 36–41.

nay), a mechanic (Jean Gabin), and a Jewish banker (Marcel Dalio)—are captured by the Germans and ceremoniously welcomed into the enemy officers' mess. They are subsequently transferred to a series of prison-camps—each one a microcosm of European society—and finally to the impregnable fortress of Wintersborn, commanded by the sympathetic Prussian aristocrat von Rauffenstein (Erich von Stroheim). The French aristocrat Boieldieu and von Rauffenstein become close friends because they are of the same caste, and they pursue a long intellectual dialogue on the role of their dwindling class in European society. Despite the cultural barrier between Boieldieu and his two compatriots, he has earlier assisted them in digging a tunnel under a prison wall in the dead of winter—the whole film takes place in this season—because it is his duty as an officer to help them escape. Equally trapped by his officer's code, von Rauffenstein must later shoot Boieldieu during an escape attempt at Wintersborn in which he willingly plays the decoy. Boieldieu dies painfully in von Rauffenstein's quarters, and the German commander, full of remorse, places a flower from his much-cherished geranium plant on the corpse. Both men have been victims of a rigid code of behavior which has left them no option but mutual destruction despite their friendship; Renoir suggests that the old ruling class of Europe is doomed for precisely the same reasons (which are also the same reasons for the "grand illusion" of war). The future of Europe seems to lie with the Jew, Rosenthal, and the mechanic, Maréchal—representatives of the bourgeoisie and working class, respectively—who have escaped together over the castle wall. After a grueling trek across Germany during which they argue continuously and nearly desert one another, Rosenthal and Maréchal finally cross the border to Switzerland, and freedom, as a result of their cooperation.

This extraordinarily rich and humane film contains magnificent ensemble playing by all of its leading actors, as well as the best performance of von Stroheim's career, perhaps because he played a character whose

9.52 *La grande illusion* (Jean Renoir, 1937): von Rauffenstein welcomes Boieldieu, Maréchal, and the other French prisoners-of-war to Wintersborn.

9.53 Brother aristocrats: Boieldieu (Pierre Fresnay) and von Rauffenstein (Erich von Stroheim). Note the potted geranium between them, a small symbol of hope in the arid environment of the prison camp.

9.54 An alliance of the working class and the bourgeoisie: Maréchal (Jean Gabin) and Rosenthal (Marcel Dalio) plan their escape.

demeanor and doomed idealism so closely resembled his own. But the most striking aspect of *La grande illusion* is Renoir's use of the *long take,* or *sequence shot*—unedited shots made from a single camera set-up which generally (but not always) constitute entire dramatic sequences within a film. Dramatic tension in such shots is created through *composition in depth,* or the arrangement of dramatically significant action and objects on several spatial planes within the frame at once. Composition in depth is essentially an attempt to make the two-dimensional space of the cinema screen three-dimensional, and it can be achieved only through what is known as *deep-focus* photography—a mode of filming in which the foreground, middleground, and background of a shot are all in sharp focus simultaneously. Technically, deep-focus photography is the achievement of a nearly perfect *depth of field* (the range of distances within which objects will be in sharp focus) within the frame; it should not be confused with *depth of focus,* a term used in describing the relationship between the lens and the surface of the film. Aesthetically, deep-focus photography provides a way of incorporating a close shot, medium shot, and long shot within a single frame, and of linking character with background. It also *appears* to reproduce the field of vision of the human eye, although in fact the eye does not possess extreme depth of field but rather is able to alter focus within a depth perspective so rapidly that we are never aware of the discontinuity.

The earliest film stock—that used by all film-makers until 1918—had possessed an extraordinary capacity for deep focus, or depth of field, in that it was relatively "fast," or sensitive to light, enabling cameramen to use small lens apertures* which kept both the foreground and background of their shots in focus (see, for example, the still from Griffith's *Musketeers of Pig Alley* [1912]). But this early stock was *monochromatic,* i.e., sensitive to *one part* of the color spectrum only (blue), and was therefore incapable of reproducing a realistic gradation of tones in black-and-white. The introduction of *orthochromatic* stock around 1918 added new areas of color registry (blue to green) but still left the cinema with a range of black-and-white visual tones that was far from naturalistic. Yet orthochromatic stock, like monochromatic, was "fast" and therefore permitted the use of small lens apertures to achieve great depth of field. Ultimately, both monochromatic and orthochromatic stock depended for their depth of field upon a strong, penetrating source of light to strike the negative through the narrow aperture of the lens—the sun during the cinema's first two decades, and mercury vapor lamps and then carbon arc lamps during the third. In 1927, concurrently with the arrival of sound, orthochromatic was replaced by *panchromatic* stock, a film sensitive to all parts of the spectrum from blue to red but much "slower" than the earlier films. Simultaneously, the carbon arc lamps, which sput-

---

* The lens aperture is the iris-like diaphragm at the optical center of the lens, a point midway between the front and rear elements. Varying the diameter of this opening, which is measured in "*f*-stops" (e.g., $f\,1, f\,1.4, f\,2, f\,2.8, f\,4, f\,5.6, f\,8, f\,11, f\,16, f\,22, f\,32, f\,45, f\,64$), determines how much light the lens will transmit to the emulsion surface of the film and therefore determines the visual quality of the image imprinted on the negative stock.

tered and popped noisily in operation, were replaced by incandescent lighting, which was soundless. The new incandescent light, however, was softer and less penetrating than the light provided by the arc lamps, so cameramen were forced to widen their lens apertures and decrease the depth of field of the image. Thus, early panchromatic focus was shallow; the backgrounds of close shots would blur and a face in close-up would become detached from its environment. With few exceptions (such as James Wong Howe's photography for *Transatlantic* [1931]),* this deficiency plagued the sound film until 1940, when technical innovations in lenses, film stock, and lighting, and the creative genius of Orson Welles and Gregg Toland, restored the cinema's physical capacity for deep focus (see Chapter 10).

Despite underdeveloped technology, however, Renoir was the first major director of the sound film to compose his shots in depth, even though the depth was achieved artificially by constantly adjusting the focus of his camera to follow dramatic action within a given take.† He had experimented with this technique in many of his early sound films, most successfully in *Toni* (1934), but *La grande illusion* was his first film based consistently on the principle of the long take or sequence shot. Generally, Renoir's films include realistic and dramatically significant background and middleground activity in every sequence shot. Actors range about the set transacting their business while the camera shifts its focus from one plane of depth to another and back again. Significant off-frame action is often followed with a moving camera, characteristically through a series of pans within a single continuous shot. The scene of Boieldieu's death in *La grande illusion,* for example, is rendered through three evocative panning shots. Von Rauffenstein has just finished a bedside conversation with the dying Frenchman in which both have agreed that their caste is doomed to extinction. In a single shot, the camera follows von Rauffenstein as he rises from his chair, walks some distance to his liquor cabinet, takes a drink, and returns to the bedside when a nurse calls off-frame. In the next shot, the camera moves with von Rauffenstein's hand in close-up as it reaches toward Boieldieu's eyes to close them. Finally, the camera observes von Rauffenstein at some distance as he walks from the bedside to the window, gazes at the falling snow, and, at last, cuts the flower from his prized geranium with a pair of scissors. Renoir makes the transition to his next scene with yet another pan: his camera moves slowly over the snowy German countryside in long shot to discover Rosenthal and Maréchal, dressed in dirty civilian clothes, hiding in a ditch at the end of the pan. *La grande illusion* is composed

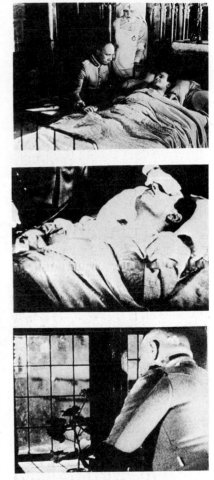

9.55 Stills from the sequence shots of Boieldieu's death.

* In Charles Higham's *Hollywood Cameramen* (Bloomington, Ind., 1970), Howe claims that for William K. Howard's *Transatlantic,* "I used wide angles, deep focus throughout, long before *Kane.* Eighty percent of the picture was shot with a twenty-five millimeter lens. . . . I carried focus from five feet back to twenty, thirty feet" (p. 84).

† For a carefully researched study of the use of depth of field before Renoir (and for an argument that this use was *not* limited by existing technology), see Charles H. Harpole, *Gradients of Depth in the Cinema Image* (New York, 1978). See also Harpole's article "Ideological and Technological Determinism in Deep-Space Cinema Images," *Film Quarterly,* 33, 3 (Spring 1980), 11–21.

almost completely of such moving sequence shots, but Renoir and his cinematographer, Christian Matras (b. 1903) never permit them to become flashy or self-conscious.

In the year of its release, *La grande illusion* won both an Academy Award in the United States and a Golden Lion at the prestigious Venice Film Festival, even though it was banned from commercial exhibition in Italy and Germany. In 1957, together with *Potemkin* and *Mother, La grande illusion* was voted one of the twelve greatest films of all time at the Brussels World's Fair.

9.56 Depth: Renoir's *La Marseillaise* (1937).

Renoir's next project was *La Marseillaise* (1937), a semi-documentary reconstruction of some major episodes from the French Revolution, financed by the trade unions and flavored with the politics of the Popular Front. Next came *La bête humaine* (*The Human Beast*, 1938), an adaptation of Zola's naturalistic novel about an alcoholic railroad engineer (played by Jean Gabin) cast in modern terms.* Renoir's final French film of the period was his greatest masterpiece and one of the great works of the cinema, *La règle du jeu* (*The Rules of the Game*, 1939). Like *La grande illusion,* it is about a culture teetering on the brink of collapse, but it is a much more complicated film in both attitude and technique.

Informed by the gracious rhythms of Mozart, Johann Strauss, and Chopin, and patterned on the classical French theater of Marivaux and Beaumarchais,† *La règle du jeu* is an elegant tragicomedy of manners whose intricacy of plot defies easy summarization. Briefly, the young aviator André Jurieu, who has just completed a daring transatlantic flight, is in love with Christine, the wife of a wealthy Jewish land-owner, the Marquis Robert de la Chesnaye (Marcel Dalio). La Chesnaye organizes a large weekend hunting party at his country estate, La Colinière, to which he invites Jurieu, Octave (a mutual friend of Jurieu and Christine, played by Renoir), and his own mistress. After a day of hunting in which hundreds of rabbits and birds are slaughtered and maimed, we are treated to a series of love intrigues among the *haut bourgeoisie* above-stairs and among the servants below-stairs—who, in their snobbery, insincerity, and pride, are the precise mirror images of their masters. The major characteristic of these intrigues is that not a single one is serious, and Jurieu has broken an important "rule of the game" by sincerely declaring his love for Christine in the most public way imaginable—in a radio broadcast from Orly airport just after his transatlantic flight. Later, during a gala evening fête featuring extravagant theatrical entertainment and a fancy-dress ball, a jealous gamekeeper attempts to shoot his wife's would-be lover (a poacher whom the kindhearted marquis has hired as a servant). After a comic chase through the ballroom reminiscent of a Marx Brothers film, the gamekeeper—in a classical case of mistaken identity—kills Jurieu instead. A model of civilized restraint, the marquis

---

* Fritz Lang directed another adaptation of Zola's novel in 1954, under the title *Human Desire.*

† Renoir, in fact, conceived of the film as an updated version of the comedy *Le caprices de Marianne* by the Romantic poet and playwright Alfred de Musset (1810–57).

9.57 *La règle du jeu* (Jean Renoir, 1939): Christine de la Chesnaye (Nora Grégor) questions her maid, Lisette (Pauline Dubost) about her own marriage.

9.58 Christine (Nora Grégor) and Octave (Jean Renoir) by moonlight at La Colinière.

takes immediate command of the situation, apologizes to his guests for the "regrettable accident," and takes all appropriate steps to restore equilibrium to the world of La Colinière.

Witty, elegant, and profoundly pessimistic, *La règle du jeu* is ultimately concerned with social breakdown and cultural decadence at a particularly critical moment in European history. Renoir presents us with a world in which feeling has been replaced by manners and all that remains of civilized values is their external form—a form which will itself soon crumble. Society has become a vast collective lie, and those, like Jurieu, who break its "rules" by telling the truth come to no good. *La règle du jeu* has the moral and intellectual depth of a great novel, but it is also a brilliant piece of film-making. Renoir had never used the long take and deep focus to such striking dramatic effect. Sequence shots dominate nearly every major scene, and the camera moves continuously to follow significant action within the frame. Fluid, graceful, and exquisitely precise are terms which describe Renoir's camera style in *La règle du jeu*. He resorts to expressive montage only once in the entire film— appropriately, to render the mindless organized violence of the hunt.

Renoir expected *La règle du jeu* to be controversial, but he could hardly have anticipated the extremity of the reaction. The film provoked a political riot at its Paris premiere, was cut and re-edited by its distributor from 113 to 80 minutes, and was finally banned in late 1939 by French military censors as "demoralizing." The Nazis banned it during the Occupation, and Allied bombing destroyed the original negative in 1942. Happily, the integral version of *La règle du jeu,* minus one short scene, was reconstructed under Renoir's supervision by two French film producers in 1956 and has enjoyed a prestigious international reputation ever since. In 1962 and 1972 an international poll of film critics ranked it among the ten greatest films ever made.

9.59 Guests at La Colinière on their way to the hunt.

9.60 Shots from the hunting sequence in *La règle du jeu*.

9.61 The marquis (Marcel Dalio) and his gamekeeper (Gaston Modot) encounter a poacher (Julien Carette).

In the summer of 1939, Renoir accepted an invitation to teach at the Centro Sperimentale in Rome (Italy's national film school) and to direct there a version of Puccini's opera *La Tosca*, with the assistance of Luchino Visconti (see Chapter 11).* The film was begun by Renoir's crew but completed by others, because Italy joined Hitler's war against France on June 10, 1940, and Renoir, who was on the Nazis' extermination list because of his Leftist politics, was forced to emigrate to the United States. Here he went to work for a variety of studios, filming in rapid succession *Swamp Water* (1941)—a sort of commercial, American *Toni* shot on location in the swamps of Georgia—and two war propaganda films— *This Land Is Mine* (1943) and *Salute to France* (1944). Renoir's most distinguished American film was *The Southerner*, made in 1945 for United Artists. This austere, semi-documentary account of the lives of poor white farmers in the deep South was shot on location with complete creative freedom; more than any other of Renoir's American films, it harks back to the poetic realism of the thirties. With *The Diary of a Chambermaid* (1946) Renoir returned to French sources (Octave Mirbeau's novel, which Luis Buñuel would also film, in 1964), but moved away from the realism of his greatest period. Independently produced and shot entirely in the studio, this film about the decadence of French bourgeois society in the late nineteenth century resembled *La règle du jeu* in theme, but it lacked the great depth of the earlier work and was universally condemned in Europe, where Renoir's pre-war reputation had declined. His last American film was *The Woman on the Beach* (1947), a tale of romantic obsession in a wild coastal setting. The film failed commercially and aesthetically, in large part because RKO re-edited it no fewer than three times.

At this point Renoir became increasingly interested in theater and spectacle, as they contrasted with his earlier "realistic" style. He left Hollywood to make *The River* (1951), a British co-production, on the banks of the Ganges River. This beautiful film—Renoir's first in color—was strikingly photographed by the director's nephew, Claude Renoir, and concerns the response of a fourteen-year-old British girl to India. Renoir next went to Italy to make *Le carrosse d'or* (*The Golden Coach*, 1952), a color film about a *commedia dell'arte* theater troupe in eighteenth-century Peru which attempted to explore the relationships among film, theater, and reality. Renoir appropriately abandoned composition in depth and the moving camera for *Le carrosse d'or* in favor of a more theatrical *mise-en-scène* using long takes from a relatively stationary camera.

In 1954 Renoir returned to his native land for the first time since the war and began his last important series of French films. *French CanCan* (1954) is set in Montmartre in the late 1890's of Renoir's childhood and

9.62   *The River* (Jean Renoir, 1951).

---

* The invitation, sent through diplomatic channels, came from Mussolini himself, who greatly admired Renoir as a film-maker despite his politics (Il Duce was said to own a private copy of *La grande illusion*, although it was officially banned by his Fascist government). Renoir accepted the invitation at the behest of the French government, which was anxious to preserve Italy's neutrality in the "phony war" with Germany, which began on September 3, 1939, and ended on May 10, 1940, when SS Panzer divisions smashed through the Maginot Line.

tells the story of the impresario who founded the famous Moulin Rouge theater. Its brilliant use of color in motion evokes the paintings of the Impressionists but goes beyond them, reaching its height in the spectacular twenty-minute cancan dance with which the film concludes. *Elena et les hommes* (English title: *Paris Does Strange Things*, 1957), a romantic costume drama set during the Franco-Prussian War, showed signs that Renoir's creative power was waning; his next two films seemed to many to confirm this. *Le testament du Dr. Cordelier* (1959) is a modern adaptation of Robert Louis Stevenson's *Dr. Jekyll and Mr. Hyde* shot in black-and-white for French television. *Le déjeuner sur l'herbe* (*Picnic on the Grass*, 1959) is a rather silly futuristic fantasy whose visual texture is nevertheless closer to that of French Impressionist painting than anything Renoir had ever filmed. In his final feature film, *Le caporal epinglé* (*The Elusive Corporal*, 1962), Renoir returned to the subject of prisoners-of-war with a lightweight comedy about the multiple escape attempts of a French corporal from a German prison-camp during World War II. Renoir's film-making career ended in 1969 with a series of short plays for French television entitled *Le petit théâtre de Jean Renoir* (*The Little Theater of Jean Renoir*, 1969). Later, Renoir retired to Southern California, where he wrote plays, a biography of his father, seven novels, and, finally, his own memoirs.

Jean Renoir, indisputably one of the great masters of world cinema, resolutely refused to be compromised by his own success. In a career that spanned forty-six years of cinema, he never ceased to experiment and explore, to consistently renew his creative vitality by striking out in new directions. *La règle du jeu* (1939) is as different from *La carrosse d'or* (1954) as both are from *Toni* (1934) and *The Southerner* (1945), and yet all four of these films are masterworks on their own terms. Renoir was also the pioneer of composition in depth in the sound film, and, according to André Bazin, he became the father of a new aesthetic: "He alone in his searchings as director prior to *La règle du jeu* . . . forced himself to look back beyond the resources provided by montage and so uncovered the secret of film form that would permit everything to be said without chopping the world up into little fragments, that would reveal the hidden meanings in people and things without disturbing the unity natural to them."[15] Renoir's influence on Orson Welles, who brought the technique of composition in depth to its ultimate perfection in *Citizen Kane*, is well known,* and his impact on Italian neo-realism was strong. His technical genius notwithstanding, Renoir was perhaps the most humanistic of all the Western cinema's major figures. He wrote: "I'm not a director—I'm a story-teller. . . . The only thing I bring to this illogical, irresponsible, and cruel universe is my love."[16] An artist of strong and uniquely personal vision, Jean Renoir also represents the flowering of the period of poetic realism (1934–1940), when French films were generally regarded as the most important and sophisticated in the world.

---

* Welles wrote a moving eulogy when Renoir died on February 12, 1979, at his home in Beverly Hills, after a long illness. It appeared in the *Los Angeles Times* on February 18, 1979.

Orson Welles and the Modern Sound Film

At the very moment that France was being occupied by the Nazis and the rest of Europe was engulfed in war, a young American director made a film which was to substantially transform the cinema. In 1939 Orson Welles (b. 1915) was brought to Hollywood by the financially troubled RKO Pictures under an unprecedented six-film contract which gave him complete control over every aspect of production. At twenty-four, Welles' experience in radio and theater was vast. From 1933 to 1937 he directed and acted in numerous Broadway and off-Broadway plays, including a production of *Macbeth* with a voodoo setting and an anti-Fascist *Julius Caesar* set in contemporary Italy; in 1937, with John Houseman (b. 1902), he founded the famous Mercury Theater company; and between 1938 and 1940 he wrote, directed, and starred in the weekly radio series *Mercury Theater of the Air,* whose pseudo-documentary broadcast based on H. G. Wells' *War of the Worlds* caused a nationwide panic on Halloween night in 1938. Welles had made several short films in connection with his theatrical productions (such as *Too Much Johnson* [1938]),* but he had never been on a soundstage in his life. His first feature film was to be an adaptation of Joseph Conrad's *Heart of Darkness* filmed with a subjective camera from the point of view of the narrator (who is also a participant in the action), but this project was abandoned indefinitely due to the outbreak of the war in Europe and the internment of its female lead, the German actress Dita Parlo.† Next, Welles undertook to film a script written by himself and Herman J. Mankiewicz (1898–1953) about the life and personality of a great American entrepreneur. Originally entitled simply *American,* the Welles-Mankiewicz scenario ultimately became the shooting script for *Citizen Kane* (1941),‡

---

* See Frank Brady, "The Lost Film of Orson Welles," *American Film,* 4, 2 (November 1978), 63–69.

† Dita Parlo (1906–71) was working in the French film industry when the war began (she had played featured roles in Vigo's *L'Atalante* [1934] and Renoir's *La grande illusion* [1937], among other films). Military officials had her arrested as an alien and, ultimately, deported to Germany.

† Since the publication of Pauline Kael's essay "Raising Kane" in *The New Yorker* (February 20 and 27, 1971) and its subsequent appearance as the introduction to *The Citizen*

the now legendary crypto-biography of America's most powerful press lord, William Randolph Hearst (1863–1951).

CITIZEN KANE

Production

Welles has claimed that his only preparation for directing *Citizen Kane* was to watch John Ford's *Stagecoach* (1939) forty times. Ford's influence on the film is pronounced, but it is equally clear that Welles was steeped in the major European traditions, especially those of German Expressionism and the *Kammerspielfilm,** and French poetic realism. If *Kane*'s narrative economy owes much to the example of Ford, its visual texture is heavily indebted to the chiaroscuro lighting of Lang, the fluid camera of Murnau, the baroque *mise-en-scène* of von Sternberg, and the deep-focus realism of Renoir. Credit is also due Welles' remarkably talented collaborators—Mankiewicz; the Mercury Theater players; the composer Bernard Herrmann; the editor Robert Wise; and RKO's art director, Van Nest Polglase. But Welles' greatest single technical asset in the filming of *Kane* was his brilliant director of photography, Gregg Toland (1904–48). Toland had earned a distinguished reputation as a cinematographer in Hollywood in the thirties and had experimented with deep-focus photography and ceilinged sets (see below) in his two most recent films, *Wuthering Heights* (William Wyler, 1939) and *The Longest Voyage* (John Ford, 1940). Welles (or Mankiewicz) had conceived *Kane* as a film which occurs largely in flashback as characters recall their acquaintance with the great man after his death, and he wanted the narrative to flow poetically from image to image in a manner analogous to the

---

Kane Book (New York, 1971) there has been much controversy over the authorship of the script of *Citizen Kane*. On the basis of what later proved to be largely unconfirmed evidence, Kael maintained that Welles did not write a single line of the script and that he consciously contrived to steal the credit from Mankiewicz after the fact. More recently, a substantial body of convincing evidence to the contrary has been mounted by such film scholars as Peter Bogdanovich ("The Kane Mutiny," *Esquire,* October 1972) and Andrew Sarris ("The Great Kane Controversy," *World,* January 16, 1973). But, as Joseph McBride points out in his crucial book *Orson Welles* (New York, 1972), the argument may well be irrelevant, since the script contains virtually no provision for shooting, direction, or *mise-en-scène.* The truth seems to be that the concept, scenic arrangement, and most of the dialogue are Mankiewicz's, while the cinematic visualization of the script—which is to say the film *Citizen Kane*—belongs entirely to Welles and his technicians. Robert Carringer has recently examined a complete set of script records in the archives of RKO General in Hollywood and reached the conclusion that principle authorship belongs to Welles: "In the eight weeks between the time [Mankiewicz's original script] passed into Welles' hands and the final draft was completed, the *Citizen Kane* script was transformed, principally by him, from a solid basis for a story into an authentic plan for a masterpiece." (Robert Carringer, "The Scripts of *Citizen Kane,*" *Critical Inquiry,* Winter 1978, p. 400.)

* As John Russell Taylor has observed, "*Citizen Kane* may be the best American film ever made; but it just might be also the best German film ever made." (Quoted in *German Film Directors in Hollywood: Catalogue of an Exhibit of the Goethe Institutes of North America* [San Francisco, 1978], p. 5.)

10.1 Gregg Toland and Orson Welles shooting *Citizen Kane* (Orson Welles, 1940): the *Inquirer* set.

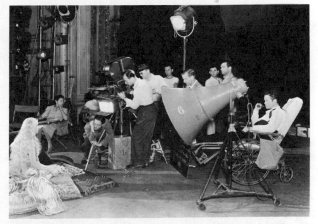

10.2 Welles directing Toland and Dorothy Comingore in an opera sequence near the end of the principal photography. (He had broken his ankle running down the stairs in pursuit of "Boss" Jim Gettys in the scene depicted by 10.29.)

process of human memory. Thus he used straight cuts only for shock effect and made most of his narrative transitions through lingering lap dissolves. More important, Welles planned to construct the film as a series of long takes, or sequence shots, scrupulously composed in depth to eliminate the necessity for narrative cutting within major dramatic scenes.

To accomplish this, Toland developed for Welles a method of deep-focus photography capable of achieving an unprecedented depth of field. Also called "pan focus" photography, this method used the newly available Eastman Super XX film stock (an ultra-"fast" film—one with a very high sensitivity to light) in combination with a 24mm wide-angle lens whose aperture was stopped down to $f8$ or less—a radical reduction in its size (see Chapter 9, note). The scenes were lit by the high-intensity arc lamps normally used only in Technicolor productions and the lenses coated with a clear plastic substance to reduce glare. By this method Toland was able to achieve something very close to "universal" focus within the frames of *Citizen Kane,* and Welles was able to distribute dramatic action across a depth perspective unlike anything ever used in a sound film. Since the early nineteen-sixties, improvements in lenses, lighting, and film emulsions have made the achievement of deep focus a much simpler matter than it was for Welles and Toland in 1940, but the technical principles remain much the same. Welles' use of the deep-focus sequence shot in *Kane* demonstrated an absolute mastery of composition in depth. Like Renoir, he used the deep-focus format functionally, to develop scenes without resorting to montage, but he also used it expressively—as Eisenstein had used montage—to create metaphors for things which the cinema cannot represent directly on the screen.

At the height of his arrogance and power, for example, Kane often looms like a giant in the foreground of the frame, dwarfing other characters in the middleground and background, and towering over the audience, often from a low camera angle. Later, Kane's self-absorbed alienation from the world and everyone in it is conveyed by the growing

10.3 Charles Foster Kane (Orson Welles) and his first wife, Emily Norton (Ruth Warrick), at breakfast: the growing distance. (From Leland's narrative.)

10.4 The aging Kane with his second wife, Susan Alexander (Dorothy Comingore), at Xanadu. The depth perspective which separates them suggests an unbreachable gap. (From Susan's narrative.)

10.5 Depth as fate: Mrs. Kane (Agnes Moorehead) and Thatcher (George Coulouris); Mr. Kane (Harry Shannon); Charlie (Buddy Swan) outside, framed by the window. (From Thatcher's narrative.)

distance which separates him from all other characters within the frame. In these instances, Welles' use of depth perspective involves an expressive distortion of space which creates a metaphor for something in Kane's psychology. At other times, Welles uses deep focus both to achieve narrative economy and to echelon characters dramatically within the frame. Early in the film we are presented with a sequence shot in the front room of a boarding-house in which Charlie Kane's mother signs the agreement that will permit her son to be taken to the East and later inherit a fortune. In exchanging her son's childhood for an adult life of fantastic wealth, she is selling him, and she knows it. Welles set the shot up like this: In the foreground of the frame, Mrs. Kane and Mr. Thatcher, whose bank is the executor of the estate, sign the agreement. The middleground is occupied by Charlie's weak-willed father, whose vacillation about the agreement is rendered visible as he paces back and forth between foreground and background. In the back of the room is a window through which, in the extreme background of the frame, we see Charlie, who in the foreground of the same shot is being indentured to his own future, playing unsuspectingly in the snow with his sled and shouting "The Union forever!" Thus, in a single shot, Welles is able to communicate a large amount of narrative and thematic information which would require many shots in a conventionally edited scene.

Kane is a film of much fluid intra-frame movement. The sequence described above, for instance, actually begins with a medium long shot of Charlie at play in the snow through the open window of the boarding-house; then the camera pulls back rapidly to reveal the other characters and elements in the composition. But there are three virtuoso moving camera shots in the film, each of which is a tour-de-force of fluidity and continuity. In the first, from a shot of a poster announcing the appearance of Kane's second wife at the El Rancho nightclub, the camera cranes up vertically to the flashing neon sign of the club itself, then tracks horizontally *through* it and down onto the rain-spattered glass of a skylight. The movement continues after a quick dissolve (made invisible by flashing lightning and distracting thunder), as the camera descends to a medium shot of Susan Alexander Kane and a newsman talking together at a table in the club's interior. In another shot, near the middle of the film, the camera cranes up vertically from a long shot of Susan Alexander Kane singing on the stage of the Chicago Municipal Opera House to a catwalk some four stories above it, where a stagehand makes a vulgar but richly deserved gesture of contempt for her performance. Finally, there is the long swooping crane shot with which the film concludes, as the camera tracks slowly across the great collection of artifacts that Kane has amassed in a lifetime of collecting, finally coming to rest on the object of the search for "Rosebud" which gives the film its narrative impulse or motive.

Other remarkable aspects of this wholly remarkable film are its expressive chiaroscuro lighting and its frequent use of extreme low-angle photography in connection with the figure of Kane. The latter necessitated the use of many ceilinged sets, which had been done in Hollywood before but never so consistently and effectively to suggest a sense of claustration and enclosure. (Film-makers have conventionally left their interior sets roofless in order first to admit the sunlight and later to facilitate artificial lighting and the free movement of the boom crane and microphone.) Finally, and most significantly, attention must be called to *Kane*'s innovative use of sound.

Welles' experience in radio served him well in recording the soundtrack for *Kane*. He invented for his few montage sequences a technique he called the "lightning mix," in which shots were rapidly linked together not by the narrative logic of their images but by the continuity of the soundtrack. Kane's growth from child to adult is managed in a matter of seconds as a shot of his guardian giving him the present of a sled and wishing him "a Merry Christmas" is cut together with a shot of the same man some fifteen years later completing the sentence—"and a Happy New Year"—again addressing Kane, but in a different dramatic context. Another lightning mix conveys the entire progress of Kane's campaign for governor of New York State in three brief shots. First we see Kane listening to Susan Alexander sing at the piano (wretchedly) in the parlor of the boarding-house in which she lives. At the end of the performance Kane claps, and the shot is dovetailed with another of a friend addressing a small street rally in Kane's behalf. The applause, which has been continuous on the soundtrack since the parlor shot, grows louder and multiplies in response to the speaker's words: "I am speaking for Charles Foster Kane, the fighting liberal . . . who entered upon this campaign with one purpose only—." We cut finally to a long shot of Kane himself addressing a huge political rally in Madison Square Garden and completing the sentence as the camera begins to track toward the speaker's platform: "—to point out and make public the dishonesty, the downright villainy of Boss Jim Gettys' political machine." The address continues, and the narrative resumes a more conventional form.

10.6 Jed Leland (Joseph Cotten) confronts Kane after the lost election. The low camera angle and expressive lighting create a sense of menace and tension. Note that the camera shoots into the ceiling. (From Raymond's narrative.)

10.7 Kane alone, after wrecking Susan's bedroom. The extreme low camera angle and sinister backlighting characterize an alienated, destructive (and, finally, self-destructive) personality. Again, note the ceiling. (From Raymond's narrative.)

Another device introduced by Welles in *Kane* was the overlapping sound montage in which—as in reality—people speak not one after another (as they do on the stage) but virtually all at once, so that part of what is said is lost. Overlapping dialogue between major players in a film had been used as early as 1931 by Lewis Milestone in *The Front Page,* but it had not been used to produce a sense of realistic collective conversation as in *Kane*. A good example in the film (and there is an example in almost every major sequence) occurs in the screening room after the projection of the "News on the March" newsreel. So many persons are speaking on the track simultaneously that one has the distinct sense of having accidentally stumbled into the aftermath of a board meeting. Welles continued to use this technique in his later films, and it has influenced many other film-makers—both his contemporaries, like Carol Reed, and more recent directors, like Robert Altman, who has been so firmly committed to overlapping sound montage that unknowledgeable critics complain about the "poor quality" of his soundtracks.*

A final example of Welles' subtle refinement of sound occurs in one of his best deep-focus set-ups. In a newsroom, Kane is seated at a typewriter in the extreme foreground of the frame finishing a bad review of Susan Alexander Kane's Chicago opera debut which his ex-friend Jed Leland has written. Correspondingly, we hear the tapping of the typewriter keys on the "foreground" of the soundtrack. From a door in the background of the frame, Leland emerges—barely recognizable, so great is the distance—and begins to walk slowly towards Kane. As he moves from the background to the foreground of the frame, Leland's footsteps move from the "background" to the "foreground" of the soundtrack—from being initially inaudible to having nearly an equal volume with the keys. Similarly, in the Chicago Opera House shot mentioned above, as the camera dollies up from the stage to the catwalk, Susan's voice grows ever more distant on the track, creating once more a precise correspondence of visual and aural "space."

10.8 Kane finishing Leland's review: visual and aural depth combined. (From Leland's narrative.)

Structure

The formal organization of *Citizen Kane* is extraordinary. Like a Jorge Luis Borges story, it begins with the death of its subject. Through an elaborate series of lap-dissolved stills, we are led from a "No Trespassing" sign on a wire fence farther and farther into the forbidding Kane estate of Xanadu, as if by the tracking movement of a camera, until at last we approach a lighted window high in a Gothic tower. The light is suddenly

---

* It should be noted, though, that Altman's method of recording overlapping sound differs markedly from Welles' in *Kane*. Altman usually has his actors arranged in large, spread-out groupings, and he initially recorded his sound "wild" on location—i.e., separately from the film strip, on magnetic tape. Since *California Split* (1974), however, he has used a wireless eight-track recording system in which each performer is equipped with a small microphone which broadcasts sound to a receiving unit. Each actor has one channel whose sound can be individually controlled while shooting, and all the actors can speak at once without grouping around a centrally located microphone. On the soundtrack, the effect is frequently an indistinct blur or hum which Altman uses deliberately to characterize an environment rather than to evoke individual personalities (see *M.A.S.H.* [1970]; *Nashville* [1975]; *Three*

10.9 Reality frame: the opening shots of *Citizen Kane*. The camera pans up the fence from the "No Trespassing" sign and slowly dissolves to the crested gate and then into Xanadu.

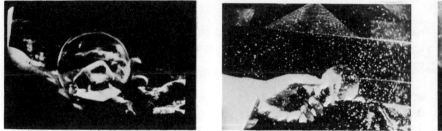

10.10 Reality frame: as Kane dies, the glass globe drops from his hand and shatters.

10.11 Reality frame: the nurse, shot through broken glass.

extinguished, and Welles cuts to the interior of the room, where Charles Foster Kane (played by Welles himself) dies in state, clutching a small glass globe which contains a swirling snow scene and whispering "Rosebud"—the word that motivates the film and echoes through it until the final frames. Kane drops the globe in dying; it rolls down the steps and breaks in close-up. Through the distorting lens of the convex broken glass, we watch a nurse enter the room from a door in the background in long shot; she walks to the foreground in close shot, folds Kane's arms, and pulls the covers up to his chest. After a fade to a medium shot of Kane's body silhouetted against the window, we suddenly cut to a logo projected obliquely on a screen, and the soundtrack booms the title "News on the March!"—introducing a sophisticated parody of a "March of Time" newsreel* on Kane's life and death. Welles is thus able

Women [1977]). Welles, on the other hand, produced his carefully modulated soundtrack for *Kane* in 1940 using the full resources of a sophisticated studio recording system, complete with its own orchestra. Furthermore, because Welles is primarily concerned with individual character, one never loses the individual identity of speaker and voice in his overlapping dialogue sequences, as one does in some of Altman's films. (See Chapter 17.)

* "The March of Time" was a popular series of skillfully (some would say slickly) produced film news journals released monthly in the United States between 1935 and 1951. Each issue was twenty minutes long, and, generally, focused on a single subject. These films were usually shown as preludes to features, so that *Citizen Kane's* original audiences might well have watched an authentic "March of Time" newsreel just before seeing the parodic "News on the March" in *Kane*. "The March of Time" series was politically conservative, reflecting the editorial policies of its financial backer, Time-Life, Inc., and of Time-Life's director, Henry R. Luce (1898–1967). Time-Life succeeded the Hearst empire, which was badly crippled by the Depression, to become a major shaper of public opinion during the thirties, forties, and fifties. The identification in *Citizen Kane* of Ralston's news organization with the Luce press is entirely deliberate, since it extends the Kane/Hearst analogy.

10.12 "News on the March": logo.

10.13 "News on the March": Teddy Roosevelt and Charles Foster Kane.

10.14 "News on the March": Kane in exile at Xanadu, shot candidly by a hidden cameraman.

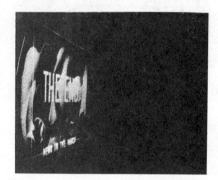

10.15 Reality frame: a startling change of camera angle at the newsreel's conclusion takes us out of the film within the film and places us unexpectedly in a projection room.

10.16 Reality frame: Thompson (William Alland) is dispatched to find "Rosebud—dead or alive. . . ."

to give a brief and coherent, if asequential, overview of the major events in Kane's life before they become jumbled like the pieces of a jigsaw puzzle in the succeeding narratives.

In a sense, the newsreel is *Citizen Kane* itself in miniature. Like the larger film, it begins with Kane's death (or his funeral), covers the same events in a similar overlapping, achronological manner, and ends with the mystery of Kane's character unresolved. We learn from the newsreel that Kane was an enormously controversial figure, hated and loved by millions of Americans, whose vast wealth was inherited by fluke: a supposedly worthless deed left to his mother in payment for a boarding-house room gave him sole ownership of the priceless Colorado Lode. We learn that in an earlier period of American history, near the turn of the century, Kane's wealth and the influence of his newspapers were incalculable. We learn that he was married twice—first to a president's niece, then to Susan Alexander, "singer," for whom he built the Chicago Municipal Opera House and Xanadu. We learn that Kane's promising and apparently nonstop political career was destroyed during a campaign for the governorship of the State of New York by a "love-nest" scandal involving Susan Alexander. We learn finally that Kane's newspaper empire was crippled by the Depression and that he subsequently exiled himself to the solitude of Xanadu, where, after many years of seclusion, he died in 1940. The newsreel ends, and the camera discovers a dimly and expressionistically lit projection room, where the contemporary media journalists (successors of the Kane/Hearst empire and identified with the Luce press) who produced the film discuss it. The executive in charge thinks it needs an "angle" that will somehow explain the paradoxical figure of Kane. Someone seizes upon the man's dying words, the film's release is postponed, and a journalist named Thompson (played by William Alland) is sent out to interview all of Kane's intimate acquaintances to discover the meaning of "Rosebud" and, it is hoped, of Kane himself.

The rest of the film is contained in a series of five narratives—told in flashback by each of the people Thompson talks to—and a balancing epilogue of sorts. The narratives overlap with each other and with the "News on the March" newsreel at certain points, so that some of the events in Kane's life are presented from several different points of view within the total film. From the screening room, a shock cut takes us to a poster on a brick wall, suddenly illuminated by lighting, which announces the El Rancho nightclub appearance of the second Mrs. Kane. Through the elaborate craning movement described above, we are brought into the interior of the club, where a drunk and hostile Susan Alexander Kane (Dorothy Comingore) refuses to talk to Thompson. He can get no information from the headwaiter either, and the screen fades out and fades into a daytime sequence at the Walter P. Thatcher Memorial Library. (Thatcher, we come to understand later in the sequence, was Kane's guardian and executor of the Colorado Lode estate.) Here, Thompson is grudgingly given access to Thatcher's memoirs, and, as he reads the words "I first encountered Mr. Kane in 1871 . . . ," the screen dissolves from a close-up of Thatcher's longhand to a lyrical shot of a boy playing with a sled in a snowstorm in front of Mrs. Kane's boarding-house somewhere in Colorado.

10.17 Thatcher's narrative: Thatcher meets young Charles for the first time outside his mother's boarding-house.

In the long deep-focus shot mentioned above, Mrs. Kane (Agnes Moorehead) signs the papers making Thatcher's bank the boy's guardian and certifying his inheritance. Outside, young Kane is told of his imminent departure for the East; he pushes Thatcher (George Coulouris) into the snow with his sled. We dissolve to a medium shot of the sled, some time later, covered with drifting snow, and then into the "Merry Christmas— Happy New Year" lightning mix, which places us in New York City many years later on the occasion of Kane's twenty-first birthday. We learn that of all the holdings in "the world's sixth largest private fortune," which Kane is about to inherit, the only thing that interests him is a financially failing daily newspaper, the *New York Inquirer,* because he thinks "it would be fun to run a newspaper." Next, in a brief but potent montage sequence, we see Thatcher increasingly outraged by the *Inquirer*'s populist, muckraking (and anti-Republican) headlines, until he finally confronts Kane in the *Inquirer* office. Their antipathy for one another—both ideological and personal—is apparent, and Thatcher warns Kane of financial disaster. As if to confirm this prophecy, the following sequence, composed in depth, shows Kane, much older, signing his now vast but bankrupt newspaper chain over to Thatcher in the midst of the Depression, and here Thatcher's narrative ends.

10.18 Thatcher's narrative: the Kane-Thatcher confrontation in the *Inquirer* office.

Thompson next visits Mr. Bernstein (Everett Sloane), once Kane's right-hand yes-man and now the aging chairman of the board of the Kane Corporation. Bernstein's narrative begins by recalling in flashback the first day at the *Inquirer* office, when he, Kane, and Kane's old college buddy Jedediah Leland (Joseph Cotten) arrived to claim the paper in what was clearly to be a lark for all three young men. But the playfulness is mitigated a few scenes later when Kane composes a "Declaration of Principles" in the presence of Bernstein and Leland for his first front page, the manuscript of which Leland asks to keep, comparing it facetiously to the Declaration of Independence. In this sequence, the twenty-one-year-old Kane is revealed to be the romantic idealist of the crusading populist headlines so repugnant to Thatcher, and Leland's admiration for him is unqualified. In the next sequence, Kane, Leland, and Bernstein are seen reflected in the window of the *New York Chronicle* Building gazing at a photograph of the *Chronicle*'s top-flight staff, which, they admit, has

10.19 Thatcher's narrative: some twenty years later, Thatcher takes the Kane papers into receivership. Bernstein (Everett Sloane) is in the foreground of the frame.

10.20 Bernstein's narrative: youthful exuberance. Leland, Kane, and Bernstein on their first day at the *Inquirer*.

10.21 Bernstein's narrative: youthful idealism. Kane composes his "Declaration of Principles."

10.22 Bernstein's narrative: depth as character. The banquet for the former *Chronicle* staff. Twin ice sculptures of Bernstein and Leland in the extreme foreground frame the real Bernstein and Leland in the middle foreground; the former *Chronicle* men stretch away from them toward the extreme background; Kane stands in the middle distance bantering with Bernstein. The shot renders in compositional terms what Leland will moments later suggest to Bernstein verbally—that Kane will become increasingly distanced from his old friends and his liberal ideals by the intervention of all the new men from the *Chronicle*.

made it the most successful newspaper in the city. The camera moves in close upon the picture and then back out to reveal the group, suddenly animated and sitting for another photograph six years later—this time to commemorate their joining the staff of the *Inquirer* en masse. A raucous banquet sequence follows, in which the dining table is photographed in extreme depth, with ice sculptures of Leland and Bernstein in the foreground at one end, Kane in the background at the other, and the new staff members occupying the space in between. During the revelry, Leland expresses to Bernstein his concern that these new men so fresh from the *Chronicle* and its policies will change Kane, and the scene dissolves into another one of Bernstein and Leland uncrating boxes of sculpture which Kane has been collecting on a European tour. It is revealed by Bernstein that Kane may also be "collecting" something (or someone) else. A dissolve brings us to the interior of the *Inquirer* office some time

10.23 Bernstein's narrative: chorus girls enliven the celebration as Leland worries about the future.

10.24 Bernstein's narrative: Leland uncrates statues while Bernstein reads a cable from Kane hinting at a romantic involvement.

later, on the day of Kane's return from Europe. The staff attempts to present him with an engraved loving cup, and he awkwardly leaves them a notice announcing his engagement to Miss Emily Monroe Norton, the niece of the President of the United States. The staff watches from the windows of the *Inquirer* Building as Kane and his fiancée drive off in a carriage; and the second narrative draws to a close with Bernstein speculating to Thompson that maybe "Rosebud" was "something he lost."

Thompson next pays a visit to Leland, who has become a somewhat senile (but still intelligent) old man confined to a nursing home. Indeed, the dissolves into the Leland narrative flashback are among the most lingering in the whole film, as if to suggest the sluggishness of his memory; and not a little of the film's impact derives from this flashback technique of narration, which permits us to see all of its major characters in youth and age almost simultaneously. Like those of the other characters, Leland's narrative is chronological but not continuous. Initially, he relates the story of Kane's first marriage in a sequence which convincingly compresses the relationship's slow decline into a series of brief breakfast-table conversations linked by swish pans* and overlapping sound—that is, a lightning mix. Next, in a much longer flashback, Leland describes

---

* Rapid panning movement which blurs the image from point to point; used as a transitional device.

10.25 Leland's narrative: Leland's memory dissolves to Kane and Emily in the breakfast-table sequence. (How Leland could recount these intimate details without having been present at the table is never made clear, and his ability to do so verbatim constitutes one of several violations of dramatic point of view in the film. The cinematic logic of the narratives is so perfect, however, that we scarcely notice.)

10.26 Leland's narrative: Kane's first meeting with Susan Alexander. She sings for him in the parlor of her boarding-house at 185 West 74th Street.

10.27 Leland's narrative: candidate Kane addresses a huge rally in Madison Square Garden on the eve of what should be a smashing victory over his opponent, Jim Gettys.

Kane's first meeting with Susan Alexander and Kane's subsequent political ruin at the hands of his opponent, "Boss" Jim Gettys (and as a result of his own stubborn, egomaniacal refusal to withdraw from the race.) Of particular note is the scene in which Leland confronts Kane after he has lost the election. The entire sequence is shot in depth from an extremely low angle (the camera was actually placed in a hole in the floor to make the shot), so that Kane looms above both Leland and the audience, a grotesque, inflated parody of the politically powerful figure he has so desperately tried (and failed) to become. Drunk, and disillusioned with his idol,

10.28 Leland's narrative: Kane betrayed. After the rally, Kane accompanies his wife to Susan's boarding-house, where she discloses the contents of a blackmail note dictated to Susan by Gettys.

10.29 Leland's narrative: from the staircase of the boarding-house, Kane rains empty threats on Gettys (Ray Collins) in a low-angle, deep-focus shot.

10.30 Leland's narrative: after his election defeat, Kane still looms large, in a low-angle, deep-focus shot.

10.31 Leland's narrative: Susan Alexander's debut as a singer, from Leland's perspective.

10.32 Leland's narrative: roused from a drunken stupor, Leland is informed by Bernstein that Kane is in the next room finishing Leland's review of Susan's debut "just the way you started it."

10.33 Susan's narrative: the debut from her own point of view.

Leland insists that he be transferred to the Chicago office, and Kane reluctantly consents. The final section of Leland's narrative concerns Kane's marriage to Susan Alexander and her singing debut at the opera house he has built for her. The lengthy vertical craning shot from Susan performing abjectly on the stage to the stagehand holding his nose occurs here, as does Leland's long, deep-focus walk from the back of the *Chicago Inquirer* newsroom to the extreme foreground of the frame, where an embittered Kane finishes Leland's bad review of the performance, and summarily fires him.

Here Leland's narrative ends, and Thompson returns once more to the El Rancho nightclub. Again the camera travels up from the poster of Susan Alexander, cranes through the sign, and dissolves through the skylight to a medium close shot of Thompson and Susan sitting at a table. Susan, who has finally agreed to talk, begins her story with a flashback to a session with her voice coach, Signor Matisti, which occurred shortly after her marriage to Kane. Susan, Matisti, and a pianist occupy the foreground of a deep-focus shot of a large, expensively decorated room. So bad is Susan's voice that Matisti refuses to continue the lesson, but at this point Kane emerges from a door in the back of the room and walks toward the group, becoming larger and larger as he moves toward the lens. When he reaches the foreground, he browbeats both Matisti and Susan into continuing the humiliating session, until a dissolve brings us to the second version of Susan's singing debut at the Chicago Municipal Opera House. We have already seen her performance from Leland's point of view in his narrative, and now we see virtually the same events from Susan's perspective as she looks out into the vast and terrifying void of the audience, invisible beyond the footlights. Her aria begins, and as she attempts to fill the huge theater with her frail voice,* Welles intercuts subjective shots of Matisti frantically coaching her with audience reaction shots (contempt, boredom, disbelief) and close-ups of an aging Kane peering grimly toward the stage. When the performance ends with very light applause, Kane claps loudly, as if to fill the hall with his solitary accolade. A dissolve brings us to Kane and Susan the morning after in a Chicago apartment, where Susan shrilly denounces Leland for his bad review—actually completed by Kane. We learn that Kane has fired Leland and sent him a check for twenty-five thousand dollars, which Leland has returned along with the pompously idealistic "Declaration of Principles" that Kane had printed in his first issue of the *New York Inquirer* years before. We also learn that Susan's singing career has been imposed upon her by Kane, who insists that it continue.

There follows a rapid montage of dissolves, overlaid on the soundtrack

---

* In 1973, at a symposium at the George Eastman House in Rochester, New York, Bernard Herrmann pointed out that Susan (or, rather, the singer dubbing her voice) actually *can* sing, but only modestly. The high tessitura overture to *Salammbô*, the fake opera Herrmann composed for her debut, was purposely designed to exceed the capacity of her voice and create "that terror-in-the-quicksand feeling" of a singer hopelessly out of her depth at the very outset of a long performance. (Quoted in *Sound and the Cinema*, ed. Evan William Cameron [Pleasantville, N.Y., 1980], p. 128.)

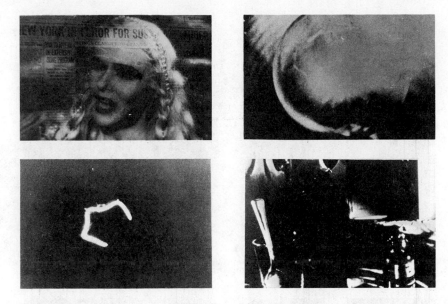

10.34 Susan's narrative: shots from the montage showing her rapid rise to stardom through media hype, her collapse, and the half-empty glass of poison after her suicide attempt.

by Susan's voice, in which *Inquirer* headlines from cities around the country acclaiming Susan Alexander's meteoric rise to stardom are lap-dissolved alternately with shots of flashing call lights, Susan onstage, Matisti in the prompter's box, and Susan receiving flowers at an ever-increasing rate until a klieg light suddenly fizzles and goes out, cutting off Susan's voice and leaving us in total darkness. Moments later, we fade slowly in on a deep-focus shot of a darkened room: in the extreme foreground is a half-empty glass of liquid and a spoon (this particular foreground object is reproduced not through deep focus but through photographic superimposition); in the middleground Susan tosses in bed, breathing heavily; in the background a door flies open and Kane bursts into the room, barely foiling a suicide attempt. Susan is treated by a discreet doctor, and Kane promises that she needn't sing again.

Now we fade to Xanadu, some time later, where the final portion of Susan's narrative takes place. Here, in deep-focus shots which distance them grotesquely from one another across the breadth of a palatial chamber, Kane and Susan pursue a series of conversations which show them to be utterly at odds. Kane has become a cynical domestic tyrant and Susan a virtual prisoner of the estate; she passes the time endlessly working and re-working jigsaw puzzles—a metaphor for the mystery of identity in the film. Against Susan's will, Kane arranges a spectacularly extravagant weekend "picnic" in the Everglades, where the two break openly and he slaps her. The next day at Xanadu, Susan announces to Kane that she is leaving him for good; he begs her to stay, but, realizing Kane's nearly constitutional inability to return love, she refuses and walks out the door. Susan concludes her narrative by advising Thompson to talk to Raymond the butler, who "knows where all the bodies are buried," when he visits Xanadu. The camera moves back and up, dissolves through the skylight, and pulls back through the El Rancho sign, reversing the movement of its entry.

10.35 Susan's narrative: working puzzles interminably at Xanadu, increasingly estranged from Kane.

10.36 Susan's narrative: in the Everglades, a bloated, domineering Kane as he appears to Susan after slapping her.

10.37 Susan's narrative, conclusion: in her bedroom at Xanadu, Kane pleads with Susan to stay, but she refuses.

Dissolves bring us to the gate of Xanadu and then to the interior for Raymond's brief narrative, which begins where Susan's ended. It opens not with a dissolve but with a shocking straight cut from Raymond (Paul Stewart) and Thompson on the stairs to a close shot of a shrieking cockatoo, behind which we see Susan in the middleground emerging from the same door she has begun to walk through (from the other side) at the end of her own narrative as she leaves Kane and Xanadu. Raymond's flashback then depicts the violent tantrum Kane throws as she departs: he staggers about Susan's bedroom like some mechanized madman, smashing furniture, mirrors, cosmetic jars, and all manner of trinkets and bric-a-brac until his hand finally comes to rest on the glass globe with the snow scene that we first saw at his death in the beginning of the film and later saw in Susan's apartment when they meet. We hear Kane whisper

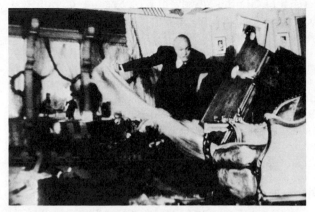

10.38 Raymond's narrative: Kane, berserk, destroying Susan's room.

10.39 Raymond's narrative, conclusion: Raymond (Paul Stewart) watches a now totally isolated Kane vanish as he walks down the hall of mirrors at Xanadu.

10.40 Reality frame: Thompson and Raymond in the great hall.

10.41 Reality frame: an extreme high-angle shot of the hall, replicating a news photographer's point of view.

10.42 Reality frame: a high-angle shot of the newspeople preparing to leave Xanadu; Thompson (slightly right of center) admits that his quest has failed.

10.43 Reality frame: a still from the long, slow track of Kane's vast collection of "things."

"Rosebud!" and watch him shuffle slowly out of Susan's demolished room, past a gauntlet of staring servants and guests, and down a huge hall of mirrors as Raymond's narrative concludes.

Now Thompson and Raymond move down the central staircase into the great hall of Xanadu, where we see in long shot that a multitude of reporters, photographers, and workmen have assembled in a mass effort to catalogue and liquidate Kane's huge collection of objects. The camera pulls back to follow the two men as they pass through the hall, discovering as it does so newspeople photographing both the treasures and trash of the Kane collection—Renaissance sculpture, Kane's mother's pot-bellied stove, Oriental statuary, the trophy cup presented to Kane by the *Inquirer* staff on his return from Europe, priceless paintings, a myriad of jigsaw puzzles. Thompson's colleagues ask him whether he has discovered the meaning of "Rosebud." He replies that he hasn't and that, in any case, he no longer believes in the quest: "I don't think any word can explain a man's life. No, I guess 'Rosebud' is just a piece in a jigsaw puzzle, a missing piece." Thompson and the others leave to catch the train back to New York, and a lap dissolve brings us to an aerial view of the hall, with the camera shooting down over the vast collection which stretches away into the distance. Another lap dissolve brings the camera a little closer to the collection as it begins to track slowly over the entire mass of crates, statues, boxes, and belongings—the ruins and relics of Kane's loveless life—which, from our aerial perspective, resemble nothing so much as the pieces of a jigsaw puzzle. The shot continues for some time until the camera reaches the humble possessions of Mrs. Kane and dollies down gracefully into an eye-level shot of her things. We see a man grab a sled and, in the next shot, throw it into a furnace at Raymond's command. We dissolve to a close-up of the burning sled and can read on it the word "Rosebud" just before the letters melt away in flames. A dissolve brings us to an exterior long shot of Xanadu at night, as we first encountered it, with smoke billowing from its chimneys. The camera tilts up to follow the smoke, dissolves to the wire fence surrounding the estate, and pans down slowly to the "No Trespassing" sign with which the film began.

Thus, *Citizen Kane* concludes with the mystery of its central figure unresolved. The identity of "Rosebud" is clearly inadequate to account for the terrible emptiness at the heart of Kane, and of America, and is meant to be. Its power as a symbol of lost love and innocence lies in its very insufficiency, for the "missing piece" of the jigsaw puzzle of Kane's life, the "something he lost," turns out to be an inanimate object, and a regressive one at that. In its barrenness, "Rosebud" becomes a perfect symbol of Kane's inability to relate to people in human terms, or to love, and the ultimate emblem of his futile attempt to fill the void in himself with objects. In the film's two-hour running time we have seen Kane from seven separate perspectives—those of the newsreel, the five narrators, and the concluding reprise—and we probably have come to know more about the circumstances of his life than the man would have known himself. We know what he did and how he lived and died, but we can never know what he *meant*—perhaps, Welles seems to suggest, because, like

10.44 Reality frame: the burning sled in Xanadu's incinerator.

10.45 Reality frame: "Rosebud."

"Rosebud," he was ultimately meaningless, or perhaps because reality itself is ambiguous and unreliable. In any case, it is the quest for meaning rather than its ultimate conclusion that makes *Citizen Kane* such a rich and important film.

Influence

10.46 Reality frame: Xanadu, scattering the ashes.

In the year of its release, *Citizen Kane* was a radically experimental film—fully twenty years ahead of its time. But it failed at the box office less because of its experimental nature than because of an aura of fear in Hollywood created by attacks on Welles and RKO in the Hearst press. Hearst was still living, and his vassals attempted to suppress what they correctly took to be an unflattering portrait of their master. Though they were unsuccessful in preventing the film's release, the adverse publicity made it difficult for *Kane* to get bookings and advertising. As a result, the film did poorly outside of New York City and was withdrawn from circulation until the mid-fifties, when it played the art house circuit* and began to acquire a more sophisticated audience. Since 1958, *Kane* has been voted the "Best Film of All Time" in three successive international polls, most recently in 1971, and there is every indication that its critical reputation continues to grow. The influence of *Citizen Kane* upon the cinema has been enormous and nearly universal. The film's impact did not begin to be felt until after the war, when its use of low-key lighting and wide-angle lenses to achieve greater depth of field influenced the visual style of American *film noir* and its flashback narrative technique began to be imitated in more conventional films like Robert Siodmak's *The Killers* (1946). There were also imitations of *Kane*'s structure and/or theme: George Cukor's *Keeper of the Flame* (1942), Max Ophüls' *Caught* (1949), and, after the revival, José Ferrer's *The Great Man* (1957). Directors like Britain's Carol Reed (*Odd Man Out* [1947]; *The Third Man* [1949]; *An Outcast of the Islands* [1952]—all highly Wellesian films) absorbed much of the film's visual and aural texture; and, according to François Truffaut, the young French *cinéastes* who would later form the New Wave found in *Kane*'s 1946 Paris premiere the ultimate justification of their reverence for American cinema.[1]

Kane's most important and pervasive influence, however, did not begin to be felt until the mid-fifties, after the advent of the widescreen processes, when European critics—notably Bazin—discovered in it (and, less emphatically, in Renoir's films) the model for a new film aesthetic based not upon montage but upon the "long take," or sequence shot. The

---

* "Art houses" were small theaters which sprang up in the major cities of the United States during the nineteen-fifties to show "art films" (foreign films with intellectual and aesthetic aspirations) as opposed to "commercial films" (all American films, with the exception of an occasional experimental production like *Citizen Kane*). The distinction between art films and commercial films can hardly be made today, in an era in which an "arty" film like Bernardo Bertolucci's *Last Tango in Paris* (1973; see Chapter 14) becomes a box-office smash and a calculated big-budget spectacular like *Star Wars* (George Lucas, 1977; see Chapter 17) is hailed as a major aesthetic achievement.

10.47 Welles in a studio publicity still for *Kane*.

10.48 Economy of means: the matte used for the exterior of Xanadu, painted for RKO by former Disney artists.

primary concern of the long take aesthetic is not the *sequencing of images,* as in montage, but the *disposition of space within the frame,* or *mise-en-scène.* Welles is today regarded for all practical purposes as the founder and master of this aesthetic (in the same way that Eisenstein is regarded as the founder and master of montage), though its lineage can be traced as far back as Louis Feuillade. Finally, *Kane* was the first recognizably modern sound film; and it stood in the same relationship to its medium in 1941 as did *The Birth of a Nation* in 1914 and *Potemkin* in 1925—that is, it was an achievement in the development of narrative form, years in advance of its time, which significantly influenced most of the important films that followed it. *La règle du jeu* (1939), the only close competitor for this honor, not only lacked the technology available to Welles but was deliberately conservative, or classical, in narrative form, while *Citizen Kane* is very much our contemporary in both regards. Through deep-focus photography, it attempts to technically reproduce the actual field of vision of the human eye in order to structure our visual perception of screen space by means of composition in depth. Through its innovative use of sound, it attempts to reproduce the actual aural experience of the human ear and then to manipulate our aural perception of screen space by distorting and qualifying this experience.* And in both respects, though the technology is not the same, it brilliantly anticipates the contemporary cinema of widescreen photography and stereophonic sound.

Contrary to popular belief, *Kane* was anything but a financially extravagant production. The entire film—ceilinged sets and all—was made for $686,033,† with a remarkable economy of means: for many scenes Welles converted standing sets from other RKO pictures, and, in the Everglades sequence, he actually used jungle footage from *Son of Kong* (1933),

---

*See Phyllis Goldfarb, "Orson Welles's Use of Sound," in *Focus on Orson Welles,* ed. Ronald Gottesman (Englewood Cliffs, N.J., 1976), pp. 85–94.

†In *The Magic World of Orson Welles* (New York, 1978), James Naremore uses the figure $749,000, which includes post-production costs.

complete with animated bats. Nevertheless, the financial failure of the film stigmatized Welles as a loser in Hollywood, and he was never again permitted to have total control of an industry production.*

WELLES AFTER *KANE*

Welles' second film, *The Magnificent Ambersons* (1942), is one of the great lost masterworks of the cinema. Like von Stroheim's *Greed* (1924) and Eisenstein's *Que viva México!* (1929–31), *The Magnificent Ambersons* was taken out of its director's hands and radically re-cut to satisfy imagined commercial demands. While Welles was in Brazil shooting footage for a semi-documentary to be entitled *It's All True*, RKO cut *The Magnificent Ambersons* from 131 to 88 minutes and provided it with a totally incongruous happy ending shot by the editor, Robert Wise.†

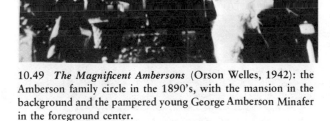

10.49 *The Magnificent Ambersons* (Orson Welles, 1942): the Amberson family circle in the 1890's, with the mansion in the background and the pampered young George Amberson Minafer in the foreground center.

10.50 Eugene Morgan (Joseph Cotten), inventor of horseless carriages, who knows implicitly that automobiles will "change men's minds."

Flawed though it is, *The Magnificent Ambersons* remains a great and powerful film. Adapted by Welles from Booth Tarkington's novel, it parallels the decline of a proud and wealthy provincial family at the turn of the century with the rise of the modern industrial city of Indianapolis. It is an unabashedly nostalgic film whose *mise-en-scène* is carefully calculated to create a sense of longing for the past. The cinematographer Stanley Cortez's high-contrast lighting and deep-focus photography of the interior of the Amberson mansion produced some of the most beautiful sequence shots ever to appear on the American screen. Like *Citizen*

---

* Welles' notoriously difficult personality also figured in his alienation from (and of) the American film industry.

† The forty-three minutes of footage cut from *The Magnificent Ambersons* is said to exist intact in the film vaults of Paramount Pictures, which bought portions of the RKO feature library in 1958. These cuts have all been documented by Charles Higham in *The Films of Orson Welles* (Berkeley, 1970), so there is at least a *possibility* of the restoration of *The Magnificent Ambersons*.

10.51 The Amberson ball, "the last of the great, long-remembered dances that everybody talked about": Eugene Morgan and Isabel Amberson (Dolores Costello).

10.52 A grown George Amberson Minafer (Tim Holt) confronts his spinster aunt Fanny (Agnes Moorehead) on the main staircase of the Amberson mansion, an emblem of splendor and the central dramatic locus of the film.

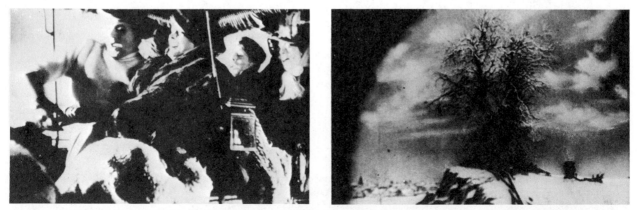

10.53 A Morgan Motors "Invincible" rides into a Currier and Ives landscape self-consciously framed by a Griffith-like iris.

10.54 Secure behind a window of the mansion, Fanny confronts the bad opinion of the town.

10.55 George is enjoined by his bachelor uncle Jack (Ray Collins) in deep focus.

10.56 Shortly before his death, old Major Amberson stares into the fire and remembers things past: "The sun. It must be the sun."

Kane, the film is constructed largely of long takes, with much spectacular tracking movement of the camera, and Welles' revolutionary use of the lightning mix and sound montage exceeds even his own earlier work. Though the eighty-eight-minute version which has survived can only hint at the epic sweep of the original, *The Magnificent Ambersons* as it stands today is a masterpiece of mood, decor, and composition in depth. It is also a remarkably intelligent and prophetic film which suggests (in 1942, and in a story set in 1905) that the quality of American life will ultimately be destroyed by the automobile and urbanization.

The Magnificent Ambersons, distributed on a double bill with a Lupe Velez comedy, was a commercial disaster. So was *Journey into Fear* (1943), a stylish adaptation of an Eric Ambler espionage novel set in the Middle East, starring Welles and the Mercury Players, and co-directed by Welles (uncredited) and Norman Foster (1900–1976). With his third box-office failure behind him, Welles was recalled from Brazil and removed from *It's All True,* which was never completed; the Mercury Players were given forty-eight hours to clear off the RKO lot. This was the beginning of a long-standing antagonism between Welles and those who run the American film industry which has never been fully resolved. Welles returned to broadcasting and the theater for the remainder of the war, though his striking performance as Rochester in *Jane Eyre* (Robert Stevenson, 1943), whose direction he seems to have influenced, did much to establish him as a popular film actor (a circumstance which would later permit him to finance his own productions when times got hard, as they frequently did).

10.57 A Wellesian low-angle shot from *Journey into Fear* (Orson Welles and Norman Foster, 1943): Joseph Cotten.

In 1945, Welles returned to Hollywood to direct and star in *The Stranger* (1946) for RKO on the condition that he use an existing script and a pre-arranged editing schedule, following both of them precisely. Welles submitted to the condition, and the resulting film is an intentional if preposterous self-parody about the tracking down of a Nazi war criminal (Welles) who is, somehow, posing as a master at a New England prep school and is married to the headmaster's daughter (Loretta Young). Technically, the film is fairly conventional, and Welles regards it as his worst. Nevertheless, its commercial success helped him to land a job at Columbia directing his brilliant and exotic essay in *film noir, The Lady from Shanghai* (1948), which starred Welles and his second wife, Rita

10.58 Welles as the Nazi war criminal Franz Kindler in *The Stranger* (Orson Welles, 1945).

10.59 *The Lady from Shanghai* (Orson Welles, 1947): the fantastic love scene before the aquarium tanks. Welles as Michael O'Hara, Rita Hayworth as Elsa Bannister.

10.60 *The Lady from Shanghai:* Elsa in Chinatown.

10.61 Lost in the fun-house: O'Hara plunges toward the hall of mirrors.

Hayworth (b. 1918). This bizarre film of corruption, murder, and betrayal is cast in the form of a thriller, but its theme is the moral anarchy of the post-war world. Though its intricate, rambling plot is almost impossible to follow,* cinematically the film is one of Welles' finest achievements: the haunting sequence shots of the assignation between Welles and Hayworth in the San Francisco Aquarium, the perfectly cut chase in the Chinese theater, and, most of all, the montage of the three-way shootout in the hall of mirrors which concludes the film have become textbook examples of Welles' genius. Because of the obscurity of its narrative, *The Lady from Shanghai* was a financial failure, and Welles became *persona non grata* in Hollywood for nearly a decade. In order to continue making films, he was forced to exile himself to Europe, but before he left, he turned out a final Mercury Theater production—a

---

* A fact abetted by Harry Cohn, president of Columbia Pictures, who held up the film's release by a year (it was originally completed in 1946) while it was re-edited, re-dubbed, and re-scored under Welles' supervision.

10.62 A studio publicity still, followed by frames from the final shoot-out in *The Lady from Shanghai:* O'Hara; Elsa; and her husband, Arthur Bannister (Everett Sloane).

nightmarishly expressionistic version of *Macbeth* (1948) shot in twenty-three days on *papier mâché* and cardboard sets for the B-studio Republic Pictures. More Welles than Shakespeare, with Welles playing Macbeth, the film still manages to convey an atmosphere of brooding evil and to create a convincing portrait of a man driven by ambition beyond the bounds of the moral universe (a characteristic theme of both Shakespeare and Welles) in a culture which has only just emerged from barbarism.*

In moving to Europe, Welles lost the great technical and financial resources of the Hollywood studios, but he gained much in creative freedom. As a result, his European films tend to be technically imperfect and imaginatively unrestrained. The first of these was another Shakespeare adaptation, *Othello* (1952), with Welles in the title role; the film was

10.63 *Macbeth* (Orson Welles, 1948): "The Three"—Druidic sorceresses who control Macbeth's destiny.

---

* Originally 107 minutes long, *Macbeth* was cut to 86 minutes by its producers after Welles had left for Europe, and the soundtrack—in which the actors spoke with Scottish burrs for verisimilitude—was re-recorded to "Americanize" the accents. This re-cut, re-dubbed version was the only one known in the United States until 1979, when a UCLA archivist discovered the original among the university's collection of NTA Film Services (Republic's distributor) nitrate prints. In 1980, *Macbeth* was restored to its original form, complete with the Scottish accented soundtrack and an eight-minute overture by the film's composer, Jacques Ibert. Among the most startling discoveries within the missing footage was a ten-minute-long take of continuous dramatic action, probably the first ever attempted in a theatrical film (Hitchcock's *Rope* went into production a few months after Welles' film was completed).

10.64 Macbeth (Welles) confronts the murdered Banquo's ghost.

10.65 Iconographic violence: Lady Macbeth (Jeanette Nolan) tormented by blood-guilt.

10.66 Macbeth prepares for his climactic battle with Macduff.

10.67 *Othello* (Orson Welles, 1952): Othello's ship arrives in Cyprus (Mogador) after an engagement with the Turks.

10.68 Othello (Welles) and Desdemona (Suzanne Cloutier) on the castle ramparts.

10.69 The Moor prepares to murder his bride.

10.70 Welles in *Mr. Arkadin* (Orson Welles, 1955).

made over a period of four years from 1948 to 1952, while Welles financed the production by acting in other people's films. With interiors shot all over Europe and exteriors shot in the ancient citadel at Mogador, Morocco, *Othello* is a film of light and openness—of wind, sun, and sea—as opposed to the brooding darkness of *Macbeth* and *The Lady from Shanghai.* Continuously re-cast, re-shot, re-cut, and re-dubbed, *Othello* nevertheless won the Grand Prix at the Cannes Film Festival when it was finally completed in 1952. Welles' next film, *Mr. Arkadin* (British title: *Confidential Report,* 1955), a failed attempt to remake *Citizen Kane* in European terms, was shot on an extremely low budget during an eight-month period in Spain, Germany, and France. On the French Riviera, a down-at-the-heels adventurer named Van Stratten is hired by the mysterious European business tycoon Gregory Arkadin (based on the real-life war profiteer Miles Krueger, and played by Welles) to piece together the details of his buried past. Van Stratten's Kafkaesque quest takes him all over Europe as he interviews the people who possess the secrets of Arkadin's past life, only to discover at the end of the film that he is the finger-man in a murder plot whereby the tycoon is systematically destroying all who can reveal his criminal past as soon as they are identified. Poorly acted, written, and recorded, with Welles himself dubbing in the voices of most of the other characters, *Mr. Arkadin* is an ambitious and intermittently brilliant failure.

No such difficulties attend *Touch of Evil* (1958), for which Welles returned to Hollywood for the first time in ten years. Universal, still a

10.71 From the conclusion of the lengthy tracking shot which opens *Touch of Evil* (Orson Welles, 1958): Charlton Heston, Janet Leigh.

10.72 Welles as Hank Quinlan in *Touch of Evil*.

minor studio, had signed Welles and Charlton Heston to play the leads in what was to be a conventional police melodrama, and Heston insisted that Welles also direct. Welles accepted the job and was permitted to rewrite the script, turning it into a nightmarish parable of the abuse of power in a dark and sinister world. Shot against the garish background of Venice, California, *Touch of Evil* is another study of a man like Kane, Macbeth, and Arkadin whose obsession with control causes him to transgress the laws of the moral universe. Hank Quinlan (Welles), a police captain in a seamy Mexican-American border town, has spent thirty years framing murder suspects about whose guilt he has "a hunch" in order to insure their conviction. He ultimately runs afoul of an honest Mexican narcotics agent (Heston) who exposes his practices and indirectly causes his death. The grotesque, inflated, and yet somehow sympathetic Quinlan is superbly played by Welles as a man whose once strong character has been utterly corrupted by an obsession. As a director, Welles demanded the impossible from the cinematographer Russell Metty (*The Stranger* [1946]) and got it. The film opens with a continuous moving crane shot (unfortunately obscured in the release print by the credits) which begins with a close-up of a time bomb and ends with the explosion of the device in a car nearly three minutes later, making it one of the longest unbroken tracking shots attempted to date. Later, Metty was required to track his camera from the exterior of a building through a lobby and into a crowded elevator, and then ride up five floors to shoot Heston greeting the occupants as the doors slide open from within. There is also significant use of deep-focus photography and sound montage for the first time since *The Lady from Shanghai* (1947). Like Welles' previous films, *Touch of Evil* was shot in high-contrast black-and-white. Ignored in every country but France (where it won the Cannes Grand Prix) in the year of its release, *Touch of Evil* is today considered a Welles masterpiece whose technical brilliance and thematic depth bring it close to the stature of *Kane*. When it was released, the film was cut from 108 to 93 minutes by Universal editors to make its narrative easier for contemporary audiences to follow. In 1976, the deleted footage was restored by Universal, and Welles' original version was released for distribution in 16mm. The restoration resolves certain obscurities of dialogue in the

10.73 Quinlan with his once-devoted henchman, Lieutenant Menzies (Joseph Calleia).

10.74 *The Trial* (Orson Welles, 1962): Anthony Perkins as "K."

10.75 Welles as Falstaff in *Chimes at Midnight* (Orson Welles, 1966).

10.76 *Chimes at Midnight:* Prince Hal (Keith Baxter) with Falstaff before his father's castle.

10.77 *Chimes at Midnight:* from the Battle of Shrewsbury sequence.

1958 version and provides for a fuller characterization of the film's protagonists.*

But the film's financial failure in 1958 confirmed Welles' status as a pariah in Hollywood; he returned to Europe, where French producers offered him an opportunity to direct a film based on a major literary work of his choice. He selected Kafka's novel *The Trial,* published in 1925. Despite budgeting problems, *The Trial* (1962) became the only one of his films since *Kane* over which Welles exercised total control. His customary visual complexity notwithstanding, the results are disappointing. Shot in black-and-white in the streets of Zagreb, Yugoslavia, and in the fantastic Gare d'Orsay in Paris, the film finally fails to evoke the antiseptic modern hell of Kafka's novel, perhaps because of some disparity between the world-views of the two artists.

Welles' next European film and his last feature to date, *Chimes at Midnight* (British title: *Falstaff,* 1966), is widely regarded as a masterpiece. Returning to an idea that he had first tried in his 1938 Theater Guild production *Five Kings,* Welles assembled all the Falstaff parts from *Henry IV, Parts I* and *II, The Merry Wives of Windsor,* and *Henry V,* and linked them together with a narration from Holinshed's *Chronicles* (the medieval source of Shakespeare's history plays) to create a portrait of the character as his privileged friendship with Prince Hal passes gradually from affection to bitterness, disillusionment, and decay. Like *Citizen Kane,* it is film about decline and loss, and like *The Magnificent Ambersons,* it is full of nostalgia for a vanished past; but it is as much the work of an older man as *Kane* and *The Magnificent Ambersons* are the work of a younger one. Shot in Spain (for financial reasons) over a period of several years, *Chimes at Midnight* is superbly photographed and acted, with Welles at his best in the title role. Its moving crane shots have been widely praised, and the lengthy montage sequence depicting the Battle of Shrewsbury has been favorably compared to Eisenstein's Odessa Steps sequence in *Potemkin* (1925) and the Battle on the Ice in *Alexander Nevsky* (1938). Yet *Chimes at Midnight* is anything but technically extravagant. It is rather a quiet, elegiac, and dignified film whose restrained style and austere black-and-white photography correspond perfectly with its sober themes of human frailty, mortality, and decay.

It is no longer possible—as it was, perhaps, even several years ago—to speak of Orson Welles as a director important for a single, if monumental and awe-inspiring, film. Welles has produced five masterpieces— *Citizen Kane, The Magnificent Ambersons, The Lady from Shanghai, Touch of Evil,* and *Chimes at Midnight*—and his Shakespearian films, extravagant and eccentric as they sometimes are, represent major contributions to the genre. In *Citizen Kane* he gave us the first modern sound film and effectively pioneered the aesthetic of the long take, or composition in depth. All of his films of the forties significantly anticipated the

---

* On the basis of reminiscences by the film's producer, Albert Zugsmith (b. 1910), James Naremore submits that the longer version of *Touch of Evil* contains footage shot by the Universal contract director Harry Keller (b. 1913) and that "the original release is probably a purer, if less coherent, example of Welles's work" (*The Magic World of Orson Welles* [New York, 1978], p. 179).

contemporary cinema of widescreen photography and stereophonic sound. But technological wizardry notwithstanding, Welles has produced a body of work which deserves to be ranked with the great narrative art of our century. Welles is a traditional moralist whose major themes have characteristically been those of classical Western literature: the corrupting nature of ambition; the disparity between social and psychological reality; the destructive power of self-delusion, appetite, and obsession; and the importance of a sense of the past. These thematic concerns are confirmed by the fact that he has for over a decade been working to complete a version of *Don Quixote* set in modern times. Stylistically, however, Welles has always been an innovator and a radical experimenter—an authentic American expressionist with a decidedly baroque sense of form which has profoundly influenced the course of Western cinema. And in his mid-sixties he is still very much a part of that cinema. In a tribute presented to him by the American Film Institute in 1975, Welles showed some provocative footage from a feature film he is making in color in Los Angeles entitled *The Other Side of the Wind,* which he claimed in 1979 was "ninety-six-percent finished"[2] in both shooting and editing. Recently he has embarked upon a venture with Northstar International to film *The Dreamers,* a romantic adventure story based upon Isak Dinesen's *Gothic Tales.* Welles is also at work on an independent film of his own memoirs for the BBC. And so, as this book goes to press, we may hope for further masterpieces from the director who is perhaps the single most important architect of the modern film.*

---

* Welles has also made several important films of less than feature length which have not been mentioned in the text. *The Immortal Story* (*Histoire immortelle,* 1968), based on a novella by Isak Dinesen, was written and directed by Welles for the nationalized French television company ORTF. Running fifty-eight minutes, it was Welles' first film in color and starred Welles, Jeanne Moreau, and Fernando Rey. *The Deep* (also called *Dead Calm* or *Dead Reckoning*), was written and directed by Welles, and was shot off the Dalmatian coast of Yugoslavia between 1967 and 1969. Based on the novel *Dead Calm* by Charles Williams, the film starred Welles, Jeanne Moreau, and Laurence Harvey. There is a useful plot summary of *The Deep,* based on an early version of the script, in James Naremore's *The Magic World of Orson Welles* (New York, 1978); outside of this, there is no information on the film, which remains unreleased. Finally—and most significant—Welles has written and directed *F for Fake* (1976), a hybrid documentary about the dynamics of fakery which focuses on the famous art forger Elmyr de Hory, his biographer (and the fraudulent pseudo-biographer of Howard Hughes) Clifford Irving, and Welles himself, who, as director of the film, is the chief illusionist among them. According to William Johnson in his *Film Quarterly* review of *F for Fake* (Summer 1976), the film provides a "commentary on the ontology of the film medium" and that medium's "specious realism."

10.78 *The Immortal Story* (Orson Welles, 1968): Jeanne Moreau as Virginie.

10.79 Orson Welles playing himself in *F for Fake* (1976).

War-Time and Post-War Cinema: Italy and America, 1940–1951

THE EFFECTS OF WAR

World War II left the national cinemas of Western Europe in a state of economic, physical, and psychological paralysis. Cinema is an industry, and industries are dependent for their survival upon the stability of the economic systems in which they function. The Nazis had destroyed the shaky pre-war economy of Europe and set up another in its place, which had in turn been destroyed by the Allied victory in the spring of 1945. Until the Marshall Plan for the economic rehabilitation of Europe began to take effect in 1948–49, national industries of all types found it impossible to resume production on a large scale. Furthermore, the physical devastation wreaked upon the European film industries by the war was immense. In England alone, air raids has destroyed 330 film theaters, or close to 25 percent of the total number; Germany lost nearly 60 percent of its production facilities in the fire-bombing of Berlin; and the French industry, which had managed to maintain fairly high standards of production during the German Occupation, was reduced to a state of chaos by Allied bombardment and street-fighting during the liberation of Paris in August 1944. In all of Europe, only the Italian industry was left with reasonably full production facilities intact, a result of Italy's early surrender and the unique circumstances of its liberation.

More devastating to the cinema than either economic instability or physical wreckage, however, was the state of psychological and moral collapse in which Europe found itself immediately following the Nazi surrender. It is estimated that World War II killed over forty-eight million people in Europe and created more than twenty-one million refugees. Whole cities, with their entire civilian populations, had been wiped out in minutes by fire-bombing and artifacts of a centuries-old civilization reduced to rubble. Indeed, at least 35 percent of all permanent dwellings in Western Europe had been destroyed by the end of the war. Liberation was joyful when it came, but the experience of Nazi barbarism left a dark imprint upon the European consciousness; and the revelation of the true extent of Nazi atrocities in the occupied territories was nothing less than shattering. In one large province of the Soviet Union, for example, 40 percent of the inhabitants had been deported to death camps, and Poland had lost 25 percent of its entire population to the camps. The

German-born sociologist and philosopher Theodor Adorno, himself a refugee from Hitler, was moved to state that there could be "no poetry after Auschwitz."* and indeed, for a while, there could not. The human spirit rekindles quickly, however (too quickly, some have felt, given the magnitude of this particular horror); economies most frequently do not, and until the benefits of the Marshall Plan began to be felt, the European national cinemas were unable to approach anything like their pre-war levels of production.† Italy was the sole exception, both because its industry had not been physically ravaged by bombing and because the forces which were to revitalize the Italian cinema had been set in motion during the war itself.

ITALY

The Italian Cinema Before Neo-Realism

When the Fascists, under Benito Mussolini, seized power in 1922, the Italian cinema had already fallen far from the position of international leadership it had assumed in the early silent period (see Chapter 2). Epic spectacles like Enrico Guazzoni's world-famous *Quo vadis?* (1913) and Giovanni Pastrone's *Cabiria* (1914) were a thing of the past; and by the time sound arrived in 1930, Italian studios were producing fewer than thirty features per year, the majority of which were either stagily photographed operas or *"telefono bianco"* ("white telephone") films—trivial romantic comedies set in blatantly artificial studio surroundings. At this point, however, the Fascists became aware of the immense propaganda potential of film and began to take a keen interest in the progress of the Italian industry.

In 1935, Mussolini ordered the establishment of a national film school (unprecedented outside of the Soviet Union), the Centro Sperimentale della Cinematografia, and authorized the construction of the vast Cinecittà studios in Rome, whose size and technical facilities rivaled those of UFA-Neubabelsberg: sixteen soundstages, 600,000 square meters for exteriors, and corridor upon corridor of dressing-rooms. In its first year of operation, 1938, Cinecittà doubled the rate of Italian film production over the previous year by releasing more than eighty films. Meanwhile, the Centro Sperimentale, under the direction of the film-maker Luigi Chiarini (1900–1975), a covert Marxist, had attracted such promising students as Roberto Rossellini, Luigi Zampa, Pietro Germi, Giuseppe De

---

* The streamlined mass-extermination complex built by the Nazis in eastern Poland, where over one million people died in two years of operation.

† In the United States, by contrast, 1946 was the most profitable year in the history of Hollywood before 1973. Box office receipts exceeded 1.7 billion dollars, no small part of which derived from the exhibition of American films in Europe (people *will* have movies—in the worst of times probably more than in the best); and it is arguable that the regeneration of the European national cinemas was substantially and deliberately retarded by a massive influx of American films in the immediate post-war period. It is also arguable, however, that the superior craftsmanship exhibited by the Hollywood productions inspired the European cinemas to new levels of technical competence when that renewal finally began.

Santis, and Michelangelo Antonioni—all to become major directors of the post-war cinema—and had begun to publish its own theoretical journal, called *Bianco e nero* ("black and white"). A rival journal called *Cinema* was soon founded, under the editorship of Vittorio Mussolini, son of *Il Duce,* which published translations of the major theoretical writings of Eisenstein, Pudovkin, and Béla Balász (see Chapters 5 and 15) and contributions from native talents like the young Luchino Visconti. Finally, to further upgrade and increase production Mussolini attempted to establish a wholly protected industry by imposing strict import quotas on foreign films and banning American films altogether when Italy entered the war in 1940. (Before this date, he had contented himself with rather childishly maligning American films through "imperial edict." In 1933, for example, Italian audiences had been forbidden to laugh at the Marx Brothers in *Duck Soup,* but the film itself was not banned.)

For all of Mussolini's efforts, as Roy Armes has observed, the Italian cinema under Fascism was in practice a distinctly mediocre commodity.*[1] Its basic distinguishing feature between 1940 and 1942 was designated by the film critic and director Giuseppe De Santis (b. 1917) as "calligraphism"—a sort of reactionary formalism which dwelled upon literary subjects of the past. Mario Soldati's *Piccolo mondo antico* (*Little Old-Fashioned World,* 1940), a tale of passion set in the nineteenth century, and Renato Castellani's *Un colpo di pistola* (*A Pistol Shot,* 1941), a version of Pushkin's 1831 short story *The Shot,* are prime examples of the type. In the Fascist propaganda documentary of the period, however, certain roots of the movement which was to become neo-realism are discernible.

11.1 Calligraphism: Renato Castellani's *Un colpo di pistola* (1941). Fosco Giachetti, Massimo Serato.

Francesco De Robertis (1902–59), as head of the film section of the naval ministry, was responsible for several semi-documentary feature films which anticipate neo-realism in their use of non-professional actors, on-location shooting, and a photographic style similar to that of contemporary newsreels. In *Uomini sul fondo* (English title: *S.O.S. Submarine*), which he directed as his first feature in 1941, De Robertis recreated the undersea rescue of a disabled Italian submarine in a fashion so authentic that critics all over the country took note. In the same year, he supervised the production of *La nave bianca* (*The White Ship*), which realistically reconstructed life aboard an Italian battleship and gave Roberto Rossellini (1906–77) his first job of directing a feature film. The influence of De Robertis was purely technical, however, for he was a devout Fascist whose world-view was in no way compatible with the liberal humanism which neo-realism came to espouse. More conceptually attuned to neo-realism was the middle-class comedy of manners as practiced by Alessandro Blasetti (b. 1900) in *Quattro passi fra le nuvole* (*Four Steps in the*

* But a 1978 showing of forty-four feature films from the period at the Museum of Modern Art ("Before Neo-Realism: Italian Cinema, 1929–1944") produced some second opinions. According to Ted Perry, for example, "the fifteen years from the coming of sound to the end of Mussolini's reign provided . . . an entertainment industry that rivaled Hollywood in the charm and sophistication of its narratives, its acting and direction" ("The Road to Neo-Realism," *Film Comment,* 14, 6 [November–December 1978], 13).

Clouds, 1942) and Vittorio De Sica in *I bambini ci guardano* (*The Children Are Watching Us,* 1942). Although both films were elaborations of an older genre perfected by Mario Camerini in the thirties, and slightly flawed by sentimentality, they were notable for their studied social observation and their realistic scripts by the Marxist screenwriter Cesare Zavattini (b. 1902), who was shortly to become to neo-realism what Carl Mayer had been to the *Kammerspielfilm*— its chief ideological spokesman and its major scenarist.*

The Foundations of Neo-Realism

Zavattini was in fact the theoretical founder of neo-realism. In 1942 he called for a new kind of Italian film—one which would abolish contrived plots, do away with professional actors, and take to the streets for its material in order to establish direct contact with contemporary social reality. Plot was inauthentic, according to Zavattini, because it imposed an artificial structure on "everyday life," and professional actors simply compounded the falsehood since "to want one person to play another implies the calculated plot." It was precisely the dignity and sacredness of the "everyday life" of ordinary people, so alien to the heroic ideal of Fascism, that Zavattini demanded the new realism capture when it emerged. As he was to write later of this emergence: "The reality buried under the myths slowly reflowered. The cinema began its creation of the world. Here was a tree; here an old man; here a house; here a man eating, a man sleeping, a man crying. . . . The cinema . . . should accept, unconditionally, what is contemporary. *Today, today, today.*" In early 1943, Umberto Barbaro (1902–59), an influential critic and lecturer at the Centro Sperimentale, published an article which attacked the reactionary conventions of the Italian film and invoked the term "neo-realism" to refer to what was lacking. Barbaro's specific allusion was to French poetic realism—the thirties cinema of Renoir, Carné, Duvivier, and Clair— but the term was soon picked up by Giuseppe De Santis and other progressive critics at *Bianco e nero* and *Cinema* to designate the revolutionary agitation for a popular and realistic national cinema which was soon to sweep the Italian film schools, cinema clubs, and critical journals.

The influences on the young men demanding a "new realism" were many and varied. For one thing, most of them were clandestine Marxists in addition to being professionally trained film critics, and the "realism" they wished to renew was quite specifically the Soviet expressive realism of Eisenstein, Pudovkin, and Dovzhenko. This influence was less technical than ideological, however, and the stylistic resemblances between Italian neo-realism and Soviet expressive realism, although they do exist,

---

* Zavattini continued to write screenplays well into the seventies, long after neo-realism's decline (recently, for example, *Un cuore semplice* [*A Simple Heart*—from Flaubert, directed by Giorgio Ferrara, 1978] and *Ligabue* [directed by Salvatore Nocita, 1978]). His autobiography is *Sequences from a Cinematic Life,* trans. William Weaver (Englewood Cliffs, N.J., 1970).

are slight. A more direct and practical influence on the neo-realist movement was French poetic realism, which had achieved international preeminence by 1939. In addition to being technically brilliant, the films of poetic realism espoused a kind of socialist humanism which Italians found at least as appealing as the strident Soviet Marxism. Furthermore, several major directors of the neo-realist cinema actually served their apprenticeships under French film-makers. Luchino Visconti (1906–76), for example, had been third assistant director and costume designer for Renoir's *Une partie de campagne* (1936; released 1946), and Michelangelo Antonioni (see below) had worked as an assistant to Carné on *Les visiteurs du soir* (1942). Most significant of all, perhaps, is the fact that the cinema of poetic realism represented aesthetic and intellectual freedom to young Italian artists trapped in the hot-house atmosphere of the Fascist studios. Many, like Rossellini, had begun their careers as government loyalists but turned bitterly against the regime as they were forced to make compromise after compromise to Fascist policy and public taste. In fact, as Roy Armes has suggested, by strait-jacketing Italy's film artists Fascism probably contributed more to the rise of neo-realism than any other single historical force.[2]

Indeed, Italian Fascism had always contained the seeds of its own destruction, and in 1943 political and historical events conspired to liberate the forces of neo-realism from the journal pages. The Allies invaded Sicily in July, and Mussolini was turned out of office by his own party. An armistice was then signed with the Allies, whose forces landed on the mainland and began their sweep up the peninsula. To add to the confusion, the new Italian government, under Marshal Badoglio, declared war on Germany, while Mussolini was installed as the head of a Nazi puppet-state, called the Salò Republic, in the northern part of the country. Partisan fighting erupted everywhere, and the Allied movement northward was slowed. Rome did not fall until June 1944, and even then it took another year of heavy fighting to effect the Germans' unconditional surrender. But in the midst of this chaos, Fascist control of the Italian film studios relaxed somewhat, and the armistice of 1943 had no sooner been signed than neo-realism was heralded by the release of Luchino Visconti's grim tale of passion and murder in modern Italy, *Ossessione* (*Obsession*).

Ossessione was based (without permission) on the American thriller *The Postman Always Rings Twice,* by the pulp-novelist James M. Cain; it could not be shown outside of Italy until 1976 because of copyright infringement.* The novel is a violent tale of sexual obsession and corruption in which a young drifter contracts an affair with the sensual wife of

---

* It was Renoir who brought *The Postman Always Rings Twice* to Visconti's attention and gave him a French typescript of the book during the shooting of *Une partie de campagne* in 1936. Appropriately, the American version of Cain's novel, directed by Tay Garnett in 1946, is one of the great classics of *film noir,* a type discussed later in this chapter. There is also a 1937 French version directed by Pierre Chenal, entitled *Le dernier tournant,* but Visconti had not seen it at the time of directing *Ossessione.* A second American version was directed by Bob Rafelson in 1980.

11.2 *Ossessione* (Luchino Visconti, 1943): Giovanna (Clara Calamai) in her kitchen.

11.3 *Ossessione:* character as fate.

the owner of a roadside cafe. Together they murder the husband for his insurance money, but they are later trapped in their own deceptions. Visconti retained the melodramatic plot and brutal characters but transferred the setting to the contemporary Italian countryside near Ferrara, whose bleakness, provinciality, and poverty he captured with great fidelity. In 1948, the co-scenarist (with Giuseppe De Santis) of *Ossessione*, Angelo Pietrangeli, offered this description of the film's visual texture: "Ferrara, its squares, its grey and deserted streets; Ancona and its San Ciriaco Fair; the Po and its sandy banks; a landscape streaked with a rubble of cars and men along the network of highways. Against this backdrop are silhouetted the wandering merchants, mechanics, prostitutes and inn boys . . . beset by violent proletarian love affairs, primitive anger, and the sins that flesh is heir to."[3] Clearly, the technical virtuosity of *Ossessione* would make it an important film under any circumstances, but coming as it did upon the heels of the neo-realist manifestoes of Zavattini and Barbaro, it seemed to validate their notion that a new Italian cinema was about to be born—one which would take its cameras out of the studios and into the streets and countryside to probe the lives of ordinary men and women in relation to their environment. Thus, *Ossessione* can be said to have provided the blueprint for neo-realism. It anticipated some of the movement's themes and styles (popular setting, realistic treatment, social content), though lacking the neo-realist political commitment and historical perspective. But, unfortunately, political and economic circumstances intervened to make the film less immediately influential than it might have been. The Fascist censors still controlled the industry, and though they had originally approved the project they were shocked at the harsh portrait of Italian provincial life Visconti had painted. Their response was to ban the film and subsequently release it in a version cut to less than half its original length. Visconti reconstructed *Ossessione* after the war, but even then the film could not be shown abroad due to copyright infringement; for this reason, the first Italian neo-realist film to reach the other countries of the West was Roberto Rossellini's *Roma, città aperta (Rome, Open City,* 1945).

Neo-Realism: Major Figures and Films

A remarkable film of Italian resistance and Nazi reprisal, *Roma, città aperta* was based upon actual events which occurred in Rome in the winter of 1943–44, when the city was declared "open"* by the Germans. It tells the story of a Communist underground leader who brings death to himself and to his friends in a vain but heroic attempt to outlast a Gestapo manhunt. The film was planned by Rossellini and his associates (Sergio Amidei, Anna Magnani, Aldo Fabrizi, and Federico Fellini—several of whom were actively involved in the Resistance movement at the time) in the midst of the Nazi Occupation, and shooting began only two months after Rome's liberation in June 1944. Only two

---

* Meaning not to be fought through or bombed—in this case, partially ironic.

studio sets were used in the entire film, and the rest was shot on location in the streets of Rome, where the events it dramatized had actually taken place. In the interest of speed, Rossellini shot *Roma, città aperta* silent and dubbed in the actors' voices after it was edited.* Moreover, because his film stock was of relatively low quality, the finished film had the look of a contemporary newsreel. Indeed, many who saw *Roma, città aperta* when it was first released in 1945 thought that they were watching a record of actual events unfolding before the cameras and were astonished that Rossellini could have been permitted to reveal so much of Nazi brutality with the Germans still in Rome. They were equally amazed at the intelligence, integrity, and technical ingenuity of the film because, as far as international audiences were aware, these qualities had been absent from the Italian cinema since the Fascists came to power in 1922.

For all of these reasons, and because it has an appealing melodramatic plot line, *Roma, città aperta* enjoyed immense success in almost every country in the Western world. In the United States alone its distributors grossed over half a million dollars, and in Italy it was the most profitable film released since the outbreak of the war. Furthermore, *Roma, città aperta* won major prizes in a number of international film festivals, including the Grand Prix at Cannes in 1946, and critical acclaim for it was very nearly universal. The American critic James Agee, for example, was so awed by the film that he publicly refused to review it. Only in Italy was *Roma, città aperta* coldly received by the established critics, and this was less for aesthetic reasons than for ideological and political ones. It is true, of course, that the film has a number of structural flaws and that these relate at least as much to Rossellini's limitations as a director as to the difficult conditions under which it was made; but in spite of these defects, *Roma, città aperta* is one of those watershed films, like *The Birth of a Nation, Das Kabinett des Dr. Caligari, Potemkin,* and *Citizen Kane,* whose appearance changed the entire course of Western cinema. Rossellini's film became the paradigm for Italian neo-realism and set the standard for everything that succeeded it—in its achievement of a documentary surface through on-location shooting and post-synchronization of sound, its mixture of professional performers (Magnani and Fabrizi) and non-professionals, its references to contemporary national experience (or at least very recent national history), its social commitment and humanistic point of view, and, above all, what Penelope Houston has called its "driving urge" to rehabilitate the national reputation.[4] It could be argued that its primacy is the result of an historical accident given the suppression of *Ossessione,* but that primacy itself is indisputable.

11.4 *Roma, città aperta* (Roberto Rossellini, 1945); Pina (Anna Magnani) murdered by the Gestapo.

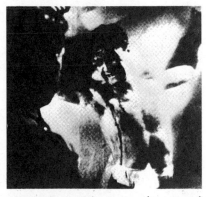

11.5 *Roma, città aperta:* the tortured Communist (Marcello Pagliero).

Rossellini's next two films confirmed his mastery of the neo-realist mode and extended his commitment to his country's recent past. *Paisà* (*Paisan,* 1946), like its predecessor, was written by Rossellini, Amidei, and Fellini. It recounts six unrelated episodes in the liberation of Italy, from the American landing in Sicily in 1943 to the Nazi evacuation of the Po Valley in 1945, and was shot on location all over the country, in Sicily, Naples, Rome, Florence, and the Po Delta. Unlike *Roma, città*

---

* Post-dubbing has become standard Italian practice since the war.

11.6 Three episodes from Rossellini's *Paisà* (1946): Sicily, Naples, the Po Valley.

aperta, Paisà was a rather costly venture (in fact, the most expensive Italian film of 1946). Nevertheless, Rossellini once again combined professional and non-professional actors—an American black man playing a GI, and people from the district in which the director happened to be shooting—and improvised part of his script to create what James Agee called in a contemporary review of *Paisà* "the illusion of the present tense." Like *Roma, città aperta*, Rossellini's second film contains flaws of structure (which Agee, incidentally, had recovered sufficiently from the first film to point out), but in its authentic representation of common people caught up in the madness and horror of war, *Paisà* validates the broadly humanistic world-view of neo-realism and confirms the effectiveness of its improvisatory techniques.

Rossellini's third film, the final part of what is often called his "war trilogy," was *Germania, anno zero* (*Germany, Year Zero*, 1947). Shot on location in bombed-out Berlin and acted entirely by non-professionals, the film is an attempt to probe the social roots of Fascism through the rather contrived story of a young German boy corrupted by Nazism who murders his bedridden father and commits suicide in the wake of the

German defeat. It is generally agreed that *Germania, anno zero* represents a personal failure for Rossellini (who, in addition to directing, wrote the script), but its specifically neo-realistic elements have been widely praised. For example, the long, nearly wordless concluding sequence in which the boy wanders through a gutted Berlin toward his personal *Götterdämmerung* is frequently cited as one of the glories of Italian neo-realist cinema. In the end, however, that cinema proved nontransplantable in alien soil, and the relative failure of *Germania, anno zero*—both commercially and critically—foreshadowed the larger failure of the neo-realist movement generally to transcend its specific social and historical contexts. Rossellini himself did not attempt another film in the neo-realist vein, and he outlasted the movement to become a major figure in world cinema.*

11.7 Rossellini's *Germania, anno zero* (1947): Edmund Moeschke as the boy.

The second major director of the Italian neo-realist movement, and one who worked within it until its demise in the fifties, was Vittorio De Sica (1901–74). A matinee idol during the "white telephone" era of the thirties, De Sica began his directing career near the end of that decade with a number of conventional middle-class comedies, at least one of which (*I bambini ci guardano* [1942]), anticipates the neo-realist concern with social problems. This film began De Sica's collaboration and life-long friendship with his scriptwriter, Cesare Zavattini, the leading theoretician of neo-realism at the time. Though De Sica's sensibility was essentially comic, he apparently fell under the influence of Zavattini's ideas sometime during the war, for in 1946 the two men began a series of films concentrating on the urban problems of post-war Italy.

Sciuscià (*Shoeshine*, 1946), is a bleak tale of the corruption of innocence in Nazi-occupied Rome. Two young shoeshine boys who are best friends become involved in a black-market deal, in an effort to buy a horse. They are caught and sent to prison, where one inadvertently betrays the other and is later killed by him in revenge. Like *Roma, città aperta*, *Sciuscià* was not well received in Italy but proved highly successful in the United States, where it won the Academy Award for the Best Foreign Film of 1946. De Sica's next film with Zavattini, *Ladri di biciclette* (*Bicycle Thieves/The Bicycle Thief*, 1948), received even greater international acclaim and is thought by some critics to be the most important film of the post-war era. In it, a family man who has been out of

---

* Rossellini's major films after 1948 were *Francesco giullare di Dio* (released in America as *The Flowers of St. Francis*, 1950); *Europa '51* (1952); *Viaggio in Italia* (released as *Strangers*, 1953); *India* (1958); *Il generale Della Rovere* (*General Della Rovere*, 1959; starring Vittorio De Sica); *Viva Italia!* (1960); *Vanina Vanini* (*The Betrayer*, 1961); *La prise de pouvoir par Louis XIV* (*The Rise of Louis XIV*, 1966; made for French television but theatrically distributed abroad); *Socrate* (*Socrates*, 1970; made for Italian television); *Augustino di Ippona* (*St. Augustine of Hippo*, 1972); *Blaise Pascal* (1972; made for Italian television); and *Il Messia* (*The Messiah*, 1978). Through his films of the fifties Rossellini exercised an important influence on the young directors of the French New Wave (see Chapter 13), which is wholly appropriate given his own reverence for the French masters of the thirties. Furthermore, as Andrew Sarris has said (in *The American Cinema* [New York, 1968], p. 152), Rossellini's biographical films are the most impressive in the history of the cinema.

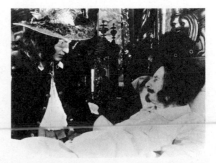

11.8 Rossellini's documentary-like *La prise de pouvoir par Louis XIV* (1966).

11.9 Vittorio De Sica's *Sciuscià* (1946): Rinaldo Smordoni and Franco Interlenghi.

11.10 De Sica's *Ladri di biciclette* (1948): Antonio (Lamberto Maggiorani) with his son (Enzo Staiola).

work for almost two years (unemployment in post-war Italy had reached 22 percent by 1948) finds a job as a municipal bill poster, for which he must provide his own transportation. He pawns the family's sheets in order to buy a bicycle, which is stolen his first day out. For the rest of the film he and his little boy search in vain for the thief, and near its conclusion the man is driven to steal a bicycle himself but is caught in the act. Shot on location in Rome with non-actors in the leading roles (the protagonist was played by a factory worker brilliantly coached by De Sica), *Ladri di biciclette* was an international success, and its rambling narrative form was widely imitated by other directors. As was recognized at the time, the film actually has meaning on several different planes: it is a powerful social document firmly committed to the reality it portrays, a poignant story of the relationship between a father and his son, and a modern parable of alienated man in a hostile and dehumanized environment. De Sica and Zavattini were to collaborate on two more neo-realist endeavors, mixing social protest with fantasy in *Miràcolo a Milano* (*Miracle in Milan,* 1951) and giving neo-realism its final masterpiece in *Umberto D.* (1952). But before we examine the decline of the movement, it is necessary to mention a film which will probably prove to be the single most enduring legacy of neo-realism to world cinema, though its own neo-realist traits are of a paradoxical nature: Luchino Visconti's *La terra trema* (*The Earth Trembles,* 1948).

La terra trema was the first part (*L'episòdio del mare:* "The Sea Episode") of a never-completed trilogy Visconti had planned on the economic problems of fishing, mining, and agriculture in post-war Sicily. It was the first film he had directed since the Fascist assault on *Ossessione* (in the interim, he had worked for the Resistance and directed theater in Rome), and it was shot entirely on location in the Sicilian fishing village of Aci Trezza with a cast of non-professionals recruited from the local populace. Initially financed by the Italian Communist Party but modestly subsidized later by a commercial company, *La terra trema* was adapted

11.11 *La terra trema* (Luchino Visconti, 1948).

by Visconti from a novel by the nineteenth-century realist Giovanni Verga (*I malavoglia* [*The House by the Medlar Tree,* 1881]) which relates the story of the downfall of a proud family of peasant fishermen through economic exploitation by wholesalers and market-men. By transferring the tale from 1881 to 1947 and giving it a Marxist interpretation, in addition to shooting the film on location with non-actors, Visconti was clearly working within the neo-realist conventions he had helped to establish in *Ossessione.* But despite its neo-realist attributes, *La terra trema* is not a purely neo-realist film, because Visconti was a paradoxical artist whose work always hovers somewhere between realism and aestheticism—some would say between realism and decadence. For one thing, though much of the Sicilian dialogue was improvised on the spot, every other aspect of the film was elaborately planned in advance and carefully controlled in the production process itself. *La terra trema*'s formal structure is masterful, and most of its shots are so sumptuously composed and photographed by the veteran cinematographer G. R. Aldo (1902–53) that Orson Welles (perhaps in a fit of professional jealousy) once remarked that Visconti was the only director in the history of the cinema to photograph starving peasants like fashion models in *Vogue.* But realism in cinema (and in any art form) is a style, not an ideology, and it is an error to equate it with ugliness or desolation. Rather, in his sweeping, stately camera movements, his rhythmic editing, and above all the beautiful and elaborate composition of his shots, Visconti achieves for his peasant tragedy a visual grandeur which is not at all at odds with its social polemic but which lends it an almost mythic resonance. One critic has called the style of *La terra trema* "a kind of operatic *cinéma vérité,*" and the tension between visual lushness and social realism which this term suggests characterizes all of Visconti's work from *Ossessione* (1943) to the posthumously released *L'innocente* (*The Innocent,* 1979). It has frequently been remarked that this tension was the product of ambiguities within the artist himself—an aristocrat by birth, a Marxist by philosophy, and a director of grand opera several months out of each year by choice. Nonetheless, it is important to recognize that in the course of his career Visconti proved himself to be one of the world's greatest directors, and that *La terra trema* is one of his most significant works. Like *Ossessione,* unfortunately, *La terra trema* had little immediate impact upon contemporary cinema. Running over two and a half hours and spoken in a dialect all but incomprehensible to mainland Italians, the film was a commercial disaster on the domestic market and suffered the same fate as its predecessor under Fascism: it was drastically cut and dubbed into Italian for re-release. *La terra trema* was exported only to France, where a voice-over narration completely destroyed its ideological content but where the film critic and theorist André Bazin saw it and communicated its importance to the generation of young film enthusiasts from whose ranks would soon be drawn the directors of the French New Wave. Visconti himself temporarily abandoned the cinema once more for the theater, returning in 1951 to direct Anna Magnani in *Bellissima,* a melodrama with few roots in neo-realism, and to begin thereby a new phase of his career.*

If the relationship of *La terra trema* to neo-realism is problematic, it is because Visconti as an artist has never been comfortable within the confines of a single perspective or cinematic mode, and has informed all of his work with a uniquely personal vision whether he was adapting American pulp fiction, Giovanni Verga, or Thomas Mann. But other Italian directors of the post-war period identified more closely with the new movement, and the years 1946 to 1949 witnessed a number of neo-realist films by relatively minor figures who nevertheless deserve mention. Inspired by the successes of Rossellini and De Sica, the Italian partisan organization (ANPI) produced two films between 1946 and 1947, both collectively written,† which examined the war and its aftermath from the point of view of the partisan Left. Aldo Vergano's *Il sole sorge ancora*

---

* Visconti continued to produce eccentric, operatic masterpieces after his neo-realist phase. The most significant of these are elaborate historical dramas (*Senso* [1954]; *Il caduta degli dei* [English title: *The Damned,* 1969]; *Ludwig* [1973]) and literary adaptations (*Il gattopardo* [*The Leopard,* 1962; from the novel by Giuseppe Tomasi di Lampedusa]; *Lo straniero* [*The Stranger,* 1969; from the novel by Albert Camus]; *Morte a Venezia* [*Death in Venice,* 1970; from the novella by Thomas Mann]). *Rocco e i suoi fratelli* (*Rocco and His Brothers,* 1960) was conceived by Visconti as a sequel to *La terra trema;* it is a loosely structured epic about the migration of a peasant family from southern Italy to the industrial north. Most of these films were shot in color by Giuseppe Rotunno (b. 1923), Visconti's close collaborator and one of the world's great cinematographers. In the last twenty years of his career, Visconti became increasingly famous for his expressive use of color and decor. His final films—*Conversation Piece* (1975) and *L'innocente* (1979; from the novel by Gabriele D'Annunzio) were released posthumously. See Donald Lyons, "Visconti's Magnificent Obsession," *Film Comment,* 15, 2 (March–April 1979), 9–13; and James McCourt "*The Innocent:* Visconti's Last Fresco," same issue, 14–16. See also Monica Stirling's critical biography, *A Screen of Time: A Study of Luchino Visconti* (New York, 1979).

† Although Giuseppe De Santis, Michelangelo Antonioni, Umberto Barbaro, Cesare Zavattini, and others contributed, the principle author of both film scripts was the Marxist intellectual Carlo Lizzani (b. 1922). Lizzani functioned in the same capacity for many other neo-realist films, including De Santis' *Riso amaro* (1948) and *Non c'e pace tra gli ulivi* (1949), and Rossellini's *Germania, anno zero* (1947). Since 1951 (*Achtung banditi!*), he has been

(*The Sun Rises Again,* 1946) tells of the formation of the Resistance in Lombardy through the adventures of a young Italian soldier who has deserted in order to join it; Giuseppe De Santis' *Caccia tragica* (*The Tragic Hunt/Pursuit,* 1947) shows the continuation of the partisan spirit after the Liberation, as the members of a collective farm pursue and capture a gang of thieves which has robbed them. Alberto Lattuada (b. 1914), the master of "calligraphism" in the early forties, made three films between 1946 and 1949 which, while unmistakably commercial, are essentially neo-realist in method and theme. His *Il bandito* (*The Bandit,* 1946) is the story of a former Italian prisoner-of-war who cannot find a place for himself in the corrupt society of post-war Turin and turns in desperation to a life of crime. In *Senza pietà* (*Without Pity,* 1949), written by Federico Fellini and Tullio Pinelli, with Luigi Comencini (b. 1916),* two lovers, both displaced persons, are corrupted by their involvement in black-market activities in Livorno. Lattuada's final film with neo-realist affinities was *Il mulino del Po* (*The Mill on the Po,* 1948), also written by Fellini and Pinelli, which uses the events of a farm-workers' strike in the Po Valley in 1876 to depict the plight of contemporary agricultural workers.

11.12 Alberto Lattuada's *Senza pietà* (1948): John Kitzmiller and Carla del Poggio.

At the other end of the country, Pietro Germi (b. 1914) traveled to Sicily to direct the neo-realist *In nome della legge* (*In the Name of the Law,* 1948), which explores the pervasive influence of the Mafia upon contemporary Sicilian life, and *Il cammino della speranza* (*The Road to Hope,* 1950), which dramatizes the hardships of post-war emigrants from the poverty-stricken island as they struggled across the length of Italy on their way to France. In the same period, the former critic Giuseppe De Santis directed two noteworthy neo-realist films on agrarian themes. His *Riso amaro* (*Bitter Rice,* 1948) initially concerns the economic exploitation of itinerant female rice-workers in the Po Valley but degenerates rapidly into the sensational melodrama and eroticism which brought international fame to its two leading performers, Silvana Mangano and Vittorio Gassman, and which some believe marked the beginning of neo-realism's ultimate decline into commercialism. De Santis' *Non c'e pace tra gli ulivi* (*No Peace Among the Olives,* 1949) is less ideologically equivocal in its tale of a young soldier who returns from the war to find both his girlfriend and his farm stolen by a powerful provincial bourgeois and who must take the law into his own hands to regain them. Finally, a list of minor neo-realist works should not omit the comedies of Luigi Zampa (*Vivere in pace* [*Living in Peace,* 1947]), Renato Castellani (*Sotto il sole di Roma* [*Under the Roman Sun,* 1947]), and Luciano Emmer (*Domenica d'agosto* [*Sunday in August,* 1949]), all of which borrowed the production techniques of the movement without

11.13 Giuseppe De Santis' *Riso amaro* (1948): Silvana Mangano (center).

---

writer-director for his own films, most recently *Fontamara* (1980), and today, with thirty features to his credit, Lizanni is a ranking figure within the Italian film industry. He is also the author of the first major history of Italian post-war cinema, *Il cinema Italiano* (1953), which is, to date, unavailable in the United States.

* Now a highly respected director within the Italian commercial cinema (e.g., *L'ingorgo* [*Bottleneck,* 1979]).

11.14 *Umberto D.* (Vittorio De Sica, 1952): Carlo Battisti.

adopting its themes. Like *Riso amaro,* these works in their lack of serious social commitment foreshadowed the collapse of neo-realism into the slick sensationalism of the fifties. But before that collapse occurred, neo-realism produced its last masterpiece through the final collaboration of Vittorio De Sica and Cesare Zavattini in *Umberto D.* (1952).

Umberto D. probably comes as close to realizing Zavattini's ideal of a pure cinema of everyday life as any film the neo-realist movement produced. It has no plot but is structured around a series of loosely connected incidents in the title character's life. Although most of these incidents are generated by a single circumstance (Umberto D. is poor and can't pay his rent), the film begins and ends *in medias res* because it is about a condition rather than about a series of events. Filmed on location in Rome with an entirely non-professional cast, *Umberto D.* offers a portrait of an old-age pensioner attempting to eke out a meager existence for himself and his dog in a furnished room, while retaining a modicum of personal dignity. The fragile equilibrium Umberto has managed to maintain between mere want and degrading poverty is destroyed when his callous landlady, in an effort to drive him out, demands that he pay his back rent in a lump sum. Umberto sells what few possessions he has, attempts to borrow money from ex-colleagues (he is apparently a retired civil servant), and even tries to beg, but he finds it impossible to raise the amount he needs. Finally, after the landlady has publicly humiliated him by letting his room to prostitutes and has all but thrown him out into the street, Umberto resolves to commit suicide. He ultimately fails, however, because he can't bring himself to abandon his dog. The conclusion leaves the two alive together, but with no place to go and no prospects for the future.

Obviously, a film about a downtrodden old man and his dog is prone to be sentimental by its very nature, and *Umberto D.* does not avoid this pitfall (no neo-realist film about victimized people ever did). But most of the emotion the film contains is honest enough, because De Sica and Zavattini do not attempt to make their protagonist seem better or nobler than he is. Umberto can be thoroughly disagreeable, and he is in most respects an average person. Roy Armes suggests that as a character he is Chaplinesque (and De Sica admired Chaplin extravagantly)—a little man adrift in an alien environment which continually threatens him.[5] It is true, of course, that *Umberto D.* is a closely observed social document which comments on the hypocrisy, cruelty, and indifference of bourgeois society toward its own aged members, but, as in the earlier De Sica-Zavattini collaborations, an examination of emotional relationships lies at the center of the film. In *Sciuscià* the crucial relationship was that between the two young shoeshine boys, in *Ladri di biciclette* between the father and son. In *Umberto D.,* however, the only significant relationship is that of the protagonist and his dog, as if to imply that relationships between human beings have become increasingly difficult or even impossible in our emotionally attenuated modern society. Others have found *Umberto D.* less pessimistic than this comment suggests, but it seems clear that its commercial failure was a direct result of the grim view it took of contemporary life.* In the year of its release, in fact, some Italian politicians attempted to prohibit the film's exportation on the grounds that it presented a falsely gloomy picture of Italian society.

The Decline of Neo-Realism

Neo-realism in Zavattini's ideal sense ("the ideal film would be ninety minutes of the life of a man to whom nothing happens") probably never existed. In practice, it was a cinema of poverty and pessimism firmly rooted in the immediate post-war period. When times changed and economic conditions began to improve, neo-realism lost first its ideological basis, then its subject matter. As Penelope Houston puts it, neo-realism was a revolutionary cinema in a non-revolutionary society, and certainly the movement could never have outlasted the prosperity and affluence of the fifties.[6] But even if Italy had remained unchanged from *Roma, città aperta* to *Umberto D.* the neo-realist cinema would have failed for other reasons. In the first place, for all of its collectivist aspirations neo-realism had never been a popular cinema in Italy and was dependent for its survival upon foreign markets—especially the United States. When the Italian film industry experienced a major crisis in 1949 due to the wholesale importation of American films (the sociologist George Huaco has found that only 10 percent of the feature films exhibited in Italy in 1949 were Italian, while 71 percent were American[7]), the government passed the protective Andreotti Law, which, among its provisions, gave censors the right to ban from exportation any Italian film which might present the country in a bad light. The mere threat of enforcement was enough to frighten most producers away from neo-realism, but when the government became openly hostile to the movement in the early fifties, backing for projects dried up altogether. Since Italy joined the NATO Pact in March 1949, some have speculated that the Andreotti Law was enacted with the implicit purpose of slowly strangling neo-realism, whose ideological orientation was Marxist. This is quite possible, given the general stupidity of governments in their relations with the arts, but it also seems clear that neo-realism had burned itself out internally before the Andreotti Law had any significant effect on production.

In their desire to achieve "the illusion of the present tense" which James Agee had noted in Rossellini's *Paisà,* the neo-realist directors frequently ignored the narrative elements of their films or treated them as irrelevant, causing the plots to degenerate into stereotypes. The same concentration on methodology also created the lapses into sentimentality

---

* As if to validate his own pessimistic premise, De Sica did little serious work after this film, turning to romantic melodrama (*La ciociaria* [English title: *Two Women,* 1960]) and slick sex comedies (*Ieri, oggi, domani* [*Yesterday, Today, and Tomorrow,* 1963]). The beautiful and poignant *Il giardino dei Finzi-Contini* (*The Garden of the Finzi-Continis,* 1971) helped to re-establish his critical reputation and re-affirm his essentially tragic vision of human experience, as did the posthumously released *Una breva vacanza* (*A Brief Vacation,* 1974) and *Il viaggio* (*The Journey,* 1975), but De Sica was clearly an artist in eclipse before his death in 1974.

which led the British critic Raymond Durgnat to label neo-realist films the "male weepies," as opposed to the "female weepies" of Hollywood melodramatists like Vincent Sherman, Irving Rapper, and Daniel Mann.[8] To all of this it might first be replied that the neo-realists were interested not so much in constructing narratives as in reconstructing the atmosphere and ambiance of a contemporary reality, something they achieved admirably. And, as André Bazin suggests in his essay on neo-realism, "An Aesthetic of Reality,"[9] it is not at all unrespectable or even unusual for an innovative movement in cinema to dissipate its creative energies in a brief span of time. Innovation in an art form whose medium is photographic reproduction and whose influence literally travels with the speed of light is bound to be short-lived (as innovation, that is) and to produce its own reaction rapidly. But the real vindication of the neo-realist movement has been in its influence on the international cinema, and this has been enormous.

The Impact of Neo-Realism

Neo-realism completely revitalized Italian film, so that today it has become one of the major creative forces in world cinema. Not only did neo-realism produce masterpieces in its own right and become the temporary medium for great directors like Rossellini and Visconti, but it provided training for two men currently thought to be among the international cinema's greatest artists—Federico Fellini (b. 1920), who had worked extensively as a scriptwriter on neo-realist films (*Roma, città aperta; Paisà; Senza pietà; Il mulino del Po; In nome della lègge; Il cammino della speranza*), and Michelangelo Antonioni (b. 1912), who was writing criticism for *Cinema* and directing documentaries during the same period (e.g., *Gente del Po* [*People of the Po*, 1943; 1947], *N.U./Nettezza urbana* [*Dustmen*, 1948], *La villa dei mostri* [*The House of Monsters*, 1950]). In their films of the fifties, especially Fellini's *I vitelloni* (1953) and Antonioni's *Le amiche* (1955), both directors may be said to have continued the neo-realist mode by turning it inward, so that the object of attention becomes not society but the human self. This element of what might be called "introspective neo-realism" largely disappeared from their work in the sixties, but it is not far-fetched to see in their mature images of modern alienation and disorder vestiges of the bombed-out, fragmented neo-realist landscapes of the late forties. Indeed, Penelope Houston suggests that the strength of the Italian cinema lies precisely in its *in*ability to escape the neo-realist heritage, so that even the generation of film-makers which succeeded that of Fellini and Antonioni has felt compelled to confront and come to terms with the neo-realist tradition (see Chapter 14).[10] Francesco Rosi (b. 1922), Pier Paolo Pasolini (1922–75), Ermanno Olmi (b. 1939), Elio Petri (b. 1929), Lina Wertmuller (b. 1930), Vittorio De Seta (b. 1923), Marco Bellocchio (b. 1939), and Bernardo Bertolucci (b. 1940) have responded variously to that tradition by adopting its techniques while modifying or rejecting its vision (see Rosi's *Salvatore Giuliano* [1961], Pasolini's *Accattone* [1961], Olmi's *Il posto* [1961], De Seta's *Banditi a Orgosolo* [1961], Bertolucci's

Prima della rivoluzione [1964], Wertmuller's *I basilischi* [1963], and Bellocchio's *I pugni in tasca* [1966]).

Neo-realism was the first post-war cinema to liberate film-making from the artificial confines of the studio and, by extension, from the Hollywood-originated studio system. On-location shooting, the use of non-professional actors, and improvisation of script, which have all become a part (though not always a large part) of conventional film-making today, were techniques almost unknown to the narrative sound film before neo-realism. The movement's influence on the French New Wave directors in this regard is a matter of record, but its impact on the American cinema has been generally ignored: in the post-war work of American directors as diverse as Nicholas Ray (*They Live by Night* [1947]), Elia Kazan (*Boomerang!* [1947]), Jules Dassin (*Naked City* [1947]), Joseph Losey (*The Lawless* [1949]), Robert Rossen (*Body and Soul* [1947]), and Edward Dmytryk (*Crossfire* [1948]) substantial elements of neo-realism can be found, including a political commitment to the Left.* Finally, several scholars have pointed out the profound influence of neo-realism on film-makers in countries which lack strong national cinemas of their own—Michael Cacoyannis (b. 1922—*Zorba the Greek* [1964]) in Greece, Luis Garcia Berlanga (b. 1921—*Las pirañas* [1967]) and Juan Antonio Bardem (b. 1922—*Muerte de un ciclista* [1955]) in Spain, and Satyajit Ray (b. 1921—the Apu trilogy: *Pather Panchali* [1955], *Aparajito* [1956], *Apur sansar* [1957]) in India have all testified to the enormous influence of neo-realism upon their work (see Chapters 14 and 16). Indeed, Ray has claimed that a single viewing of De Sica's *Ladri di biciclette* in London in 1950 led him to film his trilogy according to neo-realist methods. It is clear that neo-realism was a great deal more than a localized national phenomenon; its formative influence extended well beyond the Italian cinema. There can be no question today that, whatever its limitations of vision and form, Italian neo-realism was one of the great innovative movements in the history of the cinema, whose importance and impact is comparable in degree to that of Soviet silent realism or the French New Wave, which it most appropriately mediates between.

AMERICA

Hollywood at War

Like the Italian, the American cinema too had been moving toward a heightened kind of realism in the early forties, when the war interrupted and Hollywood was pressed into the service of the federal government. On December 18, 1941, immediately following the attack on Pearl Harbor and our declaration of war upon Japan, President Roosevelt

---

* It is no coincidence that all of these American directors except Ray were implicated in the anti-Communist witch-hunt of the late forties and fifties (described in the second part of this chapter). Losey and Dassin exiled themselves to Europe, Kazan turned informer, Dmytryk recanted after serving time for contempt of Congress (as one of the "Hollywood Ten"), and Rossen recanted after being blacklisted from 1951 to 1953.

established a Bureau of Motion Picture Affairs within the Office of War Information to mobilize the studios for the national defense effort. Hollywood responded by creating the War Activities Committee, comprised of studio executives, distributors, exhibitors, actors, and labor union officials, to coordinate American film-making activity with the propaganda and morale-boosting programs of the government.* The government suggested six thematic categories for Hollywood films which would be consonant with its war-aims information campaign but which would not preclude conventional entertainment values. As listed by Lewis Jacobs, these were: 1) The Issues of the War: what we are fighting for, the American way of life; 2) The Nature of the Enemy: his ideology, his objectives, his methods; 3) The "United Nations": i.e., our allies in arms; 4) The Production Front: supplying the materials for victory; 5) The Home Front: civilian responsibility; 6) The Fighting Forces: our armed services, our allies and our associates.[11] Hollywood complied at first by producing a raft of fatuous, super-patriotic melodramas of the battlefield and homefront which glorified a kind of warfare that had never existed in the history of the human race, much less in the current upheaval. With titles like *Salute to Courage, Dangerously We Live, Captain of the Clouds, To the Shores of Tripoli, United We Stand, The Devil with Hitler,* and *Blondie for Victory,* these unsophisticated films disappeared rapidly from the American screen when Hollywood and the general public were confronted with an infinitely more authentic version of the war, contained in newsreels from the battlefronts and government-produced information films.

From 1941 to 1945, the War Department, the Army Pictorial Services, the Army Educational Program, the American Armed Forces (AAF) First Motion Picture Unit, the Signal Corps of the combined services, the U.S. Navy, the U.S. Marine Corps, and the Overseas Branch of the Office of War Information (OWI) were involved in the production of documentary films designed to explain and justify the war to the servicemen fighting it and the civilian populace actively supporting it. Major Hollywood directors like Frank Capra, John Huston, John Ford, and William Wyler had been recruited into the armed forces, together with professional documentarists like Willard Van Dyke (b. 1906) and Irving Lerner (1909–76), to operate these programs, and the films they produced collectively are among the most outstanding documentaries in the history of the form. The seven films of the *Why We Fight* series produced by Frank Capra, for example—*Prelude to War* (Frank Capra, 1942), *The Nazis Strike* (Frank Capra and Anatole Litvak, 1942), *Divide and Conquer* (Capra and Litvak, 1943), *The Battle of Britain* (Capra and Litvak, 1943), *The Battle of Russia* (Litvak, 1943), *The Battle of China* (Capra and Litvak, 1943), *War Comes to America* (Litvak, 1944)—were documentaries edited from stock footage which persuasively and unromantically explained the necessity of America's involvement in the war. Other information films, like Wyler's *Memphis Belle* (1944) and *The Fighting Lady*

11.15 *The Nazis Strike* (Frank Capra and Anatole Litvak, 1942) and *Divide and Conquer* (Capra and Litvak, 1943).

---

* Hollywood's cooperation with the war effort was encouraged considerably by the Selective Service System's 1942 ruling that the movies were an essential industry.

(1945), Ford's *The Battle of Midway* (1944) and *The Battle of the Marianas* (1944), and Huston's *Report from the Aleutians* (1943) and *The Battle of San Pietro* (1944), were shot on location in every theater of operations in the war and constitute masterly pieces of reporting. The characteristic feature of these films was their sobriety. War was shown to be a brutal, unglamorous, and murderous business which was pursued out of utter necessity and which had nothing to do with the Yankee-Doodle-Dandy heroics of Hollywood. Vast numbers of Americans saw these documentaries at home and overseas, and there can be little doubt that they did much to upgrade the realism and honesty with which Hollywood approached the war.

11.16 *The Battle of San Pietro* (John Huston, 1944).

The years 1943 and 1944 witnessed many films whose presentation of the war and attendant themes was much more convincing than that of their predecessors. Whereas earlier films had caricatured Fascists as either cowardly buffoons or stock villains, Frank Capra's *Meet John Doe* (1943), Herman Shumlin's *Watch on the Rhine* (1943; adapted by Lillian Hellman from her own play), George Cukor's *Keeper of the Flame* (1943), Edward Dmytryk's *Hitler's Children* (1943) and *Behind the Rising Sun* (1943), Fritz Lang's *Ministry of Fear* (1943), Leslie Fenton's *Tomorrow the World* (1944), John Farrow's *The Hitler Gang* (1944), Herbert Biberman's *The Master Race* (1944), William Cameron Menzies' *Address Unknown* (1944), and Alfred Hitchcock's semi-allegorical *Lifeboat* (1944) all portrayed the dangers of Fascism abroad and on the home front with a sophisticated understanding of the ruthlessness, intelligence, and actual power of the enemy.* Another group of films provided a more realistic treatment than heretofore of "our allies in arms."

11.17 *The Hitler Gang* (John Farrow, 1944): Robert Watson as the *Führer*.

Abjuring the formulaic platitudes of Henry King's *A Yank in the R.A.F.* (1941) and the saccharine stereotypes of William Wyler's *Mrs. Miniver* (1942), these films attempted with varying degrees of success to show what life was like inside the occupied countries and to promote a bond of sympathy with them. Though a far cry from Rossellini's *Roma, città aperta*, Frank Tuttle's *Hostages* (1943), Irving Pichel's *The Moon Is Down* (1943), Jean Renoir's *This Land Is Mine* (1943), Fritz Lang's *Hangmen Also Die* (1943), Lewis Milestone's *Edge of Darkness* (1943), and Tay Garnett's *The Cross of Lorraine* (1943) offered fairly convincing representations of oppression and resistance in Nazi-occupied Europe (specifically in Norway, Czechoslovakia, Hungary, and France). Other films, like Lewis Milestone's *North Star* (1943), Jacques Tourneur's *Days of Glory* (1944), and Michael Curtiz's *Mission to Moscow* (1943), attempted to promote good will between America and its incongruous new ally, the Soviet Union—in the case of *Mission to Moscow*, by trying to rationalize Stalin's purge trials of the thirties. (It is one of the

11.18 Fredric March plays a German who rejects Nazism and must flee his country in *So Ends Our Night* (John Cromwell, 1941).

---

* A handful of intelligent anti-Fascist films were made between 1940 and Pearl Harbor: for instance, Alfred Hitchcock's *Foreign Correspondent* (1940), Frank Borzage's *The Mortal Storm* (1940), and John Cromwell's *So Ends Our Night* (1941). For a full account of how the image of the Nazis has evolved historically in American films since the war, see John Mariani, "Let's Not Be Beastly to the Nazis," *Film Comment*, 15, 1 (January–February 1979), 49–53.

11.19 Stalin (Mannart Kippen) and Churchill (Dudley Field Malone) in the film version of Ambassador Joseph E. Davies' memoir, *Mission to Moscow* (Michael Curtiz, 1943).

bitterest ironies of recent American history that many of the people who worked on these *government-authorized* propaganda films were subjected to vicious accusations of disloyalty and treason during the late forties and early fifties; see below.)

Perhaps the most telling index of the documentary influence upon American cinema during the war years was the increasing number of serious-minded and realistic combat films which portrayed the war very much as it must have seemed to the men who were fighting it. Indeed, one of the reasons that Hollywood outgrew its post–Pearl Harbor romanticism so quickly was a massive GI reaction against the patent phoniness of the early war films, but by 1944 the true horror and anguish of warfare devoid of flag-waving jingoism was being brought home to Americans in films like Tay Garnett's *Bataan* (1943) and Lewis Seiler's *Guadalcanal Diary* (1944). Lewis Jacobs notes another significant category of late combat films, such as Lloyd Bacon's *Action in the North Atlantic* (1943), Delmer Daves' *Destination Tokyo* (1943) and *Pride of the Marines* (1945), Zoltán Korda's *Sahara* (1944), Howard Hawks' *Air Force* (1944), Lewis Milestone's *The Purple Heart* (1944) and *A Walk in the Sun* (1945), Henry King's *A Bell for Adano* (1945), and William Wellman's *The Story of GI Joe* (1945), in which the battlefield action becomes a vehicle for a more personal kind of cinema—one concerned with "the deep emotional crisis and individual agony of the average Joe, anxiously examining his own conscience."[12] In their focus on the individual American in conflict with himself, these productions anticipate the searching, introspective, and ultimately disillusioned films of the immediate post-war period, in which the democratic ideals for which so many Americans fought and died are brought into serious question.*

In 1945, however, with the end of the war clearly in sight, Hollywood was more concerned with empirical victory than metaphysical defeat, and had already begun its search for buoyant post-war subject matter. War themes were jettisoned for lighter material which would coincide with the momentary mood of public euphoria, and for a brief season on the American screen, following August 14, 1945, it was as if the war had never taken place at all.† But the war had not been unkind to Hollywood, even though it had lost its foreign markets and had devoted nearly one-third of its production between 1941 and 1945 to the war effort

---

* Two other categories of American war-time cinema deserve mention here: films of women coping on the home front, such as *Tender Comrade* (Edward Dmytryk, 1943) and *Since You Went Away* (John Cromwell, 1944), and morale-boosting "service musicals," which featured radio and film celebrities and "bevies of beautiful girls" in service settings; *Hollywood Canteen* (Delmer Daves, 1944) epitomizes the latter type.

† Box-office figures tell the tale. In fiscal year 1941–42, six out of twenty-one top-grossing films had had some connection with the war. In 1942–43, 1943–44, 1944–45, 1945–46, and 1946–47, the ratio rose and fell as follows: thirteen out of twenty-four, twelve out of twenty-five, six out of thirty-four, two out of thirty-six, and one (*The Best Years of Our Lives*) out of twenty-six. So strong, in fact, was the national revulsion against the war and all things military that the AAF film unit suppressed many of its own late productions, including John Huston's *Let There Be Light,* which dealt uncompromisingly with the treatment of battle neuroses.

11.20 The crew of a downed bomber are tried for war crimes against the Japanese in *The Purple Heart* (Lewis Milestone, 1944): Dana Andrews, Farley Granger, Sam Jaffe.

11.21 The realities of war: Lewis Milestone's *A Walk in the Sun* (1945): Dana Andrews.

(according to Lewis Jacobs, more than five hundred out of the seventeen hundred films made during this period were directly concerned with Fascism and war[13]). It had even complied with the government's discomfiting request to reduce the length of A-films on double bills to economize on theater lighting—a measure which caused at least one catastrophe for the international cinema when RKO cut Orson Welles' second masterpiece, *The Magnificent Ambersons* (1942), by forty-three minutes and made it the second half of a double bill with the comedy *Mexican Spitfire Sees a Ghost* (see Chapter 10). Nevertheless, Hollywood enjoyed the most profitable four-year period in its history during the war, with weekly attendance estimated at eighty-five million persons (four times the current figure), despite the restrictions imposed upon it by the government and its own errors of judgment about what the public wanted to see. For one thing, all of its combat films were (and, with few exceptions, still are) produced with the "technical assistance" of the armed forces, which can be worth up to 50 percent of a motion picture's budget in free production values* For another, the government had cleverly levied a special war tax on theater tickets in 1942, so that going to the movies

---

* For the purpose of public relations, the American military establishment has traditionally cooperated in helping Hollywood to produce films which glorify the armed forces. The military can help production companies by providing them with free historical and technical research, heavy equipment and armaments, large casts of uniformed extras, and authentic locations for shooting. (It is rumored, for example, that the maneuvers required of the combined services in re-staging the 1944 Allied invasion of Normandy for Twentieth Century–Fox's *The Longest Day* [Ken Annakin and Bernhard Wicki, 1962] were more complicated than those of the actual event and were worth well over one million dollars to the studio.) That this relationship, probably a necessity in war-time, can become corrupt was demonstrated by the 1972 CBS television documentary "The Selling of the Pentagon." It should be noted, though, that an equally close relationship exists between the military establishments and national cinemas of certain Communist countries, where the relationship is mediated

during the war years took on the character of a patriotic act. Full employment and unprecedented prosperity after a decade of economic depression also helped to keep attendance high. (In most industrial centers the theaters stayed open twenty-four hours a day to accommodate shift workers.) But most important of all in determining Hollywood's high war-time profits was the perennial therapeutic function that films assume in periods of social stress. It is almost literally true that, since the inception of the medium, the worst of times for human history have been the best of times for the cinema, even bad cinema, because there is no fantasy realm within our waking experience which renders its make-believe so inescapably and ineluctably real.

The Post-War Boom

For all of these reasons, Hollywood came through the war years with its powerful studio production system and time-tested film genres pretty much intact, making the American the only major national cinema in the West to preserve a direct continuity of tradition with its past after 1945. In Europe—even in Italy—national cinemas had to be entirely rebuilt, which in most cases involved a beneficial process of rejuvenation, and a subsequent influx of new talent and ideas. But Hollywood had survived the war with a mere change of pace, and the industry gave every indication that it intended to march into the post-war period in the same way that it had marched out of the Depression—by avoiding the depiction of any of the unpleasant realities of American life. In 1946 there was much cause for confidence. Hollywood had already resumed its economic domination of the international cinema, because only America was in a material position to provide high-quality films to a world hungry for diversion. Moreover, the domestic audience had reached its highest peak ever, at an estimated one hundred million per week (two-thirds of the population), and the yearly box office receipts of 1.75 billion dollars broke all previous records. Thus, by the end of 1946 it seemed that Hollywood's most lucrative path lay in maintaining the pre-war status quo; but no sooner had the industry charted this course than serious obstacles began to appear.

An eight-month studio union strike in 1945 had led to a 25-percent pay increase for studio personnel in the following year.* Moreover, Hollywood's major overseas market, Great Britain, from which it drew approximately one-quarter of its net income, levied a 75-percent protective tax on all foreign film profits, and this reduced the American industry's

---

by the state rather than by mutual self-interest. Sergei Bondarchuk's eight-hour adaptation of Tolstoi's *War and Peace* (1965–67) involved the entire Red Army in re-staging the Battle of Borodino, as Eisenstein and Pudovkin had used the Soviet armed forces in their epics of the Revolution. (For an excellent historical account of U.S. military influence on the production of American war films, see Lawrence H. Suid, *Guts and Glory: Great American War Movies* [New York, 1978].)

* Many of those active in the strike fell victim to the witch-hunt of the late forties and early fifties (see below).

annual British revenue from sixty-eight million dollars in 1946 to under seventeen million dollars in 1947. Other Commonwealth countries and European nations followed suit (Italy, for example, with the Andreotti Law), and though in some cases Hollywood was able to retaliate successfully with boycotts, the damage was significant. Most disastrous of all from a financial standpoint, however, was the adjudication of the anti-trust suits begun by the federal government against the five major and three minor studios in 1938, resulting in the "Paramount decrees" or "consent decrees" of May 1948. These were court orders which forced the companies to divest themselves of their distribution and exhibition circuits according to a mutually agreed-upon schedule over the next five years.* Most immediately, divestiture meant the end of block booking and of the automatic box office receipts which this practice had created; ultimately, it meant the end of the powerful studio system which had been the shaping force of the American film industry for thirty years. Hollywood was faced with the task of restructuring its entire production and delivery system in the midst of the most severe financial crisis it had experienced since the coming of sound. Even worse was to follow, but at the beginning of 1948 things were bad enough: in the major studios unemployment had risen by 25 percent; the independent B-film production companies Rainbow, Liberty, and Eagle-Lion had failed completely; and Warner Brothers was preparing for a temporary shutdown. As early as 1947, radical economizing had begun. Shooting budgets were cut, and expensive projects like spectacles, costume films, and grade-A musicals were abandoned altogether. Only months after the American film industry's banner year of 1946, Hollywood people were starting to ask themselves how the bubble had burst, unaware that their bad luck had only just begun.

But for a while, at least, the urgent necessity to cut back on production costs had a vitalizing and invigorating effect upon the American cinema. As Charles Higham and Joel Greenberg point out, efficiency became the order of the day.[14] The industry's perpetual obsession with lavish production values temporarily gave way to a new concern for high-quality scripts and pre-planning at every stage of the shooting process to avoid expensive re-takes. For the first time in Hollywood's history, studios gave high priority to projects that could be shot on location with small casts and crews, and the content of films thus took on a greater social and psychological realism than ever before. The influence of the war-time documentary tradition and of Italian neo-realism, which had earned a high reputation among American film-makers by 1947, had a great deal to do with this sudden rejection of escapist subject matter, but much of the

---

*A federal court modified the thirty-two-year-old decision in March 1980 to permit Loew's, Inc., to produce and distribute films once more. The decision was rendered by Judge Edmund L. Palmieri in recognition of the fact that in the present film-industry economy (one in which as few as twenty films can account for 85 percent of the rentals in any given year), "Loew's entry into production and distribution will represent the entry of a new competitor and a probable increase in the supply of successful feature films." (Palmieri, quoted in *Variety*, March 5, 1980.)

credit must go to the cultural impact of the war itself upon the American people.

After the elation of victory had passed, a mood of disillusionment and cynicism came over the nation which had at least as much to do with America's image of itself as with the distant horror of the war abroad. The federal government's war-time propaganda machine, of which Hollywood was the most essential component, had created an image of an ideal America of white picket fences, cozy bungalows, and patiently loyal families and sweethearts—a pure, democratic society in which Jews, Blacks, Italians, Irish, Poles, and WASP farmboys could all live and work together, just as they had done in the ethnically balanced patrol squads of so many war-time combat films. This America, of course, had never existed, but a nation engaged in a global war of survival had an overwhelming need to believe that it did. When the war ended and the troops returned home, however, people began to discover that the basic goodness and decency of American society was more difficult to find than, for example, John Cromwell's slickly directed domestic fantasy *Since You Went Away* (1944) had made it appear—more difficult even than William Wyler's relatively sophisticated *The Best Years of Our Lives* (1946), which dealt with the successful attempts of three returned combat veterans to re-integrate themselves into civilian life, made it seem. Less difficult to locate in post-war America were social inequities and racial prejudices in every part of the country, profiteering in big business, and corruption in state and local government. What is more, many of our "boys"—especially those who had been maimed in defense of their country—came home to discover that they couldn't get jobs, secure loans, or even resume their educations. The film critic and director Paul Schrader has recently suggested that post-war disillusionment was in many ways a delayed reaction to the thirties and to the socio-economic imbalances which had helped to cause the Depression.[15] Whatever the reasons, when the euphoria of victory had passed, America suddenly found itself in worse shape internally than Hollywood or any other element of American society would have dared to suggest during the war.

11.22 Coming home: William Wyler's *The Best Years of Our Lives* (1946). Dana Andrews.

The war was over now, however, and as a result of its self-imposed economies Hollywood had become increasingly dependent upon the talents of individual writers and directors—people whose vision of things was frequently less sanguine than the studio system, under normal circumstances, would permit them to express. But circumstances were not normal for either the industry or the nation, and soon manifestations of America's social malaise began to appear on screens all over the country.

Post-War Genres: "Social-Consciousness" Films and Semi-Documentary Melodramas

The Hollywood films generated by post-war disenchantment with American life were of several basic types.* The least complex were those which dealt melioristically with contemporary social problems and their resolution. Often called "social-consciousness," or "problem," pictures, these films enjoyed a tremendous vogue in the late forties (in 1947, for example, nearly one-third of the films produced in Hollywood had a "problem" content of some sort) and concerned themselves with such subjects as racism, political corruption, and other inequities within our social institutions. In this category, Edward Dmytryk's *Crossfire* (1948), a tersely directed melodrama of murderous anti-Semitism in post-war America, is outstanding for both its thematic candor and its cinematic excellence. Elia Kazan's *Gentleman's Agreement* (1947) provides a much less honest treatment of the same theme, and his *Pinky* (1949), the sentimental tale of a young black woman who tries to pass for white, is even less credible. Nevertheless, 1949 was a good year for films on racial intolerance. Mark Robson's *Home of the Brave* (1949, produced by Stanley Kramer), sympathetically portraying the psychiatric odyssey of a black veteran, initiated what has come to be known as the "Negro cycle" of that year, which included Clarence Brown's restrained and dignified version of William Faulkner's *Intruder in the Dust,* shot on location in Oxford, Mississippi, as well as Alfred Werker's *Lost Boundaries* (produced by the documentarist Louis de Rochemont), which was based on the true story of an ostensibly "white" man's shattering discovery of his black

---

* This, and what follows, is not meant to suggest that the traditional genres faired poorly in post-war Hollywood. On the contrary, the late forties produced major films in every genre except comedy (assuming Chaplin's *Monsieur Verdoux* [1947] and the films of Preston Sturges to be in a class by themselves), including conventional melodrama (Max Ophüls' *Letter from an Unknown Woman* [1948], *Caught* [1949], and *The Reckless Moment* [1949]); fantasy (Frank Capra's *It's a Wonderful Life* [1947], William Dieterle's *Portrait of Jennie* [1949]); horror (Robert Florey's *The Beast with Five Fingers* [1947]); suspense (Hitchcock's *Notorious* [1946]); adventure (Vincent Sherman's *The Adventures of Don Juan* [1949] and Henry King's *Captain from Castile* [1947]); the Western (John Ford's *My Darling Clementine* [1946], King Vidor's *Duel in the Sun* [1946], Howard Hawks' *Red River* [1947], William Wellman's *Yellow Sky* [1948]); the musical (Vincente Minnelli's *The Pirate* [1947]; Gene Kelly's *On the Town* [1949]); and what were known in studio parlance as "women's pictures"—romantic melodramas designed to appeal to female audiences and constructed around a popular female star (John M. Stahl's *Leave Her to Heaven* [1945, Gene Tierney], Edmund Goulding's *The Razor's Edge* [1946, Gene Tierney], Irving Rapper's *Deception* [1946, Bette Davis], Jean Negulesco's *Humoresque* [1947, Joan Crawford]).

11.23 Juano Hernandez in *Intruder in the Dust* (Clarence Brown, 1949).

11.24 Broderick Crawford as Willie Stark in *All the King's Men* (Robert Rossen, 1949).

11.25 *The Lost Weekend* (Billy Wilder, 1945): Ray Milland.

11.26 *The Set-Up* (Robert Wise, 1949): Robert Ryan, down for the count.

parentage. The latter was also shot on location (in Maine and New Hampshire) with a largely non-professional cast. This same technique was practiced in the "problem" cycle's most elaborate exposé of political corruption, Robert Rossen's adaptation of Robert Penn Warren's novel *All the King's Men* (1949), a portrait of an authentic American demagogue based upon the career of Louisiana governor Huey Long. Other social-consciousness films dealt realistically for the first time in Hollywood history with the problems of alcoholism (Billy Wilder's *The Lost Weekend* [1945]; Stuart Heisler's *Smash-Up* [1947]), mental illness (Anatole Litvak's *The Snake Pit* [1948]), juvenile delinquency (Nicholas Ray's *Knock on Any Door* [1949]), prison injustice (Jules Dassin's *Brute Force* [1947]; Crane Wilber's *Cañon City* [1948]), war profiteering (Irving Reis' *All My Sons* [1948]; from the play by Arthur Miller), and the rehabilitation of paraplegic veterans (Fred Zinnemann's *The Men* [1950]). Moreover, though they can scarcely be described as problem pictures, there were several other films of the post-war era which employed various forms of social corruption as metaphors for more serious disorders in the cosmos and in the human soul. Robert Rossen's *Body and Soul* (1947) and Robert Wise's *The Set-Up* (1949), for example, both used corruption in the prize-fighting business and the brutality of the "sport" itself to suggest something about the nature of human evil; while Abraham Polonsky's poetic and Kafkaesque *Force of Evil* (1948) used the numbers racket in New York City to reflect a world collapsing internally from its own rottenness.

Closely related to the problem pictures was a series of semi-documentary crime melodramas which frequently had social overtones. These films were usually based upon true criminal cases and shot on location with as many of the original participants in the cast as it was feasible to assemble. The first was Henry Hathaway's *The House on 92nd Street* (1945), a dramatic re-enactment of an authentic case of domestic espionage based entirely on FBI files and produced for Twentieth Century-

Fox by Louis de Rochemont (1899–1978), creator of the "March of Time" newsreels (1935–43). De Rochemont followed this film with three other semi-documentary productions which gave Fox clear leadership in the field: Hathaway's *13 Rue Madeleine* (1946), a re-creation of OSS* activity in Montreal during the war; Elia Kazan's critically acclaimed *Boomerang!* (1947), based on the true story of a state's attorney who faced the wrath of an entire Connecticut town to clear an accused man of murder; and Hathaway's *Kiss of Death* (1947), an unglamorized account of criminals and cops in New York City's underworld. The outstanding commercial success of these films produced many others using the same formula of a fictionalized story based on fact and shot on location with non-professional actors; Jules Dassin's *Naked City* (1948) is among the best of these (but see also Dassin's *Brute Force* [1947], William Keighley's *The Street with No Name* [1948], Robert Siodmak's *The Killers* [1946], and Anthony Mann's *T-Men* [1948]). In *Naked City,* Dassin used a conventional crime melodrama as the vehicle for an uncompromisingly naturalistic portrait of the brutal and impersonal modern city, much of which was shot by cinematographer William Daniels (1895–1970) in *cinéma vérité* fashion with hidden cameras. After 1948, the semi-documentary melodrama largely degenerated into stereotype, and most critics consider that the final collaboration of Hathaway and De Rochemont, *Call Northside 777* (1948), based on the true case of a Chicago reporter (played by James Stewart) who attempted to clear a Polish-American of a murder charge, was the last important film of its type. Nevertheless, the influence of these motion pictures continued well into the fifties, as the documentary surfaces of fiction films like John Huston's *The Asphalt Jungle* (1950), Elia Kazan's *On the Waterfront* (1954), and Alfred Hitchcock's *The Wrong Man* (1957) attest.

11.27 *Call Northside 777* (Henry Hathaway, 1948): James Stewart.

Post-War Genres: *Film Noir*

For a while, both the problem pictures and the semi-documentary crime thrillers made it seem that Italian neo-realism had found a home in an uneasy, if affluent, America. The critic James Agee wrote in 1947, "One of the best things that is happening in Hollywood is the tendency to move out of the place—to base fictional pictures on fact and, more importantly, to shoot them not in painted studio sets but in actual places."[16] But there was another variety of post-war American film which depended on the controlled environment of the studio as well as upon real locations for its depiction of the seamy underside of American life. This was *film noir* (literally, "black film"), discovered and named by French critics in 1946 when, seeing American motion pictures for the first time since 1940, they perceived a strange new mood of cynicism, darkness, and despair in certain crime films and melodramas. These were films which carried post-war American pessimism to the point of nihilism

---

* The abbreviation for Office of Strategic Services, the American intelligence operation during World War II. The OSS provided the model and much of the personnel for the Central Intelligence Agency (CIA) when it was established in 1947.

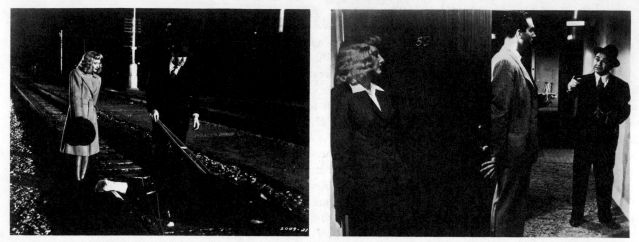

11.28 The prototypical *film noir: Double Indemnity* (Billy Wilder, 1944). Barbara Stanwyck, Fred MacMurray, Edward G. Robinson.

by assuming the absolute and irredeemable corruption of society and of everyone in it. Billy Wilder's corrosive *Double Indemnity* (1944), which startled Hollywood in the year of its release and was almost banned by the Hays Office, may be regarded as the prototype for *film noir,* although some critics trace the origins back to John Huston's tough but considerably less cynical *The Maltese Falcon* (1941).* Adapted by Wilder and Raymond Chandler from a James M. Cain novel, *Double Indemnity* is the sordid story of an insurance agent (Fred MacMurray) seduced by a client's wife (Barbara Stanwyck) into murdering her husband for his death benefits; it has been called "a film without a single trace of pity or love." [17]

Indeed, these are qualities notably absent from all *films noir,* as perhaps they seemed absent from the post-war America which produced them. Like *Double Indemnity,* these films thrived upon the unvarnished depiction of greed, lust, and cruelty because their basic theme was the depth of human depravity and the utterly unheroic nature of human beings—lessons that were hardly taught but certainly re-emphasized by the unique horrors of World War II. Most of the dark films of the late forties take the form of crime melodramas because (as Dostoievski and Dickens knew), the mechanisms of crime and criminal detection provide a perfect metaphor for corruption that cuts across conventional moral categories, and it is precisely this kind of universal corruption with which *film noir* is ultimately concerned. The protagonists of this cinema are all unsympathetic anti-heroes who pursue their base designs or simply drift aimlessly

---

* It is possible, as Paul Schrader has argued ("Notes on *Film Noir,*" *Film Comment,* 8, 1, Spring 1972), that *film noir* would have evolved naturally out of the late thirties and early forties had the war not interrupted its course. But it also seems likely that the anti-heroic vision of *film noir* was generated specifically in response to the actual horrors of the war and the multiple hypocrisies of post-war American society. See James Damico, *"Film Noir: A Modest Proposal,"* and Raymond Borde and Etienne Chaumeton, "The Sources of *Film Noir,*" (trans. Bill Horrigan), both in *Film Reader 3,* ed. Bruce Jenkins et al. (Evanston, Ill. 1978), 48–57, 58–66.

through sinister night-worlds of the urban American jungle,* re-created on the soundstages of Hollywood by the great *noir* cinematographers John Alton, John F. Seitz, Lee Garmes, Tony Gaudio, Sol Polito, Ernest Haller, Lucien Ballard, and James Wong Howe. Moral ambiguity is translated into visual style by these technicians through what has been called "anti-traditional" cinematography.[18] The pervasive use of wide-angle lenses permits greater depth of field but causes expressive distortion in close-ups; low-key lighting and night-for-night shooting (that is, actually shooting night scenes at night rather than in bright daylight with dark filters) both create harsh contrasts between the light and dark areas of the frame, in which the dark predominates, paralleling the moral chaos of the world they represent.

If all of this seems reminiscent of the artificial studio technique of German Expressionism, it should, because—like the Universal horror cycle of the thirties—*film noir* was created to a large extent by German and Eastern European expatriates, many of whom had received their basic training at UFA in the twenties and early thirties. The *noir* directors Fritz Lang, Robert Siodmak, Billy Wilder, Otto Preminger, John Brahm, Anatole Litvak, Max Ophüls, Douglas Sirk, Edgar G. Ulmer, and Curtis Bernhardt; the director-cinematographer Rudolph Maté; the cinematographers Karl Freund and John Alton; and the composers Franz Waxman and Max Steiner had all been associated with or influenced by the UFA studio style. Nevertheless, given its subject matter, *film noir* could scarcely escape the general realistic tendency of the post-war cinema, and *noir* directors frequently shot exteriors on location. For this reason, it has

11.29 *The Blue Dahlia* (George Marshall, 1946): Alan Ladd, Veronica Lake.

11.30 *The Big Heat* (Fritz Lang, 1953): Glenn Ford.

11.31 The image of post-war *angst: In a Lonely Place* (Nicholas Ray, 1950). Humphrey Bogart, Gloria Grahame.

---

* And they are anti-heroes in the most extreme sense of the term: murderous *femmes fatales* (*Double Indemnity;* Tay Garnett's incisive *The Postman Always Rings Twice* [1946]; Orson Welles' darkly brilliant *The Lady from Shanghai* [1948]; Lewis Milestone's *The Strange Loves of Martha Ivers* [1946]; Fritz Lang's two tributes to Renoir, *Scarlet Street* [1945] and *Human Desire* [1954]); down-at-the-heels and/or paranoid private eyes (Howard Hawks' *The Big Sleep* [1946], Edward Dmytryk's *Murder, My Sweet* [1945], George Marshall's *The Blue Dahlia* [1946], Henry Hathaway's *The Dark Corner* [1946], John Brahm's *The Brasher Doubloon* [1947], Jacques Tourneur's *Out of the Past* [1947]); fugitive criminals (Robert Siodmak's *The Killers* [1946] and *Cry of the City* [1948], Gordon Douglas' *Kiss Tomorrow Goodbye* [1950], Nicholas Ray's *They Live by Night* [1949], Delmer Daves' *Dark Passage* [1947]); ruthless con-men (Edmund Goulding's *Nightmare Alley* [1947]; Abraham Polonsky's *Force of Evil* [1949]); two-bit chiselers on the run (Jules Dassin's *Night and the City* [1950]); psychopathic killers (Robert Siodmak's *The Spiral Staircase* [1946] and *The Dark Mirror* [1946], Joseph H. Lewis' *Gun Crazy* [1949], and—quintessentially—Raoul Walsh's *White Heat* [1949]); corrupt, victimized, or simply neurotic cops (Rudolph Mate's *D.O.A.* [1949], Otto Preminger's *Where the Sidewalk Ends* [1950], John Cromwell's *The Racket* [1952], William Wyler's *Detective Story* [1951], Fritz Lang's *The Big Heat* [1953]); and, into the fifties, assorted punks, madmen, mobsters, and degenerates (Billy Wilder's *Ace in the Hole* [1951], Nicholas Ray's *In a Lonely Place* [1950] and *On Dangerous Ground* [1951], Fritz Lang's *Clash by Night* [1952], Otto Preminger's *Angel Face* [1952], Henry Essex's *I the Jury* [1953], Samuel Fuller's *Pickup on South Street* [1953], Joseph H. Lewis' *The Big Combo* [1955], and Robert Aldrich's *noir* masterpiece *Kiss Me Deadly* [1955]). Significantly, many stars of *film noir* (such as Dick Powell, Barbara Stanwyck, Fred MacMurray, John Garfield, Lana Turner, Alan Ladd, Joan Bennett, and Tyrone Power) were playing totally unsympathetic characters for the first time in their careers—playing, that is, against their established box-office images, which added yet another touch of eeriness to the form.

11.32 *The Big Combo* (Joseph H. Lewis, 1955).

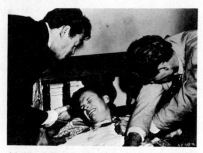

11.33 *Kiss Me Deadly* (Robert Aldrich, 1955): Ralph Meeker.

become fashionable to speak of *film noir* as a type—some believe it is a genre—of "romantic" or "expressive" realism; but its heritage includes such a wide range of cultural forces (the Warner gangster films of the thirties, Sternbergian exoticism and decadence, the poetic realism of Carné and Duvivier, the "hard-boiled" tradition of American fiction, post-war American disillusionment and the wave of cinematic realism it engendered, and, of course, *Citizen Kane*) that it seems better not to characterize it at all lest we delimit its boundaries too rigidly.

Furthermore, as several critics have recently suggested, *film noir* describes a period as well as a style or a genre, for darkness and cynicism invaded *all* genres in the late-forties cinema, not simply that of the crime thriller and melodrama. Raymond Durgnat points out that films as disparate as John M. Stahl's bizarre romance *Leave Her to Heaven* (1945) and King Vidor's epic western *Duel in the Sun* (1946) have distinctly *noir* elements, and there was a whole series of late-forties melodramas which may be said to range from off-black to gray (for example, George Cukor's *Gaslight* [1944], John Brahm's *Hangover Square* [1945], Irving Pichel's *Temptation* [1946], Sam Wood's *Ivy* [1947], Hitchcock's *The Paradine Case* [1948], Lewis Allen's *So Evil My Love* [1948]). In the end, perhaps the most categorical thing we can say about *film noir* is that both thematically and stylistically it represents a unique and highly creative counter-tradition in the American cinema, derived from eclectic sources and motivated by the pervasive existential cynicism of the post-war era. With several significant exceptions (*very* significant—for example, Mervyn LeRoy's *I Am a Fugitive from a Chain Gang* [1932], Fritz Lang's *Fury* [1936] and *You Only Live Once* [1937], Orson Welles' *Citizen Kane* [1941], John Huston's *The Maltese Falcon* [1941]), most American films of the pre-war period—and most American films, for that matter—had been optimistic, affirmative, and generally supportive of the status quo. We have seen, however, that post-war America produced in the problem picture and semi-documentary melodrama a cinema of disillusionment and searching which rejected the epic heroics and callow idealism of the World War II film—but rejected them in fairly conventional terms, always suggesting that the inequities of American society could be resolved through good faith and work. Yet *film noir* rejected all human values as ultimately corrupt and sneered at the prospects for change (perhaps, as some suggest, because the atomic future was too frightening to contemplate). Never before had the American cinema handed down such extreme indictments of American or any other society, and it would not again until the late sixties, when the indictments would be mitigated by libertarian idealism. However briefly, then, *film noir* held up a dark mirror to post-war America and reflected its moral anarchy.* Not surprisingly, a number of important and powerful Americans did not like what they saw.

---

* The revival of the genre in the Watergate era (*The Long Goodbye* [Robert Altman, 1973]; *Chinatown* [Roman Polański, 1974]; *Farewell, My Lovely* [Dick Richards, 1975; a remake of Dmytryk's 1945 *Murder, My Sweet*]; *Night Moves* [Arthur Penn, 1975]) suggests that the reflection has changed little in the past thirty years.

The Witch-Hunt and the Blacklist

Our "cold war" with the Soviet Union began officially in July 1947 when Stalin refused to accept the Marshall Plan for the Soviet Union or any of its satellites (of course, Soviet-American tensions, briefly relaxed during the alliance to defeat Hitler, had been mounting ever since the Bolshevik Revolution). Among other things, this meant that in the public mind the menace of Nazi agents and fifth columnists was replaced by the menace of Communist spies and "fellow travelers," doubly sinister since they looked just like everyone else and didn't speak with an accent. Accordingly, in the spring of 1947 the House Committee on Un-American Activities (HUAC), which had been inactive since the hot war ended, decided to undertake a full-scale investigation of what its chairman, J. Parnell Thomas, called "Communism in motion pictures." As John Howard Lawson, one of the victims of this investigation, later wrote, the charge that American films contained "Communist propaganda" in the late forties or at any other time was wholly laughable, because the American film industry was one of the most conservative elements in the country.[19] There were, however, recent films of predominantly liberal sentiment, such as the problem pictures and the semi-documentary melodramas, and there were the apolitical *films noir,* which did not take a very sanguine view of life under any system of government. There were also all of those pro-Russian films made during the war, when the Soviet Union had been our ally. But most damaging of all, because there was at least factual substance to the charge, there were a number of famous Hollywood directors, screenwriters, and actors who had joined the Communist Party or contributed funds to its cause during the Depression, when it had seemed to offer a viable alternative to starving under capitalism. Some had merely supported causes (such as relief for refugees from Franco's Spain) that also were supported by Communists. Most of these people had dropped their affiliations years before the Committee convened, but it was among their ranks that HUAC was able to do the most damage.*

In September 1947 the tragicomedy began. The Committee summoned twenty so-called friendly witnesses who proved their patriotism by naming people who, they claimed, were Leftists, and generally telling the congressmen what they wanted to hear ("Hollywood," claimed the Right-wing actor Adolphe Menjou, "is one of the main centers of Communist activity in America"). On the strength of this cooperative testimony, some forty film-makers suspected of Leftist sympathies were subpoenaed to appear before HUAC in late October, including "ten prominent figures in Hollywood whom the Committee had evidence were members of the Communist Party"[20] (among them the screenwriters Alvah Bessie, Lester Cole, Ring Lardner, Jr., John Howard Lawson, Albert Maltz, Samuel Ornitz, Adrian Scott, and Dalton

---

* On the true nature of Communist activity and influence within the American film industry, see Larry Ceplair and Steven Englund, *The Inquisition in Hollywood: Politics in the Film Community, 1930–1960* (Garden City, N.Y., 1980).

11.34 Subpoenaed film-makers leaving the HUAC hearing-room in October 1947; ten would soon go to jail for contempt of Congress. Left to right: (front row) Lewis Milestone, Dalton Trumbo, John Howard Lawson, and attorney Bartley Crum; (center row) Gordon Kahn, Irving Pichel, Edward Dmytryk, and Robert Rossen; (back row) Waldo Salt, Richard Collins, Howard Koch, Albert Maltz, Herbert Biberman, Lester Cole, Ring Lardner, Jr., and attorney Martin Popper.

Trumbo, and the directors Herbert Biberman and Edward Dmytryk). Hollywood liberals responded by forming the Committee for the First Amendment to fight for the constitutional rights of the "accused witnesses" (a contradiction in the terms of jurisprudence, if there ever was one), but opposition collapsed when the now-famous "Hollywood Ten" listed above defied HUAC by refusing to testify and were given prison sentences of six months to a year for contempt of Congress.* The Committee's action was scandalous, but its meaning was crystal clear: HUAC wished to purge Hollywood and, if possible, the entire country of any and all liberal tendencies by creating and then exploiting anti-Communist hysteria. The threat of state censorship loomed, and panic broke out in the nation's most image-conscious industry, which was already plagued by anti-trust actions, unemployment, and rapidly declining profits.

On November 24, 1947, Hollywood closed ranks against some of the most talented artists it had ever known when the fifty members of the Association of Motion Picture Producers† (including Eric Johnston,

---

* Since the hearings were not a court of law, "unfriendly" witnesses were not allowed to be accompanied by their lawyers or to examine other witnesses. The Ten tried to read prepared statements but were silenced. When questioned about their own activities and beliefs—and those of their friends and casual acquaintances—they refused to answer (Ring Lardner, Jr., quipped: "I could answer that question, but I would hate myself in the morning"), invoking their rights under the First and Fifth Amendments to the U.S. Constitution. The double-bind they faced was that if they answered even one question they admitted the Committee's right to question them at all, and a refusal to answer any further questions would open them to a charge of contempt. If, on the other hand, they refused to answer a single question (the course they chose), they were also liable to be charged with contempt. After the appellate process had been exhausted, the Ten served their sentences in 1949—along with the chairman of the Committee, who had, in the interim, been convicted of mishandling public funds. See Ceplair and Englund (cited above), and Victor S. Navasky, *Naming Names* (New York, 1980).

†The business and public relations component of the Motion Picture Association of America (MPAA), now the Association of Motion Picture and Television Producers (AMPTP). Among other functions, the AMPTP negotiates labor contracts for its members and maintains Central Casting Corporation as a means of supplying extras.

Nicholas M. Schenck, Harry Cohn, Joseph M. Schenck, Walter Wanger, Samuel Goldwyn, Henry Ginsberg, Albert Warner, Louis B. Mayer, Dore Schary, Spyros Skouras, and William Goetz) published the "Waldorf Declaration" supporting HUAC, denouncing and firing the ten "un-friendly" witnesses, and refusing to re-employ any one of them "until such time as he has purged himself of contempt and declares under oath that he is not a Communist." This was the beginning of the infamous practice of blacklisting, which brought to an end one of the most creative periods in the history of American film and made Hollywood a wasteland of vapidity, complacency, and cowardice for well over a decade. Between 1947 and 1951, hundreds of persons were called before the Committee and impugned upon the slenderest of evidence. The industry put tremen-dous pressure on these people to "come clean"—a process of self-abasement which involved denouncing one's friends (even if they had al-ready been denounced by previous witnesses), confessing one's own guilt by association, and groveling not only before HUAC but before any number of self-appointed Grand Inquisitors in the private sector, such as the American Legion and American Business Consultants, editors of the scurrilous public blacklists *Counterattack* and *Red Channels*.

Some refused to cringe, and at the end of the process in 1951 (which was resumed when Senator Pat McCarran's Internal Security Subcom-mittee re-opened the hearings in 1952, subpoenaing Judy Holiday, Burl Ives, and others), 324 persons had been fired by the studios and were no longer permitted to work in the American film industry. Among them were some of the most talented directors, writers, and actors of the post-war cinema: Joseph Losey (*The Lawless* [1950]), Jules Dassin (*Naked City* [1948]), Abraham Polonsky (*Force of Evil* [1948]), and Herbert Biberman (*The Master Race* [1944]); Carl Foreman, Gordon Kahn, Howard Koch, Sidney Buchman, Ring Larner, Jr., John Howard Law-son, Dalton Trumbo, Lester Cole, Richard Collins, Samuel Ornitz, Adrian Scott, and Waldo Salt; Gale Sondergaard, Karen Morley, Zero Mostel, Lionel Stander, Anne Revere, Larry Parks, Paul Muni, John Gar-field, Jeff Corey, Will Geer, Howard Da Silva, and others.

Some of the writers were able to make a living by selling their scripts on the black market under the names of real people, or "fronts." * (The 1956 Academy Award for the Best Original Screenplay, for ex-ample, went to a mysterious "Mr. Robert Rich" for Irving Rapper's *The Brave One*—the Oscar has never been picked up because Rich was actually Dalton Trumbo.) But the highly visible actors and directors were doomed to unemployment or exile (Muni; Losey and Dassin). Some lost their lives: Philip Loeb, one of the stars of the popular television series *The Goldbergs,* committed suicide; the screen actors John Gar-field, Canada Lee, J. Edward Bromberg, and Mady Christians died as a result of the stress they were subjected to. Hundreds of other film people were maligned by HUAC but managed to survive under the cloud of ei-ther marginal blacklisting (Lewis Milestone, Fredric March, Edward G.

---

* As in *The Front* (Martin Ritt, 1976), a film about television blacklisting made by a for merly blacklisted writer, director, and producer, with Woody Allen in the title role.

Robinson) or their own collaboration with the investigating body (Elia Kazan, Clifford Odets, Lee J. Cobb, Sterling Hayden, and, ultimately, Edward Dmytryk and Robert Rossen). For many in the latter category, the moral catastrophe of informing proved as destructive as the practical effects of being blacklisted, and few of them went on to equal their work of the immediate post-war period.

The practice of blacklisting in the American film industry continued well into the fifties, and its impact was felt throughout the sixties.* Abraham Polonsky, for example, was not able to direct again in Hollywood until 1968, when his *Tell Them Willie Boy Is Here* appeared—twenty-one years after *Force of Evil.* But as damaging to the American cinema as the loss of individual talent was the pervasive mood of fear, distrust, and self-loathing that settled over Hollywood in the wake of the hearings. Everyone was scared of the government and of everyone else, and the industry tacitly imposed a form of self-censorship more repressive and sterile than anything HUAC could have devised. As early as 1948, William Wyler speculated that a modestly progressive film like his own *The Best Years of Our Lives* (1946) could not be made in America again, adding, "In a few months we won't be able to have a heavy who is an American." Wyler was right. No one in Hollywood was willing to take the slightest chance on anybody or anything; the industry had had its fill of trouble and wanted no more of it. Safety, caution, and respectability were the watchwords of the studio chiefs, and controversial or even serious subject matter was to be avoided at all costs. Thus, vitiated, frightened, and drained of creative vitality, Hollywood experienced in miniature what the whole of American society was to experience during the McCarthy-era witch-hunts—intellectual stagnation and moral paralysis.

The Arrival of Television

Finally, as if the devastating impact of the hearings were not enough to sink Hollywood's already foundering ship, a new entertainment medium suddenly emerged which threatened to do the job all by itself. This, of course, was television—a system for transmitting moving images based upon the process of electronic image analysis and synthesis.† Perfected in America in the mid-thirties, television was quickly bought up by the major radio networks, NBC and CBS, which began telecasting on a commercial basis (about fifteen hours per week) in July 1941. Hollywood didn't pay much attention to its potential new rival then because wartime restrictions soon put a halt to the manufacture of television trans-

---

* In the American theater, blacklisting continued until the late fifties. In radio and television, it did not end until the mid-sixties.

† In this process, simply put, the image to be transmitted is broken down into 100,000 to 200,000 "bits" of discrete audio-visual information, or "picture elements," by a camera tube; these are broadcast as FM electronic signals to video receivers where they are resynthesized as images by picture tubes. (See note, p. 644.)

mission equipment and receivers, and the networks were forced to sharply curtail their telecasts. When the war ended, however, regular daily telecasting was resumed, and the production of transmitters and receivers burgeoned on a large scale. By 1949 there were one million TV sets in use in the United States, and the television broadcasting industry had begun in earnest. Only two years later, there were ten times that many sets in use, and by 1959 the number had risen to fifty million. In 1946, when two-thirds of the total population of the country went to the movies weekly, attendance had been guaranteed by the nearly complete lack of alternate sources of audio-visual entertainment. Now that lack was met with a vengeance.*

At first, Hollywood attempted to diminish the entertainment value of its competitor by barring its films and its stars from television appearances, but this simply stimulated the new medium to develop narrative programs and star personalities on its own, and by 1949 the American film industry was seriously threatened by television. In that year, attendance dropped to seventy million, from ninety million in 1948, and it continued to decline in direct proportion to the number of television sets in use. In the first quarter of 1949, only twenty-two features, or half the normal number, were in production in Hollywood, and by the end of the year the major studios were ordering large layoffs and salary reductions, star contracts were being permitted to lapse, and all over the country the great movie palaces had begun to close their doors. In the

11.35 As the fifties begin, America's dream palaces succumb to television.

wake of three years of unprecedented bad luck, a spiritual torpor descended upon Hollywood (some critics have speculated that the most manic of the late *films noir* are unconscious reflections of this malaise). From the pinnacle of its creative and commercial power in 1946–47, the American cinema, assisted by labor disputes, anti-trust actions, political investigations, and television, had been brought very low indeed, and in 1949 many people took it for granted that Hollywood could never recover its losses. But those who predicted the demise of Hollywood overlooked the American film industry's most quintessential feature: its nearly protean capacity for adaption. Though Hollywood was never to recover its immediate post-war status or to recapture its once vast audiences from television, in the decade of the fifties it adapted, counterattacked, and—as always (to date, at least)—survived.

---

* For a challenging counter-argument, see Michael Pye and Lynda Myles, *The Movie Brats: How the Film Generation Took Over Hollywood* (New York, 1979). The authors maintain that it was neither the rapid growth of television nor the divestiture orders of 1948 which caused the steady decline in film attendance and the crumbling of the studio system throughout the late forties and fifties, but rather a basic change in the organization of American society in the years following World War II. As Americans turned from the business of war to a preoccupation with home and *suburban* family life, they argue, the solitary and *urban*-centered experience of attending theatrical motion pictures gave way to forms of entertainment—such as spectator sports, recreational travel, and, of course, watching television—more symbolic of community and family. Whatever the case, one thing is clear: in 1946, 20 percent of every dollar spent on recreation in the U.S. went for motion-picture entertainment; by 1950, the figure had dropped to 12 percent; in 1974, it accounted for less than 4 percent.

THE CONVERSION TO COLOR

Television threatened Hollywood with a new technology, and Hollywood fought back in kind by isolating the technological advantages which film possessed over television, and exploiting them. The cinema had two such advantages in the early fifties—the vast size of its images, and the capacity to produce them in color. (Soon, the capacity for stereophonic sound would also be added to the list.) It was the competition with television that resulted in Hollywood's rapid conversion from black-and-white to color production between 1952 and 1955. In 1947, only 12 percent of American feature films were made in color; by 1954 the figure had risen to over 50 percent.* The changeover was made possible largely through a 1950 federal anti-trust decree which broke up the Technicolor Corporation's monopoly on color cinematography and ordered it to release its basic patents to all producers. When this occurred, new color systems were developed rapidly, facilitated by the war-time development of a new type of color film stock called "integral tripak" (the Nazis' Agfacolor, used by Eisenstein to shoot the color sequence in *Ivan the Terrible, Part II,* was the predecessor of tripak). Like Technicolor, tripak used a three-color subtractive process, but it eliminated the need for separate negatives by containing its three layers of color dye within the same emulsion and "coupling" them in the developing process, which in turn eliminated the necessity of using special color cameras. By 1952, the Eastman Kodak Corporation had developed the Eastmancolor system, a dye-coupler printing process which featured a low-cost negative

---

* Ironically, color production declined to about 25 percent of the total between 1955 and 1958, when Hollywood began to sell recent features to television and created an important second market for its theatrical films. At this point, using black-and-white became an effective way to cut production costs (at least for the television market), since almost all television broadcasts of the day were in black-and-white. But as American television converted to full-color broadcasting between 1965 and 1970, color films became an attraction for both the theatrical *and* the television market, causing Hollywood color production to increase dramatically until it had reached 94 percent of the total by 1970. See Gorham A. Kindem, "Hollywood's Conversion to Color: The Technological, Economic, and Aesthetic Factors," *Journal of the University Film Association,* 31, 2 (Spring 1979), 29–36. See also Edward Branigan, "Color and Cinema: Problems in the Writing of History," *Film Reader 4,* ed. Blaine Allan et al. (Evanston, Ill., 1979), 16–33.

tripak stock capable of seemingly excellent color contrast.* Though the system has since come to be known by the trade names of the studios who pay to use it (Warnercolor, Metrocolor, Pathécolor) or the labs that do the processing (Movielab, Technicolor, Deluxe), it was Kodak Eastmancolor which inaugurated and sustained the full-color age with dye-coupler printing, and by 1975 even the Technicolor Corporation had converted to an Eastman-based process.† Since the fifties, color has become an infinitely more subtle medium than black-and-white, and color cinematography has today reached an unparalleled degree of sophistication. By 1979, 96 percent of all American feature films were being made in color.

WIDESCREEN

Multiple-Camera Widescreen Cinerama

In a simultaneous attempt to exploit the *size* of the screen image, Hollywood began to experiment with new optical systems that lent the image greater width and depth. The earliest of the new formats was a multiple-camera widescreen process called Cinerama, introduced in September 1952, which was adapted from the Polyvision process Abel Gance had invented for *Napoléon* (1927) some twenty-five years before. In Cinerama, three synchronized 35mm cameras linked together in an arc would simultaneously record a wide-field image, which three similarly linked projectors would later cast upon a vast "wrap-around" screen

---

* For a detailed account of these events, focusing on the French film industry, see Dudley Andrew, "The Postwar Struggle for Color," *Cinema Journal,* 18, 2 (Spring 1979), 41–52.

† The problem with the Eastman-based systems, unforeseen at the time of their introduction and not manifest until a decade after, is that dye-coupling produces color much less stable (i.e., more subject to fading) than Technicolor's older imbibition process. (Ironically, the only Technicolor imbibition printing plant in operation in the world today is in the People's Republic of China.) While all color prints are subject to fading, most color films and negatives made in dye-coupler processes—that is, most American films made between 1955 and the present—are in imminent danger of extinction, and preserving them is the number-one problem facing film archivists today. Depending on how it is processed, a color print may have a lifetime as short as five years (dye-coupling, at its worst) or as long as forty (imbibition). Preservation is possible through black-and-white separations but is prohibitively expensive (twenty-five thousand to thirty-five thousand dollars per feature); cold storage is effective but impractical. Nevertheless, a new technique invented by Dr. Charles S. Ih at the University of Delaware in 1977 promises nearly perfect preservation through holography, or lensless photography. Using laser beams at three different wavelengths, the process superimposes the red, green, and blue color elements on a single black-and-white film strip. Since the ratio between the three different wavelengths is established when the hologram is made, the original color can always be duplicated from the black-and-white print. For long-term preservation, the hologram could even be imprinted on metal. (See Dr. Charles S. Ih, "Holographic Process for Color Motion Picture Preservation," *Society of Motion Picture and Television Engineers Journal,* 87, 2 [December 1978]). Other hope springs from the Ciba-Geigy Company and from Eastman Kodak itself, both of which are experimenting with new color stocks whose dye stability exceeds that of Technicolor imbibition prints by many times. (See Bill O'Connell, "Fade Out," *Film Comment,* 15, 5 [September–October 1979], 11–18; and Paul C. Spehr, "Fading, Fading, Faded: The Color Film Crisis," *American Film* [November 1979], 56–61.)

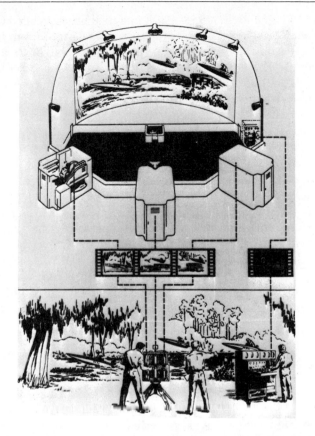

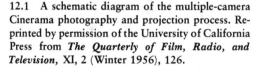

12.1 A schematic diagram of the multiple-camera Cinerama photography and projection process. Reprinted by permission of the University of California Press from *The Quarterly of Film, Radio, and Television*, XI, 2 (Winter 1956), 126.

(actually a three-screen triptych). The projected image was thus three times as wide as the standard 35mm image; it was also nearly twice as tall because of two extra sprocket holes (six instead of four) per frame on the film strip. The seams between the three images were concealed by a slight overlapping of the camera lenses and by floating metal combs in the projectors, which never proved wholly satisfactory. Nevertheless, the Cinerama image was six times the standard size, and its curvilinear shape added the phenomenon of peripheral vision to the screen. Cinerama also surrounded its audience with six-track stereophonic sound, recorded magnetically rather than optically, which permitted a directional use of sound appropriate to its sprawling image. All these factors combined to create an illusion of depth and spectator involvement which was quite thrilling to audiences accustomed to the flat rectilinear screen of decades past, and for a time Cinerama became immensely popular.

But the process was cumbersome and very expensive for both filmmaker and exhibitor, and, therefore, for the paying public. Only theaters in large cities could afford to install the complicated projection equipment and the huge three-panel screens (the installation cost seventy-five thousand dollars), and so it was as a costly urban novelty that Cinerama enjoyed its initial success. Accordingly, it offered its audiences circus rather than narrative. Films like *This Is Cinerama* (1952), *Cinerama Holiday* (1955), *Search for Paradise* (1957), *Cinerama South Seas Adventure*

(1958), and *Windjammer* (1958—shot in a rival process called Cinemiracle, which had been bought out by the Cinerama Corporation) featured a succession of wild rides, extravagant spectacles, and exotic travelogues, but no stories. The first story films made in Cinerama, *How the West Was Won* (1962) and *The Wonderful World of the Brothers Grimm* (1962), proved that the multiple-camera process was simply too clumsy and costly for the production of narratives. *How the West Was Won,* for example, required the services of three directors (John Ford, Henry Hathaway, and George Marshall) and four cinematographers, and cost over fourteen million dollars to shoot.

In 1963, driven by economic necessity, Cinerama switched to a wide-film widescreen system (Ultra Panavision) of the type described below, keeping its deeply curved screen. Given its great expense and peculiar technology, multiple-camera Cinerama never really had a chance of becoming a widely used process. At the height of its popularity, only a hundred cities all over the world were equipped to show Cinerama films. But the astounding success of Cinerama in the early fifties was the catalyst which started the widescreen revolution and brought audiences back into the theaters again in large numbers for the first time since 1946. For this reason alone, Cinerama holds a special place in the history of film.

Depth: Stereoscopic 3-D

Hollywood's next experiment with new optical formats was considerably less successful. In 1953, a three-dimensional stereoscopic process which had been used in films as early as 1930 (for example, George Seitz's *Danger Lights*) was revived, revamped, and marketed to novelty-hungry producers. In it, two interlocked cameras whose lenses were positioned to approximate the distance between the human eyes recorded a scene on two separate negatives. (Later in the year, a system which recorded the images on two layers of a single film strip was evolved.) In the theater, the two positive prints were projected onto the screen simultaneously from the same angles as the camera lenses, and spectators wearing disposable glasses with polarized lenses would perceive them as a single three-dimensional image.* The system, dubbed Natural Vision, was introduced in Arch Oboler's highly successful jungle adventure *Bwana Devil* in November 1952. The studios were so impressed that most of them rushed into 3-D production, using either Natural Vision or some older version of the process. As Arthur Knight points out, the great appeal of Natural Vision for Hollywood was that it required no large-scale conversion of existing equipment, as did Cinerama, but only the addition of a twin-lens Natural Vision camera.[1] Similarly, the cost of projector installation to exhibitors was less than two thousand dollars, a bargain compared with Cinerama's seventy-five thousand dollars. So, between 1953 and 1954 Hollywood produced sixty-nine features in 3-D, mostly

---

* In stereoscopy, as in reality, depth perception is a function of the brain's ability to combine the separate optical perspectives of our eyes into a single image. See Michael Kerbel, "3-D or Not 3-D," *Film Comment,* 16, 6 (November–December 1980), 11–20.

12.2   A contemporary advertisement for *Kiss Me Kate* (George Sidney, 1953), giving a fanciful impression of 3-D illusion: Howard Keel, Ann Miller, Kathryn Grayson.

12.3   A 1953 audience wearing 3-D glasses.

action films which could exploit the depth illusion—Westerns like *Charge at Feather River* (Gordon Douglas, 1953) and *Hondo* (John Farrow, 1953), science-fiction films like *It Came from Outer Space* (Jack Arnold, 1953) and *The Creature from the Black Lagoon* (Jack Arnold, 1953), and horror films like *House of Wax* (André de Toth, 1953) and *Phantom of the Rue Morgue* (Roy del Ruth, 1954). Two high-quality productions, George Sidney's *Kiss Me Kate* (1953) and Alfred Hitchcock's *Dial M for Murder* (1954), were shot in 3-D in late 1953 but released flat in 1954, by which time the craze had completely run its course and Natural Vision was, in the Hollywood phrase, "box-office poison." The 3-D process died largely because producers found it impossible to make serious films in such a gimmicky process. Most of the 3-D films of 1953–54 were blatant attempts to exploit the illusion of stereoscopic depth by having animals leap and people hurl objects into the Natural Vision camera lens. Another problem was that the illusion of depth created by 3-D was not particularly authentic or satisfying, because the planes of depth within the image were highly stratified. Things appeared not in the round, as they do in a hologram,* but as a series of stratified two-dimensional planes. In fact, deep-focus widescreen photography is actually capable of producing a greater illusion of depth than stereoscopic 3-D. Finally, people disliked wearing the polarized glasses necessary to achieve the 3-D effect; many complained of eye strain and headaches. Various attempts to revive stereoscopic 3-D in the last two decades have been fruitless, but the notion of an authentically three-dimensional cinema continues to fascinate both film-makers and audiences, as recent studio experiments with holography indicate. (*Logan's Run* [Michael Anderson, 1976] and *Star Wars* [George Lucas, 1977] both contained brief sequences using holographic photography.)

---

* An image produced through holography—a new process of photography which uses lasers to create perfect three-dimensional facsimiles of the objects photographed.

12.4 Cinemascope: *The Robe* (Henry Koster, 1953): Richard Burton and foe.

12.5 When "unsqueezed" in projection, this close shot of Marilyn Monroe in Fox's Cinemascope production of *How to Marry a Millionaire* (Jean Negulesco, 1953) reveals distortion and lots of wasted space.

The Anamorphic Widescreen Processes

The new optical format that came to stay during the war with television was Cinemascope, which arrived in September 1953 with Twentieth Century–Fox's Biblical epic *The Robe* (Henry Koster). This system was based upon the anamorphic distorting lens invented by Dr. Henri Chrétian (1879–1956) for tank periscopes during World War I and first used in film as early as 1928 (in Claude Autant-Lara's *Pour construire un feu*). In it, a wide-field image is "squeezed," or condensed, by distortion onto conventional 35mm film stock and redeemed as a widescreen image by a compensating lens in projection. The conventional *aspect ratio* of the cinema screen (the ratio of width to height), known as the "Academy aperture," had been standardized at 4:3, or 1.33:1, in 1932 by the Academy of Motion Picture Arts and Sciences.* Cinemascope offered a radically new ratio of 2.55:1 (approximately 8:3), which gave the screen image a broadly oblong shape like that of Cinerama, without the enhanced peripheral vision made possible by its somewhat larger image and its curved screen. The process also featured four-track stereophonic sound. Cinemascope had the distinct advantage that it required no special cameras, film stock, or projectors, only special lenses and a wide screen available to exhibitors in a package costing less than twenty thousand dollars. Its initial disadvantages were certain distortions of focus and composition caused by the early Bausch and Lomb Cinemascope lenses. Textures could become grainy and colors indistinct through the blowing-up process, and spatial distortion in close-ups was common. Nevertheless, Cinemascope brought the widescreen revolution to the everyday world of functional film-making because, unlike Cinerama and 3-D, it was cheap, flexible, and simple enough to be used on a regular basis in the commercial cinema.

Most important, the public adored it. *The Robe* was an indifferent DeMille-like spectacle, but its box office receipts of over seventeen million dollars in the year of its release made it the third most lucrative production in the history of American film, after *The Birth of a Nation* (1915) and *Gone with the Wind* (1939). In the next year, the anamorphic process took Hollywood by storm as Fox agreed to lease its Cinemascope lenses to rival production companies. (Fox insisted that all Cinemascope productions be shot in full color and four-track stereo—conditions which it later relaxed.)†

By mid-1954, every studio in Hollywood except Paramount had adopted some form of the Cinemascope process (often under a different trade name—for example, Warnerscope and Vistarama), seventy-five full-color anamorphic features were in production, and five thousand

---

* This was done to achieve a uniform international standard for the gauge of sound film, although in practice most films had conformed to the 4:3 ratio since the early 1890s, when Edison standardized the width of theatrical film at 35 mm.

† For an informative account of the introduction of Cinemascope, plus an annotated filmography of every Fox production shot in the process, see Derek J. Southall, "Twentieth Century–Fox Presents a Cinemascope Picture," *Focus on Film*, 31, pp. 8–26, 47.

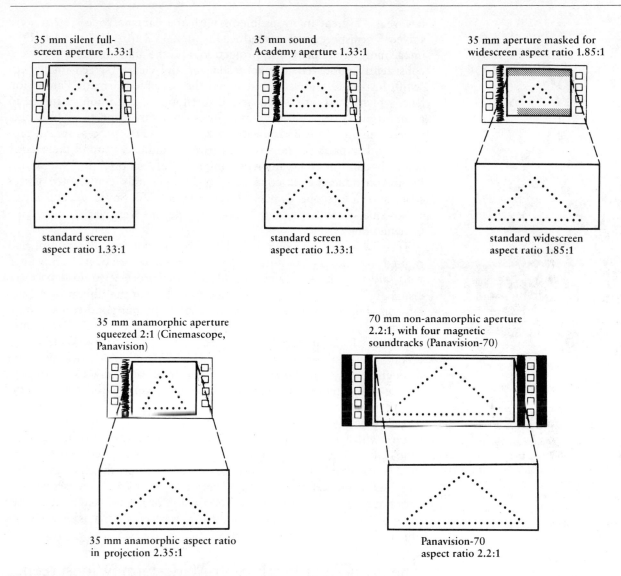

35 mm silent full-
screen aperture 1.33:1

35 mm sound
Academy aperture 1.33:1

35 mm aperture masked for
widescreen aspect ratio 1.85:1

standard screen
aspect ratio 1.33:1

standard screen
aspect ratio 1.33:1

standard widescreen
aspect ratio 1.85:1

35 mm anamorphic aperture
squeezed 2:1 (Cinemascope,
Panavision)

70 mm non-anamorphic aperture
2.2:1, with four magnetic
soundtracks (Panavision-70)

35 mm anamorphic aspect ratio
in projection 2.35:1

Panavision-70
aspect ratio 2.2:1

12.6   A schematic diagram of standard film gauges and screen aspect ratios for silent, sound, and widescreen cinema.

theater installations had been performed. A year later, the latter figure had quadrupled, and the widescreen look had become so popular that films still shot in the old ratio of 1.33:1 were "cropped" for exhibition—that is, their tops and bottoms were masked in projection and the image was cast over a wider area of the screen, which was ultimately standardized at 1.85:1. (This unfortunate practice forced directors working in the old format or, later, in VistaVision to compose their shots "loose," so that action would be kept away from the top and bottom of the frame. Many directors today, painfully conscious that their widescreen films will eventually appear on television screens whose shape was modeled on the Academy frame, attempt to keep significant action in the mid-frame, "TV-safe," area, which imposes similar artistic constraints.) In the next few years, a great many problems with the Cinemascope system were solved. The aspect ratio was reduced from 2.55:1 to 2.35:1 to permit the image more visual density in projection, and the anamorphic lenses were consistently improved to give a sharper and clearer screen image. (In 1960, Robert E. Gottschalk invented the variable prismatic Panavision lens, which today offers a nearly distortion-free definition of image to anamorphic systems.) By the mid-fifties, the conversion to anamorphic widescreen films in America was nearly total, and the process spread rapidly to other parts of the world as foreign audiences found themselves suddenly confronted by a bewildering array of "scopes." In 1956 alone, France introduced Franscope and Dyaliscope, Italy contributed Ultrascope and Colorscope, Sweden Agascope, the USSR Sovscope, and Japan Tohoscope, Daieiscope, and Nikkatsuscope; all were variations of the Cinemascope system.

There was a single holdout in Hollywood, however. Paramount had refused to adopt an anamorphic process on the advice of its technicians, who said that the squeezing and blowing-up process would debase the visual quality of the image. They also thought that the ribbon-like Cinemascope image was too long and narrow to permit good composition. Accordingly, in 1954, in *White Christmas* (Michael Curtiz), Paramount introduced its own widescreen system, called VistaVision. This was a unique non-anamorphic process in which 35mm film stock was run through the camera *horizontally* rather than vertically to produce a double-frame image (eight sprocket holes per frame) twice as wide as the conventional 35mm frame, and slightly taller. The positive print could be projected horizontally with special equipment to cast a huge image on the screen, which Paramount recommended masking down to the "golden ratio" of 1.85:1, or the print could be anamorphically reduced for standard (vertical) 35 mm projection. In either case, it produced large images of a clarity and definition much superior to those of Cinemascope, and Paramount continued to use the VistaVision process throughout the decade. In 1961, the studio converted to the perfected Panavision anamorphic process for financial reasons.

12.7 Though cropped by the studio for publicity distribution, this still from the VistaVision production *To Catch a Thief* (Alfred Hitchcock, 1955) illustrates the crisp resolution which the Paramount process was capable of achieving on nearly every plane of depth: Cary Grant, Grace Kelly.

The Non-Anamorphic, or Wide-Film Widescreen, Processes

As theater screens grew increasingly large in response to public demand (many measuring three to four times their original size), one of the reasons for Paramount's dissatisfaction with Cinemascope became apparent. The anamorphic image cast on a sixty-by-thirty-foot screen lost clarity and brightness because its visual information was distributed across too large a field through the magnification process. The only technical answer to this problem was to increase the actual width of the film stock itself so that it would correspond to the wide field of the camera lens. Then the visual information from the photographic field and the visual information recorded on the negative film stock would be approximately proportional in scale, and the positive print would reproduce the density of the photographic field in projection. But the introduction of wide-gauge film would require special wide-gauge projectors, and the studios were loath to force another expensive conversion upon the exhibitors, with whom relations had become increasingly strained since the "Paramount decrees" of 1948 (see Chapter 11). One way to meet the problem was to shoot a wide-film negative and reduce it photographically to 35mm for projection, which would increase the visual density of the image without altering its shape. This was the method used most often by VistaVision and Fox's experimental wide-film process, Cinemascope 55.

Nevertheless, in 1955 a 70mm* wide-film process was introduced to selected American theaters in a film version of the Rodgers and Hammerstein stage hit *Oklahoma!* (Fred Zinnemann), independently produced by Michael Todd (1907–58). The process, called Todd-AO, was developed by the American Optical Company and designed to compete not only with Cinemascope but with Cinerama as well, since its wide-gauge film and wide-angle lenses offered the "wrap-around" visual coverage of that process without resorting to its multiple cameras and projectors. Todd-AO proved to be a beautifully precise optical system, and *Oklahoma!*, which also featured seven-track stereophonic sound, was a huge financial success. Todd produced two more blockbusters using the process—the elephantine *Around the World in Eighty Days* (Michael Anderson, 1956) and the spectacularly garish *South Pacific* (Joshua Logan, 1957)—before his death in a plane crash in 1958. Fox purchased the rights to the system at that time and has produced eight films in Todd-AO since, including the multi-million-dollar *Cleopatra* (1963) and *The Sound of Music* (1965).

12.8 Todd-AO: *Oklahoma!* (Fred Zinneman, 1955). Gordon MacRae.

Other fine wide-film systems were evolved simultaneously with Todd-AO—Panavision-70, for example, and the Technicolor Corporation's Technirama-70—but all of them were subject to the same severe limitations as Todd's process. Wide-film cameras are bulky (at least twice the normal size) and difficult to move, especially since wide-angle lenses are subject to distortion in panning. And, like Cinerama, the wide-film processes are very expensive to use; film stock, shooting, processing, exhibition—everything—costs about twice as much as it would in a conventional 35mm film. For these reasons, the wide-film systems and Cinerama in the past few decades have been used almost solely for spectacular productions like *Spartacus* (Stanley Kubrick, 1960), *El Cid* (Anthony Mann, 1961), *Lawrence of Arabia* (David Lean, 1962), *Dr. Zhivago* (David Lean, 1965), *Grand Prix* (John Frankenheimer, 1966), and *2001: A Space Odyssey* (Stanley Kubrick, 1968), which can be "roadshown"—toured from city to city for exclusive engagements at inflated admission prices to recoup high production costs. Wide-film systems continue to provide the most optically flawless widescreen image, but today the vast majority of widescreen films—which is to say the vast majority of films—are made in an anamorphic process.

An important footnote to the coming of the widescreen processes is that it produced a nearly total conversion from optical to magnetic sound

---

* Sixty-five millimeters were used for the image and five millimeters for the magnetic stereophonic soundtrack.

recording (though sound was still played back optically in exhibition). As already noted, most early widescreen films—whatever their process— were accompanied by multiple-track stereophonic sound recorded magnetically on the film strip. Multiple-track stereo not only inundated the audience with realistic sound but allowed early widescreen filmmakers to use sound *directionally* by having dialogue and naturalistic effects emanate from that portion of the huge screen appropriate to the image at a given moment. Thus, stereophonic sound permitted a director to differentiate aurally what was undifferentiated visually within the vast space of the early widescreen frame. Most theaters outside of large cities could not afford the conversion to stereophonic speaker systems in the fifties, and many still use optical playback equipment. But after the widescreen revolution, magnetic sound become the preferred means of recording and mixing in all segments of the industry because of its flexibility, its accuracy, and the compactness of its equipment. By the late seventies, the use of a wireless eight-track recording system which employs miniature radio microphones and the non-magnetic stereo-optical Dolby noise reduction system (see Glossary) for playback in exhibition was increasingly common.

Adjusting to Widescreen

The advent of the widescreen processes in many ways parallels the introduction of sound. Once again, a financially troubled industry had gambled on a novelty long implicit in the medium, and once again the novelty produced a technological and aesthetic revolution which changed the narrative form of the cinema. As with sound, the new technology of widescreen photography presented many difficulties to film-makers used to an older, more conventionalized mode of production. Close-ups were suddenly problematic, given the vast new size of the image. On a sixty-foot screen, they would frequently appear ludicrous, menacing, or both, which made critics wonder whether intimate scenes would be possible in the widescreen medium at all. Montage became problematic for the same reason: the perceptual disorientation produced by the rapid intercutting of widescreen images was less exciting than simply confusing. Finally, composition and lighting for the widescreen image was difficult for directors and cameramen accustomed to the rectangular Academy frame. There was, for example, the purely practical problem of how to fill all that newly available space. For these reasons, many felt that the widescreen processes would destroy the cinema as an art form, and it is true that, like the first sound films, the first widescreen films were static and theatrical, with a heavy-handed emphasis on spectacle.

But as widescreen film-making was refined throughout the fifties and into the sixties, it became apparent that many of the initial assumptions about the limitations of widescreen were false. With certain stylistic modifications, close-ups and montage were not only possible but more effective in widescreen than in the old format; intimate scenes *could* be played with total authenticity in widescreen; and the cinema did *not* ultimately succumb to circus spectacle as a result of its new shape and size. For one thing, a director using widescreen could bring his characters into a tight close-up without eliminating the background and middleground of the shot, as often happened in Academy ratio close-ups of the thirties and forties. He could also have two or even three speaking characters in close-up, with ample space between their faces, instead of having to cut back and forth from one to the other or to squeeze them together artificially within the narrow borders of the Academy frame. Furthermore, the critics of widescreen in the fifties failed to recognize that the process greatly enhanced the image's capacity for depth (and thus for spectator involvement) as well as width due to the increased peripheral vision, forgetting that the industry had initially adopted the process for this very reason. Early pioneers of widescreen composition like Otto Preminger (*River of No Return* [1954]), Elia Kazan (*East of Eden* [1955]), and Nicholas Ray (*Rebel Without a Cause* [1956]) exploited this new capacity for depth by using big, brightly lit sets, or by shooting out of doors in direct sunlight, which enabled them to stop down their lens apertures and achieve great depth of field for their images (see note, Chapter 9). For all practical purposes, this meant that the deep-focus capacity Welles and Toland had labored so hard to attain in *Citizen Kane* (1941) had suddenly become available to any director who possessed the imagination to use it. And it seems clear today that the widescreen processes created the functional grounds for a new film aesthetic based upon composition in width and depth, or *mise-en-scène,* rather than upon montage.

12.9 Widescreen potential: dialogue in close-up without cutting in *The Wild Bunch* (Sam Peckinpah, 1969). William Holden, Ernest Borgnine.

In this new aesthetic, which might be called the "long take," or *mise-en-scène,* aesthetic, the major emphasis would shift from editing to shooting, since a long take composed in width and depth is capable of containing long shot, medium shot, and close-up, action and reaction, within a single frame without resort to fragmentation of the image. At least one veteran Hollywood director recognized this as early as 1955. In an interview with the British film journal *Sight and Sound,* Henry King said: "This lens [the anamorphic] enables the director . . . for the first time to show on the screen cause and effect in the same shot, whereas before we used to have to *cut* from cause to effect in a story." [My italics.][2] Obviously, film narratives would continue to be assembled through the editing process, but the primary unit of narration would no longer be the shot (or "montage cell," in Eisenstein's phrase) but the long take or sequence shot composed in width and depth and/or constantly moving to re-frame significant dramatic action. Theorists of the long-take aesthetic like André Bazin[3] and his follower Charles Barr[4] would later maintain that the long take preserves the integrity of time and space by linking foreground, middleground, and background within the same shot, whereas montage destroys it. The close-up is a case in point (ironically, since early critics thought widescreen incapable of close-ups). In montage, the figure in close-up is divorced from its background by virtue of both focal limitations and the rapidity with which images flash upon the screen. In the long-take close-up, the figure in close-up is temporally and spatially linked with its environment by virtue of the shot's *mise-en-scène,* and for Bazin and Barr, at least, this constitutes a more authentic mode of representation than the dissociated close-up of montage.

12.10 Using widescreen to link character and environment: *Rebel Without a Cause* (Nicholas Ray, 1955) and *Wild River* (Elia Kazan, 1960). James Dean; Jo Van Fleet.

12.11 The "democratic" perspective of widescreen, preserving the integrity of real time and space: *Bad Day at Black Rock* (John Sturges, 1955). Spencer Tracy.

According to the long-take theorists, montage evolved historically because it was the first technologically feasible way to structure film, or to give it "speech." But in our era, they argue, the technology of cutting has been usurped by the technology of shooting, so that the radical fragmentation of montage should now be replaced by the organization of complex images within the frame. The widescreen image composed in depth is clearly capable of containing much more visual information than the old Academy frame, and this greater visual density makes it the perfect medium for rendering detail, texture, and atmosphere in relation to character within the shot. Finally, both Bazin and Barr insist that the width and depth perspective created by the widescreen long take offer the viewer a "democratic" and "creative" alternative to the manipulative process of montage. Though shot composition can guide his seeing to some extent, the viewer of a long take can choose which details or actions to concentrate upon within a given shot, rather than have them pointed out to him by close-ups or be drawn to some inexorable conclusion through a montage sequence like Eisenstein's massacre on the Odessa steps. Although montage was the "traditional" aesthetic of the cinema, Bazin and his followers were able to construct an historical tradition for the long-take aesthetic stretching back to Feuillade and including the "integral style" of von Stroheim and Murnau, the deep-focus "realism" of Renoir and Welles, and the post-war "neo-realism" of Rossellini and De Sica. Welles began the revolution in favor of the long take with *Citizen Kane* in 1941, and the arrival of widescreen technology in the early fifties assured its permanent success. But it took the new aesthetic a decade more to evolve, and the years 1953–60, like the years 1928–35, witnessed much experimental blundering before the major artists of the wide-screen cinema could emerge.

The Widescreen "Blockbuster"

In Hollywood, this emergence was delayed by the sudden proliferation of a venerable film type known as the "blockbuster,"* newly renovated to exploit the physical novelty of the big screen. These inflated multi-million-dollar productions were the widescreen counterparts of the "100 percent all-talking, all-singing, all-dancing" films of the early sound period—lavish and excessively lengthy super-spectacles in the DeMille tradition, every element of which was made to subserve sheer visual magnitude. The blockbuster craze started in 1956, when King Vidor's *War and Peace* (VistaVision; 3 hrs., 28 min.), Michael Anderson's *Around the World in 80 Days* (Todd-AO; 3 hrs., 30 min.), and C. B. DeMille's remake of his own *The Ten Commandments* (VistaVision; 3 hrs., 39 min.) were all released simultaneously in wide-film widescreen processes and full stereophonic sound. Because the production costs for block-

---

* A term traditionally used in Hollywood to designate any large-scale, big-budget production. *Intolerance* (1916) and *Gone with the Wind* (1939) were both called "blockbusters" in their day.

busters were abnormally high, the films had to have a correspondingly high box-office gross simply to break even, and this factor, combined with their artistic unwieldiness, would ultimately destroy them. But for a while they reigned supreme. *Around the World in 80 Days,* for example, which cost six million dollars to produce, grossed over twenty-two million in the year of its release, and *The Ten Commandments,* which cost thirteen-and-a-half million dollars, grossed nearly forty-three million.

Other major blockbusters of the era were Joshua Logan's *South Pacific* (1957—Todd-AO; 3 hrs.), William Wyler's *Ben-Hur* (1959—Camera-65; 3 hrs., 37 min.), Stanley Kubrick's *Spartacus* (1960—Technirama-70; 3 hrs., 16 min.), Otto Preminger's *Exodus* (1960—Panavision-70; 3 hrs., 33 min.), Anthony Mann's *El Cid* (1961—Technirama-70; 3 hrs., 6 min.), Lewis Milestone's *Mutiny on the Bounty* (1962—Panavision-70; 3 hrs., 5 min.), and David Lean's *Lawrence of Arabia* (1962—Panavision-70; 3 hrs., 42 min.). By the early sixties, production budgets for blockbusters had grown so large through inflation that most were produced abroad in Italy (by Dino De Laurentiis at Rome's Cinecittà studios), Spain (at Samuel Bronston's vast studio complex on the outskirts of Madrid), and Yugoslavia (at the Zagreb studios) to cut costs. Even so, many—such as *El Cid* and *Mutiny on the Bounty*—went down to ruin at the box office, alerting producers to the fact that the blockbuster trend had exhausted itself with the public. But the film that demonstrated this most graphically was Joseph L. Mankiewicz's disastrous *Cleopatra* (1963—Todd-AO; 4 hrs., 3 min.), which took four years and forty million dollars to produce, nearly destroying Twentieth Century–Fox, and which has still not returned its negative cost despite several revivals and its sale to network television. Other blockbusters have been made since, including the fantastically successful *The Sound of Music* (Robert Wise, 1965), but few were able to recover their production costs before sale to television, and producers turned away from the blockbuster policy until it was revived, with substantial modifications, in the mid-seventies.

12.12 A shot from the chariot race in the blockbuster *Ben Hur* (William Wyler, 1959): Charlton Heston.

12.13 *Lawrence of Arabia* (David Lean, 1962): exploiting the new width and depth for spectacle. Peter O'Toole.

12.14 A scene from *Cleopatra* (Joseph L. Mankiewicz, 1963), the blockbuster that nearly sank Twentieth Century–Fox.

AMERICAN WIDESCREEN PIONEERS

Some American directors who pioneered widescreen composition in the fifties and early sixties, despite the blockbuster phenomenon, were: Robert Aldrich (*Vera Cruz* [1954]); Stanley Donen (*Seven Brides for Seven Brothers* [1954]; *It's Always Fair Weather* [1955]); John Sturges (*Bad Day at Black Rock* [1955]; *Gunfight at the OK Corral* [1957]); Elia Kazan (*East of Eden* [1955]; *Wild River* [1960]); Otto Preminger (*River of No Return* [1954]; *Bonjour Tristesse* [1958]; *Exodus* [1960]); Nicholas Ray (*Rebel Without a Cause* [1955]; *The True Story of Jesse James* [1957]; *Bitter Victory* [1958]); George Stevens (*Giant* [1955]); Raoul Walsh (*The Tall Men* [1955]); Alfred Hitchcock (*To Catch a Thief* [1955]; *The Man Who Knew Too Much* [1956]; *Vertigo* [1958]); Douglas Sirk (*Written on the Wind* [1957]; *The Tarnished Angels* [1958]); Budd Boetticher (*Seven Men from Now* [1956]; *Ride Lonesome* [1959]); Anthony Mann (*Man of the West* [1958]); Vincente Minnelli (*Some Came Running* [1959]; *The Courtship of Eddie's Father* [1963]); Howard Hawks (*Land of the Pharaohs* [1955]; *Rio Bravo* [1959]; *Hatari!* [1962]); and Sam Peckinpah (*Ride the High Country* [1962]). Some of these films were less important in themselves than for their purely formal achievements. But most of their directors were major talents who made other significant films during the fifties and early sixties.

Robert Aldrich (b. 1918) emerged at this time as America's most powerful practitioner of *film noir* in *Kiss Me Deadly* (1955), *The Big Knife* (1955), *Attack!* (1959), and *Whatever Happened to Baby Jane?* (1962). In *A Streetcar Named Desire* (1951), *Viva Zapata!* (1952), and *On the Waterfront* (1954), all starring Marlon Brando, Elia Kazan (b. 1909) gave the fifties three of its most persuasive and characteristic films. Otto Preminger (b. 1906), who had made his first film in Vienna in 1932 and emigrated to Hollywood in 1936, challenged the already moribund Pro-

12.15 Composition for widescreen: *Wild River* (Elia Kazan, 1960) and *Exodus* (Otto Preminger, 1960). Both films were conventional narratives distinguished by their creative use of the widescreen frame.

duction Code with *The Moon Is Blue* (1953), a sex farce; *The Man with the Golden Arm* (1957), a film about narcotics addiction; and *Anatomy of a Murder* (1959), a courtroom drama about rape. Moreover, his haunting *film noir* of 1945, *Laura,* and the semi-documentary *Where the Sidewalk Ends* (1950) are minor classics of their respective genres. In his film of the fifties, especially *Rebel Without a Cause* (1955), Nicholas Ray (1911–79) provided a definitive statement of the psychic and emotional ills that beset America during the period. Douglas Sirk (b. 1900) proved himself to be a master stylist of the widescreen color film in *Magnificent Obsession* (1954), *All That Heaven Allows* (1956), and *Written on the Wind* (1957)—a series of visually stunning motion pictures whose content bordered on soap opera.

12.16 Alienated youth: *Rebel Without a Cause* (Nicholas Ray, 1955). Jim Backus, James Dean, Ann Doran.

OTHER AMERICAN DIRECTORS

Boetticher and Mann were the architects of the modern adult Western, while Minnelli continued his practice of making potboilers into gorgeously stylish films like *The Cobweb* (1955), *Lust for Life* (1956), *Some Came Running* (1959), *Home from the Hill* (1960), and *Two Weeks in Another Town* (1962). Other important figures whose achievement peaked in the fifties and who are not mentioned elsewhere in the text of this volume are: John Huston (b. 1906—*The Treasure of the Sierra Madre* [1948]; *Key Largo* [1948]; *The Asphalt Jungle* [1950]; *The Red Badge of Courage* [1951]; *The African Queen* [1952]; *Moulin Rouge* [1953]; and *Beat the Devil* [1954]); Fred Zinnemann (b. 1907—*The Men* [1950], *High Noon* [1952], *From Here to Eternity* [1953], *A Man for All Seasons* [1966]); Robert Rossen (1908–66—*Body and Soul* [1947]; *All the King's Men* [1949]; *The Hustler* [1961]; *Lilith* [1964]); and the important action directors Don Siegel (b. 1912—*Riot in Cell Block 11*

12.17 Interracial fraternity: *The Defiant Ones* (Stanley Kramer, 1958). Sidney Poitier, Tony Curtis.

12.18 Sex: *Cat on a Hot Tin Roof* (Richard Brooks, 1959). Paul Newman, Elizabeth Taylor.

[1954]; *Invasion of the Body Snatchers* [1956];* *Baby Face Nelson* [1957]; *The Line-Up* [1958]; *The Killers* [1964]; *Madigan* [1968]; *The Beguiled* [1970]; *Dirty Harry* [1972]) and the more primitive Samuel Fuller (b. 1911—*I Shot Jesse James* [1949]; *The Steel Helmet* [1950]; *Pickup on South Street* [1953]; *House of Bamboo* [1955]; *China Gate* [1957]; *Run of the Arrow* [1957]; *Underworld USA* [1961]; *Shock Corridor* [1963]; *Shark!* [1969]; *Dead Pigeon on Beethoven Street* [1972]; *The Big Red One* [1979]). A more seasoned action director with decades of industry experience, Raoul Walsh (1892–1981), continued to make important films in the fifties (*Battle Cry* [1955]; *The Tall Men* [1955]; *Band of Angels* [1957]).

George Stevens (1905–75), a veteran studio director who had made some fine films in the thirties and forties (*Swing Time* [1936]; *Gunga Din* [1939]; *Woman of the Year* [1942]; *The More the Merrier* [1943]), did his best work in the fifties, though sententiousness sometimes got the better of his scripts. *Shane* (1953); *Giant* (1956); and, above all, *A Place in the Sun* (1951), his poetic rendition of Theodore Dreiser's novel *An American Tragedy* (1925), are all films that American cinema would be the poorer without. Sententiousness was also a problem in the films directed during this period by Stanley Kramer (b. 1913), which tended to be visually limp and heavily laden with social commentary. Still, a few Kramer films, like *The Defiant Ones* (1958), *Inherit the Wind* (1960), *Judgment at Nuremberg* (1961), and the later *Ship of Fools* (1969) and *Oklahoma Crude* (1973), are notable despite their flaws. A similarly erratic producer-director is Richard Brooks (b. 1912), who has specialized in literary adaptation for which he writes the scripts himself. His successes (*The Blackboard Jungle* [1954]; *Cat on a Hot Tin Roof* [1959]; *Elmer Gantry* [1961]; *Sweet Bird of Youth* [1962]; *The Professionals* [1966]; *In Cold Blood* [1967]) balance out pretty evenly with a number of failures (*Something of Value* [1957]; *The Brothers Karamazov* [1958]; *Lord Jim* [1964]; *Looking for Mr. Goodbar* [1977]).

Finally, after the Hollywood witch-hunts had destroyed their American careers, Jules Dassin (b. 1911—*Brute Force* [1947]; *The Naked City* [1948]) and Joseph Losey (b. 1909—*The Boy with Green Hair* [1948]; *The Prowler* [1951]) emigrated to Europe (France and Britain, respectively) where both have since become important figures. Dassin, influenced by Lang, once specialized in thrillers and sophisticated comedies (*Rififi* [1956]; *Never on Sunday* [1960]; *Topkapi* [1964]), but he has also made such serious films as a modern version of *Phaedra* (1961), an all-black version of John Ford's *The Informer* entitled *Up Tight* (1969), and *A Dream of Passion* (1978), a contemporary meditation on the Medea legend shot in Greece. Losey is a stylish and somewhat strained student of contemporary alienation who often collaborates with British playwright Harold Pinter on his screenplays (*The Servant* [1964]; *These Are the Damned* [1965]; *Eva* [1966]; *Accident* [1967]). (Losey's more recent work is discussed in Chapter 14.)

---

* Remade by the director Philip Kaufman in 1978, with appearances by Siegel and by Kevin McCarthy, star of the original version.

FIFTIES GENRES

Despite the balanced work of these fine craftsmen, Hollywood's mania for producing films on a vast scale in the fifties blighted even the conventional dramatic feature. For one thing, the standard feature length rose from ninety minutes to an average of three hours before stabilizing itself at a more manageable two hours in the mid-sixties. Moreover, there was a tendency on the part of the studios to package every class-A production as a splashy big-budget spectacle whether or not this format suited the material. Thus, from 1955 to 1965 most traditional American genres experienced an inflation of production values that destroyed their original forms and caused them to be recreated in new ones.

The Musical

The Hollywood musical had reached an exquisitely high point of sophistication and color at the turn of the decade under the auspices of the MGM directors Stanley Donen (b. 1924) and Vincente Minnelli (b. 1910), and the dancer-choreographer-director Gene Kelly (b. 1912), in medium-budget films like *The Pirate* (Minnelli / Kelly, 1948), *On the Town* (Kelly / Donen, 1949), *An American in Paris* (Minnelli / Kelly, 1951), and *Singin' in the Rain* (Kelly / Donen, 1952). But the genre contracted a fifteen-year case of elephantiasis around 1955, as well as a compulsion to abandon original scripts in favor of adapting successful stage plays. Such Broadway vehicles as *Oklahoma!* (Fred Zinnemann, 1955), *Guys and Dolls* (Joseph L. Mankiewicz, 1955), *The King and I* (Walter Lang, 1956), *South Pacific* (Joshua Logan, 1957), *West Side Story* (Robert Wise, 1962), *The Music Man* (Morton da Costa, 1962), *Gypsy* (Mervyn LeRoy, 1963), and *My Fair Lady* (George Cukor, 1964) proved successful with the public, although many of them employed stars who could neither sing nor dance (their voices were dubbed in by professional singers, and professional dancers stood in for the production numbers) and were directed by men who had never made a movie musical before. These new musicals, often versions of concurrently running hits, were "integrated"—that is, they attempted to integrate their production numbers into relatively realistic plots, which generated the totally unrealistic convention of a character's bursting into song at the slightest dramatic provocation. This tendency peaked with the release of the astoundingly popular film *The Sound of Music* (Robert Wise, 1965), the ultimate big-budget super-musical, which grossed more money (seventy-nine million dollars in domestic rentals) than any American film produced before *The Godfather, Part I* (Francis Ford Coppola, 1972), *Jaws* (Steven Spielberg, 1975), and *Star Wars* (George Lucas, 1977). *The Sound of Music* (subsequently known in the industry as "The Sound of Money") was a glossily professional adaptation of a Rodgers and Hammerstein stage musical based on the true story of the Trapp family singers and their heroic escape from Nazi-occupied Austria. The production, shot on location in Salzburg, was one of Hollywood's last great escapist confections

12.19 *Singin' in the Rain* (Gene Kelly and Stanley Donen, 1952): Gene Kelly.

12.20 *West Side Story* (Robert Wise, 1962): George Chakiris as the leader of the "Sharks."

12.21 *The Sound of Music* (Robert Wise, 1965): Julie Andrews.

—a sort of conflation of *The Bells of St. Mary's, The Wizard of Oz,* and *Gone with the Wind.* The great success of this film gave rise to a host of multi-million-dollar descendants—*Camelot* (Joshua Logan, 1967), *Star!* (Robert Wise, 1968), *Dr. Dolittle* (Richard Fleischer, 1968), *Funny Girl* (William Wyler, 1968), *Good-bye, Mr. Chips* (Herbert Ross, 1969), *Oliver!* (Carol Reed, 1969), *Hello Dolly!* (Gene Kelly, 1969)—which nearly destroyed the fortunes of their respective studios, glutted the public on musicals, and virtually killed the form of the genre as it had evolved since the thirties by blowing it out of all proportion. Bob Fosse's intelligent, socially conscious, and masterfully crafted film version of the stage success *Cabaret* (1971) seemed to signal a resurrection of the genre in a form more appropriate to the seventies—one which features increased realism, serious subject matter, a re-segregation of musical numbers and plot, and renewed emphasis on the authentic musical talent of its stars. Indeed, Fosse's *All That Jazz* (1979) and Miloš Forman's *Hair* (1979) would confirm that resurrection at the decade's end.

12.22 *Cabaret* (Bob Fosse, 1972): Joel Grey as the master of ceremonies.

Comedy

12.23 *Scared Stiff* (George Marshall, 1953): Jerry Lewis, Lizabeth Scott, Dean Martin.

Comedy was another genre that suffered seriously from widescreen inflation and the generally depressed social ambience of the McCarthy–Cold War era. The big-budget widescreen comedy was represented by films like *How to Marry a Millionaire* (Jean Negulesco, 1953), *The Long Long Trailer* (Vincente Minnelli, 1954), *High Society* (Charles Walters, 1956—a widescreen color remake, with music by Cole Porter, of George Cukor's 1940 *Philadelphia Story*), and *A Hole in the Head* (Frank Capra, 1959). The strong point of film comedies like these was less verbal or visual wit than excellent production values. This was, after all, the major strategic element in Hollywood's war on television, and for a while the strategy worked, although the new medium continued to woo both audiences and comedians away from the cinema as the decade progressed. Bob Hope (b. 1903—*Son of Paleface* [Frank Tashlin, 1952]) and Danny Kaye (b. 1913—*The Court Jester* [Norman Panama, 1956]), whose film careers had begun in the decade past, were both popular in class-A productions throughout the fifties, as was the slapstick team of Dean Martin and Jerry Lewis (b. 1917; 1926—*The Stooge* [Norman Taurog, 1953]; *Scared Stiff* [George Marshall, 1953]; *Artists and Models* [Frank Tashlin, 1955]), which had succeeded that of Abbott and Costello. When this new team split up in 1956, Lewis went on to become a major comic star by himself in films like *The Delicate Delinquent* (Don McGuire, 1957) and finally began to direct his own films in the sixties (*The Bellboy* [1960]; *The Errand Boy* [1961]; *The Nutty Professor* [1963]). Today he is regarded by the French as a major *auteur,* but his idiotic comic persona has not found much favor with American critics.

12.24 *Born Yesterday* (George Cukor, 1950): Judy Holliday, Broderick. Crawford.

Much more sophisticated than Lewis, or even Hope and Kaye, were the era's two major comediennes: Judy Holliday (1922–65—*Born Yesterday* [George Cukor, 1950]; *The Marrying Kind* [George Cukor, 1952]; *The Solid Gold Cadillac* [Richard Quine, 1956]) and Marilyn Monroe

(1926–62—*The Seven Year Itch* [Billy Wilder, 1955]; *Some Like It Hot* [Billy Wilder, 1959]); both of them appeared in a number of witty, adult comedies before their early deaths cut short their careers. These films were succeeded by the sanitized sexiness of the expensively produced Rock Hudson/Doris Day battle-of-the-sexes cycle, beginning with *Pillow Talk* (Michael Gordon, 1958) and continuing through *Lover Come Back* (Delbert Mann, 1961) and *Send Me No Flowers* (Norman Jewison, 1964). These films and their imitators were in turn succeeded by a cycle of more cynical big-budget sex comedies concerned with the strategies of seduction (David Swift's *Under the Yum-Yum Tree* [1963]; Richard Quine's *Sex and the Single Girl* [1965] and *How to Murder Your Wife* [1965]; Gene Kelly's *A Guide for the Married Man* [1967]) which reflected, sometimes rather perversely, the "sexual revolution" of the late sixties. Related to the amoral cynicism of this cycle was what might best be called the "corporate comedy" of films like *Cash McCall* (Joseph Pevney, 1960) and the *Wheeler Dealers* (Arthur Hiller, 1963), which dealt openly and humorously with business fraud and pre-figured the morass of corporate and governmental deceit underlying the Watergate and "Koreagate" scandals of the seventies. The elegant big-budget comedies of Blake Edwards (*The Pink Panther* [1964]; *A Shot in the Dark* [1964]; *The Great Race* [1965]; *The Party* [1968]) relied on sight gags to provide a lighter kind of humor.

12.25 *The Seven Year Itch* (Billy Wilder, 1955): Tom Ewell, Marilyn Monroe.

The dark genius of American comedy during this period was the German émigré director Billy Wilder, whose *Double Indemnity* (1944) had been the original *film noir*. In the fifties, Wilder began increasingly to specialize in *comédie noir*. In *Sunset Boulevard* (1950) he served up the decadence of Hollywood, old and new, in a tale of the bitterly symbiotic relationship which develops between an aging silent-film star and a fortune-hunting young writer. *Stalag 17* (1953) was a perverse satire on heroism set in a German POW camp during World War II; *The Seven Year Itch* (1955) was a send-up of American sexual mores and advertising practices; *Witness for the Prosecution* (1958) was a sardonic Hitchcockian courtroom thriller derived from a play by Agatha Christie; and *Some Like It Hot* (1959) was a torrid, fast-paced sex farce set amidst gangster wars and an "all-girl" band during Prohibition. Wilder entered the sixties with *The Apartment* (1960), a film about the battle of the sexes made in dark parody of the Hudson/Day cycle. *One, Two, Three* (1961) satirized the Cold War and American corporate imperialism, while in *Irma La Douce* (1963) and *Kiss Me, Stupid* (1964) Wilder brought the cynical sex comedy *à la* Lubitsch into the contemporary American film. By the end of the decade, he was spoofing the most revered of Victorian detectives in *The Private Life of Sherlock Holmes* (1969).* Through the influence of Wilder and others (for instance,

12.26 *Sunset Boulevard* (Billy Wilder, 1950): Gloria Swanson.

---

* In the seventies, Wilder directed, among other films, a contemporary version of Lewis Milestone's *The Front Page* (1974) and an elegant reworking of the *Sunset Boulevard* theme in *Fedora* (1979). Wilder has always co-authored his own screenplays, in close collaboration with such professional scriptwriters as Charles Brackett, Raymond Chandler, George Axelrod, and, since 1959, I. A. L. Diamond (Wilder began his film career as a scriptwriter for UFA).

12.27 *Love and Death* (Woody Allen, 1975): Woody Allen with the Grim Reaper.

12.28 The "adult Western": *High Noon* (Fred Zinneman, 1952). Gary Cooper.

12.29 *Gunfight at the OK Corral* (John Sturges, 1957).

Stanley Kubrick in *Dr. Strangelove* [1963], a film far in advance of its time), American comedy became increasingly sophisticated in the fifties and sixties, until it emerged in the seventies as a wholly adult genre. Films like *M.A.S.H.* (Robert Altman, 1970), and the work of comic *auteurs* like Woody Allen (b. 1935—*Take the Money and Run* [1969]; *Bananas* [1971]; *Play It Again, Sam* [1972]; *Sleeper* [1973]; *Love and Death* [1975]) and Mel Brooks (b. 1927—*The Producers* [1968]; *Blazing Saddles* [1973]; *Young Frankenstein* [1974]; *Silent Movie* [1976]; *High Anxiety* [1977]) all bear testimony to the increasing maturity of American film comedy—much of it undertaken in parody of other traditional genres. Allen, especially, has emerged as an important and extremely intelligent film-maker, moving from the broad social satire of his earlier works to the pointed social commentary of *Annie Hall* (1977), *Interiors* (1978), and *Manhattan* (1979).

The Western

The genre which seems to have best survived the widescreen inflation of the fifties and sixties is the Western, although it too has experienced some major changes in attitude and theme corresponding to changes in American society. The heroic, idealized, epic Westerns of John Ford and his imitators remained popular in the fifties but were gradually usurped by what was called the "adult Western." This genre, whose prototypes were *The Gunfighter* (Henry King, 1950) and *High Noon* (Fred Zinnemann, 1952), concentrated on the psychological or moral conflicts of the individual protagonist in relation to his society rather than creating the poetic archetypes of order characteristic of Ford. The directors Delmer Daves (*Jubal* [1956]; *3:10 to Yuma* [1957]; *Cowboy* [1958]) and John Sturges (*Gunfight at the O.K. Corral* [1957]; *Last Train from Gun Hill* [1958]) both contributed to the new "psychological" style during this period and helped to resolve some problems of widescreen composition in the process. But the foremost director of adult Westerns in the fifties was Anthony Mann (1906–67), who made eleven such films between 1950 and 1960, eight in close collaboration with the actor James Stewart. Mann's Westerns tended to be more intensely psychological and violent than those of his peers, and he was among the first to discover that the topography of the genre was uniquely suited to the widescreen format. In films like *The Naked Spur* (1953), *The Far Country* (1955), *The Man from Laramie* (1956), and *Man of the West* (1959), Mann carried the genre permanently into the realm of adult entertainment and created an austere visual style which, according to Andrew Sarris, closely resembles that of Michelangelo Antonioni.[5]

Mann's successor was Budd Boetticher (b. 1916), who directed a series of adult Westerns in collaboration with producer Harry Joe Brown and actor Randolph Scott for Ranown Productions in the late fifties. In such films as *Seven Men from Now* (1957), *Decision at Sundown* (1957), *The Tall T* (1957), *Buchanan Rides Alone* (1958), and *Ride Lonesome* (1959), Boetticher forged elemental and even allegorical dramas of ethical heroism in which men alone are forced to make moral choices in a moral vacuum. The Fordian tradition of the epic romance was carried on, of course, by Ford himself (see Chapter 8) and by the makers of such "big" widescreen Westerns as *Shane* (George Stevens, 1953)—a film shot in the old ratio and disastrously blown-up for widescreen exhibition; *The Big Country* (William Wyler, 1958); *The Alamo* (John Wayne, 1960); *How the West Was Won* (John Ford, Henry Hathaway, George Marshall, 1962—Cinerama); and the inflated big-budget Westerns of Andrew V. McLaglen (*McLintock!* [1963]; *Shenandoah* [1965]; *The Rare Breed* [1966]). It was the Mann-Boetticher tradition that won out in the sixties, as the early films of Sam Peckinpah (*Deadly Companions* [1961]; *Ride the High Country* [1962]) clearly demonstrate. But this new tradition was itself soon deeply influenced from an unexpected source—the Japanese *samurai* film, with its heavy emphasis on honor, fatality, and violence (see Chapter 16).

12.30 *Ride Lonesome* (Budd Boetticher, 1959): Randolph Scott.

This influence was first demonstrated in John Sturges' violent and popular *The Magnificent Seven* (1960), a version of Akira Kurosawa's *The Seven Samurai* (1954) set in the American West. In both films, seven hardened warriors (gunmen in Sturges) are inexplicably driven to risk their lives to defend the inhabitants of a small rural village from bandits. *The Magnificent Seven* was a popular success and sparked an international trend toward *samurai* imitations which ultimately produced the "spaghetti Western"—violent films of the American West starring American actors but shot in Italy or Yugoslavia by Italian film-makers. The master craftsman of the spaghetti Western was Sergio Leone (b. 1921), whose *A Fistful of Dollars*—a direct, almost shot-for-shot copy of Kurosawa's *Yojimbo* (1961)—started the cycle in 1964. Leone, who turned out to have talent of his own, followed up with *For a Few Dollars More* (1965), *The Good, the Bad, and the Ugly* (1966), and, finally, *Once Upon a Time in the West* (1967)—a bold and brilliant parody of all the mythic/romantic themes of the traditional American Western. The films of Leone and his many imitators tended to be stylish, colorful, and excessively bloody—the latter achieved through the practice of graphically depicting, for the first time on the screen, impact and exit wounds produced by bullets. For this reason mainly, one fears, the spaghetti Westerns were enormously successful in the United States and produced a number of American-made imitations (e.g., Ted Post's gratuitously brutal *Hang 'Em High* [1968]). They also played a major role in conditioning American audiences to the new levels of violence that were to emerge at the end of the decade in the non-Western gangster film *Bonnie and Clyde* (Arthur Penn, 1967) and in Sam Peckinpah's apocalyptic *The Wild Bunch* (1969; see Chapter 17). This latter work probably did more to demythologize the American Western than any single film of its era, but the process had been going on since Anthony Mann's *The Naked Spur* (1952).

12.31 *Ride the High Country* (Sam Peckinpah, 1962): (above) Randolph Scott, Mariette Hartley, Joel McCrea; (below, clockwise) L. Q. Jones, John Anderson, Warren Oates, John Davis Chandler.

In the years since then, Mann, Boetticher, Sturges (in *The Magnificent Seven*), the Italians, and Peckinpah had evolved a Western tradition counter to that of Ford—one which was anti-heroic, was realistic, and exhibited utter disillusionment with the conventional mythology of the American West. One important index of this change was a complete

12.32 Eastern Western: from the showdown which concludes *Yojimbo* (Akira Kurosawa, 1961). Toshiro Mifune.

reversal of the genre's attitude toward Indians. The hostile savages of the thirties, the forties, and most of the fifties were suddenly seen to be a race of gentle, intelligent people upon whom the U.S. military establishment had committed genocide. Two films of the period, Ralph Nelson's *Soldier Blue* (1970) and Arthur Penn's *Little Big Man* (1971), graphically depicted the massacre of defenseless Indians by U.S. cavalry troops (the analogy with the My Lai massacre in both films was inescapable and deliberate). Good "classical" Westerns continued to be made in the sixties by such Fordian craftsmen as Henry Hathaway (*The Sons of Katie Elder* [1965]; *True Grit* [1969]) and by maverick individualists like Howard Hawks (*Rio Bravo* [1959]; *El Dorado* [1967]), but the prevailing trend was toward graphic realism (*Will Penny* [Tom Gries, 1967]; *Monte Walsh* [William Fraker, 1970]) or parody (*Cat Ballou* [Eliot Silverstein, 1965]; *Waterhole No. 3* [William Graham, 1967]; *Butch Cassidy and the Sundance Kid* [George Roy Hill, 1969]). From *Fort Apache* (John Ford, 1948) and *Red River* (Howard Hawks, 1948) to *Soldier Blue* (Ralph Nelson, 1970) and *The Wild Bunch* (Sam Peckinpah, 1969), the external form of the American Western did not significantly change. The Ford and Nelson films, for example, have precisely the same subject, the same landscape, and very nearly the same plot; and *The Wild Bunch* duplicates many of the mythic elements of *Red River* without parody. It is the way in which these elements are viewed by American film-makers and their audiences which has changed. That change is profound, but it has more to do with alterations in the way America perceives itself and its past than with the evolution of film genres.

The Gangster Film and the Anti-Communist Film

The gangster film, which had been replaced by the domestic espionage film during the war, re-emerged in the late forties in shades of black. At that time, "dark" crime films like *The Killers* (Robert Siodmak, 1946), *Kiss of Death* (Henry Hathaway, 1947), *I Walk Alone* (Byron Haskin, 1947), *The Naked City* (Jules Dassin, 1948), *Force of Evil* (Abraham Polonsky, 1948), *They Live by Night* (Nicholas Ray, 1949), *Gun Crazy* (Joseph H. Lewis, 1949), *White Heat* (Raoul Walsh, 1949), *Kiss Tomorrow Goodbye* (Gordon Douglas, 1950), and *Where the Sidewalk Ends* (Otto Preminger, 1950) tended to concentrate upon the individual criminal in his relationship to the underworld. In the paranoid fifties, the emphasis shifted from the individual wrongdoer to the existence of a nationwide criminal conspiracy, commonly known as "the syndicate," which was responsible for many of America's social ills—murder, gambling, prostitution, narcotics, and labor racketeering. Since Prohibition, American gangster films have been firmly rooted in the reality of American crime, and—paranoia notwithstanding—that such a criminal conspiracy did exist and that it was closely connected with the Sicilian secret society known as the Mafia was demonstrated by the findings of the Senate Special Committee to Investigate Organized Crime, headed by Senator Estes Kefauver, in 1951. Based upon the revelations of the Kefauver Committee, *The Enforcer* (also called *Murder, Inc.*; Bretaigne

Windust, 1951) was the first film to posit such an organization on the screen, but it became the major component in *The Big Heat* (Fritz Lang, 1953), *On the Waterfront* (Elia Kazan, 1954), *New York Confidential* (Russell Rouse, 1954), *The Big Combo* (Joseph Lewis, 1955), *The Brothers Rico* (Phil Karlson, 1957), *The Phenix City Story* (Phil Karlson, 1955), *The Garment Jungle* (Vincent Sherman, 1957), *Murder, Inc.* (Stuart Rosenberg, 1960), *Underworld USA* (Samuel Fuller, 1960), and many other gangster films of the decade. The syndicate cycle experienced a decade-long hiatus in the sixties—except for Martin Ritt's *The Brotherhood* (1968)—only to re-emerge with unprecedentedly graphic violence in the blood-soaked seventies with *The Godfather, Parts I* and *II* (Francis Ford Coppola, 1972 and 1974), *The Valachi Papers* (Terence Young, 1972), *The French Connection, Part I* (William Friedkin, 1972) and *Part II* (John Frankenheimer, 1974), and *Honor Thy Father* (Paul Wendkos, 1973).

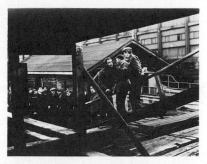

12.33 *On the Waterfront* (Elia Kazan, 1954): Marlon Brando.

Another type of gangster film, the biography of the Prohibition and/or Depression criminal, was initiated by Don Siegel's *Baby Face Nelson* (1957). Films in this cycle—*The Bonnie Parker Story* (William Witney, 1958), *Machine-Gun Kelly* (Roger Corman, 1958), *Al Capone* (Richard Wilson, 1959), *The Rise and Fall of Legs Diamond* (Budd Boetticher, 1960), *Mad Dog Coll* (Burt Balaban, 1961), *Portrait of a Mobster* (about Dutch Schultz; Joseph Pevney, 1961)—tend to rely on period reconstruction, and their apotheosis came in the late sixties with Arthur Penn's *Bonnie and Clyde* (1967), Roger Corman's *The St. Valentine's Day Massacre* (1967) and *Bloody Mama* (1969), and—more recently—John Milius' *Dillinger* (1973).

Two interesting sub-types of the gangster film which appeared in the fifties were the "caper" film and the "anti-Red" action thriller. The caper film, which began with John Huston's *The Asphalt Jungle* (1950), concentrates on the mechanics of pulling off a big heist and is still a very popular type. It is sometimes deadly serious, sometimes light and witty. Subsequent manifestations both in America and abroad include *Rififi* (Jules Dassin, 1955), *The Killing* (Stanley Kubrick, 1956), *Odds Against Tomorrow* (Robert Wise, 1959), *Seven Thieves* (Henry Hathaway, 1960), *Big Deal on Madonna Street* (Mario Monicelli, 1960), *The League of Gentlemen* (Basil Dearden, 1960), *Topkapi* (Jules Dassin, 1964), *Grand Slam* (Giuliano Montaldo, 1967), and *They Came to Rob Las Vegas* (Antonio Isasi, 1968). The anti-Red action film was a localized, primitive type endemic to the early fifties and exemplified by Gordon Douglas' *I Was a Communist for the FBI* (1951) and Samuel Fuller's *Pickup on South Street* (1953). In this type, the criminal figure is a Communist spy and the "syndicate" is the "international Communist conspiracy," but the traditional iconography of the gangster film is maintained.

12.34 *The Asphalt Jungle* (John Huston, 1950): Louis Calhern, Sam Jaffe.

The Communist-as-gangster film made its last American appearance in *The FBI Story* (Mervyn LeRoy, 1959), which also dealt with Prohibition/Depression gangsters and Nazi spies, but it is possible to see its central impulse preserved in the James Bond espionage thrillers of the sixties, produced by Harry Saltzman and Albert Broccoli for the London branch of United Artists. These immensely popular films and their imitators in effect usurped the gangster genre between 1962 and 1966 by positing criminal conspiracy on a world-wide scale and offering violent gangsterism on the part of both the conspirators and the super-hero ("licensed to kill") sent to stop them. In the James Bond films—*Dr. No* (Terence Young, 1962), *From Russia with Love* (Terence Young, 1964), *Goldfinger* (Guy Hamilton, 1964), and *Thunderball* (Terence Young, 1965),* *You Only Live Twice* (Lewis Gilbert, 1967), and *On Her Majesty's Secret Service* (Peter Hunt, 1969); the two Derek Flint films (*Our Man Flint* [Daniel Mann, 1966] and *In Like Flint* [Gordon Douglas, 1967]) and the Matt Helm series (*The Silencers* [1966]; *The Wrecking Crew* [1969]—both Phil Karlson), the gangster-as-international-conspirator vs. the gangster-as-government-agent sank the espionage thriller into a state of moral confusion from which it never emerged.†

In the late fifties and early sixties the young directors of the French New Wave borrowed heavily from the conventions of the American gangster film in works like *Breathless* (Jean-Luc Godard, 1959) and *Shoot the Piano Player* (François Truffaut, 1960), but the genre remained dormant in America itself until 1967, when Arthur Penn's *Bonnie and Clyde* appeared and re-vitalized it for the seventies. Penn's film, very much a product of the rebellious spirit of the late sixties, owed a great deal stylistically to the example of the French New Wave, but *Bonnie and Clyde* also restored the gangster to his traditional position as tragic hero and unified the genre by borrowing motifs from three great crime films of the past—Fritz Lang's *You Only Live Once* (1937), Nicholas Ray's *They Live by Night* (1949), and Joseph Lewis' *Gun Crazy* (1949). Since *Bonnie and Clyde,* the gangster film, like the Western, has re-entered the mainstream of American cinema both as a generic form and, increasingly, as a vehicle for serious artistic and social expression (e.g., *The Godfather, Parts I* and *II*).

Science Fiction

Another interesting development of the fifties was the emergence of the science fiction film as a distinct genre. There had been films of science fantasy long before World War II. One of the first important narrative

---

* The series continued into the seventies with such stylish entries as *The Spy Who Loved Me* (Lewis Gilbert, 1977) and *Moonraker* (Lewis Gilbert, 1979).

† It is possible, of course, to see the anti-Red and James Bond–type films as part of a larger category of spy films. In the sound era, this category would include films as diverse as *Dishonored* (Josef von Sternberg, 1931), *Mata Hari* (George Fitzmaurice, 1932), *The Man Who Knew Too Much* (Alfred Hitchcock, 1934; remade 1956), *The Scarlet Pimpernel* (Harold Young, 1935), *The Thirty-Nine Steps* (Alfred Hitchcock, 1935), *The Lady Vanishes* (Alfred Hitchcock, 1938), *Confessions of a Nazi Spy* (Anatole Litvak, 1939), *Across the Pacific* (John Huston, 1942), the Sherlock Holmes and Charlie Chan espionage cycles (1940–45), *The House on 92nd Street* (Henry Hathaway, 1945), *13 Rue Madeleine* (Henry Hathaway, 1946), *Notorious* (Alfred Hitchcock, 1946), *The Iron Curtain* (William Wellman, 1948), *The Man Between* (Carol Reed, 1960), *The Manchurian Candidate* (John Frankenheimer, 1962), *The Ipcress File* (Sidney J. Furie, 1965), *The Quiller Memorandum* (Michael Anderson, 1966), and *The Spy Who Came in from the Cold* (Martin Ritt, 1966). But though the spy film is a useful classification, I prefer to regard it as a subtype of the gangster film genre.

films, Georges Méliès' *Le voyage dans la lune* (1902), fits the description, as do Fritz Lang's *Metropolis* (1926) and *Die Frau im Mond* (*The Woman in the Moon*, 1929). But with the exception of William Cameron Menzies' futuristic fantasy *Things to Come* (1936) and Lothar Mendes' *The Man Who Could Work Miracles* (1937)—both based on works by H. G. Wells, science fiction before World War II concentrated on individual conflicts rather than global ones. With the war and the threat of nuclear holocaust came a widespread recognition that science and technology were in a position to affect the destiny of the entire human race, and, shortly after, the modern science fiction film, with its emphasis on global catastrophe and space travel, began to take shape. The first important example of the form was *Destination Moon* (Irving Pichel, 1950), which was followed rapidly by *Rocketship XM* (Kurt Neumann, 1950), *Five* (Arch Oboler, 1951), *The Thing* (Christian Nyby, 1951), *The Day the Earth Stood Still* (Robert Wise, 1951), *When Worlds Collide* (Rudolph Maté, 1951), *Red Planet Mars* (Harry Horner, 1952), *War of the Worlds* (Byron Haskin, 1954), *This Island Earth* (Joseph Newman, 1955), *Forbidden Planet* (Herbert Wilcox, 1956), and *Invasion of the Body Snatchers* (Don Siegel, 1956). All of these films were well-produced, and the element common to most was some form of world-threatening crisis produced by nuclear war or alien invasion (and, in the Siegel film, an invasion which threatens not destruction but conversion). But *The Thing*, which concerned the arrival of a dangerous creature from another galaxy, started an immensely popular cycle of films about monsters and mutations produced by nuclear radiation or materialized from outer space.

Science fiction purists argue that the monster films of the fifties were less science fiction than horror, but the line between the two categories is sometimes quite difficult to draw. The films of the Universal horror cycle of the thirties (*Dracula, Frankenstein,* etc.—see Chapter 8) and the imaginative widescreen color remakes of them produced by England's Hammer Films in the late fifties and the sixties,* for example, are clearly distinguishable in iconography and theme from science fiction classics like *Invasion of the Body Snatchers* and *Forbidden Planet.* Here science fiction seems to be concerned with the catastrophic impact of technology on civilization—an impact which means the end of evolution—while horror focuses upon the potential evil within the human heart. But monster films pose the specifically modern (that is, post-war) problem of how human evil and technology *combine* to threaten the existence of the race, and therefore they seem to straddle the generic fence between science fiction and horror. With the exception of Warner Brothers' *The Beast from 20,000 Fathoms* (Eugene Lourie, 1953) and the masterfully directed *Them* (Gordon Douglas, 1954), the monster films were cheaply produced and tended to decrease in quality as the decade wore on. Characteristic

* For an eccentric, inflated, but ultimately rewarding analysis of the Hammer phenomenon, see David Pirie, *A Heritage of Horror: The English Gothic Cinema, 1946–1972* (New York, 1974). The best available history of the science fiction film is John Brosnan, *Future Tense: The Cinema of Science Fiction* (New York, 1978).

12.35 Part of a theater lobby display for *Destination Moon* (Irving Pichel, 1950).

12.36 *Rocketship XM* (Kurt Neumann, 1950): an accidental landing on Mars.

12.37 *The Thing* (Christian Nyby, 1951): earthlings measure an alien craft embedded in ice at a remote Arctic air base.

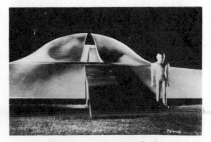

12.38 *The Day the Earth Stood Still* (Robert Wise, 1951): a flying saucer lands in Washington, D.C.

12.39   Visions of a catastrophic future: *When Worlds Collide* (Rudolph Maté, 1951).

12.40 *Invasion of the Body Snatchers* (Don Siegel, 1956): Dana Wynter and Kevin McCarthy pursued by pod-people.

12.41 *It Came from Outer Space* (Jack Arnold, 3-D, 1953)—and Steven Spielberg must have watched it over and over again.

titles are *Kronos* (Kurt Neumann, 1954); *It Came from Beneath the Sea* (Richard Gordon, 1955); *It Conquered the World* (Roger Corman, 1956); *The Deadly Mantis* (Nathan Juran, 1957); *20 Million Miles to Earth* (Nathan Juran, 1957); *The Black Scorpion* (Edward Ludwig, 1957); *The Amazing Colossal Man* (Bert I. Gordon, 1957); *The Blob* (Irvin S. Yeaworth, 1958); *Attack of the Giant Leeches* (uncredited, 1958); *The Brain Eaters* (Edwin Nelson, 1958). The technical wizardry of Universal's Jack Arnold (b. 1916) redeemed his fifties monster films— *It Came from Outer Space* (1953, 3-D); *Creature from the Black Lagoon* (1954, 3-D); *Tarantula* (1955); and his masterpiece, *The Incredible Shrinking Man* (1957)—for serious cinema, as did Kurt Neumann's direction of *The Fly* (1958). The Japanese, recent witnesses to nuclear horror, entered the atomic monster field with a well-crafted series of color films by Inoshiro Honda beginning in 1955 with *Godzilla,* and continuing through *Rodan* (1957), *The Mysterians* (1957), and *Mothra* (1959). The special effects and model work in the Japanese films were initially stunning but became increasingly slipshod through a rash of third-rate sequels (see Chapter 16).

Most of the American low-budget science fiction quickies of the fifties were made by Allied Artists (AA) and American International Pictures (AIP), the successors to the B-film studios of the thirties and forties, and most of them were trash.* Yet at least one important figure in the American cinema came to artistic maturity in this environment. Working first for AA and later for AIP, producer-director Roger Corman (b. 1926) got his start making monster/horror quickies (some reputedly in less than three days) like *Not of This Earth* (1957), *Attack of the Crab Monsters* (1957), and *Bucket of Blood* (1959), and progressed in the early sixties to

---

* Unique to the period, for example, was the preposterous if intriguing phenomenon of the "teenage monster" film—*I Was a Teenage Werewolf* (1957), *I Was a Teenage Frankenstein* (1957), *Meteor Monster* (or *Teenage Monster,* 1958), *Teenage Zombies* (1960), etc.—in which rebellious youth fell prey to experimental medicine.

a series of moody, stylish adaptations of Edgar Allan Poe works, including *The Fall of the House of Usher* (1960); *The Pit and the Pendulum* (1961); *The Premature Burial* (1962); *Tales of Terror* (1962); *The Raven* (1963); *The Haunted Palace* (1963); *The Masque of the Red Death* (1964); and *The Tomb of Ligeia* (1965). Corman directed two visually imaginative films for the youth market, *The Wild Angels* (1966) and *The Trip* (1967), and with *The St. Valentine's Day Massacre* (1967) and *Bloody Mama* (1970) he made significant entries in the gangster genre. Perhaps Corman's greatest contribution to American cinema, however, has been his backing of talented but unknown young directors in their first feature films. Francis Ford Coppola, Peter Bogdanovich, Martin Scorsese, and George Lucas, for example, were all given their first chance to direct by Corman's independently owned New World Production Company, and Corman continues to exercise an important influence upon the course of American film in his combined role as director, producer, and, most recently, distributor of significant foreign films (*Cries and Whispers* [Ingmar Bergman, 1973]; *Amarcord* [Federico Fellini, 1974]; *L'histoire d'Adèle H.* [François Truffaut, 1975]).*

In the sixties, two things happened to the science fiction film. For one thing, the low-budget, quickie monster films were replaced by medium-to-high-budget science fiction films like *The Time Machine* (George Pal, 1960), *Robinson Crusoe on Mars* (Byron Haskin, 1964), *Fantastic Voyage* (Richard Fleischer, 1966), *Planet of the Apes* (Franklin Schaffner, 1967), *The Omega Man* (Boris Sagal, 1971), *The Andromeda Strain* (Robert Wise, 1971), *Soylent Green* (Richard Fleischer, 1973), and, more recently, *Rollerball* (Norman Jewison, 1975). Secondly, serious filmmakers became interested in the genre as a vehicle for personal expression for the first time since its birth. This is demonstrated by Joseph Losey's *These Are the Damned* (1961), Jean-Luc Godard's *Alphaville* (1965), François Truffaut's *Fahrenheit 451* (1966), Elio Petri's *The Tenth Victim* (1965), Joseph Sargent's *Colossus: The Forbin Project* (1970), George Lucas's *THX 1138* (1971), Douglas Trumbull's *Silent Running* (1972), John Boorman's *Zardoz* (1974) and—the apotheosis of the science fiction film, with its multi-million-dollar budget and spectacular special effects—Stanley Kubrick's *2001: A Space Odyssey* (1968). In the wake of *Star Wars* (George Lucas, 1977), *Close Encounters of the Third Kind* (Steven Spielberg, 1977), *Alien* (Ridley Scott, 1979), and *Star Trek: The Motion Picture* (Robert Wise, 1979), it seems clear today that, like the Western and the gangster film, science fiction has been recognized as a form which transcends its generic boundaries. And, as one might expect of a genre whose focal point is technology, the science fiction film has grown increasingly strong through the advanced technology of widescreen color cinematography, electronically generated special effects, and stereo-optical Dolby sound (see Chapter 17).

---

* In 1979, a documentary about Corman's unique contributions, *Roger Corman, Hollywood's Wild Angel*, was produced and directed by Christian Blackwood.

The "Small Film": American *Kammerspiel*

The final generic development of the American fifties was the brief appearance of the "small film," a low-budget black-and-white film shot in the Academy frame format with television techniques and concerned with the everyday lives of ordinary people. Clearly influenced by Italian neo-realism, these films were independently produced, shot largely on location, and usually adapted from original teleplays for live drama by writers like Rod Serling, Paddy Chayefsky, and Reginald Rose. The first small film was *Marty* (Delbert Mann, 1955), based on a downbeat Chayefsky teleplay about the life of a shy, unattractive butcher in New York City. It was produced by the independent Hecht-Lancaster organization (see below) and was an unprecedented critical success, winning both the Grand Prix at Cannes and the American Academy Award for Best Actor (to Ernest Borgnine) in the year of its release. *Marty* was also a great commercial success, and this encouraged the production of other small films adapted from teleplays. Rod Serling's tense drama about the viciousness of corporate power struggles, *Patterns of Power,* was adapted by Fielder Cook as *Patterns* (1956), while Hecht-Lancaster attempted to repeat the success of *Marty* in *The Bachelor Party* (1957), written by Chayefsky and directed by Delbert Mann. Reginald Rose's *12 Angry Men* (Sidney Lumet, 1957), Serling's *Requiem for a Heavyweight* (Ralph Nelson, 1962), and Chayefsky's *The Catered Affair* (Richard Brooks, 1956) and *Middle of the Night* (Delbert Mann, 1959), were all adapted for the screen as "small films," but as live drama began to disappear from television in the late fifties, to be replaced by weekly filmed series, the small-film movement vanished too. The barrier between cinema and television had been broken by the small film, however, and the relationship was to remain an open one, so that ultimately the two media learned to co-exist and even to subsist upon one another. By the late fifties, for instance, the major studios were devoting a substantial percentage of their production facilities to the filming of weekly television series modeled on the B-pictures of the thirties and forties. And by the mid-sixties some of the American cinema's most important new directors—John Frankenheimer, Irvin Kershner, Sidney Lumet, and Sam Peckinpah, to name a few—had begun their careers in studio television production.

12.42 The "small film": *Marty* (Delbert Mann, 1955). Ernest Borgnine.

12.43 The "small film": *Middle of the Night* (Delbert Mann, 1959). Fredric March.

INDEPENDENT PRODUCTION AND THE DECLINE OF THE STUDIO SYSTEM

As this account of the small film suggests, independent production outside of the studio was on the rise in the fifties. Four of the decade's most brilliant American films—*Kiss Me Deadly* (Robert Aldrich, 1955), *The Night of the Hunter* (Charles Laughton, 1955—the actor's only film as a director), *The Sweet Smell of Success* (Alexander Mackendrick, 1957), and *Paths of Glory* (Stanley Kubrick, 1957)—were independently produced, as were seven of the films given the Academy Award for Best Picture between 1954 and 1962. Stanley Kramer started his independent production activities as early as 1948, producing *Home of the Brave* (Mark Robson, 1949), *Champion* (Mark Robson, 1949), *The Men* (Fred Zinnemann, 1950), and *High Noon* (Fred Zinnemann, 1952) on modest budgets in rapid succession. While Kramer's status as a director is equivocal, his production record is distinguished; it also includes the film version of Arthur Miller's play *Death of a Salesman* (Laslo Benedek, 1952), *The Member of the Wedding* (Fred Zinnemann, 1953), and *The Wild One* (Laslo Benedek, 1954). United Artists, which distributed most of Kramer's films, found that its liabilities of the thirties and forties became assets during the fifties and sixties. Having no expensive production facilities to maintain in an era of ever-increasing location shooting, and no theater circuits to lose to the consent decrees, United Artists had become the most important independent producer in Hollywood by 1956. In this capacity, among other things, it provided financial backing for some of John Huston's most important fifties and sixties films—*The African Queen* (1952), *Moulin Rouge* (1953), *Beat the Devil* (1954), *The Unforgiven* (1960), *The Misfits* (1961), *Freud* (1962), and *The List of Adrian Messenger* (1963). The Hecht-Lancaster Company, organized in 1947 by producer Harold Hecht and actor Burt Lancaster, was another successful independent. From the early fifties, it specialized in sophisticated action films such as *The Crimson Pirate* (Robert Siodmak, 1952), *Apache* (Robert Aldrich, 1954), *Vera Cruz* (Robert Aldrich, 1954), *The Professionals* (Richard Brooks, 1966), and *The Dirty Dozen* (Robert Aldrich, 1967). Other notable independent production companies born in the fifties were the Walter Mirisch Corporation, Seven-Arts, and actor Kirk Douglas' Bryna Productions.

The old studio production system remained intact throughout the fifties but continued to crumble under the combined threats of political reaction, television, rising independent production, and, perhaps most serious, the studios' loss of their exhibition chains. By mid-decade, steadily increasing monetary inflation could be added to this catalogue of woes, and all of these forces spelled the beginning of the end for Hollywood as it had been structured since the twenties. From the peak year of 1946, when American theaters had averaged nearly one hundred million admissions per week, film attendance dropped to forty-six million in 1955. In that year, production fell to 254 features per year, from 383 in 1950 and nearly 500 per year throughout the thirties. Universal Pictures was absorbed by Decca Records in 1952, which was absorbed in turn by the huge entertainment conglomerate MCA in 1959, and RKO ceased production entirely in 1953 (although the famous name survives in "RKO General," the broadcast ownership division of the General Tire and Rubber Corporation). American film attendance and production continued to decline as production costs soared, until, by 1966, 30 percent of all films made in the United States were independently produced, and 50 percent of all American films were "runaway" productions—films shot on location in foreign countries (usually Italy, Yugoslavia, or Spain) to economize on sets and labor (non-union, and therefore cheaper). In other words, by the mid-sixties, 80 percent of all American films were made outside of the once iron-clad studio system. Moreover, as we shall see in the next chapter, the foreign industries had recovered from the war by the late fifties and were starting to provide Hollywood with vigorous commercial competition for the first time in its history. Stiff post-war import duties on non-domestic productions had severely restricted Hollywood's most profitable European markets—especially England, Italy, and France—while the American demand for foreign films had been growing steadily since the divestiture order of 1948 first permitted U.S. exhibitors to show what they chose rather than what the studios had chosen for them. In fact, between 1958 and 1968, the number of foreign films in distribution in the United States would actually exceed the number of domestic productions, often by a ratio of two (and, sometimes, three) to one.

As the studio system declined throughout the fifties, so too did the star system with which it had been intimately linked for over thirty years. As studios were forced to cut back on production due to the inroads of television, inflation, and other blights, expensive promotional campaigns were abandoned and star contracts went from long-term to short-term, and finally to simple profit-sharing options on individual films. This made the stars increasingly independent of the studios, and some, like Burt Lancaster and Kirk Douglas, even formed their own production companies. There were American stars in the fifties, to be sure, and many whose careers had begun under the studio system—among them, Lancaster, Douglas, James Stewart, Cary Grant, Henry Fonda, John Wayne, Rock Hudson, Tony Curtis, Charlton Heston, Montgomery Clift, Robert Mitchum, William Holden, Frank Sinatra, Yul Brynner, Glenn Ford, Gregory Peck, Gary Cooper, Ava Gardner, Jean Simmons, Grace Kelly, Audrey Hepburn, Susan Hayward, Gina Lollobrigida, Sophia Loren, Deborah Kerr, Debby Reynolds, Elizabeth Taylor, Kim Novak, Doris Day, and—quintessentially—Marilyn Monroe, Marlon Brando, and James Dean. But they worked more independently of the system than ever before, and, to quote Alexander Walker, the fifties in general were the transitional period "from studios who owned stars to stars who owned pictures."[6]

THE SCRAPPING OF THE PRODUCTION CODE

A final important development of the American fifties was the breaking of the Production Code and the achievement of an unprecedented freedom of expression for the American cinema. Ever since a U.S. Supreme Court decision of 1915 involving D. W. Griffith's *The Birth of a Nation* (*Mutual* v. *Ohio*), the movies had not been considered a part of the press, whose freedom is guaranteed by the First Amendment to the Constitution. For this reason, six states and hundreds of local communities had film censorship boards, and, of course, through the Production Code, Hollywood had imposed an extreme form of censorship upon itself. But this situation changed in 1952, after the State of New York attempted to prevent the exhibition of the Italian film *Il miracolo* (*The Mir-*

acle, Roberto Rossellini, 1947; written by Federico Fellini) on the grounds that it committed "sacrilege." Producer-distributor Joseph Burstyn took the case to the U.S. Supreme Court, which ruled in May 1952 that movies were protected against the charge of sacrilege by both the First and Fourteenth Amendments. Subsequent court rulings between 1952 and 1958 clarified the *Miracle* decision, and by the early sixties films were guaranteed full freedom of expression.*

Simultaneously with these legal battles, the Production Code was being challenged from within by the influx of "unapproved" foreign films and, especially, by the rise of independent production. Since the studios no longer owned America's theaters, they could no longer force them to accept their product exclusively. Shrewdly realizing this, director Otto Preminger openly challenged the Code by producing two films of sensational (for that era) content—*The Moon Is Blue* (1953), which used the forbidden word *virgin,* and *The Man with the Golden Arm* (1955), in which Frank Sinatra portrayed a heroin addict—for United Artists. As Preminger had anticipated, both films were denied the Production Code's "Seal of Approval," and both were released independently to great commercial success. It didn't take long for the studios to find out which way the wind was blowing: Elia Kazan's *Baby Doll,* released by Warner Brothers in 1956 to a storm of protest, was the first motion picture of a major American studio ever to be publicly condemned by the Legion of Decency, the Catholic organization responsible for instituting the Production Code in the first place. The financial success of these three films sounded the death knell for the Legion's influence in Hollywood, and the Production Code was scrapped altogether in the sixties, in favor of a liberal ratings system administered by the Motion Picture Association of America (MPAA).†

The change meant that around 1955 human sexuality began to make its first overt appearance on the American screen since the Code's imposition some twenty years before, and, more generally, a fascination with veiled (and increasingly unveiled) eroticism came to pervade American films of the late fifties and early sixties. This more than any other single factor accounts for the vast popularity of the *Pillow Talk* cycle and the seven adaptations from the exotic plays of Tennessee Williams during

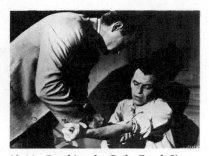

12.44 Breaking the Code: Frank Sinatra shooting dope in *The Man with the Golden Arm* (Otto Preminger, 1955).

---

* This trend is currently being reversed in federal and state court cases dealing with obscenity. The U.S. Supreme Court ruling of 1973, which left the definition of obscenity to elusive "community standards," has confused the whole issue of film and freedom of speech, since the Court did not specify what it meant by "community." Thus, films like Just Jaeckin's *Histoire d'O* (*The Story of O,* 1976)—the softest of soft-core erotica—have been successfully prosecuted in cities like Detroit on the grounds that they are offensive to "communities" which may be no larger than several blocks.

† Instituted in 1968 and revised in 1972, the MPAA Ratings System uses the following four classifications for films: G (General audience); PG (Parental Guidance suggested for children); R (Restricted to persons under seventeen unless accompanied by an adult); and X (Prohibited to persons under seventeen). Many persons believe that the ratings system has contributed significantly to the decline of high-quality films in the G and PG range and to the sharp increase in exploitative sex and violence in the R and X classifications. As with the concept of "Family Viewing Time" on network television, it would seem that a system designed to protect children from debasing entertainment has served to debase the entertainment of both children and adults.

this period. But other taboos were broken too, as a new realism of content entered the American cinema after a long period of repression. Social problems like juvenile delinquency (*Rebel Without a Cause* [1955]; *Blackboard Jungle* [1955]), alcoholism, drug addiction, and even race were suddenly fair game for film-makers working both inside and outside the studios.* Crime began to be treated less moralistically and melodramatically, so that it became possible by the end of the decade to sympathize with criminals as human beings, though they did not become wholly admirable ones until Arthur Penn's *Bonnie and Clyde* (1967). The next cultural taboo† the American cinema was to overcome (simultaneously with Italy and preceded slightly by Japan) was the convention against the graphic, excessive, and/or poetic depiction of brutality and violence. This, however, could not occur until President Kennedy and his assassin had been gunned down before running movie cameras in Dallas in 1963 and the war in Vietnam was brought nightly into American living rooms between 1965 and 1968.

---

* Important films on these themes made outside of the system during the sixties include the *cinéma-vérité* work of Shirley Clarke (b. 1925)—*The Connection* (1961), which deals with drug addiction; *The Cool World* (1964), focusing on the lives of young blacks in the ghetto; and *Portrait of Jason* (1967), an extended monologue by a black homosexual prostitute— and the improvisational dramas of John Cassavetes (b. 1929) on race (*Shadows,* 1961) and middle-class malaise (*Faces* [1968]; *Husbands* [1970]). Clarke now works primarily in video, but Cassavetes has continued to make films (*Minnie and Moskowitz* [1971]; *A Woman Under the Influence* [1974]; *Opening Night* [1978]; *Gloria* [1980]) in collaboration with his wife, the brilliant actress Gena Rowlands (b. 1934).

† But not the last: see Amos Vogel, *Film as a Subversive Art* (New York, 1974).

The French New Wave and Its Native Context

THE OCCUPATION AND POST-WAR CINEMA

During the German Occupation of 1940–45, with Feyder, Renoir, Duvivier, and Clair all in exile, a new generation of French directors emerged, most of whom had worked as scriptwriters or assistants under the major figures of poetic realism in the thirties.* Claude Autant-Lara (b. 1903), who had worked as a designer for L'Herbier and as an assistant to Clair, directed a number of sophisticated period films during the Occupation, including *Le mariage de Chiffon* (1942), *Lettres d'amour* (1942), and the satirical *Douce* (1943). Autant-Lara's critical reputation rests most firmly, however, upon a series of stylish literary adaptations, written by Jean Aurenche (b. 1904) and Pierre Bost (b. 1901), which he made in the post-war era—especially *Le diable au corps* (*The Devil in the Flesh*, 1947; from the Raymond Radiguet novel), *L'auberge rouge* (*The Red Inn*, 1950; from Aurenche), *Le blé en herbe* (*The Ripening Seed*, 1954; from Colette), *Le rouge et le noir* (*The Red and the Black*, 1954; from Stendhal), and *Le joueur* (*The Gambler*, 1958; from Dostoevsky). Writing as a team, Aurenche and Bost became specialists in tightly scripted films; they also worked closely with the director René Clément (b. 1913), whose first film had been a neo-realistic account of the activities of the French Resistance, *La bataille du rail* (*The Battle of the Rails*, 1945).

Clément also co-directed *La belle et la bête* (*Beauty and the Beast*, 1946) with the playwright Jean Cocteau and made the suspenseful anti-Nazi thriller *Les maudits* (*The Damned*, 1947). But his two greatest films of the post-war era, both written by Aurenche and Bost, were the poetic anti-war drama *Jeux interdits* (*Forbidden Games*, 1952) and a strikingly evocative adaptation of Zola's *L'assommoir* entitled *Gervaise* (1956). His *Monsieur Ripois* (*The Knave of Hearts*), shot in England in 1954, is a

---

* Perhaps the most important film event of the Occupation was the foundation of the Institut des Hautes Études Cinématographiques (IDHEC) by Marcel L'Herbier in 1943. This government-subsidized film school today offers professional training in every aspect of film production as well as in history and aesthetics. It provides certification for persons wishing to enter the French film industry, and its high standards have attracted students from all over the world.

13.1 *Les jeux interdits* (René Clément, 1952): Brigitte Fossey, Georges Poujouly.

13.2 *La belle et la bête* (Jean Cocteau and René Clément, 1946): Josette Day, Jean Marais.

comic masterpiece, but after it Clément turned to big-budget international co-productions like *Is Paris Burning?* (1966) and *Rider on the Rain* (1969).* Jean Grémillon (1902–59), who had made important films in the silent era (*Un tour au large* [1926]; *Maldone* [1927]), produced his greatest work during the Occupation—*Lumière d'été* (1943), a Renoir-esque portrait of the decadent French ruling classes written by Jacques Prévert, and *Le ciel est à vous* (English title: *The Woman Who Dared*, 1944), a beautiful film about a provincial woman who breaks the world record for long-distance flying with the help of her husband and the people of her town. After the war, Grémillon turned to the documentary but continued to exercise great influence upon the French cinema as president of the Cinémathèque Française (see below).

Jean Cocteau (1889–1963), who had confined himself to writing scripts during the Occupation (for Jean Delannoy's modernized version of the Tristan and Isolde legend, *L'éternel retour* [*The Eternal Return*, 1943]; for Robert Bresson's *Les dames du Bois de Boulogne* [*The Ladies of the Bois du Boulogne*, 1945]; see below), returned to the practice of film-making in the post-war years. Perhaps more than any other figure he incarnated the literary tendency of French cinema during this period. In 1946, he wrote and co-directed (with Clément) an enchantingly beautiful version of the Flemish fairy tale *La belle et la bête* (*Beauty and the Beast*) in a visual style based upon the paintings of Vermeer; it stands today as perhaps the greatest example of the cinema of the fantastic in the history of film.† Next, Cocteau directed two film versions of his own plays, the

---

* Like Autant-Lara, Clément continued to contribute traditional narrative films to the French cinema well into the seventies.

† Remade in 1979 by the Slovak surrealist Juraj Herz (b. 1934), mixing French and Middle European folk traditions (see Chapter 15).

satirical *Ruy Blas* (1947) and *Les parents terribles* (English title: *The Storm Within,* 1948), a domestic tragicomedy set within the confines of a single room. With *Orphée* (1950), a modern version of the Orpheus legend, Cocteau returned to the surreal, psycho-mythic regions of *Le sang d'un poète* (*Blood of a Poet,* 1930) to create his most brilliant film. He adapted his play *Les enfants terribles* (*The Terrible Children,* directed by Jean-Pierre Melville) for the screen in 1950 and gave the cinema his final artistic testament in *Le testament d'Orphée* (*The Testament of Orpheus,* 1959), a surrealistic fable replete with personal symbols which attempts to suggest the relationships among poetry, myth, death, and the unconscious mind.

Jacques Becker (1906–60) is another figure who emerged during the Occupation and came to prominence in the post-war years. As assistant to Renoir from 1931 to 1939, Becker tended to direct films which cut across the traditional class barriers of French society. *Goupi Mains-Rouge* (English title: *It Happened at the Inn,* 1943) is a realistic portrait of peasant life; *Falbalas* (English title: *Paris Frills,* 1945) is a drama set in the Parisian fashion houses; *Antoine et Antoinette* (1947) is a tale of young love in a working-class milieu; *Rendez-vous de juillet* (1949) offers a sympathetic study of the attitudes and ambitions of post-war youth; and *Edouard et Caroline* (1951) examines young married life in high society. But Becker's masterpiece is unquestionably *Casque d'or* (*Golden Helmet/Golden Marie,* 1952), a visually sumptuous tale of doomed love set in turn-of-the-century Paris and written by Becker himself. Cast in the form of a period gangster film and based upon historical fact, *Casque d'or* is a work of great formal beauty whose visual texture evokes the films of Feuillade and engravings from *la belle époque. Touchez pas au grisbi* (English title: *Honor Among Thieves,* 1954), adapted from an Albert Simonin novel, was a sophisticated tale of rivalry between contemporary Montmartre gangs which started the vogue for gangster films and thrillers that typified French cinema in the late fifties (for instance, the American émigré Jules Dassin's *Rififi* [1955]). After making three commissioned films of uneven quality, Becker directed his final masterpiece, *Le trou* (*The Hole/The Night Watch*), shortly before his death in 1960. Like Bresson's *Un condamné à mort s'est échappé* (*A Man Escaped,* 1956; see below), this film, set entirely in a prison cell where five men plot an ill-fated escape, is a restrained exploration of loyalty, freedom, and human dignity.

Another important director whose career began during the Occupation was Henri-Georges Clouzot (1907–77), a former scriptwriter for E. A. Dupont and Anatole Litvak at UFA. Clouzot's first feature was unremarkable, but his second, *Le corbeau* (*The Raven,* 1943), established him as the chief progenitor of French *film noir.* This darkly pessimistic tale of a town destroyed by poison-pen letters is a masterpiece of psychological suspense, but because it was produced by the Nazi-owned Continental Corporation and seemed to be anti-French (although it was simply misanthropic), both Clouzot and his co-scenarist, Louis Chavance (b. 1907), were accused of collaboration and briefly suspended from the French film

13.3 *Le trou* (Jacques Becker, 1960): Jean Keraudy.

13.4 *Le salaire de la peur* (Henri-Georges Clouzot, 1953): Charles Vanel.

13.5 *Justice est faite* (André Cayatte, 1950): Valentine Tessier.

industry after the Liberation. Clouzot, in fact, was apolitical, but his films typically deal with the brutal, the sordid, and the neurotic, and his entire career was marked by an aura of scandal. His first post-war film, *Quai des orfèvres* (English title: *Jenny Lamour,* 1947) was a violent thriller which transcended its genre by creating Hitchcockian suspense. In *Manon* (1949), Clouzot modernized the Abbé Prévost's eighteenth-century classic, *Manon Lescaut,* by setting it in the post-Liberation context of the Paris black market and the illegal emigration of Jews to Palestine. And with *Le salaire de la peur* (*The Wages of Fear,* 1953),* Clouzot achieved a masterpiece of unrelenting horror and alienation in a film about a group of down-and-out European expatriates, trapped in a miserable South American town, who are driven by despair and greed to undertake the suicidal mission of hauling nitroglycerine for an American oil firm.

Always a meticulous and professional craftsman in the French studio tradition, Clouzot became increasingly shallow as the fifties progressed. The film which confirmed his international reputation, *Les diaboliques* (*Diabolique,* 1955), is an intensely manipulative exercise in horrific suspense involving a complicated murder plot in a boarding school. *Les espions* (*The Spies,* 1957), set in a psychiatric clinic, is a failed attempt to combine the bitter naturalism of his earlier films with surrealistic fantasy, and *La vérité* (*The Truth,* 1960) is a professional but glib film cast in the form of a murder trial and narrated in flashbacks. A projected film on the destructive effects of jealousy, *L'enfer* (1964), was scrapped because of Clouzot's ill health, and he was able to complete only a single feature before his death in 1977—the controversial and somewhat experimental *La prisonnière* (*The Prisoner,* 1968), which returns to the perverse and pathological mode of *Le corbeau* to examine the dynamics of sexual degradation.

Mining the same dark vein as Clouzot in the post-war period was Yves Allégret (b. 1907), who became something of a specialist in *film noir* with *Dédée d'Anvers* (*Dedee,* 1947), *Une si jolie petite plage* (*Riptide/Such a Pretty Little Beach,* 1948) and *Manèges* (English title: *The Cheats,* 1950), all written by Jacques Sigurd (b. 1920). The former lawyer André Cayatte (b. 1909) was another popular director of dark films in the late forties. But his major claim to significance rests upon his four "judicial" films scripted by Charles Spaak—*Justice est faite* (*Justice Is Done,* 1950), *Nous sommes tous des assassins* (*We Are All Murderers,* 1952), *Avant le déluge* (*Before the Deluge,* 1953), and *Le dossier noir* (*The Black File,* 1955)—a series of scathing attacks upon the French legal system.† The same period witnessed the best work of Jacqueline Audry (1908–77), who collaborated closely with her husband, the scriptwriter Pierre Laroche (1902–62), to produce several tasteful adaptations of the works of Sartre (*Huis clos* [*No Exit,* 1954]) and Colette (*Mitsou,* 1956).

---

* Remade by William Friedkin in 1977 as *Sorcerer.*

† More recently, Cayatte has made *La raison d'état* (*State Reasons,* 1978), a polemical film on the corrupt practices of the French government in its arms sales to terrorists.

Robert Bresson and Jacques Tati

The foregoing account should make it clear that, except for *film noir,* the prevailing mode of the post-war French cinema was literary adaptation, and this caused French films of the era to become increasingly verbal and theatrical. The war, in short, had not produced a break with the cinematic traditions of the past in France as it had done in other European nations, most notably Italy. Two important exceptions to this statement are to be found in the quite disparate work of Robert Bresson and Jacques Tati.

Robert Bresson (b. 1907), a former scriptwriter, was the more important of the two. His two Occupation films, *Les anges du péché (The Angels of Sin,* 1943), written with the playwright Jean Giraudoux, and *Les dames du Bois de Boulogne (The Ladies of the Bois du Boulogne,* 1945), freely adapted by Bresson and Jean Cocteau from a story by the eighteenth-century writer Jacques Diderot, established him as a serious and disciplined artist within the "scenarist," or literary, tradition of French cinema. But in *Le journal d'un curé de campagne (The Diary of a Country Priest,* 1950), adapted from the novel by Georges Bernanos, Bresson displayed a highly personalized style whose psychological realism is predicated upon an absolute austerity of acting, dialogue, and *mise-en-scène.* All of Bresson's later films display this austerity and precision of style, which has led some critics to call him a "classicist," although he prefers to be thought of as a realist practicing close to the borderline of abstraction. His masterpiece, *Un condamné à mort s'est échappé (A Man Escaped,* 1956), concerns the arrest, escape, and recapture of a young Resistance fighter during the Occupation, and it takes place almost entirely in the condemned man's cell. Most of Bresson's subsequent films—*Pickpocket* (1959), *Le procès de Jeanne d'arc (The Trial of Joan of Arc,* 1961—like Dreyer's film, based upon the actual trial records), *Au hasard, Balthasar* (1966), *Mouchette* (1966), *Un femme douce (A Gentle Creature,* 1969), and *Quatre nuits d'un rêveur (Four Nights of a Dreamer,* 1971; an adaptation of Dostoevsky's novella *White Nights*)—have been derived from literary sources and deal with humanist themes. Others are more pessimistic: *Lancelot du lac (Lancelot of the Lake,* 1976) offers a dark, ascetic vision of a Camelot which has outlived its own ideals; in *Le diable probablement (The Devil Probably,* 1977), it is our own society which has outlived its ideals and its promise. All of Bresson's films are painstakingly crafted attempts to materialize the spiritual dilemmas of the race through the moral struggles of individuals, which makes Bresson a kind of contemporary Carl Dreyer. And, indeed, André Bazin often suggested that Bresson, more than any practicing director, had succeeded in fusing the values of the silent cinema with those of sound.

13.6 *Le journal d'un curé de campagne* (Robert Bresson, 1950): Claude Laydu, Nicole Maurey.

Jacques Tati (b. 1908), a former music-hall entertainer and pantomimist, became one of the international cinema's greatest comic talents in the post-war era, rivaling the achievements of Max Linder, Chaplin, and Keaton in the silent film. In his first feature, *Jour de fête* (*The Big Day*/*The Village Fair*, 1949), which took him several years to complete, Tati plays a French postman who is seduced by a documentary into employing then-sophisticated American Postal Service technology in his small village, with disastrous results. As in all of Tati's films, the humor, largely visual, is achieved through scrupulous planning and brilliant mime. In *Les vacances de M. Hulot* (*Mr. Hulot's Holiday,* 1953), Tati created a new comic character, M. Hulot, a vague, wacky middle-class Frenchman who goes to spend his holiday at a seaside resort in Brittany. Hulot's misadventures there are presented to us as a series of meticulously worked-out sight gags, in which things simply "happen" to the character with no particular logic or cause. With *Mon oncle* (*My Uncle,* 1958), his first film in color, Tati turned to the more serious vein of satire. Here, Hulot's traditional and somewhat archaic lifestyle in an old quarter of Paris is contrasted with the antiseptic and mechanistic environment of his brother-in-law, Arpel, who lives in an ultra-modern house in the city's new suburban wasteland and works as an executive in a plastics factory. The humanistic impact of the satire is not unlike that of Clair's *À nous la liberté* (1931) or Chaplin's *Modern Times* (1936), although its appeal is totally unsentimental.

13.7 Jacques Tati as M. Hulot in *Mon oncle* (Jacques Tati, 1958).

Tati's next film, *Playtime* (1967), took him three years to complete and was shot in color and 70mm Panavision with stereophonic sound. Using the full resources of the widescreen format to create spectator involvement, Tati offers in *Playtime* a series of quietly humorous vignettes about a group of American tourists who come to see the "real" Paris and end up experiencing a space-age city of steel, glass, chrome, and plastic. It is a film not of belly-laughs but of sustained, intelligent humor, and it represents Tati's finest effort to date. His latest film, *Traffic* (1971), is a minor work which comments upon the auto-mania of modern industrial society. Tati has made only five features * in his entire career, because he is a painstaking craftsman who plans every detail of his films far in advance of production. For this reason, it has been difficult for him to get financing and distribution. He is a master cinematic humorist whose concept of comedy is almost purely visual, and he deserves to be ranked with the greatest of the silent comedians for the breadth of his humanity and restrained brilliance of his comic achievement.

Max Ophüls

Another major figure working in the French cinema in the fifties, and one who was to have a profound influence on the New Wave generation which succeeded him, was Max Ophüls (b. Max Oppenheimer, 1902--57). Ophüls was a German Jew who had directed films for UFA between 1930 and Hitler's rise to power in 1933 (*Die verkaufte Braut* [*The Bartered Bride,* 1932]; *Liebelei* [1933]). For the next seven years he

---

* In 1977, Tati announced plans for a new feature, to be entitled *Confusion;* it remains uncompleted at this writing.

made films in Italy, the Netherlands, and France, where he ultimately became a citizen 1938. Ophüls was forced to flee to Hollywood when France fell to the Nazis in 1940, and, after four years of anonymity, he was finally able to make a series of stylish melodramas for Paramount: *The Exile* (1947), *Letter from an Unknown Woman* (1948), *Caught* (1949), and *The Reckless Moment* (1949). Returning to France in 1949, Ophüls entered the period of his greatest creativity, making four elegant, masterful films in succession between 1950 and 1955, before he died in 1957. In the course of his career, Ophüls had always worked within the studio system, so that the subject matter of his films—often light and operetta-like—was never as important to him as visual style. And it is for their dazzling *mise-en-scène* that Ophüls' last four films, all photographed by the great French cameraman Christian Matras (b. 1903), are most remarkable.

13.8 *Le plaisir* (Max Ophüls, 1952): Simone Simon.

La ronde (1950) is an adaptation of an Arthur Schnitzler play set in turn-of-the-century Vienna. Its ten separate episodes posit that love is a perpetual roundabout in which one partner is regularly exchanged for another until the pattern comes full circle, like the movements of a waltz, only to begin again. This unbroken circle of affairs is presided over by a master of ceremonies who manipulates and comments on the behavior of the characters, becoming a surrogate for Ophüls himself. *Le plaisir* (English title: *House of Pleasure,* 1952) is derived from three Maupassant stories, linked by a narrator, which illustrate the theme that pleasure may be easy to come by but happiness is not. Like all of Ophüls' work, the film is marked by meticulous attention to period detail and by an incessantly moving camera. In one famous sequence, the camera circles the exterior of a brothel time and time again, never entering the set but peering voyeuristically through windows at significant dramatic action taking place within. In *Madame de . . .* (English title: *The Earrings of Madame de . . . ,1953*), also set at the turn of the century, Ophüls constructs yet another circular narrative turning around a central axis of vanity, frivolity, and lust. Here, the passage of a pair of earrings from a husband to his wife to the husband's mistress to the wife's lover and finally back to the husband again constitutes a single perfect revolution in the roundabout of infidelity. The characters are ultimately shallow, because everything in *Madame de . . .* is subordinate to its aesthetic design. As if to mirror the movement of the waltzes on the soundtrack, the camera whirls and pirouettes continuously to follow the film's principals through its glittering period decor, suggesting that life is itself a kind of waltz in which all of us are caught up while the music plays.

13.9 *Madame de . . .* (Max Ophüls, 1953): Danielle Darrieux.

Lola Montès (1955) is generally considered to be Ophüls' masterpiece and the consummation of his entire life's work. Conceived by its producers as a big-budget super-spectacle in Eastmancolor and Cinemascope with an international cast of stars, it was based on the scandalous life of a mediocre nineteenth-century dancer who became the mistress of the composer Franz Liszt and of Ludwig II, the mad king of Bavaria, during the revolutions of 1848, finally ending as a circus performer who must sell kisses to earn her keep. Ophüls cared nothing for the subject, remarking

13.10 *Lola Montès* (Max Ophüls, 1959): Martine Carol.

of Lola herself, "Her rôle is roughly the same as that of our pair of earrings in *Madame de. . . .*"[1] That is, he merely used her story to create a dazzling exercise in visual style, and *Lola Montès* became one of the most intricate, opulent, and elaborate films to appear on the French screen since Abel Gance's *Napoléon* (1927). Ironically, Ophüls was initially opposed to the use of Cinemascope, but his sense of visual patterning was such that he turned *Lola Montès* into a stunning exhibition of composition for the widescreen frame. He would frequently break the horizontal space of the screen with vertical dominants and frame shots through arches, columns, and drapery. He learned to compose close-ups by balancing both sides of the frame, and at other times—as during the circus scenes—he would fill the entire Cinemascope frame with significant dramatic action. The film begins and ends within the circus tent, where the ringmaster introduces Lola's act by recalling the circumstances of her past life, which is then represented on the screen in a series of achronological flashbacks. Ophüls uses color non-naturalistically throughout the film, especially in these flashback sequences, where each is tinted according to its prevailing emotional tone. Finally, the camera seems never to stop its circular tracking around some invisible axis, in or out of the tent, making the circularity of things seen on the screen a metaphor for life itself. As Andrew Sarris has remarked, "With Ophüls it is movement itself that is emphasized rather than its terminal points of rest."[2]

As with *Intolerance* (1916) and *Citizen Kane* (1941), the narrative technique of *Lola Montès* was so unconventional that audiences stayed away from it. In response, its producers, the Gamma Company, first cut the film from 140 to 110 minutes, and finally re-edited the story in chronological sequence for release in a ninety-minute version. Still, the film's commercial failure was so complete that Gamma was eventually bankrupted by it, and it seems likely that Ophüls' death from a rheumatic heart condition in 1957 was hastened by the mutilation of his masterpiece. In 1969, however, the original version was reconstructed and released, to great critical acclaim. The key to Ophüls' style is his mastery of the long take and, especially, of the continuously moving camera. Ophüls was also a genius at composition within the frame, and the influence upon him of both German Expressionism and French pictorial Impressionism was profound. In his passion for decor and his obsession with the sensuous surfaces of reality, Ophüls most closely resembles von Sternberg. In his cynicism and worldly wit, he is close to Ernst Lubitsch. That his films are devoid of content—a charge frequently leveled against both von Sternberg and Lubitsch—is quite true, if we mean by the term *verbal* or *conceptual* substance. But as the New Wave generation was to argue and to demonstrate time and again, the substance of cinema is *audio-visual,* not verbal, and it exists on a level of discourse—like that of the circular tracking shots in *Lola Montès*—where perception and conceptualization become one.

THE INFLUENCE OF THE FIFTIES DOCUMENTARY MOVEMENT AND INDEPENDENT PRODUCTION

By 1955, the French commercial cinema had reached a dangerous point of stagnation. The new generation of directors which emerged during the Occupation had for the most part simply continued pre-war trends, and by the mid-fifties many of its members were firmly ensconced within the studio system or working on big budget spectacles and international co-productions. The cinematic individualism of Bresson and Tati, and also of Cocteau, offered a succeeding generation of French directors an example of the way in which film could be used as a medium of personal expression; and Ophüls had forecast the possibility of a purely audio-visual language for the screen. But the major stylistic influences upon this younger generation of film-makers came from the French documentary movement of the fifties, which was their training-ground, and from the films of independent directors working outside the studio system of production.

13.11 *Farrebique* (Georges Rouquier, 1948).

This documentary movement can be said to have begun in 1948 with Georges Rouquier's *Farrebique,* a lyrical feature-length documentary about peasant life on a farm through the four seasons. Jean Grémillon (*Le six juin à l'aube* [*The Sixth of June at Dawn,* 1945]) and Roger Leenhardt (*Les dernières vacances*) [*The Last Holiday,* 1947]) both made countless short documentaries throughout the fifties on art and the lives of great men. But the master of French documentary cinema during this period was Georges Franju (b. 1912), a totally original film-maker who was deeply influenced by German Expressionism and has often been called a surrealist. Franju had been working in cinema since 1937, when he made a 16mm amateur film with Henri Langlois (with whom he would later establish the important and influential Cinémathèque Française), but his first major film was *Le sang des bêtes* (*The Blood of the Beasts,* 1949), a brutally graphic documentary short about the daily activity of a slaughterhouse in a quiet Parisian suburb, whose butchery

13.12 *Le sang des bêtes* (Georges Franju, 1949).

was made deliberately resonant of the horrors of the Nazi death camps. *En passant par la Lorraine* (*Passing by Lorraine*, 1950) depicted the steel mills of that peaceful region as furnaces consuming the lives of the men who work them; and in *Hôtel des invalides,* possibly his finest film, Franju turned an ostensibly objective account of the French War Museum into a devastating anti-war statement by exposing the human suffering that underwrites the myths of heroism and glory enshrined by the institution. Other important Franju shorts were *Le grand Méliès* (1952) and *Monsieur et Madame Curie* (1953), documentary tributes to the great pioneers of modern cinema and modern science, respectively. In 1958 Franju directed his first feature, *La tête contre les murs* (English title: *The Keepers*), a half-documentary, half-surrealist account of a sane man who is committed to a French lunatic asylum; the film is often cited as a forerunner of the New Wave. The grisly horror film *Les yeux sans visage* (*Eyes Without a Face,* 1959; released—cut and dubbed—in the U.S. as *The Horror Chamber of Dr. Faustus*) concerns a mad doctor who kidnaps young girls in a futile effort to transplant their faces onto the head of his own disfigured daughter, and *Pleins feux sur l'assassin* (*Spotlight on the Murderer,* 1961) is an atmospheric thriller adapted from a novel by Boileau and Narcejac. Franju's next two films were an adaptation of François Mauriac's *Thérèse Desqueroux* (1962) and *Judex* (1963), an *hommage* to Louis Feuillade's twelve-part serial of 1916. Since 1963, Franju has made five other features—*Thomas l'imposteur* (*Thomas the Imposter,* 1965), *Les rideaux blancs* (*The White Curtains,* 1966), *Marcel Allain* (1966), *La faute de l'Abbé Mouret* (*The Sin of Abbé Mouret,* 1970), and *L'homme sans visage* (*Man Without a Face,* 1974)—all but one of them intensely poetic visualizations of literary works, which have little in common with the style of the New Wave that his own documentaries helped to create.

Alain Resnais (b. 1922), whose first feature, *Hiroshima, mon amour* (1959), became the clarion call of the New Wave, was another important figure in the French documentary movement. He made documentary shorts for the first eleven years of his career, beginning with a series of art films—*Van Gogh* (1948), *Gauguin* (1950), *Guernica* (1950)—and progressing to *Nuit et brouillard* (*Night and Fog,* 1955), a profoundly disturbing meditation upon the horrors of the death camps ten years after, and upon the effects of time and memory on the way we perceive them. *Toute la mémoire du monde* (*The Memory of the World,* 1956), a study of the books "imprisoned" in the French National Library, has a similar temporal theme, as do most of Resnais' features. Other figures associated with the documentary short in the fifties were Chris Marker (see below), an original and highly personal film-maker who organized the radical production cooperative SLON (Société pour le Lancement des Oeuvres Nouvelles) in 1967; Jean Rouch (b. 1917), who became the apostle of *cinéma-verité* in the sixties (he invented the term by translating Dziga Vertov's *kino-pravda* into French for his co-production, with the sociologist Edgar Morin, *Chronique d'un été* [*Chronicle of a Summer,* 1961]); and Agnès Varda (b. 1928), a former photographer whose first

13.13 *Les yeux sans visage* (Georges Franju, 1959): Edith Scob.

feature, the independently produced *La Pointe-Courte* (1955), was a distinct forerunner of the New Wave.

The example of independent production outside of the traditional studio system was another important influence upon the emergent New Wave generation, and Jean-Pierre Melville (b. Jean-Pierre Grumbach, 1917–73) was a vastly significant figure in this regard. A lover of cinema from an early age, Melville founded his own production company in 1945. His first feature, *Le silence de la mer* (*The Silence of the Sea,* 1947), earned him the admiration of Cocteau, who commissioned him to direct *Les enfants terribles* in 1949. The commercial success of *Quand tu liras cette lettre* (*When You Read This Letter,* 1952) allowed Melville to purchase his own studio and move into totally independent production. The result was the much-admired gangster film *Bob le flambeur* (1955), a highly personalized work whose production methods—location shooting, small crew, use of unknown actors—became the model for those of the New Wave. Melville's work itself became increasingly commercial after he directed *Léon Morin, prêtre* (*Léon Morin, Priest,* 1961), a star vehicle for Jean-Paul Belmondo, but his fascination with the iconography of the American gangster film and the underworld of urban crime caused him to produce a trilogy of popular gangster films in the sixties which are among the most admired in the genre—*Le Doulos* (*The Fingerman,* 1962), *Le deuxième souffle* (*Second Breath,* 1965), and *Le samouraï* (*The Samurai,* 1967).

Another independent production which influenced the New Wave—and which some critics have called its first manifestation—is Agnès Varda's *La Pointe-Courte* (1955). This film about the dissolution and reconstruction of a marriage in a small fishing village, produced by a collective of crew and actors, was edited by Alain Resnais, and it is considered to be a direct antecedent of Renais' *Hiroshima, mon amour* (1959).

It was the early films of Roger Vadim (b. 1928), however, which contributed most to the economic development of the New Wave. The spectacular commercial success of his independently produced first feature, *Et Dieu créa la femme* (*And God Created Woman,* 1956), demonstrated to the stagnant French film industry that young directors and new themes could attract large audiences. A visually sumptuous production in widescreen and color, *Et Dieu créa la femme* was a sensitive examination of the vagaries of amoral youth set aginst the luxurious background of St. Tropez. It starred Vadim's wife, Brigitte Bardot, and featured a number of explicit love scenes which made it an international hit. In subsequent films, such as *Les liaisons dangereuses* (*Dangerous Connections,* 1959), *Et mourir de plaisir* (English title: *Blood and Roses,* 1960), *La ronde* (English title: *Circle of Love,* 1964—a remake of the Ophüls film), *Barbarella* (1968), and *Pretty Maids All in a Row* (U.S.A., 1971), Vadim's commercialism and exploitativeness increased, but he remains an impeccable craftsman and elegant stylist of the widescreen color film. Moreover, it was Vadim, more than any other single figure in the French cinema, who opened the doors of the industry to his generation of film-makers and provided the economic justification for the New Wave.

13.14 *Le Doulos* (Jean-Pierre Melville, 1962): Jean-Paul Belmondo.

13.15 *Et Dieu créa la femme* (Roger Vadim, 1956): Jean-Louis Trintignant, Brigitte Bardot.

THEORY: ASTRUC, BAZIN, AND *CAHIERS DU CINÉMA*

Its theoretical justification came from another source: the film critic Alexandre Astruc (b. 1923), who wrote a highly influential article in 1948 on the concept of the *"caméra-stylo,"* which would permit the cinema "to become a means of expression as supple and subtle as that of written language" and would therefore accord film-makers the status of authors, or *auteurs.* Astruc's notion was to break away from the tyranny of narrative in order to evolve a new form of audio-visual language. He wrote: "The fundamental problem of the cinema is how to express thought. The creation of this language has preoccupied all the theoreticians and writers in the history of cinema, from Eisenstein down to the scriptwriters and adaptors of the sound cinema."[3] Like Bazin, Astruc questioned the values of classical montage and was an apostle of the "long take," as exemplified in the work of Murnau. Astruc later became a professional director after apprenticing himself to Marc Allégret (1900–1973), but his own films (*Le rideau cramoisi* [*The Crimson Curtain;* English title: *End of Desire,* 1952]; *Une vie* [*A Life,* 1958]) do not attempt to realize the ideal of the *caméra-stylo.* Following the example of German Expressionism, Astruc's films tend to be highly stylized elaborations of visual imagery which make excessive use of mannered composition and camera angles.

13.16. *Le rideau cramoisi* (Alexandre Astruc, 1952): Anouk Aimée.

Astruc was succeeded as a theorist by the vastly influential journal *Cahiers du cinéma* (literally, "cinema notebooks"), founded in 1951 by André Bazin (1918–58) and Jacques Doniol-Valcroze (b. 1920), which gathered about it a group of young critics—François Truffaut, Jean-Luc Godard, Claude Chabrol, Jacques Rivette, and Eric Rohmer—who were to become the major directors of the New Wave. These young men were *cinéphiles,* or "film-lovers." They had all grown up in the post-war years watching great American films of the past and present decades (most available for the first time since the Occupation) and classical French films at the amazing Cinémathèque Française in Paris. This is the magnificent film archive and public theater founded in 1936 by Georges Franju and Henri Langlois to promote cinema study and cinema culture in France and throughout the world. During the Occupation, Langlois kept the enterprise in operation secretly, at great personal risk, and afterward, through André Malraux, minister of culture, he obtained a large government subsidy for it. Today the Cinémathèque is the largest public film archive in the world, housing over fifty thousand films, three theaters, and a museum devoted entirely to film history. It was Langlois who preserved the works of Griffith, Keaton, Gance, Vigo, and Renoir for the post-war generation of *cinéphiles* and introduced them to the then-unrecognized genius of directors like Ingmar Bergman and the great Japanese masters Akira Kurosawa and Yasujiro Ozu (see Chapters 14 and 16). Under Langlois' tutelage, these young men came to love film and desperately wanted to become film-makers themselves, but they found the French commercial cinema inaccessible to them because of the powerful influence exerted by the trade unions. So, since they knew more about film, based on the experience of actual viewing, then any other generation in history, they became critics and theorists instead.

The *Cahiers* critics had two basic principles. The first, deriving from Bazin, was a rejection of montage aesthetics in favor of *mise-en-scène,* the long take, and composition in depth. *Mise-en-scène,* the "placing-in-the-scene," is probably best defined as the creation of mood and ambience, though it more literally means the structuring of the film through camera placement and movement, blocking of action, direction of actors, etc.—in other words, everything that takes place on the set prior to the editing process. Integral to the concept of *mise-en-scène* is the notion that film should be not merely an intellectual or rational experience but an emotional and psychological one as well. The second tenet of the *Cahiers* critics, derived from Astruc, was the idea of personal authorship which François Truffaut expressed in a 1954 essay entitled "A Certain Tendency in French Cinema" as *"la politique des auteurs."*[4] This "policy of authors," christened "the *auteur* theory" by the American critic Andrew Sarris,[5] states that film should ideally be a medium of personal artistic expression and that the best films are therefore those which most clearly bear their maker's "signature"—the stamp of his individual personality, controlling obsessions, and cardinal themes. The implicit assumption was that with each successive film an *auteur* grows increasingly proficient and mature of vision, an assumption which is not always borne out by fact.

As a critical premise, the *auteur* theory led to a rejection of the "tradition of quality" in French cinema, that is, the commercial scenarist tradition of Aurenche and Bost, Spaak, and directors such as Clair, Clément, Clouzot, Autant-Lara, Cayatte, and Allégret, with its heavily literary/theatrical orientation. In its stead was offered the example of Gance, Vigo, Renoir, Bresson, and Ophüls, and of numerous American directors—both major and minor—who had somehow managed to make personal statements despite the restrictions imposed upon them by the studio system. Some of the American choices—Welles, Hitchcock, Hawks, Lang, Ford, Nicholas Ray, and Anthony Mann, all masters of *mise-en-scène*—made perfect sense. Others—Jerry Lewis, Otto Preminger, Roger Corman—did not. And the unquestioning allegiance which the *Cahiers* group gave to the figures in its pantheon made many skeptics wonder whether one form of iron-clad dogmatism had not simply been exchanged for another. But for all its deficiencies (and a proneness to fanaticism and cultism seems to be a major one), the *auteur* theory does offer a valuable schematic model for interpreting the film-making process and goes some way toward solving a very basic methodological problem of film criticism; that is, to whom or what does one attribute cinematic creation? Furthermore, the *Cahiers* critics were able to partially vindicate the *auteur* theory by becoming film-makers themselves and practicing it.

THE NEW WAVE: THE FIRST FILMS

The first films of this "new wave" (*nouvelle vague*) of French directors were independently produced dramatic shorts, many of them shot in 16mm and subsequently blown-up for exhibition. Jacques Rivette's *Le coup du berger* (*Fool's Mate*, 1956), François Truffaut's *Le mistons* (*The Mischief-Makers*, 1957), and Jean-Luc Godard's *Tous les garçons s'appellent Patrick* (*All Boys Are Named Patrick* 1957) all fall into this category. But the first feature-length success of the New Wave is generally acknowledged to be Claude Chabrol's first film, *Le beau Serge* (*Handsome Serge/Bitter Reunion*, 1958), though Varda's *La Pointe-Courte* preceded it by three years. While still a *Cahiers* critic, Chabrol (b. 1930) shot *Le beau Serge,* about the rehabilitation of a village drunkard, on location with a low budget provided by an inheritance. The success of *Le beau Serge* enabled Chabrol to follow it with *Les cousins* (*The Cousins,* 1959), an ironic study of sexual intrigue and murder set against the backdrop of Parisian student life. The influence of Hitchcock became increasingly apparent in *A double tour* (English title: *Leda/Web of Passion,* 1959), a highly stylized tale of pathological murder, and the darkly satiric *Les bonnes femmes* (*The Good Women,* 1960), a film about the lives (and, in one case, the death) of Parisian shopgirls whose huge commercial failure caused Chabrol to turn for a while from the New Wave mode to more conventional thrillers like *Landru* (English title: *Bluebeard,* 1962) and *Le scandale* (English title: *The Champagne Murders,* 1966).

Nevertheless, 1959 was the *annus mirabilis* for the New Wave because in that year each of the three major figures to emerge from the movement, exclusive of Chabrol, released his first feature. François Truffaut's *Les quatre cents coups* (*The 400 Blows*), made when its director was twenty-seven years old, is a lyrical but wholly unsentimental account of an adolescent delinquent, shot on location in Paris. Photographed by the talented New Wave cinematographer Henri Decae (b. 1915), the film contains many deliberate visual echoes of Vigo's *Zéro de conduite* (1933). It won the prize for direction at Cannes in the year of its release. It was also the first film in Truffaut's Antoine Doinel series, a kind of continuing cinematic autobiography starring Jean-Pierre Léaud (b. 1944), an actor who physically resembles Truffaut. The series includes *Antoine et Colette* (a contribution to an international compilation film entitled *L'amour à vingt ans* [*Love at Twenty,* 1962]), *Baisers volés* (*Stolen Kisses,* 1968), *Domicile conjugal* (*Bed and Board,* 1970), and *L'amour en fuite* (*Love on the Run,* 1979). More remarkable in structure and theme was Alain Resnais' first feature, *Hiroshima, mon amour* (1959), which, like *Nuit et brouillard,* examines the relationship between time and memory in the context of a terrible atrocity. With a brilliant script by the novelist Marguerite Duras (who was to become an important director herself in the seventies), the film concerns a love affair between a French actress working in Hiroshima and a Japanese architect, in the course of which both recall their memories of the past war in Asia and Europe. Resnais

13.17 Jean-Pierre Léaud in *Les quatres cents coups* (François Truffaut, 1959), the first Antoine Doinel film.

13.18 *Hiroshima, mon amour* (Alain Resnais, 1959): Emmanuele Riva, Eiji Okada.

maintains the counterpoint between present and past by continuously shifting narrative modes from objective to subjective and, in several extraordinary sequences, by combining dramatic footage of the couple making love with documentary footage of the aftermath of the Hiroshima blast. *Hiroshima, mon amour,* like *Les quatre cents coups,* was a great commercial success and conferred worldwide prestige upon the New Wave by winning the International Critics' Prize at Cannes in 1959. (In the same year, the highly coveted Cannes Grand Prix went to the work of yet another young and unconventional French director, Marcel Camus' *Orphée noir* [*Black Orpheus,* 1958]).

The third important New Wave film of 1959, Jean-Luc Godard's *À bout de souffle* (*Breathless*), was in many ways the most characteristic and influential film of the movement. *Breathless,* which was written by Godard after a story by Truffaut and shot in four weeks for less than ninety thousand dollars, is dedicated to Monogram Pictures, the best of the American B-film studios of the thirties and forties, which were famous for their ability to turn out tightly-paced films on short shooting schedules and poverty-line budgets. This was precisely the ideal of the New Wave, but instead of making cheap films in order to make a quick profit, the New Wave directors made cheap films in order to be able to make films at all, since their productions were necessarily independent of the industry. (Happily, many of the first New Wave films, including *Breathless,* made a great deal of money, which temporarily insured the future of the movement.) Modeled on the American gangster film in a simultaneous spirit of parody and *hommage, Breathless* is about an amoral young thug on the run who is finally betrayed to the police by his American girlfriend (deliberate shades of *Pépé le Moko* [1936] and *Quai des brumes* [1938]), and it contains virtually every major technical characteristic of the New Wave film. These include the use of shaky hand-held 35mm cameras, location settings, natural lighting, improvised plot

13.19 *À bout de souffle* (Jean-Luc Godard, 1959):
Jean-Paul Belmondo, Jean Seberg.

13.20. Belmondo in *À bout de souffle*.

and dialogue, and direct sound recording—recording sound directly on location with portable tape machines which are electronically synchronized with the camera.

But the most important technical characteristic of the New Wave film was its jagged, elliptical style of editing, which employed a high percentage of jump cuts within scenes to destroy the spatial and temporal continuity of the viewing experience. As *Breathless* begins, for example, we witness the following sequence of events: Michel, the young hood, steals a car in Paris with the help of his French mistress and speeds out into the countryside alone; he passes several other vehicles on his side of the road at high speed; he briefly contemplates picking up two female hitch-hikers; and he talks to himself and to the audience about a variety of subjects, to occupy the time. Next, he passes a large truck at a road construction site and suddenly finds himself pursued by two motorcycle cops; he pulls off the road into a small wooded area and pretends to be having car trouble. One cop passes him by, the second spots him and pulls into the wood. At this point, Michel reaches into the car, removes a revolver, and guns down the cop. He then flees across an open field and hitch-hikes his way back to Paris. In a conventional commercial film of the day—French, American, British, or Italian—this sequence would have been rendered in many separate shots fully depicting each of the actions. In *Breathless,* the whole sequence is conveyed in only several brief shots: alternating close-ups of Michel and his mistress on a Paris street; a quick take of the car theft at eye level; medium close shots of Michel driving the car, taken from the passenger's seat; medium long shots of the road and later the hitch-hikers passing away rapidly through the windshield; a shot of the motorcycle cops appearing in the rear-view mirror, followed by one of Michel pulling off the road and opening the hood of his car as the cop discovers him; an extreme close-up of the revolver, followed by a medium long shot of the murder; a long shot of Michel running across a field and a medium shot of him arriving in Paris as a passenger in the back seat of an unidentified car. Later in the film, Godard would frequently begin a scene with a huge disorienting close-up and only later cut or pull his camera back to reveal the context of the action—which completely reversed conventional practice of the day.

Most radical of all, however, was Godard's use of the jump cut, in which a section of a single continuous shot is eliminated and then what remains is spliced together, creating a completely non-naturalistic ellipsis in the action and calling attention to the director's power to manipulate all aspects of his medium. This radical elimination of transitional scenes (of what Hollywood calls "establishing shots"—medium or long shots of exteriors which indicate changes in dramatic space) and even of continuity *within* the shot itself was thought extremely confusing when Godard and his peers first practiced it on a large scale, and yet it is no more than a logical extension of the discoveries of Méliès, Porter, and Griffith that cinematic narrative is by its nature *dis*continuous, or, as Eisenstein discovered, that spatial and temporal continuity in the cinema reside not on the screen but in the viewer's mind as it makes the connections which the images on the screen, by their arrangement, suggest. In the conventional "invisible" editing style that Hollywood (and, therefore, all of Western cinema) employed in the first three decades of the sound era, orderly narrative transitions were felt to be crucial. As late as 1957, Orson Welles was forced by Universal to shoot additional "establishing" scenes for his *Touch of Evil* so that his fast-paced editing would not confuse contemporary audiences. Today, elliptical editing and the jump cut have passed into our conventional cinematic lexicon so pervasively that it is not unusual to find them in abundance in any television series. But in 1959 elliptical editing was thought radically innovative, and it became paramount among the stylistic conventions associated with the New Wave.

THE NEW WAVE: THE ORIGINS OF STYLE

These conventions, like all film conventions, sprang from two sources—theoretical conviction and material circumstances (not necessarily in that order). The material circumstances were these: The young directors of the New Wave were the first *film*-educated generation of film-makers in history. They approached the cinema from the experience of having viewed almost the whole of its history at Langlois' Cinémathèque Française and from having written about it theoretically and critically in *Cahiers du cinéma* for nearly a decade. When they finally came to practice cinema, they knew more about the medium as an art form and less about the practical aspects of production than anyone who had ever made films before them. Consequently, they made many mistakes which their low budgets and tight shooting schedules would not permit them to correct. Like the Soviet film-makers during the film stock shortage that followed the 1917 Revolution, the New Wave directors could not afford to re-take shots, so they relied on elliptical editing to conceal technical defects on the screen. Jump cuts, for example, were a means not only of creating perceptual dislocation in the audience but also of restoring botched scenes by excising some actor's or cameraman's blunder from the middle of a take. But there were sound theoretical reasons for the stylistic conventions of the New Wave as well as budgetary ones. If location shooting with hand-held cameras was inexpensive, it was also totally at odds with the fluid, studio-bound cinematography of the contemporary commercial film. If jagged editing and jump-cutting were useful in concealing defective footage, they also eliminated all the smooth transitions which permit an audience to forget that it is watching a film—that is, a consciously crafted product of the human imagination rather than some "found" reality.

The psychological effect of these conventions—and it must be considered a calculated effect on the directors' part as well as a function of economic necessity—is to establish aesthetic distance between the audience and the film. New Wave films are constantly reminding us that we are watching a film, and *not* the reality which a film inevitably resembles, by constantly calling attention to their "filmicness," to their own artificially created nature. The abrupt and, above all, obvious manipulation of our perception in these films through the use of the jump cut, shaky hand-held cameras, and the like jolts us out of our conventional involvement with the narrative and our traditional identification with the characters, who are often less recognizable as characters than as actors playing characters. This is because New Wave cinema is, in a sense, *self-reflexive cinema,* or *meta-cinema*—film about the process and nature of film itself. According to the New Wave *cinéastes* (loosely, "film artists"), the conventional cinema had too faithfully and for too long reproduced our normal way of seeing things through its studiously unobtrusive techniques. The "invisible" editing and imperturbably smooth camera styles of the commercial cinema of the thirties, forties, fifties, and much of the sixties were designed to draw the spectator's attention away from the fact that he was watching a consciously crafted artifact. But the disruptive editing and camera styles of the New Wave say to us constantly, "Look, there's a film being made right before your eyes," and to emphasize the point a director or his technical crew will sometimes appear just inside the frame of a narrative sequence, as if by accident, to remind us that whenever we watch a film a handful of artists are controlling the process immediately beyond the borders of the frame.

The theoretical position of the New Wave film-makers is therefore that film must constantly call attention to the process of its own making and to its own unique variety of language. And thus the unparalleled cinematic *éclat,* or explosiveness, of the New Wave, its emphasis upon "magical" cinematic tricks like the jump cut, the iris-in and iris-out, decelerated and accelerated motion, and optically violent camera movement—all devices of which film and no other medium is capable. In this sense, the New Wave represents a return to Méliès and his conspicuously cinematic brand of conjuring. It envisions film as a special kind of magic which requires of its viewers a uniquely cinematic way of seeing in order to comprehend. On the other hand, the New Wave reaches back equally to Lumière because its most characteristic techniques are essentially documentary in practice. In fact, *cinéma-vérité,* the chief documentary mode of the sixties and seventies, constitutes an application of New Wave shooting and recording practices to real events rather than staged ones. Furthermore, Jean-Luc Godard, the most innovative and radical director to emerge from the New Wave, has virtually rejected narrative cinema in favor of cinematic "essays" on ideology and social praxis. New Wave cinema is aware of this paradox because it is aware of its history and conscious of the mediating position it holds between the narrative and documentary traditions of Western film. The allusions to and "quotations" from films of the past (sometimes called *hommages*) with which New Wave films are replete are no mere mannerism but rather a testament to the critical-historical cinema consciousness out of which the movement grew.

MAJOR NEW WAVE FIGURES

The critical and commercial success of the New Wave in 1959 was so great that between 1960 and 1962 over one hundred new French directors were able to find funding for their first features—an extraordinary thing in an industry so recently conservative. In some cases, the director of a commercial hit like Godard or Truffaut would produce for a less fortunate friend. In many others, a French commercial studio would produce, hoping to come up with a smash hit like *Breathless* on a B-film budget. In fact, the climate of creative and commercial enthusiasm during these two years was such that virtually anyone with the will to do so could obtain financial backing to make a low-budget film, though many who turned to directing lacked either the talent or the discipline to bring their projects to a successful conclusion. The commercial failures of the less talented began en masse in 1962, and by 1964 the studios had been so badly disappointed in well-intentioned amateurs that production money for first features was more difficult to raise than in the fifties. By this time, the New Wave as a collective phenomenon was over, and the French film industry had resumed its conventionally rigid contours. But French cinema continued to be dominated creatively by the handful of young *cinéastes* who had initiated the movement and who emerged from it as distinctly major figures—François Truffaut, Jean-Luc Godard, Alain Resnais, Claude Chabrol—and by a small group of sophisticated but less spectacular talents, such as Louis Malle, Eric Rohmer, Jacques Demy, Jacques Rivette, and Agnès Varda.

François Truffaut

François Truffaut (b. 1932), the most commercially successful of the post–New Wave group, has been able to maintain his independence by forming his own production company, Les Films du Carrosse (1961), named in *hommage* to Renoir's *Le carrosse d'or* (1952). His major cinematic influences have been the American B-film, and the work of Alfred Hitchcock and Jean Renoir. He followed *Les quatre cents coups* (1959) with what he called "a respectful tribute to the Hollywood B-film," *Tirez sur le pianiste* (*Shoot the Piano Player*, 1960), based on an American

13.21 *Tirez sur le pianiste* (François Truffaut, 1960): Charles Aznavour as Charlie/Edouard, Marie Dubois as Lena.

gangster thriller by David Goodis. The film concerns Charlie, a timid honky-tonk piano player in a sleazy Parisian bar who, we learn in a series of extended flashbacks, was once the great concert pianist Edouard Saroyan. He and his girlfriend, Lena, become involved with two gangsters who are after his younger brothers, and the couple is forced to flee the city when Charlie accidentally kills his employer in self-defense. The film ends with a shoot-out between the three brothers and the gangsters at a farmhouse in the snow, in which Lena is killed. Criticized on its release for its radical shifts in mood from comedy to melodrama to tragedy, and for the manipulativeness of its disjointed narrative style, *Shoot the Piano Player* was nevertheless Truffaut's *Breathless*—a quintessentially New Wave film replete with bizarre visual puns, allusions to other films, a mixture or "explosion" of genres, and all the self-reflexive anti-conventions of the movement. Like *Breathless,* it was stunningly photographed by the innovative New Wave cinematographer Raoul Coutard (b. 1924).

Truffaut's third feature, *Jules et Jim* (1961), stands as a tribute to the influence of Renoir and the French lyrical tradition.* As in Renoir's work, the basic themes of *Jules et Jim* are friendship and the impossibility of achieving true freedom in love (or, as Truffaut himself put it, "monogamy is impossible, but anything else is worse"). Adapted from a novel by Henri-Pierre Roché, this beautiful and sensitive film concerns two close friends—one French, the other Austrian—who fall in love with the same woman (Catherine), are separated by World War One, and afterward attempt to live together in a *ménage à trois.* Intellectually sound, the situation proves emotionally impossible for all three, and at the end of the film Catherine drowns herself with Jim, leaving Jules to cremate and bury them. The film is striking in its re-creation of the period through natural settings and in the remarkable performances of its principals—

---

* Truffaut has also claimed the influence of Edgar G. Ulmer's B-Western *The Naked Dawn* (1956); it too concerns the psychological and emotional vagaries of a sexual triangle.

13.22 The triad in Truffaut's *Jules et Jim* (1961): Jeanne Moreau, Henri Serre, Oscar Werner.

especially Jeanne Moreau* as the manic, enigmatic Catherine. While it appropriately avoids the self-conscious pyrotechnics of *Shoot the Piano Player*, *Jules et Jim* is gorgeously composed and photographed in Franscope by Raoul Coutard and sustains its emotional lyricism through the unconventional use of telephoto zooms, slow motion, freeze frames, and even a helicopter shot. After directing *Antoine et Colette* for the anthology film *L'amour à vingt ans* (1962), Truffaut produced a restrained and sympathetic study of middle-aged adultery, *Le peau douce* (*The Soft Skin*, 1964), which was marred by an overly melodramatic ending. His erratic adaptation of Ray Bradbury's *Fahrenheit 451* (1966), Truffaut's first film in color and English, is generally regarded as a failure because it played down traditional science fiction themes, but its portrait of a near-future society of emotionless, hedonistic people mindlessly tripped-out on big-screen color television seems chillingly prophetic today.

In 1967, Truffaut published a book-length interview with Alfred Hitchcock in which he demonstrated his reverence for the American director by comparing him not only to Griffith, Hawks, and Ford, but to Kafka, Dostoevsky, and Poe. Appropriately enough, Truffaut's next two features were conceived as direct tributes to the Hitchcock thriller. *La mariée était en noir* (*The Bride Wore Black*, 1967) is a suspenseful tale of vengeance in which a woman (Jeanne Moreau) relentlessly tracks down and kills the five men responsible for the accidental shooting of her husband on their wedding day. Adapted from a novel by William Irish—the author of the novel on which the film *Rear Window* (Hitchcock, 1954) is based—and with a musical score by a frequent Hitchcock collaborator, Bernard Herrmann, Truffaut's film contains a dense pattern of allusions to specific Hitchcock films, uses Hitchcockian plot construction, and is

13.23 Jeanne Moreau and her dead bridegroom in *La mariée était en noir* (François Truffaut, 1967).

* Moreau (b. 1928) has recently become a director in her own right, making an impressive debut with the semi-autobiographical *Lumière* (1977), a film about women and the dynamics of stardom, followed by *L'adolescente* (*The Adolescent*, 1979), which deals with a young girl's passage from childhood to adolescence.

13.24 Truffaut's *Baisers volés* (1968), the second Antoine Doinel film: Jean-Pierre Léaud, Claude Jade.

13.25 *L'enfant sauvage* (François Truffaut, 1969): Jean-Pierre Cargol.

intensely manipulative of audience expectations in order to generate suspense. *La sirène du Mississippi (Mississippi Mermaid,* 1969), also adapted from a William Irish novel, is dedicated to Jean Renoir and contains many allusions to his films (especially in its "open" ending, which is a visual *hommage* to the conclusion of *La grande illusion* [1932]), but in terms of style and construction, this minor thriller about the degradation of an honest man by a *femme fatale* is pure Hitchcock.

Between *La mariée était en noir* and *La sirène du Mississippi,* Truffaut made his second Antoine Doinel feature, *Baisers volés (Stolen Kisses,* 1968), a tender and affectionate portrait of Antoine's coming to adult consciousness through a series of affairs and, finally, his engagement to Christine (Claude Jade). *Domicile conjugal (Bed and Board,* 1970), the third feature in the Doinel series, examines the first few years of Antoine and Christine's marriage, its deterioration under the pressure of an affair, and its ultimate, uneasy reconstitution. The film is light and humorous, and its comedy is quite successful, but like *Jules et Jim* it also raises some serious questions about the institution of marriage and its alternatives. The last of the Doinel films, *L'amour en fuite (Love on the Run,* 1979), begins with Antoine's uncontested divorce from Christine and proceeds to recapitulate the entire cycle through flashbacks to earlier films and through Antoine's chance encounters with figures from his past. Truffaut intends *L'amour en fuite* to conclude the Doinel series begun with *Les quatre cents coups* twenty years before.

For *L'enfant sauvage (The Wild Child,* 1969), based upon the true account of a "wolf-boy" captured in the forests of central France in 1806, Truffaut both directed and played the part of Dr. Itard, the eighteenth-century rationalist who undertakes the painstakingly gradual education of the wild child. Set in its period and shot in quasi-documentary style by the award-winning cinematographer Nestor Almendros,* *The Wild Child* allowed Truffaut to explore more intensively those themes of confinement versus freedom and social conditioning versus nature which he had first broached in *Les quatre cents coups. Les deux Anglaises et le continent (Two English Girls,* 1971), adapted from another novel by Henri-Pierre Roché and set at the turn of the century, inevitably evokes comparison with *Jules et Jim,* of which it contains many deliberate echoes. The story of a young Frenchman's love for two English sisters, it is Truffaut's most visually sensuous work to date. Its sumptuous recreation of *la belle époque* is conveyed in shots composed after Impressionist paintings of the period, and its use of color is the most subtle Truffaut has achieved so far.

Une belle fille comme moi (Such a Gorgeous Kid Like Me, 1972) is a sardonic portrayal of a murderous nymphomaniac which failed, on the whole, to break new ground. But *La nuit américaine (Day for Night,*

---

* Almendros, a native of Cuba who won the American Academy Award for Cinematography in 1978 for *Days of Heaven* (Terrence Malick, 1978), continued to work closely with Truffaut on many of his subsequent films. He also collaborates regularly with Eric Rohmer and Barbet Schroeder (see below).

13.26 The set within the set of Truffaut's *La nuit américaine* (1973).

13.27 *L'histoire d'Adèle H.* (François Truffaut, 1975): Isabelle Adjani.

1973) provided the ultimate in self-reflexive cinema: a film starring Jean-Pierre Léaud (the Truffaut figure in the Antoine Doinel series) and directed by Truffaut, about the making of a film starring Léaud and directed by Truffaut. "Day for night" (or *la nuit américaine*) is the technical term for shooting night scenes in daylight through a filter; by choosing it as his title Truffaut intended to evoke the entire arsenal of cinematic tricks of which it is merely typical. Dedicated to Dorothy and Lillian Gish, the great Griffith actresses, the whole film is predicated upon cinematic illusion, and in this respect it recalls Fellini's *8½* (1963) and Bergman's *Persona* (1966). It is difficult from the outset to tell whether a scene is occurring in the film or in the film *within* the film, because the cast and crew live so closely together that there is little distinction between their work and their personal lives. The film is funny, affectionate, and strangely disquieting in its gradual revelation that the same people making the film within the film are simultaneously making *Day for Night* and that confusion between illusion and reality is the very essence of the cinema.

Day for Night was in many ways a consummation for Truffaut. It combined the stylistic influence of American realism with that of French lyricism and drew together his dual thematic obsessions with autobiography and psychology in a hymn of praise to the cinema—an art form to which he has passionately devoted his entire life. It answered the question posed by its own director-character—"Are films more important than life?"—with an emphatic "Yes!" Truffaut's next project was *L'histoire d'Adèle H.* (*The Story of Adèle H.*, 1975). Based upon the diary of Victor Hugo's youngest daughter, this is a subtle and powerful film about the psychology of a woman in the grip of a romantic obsession. Adèle's romantic fascination with a young English lieutenant leads her to follow him all over the world until she finally goes mad in Barbados and must spend the last forty years of her life in an asylum. The film begins like a conventional romantic melodrama, but as it progresses we are drawn into the increasingly demented world of the heroine with an impact which is both shocking and hauntingly beautiful. In *The Story of Adèle H.*, Truffaut demonstrates a total mastery of the new cinematic language which he helped to create and triumphantly confirms his status as one of the most important film artists of our time. His recent films include the comedies *L'argent de poche* (*Small Change*, 1976) and *L'homme qui amait les femmes* (*The Man Who Loved Women*, 1977); *La chambre verte* (*The Green Room*, 1978), based on several short stories by Henry James; and *Le dernier métro* (*The Last Subway*, 1980), a fascinating account of life in a small Paris theater under the Nazi Occupation, inspired by the autobiography of the stage and film actor Jean Marais (b. 1913). In 1979, Truffaut was honored with an extraordinary twenty-year retrospective by the American Film Institute and the Los Angeles County Museum of Art.

Jean-Luc Godard

Jean-Luc Godard (b. 1930) is the most prolific and stylistically radical of all the directors who came to prominence during the New Wave. He has made some twenty-eight feature films since *Breathless* (1959), working closely with Raoul Coutard as his director of photography* on most of them, and he is among the most influential figures in world cinema today. Unlike Truffaut, Godard is a militantly intellectual and ideologically committed film-maker whose films almost always involve some form of *autocritique* or interrogation of cinema itself. In a certain sense, they collectively constitute a *theory* of cinema because, better than any of his peers, Godard understood the essential impulse of the New Wave: "The whole New Wave," he wrote in *Cahiers,* "can be defined, in part, by its new relationship to fiction and reality." Godard's films have consistently tested this relationship by rejecting narrative in favor of *praxis,* the working out of social or political theory within the cinematic process. Since the early sixties, his films have become increasingly dialectical and rhetorical in structure, and Godard himself calls them "critical essays." Most of these "essays" are personal to the point of being idiosyncratic, and Godard has maintained his independence by producing them quickly and cheaply. His films are therefore not as carefully crafted as those of Truffaut and his other peers, and they frequently give the appearance of being less finished films than unvarnished journals about the making of a film, full of technical blunders and undigested facts. And, unlike his peers, Godard is still in the business of breaking every known cinematic convention—even the more recent conventions established by the New Wave itself—in a ceaseless attempt to expand the medium's form and pursue its potential for artistic, intellectual, and political self-expression.

Several of Godard's early films were characteristic New Wave tributes to the American cinema. *À bout de souffle* (*Breathless*, 1959) was mod-

---

* Coutard (b. 1924) would later try his hand at direction in the polemical documentaries *Hoa Binh* (1970), shot in Vietnam, and *Le legion saute sur Kolwezi* (English title: *Operation Leopard,* 1980), shot in Zaire.

eled on the B-film gangster thriller. *Une femme est une femme* (*A Woman Is a Woman*, 1961) was a studio-produced tribute to the American musical comedy, made in Cinemascope and color. *Le petit soldat* (*The Little Soldier*, 1960), made between these two films, was banned by the French government for three years because it commented on the Algerian War. Like *Breathless*, it has the form of a gangster film and turns on the theme of betrayal; but its protagonist belongs to a Fascist terrorist organization fighting the Algerian liberation front in Geneva, and the film graphically depicts the use of torture by both sides. Both *Le petit soldat* and *Une femme est une femme* starred Godard's sensuously beautiful first wife, Anna Karina, and his fourth film seemed intended as a kind of portrait of her. *Vivre sa vie* (*My Life to Live*, 1962), a study of a woman who chooses to be a prostitute, is constructed in the form of a twelve-part sociological tract on the problem of prostitution, complete with statistics and pseudo-clinical jargon.

13.28 *Une femme est une femme* (Jean-Luc Godard, 1961): Anna Karina, Jean-Paul Belmondo.

With *Les carabiniers* (*The Soldiers*/*The Riflemen*, 1963), Godard created a fable about the nature of war in a style which is both a parody of and an *hommage* to the early documentary style of Lumière. The film, whose narrative line is often fragmented to the point of breaking down, achieves an almost Brechtian detachment from its subject and is clearly among Godard's most important works. It is the first of his "critical essays," for, as one critic has said, *Les carabiniers* is less a war movie than "a series of propositions about war." *Le mépris* (*Contempt*, 1963), based upon Alberto Moravia's novel *A Ghost at Noon*, was Godard's sixth feature. It was an international co-production shot in widescreen and color, and like Truffaut's *Day for Night* it concerns the making of a movie. This film within the film is a version of Homer's *Odyssey* being shot in Rome by Fritz Lang, who plays himself. The narrative portion of *Le mépris*, which concerns the dissolution of the scriptwriter's marriage, is less important than Godard's use of the self-reflexive conceit.

13.29 An *hommage* to Lumière in Godard's *Les carabiniers* (1963).

Godard had disputes with the producers of *Le mépris* over the editing and scoring of the film, and for his seventh feature he formed his own production company, Anouchka Films. *Bande à part* (*Band of Outsiders*, 1964) is based upon an American pulp thriller and constitutes Godard's first return to the gangster genre since *Breathless*. It deals with a burglary attempt on the part of three Parisian students—two men and a woman—

13.30 Image and reality merge in *Les carabiniers*.

13.31 *Le mépris* (Jean-Luc Godard, 1963): images of image-making. Jack Palance, Brigitte Bardot, Michel Piccoli.

13.32 Allusion (to *Jules et Jim*) and pulp violence in Godard's *Band à part* (1964)—a film, the credits tell us, by "Jean-Luc/Cinema/Godard": Sami Frey, Anna Karina, Claude Brasseur.

13.33 *Une femme mariée* (Jean-Luc Godard, 1964): Macha Meril.

13.34 Godard's *Alphaville* (1965): Eddie Constantine as Lemmy Caution, with Anna Karina.

which ends in tragic farce when one of the would-be criminals is killed. The narrative is filmed straightforwardly, but our experience of it is strangely distanced through a running commentary spoken by Godard in which he summarizes the plot for latecomers, tells us what the characters are thinking, makes observations upon the drab suburban setting, or simply reads newspaper headlines. In *Une femme mariée* (*A Married Woman,* 1964), ironically subtitled "Fragments of a Film Shot in 1964," Godard mixed a wide range of narrative and documentary styles to create a sociological study of woman's role in modern culture. The film portrays twenty-four hours in the life of a married woman who is having an affair, and its visual texture is quite complex: straightforward narration is broken up by three highly stylized scenes of love-making, seven *cinéma-vérité*–type interviews with the people around the protagonist, a typically Godardian dissertation upon advertising for women's underwear, and a clip from Resnais' *Nuit et brouillard* (1955), which two of the characters watch in a theater.

In *Alphaville* (1965) Godard used the form of the science fiction thriller to create a parable about the alienating effects of technology. At some time in the future, secret agent Lemmy Caution (played by the pop thriller star Eddie Constantine) travels through intergalactic space from the Outer Countries to the city of Alphaville, where his mission is to destroy Dr. von Braun. Von Braun is the inventor and operator of Alpha-60, the computer which runs the desensitized, lobotomized society of Alphaville. Caution succeeds in destroying them both and escapes the crumbling Alphaville with von Braun's daughter. Originally entitled *Tarzan vs. IBM, Alphaville* is one of Godard's most sustained and disciplined performances. He makes brilliant use of contemporary Paris to evoke the future in a way which serves to remind us that the world of Alphaville is already upon us.

In *Pierrot le fou* (*Crazy Pete,* 1965), Godard returned to the disjointed and self-reflexive narrative style of *Les carabiniers* and to the generic model of the gangster film: a man (Jean-Paul Belmondo) and a woman (Anna Karina) run away from a Parisian gang to live an idyllic, desert-island–like existence in the south of France, until mutual betrayal causes their horribly violent deaths.* Scriptless and virtually plotless, the film comes close to realizing the Godardian ideal of "a film where there has been no writing, no editing, and no sound mixing." *Masculin/féminin* (1965) marks a definitive turning away from narrative. Like *Vivre sa vie* and *Une femme mariée,* it is a film of sociological inquiry hung upon a slender plot, but here the plot is almost irrelevant to the inquiry. The film is concerned with illustrating fifteen distinct problems of the younger generation, the "children of Marx and Coca-Cola," members of which

---

* The idea for *Pierrot le fou* was almost certainly implanted by David Newman and Robert Benton's screenplay for *Bonnie and Clyde* (Arthur Penn, 1967), which had been submitted for consideration to Truffaut and then passed on to Godard in mid-1965. Godard actually wanted to direct the American script, but only if he could begin shooting immediately—a condition unacceptable to the producers.

are interviewed and interview one another in *cinéma-vérité* fashion. Godard shows that their idealism is belied by the world of cynical sex and violence which surrounds them. Since *Masculin/féminin,* Godard's films have become increasingly ideological and structurally random. As he wrote in 1966: "Cinema is capitalism in its purest form. . . . There is only one solution, and that is to turn one's back on the American cinema."[6] The ironic result of this logic was *Made in U.S.A.* (1966).

Though it is loosely based on a detective thriller, *Made in U.S.A.* has no narrative thread at all and is a film intent upon destroying virtually every illusion of which cinema—especially traditional American cinema—is capable. Ostensibly a re-make of Hawks' *The Big Sleep* (1946) with Karina in the Bogart role, the film is so self-reflexive as to have no content: characters speak to the audience, explaining their behavior and commenting on the triviality of the plot, the dialogue is nonsensical and sometimes deliberately rendered inaudible on the soundtrack. The film's meaning lies at its periphery, in its comment upon political violence, the viciousness and stupidity of the Right, the sentimentality and fecklessness of the Left. *Deux ou trois choses que je sais d'elle (Two or Three Things I Know About Her,* 1966) is a collage of images and interviews centering around a Parisian housewife who has turned to casual prostitution in order to keep herself in middle-class luxury. The film is a radical indictment of Western capitalist technocracy, which, Godard holds, makes prostitutes of us all through its system of economic constraints. So too is *La Chinoise* (1967), subtitled "A Film in the Making," which depicts five students who set up a Maoist cell and fail, each in his or her separate way, to achieve cultural revolution. Godard also contributed a long, single-take monologue to the collective polemic *Loin de Vietnam (Far from Vietnam),* produced by SLON in 1967.

But Godard's most savage attack upon the values of Western capitalist society is *Weekend* (1967), a film which begins as a recognizable, if violent, narrative and ends as an apocalyptic vision of the collapse of civilization in the West. A young bourgeois couple sets out to visit the woman's mother in Normandy in order to borrow some money from her. They become trapped in a monumental weekend traffic jam, which Godard renders in a single slow lateral tracking shot lasting fully four minutes on the screen. Gradually, we pass from a real landscape into a symbolic one in which the highway becomes littered with burning automobiles and the bloodied, mutilated bodies of crash victims. From this point on, the film is dominated by images of mindless slaughter and mayhem from which the thin veneer of civilization has been stripped away. When the couple reaches the mother's house and are refused the money, they hack her to pieces and steal it. As they return to Paris, they are overtaken by a band of Maoist renegades armed with submachine guns, who have turned to cannibalism—the mirror image of capitalism, for Godard—to survive. The husband is killed, and his wife joins the group in eating him. *Weekend* is a harsh and brutal film which uses vivid color photography and tight dramatic construction to drive home the point that Western

13.35 Lyricism in *Pierrot le fou* (Jean-Luc Godard, 1965): Anna Karina.

13.36 Godard's *La Chinoise* (1967): Anne Wiazemsky about to be napalmed by the Esso tiger.

13.37 Capitalist apocalypse: Godard's *Weekend* (1967), alternately subtitled "A Film Lost in the Cosmos" and "A Film Found on the Scrap-Heap." Jean Yanne, Mireille Darc.

civilization is merely a façade elaborated by technology to conceal a hard core of bestiality and cannibalism.

After *Weekend* and the political "events of May" 1968,* Godard abandoned narrative altogether, considering it a bourgeois form. *Le gai savoir* (1968) is a rambling cinematic essay on language as an instrument of social conditioning and control, based on the philosophical assumptions of structural linguistics. All of Godard's films between 1968 and 1973 were produced by the Dziga-Vertov Group (actually an uneasy creative partnership between Godard and the ideologist Jean-Pierre Gorin), and Godard came to make increasing use of the arsenal of agitational techniques employed by the Soviet revolutionary cinema of 1924–28. *Un film comme les autres* (*A Film Like the Others,* 1968), for example, is a

---

* French society was thrown into an unexpected political crisis in May 1968. Early in the month, a series of rallies by student radicals on the campuses of Parisian universities mushroomed into civil disorder (the catalyst for the demonstrations was the firing of Henri Langlois as director of the Cinémathèque Française by Gaullist minister of culture André Malraux). Quarters of the city were barricaded, there was bloody street-fighting, and the Sorbonne section of the University of Paris was occupied by students and turned into a commune. By the middle of May, the disturbance had spread beyond Paris to other universities and to the unionized workers, some ten million of whom participated in a series of strikes which paralyzed the country. By late May, the most extreme of the radicals were making plans for a Marxist-style revolution against the Fifth Republic, but on May 30, President Charles de Gaulle (1890–1970) managed to turn the workers against the students by appealing for law and order on national television. He dissolved the legislature and called for new national elections on June 23. On that day, faced with a choice between what the president called "de Gaulle and anarchy," the French people chose for de Gaulle and his lieutenants. Though abortive in practical terms, the "events of May" 1968 left many thoughtful Frenchmen in doubt about the legitimacy of their government and had the ultimate effect of strengthening support for the Left. See Sylvia Harvey, *May '68 and Film Culture* (London, 1978). And, for a personal summary of Leftist politics during the sixties by an intensely committed film-maker who participated in them, see Chris Marker's *Le fond de l'aire est rouge* (Paris, 1979).

16mm record of an elementary political discussion which takes place between several people lying in tall grass, none of whom is clearly distinguishable. Godard makes a point of its randomness by suggesting that a coin be tossed to determine which of its two hour-long reels to screen first. *One Plus One* (*Sympathy for the Devil*, 1968) is a film of seemingly unrelated fragments: a Bolivian revolutionary hiding out in a London men's room, the Rolling Stones rehearsing the song "Sympathy for the Devil," Black Power militants plotting revolution in a junkyard, a television interview with the lobotomized fairy godmother "Eve Democracy," a man reading *Mein Kampf* in a Soho porno shop, etc.

At one point in *One Plus One* a character remarks: "There is only one way to be an intellectual revolutionary, and that is to give up being an intellectual." Some critics believe that Godard has followed the logic of this statement in his films and that he has in his most recent work approached a state of nihilism. All of his films for the now-defunct Dziga-Vertov Group 1969—*British Sounds* (*See You at Mao*, 1969), *Pravda* (1969), *Le vent d'est* (*Wind from the East*, 1969), *Luttes en Italie* (*Struggles in Italy*, 1969), *Vladimir et Rosa* (1970), *Tout va bien* (1972),* and *Letter to Jane* (1972)—show Godard concerned with the nature and function of ideology, regardless of its medium. Although his later work shows a renewed interest in narrative, it has been suggested that Godard's cinematic "essays" are no longer films at all. Nevertheless, Godard's impact upon the contemporary cinema generally, as distinct from his importance to the French New Wave, has been immense. As Roy Armes puts it: "He has made a whole generation question the accepted conventions of filmmaking, and his spontaneous, semi-improvised methods of direction have been widely imitated. But he himself remains a solitary, independent figure, pursuing the logic of his own development, totally indifferent to fashion."[7] Since the end of his association with Gorin in 1973,† Godard has been experimenting with a combination of film and videotape which permits him to superimpose two or more images on the screen simultaneously. In film/tapes like *Numéro deux* (*Number Two*, 1975), *Comment ça va?* (*How Goes It?*, 1975), *La communication* (1976), *Ici et ailleurs* (*Here and There*, 1970; 1976), and *Six fois deux* (*Six Times Two*, 1976),‡ he has pioneered a new means of interrogating the cinematic image by offering us two contradictory perspectives on "reality" at once.** In 1980, Godard produced his first theatrical feature in nearly eight years. Technically evocative of his late-sixties films, *Sauve qui*

13.38 Combining video and film in *Numéro deux* (Jean-Luc Godard, 1975).

---

* The uncharacteristic two-year interval in Godard's normally breathless production schedule was occasioned by a nearly fatal motorcycle accident in June 1971. By entitling the first film he made after his recovery *Tout va bien,* Godard told his audience that "All goes well."

† Gorin, who frequently co-directed with Godard during this period, has since become a film-maker in his own right with the U.S.–West German feature *Poto and Cabengo* (1979), a fascinating documentary about the effects of language on children.

‡ The last two were made in collaboration with Anne-Marie Miéville.

** Although its breadth is literally incalculable, Godard's most discernible influence in the seventies has been upon the materialist cinema of Jean-Marie Straub and his wife, Danièle Huillet (discussed in Chapter 17), upon the omnibus film essays of Hans-Jürgen Syberberg, and upon the extraordinary work of Belgian film-maker Chantal Akerman (b. 1950)—

peut/La vie (*Every Man for Himself/Slow Motion*) is an essay on the metaphysics of survival shot on location in Switzerland, that paradigm of Western capitalist survivorship, which characteristically constructs a sustained analogy between sexual degradation and economic exploitation.

Alain Resnais

Alain Resnais is identified with the New Wave because his first major successes, *Hiroshima, mon amour* (1959) and *L'année dernière à Marienbad* (*Last Year at Marienbad,* 1961), both appeared during its height. But Resnais is a generation older than the *Cahiers* group, and he began his film career not as a critic but as an editor and director of short films in the scenarist tradition. Unlike his New Wave counterparts, he likes to work from an original script, usually one written especially for the screen by a major novelist like Jean Cayrol, Marguerite Duras, Alain Robbe-Grillet, or Jorge Semprun. He also works slowly and plans his films meticulously in advance of production, in close collaboration with his writers and technicians, believing that film is basically a collective art. Yet Resnais is an avant-garde intellectual who has been strongly influenced by the philosophy of Henri Bergson.* And because his major theme is the effect of time on human memory, he communicates by exploding the conventional boundaries of narrative form. His almost Proustian fascination with time and memory leads Resnais to create remarkable structures for his films, in which past, present, and future are perceived upon the same spatial and temporal plane, and in which objectivity and subjectivity are never clearly distinguishable.

In *L'année dernière à Marienbad* (1961), written by the modernist French novelist Alain Robbe-Grillet, a man, X, meets a woman, A, at a baroque chateau which seems to be a resort for the very rich and which may or may not be Marienbad (a spa in Czechoslovakia). He claims to have met her, or a woman like her, with a man, M, who was perhaps her husband, "last year at Marienbad." She claims the contrary, and their debate, which is a debate about the nature of reality itself, recurs endlessly through the film as labyrinthine images of past, present, and future seem to merge into the same visual continuum of highly stylized tracking shots (a Resnais trademark) and frozen geometric compositions. X and A seem to have had or to be having or to desire to have an affair, the end of which is A's death at the hands of her husband. Whether the film represents an attempt to re-create the process of memory in the mind of X, a long interior monologue on the part of A, or an exercise in sheer visual abstractionism is impossible to say. But, like Bergson's philosophy, the film is clearly concerned with mental process rather than narrative. As Resnais remarked, *Marienbad* represents "an attempt, still crude and

13.39 *L'année dernière à Marienbad* (Alain Resnais, 1961): human geometry.

Jeanne Dielman, 23 quai de Commerce, 1080 Bruxelles (1977); *News from Home* (1977); and *Les rendez-vous d'Anna* (*The Meetings of Anna,* 1978), which won the Best Director Prize at the 1978 Paris Film Festival.

* Henri-Louis Bergson (1859–1941) was a French philosopher whose theories of time and "creative evolution" have had considerable impact upon twentieth-century thought.

primitive, to approach the complexity of thought and its mechanisms."[8] The film won the prestigious Golden Lion at the Venice Film Festival in 1962.

In *Muriel, ou le temps d'un retour* (English title: *Muriel*, 1963), written by Jean Cayrol, Resnais returned to the material world for a film about a mother and son haunted by the past. The mother must confront her lover of twenty-two years past who arrives for a visit accompanied by his most recent mistress, and the son is tormented by the memory of Muriel, a young Algerian girl whom he tortured and killed during the French-Algerian War. Though in terms of content *Muriel* is the least complex of Resnais' features, its elliptical narrative technique brings it close to what has been called "the cinema of pure association."

With *La guerre est finie* (*The War Is Over*, 1966), written by the Spanish novelist Jorge Semprun, Resnais entered the arena of political commitment. More conventional in narrative structure and more realistic than his other features, this film still manages to suggest the overlapping of memory and imagination and the relationship which necessarily exists between an individual's past, his present, and his identity. *La guerre est finie* concerns three days in the life of a middle-aged revolutionary named Diego (Yves Montand), who, some thirty years after the Spanish Civil War, still works for the overthrow of the Franco regime. Diego has come to Paris to plan strategy and see his mistress, but he also has a chance affair there with a radical young student. His sense of identity is called into question by her revolutionary friends, who challenge Diego's methods and his commitment to the struggles of the past. As he re-crosses the border into Spain at the end of the film, he imagines his arrest by Spanish secret police, which is in fact about to occur.

13.40 Resnais' *La guerre est finie* (1966): Yves Montand.

After contributing to the 1967 collective film *Loin de Vietnam*, Resnais produced *Je t'aime, je t'aime* (*I Love You, I Love You*, 1968), a science-fiction–like fantasy about a man, projected into the past after an unsuccessful suicide attempt, who becomes lost within the structure of time itself.

During the sixties, Resnais' films, like Godard's, had become increasingly unfashionable and unconventional as he pursued the logic of his own artistic development at the expense of financial gain. If Godard's films became critical essays on ideological praxis, Resnais' became philosophical investigations into the workings of the human mind, and this meant the loss of a popular audience after his initial success with *Hiroshima, mon amour*. As a result, Resnais was unable to make a film between 1968 and 1974 for lack of financial backing. But in 1975 his *Stavisky* was released to international critical acclaim. Written by Jorge Semprun, *Stavisky* is a political period film about a colossal financial scandal which toppled the French government in 1934. The sheer cinematic beauty of the film is matched by Resnais' complex portrayal of the paradoxical figure of Stavisky, expertly played by Jean Paul Belmondo as both swindler and saint, and many critics consider it to be his greatest achievement to date, although *Providence* (1977), which takes place entirely within the mind of a dying novelist, also has a critical following. In 1980, Resnais won a unanimous Special Jury Prize at Cannes for *Mon*

13.41 *Stavisky* (Alain Resnais, 1975): Jean-Paul Belmondo as Stavisky, Charles Boyer as Baron Raoul.

13.42 John Gielgud as the novelist Clive Langham in Resnais' *Providence* (1977).

oncle d'Amérique (My Uncle in America), a narrative of interpersonal relationships poisoned by ambition, based upon the behaviorist theories of the French biologist Henri Laborit, who appears in his laboratory at several points during the film to offer short discourses on the science of "aggressiology."

Frequently accused of coldness and abstractionism, Resnais is a serious, committed film-maker whose technical mastery of his medium has enabled him to create a handful of films of great visual beauty and intellectual depth which rank among the masterworks of French cinema. When asked, in a recent interview,[9] about the film-makers who had most influenced him, Resnais mentioned Griffith, Pudovkin, and Eisenstein. He also spoke of the Czech-born British director Karel Reisz (see Chapter 14) as his "real teacher" through Reisz's book *The Technique of Film Editing*.[10] In other words, Resnais clearly sees his work as growing out of the tradition of classical montage. And in his fascination with the manipulation of the space-time continuum Resnais serves to remind us that montage aesthetics are still alive and well in an era and a film culture which looks to *mise-en-scène* as a kind of cinematic god.

Claude Chabrol

Claude Chabrol (b. 1930), who had been forced to make a series of commercial thrillers after the financial failure of *Les bonnes femmes* in 1960, returned to the top of his form with *Les biches (The Does,* 1968), a subtle, visually exquisite study of lesbian sexual obsession and domination set in St. Tropez in winter. In the same year, Chabrol achieved absolute mastery of his medium with *La femme infidèle (The Unfaithful Wife,* 1968), an investigation into the violent consequences of adultery upon a typical French bourgeois family, which owes much technically to the example of Hitchcock. Like Truffaut, Chabrol had written a book on Hitchcock* during his apprenticeship, and he was stylistically influenced by the older director more than any other figure of the New Wave generation. One critic sees the whole body of Chabrol's work as an extended *hommage* to Hitchcock. But while Chabrol frequently employs Hitchcockian structures and metaphors (such as the simultaneous tracking out and zooming in which characterize the final shots of both *Vertigo* [1958] and *La femme infidèle),* he has a theme that is very much his own—the impact of a crime of passion on a small but intimate network of human relationships, such as those which exist within a middle-class family, a love triangle, or even a small community. Chabrol dissects the psychological complexities of these relationships with clinical precision, yet in his mature films this ironic detachment from his material never becomes indifference or coldness, and at its best can evoke a true sense of tragedy and compassion devoid of sentiment. Perhaps it is Fritz Lang and his deterministically plotted cinema of destiny (*M*[1931]; *Fury* [1936]; *The*

13.43 *Les biches* (Claude Chabrol, 1968): Stéphane Audran, Jacqueline Sassard.

---

* The book, written in collaboration with Chabrol's *Cahiers* associate Eric Rohmer, was published in Paris in 1957. It is now available in English as *Hitchcock: The First Forty-Four Years*, trans. Stanley Hochman (New York, 1979).

Big Heat [1953]), rather than Hitchcock, whom Chabrol most resembles in this respect.

Que la bête meure (*Killer*/*The Beast Must Die*, 1969), a revenge tragedy about a man who relentlessly tracks down the driver of an automobile which has killed his young son in a hit-and-run accident, is a fine contribution to Chabrol's continuing probe of the violence and bestiality which lie just beneath the surface of everyday life. But Chabrol's masterpiece to date is undoubtedly *Le boucher* (*The Butcher*, 1969), which one Parisian critic hailed as the best French film since the Liberation and which is clearly among the best two or three works to emerge from the post–New Wave period. Told with a remarkable economy and purity of cinematic style, *Le boucher* is essentially a love story set in a small French village in which one of the lovers is a sexual psychopath given to murdering young women and mutilating their bodies. This "butcher," however, is made the most sympathetic character in the entire film, and the compassionate psychological study of his relationship with a young schoolteacher, who loves him even as she becomes increasingly convinced of his guilt, represents a high point in contemporary French cinema.

13.44 Chabrol's *Le boucher* (1969): Stéphane Audran, Jean Yanne.

Since *Le boucher,* Chabrol has directed approximately one film a year: *La rupture* (*The Break-Up*, 1970); *Juste avant la nuit* (*Just Before Nightfall*, 1971); *Le décade prodigieuse* (*Ten Day's Wonder*, 1972); *Les noces rouges* (*Blood Wedding*, 1973); *Le banc de désolation*/*De Grey,* two hour-long telefilms based on Henry James stories (1973); *Nada* (English title: *The Nada Gang*, 1974); *La parti de plaisir* (*A Piece of Pleasure*, 1974) and *Les innocents aux mains sales* (English title: *Dirty Hands,* 1974); *Les magiciens* (*The Magicians*) and *Folies bourgeoises* (*Bourgeois Madness*), both 1975; *Alice, ou la dernière fugue* (*Alice, or the Last Escapade*) and *Les liens de sang* (*Blood Relations*), both 1977; and *Violette Nozière* (English title: *Violette,* 1978), a macabre film of parricide based on the true story of an eighteen-year-old girl who poisoned her parents in 1933. Like Resnais, Chabrol believes that film-making is a collective enterprise, and since *Les biches* he has gathered about him a team of collaborators who work with him on every film. These include his co-scenarist, Paul Gégauff; his director of photography, Jean Rabier; his art director, Guy Littaye; his editor, Jacques Gaillard; and his leading actress (and his wife), Stéphane Audran. Like Truffaut, Godard, and Resnais, Chabrol is a major figure in contemporary French cinema and among the most promising and exciting directors working anywhere in the world today. We are likely to receive many other fine films (e.g., *Le cheval d'orgueil* [*Horse of Pride*, 1980]) from him as his vision and technical mastery continue to expand.

Louis Malle

Louis Malle (b. 1932), a former assistant to Bresson and the celebrated underwater film-maker Jacques-Yves Cousteau (with whom he co-directed *Le monde du silence* [*The Silent World*, 1955]), began his career as a director two years before the debuts of Godard and Truffaut, with the taut suspense thriller *L'ascenseur pour l'echafaud* (*Frantic*/*Lift to the*

Scaffold, 1957) and earned an international reputation the following year with *Les amants* (*The Lovers,* 1958). This lyrical film about a brief love affair between a bored socialite and a young student for whom she leaves her husband was beautifully photographed by Henri Decae. *Zazie dans le métro* (1960) was an anarchic adaptation of Raymond Queneau's novel about a foul-mouthed ten-year-old girl who comes to visit her uncle in Paris and wreaks havoc everywhere she goes. The film is a technically exciting attempt to find visual equivalents for Queneau's neo-Joycean puns through the use of trick shots, superimposition, variable camera speeds, jump cuts, and multiple allusions to other books and films (especially Resnais' *Hiroshima, mon amour,* Fellini's *La dolce vita,* and Malle's own *Les amants*). Malle continued his experiments in narrative form in *Vie privée* (*Private Life,* 1961), a film about a young provincial girl's rise to stardom based loosely on the experience of its own star, Brigitte Bardot.

13.45 *Le feu follet* (Louis Malle, 1963): Maurice Ronet.

But *Le feu follet* (*The Fire Within/Will o'the Wisp,* 1963), adapted by the director from a novel by Drieu La Rochelle, with a piano score by Erik Satie, is regarded as Malle's masterpiece of the sixties. It depicts the last forty-eight hours in the life of an alcoholic playboy who is relentlessly driven to suicide by his disgust at the world around him. Many critics feel that the film's mood of psychological intensity and Malle's sureness of touch in sustaining it bring *Le feu follet* close to the best work of Bresson. As a change of pace from the brooding atmosphere of *Le feu follet,* Malle turned to colorful romantic spectacle in *Viva Maria* (1965), a film set at the turn of the century, in which Jeanne Moreau and Brigitte Bardot, as traveling entertainers, invent the striptease and foment a revolution in the imaginary South American republic of San Miguel. In *Le voleur* (*The Thief,* 1967), Malle used a period setting to create a portrait of a wealthy young bourgeois driven to burglary by his hatred of society. His "William Wilson" episode (based on a Poe story) in the anthology film *Histoires extraordinaires* (*Spirits of the Dead,* 1968) hauntingly examines the phenomenon of the *döppelganger,* or "double."

After contributing, with Godard and Resnais, to the 1967 collective film *Loin de Vietnam,* Malle journeyed to the East to film the feature-length *Calcutta* (1969), part of his brilliant six-hour documentary essay *Phantom India* (1970), for French television. This film, which has also been shown theatrically, offers a marvelously complex vision of the paradoxical subcontinent which has always so fascinated and puzzled the West. Using his own consciousness as a sounding-board, Malle ultimately fails to penetrate the Indian mystery, ostensibly by refusing to interpret it through Western eyes. In 1971, Malle produced a masterpiece equal to *Le feu follet* in the remarkable *Le souffle au coeur* (*Murmur of the Heart*), a delicate and irresistibly funny tale of casual incest among the bourgeoisie of Dijon in 1954—the time of the fall of Dien Bien Phu. Scripted by Malle and sumptuously photographed by Decae, this film offers an amiable, intelligent, and perversely humorous portrait of middle-class French family life in the post-war era, as well as a sensitive study of the sexual and social agonies of adolescence. Malle's next film,

13.46 Mother and son in Malle's *Le souffle au coeur* (1971): Lea Massari, Benoît Ferreux.

Lacombe Lucien (1974), received international acclaim for its subtle portrayal of a seventeen-year-old peasant boy who joins the French Gestapo during the Occupation for no particular reason and is subsequently torn between destroying and protecting a Jewish family with whose daughter he has fallen in love. With *Black Moon* (1975), photographed by the Swedish cinematographer Sven Nykvist, (a frequent collaborator of Ingmar Bergman; see Chapter 14), Malle moved from realism to symbolism in a film which the Paris newspaper *L'express* described as existing "at the crossroads of fantasy and science fiction." More recently, Malle has directed *Pretty Baby* (1978) in the United States. Shot entirely on location in New Orleans by Nykvist, this controversial film deals with a love affair between an eccentric photographer and a child prostitute in a turn-of-the-century Storyville brothel. In 1980, Malle turned north to direct an ironic drama of small-time hoods, *Atlantic City, U.S.A.*

Malle, unquestionably an important film-maker, is frequently accused of eclecticism because of his wide range of subjects and styles. Pauline Kael has pointed out that had Malle chosen a single theme and stuck with it—as Chabrol has done, say, since 1968—he would have been acclaimed as a major figure long ago.[11] But Malle's intellectual restlessness and his remarkable ability to present material from simultaneously opposing points of view have lead some critics to dismiss him as an elegant stylist with little substance at the core. *Le feu follet, Phantom India, Le souffle au coeur, Lacombe Lucien,* and *Pretty Baby* offer ample proof that only the first part of this proposition is true.

Eric Rohmer and Jacques Rivette

The former *Cahiers* critic Eric Rohmer (b. Jean-Marie Maurice Schérer, 1920) began to blossom as a director in the late sixties. His first feature, *Le signe du lion* (*The Sign of Leo*, 1959), received virtually no notice in the year of its release, but between 1962 and 1963 Rohmer made the first two of his six "Moral Tales," or *"Contes moraux,"* whose basic theme is the antagonism which exists between personal identity and sexual temptation, or between the spiritual and passional sides of man's nature.* *Le boulanger de Monceau* (*The Baker of Monceau,* 1962) and *La carrière de Suzanne* (*Suzanne's Vocation,* 1963) were both shorts shot in 16mm and produced by Barbet Schroeder, who produced the entire series.† *Ma nuit chez Maud* (*My Night at Maud's,* 1967), *La collectionneuse* (*The Collector,* 1968), *Le genou de Claire* (*Claire's Knee,* 1969), and *L'amour, l'après midi* (English title: *Chloe in the Afternoon,* 1972) are the 35mm features which complete the *"Contes moraux,"* providing four more variations on Rohmer's single theme. Abstract,

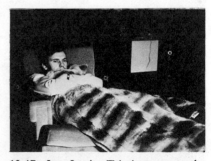

13.47 Jean-Louis Trintignant as the protagonist and narrator of *Ma nuit chez Maud* (Eric Rohmer, 1967).

* Rohmer wrote the *"Contes moraux"* as short stories in the late fifties before filming them. They have recently been published in English as *Six Moral Tales,* trans. Sabine d'Estrée (New York, 1979).

†Schroeder (b. 1941) became an important director himself in the seventies with *More* (1969); *Maitresse* (*Mistress,* 1976); *Idi Amin Dada* (1976); and *Koko, le gorilla qui parle* (*Koko, the Talking Gorilla,* 1978).

intellectual, supremely ironic, these inquiries into the nature of human passion are constructed with all the precision of Cartesian logic, and they have been hailed internationally as components of a philosophical masterpiece. Subsequently, Rohmer made a beautiful and ambiguous version of Heinrich von Kleist's *Die Marquis von O.* (*La marquise d'O.*, 1975) which continues his metaphysical probing of human sexuality in the story of a young noblewoman who awakes one day to find herself inexplicably pregnant. With *Perceval le Gallois* (English title: *Perceval,* 1978), he attempted to evoke the consciousness of the Middle Ages in his own adaption of a twelfth-century poem by Chrétien de Troyes set in the time of King Arthur.

Jacques Rivette (b. 1928), another former *Cahiers* critic, and former assistant to both Renoir and Becker, also directed a handful of important films in the sixties which show a marked predilection for literature and the theater. *Paris nous appartient* (*Paris Belongs to Us,* 1960) concerns the members of a Parisian acting troupe who are rehearsing a version of Shakespeare's *Pericles,* and who, through a series of coincidences and insinuations, come to believe themselves enmeshed in a Fascist conspiracy to destroy the world. At the end of the film, this "conspiracy" turns out to be the invention of a paranoid American novelist, but the confusion has caused two deaths and wrecked the lives of everyone involved. Rivette shot *Paris nous appartient* on a day-to-day basis between 1957 and 1959 with money for film stock borrowed from Truffaut and a camera borrowed from Chabrol. None of the cast or crew was paid until after the film's release, at which time the *Cahiers* group issued a joint statement concerning its crucial importance to *la politique des auteurs.* Rivette's film, they wrote, was "primarily the fruit of an astonishing persistence over several years to bring to the screen a personal vision of the world as rich and diverse *as if expressed by any other means*" [my italics].[12]

13.48 *Le religieuse* (Jacques Rivette, 1965): Anna Karina as the novice Suzanne Simonin.

Rivette's second feature, *La religieuse* (*The Nun,* 1965), was based upon Denis Diderot's eighteenth-century novel about a woman driven to prostitution and suicide through the hypocrisy of religious orders. This bleak film acquired something of a sensational reputation due to its suppression in France, but its sober camera style and rather conventional narrative structure lend it a seriousness that no amount of scandal can belie. Rivette's third film is his greatest to date, and it too reveals his literary tastes. *L'amour fou* (*Crazy Love,* 1968) is a four-hour study of the slow disintegration of a marriage set against the filming of a television production of Racine's tragedy *Andromaque,* in which the protagonist of the film plays the lead. Cold, austere, and agonizingly slow, *L'amour fou* provides Rivette with a laboratory in which to explore questions about the nature of film and stage illusion, as Renoir did in *Le carrosse d'or* (1952). Rivette has made six features since this one—*Out One* (1971), which exists only as a thirteen-hour work print; *Out One: Spectre* (1972), a four-and-one-half-hour abridgment, or "spectre," of *Out One; Céline et Julie vont en bateau* (*Céline and Julie Go Boating,* 1974); *Duelle* (1976); *Noroit* (1977); and *Merry Go Round* (1978)—but none save *Duelle* has been distributed outside of France.* Because of his obscurity and artistic integrity, Rivette has had little commercial success with his films, but as to the seriousness of his intent to become a great "novelist" in film there can be no question.

Agnès Varda, Jacques Demy, and Others

Agnès Varda, whose *La Pointe-Courte* (1955) had been something of a New Wave landmark, continued to make fine films in the sixties. Her second feature, *Cléo de cinq à sept* (*Cleo from Five to Seven,* 1962) depicts exactly ninety minutes (the running time of the film) in the life of a young pop singer who is waiting for a lab report that will tell her whether or not she has cancer. *Le bonheur* (*Happiness,* 1965) is a strangely detached film about a happily married family-man whose affair with another woman causes his wife to commit suicide and who proceeds to lead a happy existence with his mistress after his wife's death. The film is highly decorative but ambiguous in terms of psychological and moral considerations. In *Les créatures* (*The Animals,* 1966), Varda examined the relationship between fantasy and reality in the mind of a writer who talks to animals and cannot distinguish real people from the characters in his novels. Like Godard, Resnais, and Malle, Varda contributed to the collective *Loin de Vietnam* (1967) before coming to America to make the improvisational feature *Lion's Love* in 1969. Most recently, she has directed the semi-documentary *Daguerréotypes* (1976), and *L'une chante, l'autre pas* (*One Sings, the Other Doesn't,* 1977), a study of two women-friends pursuing totally different lifestyles.

13.49 *Cléo de cinq à sept* (Agnes Varda, 1962): Corinne Marchand.

13.50 Varda's *Le bonheur* (1965): François (Jean-Claude Drouot) and his mistress Emilie (Marie-France Boyer).

Varda's husband, Jacques Demy (b. 1931), became a specialist during the sixties in colorful, bittersweet melodrama reminiscent of poetic realism and the work of Max Ophüls. His *Lola* (1960), which is dedicated to Ophüls, is a gay, light-hearted film about love, set in Nantes, similar in style to *La ronde.* It has been called "a musical without songs or dances," and it earned Demy an international reputation. *Les parapluies de Cherbourg* (*The Umbrellas of Cherbourg,* 1964) is an actual musical about a romance between a shopgirl and a service-station attendant in which the dialogue is sung, as in an operetta. *Les demoiselles de Rochefort* (*The Young Girls of Rochefort,* 1966) is a lively *hommage* to the Hollywood musical directed in collaboration with Gene Kelly. After the American-made *Model Shop* (1968), Demy's work declined into such frivolity as *L'événement le plus important depuis que l'homme a marché sur la lune* (*The Most Important Event Since Man Walked on the Moon,* 1973), a film about a pregnant man. But his strong showing in the Japanese-French co-production *Lady Oscar* (1979), a period romance set during the French Revolution and based on a popular comic-strip, suggests Demy's return to artistic power.

13.51 *Les demoiselles de Rochefort* (Jacques Demy, 1966): Catherine Deneuve, Gene Kelly, Françoise Dorleac.

* *Duelle* and its companion-piece, *Sérial* (1976), a deliberate exercise in mystification directed by Rivette's scenarist Eduardo de Gregorio, were featured together at the 1976 New York Film Festival and later released commercially on the East and West coasts.

Other noteworthy French film-makers of the sixties and seventies who have ties with the New Wave are Phillipe de Broca (b. 1933), a former assistant to Chabrol and Truffaut, who has become a master of sophisticated comedy and satire (*Cartouche* [1961]; *L'homme de Rio* [*Our Man in Rio*, 1964]; *Le roi de coeur* [*King of Hearts*, 1966]; *Dear Detective* [1978]; *Le cavaleur* [*The Skirt-Chaser*, 1979]; *On a volé la cuisse de Jupiter* [*Someone Has Stolen Jupiter's Thigh*, 1980]), and Pierre Étaix (b. 1928), a former circus clown and gag-writer for Jacques Tati, who has directed a number of excellent comic films (*Le soupirant* [*The Suitor*, 1962]; *Yoyo* [1965]) in the tradition of Max Linder and Buster Keaton. The former actor Jean-Pierre Mocky (b. 1929) became a fine director of iconoclastic comedy in films like *Les snobs* (1961) and *Les vierges* (*The Virgins*, 1963). Alain Robbe-Grillet (b. 1922), the major practitioner of the French *nouveau roman*,* and the scriptwriter for Resnais' *L'année dernière à Marienbad*, turned to directing in the sixties with *L'immortelle* (*The Immortal*, 1963), *Trans-Europe express* (1967), and *L'homme qui ment* (*He Who Lies*, 1968). His films are all narratives about the mental process of constructing narratives, and he makes no distinction between them and his novels, calling both *ciné-romans* ("film novels").

Alain Jessua (b. 1932) produced several important films during the sixties, including the remarkable *La vie à l'envers* (*Life Upside Down*, 1963), a subjective portrait of the inception of madness, and *Jeu de massacre* (*The Killing Game*, 1967), in which the protagonist becomes so obsessed with the heroes of his favorite comic-strip that he can no longer distinguish fantasy from reality. More recently, Jessua has directed *Traitement de choc* (*Shock Treatment*, 1974), a horror film by genre but thematically a parable of capitalist exploitation of the underdeveloped nations (Portuguese workers are murdered so that their blood may be given to a rich Frenchman undergoing an exotic medical treatment). *Les chiens* (*The Dogs*, 1979) is a parable of the violence of modern life focusing on the increased use of guard-dogs for self-protection by citizens of contemporary France. The single New Wave feature by Jacques Rozier (b. 1926), *Adieu Philippine* (1962), has acquired the reputation of a minor masterpiece, although it is really something less than that: an engagingly improvised narrative about Parisian youth in the sixties filmed in *cinéma-vérité* fashion, which contains a hilarious parody of French television. Rozier's only other significant feature, *Du côté d'Oroüet* (1973), is a hyper-realistic film about the experience of three girls on holiday in Brittany. The Greek-born director Constantine Costa-Gavras (b. 1933), formerly associated with conventional thrillers, developed into a masterful director of political films in the seventies

---

* Literally, the "new novel"—an influential form of avant-garde fiction practiced in France in the fifties and sixties by such writers as Robbe-Grillet, Marguerite Duras (now a film-maker herself), Nathalie Sarraute, and Michel Butor. Formally influenced by the cinema, the *nouveau roman* was anti-humanist in its concentration on the objective, even clinical, description of material phenomenon at the expense of character, motivation, and plot. The *nouveau roman* was often "meta-fictional," in that it created narrative metaphors for the process of its own writing (see Robbe-Grillet's *Dans la labyrinth* [*In the Labyrinth*, 1959]).

with *Z* (1969), *L'aveu* (*The Confession,* 1971), *L'état de siège* (*State of Siege,* 1973), *Section spéciale* (*Special Section,* 1975), and *Clair de femme* (*Womanlight,* 1979), all starring Yves Montand.

Much interesting work whose origins are traceable to the New Wave appeared during the seventies in the French-speaking Swiss cinema. The director Alain Tanner's first feature, *Charles mort ou vif* (*Charles Dead or Alive,* 1969), was a characteristic product of the sixties in which a middle-aged businessman drops out of bourgeois society, goes to live with some young intellectuals, and is subsequently committed to an asylum by his family. Tanner's *Le salamandre* (*The Salamander,* 1971) and *La milieu du monde* (*The Middle of the World,* 1974), both concerned with day-to-day existence in modern industrial society, have been compared to the best work of Rohmer, while his *Retour d'Afrique* (*Return from Africa,* 1974) is as experimental and politically committed as anything attempted by Godard. With the critical success of *Jonah qui serais 25 dans l'année 2000* (*Jonah Who Will Be 25 in the Year 2000,* 1976), Tanner has been proclaimed a major European film-maker—a status confirmed by his harrowing dissection of Swiss society in *Messidor* (1979). Other Swiss directors with a marked personal style are Claude Goretta (*L'invitation* [*The Invitation,* 1972]; *Pas si méchant que ça* [*Not as Wicked as That/The Wonderful Crook,* 1975]; *La dentellière* [*The Lacemaker,* 1977]; *La provinciale* [1980]); Michel Soutter (*L'escapade* [*The Escapade,* 1973]); *Repérages* [English title: *Location Hunting,* 1978]); Daniel Schmid (*Violanta,* 1978); Clarisse Gabus (*Melancholy Baby,* 1979); and Yves Yersin (*Les petites fuges* [*The Little Escapes,* 1979]).

13.52 *La salamandre* (Alain Tanner, 1971): Jacques Denis, Bulle Ogier.

The work of Claude Lelouch (b. 1937) is more controversial than that of these other film-makers because of its blatant appeal to the mass audience. Lelouch uses all the modern narrative techniques of his New Wave counterparts, and he is an *auteur* in the most comprehensive sense of the term in that he produces, directs, writes, photographs, and edits all of his own films (such as *Un homme et une femme* [*A Man and a Woman,* 1966]; *Vivre pour vie* [*Live for Life,* 1967]). But while these films are visually engaging, they lack emotional depth and have the quality of extended television commercials. Recent exceptions are the ingenious comedy-thriller *Cat and Mouse* (1978), and the picaresque *À nous deux* (*Us Two/An Adventure for Two,* 1979).

Another French director whose films were largely unaffected by the New Wave but whose recent work has become too prominent to ignore is Claude Sautet (b. 1924). After graduating from IDHEC in 1950 and working as an assistant to both Georges Franju and Jacques Becker, Sautet began his career as a director with a series of *Rififi*-style thrillers (*Classe tous risques* [English title: *The Big Risk,* 1960], *L'arme à gauche* [English title: *Guns for the Dictator,* 1965]). But lately he has become an astute observer of French bourgeois society, famous for his direction of ensemble-playing. Sautet's *Les choses de la vie* (*The Things of Life,* 1970), *Max et les ferrailleurs* (*Max and the Junkmen,* 1971), *César et Rosalie* (*César and Rosalie,* 1972), *Vincent, François, Paul, et les autres* (*Vincent, François, Paul, and the Others,* 1974), *Mado* (1977), and *Une* *histoire simple* (*A Simple Story*, 1978) all deal with middle-class people trapped at mid-life by the patterns of their own routines, and the films have been much admired for their sympathetic understanding of a class which it has become almost obligatory for contemporary European directors to malign.*

In the field of documentary cinema, Chris Marker (b. Christian François Bouche-Villeneuve, 1921) has produced a number of brilliant film essays (*Cuba si!* [1961]; *Le joli mai* [1963]; *Le mystère Koumiko* [1965]), as well as the Bergsonian science fiction short *La jetée* (1962), composed almost entirely of still photographs. Marker is a close associate of Resnais and the chief organizer of SLON (Société pour le Lancement des Oeuvres Nouvelles), the film cooperative which produced *Loin de Vietnam* (1967) and several other political documentaries of the

---

* Other recent French directors of note who are less involved with the New Wave are: Jacques Deray (b. 1929): *Borsalino* (1974); *Un papillon sur l'épaule* (*A Butterfly on the Shoulder*, 1978); *Un printemps en hiver* (*A Springtime in Winter*, 1980); Yves Boisset (b. 1939): *L'attentat* (*The Outrage/The French Conspiracy*, 1972); *Un taxi mauve* (*A Mauve Taxi*, 1977; shot in Ireland); *La clé sur la porte* (*The Key in the Door*, 1978); *La femme flic* (*The Female Cop*, 1979); Jean Eustache (b. 1939): *La mamam et la putain* (*The Mother and the Whore*, 1973); *Mes petites amoureuses* (*My Little Lovers*, 1975); *Une sale histoire* (*A Dirty Story*, 1979); Maurice Pialat (b. 1925): *Nous ne vieillirons pas ensemble* (*We Won't Grow Old Together/Breaking Up*, 1972); *La gueule ouverte* (*The Mouth Agape*, 1974); *Loulou* (1980); Bertrand Tavernier (b. 1941): *L'horloger de Saint-Paul* (English title: *The Clockmaker*, 1974); *Que la fête commence* (English title: *Let Joy Reign Supreme*, 1975); *Le jugé et l'assassin* (*The Judge and the Murderer*, 1975); *Des enfants gâtes* (*Spoiled Children*, 1977); *La morte en direct* (English title: *Deathwatch*, 1980); André Téchiné (b. 1943): *Souvenirs d'en France* (English title: *French Provincial*, 1975); *Barocco* (1977); *Les soeurs Brontë* (*The Brontë Sisters*, 1978); Jean-Charles Tacchella (b. 1926): *Cousin, cousine* (1976); *Le pays bleu* (*Blue Country*, 1977); *Il y a longtemps que je t'aime* (*It's a Long Time I've Loved You*, 1979); *Soupçon* (1980); Jean-Jacques Annaud: *La victoire en chantant* (English title: *Black and White in Color*, 1976); *Coup de tête* (English title: *Hothead*, 1979); *The Quest for Fire* (U.S.A., 1980); Bertrand Blier (b. 1939): *Les valseuses* (English title: *Going Places*, 1974); *Calmos/Femmes fatales* (1976); *Preparez vos mouchoirs* (*Get Out Your Handkerchiefs*, 1978); *Buffet froid* (*Cold Cuts*, 1979); Marguerite Duras (b. 1914): *India Song* (1975); *Des journées entières dans les arbres* (*Days in the Trees*, 1976); *Le camion* (*The Truck*, 1977); *Le navire night* (1980); Michel Deville (b. 1931): *Le mouton enragé* (English titles: *Love at the Top/The French Way*, 1974); *L'apprenti salaud* (*The Apprentice Bastard*, 1977); *Le dossier 51* (1978—a film about surveillance shot entirely with a subjective camera); *Le voyage en douce* (English title: *Sentimental Journey*, 1979); Gérard Blain (b. 1930): *Les amis* (*The Friends*, 1971); *Le pélican* (*The Pelican*, 1973); *Un enfant dans le foule* (*A Child in the Crowd*, 1976); *Utopia* (1978); Pierre Kast (b. 1920): *Le soleil en face* (*Face to the Sun*, 1980); Alain Corneau (b. 1943): *France société anonyme* (*France, S.A.*, 1974); *Police Python 357* (1977); *Série noire* (1979); Jacques Doillon: *La femme qui pleure* (*The Crying Woman*, 1979); *La drôlesse* (*The Hussy*, 1980); Coline Serreau: *Pourquoi pas!* (*Why Not!*, 1979); *Mais qu'est-ce qu'elles veulent?* (*But What Do These Women Want?*, 1979); Christine de Chalonge (b. 1937): *L'argent des autres* (*Other People's Money*, 1978): Pierre Schoendoerffer (b. 1928): *Le crabe tambour* (*The Crab Drum*, 1977); Diane Kurys: *Diabolo menthe* (English title: *Peppermint Soda*, 1979); *Cocktail Molotov* (1980); René Allio (b. 1924): *La vieille dame indigne* (*The Shameless Old Lady*, 1964); *Moi, Pierre Rivère, ayant égorgé ma mere, ma soeur, et mon frere* (*I, Pierre Rivère, Have Butchered My Mother, My Sister, and My Brother*, 1978); Claude Miller: *Dite-lui que je l'aime* (*Tell Her That I Love Her*, 1979); Yannick Bellon (b. 1924): *Un viol d'amour* (*A Rape of Love*, 1977); René Gainville: *L'associé* (*The Associate*, 1979); Alain Cavelier (b. 1931): *Ce répondeur ne prend pas de*

era.* The work of the *cinéma-vérité* documentarists Jean Rouch (b. 1917—*Chronique d'un été* [*Chronicle of a Summer*, 1961]; *La punition* [*Punishment*, 1963]) and Mario Ruspoli (b. 1925—*Les inconnus de la terre* [*The Unknown of the Earth*, 1961]) had wide influence during the sixties on both the documentary (in the films of the Americans D. A. Pennebaker, Albert and David Maysles, and Frederick Wiseman) and the narrative cinema (in the work of Rozier, Godard, and Tanner, and in countless individual French, Swiss, Italian, West German, British, and American films). In the seventies, Rouch continued to produce distinguished ethnographic films, focusing mainly on black African culture (*Funérailles à Bongo: le vieux Anai, 1849–1971* [*Funeral in Bongo: Old Anai, 1849–1971*, 1979]).

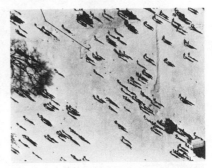

13.53 Citizens of Paris in *Le joli mai* (Chris Marker, 1963).

The most prominent French documentarist, however, is Marcel Ophüls (b. 1927), the son of the great post-war director Max Ophüls. Marcel Ophüls' masterpiece is the four-and-a-half-hour *Le chagrin et la pitié* (*The Sorrow and the Pity*, 1971), a shattering documentary which mixes newsreel footage with contemporary interviews in an attempt to assess the impact of the Nazi Occupation on the provincial city of Clermont-Ferrand and, by extension, on the whole of France. The verdict is that, except for the systematic murder of Jews, and of those non-Jews who openly opposed the Nazis, business went on very much as usual during the Occupation, largely because the Nazis obtained the cooperation of most of the French bourgeoisie and because the existence of a large, efficiently coordinated Resistance movement was a myth propagated after the war. Originally made for Swiss and West German television companies, *Le chagrin et la pitié* has still (as of this writing) not been shown on French television, a state monopoly, but as a theatrical release in France and abroad it received much attention.† Ophüls' more recent films are *A Sense of Loss* (1974), which chronicles the plight of Northern Ireland, and *A Memory of Justice* (1976), a remarkable documentary meditation on collective guilt which counterposes the question of the Nazi death camps and the Nuremberg war crimes trials with that of French atrocities in Algeria and American atrocities in Vietnam.

13.54 *Le chagrin et la pitié* (Marcel Ophüls, 1971): Hitler admiring the Eiffel Tower after his troops have occupied Paris.

---

message (*This Answering Service Takes No Messages*, 1979); Jean-Louis Comolli: *La Cecilia* (1978); Édouard Molinaro (b. 1928): *L'homme pressé* (*Man in a Hurry*, 1977); *La cage aux folles* (English title: *Birds of a Feather*, 1978); Paul Vecchiali: *Corps à coeur* (*Body to Heart*, 1979); Michel Drach (b. 1930): *Les violons du bal* (*Violins of the Ball*, 1974); *Le passé simple* (English title: *Replay*, 1977); *Le pull-over rouge* (*The Red Sweater*, 1979); Christine Pascal: *Félicité* (1979); Nelly Kaplan (b. 1934): *La fiancée du pirate* (English title: *A Very Curious Girl* (1969); *Néa* (1976); *Le satellite de Vénus* (*The Satellite of Venus*, 1977); *Au bonheur des dames* (*To the Good Luck of Ladies*, 1979); Eduardo de Gregorio: *La mémoire courte* (*Short Memory*, 1979); Luc Béraud: *La tortue sur le dos* (*Turtle on Its Back*, 1979); Jean-François Stevénin: *La passe-montagne* (*The Mountain Pass*, 1979); Jean-Pierre Denis: *Histoire d'Adrien* (*The Story of Adrien*, 1980); Jacques Bral: *Exteriur nuit* (*Exterior Night*, 1980); and, perhaps most impressive, the great contemporary stage director Ariane Mnouchkine: *1789* (1977); the four-hour *Molière* (produced by Claude Lelouch, 1978).

* The best information in English on this little-known but important group is William F. Van Wert, "Chris Marker: The SLON Films," *Film Quarterly*, 32, 3 (Spring 1979), 38–46.

† See Stanley Hoffmann, Introduction to *The Sorrow and the Pity* (New York, 1972).

THE SIGNIFICANCE OF
THE NEW WAVE

The impact of the French New Wave upon world cinema would be difficult to overestimate. The movement can be credited with almost single-handedly revitalizing the stagnant British and American cinemas during the sixties, and it produced similar chain reactions in Italy, West Germany, and Eastern Europe, and indeed around the world. To suggest that the New Wave was a monolithic phenomenon is simplistic. Varda, Resnais, Marker, and Malle, for example, evolved from a completely different context than did Truffaut, Godard, Chabrol, Rivette, and Rohmer. The former had begun their film-making careers as assistants and editors within the established industry; the latter had begun theirs as theorists and critics in total revolt against the industrial system.* And all of them, of course, went their separate artistic ways in the later sixties and seventies. But two common notions bound them together and made their films vastly important to the evolution of narrative cinema. First, they believed that film was an art form which could provide an artist with a medium of personal expression as rich, as varied, and as sensitive as any other. This assumption is implicit in the concept of personal authorship, or *la politique des auteurs,* according to which film directors are not simply analogous to writers of novels but are literally capable of "writing novels" in the audio-visual language of film. Second was the commonly shared belief that the narrative conventions they had inherited from the thirties and forties were insufficient to achieve these ends, that in fact many of these conventions prevented the audio-visual language of film from approaching its full range of expression. So they broke the old conventions and established new ones in the process, elaborating an audio-visual language which could express a whole gamut of internal and external states. This is implicit in the notion of *mise-en-scène,* according to which a film should be not simply a succession of meaningful images telling a story but an all-engrossing, mind- and sense-engaging experience. The number of major film-makers who emerged from the New Wave and who are still in the process of making ever greater and more influential features is astounding. But even more astounding is the impact that these new ideas about audio-visual language and its operations have had and continue to have upon the international cinema at large. By calling into question the very form and process of narrative cinema, the film-makers of the New Wave insured that the cinema could never again rely upon the easy narrative assumptions of its first fifty years.

---

* Rivette alone among the *Cahiers* group had received some practical training as an assistant director to Renoir and Becker in the early fifties.

European Renaissance: West

BRITAIN

Post-War British Cinema and Its Context

While the French were experiencing the New Wave, the British cinema was enjoying a renaissance of its own. Before World War II, Britain had produced a vastly important contribution to the documentary cinema in the government-funded work of John Grierson (1898–1972—*Drifters* [1929]; *Industrial Britain* [co-directed with Robert Flaherty, 1932]); Alberto Cavalcanti (b. 1897—*Coalface* [1935]); Paul Rotha (b. 1907—*Shipyard* [1933]); Basil Wright (b. 1907—*Song of Ceylon* [1934]); Harry Watt (b. 1906—*Night Mail* [co-directed with Basil Wright, 1936]); and Humphrey Jennings (1907–50—*Words for Battle* [1941]; *Listen to Britain* [1941]; *Fires Were Started* [1943]). But after the innovations of the Brighton school at the turn of the century, Britain had produced little significant narrative cinema outside of the work of Alfred Hitchcock; the films either directed or produced by Alexander Korda (1893–1956—*The Private Life of Henry VIII* [1933]; *Rembrandt* [1936]; *Things to Come* [directed by William Cameron Menzies, 1936]; *The Thief of Bagdad* [co-directed by Tim Whelan, Ludwig Berger, and Michael Powell, 1940]); and the stage adaptations of Anthony Asquith (1902–68—*Pygmalion* [co-directed with Leslie Howard, 1938]). This was because the British film industry had long been dominated by the American, due to their common language, and most British commercial production was geared toward making second features to accompany Hollywood films on double bills.

During and after World War II, however, a traditional staple of native British cinema—literary adaptation—experienced a sharp upswing. The actor-director Laurence Olivier (b. 1907) offered distinguished adaptations of three plays by Shakespeare—*Henry V* (1944), *Hamlet* (1948), and *Richard III* (1955)—and David Lean (b. 1908) produced carefully crafted, atmospheric adaptations of Charles Dickens' *Great Expectations* (1946) and *Oliver Twist* (1947), both models of their form. Anthony Asquith's stylish adaptations of Terence Rattigan's plays *The Winslow Boy* (1948) and *The Browning Version* (1951), and of Oscar Wilde's play *The Importance of Being Earnest* (1952), were matched by a brilliant expressionistic version of Alexander Pushkin's story *The Queen of Spades* (1949), directed by Thorold Dickinson (b. 1903). Carol Reed (b.

14.1 Part of the futuristic "Everytown" set in *Things to Come* (William Cameron Menzies, 1936).

14.2 Anthony Asquith's adaptation of Shaw's *Pygmalion* (1938): Leslie Howard and Wendy Hiller as Henry Higgins and Eliza Dolittle.

14.3 Laurence Olivier in his production of *Hamlet* (1948).

14.4 Pip confronts Magwitch in David Lean's adaptation of Dickens' *Great Expectations* (1946): John Mills, Finlay Currie.

1906) directed *Odd Man Out* (1946), *The Fallen Idol* (1948), *The Third Man* (1949; adapted from a story by Graham Greene), and *Outcast of the Islands* (1951; adapted from Joseph Conrad's novel), all finely wrought dramatic narratives, resonant at their best of French poetic realism and the films of Orson Welles. *The Red Shoes* (1948) and *Tales of Hoffman* (1951), the extravagant ballet spectaculars made by Michael Powell (b. 1905)* and Emeric Pressburger (b. 1902) for Gainsborough Pictures, also appeared during this period, as did the best work of the Boulting brothers, John and Roy (both b. 1913), who alternated as producer and director on such fine post-war films as *Brighton Rock* (1947; adapted from the Graham Greene novel), *The Magic Box* (1951; the story of William Friese-Greene, the putative inventor of the first British cinema machines), *Lucky Jim* (1957; adapted from the Kingsley Amis novel), and *I'm All Right, Jack* (1959).

Among the most important British films of the post-war era was a series of intelligent and witty comedies made for Michael Balcon's family-run Ealing Studios by Charles Crichton (b. 1910—*Hue and Cry* [1947]; *The Lavender Hill Mob* [1951]; *The Titfield Thunderbolt* [1953]); Alexander Mackendrick (b. 1912—*Whisky Galore/Tight Little Island* [1949]; *The Man in the White Suit* [1951]; *The Lady Killers* [1955]); Henry Cornelius (1913–58—*Passport to Pimlico* [1948]; *Genevieve* [1953]); and Robert Hamer (1911–63—*Kind Hearts and Coronets* [1949]; *Father Brown* [1954]). The splendid work of the actor Alec Guinness (b. 1914) in a number of these films made him an international star. The omnibus film *Dead of Night* (1945), co-directed by Alberto Cavalcanti, Robert Hamer, Charles Crichton, and Basil Dearden, is also a landmark of British post-war cinema because of its convincing *mise-en-scène* and circular narrative structure.

By the mid-fifties British cinema had begun to decline into cliché, and Britain was once again in danger of becoming a Hollywood colony. As early as 1947, the Oxford University film journal *Sequence* (1947–52), edited by the future directors Lindsay Anderson (b. 1923) and Karel Reisz (b. Czechoslovakia, 1926), had attacked the controlling assumption of British cinema: "The British commercial cinema has been a bourgeois rather than a revolutionary growth; and it is not a middle-class trait to examine oneself with the strictest objectivity, or to be able to represent higher or lower levels of society with sympathy and respect."[1] Anderson and Reisz went on to act upon their beliefs in 1954–55 by organizing the "Free Cinema" movement, which, like Italian neo-realism, celebrated, as a manifesto put it, "the importance of the individual and . . . the significance of the everyday." Like the French New Wave, the

---

* Powell (and, to a lesser extent, Pressburger) is currently enjoying a renaissance of critical interest. See John Russell Taylor, "Michael Powell: Myths and Supermen," *Sight and Sound,* 47, 4 (Autumn 1978), 226–29; David Badder, "Powell and Pressburger: the War Years," *Sight and Sound,* 28, 1 (Winter 1978–79), 8–13; Harlan Kennedy and Nigel Andrews, "Peerless Powell," *Film Comment,* 15, 3 (May–June 1979), 49–55; Eliott Stein, " 'A Very Tender Film, a Very Nice One': Michael Powell's *Peeping Tom,*" *Film Comment,* 15, 5 (September–October 1979), 57–59; and Ian Christie, ed., *Powell, Pressburger, and Others* (London, 1978).

14.5 *The Red Shoes* (Michael Powell and Emeric Pressburger, 1948): Moira Shearer, Robert Helpmann, Leonide Massine.

14.6 *Kind Hearts and Coronets* (Robert Hamer, 1949): Alec Guinness surrounds Valerie Hobson with six of his eight incarnations in Ealing Studios' most famous comedy.

Free Cinema movement was also dedicated to the belief that film should be a medium of personal expression for the film-maker, who should be socially committed to illuminating the problems of contemporary life.

In practice, Free Cinema meant the production of short, low-budget documentaries like Anderson's *O Dreamland* (1954), a satirical assault on the spiritual emptiness of working-class life set in an amusement park, and Reisz's and Tony Richardson's *Momma Don't Allow* (1956), a study of post-war youth in the environment of a London jazz club. Between February 1956 and March 1959, the Free Cinema movement presented a series of six programs at the National Film Theater which featured most prominently *O Dreamland; Momma Don't Allow; Every Day Except Christmas* (1959)—Anderson's poetic study of Covent Garden flower and vegetable vendors; *We Are the Lambeth Boys* (1958)—Reisz's sensitive portrait of a South London youth club; and a number of recent Continental films: Franju's *Le sang des bêtes* (1949), Roman Polański's *Two Men and a Wardrobe* (*Dwaj ludzie z szafa,* 1958; see Chapter 15), Truffaut's *Les mistons* (1957), and Chabrol's *Le beau Serge* (1958).

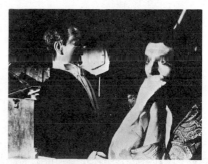

14.7 Alberto Cavalcanti's "The Ventriloquist's Dummy" episode in *Dead of Night* (Cavalcanti, Hamer, Crichton, and Dearden, 1945): Michael Redgrave, with John Maguire as Hugo the dummy.

At the same time that the Free Cinema movement emerged, a revolution was underway in the British theater and novel in which liberal working-class values emanating from the provinces and the East End of London overturned the established bourgeois tradition of the preceding decades. John Osborne's anti-establishment diatribe *Look Back in Anger* rocked the world of traditional culture when it was staged at the Royal Court Theater in May 1956, by calling into question the whole class structure of British society and assailing the moral bankruptcy of the welfare state. The following years witnessed the appearance of a new group of young, anti-establishment, working-class novelists, such as David Storey, John Braine, Alan Sillitoe, and Shelagh Delaney, who treated similar themes in a style which can be accurately characterized as "social realism." By 1959—significantly, the year that the French New Wave won a great number of the prizes at Cannes—the time was ripe for the overthrow of the class-bound British feature cinema in favor of working-class social realism.

In that year, the industry itself produced two films which announced the revolution: Jack Clayton's (b. 1921) adaptation of John Braine's novel *Room at the Top* and Tony Richardson's adaptation of *Look Back in Anger*. Both films were big-budget commercial productions with well-known stars which nevertheless dealt seriously with the disillusionments and frustrations of the British working classes, and both were international hits. *Look Back in Anger* was so successful, in fact, that Richardson (b. 1928) and Osborne (b. 1929) were able to form their own production company, the short-lived but influential Woodfall Films (1959–63), with the financial backing of producer Harry Saltzman (later responsible for the slick James Bond series). Woodfall's first independent production, Karel Reisz's *Saturday Night and Sunday Morning* (1960), a version of the Alan Sillitoe novel, was shot on location in Nottingham with unknown actors for a budget of under three hundred thousand dollars, or less than one-third of the standard feature allocation. But it recovered this figure in the first two weeks of its London run alone and went on to become the biggest international success the British film industry had known since the thirties.

14.8 *Look Back in Anger* (Tony Richardson, 1959): Richard Burton, Mary Ure.

British "New Cinema," or Social Realism

Saturday Night and Sunday Morning became the prototype for what may be fairly labeled as British "New Cinema," a social-realist film movement whose themes were borrowed from Italian neo-realism and whose techniques were modeled upon the Free Cinema documentary of the late fifties and, more currently, the films of the French New Wave. The movement's films were generally set in the industrial Midlands and shot on location in black-and-white against the gloomiest backgrounds their makers could find. They prominently featured unknown young actors, because their protagonists were typically rebellious working-class youths like Richardson/Osborne's Jimmy Porter and Reisz/Sillitoe's Arthur Seaton—men who have learned contempt for the spiritual torpor induced in their parents and friends by the welfare state and by mass communications as exemplified by the BBC. They spend a good deal of their time in pubs, drinking and brawling, and use a tough vernacular speech until then unheard in British cinema. Some major films from the New Cinema are Tony Richardson's *A Taste of Honey* (Woodfall, 1961; script by Shelagh Delaney) and *The Loneliness of the Long Distance Runner* (Woodfall, 1962; adapted from a Sillitoe novel); John Schlesinger's *A Kind of Loving* (1962) and *Billy Liar* (1963); Lindsay Anderson's *This Sporting Life* (produced by Reisz, 1963); Canadian-born Sidney J. Furie's *The Leather Boys* (1963); and Karel Reisz's *Morgan: A Suitable Case for Treatment* (1966).

Like the French New Wave, British New Cinema reached its peak

14.9 *Saturday Night and Sunday Morning* (Karel Reisz, 1960): Shirley Anne Field, Albert Finney, Norman Rossington.

around 1963 and then rapidly declined as a movement while its directors went their separate ways. During the mid-sixties, in fact, a reaction to the bleakness of social realism set in, and the depressing images of the industrial Midlands were replaced by those of "swinging London" in big-budget widescreen color productions like *Alfie* (Lewis Gilbert, 1966), *Smashing Time* (Desmond Davis, 1967), and *Joanna* (Michael Sarne, 1968), all of which, however, did have working-class protagonists. Nevertheless, Lindsay Anderson continued to pursue anti-establishment themes in *If . . .* (1968), a brilliant film about the nature of individualism and authority cast in the form of a surrealist satire on the British public-school system. One of the sixties' most important films, *If . . .* can be favorably compared with Vigo's *Zéro de conduite* (1933), to which it contains several explicit allusions; it established Anderson as the most important and influential figure to emerge from the New Cinema movement. In Anderson's more recent work, the powerful *O Lucky Man!* (1973), whose mock-poetic title refers back to his first film, *O Dreamland,* the protagonist of *If . . .* continues his education through the various levels of corruption in London society, only to be totally corrupted himself at the end of the process—by being "discovered" by the director Lindsay Anderson to star in a motion picture entitled *O Lucky Man!*

14.10 Anarchic violence at the conclusion of *If . . .* (Lindsay Anderson, 1968).

After an impressive start in *Saturday Night and Sunday Morning,* the work of Karel Reisz generally declined during the sixties, with the exception of *Morgan* (1966), a subtle and painfully funny film about mental breakdown, but his intelligent, American-made *The Gambler* (1975) signaled renewed vigor. Reisz's second American feature, *Who'll Stop the Rain?* (1978), marked his return to prominence with a corrosive adaptation of Robert Stone's best-selling novel *Dog Soldiers,* an allegorical chase-thriller about heroin smuggling during the Vietnam war. He is currently at work on an adaptation of John Fowles' "Victorian" novel *The French Lieutenant's Woman.* Whatever the future course of Reisz's career, it should be noted that his important book *The Technique of Film Editing* has greatly influenced such major film artists as Alain Resnais. The same general falling-off was seen in the work of Tony Richardson, who, after a series of three excellent working-class films and the flamboyant period comedy *Tom Jones* (1963; adapted from Henry Fielding's novel), abandoned social commitment for the big-time commercial cinema. Since then, most of his films, like the American-made *The Loved One* (1965), have been failures, but a film-maker of substantial verve is still perceptible in *The Charge of the Light Brigade* (1968), *Ned Kelly* (1970), and, more recently, his second Fielding adaptation, *Joseph Andrews* (1977). John Schlesinger (b. 1926), who began his career as a BBC documentarist, has been much more successful artistically than either Reisz or Richardson since he made his first feature, *A Kind of Loving,* in 1962. After *Billy Liar* (1963), he achieved great commercial success with *Darling* (1965), a modish examination of upper-class decadence filmed *à la nouvelle vague,* which brought Julie Christie to stardom. Since then, Schlesinger has specialized in stylish and cinematically intelligent films

14.11 *The Charge of the Light Brigade* (Tony Richardson, 1968): Ben Aris, Corin Redgrave.

14.12 *Sunday, Bloody Sunday* (John Schlesinger, 1971): Glenda Jackson, Murray Head.

14.13 *Privilege* (Peter Watkins, 1967): Paul Jones as the messianic rock star Steve Shorter.

such as *Far from the Madding Crowd* (1967; from the Thomas Hardy novel), *Midnight Cowboy* (1969), *Sunday, Bloody Sunday* (1971), *The Day of the Locust* (1975; from the novel by Nathanael West), *Marathon Man* (1976), *Yanks* (1979), and *Honky-Tonk Freeway* (1980). Jack Clayton, whose *Room at the Top* (1959) is often credited with having begun the movement, turned away from social realism in his second feature, *The Innocents* (1961), a beautiful, terrifying, and appropriately ambiguous visualization of Henry James' novel *The Turn of the Screw,* but he continued to make distinctly individual films such as *The Pumpkin Eater* (1964; script by Harold Pinter) and *Our Mother's House* (1967). Clayton's career as a director seems to have ended with the commercial and critical failure of his opulent, Hollywood-produced version of F. Scott Fitzgerald's *The Great Gatsby* (1974), which nevertheless remains an interesting film.

Other important British film-makers of the sixties were Bryan Forbes (b. 1926), whose *Whistle Down the Wind* (1961), *The L-Shaped Room* (1963), *Seance on a Wet Afternoon* (1964), *King Rat* (1965), *The Wrong Box* (1966), *The Whisperers* (1967), *Deadfall* (1967), and *The Raging Moon* (1970) demonstrate a remarkably subtle sense of atmosphere and *mise-en-scène,* and the more traditional Basil Dearden (1911–71— *Sapphire* [1959]; *The League of Gentlemen* [1960]; *The Mind Benders* [1963]; *Khartoum* [1966]) and Ronald Neame (b. 1911—*The Horse's Mouth* [1958]; *Tunes of Glory* [1960]; *The Prime of Miss Jean Brodie* [1969]).* During the same years, the television director Peter Watkins (b. 1935) made two brilliant pseudo-documentary films for the BBC— *Culloden* (1964), an historical re-creation of the bloody suppression of the 1746 Jacobite rebellion, and *The War Game* (1965), a projection of what would happen to Britain in the aftermath of a nuclear attack which was shown in restricted screenings because of its horrific content. Watkins' first theatrical feature, *Privilege* (1967), offered a strikingly original vision of England as a totalitarian state, but could not be compared with his television work; his more sophisticated *Punishment Park* (1971) depicted a Fascist America in the wake of the Vietnam war, while *Edvard Munch* (1976) used documentary techniques to dramatize the life, milieu, and creative agonies of the Norwegian Expressionist painter. The British stage director Peter Brook (b. 1925) made several fine films during the sixties, including versions of William Golding's novel *The Lord of the Flies* (1962), Peter Weiss' drama *Marat/Sade* (1966), and Shakespeare's *King Lear* (1969; released 1971), and *Tell Me Lies* (1967), a bitter and incisive polemic against American involvement in Vietnam. Also notable was a film directed by Kevin Brownlow (b. 1938) and Andrew Mollo

---

* The seventies films of both Forbes and Neame, the majority made for American studios, have been uneven but continue to demonstrate skilled craftsmanship. Forbes has made *The Stepford Wives* (1975), *The Slipper and the Rose—Story of Cinderella* (1976), and *International Velvet* (1978); Neame directed *Scrooge* (1970; a musical based on Dickens' *A Christmas Carol*), *The Poseidon Adventure* (1972), *The Odessa File* (1974), *Meteor* (1978), and *Hopscotch* (1980).

(b. 1941) and independently produced, *It Happened Here* (1964; released 1966), a "documentary" reconstruction of an imagined German occupation of England during World War II.*

British cinema was further enhanced in the sixties and seventies by the presence of two American expatriates, Joseph Losey (b. 1909) and Richard Lester (b. 1932). Losey, who became a British citizen after being hounded out of Hollywood during the McCarthy era, produced some of the most significant British films of the decade, in collaboration with absurdist playwright Harold Pinter (b. 1930): *The Servant* (1963); *Accident* (1967); and *The Go-Between* (1971), adapted from the novel by L. P. Hartley.† A subtle stylist whose major themes are the destructiveness of the erotic impulse and the corrupting nature of technocracy, Losey has also produced important films from his own scripts, notably *Eve* (1962), totally mutilated in its commercial version, and the remarkable anti-war drama *King and Country* (1964). Losey's recent films are *The Assassination of Trotsky* (1972); a version of Henrik Ibsen's *A Doll's House* (1973); *The Romantic Englishwoman* (1975), an elegant and witty film about modern marriage scripted by the playwright Tom Stoppard; *M. Klein* (1976), a study of anti-Semitism in occupied France; a version of Mozart's opera *Don Giovanni* (1979), shot on location in northern Italy; and *Les routes du sud* (*Roads of the South*, 1979), an intimate portrait of a father-son relationship, set in rural France, which contains autobiographical elements.

14.14 *The Servant* (Joseph Losey, 1963): Dirk Bogarde, James Fox.

Richard Lester came to fame and fortune through his two Beatles films, *A Hard Day's Night* (1964) and *Help!* (1965), which employ the full cinematic arsenal of the New Wave—telephoto zooms and swoops, flashbacks, jump cuts, and every conceivable device of narrative displacement—to create a dazzling new kind of audio-visual comedy. His subsequent films—*The Knack* (1965), *How I Won The War* (1967), *Petulia* (1968), and *The Bed-Sitting Room* (1969)—use the same techniques

14.15 An archetypal image of the sixties: the Beatles in *A Hard Day's Night* (Richard Lester, 1964).

---

* Since that time, Brownlow and Mollo have made only one other film, *Winstanley* (1975), another "imaginary documentary" based on David Caute's novel about the seventeenth-century English "Digger" movement. But unlike *It Happened Here,* which was personally financed by the film-makers and took seven years to complete, *Winstanley* was subsidized by the British Film Institute (BFI) Production Board. Since the mid-sixties, this institution has made limited funds available to independent film-makers such as Don Levy (b. 1932—*Herostratus* [1967]), the American-born Steve Dwoskin (b. 1939—*Central Bazaar* [1976]), David Gladwell (*Requiem for a Village* [1974]), Peter Smith (*A Private Enterprise* [1974]), and Nick Broomfield and Joan Churchill (*Juvenile Liaison* [1975]). By far the most impressive work made with BFI support is Bill Douglas' autobiographical trilogy *My Childhood* (1972), *My Ain Folk* (1974), and *My Way Home* (1978). This series of bleakly beautiful films tells the story of a poor and unwanted boy coming of age in a Scottish mining town; some critics feel that it is the greatest achievement of British cinema in the seventies. The most recent (and, to date, most expensive) BFI production is Richard Woolley's metaphysical murder mystery *Brothers and Sisters* (1980).

† For a detailed account of this collaboration, see Beverle Houston and Marsha Kinder, "The Losey-Pinter Collaboration," *Film Quarterly,* 32, 1 (Fall 1978), 17–30. See also Christopher C. Hudgins, "Inside Out: Filmic Technique and the Creation of Consciousness in Harold Pinter's *Old Times,*" *Genre,* 13, 3 (Fall 1980), 355–76.

to more serious dramatic purpose, often with less success, though *Petulia*'s disjointed narrative style works perfectly to embody the psychological disintegration of its principle characters. Lester's most recent films have been the highly successful swashbucklers *The Three Musketeers* (1973), *The Four Musketeers* (1975), and *Royal Flash* (1975); the historical romance *Robin and Marion* (1976); an adaptation of the Broadway comedy *The Ritz* (1977); the comic Western "prequel" *Butch and Sundance: The Early Days* (1979); and *Cuba* (1979), a political thriller set in the last days of the Batista regime.

The End of Social Realism

With the decline of social realism and the increasing influence of American investment in the now lucrative British cinema (90 percent by 1968), the distinctly national flavor of British films was lost in the late sixties. Many American directors (such as Billy Wilder, Richard Fleischer, Sidney Lumet, Delbert Mann, Stanley Donen, George Stevens, Otto Preminger, Anthony Mann, Richard Brooks, William Wyler, Fred Zinneman, John Huston, and Stanley Kubrick) came to work in British studios during these years, as did such major Continental figures as Roman Polański (*Repulsion* [1965]; *Cul-de-sac* [1966]); François Truffaut (*Fahrenheit 451* [1966]); and Michelangelo Antonioni (*Blow-Up* [1966]). Furthermore, the British-based directors Richardson, Lester, and Schlesinger—not to mention David Lean (*The Bridge on the River Kwai* [1957]; *Lawrence of Arabia* [1962]; *Dr. Zhivago* [1965]; *Ryan's Daughter* [1970]) and Carol Reed (*The Agony and the Ecstasy* [1962]; *Oliver!* [1968])—had all begun to make films within the American industry, and Reisz (*Isadora* [1968]) and Forbes (*The Madwoman of Chaillot* [1969]) both became involved in big-budget international co-productions.

Nevertheless, in the late sixties a new, more visually oriented generation of British directors began to appear: Clive Donner (b. 1926—*Here We Go Round the Mulberry Bush* [1967]; *Alfred the Great* [1969]; *Vampira* [1974]); Peter Yates (b. 1929—*Bullitt* [1968]; *John and Mary* [1969]; *The Friends of Eddie Coyle* [1973]; *Mother, Jugs, and Speed* [1976]; *Breaking Away* [1979]); John Boorman (b. 1933—*Point Blank* [1967]; *Hell in the Pacific* [1969]; *Leo the Last* [1970]; *Deliverance* [1972]; *Zardoz* [1974]; *The Exorcist II: The Heretic* [1977]); the Hungarian-born Peter Medak (*Negatives* [1968]; *A Day in the Death of Joe Egg* [1970]; *The Ruling Class* [1972]; *Evening Flight* [1979]); Ken Loach (b. 1936—*Poor Cow* [1967]; *Kes* [1969]; *Family Life* [1972]; *Black Jack* (1979); Alan Bridges (b. 1927—*The Hireling* [1973]; *Phobia* [1979]); Ken Russell (b. 1927—*Women in Love* [1969]; *The Music Lover* [1970]; *The Devils* [1971]; *The Boy Friend* [1972]; *Savage Messiah* [1972]; *Mahler* [1974]; *Tommy* [1975]; *Lisztomania* [1975]; *Valentino* [1977]); and Nicolas Roeg (b. 1928—*Performance* [1970]; *Walkabout* [1971]; *Don't Look Now* [1973]; *The Man Who Fell to Earth* [1976]; *Bad Timing* [1980]). The latter two, especially, seem to represent the wave of the future for British cinema. Russell oscillates between the outrageously vulgar and the outrageously brilliant, but he is engaged in creating a distinctly individual body of work in which the borderline between reality and fantasy is not simply blurred but totally destroyed. Roeg, who has worked as a cameraman for Lester, Schlesinger, and Truffaut, and who photographs all of his own films, is a more consistent artist than Russell. His beautiful and enigmatic, if frequently pretentious, films go far beyond conventional narrative to immerse the viewer in a fluent stream of audio-visual images whose most legitimate meaning is their psychological affect. The most impressive British talent to emerge since Roeg is Ridley Scott—also a former cameraman—whose first feature, *The Duellists* (1977), adapted from a short story by Joseph Conrad, won high praise at Cannes in the year of its release. Scott's second film, *Alien* (1979), made for Twentieth Century–Fox in the United States, has been hailed as a minor masterpiece of science fiction and visceral horror.*

Like the French New Wave, from which it partially sprang, the British social realist cinema disappeared along with the social context which had motivated it. But its formal and thematic legacy to British national cinema was great. It bequeathed the then radical stylistic conventions of the New Wave to a cinema stagnant with archaic narrative traditions carried over from the pre-war era. And in its new concern for the aesthetics of everyday life and its new outspokenness about the dynamics of sex, class, and power in the post-industrial world, it gave the class-ridden, hidebound British film a vastly wider range of themes than it had ever known before. Social realism also produced a handful of important directors, like Lindsay Anderson, John Schlesinger, Tony Richardson, and Karel Reisz, and a new pool of international acting talent in the person of young and previously unknown stars such as Albert Finney, Rita Tushingham, Rachel Roberts, Alan Bates, Tom Courtenay, Susannah York, Richard Harris, Oliver Reed, Michael Caine, David Warner, Julie Christie, Glenda Jackson, James Fox, Terence Stamp, David Hemmings, Michael York, Vanessa Redgrave, and Lynn Redgrave.

It is important to remember that, except for brief intervals like the period of social realism, the British film has rarely been a major force in world cinema. This is partially because of America's domination of the English-language film market, and partially because there is an innately conservative component in British visual and aural culture. Nevertheless, it is possible to hope for a resurgence of British cinema in the recent work of John Schlesinger, Ken Loach, Ridley Scott, and Nicolas Roeg, as well as that of such relative newcomers as Derek Jarman (*The Tempest* [1979]), Franc Roddam (*Quadrophenia* [1979]), Franco Rosso (*Babylon* [1980]), Christopher Petit (*Radio On* [1979]), Brian Gibson (*Breaking Glass* [1980]), Alan Clarke (*Scum* [1979]), and Monty Python (Terry Jones and Terry Gilliam directing—*Monty Python and the Holy Grail*

---

* Other British directors currently working in the American industry include Michael Apted (*Coal Miner's Daughter* [1980]), Alan Parker (*Fame* [1980]), and Adrian Lyne (*Foxes/Ladies of the Valley* [1980]).

14.16 *Picnic at Hanging Rock* (Peter Weir, 1975): Anne Lambert.

14.17 *The Last Wave* (Peter Weir, 1977): Richard Chamberlain.

14.18 *My Brilliant Career* (Gillian Armstrong, 1979): Judy Davis, Sam Neill.

[1975]; *Monty Python's Life of Brian* [1979]). Observers note a renewed exuberance and intelligence in these films which may signal a turning toward that absurdist tradition of British art associated in literature with Laurence Sterne, Lewis Carroll, Virginia Woolf, and James Joyce.*

COMMONWEALTH CINEMA: AUSTRALIA AND CANADA

A recent and most unexpected development in English-language cinema has been the emergence of Australian film from nearly total obscurity into international prominence with the work of director Peter Weir (b. 1944—*Picnic at Hanging Rock* [1975]; *The Last Wave* [1977]; *The Plumber* [1978]) and such compatriots as Phillip Noyce (*Backroads* [1977]; *Newsfront* [1978]); Fred Schepisi (*The Devil's Playground* [1976]; *The Chant of Jimmy Blacksmith* [1978]); Ian Coughlin (*Alison's Birthday* [1978–79]); Don Crombie (*Caddie* [1976]; *The Irishman* [1978], *Cathy's Child* [1978–79]); Ken Hannam (*Sunday Too Far Away* [1975]; *Dawn!* [1978–79]); John Duigan (*The Tresspassers* [1976]; *Dimboola*, 1978–79); Ebsen Storm (*In Search of Anna*, 1978–79); Tim Burstal (*Eliza Frazer* [1976]; *The Last of the Knucklemen* [1978–79]); George Miller (*Mad Max* [1978–79]); Michael Thornhill (*The Journalist* [1978–79]); Bruce Beresford (b. 1940—*The Getting of Wisdom* [1977]; *The Money Movers* [1978–79]; *Breaker Morant* [1980]); Jim Sharman (*The Night the Prowler* [1978–79]); Tom Jeffrey (*Weekend of Shadows* [1978]; *The Odd Angry Shot* [1978–79]); Albie Thoms (*Palm Beach* [1978–79]); Simon Wincer (*Snapshot* [1978–79]; *Harlequin* [1980]; Paul Cox (*Kostas* [1979]); Michael Pate (*The Mango Tree* [1977]; *Tim* [1978–79]); Linda Blagg (*Just Out of Reach* [1979]); and Gillian Armstrong (*My Brilliant Career* [1979]). Almost all of these films were financed by the state-operated Australian Film Commission, established to stimulate development of the industry in the early seventies; or by semi-official bodies such as the South Australian Film Corporation or the New South Wales Film Corporation. That goal has apparently been achieved, since many critics believe that the New Australian Cinema promises to become as distinctive and influential a phenomenon as the French and Czechoslovak New Waves (see Chapters 13 and 15).†

---

* See Harlan Kennedy, "The British Are Coming," *Film Comment,* 16, 3 (May–June 1980), 57–60; and Joseph Coencas, "British Film Renaissance," *Millimeter,* 8, 5 (June 1980), 118–23. The 1980 New York Film Festival featured a special section entitled "British Film Now" to demonstrate the rebirth forecast in these articles.

† See David Stratton (director of the Sidney Film Festival), *The New Australian Cinema* (New York, 1980); Ross Cooper and Andrew Pike, *Australian Film 1906–1977* (New York, 1980); Gideon Bachman, "Films in Australia," *Sight and Sound,* 46, 1 (Winter 1976–77), 32–35; Robin Bronby, "Test for Australia," *Sight and Sound,* 48, 2 (Spring 1979), 85–87; and Diane Jacobs, "Australian Originals," *American Film,* 4, 7 (May 1979), 52–57. See also Sylvia Lawson, "Towards Decolonization: Some Problems and Issues for Film History in Australia," *Film Reader 4,* ed. Blaine Allan et al. (Evanston, Ill., 1979), 63–71; and Eric Reade, *History and Heartburn: The Saga of Australian Film, 1896–1978* (East Brunswick, N.J., 1981).

Canada is another commonwealth nation whose cinema has experienced sudden and unexpected growth. Although Canada is one of the largest and wealthiest countries in the world, its film market was dominated until very recently by American productions, much as the British had been during the thirties. Before 1978, film production in Canada was basically a cottage industry under the tight control of the National Film Board (NFB). Founded in 1939 by the British documentary producer John Grierson, the NFB coordinated all government film activities in an attempt to end Hollywood dominance and establish a national cinema which would "interpret Canada to Canadians and the world" (Grierson). For this purpose, Grierson gathered about him a group of talented documentarists (Stuart Legg, Stanley Hawes, Raymond Spottiswoode, Joris Ivens, John Fernhout, and Irving Jacoby), and during World War II Canada became the world's leading producer of Allied war propaganda (the *World in Action* series [1942–45], and *Canada Carries On* [1940–45]) and other types of non-fiction film. After the war, Grierson returned to England, but the NFB continued to produce distinguished documentary and animated shorts (in the brilliant experimental work of Norman McLaren* [b. 1914]), turning increasingly, with the arrival of television, to the use of *cinéma-vérité* techniques (the *cinéma-direct* movement, in fact, was founded in the early sixties by French Canadian film-makers at the NFB, including Michel Brault, Pierre Perrault, and Claude Jutra, under the influence of Jean Rouch—see Chapter 13).

For all of Canada's success with documentary and animated cinema, feature film-making was left almost exclusively to the Americans until 1962, when the NFB produced Don Haldane's *Drylanders,* a semi-documentary account of the harsh existence of a Canadian farming family during the first thirty years of the century. By 1964, the NFB was supporting feature production in both French (Gilles Groulx's *Le chat dans le sac* [*The Cat in the Sack*]) and English (Don Owen's *Nobody Waved Goodbye*), but Canadian feature production averaged only four films per year, and many Canadian directors (e.g., Norman Jewison, Sidney J. Furie, Arthur Hiller, Silvio Narizzano, Ted Kotcheff) and actors (Donald Sutherland, Christopher Plummer, Michael Sarrazin, Joanna Shimkus) were migrating south to work in the American industry. And it was a rare Canadian feature indeed—such as Irvin Kershner's *The Luck of Ginger Coffey* (U.S.-Canada [1964]), shot on location in Montreal—that enjoyed even modest success beyond its own borders. In an effort to reverse this trend, the Canadian Film Development Corporation (CFDC) was established by an Act of Parliament in 1967 with a fund of $10 million (now a revolving annual fund of $4.5 million) to promote the national feature industry through grants and guaranteed loans. By 1972, the annual feature output had risen to twelve and included such notable French- and English-language films as Michel Brault's *Entre la mer et l'eau douce* (*Between the Sea and the Still Waters* [1967]); Gilles Carle's

---

* McLaren developed and perfected the technique of the cameraless film, originated by Len Lye (1901–80) in 1934, painting and drawing his images directly on the celluloid, regardless of frame divisions.

14.19 *The Apprenticeship of Duddy Kravitz* (Ted Kotcheff, 1974), the first Canadian feature to achieve international distribution: Richard Dreyfuss, Micheline Lanctôt.

Le viol d'une jeune fille douce (*The Rape of a Sweet Young Girl* [1968]) and *La vraie nature de Bernadette* (*The True Nature of Bernadette* [1972]); Gilles Groulx's *Entre tu et vous* (*Between Yourselves* [1969]); Claude Jutra's *Mon oncle Antoine* (*My Uncle Antoine* [1971]); Denys Arcand's *Réjeanne Padovani* (1972); Paul Almond's *Isabel* (1968); Don Owen's *The Ernie Game* (1968); Allan King's *Warrendale* (produced for the CBC) and *A Married Couple* (1969); Don Shebib's *Goin' Down the Road* (1970); Jean Chabot's *Mon enfance à Montréal* (*My Childhood in Montreal* [1972]); William Fruet's *Wedding in White* (1972); and Eric Till's *A Fan's Notes* (1972). In 1974, the CFDC scored an unprecedented international success with Ted Kotcheff's *The Apprenticeship of Duddy Kravitz*. Nevertheless, by 1977 less than $6 million in private funds were being invested in Canadian feature films.

But in 1978 two things occurred which radically changed the nature of the Canadian industry. The first was a policy change at the CFDC in which the seed money for Canadian feature projects was lent to producers rather than directors, increasing investment incentive within the business community. Second, and infinitely more important, the Canadian government enacted wide-ranging tax shelter legislation for film investment, which has rapidly become the second most popular form of tax relief in the country (after oil depletion allowances). The result has been a boom in the production of commercial features the like of which few nations have experienced in modern times: $6 million was invested in Canadian feature production in 1977 but over $150 million in 1979, with $300 million predicted for 1980. Co-production with the United States, France, Italy, and Japan, as well as domestic production on a previously unthinkable big-budget scale, have combined to produce one of the most commercially lucrative production environments anywhere in the world today (among the recent big winners was Irving Reitman's *Meatballs,* with $40 million in receipts for 1979). That the environment and the films lack a specifically Canadian character has troubled some observers, but there can be no question that much of the film-making activity being financed in Canada today represents a solid contribution to world cinema. For example, between 1978 and 1981, Canada produced or co-produced all of the following: *Caro Papa* (*Dear Papa* [Dino Risi, 1978]), *Una giornata speciale* (*A Special Day* [Éttore Scola, 1978]), *Why Shoot the Teacher?* (Silvio Narizzano, 1978), *Le soleil se leve en retard* (*The Sun Rises Late* [André Brassard, 1978]), *A nous deux* (*Us Two* [Claude Lelouch, 1979]), *Outrageous* (Richard Brenner, 1979), *Skip Tracer* (Zale Dalen, 1979), *A Man, a Woman, and a Bank* (Noel Black, 1979), *Silent Partner* (Daryl Duke, 1979), *Mourir à tue-tête* (English title: *Primal Fear* [Anne-Clair Poirier, 1979]), *Out of the Blue* (Dennis Hopper, 1980), *Circle of Two* (Jules Dassin, 1980), *Atlantic City, U.S.A.* (Louis Malle, 1980), *L'affair Coffin* (*The Coffin Affair* [Jean-Claude Labrecque, 1980]), *L'arrache coeur* (*The Broken Hart* [Mireille Dancereau, 1980]), *Les bon débarras* (*Good Riddance* [Francis Mankiewicz, 1980]), *The Lucky Star* (Max Fischer, 1980), *Fantastica* (Gilles Carle, 1980), *Keiko* (Claude Gagnon, 1980), *Shades of Silk* (Mary Stephen, 1980), *L'homme à tout faire* (*The Handyman* [Micheline Lanctôt, 1980]), *Scanners* (David

14.20 Anne-Claire Poirier's *Mourir à tue-tête*, Quebec's biggest commercial success of 1978.

Cronenberg, 1981), and *Surfacing* (Claude Jutra, 1981). In fact, with twenty-four entries at the 1980 Cannes Festival, Canada has announced its intention to become a "world class" force in cinema.

But while the country at large bids to become a major center for international production, a truly national Canadian cinema can be said to exist in the work of several young *québecois* directors, protégés of the somewhat older revolutionary film-maker Jean-Pierre Lefebvre (b. 1941—*La révolutionnaire* [*The Revolutionary*, 1965]; *Las dernières fiançailles* [*The Last Betrothals*, 1973]; *L'amour blessé* [*Wounded Love*, 1975]; *Le vieux pays où Rimbaud est mort* [*The Old Country Where Rimbaud Died*, 1977]); Denys Arcand (*La maudite galette* [*Dirty Money*, 1971]; *Gina* [1971]); Jean Chabot (*Une nuit en Amérique* [*A Night in America*, 1973]; *La fiction nucléaire* [*The Nuclear Lie*, 1979]); Jean-Guy Noël (*Ti-cul Tougas* [1976]); and Jacques Leduc (*La tendresse ordinaire* [*Ordinary Tenderness*, 1975]; *Chroniques de la vie quotidienne* [*Chronicles of Daily Life*, 1978]). Whether *québecois* cinema can survive as a national entity in the face of the CFDC's "world class" aspirations for the industry as a whole is perhaps the most crucial question for the Canadian film in the eighties.

14.21 *Cinéma québecois: On est au coton* (Denys Arcand, 1970), a feature-length documentary about the economic oppression of Canadian textile workers by American mill-owners, made for the National Film Board and then suppressed by the government.

THE SECOND ITALIAN FILM RENAISSANCE

Like the American, French, and British cinemas, the Italian cinema experienced a creative decline during the fifties as the neo-realist impulse died out and the studios returned to the business of producing mass entertainment. Visconti, Rossellini, and De Sica (see Chapter 11) continued to make serious films, but, as elsewhere, the industry's emphasis was on spectacle and mildly titillating sex. The fifties was largely a period of "rosy realism" in the Italian film—a mode which might best be understood as a merging of *telefono bianco* and neo-realism—and the decade witnessed the appearance of such international sex symbols as Sophia Loren, Gina Lollobrigida, and Marcello Mastroianni. But two figures were working within the domestic cinema at this time who would create the second post-war Italian film renaissance—Federico Fellini (b. 1920) and Michelangelo Antonioni (b. 1912).

Federico Fellini

Formerly a newspaper cartoonist, Fellini had begun his career as a scriptwriter for Rossellini (*Roma, città aperta* [1945]; *Paisà* [1946]), Pietro Germi (*In nome della lègge* [1949]; *Il cammino della speranza* [1950]), and Alberto Lattuada (*Senza pietà* [1948]), and his early films are very much in the orthodox neo-realist tradition. *Luci del varietà* (*Variety Lights*, 1950), co-directed with Lattuada, provides an ironic portrait of a seedy itinerant vaudeville troupe. Fellini's first solo film, *Lo sceicco bianco* (*The White Sheik*, 1952), is a sardonic account of a young bride's infatuation with the hero of a *fumetto,* or popular photo-

14.22 *I vitelloni* (Federico Fellini, 1953): Vira Silenti, Franco Interlenghi, Alberto Sordi.

14.23 Fellini's *La strada* (1954): Giulietta Masina, Anthony Quinn.

magazine strip. But *I vitelloni* (*The Loafers/The Young and the Passionate,* 1953) was the first film to reveal the director's remarkable feeling for character and atmosphere. This episodic study of aimless young loafers in the seaside resort town of Rimini, where Fellini grew up, contains semi-autobiographical elements, and it remains one of his finest achievements.

With *La strada* (*The Road,* 1954), produced by Dino De Laurentiis and Carlo Ponti,* Fellini made a break with neo-realism to tell the story of a simple-minded peasant girl who is sold to a circus strongman for a plate of pasta. He treats her brutally and, after a series of misadventures, finally abandons her. Years later, he learns of her death and collapses in a

---

* De Laurentiis (b. 1919) and Ponti (b. 1910) both began their careers as producers during the neo-realist period, the former with *Riso amaro* (1948—whose star, Silvana Mangano, De Laurentiis married in 1949), the latter with *Senza pietà* (1948) and *Il mulino del Po* (1949). In 1950 they formed Ponti–De Laurentiis Productions, which produced some of the most important Italian films of the decade—Rossellini's *Europa '51* (1952) and Fellini's *La strada* (1954) and *Le notti di Cabiria* (1956), among them—as well as the epic U.S./Italian co-production *War and Peace* (King Vidor, 1956). The partnership was dissolved in 1957, when Ponti married Sophia Loren and began to produce films for her (*The Black Orchid* [Martin Ritt, 1958]; *That Kind of Woman* [Sidney Lumet, 1959]; *Heller in Pink Tights* [George Cukor, 1960]; *Two Women* [Vittorio De Sica, 1960]). In the sixties, De Laurentiis turned to the production of epic spectacles, such as *Barabbas* (Richard Fleischer, 1962), *The Bible* (John Huston, 1966), and *Waterloo* (Sergei Bondarchuk, 1970), at his vast studios near Rome (also producing Visconti's *Lo straniero* [1967] and Roger Vadim's *Barbarella* [1968]), but he liquidated the property and moved to the United States in the early seventies, where he has since produced such notable and/or infamous films as *Serpico* (Sidney Lumet, 1973), *Death Wish* (Michael Winner, 1974), *King Kong* (John Guillermin, 1976), *The Serpent's Egg* (Ingmar Bergman, 1977), and *King of the Gypsies* (Frank Pierson, 1979). During the same period, Ponti became a French citizen and produced for Godard (*Une femme est une femme* [1961]; *Les carabiniers* [1963]), Varda (*Cleo de cinq à sept* [1962]), Demy (*Lola* [1960]), and Chabrol (*Landru* [1962]), as well as for David Lean (*Dr. Zhivago* [1965]), Elio Petri (*La dècima vittima* [1965]), Antonioni (*Blow-Up* [1966]; *Zabriskie Point* [1970]; *The Passenger* [1975]), Andy Warhol (*Andy Warhol's Frankenstein* [1974]; *Andy Warhol's Dracula* [1974]), and Éttore Scola (*Brutti, sporchi, e cattivi* [1976]; *Una giornata speciale* [1977]).

fit of weeping. Realist in form but essentially allegorical in content, *La strada* was attacked by Leftist critics, including Zavattini (see Chapter 11), as betraying the social commitment of neo-realism, but it attracted worldwide attention and won a Silver Lion, the second highest honor, at the prestigious Venice Film Festival in 1954. By the time he made *La strada,* Fellini had assembled about him the group of collaborators with whom he was to work for most of his career: his co-scenarists, Ennio Flaiano and Tullio Pinelli; his director of photography, Otello Martelli; his composer, Nino Rota; and his leading lady, Giulietta Masina, who is also his wife. Fellini's next film was *Il bidone* (*The Swindle,* 1955); like *La strada,* it was realist in style but symbolic in content. This tale of two-bit swindlers who victimize the poor has an aura of tragedy about it and contains a number of surreal touches which adumbrate Fellini's later concern with psychology and myth. *Le notti di Cabiria* (*Nights of Cabiria,* 1956), which Fellini wrote with the Marxist poet and future director Pier Paolo Pasolini, again has Giulietta Masina as the central figure. Here she plays a plucky, indomitable Roman prostitute who is betrayed and robbed by the young man she loves, but who nevertheless has the spirit to begin life anew.

14.24 Christ transported by helicopter in the opening shot of Fellini's *La dolce vita* (1960).

After a hiatus of nearly four years, Fellini produced *La dolce vita* (1960), his first film in widescreen and a turning-point in his work. This film concerns the life of a Roman journalist and press agent (Marcello Mastroianni) as he seeks sensational stories and hobnobs with the international jet set. Its superficially realistic mileau is corruption and decadence, and its visual extravagance borders on the fantastic. The film begins with a long traveling shot of a statue of Christ being flown by helicopter over the city and ends at the seashore with the capture of a monstrous dead fish. *La dolce vita* was a huge commercial success because of its sexual explicitness, but it brought Fellini international recognition as a major artist and a new master of widescreen composition.

With *Otto e mezzo* (*8½,* 1963)—so named because it was his eighth-and-a-half film, the "half" being his contributions to the anthology films *Amore in città* (1953) and *Boccaccio '70* (1962)—Fellini moved directly into the world of self-reflexive fantasy. In *8½,* Guido (Mastroianni), a film director who represents Fellini himself, has undertaken a large-scale production but runs out of creative energy in the process. To escape, he lapses into a dream-world of adolescent sexual fantasy and childhood memory, from which he ultimately emerges to accept defeat. In the film's final image, all of the major characters in his life (and in the film) link hands to dance around the rim of a circus ring as Guido stands in the middle and directs them confidently through a megaphone. This surrealistic parable of the agony of artistic creation won many international awards; though it has been called a twentieth-century version of Dante's *Inferno,* *8½* is ultimately about the process of its own making.

14.25 Fellini's *Otto e mezzo* (1963): Marcello Mastroianni, Edra Gale.

In *Giulietta degli spiriti* (*Juliet of the Spirits,* 1965), his first feature in color, Fellini focused on a woman (played by Masina) who, like Guido in *8½,* collapses into a world of fantasy under the pressure of an unpleasant external reality (her husband's infidelity, the dominance of her glamorous mother and sisters) and who struggles out of it towards identity. Like

14.26 *Fellini Satyricon* (1969).

8½, this basically non-narrative film is concerned with the psychodynamics of memory, obsession, fantasy, and dream. After contributing a characteristically haunting episode ("Toby Dammit") to the French anthology film *Histoires extraordinaires* (English title: *Spirits of the Dead*, 1968), Fellini embarked on his most ambitious project to date—*Fellini Satyricon* (1969), a flamboyant and personalized version of Petronius' epic paean to hedonism. In this lavish costume extravaganza based on a script by the director himself, he created a nightmarish portrait of the decadence of ancient Rome. Lacking any specific point of view or human reference, the film was felt by many critics to be purely a feast for the eye, as decadent and grotesque as its subject-matter. But others maintained that Fellini had created a unique audio-visual language which transcended traditional narrative to suggest the continuity of depravity throughout human history.

I clowns (*The Clowns*, 1970) was a cinematic essay on the circus, a favorite Fellini metaphor, made on a low budget for Italian television, and it is a decidedly minor work. In *Fellini Roma* (1972), stunningly photographed by Giuseppe Rotunno, the director continued his preoccupation with subjective history in an impressionistic study of Rome which combined stylized documentary with Fellini's own memories of the city as a youth. *Amarcord* (1974; the title is regional dialect for "I remember"), his next major work, is an autobiographical film about a young man growing up in the seaside town of Rimini some forty years ago. More directly autobiographical than *I vitelloni* and far less mannered and extravagant than its immediate predecessors, the film has been viewed by some critics as a return to Fellini's neo-realist roots. It is actually a restrained and muted elegy for the director's youth which provided Fellini with a breathing-space before undertaking a spectacular English-language version of Casanova's *Memoirs* (*Casanova*, 1976)—a film more controversial with the critics for its glacially sumptuous tableaux than even *Fellini Satyricon*. But *Prova d'orchèstra* (*Orchestra Rehearsal*, 1979), which uses the metaphor of a discordant symphony orchestra to comment on the dangerously chaotic state of modern democracy, has been widely praised for its cinematic beauty and intellectual depth. And the episodic *La città delle donne* (*City of Women*, 1980) offers an intelligent, if fanciful, vision of contemporary sexual warfare within the framework of its male protagonist's dreams.

Deeply influenced by neo-realism in the formlessness and circularity of his narratives, Fellini has chosen to structure his work through the sheer force of his own personality and obsessions. To use one of his favorite images, Fellini is first and foremost a great ringmaster whose circus is the human comedy as it exists both inside and outside himself. His theme is the mystery of identity (often his own or that of the characters played by Giulietta Masina), and he has learned to tap a large portion of the cinema's vast but generally unrealized potential to objectify subjective states, and vice versa. Fellini's rich frescoes and intoxicating images create a stylized world of mental fantasy in which reality is re-interpreted and made significant by the imagination of the artist. As Foster Hirsch has put it, "In his own way, [Fellini] combines the two strains that have always dominated Italian movies: the epic tradition, with its fondness for spectacle and operatic gesture, and the humanist tradition, with its deep feeling for the outcast and the oppressed."[2]

Michelangelo Antonioni

Michelangelo Antonioni, like Fellini, began his career in film as a neo-realist. The son of a wealthy Ferrara businessman, he attended the Centro Sperimentale in Rome and wrote criticism for *Cinema,* after receiving a degree in political economy from the University of Bologna. In 1942 he collaborated on the script of Rossellini's *Un pilota ritorna* and served as an assistant to Marcel Carné on *Les visiteurs du soir.* His first films as a director were bleak and uncompromising neo-realist documentary shorts like *Gente del Po (People of the Po,* 1943; 1947), *N.U./Nettezza urbana (Dustmen,* 1948), and *La villa dei mostri (The House of Monsters,* 1950). But Antonioni's first features broke away from neo-realist conventions to examine the middle-class milieu with which he was most familiar. *Cronaca di un amore (Story of a Love Affair,* 1950) depicts the consequences of an affair between a wealthy housewife and a car salesman. *I vinti (The Vanquished,* 1952) is an episodic film which examines violence among the restless youth of post-war Europe. *La signora senza camelie* (English title: *Camille Without Camellias,* 1953) concerns the rise and fall of a young movie star. All three films deal with social displacement and alienation, major themes in Antonioni's later work.

Antonioni continued to examine middle-class malaise in his first major feature, *Le amiche (The Girl Friends,* 1955), based on a novel by Cesare Pavese. In this pessimistic study of the alienated bourgeois women of Turin, Antonioni announced a new style, one which abandoned traditional plotting for a series of seemingly random events and which connected his characters intimately with their environment through the long take, or sequence shot, as opposed to montage. Use of the long take in *Le amiche,* which won the Silver Lion at Venice in 1955, enabled Antonioni to render the duration of real time on the screen and to emphasize the overwhelming importance of the material environment on the interior lives of his characters—the two major components of his mature style. In *Il grido (The Cry,* 1957), Antonioni turned briefly from the bourgeois milieu to portray the doomed journey of a factory worker and his daughter across the desolate wasteland of the Po Valley. Here, as in *Le amiche,* Antonioni used the physical environment of his film to express the psychology of the characters. But it was with *L'avventura (The Adventure,* 1959) that Antonioni achieved his first great masterpiece of *mise-en-scène.*

The first film in his brilliant trilogy about displacement and alienation in the modern world, and his first film in widescreen, *L'avventura* concerns a yachting party of rich Italians who land on a deserted volcanic island in the Mediterranean. A young woman, Anna, quarrels with her lover, Sandro, the leader of the party, and then mysteriously disappears. Anna's best friend, Claudia (played by Monica Vitti, who starred in

14.27 Lost in space: Monica Vitti in *L'avventura* (Michelangelo Antonioni, 1959).

14.28 Ennui: Jeanne Moreau as the novelist's wife in Antonioni's *La notte* (1960).

14.29 Madness on the floor of the Milan stock exchange in Antonioni's *L'eclisse* (1962): Alain Delon.

Antonioni's next three films), and Sandro, both of whom have been marginal figures in the film up to this point, search the island for her and can find no trace. At Claudia's instigation, they return to mainland Sicily and continue their search, but they ultimately forget the missing woman and become lovers. The lack of final resolution and the seeming aimlessness of the narrative caused *L'avventura* to be jeered at the 1960 Cannes Festival, but it received the Jury Prize, and the impact of its revolutionary style was soon felt around the world.

For one thing, Antonioni used the sequence shot in *L'avventura* to equate film time with real time: every scene in the film, whether edited or not, takes the same amount of time to occur on the screen as it would in empirical reality. He also employed widescreen deep focus to link his characters inexorably with their oppressive surroundings. Both techniques have the effect of transferring the psychological experience of the characters to the audience, since both groups are required to perceive time and space in precisely the same terms, unmediated by expressive montage. Thus, we experience the long and tedious search for Anna, first on the island and later on Sicily, very much as do Sandro and Claudia— at first with interest and anticipation, then with desperation, and finally with disgust and boredom, which leads us to forget the object of the search altogether and concentrate on the relationship of the searchers, just as do the searchers themelves. From one moment to the next, Antonioni never permits us to know any more about the mystery of Anna's disappearance (or about the mystery of their own relationship) than do Sandro and Claudia, and when the film ends with these mysteries unresolved, we realize that the psychological "adventure" of the characters has been made our own.

Antonioni continued his trilogy on what he calls "the great emotional sickness of our era" with *La notte* (*The Night,* 1960), a film about the growing estrangement of a successful novelist and his wife, and the alienation of both from the vacuous environment of modern industrial Milan. *L'eclisse* (*The Eclipse,* 1962), a brilliant conclusion to the trilogy, offered Antonioni's most sustained vision of the disorder and incoherence of modern existence. In Rome, two lovers conclude an affair, having "nothing left to say to each other," and the woman drifts into another affair with her mother's handsome young stockbroker. This affair, too, leads toward estrangement, and the film concludes with a seven-minute montage sequence of fifty-eight shots showing places in the city from late afternoon to nightfall where the lovers have met regularly during the course of the film, but in which neither of them now appears. Their unexplained disappearance (and our mute acceptance of it) is a chilling reminder of the fragility and impermanence of personal relationships and provides the perfect *coda* for a trilogy whose theme is the hopelessness of love in the modern age.

14.30 A frame from the concluding sequence of *L'eclisse*.

In *Deserto rosso* (*Red Desert*, 1964), his first color film and winner of the Venice Golden Lion in 1964, Antonioni portrayed the neurotic wife of a wealthy engineer searching for meaning in the industrial wasteland of Ravenna. Her sense of personal dislocation and the chaotic impingement of industry upon nature are both heightened by Antonioni's expressionistic use of color. Great poisonous clouds of yellow smoke billow from the factories, ships pass continuously in the background through the gray mists of the harbor, and chemical dyes give a nightmarish cast to the industrial wastes and slag heaps that intrude upon the natural landscape of the town.

Antonioni also used color symbolically in *Blow-Up* (1966), an abstract and mystifying film about a fashion photographer in "swinging" London who seems to have inadvertently photographed a murder in the background of some random shots he has taken of an anonymous woman in a park. As he "blows up" the telltale prints to greater and greater scale, objective reality becomes pure abstraction, and the film ends by suggesting that modern experience, even (or, perhaps, especially) when rendered visible on film, is not subject to interpretation and is therefore meaningless.

Blow-Up was Antonioni's first film to reach a large popular audience, and its commercial success led to his filming of *Zabriskie Point* for MGM in America in 1969. Shot partly on location in Death Valley, this beautiful color film was an attempt to suggest the utter decadence of American society through the fantasies of the revolutionary young, but it failed due to Antonioni's misunderstanding of the American idiom and American culture. (Some critics had charged *Blow-Up* with a similar distortion of British society, but context was subordinate to concept in that particular film.) For a director to whom milieu is so crucial to meaning, a misunderstanding of this sort can be fatal.

14.31 *Deserto rosso* (Michelangelo Antonioni, 1964): Monica Vitti, Richard Harris.

After the commercial failure of *Zabriskie Point,* Antonioni went to China for five weeks to film a 220-minute documentary for Italian television. This poetic color film, entitled *Chung kuo* (1972), is among Antonioni's finest documentary achievements, but it has been inexplicably attacked by the Chinese for denigrating their revolution (which it most certainly does not). For two years after his return from China, Antonioni worked on a project entitled *Technically Sweet,* a feature film to be shot on location in the Amazon jungles with a new color telecamera system which would permit him to experiment still further with expressionistic color. The film's producer, Carlo Ponti, finally vetoed the project and asked Antonioni to consider filming a suspense thriller, based on an original story by Mark Peploe about a man who changes his identity. The

14.32 David Hemmings takes the crucial photograph in Antonioni's *Blow-Up* (1966).

14.33 A scene from the conclusion of Antonioni's *The Passenger* (1975): Maria Schneider, Jenny Runacre, Angel del Pozo, José Maria Cafarel, and Jack Nicholson (partially off-frame) as the murdered reporter.

result was not a thriller at all but a despairing existential meditation on the uselessness of human individuality entitled *Professione: Reporter* (English title: *The Passenger*, 1975). Set in exotic international locations, *The Passenger* concerns a television news reporter at mid-life who finds a corpse in a Moroccan hotel and assumes the identity of the dead man. This desperate bid for self-liberation ends in disaster when the dead man turns out to have been a political operative dangerously involved in a Third World guerrilla war. Filmed as a series of long takes, and concluding with an elaborate seven-minute zoom-and-tracking shot in which the death of the reporter is obliquely implied rather than observed, *The Passenger* has been acclaimed as a masterpiece, although its clinical detachment from its subject verges on the inhuman.

Now in his late sixties, Antonioni is one of the world's greatest living film artists. He has tenaciously maintained his integrity and independence through a difficult career, to become a poet of the modern individual's estrangement from his environment and of his tragic inability to communicate with others and with himself. His films from *L'avventura* (1959) through *The Passenger* (1975) contain little dialogue and less music, implying the virtual irrelevance of human communication, but they make brilliant use of naturalistic sound and silence to emphasize his characters' isolation in a seemingly random, if not hostile, universe. Antonioni has, by his own account, been concerned with behavior rather than story, and he lets the situations of his films grow out of the personalities and surroundings of his characters, rather than imposing situations through plot. His oblique and languorous narrative style, with its simultaneous capacity for distancing and involvement, has decisively influenced the development of the modern widescreen cinema. What he said of *L'avventura* after its Cannes premiere speaks for all that he has done since:

> I have rid myself of much unnecessary technical baggage, eliminating all the logical narrative transitions, all those connective links between sequences where one sequence served as a springboard for the one that followed. . . . Cinema today should be tied to the truth rather than logic. . . . The rhythm of life is not made up of one steady beat; it is, instead, a rhythm that is sometimes fast, sometimes slow. . . . There are times when it appears almost static. . . . I think that through these pauses, through this attempt to adhere to a definite reality—spiritual, internal, and even moral—there springs forth what today is more and more coming to be known as modern cinema, that is, a cinema which is not so much concerned with externals as it is with those forces that move us to act in a certain way and not in another.[3]

Antonioni is currently at work on an adaptation of Jean Cocteau's *L'aigle à deux têtes* (*The Eagle with Two Heads*) for Italian television entitled *Il mistero di Oberwald* (*The Mystery of Oberwald*) and starring Monica Vitti. We may anticipate that working with his former collaborator in an Italian setting for the first time since 1964 will inaugurate a prolific new decade for this great contemporary *ciné*-poet of our alienation, our illogic, and our ennui.

Olmi, Pasolini, and Bertolucci

While Fellini and Antonioni were becoming acknowledged masters of the international cinema during the sixties, a second generation of post-war Italian directors was coming to prominence. Ermanno Olmi (b. 1931) was the young film-maker most clearly in the neo-realist tradition, though the slow-paced, elliptical style of his narratives brings him close to the later Antonioni. After making some forty documentaries in Milan between 1952 and 1959, Olmi established an international reputation in his narrative feature *Il pòsto* (*The Job/The Sound of Trumpets*, 1961). This sympathetic, insightful, and wistfully comic film concerns a young man from the provinces who takes a tedious job as a clerk with a large industrial firm in Milan. It contrasts the systematically dehumanizing nature of the job with his own naïve happiness at finding a place for himself in a complex, urbanized world. Like the films of Olmi's neo-realist predecessors, *Il pòsto* was shot entirely on location with a cast of non-professional actors, and it is virtually plotless. *I fidanzati* (*The Fiancés*, 1963) confirmed Olmi's talent for the sympathetic and sophisticated treatment of the lives of ordinary working people. In it, an engaged couple is forced to separate so that the man can pursue his job in faraway Sicily, but they manage to endure and to sustain their relationship.

14.34 *Il posto* (Ermanno Olmi, 1961): Sandro Panzeri.

After an uncharacteristically pedestrian film about the life of Pope John XXIV, *E venne un uomo* (English title: *A Man Named John*, 1965), Olmi produced his finest work to date, *Un certo giorno* (*One Fine Day*, 1968). This film concerns a successful advertising executive who kills a man in an automobile accident and is forced to re-examine the course of his entire life in an attempt to make some sense of it. In the end, he is acquitted of his crime through the services of a smart lawyer and once more succumbs to bourgeois insensitivity. *I ricuperanti* (*The Scavengers*), made for Italian television in 1969, is about the vagrant life of battlefield scavengers in post-war Italy. But with *Durante l'estate* (*In the Summertime*, 1971), also made for television, Olmi moved toward romantic fantasy in the visually sumptuous tale of a forger whose rich inner life lends him dignity and significance. As always, Olmi's surface realism here is informed by a sense of the sad and absurd comedy of everyday life. His most recent films are *La circostanza* (*The Circumstance*, 1974) and *L'albero degli zoccoli* (*The Tree of Wooden Clogs*, 1978)—the latter filmed as a three-part, 180-minute television series on peasant survival in the late nineteenth century, which Olmi produced, wrote, directed, photographed, and edited himself.

The Marxist novelist, poet, and essayist Pier Paolo Pasolini (1922–75), who had worked with Fellini on the script of *Le notti di Cabiria* (1956), made his first two films in the neo-realist tradition but later rejected it in favor of what he called an "epical religious," or mythic, vision of experience. *Accattone* (*The Beggar*, 1961) and *Mama Roma* (1962) were tough, uncompromising studies of Roman low-life, filmed on location with non-professional actors, which contained none of the sentimentality that sometimes marred the neo-realist films of Rossellini and De Sica.

14.35 *Il vangelo secondo Matteo* (Pier Paolo Pasolini, 1964): Enrique Irazoqui, a non-professional actor, as Christ.

14.36 Pasolini's *Porcile* (1969): Pierre Clementi as the leader of the cannibals.

The magnificent *Il vangèlo secondo Matteo* (*The Gospel According to St. Matthew*, 1964) was a semi-documentary reconstruction of the life of Christ from the Annunciation to the Resurrection which implicitly examined the relationship between the Marxist dialectic and Christian myth. This stark but brilliant work, shot in *cinéma-vérité* style with non-professional actors, stands today as the most dynamic version of the gospel story ever filmed.

As the sixties progressed, Pasolini turned more and more to allegory and myth. *Uccellacci e uccellini* (English title: *Hawks and Sparrows*, 1966) was, to use Pasolini's term, an "ideo-comic" film about the course of Italian Marxism. In *Edipo re* (*Oedipus Rex*, 1967), shot on location in Morocco, Pasolini set Sophocles' tragedy in a primitive region analogous to the unconscious mind and framed it with a contemporary Freudian prologue and epilogue in order "to project psychology onto myth." *Teorèma* (*Theorem*, 1968) and *Porcile* (*Pigsty*, 1969) were both major works in Pasolini's mythico-ideological mode, establishing him as a film-maker of great intellectual importance. *Teorèma* is a mythical allegory set among the bourgeoisie which equates religious experience with sex: a bisexual, extraterrestrial Christ-figure visits an Italian middle-class family and causes it to disintegrate under the pressure of his mysterious sexual attraction. *Teorèma* scandalized the Catholic Church, but its companion-piece, *Porcile*, goes even farther in its attack upon the religious and political hypocrisies of bourgeois culture. The film proceeds by intercutting two savage and revolting parables of capitalism—one about a band of medieval cannibals who live in the hills and eat the flesh of kidnapped travelers, the other about a wealthy contemporary West German industrialist who has made his fortune from the Holocaust and whose demented son loves intercourse with pigs. At the end of the film, the cannibals are ripped apart by wild dogs at the instigation of the local police authorities, and the German youth is eaten by his pigs.

After shooting a version of Euripides' *Medea* (1969) in Turkey, Pasolini abandoned the surrealist satire of the sixties to make a "trilogy of life," as he called it, by adapting the world's three greatest works of omnibus literature: Boccaccio's *Decameron* (*Il decamerone*, 1971), Chaucer's *Canterbury Tales* (*I racconti di Canterbury*, 1972), and *A Thousand and One Nights/The Arabian Nights* (*Il fiore delle mille e una notte*, 1974), shot on location in Italy, England, and Persia respectively. His last film was *Salò* (English title: *The 120 Days of Sodom*, 1975), a version of de Sade's bizarre pornographic epic, which Pasolini updated and set in the Salò Republic of Italy during the last days of Fascist rule. An important theoretician of film in many published essays, as well as a brilliant director, Pasolini at his best succeeded in creating an intellectual cinema in which metaphor, myth, and narrative form all subserved materialist ideology. By a grim irony, given his vision of the human race as a "pigsty," Pasolini's remarkable career was cut short in the fall of 1975 when he was murdered by a young thug who claimed that the director had made sexual advances toward him.

Bernardo Bertolucci (b. 1940), Pasolini's assistant on *Accattone*, has gone on to become the most significant new director to emerge from the

Italian cinema in the sixties. His film *La commare secca* (*The Grim Reaper,* 1962), made from a script by Pasolini when Bertolucci was only twenty, is a documentary-style investigation into the murder of a prostitute which was extremely well received at the Venice Festival. But it was *Prima della rivoluzione* (*Before the Revolution,* 1964) that brought the young director to international attention. This visually complex and intelligent film concerns a young man's inability to break away from bourgeois values and fully commit himself to Marxist ideals. *Partner* (1968) is an uneven film, overtly derivative of Godard, about a modern intellectual who meets his double. But with his dense philosophical investigations into the roots of Fascism, *La strategia del ragno* (*The Spider's Strategy,* 1970) and *Il conformista* (*The Conformist,* 1970), Bertolucci forged a complex and elliptical visual style bordering on surrealism but still very much his own.

In *La strategia del ragno,* produced for Italian television, a young man seeks to discover the truth behind his father's death during the Fascist period. *Il conformista,* from the novel by Alberto Moravia, explores the psychology of a young man who is hired by Italian Fascists to assassinate his former professor in France, and it makes a remarkable equation between sexual disorder, social decadence, and the authoritarian personality. Both films employ intricate narrative structures which move freely back and forth through time and emphasize its relativity. *Il conformista,* Bertolucci has said, is a film not of the past but of the present, because "however the world has changed, feelings remain the same." Bertolucci's controversial *Last Tango in Paris* (*Ultimo tango a Parigi,* 1972) is less complex than *Il conformista,* but like its predecessor it employs an expressionistic color scheme and a disjointed narrative style to take us into the mind of a man deranged by grief, where sex, pain, and death have all melded into the same sensation. The six-hour epic *Novecento* (*1900,* 1976)—reputedly the most expensive feature ever made in Italy—employs a cast of international stars to tell the stories of two families,

14.37 *Il conformista* (Bernardo Bertolucci, 1969): Jean-Louis Trintignant, Dominique Sanda.

14.38 Bertolucci's *Last Tango in Paris* (1973): Maria Schneider, Marlon Brando.

14.39 The fruits of political violence: *Novecento* (Bernardo Bertolucci, 1976). Donald Sutherland.

one rich and one poor, through the first fifty years of the twentieth century in a paean to the political consciousness of the Italian agricultural classes. Influenced by Pasolini, Godard, and the later Visconti rather than the neo-realist tradition, Bertolucci is clearly a film-maker of major importance to the future of narrative cinema, and we may justly expect from him increasingly sophisticated and significant work, although *La luna* (*Luna*, 1979), his sensuous film about an incestuous mother-son relationship, has disappointed some critics.

Other Italian *Auteurs*

Other important figures in the new Italian cinema are Marco Bellocchio (b. 1940), Francesco Rosi (b. 1922), Vittorio De Seta (b. 1923), Elio Petri (b. 1929), and Gillo Pontecorvo (b. 1919). Bellocchio's savage *I pugni in tasca* (*Fists in the Pocket*) shocked Italy in 1965 with its portrait of a young epileptic who makes a rational choice to murder off the members of his diseased bourgeois family. The director's complex and outrageously funny political satire *La Cina é vicina* (*China Is Near*, 1967) launched another frontal assault on bourgeois values and shared the Venice Jury Prize in 1967 with Godard's *La Chinoise*. With *Nel nome del padre* (*In the Name of the Father*, 1971), Bellocchio offered a stylized autobiographical account of life in a provincial Jesuit college in the late fifties. Like Vigo in *Zéro de conduite* (1933) and Lindsay Anderson in *If . . .* (1968), Bellocchio uses school as a microcosm for the oppressive, joyless, and class-ridden society which creates and sustains it. Characteristically, his fourth feature, *Marcia trionfale* (*Triumphal March*, 1976) is set in a military academy, but as in Bellocchio's subsequent films (for example, *Il gabbiano* [*The Seagull*, 1977]; *Salto nel vuoto* [*Leap into the Void*, 1979]), its formal qualities are frequently obscured by a heavy overlay of Marxist ideology.

Francesco Rosi, a former assistant to both Visconti and Antonioni, came into his own with *Salvatore Giuliano* (1962), a semi-documentary account of the real-life career of a bandit and folk-hero and his murder by the authorities in post-war Sicily. Shot on location with non-professional actors, the film has an extremely elliptical narrative structure which moves back and forth in time with the facility of Bertolucci's *Il conformista*. Rosi has since proven himself to be a director of great social commitment and a legitimate heir to neo-realism. His *Le mani sulla città* (*Hands Over the City*, 1963) is a powerful political film, shot on location in documentary style, about the corrupt relationship between real-estate development and modern city-planning, while *Il momento della verità* (*Moment of Truth*, 1965) is a critical analysis of the collective psychology of bullfighting. Rosi's next films were *Uomini contro* (*Men Against*, 1970), a diatribe against Italy's involvement in World War I, and *Il caso Mattei* (*The Mattei Affair*, 1972), yet another documentary reconstruction of an historical event, in this case the mysterious murder of a government official. *A propòsito di Lucky* (English title: *Lucky Luciano*, 1973) attempts to show the link between American and Sicilian gangsters and governments, and *Cadaveri eccellenti* (*Illustrious Corpses*,

14.40 *Salvatore Giuliano* (Francesco Rosi, 1961).

1976), a characteristic film of political murder and intrigue, won many international prizes. Rosi has just completed work on a four-hour television film (which has also been released as a two-and-a-half-hour theatrical feature) based on Carlo Levi's 1945 memoir *Cristo si è fermato ad Eboli* (*Christ Stopped at Eboli;* English title: *Eboli,* 1980).

The Sicilian-born director Vittorio De Seta, who writes and photographs his own films, made independent documentaries before directing *Banditi a Orgosolo* (*Bandits of Orgosolo,* 1961) a semi-documentary feature about a Sardinian shepherd who joins a group of revolutionary bandits, shot on location with non-actors. The film influenced the development of *cinéma-vérité* camera styles in both Italy and France, but, with the exception of the four-hour semi-documentary *Diario d'un maestro* (*Diary of a Schoolmaster,* 1973), De Seta has done little significant work since.

Elio Petri began his career as a scriptwriter for Giuseppe De Santis and Carlo Lizzani during the last days of the neo-realist movement, but he has since developed into a subtle film-maker with a sensuous and elliptical visual style of his own. Petri is a Marxist, and his most characteristic films are social satires cast in the form of conventional genre-pieces like *L'assassino* (*The Assassin,* 1961), *La dècima vittima* (*The Tenth Victim,* 1965), *Un tranquillo pòsto di campagna* (*A Quiet Place in the Country,* 1968), and his flamboyant analysis of the contemporary Fascist personality, *Indagine su un cittadino al di sopra di ogni sospetto* (*Investigation of a Citizen Above Suspicion,* 1970). Recently, Petri has become more aggressively political, in films like *La classe operaia va in paradiso* (*The Working Class Goes to Heaven,* 1972), winner of the Cannes Grand Prix; *Todo modo* (*All Roads . . . ,* 1976); and *Buone notizie* (*Good News,* 1979).

Gillo Pontecorvo was a film journalist and an assistant to Yves Allégret before turning to narrative cinema in 1960 with *Kapo,* a semi-documentary account of a young Jewish girl in Auschwitz who collaborates with the S.S. Since then, most of Pontecorvo's films have been scrupulously researched documentary reconstructions of historical events using authentic locations and non-actors. His most significant work to date is the remarkable *La battaglia di Algeri* (*The Battle of Algiers,* 1965), which employed the whole city and most of its population to reconstruct with complete verisimilitude the horrific events leading up to the liberation of Algeria. Financed by the Algerian government, the film won the Golden Lion at Venice in 1966. Impressive but less successful was *Queimada!* (*Burn!,* 1968), an attempt to probe the dynamics of colonial exploitation in the context of a nineteenth-century slave revolt on a Caribbean sugar plantation.

14.41 *La battaglia di Algeri* (Gillo Pontecorvo, 1966): Mohamed Ben Kassen, Brahim Haggiag.

Finally, some note should be taken of the important role played by state-operated Italian television, Radiotelevisione Italiana (RAI), in the production of major feature films. Since 1969, distinguished directors like Fellini (*I Clowns* [1970]), Antonioni (*Chung kuo* [1972]), Bertolucci (*La strategia del ragno* [1970]), Olmi (*I recuperanti* [1969]), and Rossellini (*Socrate* [1970]) have made films for RAI, often in collaboration with foreign television networks. RAI has also commissioned features from such promising young directors as Nelo Risi, Liliana Cavani, Giovanni Amico, and Adriano Apra. Cavani (b. 1936) emerged as a filmmaker of some importance with the notoriety of *Il portiere di notte* (*The Night Porter*, 1974), a sadomasochistic love story which attempts to dissect the culture of Fascism, and *Al di là del bene e del male* (*Beyond Good and Evil*, 1977), which re-creates the last, mad years of the German philosopher Friedrich Nietzsche in scatological detail.

Other notable Italian film-makers of the seventies are Marco Ferreri (b. 1928), a surrealist social critic in the mode of Buñuel who currently lives and works in France (*Dillinger è morto* [*Dillinger Is Dead*, 1968]; *La grande bouffe* [*Blow-Out*, 1973]; *La dernière femme* [*The Last Woman*, 1977]; *Bye Bye Monkey* [1979, U.S.A.]); *Chièdo asilo* (English title: *No Child's Land*, 1979); Èttore Scola (b. 1931—*Brutti, sporchi, e cattivi* [English title: *Down and Dirty*, 1976]; *C'eravamo tanto amati* [*We All Loved Each Other So Much*, 1975]; *Una giornata speciale* [*A Very Special Day*, 1977]; *La terrazza* [*The Terrace*, 1980]; Paolo (b. 1931) and Vittorio (b. 1929) Taviani (*Allonsanfàn* [1974]; *Padre padrone* [*Father, Master*, 1977; winner of the Cannes Grand Prix]; *Il prato* [*The Meadow*, 1979]); Mario Monicelli (b. 1915—*I compagni* [English title: *The Organizer*, 1963]; *Un borghese piccolo piccolo* [*A Very Petty Bourgeois*, 1977]; *Travels with Anita* [1979]); Mauro Bolognini (b. 1923—*La grande bourgeoise/Fàtti di gente perbene* [English title: *The Drama of the Rich*, 1974]; *Dove vai in vacanza?* [*Where Are You Going on Holiday?*, 1978]); Valerio Zurlini (b. 1926—*Il deserto dei tartari/Le désert des tartares* [*The Desert of the Tartars*, 1976]); Franco Brusati (*Pane e cioccolata* [*Bread and Chocolate*, 1974—released 1978]; *Dimenticare Venezia* [*To Forget Venice*, 1980]); Maurizio Nichetti (*Ratataplan* [1979]); Nanni Moretti (*Ecce Bombo* [1980]); and Marco Vicario (*Wife-Mistress* [1979]; *Il cappòtto di astrakan* [*The Persian Lamb Coat*, 1980]).

14.42 *Padre, padrone* (Paolo and Vittorio Taviani, 1977): Omero Antonutti as Gavino Ledda, a Sardinian shepherd, raised in brutish isolation, who ultimately becomes a professor of linguistics.

But perhaps the most important director to emerge from Italy during the seventies was Lina Wertmuller (b. 1928), who has become a controversial cult figure in the United States. Wertmuller worked as an assistant director in legitimate theater in Rome before she was chosen by Fellini to assist him on *8½* in 1963. That year she directed her first feature, a socio-comedy of Italian provincial life entitled *I basilischi* (*The Lizards*). She continued to make intelligent comic films for the domestic market until she scored her first international success with *Film d'amore e d'anarchia* (*Love and Anarchy*, 1973), an ironic examination of sex and politics in Fascist Italy focusing on the attempts of a bungling anarchist (played by Giancarlo Giannini—a Wertmuller regular) to assassinate Mussolini. *Mimi metallurgo ferito nell'onore* (*Mimi the Metalworker/The Seduction of Mimi*, 1972) and *Tutto a pòsto e niente in ordine* (*Everything's in Order But Nothing Works/All Screwed Up*, 1974) also deal with the situations of hopeless underdogs (both played by Giannini) pitted against the system and carry the connection between sex and politics one step further. The ultimate statement of that connection, however, is *Travòlti da un insòlito destino nell'azzurro mare d'Agosto* (*Swept Away by an Unusual Destiny on an Azure August Sea/Swept*

Away, 1974), in which a wealthy woman and a deck-hand are swept away by a storm from a pleasure yacht to a desert island, where their roles as master and slave are temporarily reversed. Eventually the two fall in love, but when they return to society their old roles re-assert themselves. Many feminist critics were disturbed by the film's ironic balance, but such irony is precisely Wertmuller's stock in trade as an artist. As proof, we have *Pasqualino settebellezze* (English title: *Seven Beauties,* 1976), a physically sumptuous paean to survival ethics set largely in a Nazi concentration camp where the Giannini character, an Italian army deserter, spends the duration of World War II. This complex film is by turns beautiful and repellent, since we are asked to identify with a protagonist who possesses the moral sensibility of a cockroach as well as the knack of surviving like one. The moral relativism of *Seven Beauties* outraged as many liberal critics as *Swept Away* did feminists. To the doctrinaire, both films seemed to endorse patriarchal Fascism. But for Wertmuller the phenomena of existence are more complex and disordered than doctrine of any sort will allow. As Diane Jacobs has written so acutely, "Wertmuller is a political film-maker in the tradition of Chaplin rather than Costa-Gavras: which is to say that she deplores Fascism and is out of sorts with any system that traps her little man . . . somewhere between freely willed and predestined chagrin."[4] Given her extraordinary technical mastery of the film medium and her broadly humane intelligence as an artist, there can be little doubt that Wertmuller will become a major figure of the international cinema of the nineteeneighties, although her last two films of the seventies, *The End of the World in Our Usual Bed on a Night Full of Rain* (1978) and *Blood Feud* (1979), disappointed some critics.

14.43 *Swept Away* (Lina Wertmuller, 1974): Mariangela Melato, Giancarlo Giannini.

CONTEMPORARY WIDESCREEN TECHNOLOGIES AND STYLES

The French and Italian film revolutions of the sixties paved the way for a new era of cinematic expression in the seventies and eighties, one in which narrative is no longer an end in itself but a medium for audio-visual essays in philosophy, psychology, ideology, and social criticism —essays, that is, on the human condition. In short, the cinema has become today at the level of general practice what it has always been for its greatest individual *auteurs,* regardless of their particular aesthetic: a form of audio-visual literature. But contemporary widescreen cinema is as formally distinct from the post-war sound film as the post-war sound film was from the silent film. Aesthetically, the new cinema is one of subjective involvement and *mise-en-scène* predicated upon the widescreen sequence shot.

This was the future cinema of the "integral style" announced by André Bazin before his death in 1958. Its predecessors were early masters of the long take—Feuillade, von Stroheim, and Murnau in the silent cinema; Renoir, Rossellini, and Welles in the sound film. These *mise-en-scène auteurs* had been forced to do their pioneer work within the black-and-white rectangle of the Academy frame and were recognizably eccentric to the mainstream tradition of narrative and expressive montage. The introduction of the widescreen processes and the improvement of color film stock in the fifties were the technological pre-conditions for a full-scale revolution in favor of *mise-en-scène* aesthetics, and Bazin recognized this in his last essays. But Bazin could not have foreseen two vastly significant technological developments of the sixties: 1) the perfection and widespread use of hand-held 35mm cameras which permit continuous and spontaneous on-location shooting, and 2) the rapid refinements within the optical industries, achieved through computer technology, which perfected the wide-angle and telephoto lenses, and ultimately produced the zoom lens. This latter development was especially significant, since by the mid-sixties all three types of lenses were standard equipment for Western and Eastern film-makers alike, and lens optics had become an essential component of the integral style.

The wide-angle lens is a lens of short focal length,* as low as 12.5mm, which covers a greater angle of vision than a conventional lens (the normal focal length for 35 mm film-making is 35 to 50 mm). It is used by cinematographers to shoot relatively large subjects at short range, under the kinds of physical restrictions that obtain, for example, in small rooms and in automobiles. Since the wide-angle lens works like an inverted telescope, it gives its images an exaggerated depth of field. The telephoto lens, on the other hand, is a lens of great focal length, up to 500mm, capable of achieving a variety of long-distance, telescopic close-ups. As the optical opposite of the wide-angle lens, the telephoto produces images which have little or no depth of field. The "zoom" lens, finally, is a lens of variable focal length which can move continuously from an extreme wide-angle long shot to an extreme telephoto close-up, traversing all positions in between (optically, for example, from a focal length of 25 to 250mm—a fairly standard zoom ratio of 10:1).†

The zoom lens introduced the important capacity for tracking *optically* without moving the camera. When such a lens is advanced toward its telephoto setting, the field of the image decreases radically and the camera seems to move toward its subject, and vice versa. Countless shots in Stanley Kubrick's *Barry Lyndon* (1975), for which a special 20:1 zoom lens was designed (the Cine-Pro T9 24–480 mm), are structured according to this principle. Similarly, if the camera pans slightly in its telephoto setting, the effect on the screen will be that of a lateral tracking shot. An

---

* Focal length is the distance in millimeters from the optical center of the lens (a point midway between the front and rear elements) to the emulsion surface of the film stock when the lens is sharply focused on "infinity," that is, an extremely distant object.

†A lens of variable focal length—the Taylor-Hobson 40–120mm "Varo," with a zoom ratio of 3:1—was introduced in Hollywood in 1932 and used in films intermittently through 1935, as can be noted, for example, in the opening scene of Rouben Mamoulian's *Love Me Tonight* (1932) and the shipboard dance sequence in Harry Lachman's *Dante's Inferno* (1935). Cumbersome in size and shape, the "Varo" also had serious optical limitations which caused it to be abandoned. The "zoom" lens re-appeared under its current name in 1955, but it was not sufficiently refined to maintain constant focus and *f*-stop (see Chapter 9 and Glossary) until the mid-sixties.

14.44 Two wide-angle lens shots from *Barry Lyndon* (Stanley Kubrick, 1975); director of photography, John Alcott. Note the great depth of field.

14.45 An extreme wide-angle lens shot from *Barry Lyndon* and the same subject shot from head on through a telephoto lens (actually, a zoom lens which has moved from its wide-angle position to its telephoto position, so that these two stills are the beginning and end of the same shot). Note the loss of depth of field—the "flattening-out" of the image in the telephoto setting.

outstanding example of this latter technique occurs near the end of Arthur Penn's *Bonnie and Clyde* (1967), when the camera pans a long row of shops in slightly out-of-focus close-up before coming to rest and refocusing on C.W. Moss' father, as he betrays the two outlaws to a Texas ranger, through the window of an ice-cream parlor. Visconti's *Morte a Venezia* (1971) is an excellent example of a film which consistently employs telephoto and zoom shots as a substitute for tracking, as are virtually all of the films of Robert Altman. But perhaps the most stunning use of optical traveling in recent cinema occurs at the end of Ján Kadár's *Adrift* (1971; see Chapter 15), when the anguished and apparently deranged protagonist, who has been standing under a tree outside of his house at evening, attempts to return to the house. At the beginning of the shot, the camera is behind the man with the zoom lens in its telephoto setting, so that there seems to be very little distance between either him and the house or him and the camera. But as he starts to walk toward the house, the lens begins to zoom slowly backward toward its wide-angle position, putting ever greater distance between both man and house and man and camera. As he sees his house recede before him, the man starts to run wildly toward it, and the lens zooms backward at an ever-increasing pace, paralleling his headlong flight, until finally the runner is left optically adrift, hanging suspended in space as both camera and house

14.46 The conclusion of the optical tracking shot in *Bonnie and Clyde* (Arthur Penn, 1967); director of photography, Burnett Guffey.

14.47 Optical hovering in *The Wild Bunch* (Sam Peckinpah, 1969); director of photography, Lucien Ballard.

14.48 Giuliana (Monica Vitti) and her son in Antonioni's *Deserto rosso* (1964); director of photography, Carlo Di Palma. The diminished depth perspective of the telephoto lens forces the two humans into the same plane as the abstracted industrial landscape.

recede toward infinity. This powerful image of madness and horror would have been impossible to achieve without a lens of variable focal length.

Another effect of which the zoom lens is capable is that of hovering or searching, as if the camera were trying to decide which element of a scene to focus upon from moment to moment—an especially valuable device for composing mass scenes like the mess-hall sequences in Robert Altman's *M.A.S.H.* (1970) or the outlaws' long walk through the teeming village of Agua Verde which precedes the final massacre in Sam Peckinpah's *The Wild Bunch* (1969). The zoom lens can also cause the camera to seem to leap backward or forward in space to isolate a significant detail in close-up without a cut. Thus, lenses of variable focal length permit a film-maker to move back and forth from long shot, medium shot, and close-up without the loss of continuity imposed by montage. It has even been suggested that Griffith would not have developed the syntax of narrative editing if zoom lenses had been available to him when he made his pioneering masterworks. This seems unlikely, since editing of some sort will always be an essential component of cinematic expression and since Griffith was too innovative a genius not to have recognized the fact; but in principle, at least, the suggestion is a valid one.

Of course, the possibilities for cutting on movement have been greatly increased by the cinema's new capacity for optical traveling, and the action sequences in Peckinpah's *The Wild Bunch* and *Junior Bonner* (1972) provide fine examples of the powerful kinetic impact that cutting on optical movement can achieve (see Chapter 17). Furthermore, unique visual effects can be obtained by intercutting telephoto and zoom shots with shots made through conventional lenses which possess greater depth of field. This is because lenses of variable focal length have a distorting characteristic which makes optical movement qualitatively different from real camera movement; that is, they destroy depth of field. As Paul Joannides has written: "Unlike a tracking shot a zoom represents a denial of perspective. The effect is not one of moving *through* space, but of space warping towards or away from the camera."[5] For this reason, lenses of variable focal length can in some sense be said to eliminate the third dimension and to deny the reality of space by abstracting it. In Antonioni's *Deserto rosso* (1964), for example, recurring telephoto close shots of the heroine depict a lone figure against an abstracted and flattened array of shapes, forms, and patterns—in reality the industrial landscape of Ravenna—which not only connects the character with her environment but emphasizes its meaninglessness.

This expressive effect could have been achieved only by shooting the scene through a wide-open telephoto or zoom lens, and it plainly illustrates how variable-focus lenses have become an important new aesthetic resource for contemporary film-makers who practice the integral style. In fact, the recent refinement of lens optics, more than any technological development since the introduction of widescreen, has made possible the new cinema of subjective involvement and psychological affect—a cinema of *mise-en-scène,* whose surface is often as abstractly expressionistic as it is realistic. Writing of this future cinema in 1970, Paul Joannides

14.49 A shot composed for the variable-focus lens in *The Red and the White* (Miklós Jancsó, 1967); director of photography, Tamás Somló.

14.50 A frame from a zoom lens sequence shot in Jancsó's *Red Psalm* (1972); director of photography, János Kende.

noted: "The camera will . . . play a more passive role dramatically, but a more potent one visually. Rather than being placed to *construct* the scene, it will treat the scene as a formal entity. Thus observation and group composition will be more important than the dialectic of 'significant' detail which usually makes up drama. Dialogue will tend to be replaced by conversation and will be arranged differently, in set-pieces rather than by cross-cutting."[6] Today, this cinema has arrived. As the French and Italian cinema revolutions demonstrate, for almost a decade the world's most advanced film-makers have been composing for the lens rather than for the frame. It is wholly typical of this phenomenon that the most talented *auteur* to emerge from Eastern Europe in the past ten years, the Hungarian Miklós Jancsó (b. 1921—*The Round-Up* [*Szegénylegények*, 1965]; *The Red and the White* [*Csillagosok, katonák*, 1967]; *Red Psalm* [*Még kér a nép*, 1972]), characteristically makes epic films of great visual complexity, some of which are composed of as few as a dozen long takes of ten minutes each (see Chapter 15).*

Unassociated with a distinct aesthetic movement or technological trend, or even with a specifically defined period, are two European film artists whose bodies of work are so unique as to constitute schools unto themselves. Both Ingmar Bergman and Luis Buñuel are practicing directors whose careers span much of film history, and both were true *auteurs* long before that term had currency for the cinema. Bergman and Buñuel have always attempted to exercise a high degree of control over the various components, technical and intellectual, which make up their films. Yet one has worked most of his life within the structure of a state-subsidized film industry where financial failure is virtually impossible, and the other has spent his entire career as an international free-lancer in commercial industries notoriously resistant to ideas. That both have succeeded as artists on their own terms in such dissimilar environments testifies to the nearly limitless aesthetic potential of film.

* See John Belton and Lyle Tector, "The Bionic Eye: The Aesthetics of the Zoom," *Film Comment,* 16, 5 (September–October 1980), 11–17: "Symptomatic of the evolution of film language since the New Wave, spatially distorting and inherently self-conscious, the zoom reflects the disintegration of cinematic codes developed before the Second World War."

INGMAR BERGMAN

Ingmar Bergman (b. 1918), the son of a Lutheran pastor to the Royal Court, was trained in the Swedish theater and opera. Between 1940 and 1944 he worked on scripts for Svensk Filmindustri, the Swedish national film trust, and received his first screenplay credit for Alf Sjöberg's *Torment (Hets,* 1944), a film about a sadistic schoolmaster. Sjöberg (1903–80)—*The Road to Heaven* [*Himlaspelet,* 1942]; *Miss Julie* [*Fröken Julie,* 1951]) was a director very much in the Sjöstrom/Stiller tradition of poetic naturalism (see Chapter 4), and Bergman's earliest films reflect his influence. Between 1945 and 1955 Bergman wrote and directed thirteen somber films which explored the themes of loneliness, alienation, and the sheer difficulty of being alive, the best of which were *Thirst (Törst,* 1949), *Summer Interlude (Sommarlek,* 1951), *Summer with Monika (Sommaren med Monika,* 1952), and *Sawdust and Tinsel/The Naked Night (Gycklarnas afton,* 1953). It was during this apprenticeship that Bergman discovered a long-term collaborator, the cinematographer Gunnar Fischer (b. 1910), and built up his first stock company of distinguished performers: Max von Sydow, Gunnar Björnstrand, Ingrid Thulin, Gunnel Lindblom, Harriet Andersson, Bibi Andersson, and Eva Dahlbeck (Liv Ullmann and Erland Josephson joined him later). He also evolved his characteristic working method of first writing his films as novels and then distilling them into screenplays and, finally, audio-visual images.

It was *Smiles of a Summer Night (Sommarnattens leende,* 1955) that first brought Bergman to worldwide attention, although few critics recognized beneath the surface of this sophisticated farce a Swedish version of Renoir's *La règle du jeu* (1939). In *The Seventh Seal (Det sjunde inseglet,* 1956), a poetic allegory of a medieval knight caught up in a losing chess match with Death, Bergman brilliantly evoked the Middle Ages and posed the first of a series of metaphysical questions about the relationship of man to God which was to occupy him for a decade. *The Seventh Seal* established Bergman as an important artist, but *Wild Strawberries (Smultronstället,* 1957), the film which followed, was clearly his greatest work of the fifties. This beautifully lyrical film is constructed around dreams and memories as they assail the elderly Isak Borg, a distinguished professor of science (superbly played by Bergman's greatest predecessor in Swedish cinema, Victor Sjöström) who is being driven across contemporary Sweden by his daughter-in-law to receive an honorary doctorate at the University of Lund. Borg's journey occasions a descent into the unconscious mind in which he is forced to confront all that he has been and become in the course of his life to his parents, his siblings, his children, and himself. Structurally, Bergman makes his transitions from the present to the past and back again in single shots, so that one constantly has the impression of being in both time frames simultaneously. In its broad grasp of the basic philosophical problems of existence, *Wild Strawberries* is an even more important film than *The Seventh Seal,* and it holds a high place among Bergman's masterworks.

14.51 The Dance of Death at the conclusion of *The Seventh Seal* (Ingmar Bergman, 1956).

14.52 Victor Sjöstrom in Bergman's *Wild Strawberries* (1957).

The Magician/The Face (*Ansiktet,* 1958) told a cryptic tale of a magic lanternist and prestidigitator (Bergman himself?) who dupes a bourgeois family (the audience?) into believing an elaborately contrived nightmare of murder and mayhem which has absolutely no substance. A stylistic tour-de-force, *The Magician* was somehow empty at the core, and in the sixties Bergman strove to chasten his style in an austere trilogy about the difficulty of existing in a Godless universe. Before he began this trilogy, however, Bergman concluded his important work of the fifties with *The Virgin Spring* (*Jungfrukällen,* 1959), a powerful film based on a thirteenth-century ballad. In it, a beautiful young girl on her way to church is brutally raped and murdered in the woods by three herdsmen, who later seek refuge at her father's fortress. He discovers their guilt and butchers them like pigs in a sequence of nearly apocalyptic violence. When the girl's body is discovered later in the woods, the father vows to build a church on the spot, and a spring wells up miraculously from the ground, signifying divine forgiveness. This devastating film concludes on an uncharacteristic note of hope (probably because Bergman was adapting someone else's material), but the films of the trilogy present a universe wholly unredeemed by the presence of God.

Through a Glass Darkly (*Sasom i en spegel,* 1961) is a starkly unappealing film about a schizophrenic woman living on a remote Baltic island with her physician husband, her father, and her teenage brother. When she comes to realize that her father is keeping a clinical journal of her breakdown for the purpose of writing a novel about it, she deteriorates altogether, commits incest with her brother, and is flown off the island by helicopter. In the plotless *Winter Light* (*Nattsvardsgästerna,* 1961), the austerity of Bergman's relentless spiritual probing becomes almost unbearable: a widowed village pastor celebrates Communion regularly but can do nothing to assuage the real spiritual suffering of his communicants because he lacks literally what the Church gives him officially—the ability to make sense of a senseless universe by mediating

14.53 Bergman's *The Virgin Spring* (1959): Max von Sydow.

14.54 *Winter Light* (Ingmar Bergman, 1962): Gunnar Björnstrand, Ingrid Thulin.

14.55 Bergman's *The Silence* (1963): Gunnel Lindblom, Ingrid Thulin.

14.56 Bergman's *Persona* (1966): Liv Ullmann, Harriet Andersson.

between man and God. Much of *Winter Light* is constructed from extreme close-ups of the characters' faces, a technique which Bergman came to use more and more as a means of suggesting psychological torment. With the final film of what might be called his "religious" trilogy, *The Silence* (*Tystnaden,* 1963), Bergman succeeded in creating another masterpiece. In it, two women who are engaged in a sexual relationship, and who are also sisters, come to a Central European city accompanied by one of the women's small son. The language of the city's inhabitants and even the natural sounds on the brilliantly edited soundtrack are incomprehensible both to the travelers and to ourselves, and so—like most of us—they are forced to move through a meaningless world in relative isolation from their peers. Speech finally becomes irrelevant for the three travelers, as images of perverse eroticism and impending disaster come to dominate the film—visually the most striking of the trilogy. For Bergman, as for Antonioni, it seems that modern alienation has reduced human communication to a series of desperate sexual encounters which can only end in chaos.

The Silence was brilliantly photographed by Sven Nykvist (b. 1922), who had been Bergman's cinematographer since *The Virgin Spring.* Working with Bergman from 1959 through the present, Nykvist has become one of the world's leading color cinematographers. Together, since the mid-sixties Bergman and Nykvist have incorporated some of the more boldly experimental techniques of the French and Italian cinema revolutions into their work, and this change in style signaled a new thematic concern with the nature of human psychology, perception, and identity in the director's second great trilogy of the sixties: *Persona* (1966), *Hour of the Wolf* (*Vargtimmen,* 1968), and *Shame* (*Skammen,* 1968).

Framed by sequences which seemingly depict the projection and photographing of the film itself, *Persona* collapses virtually every narrative convention of the cinema to suggest the illusory character of both the medium and the human personalities it seems so realistically to incarnate.

14.57   *Hour of the Wolf* (Ingmar Bergman, 1968).

14.58   *Shame* (Ingmar Bergman, 1968): Max von Sydow, Liv Ullmann.

The film is essentially about a transference of identity between nurse and patient which concludes with their two faces merging, with perfect visual logic, into one. But its narrative style is so elliptical, disjointed, and self-reflexive that *Persona* ultimately suggests that the cinema is no more illusory than the reality which it pretends to record.

Hour of the Wolf is an hallucinatory parable of the agonies of artistic creation, reminiscent of Fellini at his most serious best. An artist and his wife live on a remote island and are one day invited to dinner at the castle of the island's owner, where the artist is humiliated by his host. The wife later discovers her husband's secret diary, which recounts trysts with his former mistress and the strange death of a boy. The artist goes mad and returns to the castle, where he finds his former mistress lying nude on a bier. He is invited to make love to her corpse, but she awakes and kisses him, to the raucous laughter of the ghoulish castle guests, and the artist flees madly into a swamp, where he is pursued by the entire company and finally done to death by a huge bird of prey. This bizarre but visually arresting allegory of a creative artist and his wife fallen into the ever-threatening grip of madness is less successful than *Persona,* but *Shame,* the final film of the second triology, is an utterly unique masterpiece.

Shame is about the hopelessness of maintaining human values and relationships in a state of perpetual war (which, Bergman seems to suggest, is the state of the modern world). In a nameless country, in the midst of a long and bloody civil war on the mainland, two married but childless artists have chosen to live an isolated existence on a relatively secure island off the coast. Former philharmonic musicians, they attempt to remain detached from the war which rages everywhere about them but are drawn irrevocably into it when their island is invaded and they are accused of collaborating with the enemy, by both sides. The woman is strong and capable, but the husband proves himself to be a coward and, finally, a murderous turncoat. War devastates the beautiful island, turning it into a landscape of hell, and the couple—hating each other—escape together in a boat of refugees which drifts aimlessly in a sea of death. As the film concludes, the woman dreams hopelessly of having a child after the war, which we know will never end. Relying on close-ups of the faces of his protagonists, Bergman created in *Shame* a terrifying parable about the way war inevitably destroys all things valuable and human.

In *The Passion of Anna* (*En passion*, 1969), his first important color film, Bergman depicted the tense psychic interplay of four persons living on the small Swedish island where he himself resided. Characteristically, it is a drama of guilt, anguish, and finally rage, in which each of the four characters is caught up in his own unique kind of spiritual martyrdom. *The Passion of Anna* is unique in that it employs the Brechtian (and Godardian) distancing device of stopping the drama at moments of highest tension and having each of the four principals step briefly out of his role to discuss the character he is playing with the audience. The film is also brilliantly photographed by Nykvist and makes expressive use of color, sound, and the telephoto lens.

The Touch (*Beroringen,* 1970) probed the disintegration of a middle-class marriage through the story of a model Swedish housewife who leaves her comfortable but conventional surroundings for a life with an unstable American archaeologist. The focal-point of the film was the neurotic pathology of the conventionally "normal" housewife as it opposed the relative emotional health of the "abnormal" archaeologist, and to emphasize this conflict Bergman deliberately clogged his dialogue with the platitudes and clichés which make normal social intercourse as meaningless as the foreign speech of *The Silence. The Touch,* Bergman's first English-language film, was not generally regarded as a success due to the miscasting of Elliott Gould in the part of the archaeologist, but his next endeavor, *Cries and Whispers* (*Viskingar och rop,* 1972), was hailed as a masterpiece.

This highly stylized film about the nature of death and dying is a work of excruciating beauty in which reality, memory, and fantasy become one. Superbly photographed by Nykvist in rich autumnal hues, *Cries and Whispers* concerns the inter-relationship of four women who are brought together by death in a gorgeously-appointed manor house at the turn of the century. One is a spinster, dying slowly and painfully of cancer; two others are her wealthy married sisters, who have returned to their former home to attend her death; the fourth is the peasant servant, Anna, the only true "sister" of the dying woman because she can minister to her failing spirit with a warm, fleshly love. Eerie, enigmatic, and intense beyond measure, *Cries and Whispers* is constructed like a Strindberg dream-play, but it is also quintessential Bergman, a brilliant distillation of all his greatest stylistic and thematic obsessions.

Bergman's next film, *Scenes from a Marriage* (*Scener ur ett aktenskap,* 1974), was originally made in six fifty-minute installments for Swedish television but was cut to two hours and forty-eight minutes for theatrical release. (The six installments were shown uncut on American public television in 1977.) The theatrical version retains Bergman's original episodic structure: six scenes from a middle-class marriage spanning a decade. During this period, the relationship slowly disintegrates and ends in

14.59 Bergman's *Cries and Whispers* (1972): Ingrid Thulin, Harriet Andersson, Liv Ullmann, Lena Nyman.

divorce, but the two individuals become progressively stronger in separation, and by the end of the film both are married to other people. As usual, Bergman relies heavily on the close-up to convey anguish, but his characteristic psychological realism is pursued with uncharacteristic verisimilitude in this film, minus fantasy, memory, and metaphor. Open-ended, slow-paced, and involving multiple dramatic climaxes, *Scenes from a Marriage* is actually structured like a soap opera but possesses a depth of feeling and intelligence usually alien to the form.

The Magic Flute (1975) is the triumphal realization of Bergman's life-long ambition to adapt the Mozart opera about the transcendent power of love and art. Light-hearted and exuberant, the film shows a playful, sprightly side of Bergman rarely seen in the decade of the trilogies, *The Passion of Anna,* and *Cries and Whispers.* Bergman mounted the film like an eighteenth-century stage production, and his obsession with the machinery of stage illusion in *The Magic Flute* links it implicitly with both *Persona* and *The Magician.* *

14.60 Bergman's *Scenes from a Marriage* (1974): Erland Josephson, Liv Ullmann.

Face to Face (*Ansikte mot ansikte,* 1976) and *The Serpent's Egg* (1977) were not critically successful, but with *Autumn Sonata* (*Herbstsonate,* 1978), an intense study of the relationship between a concert pianist and her middle-aged daughter filmed on location in Norway, and *From the Life of the Marionettes* (1980), a searing account of psychosexual breakdown made in Germany, Bergman returned successfully to the tangled human relationships which he has illuminated so well in the past.

Bergman is an artist of vast and unusual talent, and he is clearly among the most important film-makers in the history of Western cinema. His vision of the human condition is as gloomy as that of his great predecessors in Swedish cinema, Mauritz Stiller and Victor Sjöström—and of the two Scandinavian giants of late-nineteenth-century drama, Ibsen and Strindberg—but that vision is not wholly unredeemed. Despite his cosmic nihilism, Bergman is essentially a religious artist whose films concern the fundamental questions of human existence: the meaning of suffering and pain, the inexplicability of death, the solitary nature of being, and the difficulty of locating meaning in a seemingly random and capricious universe. With the possible exception of *Persona,* Bergman has never been a great innovator in narrative form like Welles, Antonioni, or Godard, but he has been quick to assimilate the important innovations of others. His experiments have been intellectual and metaphysical rather than formal, for he has risked alienating his audiences time and again to ask difficult questions and to pursue inherently disturbing themes. Bergman has been able to follow his dark vision of experience with such integrity and independence largely due to the economic structure of Svensk Filmindustri,

* In 1976 Bergman emigrated from Sweden to France because of harassment by the Swedish government, which claimed that he owed hundreds of thousands of dollars in income taxes and even had him arrested and incarcerated briefly. Bergman and his supporters maintain that he has been driven out of the country because of the criticism of Swedish society implicit in films like *The Touch* and *Scenes from a Marriage.* Ironically, Swedish film critics have for decades attacked Bergman for his supposed detachment from contemporary Swedish life.

through which he has produced all but three of his thirty-eight features.*
This organization guarantees to underwrite the production and distribution costs of any approved project which does not return a domestic
profit, so it is fair to say that Bergman has rarely had to work under the
extreme economic pressures which afflict most other film-makers. But
Bergman would surely have pursued his vision under any circumstances,
no matter how difficult, because as he has declared many times, "To
make films is for me a natural necessity, a need similar to hunger and
thirst."[7] Bergman has also helped to maintain his independence by producing his films with a remarkable economy of means: he uses small casts
and crews, and he shoots in natural locations whenever possible. Gunnar
Fischer and Sven Nykvist, for instance, have between them photographed
virtually all of his films, and Bergman often writes his scripts with specific
actors from his stock company in mind. In a very important sense, Bergman views film-making as an essentially collective art form. He has often
compared it to the process of building a medieval cathedral, in which
each individual artisan dedicated the maximum skill of his craft

---

*The Swedish film industry is small, state-subsidized, and oriented largely toward the
domestic market. Bergman is its sole international giant, but other Swedish directors who
have recently achieved reputations outside of their native land are Bo Widerberg (b.
1930—Raven's End [Kvarteret korpen, 1963]; Elvira Madigan [1967]; Adalen 31 [1969];
The Ballad of Joe Hill [Joe Hill, 1970]; Fimpen [Stubby, 1974]; Victoria [1979]); the
former actress Mai Zetterling (b. 1925—Loving Couples [Alskande par, 1966]; Night
Games [Nattlek, 1967]; Dr. Glas [Doktor Glas, 1968]; The Girls [Flickorna, 1968]); Vilgot
Sjöman (b. 1924—My Sister, My Love [Syskonbädd, 1966]; I Am Curious—Yellow [Jag är
nyfiken—gul, 1967]; I Am Curious—Blue [Jag är nyfiken—blå, 1968]; Linus [1979]); Jan
Troell (b. 1931—The Emigrants [Utvandrarna, 1972]; The New Land [Nybyggarna, 1973];
Zandy's Bride [1974]; The Hurricane [1979]); the former Bergman actress Gunnel
Lindblom (b. 1931—Summer Paradise [1978]); Christer Dahl (The Score [Lyftet, 1978]);
and Jonas Cornell (b. 1938—Bluff Stop [1978]). The Finnish writer/director Jörn Donner
(b. 1933) played an important role in Swedish cinema during the sixties: as film critic for
the Stockholm paper Dagen nyheter he ran a series of scathing attacks on Bergman; then he
married one of Bergman's talented actresses, Harriet Andersson, and cast her in four features which he directed for Svensk Filmindustri (A Sunday in September [En sondag i
september, 1963]; To Love [Att älska, 1964]; Adventure Starts Here [Här börjar äventyret,
1965]; and Roof-Tree [Tvarbalk, 1967]). In 1967, Donner returned to Finland, where he
directed several striking features (Black on White [Mustaa valkoisella, 1967]; 69 [1969];
Fuck Off! Images from Finland [Perkele! Kuvia suomesta, 1971]) in the manner of Godard
and inspired a brief New Wave in the state-subsidized Finnish cinema, in the work of such
young film-makers as Risto Jarva (1934–77—Worker's Diary [Työmiehen päiväkirja,
1967]; Rally [Bensaa suonissa, 1970]; The Year of the Hare [Jäniksen vuosi, 1977]); Rauni
Mollberg (b. 1929—Earth Is a Sinful Song [Maa on syntinen laulu, 1973]; Pretty Good for
a Human Being [Aika hyvä ihmiseksi, 1978]); Erkko Kivikoski (b. 1936—Gunshot in the
Factory [Laukaus tehtaala, 1973]); Jaakko Pakkasvirta (b. 1934—Home for Christmas
[Jouluksi kotiin, 1975]; The Elegance of Life [Elämän koreus, 1979]; Poet and Muse
[Runoilija ja muusa, 1979]); and Eija-Elina Bergholm (Poor Maria [Marja pieni!, 1972]).
Donner returned to Stockholm in 1972 and served as director of the Archive at the Swedish
Film Institute until 1975. He has since completed a feature-length documentary on Berg-
man (The Bergman File [1976]) and has become a producer for several young Swedish and
Finnish film-makers. In 1978 Donner was named president of the Swedish Film Institute;
his most recent film as a director is the satiric Swedish-Finnish co-production Men Can't Be
Raped (Män kan inte våldtas/Meistä ei voi raiskata, 1979). See Stig Björkman, Film in
Sweden: The New Directors (London, 1976); Jim Hillier, Cinema in Finland: An
Introduction (London, 1975); and Peter Cowie, Finnish Cinema (London, 1976).

anonymously to the greater glory of God; as he has written, "Regardless of whether I believe or not, whether I am Christian or not, I would play my part in the collective building of the cathedral."[8] Ingmar Bergman is an artist of great moral integrity and spiritual courage whose long and productive career continues to affirm the necessity of being human in the face of death, disorder, and despair. He regards our darkness in an even darker universe and redeems them both through art.

LUIS BUÑUEL

After making the bitter and sardonic documentary *Las Hurdes* (1932; see Chapter 9)—which was banned by the Spanish Republican government of 1933–35 as "defamatory" but later released by the Popular Front government during the Civil War—Buñuel did not direct another film for fifteen years. He worked sporadically as a producer in Paris, Hollywood, and Madrid, before emigrating to America in 1938 to escape Fascism. Here he edited war documentaries for the Museum of Modern Art in New York and supervised the Spanish-language versions of films for Warner Brothers and MGM. In 1947 he was given a chance to direct two popular comedies for the Mexican producer Oscar Dancigers, *Gran casino* (*Grand Casino,* 1947) and *El gran calavera* (*The Great Madcap,* 1949), and on the strength of their commercial success he was permitted to make *Los olvidados* (*The Forgotten Ones*/*The Young and the Damned,* 1950), the film which restored his reputation as an important international artist.

Ostensibly a neo-realist portrayal of juvenile delinquency in modern Mexico City, *Los olvidados* is actually a disturbing catalogue of man's darkest and most destructive impulses, as subversive in its way as Buñuel's earlier surrealist films. The corrupted slum youth of the city are condemned to live in a nightmarish world of violence, brutality, and degradation, not only through the poverty imposed on them by bourgeois capitalism (whose image is ever-present in the rising skyscrapers which dominate the film's background) but through the wretchedness of reality itself. Images of horror abound, all recorded with documentary-like objectivity: a limbless cripple is tipped off his cart and sent sprawling on his back like a turtle, a blind man is tormented and robbed by a gang of young thugs, a boy is bludgeoned to death with a rock by his companion, an old degenerate fondles the bare legs of a little girl, and finally the film's pathetic young protagonist is slashed to death and his body dumped on a garbage heap. Austerely photographed by the Mexican cinematographer Gabriel Figueroa (b. 1907), who was to work on all of Buñuel's Mexican masterpieces, *Los olvidados* achieves an almost hallucinatory quality through the relentless exposition of an external reality which is literally hell on earth. The extraordinary quality of this film was recognized when it won Buñuel the Cannes Director's Prize in 1951, and he continued to work within the Mexican commercial cinema for the next five years, producing a series of unique and expertly crafted films on low budgets and short production schedules.

14.61 *Los olvidados* (Luis Buñuel, 1950): Roberto Cobo (center).

14.62 *Cumbres borrascosas* (Luis Buñuel, 1952).

14.63 Buñuel's *Subida al cielo* (1951): Lilia Prado.

14.64 *Él* (Luis Buñuel, 1952): Arturo de Cordova, Delia Garces.

Some of these were neo-realistic melodramas of sexual passion, like *Susana* (1951) and *El bruto* (*The Brute,* 1952); others were whimsical and sometimes fantastic comedies, like *Subida al cielo* (English title: *Mexican Bus Ride,* 1952) and *La ilusión viaja en tranvía* (*Illusion Travels by Streetcar,* 1954). Buñuel also made remarkable versions of two important English novels—an English-language *Robinson Crusoe* (1952), which turns Defoe on his ear to suggest the total uselessness of bourgeois civilization, and a Spanish-language *Wuthering Heights* (*Cumbres borrascosas/Abismos de pasión,* 1952), which ends with the Heathcliff character ripping open his beloved's recently interred coffin and attempting to make love to her corpse. Buñuel's most characteristic and personal films of this period, however, were *Él* (English titles: *This Strange Passion/Torment,* 1952) and *Ensayo de un crimen* (*Rehearsal for a Crime/The Criminal Life of Archibaldo de la Cruz,* 1955).

Él is a tale of pathological erotic obsession in which fantasy and reality, photographed from equally objective points of view, are constantly threatening to merge. A wealthy, repressed, middle-aged landowner who is a pillar of society and a secret foot fetishist (a Buñuel trademark) woos and wins a beautiful girl. After the marriage, he turns his oppressive rococo villa into a hothouse of sexual neurosis, as his own impotence drives him to become insanely jealous of his perfectly innocent bride. The young woman begins to fear for her life, and one night she awakes to find her husband stealthily preparing to suture her vagina. She runs away and he goes totally mad, ultimately attempting to strangle his priest. But the Church takes him to her bosom and imprisons him in a monastery, where he becomes a monk. Years later, his former wife visits him and discovers that despite his exterior calm he is as lunatic as before. *Él* is among Buñuel's most savage attacks on the Catholic Church and the repressive mechanisms of bourgeois culture. It was booed from the screen at Cannes but terrifically popular in Mexico, where audiences accepted it as a sympathetic study of a man driven crazy by jealousy.

Ensayo de un crimen is another film about a man in the grip of an overpowering erotic obsession. It is a black comedy—as, in some sense, are all of Buñuel's best films—but it is considerably lighter than *Él*. As a young boy, the film's hero has been told that his music box has the magical power to kill anyone he desires. The boy experiments on his governess, who is immediately shot dead by a stray bullet from a street riot, and he carries an erotic fascination with murder into adulthood. He attempts to become a sadistic murderer of young women but bungles every attempt, finally loses his obsession, and goes on to lead a normal life.

After 1955 Buñuel went to Paris, where he directed three international co-productions which are openly political in theme. As Raymond Durgnat observes, *Cela s'appelle l'aurore* (*It Is Called the Dawn*, Italy/France, 1955), *La mort en ce jardin* (English title: *Evil Eden*, France/Mexico, 1956), and *La fièvre mont à El Pao/Los ambiciosos* (English title: *Republic of Sin*, France/Mexico, 1959) together form a triptych which explores the morality of armed revolt against Fascist dictatorships.[9]

Buñuel returned to Mexico in 1958 to direct *Nazarín*, the masterpiece which marked the beginning of his greatest period. Based on a nineteenth-century Mexican novel set during the dictatorship of Porfirio Díaz, this film concerns the spiritual pilgrimage of a saint-like priest who makes the error of sincerely attempting to follow Christian doctrine and imitate the life of Christ. Cast out and reviled by his church, Father Nazarín journeys into the wilderness, followed by a band of female protégées whose attraction for him, it turns out, is less spiritual than fleshly. Like the Biblical story of Jesus, the film has an episodic structure, and, as Nazarín moves from one parabolic incident to the next, he becomes increasingly disillusioned with his mission. He is finally hunted down by police for his part in fomenting a workers' rebellion and is tossed into jail. The film ends with Nazarín chained to a wall between two thieves; but he is seemingly brought new hope when a peasant woman offers him a pomegranate. *Nazarín* was mistaken by many Catholic critics as signaling Buñuel's return to the fold, and in a fine irony the film was nearly awarded the Prize of the International Catholic Cinema Office. But the point of this intentionally ambiguous film is that Nazarín, who undertakes his quest with sincerity, humility, and great moral courage, manages to achieve absolutely nothing in the course of it but his own destruction. As Buñuel has said in another context, "One can be *relatively* Christian, but the absolutely pure being, the innocent, is condemned to defeat."

14.65 Buñuel's *Nazarín* (1958): Rita Macedo, Francisco Rabal.

This attitude was given its most brilliant exposition in *Viridiana* (1961), an anti-Catholic, anti-Fascist parable which Buñuel shot in Catholic Spain under the very noses of Fascist censors, who approved the script.* Like *Nazarín*, *Viridiana* concerns a devout and saintly person whose attempts to lead a truly Christian life end in disaster for herself

---

* Between *Nazarín* and *Viridiana*, Buñuel made his second English-language film, *The Young One* (Mexico, 1960), a relatively light work (for Buñuel) about an American black man, unjustly accused of rape, who flees to an offshore island to escape a lynch mob and becomes dangerously entangled there with a fourteen-year-old white girl and the man who loves her.

and everyone around her. Viridiana (the name derives from that of a little-known medieval saint), a beautiful young woman about to enter a convent, is advised by her mother superior to visit the country estate of an elderly uncle whom she barely knows. The uncle is overwhelmed by Viridiana's resemblance to his wife, who died years ago on their wedding night, and he falls madly in love with her. She gently rebuffs him, and finally (in a sequence highly reminiscent of *Él*), he has her drugged and laid out like a corpse in his wife's wedding gown. He nearly rapes her, and the next day, as Viridiana is about to flee for the convent, she learns that her uncle has hanged himself with a jump rope. Feeling herself responsible for the old man's death, she stays on to help run the estate with her uncle's illegitimate son, Jorge; and in a Nazarín-like act of contrition she invites a group of diseased beggars from a nearby town to come live in some deserted cottages on her uncle's property. A famous montage sequence contrasts her futile efforts to save these villainous wretches through prayer with Jorge's strenuous practical endeavors to restore order to the estate. One day Viridiana and Jorge go to town on business, and the beggars break into the manor house and stage a riotous feast which Buñuel composed in grotesque parody of Leonardo da Vinci's fresco *The Last Supper.* The beggars' banquet ends in a frenzied orgy accompanied by the strains of Handel's *Messiah,* and, when Jorge and Viridiana return, the girl is all but raped by a leper. This obscenity finally breaks her spiritual pride, and the final sequence of the film shows her joining Jorge and his mistress in a three-handed game of cards.

Blasphemous, ironic, and masterfully constructed, *Viridiana* is quintessential Buñuel—and all the more so for its being an outrageous practical joke on the Fascist state which permitted its production. No sooner was the film released than Spanish authorities realized its subversive nature and attempted to destroy all copies. But it was too late: prints had already reached Cannes, where the film was accepted as the official Spanish entry in the Festival and awarded the highest honors,* to the everlasting

---

* The Palme d'Or—the first major prize ever won by the Spanish cinema. With the exception of the work of Buñuel, that cinema has been almost uniformly undistinguished due to the repressive nature of the Franco regime. There was some hope in the early fifties, when the collaboration of Juan Antonio Bardem (b. 1922) and Luis Garcia Berlanga (b. 1921) produced *Bienvenido, Mr. Marshall!* (*Welcome, Mr. Marshall!,* 1952), a satire about the enrichment of a small Spanish village by the Marshall Plan. Both directors have since made interesting satirical films (*Muerte de un ciclista* [*Death of a Motorcyclist,* Bardem, 1955]; *El verdugo* [*The Executioner,* Berlanga, 1963]), but neither could effect the rejuvenation of Spanish national cinema for which they had hoped, although Berlanga has recently returned from self-imposed exile in France to direct *La escopeta nacional* (*The National Shotgun,* 1979), a satire on the final years of the Franco dictatorship. During the sixties, Carlos Saura (b. 1932) established himself with a series of black comedies clearly influenced by Buñuel (*La caza* [*The Hunt,* 1965]; *Peppermint Frappé* [1967]; *El jardín de las delicias* [*The Garden of Delights,* 1970]), and he is today regarded as Spain's leading resident director, although he lacks the artistic vision of his master. Recent Saura films include *La prima Angélica* (*Cousin Angelica,* 1973), *Cría cuervos* (*Raise Ravens,* 1975), *Elisa, vida mia* (*Elisa, My Life,* 1977), *Los ojos vendados* (*Blindfolded Eyes/Blindfolded,* 1978), and *Mama cumple 100 años* (*Mama Turns 100,* 1979). The gradual return of parliamentary democracy to Spain since Franco's death in 1976 may well permit the rise of a new and vital Spanish cinema of the type forecast by Victor Erice's *El espíritu de la colmena* (*The Spirit of*

14.66 The parody of *The Last Supper* in Buñuel's *Viridiana* (1961).

14.67 *L'univers concentrationnaire:* the trapped bourgeoisie of Buñuel's *El ángel exterminador* (1962).

chagrin of the Franco regime. Moreover, there was so little ambiguity about the film's anti-clericalism that it was officially denounced by the Vatican as "an insult to Christianity."

If *Viridiana* truly is Buñuel's ultimate insult to Christianity, then its successor, *El ángel exterminador* (*The Exterminating Angel,* Mexico, 1962), is clearly his ultimate insult to conventional bourgeois morality. In this film, which many critics regard as Buñuel's greatest, a group of wealthy people gather at an elegant villa for a sumptuous dinner party. After the meal they retire to a drawing-room, but when it is time to go home they find themselves mysteriously unable to leave the room—and, just as strangely, no one from outside can get in. The situation, initially humorous, persists for weeks and becomes a nightmare as the drawing-room is transformed into a miniature concentration camp. To eat, the inmates are forced to slaughter stray sheep which roam the villa in the aftermath of an elaborate practical joke. They cannot bathe, and they have no toilet facilities. When an old man dies and two lovers commit suicide, their corpses are stuffed into a closet for possible future use, it is darkly hinted, should the supply of sheep run out. Filthy, foul-smelling, and driven to the brink of madness by their extreme situation, the prisoners finally attempt to reconstruct the circumstances leading up to their imprisonment. Miraculously, the tactic works, and they stumble out of the villa toward an anxiously waiting public like the emaciated survivors of a death camp. The film ends in a cathedral where the survivors have come to give thanks for their salvation. After a solemn *Te Deum,* the entire

the Beehive, 1973) and José Luis Borau's *Furtivos* (*The Poachers,* 1975), and seemingly confirmed by films like Jaime Chavarri's *A un Dios desconocido* (*To an Unknown God,* 1977), Jaime Camino's *La vieja memoria* (*The Old Memory,* 1978) and *Las largas vacaciones del '36* (*The Long Vacation of '36,* 1979), Ricardo Franco's *Los restos del naufragio* (*The Remains of the Shipwreck,* 1978), Manuel Gutiérrez Aragón's *Camada negra* (*Black Brood,* 1978) and *Sonámbulos* (*Sleepwalkers,* 1979), Josep Maria Forn's *Companys, procés a Catalunya* (*Companys, Catalonia on Trial,* 1979), and Pilar Miró's *El crimen de Cuenca* (*The Cuenca Crime,* 1980). See Vicente Molina-Foix, *New Cinema in Spain* (London, 1978); Marsha Kinder, "Carlos Saura: The Political Development of Individual Consciousness," *Film Quarterly,* 32, 3 (Spring 1979), 14–25; and Annette Insdorf, "Spain Also Rises," *Film Comment,* 16, 4 (July–August 1980), 13–17.

14.68 Buñuel's *Le journal d'une femme de chambre* (1964): Jeanne Moreau.

14.69 *Simón del desierto* (Luis Buñuel, 1965): Claudio Brook as Saint Simeon Stylites, tempted by Silvia Pinal in the guise of Christ the Good Shepherd.

congregation finds itself unable to leave the church, and a flock of sheep suddenly enters the building, while anarchic violence erupts in the streets outside. As Raymond Durgnat has suggested, "the exterminating angel" of this film is the bourgeois ethos of conformity and convention which traps the dinner guests and, finally, everyone in the culture in their social roles.[10] In this brilliant surrealist parable Buñuel suggests that bourgeois concepts of self are as systematically delimiting and destructive of human freedom as the Nazi death camps, and that liberation can be achieved only by thinking ourselves back to the beginning of things.

With *Le journal d'une femme de chambre* (*Diary of a Chambermaid*, 1964; also filmed by Renoir [1946]), Buñuel returned to France to make his most political film, and his first in widescreen. He transposed the setting of Octave Mirbeau's decadent novel of erotic obsession among the French upper classes from the turn of the century to 1928, a time when French Fascism was gathering the force which would ultimately permit the collapse of the Third Republic and the Nazi Occupation. A Parisian chambermaid (Jeanne Moreau) quits her post to take a job in the manor house of a large provincial estate which proves to be a hotbed of political reaction and sexual pathology. Her elderly employer is a boot fetishist whose frigid married daughter is similarly obsessed with internal hygiene. The estate's gamekeeper, Joseph, a surly Right-winger committed to the "moral rebirth of France," is a psychopathic sadist who likes to torture the farm animals and who rapes and murders a little girl with whom the maid has become friends. The maid suspects Joseph immediately and has an affair with him in order to gather enough evidence to avenge her little friend. She does so, and finally denounces him to the police, for which she is fired. Joseph is not prosecuted, and the film ends years later in Marseille, with the former gamekeeper, now a prosperous cafe-owner, shouting slogans in support of a large Fascist rally. Buñuel cuts to a bolt of lightning rending the sky, an unequivocal reminder that brutality will continue to triumph over decency and innocence in the coming storm of war. Buñuel's equation of Fascism, decadence, and sexual perversion in *Le journal* is perfectly made, and it brings the film close in spirit to Bertolucci's *Il conformista* (1970).

Buñuel's next film, *Simón del desierto* (*Simon of the Desert,* Mexico, 1965) is a forty-two-minute feature based on the temptations of St. Simeon Stylites, the fifth-century anchorite who spent his life perched atop a sixty-foot column in the desert, preaching and performing miracles for devout Christians who came to supplicate him. Written by the director himself and shot in Mexico in twenty-five days, the film is a jovial catalogue of Buñuelian obsessions and motifs: crowds of spectators rate Simon's miracles ("not bad"); local merchants attempt to corrupt him, while local priests try to do him in; Simon lavishes equal care on restoring the chopped-off hands of a convicted thief (who immediately uses them to beat his child) and on blessing a piece of food picked from between his teeth; the Devil appears to him as a little girl in a sailor suit and as a sexy young woman unconvincingly disguised as Christ. Finally, the Devil whisks him off to New York City on a jet-propelled coffin and leaves him sipping Coke in a discothèque crowded with teenagers doing a fashionable new dance ("the latest and the last," the Devil tells him) dubbed the "Radioactive Flesh." Subtly photographed in atonal black and white by Gabriel Figueroa and playfully pessimistic in mood, *Simón del desierto* won a special Jury Prize at Venice in 1965.

In 1967, at the age of sixty-seven, Buñuel returned to France to make *Belle de jour,* the film which he claimed would be his last (although he has directed four unequivocal masterpieces since). His first film in color, *Belle de jour* is another Buñuelian classic of erotic obsession: Séverine, the beautiful wife of a successful surgeon who is also a kind husband, has a secret compulsion for sexual degradation. She attempts to realize her masochistic fantasies by working afternoons in Madame Anaïs' brothel, where she is christened "Belle de jour" (a play on *belle de nuit,* a French euphemism for "prostitute"). Here she caters to a whole range of perversions from simple fetishism to necrophilia, and her fantasy life grows apace. For Buñuel, the old surrealist, the brothel is a place of absolute freedom precisely because it *is* a region where fantasy interpenetrates the real. As the film progresses, it becomes increasingly difficult to distinguish Séverine's fantasies from the linear narrative, which now involves a sadistic young gangster who has fallen in love with Belle at the brothel. The gangster attempts to murder her husband and paralyzes him, we are told, for life. In an act of atonement, Séverine quits the brothel and becomes her husband's devoted nurse, until a jealous family friend tells him of her past existence as Belle de jour. At this, he first seems to die of shock and then rises from his wheelchair, miraculously cured. An empty black carriage with jingling bells which has been associated with Séverine's fantasy world throughout the film passes by in the park beneath the window of their fashionable apartment, and we are left to wonder whether the whole film has not been a dream or an extended fantasy in the mind of its heroine. *Belle de jour* is a hypnotically engaging film, as beautiful in its artistic intelligence as in its visually exquisite surface, and it was justly awarded the Golden Lion at the Venice Festival in 1967.

14.70 Buñuel's *Belle de jour* (1967): Catherine Deneuve.

As if to contradict himself with all due haste, Buñuel turned to his next project immediately after the release of *Belle de jour. La voie lactée (The Milky Way,* France, 1969) is a symbolic history of the Roman Catholic Church with all its heresies and schisms, told in the form of an episodic narrative about two tramps journeying from Paris to the shrine of the Apostle James at Santiago de Compostela ("St. James of the Field of Stars") in Spain. The road they follow is popularly known in Europe as "The Milky Way," but for Buñuel the term also signifies the supposedly celestial path of Christianity through the ages. Thus, in the course of their journey the tramps encounter figures from the past who either dramatize Church history (for instance, an eighteenth-century Jansenist fencing with a Jesuit) or incarnate it (Christ, the Virgin Mary, the Devil). The film is less savage than impudently funny, although we are treated to the usual assortment of Buñuelian horrors: leprous blind beggars, the Marquis de Sade flogging a victim, a crucified nun, etc. Beautifully photographed in color by the veteran French cinematographer Christian Matras, *La voie lactée* was not well received by some critics, who thought its exposition (and deflation) of Catholic theological doctrine too arcane.

About *Tristana* (1970), however, there were no doubts at all. This French/Italian co-production is set in the ancient Spanish city of Toledo in the twenties and concerns a decadent aristocrat, Don Lope, who systematically corrupts and enslaves his innocent young ward, Tristana (from *triste*, "sad"). Tristana, for her part, attempts to resist by running away from her guardian with an artist who wishes to marry her. But she returns two years later with a crippling illness which has made it necessary for a leg to be amputated, confining her permanently to a wheelchair. Totally dependent now upon Don Lope, Tristana begins to internalize his perversity, taking as her own victims the half-witted deaf-mute who pushes her wheelchair, and finally Don Lope himself: the old man dies of a heart attack while she callously refuses to call a doctor. Subtly photographed by José Aguayo in autumnal hues, this film is as much about the decay of Spain as about the inter-relationship of its characters. Tristana is the victim not simply of Don Lope but of the corrupt and impotent moral code which he embodies and which was to be institutionalized by Franco (although Don Lope is himself a sort of liberal) after the Civil War.

Buñuel's next film, *Le charme discret de la bourgeoisie* (*The Discreet Charm of the Bourgeoisie*, France, 1973), is a legitimate successor to both *L'âge d'or* (1930) and *El ángel exterminador* (1962) but exchanges their savage bite for gently mocking irony. It is a buoyant satire about the foibles and follies of the privileged class, structured as an extended dream in the mind of Don Rafael, the ambassador to France from the Latin American country of Miranda, a military dictatorship which has the highest homicide rate in the world. Don Rafael's dream, which includes the dreams of others and dreams within dreams, concerns the constantly frustrated efforts of six friends to dine together in a civilized manner. Every time the attempt is made, the dinner is interrupted by some twist of dream logic or by another dream, which will in turn be interrupted by a dream or another attempted dinner party as soon as the situation has become engaging. The film, in fact, is one long pattern of interrupted episodes, and in this sense Buñuel has created a delightful parody of the mechanisms of narrative cinema. As soon as he draws us into a story, he cuts away to another, and the charming, civilized, self-indulgent bourgeoisie never do get to eat their dinner. A couple is overcome by sexual passion and have coitus on the table; a member of the party vomits just as the meal begins; the diners suddenly discover themselves upon a stage before a live audience and forget their lines; the whole group is arrested for being accomplices in a heroin-smuggling ring (an in-joke, since Fernando Rey, who plays Don Rafael, had played the heroin kingpin in William Friedkin's *The French Connection* a year before). Other dreams are darker and concern loss of identity and death, but the good bourgeoisie manage to meet most situations with composure and a kind of bemused tolerance toward the shallowness of their own existence. Buñuel himself seems uncharacteristically mellow toward the confusion of values embodied in his characters, as if a kind of serene compassion for a long-hated enemy had set in. *Le charme discret de la bourgeoisie* is a good-

14.71 *Tristana* (Luis Buñuel, 1970): Fernando Rey, Lola Gaos, Catherine Deneuve.

14.72 Roused from a poker game in Buñuel's *Le fantôme de la liberté* (1974), two priests, two monks, and a nurse witness an act of sexual perversion: Paul Le Person, Milena Vukotic, Gilbert Montagne, Bernard Musson, Marcel Pérès.

humored and frequently hilarious film whose technical virtuosity demonstrates Buñuel's mastery of his medium. As in so many of his other films, notably *Belle de jour* and *Tristana,* Buñuel uses no musical score, which contributes to the eerie surreality of the piece.

Le fantôme de la liberté (*The Phantom of Liberty*, France, 1974) continues the experiments begun in *Le charme discret* and may well be Buñuel's most stylistically revolutionary work since *Un chien andalou* and *L'âge d'or.* In it, the director combines virtually every known storytelling device—narrative painting, the Gothic mode, the epistolatory mode, omniscient narration, the flashback, the exemplary tale, the dream sequence, and a dense pattern of allusions to his other films—to create an episodic narrative which is simultaneously circular and self-reflexive. As Marsha Kinder has noted, *Le fantôme de la liberté* is about the impossibility of escaping convention in society, politics, and art—and, ultimately, in the process of its own narrative, however radical that narrative may appear.[11] There is no recurrent motif to bind together the separate episodes such as the dinner party in *Le charme discret,* only the dream-logic of continuous interruption and circularity. By interweaving episodes from the past and present which constantly disappoint our narrative expectations, Buñuel has produced an authentically surrealist essay on the political violence, necrophilia, and sadism that underlie bourgeois cultural conventions and make an elusive phantom of personal freedom.

For his most recent film, Buñuel chose to adapt Pierre Louÿs' short novel *La femme et le pantin* (1896), which was also the source of von Sternberg's *The Devil Is a Woman* (1935) and Duvivier's *A Woman Like Satan* (1958). *Cet obscur objet du désir* (*That Obscure Object of Desire,* 1977) is an urbane and coolly ironic film about a young Spanish girl who teases and ultimately fleeces a middle-aged French widower. Buñuel compounds the irony by having two actresses with distinctly different physical appearances play the single "object" of the title, as if to suggest the polymorphous nature of desire itself.

From *Un chien andalou* to *Cet obscur objet du désir,* Buñuel, now in his eighties, has proven himself to be the most experimental and anarchistic film-maker in the history of the cinema. He is fundamentally a brilliant satirist, comparable to Swift and Goya, who uses sexual pathology as a metaphor for the distorting nature of bourgeois Christian culture. Necrophilia, sadomasochism, fetishism, cannibalism, and bestiality are for Buñuel at once both cause and effect of the mass psychosis which we call "Western civilization." Like all great satirists, Buñuel is simultaneously a moralist, a humorist, and a savage social critic, who hopes that by exposing the nauseating inhumanity of human beings he will somehow make us more human. Until very recently, Buñuel has always employed a restrained and uncomplicated visual style, which has led some critics to charge him with cinematic "indifference." We should remember, however, that for most of his career Buñuel has been forced to make films for other people on other people's terms, or not make films at all. This has often meant shooting on low budgets with production schedules as short as three or four weeks. It has also meant that Buñuel could not make his first film in widescreen until 1964 nor his first film in color until 1967, and it would be fair to argue that, while an artist in Bergman's position can afford style, one in Buñuel's cannot.

But this would be to disregard the crucial fact that Buñuel's "indifference" to style is actually a style in itself. John Russell Taylor has written: "[S]tyle is for him the best and most economical way of saying a thing. . . .[T]he highest tribute one can pay to Buñuel's direction is to say that one is hardly ever conscious of it."[12] This is as it should be for an artist who deals so consistently in the blasphemous, sardonic, and perverse. The invisibility of Buñuel's style is in fact the deliberate artistic strategy of a master ironist: what we see is so clearly what we get in Buñuel that we trust him not to dupe us, which enables him to dupe us every time. But he always dupes us for our own good, by forcing us to acknowledge what we really are instead of what we would like to be, and the jokes he makes at our expense are most often hilariously funny. Buñuel's ironic vision of human experience is perhaps best summed up in a statement he made once when asked if he had ever been a religious person. "I have always been an atheist," he responded, "thank God. . . ."

European Renaissance: East

With the exception of the Soviet Union, all of the countries of Eastern Europe either were occupied by the Nazis or collaborated with them during World War II, and those which had strong national film industries, such as Czechoslovakia and Hungary, saw them subverted for the purpose of propaganda. When the war ended, these countries were "liberated" by the Soviet army and found themselves once again occupied by a foreign totalitarian power. Gradually, but with much brutality, the Soviet government placed its own puppets at the heads of the Eastern European states, Stalinized the national governments, and forced the entire area into the Soviet bloc—a move formalized by the Warsaw Pact of 1955. Among the first acts of the new regimes was to nationalize the Eastern European film industries in order to use them, as the Nazis had, for the production of political propaganda. In Czechoslovakia and Poland, nationalization took place in conjunction with the establishment of state-supported film schools, repeating the pattern of the Soviet Union just after the Revolution. The Czech film school, the Film (later, Film and Television) Faculty of the Academy of Dramatic Arts, or FAMU, was founded in Prague in 1947; the Polish version, the Leon Schiller State Film School, was established at Lódź in 1948. Ultimately, all of the major Eastern European nations would have their state-operated film schools—Hungary its Academy for Cinematographic Art in Budapest (1948), Yugoslavia its Film Institutes in Belgrade and Zagreb (1970), and Romania its Institute of Theater and Film Art (IATC, 1950) in Bucharest. The thoroughness of the post-war nationalization meant that there would always be a close relationship between film and politics in Eastern Europe. Generally speaking, in times of oppression the Eastern European cinemas have been used for the purpose of political indoctrination; during periods of liberalization (Poland, 1954–63; Czechoslovakia, 1963–68; Hungary, 1963 to the present), the cinema has become a vehicle for social criticism and ideological debate. For this reason, the cinema has always been one of the most important arts for the Eastern European intelligentsia, while in the West this has only very recently become true.

During the repressive post-war years 1945–53, few Eastern European countries produced significant films. Most adopted the official Soviet style of "socialist realism" decreed at the Twentieth Party Congress in 1932 (see Chapter 5). The nemesis of the great Soviet directors of the twenties, this style demanded that the everyday life of the socialist worker be glorified at the expense of subjective analysis and formal experiment. When Stalin died in 1953, however, there was a brief period of liberalization, followed by an official policy of de-Stalinization which witnessed a distinct move away from the style of socialist realism in many Eastern European cinemas. The first to change was the cinema of Poland.

POLAND

The "Polish School"

Before World War II, the Polish cinema had been a rather modest affair. Perhaps the most significant pre-war development was the founding in 1929 of the radical avant-garde film society, Society of the Devotees of the Artistic Film, or START, which included the future directors Wanda Jakubowska (b. 1907) and Alexander Ford (b. 1908), whose *Knights of the Teutonic Order* [*Krzyżacy,* 1960] was to become the first great Polish film epic, as well as the film historian Jerzy Toeplitz (b. 1909). During the war, the Nazis forbade domestic production, but the material base of Polish cinema was kept alive by the Polish Army Film Unit under the direction of Aleksander Ford. With the establishment of the socialist state after the war, the provisional government nationalized the film industry under a single centralized authority, Film Polski. The first post-war films were about the horrors that the country had endured during the Nazi Occupation. Of these, the best were Jakubowska's *The Last Stage* (*Ostatni etap,* 1948), a semi-documentary account of her own experiences in Auschwitz, and Ford's *Border Street* (*Ulica Graniczna,* 1948), a fictionalized version of the Warsaw Ghetto uprising of 1943. Ford's neo-realistic *Five Boys from Barska Street* (*Piatka z ulicy Barskiej,* 1952), the first major Polish color film, was also notable. But in general the rigid dogma of socialist realism kept the standards of Polish film at a relatively low level until after the death of Stalin in 1953. In 1954, things began to change. At a meeting of the Polish Association of Cinema and Theater, Jerzy Toeplitz, then director of the Lódź Film School, attacked the tenets of socialist realism and called for a new national cinema. A year later, Film Polski was re-organized as a group of individual, self-sustaining production units known collectively as the United Groups of Film Producers. Simultaneously, the first generation of trained directors emerged from Lódź, and the Communist Party chief, Wladislaw Gomulka, decreed a thorough de-Stalinization of Poland. Thus the way was cleared for the Polish film movement known as the "Polish school," whose influence would be international in scope from 1954 to 1963.

The first major talents to rise from the Lódź Film School were Jerzy Kawalerowicz (b. 1922), Andrzej Munk (1921–61), and Andrzej Wajda (b. 1926). Kawalerowicz was the least characteristic of the group. His first films, *A Night to Remember* (*Celuloza,* 1953) and *Under the*

15.1 *Five Boys from Barska Street* (Aleksander Ford, 1953): Tadeusz Janczar.

15.2 *Under the Phrygian Star* (Jerzy Kawalerowicz, 1954).

Phrygian Star (*Pod gwiazda frygijska,* 1954), comprised a two-part epic about the gradual radicalization of a young peasant between the wars. In *Night Train* (*Pociag,* 1959), he turned what might have been a conventional murder mystery into an impressive parable of intolerance and mob violence. But his two most significant films are visually stylized historical dramas, written by the director/writer Tadeusz Konwicki (b. 1926), which reveal a highly developed sense of compositional form. Based on the famous French case of the "devils of Loudon"—which also provided the raw material for Ken Russell's *The Devils* (1971)—*Mother Joan of the Angels* (*Matka Joanna od Aniolów,* 1961) is a tension-charged film about the demonic possession of a nun in a seventeenth-century Polish convent. *Pharoah* (*Faraon,* 1966) is an expensively produced spectacle set in the Egypt of Ramses XIII, whose underlying theme is the corrupting nature of political power. For a decade after *Pharoah,* Kawalerowicz made only two films, *Game* (*Gra,* 1965) and *Maddalena* (1970), neither of which was a critical success. But he was one of the most serious and influential artists of the Polish school during the height of its power, and his first film since 1970, *Death of the President* (*Śmierć prezydenta,* 1978), displays a newly spontaneous style in probing the 1922 asassination of Poland's first elected president.

15.3 Kawalerowicz's *Mother Joan of the Angels* (1961).

After graduating from Lódź, Andrzej Munk worked for several years in the documentary field and continued to do so often after he directed his first feature, *Man on the Track* (*Czlowiek na torze,* 1955), which many critics believe to be his greatest finished film. Working closely with the scriptwriter Jerzy Stefan Stawiński (b. 1921), a co-founder of the Polish school, Munk completed only two other films before his death in an automobile accident in September 1961—the anti-heroic war film *Eroica* (*Heroism,* 1957), which satirized the Polish national devotion to lost causes, and *Bad Luck* (*Zezowate szczeście,* 1959), an ironic look at opportunism in post-war Polish society. At the time of his death, Munk had nearly finished shooting *The Passenger* (*Pasażerka*), which would surely have been his masterpiece. In it, a former SS guard traveling on an ocean liner is forced to relive her relationship with a young Jewish

15.4 *Eroica* (Andrzej Munk, 1957): Josef Nowak.

15.5 Munk's *The Passenger* (1963).

woman in Auschwitz through a series of flashbacks. In the process, we come to see the death camp from the guard's point of view as well as from the prisoner's, and an extraordinary humanistic comment is made upon the nature of guilt and suffering. The film was released in 1963 in a sixty-two-minute version pieced together by Munk's assistant, Witold Lesiewicz, and it was hailed as a classic, giving Munk posthumous international status. Today, on the strength of four features and a score of documentaries, there can be no question that the cinema has been impoverished by Munk's loss.

15.6 *A Generation* (Andrzej Wajda, 1954): Roman Polański (center).

Though his subject matter (unlike that of Kawalerowicz) was always Poland's present and her recent past, in his ironic and anti-heroic attitude toward it Munk was outside the basically Romantic vision of the Polish school as it finally evolved. Much more characteristic and formative was the work of Andrzej Wajda, the first Eastern European director whose films were widely shown in the West. The son of a Polish Cavalry officer, Wajda studied painting at the Fine Arts Academy in Kraków before attending the Łódź Film School. After graduating, he assisted Aleksander Ford on *Five Boys from Barska Street,* and in 1954 he made his first feature, *A Generation (Pokolenie).* This film was the first in a trilogy about his country's horrific experience of the war which established Wajda as a major European director and brought the Polish cinema to international attention. An essentially Romantic film in neo-realist form, *A Generation* was about a group of teenagers who become radicalized during the Occupation, join a Left-wing resistance movement, and are ultimately tracked down by the Gestapo. Wajda meant it to capture the mood and attitudes of the "lost generation" of young Poles (his own) who had come of age in the crucible of World War II. The second part of the trilogy was the unrelievedly grim *Kanal (Canal,* 1956), adapted by Jerzy Stefan Stawiński from his own novel. The film deals with hundreds of Home Army resistance fighters who find themselves trapped beneath the streets in the city's sewer system during the brutally suppressed Warsaw Uprising of 1944.* Utterly devoid of hope from the outset, they wander through a watery labyrinth of excrement and carrion while the Nazis leisurely pick them off from above with explosives and automatic weapons. Wajda's

15.7 *Canal* (Andrzej Wajda, 1956): Wienczjslaw Glinski.

---

* When Poland was invaded and occupied by the Nazis in September 1938, the Polish cabinet fled to Paris and set up a government-in-exile. (After the Nazi invasion of France in 1940, the Poles moved to London.) They left behind them in Warsaw a large but ill-equipped resistance force dubbed the "Home Army," which was charged with effecting an uprising against the Nazis when the time came. The moment arrived in July 1944, when the Red Army approached Warsaw from the east across the Vistula River and liberation seemed imminent. But the Soviet troops were as hostile to the Poles as were the occupying Nazis, so the Home Army rose up unaided against both factions in late July. It was a hopeless if heroic struggle against superior manpower, airpower, and weaponry. The Poles had only enough ammunition, food, and supplies for five days, but they stretched these out among themselves until the inevitable surrender on October 4, 1944. At the end of the battle, many resistance fighters actually did die while attempting to escape the Nazis through the Warsaw sewer system. After the surrender, Hitler ordered that the city be razed, so that virtually nothing of old Warsaw survives today. Over 200,000 Poles, most of them noncombatants, lost their lives in the uprising; German and Soviet losses were insignificant.

15.8 *Ashes and Diamonds* (Andrzej Wajda, 1958): Zbigniew Cybulski, Adam Pawlikowski.

15.9 Maciek's death in *Ashes and Diamonds*.

despairing vision of heroes doomed to die like sewer rats is the very prototype of the Romantic fatalism which came to characterize the Polish school.

So too is the last and greatest film in Wajda's war trilogy, *Ashes and Diamonds* (*Popiół i diament*, 1958). It depicts a few hours in the life of a young resistance fighter, Maciek, on May 9, 1945, the first day after the war. Maciek has been ordered by the military commander of his nationalist underground unit to go to a provincial city and assassinate the new Communist Party district secretary. He has no real political commitment to his mission, and he begins to vacillate when he discovers his victim to be only a tired and rather kindly old man. But he carries out his orders like a good soldier, is himself shot in reprisal, and dies in agony on a rubbish heap. The film's rich visual symbolism lends it universality of theme and should remind us that Wajda studied painting for four years before he entered the cinema. But *Ashes and Diamonds* also contains an implicit comment on some specific difficulties of a traditional society's adjustment to a revolution, and it offers Wajda's most disillusioned view of the futility of heroism in the modern world. Significantly, the part of Maciek was the first major role of Zbigniew Cybulski (1927–67), the brilliant and versatile young actor who became the icon of the Polish school's Romantic pessimism from 1958 until his accidental death in 1967.

Wajda made two more films set in the war period and one with a contemporary context before turning to historical themes in the sixties. *Lotna* (1959) deals with the suicidal charge of the Polish mounted cavalry against a German Panzer division during the Nazi invasion of September 1938; *Samson* (1960) is the story of a Jew who attempts to escape the Warsaw Ghetto. *Innocent Sorcerers* (*Niewinni czarodzieje*, 1961), written by the future New Wave director Jerzy Skolimowski (see below), moved away from the war-time obsessions of the Polish school to examine the attitudes, problems, and values of the generation which succeeded Wajda's own. It is generally agreed that Wajda's historical films of the sixties constitute a falling-off from his previous level of achievement.

15.10 Wajda's *A Siberian Lady Macbeth* (1962).

15.11 *Everything for Sale* (Andrzej Wajda, 1968): the film within the film. Elzbieta Czyzewska.

15.12 Wajda's *Landscape After Battle* (1970): Daniel Olbrychski.

A *Siberian Lady Macbeth* (*Sibirska Ledi Magbet*, 1962), shot in Yugoslavia with a Yugoslav cast and crew, was an uneven, stylized melodrama set in a nineteenth-century Russian village; *Ashes* (*Popioly*, 1965) was a large-scale epic account of the Polish involvement in the Napoleonic Wars; and *Gates of Paradise* (*Bramy raju*), also shot in Yugoslavia, was an unsuccessful (and, to date, unreleased) study of the moral issues surrounding the thirteenth-century Children's Crusade. The only totally satisfying work Wajda produced during this period was his short contribution to the French anthology film *L'amour à vingt ans* (1962), which starred Zbigniew Cybulski as a former Resistance fighter who rescues a child from the bear pit at the Warsaw zoo.

With *Everything for Sale* (*Wszystko na sprzedaż*, 1968), however, Wajda again hit his stride and made his most personal film. Like Fellini's *8½* (1963) and Truffaut's *Day for Night* (1973), *Everything for Sale* is about a film-maker in the process of making a film and therefore about the relationship between cinematic illusion and reality. The film was inspired by the gruesome death of Cybulski, who was run over by a train he was attempting to board in January 1967. Cybulski was not only Wajda's close personal friend and Poland's most popular star, but—like James Dean in America—he was an important cultural symbol of a whole generation's attitude toward life; his senseless death shocked the nation. *Everything for Sale* memorializes that death and poses some disturbing questions about the morality of art: A film crew has prepared itself to shoot a scene in which an actor is to fall under a train at the Wroclaw station (where Cybulski was killed), but the actor fails to arrive for the take. The crew searches for him and discovers that he has in fact been accidentally killed. The director then makes the decision to finish the film using a stand-in, thereby committing the crew to killing its former friend and colleague on film in the same way that he has been killed in reality. At times the reality of the film *Everything for Sale* and the film within the film overlap and merge, so that it is difficult for the viewer to distinguish them. And this, of course, is played off against the "real" reality outside both films—the reality of Cybulski's horrible death and its impact upon the Polish film community. Ultimately, *Everything for Sale* asks the same question posed by the director Ferrand (Truffaut) in *Day for Night:* "Are films [or art] more important than life?" The painful answer in both cases is: "Yes, for film artists, they must be and they are."

Most of Wajda's films since 1968, except the lightweight sex comedy *Hunting Flies* (*Polowanie na muchy,* 1969), have been characterized by the kind of stylized impressionism announced in *Everything for Sale.* *Landscape after Battle* (*Krajobraz po bitwie,* 1970), *The Birch-Wood* (*Brzezina,* 1970), *Pilatus and Others* (*Pilatus und Andere,* 1972), and *Wedding* (*Wesele,* 1972) are all technically innovative, visually baroque meditations on the great themes of time, art, love, and death, regardless of historical context. But *The Promised Land* (*Ziemia obiecana,* 1976), which offers a vibrant account of the brutal industrialization of Poland by foreigners in the early twentieth century, marked a return to the political themes of the fifties. Both *Man of Marble* (*Czlowiek z marmury,*

1977)* and *Without Anesthetic/Rough Treatment* (*Bez znieczulenia,* 1978) concern political corruption in the Polish news media (and both films were threatened with official censorship but eventually reached the United States intact). Wajda recently completed *The Young Girls of Wilko* (*Panny z Wilka,* 1979; a Polish-French co-production), a poetic film of love and memory set on a country estate between the world wars, and *The Conductor* (*Dyrygent,* 1980), in which an internationally famous conductor (Sir John Gielgud) returns to his native Poland in pursuit of lost love and youth in the person of a former mistress' daughter. He is currently working on a version of André Malraux's novel *L'espoir* (*Man's Hope*). Thus Andrzej Wajda, the internationally prominent visionary artist, remains faithful to his roots long after the excitement created by the Polish school has disappeared. Despite his aesthetic preoccupation with introspection and symbolic form, Wajda is still very much a national film artist who has spent most of his life working within the context of Polish history, culture, and society.

15.13   Wajda's *Wedding* (1972): Daniel Olbrychski.

The Second Generation

The so-called Polish school came to an end in the early sixties when the Gomulka regime began to attack the national cinema for presenting a negative view of everyday Polish life. † At the Thirteenth Party Congress in July 1964, Wajda's *Innocent Sorcerers* (1961) and Roman Polański's *Knife in the Water* (*Nóż w wodzie,* 1962) were singled out for special abuse as examples of this tendency. The Lódź Film School came under fire too, since four-fifths of the country's forty-eight professional directors had been trained there. Thus, the generation of film-makers which succeeded Wajda's made their first features in Poland, but as social and political conditions became increasingly repressive they left one by one to work in the West.

The two most prominent members of this generation are Roman Polański (b. 1933) and Jerzy Skolimowski (b. 1938), both of whom attended the Lódź Film School and were decisively influenced by the French New Wave. Polański began his career as an actor in Wajda's *A Generation* (1954), and his first films were the absurdist shorts *Two Men and a Wardrobe* (*Dwaj ludzie z szafa,* 1958), *The Fat and the Lean* (*Le gros et le maigre,* shot in France, 1961), and *Mammals* (*Ssaki,* 1962), all of which contain dark undertones reminiscent of the plays of Samuel Beckett. Polański's first feature—and the only one of his features shot in Poland—was *Knife in the Water,* an economical, tension-charged account of sexual rivalry between a husband, a wife, and a young stranger

15.14   *Knife in the Water* (Roman Polański, 1962): Jolanta Umecka, Zygmunt Malanowicz.

* Regarded by Wajda, after *Ashes and Diamonds,* as his most important film, *Man of Marble* won the International Critics' Prize at Cannes in 1978.

† Other significant members of the Polish school had been Kazimierz Kutz (b. 1929— *Cross of Valor* [*Krzyż walecznych,* 1959]; *Nobody Is Calling* [*Nikt nie wola,* 1960]; *People on a Train* [*Ludzie z pociagu,* 1961]; *Salt of the Black Earth* [*Sól ziemi czarnej,* 1970]; *Pearl in the Crown* [*Perla w koronie,* 1971]) and Wojciech Has (b. 1925—*The Noose* [*Petla,* 1957]; *Farewells* [*Pożegnania,* 1958]; *How to Be Loved* [*Jak być kochana,* 1963]; *The Saragossa Manuscript* [*Rekopis znaleziony w Saragossie,* 1964]; *Ciphers* [*Szyfry,* 1966]).

15.15 Polański's *Repulsion* (1965): Catherine Deneuve.

15.16 *Chinatown* (Roman Polański, 1974): Jack Nicholson menaced by hoods (Polański at left).

during a weekend sailing trip on the husband's yacht. The stranger and the wife make love aboard the boat while the husband is gone, and an electrifying sense of repressed sexual violence is sustained throughout. *Knife in the Water* achieved widespread recognition as a brilliant feature debut, and Polański subsequently made three films in England. *Repulsion* (1965) is a chillingly precise study of an individual's descent into madness under the pressure of sexual neurosis. In it, a beautiful young working-girl, superbly played by Catherine Deneuve, is driven to murder by a combination of isolation and sexual repression. Polański's masterful evocation of the hallucinated horror of psychosis, through both image and sound, makes *Repulsion* one of the classical studies of mental breakdown in modern cinema, comparable to Alain Jessua's *La vie à l'envers* (*Life Upside Down*, 1964; see Chapter 13) and Ján Kadár's *Adrift* (1971; see below). *Cul-de-sac* (1966) is a strangely engaging film about an eccentric married couple on a desolate Northumberland island whose life is dramatically altered by the arrival of two wounded gangsters from the mainland. A combination of Pinteresque black humor and forties *film noir, Cul-de-sac* is thought by many critics to be Polański's finest film, and it is the director's own favorite. *The Dance of the Vampires/The Fearless Vampire Killers,* (1967), a stylish parody of the horror film genre, is a much lighter affair but impressive nonetheless for its atmospheric evocation of Central Europe.

In 1968 Polański came to the United States to direct the most popular and commercially successful of all his films, *Rosemary's Baby,* based on the novel by Ira Levin. This tale of witchcraft and Satanism was shot on location in New York City for Paramount. The tension between its muted naturalistic style and its horrific material makes the film a classic of the genre of demonic possession. It far outdistances more contemporary manifestations like *The Exorcist* (William Friedkin, 1973) and *The Omen* (Richard Donner, 1976) in creating a sense of real evil beneath its sensationalist surface. Polański returned to England in 1971 to do a personalized, hyper-realistic version of *Macbeth* which was generally well-received but was criticized in some quarters for excessive violence. While he was in Europe he also made the poorly distributed *Che?* (*What?*, 1972), a comic account of an American virgin's encounter with a cornucopia of sexual perversions on her first visit to Italy. Ultimately, Polański returned to America to direct *Chinatown* (1974), an extremely successful essay in *film noir* set in Los Angeles during the thirties. His most conventional film in terms of structure, *Chinatown* nevertheless conveys that sense of evil, menace, and sexual tension which has become the hallmark of Polański's work. In terms of intellectual influence, it is possible to speak of surrealism and the theater of the absurd—of Kafka, Ionesco, Beckett, and Pinter. In terms of cinematic influence, Buñuel and Hitchcock clearly come to mind. But Polański's thematic obsession with cruelty, violence, and the forces which produce them must also reflect the uniquely grim circumstances of his own life. In 1941, when he was eight years old, Polański and his parents were sent to Auschwitz, where his mother died and where he was imprisoned until the end of the war. In

1969, his pregnant wife, the actress Sharon Tate, was brutally murdered and mutilated, along with several friends, by the Charles Manson gang, in one of the most repugnant crimes of the decade. More recently, Polański was himself charged with the rape of a thirteen-year-old girl in Los Angeles County and fled the country to avoid imprisonment. Since that time, he has completed a version of Thomas Hardy's tragic novel *Tess of the d'Urbervilles* (*Tess*, 1979) in England and has announced his intention to return to the United States, regardless of the consequences. The nightmare vision of human experience set forth in Polański's films should hardly surprise us, then: in his own life the director has been intimately acquainted with the nightmarish and the horrific.

Jerzy Skolimowski (b. 1938) began his career as an actor and as co-scriptwriter for Wajda's *Innocent Sorcerers* (1961). He became a student at the Lódź Film School in 1961 and the same year collaborated with Polański on the script of *Knife in the Water*. Between matriculation and graduation in 1964, Skolimowski worked continuously on his first feature, which was released as *Identification Marks: None* (*Rysopis*, 1964). This was a loosely structured account of an expelled student's last ten hours of civilian life before entering the military which freely appropriated the stylistic devices of *cinéma-vérité* and the French New Wave. Like other Skolimowski protagonists (usually played by Skolimowski himself), the student is an outsider whose alienated vision of his society is implicitly critical. In *Walkover* (*Walkower*, 1965), a feature film composed of only thirty-five long takes, an amateur boxer (Skolimowski) attempts to make it in the professional ring, knowing full well that he will

15.17 Jerzy Skolimowski (standing) as the young boxer in his *Walkover* (1965).

lose—although, ironically, he does not. Skolimowski characteristically represents this attempt as a form of rebellion against the prevailing social order. *Barrier* (*Bariera*, 1966) firmly established Skolimowski as the principal spokesman for his generation, as well as one of the most important Polish directors to emerge in the sixties. Influenced by Godard, this film is an intricately stylized account of a student's mythic journey through contemporary Poland, and its surrealist *mise-en-scène* makes it Skolimowski's most bizarre and poetic work to date. After shooting the mildly black comedy *Le départ* (*The Departure*, 1967) in Brussels, Skolimowski returned to Poland to make *Hands Up!* (*Rece do góry*, 1967), his most scathing attack yet upon the enclosure and barrenness of modern Polish society, which he personally regards as his best and most mature film. Unfortunately, the film has not been released, since it was banned by the Polish authorities on its completion. At this point, Skolimowski—like Polański before him—became an émigré. He has since made films in Czechoslovakia (*Dialogue 20-40-60*, 1968), Italy (*The Adventures of Gérard*, 1970), England (*Deep End*, 1970), and West Germany (*Konïg, Dame, Bube*, 1972—an adaptation of Vladimir Nabokov's novel *King, Queen, Knave*). While much of his non-Polish work is impressive, the critical consensus is that Skolimowski must find a receptive, stable environment for his film-making activity if he is to continue to innovate new forms. He may have found that environment recently in England, where he made *The Shout* (1978), an expressionistic tale of aboriginal sorcery,

15.18 Skolimowski's *Barrier* (1961): Jan Nowicki, Joanna Szczerbic.

15.19 *Hands Up!* (Jerzy Skolimowski, 1967).

sexual enslavement, and madness narrated in flashback during a cricket match, which makes brilliant use of Dolby sound. The film was chosen to represent Britain at Cannes in 1978, and has been highly praised by some critics in its general release.

The Third Polish Cinema

Of the third post-war generation of Polish directors, sometimes called collectively the "Third Polish Cinema," the most important is Krzysztof Zanussi (b. 1939), who is today the only rival to Wajda among those film-makers who are still regularly working in Poland. Trained as a physicist, Zanussi posits a deterministic social and biological order, while simultaneously offering the hope that human beings may somehow free themselves from it. His films tend to focus on a single contemporary problem and treat it in a highly analytic manner. In *Structure of Crystals* (*Struktura krysztalu,* 1969), for example, the focus is on the meeting of two former university classmates—one an extremely successful physicist, the other the manager of an isolated weather station. The film is a dissection of the two men's inability to communicate to one another their separate visions and values. Other important Zanussi films are *Family Life* (*Życie rodzinne,* 1971); *Behind the Wall* (*Za ściana,* 1971); *Illumination* (*Iluminacja,* 1973); *Quarterly Balance/A Woman's Decision* (*Bilans kwartalny,* 1975); *Camouflage* (*Barwy ochronne,* 1977); *Spiral* (*Spirala,* 1978); *Night Paths* (*Wege in der Nacht,* West Germany, 1979); and *Constans,* which won the Jury Prize at Cannes in 1980. All use the multiple resources of cinema, drama, and language to examine some aspect of contemporary Polish society and the individual's position within it.

The last major Polish film-maker who must be considered here is an internationally famous animator who has recently turned to the production of live-action features, with notable success. Walerian Borowczyk (b. 1923) was trained as a painter and was already an established artist when he won the Polish National Prize for his graphic work in 1953. He made his first animated shorts in collaboration with Jan Lenica (b. 1928), one of the great modern innovators in the field. These films tended to be menacing surrealistic fables like *Dom* (*House,* 1958), which portrays the paranoid hallucinations of a young girl left alone overnight in her house. In 1959 Borowczyk emigrated to Paris (Lenica followed in 1963), where he produced a series of animated shorts projecting a world of absurd violence and private nightmare. Characteristic is *Renaissance* (1963), in which a number of heaped-up disintegrated objects reconstitute themselves, only to reconstitute the source of their original destruction—a time-bomb which duly explodes at the end of the film, returning the objects to their state of chaos. In the twelve-minute *Les jeux des anges* (*Game of Angels,* 1964), Borowczyk takes us on an abstractionized tour of a concentration camp whose transmogrified horrors rival the images of Hieronymus Bosch.* In some twenty-five disquieting allegorical shorts

15.20 *Structure of Crystals* (Krysztof Zanussi, 1969): Andrzej Zarnecki, Jan Mislowicz.

15.21 Zanussi's *Illumination* (1972): Stanislaw Latallo as a young physicist plunged into confusion over the mysteries of life.

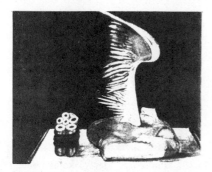

15.22 *Les jeux des anges* (Walerian Borowczyk, 1964).

---

* A Dutch painter (1450–1516) whose elaborate, hallucinatory depictions of the torments of the damned in Hell have made his work a landmark in the tradition of grotesque art.

15.23 Jan Lenica's *Labyrinth* (*Labirynt,* 1962).

and a single feature (*Le théatre de M. et Mme. Kabal,* 1967) made between 1959 and 1967, Borowczyk experimented with every known form of animation to project his vision of ironic, hallucinated horror. He has combined live action with animation, painted images directly on his film stock, and regularly employed collage, pixillation, and film loops.

When he turned to short live-action films in 1966 with *Rosalie* and *Gavotte,* Borowczyk remained essentially a graphic artist with a fine sense of the cruelty of modern existence. His first live-action feature, *Goto, l'île d'amour* (*Goto, Island of Love,* 1967), was an absurdist fable of a barbaric dictatorship on a paradisical tropical island, full of inane brutality and arbitrary destruction. More recently, Borowczyk has become preoccupied with the sexually perverse as an image of modern disorder. His *Contes immoraux* (*Immoral Tales,* 1974), a visually lush anthology film containing four separate tales of sexual perversion, became the second most popular film in France in the year of its release. *The Story of Sin* (*Dzieje grzechu,* 1975), which Borowczyk made in his native Poland and which was the most popular domestic film of 1975, is a surrealistic allegory of an innocent young girl who is drawn down into a terrible vortex of crime, perversion, and murder. Borowczyk's most recent features are *La bête* (*The Beast,* 1976), a parable of sexual obsession and insatiability concerning a hideous beast and a lovely maiden; *Zone de feu* (*Belt of Fire,* 1978), a comedy about the fifteenth-century mass murderer Gilles de Rais; and *Lulu* (1980), a graphic rendition of the Frank Wedekind sex tragedies of which Pabst's *Die Büchse der Pandora* (1928) remains the classic treatment. From both his live-action features and his animated films, it is clear that Borowczyk shares with many of his compatriots a fatalistic and absurdist vision of life. His work embodies a profound pessimism for the human heritage of dissolution, disorder, and decay. But pessimism is not cynicism and need not lead to despair. There is in Borowczyk's films a kind of affirmation in his utter outrage at human misery and in his sense of horror at the human stupidities which produce it. Borowczyk has much more in common with the Buñuel of *Un chien andalou, L'âge d'or,* and *Las Hurdes* than he does with Wajda, Polański, or Skolimowski. Nevertheless, with the latter three, Borowczyk

15.24 Borowczyk's *The Story of Sin* (1974): Grazyna Dlugolecka.

is significantly responsible for bringing the Polish cinema to the position of international prominence it has occupied since the war.

That position was temporarily weakened in the late sixties, during the political crisis which followed the student demonstrations of March 1968. In an attempt to forestall the kind of liberalization then sweeping Czechoslovakia, the Gomulka regime tightened censorship, increased police surveillance, and purged the leadership of the entire Polish film industry. The shake-up was blatantly anti-Semitic: Aleksander Ford was forced to emigrate to Israel; Jerzy Bossak, head of the highly respected Polish documentary production unit, was fired; and Jerzy Toeplitz, director of the Lódź Film School since 1949, was summarily dismissed. In 1968 Poland produced only twenty films, most of them officially sanctioned literary adaptations, and several older films, like Wajda's *Samson* (1961), were banned. By 1971, however, Gomulka had been forced from office by the more moderate Edward Gierek, who relaxed censorship and promoted the reorganization of the state production units to give them more autonomy, which in turn enabled new talents like Zanussi to appear. As the result of a steadily deteriorating economy, Poland is today in the midst of a social crisis of major proportions, but the Polish cinema remains, thirty years after its birth, as sophisticated and vital as any on the Continent.*

CZECHOSLOVAKIA

The Post-War Period

Unlike Poland, Czechoslovakia had a distinguished cinematic tradition long before World War II. One of the major pioneers of camera technology, J. E. Purkyne (1787–1869), was a Czech. Commercial production

15.25 The Nazi Occupation as envisioned in *Third Part of the Night* (Andrzej Żulawski, 1971).

---

* Among the young directors of the last decade are Janusz Majewski (b. 1931— *The Sub-Tenant* [*Sublokator*, 1967]; *The Bear* [*Lokis*, 1970]); Witold Leszczyński (b. 1933—*The Life of Matthew* [*Żywot Mateusza*, 1967]); Marek Piwowski (b. 1935—*Cruise* [*Rejs*, 1970]; *Hair* [1973]; *Foul Play* [*Przepraszam, czy tu bija?*, 1977]); Andrzej Żulawski (b. 1940—*Third Part of a Night* [*Trzecia cześć nocy*, 1971]; *Devil* [*Diabel*, 1971]); Antoni Krauze (b. 1940—*God's Finger* [*Palec Boży*, 1973]); Stanislaw Różewicz (b. 1924–*Passion* [*Pasja*, 1978]); Grzegorz Królikiewicz (b. 1939—*Through and Through* [*Na wylot*, 1973]; *Endless Complaints* [*Wieczne pretensje*, 1974]; *The Dancing Hawk* [*Tańczacy jastrzab*, 1977]); Krzysztof Kieślowski (b. 1941—*Staff* [*Personel*, 1976]; *The Scar* [*Blizna*, 1976]; *Amateur/Camera Buff* [*Amator*, 1976]); Edward Żebrowski (b. 1935—*Salvation* [*Ocalenie*, 1972]; *Hospital of Transfiguration* [*Szpital przemienienia*, 1979]); Andrzej Trzos-Rastawiecki (b. 1933—*Leprosy* [*Trad*, 1971]; *The Record of a Crime* [*Zapis zbrodni*, 1974]; *Condemned* [*Skazany*, 1976]; *Wherever You Are, Mr. President* [*Gdziekolwiek jesteś, panie prezydencie*, 1979]); Agnieszka Holland (co-scenarist of Wajda's *Without Anesthesia* [1978]—*Sunday Children* [1978]; *Test Shot/Film Test* [*Zdjecia próbne*, 1978]; *Provincial Actors* [*Aktorzy prowincjonalni*, 1980]; *Fever* [*Goraczka*, 1981]); Krzysztof Wojciechowski (*Antique* [1977]; *A Family* [1978]); Feliks Falk (*Top Dog* [*Wodzirej*, 1978]; *Chance* [*Szansa*, 1980]); and Marek Piestrak (*Test Pilot Pirx* [*Test pilota Pirxa*, 1979]). See David Robinson, "Poland's Young Generation," *Sight and Sound*, 49, 1 (Winter 1979–80), 34–35.

began in Prague in 1910, four years ahead of Berlin, and the city became a major Continental film capital in the period just before World War I. By the early thirties Prague had the most sophisticated production facilities in Europe, at the Barrandov studios. Between the wars, several Czech directors achieved international reputations—Gustave Machatý (1901–63) for his *Erotikon* (1929) and the sensational *Extase* (*Ecstasy,* 1933), which won a prize at Venice in 1934; Martin Frič (1902–68) for his Slovak folk epic *Jánošík* (1935); and Josef Rovenský (1894–1937) for his lyrical film-poem *The River* (*Reka,* 1934). During the Occupation, domestic production slumped from forty films in 1940 to nine in 1944, as the Nazis appropriated the Barrandov studios to make German-language films. But during the same period, certain Czech film-makers were already formulating plans for the nationalization of the industry when the Nazis withdrew. On August 11, 1945, the Czech president, Eduard Beneš, signed a nationalization decree which established a new production system with three major features: 1) a specially equipped studio for the production of puppet and animation films; 2) the organization of collective production groups for live-action features; and 3) the foundation of a state film school—the Prague Film ("and Television," after 1960) Faculty of the Academy of Dramatic Arts, known as FAMU. In 1947, a separate Slovak production system was organized, with its own documentary and feature studios, in Bratislava (the Slovaks were at that time culturally and religiously separate from the Czechs). Czechoslovakia thus became the first country in Eastern Europe to totally and permanently nationalize its film industry.

The first post-war Czech films dealt with the historical struggle to create a socialist state. Of these, the most impressive were Jiří Weiss' (b. 1913) *Stolen Frontier* (*Uloupená hranice,* 1947), which concerned Hitler's plundering of the Czech frontier in 1938, and Karel Steklý's (b. 1903) *The Strike* (*Siréna,* 1947), a film about an 1889 miners' rebellion which won the Golden Lion at Venice in the year of its release. Of more lasting significance were the first feature-length animated puppet films of Jiří Trnka (1912–69). His *The Czech Year* (*Špalíček,* 1947), a seven-part compilation film celebrating his country's rich folk tradition, won several festival prizes. He followed this with a magical adaptation of a Hans Christian Andersen fairy tale, *The Emperor's Nightingale* (*Císařův slavík,* 1948), and *The Happy Circus* (*Veseley cirkus,* 1950), a short which employed the nearly forgotten technique of animating paper cut-outs. Trnka made his two greatest puppet films in the fifties. *Old Czech Legends* (*Staré pověsti české,* 1953) was a folk epic comprised of seven distinct heroic tales, and it has been justly described as both "*ciné*-ballet" and "*ciné*-opera." *A Midsummer Night's Dream* (*Sen noci svatojanské,* 1958) was an enchanting widescreen adaptation of the Shakespeare play which abandoned the text for mime and dance. Three years in production, this film is widely regarded as Trnka's masterpiece, but the English-language versions have, unfortunately, been dubbed with a voice-over narration and quotations from the play which run counter to the director's intentions.

With the exception of the films of Trnka, the Czech cinema in the early

15.26 *Old Czech Legends* (Jiři Trnka, 1953).

15.27 Trnka's later work: *The Hand* (*Ruka*, 1966).

fifties was as barren as that of the other Warsaw Pact nations as a result of the official imposition of "socialist realism." Perhaps the most important event of the period was the formation in 1952 of the close association between the directors Elmar Klos (b. 1910) and Ján Kadár (1918–79), which would produce two of the greatest films of the Czech New Wave, *Shop on Main Street* and *Adrift* (see below). Klos and Kadár also collaborated on some of the most interesting Czech films of the fifties, culminating in the controversial *Three Wishes* (*Tři přání,* 1958), a veiled analysis of the mechanisms of social repression. By the year of the film's release, the post-Stalinist thaw had given Czech film-makers greater freedom to explore both contemporary and historical themes. But *Three Wishes* became the object of a neo-Stalinist attack on the industry, and, along with several other films, it was banned until 1963. This new and unexpected wave of repression caused directors to retreat to the perennially safe subject matter of the Nazi Occupation, but this time the Czech experience of the war was used as a vehicle for contemporary social comment. Jiří Weiss' *Romeo, Juliet, and the Darkness/Sweet Light in the Dark Window* (*Romeo, Julie a tma,* 1959) tells the story of a young Jewish girl sent to her death in a concentration camp through the indifference of her neighbors. Weiss' *The Coward* (*Zbabělec,* 1961) concerns a simple teacher in rural Slovakia who heroically supports his students in the face of Nazi terrorism. Vojtěch Jasný (b. 1925), a forerunner of the Czech New Wave, contributed *I Survived Certain Death* (*Přežil jsen svou smrt,* 1960), which deals with the courageous struggle of a concentration-camp prisoner to keep himself alive. But the most important of the Occupation films of the early sixties were Zbyněk Brynych's (b. 1927) *Transport from Paradise* (*Transport z ráje,* 1962), a neo-realistic account of the transfer of Jews from the "model" ghetto of Terezin (Teresienstadt) to the gas chambers of Auschwitz; and Klos and Kadár's *Death Is Called Engelchen* (*Smrt si říká Engelchen,* 1963), a formally innovative indictment of war as a corruptor of vanquished and victor alike.

Another haven from the neo-Stalinist assault on Czech film was formal

15.28 *Death Is Called Engelchen* (Elmar Klos and Ján Kadár, 1963).

experiment. The art historian František Vláčil (b. 1924) led the way with *The White Dove* (*Bílá holubice*, 1960), a formalist allegory of repression, isolation, and entrapment in the guise of a tale about a sick boy who captures a dove. In Bratislava, the young Slovak director Štefan Uher (b. 1930), whose first feature had been the unusual children's film *Form 9A* (*My z deviatej A*, 1961), made *Sunshine in a Net* (*Slnko v sieti*, 1962), which many historians identify as the first film of the Czech New Wave. Technically unconventional and highly stylized, *Sunshine in a Net* dealt primarily with the inner lives of its characters; it was attacked by the first secretary of the Slovak Communist Party for exalting subjective vision over socialist realism. Ultimately the film was banned in Bratislava, but Czech film critics organized a special premier showing in Prague and voted overwhelmingly for its artistic merit. At the same time, a major reform of the Slovak Communist Party placed the liberal Alexander Dubček at its head and prepared the way for his subsequent challenge to Czech president Novotný and the brief period of democratization that followed.

15.29 *Sunshine in a Net* (Štefan Uher, 1962).

The Czech New Wave

The official vindication of *Sunshine in a Net* helped to clear the path for the Czech New Wave. So, too, did the extraordinary experimental films of Věra Chytilová (b. 1929), a former draftsman and fashion model, who attended FAMU along with other future directors of the New Wave. Chytilová's medium-length graduation film *Ceiling* (*Strop*) was distributed commercially with her second film, *A Bag of Fleas* (*Pytel blech*), in 1962, and they established her immediately as the chief formal innovator of the New Wave. Markedly influenced by French and American *cinéma-vérité* techniques, these films were both stories of young women seeking self-actualization in the closed world of Czech urban society. Chytilová's first feature, for which she wrote the screenplay, was *Something Else/Something Different* (*O něčem jiném*, 1963), a *cinéma-vérité* portrait of the lives of two quite different women, an Olympic gymnast and a frustrated housewife. With *Daisies* (*Sedmikrásky*, 1966), however, Chytilová moved away from *cinéma-vérité* into the realm of surrealist fantasy and produced one of the outstanding films of the Czech New Wave. The film concerns two bored and self-indulgent girls (the "daisies" of the title) who embark upon an outrageous binge of destruction which ultimately destroys them as well. A bizarre and beautiful satire, *Daisies* was shot by Chytilová's husband, the brilliant cinematographer Jaroslav Kučera (b. 1929), who made free use of superimposition, collage, prismatic distortion, and expressive color to achieve dazzling visual effects for the film. It was designed and partially written by the versatile film-artist Ester Krumbachová (b. 1923), a leading figure of the New Wave who has worked in close collaboration with Chytilová, Jan Němec, and Jaromil Jireš (see below). Openly anarchic and subversive, *Daisies* was banned until 1967, when it won immense critical acclaim both at home and abroad. Chytilová, however, was denied state funds to continue her film-making activity, and her next film, another

15.30 *Daisies* (Věra Chytilová, 1966): Jitka Čerhová, Ivana Karbanová.

collaboration with Kučera and Krumbachová, was financed by a Belgian production company. Her most surrealistic film to date, *The Fruit of Paradise* (*Ovoce stromů rajských jíme*, 1969) is a complicated parable about the fantasies of women trapped in a man's world; it won several international awards. But after 1970, Chytilová, who had chosen to remain and work in her homeland despite the Soviet invasion and the overthrow of the liberal Dubček regime in 1968, was forbidden by the government to make films altogether. The ban was lifted in 1975, and she produced *The Apple Game* (*Uvadi hra o jablku*, 1976), a furiously-paced satire on the inefficiency and corruption of the Czech medical profession, followed by *Prefab Story* (*Panelstory*, 1978) and *Calamity* (*Kalamita*, 1979). Whatever her future as a film-maker, Chytilová stands today as the most influential formal innovator of the Czech New Wave.

15.31 *The First Cry* (Jaromil Jireš, 1963).

Another young formalist of note was Jaromil Jireš (b. 1935), who worked briefly with Chytilová on the script of *Daisies*. His first feature was a stylistically dazzling portrait of contemporary Czech society entitled *The First Cry* (*Křik*, 1963). It depicted a day in the life of a television repairman making his rounds from house to house while his wife lies in the hospital in labor. Clearly influenced by the French New Wave, Jireš cut back and forth at will between the repairman at work in the homes of the powerful (the only Czechs who could afford to own TV sets at this time), his wife in the hospital, and his own memories of their past life together. Between 1963 and 1968 Jireš made no feature films because all of his scripts were rejected by the censors. But in the "Prague Spring" of 1968, the brief period of democratization fostered by the Dubček regime, he was able to produce a dark, ironic masterpiece, *The Joke* (*Zert*). Based on a contemporary novel, the film provides a savage indictment of the Stalinist system in the story of a post-war philosophy student who is unjustly expelled from school and sent to serve in one of the Czech army's notoriously brutal "black units" because he made a political joke. Stylistically restrained and harshly realistic, *The Joke* contrasts sharply with Jireš' later films. *Valerie and Her Week of Wonders* (*Valerie a týden divů*, 1970), adapted from a story by the Czech surrealist poet Vítězslav Nezval, is a beautifully photographed vampire film which alternates between the erotic and the grotesque. *And Give My Love to the Swallows* (*A pozdravujte vlaštovky*, 1971) is a stylized version of the diaries of a young girl who was executed for aiding the Resistance during the Nazi Occupation, and *The Island of Silver Herons* (*Ostrov stříbrných volavek*, 1976) is a poetic meditation on honor and tradition as seen through the eyes of a young boy in a small German town at the close of World War I. (None of Jireš' more recent films have reached the West, but several have won domestic prizes.)

15.32 Jireš' *The Joke* (1968): Josef Somr.

15.33 Jireš' *Valerie and Her Week of Wonders* (1969).

The films of Chytilová and Jireš signaled the beginning of the Czech New Wave, or the "Czech Film Miracle," as it has also been called. This movement was political as well as artistic, in that its ultimate goal was to make the Czech people collectively aware that they were participants in a system of oppression and incompetence which had brutalized them all. The success of this consciousness-raising was nearly total, and there is little doubt today that the Czech cinema of 1963–68 laid much of the groundwork for liberalization. It also brought the Czech film industry into a position of international prominence which, even after the Soviet invasion of 1968, it has managed to maintain.

Though it was dominated by the youngest generation of FAMU-trained directors, the New Wave was a movement in which Czech film-makers of all generations participated, precisely because it *was* a national political phenomenon. The veterans Klos and Kadár first contributed *The Defendant* (*Obžalovaný*, 1964), an unconventional courtroom drama about a man being tried for achieving economic success within the social-ist system. They then produced an internationally acclaimed masterpiece, *Shop on Main Street* (*Obchod na korze*, 1965), which won the American Academy Award as Best Foreign Film of 1965. This film is about Tono, a carpenter in a small Slovak town, who becomes the "Aryan controller" of a button shop owned by an old Jewish woman during the early years of the Occupation. Because the woman is nearly deaf, Tono cannot ex-plain his position to her, so for practical purposes he pretends to be her shop assistant. Initially the situation and film are gently comic, but as Tono gradually comes to pity the woman he recognizes the serious and potentially dangerous nature of his commitment. When the town's Jews are finally rounded up and deported to the death camps, he must choose between protecting the old lady and saving his own skin. He tries to con-ceal her but accidentally kills her in the process, after which he commits suicide. By making the tragedy of the Jews a metaphor for the multiple tragedies of modern Europe, Klos and Kadár evoked the collective re-sponsibility of all Europeans for the existence and perpetuation of politi-cal oppression.

15.34 *Shop on Main Street* (Ján Kadár and Elmar Klos, 1965): Ida Kamińska, Josef Kroner.

In 1968 Klos and Kadár began work on their greatest film, the Czech/American co-production *Adrift/A Longing Called Anada* (*Touha zvana Anada*, 1971), based on a novel by Lájos Zihály. The shooting was interrupted by the Soviet invasion and finally completed after the interval of a year, during which Kadár came to the United States to direct *The Angel Levine* (1970), from a Bernard Malamud story. *Adrift* is an elaborately conceived parable of a man cutting himself loose from all traditional ties to his family, his culture, and his religion. Paradoxically, this liberation takes the form of madness, and its vehicle is sexual obses-sion. Catalyzed by his wife's apparently terminal illness, a simple middle-aged fisherman is overwhelmingly attracted by the image of a beautiful young woman whom he may or may not have pulled from the waters of the Danube. Except for its beginning and end—which recount the same action from different points of view—the whole film takes place in the mind of its protagonist as he stands on the brink of poisoning his sick wife and interrogates himself about the mental events which have led him to this pass. Its stylistic and structural complexity, which extends to a brilliantly modulated score by František Černý, caused many American critics to dismiss *Adrift* as incomprehensible. But the film has the circular logic of a fantasy or a dream, and to try to read it as a conventional nar-rative is to misconceive its intentions. After *Adrift*, Klos chose to remain in Czechoslovakia, but Kadár became a permanent resident of the United States, where he was made a Fellow of the American Film Institute.

15.35 *Shop on Main Street:* the round-up.

Kadár directed *Lies My Father Told Me* (1975), a moving Canadian production about a Jewish boy growing up in a Montreal immigrant neighborhood, and he did some interesting work for American television (e.g., an adaptation of Steven Crane's short story "The Blue Hotel" for PBS [1977], and the mini-series "Freedom Road" for NBC [1979]), before his death in 1979.

Another cinematic veteran who made an important contribution to the New Wave was Vojtěch Jasný, whose highly stylized fantasy *Cassandra Cat* (*Až přijde kocour,* 1963) helped to break a number of neo-Stalinist cinematic and social conventions. This balletic fable of a magic cat whose gaze makes everyone tell the truth was a modern political morality play masquerading as a fairy tale; its technical virtuosity won it a Special Jury Prize at Cannes. But Jasný's most significant film of the New Wave came at the very end of it. This was the wistfully lyrical *All My Countrymen* (*Všichni dobří rodáci,* 1968), a bittersweet paean to the inhabitants of a small Moravian village who had worked together with Jasný since the war to achieve the reform of their society so recently and brutally crushed by the Soviet invasion.

Most characteristic of the younger directors of the Czech New Wave, and ultimately the most famous, was Miloš Forman (b. 1932). Forman, who was orphaned by the Nazis during the Occupation, graduated from FAMU in 1957 and worked as an assistant to both Martin Frič and Alfred Radok (1914–76)* before making his first feature, *Black Peter/Peter and Pavla* (*Černý Petr*) in 1963. This was an ironic film about generational conflict shot in *cinéma-vérité* fashion with non-actors. A young man takes his first job as a department store detective, but he finds the work of spying on people so distasteful that it puts him at odds with his hidebound parents. The film, which won the Czech Film Critics' Prize, marked Forman's first association with his co-scenarists, Ivan Passer (b. 1933) and Jaroslav Papoušek (b. 1929), and with the cinematographer Miroslav Ondříček (b. 1933), all of whom were to collaborate on his next two films. Like *Black Peter,* these were subtle behavioral studies built upon elaborated anecdotes rather than traditional plot structures. And, like *Black Peter,* they were greeted with both popular

15.36 *Cassandra Cat* (Vojtěch Jasný 1963).

---

* Radok was already Prague's most distinguished stage director when he turned his energies to the cinema as an art consultant in 1947. In 1949, he directed his first feature, *The Long Journey* (*Daleká cesta,* 1949), an expressionistic portrait of life in the Terezin ghetto which was the first Czech film to deal with the Nazis' extermination of the Jews. (The film was later ordered withdrawn by government censors for violating the canons of socialist realism.) Radok's only other films as a director were *The Magic Hat* (*Divotvorný klobouk,* 1952), the first Czech musical, and *Old-Man Motorcar* (*Dědeček automobil,* 1956), a playfully experimental history of the automobile. Radok continued to experiment with film form in *Magic Lantern* (*Laterna Magica*), a mixed-media show which he developed for the Brussels Exposition of 1958 with the assistance of Miloš Foreman, Ivan Passer, Jaroslav Papoušek, and other young film-makers who later created the New Wave. *Magic Lantern* combined film, slides, and live action to create a new kind of theater. But its programs were too controversial for the Czech authorities, and Radok and his collaborators were forced to withdraw from the project. Radok returned to stage-directing, and emigrated to Sweden in 1968. But he left a lasting legacy to Czech cinema in his formal experimentation and in his mentorship of younger artists.

15.37 *Loves of a Blonde* (Miloš Forman, 1965): Hana Brejchová (right).

15.38 Forman's *Firemen's Ball* (1967).

acclaim and official disapproval. *Loves of a Blonde/A Blonde in Love* (*Lásky jedué plavovlásky*, 1965), which brought Forman to international attention, was the simple tale of a young factory girl who meets a touring piano-player at a local dance and ends up going to bed with him. She later visits him in his home town, to the acute embarrassment of the boy and his parents. The film is a sharply observed comedy of everyday life, and its superb sense of timing recalls the American screwball comedies of the thirties. But *Loves of a Blonde* also contained an implicit criticism of the banality of modern Czech society which did not pass unnoticed by the authorities.

Firemen's Ball (*Hoří, má panenko!*, 1967) went even farther in this direction—so far that its release was temporarily blocked by President Novotný himself. The film is a satire on Czechoslovakia's most sensitive contemporary political debate: what should be the official attitude toward the Stalinist brutality of the fifties and those still in power who perpetrated it? This issue appears in the form of a comedy about a small town's commemorative celebration for a dying fireman. The ball is interrupted by a fire, and the firemen return to discover that all of the food, gifts, and prizes have been stolen by the guests. Some are caught, and a great argument ensues over how the culprits should be treated. *Firemen's Ball* opened on December 15, 1967, just two weeks before the political crisis which was to overthrow Novotný and bring the liberal Alexander Dubček to power. When Dubček himself was toppled by the Soviet invasion, Forman, like so many of his colleagues, was forced to leave the country. With Ondříček, he came to the United States, where he has since directed *Taking Off* (1971), a social comedy about contemporary American mores; a highly acclaimed adaptation of Ken Kesey's novel *One Flew Over the Cuckoo's Nest* (1975); and a dynamic film version of the Broadway musical *Hair* (1979) shot on location in New York City. Forman's status as a major figure has been confirmed; he is currently head of the Film Division at Columbia University and is filming his own adaptation of E. L. Doctorow's novel *Ragtime*. In his concern for the texture

15.39 *Intimate Lighting* (Ivan Passer, 1965): Jan Vostrčič.

15.40 *Closely Watched Trains* (Jiří Menzel, 1966): Václav Neckar, Jitka Bendová.

15.41 Menzel in his film *Capricious Summer* (1967).

of the everyday, Forman seems to have been influenced by the British "New Cinema" (see Chapter 14) of Lindsay Anderson (*This Sporting Life*, 1963) and Karel Reisz (*Saturday Night and Sunday Morning*, 1960). His nearly perfect sense of comic timing has been attributed to the influence of Chaplin, Keaton, and Hawks. But there is something uniquely Czech in the experiential quality of his shooting and lighting, and in the black humor of his satire.

Forman's influence upon his peers in Czechoslovak cinema was great. His co-scenarists, Ivan Passer (*Intimate Lighting* [*Intimní osvětlení*, 1965]) and Jaroslav Papoušek (*The Most Beautiful Age* [*Nejkrásnějšívek*], 1968]), both made plotless, anecdotal films in the manner of Forman during the New Wave. Pavel Juráček (b. 1935), who made the highly respected, expressionistic *Josef Kilian* (*Postava k podpírání*, 1963) with Jan Schmidt (b. 1934), shot his first independent feature, *Every Young Man* (*Každy mladý muž*, 1965), in imitation of Forman. But the most important figure to adopt the anti-heroic *cinéma-vérité* style developed by Forman was Jiří Menzel (b. 1938). Menzel graduated from FAMU in 1963 and spent the next two years working as an assistant to Vera Chytilová and as an actor for Evald Schorm (see below). His first motion picture as a director was a contribution to the anthology film *Pearls of the Deep* (*Perličky na dně*, 1964), based on five short stories by Bohumil Hrabal. (Schorm, Jan Němec, Chytilová, and Jireš were the other contributors, making *Pearls of the Deep* a kind of omnibus of the Czech New Wave.) Menzel's first feature, *Closely Watched Trains* (*Ostře sledované vlaky*, 1966), was also adapted from Hrabal; it brought Menzel international fame and became the second Czech film to win an American Academy Award (as Best Foreign Film in 1967). The film is an elliptical, Formanesque study of human attitudes and behavior set in a railway town during the Occupation. An awkward youth apprentices himself to the village stationmaster, whose sexual exploits he much admires. After failing miserably in his first sexual encounter, the young man makes a suicide attempt. He finally succeeds at sex with a beautiful Resistance fighter and, in a dramatic assertion of virility, blows up a Nazi ammunition train. As he returns jubilantly to the station, he is killed by a German guard's machine-gun. *Closely Watched Trains* is both comic and deadly serious, often simultaneously, and in this regard it epitomizes an essential characteristic of Czech New Wave cinema—its ironic and often detached intermixing of dichotomous emotional responses. Menzel's other great New Wave film was *Capricious Summer* (*Rozmarné léto*, 1967), a humorous but sometimes dark fable about the sexual misadventures of three middle-aged friends in a small fishing village. Menzel's reverential parody of American musical comedy, *Crime in the Nightclub* (*Zločin v šantánu*, 1968), was an immense popular success in Czechoslovakia during the months that followed the invasion, but his *Skylarks on a String* (*Skřivánci na niti*, 1969), adapted from Hrabal, was banned, and Menzel was not permitted to make another film until the zany *Seclusion Near a Forest* (*Na samotě u lesa*, 1976). Next he directed *Those Wonderful Movie Cranks* (*Báječni muži s klikou*, 1978), commemorating the seventieth anniversary of the

Czechoslovak film industry. It is a humorous and affectionate account of the beginnings of film-making in Prague in 1907, shot in the sepia tones of the era. Menzel's most recent film is *Short Cut* (*Postřižiny*, 1981), a lyrical comedy about life in a small provincial town just before the First World War.

The two most politically controversial and morally committed directors of the Czech New Wave were Evald Schorm (b. 1931) and Jan Němec (b. 1936). Schorm, who is often called "the conscience of the New Wave," graduated from FAMU in 1962 and made his first feature, *Everyday Courage*/*Courage for Every Day* (*Odvahu pro ušední den*) in 1964. In it he eschewed both the formal experiments of Chytilová and Jireš and the *cinéma-vérité* techniques of Forman, Passer, and Menzel to make a traditional dramatic film of uncompromisingly serious intent. *Everyday Courage* is the story of an idealistic Communist organizer who gradually comes to recognize that his ideals are wrong and that they have caused much human misery. The official response to this allegory of de-Stalinization was violent condemnation. When *Everyday Courage* won the Czech Film Critics' Prize in 1965, the government refused to let Schorm accept, and attempted to sabotage the film's distribution. International outcry finally forced official acceptance of *Everyday Courage*, but Schorm's next feature, *The Return of the Prodigal Son* (*Návrat ztraceného syna,* 1966), was banned outright for several months. This film, considered to be Schorm's masterpiece, is a parable of the fate of the individual in an authoritarian society. Its protagonist, Jan, is confined to a mental institution after a suicide attempt. Jan's failure to "adjust" to the existing social structure stems from his unwillingness to compromise his personal integrity, and he is therefore certified to be mentally ill. After treatment and release, Jan is still unable to fit in, and in the film's symbolic conclusion he is hunted down by a mob that mistakes him for an assassin. In *Pastor's End*/*The End of a Priest* (*Konec faráře,* 1968), Schorm and the scriptwriter Josef Škvorecký (b. 1924)—who has also worked with Menzel and other New Wave directors*—collaborated on a farcical re-working of the Christ legend with pronounced political overtones. In a rural village, a sexton poses as a priest and accomplishes much good, but he is finally exposed and done to death by the repressive institutions of church and state. The release of *Pastor's End* was delayed by the authorities for a year, but it has now become generally available in the West. Schorm's last film, *The Seventh Day, the Eighth Night* (*Sedmý den, osmá noc,* 1969), was permanently banned in the spring of 1970, and Schorm was forbidden to work in the Czech film industry again. Since that time he has made his living by directing operas in provincial theaters—like one of his own heroes, unwilling to compromise his moral integrity or his seriousness of purpose for the comfortable security of "fitting in."

Like Schorm, Jan Němec is an ethically committed film-maker concerned with the survival of individual integrity in a repressive, regimented

15.42 *Return of the Prodigal Son* (Evald Schorm, 1966): Jan Kačer, Milan Morávec.

---

*Škvorecký's account of these years is contained in his autobiographical history of the Czech New Wave, *All the Bright Young Men and Women* (Toronto, 1973). He now lives and works in the United States and Canada.

15.43 *Diamonds of the Night* (Jan Němec, 1964).

15.44 Němec's *The Party and the Guests* (1966).

society. But unlike Schorm, he experiments boldly with form and has been on the cutting edge of the New Wave since his student days. His first feature, *Diamonds of the Night* (*Démanty noci,* 1964), was adapted by Němec and Arnošt Lustig from a story by Lustig about two young Jews who escape from a Nazi death march. Němec turned the narrative into a nightmarish representation of the mental anguish of human beings under extreme physical and psychological stress. Documentary-like footage of the four-day hunt for the boys is intercut with images from their dreams, fantasies, and hallucinations as they become increasingly desperate. The film was a great domestic success and won many international awards.

Němec's next film began a brief but fruitful collaboration with the designer Ester Krumbachová and brought the wrath of officialdom down upon the heads of them both. *The Party and the Guests/A Report on the Party and the Guests* (*O slavnosti a hostech,* 1966) was a stylized, Kafkaesque allegory about the mechanisms of repression in Czech society, and the most politically venomous film of the New Wave. The Host throws an elegant dinner party in a beautiful forest glade, assuring his guests throughout the evening that his only desire is to make them happy. As the party progresses, the guests assure The Host one by one that they are indeed supremely happy. Only one of them, The Guest Who Refused to Be Happy, resists being intimidated into contentment, and, significantly, he is played by the director Evald Schorm, whose *Return of the Prodigal Son* was then under a government ban. Eventually the unhappy guest discreetly slips away, and the crowd of remaining guests turns ugly. If a single guest refuses to join the merry-making, it spoils the party for all, so the party takes to its feet and pursues the malcontent with dogs. This sinister parable of social conformity and political dissent was brilliantly designed by Krumbachová to achieve just the proper sense of strange beauty intermixed with menace. Many of the scenes were modeled on contemporary Czech paintings and media images, giving the film a rich subtext of visual allusion. Most of the roles were played by friends of the film-makers, so at yet another level of allusion the film stands as a collective political manifesto by Prague's artists and intellectuals. When

President Novotný screened *The Party and the Guests,* he was outraged and is said to have remarked, "It's about the way we banned that fellow Schorm's film and then set the dogs on him, isn't it?" This time the dogs were set upon Němec and his friends. The film was banned for two full years and became the object of violent invective. Together with Chytilová's *Daisies,* it was used as an excuse for a denunciation of the entire New Wave in the Czechoslovak National Assembly in May 1967. Němec and Krumbachová, in the meantime, turned to the non-political theme of sexual fantasy in the three-episode *Martyrs of Love* (*Mučedníci lásky,* 1967), which recalled the hyper-visual, hallucinatory quality of *Diamonds of the Night.* When Dubček assumed power in January 1968, *The Party and the Guests* was finally released domestically, and that spring it was sent to Cannes as the official Czech entry. Němec was at work with Josef Škvorecký on a documentary about Prague when Soviet tanks entered the city on August 20–21. This film became *Oratorio for Prague* (1968), a melancholy account of the invasion which was smuggled out of Czechoslovakia for screening in the West. Němec was blacklisted immediately, and he was unable to make films from 1968 to 1974; in that year he was allowed to emigrate to France. He subsequently found work in West German television and completed *Czech Connection: Reflection of My Own Death* (1975), a forty-minute autobiographical film begun secretly in his homeland. Since 1977, Němec has lived in Santa Monica, California, where he remains virtually unknown.

The Czech film miracle came to an abrupt end with the Soviet invasion of August 1968 and the subsequent occupation of the country by Warsaw Pact troops. The liberalization of Czechoslovakia had threatened Soviet hegemony over Eastern Europe, and so it was suppressed by force. President Dubček was deposed and the "normalization" of Czechoslovakia undertaken by its new masters. Films in production were halted. Many already in release were withdrawn by Soviet censors and banned. The director of the state distribution organization, Czechoslovak Film, was arrested, and every Czech film-maker discussed in this chapter except Jireš was blacklisted and forbidden to work in the film industry indefinitely. Kadár, Jasný, Forman, Passer, and, ultimately, Němec left the country for good, and a whole rising generation of new talent was permanently quashed. By 1973 virtually every important film of the previous decade lay buried in a vault in the cellar of the Barrandov studios, and four of these had been labeled "Banned Forever"—Forman's *Firemen's Ball,* Schorm's *Pastor's End,* Němec's *The Party and the Guests,* and Jasný's *All My Countrymen.* It was as if the New Wave and everything it had accomplished had never existed. What might have happened had the New Wave cinema been allowed to grow and prosper—and what that growth might have meant for the development of international cinema— is impossible to say. Surely its significance would have been great. But, instead, "normalization" left a huge vacuum which the Czech film industry has been unable to fill ever since. Very few notable films have come from Prague in the seventies. There has been some excitement about the work of the Slovak surrealist Juraj Jakubisko (b. 1938—*Deserters and*

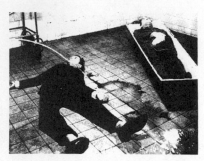

15.45 *The Cremator* (Juraj Herz, 1968): Rudolf Hrusinský.

Nomads [*Zbehovia a pútníci*, 1968]; *Birds, Orphans, and Fools* [*Vtáčkovia, siroty a blázni*, 1969]; *Build a House, Plant a Tree* [*Postav dom, zasad strca*, 1980], which has been compared to that of Dovzhenko in its violent, elemental force. The comedies of Oldřich Lipský (b. 1924—*Dinner for Adele* [*Adela ještě nevečeřela*, 1978]; *Long Live Ghosts!* [*Ať žiji duchove!*, 1979]) and the baroque allegories of the Slovak director Juraj Herz (b. 1934—*The Cremator* [*Spalovač mrtvol*, 1968]; *Kerosene Lamps* [*Petrolejové lampy*, 1971]; *The Beauty and the Beast* [1979]) have also enjoyed some international success. But the miracle is over and cannot happen again under the prevailing political conditions in Czechoslovakia. What is amazing is how very much was achieved in such a short time: In less than a decade, a nation no larger than the state of Tennessee evolved a film movement which simultaneously had a radical impact on its own socio-political structure and changed the shape of the international cinema.

HUNGARY

Like Czechoslovakia, Hungary has had a long and distinguished cinematic tradition. The Hungarians, in fact, seem to have identified film as an art form before any other nationality in the world, including the French. From the beginning, they emphasized the literary and intellectual aspects of film, and most films were adapted from classical Hungarian novels and plays. For this reason, famous authors and actors from the legitimate stage had none of the qualms about working in film which afflicted their counterparts in the West. In 1912 the radical writer Sándor Korda* (who later worked in Britain as the producer-director Alexander Korda) founded *Pesti mozi* ("Pest† cinema"), the first Hungarian film journal, and by 1920 it had been joined by sixteen others. A strong tradition of advanced film theory was founded in the teens by the philosophers Jenö Török and Cecil Bognár, and passed on to Béla Balázs (1884–1949), whose *Films—Werden und Wesen einer neuen Kunst‡* became greatly influential. As in France, film attracted the avant-garde—the painter László Moholy-Nagy (1895–1946), for example, conducted numerous experiments with film's ability to transform space and light between 1923 and 1928. Hungary also had the first nationalized film industry in history. Béla Kun's socialist revolution of March 1919 declared Hungary a "Red Council of Republics," and the cinema was nationalized in April of that year—four months before Lenin nationalized the Soviet industry. This adventure lasted only until the Rightist counter-revolution of Admiral Horthy in August, but thirty-one films were produced in

---

* Hungarian names are here given with the surname last, although in Hungary the convention is the reverse.

† The present city of Budapest was formed in 1873 by the union of Buda and Óbuda, on the right bank of the Danube River, with Pest (pronounced "Pesht"), on the left bank. Even today, many Hungarians refer to "Buda," or to "Pest," rather than to "Budapest."

‡ Berlin, 1948; published in English as *Theory of the Film: Character and Growth of a New Art*, trans. Edith Bone (London, 1952; New York, 1972).

the interim. Hungary's first important director was Mihály Kertész (1888–1962), who studied film-making at Denmark's Nordisk studios, directed a number of films in Germany in the twenties, and settled in the United States, where he worked for Warner Brothers as Michael Curtiz. Other important figures were Pál Fejös (1898–1963) and Endre Toth (b. 1900; known in the United States as André de Toth), both of whom ultimately emigrated to America.

In 1920 the Horthy regime restored film production to the private sector, and during the twenties and thirties the Hungarian industry became commercialized along American lines. Most films of the period were made on an assembly-line basis, in imitation of Hollywood. When World War II broke out, the Horthy government, which was allied with the Germans, took control of the industry through the National Film Committee and permitted it to produce only conformist entertainment and propaganda films. When the regime collapsed at the end of the war, the Academy for Cinematographic Art was founded, and Soviet and American classics were shown in Hungary for the first time. The most significant Hungarian film of this period was the privately produced *Somewhere in Europe* (*Valahol Európában,* 1947), a humanitarian fantasy about the reclamation of war orphans, written by Béla Balázs and directed by Géza Radványi (b. 1907). When a Communist government came to power early in 1948, the Hungarian film industry was nationalized for the second time. The first state-subsidized films were quite promising, but the political climate deteriorated rapidly, and the period 1949–53 was one of stolid socialist realism.

15.46 *Somewhere in Europe* (Géza Radvány, 1947): Miklós Gábor.

The death of Stalin in 1953 and the subsequent replacement of Mátyás Rákosi as the Hungarian premier by Imre Nagy marked the beginning of a brief era of liberalization. This period was one of high achievement for Hungarian cinema. It witnessed the emergence of a new generation of directors: Zoltán Fábri (b. 1917—*Fourteen Lives in Danger* [*Életjel,* 1954]; *Merry-Go-Round* [*Körhinta,* 1955]; *Professor Hannibal* [*Hannibál, tanár úr,* 1956]); Károly Makk (b. 1925—*Liliomfi* [1954]); János Herskó (b. 1926—*Under the City* [*A város alatt,* 1954]); and Felix Máriássy (b. 1919—*Spring in Budapest* [*Budapesti tavasz,* 1955]; *A Glass of Beer* [*Egy pikoló világos,* 1955]), many of whom are still active in the Hungarian cinema today (e.g., Károly Makk, *Love* [*Szerelem,* 1975]; Zoltán Fábri, *The Hungarians* [*Magyarok,* 1978]). Their films expressed the increasingly liberal sentiments of the Hungarian workers and their yearning for a true social democracy. In October 1956 this yearning began to manifest itself in demonstrations, street-fighting, and, finally, armed violence. Then, as it would do twelve years later in Czechoslovakia, the Soviet government intervened and crushed the rebellion. Imre Nagy and about five hundred of his supporters were arrested and executed. Another ten thousand persons were deported to Soviet labor camps, and an undetermined number were imprisoned for years without trial. The revolution was crushed, but the moderate János Kádár was installed as premier, and he gradually embarked upon a realistic course of liberalization which left Hungary substantially more free than any of its Warsaw Pact neighbors in the years to come.

15.47 *Merry-Go-Round* (Zoltán Fábri, 1955): Mari Töröcsik, Imre Sós.

15.48 *Catsplay* (*Macskajáték,* 1974), a recent film by Károly Makk: Margit Dayka.

The effect of the revolt upon Hungarian cinema was one of arrested development. The films of 1954–56 had been notable primarily for their content, rather than for the kind of formal innovations which liberalization would produce in Poland and Czechoslovakia. In the matter of style and structure, Hungarian film was still essentially realist (or, at most, neo-realist) when the revolution was put down. Afterwards, it could evolve in neither form nor content until Kádár's steady process of liberalization had been realized. The films of 1957–61, therefore, were unremarkable. But in 1958 the experimental Béla Balázs Studio was founded in order to give graduates of the state-operated Academy for Cinematographic Art in Budapest an opportunity to make their first films. The year 1961 saw the release of the studio's first batch of features and marked a renaissance for Hungarian cinema. The two figures of signal importance to this renaissance were András Kovács and Miklós Jancsó.

András Kovács (b. 1925) attended the Budapest Academy and made several features before undertaking a two-year period of study in Paris. There, Kovács fell under the influence of *cinéma-vérité,* whose techniques he employed in *Difficult People* (*Nehéz emberek,* 1964) on his return to Hungary. This film examines the true cases of five Hungarian inventors whose work had been opposed or ignored through bureaucratic stupidity. *Difficult People* sparked a debate throughout the country, since it was the first time since 1955 that contemporary reality had been so directly confronted on the screen. Kovács' next film, *Cold Days* (*Hideg napok,* 1966), was a visually engaging account of the massacre of some three thousand civilians by Hungarian troops in Czechoslovakia during World War II. The event is narrated in flashback by four participants who are in prison awaiting trial for the atrocity some years later. This film, too, provoked debate—this time about the collective nature of responsibility in both the national present and the national past. *Cold Days* appeared at several international festivals and attracted world attention to the new Hungarian cinema. In *Walls* (*Falak,* 1968) and *Relay Race* (*Staféta,* 1970), Kovács continued to probe the contradictions of contemporary Hungarian society with a degree of artistic freedom unprecedented in any other country in Eastern Europe. His most recent films are *The Stud Farm* (*Ménesgazda,* 1979), a tale of political terror set during the first nervous months of the new Stalinist regime in 1950, and *A Sunday in October* (*Októberi vasárnap,* 1980), an historical reconstruction of Admiral Horthy's secret attempt to abandon the Axis and negotiate a separate peace with the Soviet Union near the end of World War II.

The first major film of Miklós Jancsó (b. 1921), *Cantata* (*Oldás és kötés,* 1962), is also considered to be the first film of the Hungarian New Wave. Jancsó had studied law, ethnography, and art history before he entered the Budapest Academy, from which he graduated in 1950. For eight years he made newsreels and documentaries which were fairly conventional in both form and content, as was his first feature, *The Bells Have Gone to Rome* (*A harangok Rómába mentek,* 1958). But *Cantata,* written by his perennial collaborator, Gyula Hernádi, revealed a striking talent for visual composition and psychological analysis. Photographed

15.49 *Cold Days* (András Kovács, 1966).

in the neutralized style of Antonioni, it concerns a physician who has long ago cut himself off from reality and now attempts to establish an authentic relationship with his aged peasant father. It was *My Way Home* (*Igy jöttem,* 1964), however, which announced the style for which Jancsó would become famous—one based upon extended long takes sustained by rhythmic tracking movements of the camera and optical traveling through the zoom lens. The film is about a Hungarian captured by a young Russian soldier at the end of World War II. They live together in peace for a while, but when the Russian unexpectedly dies the Hungarian is hunted down in the hills. *My Way Home* offers a pessimistic view of a hostile universe in a structure of great formal beauty—traits strikingly present in Jancsó's next film.

15.50 *My Way Home* (Miklós Jancsó, 1964).

The Round-Up/The Hopeless Ones (*Szegénylegények,* 1965), which brought Jancsó to international prominence when it was shown at Cannes in 1966, is a chilling account of an historical incident which occurred in 1868 and the first of many Janscó films about great events from the Hungarian past. The secret police of the Austro-Hungarian Empire attempt to unmask Sándor, the leader of a rebel army group during the 1848 Revolution led by Lájos Kossuth. They do so by rounding up several hundred outlaws, rebel peasants, and herdsmen—former comrades-in-arms under Sándor—into a prison stockade on the great Hungarian plain, where they employ the classical means of political terror to force the inmates into mutual betrayal. A film of stark beauty and terrific force, *The Round-Up* introduced many of Jancsó's mature personal symbols and stylistic obsessions: the use of nudity to signify humiliation; the totally impersonal depiction of cruelty and violence; the menacing image of incessantly circling horsemen on the empty spaces of the plain; the balletic choreography of the camera and groups of actors within the frame; the replacement of characterization through dialogue with bureaucratic jargon, slogans, and songs. The film also demonstrated that Jancsó was an absolute master of the new aesthetics whose cinematic structures were dependent upon widescreen composition, the long take, and the zoom lens. *The Round-Up* was shot by the cinematographer Tamás Somló, who worked with Jancsó on his next film as well.

15.51   Openness and closure in Jancsó's *The Round-Up* (1966).

15.52 Symbolic use of nudity in Jancsó's *The Red and the White* (1967).

Jancsó continued his bold stylistic experiments in a series of films whose symbolic subject was Hungary's past but whose real theme was Hungary's present and future. All were characterized by the abstract, mythographic, and sometimes theatrical quality visible in *The Round-Up,* but they tended to extend these modes to the very limits of coherence. *The Red and the White (Csillagosok, katonák,* 1967) was concerned with Hungarians fighting in the Red Army in 1918 during the Civil War in Russia. It employed sustained lateral tracking and widescreen composition brilliantly to visualize the constantly shifting balance of power between two great armies massed against one another in empty space. *Silence and Cry (Csend és kiáltás,* 1968) was set in 1919 during the fall of the Red Council of Republics, when police were hunting down and punishing anyone suspected of radical sympathies. Like *The Round-Up,* it is a film about degradation, torture, alienation, and betrayal. *Silence and Cry* was also Jancsó's first film with the cinematographer János Kende, who has been his constant collaborator ever since. *The Confrontation (Fényes szelek,* 1969), Jancsó's first film in color, dealt with a student rebellion of 1947 but had obvious reference to contemporary student unrest. Yet it was the director's most stylized film to date, a virtual ballet for camera and soundtrack in which every gesture had ritual significance.

In *Winter Wind (Sirokkó,* 1969), a film composed of only thirteen shots, some as long as ten minutes, a group of Croatian nationalists are being trained to assassinate King Alexander of Yugoslavia on the Hungarian-Yugoslav border. Again, Jancsó's theme is the destructive effects of political terror on the individual will. In *Agnus Dei (Égi bárány,* 1970) Jancsó went farther than ever before in the direction of symbolic abstraction. This beautiful color film is essentially a celebration of the revolutionary spirit in which all dialogue takes the form of quotations from the Bible or from national songs. With *Red Psalm (Még kér a nép,* 1972), Jancsó produced his masterpiece. Composed of fewer than thirty shots, this film is a stunning symbolic analysis of the revolutionary process, its psychological and social pre-conditions, and its ultimate, necessary failure. For eighty minutes, camera and lens move incessantly, circling and encircling the choric participants in the drama—historically, an

15.53 The aesthetics of widescreen space: Jancsó's *The Red and the White* (1967) and *Red Psalm* (1970).

15.54 A frame from one of the twelve sequence shots comprising Jancsó's *Elektreia* (1974).

abortive agrarian socialist rebellion in the late nineteenth century. Music and sound, color, focus—virtually every element in the film—work in concert to make *Red Psalm* a film of nearly perfect formal beauty, great humanity, and awesome cinematic power. Jancsó's twelve-shot *Elektreia* (*Szerelmem, Elektra*, 1974) extends his abstractionist vision into the realm of Greek legend. But more recently he has returned to his national heritage with an ambitious trilogy intended to represent Hungarian history from the turn of the century to World War II, two parts of which, *Hungarian Rhapsody* (*Magyar rapszódia*, 1979) and *Allegro Barbaro* (1979), have been completed and released as a single film. Though *Hungarian Rhapsody* (the collective title) took no prizes at Cannes in 1979, Jancsó himself was awarded a Special Jury Prize for the entire body of his work.

It has often been said of Jancsó that all of his films seem to be one and the same. But this criticism against consistency of vision might apply equally to Bergman, Antonioni, Ozu, and many other masters of contemporary cinema. The mysterious, mythopoeic qualities of Jancsó's images and structures, his symbolic use of song and ritual to embody his themes of human submission and domination, his seeming closeness to the earth all remind one of Dovzhenko—but a Dovzhenko who has consciously and willfully rejected montage. Jancsó's mastery of widescreen composition and the extended long take alone would assure him a permanent place in the history of film. But Jancsó has always used this technical mastery to make films of hallucinatory beauty, profound feeling, and great intellectual depth. And it is this, above all else, that makes him one of the great artists of the modern cinema, as well as Hungary's greatest national film poet.

Other important Hungarian film-makers are: István Szabó (b. 1938—*The Age of Daydreaming* [*Álmodozások kora*, 1964]; *Father* [*Apa*, 1967]; *Love Film* [*Szerelmes film*, 1970]; *25 Fireman's Street* [*Tűzoltó utca 25*, 1973]; *Budapest Tales* [*Budapesti meszék*, 1976]; *Confidence* [*Bizalom*, 1980]); István Gaál (b. 1933—*The Falcons* [*Magasiskola*, 1970]; *Dead Landscape* [*Holt vidék*, 1971]; *Legato* [1978]); Ferenc Kósa (b. 1937—*Beyond Time* [*Nincs idő*, 1973]; *Snowfall* [*Hószkadás*, 1976]; *Portrait of a Champion* [*Küldetés*, 1979]; Sándor Sára (b. 1933—*The*

15.55 *Father* (István Szabó, 1966): Dániel Erdélyi.

15.56 *The Falcons* (István Gaál, 1970): Iván Andonov, György Bánffy.

Upthrown Stone [*Feldobott kö*, 1968]; *Pheasant Tomorrow* [*Holnap lesz fácán*, 1974]; *80 Hussars* [*80 Huszár*, 1978]); Judit Elek (b. 1937—*Lady from Constantinople* [*Sziget a szárazföldön*, 1969]; *Hungarian Village* [*Istenmezején*, 1974]; *A Simple Story* [*Egyszerű törtonét*, 1975]; *Maybe Tomorrow* [*Majd holnap*, 1980]); Márta Mészáros (b. 1931—*Girl* [*Eltávozott nap*, 1968]; *Adoption* [*Örökbefogadás*, 1975]; *Nine Months* [*Kilenc hónap*, 1976]; *The Two of Them/Women* [*Ők kétten*, 1977]; *Just Like at Home* [*Olyan, mint otthon*, 1978]; *On the Move* [*Ütközben*, 1980]); Pál Sándor (b. 1939—*Sarah, My Dear* [*Sárika, drágám*, 1971]; *The Old-Time Soccer* [*Régi idők focija*, 1974]; *Deliver Us from Evil* [*Szabadíts meg a gonosztól*, 1979]); Pál Gábor (b. 1932—*Horizon* [*Horizont*, 1971]; *Journey with Jacob* [*Utazas Jakabbal*, 1972]; *Angi Vera* [1979]); Zsolt Kédzdi-Kovács (b. 1936—*Temperate Zone* [*Mérsékelt égöv*, 1970]; *Romanticism* [*Romantika*, 1972]; *The Good Neighbor* [*A kedves szomszéd*, 1979]); Reszo Szörény (*Happy New Year* [*Búék!*, 1979]); János Zsombolyai (b. 1934—*Don't Lean Out the Window* [*Kihajolni veszélyes*, 1978]); Sándor Simó (*My Father's Happy Years* [*Apám néhány boldog éve*, 1978]); Péter Bacsó (*Electric Shock* [*Áramütés*, 1978]); Judit Ember (*Mistletoes* [*Fagyöngyök*, 1979]); Gábor Bódy (*Psyche* [1979]); Zoltán Huszárik (*Szindbad* [1971]; *Czontvary* [1980]); Péter Gothar (*A Priceless Day* [*Ajándék ez a nap*, 1980]); János Rósza (*Sunday Parents* [*Vasárnapi szülők*, 1980]); István Dárday (*Strategy* [*Harcmódor*, 1980]); Tamás Rényi (*Dead or Alive* [*Élve vagy halva*]); and Livia Gyarmathy (*Koportos* [1980]).* Until recently, few of their films have been available in the United States. But, like Kovács and Jancsó, these new Hungarian directors tend to use film as a medium for presenting positive social criticism and generating political debate. They have more freedom in this pursuit than their counterparts in any other Eastern European state, in part because the Hungarians have been committed to the gradual liberalization of their society ever since their premature rebellion in 1956.

YUGOSLAVIA

The Yugoslavs have had a national cinema only since the end of World War II. Its annual output is small, and until recently most of it was intended for domestic consumption, but one Yugoslav director has managed to achieve an international reputation. This is the Serbian Dušan Makavejev (b. 1932), who might best be described as an avant-garde satirist of great intellect. The forms of his films are experimental, and their subject is sexual and social repression, which he sees as intimately related phenomena. *Man Is Not a Bird* (*Čovek nije tica*, 1966) is about the dehumanization of the socialist worker through regimentation. In *An*

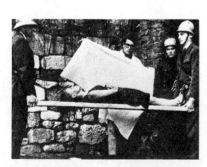

15.57 *An Affair of the Heart, or the Tragedy of the Switchboard Operator* (Dušan Makavejev, 1967): Milena Dravić.

* See Karen Jaehne, "István Szabó: Dreams of Memories," *Film Quarterly*, 32, 1 (Fall 1978), 30–41; Daniel Bickley, "Socialism and Humanism: The Contemporary Hungarian Cinema," *Cineaste*, 9, 2 (Winter 1978–79), 30–35; and Graham Petrie, *History Must Answer to Man: The Contemporary Hungarian Cinema* (London, 1979).

Affair of the Heart, or The Tragedy of the Switchboard Operator (*Ljubavni slučaj ili tragedija službenice PTT*, 1967), a film about the relationship between social structures, love, and sex, Makavejev inaugurated experiments in free association which culminated in the remarkable cinematic essay *WR—The Mysteries of the Organism* (*WR—Misterije organizma*, 1971). This film, clearly influenced by the work of Věra Chytilová in Czechoslovakia (see above), is a surrealist collage which applies the radical theories of the Austrian psychoanalyst Wilhelm Reich (1897–1957) critically to both capitalist decadence and socialist authoritarianism. Like Reich, Makavejev ultimately equates social and sexual repression. The film was temporarily banned by Yugoslav officials, and Makavejev's next film, *Sweet Movie* (1974), had to be made abroad. Like *WR*, this film uses the strategies of free association and, more especially, the manipulation of alternately attractive and repellent images to make a statement about the ugliness and craziness of the contemporary world.

Makavejev was part of an avant-garde movement within the Yugoslav cinema during the sixties known as *novi film* ("new film"). Its principal directors, with Makavejev, were the former animator Vatroslav Mimica (b. 1923—*Prometheus from Vishevica Island* [*Prometej sa otoka Viševice*, 1964]; *Monday or Tuesday* [*Pondeljak ili utorak*, 1966]; *Kaia, I'll Kill You* [*Kaja, ubit ču te*, 1967]; *Event* [*Dogadaj*, 1969]; *Nourishee* [*Hranjenik*, 1971]); Puriša Djordjević (b. 1924—*Girl* [*Devojka*, 1965]; *Dream* [*San*, 1966]; *Morning* [*Jutro*, 1967]; and *Noon* [*Podne*, 1968]; *The Cyclists* [*Biciklisti*, 1970]; *Pavle Pavlović* [1975]); Aleksandar Petrović (*Three* [*Tri*, 1965]; *I Even Met Happy Gypsies* [*Skupljači perja*, 1967], *It Rains in My Village* [*Biče skoro propast sveta*, 1969]; *The Master and Margarita* [*Majstor i Margarita*, 1972; from the novel by Bulgakov]); and Živojin Pavlović (*The Double* [*Sovražnik*, 1965; from the Dostoevsky novella]; *The Awakening of the Rat* [*Budjenje pacova*, 1966]; *When I Am Pale and Dead* [*Kad budem mrtav i beo*, 1967]; *The Ambush* [*Zaseda*, 1969]; *Red Husks* [*Rdeče klasja*, 1971]). Like the Czech New Wave, *novi film* was associated with an increasing democratization of the national culture during the late sixties, known in Yugoslavia as the "Second Revolution" (as it was called the "Prague Spring" in Czechoslovakia). Yugoslavia was spared a Soviet invasion, but the forces of reaction launched a counter-offensive against the liberal wing of the Yugoslav Communist Party which by 1972 had resulted in purges and arrests. Makavejev, Petrović, Pavlović, and other directors were expelled from the Party under the accusation of making "black films." Some, like Makavejev, went into self-imposed exile, and those who remained were encouraged to pursue the heroic historical themes canonized by socialist realism. After several years of stagnation, however, the climate for film-making in Yugoslavia improved substantially, and a new generation of stylistically conscious directors emerged, many of whom had been trained at FAMU, the Prague Film School. Among them are Goran Paskaljević (*The Beach Guard in Winter* [*Čuvar plaže u zimskom periodu*, 1976]; *The Dog Who Liked Trains* [*Pas koji je voleo vozove*, 1978]; *The Days Are Passing* [*Zemaljski dani teku*, 1979]; *Special Treatment*

15.58 Makavejev's *WR—The Mysteries of the Organism* (1971): Milena Dravić.

15.59 *WR:* Makavejev arranging Dravić's severed head(s).

15.60 *Morning* (Puriša Djordjevic, 1967).

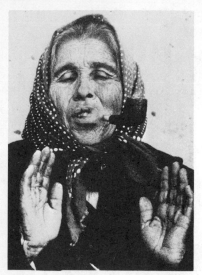

15.61 *I Even Met Happy Gypsies* (Aleksandar Petrović, 1967).

[*Poseban tretman,* 1980]); Lordan Zafranović (*Matthew's Passion* [*Mate passion,* 1977]; *Occupation in 26 Pictures* [*Okupacija u 26 skika,* 1978]); Goran Marković (*The National Class* [*Nacionalna klasa,* 1978]; *Special Education* [*Specijalno vaspitanje,* 1977]); Dejan Karaklajić (*Beloved Love/The Lovely Life· of Budimir Trajcović* [*Ljubavni život Budimira Trajcoviéa,* 1977]); Rajko Grlić (*Bravo Maestro* [1978]); Bogdan Žižić (*Don't Lean Out* [*Ne naginji se van,* 1978]); and Srdjan Karanović (*The Smell of Wild Flowers* [*Miris poljs kog cveca,* 1978]). Known collectively as the "Second Wave," these young film-makers tend to support each other's projects in the manner of the French New Wave directors; they have acquired a large and loyal domestic audience, and have won several international prizes for Yugoslav cinema. This development, coupled with the fact that several veterans of *novi film* (Makavejev, Petrović, Pavlović, and Djordjević) have returned to work within the indistry, holds promise that Yugoslavia may one day find itself in the vanguard of European cinema.*

BULGARIA

Bulgaria scarcely had a film industry at all until 1960, when annual production rose to ten features, but the next decade witnessed the appearance of some talented directors and interesting films. Binka Zhelyazkova's (b. 1923) *The Attached Balloon* (*Prevurzanyat balon,* 1966); *Side Track* (*Malko otklonenie,* 1967), co-directed by Grisha Ostrovski (b. 1918) and Todor Stoyanov (b. 1930), from a script by the poet Blaga Dimitrova; Metodi Andonov's (1932–74) *White Chamber* (*Byalata staya,* 1968); and, especially, Todor Dinov's (b. 1919) and Khristo Khristov's (b. 1926) *Iconostasis* (*Iconostassut,* 1968), similar in theme to *Andrei Rublev* (see USSR section, below), were all important films which received some distribution outside of Bulgaria. Among the younger generation, leading figures are Georgi Stoyanov (b. 1939; trained at IDHEC in Paris—*Birds and Greyhounds* [*Ptitsi i khrutki,* 1969]; *Third from the Sun* [*Tret sled sluntseto,* 1972—Bulgaria's first science fiction film]; *Panteley* [1978]); Eduard Zakhariev (b. 1938—*Hare Census* [*Prebroyavane na divite zaytsi,* 1973]; *Manly Times* [*Muzhki vremena,* 1978]; *Almost a Love Story* [*Pochti lyubovna istorya,* 1980]); Georgi Dyulgerov (b. 1943; a graduate of VGIK—*There Came the Day* [*Doyde denyat,* 1973]; *Advantage* [1978; winner of the Best Director Prize at Berlin in 1978]; *Swap* [*Trampa,* 1979]); Ivan Nichev (b. 1940—*Memory* [*Spomen,* 1974]; *Boomerang* [1979]); Stefan Dimitrov (*Hark to the Cock* [*Chui petela,* 1978]); Vladimir Yanchev (*Warmth* [*Toplo,* 1979]); and Lyudmil Kirkov (*Matriarchy* [*Matriarhat,* 1978]; *A Ray of Sunlight* [*Kratko sluntze,* 1979]). As in other Eastern European countries, the Bulgarian film industry is nationalized, but there is no state film school. Most of its film-makers are trained at FAMU in Prague and VGIK in Moscow.

15.62. *Side Track* (Grisha Ostrovski and Todor Stoyanov, 1967): Nevena Kokanova.

15.63 *Iconostasis* (Todor Dinov and Khristo Khristov, 1968): Dimiter Tashev.

---

* In one respect, it already is: the internationally famous animation studios at Zagreb have the most sophisticated facilities in the world.

ROMANIA

The Romanian film industry is more advanced than the Bulgarian by virtue of having its own film school, IATC (Institute of Theater and Film, established in 1950), and an elaborate set of studios at Buftea (completed in 1956) just outside of Bucharest. But its production output was slow until the sixties, when some important directors emerged. Among them were Sergiu Nicolaescu (b. 1930—*The Dacians* [*Dacii*, 1966]; *Michael the Brave* [*Mihai viteazul*, 1971]); Mircea Drăgan (b. 1932—*Thirst* [*Setea*, 1960—the first Romanian widescreen film]; *Lupeni 29* [1962]; [*Golgotha* [*Golgota*, 1967]); Liviu Ciulei (b. 1923—*The Danube Waves* [*Valurile Dunării*, 1959]); *The Forest of the Hanged* [*Pădurea spînzuraților*, 1965—winner of the Best Director Prize at Cannes in that year]); Lucian Pintilie (b. 1933—*Sunday at Six* [*Duminică la ora 6*, 1965]; *Reconstruction* [*Reconstituirea*, 1969]; *Ward VI* [*Pavilion VI*, 1979—made in Yugoslavia; adapted from Chekhov's novella]); and the world-famous animator Ion Popescu-Gopo (b. 1923—*The Seven Arts* [*Sapte arte*, 1958]; *Homo Sapiens* [1960]; *Kiss Me Quick* [1969]). In the seventies, Romanian cinema experienced something of a New Wave in the work of such young IATC graduates as Dan Pița (b. 1938—*Philip the Kind* [*Filip cel bun*, 1974]; *Summer Tale* [*Tanase scatiu*, 1976]; *The Prophet, Gold, and the Transylvanians* [*Profetul, aurul, si Ardelenii*, 1979]); Mircea Veroiu (b. 1941—*Seven Days* [*Sapte zile*, 1973]; *Beyond the Bridge* [*Dincolo de pod*, 1976]; *Chronicle of the Barefoot Emperors* [*Minia*, 1979]; Mircea Daneliuc (*The Race* [*Cursa*, 1976]; *Special Issue* [*Ediție speciala*, 1978]; *Microphone Test* [*Proba de microfon*, 1980]); Alexandru Tato (*The Wandering* [*Rătăcire*, 1978]); Timotei Ursu (*September* [*Septembrie*, 1978]); Stere Gulea (*The Green Grass of Home* [*Iarba verde de acasa*, 1978]); Dinu Tănase (*Dr. Poenaru* [1978]); Aleka Visarion (*Before Silence Came* [*Inainte de tačere*, 1979]); Gheorge Vitandis (*The Moment* [*Clipa*, 1979]); and Elisabeta Bostan (b. 1931—*Veronica* [1972]; *Return of Veronica* [*Veronica se întoarce*, 1973]; *Ma-Ma* [1979]). There is much hope within the Romanian industry that in the work of these young film-makers an authentic national cinema is emerging.*

15.64 *Reconstruction* (Lucian Pintilie, 1969).

THE SOVIET UNION

The Soviet Union, whose political and military presence looms so large over the other countries discussed in this chapter, has also produced

---

* Though the film industries of Yugoslavia, Bulgaria, and Romania are often treated in general studies of Eastern European cinema (such as Mira and Antonín Liehm's excellent *The Most Important Art: East European Film After 1945* [Berkeley, 1977]), there is hardly any information available in English on cinema in the non socialist Balkan countries of Turkey and Greece. The best existing sources are the International Film Guide series, published annually since 1964 by the Tantivy Press, London, and edited by Peter Cowie, and the "Balkan Film" special issue of *Variety* for October 10, 1979. Mel Schuster's *The Contemporary Greek Cinema* (Metuchen, N.J., 1979) contains some useful bibliographical and filmographical information, but it is highly suspect as a work of criticism.

some distinguished cinema since World War II. But before this could occur, it had to go through a period of Stalinist repression even darker than that experienced by its satellites. In the immediate postwar years, the Politburo, under the auspices of A. A. Zhdanov, set out to destroy the avant-garde heritage of Eisenstein, Pudovkin, and Dovzhenko, and to promote strict adherence to the tenets of socialist realism. This fanatical policy nearly destroyed the Soviet film industry as well, since standards of script approval became so rigidly ideological that only a handful of projects could be authorized for production. From nineteen fiction features in 1945, the Soviet output fell to five films in 1952.

Stalin's death in March 1953 caused a loosening of ideological criteria, and 1954 witnessed the production of forty features. By 1958, the figure had risen to 116. As the period of the political "thaw" began under Khrushchev, there was a dramatic return to the pre-Stalinist tradition of individual cinematic expression in such films as Grigori Chukhrai's (b. 1921) *The Forty-First* (*Sorok pervyi*, 1956), *Ballad of a Soldier* (*Ballada o soldate*, 1959), and *Clear Skies* (*Chistoye nebo*, 1961), and Mikhail Kalatozov's (1903–73) *The Cranes Are Flying* (*Letyat zhuravli*, 1957). When the latter took the Grand Prix at Cannes in 1958, it became the first Soviet film to win a major international award in over twenty years and gave hope that the great tradition of Soviet realism was still alive. (*Ballad of a Soldier* also took prizes at Cannes and San Francisco in 1960).

15.65 *Ballad of a Soldier* (Grigori Chukhrai, 1958): Shanna Prokhorenko, Vladimir Ivashov.

The sixties brought not a spectacular renewal but further proof that a cinema of individual expression and personal style was indeed returning to the Soviet Union. The films of Sergei Bondarchuk (b. 1920)—especially *Fate of a Man* (*Sudba cheloveka*, 1959; adapted from Mikhail Sholokhov's novel) and the four-part *War and Peace* (*Voina i mir*, 1965–67; adapted from Tolstoi)—demonstrated an impressive mixture of intimate observation and epic-scale drama. Literary adaptation was also the forte of Iosif Heifitz (b. 1906—*The Lady with the Little Dog* [*Dama s sobachkoi*, 1960] and *In the Town of S* [*V gorode "S,"* 1966]; both adapted from short stories by Chekhov), and Grigori Kozintsev (1905–73—*Don Quixote* [1956]; *Hamlet* [1964]; and *King Lear* [*Korol Lir*, 1972]). In the mid-sixties, a new generation of directors began to emerge from VGIK, the State Film School established by Lenin in 1919, where Eisenstein, Pudovkin, Dovzhenko, Yutkevich, Kozintsev, and Tisse had all been teachers (see Chapter 5). Many new directors were from the autonomous non-Russian republics: the Ukraine (Yuri Ilyenko, b. 1936—*On the Eve of Ivan Kupala Day* [*Noch nakanune Ivana Kupaly*, 1967]; *White Bird with a Black Spot* [*Belaya ptitsa s chernoy otmetinoy*, 1971]; Larissa Shepitko, 1939–80—*Heat* [*Znoi*, 1963]; *Wings* [*Krilya*, 1966]; *The Homeland of Electricity* [*Rodina electrichestva*, 1968]; *You and I* [*Ty i ya*, 1971]; *The Ascent* [*Voskhozhyeniye*, 1978]); Armenia (Sergei Paradzhanov, b. 1923—*Shadows of Forgotten Ancestors* [*Teni zabytykh predkov*, 1964—a visually beautiful retelling of Ukrainian folk-legends (photographed by Ilyenko) which won sixteen international awards]; *The Color of Pomegranates* [*Sayat Nova* [1968]); Georgia

15.66 *King Lear* (Grigori Kozintsev, 1972): Yuri Zharvet as Lear, Valentina Shendrikova as Cordelia.

15.67 Sergei Bondarchuk as Pierre in his adaptation of *War and Peace* (1965–67).

15.68 *Shadows of Forgotten Ancestors* (Sergei Paradzhanov, 1964).

(Otar Yoseliani, b. 1934—*When Leaves Fall* [*Listopad,* 1967]; *There Lived a Singing Blackbird* [*Zhil pevchiy drozd,* 1970]; Marlen Khutsiev, b. 1925—*I'm Twenty* [*Mnye dvadsat let,* 1964]; *July Rain* [*Yulskiy dozhd,* 1965]; Revaz Chkheidze, b. 1926—*Father of a Soldier* [*Otets soldata,* 1964]; Tengiz Abuladze, b. 1924—*The Appeal* [*Molba,* 1968]; *The Wishing Tree* [*Drevo zhelanya,* 1978]; Georgi Danelia, b. 1930—*The Thirty-Three* [*Tridsat tretiy,* 1965]; *Cheer Up!* [*Ne goriyu!,* 1969]; *Autumn Marathon* [*Osenny marafon,* 1979]; Georgi Shengelaya, b. 1937—*Pirosmani* [1971]); Moldavia (Emil Lotyanu, b. 1936—*Red Glades* [*Krasnye polyany,* 1966]; *The Leutary* [1972]); Lithuania (Vitautas Zhalakevichius, b. 1930—*Nobody Wanted to Die* [*Nikto nye khotiel umirat,* 1966]); Kirghizia (Bolotbek Shamshiev, b. 1941—*The Herdsman* [*Tshaban,* 1967]; *The Gunshot in the Mountain Pass* [*Vystrel na perevale,* 1969]; *Among People* [*Sredi lyudei,* 1979]); and Uzbekistan (Ali Khamraev, b. 1937—*White, White Storks* [*Belye, belye aisti,* 1967]; *Tryptych* [1978]).

15.69 *The Leutary* (Emil Lotyanu, 1972).

But the key figure among the new directors was Andrei Tarkovsky (b. 1932), whose *Andrei Rublev* (1966) won international acclaim when it was shown at Cannes in 1969. The title character is an historical figure, the Russian Orthodox monk who brought the art of religious icon painting to its zenith in the fifteenth century. Tarkovsky used Rublev's life, reconstructed in loosely connected episodes, to symbolize the conflict between Russian barbarism and idealism. The film was shelved in the Soviet Union on the grounds that it did not accurately represent history, and a substantially re-edited version was released there in 1971. Other Tarkovsky films are the much-admired science fiction film *Solaris* (1971); the autobiographical *A Mirror* (*Zerkalo,* 1974), highly reminiscent of Fellini's *Amarcord;* and *Stalker* (1979), a complex allegory of metaphysical despair.

15.70 Tarkovsky's *Andrei Rublev* (1966): Anatoli Solonitsyn in the title role.

In the seventies, progressive trends have emerged in the films of Elem Klimov (b. 1935—*Sport, Sport, Sport* [1971]; *Agony* [*Agoniya,* 1975]); Andrei Mikhalkov-Konchalovsky (b. 1937—*A Nest of Gentlefolk*

15.71 *Uncle Vanya* (Andrei Mikhalkov-Konchalovsky, 1972): Vanya (Innokenti Smoktunovski) is comforted by Sonya (Irina Kupchenko).

[*Dvoryanskoye gnezdo*, 1969; adapted from Turgenev's novel]; *Uncle Vanya* [*Dyadya Vanya*, 1970; adapted from the Chekhov play]; *In Love* [*Vlyublonnye*, 1974]);* Vasili Shukshin (1929–1974—*The Red Snowball Bush* [*Kalina krasnaya*, 1973]); Gleb Panfilov (b. 1933—*No Path Through the Flames* [*V ogne broda nyet*, 1968]; *The Debut* [*Nachalo*, 1970]; *May I Have the Floor?* [*Proshu slovo*, 1976]); Ilya Averbakh (*Confession of Love* [*Obyasnyenie v lyubovy*, 1979]); Lana Gogoberidze (*Some Interviews on Personal Questions* [*Neskolko intervyu po lichnym voprosam*, 1979]); and Nikita Mikhalkov (b. 1945—*Slave of Love* [*Raba lyubvi*, 1976]; *Five Evenings* [*Pyat' vecherov*, 1979]; *Oblomov* [1980]). But the Soviet cinema, like every other aspect of Soviet society, is still under tight state control. In the late seventies there were twenty studios producing an average of 150 films per year. Each director must graduate from VGIK or its equivalent (such as FAMU) and is assigned to a specific studio. Film scripts are no longer subject to prior approval, as in Stalin's time, but films are rated by a special commission after production, and those not approved, like *Andrei Rublev,* are either shelved or remade until they are acceptable to the censors.

As Lenin predicted in 1917, film for the Eastern Europeans has become "the most important art." It has helped to support their revolutions and to transform their societies. And it has managed to attain for itself a sophistication of form unparalleled in any other part of the world. The reasons are many, but two stand out clearly. Culturally, the countries of Eastern Europe have always had an affinity for the kind of sensuous thinking which produces great films and creates new cinematic languages. Their apprehension of art forms has historically been at once abstract and concretely structural. It is no concidence that the same milieu which produced Franz Kafka, Karel Čapek, and Eugène Ionesco also produced Věra Chytilová, Jan Němec, and Miklós Jancsó, for all of these artists fuse romanticism and cynicism into a strong sense of the existential absurd. Secondly, the countries of Eastern Europe have been plundered, colonized, occupied, or otherwise oppressed for most of film history. In situations of great social and political oppression, art often provides the only means of self-expression to which a culture can attain. And film art—"the most important art"—has traditionally served this function in Eastern Europe. As proof one has only to note the correlation between periods of political turbulence and great achievement in Eastern European film: Poland, 1954–63, for example, and Czechoslovakia, 1963–68. That so much greatness and beauty of expression should be the product of oppression is a tragedy. But that it exists at all—and has been permitted to influence the cinemas of the West—should renew our faith in the power of the human spirit not merely to survive but to prevail.

---

* Mikhalkov-Konchalovsky's epic of Siberia, *The Siberiad* (*Sibiriada*, 1979) won the Special Jury Prize at Cannes in 1979.

Wind from the East: Japan and Elsewhere

JAPAN

The Early Years

The Japanese cinema, like most other aspects of Japanese culture, evolved in nearly total isolation from the West until the end of World War II. The Edison Kinetograph had been introduced into Japan as early as 1896, and movies had almost immediately become a popular cultural form. But the Japanese cinema went through a much longer "primitive" period than the cinemas of the West (roughly 1896–1926) because of the persistence of an older, more venerable cultural form: the *kabuki* theater—ironically, the same form that had stimulated Eisenstein in elaborating his radically innovative theory of montage. *Kabuki* was a highly stylized and somewhat overwrought dramatic form deriving from the feudal Tokugawa period (1598–1867), and, because it was perennially popular, the earliest Japanese fiction films were versions of famous *kabuki* plays. As the Japanese cinema grew into a large-scale domestic industry in the first two decades of this century, the stylized conventions of *kabuki* became the mainstream conventions of Japanese narrative film, prohibiting the kind of formal experimentation then going on in the West in the work of Griffith, Eisenstein, Feuillade, and Murnau.

Two of these conventions were especially restrictive. First, all female roles in *kabuki* were played by professional female impersonators known as *onnagata* or *oyama*. This situation existed in most Japanese films until well into the twenties, militating against even the simplest sort of photographic realism. Second, and much more damaging to the formal development of Japanese film, was the convention in *kabuki* of the *benshi*—a commentator who stood at the side of the stage and narrated the action for the audience. In the cinema, the *benshi* eliminated the troublesome necessity for titles, but he also eliminated the necessity for cinematic narrative. Why use intercut close-ups, camera angles, montage, and the like, when the *benshi* could interpret screen images for the audience verbally? In short, the presence of a human, *verbal* narrator permitted Japanese *cinematic* narrative to remain at a relatively crude stage of development until 1923, when an earthquake leveled the cities of Tokyo and Yokohama and, with them, the physical facilities of the entire Japanese film industry. After the quake, the industry, like much of Japan itself, had to be rebuilt from scratch, and one result was a turning away from the past and

16.1 *A Page of Madness* (Teinosuke Kinugasa, 1926): Masao Inoue.

an increased receptivity to modern ideas. The *oyama* rapidly disappeared, and Japanese films adopted more sophisticated styles, such as the newly discovered Western modes of naturalism (in Minoru Murata's* *The Street Juggler* [*Machi no tejinashi,* 1924]) and expressionism (Teinosuke Kinugasa's *A Page of Madness* [*Kurutta ippeiji,* 1926] and *Crossways* [*Jujiro,* 1928]). The *benshi,* many of whom had become stars in their own right, would remain a potent force in Japanese cinema until 1932, some years after the introduction of sound, but their stranglehold on the industry was broken by re-organization, so that the director could finally become the major creative force in Japanese film, as he already was in most countries of the West.

By 1925 the *kabuki*-oriented cinema had been replaced by a new director's cinema consciously divided into two large genres or types which persist to this day: the *jidai-geki,* or period film set before 1868 (the year marking the beginning of the Meiji Restoration, 1868–1912, and the abolition of feudal Japan), and the *gendai-geki,* or film of contemporary life. Both genres are obviously very broad, and each has come to contain a large number of sub-types. Currently, for example, the *jidai-geki* encompasses the *chambara,* or sword-fight film, which focuses on the figure of the masterless *samurai* ("warrior") or *ronin;* the historical romance; and most ghost films. The *gendai-geki* includes such disparate types as the lower-middle-class comedy-drama (*shomin-geki*), the "children's film" (in which the inanities and corruptions of the adult world are satirized by presenting them from a child's point of view), and the *yakuza-eiga,* or modern gangster film. The years 1926 to 1932 saw the appearance of the first major works of Japanese cinema in the beautiful period films of Teinosuke Kinugasa (b. 1896) and Kenji Mizoguchi (see below), and in the *shomin-geki* of Yasujiro Shimazu (1897–1945), Heinosuke Gosho (b. 1902), Mikio Naruse (1905–69), and—above all— Yasujiro Ozu (see below). In careers that extended well into the post-war period, both Mizoguchi and Ozu became two of the three classical masters of the Japanese film; the third was Akira Kurosawa (see below), whose career did not begin until the middle years of World War II.

Sound

Sound entered the Japanese cinema more gradually and more smoothly than in the countries of the West, because it was less of a novelty for both audiences and film-makers. Japanese movies had always "talked" through the mediation of the *benshi,* and, far from retarding the formal development of Japanese cinema (as it had for a brief period in the West), the coming of synchronously recorded sound actually accelerated it by permanently liberating films from subservience to a live narrator. The first successful talkie, Gosho's comic *shomin-geki, The Neighbor's Wife and Mine* (*Madamu to nyobo,* 1931), ranked very high in formal achievement among early sound films generally. But the addition of sound was a leisurely process in Japan. In 1932 only forty-five feature-

---

* Japanese names in this chapter are given in the Western style, with the surname last.

length sound films were produced out of a total of four hundred, and silent features continued to be made until 1937 (the most important Japanese film of 1932, for example, was Ozu's silent "children's comedy" *I Was Born, But . . .* [*Umarete wa mita keredo*]). Other changes were swifter and ultimately more significant.

One important consequence of the re-organization was the complete monopolization of the Japanese film industry by three, and later five, major production companies, called *zaibatsu* (Japanese for "conglomerate"), through the Japan Motion Picture Producers' Association (founded 1925) in a pattern remarkably similar to the American studio system. As in the American system, each of the three Japanese studios during the thirties (Nikkatsu, founded 1914; Shochiku, founded 1920; and Toho, founded 1932) had been formed by the ruthless absorption of smaller companies. And, as in the American system, they existed solely for the purpose of mass-producing films for mass consumption through a highly efficient, rigidly structured production process. With some modification, this system still operates in Japan today, and until the recent economic recession it was the most productive in the world, averaging over four hundred features a year. One aspect of the Japanese studio system which differed from the American, however—and which differs to this day as part of an ingrained cultural pattern—was the hierarchical master-pupil relationship which existed between directors and their assistants. For an aspiring young film-maker to rise within the system, he had to apprentice himself to an older, more experienced one and literally prove his worth (that is, his competence to turn a profit for his studio) before being permitted to direct on his own. Thus Yasujiro Shimazu, who founded the *shomin-geki* in the early twenties, himself had been taught by the first-generation Shochiku director Kaoru Osanai, and in the course of his own long career trained ten younger directors, including the now-prominent Keisuke Kinoshita (b. 1912), Masaki Kobayashi (b. 1916), and Kaneto Shindo (b. 1912). Another unique aspect of the Japanese studio system is the paternalistic relationship of the director to his entire cast and crew. It seems clear that both the apprenticeship system of direction and the familial organization of production recapitulate an element deeply rooted in the Japanese character, which may best be described as feudalism.

The Meiji Restoration of 1868–1912 had provided a brief respite of enlightenment after eight hundred years of feudal culture. In 1868, the fifteen-year-old Emperor Meiji abolished the Tokugawa *shogunate,* a military dictatorship which had ruled Japan in the legitimate emperor's stead since 1185, and outlawed the *samurai,* or warrior, class, which had supported it. But these centuries-old feudal institutions did not disappear. Instead, they translated themselves into modern terms and emerged in the late nineteen-twenties as the general staff and officer corps of Japan's powerful military establishment, and by the end of 1931 they had virtually re-asserted their control of the government. As sound came to the Japanese cinema in the early thirties, militarism, patriotism, and xenophobia pervaded every segment of Japanese society, leading first to Japan's war of aggression against China in 1937 and ultimately to its

16.2 *I Was Born, But . . .* (Yasujiro Ozu, 1932): Hideo Sugawara, Tokkan Kozo.

16.3 *Man-Slashing, Horse-Piercing Sword* (Daisuke Ito, 1930): Ryunosuke Tsukigata, Junichi Amano.

catastrophic confrontation with the United States. As the new mood of ultra-nationalism gripped Japan, a new film genre appeared, opposing it—the left-wing "tendency" film, which, in either period or contemporary guise, was devoted to social criticism of the established order. The founder of the tendency film was Daisuke Ito (b. 1898), whose violently realistic *jidai-geki* of the late twenties—*Servant* (*Gero*, 1927), *Diary of Chuji's Travel's* (*Chuji tabinikki*, 1927–28), *Ooka's Trial* (*Ooka seidan*, 1928), and the famous *Man-Slashing, Horse-Piercing Sword* (*Zanjin zamba ken*, 1930)—all attacked the feudalism of the Tokugawa period. Most tendency films, however, were *shomin-geki* dealing with contemporary social problems which availed themselves of the heightened realism made possible by sound. The most important of these social realist films were Kinugasa's *Before Dawn* (*Reimei izen*, 1931); Shimazu's *O-Koto and Sasuke* (*O-Koto to Sasuke*, 1935); Gosho's *Everything That Lives* (*Ikitoshi ikerumono*, 1936); Shiro Toyoda's *Young People* (*Wakai hito*, 1937); Tomu Uchida's *The Naked Town* (*Hadaki no machi*, 1937); Ozu's first sound film, *The Only Son* (*Hitori musuko*, 1936); and Mizoguchi's two masterpieces, thought to be the greatest of Japanese pre-war sound films, *Osaka Elegy* (*Naniwa ereji*, 1936) and *Sisters of the Gion* (*Gion no shimai*, 1936).

War

16.4 *Humanity and Paper Balloons* (Sadao Yamanaka, 1937): Sukezo Suketakaya, Chojuro Kawarazaki, Kanemon Nakamura.

In response to the tendency film and other dissident elements in the culture, the government, through its Ministry of Propaganda, imposed state censorship whose severity increased as the thirties wore on. In 1937, to the horror of the progressive film-makers grouped around Mizoguchi and Ozu, Sadao Yamanaka's (1907–38) humanistic film of life in the Tokugawa era, *Humanity and Paper Balloons* (*Ninjo kami-fusen*, 1937), was suppressed and its young director ordered to the Chinese front, where he was killed shortly after arriving. In addition to censoring what it did not like, the Ministry of Propaganda began to actively involve itself in production, demanding war films which showed Japanese military prowess in battle. Ironically, the first two films commissioned by the ministry—Tomotaka Tasaka's *Five Scouts* (*Go-nin no sekkohei*, 1938) and *Mud and Soldiers* (*Tsuchi to heitai*, 1939)—were profoundly humanistic accounts of men in battle which compare favorably with the great pre-war pacifist films of the West, G. W. Pabst's *Westfront 1918* (1930) and Lewis Milestone's *All Quiet on the Western Front* (1930). Kimisaburo Yoshimura's (b. 1911) highly regarded *The Story of Tank Commander Nishizumi* (*Nishizumi senshacho-den*, 1940) was equally humane and individualistic in its outlook. It was almost as though Japanese directors had carried the banner of social realism into the war itself. Finally, after the attack on Pearl Harbor in December 1941, the Japanese government issued strict guidelines and established quotas for the production of films on specific "national policy" themes. Then, following the example of Goebbels in Nazi Germany, it consolidated the ten existing studios into two large corporations under the Office of Public Informa-

16.5 *Five Scouts* (Tomotaka Tasaka, 1938): Isamu Kosugi (center).

tion to insure that the guidelines would be adhered to. The result was a wave of conventional war propaganda films, both narrative and documentary, with titles like *Flaming Sky* (*Moyuru ozora*, Yutaka Abe, 1941), *The Suicide Troops of the Watch Tower* (*Boro no kesshitai*, Tadashi Imai, 1942), *The War at Sea from Hawaii to Malaya* (*Hawai-Marei oki kaisen*, Kajiro Yamamoto, 1942), and *Generals, Staff, and Soldiers* (*Shogun to sambo to hei*, Tetsu Taguchi, 1943). Since little battle footage was available from the Pacific at this point in the war, these films made remarkably sophisticated use of special effects and models to replicate battle action—a practice which became common in such films as the war progressed and which helps to explain the consistently high quality of special effects in post-war Japanese science fiction films.

16.6 Expert model work and special effects were used to simulate live battle action in *The War at Sea from Hawaii to Malaya* (Kajiro Yamamoto, 1942).

As the war grew more intense, virtually all genres, including the children's film (*Chocolate and Soldiers* [*Chokoreto to heitai*, Také Sado, 1942]) and the middle-class comedy-drama (*The Daily Battle* [*Nichijo no tatakai*, Yasujiro Shimazu, 1944]), were pressed into the service of national policy. Some directors, like Ozu (*The Brothers and Sisters of the Toda Family* [*Toda-ke no kyodai*, 1941]) and Gosho (*New Snow* [*Shinsetsu*, 1942]), protested the war by more or less ignoring it. Others, like Mizoguchi (*The Story of the Late Chrysanthemums* [*Zangiku monogatari*, 1939]; *Woman of Osaka* [*Naniwa onna*, 1940] and Hiroshi Inagaki (b. 1905—*The Life of Matsu the Untamed* [*Muho Matsu no issho*, 1943]), avoided militaristic themes by turning to the *Meiji-mono* (historical dramas set in the enlightened Meiji era), but both were forced by the government to make *jidai-geki* set in the feudal Tokugawa period as well (Mizoguchi's *The Forty-Seven Loyal Ronin, Parts I* and *II* [*Genroku chushingura*, 1941–42]; Inagaki's *The Last Days of Edo* [*Edo saigo no hi*, 1941]). Akira Kurosawa began his career as a director with a *Meiji-mono* about the founder of judo, *The Judo Story* (*Sanshiro sugata*, 1943), which the Ministry of Propaganda liked so much (for the wrong reasons) that it sponsored a sequel, *The Judo Story, Part II* (*Zoku sanshiro sugata*, 1945).

Occupation

When World War II ended on August 14, 1945, much of Japan lay in ruins. The massive fire-bombing of its sixty major cities from March through June 1945, and the dropping of atomic bombs on Hiroshima and Nagasaki, had resulted in some 900,000 casualties and led to the total paralysis of civilian life. On the morning of August 15, when Emperor Hirohito broadcast to his subjects the news that the war had ended and that Japan had lost, there was widespread disbelief. Never in their history had the Japanese people been defeated or occupied, and so the circumstances of the American Occupation, 1945–52, were utterly unique.

The Occupation forces were led by General Douglas MacArthur, whose title of Supreme Commander for the Allied Powers lent his administration the acronym "SCAP." SCAP's primary objective was the "democratization" of Japan; to this end it imposed strict censorship through its Civil Information and Education Section (CI&E). Nearly half of Japan's movie theaters had been destroyed by Allied bombing (there were only 845 in operation in October 1945), but most of the studios remained intact, and films continued to be produced despite the surrender. With the officially published vow that "Japan will never in the future disturb the peace of the world," CI&E demanded that these films do nothing to glorify feudalism, imperialism, or militarism—which necessarily eliminated the whole genre of *jidai-geki* and encouraged the production of *Meiji-mono* and films of contemporary life. Of the 554 wartime and post-war films confiscated by SCAP, 225 were banned on the grounds that they promoted anti-democratic tendencies, and many of them were destroyed.

Between 1946 and 1950, the Japanese could hardly have been said to control their own film industry. In an attempt at de-monopolization, SCAP broke up the huge war-time *zaibatsu* in 1946 (they regrouped themselves into five—later six—major corporations as soon as the Occupation had ended). During these years SCAP attempted to ferret out "war criminals" within the industry and permitted CI&E to dictate the subject-matter of Japanese films. These phenomena were significant but short-lived. Of more lasting consequence was the great influx of American films into Japan for the first time since the beginning of the war—a time when domestic production had reached a very low ebb. (Only sixty-seven indigenous films were released in 1946; the figure for 1927 had been over seven hundred.) There is some evidence that the newly available films of Frank Capra, John Ford, Howard Hawks, and Orson Welles had an influence upon the first post-war generation of Japanese directors comparable to that which they had upon the *cinéastes* of the French New Wave. In any case, many Japanese studios during the Occupation found it politic to copy American styles and themes. The only domestic themes thoroughly endorsed by SCAP were those dealing with the new social freedoms made possible by democracy, especially the emancipation of women. Mizoguchi, Kinugasa, Kinoshita, Kurosawa, Gosho, Yoshimura, and Ozu all made fine films on the subject during the Occupation. During this period, Akira Kurosawa (b. 1910) made four films—*The Men Who Tread on the Tiger's Tail* (*Tora no o o fumu otoko tachi*, 1945), *No Regrets for Our Youth* (*Waga seishun ni kuinashi*, 1946), *Drunken Angel* (*Yoidore tenshi*, 1948), and *Stray Dog* (*Nora inu*, 1949)—which established him as one of the great post-war directors. But it was not until his *Rashomon* (1950) unexpectedly won the Golden Lion at the Venice International Film Festival in 1951 that the real post-war renaissance of Japanese cinema began.*

---

* For an extremely sophisticated argument that there was no post-war renaissance but rather a "regression," and that the "golden age" of Japanese film was the period 1930–45, see Noël Burch's dialectical analysis of Japanese film discourse, *To the Distant Observer: Form and Meaning in Japanese Cinema*, revised and edited by Annette Michelson (Berkeley, 1979). See also David Bordwell, "Our Dream-Cinema: Western Historiography and the Japanese Film," in *Film Reader 4*, ed. Blaine Allan et al. (Evanston, Ill., 1979), 45–62.

16.7 Akira Kurosawa's post-war detective film *Stray Dog* (1949): Toshiro Mifune, Takashi Shimura.

16.8 *Rashomon* (Akira Kurosawa, 1950): the bandit (Toshiro Mifune), the husband (Masayuki Mori), the wife (Machiko Kyo).

Rashomon, Kurosawa, and the Post-War Renaissance

Based on two short stories by Ryunosuke Akutagawa (1892–1927), *Rashomon* is a film about the relativity of truth in which four conflicting versions of the same event are offered by four equally credible (or equally incredible) narrators. In medieval Japan, three men take cover from a rainstorm under the crumbling Rashomon gate of the ancient capital of Kyoto. Two of them, a woodcutter and a priest, have just come from police headquarters, and they tell the third a strange tale which becomes the main portion of the film in flashback. The woodcutter explains how he had earlier found the body of a nobleman in the woods; the man had been stabbed to death but the weapon was missing. The priest had encountered this same nobleman traveling with his wife on the road shortly before the murder. The woodcutter and the priest met at police headquarters, where both had come to give evidence. While they were there, the police captured a bandit (played by Toshiro Mifune [b. 1920]—a brilliant actor and Kurosawa's constant collaborator) who confessed to killing the man and who gave the following account, which is related in the framing story by the woodcutter: The bandit was asleep in the woods when the nobleman passed by with his beautiful wife. Consumed with desire for her, he tricked the husband, tied him to a tree, and raped the wife. Afterwards the woman forced the two men into a duel in which the husband was killed. Next, the wife was brought to police headquarters, where she gave her version of the truth, recounted in the framing story by the priest. As she told it, the bandit left after the rape, and her husband spurned her for being so easily dishonored. She fainted from grief and awakened to find a dagger in her husband's breast. The priest and the woodcutter then inform the stranger that a third version was offered by the spirit of the dead husband, speaking through the lips of a medium. He testified that after the rape his wife begged the bandit to kill him and carry her away. The bandit refused, the wife ran off into the woods, and the husband committed suicide with the dagger, which he felt someone remove from his body after his death. Finally, the woodcutter admits to the priest and the stranger that he actually witnessed the whole sequence of events from a hiding-place in the forest: "There was no dagger in that man's breast," he says, "He was killed by a sword thrust." The woodcutter's story is that both men were cowards and had to be goaded into the duel by the shrewish woman. In the event, he says, the bandit killed the husband almost by accident, and the woman ran off into the woods. But this "objective" account of things is called into question when the stranger accuses the woodcutter of having stolen the missing dagger. Thus all four versions of the truth are shown to be relative to the perspectives of the individual participants in the action. Even the woodcutter's detached account suggests the possibility of distortion. Kurosawa seems to suggest that reality or truth does not exist independently of human consciousness, identity, and perception. It is small wonder, then, that Alain Resnais claimed *Rashomon* as the inspiration for his own film about the enigmatic nature of reality, *L'année dernière à Marienbad* (1961; see Chapter 13).

Cinematically, *Rashomon* is a masterpiece, and its release marked the emergence of Kurosawa as a major figure on the international scene. Each of the four tales has a unique style appropriate to the character of its teller, but the film as a whole is characterized by many complicated tracking shots, superbly paced editing, and thematically significant composition of the frame in depth. The camera seems to be almost constantly in motion, much of it violent, and Kurosawa uses many subjective shots to represent "reality" from the perspective of the individual narrators. Ironically, the Japanese had been somewhat reluctant to enter *Rashomon* in the Venice Festival, thinking that foreigners would misunderstand it. They were as amazed as they were pleased when the film won the Golden Lion, but their industry was quick to capitalize on its success. From 1951 through the present, the Japanese have consistently submitted entries to international film festivals, and they have achieved recognition and respect for their cinema all over the world. Between 1951 and 1965, the Japanese cinema experienced a renaissance unprecedented in the history of any national cinema, as vast new export markets opened in the West and as Japanese films won prizes in festival after festival. Established figures like Mizoguchi and Ozu produced their greatest work during this period, and relatively new figures like Kurosawa, Shindo, Ichikawa, and Kobayashi all made films that stand among the classics of the international cinema.

It was Kurosawa who was to become the most famous Japanese director in the West, perhaps because his films are more Western in construction than those of his peers. He followed *Rashomon* with an adaptation of Dostoevsky's *The Idiot* (*Hakuchi*, 1951) and the brilliant *shomin-geki Ikiru* (*Living/To Live*, 1952), a fatalistic yet ultimately affirmative account of the last months of a minor bureaucrat dying of cancer. In 1954 Kurosawa produced the epic *jidai-geki Seven Samurai* (*Shichinin no samurai*), which many critics regard as his greatest work. Over eighteen months in production, this spectacular and deeply humanistic film tells the story of a small village which hires seven unemployed *samurai* to

16.9 *Ikiru* (Akira Kurosawa, 1952): Takashi Shimura, Miki Odagiri.

16.10 *The Seven Samurai* (Akira Kurosawa, 1954): Toshiro Mifune, Yoshio Inaba, Takashi Shimura, Ko Kimura, Daisuke Kato, Seiji Miyaguchi, Minoru Chiaki.

defend it against bandit raids in sixteenth-century Japan, an era in which the *samurai* as a class were rapidly dying out (in fact, the bandits are themselves unemployed *samurai*). As an epic, *Seven Samurai* clearly ranks with the greatest films of Griffith and Eisenstein, and cinematically it is a stunning achievement. As several critics have pointed out, the entire film is a tapestry of motion. Complicated tracking shots compete with equally elaborate and fast-paced editing to create a film whose constant prevailing tempo is that of war punctuated by ever shorter intervals of peace. For the battle between bandits and *samurai* which concludes the film, Kurosawa created a montage sequence which rivals the massacre on the Odessa Steps in *Potemkin* in its unprecedented combination of rapid tracking shots with telephoto close-ups of the action at various decelerated camera speeds. *Seven Samurai* was honored on a global scale, receiving the *Kinema Jumpo* Award in Japan, the Silver Lion at Venice, and the Academy Award for Best Foreign Film in the United States. It was remade by John Sturges as *The Magnificent Seven* (1960), with its setting transposed to the American West, and it stands firmly behind the theme and style of Sam Peckinpah's classical Western *The Wild Bunch* (1969; see Chapter 17).

16.11 The *samurai* enter the village.

16.12 The three peasants who had been sent to hire the *samurai* return to find the villagers terrified of their guests.

16.13. A lyrical interlude between a village girl and the youngest *samurai:* Keiko Tsushima, Ko Kimura.

16.14 Without waiting to be attacked, the *samurai* storm the bandits' river fortress and burn it to the ground.

16.15 In the attack, one of their number is killed and many of the bandits escape.

16.16 The remaining bandits launch an all-out attack on the village.

16.17 In the final battle in the rain, all of the bandits are killed, but only three *samurai* survive. (Note the flattening of perspective produced by the telephoto lens.) On the following day, the *samurai* prepare to leave: "We've lost again . . . the farmers are the winners. Not us."

16.18 The death of Lord Washizu in Kurosawa's *Throne of Blood* (1957): Toshiro Mifune.

16.19 Kurosawa's *Red Beard* (1965): Toshiro Mifune, Yuzo Kayama.

Kurosawa's other masterpiece of the fifties was a brilliant adaptation of Shakespeare's *Macbeth* as a *jidai-geki* set in medieval Japan. Despite the cultural transposition, *Throne of Blood/Cobweb Castle* (*Kumonosu-jo*, 1957) is perhaps the greatest version of Shakespeare on film. The supernatural element of the drama was enhanced by the sparing use of ritualized conventions from classical *noh* plays* and by shooting the exteriors in the misty forests around Mount Fuji. Like *Seven Samurai*, *Throne of Blood* concludes with an elaborate montage sequence in which the Macbeth figure, Lord Washizu (Toshiro Mifune), is immolated by a hail of arrows.

In *Seven Samurai* and *Throne of Blood,* Kurosawa had succeeded in elevating the *jidai-geki* from a simple action genre to an art form. After another literary adaptation, this time of Maxim Gorki's play *The Lower Depths* (*Donzoko,* 1957), he continued the practice with three superb *chambara—The Hidden Fortress* (*Kakushi toride no san-akunin,* 1958), *Yojimbo* (*The Bodyguard,* 1961), and *Sanjuro* (*Tsubaki sanjuro,* 1962). Though these films lack the thematic depth of his earlier *jidai-geki,* they are masterworks of widescreen composition and rival their predecessors in visual richness. Kurosawa has worked slowly since the early sixties, producing *High and Low* (*Tengoku to jigoku,* 1963), a detective film based on a novel by Ed McBain; *Red Beard* (*Aka hige,* 1965), the story of a young doctor's education in late-Tokugawa Japan; and his first film in color, *Dodes'kaden* (*Dodesukaden,* 1970), an unstructured narrative

16.20 Masterful widescreen composition in Kurosawa's *The Hidden Fortress* (1958) and *Yojimbo* (1961). Compare the American and Italian-American Westerns of the same period; see Chapter 12.

about the lives of the very poor in a Tokyo slum. In 1976, after six years of silence, Kurosawa gave the cinema another masterpiece—*Dersu Uzala,* a Soviet-Japanese co-production shot in 70mm with six-track sound. Set in the forests of eastern Siberia at the turn of the century, it is a

---

* Developed in medieval Japan, *noh* is a form of ritualized drama which treats mythic, historical, or literary themes. Whereas the more popular *kabuki* theater tends towards extravagance and relates events which are in the process of occurring, *noh* theater is more intellectually refined and always deals with events that have occurred in the past. Its settings and gestures are symbolic, and its language is formal and highly allusive. Much use is made of mime and masks. Though *Throne of Blood* is Kurosawa's only film to employ *noh* elements throughout, many of his films use *noh* choruses (*The Men Who Tread on the Tiger's Tail*), music (*Seven Samurai*), and plot structure (*The Hidden Fortress*).

16.21 The famous "explosion of blood" from the final sword-fight in Kurosawa's *Sanjuro* (1962): Toshiro Mifune, Tatsuya Nakadai.

portrait of the friendship that grows between an aging hunter of the Goldi tribe and a young Russian surveyor. By 1977 the film had won the Grand Prize at the Moscow Festival and an Acadeny Award in America. In 1980 Kurosawa completed *Shadow Warrior* (*Kagemusha*), a tragic *jidai-geki* set during the sixteenth-century civil wars; this film was co-winner of the Grand Prix at Cannes in the year of its release.

Today, Kurosawa is unquestionably a giant of the international cinema. Like Bergman and Antonioni, he is the true *auteur* of his films—he sets up his own shots, does his own editing, and writes his own scripts. He is probably more conscious of Western styles of film-making than any of his Japanese peers and has always claimed a great stylistic debt to John Ford (the American cinema's recent debt to Kurosawa has already been noted). Kurosawa was also a professional student of Western painting before he entered the cinema. It would be a mistake, however, to assume that the Western "look" of his films betokens Western values. Kurosawa has sometimes been mistaken by Western critics for a humanist. He is in fact a fatalist, or at least an existentialist, in subtle but thoroughly Japanese terms. His vision of human experience is firmly rooted in the value system of feudal Japan. Zen Buddhism, the *samurai* code of *bushido* ("the way of the warrior"—loyalty and self-sacrifice), and the master-pupil relationship are all important ethical components of his films. Because of his great universality of spirit, we can recognize in Kurosawa much of ourselves, but we would also do well to remember that Kurosawa's dearest friend was Yukio Mishima, the Nobel Prize–winning novelist and founder of a large private army who committed *hara-kiri* in 1972 in disgust at the dwindling of feudalism in Japanese culture.

Kenji Mizoguchi

More clearly Oriental in form than the work of Kurosawa is that of Kenji Mizoguchi (1898–1956), a director whose career spanned thirty-four years and encompassed ninety feature films. Like Kurosawa, Mizoguchi studied Western painting as a student, but his themes and visual style were purely Japanese. He began his career as an actor for the Nikkatsu studio and became a director there in 1922. Mizoguchi's first films were mainly thrillers and melodramas adapted from popular literature (such as *Harbor in the Fog* [*Kiri no minato*, 1923]), but in 1925 he began

16.22 *Sisters of the Gion* (Kenji Mizoguchi, 1936): Isuzu Yamada, Yoko Umemura.

16.23 Mizoguchi's *Women of the Night* (1948): Kumeko Urabe, Kinuyo Tanaka. Note the dominance of diagonals relative to the borders of the frame.

to make films dealing with the impact of urbanization on Japanese life (*Tokyo March* [*Tokyo koshin-kyoku*, 1929]; *Metropolitan Symphony* [*Tokai kokyogaku*, 1929]). Few of his silent films have survived, but those which do reveal an almost painterly evocation of atmosphere and mood. After a politically committed film about the urban working class, *Nevertheless, They Go On* (*Shikamo karera wa yuku*, 1931), Mizoguchi turned increasingly to period films to avoid government censorship. Yet his two greatest films of the thirties, *Osaka Elegy* (*Naniwa ereji*, 1936— banned in 1940) and *Sisters of the Gion* (*Gion no shimai*, 1936), both have contemporary settings and announce Mizoguchi's major thematic concern: the position of women within the social order and the redemptive power of their love. The films also contain Mizoguchi's first consistent use of a technique which would become the hallmark of his later films—the extended long take composed in depth for a static camera. Critics have compared *Osaka Elegy* and *Sisters of the Gion* with Jean Renoir's pre-war films (see Chapter 9) in terms of both their humanism and their *mise-en-scène*. Like Renoir, Mizoguchi constantly sought ways to portray internal states through external means, and he felt that in the long take he had discovered what he called "the most precise and specific expression for intense psychological moments." Diagonal composition leading the eye outward toward the world beyond the frame, fluid and thematically significant moving camera shots, luminous photography (often by Kazuo Miyagawa), and minimal cutting are other characteristics of Mizoguchi's mature style which link him with the *mise-en-scène* tradition of the West.

During the war, Mizoguchi was forced to make a certain number of government-policy films, although he was able to confine them to *jidai-geki* like *The Forty-Seven Loyal Ronin, Parts I and II* (*Genroku chushingura*, 1941–42). After the surrender, he continued to examine the condition of Japanese women in films like *Women of the Night* (*Yoru no onnatachi*, 1948), which concerns prostitution during the Occupation. But in the last six years of his life, with the Occupation ended, Mizoguchi produced his greatest masterpieces. In rapid succession he shot five films which are thought to be among the most beautiful and haunting ever made. *The Life of Oharu* (*Saikaku ichidai onna*, 1952), winner of the International Director's Prize at the 1952 Venice Film Festival, is a humane critique of feudalism centered around the degraded life of a prostitute in seventeenth-century Kyoto. *Ugetsu* (*Ugetsu monogatari*, 1953), which won the Silver Lion at Venice in 1953, is set during the feudal wars of the sixteenth century. Two ambitious young men leave their wives to seek wealth and glory. In the course of a long and picaresque pilgrimage, they both come to realize that nothing they have gained on their journey is worth the love of the women they have cast away. Simultaneously realistic, allegorical, and supernatural, *Ugetsu* is the most stylistically perfect of all Mizoguchi's works, and many critics regard it as the greatest Japanese film ever made. *Gion Festival Music* (*Gion bayashi*, 1953) is a highly successful remake of *Sisters of the Gion*; but with *Sansho the Bailiff* (*Sansho dayu*, 1954), set in the eleventh century, and *Crucified Lovers/A Story from Chikamatsu* (*Chikamatsu monogatari*, 1954), set in the sev-

16.24 *Mise-en-scène* aesthetics in Mizoguchi's *Ugetsu* (1953): luminous photography, diagonal composition, the long take. Machiko Kyo, Masayuki Mori.

enteenth century, Mizoguchi continued his concentrated scrutiny of the feudal social system and its impact upon women, although neither film was the equal of *The Life of Oharu* or *Ugetsu*. *The Empress Yang Kwei-fei* (*Yokihi*, 1955) and *New Tales of the Taira Clan* (*Shin heike monogatari*, 1955) were Mizoguchi's only films in color, and although both are decidedly "popular" in their content, they show a marvelously expressive sense of the medium. Characteristically, the last film Mizoguchi completed before his death in 1956 was *Street of Shame* (*Akasen chitai*, 1956), a fictionalized account of the lives of Tokyo prostitutes.

Mizoguchi is popularly perceived in the West, which has seen only about a tenth of his total opus, as a maker of period films. Indeed, as Kurosawa remarked when the elder director died, "Now that Mizoguchi is gone, there are very few directors left who can see the past clearly and realistically."[1] But when Mizoguchi looked at the past, it was always as a mirror for the present. His lifelong critique of feudalism, his sympathetic concern for the social and psychological condition of women, his simple humanism in the face of a callous world are the thematic bridges uniting his period and his contemporary films. Furthermore, his absolute mastery of decor, the long take, and the moving camera make Mizoguchi one of the great *mise-en-scène* directors of the international cinema, a rival of Murnau, Ophüls, and Welles, to name only his contemporaries. Nevertheless, his nearly transcendental visual style finally makes Mizoguchi unique in the history of film. As the French New Wave director Jacques Rivette said of him, "Mizoguchi, alone, imposes a feeling of a unique world and language, is answerable only to himself."[2]

Yasujiro Ozu and the Use of Off-Screen Space

The Japanese director whose work most expresses traditional Japanese values is undeniably Yasujiro Ozu (1903–63), who, for that reason, was the last of the three great masters of Japanese cinema to be discovered by the West. As a boy in Tokyo, Ozu spent much of his time in moviehouses, entranced by Italian spectacles like *Quo vadis?* (1913), and by American comedy, melodrama, and romance (he particularly admired Lubitsch and Griffith). After briefly attending Waseda University, he became a script-writer at the Shochiku studio, where he was to work for the rest of his life. Here he soon became an assistant director under the tutelage of Tadamoto Okubo, a specialist in light comedies known as "nonsense-*mono*," and by 1927 Ozu had directed his first feature, a *jidai-geki* entitled *The Sword of Penitence* (*Zange no yaiba*). This film was unremarkable, except for the fact that it was written by Kogo Noda, who was to become Ozu's lifelong collaborator and friend.

For a time, Ozu specialized in nonsense-*mono* in the manner of Okubo, but he soon turned his attention to the more serious genre of *shomin-geki,* social comedies which concentrate on the daily lives and interpersonal relationships of the members of lower-middle-class families. Ozu seems to have chosen this genre because he found in the routine lives of these people—in their necessary facility for coping with hardship—a perfect expression of the Zen Buddhist conception of *mono no aware,* a "sympathetic sadness" at the harshness of the natural order which ultimately enables one to transcend it. In Western culture, the lower middle class has traditionally been considered a fit subject not for art but rather, and at best, for soap opera and low comedy. In Japan, however, the kind of simple life-style necessarily practiced by the people of this class is highly regarded as the most authentic, valid, and human way to live, unencumbered as it is by false values, pretensions, and distortions. As Barbara Wolf has put it, "After all, what could possibly be so real as to be born, make a living, bring forth a new generation and then die?"[3] Nearly all of Ozu's fifty-four films deal with the life cycles and life crises of lower-middle-class family members, and they are all very much alike. In a sense, they are all parts of the same film, often using the same actors, that the director was driven to make continuously throughout his career. Even the titles seem barely distinguishable from one another: *I Graduated, But . . .* (*Daigaku wa deta keredo,* 1929), *Life of an Office Worker* (*Kaishain seikatsu,* 1930), *I Flunked, But . . .* (*Rakudai wa shita keredo,* 1930), *The Chorus of Tokyo* (*Tokyo no gassho,* 1931), *I Was Born, But . . .* (*Umarete wa mita keredo,* 1932), *The Story of Floating Weeds* (*Ukigusa monogatari,* 1934), *Tokyo's a Nice Place* (*Tokyo yoi toko,* 1935), *College Is a Nice Place* (*Daigaku yoi toko,* 1936), *The Only Son* (*Hitori musuko,* 1936), *There Was a Father* (*Chichi ariki,* 1942), *Late Spring* (*Banshun,* 1949), *Early Summer* (*Bakushu,* 1951), *The Flavor of Green Tea over Rice* (*O-chazuke no aji,* 1952), *Tokyo Story* (*Tokyo monogatari,* 1953), *Early Spring* (*Soshun,* 1956), *Tokyo Twilight* (*Tokyo boshoku,* 1957), *Equinox Flower* (*Higanbana,* 1958), *Good Morning* (*Ohayo,* 1959), *Floating Weeds* (*Ukigusa,* 1959), *Late Autumn* (*Akibiyori,* 1960), *The End of Summer* (*Kohayagawa-ke no aki,* 1961), *An Autumn Afternoon* (*Samma no aji,* 1962).

To these films of people living restrained and minimal lives, Ozu brought a restrained and minimal cinematic style. Most of the films he made from 1936 on take place within the confines of a typical Japanese home. His camera is motionless, and it invariably assumes the low-angle position of a person seated on a *tatami* mat whose eye level is about three feet above the floor, as if it were a guest or visitor in the household. Its at-

16.25 *Good Morning* (Yasujiro Ozu, 1958): Masahiro Shimazu, Koji Shidari, Yoshiko Kuga.

16.26 Ozu shooting a scene for *The Flavor of Green Tea Over Rice* (1952). Note the low-angle, eye-level perspective.

16.27 (left) Ozu's *Late Spring* (1949): Chishu Ryu, Setsuko Hara, Haruko Sugimura. (right) Ozu's *Tokyo Story* (1953): Chishu Ryu, Cheiko Higashiyama. Note the low-angle horizontal composition, here and throughout the Ozu stills, as if the camera were a person seated on a *tatami* mat. Note also the reliance on off-screen space.

titude is one of calmness, quiescence, and repose. The composition of the frame is inevitably horizontal, and the editing style is spare, with no fades or dissolves but straight cuts only, and with little concern for traditionally fluid continuity. In fact, the characteristic Ozu film is composed of a series of static long takes in which the dialogue, always written by Ozu in close collaboration with Noda, sustains the drama. Sometimes, however, there occur in Ozu's films moments of stillness and stasis in which there are no human beings at all. These are Ozu's famed "empty scenes" or "still lifes," and they are extremely important both to his aesthetic and to the international cinema at large.

It often happens in an Ozu film that the characters leave a room to eat or go to the bathroom or to bed, and the camera will remain behind them in its stationary position to record for a while the empty space that the actors have created by their departure. This preoccupation corresponds to a concept in Zen aesthetics known as *mu,* which, technically, designates the empty space between the flowers in the Japanese art of flower arrangement, but which more generally refers to the Zen doctrine that the spaces between the materials used to create a work of art are an integral part of the work.* Will Peterson has put it this way: "The blank

* For more on the relationship between the Zen aesthetic of discontinuity and the formal qualities of Japanese cinema, see Noël Burch's *To the Distant Observer: Form and Meaning in Japanese Cinema* (Berkeley, 1979). Burch goes so far as to suggest that Japanese audiences found the flicker effect of early projections far less irritating than their Western counterparts, since their traditional aesthetic did not require the illusion of seamless continuity as do the traditional aesthetics of the West. (This, interestingly enough, even though the flicker effect in Japan was more pronounced, since until the twenties Japanese cameras and projectors operated at the rate of twelve frames per second rather than the sixteen to twenty frames common in the West.)

sheet of paper is perceived only as paper, and remains as paper. Only by filling the paper does it become empty."[4] So Ozu's "still lifes," which appear in each of his major films, are an integral part of his transcendental vision of reality. But they are also of great importance to the formal evolution of narrative film. Through his use of the "empty scene," Ozu became one of the first directors in the history of film to create "off-screen space"—a technical phenomenon which has become decisively important to the new cinema movements on the Continent and in the Third World countries in the past decade.

There are two ways of conceptualizing the cinema screen. In one, the outer edges of the screen become a framing device for the visual composition centered within it, like the frame of a painting or a still photograph. In this model, the reality of the film is contained entirely *within* the screen, and the edges of the screen are borders separating the film's reality from the categorically "real" reality outside. This way of regarding the screen and the method of composition it demands has, with a few notable exceptions (in the work of von Stroheim, Murnau, Renoir, Welles, and Rossellini), dominated the narrative cinema of the West until very recently—perhaps the last fifteen years. In the other mode of conceptualizing cinematic space, first formally articulated by André Bazin, the screen is conceived as a window on the world whose frame, if moved to the right or to the left, or up or down, would reveal more of the same spatial reality contained within the screen. Of course, the screen must contain most of the action most of the time, so this "off-screen space," as it has come to be called, must be revealed by camera movement (as in the lateral tracking shots of the films Godard made after 1968) or, more provocatively, by what can be termed "off-center" or "non-centered" framing. In this technique, the film frame is made to contain only part of the significant action, or sometimes, as in Ozu, none of it at all.

The following consecutive non-centered shots from Ozu's *Floating Weeds* (1959) will help to illustrate the concept:

16.28 Off-screen space can be created in front of the screen (and thus behind the camera) as well as beyond its linear borders. For example, classical Hollywood framing conceives an imaginary axis which positions the camera within a 180-degree semi-circle vis-à-vis the action, cutting the viewer off from the 180 degrees of filmic space behind it. Anti-traditional framing often conceives filmic space as a full circle, breaking the imaginary axis of action and creating a totally new spatial paradigm. In the shot-reverse-shot sequence above, the same actor's feet extend into the frame first from the left and then from the right, making it clear that the camera has turned 180 degrees on its axis.

16.29 Ozu's *Late Autumn* (1960): (left) Yoko Tsukasa, Setsuko Hara, Keiji Sada, Shin Saburi, Nobuo Nakamura; (right) Setsuko Hara, Yoko Tsukasa, Nobuo Nakamura, Chishu Ryu.

In traditional or centered framing, the force of the image is, in Bazin's terms, *centrifugal:* the image is composed so that our eyes are drawn inward toward the vanishing-point at the center of the frame. In anti-traditional or off-center framing, the force of the image is *centripetal:* our eyes are thrown out upon the world beyond the frame, a process which suggests the essential reality of that world. Centered framing has the effect of denying the reality of the world beyond the frame by isolating it from us, off-center framing has the effect of affirming the reality of the world beyond the frame by constantly calling our attention to it. In short, centered framing creates an illusion about the structure of reality which off-center framing seeks to destroy. Thus, the latter is an inherently more realistic technique in terms of the way we actually perceive reality. For this reason, off-center framing has become an increasingly favored device among young Marxist directors on the Continent and in the Third World, since it promises to deconstruct what is for them an essentially deceptive, illusionist way of looking at the world and one's position in it.

Ozu's use of off-screen space was somewhat differently motivated. Many Ozu films exploit off-screen space by means of "empty scenes" in which the motionless camera trains its attention for some time on dramatically insignificant objects—a vase on a night-stand, a ticking wall clock, an empty hallway—which, because they are themselves meaningless in terms of narrative and theme, draw our attention to the fact that they are surrounded by spaces containing meaningful objects and people off-screen. By showing us *nothing,* these shots draw our attention to the *something* which surrounds it, in the same way—but much more emphatically—that off-center framing makes us aware of the world beyond the frame instead of denying its existence by isolating it from us. It is generally true that the longer the screen remains empty, the more our attention is drawn to off-screen as opposed to on-screen space, and Ozu was among the first directors anywhere to realize this. Another way that Ozu uses off-screen space is by training his stationary camera on some significant action while significant action is also in progress off-screen. This

16.30 "Empty scenes" from the opening sequence of *Early Spring* (Yasujiro Ozu, 1956).

could be suggested by off-screen dialogue or naturalistic sound effects, or, as in many of Ozu's later films, by having the action oscillate between off-screen and on-screen space. In *The End of Summer* (1960), for example, the static camera trains on a mother ironing a dress in full shot while her son and her father play catch, moving in and out of the frame at random as the game grows increasingly noisy and wild.

Yet, for all this, Yasujiro Ozu was an extremely conservative director. He did not make his first sound film until 1936 or his first color film until 1958, and he never used widescreen. His films employed only the most fundamental of stylistic devices—basically those which had been available since the "primitive" period of film history before 1914. Ozu's simplicity of style derives from the fact that his art is essentially religious in nature. It is an art predicated on the Zen Buddhist reverence for the mystery of the everyday. As Donald Richie has pointed out, it assumes that it is only through the mundane and the common that the transcendent can be expressed, and, like much religious art, it is primitive in terms of technique.[5] From this elementary base, however, Ozu made films of great emotional sophistication and subtlety, and he ranks today as one of the international cinema's great *auteurs*. From 1936 until his death in 1963, he kept the writing, casting, shooting, and editing of his films tightly under his control, building up his own repertory company of trusted performers and technicians. He was also quintessentially Japanese, the reason that he has only just begun to be discovered in the West. But, like Shakespeare and Tolstoi, Ozu had a single universal subject: human nature. And he became in the course of his long career what he was recently voted by the British Film Institute—"one of the greatest artists of the twentieth century in any medium and in any country."

16.31 Ozu's *Floating Weeds* (1959): Hiroshi Kawaguchi, Ganjiro Nakamura.

The generation of Kurosawa, Mizoguchi, and Ozu also included Teinosuke Kinugasa (b. 1896), whose beautifully photographed *jidai-geki* *Gate of Hell* (*Jigokumon,* 1953) is considered one of the finest color films ever made,* and Keisuke Kinoshita (b. 1912), whose humanistic *Twenty-Four Eyes* (*Nijushi no hitomi,* 1954) traces the course of Japanese Fascism from 1927 to 1946 through the eyes of a young schoolteacher and her pupils. Tadashi Imai (b. 1912) is a politically committed critic of vestigial feudalism and a prolific exponent of neo-realism. His three-part *Muddy Waters* (*Nigori,* 1953), for example, is an exposé of political and social repression during the "liberal" Meiji Restoration.

16.32 *Twenty-Four Eyes* (Keisuke Kinoshita, 1954): Hideko Takamine.

The Second Post-War Generation

The second generation of the post-war renaissance came to prominence in the fifties and sixties and was comprised primarily of Masaki Kobayashi (b. 1916), Kon Ichikawa (b. 1915), and Kaneto Shindo (b. 1912). The work of Kobayashi and Ichikawa is probably best known in the West. Kobayashi was trained in philosophy at Waseda University,

---

* It is impossible, however, to experience *Gate of Hell* in its original form due to severe color fading of the negative. For more on this problem, see Chapter 12.

and his early films dealt mainly with social and political problems in a realistic vein. His first masterpiece was *The Human Condition* (*Ningen no joken,* 1959–61), a nine-and-one-half-hour anti-war epic of Japan's occupation and rape of Manchuria, 1943–45. Released in three parts, this humanistic but grimly realistic widescreen film tells the story of a young pacifist forced into the war and ultimately destroyed by it. Kobayashi's next important films were graphically violent *jidai-geki*—*Hara kiri* (*Seppuku,* 1962) and *Rebellion* (*Joi-uchi,* 1967), both of which used the situation of an individual's doomed revolt against the authoritarian social system of the Tokugawa period to make serious comments on the survival of feudalism in modern technological Japan. In the uncharacteristic but strikingly beautiful color film *Kwaidan* (*Kaidan,* 1964), Kobayashi made carefully controlled use of the widescreen format to tell four haunting ghost stories adapted from the writings of Lafcadio Hearn (1850–1904), an American author who became a Japanese citizen. One of the tales, "Hoichi the Earless" ("Minimachi Hoichi") draws heavily on elements of the *noh* play. Among Kobayashi's more recent works are the period gangster film *Inn of Evil* (*Inochi bo ni furo,* 1971), and the thirteen-part television series *Kaseki* (1975), a sensitive account of an elderly business executive who discovers that he is dying of cancer and must re-assess his life.

16.33 *The Human Condition, Part I* (Masaki Kobayashi, 1958): Tatsuya Nakadai.

Kon Ichikawa is widely acknowledged in the West as one of the Japanese cinema's most brilliant stylists. He began his career as an animator, but his first important film was *The Harp of Burma* (*Biruma no tategoto,* 1956), a lyrical epic about a Japanese soldier whose guilt at his complicity in the collective horrors of war drives him to become a saintly Buddhist monk. Ichikawa's other great pacifist film, *Fires on the Plain* (*Nobi,* 1959), is set during the last days of the Japanese occupation of the Philippines, when the remnants of the decimated Japanese army turned to murder and cannibalism in order to survive and face their final battle with "honor." The film offers a nightmarish vision of an inferno which goes far beyond its implicit social criticism of the feudal code of *bushido.* *Conflagration* (*Enjo,* 1958), adapted from a novel by Yukio Mishima, is a richly textured widescreen film which tells the true story of a young Buddhist novitiate who burns down the Temple of the Golden Pavillion at Kyoto in disgust at the worldly corruption which surrounds him. Other Ichikawa films known in the West include *Odd Obsession/The Key* (*Kagi,* 1959), a disturbing tale of an elderly man's sexual perversion; *Alone in the Pacific* (*Taiheiyo hitoribochi,* 1963), based on the true story of a young man who sailed the Pacific from Osaka to San Francisco in three months; and the monumental documentary *Tokyo Olympiad* (1965), which compares favorably with Riefenstahl's *Olympia* (1936). More recently, Ichikawa has produced *The Wanderers* (*Matatabi,* 1973), generically a nineteenth-century *chambara* which many critics have seen as the consummation of his sixty-film career in its combination of savage irony, technical mastery, and lush compositional beauty.

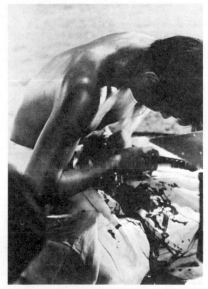

16.34 Kobayashi's *Hara kiri* (1962): Akira Ishihama.

16.35 *Fires on the Plain* (Kon Ichikawa, 1959): Eiji Funakoshi, Mickey Curtis.

Kaneto Shindo began as a scriptwriter for Kurosawa, Ichikawa, and others. His status as a film artist is less well established than that of either Kobayashi or Ichikawa, but he has made a number of important films since the war. Shindo worked as an assistant to Mizoguchi on *The Life of Oharu* and *Ugetsu,** and in 1952 he made his first major film, *Children of Hiroshima (Genbaku no ko)*, a stylized semi-documentary about the atomic holocaust and its effects upon the Japanese people. Shindo's reputation in the West rests on the international success of another semi-documentary, *The Island (Hadaka no shima, 1960)*, which concerns the struggle of a peasant farming family to survive on a barren Pacific atoll. The film is poetic in the manner of Robert Flaherty's work and some consider it self-consciously beautiful, but it has obvious authenticity as a representation of human experience, which stems from the fact that it is largely autobiographical. The only other Shindo film known outside of Japan is the folkloristic *jidai-geki Onibaba (1964)*, which concerns a mother and daughter who survive the civil wars of the sixteenth century by killing wounded *samurai* and selling their armor for rice. This strange and brutal film blends gorgeous widescreen photography with sickening violence and graphic sex, and it never achieves the poetic quality Shindo apparently sought for it. Shindo's later work has tended toward the sensational and melodramatic, but he remains a prolific scriptwriter and a figure of some importance to the post-war development of Japanese cinema.

So, too, in a more popular sense does the director Ishiro (or Inoshiro) Honda (b. 1911), whose *Godzilla* (1954) started a twenty-year cycle of formulaic monster films which demonstrated to the world the Japanese facility for special effects. Some typical titles, in translation, are *Rodan* (1956), *The Mysterians* (1957), *Mothra* (1961), *King Kong vs. Godzilla* (1962), *Ghidrah, the Three-Headed Monster* (1965), and *Destroy All Monsters* (1968). Almost all of Honda's science fiction films are parabolic: the monster is unleashed through the careless explosion of an atomic bomb, and, after wreaking havoc on the urban centers of the nation, it is finally destroyed by Japanese scientists.

16.36 *Godzilla* (Ishiro Honda, 1954) and other Japanese monster films relied on a proficiency with models and special effects acquired in the production of domestic propaganda films during World War II.

The Japanese New Wave

The third post-war generation of Japanese film-makers emerged during the late sixties and the seventies to form a kind of radical New Wave. Many of them moved away from the studios to form their own independent production companies. Some characteristic directors are Hiroshi Teshigahara (b. 1927), Susumu Hani (b. 1928), Masashiro Shinoda (b. 1931), and Nagisa Oshima (b. 1932). Teshigahara is an avant-garde abstractionist whose international reputation rests upon a single film, *Woman in the Dunes (Suna no onna, 1964)*, based on a novel by Kobo Abé and produced for less than a hundred thousand dollars. Among the premier works of the Japanese New Wave, this film is a complex allegory in which a young scientist becomes mysteriously trapped in an isolated sand-pit by the powers of a woman who has apparently been condemned to shovel away the sand interminably by hand.

16.37 *Woman in the Dunes* (Hiroshi Teshigahara, 1964): Kyoko Kishida, Eiji Okada.

---

* In 1979, Shindo produced and directed *Mizoguchi Kenji,* a documentary about the director's life and work.

Susumu Hani began his career by making documentaries, which helped to shape his later *cinéma-vérité* style. Most of Hani's feature films are shot on location with non-actors, and they typically treat the problems of the post-war generation—specifically the problems of living in a once traditional culture disintegrating under the pressures of rapid social change. Hani has also made films about what it means to be Japanese in foreign lands—for example, the semi-documentary *Bwana Toshi* (Kenya, 1965) and *Bride of the Andes* (*Andesu no hanayome,* Peru, 1966). According to many critics, Hani's best and most characteristic film is *The Inferno of First Love* (*Hatsukoi jigoku-hen,* 1968), in which two teenagers attempt through physical love to cope with the social chaos which surrounds them, only to be destroyed. Hani's former wife, Sachiko Hidari (b. 1930), one of Japan's finest actresses and the star of most of Hani's films, has recently directed her own first feature, *The Far Road* (*Toi ippono michi,* 1978), which concerns the day-to-day life of an aging railroad worker, his wife, and his family.

Masashiro Shinoda is a New Wave director similarly committed to the younger generation's struggle against society, but, unlike Hani, he is a supreme stylist whose sense of pictorial composition compares favorably with that of the "classical" directors of the fifties. He has made films on every major aspect of his country's history, as well as on contemporary life. Like those of his peers, Shinoda's films tend to be violent and nihilistic, but they are also ethically committed and formally precise. The most significant are *Assassination/The Assassin* (*Ansatsu,* 1964), *Punishment Island* (*Shokei no shima,* 1966), *Double Suicide* (*Shinju ten no amijima,* 1969), *The Scandalous Adventures of Buraikan* (*Buraikan,* 1970), *Banished Orin* (*Hanare goze Orin,* 1977), and *Demon Road* (*Yashaga ike,* 1980). Other New Wave directors of note are Yasuzo Masumura (b. 1924—*The Hoodlum Soldier* [*Heitai yakuza,* 1965]; *Red Angel* [*Akai tenshi,* 1966]; *Lovers' Suicide in Sonezaki* [*Sonezaki sinju,* 1978]); Yoshishige Yoshida (b. 1933—*Farewell to Summer Light* [*Saraba natsu no hikari,* 1968]); and Shohei Imamura (b. 1926—*The Insect Woman* [*Nippon konchuki,* 1964]; *The Pornographer* [*Jinruigaku nyumon,* 1966]; *A Man Vanishes* [*Ningen johatsu,* 1967]; *History of Japan as Told by a Bar Hostess* [*Nippon sengo shi: Madamu Omboro no seikatsu,* 1970]; *Vengeance Is Mine* [*Fukushu suruwa ware ni ari,* 1980]).

But by far the most influential film-maker of the Japanese New Wave is Nagisa Oshima (b. 1932), a militantly radical intellectual who was trained at Kyoto University in political history and law. He joined the Shochiku studios as a scriptwriter in 1955 and began directing there in 1959. When one of his films, *Night and Fog in Japan* (*Nihon no yoru to kiri,* 1960), was withdrawn for political reasons, he left the studio to form his own production company, Sozosha ("Creation"), which is still in operation. Much of his early work was in the genre of the *yakuza-eiga,* or contemporary gangster film. It tended to be violent, sexually explicit, and politically radical, in that Oshima's criminals were figures in open revolt against modern Japanese society. The malaise of this society was to become Oshima's overriding theme, making him the first major post-war director to concentrate solely on the problems of being Japanese in

16.38 The highly stylized *Double Suicide* (Masashiro Shinoda, 1969): Shima Iwashita, Kicheimon Nakamura.

the present. Appropriately, Oshima rejected his culture's cinematic past as well as its historical one, so that even his earliest films reveal the stylistic influence of the French New Wave rather than that of his great Japanese predecessors. The use of hand-held cameras, *cinéma-vérité* shooting techniques, and on-location sound recording is typical of Oshima's early work, although all of his films since 1960 have been made in widescreen and color. By the late sixties Oshima had moved away from narrative altogether, and the influence of Godard and the Yugoslav avant-gardist Dušan Makavejev became apparent in his blending of fantasy and reality and in his use of printed chapter titles, voice-over narration, extreme long shots, and audience-alienation effects. As the Japanese critic Hideo Osabe puts it, the films of Oshima have become "provocations directed at the spectators"[6]—like the work of Godard, they are audio-visual polemics designed to generate in the audience indignation and rebellion at the state of contemporary society.

Japanese society, like our own, is one in which massive industrialization, urbanization, and technocratization have accelerated social change and caused the disintegration of raditional (and, in Japan's case, centuries-old) values without offering anything in their place. As Oshima sees it in films like *Death by Hanging* (*Koshikei,* 1968), *The Diary of a Shinjuku Thief* (*Shinjuku dorobo nikki,* 1968), *Boy* (*Shonen,* 1969), *The Man Who Left His Will on Film* (*Tokyo senso sengo hiwa,* 1970), and *The Ceremony* (*Gishiki,* 1972), the Japanese family structure so dear to Ozu has degenerated into a series of empty rituals; the giant corporations have destroyed the physical and psychological environment of the entire country; Japan's cities are sinks of pollution, overcrowding, and violent crime. In response, the Japanese state has become feudal once more—authoritarian, imperialistic, racist, and politically repressive. For Oshima, then, Japan is in the midst of a nightmare of social disorder which increasingly courts a rebirth of Fascism. His films are works of aggressive, often violent, social protest. Frequently, the graphic and even pornographic depiction of sex becomes a vehicle for his radical indictment of modern, technocratized Japan, as his recent films *Empire of the Senses/In the Realm of the Senses* (*Ai no corrida,* 1976) and *Empire of Passion/The Phantom of Love* (*Ai no borei,* 1978) vividly demonstrate. Ultimately, ideas are more important to Oshima than visual surfaces, and he is often accused of having no consistent style. But critics often confuse inconsistency with versatility, and there can be no question that Oshima the social critic is also a great film artist and one of the foremost innovators of the international cinema today.

16.39 *The Man Who Left His Will on Film* (Nagisa Oshima, 1970).

The Decline of the Studios

The rise of independent production and the New Wave was a consequence of the economic decline of the Japanese studio system. Multiple-channel color television was introduced in Japan in 1960, and ever since that time there has been a steady drop in film attendance, paralleling the experience of the West. Two of the major studios—Shintoho and Daiei—have gone bankrupt, and the remaining four—Nikkatsu, Toei,

Toho, and Shochiku—have become increasingly commercial and exploitative in their output. The mid-sixties saw the rise of two new domestic exploitation genres which together have come to constitute the mainstay of the declining film industry. The first was the *yakuza-eiga,* or contemporary gangster film, which has replaced the *samurai* film in popularity among Japanese audiences. The *yakuza* is in fact a kind of latter-day *samurai,* an outlaw swordsman in the urban jungle who nevertheless lives by a traditional code, and as such he possesses considerable symbolic appeal for audiences whose traditional values have been eroded by a repressive technocracy. Moreover, *yakuza* films are invariably brutal and bloody, and they clearly provide audiences with a socially acceptable channel for their hostility and aggression—much of it directed toward society itself. In 1974, the Japanese studios produced some one hundred *yakuza* films, more than a third of the industry's annual output. The second exploitation genre to sweep Japan was the "eroduction," or "pink" film, a feature-length sex film with a high content of sadism. (Censorship in any form was illegal in Japan from 1966 to 1972.) Initially pure pornography, the eroduction has developed into a genre of some sophistication and, as is the case with the *yakuza-eiga,* has attracted some serious film-makers. Among the most notable of these sado-erotic films are Koji Wakamatsu's *Violated Angels* (1968), a graphic rendition of a mass murder that occurred in the United States early in the sixties; Yoshida's *Eros Plus Massacre (Eros + gyakusatsu,* 1969); and Oshima's *Empire of the Senses* (1976). By the early seventies the Japanese studio system was producing more "pink" films than any other kind. The situation changed slightly after censorship was re-instated in 1972, but between 1965 and 1975 the Japanese film industry devoted more than half of its total output to *yakuza-eiga* and eroductions, producing some sixteen hundred of these popular genre films in a single decade. The box-office success of *Star Wars* (George Lucas, 1977) and *Close Encounters of the Third Kind* (Steven Spielberg, 1977) in Japan has recently led to a glut of cheaply produced imitations, such as Toho's *Message from Space* (1978) and *War in Space* (1979), which recycle the special-effects techniques of the *Godzilla/Rodan* films with little imagination or style.

The Japanese cinema today is in flux. The economic recession which began in 1972 has further undermined the crumbling studio system. In July 1972, the government was forced to grant subsidies to the industry to prevent its complete collapse. The first two generations of post-war film-makers worked almost exclusively for the studios, and in the seventies their surviving members have produced few important films. Most significant production today is either independent or financed by foreign capital. Nevertheless, in the work of the New Wave—of Hani, Shinoda, Yoshida, Imamura, Masumura, and Oshima—there is great promise that the Japanese cinema will be as internationally prominent in the future as it has been in the past. But we should not assume that even now we know a great deal about that cinema, since only a small portion of it has reached the West. Kurosawa, the Japanese director most widely known outside his country, has made twenty-seven films, but some of them have still not been shown in the West. In the course of their careers, Mizoguchi directed eighty-seven films, Ozu fifty-six, Ichikawa sixty-one; and Oshima, at the age of forty-eight, had already made twenty-one. Only a handful of these works have been made available to the West, perhaps because the Japanese have traditionally been wary of being misunderstood by foreigners. Yet during the post-war period 1951–68 more than four hundred Japanese films won prizes at foreign festivals. So we must remember that we have seen a mere sampling of the great films that formed the renaissance of those years. When we can some day see the Japanese cinema whole, we will undoubtedly be amazed at the richness of our discovery.

SATYAJIT RAY AND INDIAN FILM

Because television does not exist as a mass medium in India (there are fewer than 1,000,000 receivers in a land of 632,000,000 people), cinema is still the most popular form of mass entertainment. The Indian film industry—which is centered in Bombay (Hindi-language films), with large industries in Calcutta (Bengali-language films) and Madras (Tamil, Kannada, and Telugu films)—produces over seven hundred motion pictures a year in more than sixteen different languages, the highest output of any nation in the world, including the United States and Japan. But 90 percent of these films are rigidly conventionalized musicals* and mythological romances made for consumption by a largely uneducated and impoverished domestic audience. (Significant export markets for Indian films exist only in Indonesia, Malaysia, and the United Kingdom.) The formula has been described as "a star, six songs, and three dances,"[7] preferably about three hours long and in garish color. As this formula suggests, the Indian film industry is dominated today by a star system similar to that of Hollywood's early years, and the cinematic quality of the star vehicles matters little to either the producers or their unsophisticated audiences. Despite these conditions, India has produced at least one contemporary director of major international stature, Satyajit Ray (b. 1921).

As a young man, Ray studied painting with the Bengali poet Rabindranath Tagore (1861–1941) and then worked for a while in the world of advertising as an illustrator. His job took him to London for six months in 1950; there he saw Vittorio De Sica's *Ladri di biciclette* (1948) and was tremendously impressed by the film and by the style of Italian neo-realism. On his return to Calcutta, he met Jean Renoir and was able to observe his filming of *The River* (1951). After many practical difficulties, Ray made his first film, a visualization of the first part of a long novel by the Bengali writer Bibhuttibhusan Bannerji entitled *The Song of the*

---

* The songs are not sung but lip-synchronized by the stars of the films. The singers—known as "playback singers"—often become stars in their own right by recording songs from current films and marketing the disks with their pictures on the jackets. The composers also sell records on the strength of their names, often recording their own songs. For more on Indian film audiences, see the affectionate docu-drama *Cinema Cinema* (1979) by the Indian director Krishna Shah; and Elliot Stein, "Bangalore, Mon Amour: A Voyage to India," *Film Comment*, 16, 3 (May–June 1980), 61–71. See also Chidananda Das Gupta, "New Directions in Indian Cinema," *Film Quarterly*, 34, 1 (Fall 1980), 32–42.

16.40 Family members in *Pather panchali* (Satyajit Ray, 1955): Karuna Bannerji, Runki Bannerji, Subir Bannerji.

Road (Pather panchali, 1955), which, to the astonishment of nearly everyone, won the Jury Prize at Cannes in 1956. Ray followed with two more films, *The Unvanquished (Aparajito,* 1957) and *The World of Apu (Apur sansar,* 1958), which together completed his adaptation of the novel and formed the Apu trilogy—a sensitive, humanistic story of the growth of a young Bengali boy from childhood to maturity. Ray's style was neo-realistic in its simplicity and directness, and he made brilliant use of classical Indian music with a soundtrack composed and played by Ravi Shankar (Ray now composes his own scores). He acquired a large international following on the basis of his films of the sixties—*The Music Room (Jalsaghar,* 1958; released 1963); *The Goddess (Devi,* 1960); *Two Daughters (Teen kanya,* 1961; from stories by Tagore); *Kanchenjunga* (1962); *Expedition (Abhijan,* 1962); *The Big City (Mahanagar,* 1963); *The Lonely Wife (Charulata,* 1964; adapted from a novel by Tagore); and *Days and Nights in the Forest (Aranyer din ratri,* 1970)—all of them studied accounts of some telling aspect of Bengali life.

Because his focus falls so frequently on personal relationships and the small intimacies of everyday life, Ray has sometimes been accused of ignoring India's pressingly serious problems of poverty, official corruption, and religious intolerance. In the seventies, however, he appears to have attempted to answer this criticism with more politically conscious films like *The Adversary (Pratidwandi,* 1971), which deals with unemployment among middle-class youth; *Distant Thunder (Ashanti sanket,* 1973), a depiction of the effects of famine on Bengal during World War II; *The Chess Players (Shatranj ke khilari,* 1978; Ray's first film in Urdu rather than Bengali), set during the British annexation of India's last independent princely state in 1856; and *The Middleman (Jana aranya,* 1979), a bitter satire about the Calcutta business world. But whatever his status as a social critic, Ray is a serious film artist who has for the first time in its history made the Indian cinema worthy of serious attention. He has also provided encouragement for a number of younger film-makers who gathered about him in Calcutta during the sixties, notably the American director James Ivory (b. 1928—*The Householder* [1963]; *Shakespeare*

Wallah [1965]; *Bombay Talkie* [1970]; *Savages* [U.K., 1972]; *Auto-biography of a Princess* [1975]; *Roseland* [U.S.A., 1977]; *The Europeans* [U.K., 1979; from the novel by Henry James]), whose films are in English; and the Indian directors Mrinal Sen (*The Village Story* [*Oka oorie katha*, 1977]; *Man with the Axe* [*Parasuram*, 1979]; *And Quiet Rolls the Day* [*Ekdin pratidin*, 1980]); M. S. Sathyu (*The Legendary Outlaw* [*Kanneshware*, 1977]); and Shyam Benegal (b. 1934), whose films are in Hindi (the trilogy *The Seedling* [*Ankur*, 1974], *Night's End* [*Nishant*, 1975], and *The Churning* [*Manthan*, 1976]; *The Boon* [*Anugraham*, 1978]; *Obsession* [*Junoon*, 1979]).

A NOTE ON CHINA

The glut of cheaply made martial arts (*kung-fu*) films produced in Hong Kong and Taiwan between 1970 and 1974, and voraciously consumed in the West, obscured the existence of a high-quality Chinese cinema in the work of Hong Kong directors like Li Han-hsiang (b. 1926 —*Eternal Love* [1963]) and King Hu (b. 1931), whose period film *A Touch of Zen* (1969; released 1975) was much admired at Cannes in 1975. Films from the People's Republic of China, such as *Battle Song of Taching* (Sun Yung Ping, 1966), *Island Militia Women* (Chien Chiang, Chen Huai-ai, and Wang Hao-wei, 1975), and *Breaking with Old Ideas* (Li Wen-hua, 1975), are just beginning to reach the United States and are not very sophisticated in narrative terms. But news from several European festivals where Chinese retrospectives were held in 1978 indicates that Chinese cinema may have experienced a hitherto unknown artistic flowering in the late fifties and sixties in such films as Chin Shan's *Storm* (1959), Hsie Tie-Li's *Hurricane* (1961) and *Threshold of Spring* (1963), Yi Lin's *Great Waves Purify the Sand* (1964), Li Chung's *Serfs* (1964), Lin Nung's *Naval Battle of 1864* (1961), Chang Chun-hsiang's *Dr. Norman Bethune* (1964; released 1977), and the Wan brothers' animated feature *Disturbance in Heaven* (1965).*

16.41 *Battle Song of Taching* (Sun Yung Ping, 1966).

---

* See Jay Leyda, *Dianying: An Account of Films and the Film Audience in China* (Cambridge, Mass., 1972; revised 1979).

The Shape of the Seventies

The three most important historical developments of the seventies were the emergence of Third World cinema as an international movement, the spectacular renaissance of film in West Germany, and the steady decline of Hollywood as an important center of theatrical film production.

THIRD WORLD CINEMA

The emergence of vital national film cultures in those nations of Latin America and Africa collectively known as the Third World has taken place gradually over the past fifteen years. But by the mid-seventies, Third World cinema was widely recognized as one of the most important and innovative movements in contemporary film-making, as significant historically as Italian neo-realism and the French New Wave. The uniqueness of Third World cinema is undeniable. The term covers a wide range of films produced in the countries of two continents, most of which have long histories of exploitation and colonial oppression by Western powers. Only now are these countries emerging from centuries of underdevelopment, and their struggle to do so has produced one of the most exciting creative impulses in cinema today.

Despite their great ethnic and political diversity, all Third World cinemas have several common characteristics which permit us to identify them as parts of a coherent international movement. First, Third World film-makers conceive of cinema not as an entertainment commodity produced to make a profit but as a compelling means of mass persuasion, cultural consolidation, and consciousness-raising. Second, Third World film-makers usually operate from an independent production base outside of their countries' established (and usually Western-dominated) film industries. For this reason, Third World cinema is distinguished by its use of unconventional production modes, including collective production, secret or "underground" production, on-location shooting of guerrilla warfare, and non-Western extra-national funding. Finally—and most important from an aesthetic standpoint—Third World cinema rejects the

17.1 The dark comedy *Muerte de un burócrata* (Tomás Gutiérrez Alea, 1969), which the director dedicated to Laurel and Hardy, among others: Salvador Wood, Silvia Planas.

17.2 Alea's *Memorias del subdesarrollo* (1969): pre-revolutionary consciousness. Sergio Corriere.

17.3 Alea's *La última cena* (1977): the count (Nelson Villagra) with one of the twelve slaves he has invited to his "last supper."

conventional narrative syntax of Hollywood and other Western film industries in an effort to extend the limits of film structure and teach its audiences new ways of seeing their socio-political reality. The ultimate goal of this process is the reclamation of authentic forms of national cultural expression long obscured by imposed foreign values. As the militant Argentine film-makers Fernando Solanas and Octavio Getino (*La hora de los hornos* [*Hour of the Furnaces,* 1968]) have put it, theirs is a "third cinema," which goes beyond the "first cinema" (conventional Hollywood narrative) and the "second cinema" (the auteurist cinema of personal expression) to counter

a cinema of characters with a cinema of themes, one of individuals with one of the masses, one of *auteurs* with one of operative groups, a cinema of neocolonial misinformation with a cinema of information, one of escape with one that recaptures the truth, a cinema of passivity with one of aggression. To an institutionalized cinema, it counterposes a guerrilla cinema; to movies as shows or spectacles, it counterposes a film act or action; to a cinema of destruction, one that is both destructive and constructive; to a cinema made for and by the old kind of human beings, it counterposes a cinema *fit for a new kind of human being, for what each one of us has the possibility of becoming.* [Emphasis in the original.][1]

It should be clear from this statement that Third World cinema is above all a movement in which social, political, and aesthetic concerns are closely fused.

Latin America led the Third World in the development of a distinct cinematic style in the early sixties with the emergence of *cine liberación* in Cuba and *cinema nôvo* in Brazil. Since the revolution of 1959, the Cuban government has subsidized the Cuban Institute of Cinematic Art and Industry (ICAIC—Instituto Cubano del Arte y Industria Cinematográficos), which organizes every aspect of national film activity from production through distribution to exhibition. Initially blatantly agitational and nationalistic in the manner of the early Soviet *agitki* (complete with *"cine-móviles"* which took revolutionary films to the provinces like the Bolshevik "agit-trains" of the twenties), the Cuban cinema has developed into the most sophisticated of the Third World under the auspices of ICAIC. Revolutionary ideology, advanced formal experimentation, and great compositional beauty are subtly mixed in the work

17.4 Scenes from the three parts of *Lucia* (Humberto Solás, 1969): Raquel Revuelta, Eslinda Nuñez, Adela Legra.

17.5 *La primera carga al machete* (Manuel Octavio Gómez, 1969).

17.6 *De cierta manera* (Sara Gómez, 1974), a critique of racism and sexism in contemporary Cuba.

of such talented directors as Tomás Gutiérrez Alea (b. 1928—*Muerte de un burócrata* [*Death of a Bureaucrat*, 1966]; *Memorias del subdesarrollo* [*Memories of Underdevelopment*, 1969]; *La última cena* [*The Last Supper*, 1977]; *Los sobrevivientes* [*The Survivors*, 1978]); Humberto Solás (b. 1943—*Lucia* [1969]); Manuel Octavio Gómez (b. 1939—*La primera carga al machete* [*The First Charge of the Machete*, 1969]; *La tierra y el cielo* [*The Earth and the Sky*, 1978]); Sergio Giral (*El otro Francisco* [*The Other Francisco*, 1975]; *Rancheador* [*The Bounty-Hunter*, 1978]); Sara Gómez (b. 1943—*De cierta manera* [*One Way or Another*, 1977]); Octavio Cortázar (b. 1935—*El brigadista* [*The Teacher*, 1978]); Pastor Vega (b. 1940—*Retrato de Teresa* [*Portrait of Teresa*, 1979]); and the documentarist Santiago Álvarez (b. 1919—*Las 79 primaveras de Ho Chi Minh* [*The 79 Springs of Ho Chi Minh*, 1969]).

The leader of the *cinema nôvo* ("new cinema") movement in Brazil was the director Glauber Rocha (b. 1939), whose theoretical writings laid the foundation for a new Latin American cinema—one which would acknowledge the political and social realities of a land half of whose people were unemployed and half illiterate. Rocha's major films (*Barravento* [1961]; *Deus e o diabo na terra do sol* [*White Devil, Black God*, 1964]; *Terra em transe* [*Land in Anguish*, 1967]; *Antonio das Mortes* [1968];) tended to be strangely lyrical blends of anthropology, folklore, and

17.7 A peasant turned *cangaceiro* (rebel-bandit) in *Deus e o diabo na terra do sol* (Glauber Rocha, 1964), the first *cinema nôvo* feature to be widely seen outside Brazil.

stylized political violence, and they brought the *cinema nôvo* movement to international attention. Other important *cinema nôvo* directors were Ruy Guerra (b. 1931—*Os fuzis* [*The Guns*, 1963]; *Os deuses e os mortos* [*The Gods and the Dead*, 1971]; *Mueda* [1980]); Joaquim Pedro de Andrade (b. 1932—*Macunaíma* [1969]; *Os inconfidentes* [*Conspirators*, 1969]); Carlos Diegues (b. 1940—*Os herdeiros* [*The Heirs*, 1968–69]; *Xica da silva* [*The Silver Queen*, 1969]; *Bye Bye Brazil* [1979]; *Chuvas de verao* [*Summer of Rain*, 1980]); and Nelson Pereira dos Santos (b. 1928—*Vidas sêcas* [*Barren Lives*, 1963];) *Como era gostoso o meu frances* [*How Tasty Was My Little Frenchman*, 1971]; *Tenda dos milagres* [*Tent of Miracles*, 1978]); there were many more of lesser rank.

17.8 Political violence in *Vidas sêcas* (Nelson Pereira dos Santos, 1963).

17.9 *La hora de los hornos* (Fernando Solanas and Octavio Getino, 1968): agitational cinema.

17.10 *La Patagonia rebelde* (Hector Olivera, 1974).

Indeed Brazil's contribution to Third World cinema was prolific through 1971, when the country's Right-wing dictatorship drastically curtailed freedom of expression and forced its most important film-makers into exile. (In 1968, the military government of Brazil had promulgated Institutional Act Number Five, which permits the junta to suspend all civil rights at will.)

From Brazil, the New Cinema movement spread to Argentina* (Fernando Solanas and Octavio Getino, *La hora de los hornos* [*Hour of the Furnaces,* 1968]; Hector Olivera, *La Patagonia rebelde* [*Rebellion in Patagonia,* 1974]); Bolivia (Jorge Sanjines and the Grupo Ukamau, *Yawar mallku* [English title: *The Blood of the Condor,* 1969]; Antonio Eguino, *Pueblo chico* [*Little Town,* 1974]; *Chuquiago* [1977]); and Chile (Miguel Littín, *El chacal de Nahueltoro* [*The Jackal of Nahueltoro* 1969]; *La tierra prometida* [*The Promised Land,* 1973]; *El recurso del método* [*Recourse to the Method,* 1978]; *La viuda de Montiel* [*The Widow Mon-*

---

* In addition to their Third World cinemas, both Brazil and Argentina have small commercial industries which produce films for export as well as for domestic consumption. A recent Brazilian hit was Bruno Barreto's (b. 1955) erotic comedy *Doña Flor e seus dois maridos* (*Doña Flor and Her Two Husbands,* 1978), which received international distribution. The Argentine industry, once the most productive in Latin America, is currently experiencing a serious financial crisis, as is the entire domestic economy. But in better times it produced at least one internationally prominent figure, the director Leopoldo Torre-Nilsson (b. 1924). The son of a Swedish mother and the Argentine director Leopoldo Torres-Rios (1899–1960), Torre-Nilsson's first independent production was an adaptation of a short story by Jorge Luis Borges, *Dias de odio,* in 1954. The three films which brought him to the attention of European critics—*La casa del ángel* (*The House of the Angel,* 1957), *La caída* (*The Fall,* 1959), and *La mano en la trampa* (*The Hand in the Trap,* 1961)—were all adapted from novels by his wife and frequent collaborator, Beatriz Guido. Torre-Nilsson's most recent success was *Boquitas pintadas* (*Painted Lips,* 1974), a scathing criticism of the Argentine middle classes. Like Buñuel, with whom he is often compared, Torre-Nilsson deals with the hypocrisy and repressiveness of the bourgeoisie.

tiel, 1980]); Patricio Guzmán, *La batalla de Chile* [*The Battle of Chile*, *Parts I, II, and III,* Cuba and Chile, 1973–77]), where it prospered until crushed by similar incursions of Rightist power. Bolivia's progressives were purged by General Banzer's junta in 1971; the socialist democracy of Chilean president Salvador Allende was overthrown by a brutal coup in 1973; and Argentina's tenuous experiment in democracy ended with a military putsch in 1976. Only in Venezuela, where a policy of liberal state subsidies (60 percent of costs) for domestic production was begun in the early seventies, has the effort to develop a truly national film culture been successful. Nevertheless, the New Cinema movement in Latin America, also known as "guerrilla" or "militant" cinema,* provided a model for subsequent Third World film movements in Arab and Black Africa, notably in Algeria and Senegal.

17.11 Quechua Indians exploited by the Peace Corps in *Yawar mallku* (Jorge Sanjines and the Grupo Ukamau, 1969).

During the sixties, most Algerian films concerned the savage war of liberation from France which had traumatized the country from 1954 through 1962. A few of these films (collectively known as *cinema mudjahad*—"freedom-fighter cinema"), such as Ahmed Rachedi's *L'aube des damnés* (*Dawn of the Damned*, 1965) and Mohamed Lakhdar-Hamina's *Le vent des Aurés* (*The Wind of Aurés,* 1966), were of superior quality, but it was not until the *cinema djidid* ("new cinema") movement of the seventies that Algeria established an authentic and sophisticated alternative cinema, in the work of Ali Ghalem (*Mektoub,* 1970); Mohamed Bouamari (*Le charbonnier* [*The Coal-Miner,* 1973]); Mohamed Slim Riad (*Ryah el janoub* [*The South Wind,* 1975]); and Mohamed Lakhdar-Hamina (*Chronique des années de braise* [*Chronicle of the Years of Embers,* 1975—winner of the Grand Prix at Cannes in the same year]).

17.12 *Chuquiago* (Antonio Eguino, 1977).

17.13 *La tierra prometida* (Miguel Littin, 1973).

17.14 *Chronique des années de braise* (Mohamed Lakhdar-Hamina, 1975): reflections on the Algerian war of liberation. Leila Shenna (right).

---

* It has also contributed to the recent emergence of serious and socially committed Mexican cinema; see Jesús Salvador Treviño, "The New Mexican Cinema," *Film Quarterly,* 32, 3 (Spring 1979), pp. 26–37; and B. R. Nevares, *The Mexican Cinema* (Albuquerque, N. M., 1976).

17.15 *Xala* (Ousmane Sembène, 1974): a government official (Thierno Leye) caught between neo-colonialism and the ancient curse of the evil eye.

In Senegal (independent since 1960), film production is partially subsidized by the state, and a vital ideological cinema flourishes there in the work of directors such as Ousmane Sembène (*La noire de . . .* [*Black Girl*, 1960]; *Mandabi* [*The Money Order*, 1970]; *Emitai* [*Lords of the Sky*, 1972]; *Xala* [1974]; *Ceddo* [1978]), and Mahama Traore (*Reoutakh* [*The Big City*, 1971]).

Other contributions to the African cinema have been made by Sega Coulibaly of Mali (*Kosu den*, 1979); Sarah Maldoror (a French resident of Guadeloupe parentage), whose tense film of the Angolan liberation struggle, *Sambizanga* (1972), has won several international awards; and the Ethiopian Haile Gerima (b. 1946—*Harvest: Three Thousand Years* [*Mirt sost shi amit*, 1975]), who now lives and works in the United States.

GERMANY: *DAS NEUE KINO*

Post-War Origins

Related to the Third World cinema movement through its emphatic rejection of conventional narrative syntax and its Marxist ideological perspective, *das neue Kino* ("the new cinema") has made the West German cinema among the most exciting in the world today, compensating for its long post-war eclipse. After World War II, the German cinema, like the nation itself, was split into Western and Eastern parts. Most of the production equipment was under Soviet control in the Eastern Zone, as were the former UFA studios at Neubabelsberg. In May 1946, all activities of these production facilities were nationalized under the Deutsche Film Aktiengesellschaft (German Film Company, or DEFA), which provided new production capital in the form of state subsidies.* In the Western sector, the Americans installed the former UFA producer Erich Pommer (see Chapter 4) as film commissioner for their zone and insured through various de-cartelization laws that no centralized German film industry could emerge to compete with theirs. Nevertheless, the Allies began to license individual production companies in 1946, and the years 1946–48 saw the release of several notable films dealing with immediate post-war social problems in both the Eastern and Western zones, among them *Die Mörder sind unter uns* (*The Murderers Are Among Us* [Wolfgang Staudte, East Germany, 1946]); *Freies Land* (*Free Land* [Milo Harbig, East Germany, 1946]); *Morituri* (Artur Brauner, West Germany,

17.16 *Die Mörder sind unter uns* (Wolfgang Staute, 1946).

---

* East German production is still controlled by DEFA, which devotes up to 50 percent of its output to films dealing with contemporary domestic issues. Popular genres include the literary adaptation, the children's film, and the anti-Nazi film. A few distinguished features in the latter category have recently reached the West, including Frank Beyer's film about the Warsaw Ghetto, *Jakob der Lügner* (*Jacob the Liar*, 1976), Konrad Wolf's *Mama, ich lebe* (*Mum, I'm Alive*, 1977) and *Solo Sunny* (1980), and Evelyn Schmidt's *Seitensprung* (*Escapade*, 1980). For more, see the sections on the German Democratic Republic in Mira and Antonín Liehm, *The Most Important Art: East European Film After 1945* (Berkeley, 1977), and Elaine and Harry Mensh, *Behind the Scenes in Two Worlds* (New York, 1978).

1946); *In jenen Tagen* (*In Former Days* [Helmut Käutner, West Germany, 1947]); and *Berliner Ballade* (*The Ballad of Berlin* [Robert Stemmle, West Germany, 1948]). These were known as *Trümmerfilme* ("rubble films") because of the devastated physical condition of the Germany they portrayed, and they gave some hope of a realist German film movement similar to the one being born concurrently in Italy.* But as production rose to over seventy German films a year in 1949, currency reform brought the promise of prosperity to West Germany, and the films of that sector turned away from self-scrutiny toward lightweight entertainment.

17.17 *In jenen Tagen* (Helmut Käutner, 1947).

Economic recovery proceeded rapidly through the fifties, and West Germany became the fifth largest producer of films in the world. Yet its increasingly escapist *Heimatfilme* ("homeland films") were directed exclusively at the domestic audience, and they compared unfavorably with the glossy Hollywood products which flowed ceaselessly into the market through American-owned distributors. (Although the Americans had prevented the re-emergence of a centralized German film industry during the Occupation, they had supported the rebuilding of the exhibition and distribution sectors. After a series of monetary crises during the fifties, all but one of the major West German distributors, Constantin Film, had fallen into American hands.) In East Germany, the DEFA output remained relatively small and ideologically focused, attacking Nazism as the arch-enemy of the new socialist state.†

17.18 A typical *Heimatfilm: Ich denke oft an Piroschka* (*I Often Think of Piroschka*, Kurt Hoffmann, 1956): Liselotte Pulver.

When television and increased mobility began to change patterns of leisure activity in the late fifties, West German film attendance fell off dramatically, just as it did in the rest of Europe and in the United States. Between 1956 and 1968, in fact, it dropped from 900 million to 192 million annually. Domestic production was badly hurt, and the West German film industry had no alternative but to appeal to the federal government for subsidies. These were granted at first in the form of guaranteed credits (*Ausfallbürgschaften*) but were eliminated in 1961 when the Ministry of the Interior decided to help rejuvenate German cinema by awarding production grants for feature films.

Young German Cinema

The seeds of *das neue Kino* were sown at the Oberhausen Film Festival in 1962, when twenty-six writers and film-makers who had accepted

---

* Roberto Rossellini's neo-realist classic *Germania, anno zero* (*Germany, Year Zero*, 1947) was shot on location in bombed-out Berlin (see Chapter 11).

† The rabid anti-Nazism of the East German government makes it appear that East Germans have "forgotten" less about the past than their former countrymen. For example, whereas only one concentration camp (Dachau) has been left standing in West Germany, East Germany has memorialized over thirty of them and requires that all schoolchildren visit at least one in the course of their education. But what is memorialized in the East German camps is not the history of what happened there but the myth of heroic Communist resistance against the Nazis (of which there was little, in fact). So if the West has behaved as if Nazism never happened, the East seems to have convinced itself that it happened to somebody else.

ministry grants called for the establishment of a *junger deutscher Film*, a "young German cinema," in a manifesto which concluded as follows:

> The collapse of the commercial German film industry finally removes the economic basis for a mode of film-making whose attitude and practice we reject. With it, the new film has a chance to come to life. The success of German shorts at international festivals demonstrates that the future of the German cinema lies with those who have shown that they speak the international language of the cinema. This new cinema needs new forms of freedom: from the conventions and habits of the established industry, from intervention by commercial partners, and finally freedom from the tutelage of other vested interests. We have specific plans for the artistic, formal and economic realisation of this new German cinema. We are collectively prepared to take the economic risks. The old cinema is dead. We believe in the new.[2]

Through its spokesman, the director Alexander Kluge, the Oberhausen group successfully lobbied the West German parliament (Bundestag) for the formation in 1965 of the Young German Film Board (Kuratorium Junger Deutscher Film), an institution charged with implementing the proposals of the Oberhausen manifesto. Specifically, drawing from the cultural budgets of the various federal states, the Kuratorium sponsored the first features of Kluge, Hans-Jürgen Pohland, and Werner Herzog, and seventeen other features, between 1965 and 1968. The Oberhausen group was also able to achieve the foundation of two professional film schools (at Munich and Berlin) and a German Film Archive in Berlin.

But by 1970 the successes of the "young German cinema" rang rather hollow. The passage of a Film Subsidies Bill by the Bundestag in 1967 had established a Film Subsidies Board (Filmförderungsanstalt, or FFA) that concentrated economic power in the hands of the commercial studios and distributors, and the result was a boom in the production of quick, shoddily made features which were foisted on a dwindling audience through block booking. Most of the boom productions were idiotic classroom comedies and soft-core pornographic films aimed at West Germany's two million immigrant workers. Theater owners were forced to book them as part of package deals with distributors, whether a local audience existed for the films or not. With West German production hitting an all-time high of 121 films per year in 1969 and film attendance slipping at the rate of one million per year, the late sixties and early seventies witnessed a wave of theater closings all over the country. The drivel produced by the first three years of FFA subsidies had alienated serious film-goers, bored the general public, and brought the West German film industry to the brink of another financial crisis. As recently as 1971 the *New York Times* could write, "The persistently dismal situation of German film art is unique; a list of new films comprises a greater proportion of trash than anywhere else."[3]

The New German Cinema

Nevertheless, a new German cinema was about to be born from the combined efforts of the Oberhausen group and a group of somewhat younger independent film-makers who began their careers in West German television. In 1971 this group formed the Filmverlag der Autoren (literally, the "Authors' Film-Publishing Group") as a private company to distribute the films of its members, who today include Alexander Kluge, Rainer Werner Fassbinder, Bernhard Sinkel, Peter Lilienthal, Ulli Lommel, Edgar Reitz, Hans W. Geissendörfer, Hark Bohm, Reinhard Hauff, Uwe Brandner, and Wim Wenders. The impetus of the Oberhausen group, the resources of West German television and the Kuratorium, and a liberalized FFA grant policy* have made possible the phenomenal rise of the New German Cinema. Although the films of the movement have only a small following in West Germany itself, they have created more excitement within the international cinema than anything comparable since the French New Wave. Although the young film artists whose work collectively comprises the New German Cinema are quite diverse, they do have some distinct stylistic traits in common. Thomas Elsaesser writes of

> an unusual degree of aesthetic closure towards formal beauty and abstraction, a refusal to be explicit on the level of argument and meaning. Sensuousness, colour, and emotional luxuriance to the point of morbidity lure the viewer into accepting as valid discourse a social stance that is poignantly defensive and individualistic to a vulnerable extent. A style has evolved in the German cinema of the last five or six years that vacillates between satirical realism and symbolism of almost oppressive obliqueness, a style not unconnected with the cultural limbo affecting much of Germany's intellectual life today.[4]

The last point is important, because West Germany is a country which has only just begun to come to terms with the nightmare of its own recent history, its *unbewältige Vergangenheit* ("unassimilated past"). The generation of young film-makers represented by *das neue Kino* grew up in an Americanized, economically prospering Germany, only dimly aware of the Nazi past. Cultural historians point out that since the collapse of the "Thousand-Year Reich," the German people have suffered from a kind of collective amnesia about the "brown years" of Nazi rule, 1933–45. The shock and humiliation of defeat, the appalling devastation of the material environment and the partitioning of the country itself, and collective guilt for the most terrible acts of barbarism and genocide ever committed—all conspired to rob Germany of its cultural identity by robbing it of access to its immediate past. The past was not discussed in post-war

---

* The FFA makes about $7.5 million available for film production annually by levying a six-cent (0.15 Deutschmarks) tax on every ticket sold in West Germany's three thousand cinema theaters. (In 1979 a new law raised the tax by 50 percent.) Only directors whose previous films have returned at least $500,000 may apply for funds, which gives the FFA a decidedly commercial bias. But since 1975 three million dollars annually have been earmarked for supporting worthy independent projects selected by an eleven-man committee of critics and businessmen. The committee provided up to 80 percent funding for forty-one projects between 1975 and 1978. See Charles Eidsvik, "The State as Movie Mogul," *Film Comment*, 15, 2 (March–April 1979), 60–66; Andrea Strout, "West Germany's Film Miracle," *American Film*, 5, 7 (May 1980), 37–39; and Hans-Bernhard Moeller, "New German Cinema and Its Precarious Subsidy and Finance System," *Quarterly Review of Film Studies*, 5, 2 (Spring 1980), 157–68.

German households nor dwelled upon in post-war West German schools.* Since the early seventies, however, when the post-war generation began to demographically displace the generation which had actually experienced Nazism, public curiosity and confusion about the past has steadily increased. Added to this is the fact that, through its lucrative post-war alliance with the United States, West Germany has traded off large chunks of its cultural identity to become one of the most highly technocratized countries in the world, surpassing perhaps even Japan and the United States itself in some sectors of the Gross National Product. This set of circumstances has produced in the post-war generation an acute sense of alienation and anomie (signs of which are apparent in Japan, the United States, and many other industrialized nations as well). Robbed of their past by the infamy of Nazism and of their future by American cultural imperialism, the film-makers of *das neue Kino* express the sense of psychological and cultural dislocation described by the film critic Michael Covino as "a worldwide homesickness."[5] Their films are unsettling and sometimes depressing, but there can be no question of their unique contribution to international cinema.

Volker Schlöndorff and Alexander Kluge

Historically, the New German Cinema movement can be said to date from the release of Volker Schlöndorff's independently produced *Der junge Törless* (*Young Törless,* 1966), a psychologically detailed adaptation of Robert Musil's anti-militarist novel set in a boy's school before World War I, which won the International Critics' Prize at Cannes. Schlöndorff (b. 1939), who studied at IDHEC (Paris), had worked as an assistant to Louis Malle, Alain Resnais, and Jean-Pierre Melville before

---

* In a survey of West German teenagers taken in 1970, an overwhelming majority could identify Hitler only as "the man who built the *Autobahn.*" Indeed, the Bonn government expressed open concern as recently as 1978 that the lack of understanding of Nazism among West German youth could lead to a rekindling of it. As if to certify this concern, after *Holocaust* (the NBC-produced mini-series on the Nazis' extermination of the Jews) was shown on West German television in January 1979, national polls revealed that 70 percent of viewers between the ages of fourteen and nineteen felt that they had learned more about Nazism from the American television program than from all their years of studying German history.

That telecast, in fact, was the source of great emotional upheaval in West Germany and became a cultural phenomenon akin to the first broadcast of *Roots* in the United States. Initially opposed on the grounds that it would open old wounds—and denied national broadcast on the First German Network—*Holocaust* was finally aired regionally on the Third German Network, where over half of the adult population saw all or part of it. Polls conducted by the Bonn government and the Marplan Institute in the months after the telecast indicated a profound and lasting effect. In one poll, 64 percent of the viewers said that they were "deeply shocked," and 21 percent had been moved to tears. The number of viewers who, after viewing the program, favored the 1944 plot to assassinate Hitler increased from 49 to 63 percent; over half of the viewers reported that they had learned something new about Nazi atrocities; 73 percent felt "very positive" about the experience of watching *Holocaust;* and over half of the adults and two-thirds of the teenagers said that they would like to see it again because the program was so informative. (*Variety,* May 23, 1979.) Characteristically, the East German government refused to broadcast *Holocaust* on the grounds that its people had already been thoroughly schooled about Nazism and its crimes.

directing this feature. His next independent film* was *Baal* (1969), an adaptation of Bertolt Brecht's first play, which was followed by *Der plötzliche Reichtum der armen Leute von Kombach* (*The Sudden Wealth of the Poor People of Kombach,* 1971), a bizarre parody of the *Heimatfilm* tradition in which a group of nineteenth-century peasants rebel against the degradation of rural life by becoming bandits, and are put to death by the state. Other notable Schlöndorff films are *Coup de grace* (*Der Fangschuss,* 1976), a psychological drama set among German volunteers in the Baltic states at the end of World War I, and *Nur zum Spass—nur zum Spiel, Kaleidoskop Valeska Gert* (1977), in which a famous cabaret artist reminisces about her more than sixty years in show business, shortly before her death in 1978. In 1979 Schlöndorff's adaptation of Günter Grass' novel *The Tin Drum* (*Die Blechtrommel*) shared the Grand Prix at Cannes with the American director Francis Ford Coppola's *Apocalypse Now,* and in 1980 it won the American Academy Award for Best Foreign Film. Schlöndorff has worked frequently for the commercial studios, where he has collaborated with his wife, the scenarist and actress Margarethe von Trotta (b. 1942),† on a number of important films dealing with feminism and other social and political themes—most notably *Strohfeuer* (*Summer Lightning/A Free Woman,* 1972), and *Die verlorene Ehre der Katharina Blum* (*The Lost Honor of Katharina Blum,* 1975—from the novel by Heinrich Böll).

17.19 *Der junge Törless* (Volker Schlöndorff, 1966): Matthieu Carrière, Barbara Steele.

Another founder of *das neue Kino* is Alexander Kluge (b. 1932), whose *Artisten unter der Zirkuskuppel: ratlos* (*Artists Under the Big Top: Disoriented,* 1968) provided a metaphor for the plight of the serious film artist in Germany in the Godardian parable of a young woman who inherits a circus but cannot reform its deeply embedded traditions to create a new role for it in the "media world." Kluge, a practicing lawyer, novelist, legal scholar, and social theoretician who worked as an assistant to Fritz Lang (see Chapter 4) during Lang's brief return to Germany in the late fifties, is the intellectual father of New German Cinema. As spokesman for the original Oberhausen *junger deutscher Film* group, he was responsible for convincing the federal government to establish the Kuratorium and the film schools in Munich and Berlin. Kluge's style is objective, coolly rational, and satirical. His films almost always involve the precise analysis of some social problem which besets contemporary Germany, focusing on a representative protagonist (often played by his younger sister, Alexandra Kluge). Kluge's most significant films since *Artisten* are *Gelegenheitsarbeit einer Sklavin* (*Part-Time Work of a Domestic Slave,* 1974), which examines the issues of women's liberation and political organizing, and *Strong Man Ferdinand* (*Der starke Ferdinand,* 1976), a

17.20 *Artisten unter der Zirkuskuppel: ratlos* (Alexander Kluge, 1968): Hannelore Hoger.

---

* Two commercial features intervened: a murder mystery entitled *Mord und Totschlag* (*A Degree of Death,* 1966) and the German-Czech-American co-production *Michael Kohlhass—der Rebell* (1969), an epic of a sixteenth-century German political rebellion based on an 1808 story by Heinrich von Kleist (the same story was filmed as *Michael Kohlhass* in 1979 by the director Wolf Vollmar).

† Von Trotta has recently directed two of her own films: *Das zweite erwachen der Christa Klages* (*The Second Awakening of Christa Klages,* 1978) and *Schwestern oder die Bilanz des Glucks* (*Sisters, or The Balance of Happiness,* 1979).

satirical allegory of Fascism about an industrial security guard whose paranoid quest for order results in catastrophe for everyone around him. A recent Kluge project was the bringing together of ten other New German film-makers and the Novel Prize–winning novelist Heinrich Böll to produce *Deutschland im Herbst* (*Germany in Autumn,* 1978) for the Filmverlag der Autoren. Highly reminiscent of SLON's *Loin de Vietnam* (1967), this semi-documentary cooperative feature is a rumination on the events of autumn 1977, when a public official was kidnapped and murdered by terrorists, and several of the terrorists later died under mysterious circumstances in prison. Kluge expanded his contribution to *Deutschland im Herbst* into *Die Patriotin* (*The Patriot,* 1980), a meditation on the teaching of German history both in and out of school. In another cooperative project, Kluge, Schlöndorff, and two younger directors produced *Der Kandidat* (*The Candidate,* 1980), an ironic documentary portrait of Franz Josef Strauss, the Right-wing challenger in the 1980 West German federal elections.

Schlöndorff and Kluge are both still important representatives of *das neue Kino,* but three other West German film-makers have achieved greater international acclaim for the movement during the seventies. They are Rainer Werner Fassbinder, Werner Herzog, and Wim Wenders.

Rainer Werner Fassbinder

Rainer Werner Fassbinder (b. 1946) is the best known of the three and the most prolific, having completed forty features between 1969 and 1979. Originally an actor, playwright, and theater director, he has become the undisputed leader of the New German Cinema. Fassbinder began shooting low-budget features while he was still directing experimental theater in Munich, using a stock company of actors and technicians who have stayed with him through his later work. Many of these early films were based on scenarios improvised by Fassbinder and concerned the untreated malaise beneath the affluent surface of contemporary West German society. *Katzelmacher* (1969)—the term is Bavarian slang for a foreigner from the South who is possessed of great sexual potency—is about a Greek *Gastarbeiter,* or immigrant worker (played by Fassbinder), who is lynched by a group of young toughs because he is so attractive to their girls. *Warum läuft Herr R. amok?* (*Why Does Herr R. Run Amok?,* 1969) concerns a successful technical designer who one day murders his wife, their child, and a friend, and later commits suicide at his office by hanging himself over an open toilet. In *Der amerikanische Soldat* (*The American Solider,* 1970), an extended *hommage* to the American gangster film, a young German who has just returned to Munich from service with the American Special Forces in Vietnam is hired by three cops to commit a series of murders; all of the principals, of course, are killed by the end of the film.

17.21 *Warum läuft Herr R. amok?* (Rainer Werner Fassbinder, 1969): Kurt Raab.

If the plots of these films sound melodramatic, it is because Fassbinder intends them to be. He has a high regard for melodrama as a popular form, as evinced by his admiration for the films of Douglas Sirk (b. Detlef Sierck, 1900), the German émigré director who settled in Hollywood

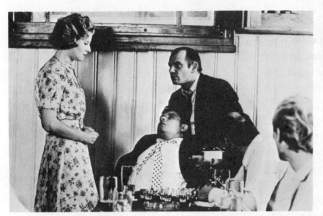

17.22 Fassbinder's *Der Händler der vier Jahreszeiten* (1971): Irm Hermann, Hans Hirschmüller, Klaus Löwitsch.

17.23 *Die bitteren Tränen der Petra von Kant* (R. W. Fassbinder, 1972): Margit Carstensen, Hanna Schygulla,

during the Nazi years and became master of the widescreen melodrama in the fifties (*Magnificent Obsession* [1954]; *All That Heaven Allows* [1956]; *Written on the Wind* [1957]; *Interlude* [1957]; *The Tarnished Angels* [1958]; *Imitation of Life* [1959]). Most of Fassbinder's films are about people who don't "make it," who have somehow failed to reap the material benefits of the German "economic miracle." For depicting the condition of these people, he sees melodrama as a form of heightened realism. He has written: "I don't find melodrama 'unrealistic'; everyone has the desire to dramatize the things that go on around him . . . everyone has a mass of small anxieties that he tries to get around in order to avoid questioning himself; melodrama comes up hard against them. . . . The only reality that matters is in the viewer's head."[6] Melodrama, in other words, is about real life. From this perspective, bourgeois culture depises melodrama because it has developed much more repressive forms of communication (for example, the high-culture forms of classical music and art, literature, and history) whose aim is to conceal process and function, and therefore to keep the bourgeoisie unaware of itself as a class in relationship to other classes. So it is as a Marxist that Fassbinder has chosen melodrama as his particular form, but it is as a humanist that he has chosen Marxism, and this is finally why he admires Sirk: ". . . Sirk has made the tenderest films I know; they are films of someone who loves people and doesn't despise them as we do."[7]

The most obvious stylistic influence on Fassbinder's early films (some of which were shot in less than ten days) was Godard, but with *Der Händler der vier Jahreszeiten* (*The Merchant of Four Seasons*, 1971) he began to develop a style of his own. The melodrama, however—stripped bare of theatrics, mock-heroics, and sentimentality, but nearly always photographed in garish color—has remained a constant in his work. In *Der Händler,* which has been extremely popular with German audiences, a failed engineer enters a loveless marriage and becomes a fruit vendor. Bullied by his wife and betrayed by his friends, he grows terminally depressed and finally drinks himself to death in a bar. In *Die bitteren Tränen der Petra von Kant* (*The Bitter Tears of Petra von Kant,* 1972),

17.24 *Angst essen Seele auf* (R. W. Fassbinder, 1973): Brigitte Mira, El Hedi Ben Salem.

17.25 *Fontane Effi Briest* (R. W. Fassbinder, 1974): Hanna Schygulla,

the title character has an affair with a younger woman who constantly betrays her and drives her to a nervous breakdown. *Wildwechsel* (*Wild Home*, 1972) deals with a sexual liaison between a fourteen-year-old girl and a nineteen-year-old boy. The boy is sent to prison for seducing a minor, and on his release the couple murders the girl's father. *Angst essen Seele auf* (*Fear Eats the Soul/Ali,* 1973), which won the International Critics' Prize at Cannes in 1974, is about the prejudice encountered by a widowed Munich charwoman when she marries a Moroccan immigrant worker some twenty years her junior. *Fontane Effi Briest* (*Effi Briest,* 1974), Fassbinder's least characteristic film, is an adaptation of a late-nineteenth-century novel by Theodor Fontane about a young middle-class woman destroyed by rigid social conventions because she is believed to have committed adultery. The film was shot in austere black-and-white, and Fassbinder used devices such as fades to white,* titles, and voice-over narration to replicate the narrative strategies of nineteenth-century fiction.

In *Faustrecht der Freiheit* (*Fist-Right of Freedom/Fox and His Friends,* 1975) a young working-class homosexual (Fassbinder) wins half a million Deutschmarks in the national lottery and is taken up by a group of corrupt bourgeois homosexuals who spend all of his money and abandon him, after which he takes an overdose of tranquilizers and dies on the floor of an ultra-modern Frankfurt subway station. In *Mutter Küsters Fahrt zum Himmel* (*Mother Küster's Trip to Heaven,* 1975), the working-class husband of a sweet little old lady goes berserk at his factory, killing himself and his foreman. The widowed Mother Küster suddenly finds herself the center of attention, as her husband's former employers, the popular press, her careerist daughter, and assorted political groups attempt to use the scandal for their own ends. Ultimately, like so many of Fassbinder's protagonists, she is used shamelessly and abandoned. *Angst vor der Angst* (*Fear of Fear,* 1975) is a study of a happily married middle-class housewife who has a psychotic breakdown, which, as Vincent Canby points out, dramatizes one possible end of capitalism, "when everything becomes perfect and, suddenly, nothing works."[8] *Die Reise ins Licht* (*Despair,* 1978), with a scenario by the British playwright Tom Stoppard, is a brilliant adaptation of Vladimir Nabokov's ironic novel about a man who tries to murder his double. Shot in Germany on a big budget (two-and-a-half million dollars) and with a predominantly

---

* Of these unusual fades to white instead of black, Fassbinder has commented:

According to [Siegfried] Kracauer [in *Theory of Film*], when it gets black, the audience begins to fantasize, to dream, and I wanted the opposite effect through the white. I wanted to make them awake. It should not function like most films through the subconscious, but through the conscious. It's . . . the first time that I know of where the audience is supposed to have its own fantasy, like reading a novel—the first normal fiction film. . . . It's like a novel that one reads where you can have your own dreams and fantasies at the same time. When you read a book, a novel, you imagine your own characters. That's just what I wanted to do in this film. I didn't want to have predetermined characters made for the audience; rather, the audience should continue the work. . . . [Quoted in Paul Thomas, "Fassbinder: Poetry of the Inarticulate," *Film Quarterly,* 30, 2 (Winter 1977–78), 6.]

17.26 *Faustrecht der Freiheit* (R. W. Fassbinder, 1975): Fox (Fassbinder) and his friends.

17.27 Fassbinder's *Die Ehe der Maria Braun* (1979): Günter Lamprecht, Gisela Uhlen, Gottfried John, Anton Schirsner, Hanna Schygulla, Elisabeth Trissenaar.

English cast, this film marked a departure from Fassbinder's usual, more improvisational, mode of production. But he returned to that mode in *Die Ehe der Maria Braun* (*The Marriage of Maria Braun*, 1979), a rambling melodrama set in war-time and post-war Berlin which has been a great commercial success in both Germany and America; *Die dritte Generation* (*The Third Generation*, 1979), a film about the relationships which exist among a group of young terrorists; and *In einem Jahr mit 13 Monden* (*In a Year of 13 Moons*, 1979), a portrait of the hellish life of a contemporary transsexual. Fassbinder also contributed to *Deutschland im Herbst* (see above) and directed *Lili Marleen* (1981). He is currently completing *Cocaine* (1981) and adapting Alfred Döblin's classic novel of working-class life, *Berlin Alexanderplatz* (1929—first filmed in 1930 by Piel Jutzi), as a thirteen-part series for German television.

Clearly, Fassbinder's is a cinema of the underdog, the exploited, and the oppressed. It is also a cinema of great formal beauty grounded in the expressive use of color, lighting, and decor. Again, Fassbinder's comments on Sirk are instructive:

> Sirk has said: you can't make films *about* things, you can only make films *with* things, with people, with light, with flowers, with mirrors, with blood, in fact with all the fantastic things that make life worth living. Sirk has also said: a director's philosophy is his lighting and camera angles.* . . . Sirk's lighting is always as unnatural as possible. Shadows where there shouldn't be any make feelings plausible which one would rather have left unacknowledged. In the same way, the camera angles in *Written on the Wind* are almost always tilted, mostly from below, so that the strange things in the story happen on the screen, not just in the spectator's head. Douglas Sirk's films liberate your head.[9]

---

* Compare Godard's "The dolly shot is a moral statement."

So Fassbinder is pictorial, even painterly, but not for the sake of pictorialism, any more than he is melodramatic for the sake of creating melodrama. Of his true ends, he has said this: "I don't want to create realism the way it's usually done in films. It's a collison between film and the subconscious that creates a new realism. If my films are right, then a new realism comes about in the head, which changes the social reality."[10] Wherever Fassbinder may go from here, he has already become the most exciting young director of the seventies, as well as the most prolific, and he is probably the most original talent to appear in the international cinema since Godard.

Werner Herzog

Werner Herzog (b. Werner H. Stipetic, 1942) studied literature and theater at the University of Pittsburg and worked briefly in American television. When he returned to Germany, Herzog became a welder in order to finance his own short documentaries, of which he made four before shooting his first feature in 1967. Produced by the Kuratorium, this was *Lebenszeichen* (*Signs of Life*), the allegorical tale of a young German soldier on a Greek island during World War II who stages a one-man rebellion against the army. But it was the bizarre *Auch Zwerge haben klein angefangen* (*Even Dwarfs Started Small*, 1970), shot on location in the Canary Islands, that first brought Herzog to international attention. The film is a black, Buñuelesque fantasy about an abortive revolt staged by the inmates of a correctional institution, played entirely by dwarfs and midgets. Its grotesque vision of human futility was matched by *Land des Schweigens und der Dunkelheit* (*Land of Silence and Darkness,* 1971), a feature-length documentary about a deaf and blind woman who attempts to liberate others similarly handicapped. Both films speak to the flawed nature of humanity itself rather than to the insufficiency of particular social institutions, and they emphasize the metaphysical, even mystical, nature of Herzog's central artistic concerns. To film *Fata Morgana* (1970), Herzog went to the Sahara Desert for what can only be described as a transcendental documentary about disintegration and alienation. The nearly hallucinatory camera style of this film, with its 360-degree pans and seemingly interminable tracking shots, is accompanied by sacred texts from Guatemalan Indian creation myths of the sixteenth century. It has no narrative line but proceeds on a poetic, visionary level to create from the material surfaces of reality images of total wreckage and decay. As Amos Vogel writes, the result is "an interior travelogue; an obsessive, hypnotic, and iconoclastic 'comment' on technology, sentimentality, and stupidity, filled with everyday objects that reveal their frightening secrets."[11]

Aguirre, der Zorn Gottes (*Aquirre, the Wrath of God,* 1972), Herzog's most powerful film to date, was shot on location in the jungles of Brazil and Peru and was based on an actual historical incident of the sixteenth century. It concerns a detachment of Spanish conquistadors in search of El Dorado in the steaming rain-forests of the Andes. The quest is suicidal from beginning to end, since the Spaniards insist on dragging the clumsy

17.28 *Auch Zwerge haben klein angefangen* (Werner Herzog, 1970).

17.29 *Fata morgana* (Werner Herzog, 1970): images of cosmic desolation.

accoutrements of "modern civilization" into the tangled wilderness with them. The film opens with the very image of futility, as about fifty conquistadors in heavy battle-dress attempt to maneuver a huge cannon down a plunging forest hillside to the river valley below. What we witness in this sequence is a concrete visualization of the characteristic which dooms all "civilized" peoples: their inability to surrender their dependence on technology in situations which render technology utterly useless.* But the folly of the Spaniards is protracted by Aguirre, a fanatical officer strikingly portrayed by Klaus Kinski, who usurps the crown of King Philip II, declaring himself to be "the Wrath of God," and drives the group ever deeper into the jungle in his mad obsession to establish a new order of civilization at El Dorado. As the quest ensues, it becomes increasingly pathological and ruthless, until it ends in the destruction of everyone but Aguirre himself, who in the final frames stands alone among the dead, on a drifting raft, shouting orders to the monkeys in the trees which line the river. The film, shot in splendidly evocative color by Thomas Mauch, is a brilliant study of idealism turned to barbarism through zealotry, and the Nazi past clearly stands behind it. But so too does the European conquest of Africa in the late nineteenth century,† the American experience in Vietnam, and all other historical tragedies in which high-minded aspirations have ended in a welter of murder, madness, and despair.

17.30 Herzog's *Aguirre, der Zorn Gottes* (1972): Klaus Kinski, Cecilia Rivera.

Herzog's next film, *Jeder für sich und Gott gegen alle* (*Every Man for Himself and God Against All/The Enigma of Kaspar Hauser,* 1974), was an equally bizarre allegory of the human condition: as the prologue announces, it was based upon an actual event and treats "the sole known case in human history in which a man was born as an adult." In 1828, a young man who has been locked in a cellar since birth, without access to memory or speech, suddenly appears in a small German town, where he is at first treated as a freak and then gradually taught to live by the systems of rational men. His acquisition of language, logic, religion, and natural philosophy plunges him into despair, and he is finally murdered by the man who had initially redeemed him from his brutish state. Reminiscent of Truffaut's *L'enfant sauvage* (1969) in terms of theme and plot, *Kaspar Hauser* is deeper and darker in its vision of the relationship between civilization and its discontents. Herzog employs a variety of unpredictable camera angles, awkward framing devices, and unusual lighting effects to transfer Kaspar's experience of perceptual disorientation to the audience. But Herzog achieved the film's most spectral and estranging effect by casting a former schizophrenic brought up in various institutions, the pseudonymous "Bruno S.," in the title role. The disaffected but strangely endearing Bruno S. also has the title role in Herzog's *Stroszek*

17.31 *Jeder für sich und Gott gegen alle* (Werner Herzog, 1974): Bruno S.

---

* Western cultural historians used to point to the fact that the Peruvian Incas had not invented the wheel as proof that their civilization was not a highly advanced one. But it was subsequently observed that the technology of the wheel would have been completely inappropriate to the mountainous terrain of the Andes.

† As elaborated, say, in Joseph Conrad's novel *Heart of Darkness* (1898), to which *Aguirre* has been aptly compared (Aguirre = Kurtz, the Amazon = the Congo, etc.). Compare *Apocalypse Now* (Francis Ford Coppola, 1979).

17.32 Herzog's *Stroszek* (1977): Bruno S., Eva Mattes.

17.33 Herzog's *Herz aus Glas* (1977): the glassworks owner's valet (Clemens Scheitz) foretells doom.

(1977), a balladic tale of three oddly assorted losers—two street musicians and a prostitute—who become friends and set out from contemporary Berlin to find the Promised Land in the backwoods of northern Wisconsin; of course, what they discover there is something altogether different. But for all its bitter irony, the film is full of a spontaneous and sympathetic humor which, Herzog seems to suggest, may be our only conceivable means of survival.

Herz aus Glas (*Heart of Glass*, 1977) is simultaneously Herzog's most beautiful and most enigmatic film. Shot in 1976 in Wyoming, Alaska, Utah, Bavaria, Switzerland, and the Skellig Islands, off the coast of Ireland, it concerns (apparently) a small medieval village whose entire economy is based upon the production of a certain "ruby glass" by its glassworks. The secret of producing this strange crystal dies with an aged glassblower, and for the rest of the film every inhabitant of the town constructs and acts out fantastic hypotheses about the missing formula. A young man who is to inherit the glassworks becomes obsessed with the notion that the secret ingredient is blood, and he murders a young girl to obtain it. In the apocalypse that follows, he burns the factory to the ground, destroying all hope for the village and plunging its inhabitants into collective madness. If *Herz aus Glas* resists any concrete allegorical interpretation, it is because the film seems to be about the nature of mystery itself, in the same way that *Aguirre* is about the nature of idealism (and, possibly, of power). More than in other Herzog films, the interpenetration of fantasy and reality is so thorough that we find it difficult to distinguish the two realms—perhaps because the people of the age he recreates did not themselves make that distinction. It is in fact this magical view of reality, so alien to the contemporary world, to which Herzog would recall us. He attempted to evoke it for *Herz aus Glas* by hypnotizing its cast every day in advance of shooting. "It was a stylistic effort," he has said. "I wanted this air of the floating, fluid movements, the rigidity of a culture caught in decline and superstition, the atmosphere of prophecy. . . . My heart is very close to the Middle Ages."[12] Herzog's *Nosferatu* (1979), a U.S.–French–West German co-production backed by Twentieth Century–Fox, is a studied remake of Murnau's 1922 classic (see Chapter 4) which uses exquisite European locations and rings some interesting changes on the vampire theme. But neither it nor the more modestly produced version of Georg Büchner's 1850 play *Woyzeck* (1979) enjoyed the critical esteem accorded Herzog's earlier films.*

In addition to his major features, Herzog has made two extraordinary documentary shorts: *Die grosse Ekstase des Bildschnitzers Steiner* (*The Great Ecstasy of the Wood-Sculptor Steiner*, 1975), about a man so obsessed with ski-jumping† that he constantly risks his life to break records, and *La Soufrière* (1977), a thirty-minute record of what hap-

---

* In 1979, a feature-length film portrait of Herzog and his work, entitled *Was ich bin, sind meine Filme* (*I Am What My Films Are*), was compiled by the New German Cinema directors Christian Weisenborn and Edwin Keusch.

† As Herzog himself is obsessed—his favorite photograph of himself shows him upside-down in mid-air, in the midst of a jump.

17.34 *Woyzeck* (Werner Herzog, 1979): Klaus Kinski, Willy Semmelrogge.

pened on Guadeloupe in 1976 when the prediction of a dire volcanic eruption caused the mass evacuation of the Caribbean island's entire population of seventy-five thousand, except for a single old peasant who refused to leave, though he was warned of certain death. Despite absolute confirmation by a team of international scientists and meteorologists, the eruption failed to materialize, and *La Soufrière* ends with Herzog peering into the depths of the smoking volcanic crater and commenting, "This, then, is a report about an inescapable catastrophe that did not take place." *La Soufrière*, at least as much as *Aguirre* and *Herz aus Glas*, epitomizes Herzog's metaphysical vision of reality. As Amos Vogel has so acutely written,

> To reveal a metaphysical element in life or art without becoming a re-actionary is one of the challenges of the day: and Herzog, compulsively, and whenever possible, rubs salt into this particular, festering wound. . . . He examines the Holy Fool . . . —the person considered a fool because outsider and eccentric, the one who dares more than any human should, and who is therefore—and this is why Herzog is fascinated by him—closer to possible sources of deeper truth though not necessarily capable of reaching them.[13]

Our twentieth-century technology and rationalism have become an infallible religion to us, Herzog warns us, no less than sixteenth-century technology and rationalism were an infallible religion to the conquistadors in Peru. And he suggests that we, no less than Aguirre, are engaged in a self-destructive process of dragging heavy artillery into jungles where there is no one to bombard but ourselves and the monkeys. As Herzog has remarked,

> We are surrounded by worn-out images, and we deserve new ones. Perhaps I seek certain utopian things, space for human honor and respect, landscapes not yet offended, planets that do not exist yet, dreamed landscapes. Very few people seek these images today which correspond to the time we live, pictures that can make you understand yourself, your position today, our status of civilization. I am one of the ones who try to find those images.[14]

Wim Wenders

Wim Wenders (b. 1945) is the newest director of *das neue Kino* to achieve an international reputation, largely on the basis of his 1976 film *Im Lauf der Zeit* (see below), which won the International Critics' Prize at Cannes in the year of its release. While studying at the Munich Film School from 1962 to 1970, Wenders worked as a critic for cinema journals and newspapers. In 1971, after making several experimental shorts, he completed his first feature, a version of Peter Handke's novel *Die Angst des Tormanns beim Elfmeter* (*The Goalie's Anxiety at the Penalty Kick*), from a script which he had written with Handke. Ostensibly a murder mystery, *Die Angst des Tormanns* is in fact a film of psychological disintegration in which a soccer goalie goes quietly mad from the fragmentation and discontinuity of his existence. Through Ozu-like camera placement and a variety of unusual subjective shots, Wenders induces in the viewer a state of anxiety similar to that experienced by the goalie. After a liberal adaptation of Hawthorne's *The Scarlet Letter* in 1972, Wenders made *Alice in den Städten* (*Alice in the Cities,* 1974), another film of existential questing. In it, a down-and-out young journalist and an abandoned nine-year-old girl meet in New York City and begin a search for the girl's European relatives which takes them across West Germany. The search becomes a symbol of futility and dislocation, since the only clue to the whereabouts of Alice's relatives is a random, unmarked snapshot of her grandmother's house.

Covino has described Wenders' major theme as "a worldwide homesickness," the anxiety-ridden sense of psychological and geographical dislocation induced by living in the modern world.[15] Wenders' next film, *Im Lauf der Zeit* (*In the Course of Time/As Time Goes By;* English title: *Kings of the Road,* 1976), provides his most brilliant exposition of this theme in the story of two men in their thirties who meet by accident on the road and begin an aimless journey across the desolate plains of northern Germany. Bruno lives in his van and survives by driving from one country town to another repairing broken movie projectors. Robert is a psycho-linguist from Geneva whose wife has recently left him; he meets Bruno in the course of an absurd attempt to commit suicide by driving his Volkswagen into a shallow river. The two men tacitly agree to travel together, and the rest of the film chronicles their movement through the stark wastelands of the East-West border regions. Strikingly photographed in crisp black-and-white by Wenders' cinematographer, Robert Müller, *Im Lauf der Zeit* is nearly three hours long (176 minutes), but the film is so carefully and uniquely composed that we barely notice the passage of time (which, as the original title announces, is what the film is really about). Nothing much happens to Bruno and Robert in the course of time, and very little is communicated between them, but Wenders has a genius for creating cinematic metaphors for the contemporary malaise afflicting the two men. Extremely long takes and slow traveling shots, unusual camera angles and framing devices, and, above all, the manipulation of off-screen space generate in the viewer a sense of perceptual dislocation corresponding to the spiritual disorientation of

17.35 *Im Lauf der Zeit* (Wim Wenders, 1976): Hanns Zischler, Rudiger Vogler.

Bruno and Robert. In this sense, *Im Lauf der Zeit,* like other Wenders films, is extremely self-contained: it can be said to describe itself by calling into question conventional modes of film structure.

After *Falsche Bewegung (Wrong Move,* 1976), another film about rootlessness from a script by Handke, Wenders made his first (relatively) big-budget production,* a version of Patricia Highsmith's novel *Ripley's Game,* entitled *Der amerikanische Freund (The American Friend;* original title: *Regel ohne Ausnahme [Rule Without Exception],* 1977), which continued the theme of dislocation in the form of an international thriller. More recently, Wenders collaborated with the late American director Nicholas Ray to produce *Lightning Over Water/Nick's Movie* (1980), a sensitive film about Ray's attempt to continue his work while dying of cancer.

17.36 Wenders' *Die amerikanische Freund* (1977): Dennis Hopper.

Unlike many of his associates in the Filmverlag, Wenders is not openly political. Yet he has said that "film language is always political: it is either exploitation or it isn't exploitation . . . not only the story that is told, but the way it is told."[16] In this regard, Wenders claims as his masters Yasujiro Ozu and the American action director Anthony Mann, both of whom had a brilliant facility for the creation of spatial metaphors. Clearly, Wenders has a similar gift, but there is something in the austerity of his vision which is reminiscent of Bresson and Dreyer. Like his frequent collaborator Peter Handke (now a director in his own right: *Die linkshandige Frau [The Left-Handed Woman,* 1978]), Wenders seems to have a clear vision of the modern world's spiritual confusion and a tremendous talent for translating that confusion into the terms of his art.

Jean-Marie Straub and Marxist Aesthetics

A final figure who must be mentioned as having inspired and influenced *das neue Kino,* although his own aesthetic concerns are independent of it, is the French-born Jean-Marie Straub (b. 1933). Straub, who has lived and worked in Germany since 1958, is the patron saint of minimal cinema—one which involves minimal dependence on the technical conventions of the medium as a narrative form. Specifically, this means the consistent use of direct sound, natural lighting, non-narrative editing and camera styles, and, of course, non-actors. (Straub worked as an assistant to Robert Bresson during the fifties† and was permanently influenced by his austerity of technique, especially that of *Les dames du Bois de Boulogne* [1945]). Philosophically, Straub regards cinema as a material rather than as a narrative form. While narrative forms tell stories which encourage audience identification with fictitious characters and events, material forms can be said to create primary experiences for their audience rather than secondary or vicarious ones. It is the difference between being told a story about a madman or a "wild child" and being

---

* $1.2 million dollars, or more than his first six films put together.

† During the same period Straub also worked as an assistant to Abel Gance (*Tour de Nesle* [1954]), Jean Renoir (*French Cancan* [1955]; *Eléna et les hommes* [1956]), Jacques Rivette (*Le coup de berger* [1956]), and Alexander Astruc (*Une vie* [1958]); see Chapters 9 and 13.

asked to participate in the experience of perceptual disorientation and disaffection which characterizes a state of madness or savagery. In a sense, it is the difference between Truffaut's *L'enfant sauvage* (1970) and Herzog's *Kaspar Hauser* (1974), or between Dennis Hopper's *Easy Rider* (1969) and Wenders' *Im Lauf der Zeit* (1976).

In pursuing his own vision of materialist cinema, Straub has created (in collaboration with his wife, Danièle Huillet) a number of extraordinary films whose structures of light, space, and sound approach the mathematical precision of musical composition. These include *Nicht versöhnt* (*Not Reconciled,* 1965); *Chronik der Anna Magdalena Bach* (*The Chronicle of Anna Magdalena Bach,* 1968—an historical study whose viewpoint is the consciousness of Bach's wife); *Othon* (1970—a version of Pierre Corneille's most rigidly formalized verse tragedy); *Leçons d'histoire* (*History Lessons,* 1972); *Moses und Aron* (1975—a severe version of Arnold Schoenberg's modernist opera); and *Fortini-Cani* (1977). As with musical composition, Straub's film's are "about" what happens to the viewer while watching them as much as they are "about" their ostensible content. That is, in their restraint his films create a vacuum which the viewer must fill with the primary experience of his or her own life, forcing introspection rather than encouraging vicarious identification with invented characters and plots.

17.37 Minimal/materialist cinema: the chorus in *Moses und Aron* (Jean-Marie Straub and Danièle Huillet, 1975).

It is this theoretical assumption which links Straub with the young film-makers of *das neue Kino,* although as an individual artist he is more clearly a member of the experimental avant-garde. Straub and his followers take the Marxist position that perception is an ideological as well as a physiological phenomenon, or at least that perception is ideologically and culturally conditioned. Cinema is a communications medium whose basic signifying unit (the shot) is a discrete unit of perception: every shot and every individual frame within a shot offer a unique perceptual perspective on some event or object. But in the conventional narrative cinema of the Western capitalist countries, those perceptual perspectives have been ideologically appropriated to create fictions about life, and we, the audience, have been ideologically conditioned to expect and receive these fictions. From the Marxist perspective, fiction or narrative is defined as a bourgeois form whose purpose is to propagate illusions about the real nature of our society and our lives within it. We must have illusions, the Marxists insist, to divert our attention from the exploitation, violence, and oppression which are the necessary by-products of our economic system; and therefore our cinema (and most of our other art forms) has traditionally been a narrative medium whose purpose is the creation of illusionist spectacle which serves the ideology of the ruling class.

What the new breed of radical film-makers is attempting, in both Europe and the Third World, is the *deconstruction* of bourgeois perceptual ideology through a deconstruction of conventional cinematic language—language which has, since its inception and throughout its history (with notable exceptions during the periods of Soviet silent realism, Italian neo-realism, and the French New Wave), been a bourgeois narrative form. J. Dudley Andrew summarizes the Marxist position:

"The Marxists call for a critical cinema which will 'deconstruct' itself at every moment. Instead of fabricating an illusion, this cinema will let the viewer see beneath the images and the story to the process of creation itself. . . . Every subject should be exposed for its socio-economic underpinnings; every signification (every image and narrative relation) should expose its own work. This way we can strive toward the conscious reshaping of the world."[17] In other words, the cinema's enslavement to a narrative code of vision has radically restricted its potential for the expression of new cultural realities. The vast range of ideas, feelings, perceptions, and experience which film is capable of communicating has barely been touched upon in the ninety-odd years of its history as a narrative form. But radical film-makers like Straub and the leaders of *das neue Kino* are now attempting to tap that potential as never before, and it is this effort—much of it successful—which lends the quality of strangeness and mystery and otherness to their films. They are groping toward a new cinematic language with which to express the formerly inexpressible, and the process demands that the audience feel, see, and think things formerly alien to the experience of film-watching.

Unfortunately, this same process can anger an audience that *wants* to be diverted by illusion rather than struggle to acquire new codes of vision and experience. And this process of audience disaffection is occurring in West Germany today, just as it occurred in France during the New Wave. With a few exceptions (such as Fassbinder's *Der Händler der vier Jahreszeiten* and Wenders' *Im Lauf der Zeit*), *das neue Kino* has not been popular with German audiences, who find the films obscure, depressing, and overly intellectual.* The largest markets are in France, Great Britain, and the United States, where many of its directors have won festival prizes and become fashionable cult figures among the intelligentsia. It is ironic that a cinema which aspires to create a new vision of the world cannot find a popular audience, while the illusionist spectacle it seeks to replace enjoys mass approval, even in West Germany itself, where the films with the biggest box-office receipts have recently been American superproductions like *The Godfather, Part II* (Francis Ford Coppola, 1974), *Jaws* (Steven Spielberg, 1975), and *Cross of Iron* (Sam Peckinpah, 1977—shot in Germany).

One major problem for the film-makers of *das neue Kino* is that of distribution. While the Film Subsidies Board generously supports independent production of all sorts, the outlets for exhibition in West Germany are few, because major distributors are unwilling to risk their capital on potentially unpopular films. A situation now exists in which the films of the New German Cinema have grown too elaborate and too numerous for the exhibition outlets available to them, and many observers believe that this will ultimately sink the movement entirely. Some *neue Kino* directors are starting to make films for large production companies in order to achieve blanket distribution. Fassbinder recently shot the two

---

* This is true for other forms as well. West Germany is currently the center of a European experimental avant-garde which extends all the way from literature (Günter Grass, Jakov Lind, Peter Handke, Peter Weiss) to electronic rock (Brian Eno, Kraftwerk).

and-a-half-million-dollar international co-production *Despair* (1978) for Bavaria Film, Herzog's *Nosferatu* (1979) was underwritten by Fox, and Wenders is currently working on *Hammett,* a fictionalized life of the crime writer Dashiell Hammett set in San Francisco and produced by Francis Ford Coppola. It may be that, like the French New Wave, the New German Cinema is doomed to expire from its own aesthetic success. At the height of the New Wave, almost anyone with the will to do so could find money to produce a low-budget film: state subsidies guarantee the same for *das neue Kino* today.* As in France, so many films are being produced by aspiring new talents that exhibition outlets are not sufficient to return the modest profits necessary to keep the movement going. As Jan Dawson has remarked, "The New German Cinema is, for the seventies, what the *nouvelle vague* was for the sixties: a questioning of received

---

* Other important figures of *das neue Kino* whose work has been subsidized by the FFA are Hans-Jürgen Syberberg (*Ludwig* [1974]; *Karl May* [1975]; *Winifred Wagner* [1976]; *Hitler—ein Film aus Deutschland* [*Hitler, a Film from Germany/Our Hitler,* 1977]); Johannes Schaaf (*Trotta* [1972]; *Dreamtown* [1974]); Hans W. Geissendörfer (*Jonathan* [1972]; *Sternsteinhof* [*Sternstein Mansion,* 1976]; *The Wild Duck* [1977]; *Die gläserne Zelle* [*The Glass Cell,* 1978]); Hark Bohm (*Nordsee ist Mordsee* [*North Sea's the Dead Sea,* 1976]; *Moritz, lieber Moritz* [*Moritz, Dear Moritz,* 1978]); Ottokar Runze (*Im Namen des Volkes* [*In the Name of the People,* 1975]; *Verlorene Liebe* [*Lost Love,* 1976]); Ulli Lommel (*The Tenderness of Wolves* [1975—a stylized remake of Fritz Lang's 1931 film *M*]); Edgar Reitz (*In Gefahr und grösster Not bringt der Mittelweg den Tod* [*In Danger and Greatest Distress, the Middle Course Brings Death,* 1976]; *Stunde null* [*Zero Hour,* 1977]; *Der Schneider von Ulm* [*The Tailor from Ulm,* 1979]); Peter Lilienthal (*Es herrscht Ruhe im Land* [*The Country Is Calm,* 1976]; *David* [1978]); Reinhard Hauff (*Die Verrohung des Franz Blum* [*The Brutalization of Franz Blum,* 1975]; *Paule Pauleander* [1976]; *Messer im Kopf* [*Knife in the Head,* 1978]); Bernhard Sinkel and Alf Brustellin (*Lina Braake* [1975]; *Berlinger* [1976]; *Mädchenkrieg* [*Three Daughters/The Maiden's War,* 1977]; *Taugenichts* [*Good-for-Nothings,* 1978]); Uwe Brandner (*Halbe-Halbe* [*Fifty-Fifty,* 1979]); Wolfgang Petersen (*Die Konsequenz* [*The Consequence,* 1978]; *Schwarz und Weiss wie Tage und Nächte* [*Black and White Like Day and Night,* 1979]); Niklaus Schilling (*Rheingold* [1978]; *Der Willi-Busch Report* [*The Willi Busch Report,* 1979]); Klaus Emmerich (*Die erste Polka* [*The First Polka*]; *Geheime Reichssache* [*State Secrets,* 1979]); Theodor Kotulla (*Aus einem deutsche Leben* [*Out of a German Life,* 1978—a biography of the commandant of Auschwitz]); Walter Bockmayer and Rolf Bührmann (*Flammende Herzen* [*Flaming Hearts,* 1978]); Jutta Bruckner (*Tue Recht und scheue niemand* [*Do Right and Fear No One,* 1978]); the Iranian-born Sohrab Shahid Saless (*Tagebuch eines Liebenden* [*Diary of a Man in Love,* 1977]; *Die langen ferien der Lotte H. Eisner* [*The Long Vacation of Lotte H. Eisner,* 1979]; *Ordnung* [*Order,* 1980]); Klaus Lemke (*Ein komischer Heiliger* [*Some Kind of Saint,* 1979]); Eberhard Schubert (*Flamme empor* [*Torch High,* 1979]); Adolf Winkelmann (*Die Abfahrer* [*On the Move,* 1979]); Helmut Dietl (*Der Durchdreher* [*It Can Only Get Worse,* 1979]); Heidi Genée (*1 + 1 = 3* [1979]); Norbert Kückelmann (*Die letzten Jahre der Kindheit* [*The Last Years of Childhood,* 1979]); Herbert Achternbusch (*Der Comanche* [*The Comanche,* 1979]); Lothar Lambert (*Tiergarten* [1980]); Christian Rischert (*Lena Rais* [1980]); Rainer Erler (*Fleisch* [*Meat,* 1979]); Rosa von Praunheim (*Armee der Liebenden oder Aufstand der Perversen* [*Army of Lovers, or Revolt of the Perverts,* 1979]); Hellmuth Costard (*Der kleine Godard* [*The Little Godard,* 1979]); Werner Schroeter (*Der Bomberpilot* [*The Bomber Pilot,* 1970]; *Salome* [1971]; *Willow Springs* [1973]; *Goldflocken/Flocon d'or* [*The Golden Fleece,* 1975]; *Neapolitanische Geschwister/Il regno di Napoli* [*The Kingdom of Naples,* 1978]; *Palermo oder Wolfsburg* [1980]); and Peter Stein (*Trilogie des Wiedersehens* [*Trilogy of Reunions,* 1979]). See Charles Eidsvik, "Behind the Crest of the Wave: An Overview of the New German Cinema," *Literature/Film Quarterly,* 7, 3 (Summer 1979), 167–81; and "West German Film in the 1970s," *Quarterly Review of Film Studies,* 5, 2 (Spring 1980 [special issue]).

values, an intoxicating burst of energy, a love affair with the cinema, and a love-hate relationship with Hollywood."[18] Whether that kind of relationship can avoid the fate of the New Wave is really a moot point; that *das neue Kino* has flourished for a decade will be enough to change the form of film language for some time to come.

HOLLYWOOD, 1965–1970

In the sixties, for the first time in its history, Hollywood had fallen behind the rest of the world—aesthetically, commercially, and even technologically (the latter because of the conservatism of its unions). Its decline resulted from the American industry's obstinate refusal to face a single fact: that the composition of the weekly American film audience was changing as rapidly as the culture itself. Between the mid-fifties and the mid-sixties, that audience shifted from a predominantly middle-aged, modestly educated, middle-to-lower-class group to a younger, better educated, more affluent, and predominantly middle-class group. The new audience in America, as all over the world, was formed by the post-war generation's coming of age. It was smaller than the older one, and its values were different. By the early sixties, the old audience had begun to stay home and watch television, venturing out occasionally for some spectacular family entertainment, but generally staying away from movie theaters. As the audience decreased, admission prices rose well above the rate of general inflation,* which had the effect of further decreasing the demand for the traditional Hollywood product. Yet the industry continued to make films according to the stylistic conventions of the forties and fifties, as if its old constituency still existed (and, of course, vestiges of it did).

The only real change was in the cost of the productions themselves, which by 1966 were averaging three million dollars apiece due to both monetary inflation and the industry's own extravagant search for a winning box-office formula. The new audience was not interested in seeing these films any more than was the old one, because as long as American cinema simply duplicated the popular entertainment function of television on a larger scale, neither audience particularly needed it. By 1962, Hollywood's yearly box-office receipts had fallen to their lowest level in history—nine hundred million dollars, or one-half of the immediate post-war figure. The studios were in serious financial trouble, which grew worse as they made increasingly desperate attempts to recapture the old audience with spectacular flops like Twentieth Century–Fox's *Cleopatra* (1963). In 1965, the unprecedented success of Warner Brothers' *The Sound of Music,* which grossed more than 135 million dollars nationwide, rekindled false hope in the spectacle formula, but a succession of stunning failures, such as Twentieth Century–Fox's *Star!* (1968), *Dr. Dolittle* (1970), and *Tora! Tora! Tora!* (1971), and Paramount's *Darling Lili* (1968), *The Molly McGuires* (1970), and *Paint Your Wagon* (1971),

---

* Between 1956 and 1972, when the general cost of living in the United States rose 53.9 percent, theater admission prices rose 160 percent.

pushed the industry to the brink of catastrophe by the early seventies.

As Hollywood's financial troubles worsened throughout the sixties, several commercial forces coalesced to bring the new American audience into the theaters. For one thing, the French and Italian New Waves had demonstrated to producers all over the world that "art" films could make money —especially if they were shot rapidly on low budgets by young directors who were willing to work for less money than older, more established ones. This realization had two profound consequences for the American cinema. In the first place, there was an increased tolerance for independent production of the type being practiced in Europe by Godard, Truffaut, Antonioni, Fellini, and others. By the mid-sixties, independent producers like Roger Corman of New World Films were able to sponsor young directors like Francis Ford Coppola (b. 1939) and George Lucas (b. 1944), who were making their first features. Independent producer-directors like Stanley Kubrick (b. 1928) and Arthur Penn (b. 1922) found themselves for the first time able to control the financing of their own films and to achieve an unprecedented degree of creative freedom. In the second place, the studios, who were turning increasingly to television production to save themselves from financial ruin,* became the willing distributors of these independent productions—a thing they would never have considered several years before—because distribution provided them with a badly-needed source of revenue. The studios also became large-scale domestic distributors of foreign films, whose circulation in the United States they had successfully managed to limit when they were powerful monopolies. By the mid-sixties, the work of Fellini, Antonioni, Bergman, and Buñuel, as well as that of French New Wave directors—which had previously been available in this country only in specialized "art houses" in major urban centers, if at all—suddenly began to appear regularly in first-run theaters all over America. By the seventies, foreign films were as readily available as American ones, not just in cities but even in many small towns.†

As the rigid structure of the studio system began to crumble, new talent entered the industry—young directors from television like Irvin Kershner (b. 1923—*The Hoodlum Priest* [1961]; *The Luck of Ginger Coffey* [1964]; *A Fine Madness* [1966]; *Loving* [1970]; *Up the Sandbox* [1972]; *The Return of a Man Called Horse* [1976]; *Eyes of Laura Mars* [1978]; *The Empire Strikes Back* [1980]); John Frankenheimer (b. 1930—*The Manchurian Candidate* [1962]; *The Train* [1965]; *Seconds* [1966]; *The Fixer* [1968]; *The Gypsy Moths* [1969]; *I Walk the Line* [1970]; *The Horsemen* [1973]; *Black Sunday* [1977]; *Prophecy* [1979]); Sidney Lumet (b. 1924—*The Pawnbroker* [1965]; *The Group* [1966]; *Bye, Bye, Braverman* [1968]; *The Seagull* [1968]; *The Anderson Tapes* [1971]; *Serpico* [1973]; *Murder on the Orient Express* [1974]; *Dog Day*

---

* Fifty percent of the approximately twenty thousand jobs in Hollywood today are in television production and distribution. At present, 90 percent of all prime-time programming is shot on film, although this situation will change as the quality of videotape improves.

† The availability of foreign films in this country has decreased recently because of the international recession and the rising domestic costs of advertising, distribution, and dubbing.

Afternoon [1975]; *Network* [1976]; *Equus* [1977]; *The Wiz* [1978]; *Just Tell Me What You Want* [1980]); Arthur Penn (b. 1926—*The Miracle Worker* [1962]; *Mickey One* [1965]; *The Chase* [1966]; *Bonnie and Clyde* [1967]; *Alice's Restaurant* [1969]; *The Appointment* [1969]; *Little Big Man* [1970]; *Night Moves* [1975]; *The Missouri Breaks* [1976]); Sam Peckinpah (b. 1926—*Ride the High Country* [1962]; *Major Dundee* [1965]; *The Wild Bunch* [1969]; *The Ballad of Cable Hogue* [1970]; *Straw Dogs* [1971]; *Junior Bonner* [1972]; *The Getaway* [1972]; *Pat Garrett and Billy the Kid* [1973]; *Bring Me the Head of Alfredo Garcia* [1974]; *The Killer Elite* [1975]; *Cross of Iron* [1977]; *Convoy* [1978])—and new cinematographers from the East Coast like Conrad Hall (b. 1926), Haskell Wexler (b. 1926), and William Fraker (b. 1923), and the Hungarian émigrés Laszlo Kovacs (b. 1933) and Vilmos Zsigmond (b. 1930). As these new film-makers, working with ever-increasing creative freedom and mobility, assimilated the French and Italian innovations, a new kind of American cinema was born for a new American audience.

This audience was composed of the first generation in history which had grown up with the visually, if not intellectually, sophisticated medium of television. Through hours of watching television as children and teenagers, its members knew the language of cinema implicitly, and when film-makers like Frankenheimer, Lumet, Penn, and Peckinpah began to move out of the studios in the mid- to late sixties and to employ the New Wave techniques of the French and Italian cinemas for the first time on the American screen, this young audience liked what it saw. A phenomenal increase in the number and quality of college and university film study courses simultaneously enabled many members of the new audience to *understand* what they saw as well as to enjoy it.* It is important to realize that the values of the new audience, like its life-styles, were radically different from those of the old. For better or worse, it had a generally permissive attitude toward such former cultural taboos as the explicit representation of sex, violence, and death. Thus, when censorship was completely abolished and replaced by a rating system in November 1968, the content of American cinema, as well as its form, was revolutionized to permit the depiction of virtually everything under the sun, including graphic sex and violent death. That this liberalization has created some disgusting abuses is inarguable, but it was necessary before the American film could achieve full maturity of content. It is difficult, for example, to imagine a director like Robert Altman (*Nashville* [1975]; *Three Women* [1977]) working at his best in the moral climate that produced *The Sound of Music* in 1965.

---

* As film studies continue to grow in the United States, more and more of the country's educated citizens are achieving a state of what could be called cinema or media literacy (Charles Eidsvik's useful term is "cineliteracy"—see his *Cineliteracy: Film Among the Arts* [New York, 1978]). The American Film Institute's *Guide to College Courses in Film and Television* for 1981 lists nearly eight thousand courses in film and television at over six hundred American colleges and universities. The majority of these schools offer programs leading to a degree in one subject or both.

17.38 Romantic revolutionaries: a touched-up publicity shot and an unretouched still from *Bonnie and Clyde* (Arthur Penn, 1967). Faye Dunaway, Warren Beatty.

A New American Cinema: The Impact of *Bonnie and Clyde*

A new American cinema and a new American film audience announced themselves emphatically with the release in 1967 of Arthur Penn's *Bonnie and Clyde*. This film, which was universally attacked by the critics when it opened in August, had by November become the most popular film of the year.* It would subsequently receive ten Academy Award nominations and win two (Best Cinematography: Burnett Guffey; Best Supporting Actress: Estelle Parsons), win the New York Film Critics' Award for Best Script (David Newman and Robert Benton), and be named the Best Film of 1967 by many of the critics who had originally panned it. Most triumphant of all, perhaps, *Bonnie and Clyde* is the only film ever to have forced the public retraction of a critical opinion by *Time* magazine, which dismissed the film in a summer issue and in its issue of December 8, 1967, ran a long cover story on its virtues. Indeed, the phenomenal success of *Bonnie and Clyde* caused many retractions on the part of veteran film critics who, on first viewing, had mistaken it for a conventional, if gratuitously bloody, gangster film. *Bonnie and Clyde* was in fact a sophisticated blend of comedy, violence, romance, and—symbolically, at least—politics, which borrowed freely from the techniques of the French New Wave (it was originally to have been directed by Truffaut and then Godard) and which perfectly captured the rebellious spirit of the times.

Based on the real-life career of Bonnie Parker and Clyde Barrow, the film tells the story of two young and attractive small-time criminals (Warren Beatty and Faye Dunaway) from the Midwest who during the

---

* The film was so popular at the time of its release that its protagonists became cult figures. Double-breasted suits and fedora hats of the type worn by Clyde were all the rage in men's clothing, and Bonnie's thirties hemlines temporarily banished the miniskirt from the world of women's fashion. You could even buy transparent decals with which to simulate bullet holes on the windshield of your car in imitation of a famous shot from the film.

17.39 Vulnerable revolutionaries: two botched jobs.

Depression fall in love, go on a spree of robberies and killings, and become national folk heroes in the process. Their victims are not the common people but the avaricious banks and the armies of police that protect them—in other words, "the system." Bonnie and Clyde were thus prototypes of the anti-establishment heroes which have come to dominate so many American films since, and as such they resonated perfectly with the revolutionary tenor of the late sixties. ("They're young! They're in love! And they kill people!" the advertising copy proclaimed.) By mid film the lovers are clearly doomed, but nothing could prepare audiences in 1967 for the apocalyptic violence of the ending, in which Bonnie and Clyde are ambushed after a romantic interlude and their bodies ripped apart by machine-gun slugs in a protracted ballet of agony and death. Penn shot this conclusion with four cameras running at different speeds and with different lenses, and intercut the footage into a complex montage sequence which gives the deaths a mythic, legendary quality: Bonnie and Clyde are not simply killed; they are destroyed. Even today the sequence has an almost unbearable intensity because our dramatic identification with the characters is so complete. In the social climate of the times, however, the new American audience identified with Bonnie and Clyde less as dramatic characters than as types of romantic revolutionaries. And the tense, nervous texture of the film, with its unpredictable shifts in mood and its graphic, sensual depiction of violent death, was as revolutionary in 1967 as were its protagonists. The form of *Bonnie and Clyde* has been imitated so many times by hundreds of "criminal couple" and "road" pictures since 1967* that it is hard for contemporary

---

* In addition to relentlessly juvenile drive-in fare like *Dirty Mary, Crazy Larry* (Larry Hough, 1974) and *Aloha Bobby and Rose* (Floyd Mutrux, 1976), the "criminal couple" format has produced such interesting films as Sam Peckinpah's *The Getaway* (1972), Robert Altman's *Thieves Like Us* (1974), Terrence Malick's *Badlands* (1974), Steven Spielberg's *Sugarland Express* (1974), and Ted Kotcheff's *Fun with Dick and Jane* (1977). *Bonnie and Clyde* also had distinguished forebears in Fritz Lang's *You Only Live Once* (1937), Nicholas Ray's *They Live By Night* (1948), and Joseph H. Lewis' *Gun Crazy* (1949).

17.40 A new aesthetic of violence: shots from the montage sequence which concludes *Bonnie and Clyde*. By intercutting footage of the death scene from several separate cameras equipped with different lenses and running at different speeds, Penn and his collaborators created an unprecedented (though now widely imitated) effect.

audiences to comprehend the originality of the film when it was released. But in 1967 it was clearly subversive in both form and content, and the angry critical debate it caused in the United States was, in many ways, less about a pair of thirties gangsters than about the morality of violent dissent against an oppressive social order.

2001: A Space Odyssey

Another film which caught the imagination of a generation in the late sixties was Stanley Kubrick's *2001: A Space Odyssey* (1968). Produced at a cost of ten-and-a-half million dollars over a period of two-and-a-half years, *2001* offered a mythic vision of the relationship between humanity and technology at a time when that relationship had crucial bearing on the future of American society and of the entire Western world. Like its Greek namesake, the film has an epic structure. In Section I, we watch a tribe of prehistoric ape-men learn how to use bones as instruments of destruction (our first technology being weaponry, preceding even

17.41 *2001: A Space Odyssey* (Stanley Kubrick, 1968): a space station transformed from a prehistoric bone; the discovery of the monolith on the moon; deep space.

language) after they have encountered an enormous monolithic slab in the middle of the desert. Immediately after the discovery, an ape crushes the skull of a rival with a bone and tosses the weapon jubilantly into the air, where it rotates in slow motion until an associative cut transforms it into the axis of a gigantic space station (actually a weapons platform) several million years later. From this station, in Section II, a space probe is launched in which scientists discover a similar monolith buried beneath the surface of the moon. Section III opens eighteen months later with a huge phallic spacecraft gliding toward Jupiter in empty space. Inside are a team of astronauts and a brand-new HAL 9000* talking computer, which guides the ship and controls all of its vital functions. The mission of this probe is unclear, but it has something to do with the appearance of yet another monolith near a moon of Jupiter.

HAL, who seems more highly evolved in emotional terms than any of the humans, suffers a paranoid breakdown when he makes a miscalculation and sets about killing all of the human witnesses to his error. He succeeds in terminating the life functions of three hibernating astronauts and in marooning another in deep space, but the lone human survivor destroys HAL as a thinking entity by disconnecting his memory bank, while HAL tries desperately to talk him out of it. As we witness the computer regress to its basic language programs and finally expire, we feel a disturbing sympathy for it—disturbing because we have been encouraged to feel so little for the coolly disaffected humans of this future world. Alone aboard the drifting spacecraft now, the final astronaut is drawn toward Jupiter and encounters the third monolith floating through space

---

* "HAL" is an acronym derived from the terms for two systems of problem-solving used in mathematics, computer science, and artificial intelligence—"*h*euristic" and "*al*gorithmic."

Suddenly he is sucked into another dimension, where he experiences an hallucinatory trip through time and space in which all perceptual relationships are blurred. Arriving as an old man in a conventional, completely white bedroom suite furnished in Louis XVI style, the astronaut ages to decrepitude before our eyes and is reborn in the film's final frames as the luminous, embryonic Star-Child—a new order of intelligence, beyond ape, man, and machine, moving through space toward the earth from which it evolved millions of years before.

Enigmatic, mystical, and profoundly sensuous, *2001* resists concrete logical interpretation because in a real sense its medium *is* its message. As Kubrick himself has pointed out, the film is "essentially a non-verbal experience. . . . It attempts to communicate more to the subconscious and to the feelings than it does to the intellect."[19] Indeed, less than half of the film contains dialogue; the rest alternates between a brilliantly scored combination of classical and avant-garde electronic music and the silence of deep space. *2001* also broke new ground in photographic special effects (supervised by Douglas Trumbull and Con Pederson), particularly in the technique of front projection* which it is credited with perfecting; it was shot by Geoffrey Unsworth (1914–78) in Super Panavision for presentation in Cinerama. Immensely popular in 1968, the film has a large cult following even today and is constantly revived. It has been ranked by the critic Fred Silva with *The Birth of a Nation* and *Citizen Kane* as an American landmark film—that is, a film which describes "a critical, unsettled area of American life"[20]—in this case, the emptiness of technology in the form of a film which is itself a great technological achievement. From any perspective, *2001* is that most rare of cinematic achievements: a big-budget, non-narrative spectacle of enormous technical sophistication which nevertheless makes an original and personal artistic statement about the human condition.†

---

*A more effective alternative to back projection (see Glossary), in which action is shot against a glass-beaded reflective screen. The background image is projected onto this screen by means of a small semi-silvered mirror, which both transmits and reflects light, situated at a forty-five-degree angle to the camera lens. Since this puts the projector and the camera in the same optical position, the camera does not record the shadows cast on the screen from the projection by actors and sets. Extremely bright studio lighting is used to drown out the background image as projected on actors and set. The process requires half the studio space of back projection and is more convincing onscreen.

The special effects for *2001* took eighteen months to produce and cost $6.5 million, over 60 percent of the film's entire budget; they have never been equaled in their verisimilitude, although *Star Wars* and subsequent films have gone beyond them in scope. The fullest account of how the *2001* effects were accomplished is contained in John Brosnan, *Movie Magic: The Story of Special Effects in the Cinema* (New York, 1976), pp. 218–29.

† Kubrick's best films have always been both technically and intellectually a decade ahead of their time. His classic anti-war statement *Paths of Glory* (1957), set in a French army unit during World War I, relentlessly exposed the type of military stupidity and callousness which would lead us into Vietnam. *Dr. Strangelove, or How I Learned to Stop Worrying and Love the Bomb* (1963) is an unsparing black comedy about the inevitability of nuclear holocaust, produced amid the starry-eyed optimism of the New Frontier; and *A Clockwork Orange* (1971), liberally adapted from the novel by Anthony Burgess, projected a vision of the alienated, drug-ridden, ultra-violent future incarnated by "Punk" culture in the late seventies. *Barry Lyndon* (1975) and *The Shining* (1980) may prove to have been similarly advanced.

The Wild Bunch: Zapping the Cong

The years 1968 and 1969, perhaps the darkest in American history since the Civil War, witnessed some of the most original American films since the late forties. Like *Bonnie and Clyde,* many of them were aimed at the new youthful audience and were either covertly or overtly concerned with the political hysteria that had gripped the nation over the war in Vietnam. If *Bonnie and Clyde* was about the type of romantic rebel who would fight the military-industrial complex to end the war and usher in the greening of America, Sam Peckinpah's *The Wild Bunch* (1969) was about America's mercenary presence in Vietnam itself. In this film, which opens with the bloody massacre of an entire Texas town in the course of a payroll robbery, a gang of aging outlaws led by Pike Bishop (William Holden) grows increasingly restless and frustrated with the closing of the American frontier, and they cross the border into Mexico in search of greener pastures. The year is 1914, and the Mexican civil war is in full swing, but the members of the Wild Bunch aren't looking for a cause, only some action. (As one of them comments after they have crossed the Rio Grande, "Just more of Texas, as far as I'm concerned.") The group falls in with Mapache, a brutish general who is leading federal troops in the fight against Pancho Villa and the insurgents. Brilliantly played by the Mexican director Emilio Fernández (b. 1904), Mapache is a sadistic thug who murders and tortures indiscriminately. His military base in the village of Agua Verde is a corrupt, barely competent dictatorship propped up by powerful foreign governments (in this case Germany and her allies) and their sophisticated weapons technology. The Bunch agrees to rob an American munitions train near the border for Mapache, who then attempts to seize the arms without paying for them. The gang outwits him, but Mapache captures one of their number—a Mexican Indian who has collaborated with the rebels—and tortures him to death before their eyes. In disgust, Pike and his men confront Mapache and kill him. The film ends in a sustained bloodbath as the Bunch seizes the *federales'* machine gun and blasts Agua Verde to pieces, all of them dying in the process.

The spectacular massacres which open and close *The Wild Bunch* are filmed in the style of the final ambush of *Bonnie and Clyde,* with a variety of lenses and different cameras running at different speeds, usually decelerated to depict the moment of death. With the death scene from Penn's film, they are among the most complex, kinetic, and shocking montage sequences in the post-war American cinema, and they are balletically choreographed in a manner reminiscent of the battle scenes from Kurosawa's *Seven Samurai.* The film is also a stunning piece of widescreen composition from beginning to end, skillfully photographed by Lucien Ballard in Panavision-70. Nevertheless, critics of the period were outraged at the extent and ferocity of the bloodshed. The final massacre has about it a sort of mad, orgasmic ecstasy, as the slaughter grows more and more intense until it reaches Eisensteinian (or Buñuelian) proportions: we see more people die than could possibly fill the small village; we see the same people die over and over again. Furthermore, the victims of this "heroic" violence are principally civilians caught in the crossfire. But a

17.42 A mercenary presence: *The Wild Bunch* (Sam Peckinpah, 1969). Ernest Borgnine, William Holden, Warren Oates. (Note the expertly balanced composition.)

17.43 Radical destruction: a shot from the massacre which concludes *The Wild Bunch*. William Holden.

year before the revelation of the My Lai massacre, the outraged critics could not know that they were watching an allegory of American intervention in Vietnam.*

As with *Bonnie and Clyde,* the violence of *The Wild Bunch was* revolutionary, *was* excessive for its time—a thing difficult to see today, when slow-motion bloodletting has passed from innovation to convention to cliché. Nevertheless, Penn and Peckinpah were committed film-makers during the time of the war. Like their counterparts in the *film noir* movement of the late forties (see Chapter 11), they were interested in exposing their audience to certain dark realities of contemporary American life which the audience had itself largely chosen to ignore. Their films introduced conventions for the depiction of violence and carnage which others exploited *ad nauseum* in the seventies. But both directors insisted for the first time in American cinema that the human body is made of real flesh and blood; that arterial blood spurts rather than drips demurely; that bullet wounds leave not trim little pin-pricks but big, gaping holes; and, in general, that violence has painful, unpretty, humanly destructive consequences. By bringing the American film closer to reality in its depiction of the human body and what high-powered modern weap-

---

* In 1969, the original release print of *The Wild Bunch* had more individual shots than any color film ever made—a difficult claim to substantiate today since the film was withdrawn by Warner Brothers after its debut and re-released in several different versions, none of them as long or elaborate as Peckinpah had intended. For example, there was apparently a third massacre sequence in the middle of the film in which Mapache's troops are attacked and routed at a railroad station by Villa's and destroy a neutral Indian village in retribution. (This was perhaps too close to the era's nightly newscasts for comfort.) During 1969, *The Wild Bunch* was shown in alternate versions of 190, 148, 145, 143, and 135 minutes. Only the 145- and 135-minute versions are available today, although Warner Brothers still owns the master print and may some day restore it for public exhibition. See Doug McKinney, *Sam Peckinpah* (Boston, 1979), pp. 88–91; and Paul Seydor, *Peckinpah: The Western Films* (Urbana, Ill., 1980), pp. 78–84.

onry could do to it, Penn and Peckinpah had overturned decades of polite convention which insisted that the body had the resilience of rubber and that death was simply a state of terminal sleep—important new knowledge for the citizens of a nation whose government was waging a savage war of annihilation in Southeast Asia by remote control.*

End of a Dream

Nineteen sixty-eight and nineteen sixty-nine may well be remembered as the years in which the violence of our lives erupted onto our screens. The veteran cinematographer Haskell Wexler's *Medium Cool* (1969) was literally *about* media representations of violence in an America divided against itself by the war. Its main character is an alienated news cameraman who learns in the course of the film how easily the "detachment" of the media blends into distortion. As if to comment on itself, *Medium Cool* was shot in *cinéma vérité* fashion with a climax staged against the very real backdrop of the police riots at the 1968 Democratic National Convention in Chicago. *Easy Rider* (Dennis Hopper, 1969) also dealt openly with the violence and paranoia of an ideologically divided nation, although like other movies of the period it was praised for its radical social perspective far beyond its value as a film. In it, two hippies score a big drug deal and set off from California to Florida on their motorcycles "in search of America." But, as the ad copy read, "they couldn't find it anywhere." Treated with unmitigated contempt because of their appearance everywhere they go, the bikers are finally gunned

17.44 The illusion of freedom: *Easy Rider* (Dennis Hopper, 1969). Dennis Hopper, Peter Fonda, Jack Nicholson.

* What *Bonnie and Clyde* and *The Wild Bunch* did for violence *The Graduate* (Mike Nichols, 1967), *I Am Curious—Yellow* (Vilgot Sjöman, 1967; U.S. release, 1969), and *Midnight Cowboy* (John Schlesinger, 1969) did for sex. All three films were enormously popular with the youth market in the late sixties, and all three dealt explicitly with human sexuality in ways unthinkable only years before. *The Graduate* concerned a sexual liaison between a recent college graduate and a middle-aged woman (his girlfriend's mother). *I Am Curious—Yellow*, which was confiscated by U.S. Customs authorities in 1967 but released by court order in 1969, contained male and female frontal nudity and simulated copulation. *Midnight Cowboy*, a fine dramatic feature which became the first X-rated film to win an Academy Award, dealt allusively with homosexual prostitution. These three films and inferior imitations opened the floodgates for the graphic representation of sex on American screens in the seventies, making possible everything from *Deep Throat* (Gerard Damiano, 1972) to *Last Tango in Paris* (Bernardo Bertolucci, 1972).

Black film was also born as a mainstream enterprise in the late sixties, with films like Robert Downey's bitter satire *Putney Swope* (1969), Gordon Parks' *The Learning Tree* (1969), Melvin Van Peebles' *Sweet Sweetback's Baadasssss Song* (1970), and Ossie Davis' *Cotton Comes to Harlem* (1970). The loosening-up and subsequent disappearance from the American cinema of taboos about racial mixing onscreen (and of *some* racial stereotypes)—probably stronger than those against sex and violence put together—produced both the black exploitation films of the seventies (*Shaft* [Gordon Parks, 1971]; *Super-Fly* [Gordon Parks, Jr., 1973]; *Hit-Man* [George Armitage, 1972]; *Slaughter*[Jack Starrett, 1972]; *Trouble Man* [Ivan Dixon, 1972]; *Coffy* [Jack Hill, 1973], *Black Caesar* [Larry Cohen, 1973]; *Blacula* [William Crain, 1972]) and such interesting features as *Sounder* (Martin Ritt, 1972); *Black Girl* (Ossie Davis, 1972); *Lady Sings the Blues* (Sidney J. Furie, 1973), *Ganja and Hess* (Bill Gunn, 1973), *Claudine* (John Berry, 1974), *Bingo Long and the Traveling All-Stars and Motor Kings* (John Badham, 1977), and *Stony Island* (Andrew Davis, 1978).

down on a southern highway by some angry rednecks. A modestly competent synthesis of *Bonnie and Clyde* and the grade-B biker film, scored with good contemporary rock, *Easy Rider* shrewdly exploited the paranoia of a generation which felt itself at war with a hostile and increasingly belligerent establishment, and it became the box-office phenomenon of the decade. Produced for $375,000, it returned $50,000,000 and convinced old-guard Hollywood that a vast new youth market was ready to be tapped.

This conviction led to a spate of low-budget "youth culture" movies about protest, drugs, and the generation gap. *Getting Straight* (Richard Rush, 1970), *The Strawberry Statement* (Stuart Hagmann, 1970), *Move!* (Stuart Rosenberg, 1970), *Joe* (John G. Avildsen, 1970), *Little Fauss and Big Halsey* (Sidney J. Furie, 1970), and *Cisco Pike* (Bill L. Norton, 1971) were probably the best of this type, while most were so bad that they couldn't even be sold to television after their theatrical release. Perhaps the only youth-oriented dramatic feature of the era to achieve any real distinction—and this on a standard production budget—was Arthur Penn's extraordinary *Alice's Restaurant* (1969), a nearly plotless film about the failed idealism of the protest movement. There was, however, a good deal of vitality in another form calculated to appeal exclusively to the youth market, the rock documentary. While films like *Monterey Pop* (D. A. Pennebaker, 1969) and *Mad Dogs and Englishmen* (Pierre Adidge, 1971) did little more than re-create the experience of a live rock concert for a movie audience, Michael Wadleigh's *Woodstock* (1970) and, especially, Albert and David Maysles' *Gimme Shelter* (1971) attempted to make serious statements about the nature of rock music by approaching their respective concerts as social metaphors.

The "youth-cult" bubble of 1969–70 was soon to burst as the youth movement itself became increasingly disoriented and confused, and Hollywood returned to more conventional modes of production. With so many important films like *Bonnie and Clyde, The Wild Bunch, 2001,* and *Medium Cool* clustered around the years 1967–69, it had seemed for a time that America was headed for a major cinematic (and social) renaissance. But neither came to pass. Significantly, not one of the directors mentioned above, with the possible exception of Stanley Kubrick, has since made a film which truly equals in stature his contribution to the late-sixties groundswell. Arthur Penn's *Little Big Man* (1970), *Night Moves* (1975), and *The Missouri Breaks* (1976) are all serious, intelligent, and cinematically sophisticated films, but they do not compare in originality and vitality with *Bonnie and Clyde*. Peckinpah's genius for depicting mass slaughter has moved from self-plagiarism (*Straw Dogs* [1971]) to self-parody (*The Getaway* [1972]; *The Killer Elite* [1975]; *Convoy* [1978]) in the seventies, although he continues to make interesting films (*Junior Bonner* [1972]; *Pat Garrett and Billy the Kid* [1973]; *Bring Me the Head of Alfredo Garcia* [1974]; *Cross of Iron* [1977]). Even Kubrick, whose reputation as a major figure seems assured, has not produced a film to rival *2001,* although some critics feel that his lavish attempt to recreate the structures of the nineteenth-century novel in *Barry Lyndon* (1975; from the novel by Thackeray) comes close. His horror

17.45   *Woodstock* (Michael Wadleigh, 1970).

17.46   *Gimme Shelter* (Albert and David Maysles, 1971).

epic of 1980, *The Shining,* did little to alter the balance of critical opinion. Haskell Wexler has turned mainly to cinematography since 1968, collaborating as director only with Saul Landau on *Interview with President Allende* (1971) and *Report on Torture in Brazil* (1971), and with Emile De Antonio on *Underground* (1976). Dennis Hopper, whose success as a director was purely circumstantial in the first place, has completed two features since *Easy Rider, The Last Movie* (1971) and *Out of the Blue* (1980), but neither approaches the vitality of his first film. There was clearly something about the political and intellectual ferment of the late sixties which produced, however briefly, a period of great creativity in the American cinema and contributed to the sweeping away of time-honored conventions of both form and content. It was comparable in kind, if not in degree, to the Czech renaissance which preceded the Soviet invasion of 1968. The hope of liberalization released a surge of creative energy whose influence continued to be felt long after the hope was crushed.

HOLLYWOOD IN THE SEVENTIES

Inflation and Conglomeration

The enormous popular success of two conventional formula films, *Love Story* (Arthur Hiller) and *Airport* (George Seaton), in 1970 restored Hollywood's faith in the big-budget, mass-appeal feature, and the seventies witnessed an inflation in the production costs of American films unparalleled in the industry's history. It was a decade of ever-bigger hits (*The Poseidon Adventure* [Ronald Neame, 1972]; *The Godfather* [Francis Ford Coppola, 1972]; *The Exorcist* [William Friedkin, 1973]; *The Sting* [George Roy Hill, 1973]; *The Towering Inferno* [John Guillermin, 1974]; *Jaws* [Steven Spielberg, 1975]; *Star Wars* [George Lucas, 1977]; *Saturday Night Fever* [John Badham, 1977]; *Grease* [Randal Kleiser, 1978]; *Superman* [Richard Donner, 1978]) and ever-bigger flops (*Jesus Christ Superstar* [Norman Jewison, 1973]; *Lucky Lady* [Stanley Donen, 1975]; *The Hindenberg* [Robert Wise, 1975]; *Gable and Lombard* [Sidney J.

Furie, 1976]; *Sorcerer* [William Friedkin, 1977]; *The Wiz* [Sidney Lumet, 1978]; *1941* [Steven Spielberg, 1979]). Between 1972 and 1977 the average production budget for a single film increased by 178 percent, or nearly four times the general rate of inflation. By the end of 1979, average production costs had nearly doubled the 1977 figure to reach the staggering sum of $7.5 million per feature. Profits rose accordingly only if the film was a huge success,* so the financial risks of production were substantially multiplied. This caused a trend toward the production of fewer and fewer films with every year that passed, plus a steady increase in the amount spent on advertising and marketing campaigns designed to insure the films' success (often rising as high as twice the production costs).

By 1975 it was not unusual for a single production company like Paramount or Twentieth Century–Fox to have all of its capital tied up in five or six films annually, every one a blockbuster with an average budget of four to seven million dollars (compare this figure with MGM's average of forty-two features per year during the thirties). In 1977 at least one company (Columbia) had all of its capital, reportedly twenty million dollars, invested in a single film (*Close Encounters of the Third Kind*), and since that time, production budgets of fifteen to twenty million dollars have not been uncommon, with Francis Ford Coppola's *Apocalypse Now* (1979) and Robert Wise's *Star Trek* (1979) topping the list at forty and forty-two million respectively. (Temporarily, at least—the combined production costs of *Superman, Parts I* and *II* (Richard Donner, 1978; Richard Lester, 1980) are estimated at more than sixty million dollars.) The profits to be reaped by a success like *Jaws* or *Star Wars* are immense,† but a single big-budget flop can threaten the solvency of an entire studio. This condition has been seen as inhibiting the creative freedom of people

---

* A Hollywood rule of thumb equates a film's breaking even with returning two-and-a-half times its "negative cost" (literally, all costs required to produce the final cut of the master negative, exluding the costs of promotion, distribution, and exhibition). This break-even figure allows for advertising, studio overhead, and distribution prints (which cost about $1,000 apiece). A low-to-medium-budget film ($750,000 to $3 million in the mid-seventies) was once regarded as a success if it returned four times its negative cost. This calculus went haywire in the late seventies, with big-budget features like *Star Wars* recouping as much as two hundred times their initial investment. The gross which returns to the producer-distributor, and which determines all profits, represents what remains after the exhibitors have taken their cut. According to *Variety* for October 22, 1980, the average production cost per feature rose to $10 million in 1980, with another $6 million in average marketing costs—this, exclusive of another $24 million per feature in national distribution costs. In 1980, in other words, the average American film had to earn $40 million simply to return its investment.

† As of January 1, 1980, *Jaws* had grossed $133 million and *Star Wars* $176 million in the domestic market alone, making them the first and second top-grossing films of all time (and Fox estimates that over $500 million worth of *Star Wars* toys were sold between the film's opening on May 25, 1977, and January 1, 1980). The films were produced for eight and ten million dollars respectively. Some idea of what this means financially to the film-makers is provided by the fact that Richard Zanuck, the producer of *Jaws,* has made more money from his share of that film's profits than his father, the veteran producer Darryl F. Zanuck, made in his entire career.

working within the industry, especially since it has become common practice for producers, directors, writers, and stars to receive a percentage of the gross profits of their films rather than a fixed salary or fee-for-service. It also creates a hit-or-miss mentality among film executives, who, as Leo Janos writes, are "trapped between the need to reap huge, ever-increasing profits and the absence of any body of professional knowledge or skill that can guarantee a hit."*[21] In this volatile fiscal environment, it is almost impossible for a new writer or director to be given a chance to work on an even modestly expensive (seven-to-ten-million-dollar) film. The fact that in 1978 there were approximately three thousand film-makers competing to make about seventy major films provides an index of the limitations this situation places upon the contemporary American cinema.

Exacerbating these constraints is the fact that during the financial and social turbulence of the sixties most of the established Hollywood studios allowed themselves to be absorbed by huge conglomerates. Universal was acquired in 1962 by the Music Corporation of America; Paramount in 1966 by Gulf and Western Industries (whose holdings include firms that supply natural resources, agricultural products, and financial services); United Artists in 1967 by Transamerica Corporation (a holding company for the Bank of America); Warner Brothers (later re-incorporated as Warner Communications) in 1969 by the vastly diversified Kinney Services; and MGM in 1970 by the Las Vegas financier Kirk Kerkorian, who liquidated the studio's land at a huge profit which he re-invested in resort hotels. (Kerkorian, however, invests regularly in the production of theatrical films, and, as of this writing, was negotiating the purchase of a large block of Columbia Pictures Industries stock.) For most of these conglomerates, film and television production accounts for only a small percentage of their annual revenues. In 1977, for example, the entire "Leisure Time" division of Gulf and Western—which owns several publishing companies and major sports franchises, in addition to Paramount—accounted for less than 11 percent of total corporate income. But as Anthony Hoffman, entertainment analyst for the investment firm of Bache Halsey Stuart Shields, has remarked: "One thing that is obvious about this industry, and what has attracted the conglomerates to it in the first place, is that if you take any recent four- or five-year period, and you match total investment in production costs with pre-tax profits, it is not unusual to come up with average rates of return of 40 to 50 percent. . . . No other industry has that rate of return, particularly one that has such a low asset base."[22] Given this compelling reason for conglomeration, only Twentieth Century–Fox, Columbia Pictures Industries, and the family-owned Disney studio, Buena Vista, remain in the control of veteran film

---

* More and more, however, production companies are resorting to the sophisticated demographic and psychographic techniques of contemporary market research to discover what the public wants to see and then to "pre-sell" it. See, for example, Thomas Simonet, "Market Research: Beyond the Fanny of the Cohn," *Film Comment*, 16, 1 (January–February 1980), 66–69.

industry management.* Hollywood is by no means dead; in fact, 1980 was the most lucrative year in its history. But with fewer than seventy major films being produced each year out of an average total output of 160 (compared with 538 in 1937), there are serious questions about the creative vitality of the American cinema.

New Film-Makers of the Seventies

Yet some critics have claimed quite the opposite: that Hollywood in the seventies experienced a renaissance of creative talent as a result of the many young directors now working in the industry who were professionally trained at American film schools. Most new directors of the sixties—Penn, Peckinpah, Irvin Kershner, John Frankenheimer, Sidney Lumet—had been trained in the medium of television, and the modes of teleproduction which they knew best emphasized economy, flexibility, and speed. As with the *cinéastes* of the French New Wave, some of their best films bore the mark of spontaneous improvisation. Many new directors of the seventies, on the other hand, had studied film history, aesthetics, and production as formal academic subjects in university graduate school programs. Francis Ford Coppola (b. 1939) and the screenwriter/director Paul Schrader (b. 1946) went to film school at UCLA; George Lucas (b. 1944) and the screenwriter/director John Milius (b. 1944) graduated from the University of Southern California; Martin Scorsese (b. 1942) and Brian De Palma (b. 1940) attended New York University; Steven Spielberg (b. 1946) studied film and dramatic arts in college and, like Peter Bogdanovich (b. 1939), was a self-taught film buff from childhood. This highly specialized training has produced a generation of young American film-makers whose visual and technical sophistication is immense but whose films are sometimes so painstakingly calculated for effect as to lack spontaneity.

Coppola, for example, is unquestionably a major American film-maker; his epic of organized crime in the United States, *The Godfather, Parts I* and *II* (1972; 1974), is one of the most significant American films of the decade. But there is something about *The Conversation* (1974) which makes it all too obviously a remake of Antonioni's *Blow-Up* (1966) in audio electronics terms. George Lucas' *Star Wars* (1977) is important historically because of its unprecedented use of computer technology to generate special photographic and auditory effects,† but it is

---

* Columbia and Fox are also rapidly diversifying. In 1977, Columbia drew 46 percent of its income from feature film production and the rest from television production and recording industry and broadcasting activities. During the same period, Twentieth Century–Fox earned 63 percent of its annual income from film production and the rest from similarly diversified acquisitions, including Coca-Cola Bottling Midwest and the Aspen Skiing Corporation. In 1979, the excess profits from *Star Wars* enabled Fox to acquire the Pebble Beach Corporation, which owns several fashionable resorts and golf courses on the Monterey peninsula, for seventy-two million dollars.

† *Star Wars* was the first widely released film to be both recorded and exhibited in Dolby stereo-optical sound (see Glossary).

17.47 The dark side of American business: *The Godfather, Part I* (Francis Ford Coppola, 1972). Robert Duvall, Marlon Brando.

17.48 High-tech fairy tale: *Star Wars* (George Lucas, 1977). Darth Vader (David Prowse) and Ben (Obi-Wan) Kenobi (Alec Guinness).

also a film intensely manipulative of its audience's perception. There is no room for interpretation or speculation in *Star Wars:* everyone who sees it has precisely the same experience. The same might be said of Steven Spielberg's *Jaws* (1975) and *Close Encounters of the Third Kind* (1977), both technically polished to a degree but so calculated in terms of effect that they have all the predictability of a Big Mac hamburger. Scorsese's *Mean Streets* (1973) is a strikingly original independent feature; but *Taxi Driver* (1976) exploits the paranoid alienation it pretends to examine, and *New York, New York* (1977), a meticulously studied effort to re-create the musicals of the Big Band era, seems more like a scholarly article than a feature film. Finally, Brian De Palma, who directed some of the most stylish and effective horror thrillers of the seventies (*Sisters* [1973]; *Phantom of the Paradise* [1974]; *Obsession* [1975]; *Carrie* [1976]; *The Fury* [1978]), admits that he approaches film from a scientific point of view and says that he tends to equate film-making with "building machines."[23] None of this is to preclude the possibility that any one of these extremely talented film-school–trained directors will produce a masterpiece. It is rather to indicate what seems at times an almost academic preoccupation with cinematic effect and audience response—the kind of attitude described by Vincent Canby when he writes of "major contemporary American film-makers, who, more and more, tend to put films together with such deliberation you might think that instead of making movies they were building arks to save mankind."*[24]

Perhaps the most important film-maker working within the American commercial system today—and this as his own producer, through Lion's Gate Films, since 1971—is Robert Altman (b. 1925). Altman came to film from television, where he directed episodes of "Alfred

* See, for example, Richard Corliss, "We Lost It at the Movies: The Generation That Grew Up on *The Graduate,* Took Over Hollywood—and Went into Plastics," *Film Comment,* 16, 1 (January–February 1980), 34–38.

17.49 The "last supper" for Painless the dentist in *M.A.S.H.* (Robert Altman, 1970): Carl Gottlieb, David Arkin, Tom Skerritt, John Schuck (Painless), Donald Sutherland (Hawkeye), and Elliott Gould (Trapper John).

17.50 *McCabe and Mrs. Miller* (Robert Altman, 1971): Warren Beatty (McCabe) in the final showdown.

17.51 Altman's *The Long Goodbye* (1973): Elliott Gould as Marlowe.

Hitchcock Presents," "Combat," "Bonanza," and "Bus Stop." His first major feature was *M*A*S*H* (1970), an iconoclastic comedy set in a mobile army surgical hospital during the Korean War, which became the basis for the popular television series. The film is characterized by a subversive combination of humor and gore, and it makes effective use of the wide-angle Panavision compositions and overlapping dialogue for which Altman has become justly famous. While *M*A*S*H* had a tough, absurdist edge and set new standards for the melding of cruelty, violence, and humor, it never pretended to be more than a hip service comedy. *Brewster McCloud* (1970), on the other hand, is a deliberate venture into social satire and Altman's personal favorite among his films. It concerns a young man who is preparing for a bird flight in the Houston Astrodome under the tutelage of a bird-woman mentor named Louise. McCloud must avoid sex, which binds him to earth, and must kill a number of reactionary characters in order to realize his dream of total freedom through flight, an equation perfectly made by Altman through subjective aerial photography. Some critics thought the film eccentric nonsense, but Andrew Sarris was closer to the mark when he called it "the first American film to apply an appropriate tone and style to the absurdist follies of our time."[25]

McCabe and Mrs. Miller (1971), Altman's next film, has become increasingly interesting in light of his later work. Beautifully photographed on location in Washington State by Vilmos Zsigmond, it is about a small-time gambler and (by his own account) gunfighter who founds the town of Presbyterian Church near the turn of the century. With the aid of an enterprising madam, he helps the town grow and prosper until representatives of a large mining conglomerate approach him and attempt to buy him out. Always something of a buffoon beneath his self-confident exterior, McCabe actually believes in the free enterprise system, and he refuses to sell his interest in the town. Naturally, agents are sent to kill him, and after a serio-comic gun battle he is shot to death in the snow. The film ends with a slow zoom into the dilating pupil of Mrs. Miller as she lies in bed stoned on opium after the murder, suggesting an option which many Americans have chosen, in order to avoid confronting the brutality of our economic system.

After *Images* (1972), an experimental feature which attempted rather unsuccessfully to probe the mind of a schizophrenic, Altman made his most cinematically elegant film, an updated version of Raymond Chandler's forties detective novel *The Long Goodbye* (1973). Shot by Zsigmond on location in Los Angeles and Malibu, the film is less a detective story than a sardonic comment on contemporary American narcissism drenched in the languid and decadent atmosphere of Southern California. Philip Marlowe, an unsuccessful private detective, helps a friend who is accused of murdering his wife and defends him staunchly, only to discover that the friend actually committed the crime and has used Marlowe shamelessly to avoid detection. Marlowe, whose throwaway line throughout the film has been "It's OK with me," is finally backed up against something that's not OK, not even in the modern Babylon of Los

Angeles, and he tracks his friend to his hideaway in Mexico and shoots him. *The Long Goodbye* was Altman's most visually elaborate film before *Three Women* (1977), and it makes striking thematic use of Zsigmond's wide-angle and telephoto zoom shots.

Thieves Like Us (1974), Altman's entry in the "Bonnie and Clyde" category, is adapted from the same novel as Nicholas Ray's *They Live by Night* (1949). It deals with three prison escapees during the Depression who set out on a spree of bank robbing, become notorious, and are finally killed by the police. *California Split* (1974), Altman's first film to use wireless eight-track sound, is an episodic story about compulsive gambling set in Las Vegas. Both it and *Thieves Like Us* are ultimately about American rootlessness, but it was in *Nashville* (1975) that Altman made his most telling comment on the nature of American society.

Nearly three hours long* and recorded in Dolby sound, *Nashville* is set in the present and has no plot in the traditional sense. It concerns the lives of twenty-four separate characters in the five-day period which precedes a rally to be given at the city's Parthenon for "Replacement Party" presidential candidate Hal Philip Walker (whose ironic campaign slogan is "New Roots for the Nation"). The characters all come from different walks of life, but they have one thing in common: all are seeking either to become or to remain celebrities in the world of country music and, by extension, of American mass-mediated culture at large. Their individual lives coalesce at the political rally which concludes the film, where a young assassin who has come there to kill Walker kills one of the celebrities instead. As Pauline Kael has remarked, *Nashville* is "a country-and-Western musical; a documentary essay on Nashville and American life; a meditation on the love affair between performers and audiences; and an Altman party."[26] But *Nashville* is also a film about the ways in which our national entertainment media and our national politics—all but indistinguishable from one another—work constantly to distract us from the massive inequalities of our society and the violence of our recent national past. Altman finds many American virtues to admire, but the most important theme of *Nashville* is how quickly we forget and gloss over such things as the terrible public violence of the sixties and the human consequences of the war in Vietnam. Its most urgent comment is that we Americans, in our blind pursuit of success and our compulsive need for social change, are leading unexamined lives.

Nashville was Altman's Bicentennial birthday present to the United States. Such is the high-risk mentality of Hollywood in the seventies that it returned $8.8 million† and was deemed a commercial failure. But Altman has continued to produce the most original and sophisticated films of anyone in the industry. *Buffalo Bill and the Indians* (1976) is, like

17.52 From the final frames of *The Long Goodbye:* Marlowe does a soft-shoe down a dusty Mexican road as the soundtrack plays "Hooray for Hollywood."

17.53 The "gang" in Altman's *Thieves Like Us* (1974): T-Dub (Bert Remsen), Chickamaw (John Schuck), and Bowie (Keith Carradine).

17.54 *Nashville* (Robert Altman, 1975): Barbara Harris as Albuquerque.

---

* Various rough cuts of *Nashville* ran between six and eight hours. A four-hour version was released theatrically, withdrawn, and pared to 161 minutes. There were originally plans to show the eight-hour version as a mini-series on television, but as of 1980 only a heavily edited theatrical print had been aired on "The ABC Sunday Night Movie."

† On the remarkably low production cost of $1.2 million.

17.55 Altman's *Three Women* (1977): Shelley Duvall as Millie Lammoreaux, Sissy Spacek as Pinky Rose.

Nashville, an attack on the hypocrisy and exploitativeness of American "show biz," as reflected in the way in which the title character sustains his own popular myth in his dealings with Chief Sitting Bull. From this completely plotless film, Altman moved confidently into the realm of dreams with *Three Women* (1977), which deals with the nature of the female psyche in mythic, surrealistic terms. The film begins as a social satire with a strong sub-text of mythic imagery and becomes progressively more allusive and mythic until it transforms itself completely in the concluding sequences, which are surely among the most harrowing in the contemporary American cinema.

From the irreverent humor of *M.A.S.H.* to the film-dreaming of *Three Women,* Robert Altman has proven himself to be one of the most innovative American film-makers of the past thirty years. If his recent films—*A Wedding* (1978), *Quintet* (1979), *A Perfect Couple* (1979)—have been ambiguous or obscure, it is because he is one of the few American directors working today who refuses to pander to the box office. Like many of his European counterparts, he has progressively abandoned conventional narrative to develop his own highly personal style. Certain hallmarks make an Altman film easy to identify: the overlapping dialogue and experimental use of sound (see note, Chapter 10); the sardonic humor; the visual lushness and density based on an uncommonly perceptive use of the wide-angle and telephoto zoom lens; the intriguingly unusual faces of his repertory company (Shelley Duvall, Michael Murphy, Bert Remsen, etc.). It is argued that style sometimes takes precedence over substance in Altman, but it seems more accurate to suggest that, in films like *Three Women,* style and substance have finally become indistinguishable. He has seen us with our raw nerves exposed at a time in American history when the conflicting demands of community and individual freedom have never been more extreme, and he has become an epic poet of that conflict. He also works with more economy and discipline than most of his contemporaries, both in Europe and in the United States. As Gary Arnold remarks, by the time Altman retires, he may be the only major film-maker of his generation with as many films to his credit as the directors who worked in Hollywood during its Golden Age.[27] Finally, a certain fashionable nihilism notwithstanding, Altman is making the most intellectually honest films about the American experience of any director since Orson Welles.*

---

* Other contemporary American directors of note who are not discussed above are, in alphabetical order (with some examples of their recent and/or most important work given in parentheses): Robert Aldrich (b. 1918—*The Dirty Dozen* [1967]; *The Legend of Lylah Clare* [1968]; *Too Late the Hero* [1970]; *The Grissom Gang* [1971]; *Ulzana's Raid* [1973]; *The Emperor of the North Pole* [1974]; *Twilight's Last Gleaming* [1977]); John A. Alonzo (*FM* [1978]); Hal Ashby (b. 1936—*Harold and Maude* [1971]; *The Last Detail* [1973]; *Shampoo* [1975]; *Bound for Glory* [1976]; *Coming Home* [1978]; *Being There* [1979]); John Avildsen (b. 1937—*Save the Tiger* [1972]; *Rocky* [1976]); John Badham (*Saturday Night Fever* [1977]; *Dracula* [1979]; *The Formula* [1980]); Ralph Bakshi (b. 1940—*Fritz the Cat* [1972]; *Heavy Traffic* [1973]; *Wizards* [1977]; *The Lord of the Rings* [1978]); Carroll Ballard (b. 1937—*The Black Stallion* [1979]); Robert Benton (b. 1932—*Bad Company* [1972]; *The Late Show* [1977]; *Kramer vs. Kramer* [1979]; *Terror* [1980]); Noel Black (b. 1937—*Pretty Poison* [1969]; *A Man, a Woman, and a Bank* [1979]); Peter Bogdanovich

17.56 *Coming Home* (Hal Ashby, 1978): Jane Fonda, Bruce Dern.

THE SHAPE OF THE FUTURE

Prediction is a risky business, but one thing seems clear: as technological forms, film and television will draw closer and closer together until the distinctions between them blur. Already, as much as 80 percent of all television programming is recorded on film, because film provides better resolution or sharpness of image than any videotape currently available.

(*Targets* [1968]; *The Last Picture Show* [1971]; *What's Up, Doc?* [1972]; *Daisy Miller* [1974]; *Nickelodeon* [1976]; *St. Jack* [1979]); Mel Brooks (b. 1926—*The Producers* [1967]; *Blazing Saddles* [1974]; *Young Frankenstein* [1974]; *Silent Movie* [1976]; *High Anxiety* [1977]); Lewis John Carlino (*The Sailor Who Fell from Grace with the Sea* [1976]; *The Great Santini* [1979]); John Carpenter (*Halloween* [1978]; *The Fog* [1979]); Michael Cimino (*Thunderbolt and Lightfoot* [1974]; *The Deer Hunter* [1978]; *Heaven's Gate* [1980]; Andrew Davis (*Stony Island* [1978]); Peter Davis (*Hearts and Minds* [1974])); Jonathan Demme (*Caged Heat* [1974]; *Citizens Band* [1977]; *Last Embrace* [1978]; *Melvin and Howard* [1980]); Stanley Donen (b. 1924—*Two for the Road* [1967]; *Bedazzled* [1968]; *Movie Movie* [1978]); Richard Donner (*The Omen* [1976]; *Superman* [1978]); Bob Fosse (b. 1927—*Cabaret* [1972]; *Lennie* [1974]; *All That Jazz* [1979]); John Hancock (b. 1941—*Bang the Drum Slowly* [1973]; *Baby Blue Marine* [1976]; *California Dreaming* [1979]); John Hanson and Rob Nilsson (*Northern Lights* [1979]); Monte Hellman (b. 1932—*The Shooting* [1966]; *Ride in the Whirlwind* [1966]; *Two-Lane Blacktop* [1971]; *Cockfighter* [1974]); George Roy Hill (b. 1922—*Butch Cassidy and the Sundance Kid* [1969]; *Slaughterhouse Five* [1972]; *The Sting* [1973]; *Slapshot* [1977]; *A Little Romance* [1979]); Walter Hill (b. 1942—*The Driver* [1978]; *The Warriors* [1979]; *The Long Riders* [1980]); John Huston (b. 1906—*Reflections in a Golden Eye* [1969]; *The Life and Times of Judge Roy Bean* [1972]; *Fat City* [1972]; *The Man Who Would Be King* [1975]; *Wise Blood* [1979]); Peter Hyams (b. 1943—*Capricorn One* [1978]; *Hanover Street* [1979]); Lamont Johnson (b. 1922—*The Mackenzie Break* [1970]; *The Last American Hero* [1973]; *Lipstick* [1977]); Jeremy Paul Kagan (*Heroes* [1977]; *The Big Fix* [1978]); Philip Kaufman (b. 1936—*The Great Northfield Minnesota Raid* [1971]; *The White Dawn* [1974]; *Invasion of the Body Snatchers* [1978]; *The Wanderers* [1979]); Barbara Kopple (*Harlan County, U.S.A.* [1976]); John Korty (b. 1941—*The Autobiography of Miss Jane Pittman* [TV-movie, 1973]; *Who Are the DeBolts? And Where Did They Get 19 Kids?* [TV-movie, 1977]; *Oliver's Story* [1978]; *Forever* [TV-movie, 1978]); Ted Kotcheff (b. 1931—*The Apprenticeship of Duddy Kravitz* [1974]; *Fun with Dick and Jane* [1977]; *Who Is Killing the Great Chefs of Europe?* [1978]; *North Dallas Forty* [1979]); John Landis (*The Kentucky Fried Movie* [1977]; *National Lampoon's Animal House* [1978]); Barbara Loden (1932–80—*Wanda* [1970]); Tony Luraschi (*The Outsider* [U.K. 1979]); Terrence Malick (b. 1945—*Badlands* [1973]; *Days of Heaven* [1978]); Elaine May (b. 1932—*A New Leaf* [1971]; *The Heartbreak Kid* [1972]; *Mikey and Nicky* [1976]); Paul Mazursky (b. 1930—*Bob & Carol & Ted & Alice* [1969]; *Alex in Wonderland* [1970]; *Blume in Love* [1973]; *Harry and Tonto* [1974]; *Next Stop: Greenwich Village* [1976]; *An Unmarried Woman* [1978]); John Milius (b. 1944—*Dillinger* [1973]; *The Wind and the Lion* [1975]; *Big Wednesday* [1978]); Floyd Mutrux (*Aloha Bobby and Rose* [1975]; *American Hot Wax* [1978]; *American Me* [1979]); Hal Needham (*Smokey and the Bandit* [1977]; *Hooper* [1978]); Mike Nichols (b. 1931—*The Graduate* [1967]; *Catch-22* [1970]; *Carnal Knowledge* [1971]; *The Fortune* [1975]); Alan J. Pakula (b. 1928—*Klute* [1971]; *The Parallax View* [1974]; *All the President's Men* [1976]; *Comes a Horseman* [1978]; *Starting Over* [1979]); Richard Pearce (*Heartland* [1979]); Frank Perry (b. 1930—*The Swimmer* [1968]; *Last Summer* [1969]; *Diary of a Mad Housewife* [1970]; *Play It as It Lays* [1972]; *Rancho Deluxe* [1974]); Sidney Pollack (b. 1934—*They Shoot Horses, Don't They?* [1969]; *Jeremiah Johnson* [1972]; *Three Days of the Condor* [1975]; *Bobby Deerfield* [1977]; *The Electric Horseman* [1979]); Bob Rafelson (b. 1935—*Five Easy Pieces* [1970]; *The King of Marvin Gardens* [1972]; *Stay Hungry* [1976]; *The Postman Always Rings Twice* [1980]); Steve Rash (*The Buddy Holly Story* [1978]); Dick Richards (b. 1936—*The Culpepper*

17.57 *Harlan County, U.S.A.* (Barbara Kopple, 1976).

17.58 *An Unmarried Woman* (Paul Mazursky, 1978): Alan Bates, Jill Clayburgh.

But as the line scan* of videotape is increased from the present 525 to 625 or 1,000, as it surely will be within the next decade, image quality will no longer be an issue. As the media futurologist Gene Youngblood told the Directors' Guild of America in a 1978 address entitled "The Impact of Video on the Film Industry," "It's absolutely clear that video *can* produce an image not only equal to that of 35 mm film but actually better."[28] One result of a conversion to tape would be an enormous reduction in the cost of making feature films, and this would mean greater access to the medium by a larger number of film-makers than has been possible at any time in cinema's ninety-year history. (Even today, crew and post-production costs are substantially less for tape than for film.) Videotape technology might free the film-maker from the constraints of an industrial system predicated on large capital investment and enable him to become more like the individual artist in other media.

If the technology of film-making is gradually evolving toward the technology of videotape, video formats are becoming increasingly receptive to the presentation of feature films. Hundreds of theatrical motion pictures are currently available for video screening in a bewildering variety of videocassette and videodisc systems, none of which is yet compatible with the others. Cable television services like Time Incorporated's

---

Cattle Company [1972]; *Farewell, My Lovely* [1975]; *Double Exposure* [1978]); William Richert (*Winter Kills* [1979]; *The American Success Story* [1979]); Michael Ritchie (b. 1939—*Downhill Racer* [1969]; *The Candidate* [1972]; *Smile* [1975]; *The Bad News Bears* [1976]; *Semi-Tough* [1977]; *An Almost Perfect Affair* [1979]; *The Island* [1980]); Martin Ritt (b. 1920—*The Brotherhood* [1968]; *Sounder* [1972]; *The Front* [1977]; *Norma Rae* [1979]; *Backroads* [1980]); Herbert Ross (b. 1926—*Play It Again, Sam* [1972]; *The Last of Sheila* [1973]; *The Seven Per Cent Solution* [1976]; *The Turning Point* [1977]; *The Goodbye Girl* [1978]; *California Suite* [1978]; *Nijinsky* [1980]); Alan Rudolph (*Welcome to L.A.* [1977]; *Remember My Name* [1978]; *Roadie* [1980]); Joseph Sargent (b. 1925—*The Forbin Project* [1969]; *The Taking of Pelham 1-2-3* [1974]); Franklin J. Schaffner (b. 1922—*Planet of the Apes* [1968]; *Patton* [1970]; *Papillon* [1973]; *Islands in the Stream* [1977]); Jerry Schatzberg (*The Panic in Needle Park* [1971]; *Scarecrow* [1973]; *The Seduction of Joe Tynan* [1979]); Paul Schrader (*Blue Collar* [1978]; *Hard Core* [1979]; *American Gigolo* [1979]); Michael Schultz (b. 1938—*Cooley High* [1975]; *Car Wash* [1976]; *Greased Lightning* [1977]; *Sergeant Pepper's Lonely Hearts Club Band* [1978]); Don Siegel (b. 1912—*Madigan* [1969]; *Dirty Harry* [1971]; *The Beguiled* [1971]; *The Shootist* [1976]; *Escape from Alcatraz* [1979]); Joan Micklin Silver (*Hester Street* [1974]; *Bernice Bobs Her Hair* [1976, for PBS]; *Between the Lines* [1977]; *Head Over Heels* [1979]); Anna Thomas (*The Haunting of M* [1979]); Joan Tewkesbury (*Old Boyfriends* [1979]); Claudia Weill (*Girlfriends* [1978]); Ira Wohl (b. 1944—*Best Boy* [1979]); Robert Young (*Short Eyes* [1977]; *Rich Kids* [1979]); Robert Zemeckis (*I Wanna Hold Your Hand* [1978, with Bob Gale]); and Howard Zieff (*Hearts of the West* [1975]; *House Calls* [1978]).

* A video image is produced by 1) electronically breaking down the televised subject into 210,000 discrete picture elements, or "bits"; 2) transmitting or recording these bits as 525 (U.S. standards) or 625 (European standards) successive horizontal lines, at rates consistent with persistence of vision—thirty times per second by U.S. standards, twenty-five by European. The resolution of a video image is the product of the number of horizontal lines scanned for each complete picture and the number of successive pictures produced per second. (These pictures are called "frames," as in film, although they are *not* individual photographic cells since they never exist as complete images at any given moment.) As videotape becomes capable of accommodating more and more scan lines, its resolution will approach the photographic clarity of the film image.

"Home Box Office" (HBO), Warner Cable's two-way "QUBE" system, and Viacom International's/Teleprompter's "Showtime" provide theatrical films in video form to monthly subscribers in many parts of the nation.* And large-screen video projection systems are presently being marketed which offer video images with the size and resolution of a 16mm film projection. As these technologies of home video delivery become more compatible and drop in price, making them available to the average consumer, the entire system of film distribution—and therefore the dynamics of film production—will be transformed. There will be a marked shift away from seeing films in theaters toward viewing them at home. In fact, a 1977 "Impact Service Report" by the consulting firm of Arthur D. Little maintains that home video delivery—by cassettes, discs, cable, or satellite—will be almost the only way to see film programming by 1985. The report further speculates that movie theaters are becoming obsolete and that in the future all films will be distributed through some form of home video technology, except for some "very specialized" projects.† Already, Sony of America has contracts with major Hollywood studios to produce films and entertainment programming for distribution exclusively through its Betamax cassettes. MCA has a similar arrangement with its wholly owned subsidiary, Universal Films, to produce original material for its DiscoVision system. And, as of early 1980, many cable and satellite network owners were preparing to enter the field of program production on their own.

Whether or not the history of film and the history of television merge in the nineteen-eighties, it is certain that the technological evolution of the two media will continue to accelerate. It has been the main argument of this volume that film is a technological art form and that every revolution in its technology has produced and will continue to produce an essential change in the form itself. We have seen how the silent film is formally distinct from the sound film, and the widescreen film from them both—all on the basis of the technology available to film-makers at any given point in time. The body of narrative conventions that Griffith worked a lifetime to discover is available today to anyone who can purchase a copy of *A Primer for Film-Making*[29] or any of a score of similar instructional manuals. Eisensteinian montage can be found in every television commercial. The fluidity of camera movement which once required all the brilliance of Murnau, Renoir, or Welles to achieve can

---

*As of this writing, Westinghouse Electric Corporation was negotiating the purchase of Teleprompter Corporation for $646 million—the largest merger in the history of electronic media—which, in addition to its broadcast holdings, would make Westinghouse a cable giant with 1.25 million subscribers. Indeed, corporate acquisitions are proceeding so rapidly in this field that ownership of the cable systems and satellite networks mentioned above may well have changed several times by the time this book is published.

†Perhaps films in some spectacular new process such as that invented by special-effects wizard Douglas Trumbull (*2001; Close Encounters of the Third Kind*). "Showscan" or "Super 70," as the process is tentatively called, produces a heightened realism for the motion picture screen by photographing and projecting 70 mm film at the rate of sixty frames per second rather than twenty-four. The sensation of a flicker-free image on the optic nerve is purportedly akin to that produced by the "feelies" of Aldous Huxley's *Brave New World*.

now be had for the rental fee of a Steadicam, the new forty-eight-pound hand-held camera that moves to record images as smoothly as if it were on a crane or a dolly. Technology obsolesces itself, art does not; that is the great paradox of a technological art form. To understand the true genius of Griffith, or Eisenstein, or Renoir, or Welles, or any other seminal figure in film history, we must think ourselves back to the technological limitations of their times, the limitations which they transcended to create an art of the moving photographic image. Otherwise, someday in the not-too-distant future, as we sit before our wall-sized holographic television screens and watch images of unprecedented sensory refinement dance before our eyes, we will be tempted to forget how very much we owe these pioneers—not only for creating and structuring our most technological of art forms, but for keeping that form meaningful, significative, and humane. Unless that commitment to the humane can be maintained by succeeding generations of film and video artists, the audio-visual environment of the future is likely to be as cold and alien as the landscape of the moon in *2001*.

CHAPTER 1. *Origins*

1. Adapted from the *Star Film Catalogue* (Paris, 1903).
2. Georges Sadoul, *Histoire du cinéma mondial* (Paris, 1949); and Kenneth Macgowan, *Behind the Screen* (New York, 1965).
3. Macgowan, p. 114.
4. *Edison Catalogue* (New York, 1904); quoted in Lewis Jacobs, *The Rise of the American Film*, rev. ed. (New York, 1948), p. 46.

CHAPTER 2. *International Expansion, 1907–1918*

1. Jacobs, p. 53.
2. Jacobs, pp. 58–59.
3. Arthur Knight, *The Liveliest Art* (New York, 1957), p. 30.
4. Macgowan, p. 163.
5. Jacobs, p. 93.
6. Vachel Lindsay, *The Art of the Moving Picture* (New York, 1915; reprinted, New York, 1970); and Hugo Münsterberg, *The Film: A Psychological Study* (New York, 1916; reprinted, New York, 1970).
7. Jacobs, p. 249.
8. Georges Sadoul, *The French Film* (London, 1953), p. 7.
9. David Robinson, *The History of World Cinema* (New York, 1973), pp. 79–80.
10. Macgowan, p. 108.
11. Robinson, p. 51.
12. Vernon Jarratt, *The Italian Cinema* (London, 1951), p. 16.
13. Jarratt, p. 18.

CHAPTER 3. *D. W. Griffith and the Consummation of Narrative Form*

1. Both quoted in *Focus on D. W. Griffith*, ed. Harry M. Geduld (Englewood Cliffs, N.J., 1971), pp. 155, 163.
2. Linda Arvidson Griffith, *When the Movies Were Young* (New York, 1927), p. 66.
3. Jacobs, p. 103.
4. Edward Wagenknecht, *The Movies in the Age of Innocence* (Norman, Okla., 1962), p. 89.
5. Quoted in Wagenknecht, p. 89.
6. Knight, p. 32.
7. Jacobs, p. 114.
8. Jacobs, p. 116.

9. Quoted in "The Making of *The Birth of a Nation*," in *Focus on "The Birth of a Nation,"* ed. Fred Silva (Englewood Cliffs, N.J., 1971), p. 47.
10. Quoted in Peter Noble, "The Negro in *The Birth of a Nation*," in *Focus on "The Birth of a Nation,"* p. 131.
11. Robert Henderson, *D. W. Griffith: His Life and Work* (New York, 1972), p. 151.
12. Theodore Huff, *A Shot Analysis of D. W. Griffith's "The Birth of a Nation"* (New York: Museum of Modern Art Film Library, 1961). Copyright © 1961. Excerpted by permission.
13. Woodrow Wilson, *A History of the American People,* 5 vols. (New York, 1902), vol. 5, pp. 58–59.
14. Lindsay, p. 41.
15. Lindsay, p. 49.
16. Geduld, p. 8.
17. Quoted in Everett Carter, "Cultural History Written with Lightning: The Significance of *The Birth of a Nation*," in *Focus on "The Birth of a Nation,"* p. 133.
18. Geduld, p. 47.
19. Iris Barry, *D. W. Griffith: American Film Master* (New York, 1940), p. 25.
20. Barry, p. 24.
21. Geduld, p. 165.
22. John Dorr, "The Griffith Tradition," *Film Comment,* 10, 2 (March–April 1974), 54.
23. Robert Henderson, *D. W. Griffith: His Life and Work* (New York, 1972), p. 209.
24. Quoted in Georges Sadoul, *Dictionary of Films,* trans. and ed. Peter Morris (Berkeley, 1972), p. 43.
25. Sergei Eisenstein, *The Film Form,* trans. and ed. Jay Leyda (New York, 1949), pp. 233, 235.

CHAPTER 4. *German Cinema of the Weimar Period*

1. Siegfried Kracauer, *From Caligari to Hitler: A Psychological History of the German Film* (Princeton, 1947), p. 31.
2. Kracauer, pp. 38–39.
3. Jacobs, p. 303.
4. Kracauer, p. 49.
5. Lotte H. Eisner, *The Haunted Screen: German Expressionism and the Influence of Max Reinhardt,* trans. Richard Greaves (Berkeley, 1969).
6. Jacobs, p. 303.
7. Knight, p. 58.
8. Paul Rotha, *The Film Till Now* (London, 1930), p. 255.
9. Kracauer, p. 88.
10. Béla Belázs, *The Visible Man, or Film Culture* (Halle, Germany, 1924); quoted in Kracauer, p. 78.
11. Lotte H. Eisner, *Murnau* (Berkeley, 1973), p. 167.
12. Jacobs, p. 307.

CHAPTER 5. *Soviet Silent Cinema and the Theory of Montage*

1. Sadoul, *Dictionary of Films,* p. 178.
2. David Bordwell, "Dziga Vertov," *Film Comment,* 8, 1 (Spring 1972), 41.
3. Barry, p. 26.
4. Jay Leyda, *Kino* (New York, 1960), p. 143.
5. V. I. Pudovkin, *Film Technique and Film Acting* (London, 1929), p. 168.
6. Ron Levaco, "Kuleshov," *Sight and Sound,* 40, 2 (Spring 1971), 88.
7. Eisenstein, *The Film Form,* p. 240.
8. Pudovkin, "Foreword" to *The Art of Cinema;* reprinted in *Kuleshov on Film,* ed. Ronald Levaco (Berkeley, 1974), p. 41.
9. Levaco, "Kuleshov," p. 86.

10. Pudovkin, *Film Technique and Film Acting*, pp. 166–67.
11. "Chaplin and Chaplinism," in *Meyerhold on the Theater*, ed. Edward Braun (London, 1969), pp. 311–12.
12. Peter Wollen, *Signs and Meaning in the Cinema*, 2nd ed. (Bloomington, Ind., 1972), pp. 46–55.
13. Reprinted in Sergei Eisenstein, *The Film Sense*, trans. and ed. Jay Leyda (New York, 1942), pp. 166–67.
14. Eisenstein, *The Film Sense*, p. 39.
15. Yon Barna, *Eisenstein* (Bloomington, Ind., 1973), p. 70.
16. Quoted in Barna, p. 78.
17. Quoted in Barna, p. 88.
18. Knight, p. 80.
19. Quoted in Barna, p. 109.
20. Quoted in Marie Seton, *Sergei M. Eisenstein* (London, 1952), p. 86.
21. Quoted in Barna, p. 104.
22. Eisenstein, "The Cinematographic Principle and the Ideogram" (excerpted from *The Film Form*); reprinted as "Collision of Ideas" in *Film: A Montage of Theories*, ed. Richard Dyer MacCann (New York, 1966), p. 36.
23. *The Film Form*, pp. 45–63, 150–78.
24. *The Film Form*, pp. 164–65.
25. *The Film Form*, p. 75.
26. *The Film Form*, p. 69.
27. *The Film Form*, p. 82.
28. André Bazin, "The Evolution of the Language of the Cinema," in *What Is Cinema?*, trans. Hugh Grey, 2 vols. (Berkeley, 1967; 1971), vol. 1, pp. 35–36.
29. Paul Seydor, "Eisenstein's Aesthetic: A Dissenting View," *Sight and Sound*, 43, 1 (Winter 1973–74), 38–43.
30. *The Film Sense*, p. 32.
31. Barna, p. 125.
32. *The Film Form*, p. 35.
33. *The Film Form*, p. 69.
34. *The Film Form*, p. 66.
35. Quoted in Barna, p. 70.
36. Quoted in Barna, p. 115.
37. Pudovkin, *Film Technique and Film Acting*, p. 95.
38. Pudovkin, *Film Technique and Film Acting*, p. 24.
39. Quoted in Georges Sadoul, *Dictionary of Film-Makers*, trans. and ed. Peter Morris (Berkeley, 1972), p. 68.
40. Quoted in *Alexander Dovzhenko: The Poet as Filmmaker*, trans. and ed. Marco Carynnyk (Cambridge, Mass., 1973), p. xv.
41. Quoted in *Alexander Dovzhenko*, p. 14.
42. Quoted in Leyda, *Kino*, p. 252.
43. Leyda, quoted in *Alexander Dovzhenko*, p. xvii.
44. Jacobs, p. 560.
45. Ivor Montagu, "Dovzhenko: Poet of Eternal Life," *Sight and Sound*, 26, 3 (Summer 1957), 47. Quoted in *Alexander Dovzhenko*, p. xxi.
46. Quoted in Richard Taylor, *The Politics of the Soviet Cinema, 1917–1929* (London: Cambridge University Press, 1979), p. 64.
47. *Marxism, Communism, and Western Society*, ed. C. D. Kernig, 8 vols. (New York, 1973), vol. 8, p. 1.

CHAPTER 6. *Hollywood in the Twenties*

1. Quoted in David Robinson, *Hollywood in The Twenties* (New York, 1970), p. 91.
2. Walter Kerr, *The Silent Clowns* (New York, 1975), p. 246.

3. Rudi Blesh, *Keaton* (New York, 1966), p. 12.
4. David Robinson, *Buster Keaton* (New York, 1969), p. 165.
5. P. Demun, quoted in Sadoul, *Dictionary of Films*, p. 51.
6. Kerr, pp. 190–92.
7. Knight, p. 113.
8. David Robinson, *Hollywood in the Twenties* (New York, 1968), pp. 38–39.
9. Benjamin Hampton, *A History of the Movies* (New York, 1931), pp. 205–7.
10. Bazin, p. 27.

CHAPTER 7. *The Coming of Sound, 1926–1932*

1. Harry M. Geduld, *The Birth of the Talkies* (Bloomington, Ind., 1975), p. 36.
2. Geduld, p. 142.
3. Geduld, p. 142.
4. Richard Griffith, *The Movies* (New York, 1971), p. 341.
5. Alexander Walker, *The Shattered Silents: How the Talkies Came to Stay* (London, 1978), p. vii.
6. Knight, p. 150.
7. Macgowan, p. 287.
8. Knight, p. 148.
9. Rotha, p. 405.
10. Quoted in Léon Moussinac, *Sergei Eisenstein,* trans. D. S. Petry (New York, 1970), pp. 154–55.
11. René Clair, "The Art of Sound" (excerpted from *Reflections on the Cinema*); reprinted in *Film: A Montage of Theories,* pp. 38–40.
12. Pudovkin, *Film Technique and Film Acting,* p. 184.
13. Lewis Jacobs, *The Movies as Medium* (New York, 1970), p. 245.
14. Knight, p. 153.

CHAPTER 8. *The Sound Film and the American Studio System*

1. Robert Warshow, "The Gangster as Tragic Hero," in *The Immediate Experience* (New York, 1962), pp. 127–34.
2. Jacobs, *The Rise of the American Film,* p. 228.
3. Robinson, *Hollywood in the Twenties,* p. 33.
4. Raymond Moley, *The Hays Office* (Indianapolis, 1945), p. 132.
5. Robinson, *The History of World Cinema,* p. 178.
6. Charles Higham, *Warner Brothers* (New York, 1975), p. 108.
7. John Baxter, *Hollywood in the Thirties* (London, 1968), p. 16.
8. Baxter, p. 34.
9. Jeffrey Richards, *Visions of Yesterday* (London, 1973), p. 254.
10. Josef von Sternberg, *Fun in a Chinese Laundry* (New York, 1965), p. 45.
11. Herman G. Weinberg, *Josef von Sternberg* (New York, 1967), p. 60.
12. Quoted in John Baxter, *The Cinema of Josef von Sternberg* (New York, 1971), p. 15.
13. Quoted in Georges Sadoul, *Dictionary of Film Makers,* trans. and ed. Peter Morris (Berkeley, 1972), p. 112.
14. Andrew Sarris, *The American Cinema* (New York, 1968), p. 57.
15. Hannah Arendt, *Eichmann in Jerusalem* (New York, 1963).

CHAPTER 9. *Europe in the Thirties*

1. Quoted in Sadoul, *Dictionary of Films,* p. 383.
2. Quoted in Sadoul, *Dictionary of Films,* p. 302.
3. Sadoul, *Dictionary of Films,* p. 6.
4. Quoted in Wollen, p. 60.

5. Quoted in Sadoul, *Dictionary of Films,* p. 162.
6. Georges Sadoul, *The French Film,* pp. 28–29.
7. Quoted in Sadoul, *Dictionary of Films,* p. 63.
8. Kevin Brownlow, *The Parade's Gone By* (New York, 1968), p. 547.
9. Sadoul, *The French Film,* pp. 33–34.
10. Quoted in Sadoul, *Dictionary of Films,* p. 276.
11. Sadoul, *The French Film,* p. 63.
12. Sadoul, *Histoire du cinéma mondial,* p. 274 (my translation).
13. Quoted in Sadoul, *Dictionary of Films,* p. 299.
14. Quoted in Sadoul, *History of Films,* p. 380.
15. Bazin, p. 38.
16. Quoted in Roy Armes, *French Cinema Since 1946,* 2 vols. (London, 1970), vol. 1, p. 46.

CHAPTER 10. *Orson Welles and the Modern Sound Film*

1. François Truffaut, "Foreword" to André Bazin, *Orson Welles: A Critical View,* trans. Jonathan Rosenbaum (New York, 1978), p. 1.
2. Quoted in "Journals: Todd McCarthy, from L.A.," *Film Comment,* 15, 2 (March–April 1979), 6.

CHAPTER 11. *War-Time and Post-War Cinema: Italy and America, 1940–1951*

1. Roy Armes, *Patterns of Realism* (London, 1972), pp. 33–34.
2. Armes, p. 49.
3. Quoted in Sadoul, *Dictionary of Films,* p. 264.
4. Penelope Houston, *The Contemporary Cinema* (London, 1963), p. 23.
5. Armes, pp. 60–61.
6. Houston, p. 29.
7. George Huaco, *The Sociology of Film Art* (New York, 1965), p. 185.
8. Quoted in Sarris, p. 110.
9. Bazin, "An Aesthetic of Reality," in *What Is Cinema?,* vol. 2, pp. 18–19.
10. Houston, p. 33.
11. Lewis Jacobs, "World War II and the American Film," *Cinema Journal,* 7, 2 (Winter 1967–68); reprinted in *The Movies: An American Idiom,* ed. Arthur F. McClure (Rutherford, N.J., 1971), p. 164.
12. Jacobs, p. 173.
13. Jacobs, p. 176.
14. Charles Higham and Joel Greenberg, *Hollywood in the Forties* (New York, 1968), pp. 15–16.
15. Paul Schrader, "Notes on *Film Noir,*" *Film Comment,* 8, 1 (Spring 1972), 9–10.
16. James Agee, *Agee on Film,* Vol. 1: *Reviews and Comments* (Boston, 1958), p. 376.
17. Higham and Greenberg, p. 28.
18. J. A. Place and L. S. Peterson, "Some Visual Motifs of *Film Noir,*" *Film Comment,* 10, 1 (January–February 1974), 30–31.
19. John Howard Lawson, *Film: The Creative Process* (New York, 1967), p. 156.
20. Stefan Kanfer, *A Journal of the Plague Years* (New York, 1973), p. 40.

CHAPTER 12. *Hollywood, 1952–1965*

1. Knight, p. 289.
2. Quoted in Robinson, *The History of World Cinema,* p. 281.
3. Bazin, *What Is Cinema?,* vols. 1 and 2.
4. Charles Barr, "Cinemascope: Before and After," *Film Quarterly,* 16, 4 (1963), 4–24.
5. Andrew Sarris, *The American Cinema,* p. 98.
6. Alexander Walker, *Stardom* (New York, 1970), p. 332.

CHAPTER 13. *The French New Wave and Its Native Context*

1. Quoted in Roy Armes, *French Cinema Since 1946*, vol. 2, *The Great Tradition* (London, 1970), p. 62.
2. "Max Ophüls: An Introduction by Andrew Sarris," *Film Comment*, 7, 2 (Summer 1971), 57.
3. Reprinted in *The New Wave*, ed. Peter Graham (New York, 1968), p. 20.
4. Reprinted in *Movies and Methods*, ed. Bill Nichols (Berkeley, 1976), pp. 224–37.
5. Andrew Sarris, "Notes on the *Auteur* Theory in 1962," in *Film Theory and Criticism*, 2nd ed., ed. Gerald Mast and Marshall Cohen (New York, 1979), pp. 650–65.
6. Quoted in Sadoul, *Dictionary of Film Makers*, p. 101.
7. Roy Armes, *French Film* (London, 1970), p. 140.
8. Quoted in Armes, *French Cinema Since 1946*, vol. 2, p. 123.
9. Quoted in Peter Harcourt, "Alain Resnais," *Film Comment*, 9, 6 (November–December 1973), 47.
10. Karel Reisz, *The Technique of Film Editing* (London, 1957).
11. Pauline Kael, *Deeper into Movies* (Boston: Little, Brown, 1973), p. 307.
12. Quoted in Sadoul, *Dictionary of Films*, p. 274.

CHAPTER 14. *European Renaissance: West*

1. Quoted in Robinson, *The History of World Cinema*, p. 292.
2. Review of *Amarcord, Film Quarterly*, 1, 29 (Fall 1975), 50.
3. Michelangelo Antonioni, *L'avventura* (New York, 1969), pp. 214–215.
4. Diane Jacobs, "Lina Wertmuller," in *International Film Guide*, ed. Peter Cowie (London, 1977), p. 59.
5. Paul Joannides, "The Aesthetics of the Zoom Lens," *Sight and Sound*, 40, 1 (Winter 1970–71), 41.
6. Joannides, p. 41.
7. Ingmar Bergman, "Self-Analysis of a Film-Maker," *Films and Filming*, September 24, 1956, p. 19.
8. Ingmar Bergman, "Introduction: Bergman Discusses His Film-Making," in *Four Screenplays*, trans. Lars Malstrom and David Kushner (New York, 1960), p. xxii.
9. Raymond Durgnat, *Luis Buñuel* (London, 1967), p. 100.
10. Durgnat, p. 128.
11. Marsha Kinder, "The Tyranny of Convention in *The Phantom of Liberty*," *Film Quarterly*, 28, 4 (Summer 1975), 20.
12. John Russell Taylor, *Cinema Eye, Cinema Ear* (London, 1964), p. 113.

CHAPTER 16. *Wind from the East: Japan and Elsewhere*

1. Quoted in Richard Tucker, *Japan: Film Image* (London, 1973), p. 64.
2. Quoted in David Thomson, *A Biographical Dictionary of Film* (New York, 1976), p. 390.
3. Barbara Wolf, *The Japanese Film* (New York, 1976), p. 38.
4. Quoted in Paul Schrader, *Transcendental Style in Film* (Berkeley, 1972), p. 27.
5. Donald Richie, *Ozu* (Berkeley, 1974), p. 64.
6. Quoted in Joan Mellen, *Voices from the Japanese Cinema* (New York, 1975), p. 255.
7. Erik Barnouw and Subramanyam Krishnaswamy, *The Indian Film*, 2nd ed. (New York, 1980), p. 155.

CHAPTER 17. *The Shape of the Seventies*

1. Quoted in Julianne Burton, "The Camera as Gun," *Latin American Perspectives*, 5, 1 (Winter 1978), 50.
2. Quoted in *Fassbinder*, ed. Tony Raynes (London, 1976), p. 4.
3. Quoted in *Time*, March 20, 1978, p. 51.

4. In *Fassbinder,* p. 13.

5. Michael Covino, "A Worldwide Homesickness: The Films of Wim Wenders," *Film Quarterly,* 30, 2 (Winter 1976–77), 16.

6. Quoted in Paul Thomas, "Fassbinder: Poetry of the Inarticulate," *Film Quarterly,* 30, 2 (Winter 1976–77), 6.

7. Thomas, p. 5.

8. "Rainer Fassbinder—the Most Original Talent Since Godard," *New York Times,* March 6, 1977, sec. 2, p. 13.

9. Thomas, pp. 4–5.

10. Thomas, p. 6.

11. Amos Vogel, *Film as a Subversive Art* (New York, 1974), p. 314.

12. Quoted in Gideon Bachmann, "The Man on the Volcano: A Portrait of Werner Herzog," *Film Quarterly,* 31, 3 (Fall 1977), 5.

13. "Herzog in Berlin," *Film Comment,* 13, 5 (September–October 1978), 38.

14. Bachmann, p. 10.

15. Covino, p. 9.

16. Quoted in Covino, p. 17.

17. J. Dudley Andrew, *The Major Film Theories* (New York, 1976), pp. 238–39.

18. Jan Dawson, *Wim Wenders* (Toronto, 1976), p. 3.

19. Sadoul, *Dictionary of Films,* p. 387.

20. Silva, p. 15.

21. "The Hollywood Game Grows Rich—and Desperate," *New York Times,* February 12, 1978, sec. 2, p. 9.

22. Quoted in "After the Moguls, a New Breed Rules Hollywood," *Washington Post,* February 5, 1978, p. M6.

23. Quoted in Gary Arnold, "De Palma's Spectacular Sleeper," *Washington Post,* November 21, 1976, p. G5.

24. *New York Times,* July 4, 1976, sec. 10, p. 11.

25. Quoted in Diane Jacobs, *Hollywood Renaissance* (New York, 1977), p. 73.

26. Pauline Kael, *Reeling* (New York, 1976), p. 447.

27. *Washington Post,* July 4, 1976, p. H3.

28. Quoted in *Action,* March–April 1978, p. 34.

29. Kenneth H. Roberts and Win Sharples, Jr. (New York, 1971).

Academy aperture   The frame size established by the Academy of Motion Picture Arts and Sciences to standardize the sound film in 1932. It indicates an aspect ratio of 4:3, or 1.33:1. See **aspect ratio; widescreen.**

accelerated montage   A sequence, made up of shots of increasingly shorter lengths, that creates a psychological atmosphere of excitement and tension. See **montage; parallel action.**

accelerated motion   See **fast motion.**

aerial shot   A shot from above, usually made from a plane, helicopter, or crane. See **crane shot.**

anamorphic lens   A lens which squeezes a wide image to fit the dimensions of a standard 35 mm film frame. In projection, an anamorphic lens on the projector reverses the process and redistributes the wide image on the screen. See **widescreen.**

animation   All techniques which make inanimate objects move on the screen, such as drawing directly on the film, individually photographing animation cells, and photographing the objects one frame at a time while the objects' positions are adjusted between frames. See **pixillation; stop-motion photography.**

arc light   The source of high-energy illumination on the movie set and in the projector. It is produced by an electric current that arcs across the gap between two pieces of carbon.

Arriflex   A light, portable camera, first used in the late fifties, essential to the mobile, hand-held photography of the New Wave and to most contemporary cinematography.

art director   The person responsible for set design and graphics.

art film   During the fifties, a term used to denote a "serious" film (usually European) as opposed to the standard Hollywood commercial product. The distinction is not often made today.

aspect ratio   The ratio of the width to the height of the cinematic image, or frame.

The Academy aperture, standard through 1952, was 1.33:1. Contemporary widescreen ratios vary, but 1.66:1 is most common in Europe and 1.85:1 in the U.S. Anamorphic processes such as Cinemascope can range from 2.00:1 to 2.55:1. See **widescreen.**

asynchronous sound   Sound which docs not procccd dircctly from thc film image. See **contrapuntal sound.**

associative editing   The cutting together of shots to establish their metaphorical or symbolic, as opposed to their narrative, relationship. The prehistoric bone which becomes a futuristic space station in Kubrick's *2001* (1968) is a prime example. See **match cut.**

audion   Lee De Forest's vacuum tube, which first permitted amplification of audio signals for large audiences.

auteur   A director with a recognizable and distinctive style who is considered the prime "author" of a film. See *politique des auteurs.*

back-lighting   Lighting directed at the camera from behind the subject, thus silhouetting it. See **key light.**

back projection   See **rear projection.**

biopic   A biographical film, especially the kind produced by Warner Brothers in the thirties and forties.

blimp   An awkward soundproofing cover for the camera first used in the early years of sound. Most cameras today are constructed with their own internal soundproofing.

blockbuster   A film that is either enormously popular or so costly that it must be enormously successful to make a profit. *Jaws* (1975) and *Star Wars* (1977) are recent examples.

booking   Film rental.

boom   The mobile arm that suspends the microphone above the actors and outside of the frame.

B-picture   A cheaply and quickly made film used to fill the bottom half of a double bill when double features were standard.

broadcast   The transmission of an electromagnetic signal over a widely dispersed area.

cable television   The transmission of television signals via wire instead of broadcast radio waves. Although it was originally developed to permit television transmission to special geographical areas, it has become a popular alternative to broadcast television.

Cahiers du cinéma   Founded by André Bazin and Jacques Doniol-Valcroze in 1951, this Paris-based film journal featured important articles by Jean-Luc Godard, François Truffaut, Claude Chabrol, Erich Rohmer, Jacques Rivette, and other future directors of the French New Wave. It is still being published.

camera angle   The perspective which the camera takes on the subject being shot. A low angle, high angle, or tilt angle are the three most common.

caméra-stylo   Literally, "camera pen": a phrase first used by Alexandre Astruc in 1948 to suggest that cinema could be as multi-dimensional and personal as the older literary arts.

chambara   Japanese "sword-fight film."

chiaroscuro   The artistic technique of arranging light and dark elements in pictorial composition.

cinéaste   An artistically committed film-maker.

Cinecittà   The largest Italian studio complex, located in Rome.

cinema nôvo   Literally, "new cinema": politically committed Brazilian cinema of the sixties.

Cinemascope   The trade name used by Twentieth Century–Fox for its anamorphic widescreen process. The word is frequently used today to refer to all anamorphic processes.

Cinémathèque Française   Established by Henri Langlois and Georges Franju in Paris in 1936, it is reputed to have the world's largest film library. By making older classics available to the public, it is also said to have influenced the style and the themes of French films in the fifties and sixties.

Cinématographe   The camera-projector-printer invented by the Lumière brothers in 1895.

cinematographer   The "director of photography," or "lighting cameraman," who is responsible for the camera technique and the lighting of a film in production.

cinematography   Motion-picture photography.

cinéma vérité   Literally, "cinema truth": originally used to describe a particular kind of cinema that utilized lightweight equipment, small crews, and direct interviews, the term is now used to refer more casually to any documentary technique. See **direct cinema** and **documentary.**

cinéphile   A person who loves cinema.

Cinerama   A widescreen process, invented by Fred Waller, that requires three electronically synchronized cameras; it was first used in the 1952 film *This Is Cinerama* and was abandoned in 1962 in favor of an anamorphic process marketed under the same name.

close-up   In its precise meaning, a shot of the subject's face alone; more generally, any close shot.

compilation film   A film whose shots, scenes, and sequences come from other films, often archival newsreel footage. *The Fall of the Romanov Dynasty* (Esther Shub, 1927) is an early example.

computer graphics   Electronically generated animation, used since the late seventies to provide credit sequences (*Superman* [1978]) and special effects (*Star*

Wars [1977]; *Close Encounters of the Third Kind* [1977]) for theatrical films. It is also used in television commercials and network logos.

continuity   The final editing structure of a completed film.

contrapuntal sound   Sound used in counterpoint or contrast to the image.

crane shot   A shot taken from a mobile crane device. See **aerial shot.**

credits   The list of the writers, cast, technical personnel, and production staff of a film.

crosscutting   Intercutting shots from two or more sequences, actions, or stories to suggest **parallel action,** as D. W. Griffith did in *Intolerance* (1916).

cutting   Moving from one image or shot to another by editing.

day-for-night   The technique used to shoot night scenes during the day. The necessary effect is created by using special camera filters or by special film processing.

deep focus   A technique that exploits **depth of field** to render subjects near the camera lens and far away with equal clarity. Orson Welles' *Citizen Kane* (1941) is one of the earliest and most famous films to use deep-focus shots as a basic structural element.

definition   A term used to describe the facility of film stock to articulate the separate elements of an image. See **resolution.**

depth of field   The varying range of distances from the camera at which an object remains in sharp focus.

diaphragm   The mechanism that regulates the amount of light that passes through a lens.

direct cinema   Since the early sixties, the predominant documentary style in the U.S. It is similar to *cinéma vérité* in that it uses light, mobile equipment, but it stringently avoids narration or participation on the part of the film-maker.

director of photography   See **cinematographer.**

direct sound   Sound that is recorded simultaneously with the image. With modern developments such as portable tape recorders and soundproofed cameras, direct sound has become common.

dissolve   Frequently called a "lap dissolve": a transition that superimposes a fade-out over a fade-in.

documentary   Coined by John Grierson in the thirties, the term broadly refers to any film not entirely fictional in nature.

Dolby   A system (named for its inventor, Ray Dolby) for audio recording and playback which reduces background noise and improves frequency response, adding two-and-a-half octaves to the range. In motion picture exhibition, it can be used to produce multi-track stereophonic sound optically rather than magnetically—an advantage since most exhibitors still use the less expensive optical playback equipment. Dolby was first used theatrically in rock concert documentaries and rock musicals (e.g., Ken Russell's *Tommy* [1975]). Francis

Ford Coppola (*The Conversation*, 1974) and Robert Altman (*Nashville*, 1975) were the first to use it for strictly aesthetic ends, and *Star Wars* (1977) was the first widely released film recorded in Dolby throughout. Since 1977, Dolby sound has played an increasingly important role, in such films as *Close Encounters of the Third Kind* (1977), *Saturday Night Fever* (1977), *The Last Waltz* (1978), *The Buddy Holly Story* (1978), *Days of Heaven* (1978), *Grease* (1978), and *Invasion of the Body Snatchers* (1978).

editor The person who supervises the splicing or cutting together of the shots of a film into their final structure.

emulsion A thin, light-sensitive coating of chemicals covering the base of the film stock.

emulsion speed A measure of a film stock's sensitivity to light. According to a scale established by the American Standards Association (ASA), the faster emulsion speeds are more sensitive to light and have a higher ASA number.

establishing shot A shot, usually a long shot, that orients the audience in a film narrative by providing visual information (such as location) for the scene that follows.

exploitation film A negative term for a film aimed at a particular audience and designed to succeed commercially by appealing to specific psychological traits in that audience.

exposure The degree of light allowed to strike the surface of a film. Film can be under-exposed to create dark, murky images, or over-exposed to create light ones.

expressionism A literary or cinematic style which expresses the author's or director's private vision or offers a distorted perspective on reality. *Das Kabinett des Dr. Caligari* (1919) is an early expressionist film.

extreme long shot A shot made from a considerable distance, sometimes as far as a quarter of a mile. It provides a panoramic view of a location without camera movement. See **long shot** and **full shot**.

fade-in A technique for beginning a scene whereby an image gradually appears on a blackened screen, finally brightening into full visibility.

fade-out The opposite of **fade-in**.

fast motion Action filmed at less than twenty-four frames per second (standard sound film speed), so that when the processed film is projected at normal speed the action appears accelerated. Most silent films were shot at close to sixteen frames per second, and so they display unintentional fast motion when projected at sound speed, as they frequently are today.

feature The main film in a program of several films, or any film over three reels (approximately 35 minutes) in length. Standard theatrical feature length is 90 to 120 minutes. See **short**.

filler light A secondary light that illuminates the subject from the side or that lights areas not lit by the **key light**.

film clip A short section of a film cut out of context, usually for the purpose of reviewing or previewing. Also used in making a **compilation film.**

film d'art A movement in French cinema, started around 1908, that attempted to produce exact records of stage productions; it featured renowned dramatic personalities such as Sarah Bernhardt.

film gauge The width of film stock, measured in millimeters: standard commercial film is 35mm, although 16mm is becoming more common; 65–70mm stocks are often used for epic productions; 16mm is standard for most other films; 8mm and super 8mm are still basically the province of amateurs.

film noir Literally, "black film": a generic term for a type of film set in a sordid urban atmosphere that deals with dark passions and violent crimes. Many American thrillers of the late forties were of this type.

filmography A listing of films, their directors, and their dates, similar to a bibliography.

film plane The front surface of the film as it lies in the camera or projector gate (i.e., the film aperture).

film stock The basic material of film, made of cellulose triacetate and coated with photographic emulsions.

filter A plate of glass, plastic, or gelatin which alters the quality of light entering a lens.

final cut A film in its completed form. See **rough cut.**

first run The distribution of a new film to a limited number of showcase theaters. On its second run the film is usually distributed to a large number of theaters in less exclusive locations.

fish-eye lens A radically distorting wide-angle lens with an angle view of nearly 180 degrees.

flashback A shot, scene, sequence, or (sometimes) a major part of a film, inserted into the narrative present in order to recapitulate the narrative past.

flash forward Like a flashback, a shot, scene, or sequence outside the narrative present, but projected into the narrative future.

f-**stop** The measure of the camera diaphragm's opening. A high *f*-stop number indicates a small opening and little light entering the camera lens.

focal length The length of the camera's lens, measured from the outside surface of the lens to the film plane. Short lenses are called **wide-angle lenses,** while long lenses are called **telephoto lenses.**

focus The clarity and sharpness of an image, limited to a certain range of distance from the camera. See **deep focus** and **shallow focus.**

focus plane The plane at which the lens forms an image when focused on a given scene, measured as the distance from the film plane. See **depth of field.**

Formalism A concentration on form rather than content. Formalism posits that meaning is a function of the strictly formal features of a discourse, and not the content or the referent of the content.

frame The smallest compositional unit of film structure, the frame is the individual photographic image both in projection and on the film strip.

Free Cinema An important documentary-style film movement in Britain started by Lindsay Anderson, Karel Reisz, and Tony Richardson in the mid-fifties.

freeze frame A shot that replicates a still photograph. The effect is achieved by printing a single frame many times in succession.

front projection An alternative to **rear projection.** While live action is filmed against a reflective backdrop, another image is projected on the backdrop by means of mirrors lying along the same axis as the camera lens. The lighting and reflective backdrop prevent shadows.

full shot A shot that includes the subject's entire body and excludes almost everything else from the frame.

gaffer The chief electrician and supervisor of all lighting on a set.

gendai-geki One of two major Japanese film genres, the *gendai-geki* deals with stories of contemporary life. A popular subtype is the *shomin-geki,* or comedy of middle-class and lower-middle-class family life. See *jidai-geki.*

genre A category used to classify a film in terms of certain general patterns of form and content, such as the Western, the horror film, or the gangster film.

glass shot A special-effects technique in which sections of a scene are painted on a glass plate which is then mounted in front of the camera for integration with live action.

grip The person who rigs up equipment such as lights and props, and makes certain they function properly.

gross The total amount of money a film makes in rental and ticket receipts before deducting costs. The word is also used as a verb.

hand-held shot A type of shot made possible by portable, single-operator cameras. See **Arriflex.**

high key A lighting **set-up** in which the **key light** is particularly bright.

highlighting The use of extremely concentrated or fine light beams to accentuate certain parts of the subject.

holography A modern photographic technique that uses laser beams to replicate three-dimensionality.

intercutting See **crosscutting.**

intertitles Printed titles which appear within the main body of a film to convey dialogue and other narrative information. Intertitles are common in (but not essential to) the silent cinema.

jidai-geki One of two major Japanese film genres, the *jidai-geki* is a period film set before the Meiji Restoration of 1868. All *samurai* films are *jidai-geki.*

jump cut A cut that is made in the midst of a continuous shot rather than between shots. Jump cuts create discontinuity in filmic time and draw attention to the medium itself, as opposed to its content.

key light The main light on a set, normally placed at a forty-five-degree angle to the camera-subject axis. See **filler light** and **back-lighting**.

key-lighting In high key-lighting, the scene is almost entirely lit by the key light; in low key-lighting, little of the scene's illumination is provided by the key light.

Kinetograph The first viable motion picture camera, invented in 1889 by W. K. L. Dickson for the Thomas Edison Laboratories. See **Cinématographe; Kinetoscope.**

Kinetophone Edison's sound film system (never successfully marketed).

Kinetoscope Edison's peepshow device, in which short, primitive moving pictures could be seen before the invention of the projector.

kino-glaz Literally, "kino-eye": an early *cinéma-vérité* approach to film aesthetics conceived by Dziga Vertov in the twenties and best typified by his film *The Man with a Movie Camera* (1928).

lap dissolve See **dissolve.**

laser An acronym for "Light Amplification by Stimulated Emission of Radiation." Developed in 1960, lasers project concentrated beams of light whose different rays are synchronized. Owing to its peculiar properties, laser light is a central factor in **holography.**

Latham loop A set of sprockets in early projection systems which looped the film to keep it from breaking as a result of its own inertia.

lens The optical device used in cameras and projectors to focus light rays by refraction.

lighting cameraman The British term for **cinematographer.**

linkage V. I. Pudovkin's description of **montage,** to which Sergei Eisenstein took exception.

location shooting Any shooting not done inside a studio.

long shot A shot that generally includes the whole figures of its subjects and a good deal of background. See **full shot** and **extreme long shot.**

long take A single unbroken shot, moving or stationary, which describes a complex action that might otherwise be represented through montage. It is essential to *mise-en-scène* aesthetics. See **sequence shot.**

mask A covering of some type placed before the camera lens to block off part of the photographed image. A mask can also refer to the shield inserted behind a projector lens in order to obtain a desired aspect ratio. See **matte shot.**

match cut A cut in which two different shots are linked together by visual, aural, or metaphorical parallelism. See **associative editing.**

matte shot A shot that is partially opaque in the frame area so that it can be printed together with another frame, masking unwanted content and allowing for the addition of another scene on a reverse matte.

medium shot A shot distanced midway between a **close-up** and a **full shot.**

microphotography Photographing or filming done through a microscope; also called photomicrography.

microphone A piece of electronic equipment which picks up sound waves and converts them into electrical signals for amplification.

minimal cinema A particularly stark, simplified kind of realism involving as little narrative manipulation as possible, associated with the films of Carl Dreyer, Robert Bresson, and, most recently, Jean-Marie Straub.

mirror shot A shot taken in a mirror, or a type of **glass shot.**

mise-en-scène Literally, "putting in the scene": a term that describes the action, lighting, decor, and other elements within the shot itself, as opposed to the effects created by cutting. Realists generally prefer the process of *mise-en-scène* to the more manipulative techniques of montage.

mix Optically, a **dissolve.** Aurally, the combination of several different soundtracks, such as dialogue and music.

mixing The work of the general sound editor, who refines, balances, and combines different soundtracks.

model shot A shot that uses miniatures instead of real locations, especially useful in disaster or science fiction films.

mogul Originally, a powerful conqueror; the word today designates the heads of the Hollywood studios in their heyday.

monogatari Japanese for "story" or "narrative." The word appears in many Japanese film titles.

monochromatic stock The earliest film stock, sensitive only to the blue area of the color spectrum but capable of great depth of field. Replaced by orthochromatic stock around 1918.

montage Its simplest meaning is "cutting." Sergei Eisenstein, however, developed an elaborate theory of montage based on the idea that contiguous shots relate to each other in a way that generates concepts not materially present in the content of the shots themselves. (**Montage** can also refer to the presentation of a great deal of narrative information through editing in a short period of time.)

narrative A story with a beginning, a middle, and an end (though—to paraphrase Godard—not necessarily in that order).

narrative film A film whose structure follows a story-line of some sort. The mainstream of film history from the medium's birth through the present has been narrative.

naturalism A concept in literature and film that assumes that the lives of the characters are biologically, sociologically, or psychologically determined. Von

Stroheim's *Greed* (1924) is a classic example of naturalism in film (as is Frank Norris' *McTeague* [1899], the novel on which the film is based, in fiction).

negative Film that inversely records the light and dark areas of a photographed scene. **Positive** prints are produced from negatives.

negative cost The cost of producing a film, exclusive of advertising, studio overhead, and distribution prints.

neo-realism A post–World War II movement in film-making associated primarily with the films of Roberto Rossellini, Luchino Visconti, and Vittorio De Sica in Italy. It was characterized by Leftist political sympathies, location shooting, and the use of non-professional actors.

das neue Kino Literally, "the new cinema" of West Germany since 1968.

newsreel Filmed news reports shown along with the main feature in American theaters in the thirties, forties, and fifties; eclipsed by television news.

nickelodeon The first permanent movie theaters, converted from storefronts. From *nickel* (the price of admission) plus *odeon* (Greek for "theater").

nouvelle vague Literally, "new wave": a school of French film-makers, originally including Godard, Truffaut, Chabrol, Rohmer, and others, who started their careers as critics for *Cahiers du cinéma* in the fifties. The year 1959 can be said to mark the beginning of this movement, since it was the release date of Truffaut's *Les quatre cents coups,* Godard's *À bout de souffle,* and Resnais' *Hiroshima, mon amour.* The phrase is also used to describe any new group of directors in any country whose approach to film-making is radically different from that of the established tradition, as in the Czech "New Wave."

off-screen space The implied filmic space beyond the borders of the film frame at any given moment in projection. In conventional modes of representation (e.g., classical Hollywood narrative), off-screen space is treated as "dead," giving the borders the status of a compositional framing device beyond which filmic reality ceases to exist. Anti-traditional modes of representation (e.g., in the films of Ozu or in contemporary materialist cinema) attempt to suggest the continuity of off-screen and on-screen space, giving the borders the status of a window frame beyond which there is more filmic reality. Off-screen space can also be created in front of the screen, as well as beyond its borders, if the camera traverses the 180-degree axis of action established by traditional practice and shoots what is, in effect, "behind" it.

optical printer The machine that duplicates film prints. Many optical processes, such as **dissolves,** color-balancing, and some **special effects,** are accomplished on an optical printer.

orthochromatic stock A kind of black-and-white film stock that reacts particularly to the blue and green areas of the color spectrum rather than the red; widely replaced by **panchromatic stock** after 1926, but still used for special applications.

out-take   A **take** that is not included in the final print of the film.

pan   Any pivotal movement of the camera around an imaginary vertical axis running through it; from "panorama." See **roll; swish pan; tilt shot.**

Panavision   The anamorphic process most commonly used today; it replaced Cinemascope in the early sixties. Panavision-70 uses 70mm film stock without squeezing the image.

panchromatic stock   Black-and-white film stock that is sensitive to all the colors of the spectrum, from red to blue, but is less capable of achieving great depth of field than the orthochromatic stock it replaced in 1927. The introduction of **widescreen** processes in the fifties greatly enhanced panchromatic **depth of field.**

parallel action   A narrative strategy that crosscuts between two or more separate actions in order to create the illusion that they are occurring simultaneously. See **accelerated montage.**

persistence of vision   The physiological foundation of the cinema: an image remains on the retina of the eye for a short period of time after it disappears from the actual field of vision; when a successive image replaces it immediately, as on a moving strip of film, the illusion of continuous motion is produced.

pixillation   An animation technique that photographs a subject so that the illusion of continuous motion is disrupted. This effect is achieved either by photographing each frame separately or by culling out particular frames from the negative of the film stock.

politique des auteurs   Literally, "authors' policy": the idea that a single person, most often the director, has the sole aesthetic responsibility for a film's form and content. François Truffaut first postulated the *politique des auteurs* in his article *"Une certaine tendance du cinéma français,"* which appeared in the January 1954 issue of ***Cahiers du cinéma.*** Other prominent exponents of this theory of film have been André Bazin in France and Andrew Sarris in the U.S.

positive   A print in which the light values of the film correspond to those of the scene recorded. Produced from a **negative.**

post-synchronization   Synchronizing sound and image after the film has been shot—an important step forward in the liberation of the early sound film camera from its glass-paneled booth.

process shot   See **special effects.**

rack focus   A **shallow-focus** technique that forcibly directs the vision of the spectator from one subject to another. The **focus** is pulled and changed to shift the **focus plane.**

ratings   A system of film classification based on the amount of violence, sex, or "adult" language in a film. The British Board of Censors has three categories: U (universal); A (adult); and X (prohibited to children). The Motion Picture Association of America has four categories: G (general); PG (parental guidance suggested); R (restricted to persons under seventeen unless accompanied by an adult); and X (prohibited to persons under seventeen).

reaction shot   A shot that cuts away from the central action to show a character's reaction to it.

realism   In cinema, realism describes a type of filming in which the subject itself is more important than the director's attitude toward it. As opposed to expressionism, there is usually a minimum of montage and **special effects.** See **formalism; minimal cinema; neo-realism.**

real time   The actual time it would take for an event to occur in reality, outside of filmic time. In the works of modernist directors like Antonioni and Jancsó, real time and filmic time often coincide for long sequences, although not usually over the entire length of the film. In rare instances, however (Robert Wise's *The Set-Up* [1949], Agnès Varda's *Cleo de 5 à 7* [1962]), real time and filmic time coincide precisely.

rear projection   A technique in which a scene is projected onto a translucent screen located behind the actors, so that it appears that they are in a specific location. It may first have been used in Porter's *The Great Train Robbery* (1903).

reel   The casing and holder for the film or tape. The feed-reel supplies the film, and the take-up reel rewinds it.

release print   The final print used for screening and distribution.

resolution   The ability of a camera lens to define visual details distinctly.

reverse-angle shot   A **shot** taken at a 180-degree angle from the preceding shot. Two-party dialogue sequences are usually constructed of alternating reverse-angle shots, in a manner that the French call *"champ-contra-champ"*: (visual) field against field.

reverse motion   A subject is shot with film running backward through the camera. When it is later projected in the normal manner, the action appears to run backward.

roll   The movement of the camera around the imaginary axis that runs between the lens and the subject.

rough cut   The first completed version of a film prepared by the **editor.** General polishing and the finer points of timing and **continuity** are accomplished later.

scenario   Either a part or the whole of a **screenplay.**

scene   A rather vague term that describes a unit of narration. In film, it may consist of a series of shots or a single sequence shot in the same location. See **shot; sequence.**

Schüfftan process   A process-photography technique that combines **mirror shots** and **model shots** to create a composite image. It was invented by the UFA cinematographer Eugen Schüfftan (later Schuftan) and was first used on a large scale by Fritz Lang to create the futuristic vistas of *Metropolis* (1926).

Scope   An abbreviation for **Cinemascope** or any other **anamorphic** process.

score   The musical **soundtrack** for a film.

screen   As a noun, the specially treated surface on which a film is projected; as a verb, the act of projecting or watching a film.

screenplay   The script of a film. It may be no more than a rough outline which the director fills in, or it may be detailed, complete with dialogue, continuity, and camera movements, as were most Hollywood studio scripts of the thirties and forties.

screwball comedy   A type of comedy, popular in American films of the thirties, characterized by frantic action and a great deal of verbal wit. The focal point of the plot is usually a couple in a bizarre predicament, as in Capra's *It Happened One Night* (1934) and Hawks' *Bringing Up Baby* (1938).

second unit   In an elaborate production, a supplementary film crew that photographs routine scenes not shot by the first unit. Background and **establishing shots,** for instance, are usually shot by the second unit.

sequence   A unit of film structure made up of one or more **scenes** or **shots** that combine to form a larger unit.

sequence shot   A long take that usually requires sophisticated camera movement. Sometimes called by the French term *plan-séquence.*

set   The location where a scene is shot, often constructed on a **soundstage.**

set-up   The position of the camera, lights, sound equipment, actors, etc., for any given **shot.** The number of different set-ups that a film requires can be an important economic factor.

shallow focus   A technique that deliberately uses a shallow **depth of field** in order to direct the viewer's perception along a shallow **focus plane.** See **deep focus; rack focus.**

short   A film whose running time is less than thirty minutes.

shot   A continuously exposed, un-edited piece of film of any length: the basic signifying unit of film structure. The average shot length (ASL) and the number of shots vary with every film.

shutter   The mechanism that opens and closes to obstruct light from individual film frames as they are moved into position for exposure in the camera and projection in the projector.

slapstick   A type of comedy that relies on acrobatic physical gags and exaggerated pantomine rather than on verbal humor. It was, obviously, the dominant comic form during the silent era.

slow motion   The camera is overcranked to film action at a speed faster than twenty-four frames per second. When the film is later projected at normal speed, the action appears much slower on the screen than it would in reality.

socialist realism   The aesthetic doctrine promulgated in the Soviet Union in the late twenties which insists that all art be rendered intelligible to the masses and, therefore, subserve the purposes of the state. It has little to do with either socialism or realism.

soft focus   By means of lens filters, special lenses, or even vaseline smeared directly on a normal lens, the definition of a subject is blurred or softened, producing a dreamy or romantic effect (and, often, making an actor or actress appear younger).

sound effects   All sounds which are not dialogue or music.

soundstage   A specially designed soundproof building in which **sets** are constructed for filming.

soundtrack   There are two basic types of soundtrack in use today: optical and magnetic. Optical soundtracks encode information on a photographic light band that widens or narrows on the edge of the film strip. Magnetic soundtracks encode information electromagnetically on specially treated surfaces.

special effects   A term used to describe a range of artificial photographic processes or devices, such as **front projection, model shots, rear projection,** etc.

split screen   Two or more images contained within a single frame which do not overlap. Abel Gance used the technique extensively in *Napoléon* (1927).

sprockets   The evenly spaced holes on the edge of the film strip that allow it to be moved forward mechanically; also, the gears that engage these holes in the camera and projector.

stereophonic sound   The use of two or more high-fidelity speakers and **soundtracks** to approximate the actual dimensionality of hearing with the two ears.

still   A single frame-enlargement from a film that looks like a photograph.

stock shot   A shot that is borrowed from a collection or library of standard, often-used shots, such as one of World War II combat or street crowds in New York City.

stop-motion photography   A technique used for trick photography and **special effects,** in which one frame is exposed at a time so that the subject can be adjusted between frames; reputedly discovered by Georges Méliès.

subjective camera   A technique which causes the viewer to observe events from the perspective of a character in the film, either empirically or psychologically.

subtitle   A printed title superimposed over the images, usually at the bottom of the frame, to translate foreign dialogue, etc.

surrealism   A movement in painting, film, and literature in the twenties; the term now suggests any fantastic style of representation.

swish pan   A **pan** that moves from one scene to another so quickly that the intervening content is blurred.

synchronization   The use of mechanical or electronic timing devices to keep sound and image in a precise relationship to each other. Also known as "sync."

synchronous sound   Sound whose source is made clear by the image track. See **asynchronous sound.**

take   A director shoots one or more takes of each shot in a given **set-up,** only one of which appears in the final version of the film.

telephoto lens   A lens with a long **focal length** that functions like a telescope to magnify distant objects. Because its angle of view is very narrow, it flattens the depth perspective.

television   A system for the broadcast transmission of moving images and sound to home receivers, invented in the thirties but not available for mass marketing until after World War II. Since that time, television has usurped the cinema as America's dominant mass medium to the point that Hollywood is kept alive today less by theatrical film-making than by the production of telefilm. The word *television* derives from the Greek for "seeing at a distance."

theatrical distribution   The distribution of films through normal commercial agencies and theaters.

theatrical film   A film made primarily for viewing in a motion picture theater rather than for television or some other specialized delivery system.

Third World cinema   A type of militant cinema now being produced in the countries of Latin America, Africa, and Asia. It is generally Marxist in ideology.

tilt shot   A shot made by turning the camera up and down so that it rotates on an axis running from left to right through the camera head. See **pan; roll.**

time-lapse photography   Used primarily as a scientific tool to photograph natural phenomena that occur too slowly for normal observation, it is a kind of extreme **fast-motion** shooting that compresses real time by photographing a subject at a rate (for example) of one frame every thirty seconds. The opposite type of time-lapse photography would rapidly expose film to capture movement that occurs too quickly to be seen by the naked eye.

track   A single recording channel on a **soundtrack** that can be mixed with others and modified to create a variety of effects.

tracking shot   A single continuous **shot** made with a moving camera.

two-reeler   A film running about twenty minutes, the standard length of silent comedies.

typage   A theory of casting actors and actresses used by Eisenstein: instead of professionals with individual characteristics, he sought "types" and representative characters.

undercrank   To run a camera at a speed of less than twenty-four frames per second. When the film is projected at normal speed, the subject appears in fast motion. See **slow motion.**

VCR   Abbreviation for "videocassette recorder" or "videocassette recording." See **videocassette.**

VHS   Abbreviation for "video home system." Any video system or combination of systems designed for home use, including VCRs, **videodisc** players, video games, and home computers with video display. More specifically, VHS is the technical designation for a popular half-inch videotape format (RCA, Panasonic, JVC, etc.) which competes on the consumer market with the Beta-format (Sony, Zenith, Toshiba, etc.).

videocassette A sealed two-reel system of three-quarter-inch or half-inch video-tape generally used for private recording and viewing.

videodisc A system for home video playback of pre-recorded discs. Audio-visual information is encoded on plastic discs by a **laser** beam for decoding by a corresponding laser beam on the playback unit.

videotape Magnetic tape for recording video images and sound; manufactured in two-inch (professional), three-quarter-inch, and half-inch (amateur) formats.

VistaVision. A non-anamorphic widescreen process developed by Paramount to compete with Fox's Cinemascope in 1954: 35mm film stock was run through the camera horizontally rather than vertically to produce a double-frame image twice as wide as the conventional 35mm frame and slightly taller. The positive print could be projected horizontally with special equipment to cast a huge image on the screen, or it could be reduced anamorphically for standard vertical 35mm projection. The process was abandoned in 1961 because it was too expensive.

VTR Abbreviation for "videotape recorder" or "videotape recording," reel-to-reel or cassette.

wide-angle lens A lens whose broad angle of view increases the illusion of depth but distorts the linear dimensions of the image. See **fish-eye lens; telephoto lens.**

widescreen Any film format with an aspect ratio of 1.66:1 or more. Most wide-screen processes are anamorphic, but some employ wide-gauge film (Panavision-70, Todd-AO) or multiple camera processes (Cinerama).

wild recording Recording sound (usually to be used later as sound effects) independently of the visuals.

wild shooting Shooting a film without simultaneously recording the soundtrack.

wild sound See **wild recording.**

wipe An optical process whereby one image appears to wipe the preceding image off the screen—a common transitional device in the thirties. See **dissolve; fade-out; iris-out.**

zoom A shot made with a variable-focus lens (one capable of focal lengths ranging from **wide-angle** to **telephoto**), often used to create optical motion without **tracking** the camera.

CHAPTER 1. *Origins*

Barnes, John. *The Beginnings of the Cinema in England.* New York: Barnes & Noble, 1976.

Benjamin, Walter. "A Short History of Photography." *Screen,* 13, 1 (Spring 1972), 5–26.

Ceram, C. W. *Archaeology of the Cinema.* London: Thames and Hudson, 1965.

Conot, Robert. *A Streak of Luck: The Life and Legend of Thomas Alva Edison.* New York: Seaview Books, 1979.

Cook, Olive. *Movement in Two Dimensions.* London: Hutchinson, 1963.

Dickson, W. K. L., and Dickson, Antonia. *History of the Kinetograph, Kinetoscope, and Kinetophone.* New York: S. Albert Bunn, 1895; reprinted, New York: Arno Press, 1970.

Gernsheim, Helmut. *The History of Photography.* New York: Oxford University Press, 1955.

Hammond, Paul. *Marvellous Méliès.* London. Gordon Fraser Gallery, 1974.

Hendricks, Gordon. *Eadweard Muybridge: The Father of the Motion Pictures.* New York: Grossman Publishers, 1965.

———. *Origins of the American Film.* New York: Arno Press, 1972. (Contains "The Edison Motion Picture Myth" [1961], "The Kinetoscope" [1966], and "Beginnings at Biograph" [1964].)

Hepworth, Cecil. *Came the Dawn: Memories of a Film Pioneer.* London: Phoenix House, 1961.

Josephson, Mathew. *Edison.* London: Eyre & Spottiswoode, 1961; New York: McGraw-Hill, 1963.

MacDonnell, Kevin. *Eadweard Muybridge.* Boston: Little, Brown, 1972.

Macgowan, Kenneth. *Behind the Screen.* New York: Delacorte Press, 1965.

Marey, E. J. *E. J. Marey, 1830–1904: La photographie du mouvement.* Paris: Musée National d'Art Moderne, 1977.

Muybridge, Eadweard. *Muybridge's Complete Human and Animal Locomotion: All 781 Plates from the 1887 "Animal Locomotion."* Introduction by Anita Ventura Mozley. 3 vols. New York: Dover Books, 1979.

Ramsaye, Terry. *A Million and One Nights: A History of the Motion Picture.* New York: Simon and Schuster, 1926; reprinted 1964.

Sanderson, Richard A. *A Historical Study of the Development of American Motion Picture Content and Techniques Prior to 1904.* New York: Arno Press, 1977.

Spehr, Paul C. *The Movies Begin: Making Movies in New Jersey, 1887–1920.* Newark, N.J.: The Newark Museum, 1977.

Wenden, D. J. *The Birth of the Movies.* New York: E. P. Dutton, 1974.

CHAPTER 2. *International Expansion 1907–1918*

Balshoffer, Fred J., and Miller, Arthur C. *One Reel a Week.* Berkeley: University of California Press, 1967.

Benjamin, Walter. "The Work of Art in the Age of Mechanical Reproduction." In *Illumina-tions*. New York: Schocken Books, 1969.

Everson, William K. *American Silent Film*. New York: Oxford University Press, 1978.

Fell, John L. *Film and the Narrative Tradition*. Norman: University of Oklahoma Press, 1974.

French, Philip. *The Movie Moguls*. London: Weidenfeld & Nicolson, 1969.

Hurt, James. *Focus on Film and Theatre*. Englewood Cliffs, N.J.: Prentice-Hall, 1974.

Jacobs, Lewis. *The Rise of the American Film*. New York: Harcourt, Brace, 1939; reprinted, New York: Teachers College Press, 1968.

Jarrat, Vernon. *The Italian Cinema*. New York: Falcon Press, 1951.

Lacassin, Francis. *Louis Feuillade*. Paris, 1964.

Lindsay, Vachel. *The Art of the Moving Picture*. New York: Macmillan, 1915; reprinted, New York: Liveright, 1970.

Macgowan, Kenneth. *The Living Stage*. Englewood Cliffs, N.J.: Prentice-Hall, 1955.

Pathé, Charles. *Souvenirs et conseils d'un parvenu*. Paris, 1926.

———. *De Pathé frères à Pathé cinéma*. Lyons, 1940.

Pratt, George C. *Spellbound in Darkness: A History of the Silent Film*. Rochester, N.Y.: University of Rochester Press, 1966; revised edition, Greenwich, Conn.: New York Graphic Society, 1973.

Rondi, Gian Luigi. *Italian Cinema Today*. London: Denis Dobson, 1966.

Slide, Anthony. *Aspects of American Film History Prior to 1920*. Metuchen, N.J.: Scarecrow Press, 1978.

———. *Early American Cinema*. Cranbury, N.J.: A. S. Barnes, 1969.

Tariol, Marcel. *Louis Delluc*. Paris, 1965.

Walker, Alexander. *Stardom*. New York: Stein & Day, 1970.

Zierold, Norman. *The Moguls*. New York: Coward-McCann, 1969.

CHAPTER 3. *D. W. Griffith and the Consummation of Narrative Form*

Aitken, Roy E. *"The Birth of a Nation."* Middleburg, Va.: William W. Denlinger, 1965.

Barry, Iris. *D. W. Griffith: American Film Master*. Edited by Eileen Bowser. New York: New York Graphic Society, 1965.

Bitzer, G. W. *Billy Bitzer: His Story*. New York: Farrar, Straus & Giroux, 1973.

Brown, Karl. *Adventures with D. W. Griffith*. New York: Farrar, Straus & Giroux, 1973.

Geduld, Harry M., ed. *Focus on D. W. Griffith*. Englewood Cliffs, N.J.: Prentice-Hall, 1971.

Griffith, D. W. *The Man Who Invented Hollywood: The Autobiography of D. W. Griffith*. Edited by James Hart. Louisville, Ky.: Touchstone, 1972.

Griffith, Linda Arvidson. *When the Movies Were Young*. New York: E. P. Dutton, 1925; reprinted, New York: Dover Books, 1969.

Henderson, Robert M. *D. W. Griffith: His Life and Work*. New York: Oxford University Press, 1972.

———. *D. W. Griffith: The Years at Biograph*. New York: Noonday Press, 1970.

Huff, Theodore. *"Intolerance": The Film by David Wark Griffith: Shot-by-Shot Analysis*. New York: Museum of Modern Art, 1966.

———. *A Shot Analysis of D. W. Griffith's "The Birth of a Nation."* New York: Museum of Modern Art Film Library, 1961.

Koszarski, Richard, ed. *The Rivals of D. W. Griffith: Alternate Auteurs 1913–1918*. Catalogue of exhibit at the Walker Art Center, Minneapolis, November–December 1976.

O'Dell, Paul. *Griffith and the Rise of Hollywood*. Cranbury, N.J.: A. S. Barnes, 1970.

Silva, Fred, ed. *Focus on "The Birth of a Nation."* Englewood Cliffs, N.J.: Prentice-Hall, 1971.

Thomas, Emory M. *The American "War and Peace."* Englewood Cliffs, N.J.: Prentice-Hall, 1973.

Wagenknecht, Edward, and Slide, Anthony. *The Films of D. W. Griffith*. New York: Crown Publishers, 1976.

Williams, Martin. *Griffith: First Artist of the Movies*. New York: Oxford University Press, 1980.

CHAPTER 4. *German Cinema of the Weimar Period, 1919–1929*

Amengual, Barthélemy. *G. W. Pabst.* Paris, 1966.

Atwell, Lee. *G. W. Pabst.* Boston: Twayne Publishers, 1977.

Baxter, John. *The Hollywood Exiles.* New York: Taplinger Publishers, 1967.

Béranger, Jean. *La grand aventure du cinéma suédois.* Paris, 1960.

Bogdanovich, Peter. *Fritz Lang in America.* New York: Frederick A. Praeger, 1967.

Bucher, Felix. *Germany: An Illustrated Guide.* Screen Series. London: A. Zwemmer, 1971.

Cowie, Peter. *Finnish Cinema.* Cranbury, N.J.: A. S. Barnes, 1977.

———. *Sweden.* Screen Series. 2 vols. Revised ed. Cranbury, N.J.: A. S. Barnes, 1969.

Eisner, Lotte H. *Fritz Lang.* New York: Oxford University Press, 1977.

———. *The Haunted Screen.* Berkeley: University of California Press, 1969.

———. *Murnau.* Berkeley: University of California Press, 1973.

Hardy, Forsyth. *Scandinavian Film.* London: Falcon Press, 1952.

Idestam-Almquist, Bengt. *Victor Sjöström.* Paris, 1965.

Jensen, Paul M. *The Cinema of Fritz Lang.* Cranbury, N.J.: A. S. Barnes, 1969.

Kracauer, Siegfried. *From Caligari to Hitler: A Psychological History of the German Film.* Princeton: Princeton University Press, 1947.

Milne, Tom. *The Cinema of Carl Dreyer.* Cranbury, N.J.: A. S. Barnes, 1971.

Neergaard, Ebbe. *The Story of Danish Film.* Copenhagen: Danish Institute, 1962.

Pensel, Hans. *Seastrom and Stiller in Hollywood.* New York: Vantage Press, 1969.

Phillips, M. S. "The Nazi Control of the German Film Industry." *Journal of European Studies* 1, 1 (1971), 37–68.

Skoller, Donald, ed. *Dreyer in Double Reflection.* New York: E. P. Dutton, 1973. (Translation of Dreyer's *Om Filmen.*)

Wollenberg, Hans H. *Fifty Years of German Film.* Edited by Roger Manvell. London: Falcon Press, 1948; reprinted, New York: Arno Press, 1972.

CHAPTER 5. *Soviet Silent Cinema and the Theory of Montage, 1917–1931*

Barna, Yon. *Eisenstein.* Boston: Little, Brown, 1973.

Bryher, W. *Film Problems of Soviet Russia.* Territet, Switzerland, 1929.

Constantine, Mildred, and Fern, Alan. *Revolutionary Soviet Film Posters.* Baltimore: Johns Hopkins University Press, 1974.

Dickinson, Thorold. *Soviet Cinema.* London: Falcon Press, 1948.

Dovzhenko, Alexander. *Alexander Dovzhenko: The Poet as Filmmaker.* Translated and edited by Marco Carynnyk. Cambridge, Mass.: MIT Press, 1973.

Eisenstein, Sergei. *The Complete Films of Eisenstein.* New York: E. P. Dutton, 1974.

———. *Film Form.* Translated and edited by Jay Leyda. New York: Harcourt Brace Jovanovich, 1969.

———. *The Film Sense.* Translated and edited by Jay Leyda. New York: Harcourt Brace Jovanovich, 1969.

———. *Notes of a Film Director.* New York: Dover Books, 1970.

Feldman, Seth R. *The Evolution of Style in the Early Work of Dziga Vertov.* New York: Arno Press, 1977.

Hough, Richard. *The Potemkin Mutiny.* Englewood Cliffs, N.J.: Prentice-Hall, 1960.

The Influence of Silent Soviet Cinema on World Cinema. Proceedings of the International Federation of Film Archives Symposium. Varna, Bulgaria, June 29–July 2, 1977.

Kuleshov, Lev. *Kuleshov on Film.* Translated and edited by Ronald Levaco. Berkeley: University of California Press, 1974.

Leyda, Jay. *Kino: A History of the Russian and Soviet Cinema.* London: George Allen & Unwin, 1960.

Marshall, Herbert, ed. *Sergei Eisenstein's "The Battleship Potemkin."* New York: Avon Books, 1978.

Mayer, David. *Eisenstein's "Potemkin."* New York: Grossman Publishers, 1972. (Shot-by-shot analysis.)

Moussinac, Léon. *Sergei Eisenstein.* Translated by D. Sandy Petrey. New York: Crown Publishers, 1970.

Nizhnii, Vladimir. *Lessons with Eisenstein.* Translated by Ivor Montagu. London: George Allen & Unwin, 1952; New York: Hill & Wang, 1962.

Pudovkin, V. I. *Film Technique and Film Acting.* London, 1929; reprinted, New York: Grove Press, 1970.

Sadoul, Georges. *Dziga Vertov.* Paris, 1971.

Schnitzer, Jean, ed. *Cinema in Revolution.* New York: Hill & Wang, 1973.

————, and Schnitzer, Luda. *Dovjenko.* Paris, 1966.

Seton, Marie. *Sergei M. Eisenstein.* New York: A. A. Wyn, 1953.

"Soviet Film." *Cinema Journal,* 17, 1 (Fall 1977 [special issue]).

Swallow, Norman. *Eisenstein: A Documentary Portrait.* London: George Allen & Unwin, 1976; New York: E. P. Dutton, 1977.

Taylor, Richard. *The Politics of the Soviet Cinema, 1917–1929.* London: Cambridge University Press, 1979.

CHAPTER 6. *Hollywood in the Twenties*

Asplund, Una. *Chaplin's Films.* Translated by Paul Britten Austin. London: David & Charles, 1971.

Barr, Charles. *Laurel and Hardy.* Berkeley: University of California Press, 1968.

Blesh, Rudi. *Keaton.* New York: Macmillan, 1966.

Brownlow, Kevin. *The Parade's Gone By.* New York: Alfred A. Knopf, 1968.

————, and Kobal, John. *Hollywood: The Pioneers.* New York: Alfred A. Knopf, 1979.

Brownlow, Kevin. *The Parade's Gone By.* New York: Alfred A. Knopf, 1968.

Byron, Stuart. *Movie Comedy.* New York: Grossman Publishers, 1977.

Calder-Marshall, Arthur. *The Innocent Eye.* New York: Harcourt, Brace, and World, 1963.

Carey, Gary. *Lost Films.* New York: Museum of Modern Art, 1970.

Carringer, Robert, and Sabath, Barry. *Ernst Lubitsch: A Guide to References and Resources.* Boston: G. K. Hall, 1978.

Chaplin, Charles. *My Autobiography.* New York: Pocket Books, 1966.

"Chaplin: Twelve Essays." *Film Comment,* 8, 3 (September–October 1972) [special issue]).

Cooke, Alistair. *Douglas Fairbanks: The Making of a Screen Character.* New York: Macmillan, 1940.

Curtis, Thomas Quinn. *Von Stroheim.* New York: Farrar, Straus & Giroux, 1971.

Dardis, Tom. *Keaton: The Man Who Wouldn't Lie Down.* New York: Charles Scribner's Sons, 1979.

Durgnat, Raymond. *The Crazy Mirror.* New York: Horizon Press, 1969.

Finler, Joel. *Stroheim.* Berkeley: University of California Press, 1968.

Gifford, Denis. *Chaplin.* Garden City. N.Y.: Doubleday, 1974.

Hall, Ben. *The Golden Age of the Movie Palace.* New York: Clarkson Potter, 1961.

Herndon, Booton. *Mary Pickford and Douglas Fairbanks.* New York: W. W. Norton, 1977.

Kerr, Walter. *The Silent Clowns.* New York: Alfred A. Knopf, 1975.

Lebel, J. P. *Buster Keaton.* Cranbury, N.J.: A. S. Barnes, 1967.

Lloyd, Harold. *An American Comedy.* New York: Dover Books, 1971.

McCabe, John. *Laurel and Hardy.* New York: E. P. Dutton, 1975.

McCaffrey, Donald W., ed. *Focus on Chaplin.* Englewood Cliffs, N.J.: Prentice-Hall, 1971.

Mast, Gerald. *The Comic Mind.* New York: Bobbs-Merrill, 1973.

Moews, Daniel. *Keaton: The Silent Features Close Up.* Berkeley: University of California Press, 1977.

Montgomery, John. *Comedy Films.* London: George Allen & Unwin, 1968.

Robinson, David. *Buster Keaton.* Bloomington: Indiana University Press, 1969.

————. *Hollywood in the Twenties.* Cranbury, N.J.: A. S. Barnes, 1968.

Rubinstein, E. *Filmguide to "The General."* Bloomington: Indiana University Press, 1973.

Schickel, Richard, and Fairbanks, Douglas, Jr. *The Fairbanks Album*. Boston: New York Graphic Society, 1975.

Sennett, Mack. *King of Comedy*. Garden City, N.Y.: Doubleday, 1954.

Sinclair, Upton. *Upton Sinclair Presents William Fox*. Los Angeles: Upton Sinclair, 1933.

Thomson, David. *Movie Man*. New York: Stein & Day, 1967.

Tyler, Parker. *Chaplin, Last of the Clowns*. New York: Horizon Press, 1972.

Wead, George. *The Film Career of Buster Keaton*. Boston: G. K. Hall, 1977.

Weinberg, Herman G. *The Complete "Greed."* New York: E. P. Dutton, 1972.

———. *The Lubitsch Touch*. New York: E. P. Dutton, 1971.

———. *Stroheim: A Pictorial Record of His Nine Films*. New York: Dover Books, 1975.

CHAPTER 7. *The Coming of Sound, 1926–1932*

Bergman, Andrew. *We're in the Money: Depression America and Its Films*. New York: New York University Press, 1971.

Cameron, Evan W., ed. *Sound and the Cinema: The Coming of Sound to American Film*. Pleasantville, N.Y.: Redgrave, 1979.

Geduld, Harry M. *The Birth of the Talkies: From Edison to Jolson*. Bloomington: Indiana University Press, 1975.

Hoffman, Charles. *Sounds for Silents*. New York: Museum of Modern Art, 1970.

Rosten, Leo C. *Hollywood: The Movie Colony, the Movie Makers*. New York: Harcourt, Brace, 1941.

Ryan, Roderick T. *A History of Motion Picture Color Technology*. New York: Focal Press, 1978.

Thorp, M. F. *America at the Movies*. New Haven: Yale University Press, 1939.

Thrasher, Frederic. *Okay for Sound*. New York: Duell, Sloan & Pierce, 1964.

Walker, Alexander. *The Shattered Silents: How the Talkies Came to Stay*. London: Elm Tree Books, 1978.

CHAPTER 8. *The Sound Film and the American Studio System*

Allen, Frederick Lewis. *Only Yesterday*. New York: Harper & Brothers, 1940.

Anderegg, Michael A. *William Wyler*. Boston: Twayne Publishers, 1979.

Balio, Tino. *United Artists*. Madison: University of Wisconsin Press, 1976.

Baxter, John. *The Cinema of John Ford*. London: Tantivy Press, 1971.

———. *The Cinema of Josef von Sternberg*. London: Tantivy Press, 1971.

———. *Hollywood in the Thirties*. Cranbury, N.J.: A. S. Barnes, 1968.

Behlmer, Rudy, ed. *Memo from David O. Selznick*. New York: Viking Press, 1972.

Benchley, Nathaniel. *Bogart*. Boston: Little, Brown, 1975.

Bogdanovich, Peter. *John Ford*. Berkeley: University of California Press, 1968.

Canham, Kingsley; Denton, Clive; Belton, John; et al. *The Hollywood Professionals,* vols. 1, 2, 3, and 4. Cranbury, N.J.: A. S. Barnes, 1974–78.

Capra, Frank. *The Name Above the Title*. New York: Bantam Books, 1971.

Croce, Arlene. *The Fred Astaire and Ginger Rogers Book*. New York: Vintage Books, 1977.

Durgnat, Raymond. *The Strange Case of Alfred Hitchcock*. Boston: M.I.T. Press, 1975.

Eames, John D. *The MGM Story: The Complete Story of Fifty Roaring Years*. New York: Crown Publishers, 1964.

Fernett, Gene. *Poverty Row*. Satellite Beach, Fla.: Coral Reef Publications, 1973.

Fielding, Raymond. *The March of Time*. New York: Oxford University Press, 1978.

Finch, Christopher. *The Art of Walt Disney*. New York: Harry N. Abrams, 1975.

French, Warren. *Filmguide to "The Grapes of Wrath."* Bloomington: Indiana University Press, 1973.

Glatner, Richard, ed. *Frank Capra*. Ann Arbor: University of Michigan Press, 1975.

Halliwell, Leslie. *Mountain of Dreams: The Golden Years of Paramount Pictures*. London: Hart-Davis, MacGibbon, 1978.

Harris, Robert A. *The Films of Alfred Hitchcock.* Secaucus, N.Y.: Citadel Press, 1976.

Higham, Charles. *Hollywood Cameramen.* Bloomington: Indiana University Press, 1970.

———. *Warner Brothers: A History of the Studio.* New York: Charles Scribner's Sons, 1975.

Hirschhorn, Clive. *The Warner Brothers Story.* New York: Crown Publishers, 1979.

Kempton, Murray. *Part of Our Time: Some Monuments and Ruins of the Thirties.* New York: Simon and Schuster, 1955.

Klingender, F. D., and Legg, Stuart. *Money Behind the Screen.* London: Lawrence & Wishart, 1937.

Koszarski, Richard. *Hollywood Directors, 1914–1940.* New York: Oxford University Press, 1976.

Lambert, Gavin. *On Cukor.* New York: Capricorn Books, 1973.

LaValley, Albert, ed. *Focus on Hitchcock.* Englewood Cliffs, N.J.: Prentice-Hall, 1972.

McBride, Joseph, ed. *Focus on Howard Hawks.* Englewood Cliffs, N.J.: Prentice-Hall, 1972.

McBride, Joseph, and Wilmington, Michael. *John Ford.* New York: DaCapo Press, 1975.

McCarthy, Todd, and Flynn, Charles. *Kings of the B's.* New York: E. P. Dutton, 1975.

Madsen, Axel. *William Wyler.* New York: Thomas Y. Crowell, 1973.

Marx, Arthur. *Goldwyn.* New York: W. W. Norton, 1976.

Marx, Samuel. *Mayer and Thalberg.* New York: Random House, 1975.

Miller, Don. *"B" Movies.* New York: Curtis Books, 1973.

Milne, Tom. *Rouben Mamoulian.* London: Thames and Hudson, 1969.

Naremore, James. *Filmguide to "Psycho."* Bloomington: Indiana University Press, 1973.

Parish, James R. *The Golden Era: The MGM Stock Company.* New Rochelle, N.Y.: Arlington House, 1974.

———. *The Great Gangster Pictures.* Metuchen, N.J.: Scarecrow Press, 1976.

Perlman, William. *The Movies on Trial.* New York: Macmillan, 1936.

Perry, George. *The Films of Alfred Hitchcock.* New York: E. P. Dutton, 1965.

Rohmer, Eric, and Chabrol, Claude. *Hitchcock: The First Forty-Four Films.* Translated and with an introduction by Stanley Hochman. New York: Frederick Ungar, 1979.

Sarris, Andrew. *The Films of Josef von Sternberg.* New York: Doubleday, 1966.

———. *The John Ford Movie Mystery.* Bloomington: Indiana University Press, 1975.

Schickel, Richard. *The Disney Version.* New York: Simon and Schuster, 1968.

Sennett, Ted. *Warner Brothers Presents.* New Rochelle, N.Y.: Arlington House, 1971.

Sinclair, Andrew. *John Ford.* New York: The Dial Press/James Wade, 1979.

Spoto, Donald. *The Art of Alfred Hitchcock: Fifty Years of His Motion Pictures.* New York: Hopkinson and Blake, 1976.

Taylor, John Russell. *Hitch: The Life and Times of Alfred Hitchcock.* New York: Pantheon Books, 1978.

Thomas, Bob. *Walt Disney.* New York: Simon and Schuster, 1976.

Thomas, Tony. *The Busby Berkeley Book.* Greenwich, Conn.: New York Graphic Society, 1969.

———, and Solomon, Aubrey. *The Films of Twentieth Century-Fox: A Pictorial History.* New York: Citadel Press, 1979.

Truffaut, François, and Scott, Helen. *Hitchcock.* New York: Simon and Schuster, 1966.

Tuska, Jon, ed. *Close Up: The Contract Director.* Metuchen, N.J.: Scarecrow Press, 1976.

———. *Close Up: The Hollywood Director.* Metuchen, N.J.: Scarecrow Press, 1978.

Vidor, King. *On Film Making.* New York: David McKay, 1972.

Weinberg, Herman G. *Josef von Sternberg.* New York: E. P. Dutton, 1967.

Willis, Donald C. *The Films of Frank Capra.* Metuchen, N.J.: Scarecrow Press, 1974.

———. *The Films of Howard Hawks.* Metuchen, N.J.: Scarecrow Press, 1975.

Wood, Robin. *Hitchcock's Films.* Cranbury, N.J.: A. S. Barnes, 1969.

———. *Howard Hawks.* Garden City, N.Y.: Doubleday, 1968.

Yacowar, Maurice. *Hitchcock's British Films.* Hamden, Conn.: Archon Books, 1977.

CHAPTER 9. *Europe in the Thirties*

Babitsky, Paul. *The Soviet Film Industry.* New York: Frederick A. Praeger, 1955.

Balcon, Michael. *Twenty Years of British Film.* London: Falcon Press, 1947.

Baxter, John. *The Hollywood Exiles.* New York: Taplinger Publishers, 1976. (European émigrés in Hollywood.)

Bazin, André. *Jean Renoir.* Edited by François Truffaut. New York: Simon and Schuster, 1973.

Birkos, Alexander S. *Soviet Cinema: Directors and Films.* Hamden, Conn.: Archon Books, 1976.

Bordwell, David. *Filmguide to "La Passion de Jeanne d'Arc."* Bloomington: Indiana University Press, 1973.

Braudy, Leo. *Jean Renoir.* Garden City, N.Y.: Doubleday, 1972.

Durgnat, Raymond. *Jean Renoir.* Berkeley: University of California Press, 1975.

Faulkner, Christopher. *Jean Renoir: A Guide to References and Resources.* Boston: G. K. Hall, 1979.

Fraigneau, André. *Cocteau on the Film.* 1954; reprinted, New York: Dover Books, 1972.

Geduld, Harry M., and Gottesman, Ronald, eds. *The Making and Unmaking of "Que Viva México!"* Bloomington: Indiana University Press, 1970.

Gilliatt, Penelope. *Jean Renoir: Essays, Conversations, Reviews.* New York: McGraw-Hill, 1975.

Gilson, René. *Jean Cocteau.* New York: Crown Publishers, 1974.

Infield, Glenn. *Leni Riefenstahl: The Fallen Film Goddess.* New York: Thomas Y. Crowell, 1976.

Ivens, Joris. *The Camera and I.* New York: International Publishers, 1969.

Hull, David Stewart. *Film in the Third Reich.* Berkeley: University of California Press, 1969.

Kulik, Karol. *Alexander Korda.* London: W. H. Allen, 1975.

Lawder, Standish D. *The Cubist Cinema.* New York: New York University Press, 1975.

Leiser, Erwin. *Nazi Cinema.* New York: Macmillan, 1974.

Leprohon, Pierre. *Jean Renoir.* New York: Crown Publishers, 1971.

Low, Rachel. *The History of the British Film, 1929–1939: Documentary and Educational Films of the 1930s.* London: George Allen & Unwin, 1979.

———. *The History of the British Film, 1929–1939: Films of Comment and Persuasion of the 1930s.* London: George Allen & Unwin, 1979.

Mast, Gerald. *Filmguide to "The Rules of the Game."* Bloomington: Indiana University Press, 1973.

Minton, David B. *The Films of Leni Riefenstahl.* Metuchen, N.J.: Scarecrow Press, 1978.

Montagu, Ivor. *With Eisenstein in Hollywood.* New York: International Publishers, 1967.

Ogle, Patrick. "Technological Influences Upon the Development of Deep Focus Photography in the United States," *Screen,* 13, 1 (Spring 1972), 45–72.

Perry, George. *The Great British Picture Show.* New York: Hill & Wang, 1974.

Petley, Julian. *Capital and Culture: German Cinema, 1933–45.* London: British Film Institute, 1979.

Renoir, Jean. *My Life and My Films.* Translated by Norman Denny. New York: Atheneum Publishers, 1974.

Sadoul, Georges. *French Film.* London: Falcon Press, 1953.

Salles Gomes, P. E. *Jean Vigo.* Berkeley: University of California Press, 1971.

Sesonske, Alexander. *Jean Renoir: The French Films, 1924–1939.* Cambridge, Mass.: Harvard University Press, 1980.

Smith, John M. *Jean Vigo.* New York: Frederick A. Praeger, 1972.

Taylor, Richard. *Film Propaganda: Soviet Russia and Nazi Germany.* New York: Barnes & Noble, 1979.

Wollenberg, Hans H. *Fifty Years of German Film.* London: Falcon Press, 1947; reprinted, New York: Arno Press, 1972.

CHAPTER 10. *Orson Welles and the Modern Sound Film*

Bazin, André. *Orson Welles: A Critical View.* Translated by Jonathan Rosenbaum. New York: Harper & Row, 1978.

Cowie, Peter. *A Ribbon of Dreams.* Cranbury, N.J.: A. S. Barnes, 1973.

France, Richard. *The Theatre of Orson Welles.* Lewisburg, Pa.: Bucknell University Press, 1977.

Gottesman, Ronald, ed. *Focus on "Citizen Kane."* Englewood Cliffs, N.J.: Prentice-Hall, 1971.

————. *Focus on Orson Welles.* Englewood Cliffs, N.J.: Prentice-Hall, 1975.

Higham, Charles. *The Films of Orson Welles.* Berkeley: University of California Press, 1970.

Kael, Pauline, ed. *The Citizen Kane Book.* Boston: Little, Brown, 1972.

Koch, Howard. *The Panic Broadcast.* Boston: Little, Brown, 1970.

McBride, Joseph. *Orson Welles.* New York: Viking Press, 1972.

Naremore, James. *The Magic World of Orson Welles.* New York: Oxford University Press, 1978.

————, ed. *Orson Welles: A Guide to References and Resources.* Boston: G. K. Hall, 1980.

CHAPTER 11. *War-Time and Post-War Cinema: Italy and America, 1940–1951*

Agel, Henri. *Romance américaine.* Paris: Éditions du Cerf, 1963.

Alloway, Lawrence. *Violent America: The Movies, 1946–1964.* New York: Museum of Modern Art, 1965.

Alton, John. *Painting with Light.* New York: Macmillan, 1950.

Armes, Roy. *Patterns of Realsim.* London: Tantivy Press, 1971.

Bohne, Luciana, ed. "Italian Neorealism." *Film Criticism,* 3, 2 (Winter 1979 [special issue]).

Calvocoressi, Peter. *Total War.* New York: Random House, 1972.

Guarner, José Luis. *Rossellini.* New York: Frederick A. Praeger, 1970.

Higham, Charles, and Greenberg, Joel. *Hollywood in the Forties.* Cranbury, N.J.: A. S. Barnes, 1968.

Hovald, P. G. *Néoréalisme.* Paris, 1959.

Huaco, George A. *The Sociology of Film Art.* New York: Basic Books, 1965.

Jones, Ken D., and McClure, Arthur F. *Hollywood at War.* Cranbury, N.J.: A. S. Barnes, 1973.

Kagan, Norman. *The War Film.* New York: Pyramid Publications, 1974.

Karimi, A. M. *Toward a Definition of the American Film Noir.* New York: Arno Press, 1976.

Leprohon, Pierre. *The Italian Cinema.* New York: Frederick A. Praeger, 1972.

Manvell, Roger. *Films and the Second World War.* Cranbury, N.J.: A. S. Barnes, 1974.

Morella, Joe, et al. *The Films of World War Two.* Secaucus, N.J.: Citadel Press, 1973.

Navasky, Victor. *Naming Names.* New York: Viking Press, 1980.

Nowell-Smith, Geoffrey. *Luchino Visconti.* Garden City, N.Y.: Doubleday, 1968.

Shindler, Colin. *Hollywood Goes to War: Films and American Society, 1939–52.* London: Routledge and Kegan Paul, 1979.

Stirling, Monica. *A Screen of Time: A Study of Luchino Visconti.* New York: Harcourt Brace Jovanovich, 1979.

Suid, Lawrence H. *Guts and Glory: Great American War Movies.* Reading, Mass.: Addison-Wesley, 1978.

Warshow, Robert. *The Immediate Experience.* Garden City, N.Y.: Doubleday, 1962; reprinted, New York: Atheneum Publishers, 1971.

Zavattini, Cesare. *Sequences from a Cinematic Life.* Translated by William Weaver. Englewood Cliffs, N.J.: Prentice-Hall, 1970.

CHAPTER 12. *Hollywood, 1952–1965*

Battcock, Gregory, ed. *The New American Cinema.* New York: E. P. Dutton, 1967.

Baxter, John. *Hollywood in the Sixties.* New York: Macmillan, 1972.

Casper, Joseph A. *Vincente Minnelli and the Film Musical*. London: Thomas Yoseloff, 1977.

Ceplair, Larry, and Englund, Steven. *The Inquisition in Hollywood: Politics in the Film Community, 1930–1960*. Garden City, N.Y.: Doubleday, 1980.

Ciment, Michel. *Kazan on Kazan*. New York: Viking Press, 1973.

Garnham, Nicholas. *Samuel Fuller*. New York: Viking Press, 1971.

Gow, Gordon. *Hollywood in the Fifties*. London: A. Zwemmer, 1971.

Halliday, Jon. *Sirk on Sirk*. New York: Viking Press, 1972.

Hardy, Phil. *Samuel Fuller*. New York: Frederick A. Praeger, 1970.

Kanfer, Stephan. *A Journal of the Plague Years*. New York: Antheneum Publishers, 1973. (Witch-hunts and blacklisting.)

Kreidl, John Francis. *Nicholas Ray*. Boston: Twayne Publishers, 1977.

Limbacher, James L. *Four Aspects of Film*. New York: Russell and Russell, 1975.

Madsen, Axel. *Billy Wilder*. Bloomington: Indiana University Press, 1969.

Manvell, Roger. *New Cinema in the U.S.A.* New York: E. P. Dutton, 1968.

Pratley, Gerald. *The Cinema of John Frankenheimer*. Cranbury, N.J.: A. S. Barnes, 1969.

———. *The Cinema of John Huston*. Cranbury, N.J.: A. S. Barnes, 1977.

———. *The Cinema of Otto Preminger*. Cranbury, N.J.: A. S. Barnes, 1971.

Ross, Lillian. *Picture*. New York: Avon Books, 1952. (On the filming of John Huston's *Red Badge of Courage*.)

Schumach, Murray. *The Face on the Cutting Room Floor*. New York: William Morrow, 1964.

Seidman, Steve. *The Film Career of Billy Wilder*. Boston: G. K. Hall, 1977.

Stern, Michael. *Douglas Sirk*. Boston: Twayne Publishers, 1979.

Sinyard, Neil, and Turner, Adrian. *Journey Down Sunset Boulevard: The Films of Billy Wilder*. London: BCW Publications, 1980.

Talbot, David, and Zheutlin, Barbara. *Creative Differences: Profiles of Hollywood Dissidents*. Boston: South End Press, 1978.

Vizzard, Jack. *See No Evil: Life Inside a Hollywood Censor*. New York: Pocket Books, 1971.

Wysotsky, Michael Z. *Wide-Screen Cinema and Stereophonic Sound*. New York: Hastings House, 1971.

Zolotow, Maurice. *Billy Wilder in Hollywood*. New York: G. P. Putnam's Sons, 1977.

CHAPTER 13. *The French New Wave and Its Native Context*

Allen, Don. *Truffaut*. New York: Viking Press, 1974.

Andrew, J. Dudley. *André Bazin*. New York: Oxford University Press, 1978.

Armes, Roy. *The Cinema of Alain Resnais*. Cranbury, N.J.: A. S. Barnes, 1968.

———. *French Cinema Since 1946*. 2 vols. Cranbury, N.J.: A. S. Barnes, 1970.

———. *French Film*. New York: E. P. Dutton, 1970.

Braudy, Leo, ed. *Focus on "Shoot the Piano Player."* Englewood Cliffs, N.J.: Prentice-Hall, 1972.

Brown, Royal S., ed. *Focus on Godard*. Englewood Cliffs, N.J.: Prentice-Hall, 1972.

Cameron Ian, ed. *Claude Chabrol*. New York: Frederick A. Praeger, 1970.

———. *The Films of Jean-Luc Godard*. New York: Frederick A. Praeger, 1969.

———. *The Films of Robert Bresson*. New York: Frederick A. Praeger, 1969.

Collet, Jean. *Jean-Luc Godard*. New York: Crown Publishers, 1968.

Crisp, C. G. *François Truffaut*. New York: Frederick A. Praeger, 1972.

Durgnat, Raymond. *Franju*. London: Studio Vista Books, 1967.

French, Philip, et al. *The Films of Jean-Luc Godard*. London: Blue Star House, 1967.

Giannetti, Louis D. *Godard and Others*. London: Tantivy Press, 1975.

Graham, Peter. *The New Wave*. Garden City, N.Y.: Doubleday, 1968.

Harvey, Sylvia. *May '68 and Film Culture*. London: British Film Institute, 1978.

Insdorf, Annette. *François Truffaut*. New York: William Morrow, 1979.

Kawin, Bruce F. *Mindscreen: Bergman, Godard, and First-Person Film.* Princeton, N.J.: Princeton University Press, 1978.

MacBean, James Roy. *Film and Revolution.* Bloomington: Indiana University Press, 1975.

Martin, Marcel. *France: Screen Guide.* New York: A. S. Barnes, 1971.

Monaco, James. *Alain Resnais.* New York: Oxford University Press, 1979.

———. *The New Wave: Truffaut, Godard, Chabrol, Rohmer, Rivette.* New York: Oxford University Press, 1976.

Mussman, Toby, ed. *Jean-Luc Godard.* New York: E. P. Dutton, 1968.

Nogueira, Rui. *Melville.* New York: Viking Press, 1971.

Petrie, Graham. *The Cinema of François Truffaut.* Cranbury, N.J.: A. S. Barnes, 1970.

Rosenbaum, Jonathan. *Rivette: Texts and Interviews.* London: British Film Institute, 1977.

Roud, Richard. *Jean-Luc Godard.* Bloomington: Indiana University Press, 1969.

Truffaut, François. *The Films in My Life.* New York: Simon and Schuster, 1979.

Van Wert, William F. *The Film Career of Alain Robbe-Grillet.* Boston: G. K. Hall, 1977.

Ward, John. *Alain Resnais or the Theme of Time.* New York: Doubleday, 1968.

Willemen, Paul, ed. *Ophüls.* London: British Film Institute, 1978.

Wood, Robin, and Walker, Michael. *Claude Chabrol.* New York: Frederick A. Praeger, 1970.

CHAPTER 14. *European Renaissance: West*

Aranda, Francisco. *Luis Buñuel.* London: Secker & Warburg, 1969.

Armes, Roy. *The Ambiguous Image: Narrative Style in Modern European Cinema.* Bloomington: Indiana University Press, 1976.

———. *A Critical History of British Cinema.* New York: Oxford University Press, 1978.

Barr, Charles. *Ealing Studios.* London: Cameron & Taylor, 1977.

Baxter, John. *An Appalling Talent: Ken Russell.* London: Michael Joseph, 1973.

———. *The Australian Cinema.* Sidney: Angus and Robertson, 1970.

Bergman, Ingmar. "Introduction: Bergman Discusses His Film-Making." In *Four Screenplays.* Translated from the Swedish by Lars Malstrom and David Kushner. New York: Simon and Schuster, 1960, p. xxii.

Bergom-Larsson, Maria. *Swedish Film: Ingmar Bergman and Society.* Cranbury, N.J.: A. S. Barnes, 1979.

Betti, Liliana. *Fellini: An Intimate Portrait.* Boston: Little, Brown, 1979.

Betts, Ernest. *The Film Business: A History of British Cinema 1896–1972.* London: George Allen & Unwin, 1973.

Björkman, Stig; Manns, Torsten; and Sima, Jonas. *Bergman on Bergman.* Translated by Paul Britten Austin. New York: Touchstone/Simon and Schuster, 1973.

Buache, Freddy. *The Cinema of Luis Buñuel.* Cranbury, N.J.: A. S. Barnes, 1973.

Butler, Ivan. *Cinema in Britain.* London: Tantivy Press, 1969.

Cameron, Ian. *Antonioni.* London: Studio Vista Books, 1969.

Christie, Ian, ed. *Powell, Pressburger, and Others.* London: British Film Institute, 1978.

Di Carlo, Carlo. *Michelangelo Antonioni.* Rome: Edizioni di Bianco e Nero, 1964.

Durgnat, Raymond. *Luis Buñuel.* Berkeley: University of California Press, 1970.

———. *A Mirror for England: British Movies from Austerity to Affluence.* New York: Frederick A. Praeger, 1971.

Feldman, Seth, and Nelson, Joyce. *Canadian Film Reader.* Toronto: Peter Martin Associates, 1977.

Fellini, Federico. *Fellini on Fellini.* Translated by Isabel Quigley. New York: Delacorte Press, 1976.

Foix-Molina, Vincente. *New Cinema in Spain.* London: British Film Institute, 1977.

Furhammar, Leif, and Isaksson, Folke. *Politics and Film.* Translated by Kersti French. New York: Frederick A. Praeger, 1971.

Gifford, Denis. *British Cinema.* Cranbury, N.J.: A. S. Barnes, 1968.

Gomez, Joseph A. *Peter Watkins.* Boston: Twayne Publishers, 1979.

Handling, Piers. *The Films of Don Shebib*. Ottawa: Canadian Film Institute, 1978.

Harcourt, Peter. *Six European Directors*. New York: Penguin Books, 1974.

Hillier, Jim. *Cinema in Finland*. London: British Film Institute, 1978.

Huss, Roy, ed. *Focus on "Blow-Up."* Englewood Cliffs, N.J.: Prentice-Hall, 1971.

Kaminsky, Stuart, and Hill, Joseph F., eds. *Ingmar Bergman: Essays in Criticism*. New York: Oxford University Press, 1975.

Krelman, Martin. *This Is Where We Came In: The Career and Character of Canadian Film*. Toronto: McClelland and Stewart, 1978.

Kulik, Karol. *Alexander Korda*. London: W. H. Allen, 1975.

Leahy, James. *The Cinema of Joseph Losey*. Cranbury, N.J.: A. S. Barnes, 1967.

Leprohon, Pierre. *Michelangelo Antonioni*. New York: Simon and Schuster, 1963.

Lyons, Robert J. *Michelangelo Antonioni's Neo-Realism*. New York: Arno Press, 1976.

Manvell, Roger. *New Cinema in Britain*. New York: E. P. Dutton, 1968.

———. *New Cinema in Europe*. New York: E. P. Dutton, 1966.

Mellen, Joan, ed. *The World of Luis Buñuel: Essays in Criticism*. New York: Oxford University Press, 1978.

Milne, Tom. *Losey on Losey*. New York: Doubleday, 1968.

Morris, Peter. *Embattled Shadows: A History of Canadian Cinema, 1895–1939*. Montreal: McGill–Queens University Press, 1979.

Murray, Edward. *Fellini the Artist*. New York: Frederick Ungar, 1976.

Perry, Ted. *Filmguide to "8½."* Bloomington: Indiana University Press, 1975.

Reade, Eric. *History and Heartburn: The Saga of Australian Film, 1896–1978*. East Brunswick, N.J.: Fairleigh Dickinson University Press, 1981.

Rosenthal, Stuart. *The Cinema of Federico Fellini*. Cranbury, N.J.: A. S. Barnes, 1976.

Salachas, Gilbert. *Federico Fellini*. New York: Crown Publishers, 1969.

Simon, John. *Ingmar Bergman Directs*. New York: Harcourt Brace Jovanovich, 1972.

Stack, Oswald, ed. *Pasolini on Pasolini*. Bloomington: Indiana University Press, 1969.

Steene, Birgitta, ed. *Focus on "The Seventh Seal."* Englewood Cliffs, N.J.: Prentice-Hall, 1972.

———. *Ingmar Bergman*. New York: Twayne Publishers, 1968.

Sussex, Elizabeth. *Lindsay Anderson*. New York: Frederick A. Praeger, 1970.

Taylor, John Russell. *Directors and Directions: Cinema for the Seventies*. New York: Hill & Wang, 1975.

Veroneau, Pierre, ed. *The Canadian Cinemas*. Ottawa: Canadian Film Institute, 1979.

Walker, Alexander. *Hollywood, U.K.* New York: Stein & Day, 1974.

Willemen, Paul, ed. *Pier Paolo Pasolini*. London: British Film Institute, 1977.

Wood, Robin. *Ingmar Bergman*. New York: Frederick A. Praeger, 1969.

Young, Vernon. *Cinema Borealis: Ingmar Bergman and the Swedish Ethos*. New York: Avon Books, 1971.

CHAPTER 15. *European Renaissance: East*

Banaszkiewicz, Wladyslaw. *Contemporary Polish Cinematography*. Warsaw: Polonia Publishing House, 1962.

Broz, Jaroslav. *The Path of Fame of the Czechoslovak Film: A Short Outline of Its History*. Prague: Československý Filmexport, 1967.

Butler, Ivan. *The Cinema of Roman Polanski*. Cranbury, N.J.: A. S. Barnes, 1970.

Dolmatovskaya, Galina, and Shilova, Irina. *Who's Who in the Soviet Cinema*. Translated by Galina Dolmatovskaya. Moscow: Progress Publishers, 1979.

Estéve, Michel. *Miklós Jancsó*. Paris: Lettres Moderne, 1975.

Fukslewicz, Jacek. *Film and Television in Poland*. Warsaw: Interpress Publishers, 1976.

Hibbin, Nina. *Eastern Europe: An Illustrated Guide*. Screen Series. Cranbury, N.J.: A. S. Barnes, 1969.

Holloway, Ronald. *Z Is for Zagreb*. Cranbury, N.J.: A. S. Barnes, 1972.

Kurzewski, Stanislaw. *Contemporary Polish Cinema*. London: Stephen Wischhusen, 1980.

Langdon, Dewey. *Outline of Czechoslovakian Cinema*. London: Informatics, 1971.

Liehm, Antonín J. *Closely Watched Films: The Czechoslovak Experience*. White Plains, N.Y.: International Arts and Sciences Press, 1974.

———. *The Miloš Forman Stories*. White Plains, N.Y.: International Arts and Sciences Press, 1975.

Liehm, Mira, and Liehm, Antonín J. *The Most Important Art: East European Film After 1945*. Berkeley: University of California Press, 1977.

Michalek, Boleslaw. *The Cinema of Andrzej Wajda*. Translated by Edward Rothert. Cranbury, N.J.: A. S. Barnes, 1973.

Nemeskürty, István. *Word and Image: History of the Hungarian Cinema*. Translated by Zsuzsanna Horn. Budapest: Corvina Press, 1968.

Petrie, Graham. *History Must Answer to Man: The Contemporary Hungarian Cinema*. London: Tantivy Press, 1979.

Škvorecký, Josef. *All the Bright Young Men and Women: A Personal History of the Czech Cinema*. Toronto: Peter Martin Associates, 1971.

Stoil, Michael. *Cinema Beyond the Danube: The Camera and Politics*. Metuchen, N.J.: Scarecrow Press, 1974.

Vronskaya, Jeanne. *Young Soviet Film-Makers*. London: George Allen & Unwin, 1972.

Whyte, Alistair. *New Cinema in Eastern Europe*. New York: E. P. Dutton, 1971.

Žalman, Jan. *Films and Film-Makers in Czechoslovakia*. Prague: Orbis, 1968.

CHAPTER 16. *Wind from the East: Japan and Elsewhere*

Anderson, Joseph L., and Richie, Donald. *The Japanese Film: Art and Industry*. Rutland, Vt.: Charles E. Tuttle, 1959.

Barnouw, Erik, and Krishnaswamy, Subramanyam. *Indian Film*. New York: Columbia University Press, 1963; second edition, New York: Oxford University Press, 1980.

Bock, Audi. *Japanese Film Directors*. New York: Kodansha International, 1978.

Burch, Noël. *Theory of Film Practice*. Translated by Helen R. Lane. New York: Frederick A. Praeger, 1973.

———. *To the Distant Observer: Form and Meaning in Japanese Cinema*. Revised and edited by Annette Michelson. Berkeley: University of California Press, 1979.

Castillon, Pierre de. *Le cinéma japonais*. Notes et études documentaire, nos. 4.158–4.159. Paris: Documentation Française, 1975.

Da Cunha, Uma. *Indian Film, '78/'79*. New Delhi: F. C. Rampal, 1979.

Eberhard, Wolfram. *The Chinese Silver Screen*. Taipei: The Oriental Cultural Service, 1972.

Iwazaki, Akira. *Kenji Mizoguchi*. Paris, 1967.

"Japanese Cinema." *Wide Angle*, 1, 4 (1977 [special issue]).

Leyda, Jay. *Dianying: Electric Shadows: An Account of Films and the Film Audience in China*. Cambridge, Mass.: MIT Press, 1972; revised edition, 1979.

Mellen, Joan. *Voices from the Japanese Cinema*. New York: Liveright, 1975.

———. *The Waves at Genji's Door*. New York: Pantheon Books, 1976.

Ray, Satyajit. *Our Films, Their Films*. Bombay: Orient Longmans, 1977.

Richie, Donald. *The Films of Akira Kurosawa*. Berkeley: University of California Press, 1965.

———. *Focus on "Rashomon."* Englewood Cliffs, N.J.: Prentice-Hall, 1972.

———. *Japanese Cinema*. Garden City, N.Y.: Anchor Books, 1971.

———. *The Japanese Movie*. Tokyo: Kodansha International, 1966.

———. *Ozu*. Berkeley: University of California Press, 1974.

Sato, Tadao. *The Art of Yasujiro Ozu*. Tokyo, 1974.

Tucker, Richard N. *Japan: Film Image*. London: Studio Vista Books, 1973.

Schrader, Paul. *Transcendental Style in Film: Ozu, Bresson, Dreyer*. Berkeley: University of California Press, 1972.

Seton, Marie. *Portrait of a Director: Satyajit Ray*. Bloomington: Indiana University Press, 1971.

Silver, Alain. *The Samurai Film*. Cranbury, N.J.: A. S. Barnes, 1977.

Svensson, Arne. *Japan: An Illustrated Guide.* Cranbury, N.J.: A. S. Barnes, 1971.

Tiedeman, Arthur E., ed. *An Introduction to Japanese Civilization.* New York: Columbia University Press, 1974.

Varley, H. Paul. *Samurai.* New York: Delacorte Press, 1970.

Vasuder, Aruna. *Liberty and License in the Indian Cinema.* New Delhi: Vikas, 1978.

Wood, Robin. *The Apu Trilogy.* New York: Frederick A. Praeger, 1971.

CHAPTER 17. *The Shape of the Seventies*

Agel, Jerome. *The Making of "2001."* New York: Signet Books, 1970.

Burton, Julianne. *The New Latin American Cinema: An Annotated Bibliography.* New York: Cineaste, 1976.

Cameron, Ian, et al. *Second Wave.* New York: Frederick A. Praeger, 1970.

Cawelti, John G., ed. *Focus on "Bonnie and Clyde."* Englewood Cliffs, N.J.: Prentice-Hall, 1972.

Chanan, Michael, ed. *Chilean Cinema.* London: British Film Institute, 1976.

Clarke, Arthur C. *Lost Worlds of "2001."* New York: Signet Books, 1972.

"Culture in the Age of Mass Media." *Latin American Perspectives,* 16, 5, 1 (Winter 1978 [special issue]).

Cyr, Helen W. *A Filmography of the Third World.* Metuchen, N.J.: Scarecrow Press, 1976.

The Education of the Film-Maker. Washington, D.C.: Unesco Press, 1975.

Geduld, Carolyn. *Filmguide to "2001: A Space Odyssey."* Bloomington: Indiana University Press, 1973.

Houston, Penelope. *The Contemporary Cinema.* Baltimore: Penguin Books, 1963; revised edition, 1971.

Jacobs, Diane. *Hollywood Renaissance.* Cranbury, N.J.: A. S. Barnes, 1977.

Johnson, Robert K. *Francis Ford Coppola.* Boston: Twayne Publishers, 1977.

Kagan, Norman. *The Cinema of Stanley Kubrick.* New York: Grove Press, 1975.

Kass, Judith. *Robert Altman: American Innovator.* New York: Popular Library, 1978.

Kolker, Robert Phillip. *A Cinema of Loneliness: Penn, Kubrick, Coppola, Scorsese, Altman.* New York: Oxford University Press, 1980.

Koszarski, Richard, ed. *Hollywood Directors, 1941–1976.* New York: Oxford University Press, 1977.

MacBean, James Roy. *Film and Revolution.* Bloomington: Indiana University Press, 1975.

Madsen, Axel. *The New Hollywood.* New York: Thomas Y. Crowell, 1975.

Manvell, Roger. *The German Cinema.* London: J. M. Dent, 1971.

McKinney, Doug. *Sam Peckinpah.* Boston: Twayne Publishers, 1979.

Monaco, James. *American Film Now: The People, the Power, the Money, the Movies.* New York: Oxford University Press, 1979.

Musun, Chris. *The Marketing of Motion Pictures.* Los Angeles: Chris Musun, 1969.

Nevares, B. R. *The Mexican Cinema.* Albuquerque: University of New Mexico Press, 1976.

Paul, William. "Hollywood *Harakiri.*" *Film Comment,* 13, 2 (March–April 1977), 40–43, 56–62.

Pye, Michael, and Myles, Linda. *The Movie Brats: How the Film Generation Took Over Hollywood.* New York: Holt, Rinehart, and Winston, 1979.

Roud, Richard. *Straub.* New York: Viking Press, 1972.

Salmane, Hala. *Algerian Cinema.* London: British Film Institute, 1977.

Sarris, Andrew. "After *The Graduate.*" *American Film,* 3, 9 (July–August 1978), 32–37.

Seydor, Paul. *Peckinpah: The Western Films.* Urbana: University of Illinois Press, 1980.

Smith, Julian. *Looking Away: Hollywood and Vietnam.* New York: Charles Scribner's Sons, 1975.

Toeplitz, Jerzy. *Hollywood and After: The Changing Face of Movies in America.* Translated by Boleslaw Sulik. Chicago: Henry Regnery, 1974.

Wake, Sandra, ed. *The "Bonnie and Clyde" Book.* London: Lorrimer, 1972.

Walker, Alexander. *Stanley Kubrick Directs.* New York: Harcourt Brace Jovanovich, 1971.

Wood, Robin. *Arthur Penn.* New York: Frederick A. Praeger, 1969.

Zuker, Joel S. *Arthur Penn: A Guide to References and Resources.* Boston: G. K. Hall, 1980.

World and American Film History

Bardèche, Maurice, and Brasillach, Robert. *A History of the Motion Pictures.* Translated and edited by Iris Barry. New York: W. W. Norton/Museum of Modern Art, 1938.

Bluem, William. *The Film Industries.* New York: Hastings House, 1973.

———. *The Movie Business.* New York: Hastings House, 1972.

Blum, Daniel. *A Pictorial History of the Silent Screen.* New York: G. P. Putnam's Sons, 1953.

Bohn, Thomas W., and Stromgren, Richard L. *Light and Shadows: A History of Motion Pictures.* 2nd edition. Sherman Oaks, Calif.: Alfred, 1978.

Brownlow, Kevin. *The Parade's Gone By.* New York: Alfred A. Knopf, 1968.

———. *The War, the West, and the Wilderness.* New York: Alfred A. Knopf, 1979.

———, and Kobal, John. *Hollywood: The Pioneers.* New York: Alfred A. Knopf, 1979.

Casty, Alan. *Development of the Film: An Interpretive History.* New York: Harcourt Brace Jovanovich, 1973.

Conant, Michael. *Antitrust in the Motion Picture Industry.* Berkeley: University of California Press, 1960.

Cowie, Peter. *A Concise History of the Cinema.* 2 vols. London: A. Zwemmer, 1971.

———. *Seventy Years of Cinema.* New York: Castle Books, 1969.

Dickinson, Thorold. *A Discovery of Cinema.* New York: Oxford University Press, 1971.

Earley, Steven C. *An Introduction to American Movies.* New York: New American Library, 1978.

Ellis, Jack C. *A History of Film.* Englewood Cliffs, N.J.: Prentice-Hall, 1979.

Fell, John L. *A History of Films.* New York: Holt, Rinehart, and Winston, 1978.

Fielding, Raymond. *A Technological History of Motion Pictures and Television.* Berkeley: University of California Press, 1967.

Fulton, A. R. *Motion Pictures: The Development of an Art from Silent Films to the Age of Television.* Norman: University of Oklahoma Press, 1960; revised edition, 1980.

Goodman, Ezra. *The Fifty Year Decline and Fall of Hollywood.* New York: Simon and Schuster, 1961.

Griffith, Richard, and Mayer, Arthur. *The Movies.* New York: Simon and Schuster, 1957; revised edition, 1970.

Hampton, Benjamin B. *A History of the American Film Industry from Its Beginnings to 1931.* Edited by Richard Griffith. New York: Covici, 1931; reprinted, New York: Dover Books, 1970. (Originally titled *A History of the Movies.*)

Hendricks, Gordon. *The Edison Motion Picture Myth.* Berkeley: University of California Press, 1961.

Hennebelle, Guy. *Quinze ans du cinéma mondial, 1960–1975.* Paris: Éditions Cerf, 1975.

Higham, Charles. *The Art of the American Film.* Garden City, N.Y.: Anchor Books, 1973.

Jacobs, Lewis, ed. *The Emergence of Film Art.* New York: Hopkinson and Blake, 1969; second edition, New York: W. W. Norton, 1979.

———. *The Rise of the American Film.* New York: Harcourt, Brace, 1939.

Jeanne, René, and Ford, Charles. *Histoire encyclopédique du cinéma.* Paris, 1947–68.

Jowett, Garth. *Film, the Democratic Art: A Social History of American Film.* Boston: Little, Brown, 1976.

Knight, Arthur. *The Liveliest Art: A Panoramic History of the Movies.* New York: Macmillan, 1957; revised edition, New York: Mentor Books, 1978.

Lacassin, Francis. *Pour une contre-histoire du cinéma.* Paris: Union Générale d'Éditions, 1972.

MacCann, Richard Dyer. *Hollywood in Transition.* Boston: Houghton Mifflin, 1962.

Macgowan, Kenneth. *Behind the Screen.* New York: Delacorte Press, 1965.

McClure, Arthur, ed. *The Movies: An American Idiom.* Rutherford, N.J.: Fairleigh Dickinson University Press, 1971.

Mast, Gerald. *A Short History of the Movies.* 3rd edition. Indianapolis: Bobbs-Merrill, 1981.

Mitry, Jean. *Histoire du cinéma: art et industrie.* Paris, 1967–73. (A three-volume account of the silent film.)

O'Connor, John E., and Jackson, Martin A., eds. *American History/American Film: Interpreting Hollywood Images.* New York: Frederick Ungar, 1979.

Pratt, George C. *Spellbound in Darkness: A History of the Silent Film.* Rochester, N.Y.: University of Rochester Press, 1966; revised edition, Greenwich, Conn.: New York Graphic Society, 1973.

Quigley, Martin. *Magic Shadows.* Washington, D.C.: Georgetown University Press, 1948.

Ramsaye, Terry. *A Million and One Nights: A History of the Motion Picture.* New York: Simon and Schuster, 1926.

Reader, Keith. *The Cinema: A History.* London: Hodder & Stoughton, 1979.

Rhode, Eric. *A History of the Cinema from Its Origins to 1970.* New York: Hill & Wang, 1976.

Robinson, David. *The History of World Cinema.* New York: Stein & Day, 1973.

Rotha, Paul, and Griffith, Richard. *The Film Till Now.* New York: Funk and Wagnalls, 1950.

Sadoul, Georges. *Histoire générale du cinéma.* Paris, 1946–54.

Schickel, Richard. *Movies: The History of an Art and an Institution.* New York: Basic Books, 1964.

Sklar, Robert. *Movie-Made America: A Cultural History of American Movies.* New York: Random House, 1975.

Taylor, Deems; Hale, Bryant; and Peterson, Marcelene. *A Pictorial History of the Movies.* New York: Simon and Schuster, 1950.

Thomson, David. *America in the Dark: The Impact of Hollywood Films on American Culture.* New York: William Morrow, 1979.

Tyler, Parker. *Classics of the Foreign Film.* New York: Citadel Press, 1962.

Vardac, Nicholas. *From Stage to Screen.* Cambridge: Harvard University Press, 1949.

Wagenknecht, Edward. *The Movies in the Age of Innocence.* Norman: University of Oklahoma Press, 1962.

Wright, Basil. *The Long View.* New York: Alfred A. Knopf, 1974.

Film History: Special Topics

Barsacq, Léon. *Caligari's Cabinet and Other Grand Illusions: A History of Film Design.* New York: New American Library, 1978.

Battcock, Gregory, ed. *The New American Cinema.* New York: E. P. Dutton, 1967.

Bazelon, Irwin. *Knowing the Score: Notes on Film Music.* New York: Van Nostrand Reinhold, 1972.

Bogle, Donald. *Toms, Coons, Mulattoes, Mammies, and Bucks.* New York: Bantam Books, 1974.

Brakhage, Stan. *Film Biographies.* Berkeley, Calif.: Turtle Island, 1977.

Brosnan, John. *Movie Magic: The Story of Special Effects.* New York: New American Library, 1976.

Cripps, Thomas. *Black Film as Genre.* Bloomington: Indiana University Press, 1978.

———. *Slow Fade to Black: The Negro in American Film.* New York: Oxford University Press, 1977.

Curtis, David. *Experimental Cinema.* New York: Universal Books, 1971.

"Film Music." *Cinema Journal,* 17, 2 (Spring 1978 [special issue]).

Gidal, Peter, ed. *Structural Film Anthology.* London: British Film Institute, 1976.

Haskell, Molly. *From Reverence to Rape: The Treatment of Women in the Movies.* Baltimore: Penguin Books, 1974.

"The Hollywood Cartoon." *Film Comment,* 11, 1 (January–February 1975 [special issue]).

Kay, Karyn, and Peary, Gerald. *Women and the Cinema.* New York: E. P. Dutton, 1977.

Klotman, Phyllis Rauch. *Frame by Frame—A Black Filmography.* Bloomington: Indiana University Press, 1979.

Limbacher, James L. *Film Music from Violins to Video*. Metuchen, N.J.: Scarecrow Press, 1974.

Matthews, J. H. *Surrealism and Film*. Ann Arbor: University of Michigan Press, 1971.

Murray, James. *To Find an Image: Black Films from Uncle Tom to Superfly*. Indianapolis: Bobbs-Merrill, 1973.

Prendergast, Roy M. *Film Music: A Neglected Art*. New York: W. W. Norton, 1977.

Renan, Sheldon. *An Introduction to the American Underground Film*. New York: E. P. Dutton, 1967.

Rosenblum, Ralph, and Karen, Robert. *When the Shooting Stops . . . the Cutting Begins*. New York: Viking Press, 1979.

Sitney, P. Adams. *Visionary Film: The American Avant-Garde*. New York: Oxford University Press, 1974; revised edition, 1979.

Stephenson, Ralph. *The Animated Film*. Cranbury, N.J.: A. S. Barnes, 1973.

General Reference Works and Bibliographies (Including Collections of Reviews and Essays)

Adler, Renata. *A Year in the Dark*. New York: Random House, 1969.

Agee, James. *Agee on Film*. Vol. 1: *Reviews and Comments*. Vol. 2: *Five Film Scripts*. Boston: Beacon Press, 1964.

The American Film Institute Catalogue of Motion Pictures Produced in the U.S. Part I: *Feature Films 1921–1930*. 2 vols. Part II: *Feature Films 1961–1970*. New York: R. R. Bowker, 1971, 1976.

Bawden, Liz-Anne, ed. *The Oxford Companion to Film*. New York: Oxford University Press, 1976.

Beattie, Eleanor. *The Handbook of Canadian Cinema*. 2nd edition. Toronto: Peter Martin, 1977.

Bellone, Julius, ed. *Renaissance of the Film*. London: Collier-Macmillan, 1970.

Bohnenkamp, Dennis R., and Grogg, Sam L., Jr., eds. *The American Film Institute Guide to College Courses in Film and Television*. Princeton, N.J.: Peterson's Guides, 1980.

Bowser, Eileen. *Film Notes*. New York: Museum of Modern Art, 1969.

Braudy, Leo, and Dickstein, Morris, eds. *Great Film Directors*. New York: Oxford University Press, 1978.

Bukalski, Peter J. *Film Research: A Critical Bibliography with Annotations and Essays*. Boston: G. K. Hall, 1972.

Cawkwell, Tim, and Smith, John, eds. *The World Encyclopedia of Film*. New York: A & W Visual Library, 1972.

Corliss, Richard. *Talking Pictures: Screenwriters in the American Cinema*. New York: Viking Press, 1973.

Cowie, Peter, ed. *Fifty Major Film Makers*. Cranbury, N.J.: A. S. Barnes, 1975.

———. *International Film Guide*. Cranbury, N.J.: A. S. Barnes, 1974–. (Issued annually.)

Crist, Judith. *The Private Eye, the Cowboy, and the Very Naked Girl*. New York: Holt, Rinehart and Winston, 1968.

Delson, Donn. *The Dictionary of Marketing and Related Terms in the Motion Picture Industry*. Thousand Oaks, Ca.: Brandson Press, 1979.

Directory of Films by and/or About Women. Berkeley: Women's Historical Research Center, 1972.

Dyment, Alan. *Literature of the Film*. London: White Lion Publishers, 1975.

Ellis, Jack D.; Derry, Charles; and Kern, Sharon, eds. *The Film Book Bibliography, 1940–1975*. Metuchen, N.J.: Scarecrow Press, 1979.

Farber, Manny. *Negative Space*. New York: Frederick A. Praeger, 1972.

Feinberg, Cobbett. *Reel Facts: The Movie Book of Records*. New York: Vintage Books, 1978.

Ferguson, Otis. *The Film Criticism of Otis Ferguson*. Edited by Robert Wilson. Philadelphia: Temple University Press, 1971.

Garbicz, Adam, and Klinowski, Jacek. *Cinema, the Magic Vehicle: A Guide to Its Achieve-*

ment. *Journey One: The Cinema Through 1949.* Metuchen, N.J.: Scarecrow Press, 1975.

———. *Cinema, the Magic Vehicle: A Guide to Its Achievement. Journey Two: The Cinema in the Fifties.* Metuchen, N.J.: Scarecrow Press, 1980.

Gerlach, John C., and Gerlach, Lana, eds. *The Critical Index: A Bibliography of Articles on Film in English, 1946–1973.* New York: Teachers College Press, 1974.

Gifford, Denis. *The British Film Catalogue, 1895–1970: A Reference Guide.* 2 vols. New York: McGraw-Hill, 1973.

Gilliatt, Penelope. *Unholy Fools.* New York: Viking Press, 1973.

Gottesman, Ronald, and Geduld, Harry. *Guidebook to Film.* New York: Holt, Rinehart and Winston, 1972.

Graham, Peter, ed. *Dictionary of the Cinema.* London: Tantivy Press, 1964.

Guback, Thomas H. *The International Film Industry.* Bloomington: Indiana University Press, 1969.

Halliwell, Leslie. *The Filmgoer's Companion.* New York: Avon Books, 1978.

Halliwell, Leslie. *Halliwell's Film Guide.* New York: Charles Scribner's Sons, 1979.

Hecquet, Marie-Claude, and McNicoll, David. *A Guide to Film and Television Courses in Canada, 1978–79.* Ottawa: Canadian Film Institute, 1978.

Hedgecoe, John. *The Photographer's Handbook.* New York: Alfred A. Knopf, 1978.

Henshaw, Richard, ed. "Women Directors: 150 Filmographies." *Film Comment,* 8, 4 (November–December 1972), 33–45.

Hochman, Stanley, ed. *American Film Directors.* New York: Frederick Ungar, 1974.

International Index to Film Periodicals. Sponsored by Fédération Internationale des Archives du Film (FIAF). Yearly. Vol. 1: *1972.* Edited by Karen Jones. New York: R. R. Bowker, 1973. Vol. 2: *1973.* Edited by Michael Moulds. New York: R. R. Bowker, 1974. Vol. 3: *1974.* Edited by Karen Jones. London: Saint James Press; New York: St. Martin's Press, 1975. Vols. 4–6: *1975–77.* Edited by Frances Thorpe. New York: St. Martin's Press, 1976–78.

Jenkins, Bruce, ed. *Film Reader 3: Film Genre/Film and the Other Arts.* Evanston, Ill.: Northwestern University Press, 1978.

Jones, Karen, ed. *International Index to Film Periodicals, 1972* and *1974.* New York: R. R. Bowker, 1973, 1975.

Kael, Pauline. *Deeper into Movies.* Boston: Little, Brown, 1973.

———. *Going Steady.* Boston: Little, Brown, 1970.

———. *I Lost It at the Movies.* New York: Atlantic, Little, Brown, 1965.

———. *Kiss Kiss, Bang Bang.* New York: Atlantic, Little, Brown, 1968.

———. *Reeling.* Boston: Little, Brown, 1976.

Kauffmann, Stanley. *Before My Eyes.* New York: Harper & Row, 1980.

———. *Living Images.* New York: Harper & Row, 1975.

———. *When the Lights Go Down.* New York: Holt, Rinehart and Winston, 1980.

———. *A World on Film.* New York: Harper & Row, 1966.

———, and Henstell, Bruce, eds. *American Film Criticism: From the Beginnings to "Citizen Kane."* New York: Liveright, 1972.

Koszarski, Richard, ed. *Hollywood Directors, 1914–1940.* New York: Oxford University Press, 1977.

Leyda, Jay, ed. *Voices of Film Experience, 1894 to the Present.* New York: Macmillan, 1977.

Luboviski, Git. *Cinema Catalogue.* Hollywood: Larry Edmunds Cinema Bookshop, n.d.

Lyons, Timothy J., ed. *The Influence of the World Cinema Heritage on the Education and Training of Film/Television Directors and Communicators.* University Film Association Monograph No. 4, Fall 1979.

MacCann, Richard Dyer, ed. *The New Film Index: A Bibliography of Magazine Articles in English, 1930–1970.* New York: E. P. Dutton, 1975.

MacDonald, Dwight. *On Movies.* New York: Berkley, 1969.

McIlroy, Susan; Beard, David; and Maunder, T. C. *Cinebooks Catalogue.* Toronto: Cinebooks, 1976.

Maltin, Leonard, ed. *TV Movies*. 1981–82 revised edition. New York: Signet Books, 1980.

Manchel, Frank. *Film Study: A Resource Guide*. Rutherford, N.J.: Fairleigh Dickinson University Press, 1973.

Manvell, Roger. *The Film and the Public*. New York: Penguin Books, 1955.

———, and Jacobs, Lewis, eds. *International Encyclopedia of Film*. New York: Crown Publishers, 1972.

Mayer, Michael F., ed. *The Film Industries*. New York: Hastings House, 1978.

Mercer, John. *Glossary of Film Terms*. University Film Association Monograph No. 2, Summer 1978.

Michael, Paul, ed. *The American Movies Reference Book: The Sound Era*. Englewood Cliffs, N.J.: Prentice-Hall, 1969.

Mitry, Jean. *Dictionaire du cinéma*. Paris: Libraire Larousse, 1963.

Monaco, James, and Schenker, Susan. *Books About Film: A Bibliographical Checklist*. New York: New York Zoetrope, 1976.

Murray, Edward. *Nine American Film Critics*. New York: Frederick Ungar, 1975.

The New York Times Film Reviews, 1913–1970. 7 vols. New York: Arno Press, 1971.

Parish, James R., and Pitts, Michael R. *Film Directors: A Guide to Their American Films*. Metuchen, N.J.: Scarecrow Press, 1974.

Parish, James R., et al. *Film Directors Guide: Western Europe*. Metuchen, N.J.: Scarecrow Press, 1976.

Pechter, William S. *Twenty-Four Times a Second: Films and Film-Makers*. New York: Harper & Row, 1971.

Potamkin, Harry Alan. *The Compound Cinema: The Film Writings of Harry Alan Potamkin*. Edited by Lewis Jacobs. New York: Teachers College Press, 1977.

Rehrauer, George. *Cinema Booklist*. Metuchen, N.J.: Scarecrow Press, 1972. *Supplement One*, 1974; *Supplement Two*, 1976.

Roud, Richard, ed. *Cinema: A Critical Dictionary*. 2 vols. New York: Viking Press, 1980.

Sadoul, Georges. *Dictionary of Film Makers*. Translated and edited by Peter Morris. Berkeley: University of California Press, 1972.

———. *Dictionary of Films*. Translated and edited by Peter Morris. Berkeley: University of California Press, 1972.

Samples, Gordon. *The Drama Scholar's Index to Plays and Filmscripts*. Metuchen, N.J.: Scarecrow Press, 1974.

Sarris, Andrew. *The American Cinema: Directors and Directions, 1929–1968*. New York: E. P. Dutton, 1968.

———. *Confessions of a Cultist*. New York: Simon and Schuster, 1971.

———. *Politics and Cinema*. New York: Columbia University Press, 1978.

———. *The Primal Screen*. New York: Simon and Schuster, 1973.

Scheuer, Steven H. *Movies on TV*. 1978–79 revised edition. New York: Bantam Books, 1977.

Silva, Fred, et al., eds. *Film Literature Index*, Vols. 1–5, *1973–77*. New York: R. R. Bowker, 1975–79.

Silver, Alain, and Ward, Elizabeth. *Film Noir: An Encyclopedic Reference to the American Style*. New York: Overlook Press, 1979.

Simon, John. *Movies into Films: Film Criticism, 1967–70*. New York: Dial Press, 1971.

———. *Private Screenings*. New York: Berkley, 1967.

Slide, Anthony. *Films on Film History*. Metuchen, N.J.: Scarecrow Press, 1979.

Smith, Sharon. *Women Who Make Movies*. New York: Hopkinson and Blake, 1975.

Speed, F. Maurice. *Film Review*. London: W. H. Allen, 1966–.

Spottiswoode, Raymond, et al. *The Focal Encyclopedia of Film and Television Techniques*. New York: Hastings House, 1969.

Thomas, Bob, ed. *Directors in Action*. Indianapolis: Bobbs-Merrill, 1973.

Thomson, David. *A Biographical Dictionary of Film*. New York: William Morrow, 1976.

Weinberg, Herman G. *Saint Cinema*. New York: Dover Books, 1970.

Willis, John, ed. *John Willis' Screen World*. London: Frederick Muller, 1949–.

World Filmography. General editor, Peter Cowie. Vols. *1967* and *1968.* London: Tantivy Press, 1977. (An annual filmography of feature releases in 49 countries, projected at 70 volumes.)

Theory and Aesthetics

Alpert, Hollis. *The Dreams and the Dreamers.* New York: Macmillan, 1962.

Andrew, J. Dudley. *The Major Film Theories.* New York: Oxford University Press, 1976.

Armes, Roy. *Film and Reality.* New York: Penguin Books, 1974.

Arnheim, Rudolf. *Art and Visual Perception: A Psychology of the Creative Eye.* Berkeley: University of California Press, 1954.

———. *Film as Art.* Berkeley: University of California Press, 1957.

———. *Visual Thinking.* Berkeley: University of California Press, 1969.

Balázs, Béla. *Theory of the Film.* Translated by Edith Bone. New York: Roy, 1953; reprinted, New York: Dover Books, 1970.

Barr, Charles. "Cinemascope: Before and After." *Film Quarterly,* 16, 4 (1963), 4–24.

Bazin, André. *What Is Cinema?* 2 vols. Selected and translated by Hugh Gray. Berkeley: University of California Press, 1967; 1971.

Bluestone, George. *Novels into Film.* Baltimore: Johns Hopkins Press, 1957.

Bordwell, David, and Thompson, Kristin. *Film Art: An Introduction.* Reading, Mass.: Addison-Wesley, 1979.

Braudy, Leo. *The World in a Frame.* New York: Anchor Books, 1976.

Burch, Noël. *Theory of Film Practice.* Translated by Helen R. Lane. New York: Frederick A. Praeger, 1973.

Buscombe, Edward, ed. *Film Reader 4: Point of View/Metahistory of Film.* Evanston, Ill.: Northwestern University Press, 1979.

Cameron, Ian, ed. *Movie Reader.* New York: Frederick A. Praeger, 1972.

Cavell, Stanley. *The World Viewed: Reflections on the Ontology of Film.* New York: Viking Press, 1971; enlarged edition, Cambridge, Mass.: Harvard University Press, 1979.

Clair, René. *Reflections on the Cinema.* London: Kimber, 1953.

Cohen, Keith. *Film and Fiction.* New Haven: Yale University Press, 1979.

Dovzhenko, Alexander. *Alexander Dovzhenko: The Poet as Filmmaker.* Translated and edited by Marco Carynnyk. Cambridge, Mass.: MIT Press, 1973.

Eco, Umberto. *The Semiotic Threshhold.* The Hague: Mouton, 1973.

———. *A Theory of Semiotics.* Bloomington: University of Indiana Press, 1976.

Eisenstein, Sergei. *Film Essays and a Lecture.* Translated and edited by Jay Leyda. New York: Frederick A. Praeger, 1970.

———. *Film Form.* Translated and edited by Jay Leyda. New York: Harcourt Brace Jovanovich, 1969.

———. *The Film Sense.* Translated and edited by Jay Leyda. New York: Harcourt Brace Jovanovich, 1969.

Geduld, Harry M., ed. *Authors on Film.* Bloomington: Indiana University Press, 1972.

———, ed. *Filmmakers on Filmmaking.* Bloomington: Indiana University Press, 1967.

Gessner, Robert. *The Moving Image: A Guide to Cinematic Literacy.* New York: E. P. Dutton, 1970.

Giannetti, Louis. *Understanding Movies.* 2nd edition. Englewood Cliffs, N.J.: Prentice-Hall, 1976.

Godard, Jean-Luc. *Godard on Godard.* Edited by Tom Milne. New York: Viking Press, 1972.

Hauser, Arnold. *The Social History of Art.* Vol. 4. New York: Vintage Books, 1960.

Henderson, Brian. *A Critique of Film Theory.* New York: E. P. Dutton, 1980.

Houston, Beverle, ed. "Feminist and Ideological Criticism." *Quarterly Review of Film Studies,* 3,4 (fall 1978 [special issue]).

Huss, Roy, and Silverstein, Norman. *The Film Experience.* New York: Delta Books, 1968.

Jacobs, Lewis, ed. *Introduction to the Art of Movies.* New York: Farrar, Straus & Giroux, 1960.

———. *The Movies as Medium.* New York: Farrar, Straus & Giroux, 1970.

Johnson, Lincoln. *Film: Space, Time, Light and Sound.* New York: Holt, Rinehart and Winston, 1974.

Jowett, Garth and Linton, James M. *Movies as Mass Communication.* Beverly Hills: SAGE Publications, 1980.

Kracauer, Siegfried. *Theory of Film: The Redemption of Physical Reality.* New York: Oxford University Press, 1960.

Kuleshov, Lev. *Kuleshov on Film.* Translated and edited by Ronald Levaco. Berkeley: University of California Press, 1975.

Lawson, John Howard. *Film: The Creative Process.* New York: Hill & Wang, 1964.

Lindgren, Ernest. *The Art of the Film.* New York: Macmillan, 1948.

Lindsay, Vachel. *The Art of the Moving Picture.* New York: Macmillan, 1915; reprinted, New York: Liveright, 1970.

Lorentz, Pare. *Lorentz on Film.* New York: Harcourt Brace Jovanovich, 1975.

MacCann, Richard Dyer, ed. *Film: A Montage of Theories.* New York: E. P. Dutton, 1966.

Manvell, Roger. *Film.* Harmondsworth, Middlesex, England: Penguin Books, 1950.

Mast, Gerald, and Cohen, Marshall, eds. *Film Theory and Criticism.* New York: Oxford University Press, 1974; second edition, 1979.

Mekas, Jonas. *Movie Journal: Rise of the New American Cinema: 1969–1971.* New York: Macmillan, 1972.

Metz, Christian. *Film Language: A Semiotics of the Cinema.* Translated by Michael Taylor. New York: Oxford University Press, 1974.

———. *Language and Cinema.* Translated by Donna Jean Umiker-Sebeok. The Hague: Mouton, 1974.

Mitry, Jean. *Esthétique et psychologie du cinéma.* 2 vols. Paris: Éditions Universitaires, 1963.

Monaco, James. *How to Read a Film.* New York: Oxford University Press, 1977.

Montagu, Ivor. *Film World.* Baltimore: Penguin Books, 1964.

Münsterberg, Hugo. *The Film: A Psychological Study.* New York: D. Appleton, 1916; reprinted, New York: Dover Books, 1970.

Nichols, Bill, ed. *Movies and Methods.* Berkeley: University of California Press, 1977.

Nilsen, Vladimir. *Cinema as Graphic Art.* New York: Hill & Wang, 1973.

Perkins, V. F. *Film as Film: Understanding and Judging Movies.* New York: Penguin Books, 1972.

Pudovkin, V. I. *Film Technique and Film Acting.* London, 1929; reprinted, New York: Grove Press, 1970.

Sitney, P. Adams, ed. *The Avant-Garde Film: A Reader of Theory and Criticism.* New York: New York University Press, 1978.

———. *The Essential Cinema.* New York: New York University Press, 1975.

Solanas, Fernando, and Getino, Octavio. "Towards a Third Cinema." *Cinéaste,* 4, 3 (1970), 1–10.

Spottiswoode, Raymond R. *Film and Its Techniques.* Berkeley: University of California Press, 1951; reprinted, 1965.

Stephenson, Ralph, and Debrix, J. R. *The Cinema as Art.* New York: Penguin Books, 1965.

Talbot, Daniel, ed. *Film: An Anthology.* Berkeley: University of California Press, 1967.

Taylor, John Russell. *Cinema Eye, Cinema Ear.* New York: Hill & Wang, 1964.

Thomson, David. *Movie Man.* New York: Stein & Day, 1967.

Tudor, Andrew. *Theories of Film.* New York: Viking Press, 1973.

Tyler, Parker. *Hollywood Hallucination.* 1944; reprinted, New York: Simon and Schuster, 1970.

———. *Magic and Myth in the Movies.* 1947; reprinted, New York: Grove Press, 1970.

———. *Sex, Psyche, Etc., in the Film.* New York: Penguin Books, 1971.

————. *The Shadow of an Airplane Climbs the Empire State Building: A World Theory of Film*. Garden City, N.Y.: Doubleday, 1973.

————. *The Three Faces of the Film*. New York: Thomas Yoseloff, 1960.

————. *Underground Film*. New York: Grove Press, 1969.

Vogel, Amos. *Film as a Subversive Art*. New York: Random House, 1974.

Wollen, Peter. *Signs and Meaning in the Cinema*. 2nd edition. New York: Viking Press, 1972.

Wollenberg, H. H. *Anatomy of Film*. London: Marsland, 1947.

Wood, Robin. *Personal Views*. London: Gordon Fraser, 1976.

Young, Vernon. *On Film*. New York: Quadrangle Books, 1973.

Youngblood, Gene. *Expanded Cinema*. New York: E. P. Dutton, 1970.

Genre Studies

Baxter, John. *The Gangster Film*. Cranbury, N.J.: A. S. Barnes, 1970.

————. *Science Fiction in the Cinema*. Cranbury, N.J.: A. S. Barnes, 1970.

Brosnan, John. *Future Tense: The Cinema of Science Fiction*. New York: St. Martin's Press, 1978.

————. *The Horror People*. New York: St. Martin's Press, 1976.

Clarens, Carlos. *Crime Movies*. New York: W. W. Norton, 1980.

————. *An Illustrated History of the Horror Film*. New York: Capricorn Books, 1967.

Davis, Brian. *The Thriller*. New York: E. P. Dutton, 1973.

Dillard, Richard H. W. *Horror Films*. New York: Monarch Press, 1976.

Everson, William K. *The Bad Guys*. New York: Citadel Press, 1964.

————. *The Detective in Film*. New York: Citadel Press, 1972.

Eyles, Allen. *The Western*. Cranbury, N.J.: A. S. Barnes, 1975.

Fenin, George N., and Everson, William K. *The Western: From Silents to the Seventies*. 2nd edition. New York: Grossman Publishers, 1973.

Folsom, James K., ed. *The Western*. Englewood Cliffs, N.J.: Prentice-Hall, 1979.

French, Philip. *Westerns*. New York: Viking Press, 1973.

Gabree, John. *Gangsters: From Little Caesar to the Godfather*. New York: Pyramid Publications, 1973.

Gifford, Denis. *Science Fiction Film*. London: Studio Vista Books, 1951.

Glaessner, Verina. *Kung-Fu: Cinema of Vengeance*. New York: Bounty, 1973.

Gow, Gordon. *Suspense in the Cinema*. Cranbury, N.J.: A. S. Barnes, 1968.

Huss, Roy, ed. *Focus on the Horror Film*. Englewood Cliffs, N.J.: Prentice-Hall, 1972.

Johnson, William, ed. *Focus on the Science Fiction Film*. Englewood Cliffs, N.J.: Prentice-Hall, 1972.

Kaminsky, Stuart M. *American Film Genres: Approaches to a Critical Theory*. New York: Dell, 1974.

Karpf, Steven. *The Gangster Film: Emergence, Variation, and Decay of a Genre*. New York: Arno Press, 1973.

Kitses, Jim. *Horizons West*. Bloomington: Indiana University Press, 1970.

Kobal, John. *Gotta Sing Gotta Dance: A Pictorial History of Film Musicals*. London: Hamlyn, 1971.

McArthur, Colin. *Underworld U.S.A.* New York: Viking Press, 1972.

McVay, Douglas. *The Musical Film*. Cranbury, N.J.: A. S. Barnes, 1967.

Menville, Douglas. *A Historical and Critical Survey of the Science Fiction Film*. New York: Arno Press, 1975.

Nachbar, Jack, ed. *Focus on the Western*. Englewood Cliffs, N.J.: Prentice-Hall, 1974.

Parish, James R. *The Great Gangster Pictures*. Metuchen, N.J.: Scarecrow Press, 1976.

————. *The Great Science Fiction Pictures*. Metuchen, N.J.: Scarecrow Press, 1977.

————. *The Great Spy Pictures*. Metuchen, N.J.: Scarecrow Press, 1974.

————. *The Great Western Pictures.* Metuchen, N.J.: Scarecrow Press, 1974.

Pilkington, William T., ed. *Western Movies.* Albuquerque: University of New Mexico Press, 1979.

Pirie, David. *A Heritage of Horror: The English Gothic Cinema 1946–1972.* New York: Avon Books, 1973.

Rosow, Eugene. *Born to Lose: The Gangster Film in America.* New York: Avon Books, 1978.

Rovin, Jeff. *A Pictorial History of Science Fiction Films.* Secaucus, N.J.: Citadel Press, 1975.

Shadoian, Jack. *Dreams and Dead Ends: The American Gangster Film.* Cambridge, Mass.: MIT Press, 1977.

Solomon, Stanley J. *Beyond Formula: American Film Genres.* New York: Harcourt Brace Jovanovich, 1976.

Steinbrunner, Chris. *Cinema of the Fantastic.* New York: Saturday Review Press, 1972.

Sterne, Lee. E. *The Movie Musical.* New York: Pyramid Publications, 1974.

Taylor, John Russell, and Jackson, Arthur. *The Hollywood Musical.* New York: McGraw-Hill, 1971.

Turan, Kenneth, and Zito, Stephen F. *Sinema: American Pornographic Films and the People Who Make Them.* New York: Frederick A. Praeger, 1974.

Tuska, Jon. *The Detective in Hollywood.* Garden City, N.Y.: Doubleday, 1978.

————. *The Filming of the West.* Garden City, N.Y.: Doubleday, 1976.

Vallance, Tom. *The American Musical.* Cranbury, N.J.: A. S. Barnes, 1970.

Wright, Will. *Six Guns and Society: A Structural Study of the Western.* Berkeley: University of California Press, 1975.

The Documentary

Barnouw, Erik. *Documentary: A History of the Non-Fiction Film.* New York: Oxford University Press, 1974.

Barsam, Richard. *Non-Fiction Film: A Critical History.* New York: E. P. Dutton, 1973.

————, ed. *Non-Fiction Film Theory and Criticism.* New York: E. P. Dutton, 1976.

Beddeley, W. Hugh. *The Technique of Documentary Film Production.* New York: Hastings House, 1963.

Beveridge, James. *John Grierson: Film Master.* New York: Macmillan, 1978.

Calder-Marshall, Arthur. *The Innocent Eye: The Life of Robert Flaherty.* London: W. H. Allen, 1963; reprinted, New York: Penguin Books, 1970.

Fielding, Raymond. *The American Newsreel: 1911–1967.* Norman: University of Oklahoma Press, 1972.

Grierson, John. *Grierson on Documentary.* Edited by Forsyth Hardy. New York: Frederick A. Praeger, 1971.

Griffith, Richard. *The World of Robert Flaherty.* New York: Duell, Sloan, and Pearce, 1953.

Jacobs, Lewis, ed. *The Documentary Tradition.* New York: Hopkinson and Blake, 1971; second edition, New York: W. W. Norton, 1979.

Levin, G. Roy, ed. *Documentary Explorations.* Garden City, N.Y.: Doubleday, 1972.

Lovell, Alan, and Hillier, Jim. *Studies in Documentary.* New York: Viking Press, 1972.

Mamber, Stephen. *Cinéma Vérité in America.* Cambridge, Mass.: MIT Press, 1974.

Marcorelles, Louis. *Living Cinema.* New York: Frederick A. Praeger, 1973.

Rosenthal, Alan. *The New Documentary in Action.* Berkeley: University of California Press, 1971.

Sussex, Elizabeth. *The Rise and Fall of British Documentary.* Berkeley: University of California Press, 1976.